VISUAL
dictionary

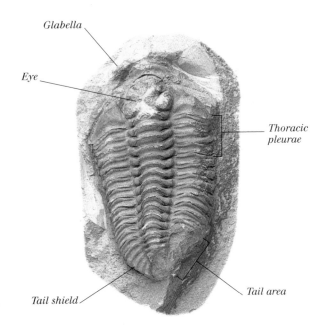

Glabella

Eye

Thoracic
pleurae

Tail shield

Tail area

PREHISTORIC TRILOBITE

DIGITAL VIDEO CAMERA

Liquid crystal display (LCD)

Viewfinder

Power switch

Cassette compartment lid

Battery

OVERHEAD VIEW OF OUR GALAXY

Location of Solar System

Nucleus

First electron shell

Second electron shell

Nucleus

ANATOMY OF A FLUORINE–19 ATOM

Fault plane

Dip of fault plane

Hade of fault plane

STRUCTURE OF A FAULT

Openable windscreen

Steering wheel

Radiator

Headlamp

Exhaust port

VELOCETTE OHV ENGINE

Floral design

MOSAIC DESIGN

MODEL T FORD

VISUAL dictionary

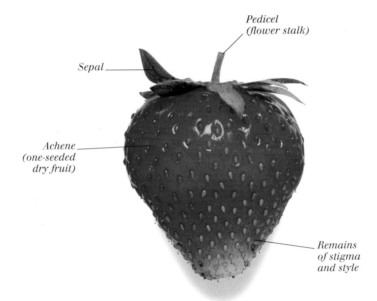

Pedicel
(flower stalk)

Sepal

Achene
(one-seeded
dry fruit)

Remains
of stigma
and style

STRAWBERRY

TED SMART

TED SMART

Original Edition (*Ultimate Visual Dictionary*)
Project Art Editors Heather McCarry, Johnny Pau, Chris Walker, Kevin Williams
Designer Simon Murrell

Project Editors Luisa Caruso, Peter Jones, Jane Mason, Geoffrey Stalker
Editor Jo Evans

DTP Designer Zirrinia Austin
Picture Researcher Charlotte Bush

Managing Art Editor Toni Kay
Senior Editor Roger Tritton
Managing Editor Sean Moore

Production Manager Hilary Stephens

Anatomical And Botanical Models Supplied By Somso Modelle, Coburg, Germany

Revised Edition
Art Editor Hugh Schermuly
Designers Phil Gamble, Simon Oon, Pamela Shiels
Jacket Designer John Dinsdale
Project Editor Cathy Meeus
Editor Paul Docherty
Jacket Editor Beth Apple
Editorial Consultant Sarah Angliss
Senior Art Editor Ina Stradins
Senior Editor Angeles Gavira
Production Manager Elizabeth Cherry
Managing Art Editor Phil Ormerod
Category Publisher Jonathan Metcalf

FIRST PUBLISHED IN GREAT BRITAIN IN 1994
UNDER THE TITLE ULTIMATE VISUAL DICTIONARY BY
DORLING KINDERSLEY LIMITED
80 STRAND, LONDON WC2R 0RL
A PENGUIN COMPANY

THIS EDITION PRODUCED FOR THE BOOK PEOPLE LTD.

HALLWOOD AVENUE, HAYDOCK, ST HELENS, WA11 9UL

REVISED EDITIONS IN 1996, 1997, 1998, 1999, 2000, 2002

COPYRIGHT © 1994, 1996, 1997, 1998, 1999, 2000, 2002 DORLING KINDERSLEY LIMITED, LONDON

A CIP CATALOGUE RECORD FOR THIS BOOK IS AVAILABLE FROM THE BRITISH LIBRARY

ISBN 0 75133 7439

REPRODUCED BY COLOURSCAN, SINGAPORE
PRINTED AND BOUND BY AGT, SPAIN
D.L. TO: 907 - 2003
See our complete catalogue at www.dk.com

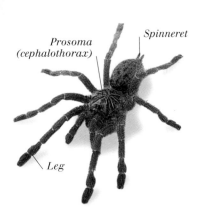

Prosoma (cephalothorax)

Spinneret

Leg

EXTERNAL FEATURES OF A SPIDER

Canopy

Fin

G-BNHB

Main landing gear

SIDE VIEW OF ARV SUPER 2 AEROPLANE

Heat shield

PAM-D upper stage booster

Launch vehicle

MARS PATHFINDER

CONTENTS

INTRODUCTION 6

THE UNIVERSE 8

PREHISTORIC EARTH 54

PLANTS 110

ANIMALS 164

THE HUMAN BODY 208

GEOLOGY, GEOGRAPHY, AND METEOROLOGY 262

PHYSICS AND CHEMISTRY 304

RAIL AND ROAD 322

SEA AND AIR 370

THE VISUAL ARTS 428

ARCHITECTURE 456

MUSIC 500

SPORTS 522

THE MODERN WORLD 564

APPENDIX 616

INDEX 624

Barrel

Permanent black ink

FOUNTAIN PEN AND INK

Retractable head light

Pause button

SONY AIBO ROBOT DOG

Parallel bands

ONYX

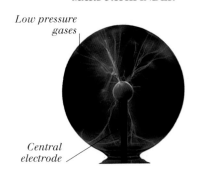

Low pressure gases

Central electrode

BALL CONTAINING HIGH TEMPERATURE GAS (PLASMA)

Non-breakable plastic

Shock absorber

AMERICAN FOOTBALL HELMET

Introduction

THE VISUAL DICTIONARY is a completely new kind of reference book. It provides a link between pictures and words in a way that no ordinary dictionary ever has. Most dictionaries simply tell you what a word means, but the *Visual Dictionary* shows you – through a combination of detailed annotations, explicit photographs, and illustrations. In the *Visual Dictionary*, pictures define the annotations around them. You do not read definitions of the annotated words, you see them. The highly accessible format of the *Visual Dictionary*, the thoroughness of its annotations, and the range of its subject matter make it a unique and helpful reference tool.

How to use the Visual Dictionary

You will find the *Visual Dictionary* simple to use. Instead of being organized alphabetically, it is divided by subject into 14 sections – The Universe, Prehistoric Earth, Plants, Animals, The Human Body, etc. Each section begins with a table of contents listing the major entries within that section. For example, The Visual Arts section has entries on *Drawing, Tempera, Fresco, Oils, Watercolour, Pastels, Acrylics, Calligraphy, Printmaking, Mosaic,* and *Sculpture.* Every entry has a short introduction explaining the purpose of the photographs and illustrations, and the significance of the annotations.

If you know what something looks like, but don't know its name, find the term you need by turning to the annotations surrounding the pictures; if you know a word, but don't know what it refers to, use the comprehensive index to direct you to the appropriate page.

Suppose that you want to know what the bone at the end of your little finger is called. With a standard dictionary, you wouldn't know where to begin. But with the *Visual Dictionary* you simply turn to the entry called *Hands* – within The Human Body section – where you will find four fully annotated, colour photographs showing the skin, muscles, and bones of the human hand. In this entry you will quickly find that the bone you are searching for is called the distal phalanx, and for good measure you will discover that it is attached to the middle phalanx by the distal interphalangeal joint.

Perhaps you want to know what a catalytic converter looks like. If you look up "catalytic converter" in an ordinary dictionary, you will be told what it is and possibly what it does – but you will not be able to tell what shape it is or what it is made of. However, if you look up "catalytic converter" in the index of the *Visual Dictionary*, you will be directed to the *Modern engines* entry on page 344 – where the introduction gives you basic information about what a catalytic converter is – and to page 350 – where there is a spectacular exploded-view photograph of the mechanics of a Renault Clio. From these pages you will find out not only what a catalytic converter looks like, but also that it is attached at one end to an exhaust downpipe and at the other to a silencer.

Whatever it is that you want to find a name for, or whatever name you want to find a picture for, you will find it quickly and easily in the *Visual Dictionary*. Perhaps you need to know where the vamp on a shoe is; or how to tell obovate and lanceolate leaves apart; or what a spiral galaxy looks like; or whether birds have nostrils. With the *Visual Dictionary* at hand, the answers to each of these questions, and thousands more, are readily available.

The *Visual Dictionary* does not just tell you what the names of the different parts of an object are. The photographs, illustrations, and annotations are all specially arranged to help you understand which parts relate to one another and how objects function.

With the *Visual Dictionary* you can find in seconds the words or pictures that you are looking for; or you can simply browse through the pages of the book for your own pleasure. The *Visual Dictionary* is not intended to replace a standard dictionary or conventional encyclopedia, but is instead a stimulating and valuable companion to ordinary reference volumes. Giving you instant access to the language that is used by astronomers and architects, musicians and mechanics, scientists and sportspeople, it is the ideal reference book for specialists and generalists of all ages.

Sections of the VISUAL DICTIONARY

The 14 sections of the *VISUAL DICTIONARY* contain a total of more than 30,000 terms, encompassing a wide range of topics:

•In the first section, THE UNIVERSE, spectacular photographs and illustrations are used to show the names of the stars and planets and to explain the structure of solar systems, galaxies, nebulae, comets, and black holes.

•PREHISTORIC EARTH tells the story in annotations of how our own planet has evolved since its formation. It includes examples of prehistoric flora and fauna, and fascinating dinosaur models – some with parts of the body stripped away to show anatomical sections.

•PLANTS covers a huge range of species – from the familiar to the exotic. In addition to the colour photographs of plants included in this section, there is a series of micrographic photographs illustrating plant details – such as pollen grains, spores, and cross-sections of stems and roots – in close-up.

•In the ANIMALS section, skeletons, anatomical diagrams, and different parts of animals' bodies have been meticulously annotated. This section provides a comprehensive guide to the vocabulary of zoological classification and animal physiology.

•The structure of the human body, its parts, and its systems are presented in THE HUMAN BODY. The section includes lifelike, three-dimensional models and the latest false-colour images. Clear and authoritative annotations indicate the correct anatomical terms.

•GEOLOGY, GEOGRAPHY, AND METEOROLOGY describes the structure of the Earth – from the inner core to the exosphere – and the physical phenomena – such as volcanoes, rivers, glaciers, and climate – that shape its surface.

•PHYSICS AND CHEMISTRY is a visual journey through the fundamental principles underlying the physical universe, and provides the essential vocabulary of these sciences.

•In RAIL AND ROAD, a wide range of trains, trams and buses, cars, bicycles, and motorcycles are described. Exploded-view photographs show mechanical details with striking clarity.

•SEA AND AIR gives the names for hundreds of parts of ships and aeroplanes. The section includes civil and fighting craft, both historical and modern.

•THE VISUAL ARTS shows the equipment and materials used by painters, sculptors, printers, and other artists. Well-known compositions have been chosen to illustrate specific artistic techniques and effects.

•ARCHITECTURE includes photographs of exemplary architectural models and illustrates dozens of additional features such as columns, domes, and arches.

•MUSIC provides a visual introduction to the special language of music and musical instruments. It includes clearly annotated photographs of each of the major groups of traditional instruments – brass, woodwind, strings, and percussion – together with modern electronic instruments.

•The SPORTS section is a guide to the playing areas, formations, equipment, and techniques needed for many of today's most popular sports.

•In THE MODERN WORLD, items that are a familiar part of our daily lives are taken apart to reveal their inner workings and give access to the language used by their manufacturers. It also includes systems and concepts, such as the Internet, that increasingly influence our 21st century world.

THE UNIVERSE

ANATOMY OF THE UNIVERSE 10

GALAXIES 12

THE MILKY WAY 14

NEBULAE AND STAR CLUSTERS 16

STARS OF NORTHERN SKIES 18

STARS OF SOUTHERN SKIES 20

STARS 22

SMALL STARS 24

MASSIVE STARS 26

NEUTRON STARS AND BLACK HOLES . . . 28

THE SOLAR SYSTEM 30

THE SUN 32

MERCURY 34

VENUS 36

THE EARTH 38

THE MOON 40

MARS 42

JUPITER 44

SATURN 46

URANUS 48

NEPTUNE AND PLUTO 50

ASTEROIDS, COMETS, AND METEOROIDS . . . 52

Anatomy of the Universe

Fireball of rapidly expanding, extremely hot gas lasting about one million years

THE UNIVERSE CONTAINS EVERYTHING that exists, from the tiniest subatomic particles to galactic superclusters (the largest structures known). Nobody knows how big the Universe is, but astronomers estimate that it contains about 100 billion galaxies, each comprising an average of 100 billion stars. The most widely accepted theory about the origin of the Universe is the Big Bang theory, which states that the Universe came into being in a huge explosion – the Big Bang – that took place between 10 and 20 billion years ago. The Universe initially consisted of a very hot, dense fireball of expanding, cooling gas. After about one million years, the gas probably began to condense into localized clumps called protogalaxies. During the next five billion years, the protogalaxies continued condensing, forming galaxies in which stars were being born. Today, billions of years later, the Universe as a whole is still expanding, although there are localized areas in which objects are held together by gravity; for example, many galaxies are found in clusters. The Big Bang theory is supported by the discovery of faint, cool background radiation coming evenly from all directions. This radiation is believed to be the remnant of the radiation produced by the Big Bang. Small "ripples" in the temperature of the cosmic background radiation are thought to be evidence of slight fluctuations in the density of the early Universe, which resulted in the formation of galaxies. Astronomers do not yet know if the Universe is "closed", which means it will eventually stop expanding and begin to contract, or if it is "open", which means it will continue expanding forever.

FALSE-COLOUR MICROWAVE MAP OF COSMIC BACKGROUND RADIATION

Pink indicates "warm ripples" in background radiation

Pale blue indicates "cool ripples" in background radiation

Deep blue indicates background radiation corresponding to -270.3°C (remnant of the Big Bang)

Red and pink band indicates radiation from our galaxy

Low-energy microwave radiation corresponding to about -270°C

High-energy gamma radiation corresponding to about 3,000°C

ORIGIN AND EXPANSION OF THE UNIVERSE

Quasar (probably the centre of a galaxy containing a massive black hole)

Universe one to five billion years after Big Bang

Protogalaxy (condensing gas cloud)

Galaxy spinning and flattening to become spiral shaped

Dark cloud (dust and gas condensing to form a protogalaxy)

Elliptical galaxy in which stars form rapidly

Universe today (10–20 billion years after Big Bang)

Cluster of galaxies held together by gravity

Elliptical galaxy containing old stars and little gas and dust

Irregular galaxy

Spiral galaxy containing gas, dust, and young stars

OBJECTS IN THE UNIVERSE

CLUSTER OF GALAXIES IN VIRGO

FALSE-COLOUR IMAGE OF 3C273 (QUASAR)

NGC 4406 (ELLIPTICAL GALAXY)

NGC 5236 (SPIRAL GALAXY)

NGC 6822 (IRREGULAR GALAXY)

THE ROSETTE NEBULA (EMISSION NEBULA)

THE JEWEL BOX (STAR CLUSTER)

THE SUN (MAIN SEQUENCE STAR)

EARTH

THE MOON

Galaxies

SOMBRERO,
A SPIRAL GALAXY

A GALAXY IS A HUGE MASS OF STARS, nebulae, and interstellar material. The smallest galaxies contain about 100,000 stars, while the largest contain up to 3,000 billion stars. There are three main types of galaxy, classified according to their shape: elliptical, which are oval shaped; spiral, which have arms spiralling outwards from a central bulge; and irregular, which have no obvious shape. Sometimes, the shape of a galaxy is distorted by a collision with another galaxy. Quasars (quasi-stellar objects) are thought to be galactic nuclei but are so far away that their exact nature is still uncertain. They are compact, highly luminous objects in the outer reaches of the known Universe: while the furthest known "ordinary" galaxies are about 10 billion light years away, the furthest known quasar is about 15 billion light years away. Active galaxies, such as Seyfert galaxies and radio galaxies, emit intense radiation. In a Seyfert galaxy, this radiation comes from the galactic nucleus; in a radio galaxy, it also comes from huge lobes on either side of the galaxy. The radiation from active galaxies and quasars is thought to be caused by black holes (see pp. 28-29).

OPTICAL IMAGE OF NGC 4486 (ELLIPTICAL GALAXY)

Globular cluster containing very old red giants

Central region containing old red giants

Less densely populated region

Neighbouring galaxy

OPTICAL IMAGE OF LARGE MAGELLANIC CLOUD (IRREGULAR GALAXY)

Tarantula Nebula

Dust cloud obscuring light from stars

Emission nebula

Light from stars

OPTICAL IMAGE OF NGC 2997 (SPIRAL GALAXY)

Glowing nebula in spiral arm

Spiral arm containing young stars

Galactic nucleus containing old stars

Dust in spiral arm reflecting blue light from hot young stars

Hot, ionized hydrogen gas emitting red light

Dust lane

**OPTICAL IMAGE OF CENTAURUS A
(RADIO GALAXY)**

**FALSE-COLOUR RADIO
IMAGE OF CENTAURUS A**

*Dust lane crossing
elliptical galaxy*

*Galactic nucleus
containing
powerful source
of radiation*

*Light from
old stars*

*Red indicates
high-intensity
radio waves*

*Blue indicates
low-intensity
radio waves*

*Radio
lobe*

*Radiation from
galactic nucleus*

*Outline of
optical image
of Centaurus A*

*Radio
lobe*

*Yellow indicates
medium-intensity
radio waves*

FALSE-COLOUR RADIO IMAGE OF 3C273 (QUASAR)

*Radiation from jet
of high-energy
particles moving
away from quasar*

Quasar nucleus

*White indicates high-
intensity radio waves*

*Blue indicates
low-intensity
radio waves*

**OPTICAL IMAGE OF NGC 1566
(SEYFERT GALAXY)**

**FALSE-COLOUR OPTICAL IMAGE OF NGC 5754
(TWO COLLIDING GALAXIES)**

*Nebula in
spiral arm*

*Compact nucleus
emitting intense
radiation*

Spiral arm

*Blue indicates low-
intensity radiation*

*Red indicates
medium-intensity
radiation*

*Spiral arm
distorted by
gravitational
influence of
smaller galaxy*

*Large spiral
galaxy*

*Smaller galaxy
colliding with
larger galaxy*

*Yellow indicates
high-intensity
radiation*

The Milky Way

THE MILKY WAY IS THE NAME GIVEN TO THE FAINT BAND OF LIGHT that stretches across the night sky. This light comes from stars and nebulae in our galaxy, known as the Milky Way Galaxy or simply as "the Galaxy". The Galaxy is shaped like a spiral, with a dense central bulge that is encircled by four arms spiralling outwards and surrounded by a less dense halo. We cannot see the spiral shape because the Solar System is in one of the spiral arms, the Orion Arm (also called the Local Arm). From our position, the centre of the Galaxy is completely obscured by dust clouds; as a result, optical maps give only a limited view of the Galaxy. However, a more complete picture can be obtained by studying radio, infra-red, and other radiation. The central bulge of the Galaxy is a relatively small, dense sphere that contains mainly older red and yellow stars. The halo is a less dense region in which the oldest stars are situated; some of these stars may be as old as the Galaxy itself (possibly 15 billion years). The spiral arms contain mainly hot, young, blue stars, as well as nebulae (clouds of dust and gas inside which stars are born). The Galaxy is vast, about 100,000 light years across (a light year is about 9,460 billion kilometres); in comparison, the Solar System seems small, at about 12 light hours across (about 13 billion kilometres). The entire Galaxy is rotating in space, although the inner stars travel faster than those further out. The Sun, which is about two-thirds out from the centre, completes one lap of the Galaxy about every 220 million years.

SIDE VIEW OF OUR GALAXY

Disc of spiral arms containing mainly young stars

Central bulge containing mainly older stars

Halo containing oldest stars

Nucleus

100,000 light years

OVERHEAD VIEW OF OUR GALAXY

Central bulge

Nucleus

Perseus Arm

Crux-Centaurus Arm

Emission nebula

Sagittarius Arm

Dust in spiral arm reflecting blue light from hot young stars

Location of Solar System

Patch of dust clouds

Orion Arm (Local Arm)

PANORAMIC OPTICAL MAP OF OUR GALAXY AND NEARBY GALAXIES

Polaris (the Pole Star), a blue-green variable binary star

Light from stars and nebulae in the Perseus Arm

Galactic plane

Milky Way (the band of light that stretches across the night sky)

Pleiades (the Seven Sisters), an open star cluster

Andromeda Galaxy, a spiral galaxy 2.2 million light years away; the most distant object visible to the naked eye

PANORAMIC RADIO MAP OF OUR GALAXY

North Galactic spur
(possibly radio emission
from a supernova remnant)

North Galactic
Pole

Red indicates
high-intensity
radio-wave emission

Galactic
plane

Blue indicates
low-intensity
radio-wave emission

South
Galactic Pole

Yellow and green
indicate medium-intensity
radio-wave emission

PANORAMIC INFRA-RED MAP OF OUR GALAXY

North Galactic
Pole

Low-intensity infra-red
radiation from interstellar
gas and dust

Galactic
plane

Galactic
plane

South Galactic Pole

High-intensity infra-red
radiation from interstellar
gas and dust

High-intensity
infra-red
radiation
from region
of starbirth

Vega, a white main
sequence star; the fifth
brightest star in the sky

North Galactic Pole

Dark clouds of dust and gas
obscuring light from part of the
Sagittarius Arm

Light from stars and nebulae in the
part of the Sagittarius Arm between
the Sun and Galactic centre

Light from stars
and nebulae in the
Perseus Arm

Galactic
plane

Orion's belt,
a row of
three bright
stars

Orion Nebula

Sirius, a white main
sequence star; the
brightest star in the sky

Canopus, a white supergiant;
the second brightest star in the sky

Dust clouds
obscuring
Galactic centre

South Galactic Pole

Small Magellanic Cloud, an irregular
galaxy 190,000 light years away; the
second nearest object to our galaxy

Large Magellanic Cloud, an
irregular galaxy 170,000 light years
away; the nearest object to our galaxy

Nebulae and star clusters

**HODGE 11, A
GLOBULAR CLUSTER**

A NEBULA IS A CLOUD OF DUST AND GAS inside a galaxy. Nebulae become visible if the gas glows, or if the cloud reflects starlight or obscures light from more distant objects. Emission nebulae shine because their gas emits light when it is stimulated by radiation from hot young stars. Reflection nebulae shine because their dust reflects light from stars in or around the nebula. Dark nebulae appear as silhouettes because they block out light from shining nebulae or stars behind them. Two types of nebula are associated with dying stars: planetary nebulae and supernova remnants. Both consist of expanding shells of gas that were once the outer layers of a star. A planetary nebula is a gas shell drifting away from a dying stellar core. A supernova remnant is a gas shell moving away from a stellar core at great speed following a violent explosion called a supernova (see pp. 26-27). Stars are often found in groups known as clusters. Open clusters are loose groups of a few thousand young stars that were born in the same cloud and are drifting apart. Globular clusters are densely packed, roughly spherical groups of hundreds of thousands of older stars.

TRIFID NEBULA (EMISSION NEBULA)

Reflection nebula

Emission nebula

Dust lane

Starbirth region (area in which dust and gas clump together to form stars)

PLEIADES (OPEN STAR CLUSTER) WITH A REFLECTION NEBULA

Wisps of dust and hydrogen gas remaining from cloud in which stars formed

Young star in an open cluster of 300–500 stars

Reflection nebula

HORSEHEAD NEBULA (DARK NEBULA)

Glowing filament of hot, ionized hydrogen gas

Alnitak (star in Orion's belt)

Dust lane

Emission nebula

Star near southern end of Orion's belt

Emission nebula

Horsehead Nebula

Reflection nebula

Dark nebula obscuring light from distant stars

ORION NEBULA (DIFFUSE EMISSION NEBULA)

Glowing cloud of dust and hydrogen gas forming part of Orion Nebula

Dust cloud

Trapezium (group of four young stars)

Red light from hot, ionized hydrogen gas

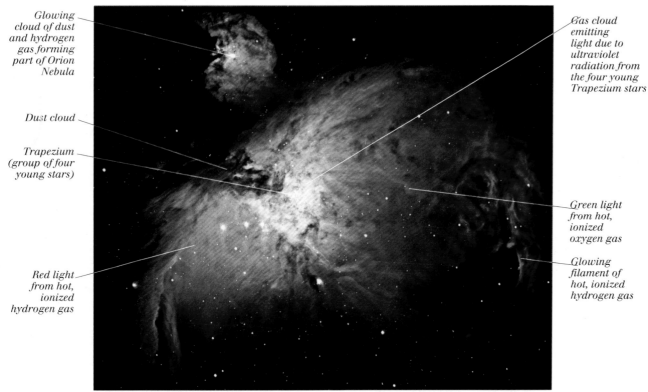

Gas cloud emitting light due to ultraviolet radiation from the four young Trapezium stars

Green light from hot, ionized oxygen gas

Glowing filament of hot, ionized hydrogen gas

VELA SUPERNOVA REMNANT

HELIX NEBULA (PLANETARY NEBULA)

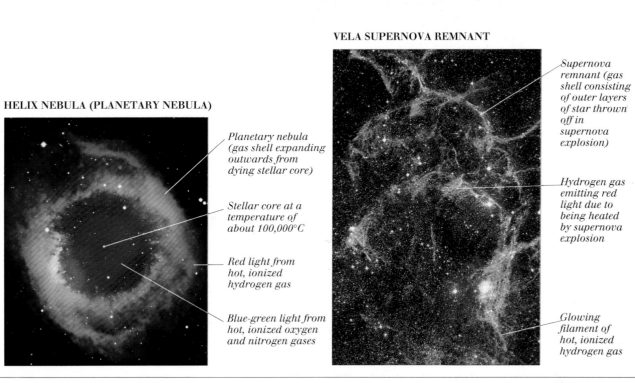

Planetary nebula (gas shell expanding outwards from dying stellar core)

Stellar core at a temperature of about 100,000°C

Red light from hot, ionized hydrogen gas

Blue-green light from hot, ionized oxygen and nitrogen gases

Supernova remnant (gas shell consisting of outer layers of star thrown off in supernova explosion)

Hydrogen gas emitting red light due to being heated by supernova explosion

Glowing filament of hot, ionized hydrogen gas

Stars of northern skies

WHEN YOU LOOK AT THE NORTHERN SKY, you look away from the densely populated Galactic centre, so the northern sky generally appears less bright than the southern sky (see pp. 20-21). Among the best-known sights in the northern sky are the constellations Ursa Major (the Great Bear) and Orion. Some ancient civilizations believed that the stars were fixed to a celestial sphere surrounding the Earth, and modern maps of the sky are based on a similar idea. The North and South Poles of this imaginary celestial sphere are directly above the North and South Poles of the Earth, at the points where the Earth's axis of rotation intersects the sphere. The celestial North Pole is at the centre of the map shown here, and Polaris (the Pole Star) lies very close to it. The celestial equator marks a projection of the Earth's equator on the sphere. The ecliptic marks the path of the Sun across the sky as the Earth orbits the Sun. The Moon and planets move against the background of the stars because the stars are much more distant; the nearest star outside the Solar System (Proxima Centauri) is more than 50,000 times further away than the planet Jupiter.

ORION

Chi₂ Orionis
Chi₁ Orionis
Nu Orionis
Xi Orionis
Heka
Mu Orionis
Bellatrix
Betelgeuse
Orion's belt
Omicron Orionis
Alnitak
Pi₂ Orionis
Pi₃ Orionis
Pi₄ Orionis
Pi₅ Orionis
Pi₆ Orionis
Saiph
Mintaka
Eta Orionis
Tau Orionis
Orion Nebula
Rigel
Alnilam

VISIBLE STARS IN THE NORTHERN SKY

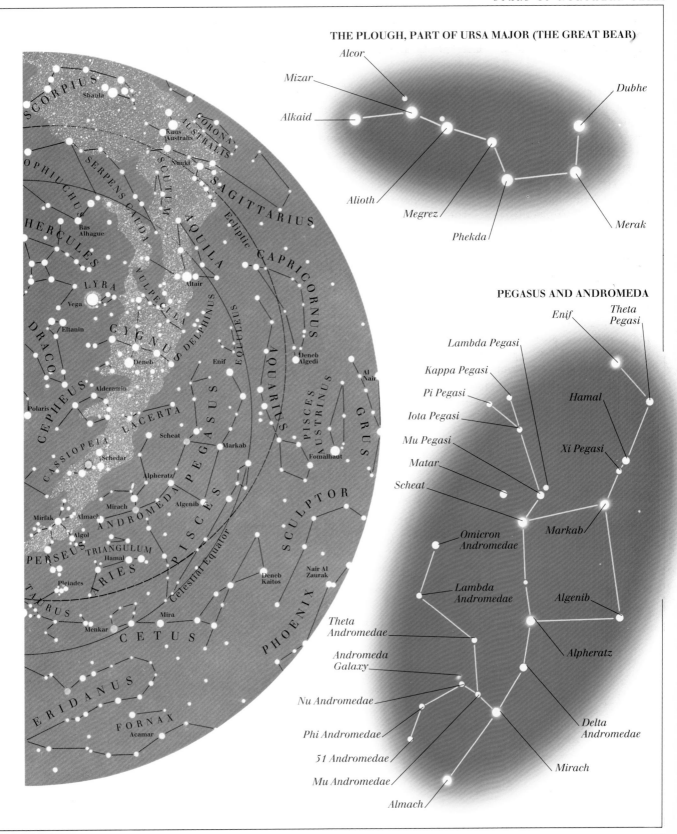

THE PLOUGH, PART OF URSA MAJOR (THE GREAT BEAR)

Alcor
Mizar
Alkaid
Alioth
Megrez
Phekda
Dubhe
Merak

PEGASUS AND ANDROMEDA

Enif
Theta Pegasi
Lambda Pegasi
Kappa Pegasi
Pi Pegasi
Iota Pegasi
Mu Pegasi
Matar
Scheat
Hamal
Xi Pegasi
Markab
Omicron Andromedae
Lambda Andromedae
Algenib
Alpheratz
Theta Andromedae
Andromeda Galaxy
Nu Andromedae
Phi Andromedae
51 Andromedae
Mu Andromedae
Almach
Delta Andromedae
Mirach

SCORPIUS
Shaula
CORONA AUSTRALIS
Kaus Australis
Nunki
SAGITTARIUS
OPHIUCHUS
SERPENS CAUDA
SCUTUM
AQUILA
Ras Alhague
CAPRICORNUS
HERCULES
LYRA
VULPECULA
Altair
Vega
Eltanin
CYGNUS
DELPHINUS
Deneb
Ecliptic
EQUULEUS
AQUARIUS
Enif
Deneb Algedi
Al Nair
PISCES AUSTRINUS
GRUS
DRACO
CEPHEUS
Alderamin
LACERTA
PEGASUS
Scheat
Markab
Fomalhaut
Polaris
CASSIOPEIA
Schedar
Alpheratz
ANDROMEDA
Algenib
SCULPTOR
Mirach
Mirfak
Almach
PERSEUS
Algol
TRIANGULUM
Hamal
ARIES
PISCES
Celestial Equator
Deneb Kaitos
Nair Al Zaurak
PHOENIX
Pleiades
TAURUS
Mira
Menkar
CETUS
ERIDANUS
FORNAX
Acamar

Stars of southern skies

WHEN YOU LOOK AT THE SOUTHERN SKY, you look towards the Galactic centre, which has a huge population of stars. As a result, the Milky Way appears brighter in the southern sky than in the northern sky (see pp. 18-19). The southern sky is rich in nebulae and star clusters. It contains the Large and Small Magellanic Clouds, which are the two nearest galaxies to our own. Stars make fixed patterns in the sky called constellations. However, the constellations are only apparent groupings of stars, since the distances to the stars in a constellation may vary enormously. The shapes of constellations may change over many thousands of years due to the relative motions of stars. The movement of the constellations across the sky is due to the Earth's motion in space. The daily rotation of the Earth causes the constellations to move across the sky from east to west, and the orbit of the Earth around the Sun causes different areas of sky to be visible in different seasons. The visibility of areas of sky also depends on the location of the observer. For instance, stars near the celestial equator may be seen from either hemisphere at some time during the year, whereas stars close to the celestial poles (the celestial South Pole is at the centre of the map shown here) can never be seen from the opposite hemisphere.

HYDRUS (THE WATER SNAKE) AND MENSA (THE TABLE)

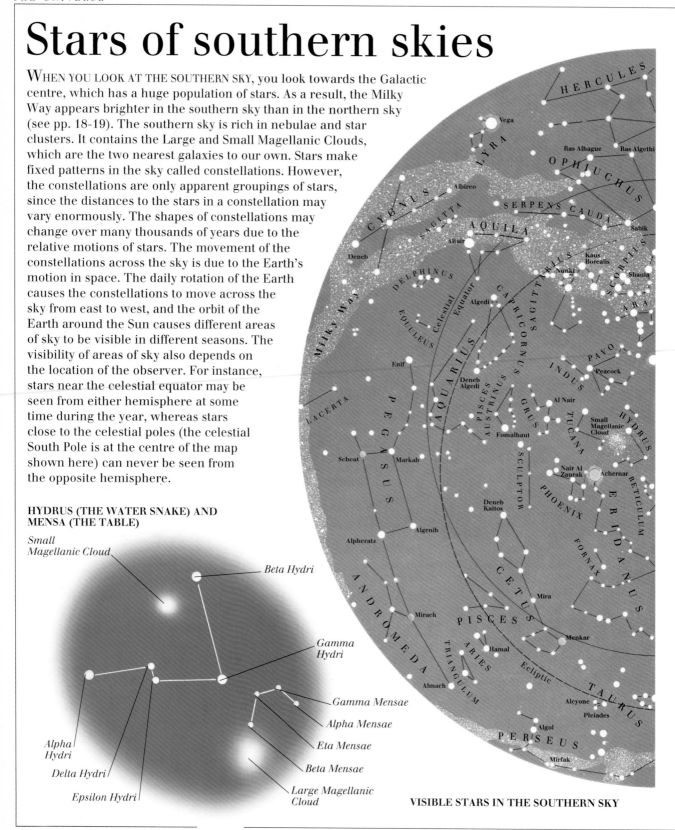

Small Magellanic Cloud

Beta Hydri

Gamma Hydri

Gamma Mensae

Alpha Mensae

Eta Mensae

Beta Mensae

Large Magellanic Cloud

Alpha Hydri

Delta Hydri

Epsilon Hydri

VISIBLE STARS IN THE SOUTHERN SKY

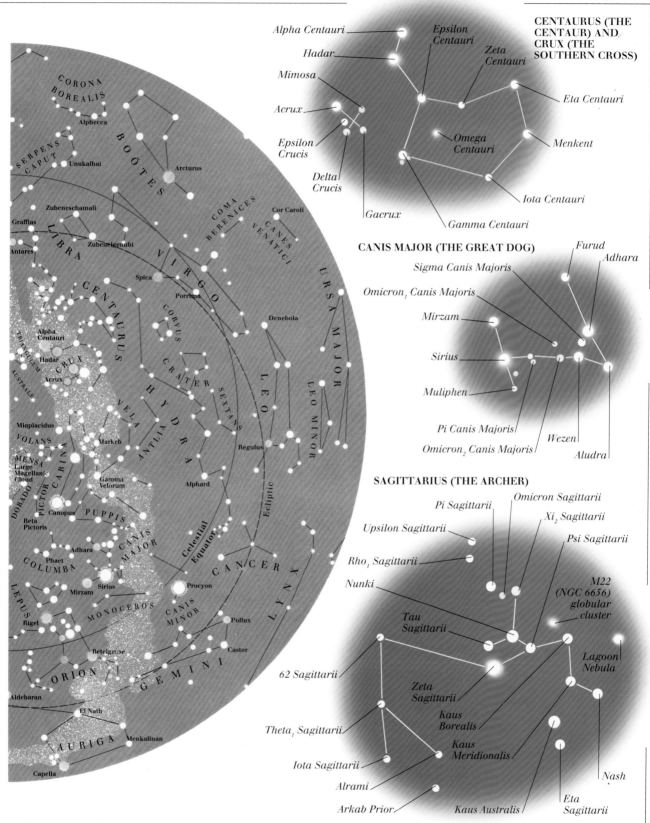

CENTAURUS (THE CENTAUR) AND CRUX (THE SOUTHERN CROSS)

Alpha Centauri
Epsilon Centauri
Hadar
Zeta Centauri
Mimosa
Eta Centauri
Acrux
Omega Centauri
Epsilon Crucis
Menkent
Delta Crucis
Iota Centauri
Gacrux
Gamma Centauri

CANIS MAJOR (THE GREAT DOG)

Furud
Adhara
Sigma Canis Majoris
Omicron₁ Canis Majoris
Mirzam
Sirius
Muliphen
Pi Canis Majoris
Wezen
Omicron₂ Canis Majoris
Aludra

SAGITTARIUS (THE ARCHER)

Pi Sagittarii
Omicron Sagittarii
Upsilon Sagittarii
Xi₂ Sagittarii
Rho₁ Sagittarii
Psi Sagittarii
Nunki
M22 (NGC 6656) globular cluster
Tau Sagittarii
Lagoon Nebula
62 Sagittarii
Zeta Sagittarii
Theta₁ Sagittarii
Kaus Borealis
Iota Sagittarii
Kaus Meridionalis
Alrami
Nash
Arkab Prior
Kaus Australis
Eta Sagittarii

CORONA BOREALIS
Alphecca
BOÖTES
SERPENS CAPUT
Unukalhai
Arcturus
Zubeneschamali
COMA BERENICES
Graffias
Cor Caroli
LIBRA
Antares
Zubenelgenubi
VIRGO
CANES VENATICI
Spica
CENTAURUS
Porrima
Denebola
URSA MAJOR
CORVUS
Alpha Centauri
CRATER
LEO
Hadar
CRUX
HYDRA
SEXTANS
Acrux
LEO MINOR
TRIANGULUM AUSTRALE
VELA
ANTLIA
Regulus
Miaplacidus
Markeb
VOLANS
CARINA
Gamma Velorum
Alphard
MENSA
Large Magellanic Cloud
DORADO
PICTOR
Canopus
PUPPIS
Beta Pictoris
CANIS MAJOR
Celestial Equator
Adhara
CANCER
Phact
COLUMBA
MONOCEROS
Sirius
Mirzam
LYNX
LEPUS
Procyon
Rigel
CANIS MINOR
Pollux
Betelgeuse
Castor
ORION
GEMINI
Aldebaran
El Nath
Menkalinan
AURIGA
Capella
Ecliptic

Stars

OPEN STAR CLUSTER AND DUST CLOUD

STARS ARE BODIES of hot, glowing gas that are born in nebulae (see pp. 24-27). They vary enormously in size, mass, and temperature: diameters range from about 450 times smaller to over 1,000 times bigger than that of the Sun; masses range from about a twentieth to over 50 solar masses; and surface temperatures range from about 3,000°C to over 50,000°C. The colour of a star is determined by its temperature: the hottest stars are blue and the coolest are red. The Sun, with a surface temperature of 5,500°C, is between these extremes and appears yellow. The energy emitted by a shining star is produced by nuclear fusion in the star's core. The brightness of a star is measured in magnitudes – the brighter the star, the lower its magnitude. There are two types of magnitude: apparent magnitude, which is the brightness seen from Earth, and absolute magnitude, which is the brightness that would be seen from a standard distance of 10 parsecs (32.6 light years). The light emitted by a star may be split to form a spectrum containing a series of dark lines (absorption lines). The patterns of lines indicate the presence of particular chemical elements, enabling astronomers to deduce the composition of the star's atmosphere. The magnitude and spectral type (colour) of stars may be plotted on a graph called a Hertzsprung-Russell diagram, which shows that stars tend to fall into several well-defined groups. The principal groups are main sequence stars (those which are fusing hydrogen to form helium), giants, supergiants, and white dwarfs.

STAR SIZES

Red giant (diameters between about 15 million and 150 million km)

The Sun (main sequence star with diameter about 1.4 million km)

White dwarf (diameters between about 3,000 and 50,000 km)

ENERGY EMISSION FROM THE SUN

Nuclear fusion in core produces gamma rays and neutrinos

Neutrinos travel to Earth directly from Sun's core in about 8 minutes

Lower-energy radiation travels to Earth in about 8 minutes

Earth

Sun

High-energy radiation (gamma rays) loses energy while travelling to surface over 2 million years

Lower-energy radiation (mainly ultraviolet, infra-red, and light rays) leaves surface

STAR MAGNITUDES

APPARENT MAGNITUDE

ABSOLUTE MAGNITUDE

Brighter stars

-9

0

+9

Fainter stars

Sirius: apparent magnitude of -1.46

Rigel: apparent magnitude of +0.12

Objects of magnitude higher than about +5.5 cannot be seen by the naked eye

Rigel: absolute magnitude of -7.1

Sirius: absolute magnitude of +1.4

NUCLEAR FUSION IN MAIN SEQUENCE STARS LIKE THE SUN

Positron

Deuterium nucleus

Proton

Neutron

Proton (hydrogen nucleus)

Neutrino

Gamma rays

Helium-3 nucleus

Helium-4 nucleus

HERTZSPRUNG-RUSSELL DIAGRAM

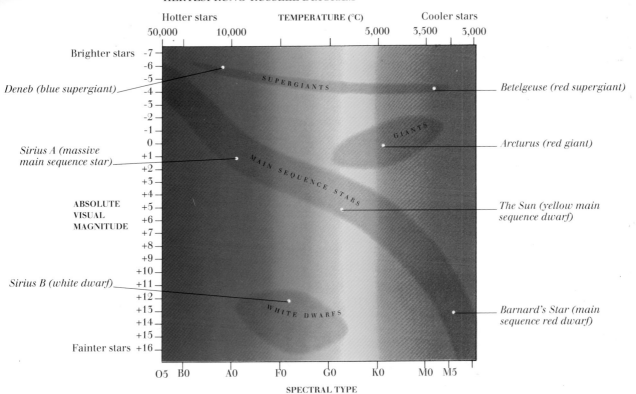

Hotter stars   TEMPERATURE (°C)   Cooler stars

50,000   10,000   5,000   3,500   3,000

Brighter stars

SUPERGIANTS

Deneb (blue supergiant)

Betelgeuse (red supergiant)

GIANTS

Sirius A (massive main sequence star)

Arcturus (red giant)

MAIN SEQUENCE STARS

ABSOLUTE VISUAL MAGNITUDE

The Sun (yellow main sequence dwarf)

Sirius B (white dwarf)

WHITE DWARFS

Barnard's Star (main sequence red dwarf)

Fainter stars

O5   B0   A0   F0   G0   K0   M0   M5

SPECTRAL TYPE

STELLAR SPECTRAL ABSORPTION LINES

Calcium line   Hydrogen gamma line   Hydrogen beta line   Helium line   Sodium lines   Hydrogen alpha line

STAR OF SPECTRAL TYPE A (e.g., SIRIUS)

STAR OF SPECTRAL TYPE G (e.g., THE SUN)

Hydrogen beta line   Magnesium lines   Sodium lines   Hydrogen alpha line

23

Small stars

REGION OF
STAR FORMATION
IN ORION

SMALL STARS HAVE A MASS of up to about one and a half times that of the Sun. They begin to form when a region of higher density in a nebula condenses into a huge globule of gas and dust that contracts under its own gravity. Within a globule, regions of condensing matter heat up and begin to glow, forming protostars. If a protostar contains enough matter, the central temperature reaches about 15 million °C. At this temperature, nuclear reactions in which hydrogen fuses to form helium can start. This process releases energy, which prevents the star from contracting further and also causes it to shine; it is now a main sequence star. A star of about one solar mass remains in the main sequence for about 10 billion years, until the hydrogen in the star's core has been converted into helium. The helium core then contracts again, and nuclear reactions continue in a shell around the core. The core becomes hot enough for helium to fuse to form carbon, while the outer layers of the star expand, cool, and shine less brightly. The expanding star is known as a red giant. When the helium in the core runs out, the outer layers of the star may drift off as an expanding gas shell called a planetary nebula. The remaining core (about 80 per cent of the original star) is now in its final stages. It becomes a white dwarf star that gradually cools and dims. When it finally stops shining altogether, the dead star will become a black dwarf.

STRUCTURE OF A MAIN SEQUENCE STAR

Core containing hydrogen fusing to form helium

Radiative zone

Convective zone

Surface temperature about 5,500°C

Core temperature about 15 million °C

STRUCTURE OF A NEBULA

Young main sequence star

Dense region of dust and gas (mainly hydrogen) condensing under gravity to form globules

Hot, ionized hydrogen gas emitting red light due to being stimulated by radiation from hot young stars

Dark globule of dust and gas (mainly hydrogen) contracting to form protostars

LIFE OF A SMALL STAR OF ABOUT ONE SOLAR MASS

Cool cloud of gas (mainly hydrogen) and dust

Dense globule condensing to form protostars

NEBULA

Glowing ball of gas (mainly hydrogen)

Natal cocoon (shell of dust blown away by radiation from protostar)

PROTOSTAR
Duration: 50 million years

About 1.4 million km

Star producing energy by nuclear fusion in core

MAIN SEQUENCE STAR
Duration: 10 billion years

STRUCTURE OF A RED GIANT

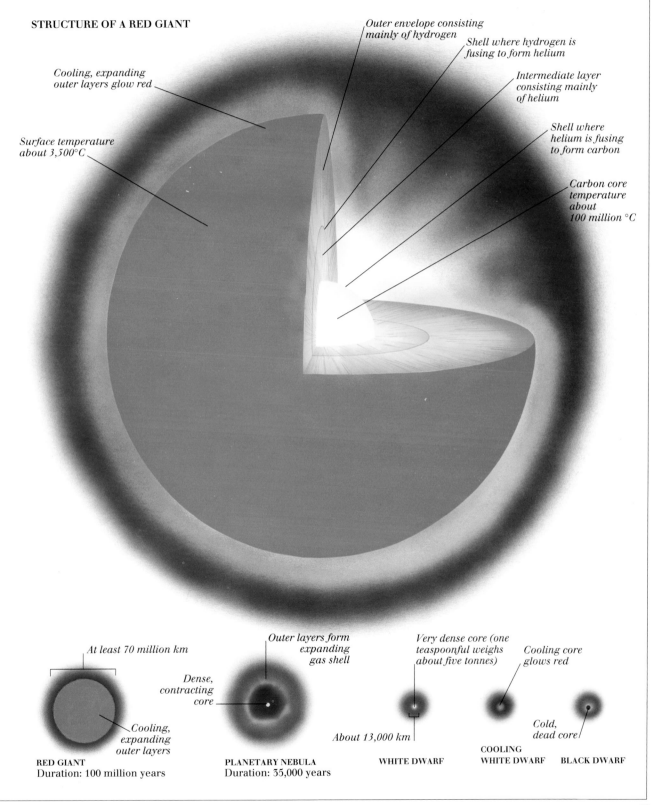

Cooling, expanding
outer layers glow red

Surface temperature
about 3,500°C

Outer envelope consisting
mainly of hydrogen

Shell where hydrogen is
fusing to form helium

Intermediate layer
consisting mainly
of helium

Shell where
helium is fusing
to form carbon

Carbon core
temperature
about
100 million °C

At least 70 million km

Cooling,
expanding
outer layers

RED GIANT
Duration: 100 million years

Outer layers form
expanding
gas shell

Dense,
contracting
core

PLANETARY NEBULA
Duration: 35,000 years

Very dense core (one
teaspoonful weighs
about five tonnes)

About 13,000 km

WHITE DWARF

Cooling core
glows red

Cold,
dead core

**COOLING
WHITE DWARF**

BLACK DWARF

Massive stars

MASSIVE STARS HAVE A MASS AT LEAST THREE TIMES that of the Sun, and some stars are as massive as about 50 Suns. A massive star evolves in a similar way to a small star until it reaches the main sequence stage (see pp. 24-25). During the main sequence, a star shines steadily until the hydrogen in its core has fused to form helium. This process takes billions of years in a small star, but only millions of years in a massive star. A massive star then becomes a red supergiant, which initially consists of a helium core surrounded by outer layers of cooling, expanding gas. Over the next few million years, a series of nuclear reactions form different elements in shells around an iron core. The core eventually collapses in less than a second, causing a massive explosion called a supernova, in which a shock wave blows away the outer layers of the star. Supernovae shine brighter than an entire galaxy for a short time. Sometimes, the core survives the supernova explosion. If the surviving core is between about one and a half and three solar masses, it contracts to become a tiny, dense neutron star. If the core is considerably greater than three solar masses, it contracts to become a black hole (see pp. 28-29).

SUPERNOVA

TARANTULA NEBULA BEFORE SUPERNOVA

STRUCTURE OF A RED SUPERGIANT

Outer envelope consisting mainly of hydrogen

Layer consisting mainly of helium

Layer consisting mainly of carbon

Layer consisting mainly of oxygen

Layer consisting mainly of silicon

Shell of hydrogen fusing to form helium

Shell of helium fusing to form carbon

Shell of carbon fusing to form oxygen

Shell of oxygen fusing to form silicon

Shell of silicon fusing to form iron core

Surface temperature about 3,000°C

Cooling, expanding outer layers glow red

Core of mainly iron at a temperature of 3–5 billion °C

LIFE OF A MASSIVE STAR OF ABOUT 10 SOLAR MASSES

Dense globule condensing to form protostars

Cool cloud of gas (mainly hydrogen) and dust

NEBULA

Glowing ball of gas (mainly hydrogen)

Natal cocoon (shell of dust blown away by radiation from protostar)

PROTOSTAR
Duration: a few hundred thousand years

About 3 million km

Star producing energy by nuclear fusion in core

MAIN SEQUENCE STAR
Duration: 10 million years

FEATURES OF A SUPERNOVA

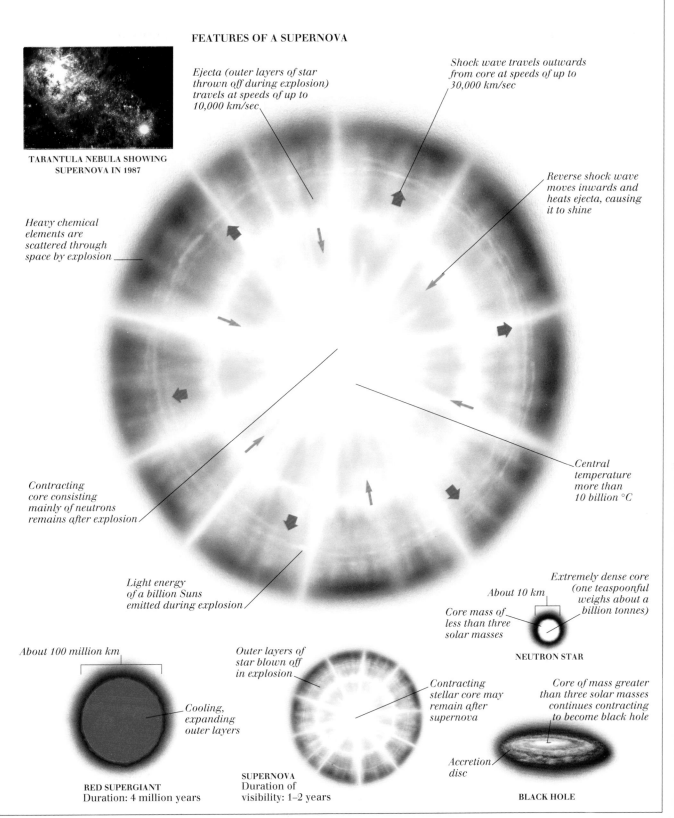

TARANTULA NEBULA SHOWING SUPERNOVA IN 1987

Ejecta (outer layers of star thrown off during explosion) travels at speeds of up to 10,000 km/sec

Shock wave travels outwards from core at speeds of up to 30,000 km/sec

Reverse shock wave moves inwards and heats ejecta, causing it to shine

Heavy chemical elements are scattered through space by explosion

Contracting core consisting mainly of neutrons remains after explosion

Central temperature more than 10 billion °C

Light energy of a billion Suns emitted during explosion

Extremely dense core (one teaspoonful weighs about a billion tonnes)

About 10 km

Core mass of less than three solar masses

NEUTRON STAR

About 100 million km

Outer layers of star blown off in explosion

Cooling, expanding outer layers

Contracting stellar core may remain after supernova

Core of mass greater than three solar masses continues contracting to become black hole

Accretion disc

RED SUPERGIANT
Duration: 4 million years

SUPERNOVA
Duration of visibility: 1–2 years

BLACK HOLE

27

Neutron stars and black holes

NEUTRON STARS AND BLACK HOLES form from the stellar cores that remain after stars have exploded as supernovae (see pp. 26-27). If the remaining core is between about one and a half and three solar masses, it contracts to form a neutron star. If the remaining core is greater than about three solar masses, it contracts to form a black hole. Neutron stars are typically only about 10 kilometres in diameter and consist almost entirely of subatomic particles called neutrons. Such stars are so dense that a teaspoonful would weigh about a billion tonnes. Neutron stars are observed as pulsars, so-called because they rotate rapidly and emit two beams of radio waves, which sweep across the sky and are detected as short pulses. Black holes are characterized by their extremely strong gravity, which is so powerful that not even light can escape; as a result, black holes are invisible. However, they may be detected if they have a close companion star. The gravity of the black hole pulls gas from the other star, forming an accretion disc that spirals around the black hole at high speed, heating up and emitting radiation. Eventually, the matter spirals in to cross the event horizon (the boundary of the black hole), thereby disappearing from the visible Universe.

X-ray emission from pulsar (neutron star rotating 30 times each second)

X-ray emission from centre of nebula

X-RAY IMAGE OF THE CRAB NEBULA (SUPERNOVA REMNANT)

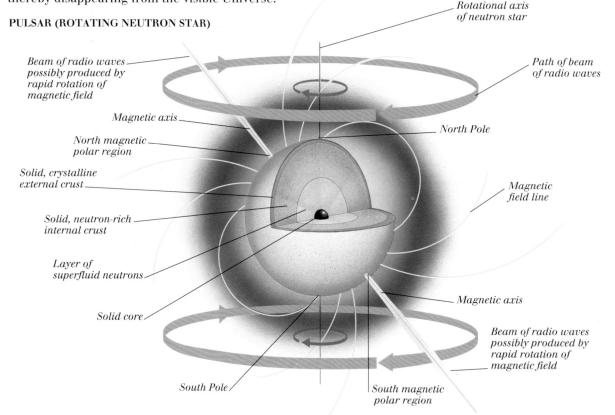

PULSAR (ROTATING NEUTRON STAR)

Rotational axis of neutron star

Beam of radio waves possibly produced by rapid rotation of magnetic field

Path of beam of radio waves

Magnetic axis

North magnetic polar region

North Pole

Solid, crystalline external crust

Magnetic field line

Solid, neutron-rich internal crust

Layer of superfluid neutrons

Solid core

Magnetic axis

Beam of radio waves possibly produced by rapid rotation of magnetic field

South Pole

South magnetic polar region

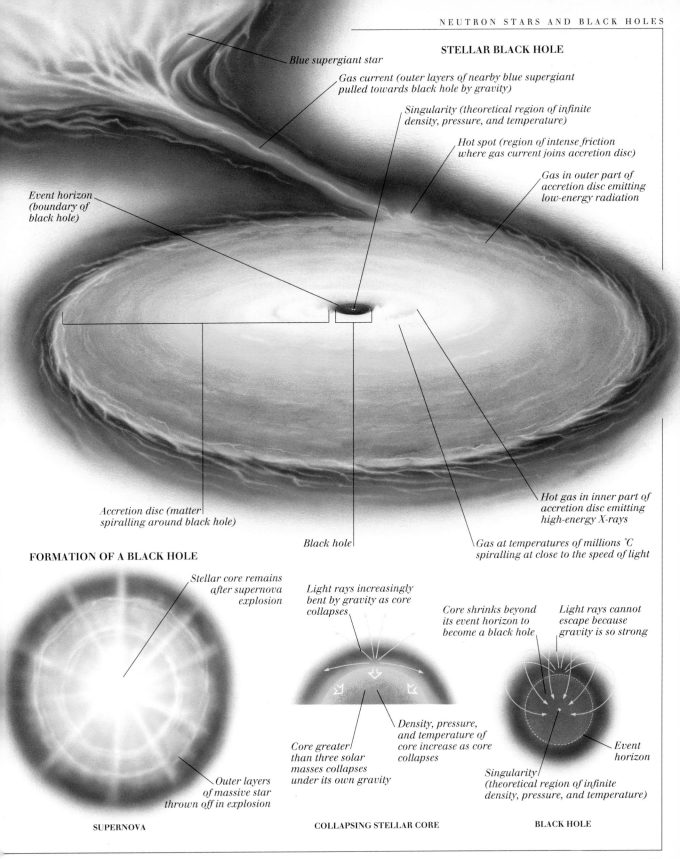

STELLAR BLACK HOLE

Blue supergiant star

Gas current (outer layers of nearby blue supergiant pulled towards black hole by gravity)

Singularity (theoretical region of infinite density, pressure, and temperature)

Hot spot (region of intense friction where gas current joins accretion disc)

Gas in outer part of accretion disc emitting low-energy radiation

Event horizon (boundary of black hole)

Accretion disc (matter spiralling around black hole)

Black hole

Gas at temperatures of millions °C spiralling at close to the speed of light

Hot gas in inner part of accretion disc emitting high-energy X-rays

FORMATION OF A BLACK HOLE

Stellar core remains after supernova explosion

Light rays increasingly bent by gravity as core collapses

Core shrinks beyond its event horizon to become a black hole

Light rays cannot escape because gravity is so strong

Density, pressure, and temperature of core increase as core collapses

Core greater than three solar masses collapses under its own gravity

Outer layers of massive star thrown off in explosion

Event horizon

Singularity (theoretical region of infinite density, pressure, and temperature)

SUPERNOVA

COLLAPSING STELLAR CORE

BLACK HOLE

The Solar System

THE SUN

THE SOLAR SYSTEM consists of a central star (the Sun) and the bodies that orbit it. These bodies include nine planets and their 61 known moons; asteroids; comets; and meteoroids. The Solar System also contains interplanetary gas and dust. Most of the planets fall into two groups: four small rocky planets near the Sun (Mercury, Venus, Earth, and Mars); and four planets further out, the gas giants (Jupiter, Saturn, Uranus, and Neptune). Pluto belongs to neither group but is very small, solid, and icy. Pluto is the outermost planet, except when it passes briefly inside Neptune's orbit. Between the rocky planets and gas giants is the asteroid belt, which contains thousands of chunks of rock orbiting the Sun. Most of the bodies in the Solar System move around the Sun in elliptical orbits located in a thin disc around the Sun's equator. All the planets orbit the Sun in the same direction (anticlockwise when viewed from above) and all but Venus, Uranus, and Pluto also spin about their axes in this direction. Moons also spin as they, in turn, orbit their planets. The entire Solar System orbits the centre of our galaxy, the Milky Way (see pp. 14-15).

PLANETARY ORBIT

Perihelion (orbital point closest to Sun)

Sun

Elliptical orbit

Planet orbiting Sun

Direction of planetary rotation

Aphelion (orbital point furthest from Sun)

Aphelion of Neptune: 4,537 million km

ORBITS OF INNER PLANETS

Average orbital speed of Venus: 35.03 km/sec

Average orbital speed of Mercury: 47.89 km/sec

Average orbital speed of Earth: 29.79 km/sec

Average orbital speed of Mars: 24.13 km/sec

Mercury

Perihelion of Mercury: 45.9 million km

Perihelion of Venus: 107.4 million km

Perihelion of Earth: 147 million km

Mars

Perihelion of Mars: 206.7 million km

Earth

Venus

Sun

Asteroid belt

Aphelion of Mercury: 69.7 million km

Aphelion of Venus: 109 million km

Aphelion of Earth: 152 million km

Aphelion of Mars: 249 million km

Aphelion of Pluto: 7,375 million km

MERCURY
Year: 87.97 Earth days
Mass: 0.06 Earth masses
Diameter: 4,878 km

VENUS
Year: 224.7 Earth days
Mass: 0.81 Earth masses
Diameter: 12,103 km

EARTH
Year: 365.26 days
Mass: 1 Earth mass
Diameter: 12,756 km

MARS
Year: 1.88 Earth years
Mass: 0.11 Earth masses
Diameter: 6,786 km

JUPITER
Year: 11.86 Earth years
Mass: 317.94 Earth masses
Diameter: 142,984 km

ORBITS OF OUTER PLANETS

Perihelion of Uranus: 2,735 million km

Inner planetary orbits

Sun

Perihelion of Saturn: 1,347 million km

Saturn

Perihelion of Jupiter: 740.9 million km

Aphelion of Saturn: 1,507 million km

Aphelion of Jupiter: 815.7 million km

Jupiter

Uranus

Average orbital speed of Jupiter: 13.06 km/sec

Aphelion of Uranus: 3,004 million km

Average orbital speed of Saturn: 9.64 km/sec

Average orbital speed of Uranus: 6.81 km/sec

Pluto

Direction of orbital motion

Neptune

Average orbital speed of Neptune: 5.43 km/sec

Average orbital speed of Pluto: 4.74 km/sec

INCLINATION OF PLANETARY ORBITS TO THE ECLIPTIC

Pluto: 17.2°
Mercury: 7°
Venus: 3.39°
Saturn: 2.49°
Mars: 1.85°
Neptune: 1.77°
Jupiter: 1.3°
Uranus: 0.77°

Ecliptic (Earth's orbital plane)

Earth: 0°

SATURN
Year: 29.46 Earth years
Mass: 95.18 Earth masses
Diameter: 120,536 km

URANUS
Year: 84.01 Earth years
Mass: 14.54 Earth masses
Diameter: 51,118 km

NEPTUNE
Year: 164.79 Earth years
Mass: 17.14 Earth masses
Diameter: 49,528 km

PLUTO
Year: 248.54 Earth years
Mass: 0.0022 Earth masses
Diameter: 2,300 km

31

The Sun

SOLAR PHOTOSPHERE

THE SUN IS THE STAR AT THE CENTRE of the Solar System. It is about five billion years old and will continue to shine as it does now for about another five billion years. The Sun is a yellow main sequence star (see pp. 22-23) about 1.4 million kilometres in diameter. It consists almost entirely of hydrogen and helium. In the Sun's core, hydrogen is converted to helium by nuclear fusion, releasing energy in the process. The energy travels from the core, through the radiative and convective zones, to the photosphere (visible surface), where it leaves the Sun in the form of heat and light. On the photosphere there are often dark, relatively cool areas called sunspots, which usually appear in pairs or groups and are thought to be caused by magnetic fields. Other types of solar activity are flares, which are usually associated with sunspots, and prominences. Flares are sudden discharges of high-energy radiation and atomic particles. Prominences are huge loops or filaments of gas extending into the solar atmosphere; some last for hours, others for months. Beyond the photosphere is the chromosphere (inner atmosphere) and the extremely rarified corona (outer atmosphere), which extends millions of kilometres into space. Tiny particles that escape from the corona give rise to the solar wind, which streams through space at hundreds of kilometres per second. The chromosphere and corona can be seen from Earth when the Sun is totally eclipsed by the Moon.

HOW A SOLAR ECLIPSE OCCURS

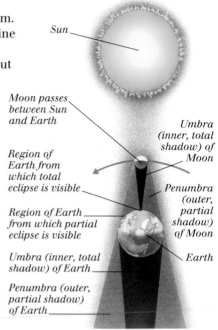

Sun

Moon passes between Sun and Earth

Umbra (inner, total shadow) of Moon

Region of Earth from which total eclipse is visible

Penumbra (outer, partial shadow) of Moon

Region of Earth from which partial eclipse is visible

Umbra (inner, total shadow) of Earth

Earth

Penumbra (outer, partial shadow) of Earth

SURFACE FEATURES

Gas loop (looped prominence)

Prominence (jet of gas at edge of Sun's disc up to hundreds of thousands of kilometres high)

Spicule (vertical jet of gas)

Photosphere (visible surface)

Chromosphere (inner atmosphere)

TOTAL SOLAR ECLIPSE

Corona (outer atmosphere of extremely hot, diffuse gas)

Moon covers Sun's disc

SUNSPOTS

Granulated surface of Sun

Penumbra (lighter, outer region) containing radial fibrils

Umbra (darker, inner region) temperature about 4,000°C

Photosphere temperature about 5,500°C

**EXTERNAL FEATURES AND
INTERNAL STRUCTURE OF THE SUN**

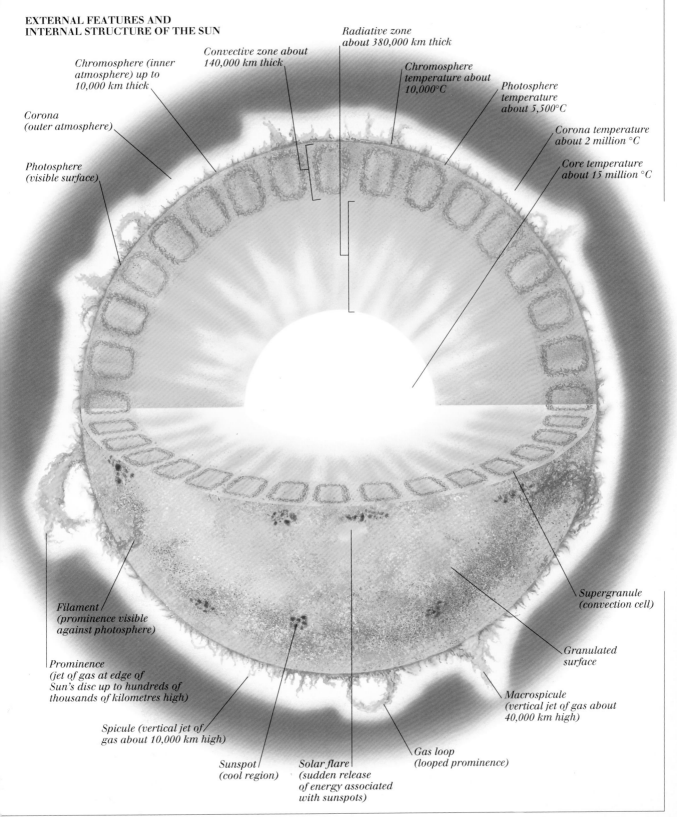

*Radiative zone
about 380,000 km thick*

*Convective zone about
140,000 km thick*

*Chromosphere (inner
atmosphere) up to
10,000 km thick*

*Chromosphere
temperature about
10,000°C*

*Photosphere
temperature
about 5,500°C*

*Corona
(outer atmosphere)*

*Corona temperature
about 2 million °C*

*Core temperature
about 15 million °C*

*Photosphere
(visible surface)*

*Filament
(prominence visible
against photosphere)*

*Prominence
(jet of gas at edge of
Sun's disc up to hundreds of
thousands of kilometres high)*

*Spicule (vertical jet of
gas about 10,000 km high)*

*Sunspot
(cool region)*

*Solar flare
(sudden release
of energy associated
with sunspots)*

*Gas loop
(looped prominence)*

*Macrospicule
(vertical jet of gas about
40,000 km high)*

*Granulated
surface*

*Supergranule
(convection cell)*

Mercury

MERCURY

MERCURY IS THE NEAREST PLANET to the Sun, orbiting at an average distance of about 58 million kilometres. Because Mercury is the closest planet to the Sun, it moves faster than any other planet, travelling at an average speed of nearly 48 kilometres per second and completing an orbit in just under 88 days. Mercury is very small (only Pluto is smaller) and rocky. Most of the surface has been heavily cratered by the impact of meteorites, although there are also smooth, sparsely cratered plains. The Caloris Basin is the largest crater, measuring about 1,300 kilometres across. It is thought to have been formed when a rock the size of an asteroid hit the planet, and is surrounded by concentric rings of mountains thrown up by the impact. The surface also has many ridges (called rupes) that are thought to have been formed when the hot core of the young planet cooled and shrank about four billion years ago, buckling the planet's surface in the process. The planet rotates about its axis very slowly, taking nearly 59 Earth days to complete one rotation. As a result, a solar day (sunrise to sunrise) on Mercury is about 176 Earth days – twice as long as the 88-day Mercurian year. Mercury has extreme surface temperatures, ranging from a maximum of 430°C on the sunlit side to -170°C on the dark side. At nightfall, the temperature drops very quickly because the planet's atmosphere is almost non-existent. It consists only of minute amounts of helium and hydrogen captured from the solar wind, plus traces of other gases.

TILT AND ROTATION OF MERCURY

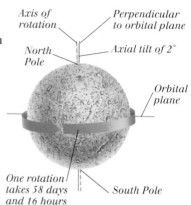

Axis of rotation

Perpendicular to orbital plane

North Pole

Axial tilt of 2°

Orbital plane

One rotation takes 58 days and 16 hours

South Pole

DEGAS AND BRONTË (RAY CRATERS)

Bright ray of ejecta (ejected material)

Brontë

Unmapped region

Degas with central peak

FORMATION OF A RAY CRATER

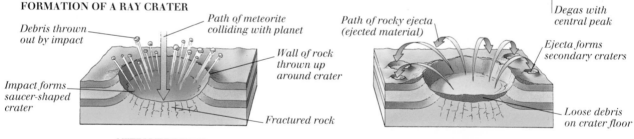

Debris thrown out by impact

Path of meteorite colliding with planet

Wall of rock thrown up around crater

Impact forms saucer-shaped crater

Fractured rock

METEORITE IMPACT

Path of rocky ejecta (ejected material)

Ejecta forms secondary craters

Loose debris on crater floor

SECONDARY CRATERING

Wall of rock forms ring of mountains

Ray of ejecta (ejected material)

Small secondary crater

Loose ejected rock

Central mountain rings form if floor of large crater recoils from meteorite impact

Falling debris forms ridges on side of wall

RAY CRATER

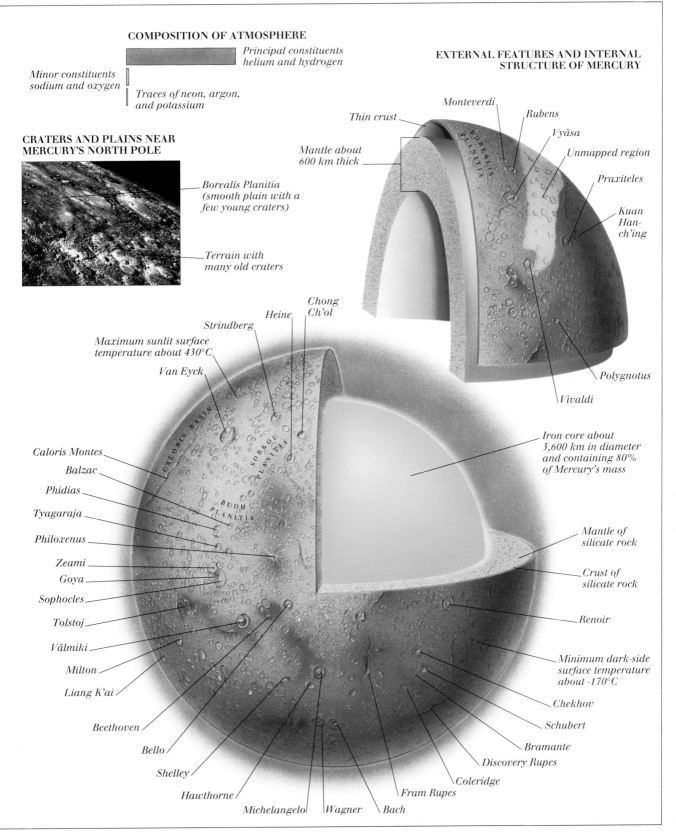

COMPOSITION OF ATMOSPHERE

Principal constituents helium and hydrogen

Minor constituents sodium and oxygen

Traces of neon, argon, and potassium

EXTERNAL FEATURES AND INTERNAL STRUCTURE OF MERCURY

Monteverdi

Rubens

Vyāsa

Thin crust

Unmapped region

Praxiteles

Mantle about 600 km thick

Kuan Han-ch'ing

CRATERS AND PLAINS NEAR MERCURY'S NORTH POLE

Borealis Planitia (smooth plain with a few young craters)

Terrain with many old craters

Polygnotus

Vivaldi

Chong Ch'ol

Heine

Strindberg

Maximum sunlit surface temperature about 430°C

Van Eyck

Iron core about 3,600 km in diameter and containing 80% of Mercury's mass

Caloris Montes

Balzac

Phidias

Tyagaraja

Philoxenus

Mantle of silicate rock

Zeami

Goya

Crust of silicate rock

Sophocles

Tolstoj

Renoir

Vālmiki

Milton

Minimum dark-side surface temperature about -170°C

Liang K'ai

Chekhov

Beethoven

Schubert

Bello

Bramante

Shelley

Discovery Rupes

Hawthorne

Coleridge

Michelangelo

Wagner

Bach

Fram Rupes

CALORIS BASIN

SOBKOU PLANITIA

BUDH PLANITIA

55

Venus

RADAR IMAGE OF VENUS

VENUS IS A ROCKY PLANET and the second planet from the Sun. Venus spins slowly backwards as it orbits the Sun, causing its rotational period to be the longest in the Solar System, at about 243 Earth days. It is slightly smaller than Earth and probably has a similar internal structure, consisting of a semi-solid metal core, surrounded by a rocky mantle and crust. Venus is the brightest object in the sky after the Sun and Moon because its atmosphere reflects sunlight strongly. The main component of the atmosphere is carbon dioxide, which traps heat in a greenhouse effect far stronger than that on Earth. As a result, Venus is the hottest planet, with a maximum surface temperature of about 480°C. The thick cloud layers contain droplets of sulphuric acid and are driven around the planet by winds at speeds of up to 360 kilometres per hour. Although the planet takes 243 Earth days to rotate once, the high-speed winds cause the clouds to circle the planet in only four Earth days. The high temperature, acidic clouds, and enormous atmospheric pressure (about 90 times greater at the surface than that on Earth) make the environment extremely hostile. However, space probes have managed to land on Venus and photograph its dry, dusty surface. The Venusian surface has also been mapped by probes with radar equipment that can "see" through the cloud layers. Such radar maps reveal a terrain with craters, mountains, volcanoes, and areas where craters have been covered by plains of solidified volcanic lava. There are two large highland regions called Aphrodite Terra and Ishtar Terra.

TILT AND ROTATION OF VENUS

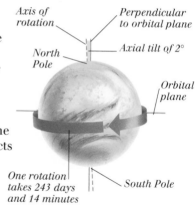

Axis of rotation
Perpendicular to orbital plane
Axial tilt of 2°
North Pole
Orbital plane
One rotation takes 243 days and 14 minutes
South Pole

CLOUD FEATURES

Polar hood
Dark, mid-latitude band
Cloud features swept around planet by winds of up to 360 km/h
Dirty yellow hue due to sulphuric acid in atmosphere
Bright polar band

VENUSIAN CRATERS

Danilova
Ejecta (ejected material)
Central peak
Howe

FALSE-COLOUR RADAR MAP OF THE SURFACE OF VENUS

Metis Regio
Maxwell Montes
Bell Regio
Tethus Regio
Atalanta Planitia
Sedna Planitia
Leda Planitia
Eisila Regio
Tellus Regio
Guinevere Planitia
Niobe Planitia
Phoebe Regio
Alpha Regio
Ovda Regio
Themis Regio
Thetis Regio
Lavinia Planitia
Aino Planitia
Helen Planitia
Lada Terra

ISHTAR TERRA
APHRODITE TERRA

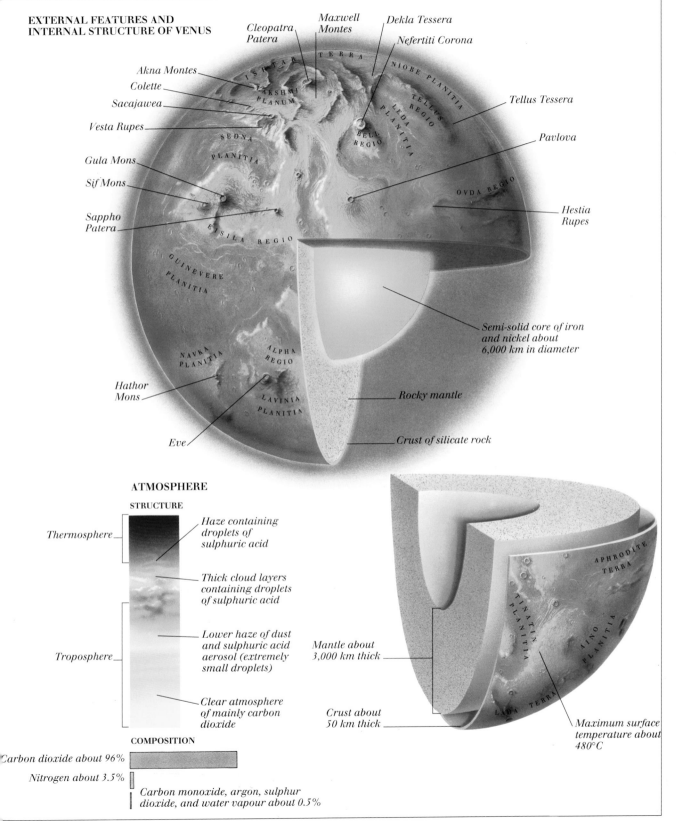

EXTERNAL FEATURES AND INTERNAL STRUCTURE OF VENUS

Cleopatra Patera

Maxwell Montes

Dekla Tessera

Nefertiti Corona

Akna Montes

Colette

Sacajawea

Vesta Rupes

Gula Mons

Sif Mons

Sappho Patera

Hathor Mons

Eve

Tellus Tessera

Pavlova

Hestia Rupes

Semi-solid core of iron and nickel about 6,000 km in diameter

Rocky mantle

Crust of silicate rock

ATMOSPHERE

STRUCTURE

Thermosphere

Troposphere

Haze containing droplets of sulphuric acid

Thick cloud layers containing droplets of sulphuric acid

Lower haze of dust and sulphuric acid aerosol (extremely small droplets)

Clear atmosphere of mainly carbon dioxide

Mantle about 3,000 km thick

Crust about 50 km thick

Maximum surface temperature about 480°C

COMPOSITION

Carbon dioxide about 96%

Nitrogen about 3.5%

Carbon monoxide, argon, sulphur dioxide, and water vapour about 0.5%

The Earth

THE EARTH

THE EARTH IS THE THIRD of the nine planets that orbit the Sun. It is the largest and densest rocky planet, and the only one known to support life. About 70 per cent of the Earth's surface is covered by water, which is not found in liquid form on the surface of any other planet. There are four main layers: the inner core, the outer core, the mantle, and the crust. At the heart of the planet the solid inner core has a temperature of about 4,000°C. The heat from this inner core causes material in the molten outer core and mantle to circulate in convection currents. It is thought that these convection currents generate the Earth's magnetic field, which extends into space as the magnetosphere. The Earth's atmosphere helps screen out some of the harmful radiation from the Sun, stops meteorites from reaching the planet's surface, and traps enough heat to prevent extremes of cold. The Earth has one natural satellite, the Moon, which is large enough for both bodies to be considered a double-planet system.

TILT AND ROTATION OF THE EARTH

Axis of rotation

Axial tilt of 23.4°

North Pole

Orbital plane

South Pole

Perpendicular to orbital plane

One rotation takes 23 hours and 56 minutes

THE FORMATION OF THE EARTH

The heat of the collisions caused the planet to glow red

The cloud broke up into particles of ice and rock, which stuck together to form planets

Micro-organisms began to photosynthesize, creating a build up of oxygen

4,600 MILLION YEARS AGO, THE SOLAR SYSTEM FORMED FROM A CLOUD OF GAS AND DUST

THE EARTH WAS FORMED FROM COLLIDING ROCKS

4,500 MILLION YEARS AGO THE SURFACE COOLED TO FORM THE CRUST

THE CONTINENTS BROKE UP AND REFORMED, GRADUALLY TAKING THEIR PRESENT POSITIONS

Solar wind enters atmosphere and produces aurora

Magnetosphere (magnetic field)

Solar wind (stream of electrically charged particles)

THE EARTH'S MAGNETOSPHERE

Van Allen radiation belt

Earth

Axis of geographic poles

Axis of magnetic poles

**EXTERNAL FEATURES AND
INTERNAL STRUCTURE
OF THE EARTH**

Greenland

Atmosphere about
500 km deep

Crust 6–40 km thick

NORTH ATLANTIC
OCEAN

Mantle about
2,800 km
thick

Outer core
about 2,300 km
thick

Cyclonic
storm

COMPOSITION OF THE EARTH

Other elements less than 1%

Aluminium 0.4%

Calcium 0.6%

Sulphur 2.7%

Nickel 2.7%

Silicon 13%

Magnesium 17%

Oxygen 28%

Iron 35%

Core temperature about 4,000°C

Surface temperature
between about -88°C
and 58°C

Molten core of iron
and nickel

Solid inner core
of iron and nickel
about 2,400 km
in diameter

Gutenberg discontinuity
(boundary between outer
core and mantle)

EUROPE

Mantle of mostly solid
silicate material

AFRICA

Atlas Mountains

Sahara (desert
region)

Mohorovicic
discontinuity
(boundary
between mantle
and crust)

Congo Basin
(tropical
rain-forest)

Crust of silicate rock

SOUTH
PACIFIC
OCEAN

SOUTH
AMERICA

SOUTH ATLANTIC
OCEAN

Amazon Basin (tropical
rain-forest region)

Land forms about
30% of surface

Andes (mountain range
near crustal plate
boundary)

Cloud typically covers
about 50% of surface

Earthquake region along
crustal plate boundary

Oceans cover about
70% of surface

The Moon

THE MOON FROM EARTH

THE MOON IS THE EARTH'S only natural satellite. It is relatively large for a moon, with a diameter of about 3,470 kilometres – just over a quarter that of the Earth. The Moon takes the same time to rotate on its axis as it takes to orbit the Earth (27.3 days), and so the same side (the near side) always faces us. However, the amount of the surface we can see – the phase of the Moon – depends on how much of the near side is in sunlight. The Moon is dry and barren, with no atmosphere or water. It consists mainly of solid rock, although its core may contain molten rock or iron. The surface is dusty, with highlands covered in craters caused by meteorite impacts, and lowlands in which large craters have been filled by solidified lava to form dark areas called maria or "seas". Maria occur mainly on the near side, which has a thinner crust than the far side. Many of the craters are rimmed by mountain ranges that form the crater walls and can be thousands of metres high.

TILT AND ROTATION OF THE MOON

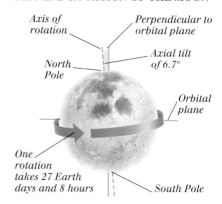

Axis of rotation

Perpendicular to orbital plane

North Pole

Axial tilt of 6.7°

Orbital plane

One rotation takes 27 Earth days and 8 hours

South Pole

CRATERS ON OCEANUS PROCELLARUM

Aristarchus

Cobra Head (head of Schröter's Valley)

Herodotus

NEAR SIDE OF THE MOON

De la Rue
Aristoteles
Aristillus
Plato
Archimedes
Montes Jura
Sinus Iridum
Bright rays of ejected material
Copernicus
Aristarchus
Kepler
Encke
Flamsteed
Fra Mauro
Grimaldi
Letronne
Gassendi
Mersenius
Pitatus
Schickard
Alphonsus
Bailly
Tycho
Clavius
Maginus
Deslandres
Stöfler
Walter
Arzachel
Ptolemaeus
Albategnius
Rupes Altai
Catharina
Furnerius
Fracastorius
Petavius
Cyrillus
Vendelinus
Langrenus
Julius Caesar
Macrobius
Cleomedes
Montes Apenninus
Atlas
Hercules

Hercules
Atlas

MARE FRIGORIS
MARE IMBRIUM
MARE SERENITATIS
MARE CRISIUM
MARE VAPORUM
MARE TRANQUILLITATIS
MARE FECUNDITATIS
MARE NECTARIS
MARE NUBIUM
MARE HUMORUM
OCEANUS PROCELLARUM

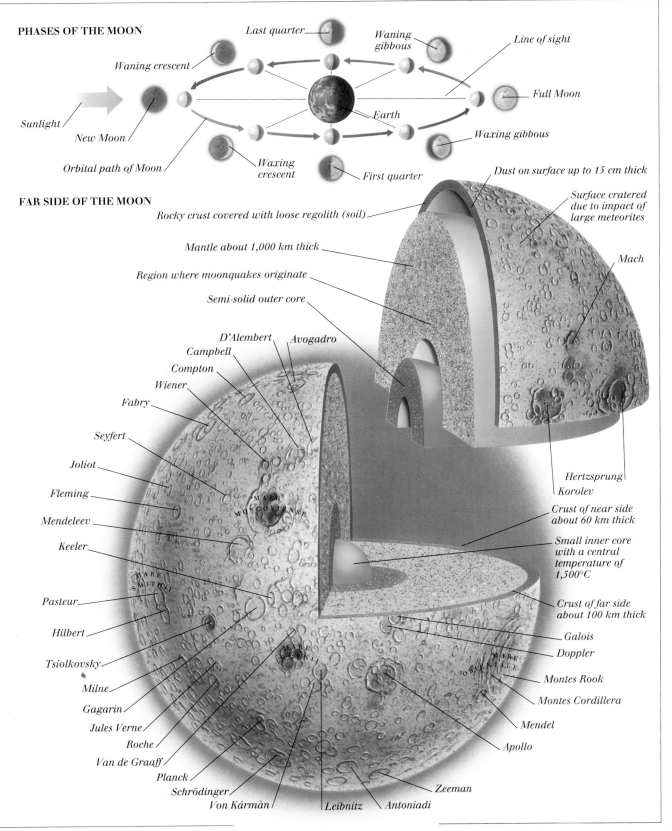

PHASES OF THE MOON

Last quarter

Waning gibbous

Waning crescent

Line of sight

Sunlight

Full Moon

New Moon

Earth

Orbital path of Moon

Waxing gibbous

Waxing crescent

First quarter

FAR SIDE OF THE MOON

Dust on surface up to 15 cm thick

Rocky crust covered with loose regolith (soil)

Surface cratered due to impact of large meteorites

Mantle about 1,000 km thick

Region where moonquakes originate

Mach

Semi-solid outer core

D'Alembert

Avogadro

Campbell

Compton

Wiener

Fabry

Seyfert

Joliot

Fleming

Mendeleev

MARE MOSCOVIENSE

Keeler

Hertzsprung

Korolev

Crust of near side about 60 km thick

MARE SMYTHII

Small inner core with a central temperature of 1,500°C

Pasteur

Hilbert

Crust of far side about 100 km thick

Tsiolkovsky

MARE INGENII

Galois

Milne

Doppler

MARE ORIENTALE

Gagarin

Montes Rook

Jules Verne

Montes Cordillera

Roche

Van de Graaff

Mendel

Planck

Apollo

Schrödinger

Von Kármàn

Zeeman

Leibnitz

Antoniadi

Mars

MARS

MARS, KNOWN AS THE RED PLANET, is the fourth planet from the Sun and the outermost rocky planet. In the 19th century, astronomers first observed what were thought to be signs of life on Mars. These signs included apparent canal-like markings on the surface, and dark patches that were thought to be vegetation. It is now known that the "canals" are an optical illusion, and the dark patches are areas where the red dust that covers most of the planet has been blown away. The fine dust particles are often whipped up by winds into dust storms that occasionally obscure almost all the surface. Residual dust in the atmosphere gives the Martian sky a pinkish hue. The northern hemisphere of Mars has many large plains formed of solidified volcanic lava, whereas the southern hemisphere has many craters and large impact basins. There are also several huge, extinct volcanoes, including Olympus Mons, which, at 600 kilometres across and 25 kilometres high, is the largest known volcano in the Solar System. The surface also has many canyons and branching channels. The canyons were formed by movements of the surface crust, but the channels are thought to have been formed by flowing water that has now dried up. The Martian atmosphere is much thinner than Earth's, with only a few clouds and morning mists. Mars has two tiny, irregularly shaped moons called Phobos and Deimos. Their small size indicates that they may be asteroids that have been captured by the gravity of Mars.

TILT AND ROTATION OF MARS

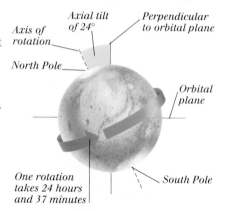

Axial tilt of 24°

Axis of rotation

Perpendicular to orbital plane

North Pole

Orbital plane

One rotation takes 24 hours and 37 minutes

South Pole

SURFACE FEATURES OF MARS

Bright water-ice fog

Fog in canyon about 20 km wide at end of Valles Marineris

Syria Planum

NOCTIS LABYRINTHUS (CANYON SYSTEM)

Summit caldera consisting of overlapping collapsed volcanic craters

Crater

Gentle slope produced by lava flow

Cloud formation

OLYMPUS MONS (EXTINCT SHIELD VOLCANO)

THE SURFACE OF MARS

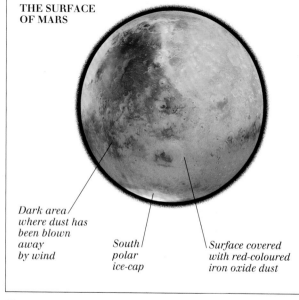

Dark area where dust has been blown away by wind

South polar ice-cap

Surface covered with red-coloured iron oxide dust

MOONS OF MARS

PHOBOS
Average diameter: 22 km
Average distance from planet: 9,400 km

DEIMOS
Average diameter: 13 km
Average distance from planet: 23,500 km

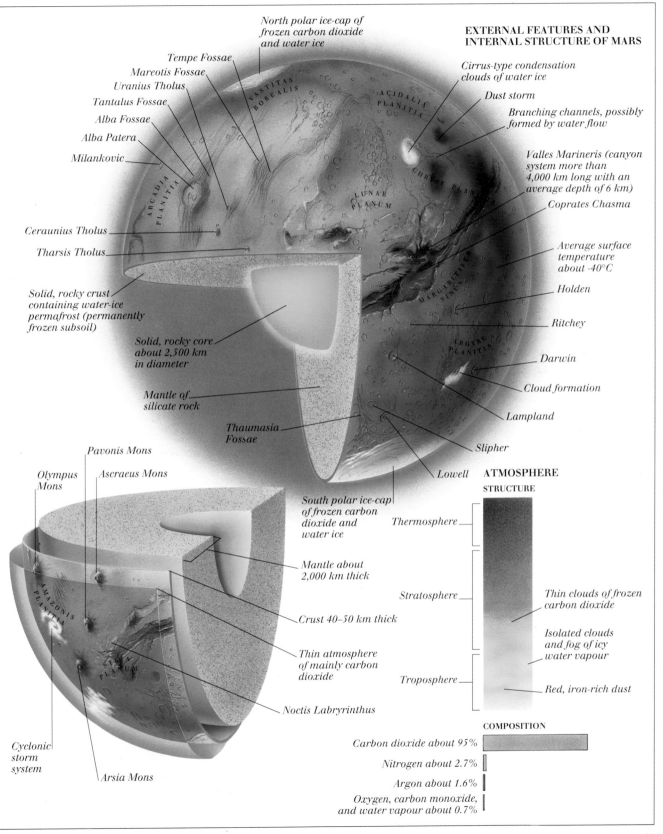

North polar ice-cap of frozen carbon dioxide and water ice

Tempe Fossae

Mareotis Fossae

Uranius Tholus

Tantalus Fossae

Alba Fossae

Alba Patera

Milankovic

Ceraunius Tholus

Tharsis Tholus

Solid, rocky crust containing water-ice permafrost (permanently frozen subsoil)

Solid, rocky core about 2,500 km in diameter

Mantle of silicate rock

Thaumasia Fossae

EXTERNAL FEATURES AND INTERNAL STRUCTURE OF MARS

Cirrus-type condensation clouds of water ice

Dust storm

Branching channels, possibly formed by water flow

Valles Marineris (canyon system more than 4,000 km long with an average depth of 6 km)

Coprates Chasma

Average surface temperature about -40°C

Holden

Ritchey

Darwin

Cloud formation

Lampland

Slipher

Lowell

South polar ice-cap of frozen carbon dioxide and water ice

Olympus Mons

Pavonis Mons

Ascraeus Mons

Cyclonic storm system

Arsia Mons

Mantle about 2,000 km thick

Crust 40–50 km thick

Thin atmosphere of mainly carbon dioxide

Noctis Labryrinthus

ATMOSPHERE

STRUCTURE

Thermosphere

Stratosphere

Troposphere

Thin clouds of frozen carbon dioxide

Isolated clouds and fog of icy water vapour

Red, iron-rich dust

COMPOSITION

Carbon dioxide about 95%

Nitrogen about 2.7%

Argon about 1.6%

Oxygen, carbon monoxide, and water vapour about 0.7%

Jupiter

JUPITER

JUPITER IS THE FIFTH PLANET from the Sun and the first of the four gas giants. It is the largest and the most massive planet, with a diameter about 11 times that of the Earth and a mass about 2.5 times the combined mass of the eight other planets. Jupiter is thought to have a small rocky core surrounded by an inner mantle of metallic hydrogen (liquid hydrogen that acts like a metal). Outside the inner mantle is an outer mantle of liquid hydrogen and helium that merges into the gaseous atmosphere. Jupiter's rapid rate of rotation causes the clouds in its atmosphere to form belts and zones that encircle the planet parallel to the equator. Belts are dark, low-lying, relatively warm cloud layers, and zones are bright, high-altitude, cooler cloud layers. Within the belts and zones, turbulence causes the formation of cloud features such as white ovals and red spots, both of which are huge storm systems. The most prominent cloud feature is a storm called the Great Red Spot, which consists of a spiralling column of clouds three times wider than the Earth that rises about eight kilometres above the upper cloud layer. Jupiter has one thin, faint, main ring, inside which is a tenuous halo ring of tiny particles extending towards the planet. There are 16 known Jovian moons. The four largest moons (called the Galileans) are Ganymede, Callisto, Io, and Europa. Ganymede and Callisto are cratered and probably icy. Europa is smooth and icy and may contain water. Io is covered in bright red, orange, and yellow splotches. This colouring is caused by sulphurous material from active volcanoes that shoot plumes of lava hundreds of kilometres above the surface.

TILT AND ROTATION OF JUPITER

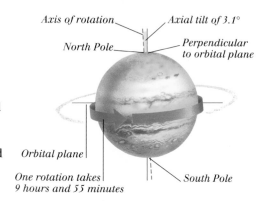

Axis of rotation

Axial tilt of 3.1°

North Pole

Perpendicular to orbital plane

Orbital plane

One rotation takes 9 hours and 55 minutes

South Pole

GREAT RED SPOT AND WHITE OVAL

Great Red Spot (anticyclonic storm system)

Red colour probably due to phosphorus

White oval (temporary anticyclonic storm system)

RINGS OF JUPITER

Main ring

Halo ring

GALILEAN MOONS OF JUPITER

EUROPA
Diameter: 3,138 km
Average distance from planet: 670,900 km

CALLISTO
Diameter: 4,800 km
Average distance from planet: 1,880,000 km

GANYMEDE
Diameter: 5,262 km
Average distance from planet: 1,070,000 km

IO
Diameter: 3,642 km
Average distance from planet: 421,800 km

ATMOSPHERE

STRUCTURE

EXTERNAL FEATURES AND INTERNAL STRUCTURE OF JUPITER

Stratosphere

Troposphere

White clouds of
ammonia crystals

Dark orange
clouds of ammonium
hydrosulphide crystals

Bluish clouds of water
ice and water droplets

COMPOSITION

Hydrogen about 90%

Helium about 10%

Traces of ammonia,
methane, and water
vapour

Atmosphere of mainly
hydrogen and helium

Outer mantle
merging into
atmosphere

Inner mantle about
30,000 km thick

Zone (high-pressure
region of rising gases)

Red
spot

Plume
(trailing
cloud)

High-altitude
white cloud

North polar
aurora

North Temperate Zone

North Temperate Belt

North Tropical
Zone

North Equatorial
Belt

Equatorial Zone

South
Equatorial Belt

South
Tropical Zone

South
Temperate Belt

South
Temperate Zone

Flash of lightning

Great Red Spot
(anticyclonic
storm system)

Outer mantle of liquid
hydrogen and helium

Inner mantle of
metallic hydrogen

Rocky core about
28,000 km in diameter

Core temperature
about 30,000°C

Belt (low-pressure
region of sinking
gases)

White oval
(temporary
anticyclonic
storm system)

Cloud-top
temperature
about -120°C

Saturn

FALSE-COLOUR
IMAGE OF SATURN

SATURN IS THE SIXTH PLANET from the Sun. It is a gas giant almost as big as Jupiter, with an equatorial diameter of about 120,500 kilometres. Saturn is thought to consist of a small core of rock and ice surrounded by an inner mantle of metallic hydrogen (liquid hydrogen that acts like a metal). Outside the inner mantle is an outer mantle of liquid hydrogen that merges into a gaseous atmosphere. Saturn's clouds form belts and zones similar to those on Jupiter, but obscured by overlying haze. Storms and eddies, seen as red or white ovals, occur in the clouds. Saturn has an extremely thin but wide system of rings that is less than one kilometre thick but extends outwards to about 420,000 kilometres from the planet's surface. The main rings comprise thousands of narrow ringlets, each made of icy lumps that range in size from tiny particles to chunks several metres across. The D, E, and G rings are very faint, the F ring is brighter, and the A, B, and C rings are bright enough to be seen from Earth with binoculars. Saturn has 18 known moons, some of which orbit inside the rings and are thought to exert a gravitational influence on the shapes of the rings. Unusually, seven of the moons are co-orbital – they share an orbit with another moon. Astronomers believe that such co-orbital moons may have originated from a single satellite that broke up.

TILT AND ROTATION OF SATURN

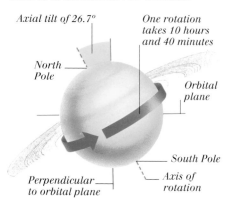

Axial tilt of 26.7°

One rotation takes 10 hours and 40 minutes

North Pole

Orbital plane

South Pole

Perpendicular to orbital plane

Axis of rotation

FALSE-COLOUR IMAGE OF SATURN'S CLOUD FEATURES

Ribbon-shaped striation caused by winds of up to 540 km/h

Oval (rotating storm system)

INNER RINGS OF SATURN

D ring

C ring ("crepe ring")

B ring

Cassini Division

A ring

Encke Division

F ring

MOONS OF SATURN

ENCELADUS
Diameter: 498 km
Average distance from planet: 238,000 km

TETHYS
Diameter: 1,050 km
Average distance from planet: 295,000 km

DIONE
Diameter: 1,118 km
Average distance from planet: 377,000 km

MIMAS
Diameter: 397 km
Average distance from planet: 186,000 km

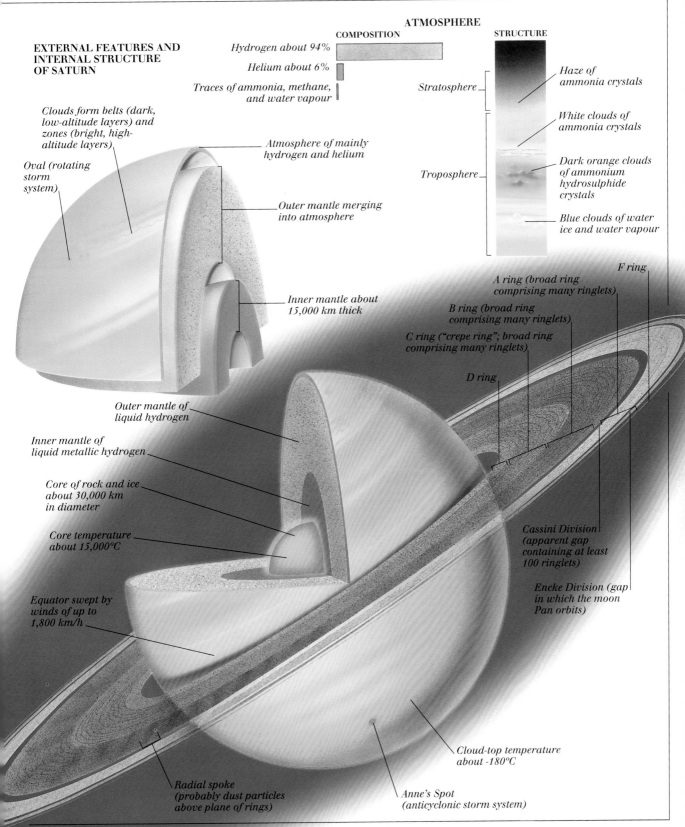

ATMOSPHERE

EXTERNAL FEATURES AND INTERNAL STRUCTURE OF SATURN

COMPOSITION

Hydrogen about 94%

Helium about 6%

Traces of ammonia, methane, and water vapour

STRUCTURE

Stratosphere

Troposphere

Haze of ammonia crystals

White clouds of ammonia crystals

Dark orange clouds of ammonium hydrosulphide crystals

Blue clouds of water ice and water vapour

Clouds form belts (dark, low-altitude layers) and zones (bright, high-altitude layers)

Oval (rotating storm system)

Atmosphere of mainly hydrogen and helium

Outer mantle merging into atmosphere

Inner mantle about 15,000 km thick

F ring

A ring (broad ring comprising many ringlets)

B ring (broad ring comprising many ringlets)

C ring ("crepe ring"; broad ring comprising many ringlets)

D ring

Outer mantle of liquid hydrogen

Inner mantle of liquid metallic hydrogen

Core of rock and ice about 30,000 km in diameter

Core temperature about 15,000°C

Cassini Division (apparent gap containing at least 100 ringlets)

Encke Division (gap in which the moon Pan orbits)

Equator swept by winds of up to 1,800 km/h

Cloud-top temperature about -180°C

Radial spoke (probably dust particles above plane of rings)

Anne's Spot (anticyclonic storm system)

Uranus

FALSE-COLOUR IMAGE OF URANUS

URANUS IS THE SEVENTH PLANET from the Sun and the third largest, with a diameter of about 51,000 kilometres. It is thought to consist of a dense mixture of different types of ice and gas around a solid core. Its atmosphere contains traces of methane, giving the planet a blue-green hue, and the temperature at the cloud tops is about -210°C. Uranus is the most featureless planet to have been closely observed: only a few icy clouds of methane have been seen so far. Uranus is unique among the planets in that its axis of rotation lies close to its orbital plane. As a result of its strongly tilted rotational axis, Uranus rolls on its side along its orbital path around the Sun, whereas other planets spin more or less upright. Uranus is encircled by 11 rings that consist of rocks interspersed with dust lanes. The rings contain some of the darkest matter in the Solar System and are extremely narrow, making them difficult to detect: nine of them are less than 10 kilometres wide, whereas most of Saturn's rings are thousands of kilometres in width. There are 15 known Uranian moons, all of which are icy and most of which are further out than the rings. The 10 inner moons are small and dark, with diameters of less than 160 kilometres, and the five outer moons are between about 470 and 1,600 kilometres in diameter. The outer moons have a wide variety of surface features. Miranda has the most varied surface, with cratered areas broken up by huge ridges and cliffs 20 kilometres high.

TILT AND ROTATION OF URANUS

Axial tilt of 97.9°

Perpendicular to orbital plane

Orbital plane

South Pole

Axis of rotation

North Pole

One rotation takes 17 hours and 14 minutes

OUTER MOONS

MIRANDA
Diameter: 472 km
Average distance from planet: 129,800 km

RINGS OF URANUS

Epsilon ring

Ring 1986 U1R

Delta ring

Gamma ring

Eta ring

Beta ring

Alpha ring

Rings 4 and 5

Ring 6

Ring 1986 U2R

RINGS AND DUST LANES

ARIEL
Diameter: 1,158 km
Average distance from planet: 191,200 km

UMBRIEL
Diameter: 1,169 km
Average distance from planet: 266,000 km

TITANIA
Diameter: 1,578 km
Average distance from planet: 435,900 km

OBERON
Diameter: 1,523 km
Average distance from planet: 582,600 km

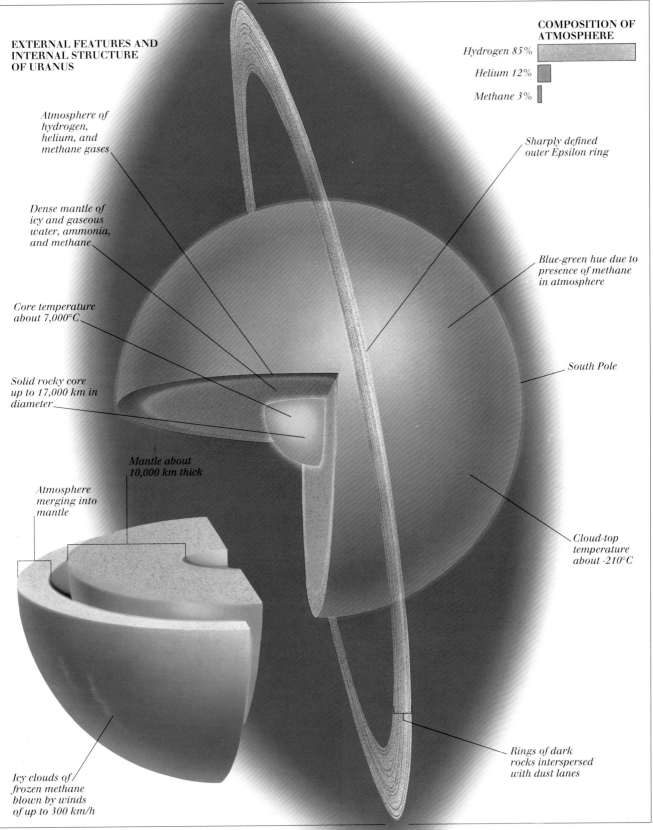

**EXTERNAL FEATURES AND
INTERNAL STRUCTURE
OF URANUS**

**COMPOSITION OF
ATMOSPHERE**

Hydrogen 85%

Helium 12%

Methane 3%

Atmosphere of
hydrogen,
helium, and
methane gases

Dense mantle of
icy and gaseous
water, ammonia,
and methane

Core temperature
about 7,000°C

Solid rocky core
up to 17,000 km in
diameter

Mantle about
10,000 km thick

Atmosphere
merging into
mantle

Icy clouds of
frozen methane
blown by winds
of up to 300 km/h

Sharply defined
outer Epsilon ring

Blue-green hue due to
presence of methane
in atmosphere

South Pole

Cloud-top
temperature
about -210°C

Rings of dark
rocks interspersed
with dust lanes

Neptune and Pluto

FALSE-COLOUR
IMAGE OF NEPTUNE

NEPTUNE AND PLUTO are the two furthest planets from the Sun, at an average distance of about 4,500 million kilometres and 5,900 million kilometres respectively. Neptune is a gas giant and is thought to consist of a small rocky core surrounded by a mixture of liquids and gases. The atmosphere contains several prominent cloud features. The largest of these are the Great Dark Spot, which is as wide as the Earth, the Small Dark Spot, and the Scooter. The Great and Small Dark Spots are huge storms that are swept around the planet by winds of about 2,000 kilometres per hour. The Scooter is a large area of cirrus cloud. Neptune has four tenuous rings and eight known moons. Triton is the largest Neptunian moon and the coldest object in the Solar System, with a temperature of -235°C. Unlike most moons in the Solar System, Triton orbits its mother planet in the opposite direction to the planet's rotation. Pluto is usually the outermost planet but its elliptical orbit causes it to pass inside the orbit of Neptune for 20 years of its 248-year orbit. Pluto is so small and far away that little is known about it. It is a rocky planet, probably covered with ice and frozen methane. Pluto's only known moon, Charon, is large for a moon, at half the size of its parent planet. Because of the small difference in their sizes, Pluto and Charon are sometimes considered to be a double-planet system.

TILT AND ROTATION OF NEPTUNE

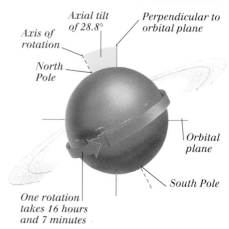

Axial tilt of 28.8°

Perpendicular to orbital plane

Axis of rotation

North Pole

Orbital plane

South Pole

One rotation takes 16 hours and 7 minutes

CLOUD FEATURES OF NEPTUNE

Great Dark Spot (anticyclonic wind storm)

Scooter (cirrus cloud)

Small Dark Spot (cyclonic wind storm)

RINGS OF NEPTUNE

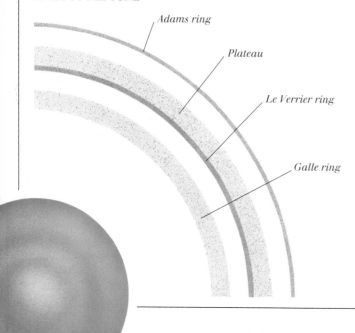

Adams ring

Plateau

Le Verrier ring

Galle ring

HIGH-ALTITUDE CLOUDS

Methane cirrus clouds 40 km above main cloud deck

Cloud shadow

Main cloud deck blown by winds at speeds of about 2,000 km/h

MOONS OF NEPTUNE

TRITON
Diameter: 2,705 km
Average distance from planet: 354,800 km

PROTEUS
Diameter: 416 km
Average distance from planet: 117,600 km

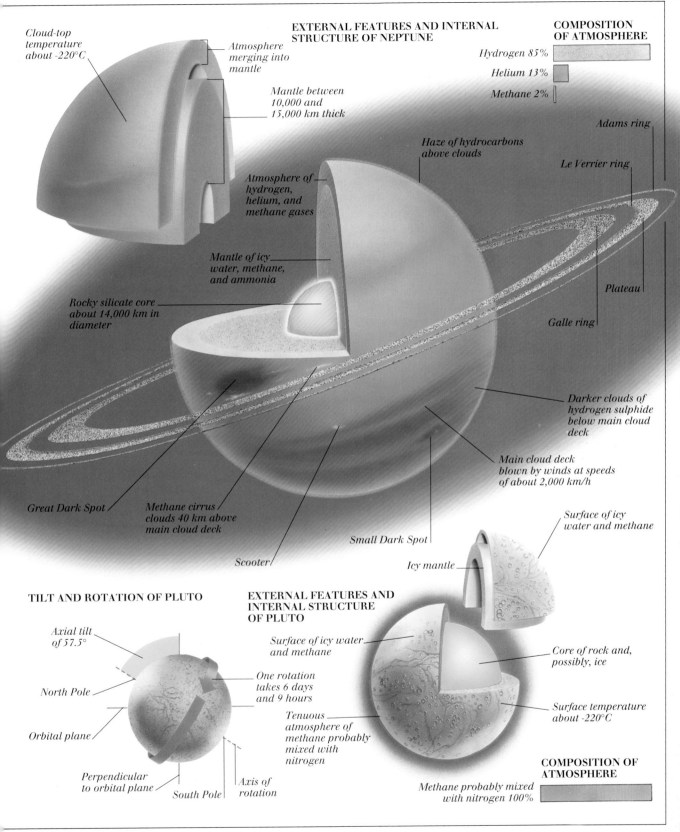

EXTERNAL FEATURES AND INTERNAL STRUCTURE OF NEPTUNE

Cloud-top temperature about -220°C

Atmosphere merging into mantle

Mantle between 10,000 and 15,000 km thick

COMPOSITION OF ATMOSPHERE

Hydrogen 85%

Helium 13%

Methane 2%

Haze of hydrocarbons above clouds

Adams ring

Le Verrier ring

Atmosphere of hydrogen, helium, and methane gases

Mantle of icy water, methane, and ammonia

Rocky silicate core about 14,000 km in diameter

Plateau

Galle ring

Darker clouds of hydrogen sulphide below main cloud deck

Main cloud deck blown by winds at speeds of about 2,000 km/h

Great Dark Spot

Methane cirrus clouds 40 km above main cloud deck

Scooter

Small Dark Spot

Surface of icy water and methane

Icy mantle

TILT AND ROTATION OF PLUTO

Axial tilt of 57.5°

North Pole

Orbital plane

Perpendicular to orbital plane

South Pole

Axis of rotation

EXTERNAL FEATURES AND INTERNAL STRUCTURE OF PLUTO

Surface of icy water and methane

One rotation takes 6 days and 9 hours

Tenuous atmosphere of methane probably mixed with nitrogen

Core of rock and, possibly, ice

Surface temperature about -220°C

COMPOSITION OF ATMOSPHERE

Methane probably mixed with nitrogen 100%

Asteroids, comets, and meteoroids

ASTEROID 951 GASPRA

ASTEROIDS, COMETS, AND METEOROIDS are all debris remaining from the nebula in which the Solar System formed 4.6 billion years ago. Asteroids are rocky bodies up to about 1,000 kilometres in diameter, although most are much smaller. Most of them orbit the Sun in the asteroid belt, which lies between the orbits of Mars and Jupiter. Comets may originate in a huge cloud (called the Oort Cloud) that is thought to surround the Solar System. They are made of frozen gases and dust, and are a few kilometres in diameter. Occasionally, a comet is deflected from the Oort Cloud to orbit the Sun in a long, elliptical path. As the comet approaches the Sun, the comet's surface starts to vaporize in the heat, producing a brightly shining coma (a huge sphere of gas and dust around the nucleus), a gas tail, and a dust tail. Meteoroids are small chunks of stone or stone and iron, some of which are fragments of asteroids or comets. Meteoroids range in size from tiny dust particles to objects tens of metres across. If a meteoroid enters the Earth's atmosphere, it is heated by friction and appears as a glowing streak of light called a meteor (also known as a shooting star). Meteor showers occur when the Earth passes through the trail of dust particles left by a comet. Most meteors burn up in the atmosphere. The few that are large enough to reach the Earth's surface are termed meteorites.

OPTICAL IMAGE OF HALLEY'S COMET

FALSE-COLOUR IMAGE OF HALLEY'S COMET

High-intensity light emission

Nucleus

Medium-intensity light emission

Low-intensity light emission

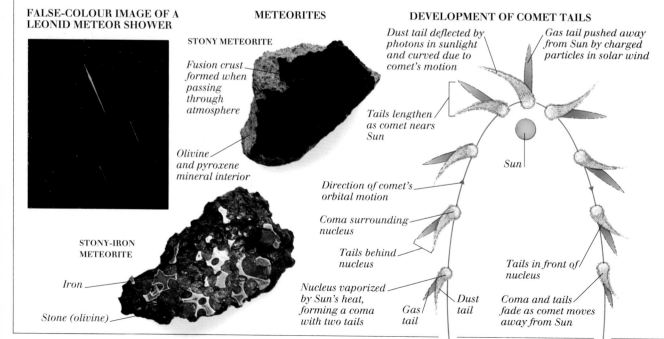

FALSE-COLOUR IMAGE OF A LEONID METEOR SHOWER

METEORITES

STONY METEORITE

Fusion crust formed when passing through atmosphere

Olivine and pyroxene mineral interior

STONY-IRON METEORITE

Iron

Stone (olivine)

DEVELOPMENT OF COMET TAILS

Dust tail deflected by photons in sunlight and curved due to comet's motion

Gas tail pushed away from Sun by charged particles in solar wind

Tails lengthen as comet nears Sun

Direction of comet's orbital motion

Coma surrounding nucleus

Tails behind nucleus

Sun

Nucleus vaporized by Sun's heat, forming a coma with two tails

Gas tail

Dust tail

Tails in front of nucleus

Coma and tails fade as comet moves away from Sun

FEATURES OF A COMET

Thin, straight gas tail

Broad, curved dust tail

Gas molecules heated by Sun and emitting light

Comet tails up to 100 million km long

Thin, straight gas tail blown by solar wind

Head (coma and nucleus)

Coma surrounding nucleus

Nucleus a few kilometres across

STRUCTURE OF A COMET

Glowing coma up to 1 million km across surrounding nucleus

Possible core of silicate dust

Crust with active areas emitting jets of gas and dust

Jet of gas and dust produced by vaporization on sunlit side of nucleus

Ices, including water ice, and frozen carbon dioxide, methane, and ammonia

Broad dust tail curved along comet's orbital path

Dust particles reflecting sunlight

53

PREHISTORIC EARTH

THE CHANGING EARTH	56
THE EARTH'S CRUST	58
FAULTS AND FOLDS	60
MOUNTAIN BUILDING	62
PRECAMBRIAN TO DEVONIAN PERIOD	64
CARBONIFEROUS TO PERMIAN PERIOD	66
TRIASSIC PERIOD	68
JURASSIC PERIOD	70
CRETACEOUS PERIOD	72
TERTIARY PERIOD	74
QUATERNARY PERIOD	76
EARLY SIGNS OF LIFE	78
AMPHIBIANS AND REPTILES	80
THE DINOSAURS	82
THEROPODS 1	84
THEROPODS 2	86
SAUROPODOMORPHS 1	88
SAUROPODOMORPHS 2	90
THYREOPHORANS 1	92
THYREOPHORANS 2	94
ORNITHOPODS 1	96
ORNITHOPODS 2	98
MARGINOCEPHALIANS 1	100
MARGINOCEPHALIANS 2	102
MAMMALS 1	104
MAMMALS 2	106
THE FIRST HOMINIDS	108

The changing Earth

THE EARTH FORMED FROM A CLOUD OF DUST and gas drifting through space about 4,600 million years ago. Dense minerals sank to the centre while lighter ones formed a thin rocky crust. However, the first known life-forms – bacteria and blue-green algae – did not appear until about 3,400 million years ago, and it was only about 700 million years ago that more complex plants and animals began to develop. Since then, thousands of animal and plant species have evolved; some, such as the dinosaurs, survived for many millions of years, while others died out quickly. The Earth itself is continually changing. Although continents neared their present locations about 50 million years ago, they are still drifting slowly over the planet's surface, and mountain ranges such as the Himalayas – which began to form 40 million years ago – are continually being built up and worn away. Climate is also subject to change: the Earth has undergone a series of ice ages interspersed with warmer periods (the most recent glacial period was at its height about 20,000 years ago).

Small mammals appeared (e.g., Crusafontia)

Dinosaurs became extinct

Global mountain building occurred

Multicellular soft-bodied animals appeared (e.g., worms and jellyfish)

Shelled invertebrates appeared (e.g., trilobites)

Marine plants flourished

Land plants appeared (e.g., Cooksonia)

Unicellular organisms appeared (e.g., blue-green algae)

Earth formed

Coral reefs appeared

Vertebrates appeared (e.g., Hemicyclaspis)

More complex types of algae appeared

Amphibians appeared (e.g., Ichthyostega)

CRETACEO

ORDOVICIAN

CAMBRIAN

PRECAMBRIAN TIME

SILURIAN

DEVONIAN

GEOLOGICAL TIMESCALE

MILLIONS OF YEARS AGO (MYA)

4,600	570	510	439	409	363	323	290

PRECAMBRIAN TIME	CAMBRIAN	ORDOVICIAN	SILURIAN	DEVONIAN	MISSISSIPPIAN (NORTH AMERICA)	PENNSYLVANIAN (NORTH AMERICA)
					CARBONIFEROUS	
	PALAEOZOIC					

EVOLUTION OF THE EARTH

Birds appeared
(e.g., Archaeopteryx)

Dinosaurs
flourished

Marine reptiles
appeared (e.g.,
Mixosaurus)

JURASSIC

TRIASSIC

Flowering plants
appeared (e.g.,
Magnolia)

Oil and gas
deposits formed

Himalayas
began to form

Coal-forming
forests flourished

Large mammals
appeared (e.g.,
Arsinoitherium)

PERMIAN

Early
desertification
occurred

Conifers
appeared

TERTIARY

CARBONIFEROUS

Last glacial
period occurred

Colorado River
began to cut out
the Grand Canyon

Uplift of the
Sierra Nevada
began

QUATERNARY

Modern humans
(Homo sapiens)
appeared

	65	56.5	35.5	23.5	5.2	1.64		0.01	0	MYA
	PALAEOCENE	EOCENE	OLIGOCENE	MIOCENE	PLIOCENE	PLEISTOCENE		HOLOCENE		EPOCH

290	245	208		146					
PERMIAN	TRIASSIC	JURASSIC		CRETACEOUS		TERTIARY		QUATERNARY	PERIOD
		MESOZOIC				CENOZOIC			ERA

57

The Earth's crust

THE EARTH'S CRUST IS THE SOLID outer shell of the Earth. It includes
continental crust (about 40 kilometres thick) and oceanic crust (about
six kilometres thick). The crust and the topmost layer of the mantle
form the lithosphere. The lithosphere consists of semi-rigid plates
that move relative to each other on the underlying asthenosphere
(a partly molten layer of the mantle). This process is known as plate
tectonics and helps explain continental drift. Where two plates move
apart, there are rifts in the crust. In mid-ocean, this movement results
in sea-floor spreading and the formation of ocean ridges; on continents,
crustal spreading can form rift valleys. When plates move towards each other,
one may be subducted beneath (forced under) the other. In mid-ocean, this causes
ocean trenches, seismic activity, and arcs of volcanic islands. Where oceanic crust
is subducted beneath continental crust or where continents collide, land may be
uplifted and mountains formed (see pp. 62–63). Plates may also slide past each
other – along the San Andreas fault, for example. Crustal movement on continents
may result in earthquakes, while movement under the seabed can lead to tidal waves.

ELEMENTS IN THE EARTH'S CRUST

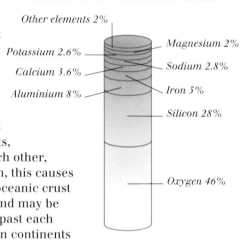

Other elements 2%
Potassium 2.6%
Calcium 3.6%
Aluminium 8%
Magnesium 2%
Sodium 2.8%
Iron 5%
Silicon 28%
Oxygen 46%

FEATURES OF PLATE MOVEMENTS

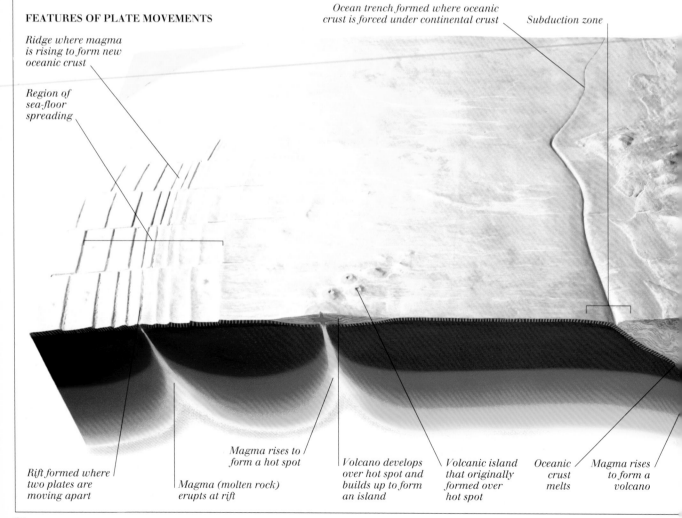

Ocean trench formed where oceanic
crust is forced under continental crust

Subduction zone

Ridge where magma
is rising to form new
oceanic crust

Region of
sea-floor
spreading

Rift formed where
two plates are
moving apart

Magma (molten rock)
erupts at rift

Magma rises to
form a hot spot

Volcano develops
over hot spot and
builds up to form
an island

Volcanic island
that originally
formed over
hot spot

Oceanic
crust
melts

Magma rises
to form a
volcano

MAJOR PLATES OF THE EARTH'S CRUST

Hellenic plate

Eurasian plate

North American plate

Plates sliding past each other

Cocos plate

Caribbean plate

Nazca plate

Pacific plate

Philippine plate

Plates converging

South American plate

African plate

Indo-Australian plate

Plates moving apart

Boundary along which two plates slide past each other

Mountain range uplifted where subducting oceanic crust compresses and deforms edge of continental crust

Lithosphere (crust and topmost layer of mantle)

Asthenosphere (upper part of mantle)

MOVEMENT OF LAND ALONG OCEANIC RIDGES

Land moves apart at a constant rate, perpendicular to ridge

STRAIGHT OCEANIC RIDGE

Land moves apart at a constant rate, perpendicular to curve

CURVED OCEANIC RIDGE

Staggered parallel ridge sections take shape of curve

Transform fault

STRESSES RESOLVE INTO SECTIONS

Faults and folds

THE CONTINUOUS MOVEMENT of the Earth's crustal plates (see pp. 58–59) can squeeze, stretch, or break rock strata, deforming them and producing faults and folds. A fault is a fracture in a rock along which there is movement of one side relative to the other. The movement can be vertical, horizontal, or oblique (vertical and horizontal). Faults develop when rocks are subjected to compression or tension. They tend to occur in hard, rigid rocks, which are more likely to break than bend. The smallest faults occur in single mineral crystals and are microscopically small, whereas the largest – the Great Rift Valley in Africa, which formed between 5 million and 100,000 years ago – is more than 9,000 kilometres long. A fold is a bend in a rock layer caused by compression. Folds occur in elastic rocks, which tend to bend rather than break. The two main types of fold are anticlines (upfolds) and synclines (downfolds). Folds vary in size from a few millimetres long to folded mountain ranges hundreds of kilometres long, such as the Himalayas (see pp. 62–63) and the Alps, which are repeatedly folding. In addition to faults and folds, other features associated with rock deformations include boudins, mullions, and *en échelon* fractures.

STRUCTURE OF A FOLD

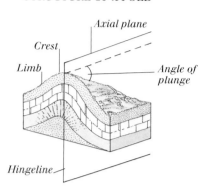

Axial plane

Crest

Limb

Angle of plunge

Hingeline

STRUCTURE OF A FAULT

Fault plane

Dip of fault plane (angle from horizontal)

Upthrow

Throw (vertical displacement of fault)

Downthrow

Hade of fault plane (angle from vertical)

STRUCTURE OF A SLOPE

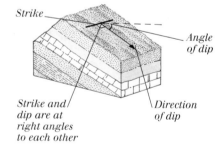

Strike

Angle of dip

Strike and dip are at right angles to each other

Direction of dip

FOLDED ROCK

Steeply dipping limbs

Crest of anticline

Plunge

SECTION THROUGH FOLDED ROCK STRATA THAT HAVE BEEN ERODED

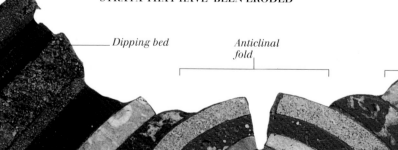

Dipping bed

Anticlinal fold

Monoclinal fold

Mineral-filled fault

Upper Carboniferous Millstone Grit

Lower Carboniferous Limestone

EXAMPLES OF FOLDS

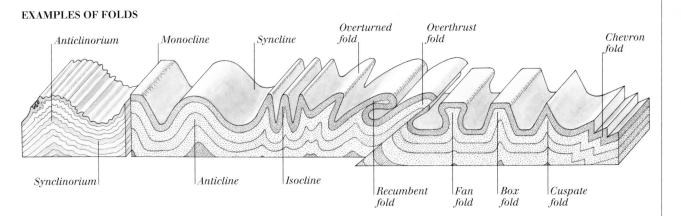

Anticlinorium

Monocline

Syncline

Overturned fold

Overthrust fold

Chevron fold

Synclinorium

Anticline

Isocline

Recumbent fold

Fan fold

Box fold

Cuspate fold

EXAMPLES OF FAULTS

Sinistral strike-slip (lateral) fault

Dextral strike-slip (lateral) fault

Horst

Tear fault

Normal dip-slip fault

Reverse dip-slip fault

Thrust fault

Oblique-slip fault

Graben

Cylindrical fault

SMALL-SCALE ROCK DEFORMATIONS

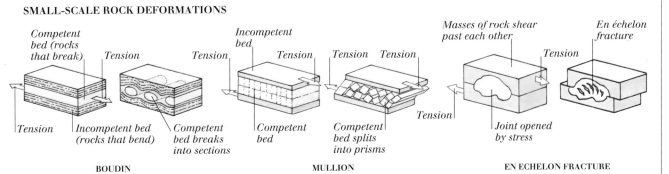

Competent bed (rocks that break)

Tension

Tension

Incompetent bed

Tension

Tension

Tension

Masses of rock shear past each other

Tension

En échelon fracture

Tension

Incompetent bed (rocks that bend)

Competent bed breaks into sections

Competent bed

Competent bed splits into prisms

Tension

Joint opened by stress

BOUDIN

MULLION

EN ECHELON FRACTURE

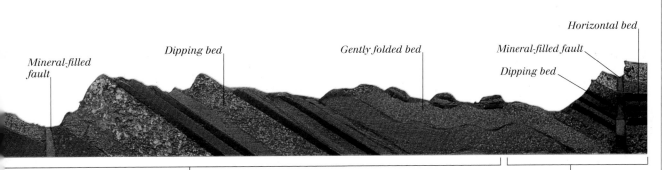

Mineral-filled fault

Dipping bed

Gently folded bed

Horizontal bed

Mineral-filled fault

Dipping bed

Upper Carboniferous Millstone Grit

Upper Carboniferous Coal Measures

Mountain building

THE PROCESSES INVOLVED in mountain building – termed orogenesis – occur as a result of the movement of the Earth's crustal plates (see pp. 58–59). There are three main types of mountains: volcanic mountains, fold mountains, and block mountains. Most volcanic mountains have been formed along plate boundaries where plates have come together or moved apart and lava and other debris have been ejected onto the Earth's surface. The lava and debris may have built up to form a dome around the vent of a volcano. Fold mountains are formed where plates push together and cause the rock to buckle upwards. Where oceanic crust meets less dense continental crust, the oceanic crust is forced under the continental crust. The continental crust is buckled by the impact. This is how folded mountain ranges, such as the Appalachian Mountains in North America, were formed. Fold mountains are also formed where two areas of continental crust meet. The Himalayas, for example, began to form when India collided with Asia, buckling the sediments and parts of the oceanic crust between them. Block mountains are formed when a block of land is uplifted between two faults as a result of compression or tension in the Earth's crust (see pp. 60–61). Often, the movement along faults has taken place gradually over millions of years. However, two plates may cause an earthquake by suddenly sliding past each other along a faultline.

BHAGIRATHI PARBAT, HIMALAYAS

Asia

Himalayas formed by buckling of sediment and part of the oceanic crust between two colliding continents

India moves north

India collides with Asia about 40 million years ago

EXAMPLES OF MOUNTAINS

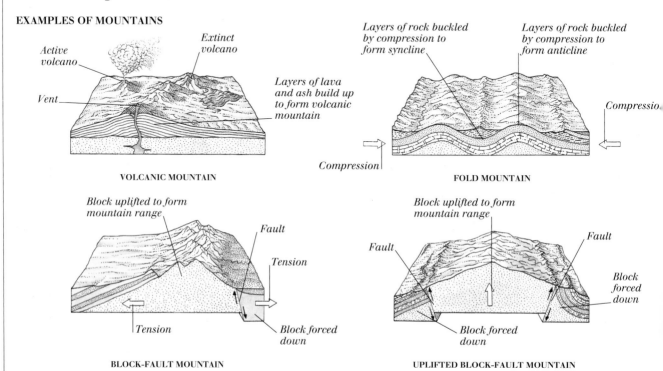

Active volcano

Extinct volcano

Vent

Layers of lava and ash build up to form volcanic mountain

VOLCANIC MOUNTAIN

Layers of rock buckled by compression to form syncline

Layers of rock buckled by compression to form anticline

Compression

Compression

FOLD MOUNTAIN

Block uplifted to form mountain range

Fault

Tension

Tension

Block forced down

BLOCK-FAULT MOUNTAIN

Block uplifted to form mountain range

Fault

Fault

Block forced down

Block forced down

UPLIFTED BLOCK-FAULT MOUNTAIN

STAGES IN THE FORMATION OF THE HIMALAYAS

60 MILLION YEARS AGO

India moves towards Asia
Sediment
Ocean area becomes smaller as plates converge
Sediment
Asia
Volcano
Continental crust
Continental crust
Oceanic crust forced under continental crust
Magma rises to form volcanoes

40 MILLION YEARS AGO

Sediment and part of oceanic crust folded by continental collision
India
Asia
Continental crust
Oceanic crust forced further under continental crust
Continental crust

20 MILLION YEARS AGO

Ganges plain
Sediment and part of oceanic crust folded and uplifted
India
Asia
Continental crust
Continental crust

TODAY

Sediment and part of oceanic crust further folded and uplifted to form Himalayas
Ripple effect of collision forms mountains and plateau of Tibet
Ganges plain
India
Asia
Continental crust
Continental crust

SAN ANDREAS FAULT

EARTHQUAKES

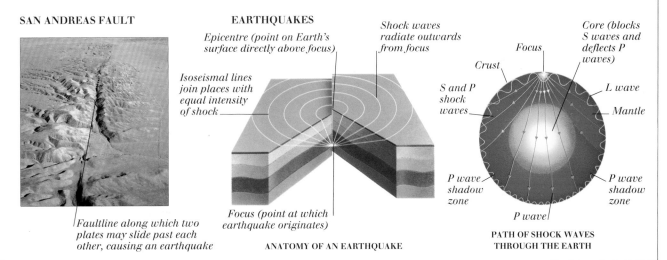

Faultline along which two plates may slide past each other, causing an earthquake

Epicentre (point on Earth's surface directly above focus)
Shock waves radiate outwards from focus
Isoseismal lines join places with equal intensity of shock
Focus (point at which earthquake originates)

ANATOMY OF AN EARTHQUAKE

Core (blocks S waves and deflects P waves)
Focus
Crust
L wave
S and P shock waves
Mantle
P wave shadow zone
P wave shadow zone
P wave

PATH OF SHOCK WAVES THROUGH THE EARTH

Precambrian to Devonian periods

WHEN THE EARTH FORMED about 4,600 million years ago, its atmosphere consisted of volcanic gases with little oxygen, making it hostile to most forms of life. One large supercontinent, Gondwanaland, was situated over the southern polar region, while other smaller continents were spread over the rest of the world. Constant movement of the earth's crustal plates carried continents across the earth's surface. The first primitive life-forms emerged around 3,400 million years ago in shallow, warm seas. The build up of oxygen began to form a shield of ozone around the earth, protecting living organisms from the sun's harmful rays and helping to establish an atmosphere in which life could sustain itself. The first vertebrates appeared about 470 million years ago, during the Ordovician period (510–439 million years ago), the first land plants appeared around 400 million years ago during the Devonian period (409–363 million years ago), and the first land animals about 30 million years later.

North America
Greenland
China
South America
Australia
South Africa
India
Africa
North East Africa
Scandinavia
Europe
Siberia
Central Asia

EXAMPLES OF PRECAMBRIAN TO DEVONIAN PLANT GROUPS

A PRESENT-DAY CLUBMOSS
(*Lycopodium sp.*)

**A PRESENT-DAY
LAND PLANT**
(*Asparagus setaceous*)

FOSSIL OF AN EXTINCT LAND PLANT
(*Cooksonia hemisphaerica*)

FOSSIL OF AN EXTINCT SWAMP PLANT
(*Zosterophyllum llanoveranum*)

EXAMPLES OF PRECAMBRIAN TO DEVONIAN TRILOBITES

ACADAGNOSTUS
Family: Agnostidae
Length: 8 mm (⅓ in)

PHACOPS
Family: Phacopidae
Length: 4.5 cm (1¾ in)

OLENELLUS
Family: Olenellidae
Length: 6 cm (2½ in)

ELRATHIA
Family: Ptychopariidae
Length: 2 cm (¾ in)

THE EARTH DURING THE MIDDLE ORDOVICIAN PERIOD

Siberia

Laurentia

China

Kazakstania

Gondwanaland

Baltica

EXAMPLES OF EARLY MARINE INVERTEBRATES

FOSSIL NAUTILOID
(*Estonioceras perforatum*)

FOSSIL BRACHIOPOD
(*Dicoelosia bilobata*)

TRACE FOSSIL
(*Mawsonites spriggi*)

FOSSIL GRAPTOLITE
(*Monograptus convolutus*)

EXAMPLES OF DEVONIAN FISH

RHAMPHODOPSIS
Family: Ptyctodontidae
Length: 15 cm (6 in)

PTERASPIS
Family: Pteraspidae
Length: 25 cm (10 in)

COCCOSTEUS
Family: Coccosteidae
Length: 35 cm (14 in)

BOTHRIOLEPIS
Family: Bothriolepidae
Length: 40 cm (16 in)

CHEIRACANTHUS
Family: Acanthodidae
Length: 30 cm (12 in)

PTERICHTHYODES
Family: Asterolepidae
Length: 15 cm (6 in)

CHEIROLEPIS
Family: Cheirolepidae
Length: 17 cm (6¾ in)

CEPHALASPIS
Family: Cephalaspidae
Length: 22 cm (8¾ in)

Carboniferous to Permian periods

North
America   Greenland   Siberia

China

South
America

Antarctica   Africa   Australia

Antarctica

India

THE CARBONIFEROUS PERIOD (363–290 million years ago) takes its name
from the thick, carbon-rich layers – now coal – that were produced
during this period as swampy tropical forests were repeatedly
drowned by shallow seas. The humid climate across northern
and equatorial continents throughout Carboniferous times
produced the first dense plant cover on Earth. During the early
part of this period, the first reptiles appeared. Their development
of a waterproof egg with a protective internal structure
ended animal life's dependence on an aquatic environment.
Towards the end of Carboniferous times, the earth's continents
Laurasia and Gondwanaland collided, resulting in the huge
land-mass of Pangaea. Glaciers smothered much of the southern
hemisphere during the Permian period (290–245 million years ago),
covering Antarctica, parts of Australia, and much of South America, Africa, and India.
Ice locked up much of the world's water and large areas of the northern hemisphere experienced
a drop in sea-level. Away from the poles, deserts and a hot dry climate predominated. As a result of
these conditions, the Permian period ended with the greatest mass extinction of life on earth ever.

EXAMPLES OF CARBONIFEROUS AND PERMIAN PLANT GROUPS

A PRESENT-DAY FIR
(Abies concolor)

FOSSIL OF AN EXTINCT FERN
(Zeilleria frenzlii)

**FOSSIL OF AN
EXTINCT HORSETAIL**
(Equisetites sp.)

**FOSSIL OF AN
EXTINCT CLUBMOSS**
(Lepidodendron sp.)

EXAMPLES OF CARBONIFEROUS AND PERMIAN TREES

PECOPTERIS
Family: Marattiaceae
Height: 4 m (13 ft)

PARIPTERIS
Family: Medullosaceae
Height: 5 m (16 ft 6 in)

MARIOPTERIS
Family: Unclassified
Height: 5 m (16 ft 6 in)

MEDULLOSA
Family: Medullosaceae
Height: 5 m (16 ft 6 in)

THE EARTH DURING THE LATE CARBONIFEROUS PERIOD

Siberia

Laurussia

China

Ural
Mountains

Caledonian
Mountains

Appalachian
Mountains

Gondwanaland

EXAMPLES OF CARBONIFEROUS
AND PERMIAN ANIMALS

SKULL OF AN EXTINCT SYNAPSID REPTILE
(Dimetrodon loomisi)

**FOSSIL TEETH OF
AN EXTINCT SHARK**
(Helicoprion bessonowi)

**MODEL OF AN EXTINCT
CARBONIFEROUS REPTILE**
(Westlothiana lizziae)

LEPIDODENDRON
Family: Lepidodendraceae
Height: 30 m (100 ft)

CORDAITES
Family: Cordaitacea
Height: 10 m (33 ft)

GLOSSOPTERIS
Family: Glossopteridaceae
Height: 8 m (26 ft)

ALETHOPTERIS
Family: Medullosaceae
Height: 5 m (16 ft 6 in)

Triassic period

THE TRIASSIC PERIOD (245–208 million years ago) marked the beginning of what is known as the Age of the Dinosaurs (the Mesozoic era). During this period, the present-day continents were massed together, forming one huge continent known as Pangaea. This land-mass experienced extremes of climate, with lush green areas around the coast or by lakes and rivers, and arid deserts in the interior. The only forms of plant life were non-flowering plants, such as conifers, ferns, cycads, and ginkgos; flowering plants had not yet evolved. The principal forms of animal life included primitive amphibians, rhynchosaurs ("beaked lizards"), and primitive crocodilians. Dinosaurs first appeared about 230 million years ago, at the beginning of the Late Triassic period. The earliest known dinosaurs were the carnivorous (flesh-eating) herrerasaurids and staurikosaurids, such as *Herrerasaurus* and *Staurikosaurus*. Early herbivorous (plant-eating) dinosaurs first appeared in Late Triassic times and included *Plateosaurus* and *Technosaurus*. By the end of the Triassic period, dinosaurs dominated Pangaea, possibly contributing to the extinction of many other reptiles.

TRIASSIC POSITIONS OF PRESENT-DAY LAND-MASSES

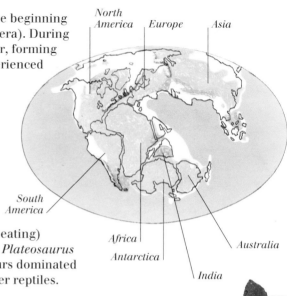

North America

Europe

Asia

South America

Africa

Antarctica

India

Australia

EXAMPLES OF TRIASSIC PLANT GROUPS

A PRESENT-DAY CYCAD
(*Cycas revoluta*)

A PRESENT-DAY GINKGO
(*Ginkgo biloba*)

A PRESENT-DAY CONIFER
(*Araucaria araucana*)

FOSSIL OF AN EXTINCT FERN
(*Pachypteris sp.*)

FOSSIL LEAF OF AN EXTINCT CYCAD
(*Cycas sp.*)

EXAMPLES OF TRIASSIC DINOSAURS

MELANOROSAURUS
A melanorosaurid
Length: 12.2 m (40 ft)

MUSSAURUS
A plateosaurid
Length: 2–3 m (6 ft 6 in–10 ft)

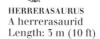

HERRERASAURUS
A herrerasaurid
Length: 3 m (10 ft)

PISANOSAURUS
A primitive ornithischian
Length: 90 cm (3 ft)

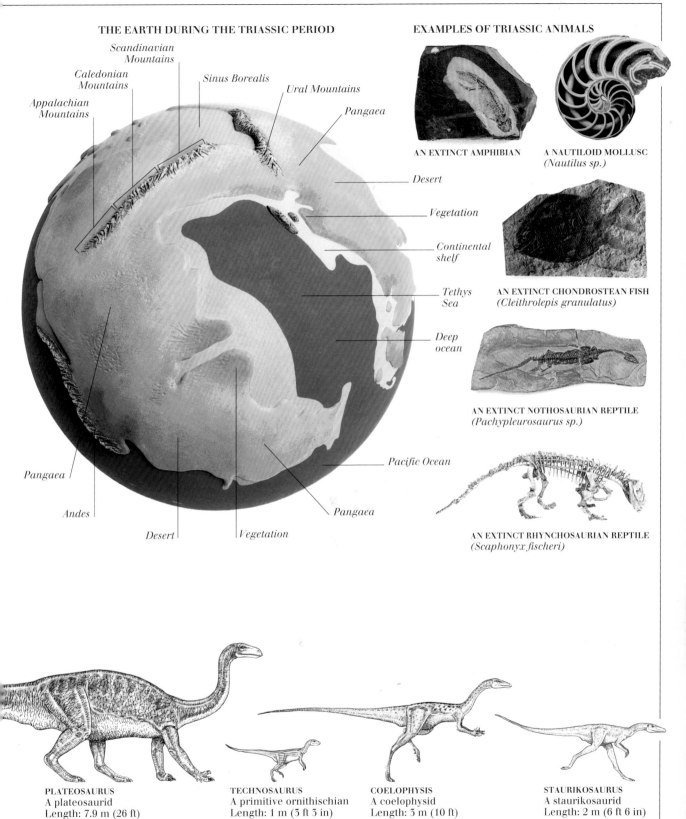

THE EARTH DURING THE TRIASSIC PERIOD

Scandinavian Mountains

Caledonian Mountains

Appalachian Mountains

Sinus Borealis

Ural Mountains

Pangaea

Desert

Vegetation

Continental shelf

Tethys Sea

Deep ocean

Pacific Ocean

Pangaea

Pangaea

Andes

Desert

Vegetation

EXAMPLES OF TRIASSIC ANIMALS

AN EXTINCT AMPHIBIAN

A NAUTILOID MOLLUSC
(Nautilus sp.)

AN EXTINCT CHONDROSTEAN FISH
(Cleithrolepis granulatus)

AN EXTINCT NOTHOSAURIAN REPTILE
(Pachypleurosaurus sp.)

AN EXTINCT RHYNCHOSAURIAN REPTILE
(Scaphonyx fischeri)

PLATEOSAURUS
A plateosaurid
Length: 7.9 m (26 ft)

TECHNOSAURUS
A primitive ornithischian
Length: 1 m (3 ft 3 in)

COELOPHYSIS
A coelophysid
Length: 3 m (10 ft)

STAURIKOSAURUS
A staurikosaurid
Length: 2 m (6 ft 6 in)

69

Jurassic period

THE JURASSIC PERIOD, the middle part of the Mesozoic era, lasted from 208 to 146 million years ago. During Jurassic times, the land-mass of Pangaea broke up into the continents of Gondwanaland and Laurasia, and sea-levels rose, flooding areas of lower land. The Jurassic climate was warm and moist. Plants such as ginkgos, horsetails, and conifers thrived, and giant redwood trees appeared, as did the first flowering plants. The abundance of plant food coincided with the proliferation of herbivorous (plant-eating) dinosaurs, such as the large sauropods (e.g., *Diplodocus*) and stegosaurs (e.g., *Stegosaurus*). Carnivorous (flesh-eating) dinosaurs, such as *Compsognathus* and *Allosaurus,* also flourished by hunting the many animals that existed – among them other dinosaurs. Further Jurassic animals included shrew-like mammals, and pterosaurs (flying reptiles), as well as plesiosaurs and ichthyosaurs (both marine reptiles).

JURASSIC POSITIONS OF PRESENT-DAY LAND-MASSES

North America

Europe

Arabia

Asia

South America

Africa

Antarctica

India

Australia

EXAMPLES OF JURASSIC PLANT GROUPS

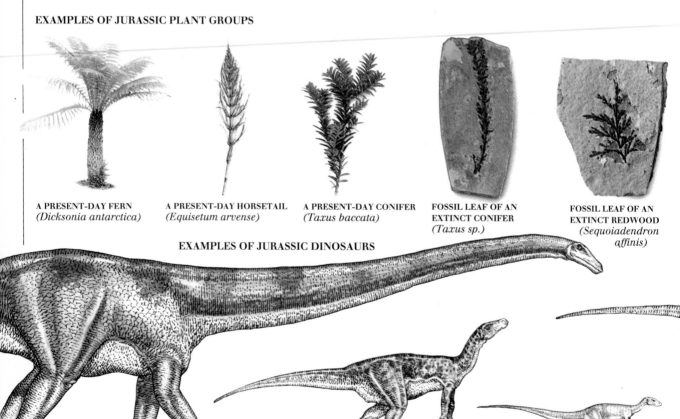

A PRESENT-DAY FERN
(*Dicksonia antarctica*)

A PRESENT-DAY HORSETAIL
(*Equisetum arvense*)

A PRESENT-DAY CONIFER
(*Taxus baccata*)

FOSSIL LEAF OF AN EXTINCT CONIFER
(*Taxus sp.*)

FOSSIL LEAF OF AN EXTINCT REDWOOD
(*Sequoiadendron affinis*)

EXAMPLES OF JURASSIC DINOSAURS

DIPLODOCUS
A diplodocid
Length: 26.8 m (88 ft)

CAMPTOSAURUS
A camptosaurid
Length: 4.9–7 m (16–23 ft)

DRYOSAURUS
A dryosaurid
Length: 3–4 m (10–13 ft)

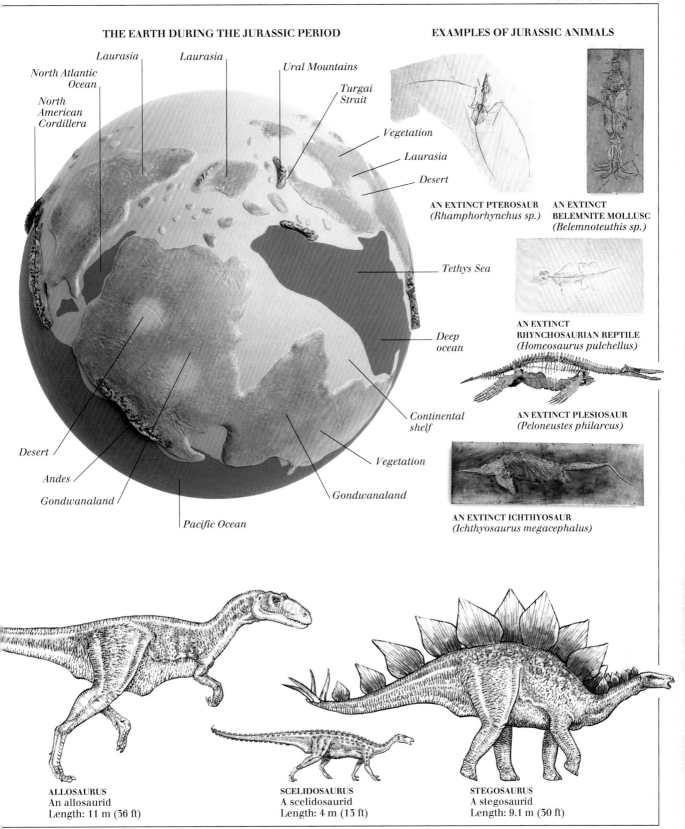

THE EARTH DURING THE JURASSIC PERIOD

Laurasia

Laurasia

North Atlantic Ocean

North American Cordillera

Ural Mountains

Turgai Strait

Vegetation

Laurasia

Desert

Tethys Sea

Deep ocean

Continental shelf

Vegetation

Gondwanaland

Desert

Andes

Gondwanaland

Pacific Ocean

EXAMPLES OF JURASSIC ANIMALS

AN EXTINCT PTEROSAUR
(*Rhamphorhynchus sp.*)

AN EXTINCT BELEMNITE MOLLUSC
(*Belemnoteuthis sp.*)

AN EXTINCT RHYNCHOSAURIAN REPTILE
(*Homeosaurus pulchellus*)

AN EXTINCT PLESIOSAUR
(*Peloneustes philarcus*)

AN EXTINCT ICHTHYOSAUR
(*Ichthyosaurus megacephalus*)

ALLOSAURUS
An allosaurid
Length: 11 m (36 ft)

SCELIDOSAURUS
A scelidosaurid
Length: 4 m (13 ft)

STEGOSAURUS
A stegosaurid
Length: 9.1 m (30 ft)

Cretaceous period

THE MESOZOIC ERA ENDED WITH the Cretaceous period, which lasted from 146 to 65 million years ago. During this period, Gondwanaland and Laurasia were breaking up into smaller land-masses that more closely resembled those of the modern continents. The climate remained mild and moist but the seasons became more marked. Flowering plants, including deciduous trees, replaced many cycads, seed ferns, and conifers. Animal species became more varied, with the evolution of new mammals, insects, fish, crustaceans, and turtles. Dinosaurs evolved into a wide variety of species during Cretaceous times; more than half of all known dinosaurs – including *Iguanodon*, *Deinonychus*, *Tyrannosaurus*, and *Hypsilophodon* – lived during this period. At the end of the Cretaceous period, however, dinosaurs became extinct. The reason for this mass extinction is unknown but it is thought to have been caused by climatic changes due to either a catastrophic meteor impact with the Earth or extensive volcanic eruptions.

CRETACEOUS POSITIONS OF PRESENT-DAY LAND-MASSES

North America
Europe
Arabia
Asia
South America
Africa
India
Antarctica
Australia

EXAMPLES OF CRETACEOUS PLANT GROUPS

A PRESENT-DAY CONIFER
(*Pinus muricata*)

A PRESENT-DAY DECIDUOUS TREE
(*Magnolia sp.*)

FOSSIL OF AN EXTINCT FERN
(*Sphenopteris latiloba*)

FOSSIL OF AN EXTINCT GINKGO
(*Ginkgo pluripartita*)

FOSSIL LEAVES OF AN EXTINCT DECIDUOUS TREE
(*Cercidyphyllum sp.*)

EXAMPLES OF CRETACEOUS DINOSAURS

SALTASAURUS
A titanosaurid
Length: 12.2 m (40 ft)

TOROSAURUS
A ceratopsid
Length: 7.6 m (25 ft)

HYPSILOPHODON
A hypsilophodontid
Length: 1.4–2.3 m (4 ft 6 in–7 ft 6 in)

THE EARTH DURING THE CRETACEOUS PERIOD

EXAMPLES OF CRETACEOUS ANIMALS

West Africa
Africa
Greenland
Europe
Continental Sea
North America
Rocky Mountains
Ural Mountains
Desert
Tethys Sea
Asia
India
Indian Ocean
Australia
Pacific Ocean
North Atlantic Ocean
Andes
South America
South Atlantic Ocean
Antarctica
Vegetation

AN EXTINCT INSECT
(*Libellulium longialatum*)

AN EXTINCT MARINE TURTLE
(*Plesiochelys latiscutata*)

AN EXTINCT CRUSTACEAN
(*Homarus sp.*)

AN EXTINCT CROCODILIAN

AN EXTINCT HOLOSTEAN FISH
(*Lepidotes maximus*)

TYRANNOSAURUS
A tyrannosaurid
Length: 12.2 m (40 ft)

DEINONYCHUS
A dromaeosaurid
Length: 2.4–3.4 m (8–11 ft)

IGUANODON
An iguanodontid
Length: 9.1 m (30 ft)

Tertiary period

FOLLOWING THE DEMISE OF THE DINOSAURS at the end of the Cretaceous period, the Tertiary period (65–1.6 million years ago), which formed the first part of the Cenozoic era (65 million years ago–present), was characterized by a huge expansion of mammal life. Placental mammals nourish and maintain the young in the mother's uterus; only three orders of placental mammals existed during Cretaceous times, compared with 25 orders during the Tertiary period. One of these 25 included the first hominid (see pp.108–109), *Australopithecus*, which appeared in Africa. By the beginning of the Tertiary period, the continents had almost reached their present position. The Tethys Sea, which had separated the northern continents from Africa and India, began to close up, forming the Mediterranean Sea and allowing the migration of terrestrial animals between Africa and western Europe. India's collision with Asia led to the formation of the Himalayas. During the middle part of the Tertiary period, the forest-dwelling and browsing mammals were replaced by mammals such as the horse, better suited to grazing the open savannahs that began to dominate. Repeated cool periods throughout the Tertiary period established the Antarctic as an icy island continent.

TERTIARY POSITIONS OF PRESENT-DAY LAND-MASSES

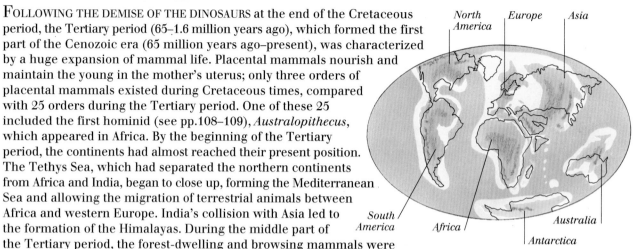

North America
Europe
Asia
South America
Africa
Australia
Antarctica

EXAMPLES OF TERTIARY PLANT GROUPS

A PRESENT-DAY OAK
(*Quercus palustris*)

A PRESENT-DAY BIRCH
(*Betula grossa*)

FOSSIL LEAF OF AN EXTINCT BIRCH
(*Betulites sp.*)

FOSSILIZED STEM OF AN EXTINCT PALM
(*Palmoxylon sp.*)

EXAMPLES OF TERTIARY ANIMAL GROUPS

HYAENODON
An hyaenodontid
Length: 2 m (6 ft 6 in)

TITANOHYRAX
A pliohyracid
Length: 2 m (6 ft 6 in)

PHORUSRHACUS
A phorusrhacid
Length: 1.5 m (5 ft)

SAMOTHERIUM
A giraffid
Length: 3 m (10 ft)

THE EARTH DURING THE TERTIARY PERIOD

EXAMPLES OF TERTIARY ANIMALS

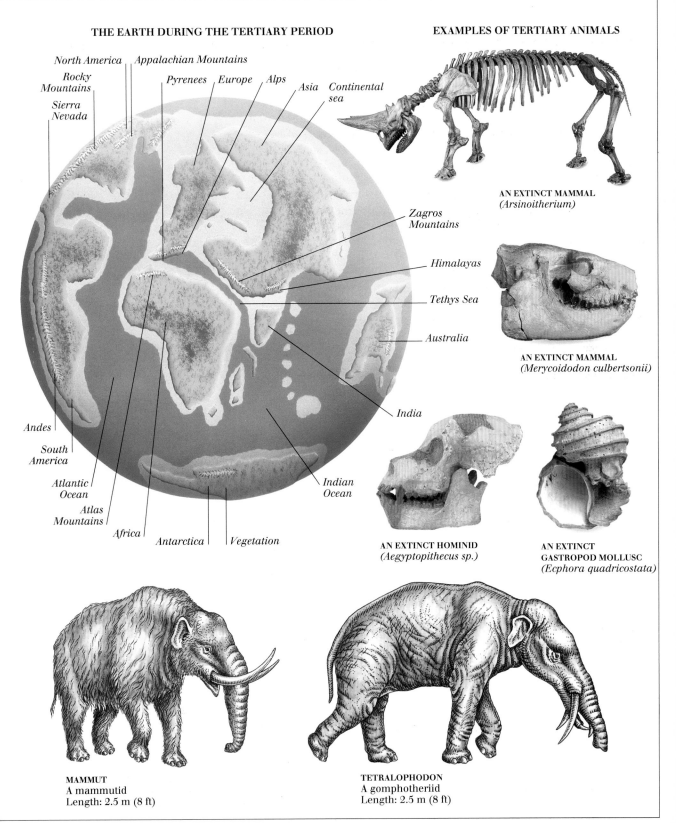

North America
Rocky Mountains
Sierra Nevada
Appalachian Mountains
Pyrenees
Europe
Alps
Asia
Continental sea
Zagros Mountains
Himalayas
Tethys Sea
Australia
India
Andes
South America
Atlantic Ocean
Atlas Mountains
Africa
Antarctica
Vegetation
Indian Ocean

AN EXTINCT MAMMAL
(*Arsinoitherium*)

AN EXTINCT MAMMAL
(*Merycoidodon culbertsonii*)

AN EXTINCT HOMINID
(*Aegyptopithecus sp.*)

AN EXTINCT GASTROPOD MOLLUSC
(*Ecphora quadricostata*)

MAMMUT
A mammutid
Length: 2.5 m (8 ft)

TETRALOPHODON
A gomphotheriid
Length: 2.5 m (8 ft)

Quaternary period

QUATERNARY POSITIONS OF PRESENT-DAY LAND-MASSES

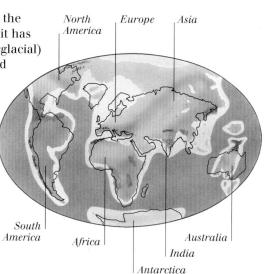

North America

Europe

Asia

South America

Africa

Australia

India

Antarctica

THE QUATERNARY PERIOD (1.6 million years ago–present) forms the second part of the Cenozoic era (65 million years ago–present): it has been characterized by alternating cold (glacial) and warm (interglacial) periods. During cold periods, ice sheets and glaciers have formed repeatedly on northern and southern continents. The cold environments in North America and Eurasia, and to a lesser extent in southern South America and parts of Australia, have caused the migration of many life forms towards the Equator. Only the specialized ice age mammals such as *Mammuthus* and *Coelodonta*, with their thick wool and fat insulation, were suited to life in very cold climates. Humans developed throughout the Pleistocene period (1.6 million–10,000 years ago) in Africa and migrated northward into Europe and Asia. Modern humans, *Homo sapiens*, lived on the cold European continent 30,000 years ago and hunted mammals. The end of the last ice age and the climatic changes that occurred about 10,000 years ago brought extinction to many Pleistocene mammals, but enabled humans to flourish.

EXAMPLES OF QUATERNARY PLANT GROUPS

A PRESENT-DAY BIRCH
(*Betula lenta*)

A PRESENT-DAY SWEEETGUM
(*Liquidambar styraciflua*)

FOSSIL LEAF OF A SWEETGUM
(*Liquidambar europeanum*)

FOSSIL LEAF OF A BIRCH
(*Betula sp.*)

EXAMPLES OF QUATERNARY ANIMAL GROUPS

PROCOPTODON
A macropodid
Length: 3 m (10 ft)

DIPROTODON
A diprotodontid
Length: 3 m (10 ft)

TOXODON
A toxodontid
Length: 3 m (10 ft)

MAMMUTHUS
An elephantid
Length: 3 m (10 ft)

THE EARTH DURING THE QUATERNARY PERIOD

Pyrenees

Alps

Appalachian
Mountains

Ice sheet

Rocky
Mountains

Asia

North
America

Vegetation

Carpathian
Mountains

Taurus
Mountains

Himalayas

India

Australia

Andes

Desert

South
America

Indian
Ocean

Atlantic
Ocean

Ice cap

Atlas
Mountains

Africa

Antarctica

EXAMPLES OF QUATERNARY ANIMALS

A MAMMAL SKELETON
(*Hippopotamus
amphibius*)

**SKULL OF AN EXTINCT
CAVE BEAR**
(*Ursus spelaeus*)

**SKULL OF AN
EXTINCT TORTOISE**
(*Meiolania platyceps*)

A MAMMOTH TOOTH
(*Mammuthus
primigenius*)

DEINOTHERIUM
A deinotheriid
Length: 4 m (13 ft)

COELODONTA
A rhinocerotid
Length: 4 m (13 ft)

AUSTRALOPITHECUS
A hominid
Length: 1.2 m (4 ft)

Early signs of life

FOR ALMOST A THOUSAND MILLION YEARS after its formation, there was no known life on Earth. The first simple, sea-dwelling organic structures appeared about 3,500 million years ago; they may have formed when certain chemical molecules joined together. Prokaryotes, single-celled micro-organisms such as blue-green algae, were able to photosynthesize (see pp. 138–139), and thus produce oxygen. A thousand million years later, sufficient oxygen had built up in the earth's atmosphere to allow multicellular organisms to proliferate in the Precambrian seas (before 570 million years ago). Soft-bodied jellyfish, corals, and seaworms flourished about 700 million years ago. Trilobites, the first animals with hard body frames, developed during the Cambrian period (570–510 million years ago). However, it was not until the beginning of the Devonian period (409–363 million years ago) that early land plants, such as *Asteroxylon*, formed a water-retaining cuticle, which ended their dependence on an aquatic environment. About 360 million years ago, the first amphibians (see pp. 80–81) crawled onto the land, although they still returned to the water to lay their soft eggs. Not until the emergence of the first reptiles would animals with backbones appear that were independent of water in this way.

STROMATOLITIC LIMESTONE

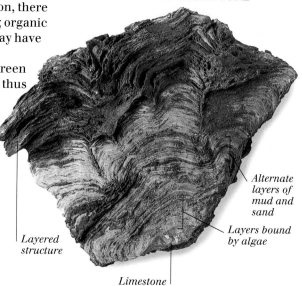

Alternate layers of mud and sand

Layers bound by algae

Layered structure

Limestone

Long, beak-like snout

Growth line

Dorsal plate

Dorsal spine base

Fixed lateral plate

Bony dorsal shield

FOSSILIZED JAWLESS FISH

Glabella

Eye

Thoracic pleurae

Tail shield

Tail area

FOSSILIZED TRILOBITE

Ambulacral groove

Small ossicles of upper surface

Central disc

Iron pyrites

FOSSILIZED STARFISH

Row of ossicles

Broad disc

UPPER SURFACE OF FOSSILIZED STARFISH

Row of ossicles

Short arm

LOWER SURFACE OF FOSSILIZED STARFISH

Jointed leg

Chelicera (jointed pincer)

Jointed leg with oar-shaped paddle

Segmented abdomen

UNDERSIDE OF FOSSILIZED EURYPTERID

Growing tip

Disc-shaped sporangium (spore-case)

Leaf-like scale

Stem

RECONSTRUCTION OF ASTEROXYLON

Telson (tail spine)

Abdominal segments

Shell contains eight somites (thoracic segments)

Hingeless, bivalved shell

FOSSIL OF AN EXTINCT SHRIMP

Amphibians and reptiles

THE EARLIEST KNOWN AMPHIBIANS, such as *Acanthostega* and *Ichthyostega*, lived about 363 million years ago at the end of the Devonian period (409–363 million years ago). Their limbs may have evolved from the muscular fins of lungfish-like creatures. These fish can use their fins to push themselves along the bottom of lakes and some can breathe at the water's surface. While amphibians (see pp. 182–183) can exist on land, they are dependent on a wet environment because their skin does not retain moisture and they must return to the water to lay their eggs. Evolving from amphibians, reptiles (see pp. 184–187) first appeared during the Carboniferous period (363–290 million years ago): *Westlothiana*, a possible early reptile, lived on land 338 million years ago. The development of the amniotic egg, with an embryo enclosed in its own wet environment (the amnion) and protected by a waterproof shell, freed reptiles from the amphibian's dependence on a wet habitat. A scaly skin protected the reptile from desiccation on land and enabled it to exploit ways of life closed to its amphibian ancestors. Reptiles include the dinosaurs, which came to dominate life on land during the Mesozoic era (245–65 million years ago).

FOSSIL SKULL OF ACANTHOSTEGA

MODEL OF ICHTHYOSTEGA

SKELETON OF ERYOPS

FOSSIL SKELETON OF WESTLOTHIANA

Pelvis

Rib

Vertebra

Flattened
skull bones

Leg

Rear foot

Caudal
vertebra

FOSSIL SKELETON OF A PAREIASAUR

Dorsal
vertebra

Scapula

Humerus

Radius

Ulna

Rib

Femur

Tail

Waterproof,
scaly skin

Eye

Mouth

Five-toed
foot

Semi-sprawling
stance

MODEL OF WESTLOTHIANA

Neural spine

Sacral vertebra

Ilium

Tri-lobed tail

Fleshy,
lobed
pelvic fin

Fleshy,
lobed
pectoral
fin

FOSSILIZED LUNGFISH

Caudal vertebra

Pubis

Femur

Ischium

Tibia

Fibula

Acetabulum

Metatarsals

Chevron

Phalanges

The dinosaurs

THE DINOSAURS WERE A LARGE GROUP of reptiles that were the dominant land vertebrates (animals with backbones) for most of the Mesozoic era (245–65 million years ago). They appeared some 230 million years ago and were distinguished from other scaly, egg-laying reptiles by an important feature: dinosaurs had an erect limb stance. This enabled them to keep their bodies well above the ground, unlike the sprawling and semi-sprawling stance of other reptiles. The head of the dinosaur's femur (thigh-bone) fitted into a socket in its pelvis (hip-bone), producing efficient and mobile locomotion. Dinosaurs are categorized into two groups according to the structure of their pelvis: saurischian (lizard-hipped) and ornithischian (bird-hipped) dinosaurs. In the case of most saurischians, the pubis (part of the pelvis) jutted forward, while in ornithischians it slanted back, parallel to the ischium (another part of the pelvis). Dinosaurs ranged in size from smaller than a domestic cat to the biggest land animals ever known. The Dinosauria were the most successful land vertebrates ever, and survived for 165 million years, until their extinction 65 million years ago.

STRUCTURE OF SAURISCHIAN PELVIS

Ilium

Hook of preacetabular process

Postacetabular process

Ilio-pubic joint

Acetabulum

Pubis

Ilio-ischial joint

Ischium

Pubic foot

GALLIMIMUS
A saurischian dinosaur

POSITION OF PELVIS IN A SAURISCHIAN DINOSAUR

STRUCTURE OF ORNITHISCHIAN PELVIS

Ilium

Preacetabular process

Postacetabular process

Ilio-pubic joint

Ilio-ischial joint

Prepubis

Acetabulum

Pubis

Ischium

HYPSILOPHODON
An ornithischian dinosaur

POSITION OF PELVIS IN AN ORNITHISCHIAN DINOSAUR

BAROSAURUS
A saurischian dinosaur

COMPARISON OF ANIMAL STANCES

SPRAWLING STANCE
The thighs and upper arms project straight out from the body so that the knees and elbows are bent at right angles.

COMMON IGUANA
(*Iguana iguana*)
A present-day reptile

ERECT STANCE
The thighs and upper arms project straight down from the body so that the knees and elbows are straight.

SEMI-SPRAWLING STANCE
The thighs and upper arms project downwards and outwards so that the knees and elbows are slightly bent.

DWARF CROCODILE
(*Osteolaemus tetraspis*)
A present-day reptile

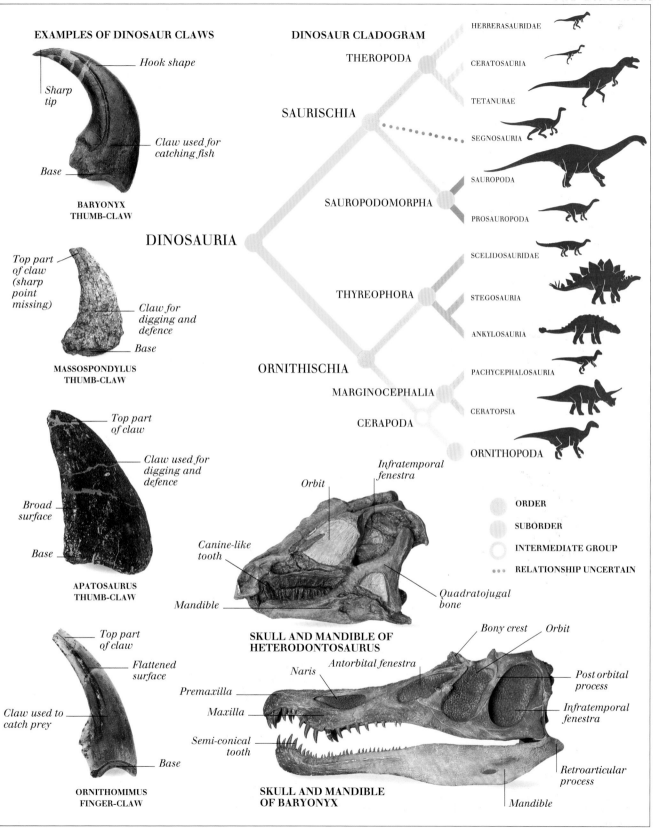

EXAMPLES OF DINOSAUR CLAWS

BARYONYX THUMB-CLAW

Hook shape

Sharp tip

Claw used for catching fish

Base

MASSOSPONDYLUS THUMB-CLAW

Top part of claw (sharp point missing)

Claw for digging and defence

Base

APATOSAURUS THUMB-CLAW

Top part of claw

Claw used for digging and defence

Broad surface

Base

ORNITHOMIMUS FINGER-CLAW

Top part of claw

Flattened surface

Claw used to catch prey

Base

DINOSAUR CLADOGRAM

THEROPODA

SAURISCHIA

DINOSAURIA

SAUROPODOMORPHA

THYREOPHORA

ORNITHISCHIA

MARGINOCEPHALIA

CERAPODA

ORNITHOPODA

HERRERASAURIDAE

CERATOSAURIA

TETANURAE

SEGNOSAURIA

SAUROPODA

PROSAUROPODA

SCELIDOSAURIDAE

STEGOSAURIA

ANKYLOSAURIA

PACHYCEPHALOSAURIA

CERATOPSIA

- ORDER
- SUBORDER
- INTERMEDIATE GROUP
- ··· RELATIONSHIP UNCERTAIN

SKULL AND MANDIBLE OF HETERODONTOSAURUS

Orbit

Infratemporal fenestra

Canine-like tooth

Quadratojugal bone

Mandible

SKULL AND MANDIBLE OF BARYONYX

Bony crest

Orbit

Naris

Antorbital fenestra

Premaxilla

Maxilla

Semi-conical tooth

Post orbital process

Infratemporal fenestra

Retroarticular process

Mandible

Theropods 1

AN ENORMOUSLY SUCCESSFUL SUBORDER of the Saurischia, the bipedal (two-footed) theropods ("beast feet") emerged 230 million years ago in Late Triassic times; the oldest known example comes from South America. Theropods spanned the whole of the Age of the Dinosaurs (230–65 million years ago) and included most of the known predatory dinosaurs. The typical theropod had small arms with sharp, clawed fingers; powerful jaws lined with sharp teeth; an S-shaped neck; long, muscular hind limbs; and clawed, usually four-toed feet. Many theropods may have been warm-blooded; most were exclusively carnivorous. Theropods ranged from animals no larger than a chicken to huge creatures, such as Tyrannosaurus and Baryonyx. The group also included ostrich-like omnivores and herbivores with toothless beaks, such as Struthiomimus and Gallimimus. Many scientists believe that birds are the closest living relatives to the dinosaurs, and share a common ancestor with the theropods. Archaeopteryx, small and feathered, was the first known bird and lived alongside its dinosaur relatives.

INTERNAL ANATOMY OF ALBERTOSAURUS LEG

Ilio-tibial muscle
Ilio-femoral muscle
Femoro-tibial muscle
Internal tibial flexor muscle
Femur
Ilio-fibular muscle
Gastrocnemius muscle
Digital flexor muscle
Fibula
Tarsal
Metatarsal
Ambiens muscle
Femoro-tibial muscle
Anterior tibial muscle
Common digital extensor muscle
Toe
Claw

Cranium
Supraoccipital crest
Orbit
Naris
Cervical vertebrae
Dorsal vertebrae
Ilium
Mandible
Serrated tooth
Cervical rib
Scapula
Shoulder joint
Ulna
Phalanges
Metacarpals
Wrist joint
Elbow joint
Coracoid
Rib
Humerus
Femur
Ischium
Hip joint
Knee joint
Pubis
Naris
Eye
Thigh
Scaly skin
Tail
Forelimb
Hand
Knee
Ankle
Toe
Claw
Foot
Hind limb
Metatarsals
Phalanges
Tibia
Fibula
Ankle joint
Hallux (first toe)

SKELETON OF TYRANNOSAURUS

EXTERNAL FEATURES OF TYRANNOSAURUS

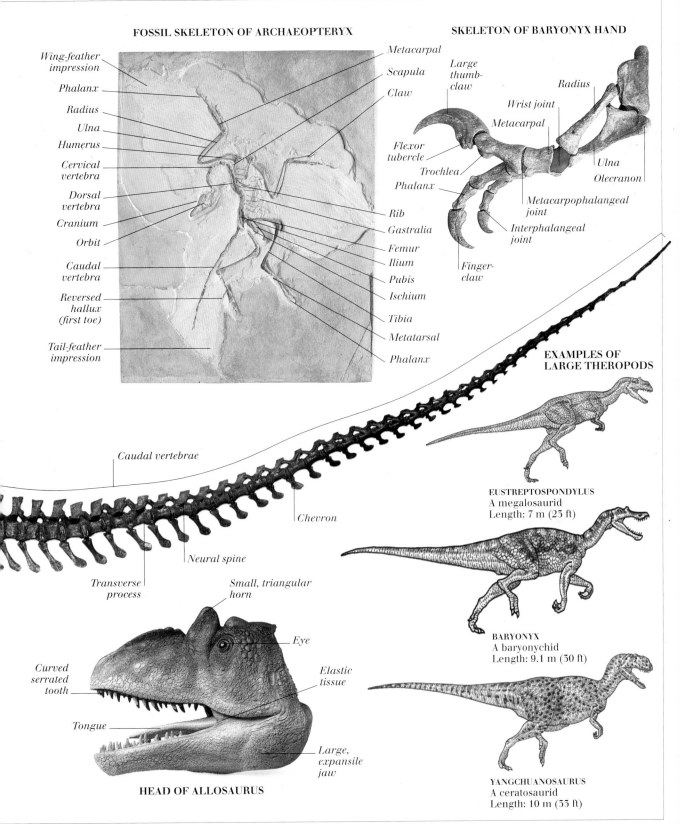

FOSSIL SKELETON OF ARCHAEOPTERYX

Wing-feather impression
Phalanx
Radius
Ulna
Humerus
Cervical vertebra
Dorsal vertebra
Cranium
Orbit
Caudal vertebra
Reversed hallux (first toe)
Tail-feather impression

Metacarpal
Scapula
Claw

Rib
Gastralia
Femur
Ilium
Pubis
Ischium
Tibia
Metatarsal
Phalanx

SKELETON OF BARYONYX HAND

Large thumb-claw
Flexor tubercle
Trochlea
Phalanx
Finger-claw

Radius
Wrist joint
Metacarpal
Ulna
Olecranon
Metacarpophalangeal joint
Interphalangeal joint

EXAMPLES OF LARGE THEROPODS

Caudal vertebrae
Chevron
Neural spine
Transverse process
Small, triangular horn
Eye
Elastic tissue
Curved serrated tooth
Tongue
Large, expansile jaw

HEAD OF ALLOSAURUS

EUSTREPTOSPONDYLUS
A megalosaurid
Length: 7 m (23 ft)

BARYONYX
A baryonychid
Length: 9.1 m (30 ft)

YANGCHUANOSAURUS
A ceratosaurid
Length: 10 m (33 ft)

Theropods 2

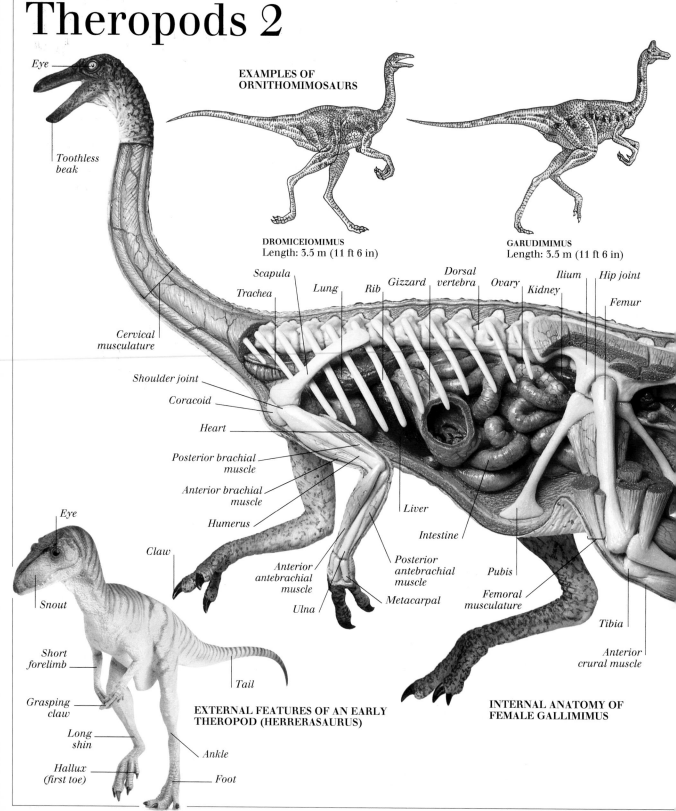

Eye

Toothless beak

Cervical musculature

EXAMPLES OF ORNITHOMIMOSAURS

DROMICEIOMIMUS
Length: 3.5 m (11 ft 6 in)

GARUDIMIMUS
Length: 3.5 m (11 ft 6 in)

Scapula

Trachea

Lung

Rib

Gizzard

Dorsal vertebra

Ovary

Kidney

Ilium

Hip joint

Femur

Shoulder joint

Coracoid

Heart

Posterior brachial muscle

Anterior brachial muscle

Humerus

Claw

Anterior antebrachial muscle

Ulna

Liver

Intestine

Posterior antebrachial muscle

Metacarpal

Pubis

Femoral musculature

Tibia

Anterior crural muscle

Eye

Snout

Short forelimb

Grasping claw

Long shin

Hallux (first toe)

Tail

Ankle

Foot

EXTERNAL FEATURES OF AN EARLY THEROPOD (HERRERASAURUS)

INTERNAL ANATOMY OF FEMALE GALLIMIMUS

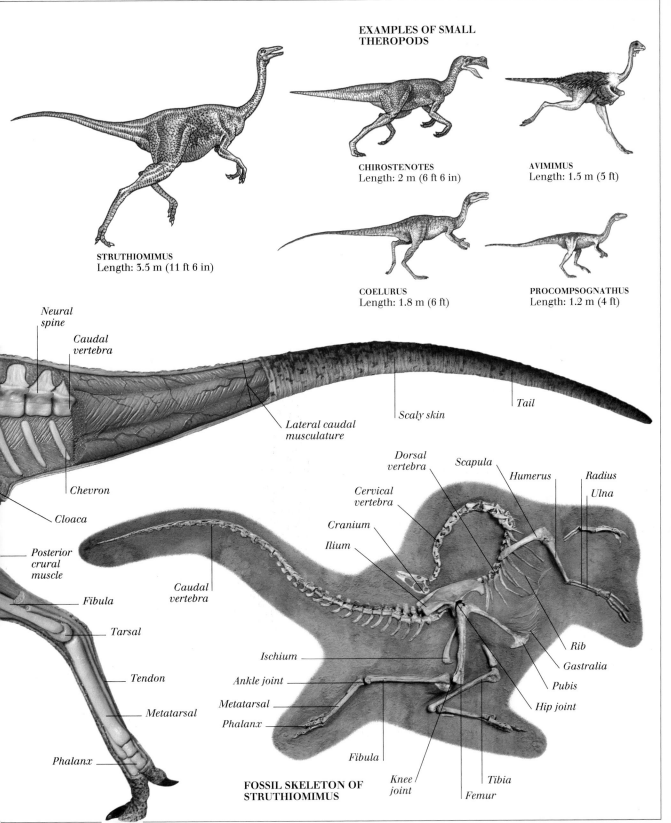

EXAMPLES OF SMALL THEROPODS

STRUTHIOMIMUS
Length: 3.5 m (11 ft 6 in)

CHIROSTENOTES
Length: 2 m (6 ft 6 in)

AVIMIMUS
Length: 1.5 m (5 ft)

COELURUS
Length: 1.8 m (6 ft)

PROCOMPSOGNATHUS
Length: 1.2 m (4 ft)

Neural spine

Caudal vertebra

Chevron

Cloaca

Posterior crural muscle

Fibula

Tarsal

Tendon

Metatarsal

Phalanx

Lateral caudal musculature

Scaly skin

Tail

Dorsal vertebra

Scapula

Humerus

Radius

Ulna

Cervical vertebra

Cranium

Ilium

Caudal vertebra

Ischium

Ankle joint

Metatarsal

Phalanx

Fibula

Knee joint

Femur

Tibia

Hip joint

Pubis

Gastralia

Rib

FOSSIL SKELETON OF STRUTHIOMIMUS

Sauropodomorphs 1

THE SAUROPODOMORPHA ("lizard-feet forms") were herbivorous, usually quadrupedal (four-footed) dinosaurs. A suborder of the Saurischia, they were characterized by small heads, bulky bodies, and long necks and tails. There were two infraorders: prosauropods and sauropods.

THECODONTOSAURUS

Prosauropods lived from Late Triassic to Early Jurassic times (225–180 million years ago) and included beasts such as the small *Anchisaurus* and one of the first very large dinosaurs, *Plateosaurus*. By Middle Jurassic times (about 165 million years ago), sauropods had replaced prosauropods and spread worldwide. They included the heaviest and longest land animals ever, such as *Diplodocus* and *Brachiosaurus*. Sauropods persisted to the end of the Cretaceous period (65 million years ago). Many of these dinosaurs moved in herds, protected from predatory theropods by their huge bulk and powerful tails, which they could use to lash out at attackers. Sauropodomorphs were the most common large herbivores until Late Jurassic times (about 145 million years ago), and appear to have survived in southern continents long after they had disappeared from the north.

SKULL AND MANDIBLE OF PLATEOSAURUS

Naris
Antorbital fenestra
Orbit
Mandible
Infratemporal fenestra
Paroccipital process
Serrated, leaf-shaped tooth
Mandibular fenestra

SKELETON OF PLATEOSAURUS

Dorsal vertebrae
Sacral vertebrae
Ilium
Cervical vertebrae
Humerus
Scapula
Shoulder joint
Rib
Pubis
Hip joint
Femur
Ischium
Thumb-claw
Elbow joint
Radius
Knee joint
Tail
Wrist joint
Ulna
Tibia
Fibula
Metacarpal
Ankle joint
Cranium
Metatarsals
Phalanx
Orbit
Mandible
Naris
Phalanges

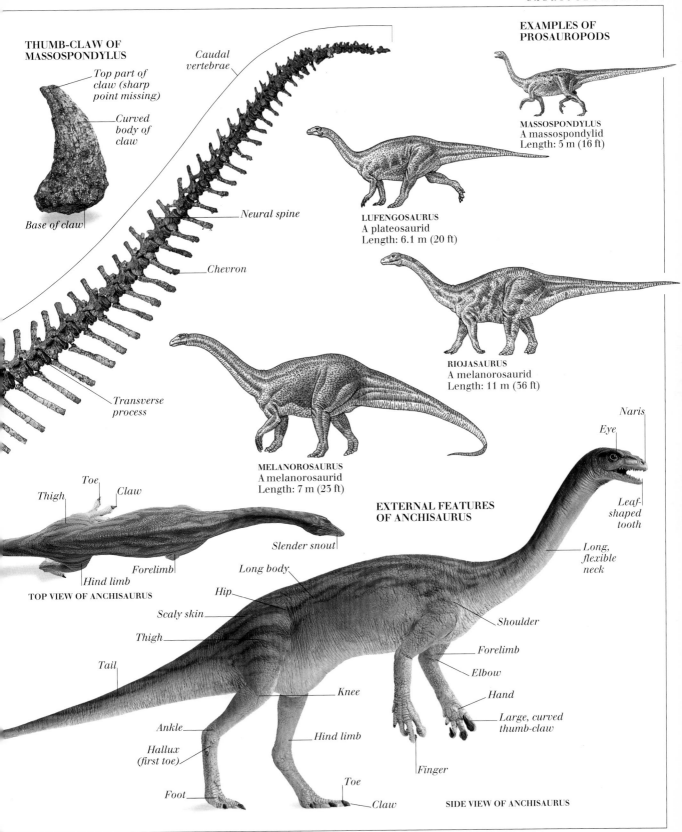

THUMB-CLAW OF MASSOSPONDYLUS

Top part of claw (sharp point missing)

Curved body of claw

Base of claw

Caudal vertebrae

Neural spine

Chevron

Transverse process

EXAMPLES OF PROSAUROPODS

MASSOSPONDYLUS
A massospondylid
Length: 5 m (16 ft)

LUFENGOSAURUS
A plateosaurid
Length: 6.1 m (20 ft)

RIOJASAURUS
A melanorosaurid
Length: 11 m (36 ft)

MELANOROSAURUS
A melanorosaurid
Length: 7 m (23 ft)

Thigh

Toe

Claw

Forelimb

Hind limb

TOP VIEW OF ANCHISAURUS

EXTERNAL FEATURES OF ANCHISAURUS

Slender snout

Long body

Hip

Scaly skin

Thigh

Tail

Ankle

Hallux (first toe)

Foot

Knee

Hind limb

Toe

Claw

Naris

Eye

Leaf-shaped tooth

Long, flexible neck

Shoulder

Forelimb

Elbow

Hand

Large, curved thumb-claw

Finger

SIDE VIEW OF ANCHISAURUS

Sauropodomorphs 2

SKULL AND MANDIBLE OF DIPLODOCUS

Orbit
Antorbital fenestra
Cranium
Maxillary fenestra
Maxilla
Peg-shaped tooth
Sclerotic ring
Infratemporal fenestra
Mandible

FOREFOOT OF ELEPHANT

Wrist
Nail

COMPARISON OF THE FOREFEET OF AN ELEPHANT AND DIPLODOCUS

FOREFOOT BONES OF ELEPHANT

Radius
Ulna
Carpals
Metacarpals
Phalanges

FOREFOOT BONES OF DIPLODOCUS

Radius
Ulna
Carpals
Metacarpals
Phalanges

MIDDLE SECTION OF DIPLODOCUS SKELETON

Coracoid
Dorsal vertebra
Scapula
Sacral vertebra
Ilium
Caudal vertebra
Hip joint
Ischium
Femur
Humerus
Rib
Elbow joint
Knee joint
Ankle joint
Ulna
Tibia
Radius
Fibula
Wrist joint
Phalanges
Metacarpals

Neural spine
Small intestine
Dorsal vertebra
Ovary
Kidney
Rib
Large intestine
Hip joint
Caecum
Pubis
Femur
Oviduct
Cloaca
Thigh musculature
Posterior crural musculature
Caudal musculature
Fibula
Ankle joint
Anterior crural muscle
Metatarsal

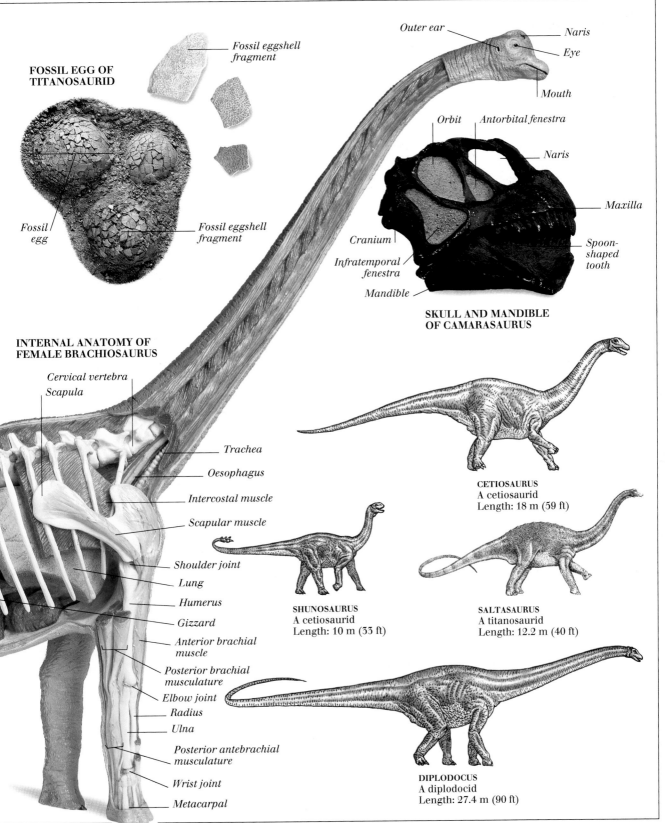

FOSSIL EGG OF TITANOSAURID

Fossil eggshell fragment

Fossil egg

Fossil eggshell fragment

Outer ear

Naris

Eye

Mouth

Orbit

Antorbital fenestra

Naris

Cranium

Maxilla

Infratemporal fenestra

Spoon-shaped tooth

Mandible

SKULL AND MANDIBLE OF CAMARASAURUS

INTERNAL ANATOMY OF FEMALE BRACHIOSAURUS

Cervical vertebra

Scapula

Trachea

Oesophagus

Intercostal muscle

Scapular muscle

Shoulder joint

Lung

Humerus

Gizzard

Anterior brachial muscle

Posterior brachial musculature

Elbow joint

Radius

Ulna

Posterior antebrachial musculature

Wrist joint

Metacarpal

CETIOSAURUS
A cetiosaurid
Length: 18 m (59 ft)

SHUNOSAURUS
A cetiosaurid
Length: 10 m (33 ft)

SALTASAURUS
A titanosaurid
Length: 12.2 m (40 ft)

DIPLODOCUS
A diplodocid
Length: 27.4 m (90 ft)

Thyreophorans 1

THYREOPHORANS ("SHIELD BEARERS") were a group of quadrupedal armoured dinosaurs. A sub-order of the Ornithischia (bird-hipped dinosaurs), they were characterized by rows of bony studs, plates, or spikes along the back, which protected some from predators and may have helped others regulate body temperature. Up to 9m (30ft) long, with a small head and small cheek teeth, Thyreophorans had shorter forelimbs than hind limbs and probably browsed on low-level vegetation. The earliest thyreophorans were small and lived in Early Jurassic times (about 200 million years ago) in Europe, North America, and China. Stegosaurs, such as Stegosaurus and Kentrosaurus, replaced these older forms. The earliest stegosaur remains come mainly from China. Several genera of stegosaurs survived into the Early Cretaceous period (146–100 million years ago), but only in India did they persist into Late Cretaceous times (97–65 million years ago). Ankylosaurs, with their toothless beaks and cheek teeth adapted for cropping vegetation, appeared later than stegosaurs. They originated in the Late Jurassic period (155 million years ago) and in North America survived until 65 million years ago.

TUOJIANGOSAURUS
A stegosaurid
Length: 7 m (25 ft)

Dorsal plate

Hip

Thigh

Cervical plate

Eye

Naris

Beak

Cheek

Neck

Outer ear

Knee

Shoulder

Short forelimb

Long hind limb

Elbow

Nail

Wrist

Ankle

Hind foot

EXTERNAL FEATURES OF STEGOSAURUS

Nail

Forefoot

EXAMPLES OF STEGOSAURS

HUAYANGOSAURUS
A huayangosaurid
Length: 4 m (13 ft)

KENTROSAURUS
A stegosaurid
Length: 4.9 m (16 ft)

WUERHOSAURUS
A stegosaurid
Length: 6.1 m (20 ft)

EXAMPLES OF STEGOSAUR SKELETONS

Scaly skin

Tail

Caudal plate

Caudal spike

Caudal spike

Prepubic process

Ilium

Caudal vertebra

Dorsal plate

Dorsal vertebra

Cervical vertebra

Cervical plate

Caudal plate

Neural spine

Pubis

Ischium

Femur

Tibia

Chevron

Humerus

Fibula

Cranium

Ulna

STEGOSAURUS

DORSAL PLATE OF STEGOSAURUS

Front edge

Pointed top

Back edge

Base

Large surface area for radiating and absorbing heat

Hole for blood vessel

SIDE VIEW OF DORSAL PLATE

SECTION THROUGH DORSAL PLATE

Dorsal plate

Ilium

Caudal spike

Caudal vertebra

Dorsal vertebra

Cervical plate

Cranium

Femur

Humerus

Cervical vertebra

Ulna

KENTROSAURUS

Dorsal plate

Ilium

Caudal plate

Neural spine

Caudal spike

Chevron

Caudal vertebra

Dorsal vertebra

Scapula

Cervical plate

Cervical vertebra

Femur

Humerus

Ulna

Cranium

TUOJIANGOSAURUS

Thyreophorans 2

EXAMPLES OF ANKYLOSAUR SKULLS

Maxilla

Orbit

Posterolateral horn

Naris

Beak

Tooth

Mandible

Cranium

Jugal plate

SKULL AND MANDIBLE OF EUOPLOCEPHALUS

Nasal bone

Maxilla

Orbit

Cranium

Posterolateral horn

Naris

Beak

Tooth

Mandible

SKULL AND MANDIBLE OF ANKYLOSAURUS

Orbit

Nasal bone

Beak

Naris

Cranium

Infratemporal fenestra

Mandible

SKULL AND MANDIBLE OF PANOPLOSAURUS

Dorsal vertebra

Small intestine

Ilio-tibial muscle

Rib

Gizzard

Ilium

Reproductive canal

Scapula

Lung

Ischium

Coracoid

Cervical musculature

Head horn

Humerus

Radius

Wrist joint

Heart

Toothless beak

Ilio-tibial muscle

Femur

Knee joint

Metacarpal

Liver

Fibula

Gastrocnemius muscle

Ventral antebrachial muscle

Ulna

Elbow joint

Large intestine

Digital extensor muscle

Ankle joint

Metatarsal

INTERNAL ANATOMY OF FEMALE EUOPLOCEPHALUS

EXTERNAL FEATURES OF EDMONTONIA

Hind
limb

Flank
spike

Dorsal
scute

Dermal
armour

Scaly
skin

Nuchal ring

Shoulder
spike

Broad, flat
snout

Ankle | Elbow

Forelimb

Naris

Caudal vertebra

Neural spine

Ureter

Forefoot

Blunt nail

Terminal
plate

Chevron

Cloaca

Lateral plate

Lateral caudal
musculature

Tail club

EXAMPLES OF ANKYLOSAURS

PINACOSAURUS
An ankylosaurid
Length: 5 m (16 ft 6 in)

MINMI
A nodosaurid
Length: 2.4 m (8 ft)

POLACANTHUS
A nodosaurid
Length: 4 m (13 ft)

**FOSSIL OF
ANKYLOSAURUS
TAIL CLUB**

Ossified caudal
vertebra

Ornithopods 1

IGUANODON TOOTH

ORNITHOPODS ("BIRD FEET") were a group of ornithischian ("bird-hipped") dinosaurs. These bipedal and quadrupedal herbivores had a horny beak, plant-cutting or grinding cheek teeth, and a pelvic and tail region stiffened by bony tendons. They evolved teeth and jaws adapted to pulping vegetation and flourished from the Middle Jurassic to the Late Cretaceous period (165–65 million years ago) in North America, Europe, Africa, China, Australia, and Antarctica. Some ornithopods were no larger than a dog, while others were immense creatures up to 15 m (49 ft) long. Iguanodonts, an ornithopod group, had a broad, toothless beak at the end of a long snout, large jaws with long rows of ridged, closely packed teeth for grinding vegetation, a bulky body, and a heavy tail. *Iguanodon* and some other iguanodonts had large thumb-spikes that were strong enough to stab attackers. Another group, the hadrosaurs, such as *Gryposaurus* and *Hadrosaurus*, lived in Late Cretaceous times (97–65 million years ago) and with their broad beaks are sometimes known as "duckbills". They were characterized by their deep skulls and closely packed rows of teeth, while some, such as *Corythosaurus* and *Lambeosaurus*, had tall, hollow, bony head crests.

SKELETON OF IGUANODON

Orbit
Cranium
Naris
Mandible
Cervical vertebra
Cervical rib
Scapula
Dorsal vertebra
Humerus
Sternal bone
Radius
Sacral vertebra
Ulna
Prepubic process
Caudal vertebra
Femur
Neural spine
Pubis
Tibia
Ilium
Chevron
Fibula
Ischium
Metatarsal

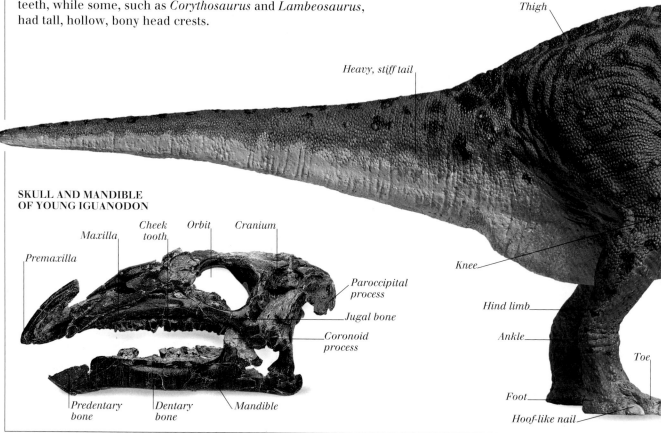

Thigh
Heavy, stiff tail
Knee
Hind limb
Ankle
Toe
Foot
Hoof-like nail

SKULL AND MANDIBLE OF YOUNG IGUANODON

Cheek tooth
Maxilla
Orbit
Cranium
Premaxilla
Paroccipital process
Jugal bone
Coronoid process
Predentary bone
Dentary bone
Mandible

EXAMPLES OF IGUANODONTS

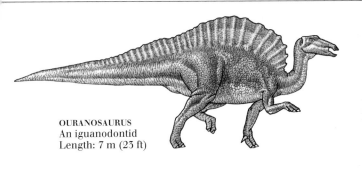

OURANOSAURUS
An iguanodontid
Length: 7 m (23 ft)

CAMPTOSAURUS
A camptosaurid
Length: 4.9–7 m (16–23 ft)

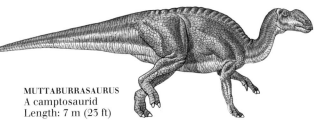

MUTTABURRASAURUS
A camptosaurid
Length: 7 m (23 ft)

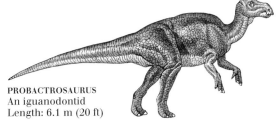

PROBACTROSAURUS
An iguanodontid
Length: 6.1 m (20 ft)

EXTERNAL FEATURES OF IGUANODON

INTERNAL ANATOMY OF HIND LEG OF IGUANODON

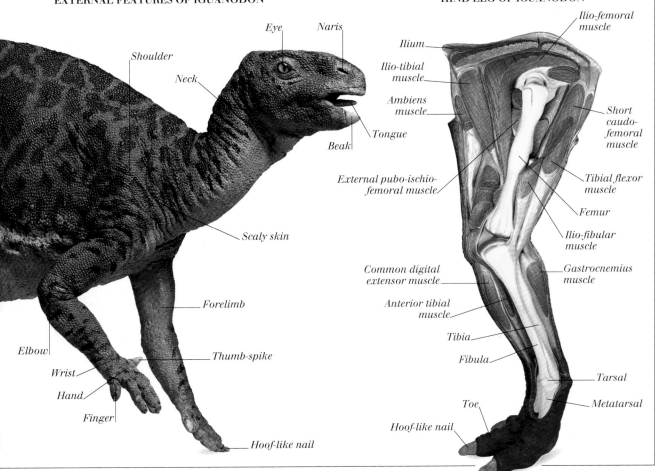

Eye

Naris

Shoulder

Neck

Ilio-femoral muscle

Ilium

Ilio-tibial muscle

Ambiens muscle

Tongue

Beak

Short caudo-femoral muscle

External pubo-ischio-femoral muscle

Tibial flexor muscle

Femur

Ilio-fibular muscle

Scaly skin

Gastrocnemius muscle

Common digital extensor muscle

Anterior tibial muscle

Forelimb

Tibia

Fibula

Elbow

Wrist

Hand

Thumb-spike

Tarsal

Metatarsal

Finger

Toe

Hoof-like nail

Hoof-like nail

Ornithopods 2

BRACHYLOPHOSAURUS
Length: 7m (23 ft)

LAMBEOSAURUS
Length: 14.9 m (49 ft)

Caudal vertebrae

Sacral vertebrae

Neural spine

Chevron

Rounded top
end of egg

Emerging
hatchling

Hatchling

Eggshell
fragment

Plant material
to protect and
warm eggs

Ilium

Unhatched
egg

Raised nest
scooped out
of soil

Ischium

Hip joint

Prepubic process

MODEL OF MAIASAURA NEST

Femur

Knee joint

Bony crest

Naris

Eye

Cheek pouch

Neck

Thigh

**FOSSIL SKELETON OF
PARASAUROLOPHUS**

Tongue

Toothless
beak

Scaly skin

Shoulder

Forelimb

Elbow

Tubercle

Long, thick
tail

Ankle joint

Wrist

Metatarsal

Knee

Hind limb

Nail

Ankle

Toe

**EXTERNAL FEATURES
OF CORYTHOSAURUS**

Nail

Foot

EXAMPLES OF HADROSAURS

HYPACROSAURUS
Length: 9.1 m (30 ft)

HADROSAURUS
Length: 7.9–10 m (26–33 ft)

GRYPOSAURUS
Length: 7.9–10 m (26–33 ft)

Dorsal vertebrae

Bony crest

Air passage

Cranium

Infratemporal fenestra

Orbit

Orbit

Infratemporal fenestra

Air passage

Naris

Cervical vertebrae

Mandible

Tooth

SKULL AND MANDIBLE OF JUVENILE LAMBEOSAURUS

Mandible

Naris

Scapula

Shoulder joint

Sclerotic ring

Bony crest

Cranium

Tibia

Orbit

Rib

Naris

Humerus

Elbow joint

Radius

Infratemporal fenestra

Mandible

Premaxilla

Fibula

Wrist joint

Ulna

SKULL AND MANDIBLE OF ADULT LAMBEOSAURUS

Phalanges

Metacarpal

Phalanges

99

Marginocephalians 1

- Thick, high-domed cranium
- Supraorbital ridge
- Orbit
- Naris
- Mandible
- Neural spine
- Cervical rib
- Humerus
- Ulna
- Radius
- Prepubis
- Wrist joint
- Metacarpal
- Phalanx
- Ilium
- Ischium
- Metatarsals
- Phalanges

HEAD-BUTTING PRENOCEPHALES

MARGINOCEPHALIA ("margined heads") were a group of bipedal and quadrupedal ornithischian dinosaurs with a narrow shelf or deep, bony frill at the back of the skull. Marginocephalians were probably descended from the same ancestor as the ornithopods and lived in what are now North America, Africa, Asia, and Europe during the Cretaceous period (146–65 million years ago). They were divided into two infraorders: Pachycephalosauria ("thick-headed lizards"), such as *Pachycephalosaurus* and *Stegoceras*, and Ceratopsia ("horned faces"), such as *Triceratops* and *Psittacosaurus*. The thick skulls of Pachycephalosauria protected their brains during head-butting contests fought to win territory and mates; their hips and spines were also strengthened to withstand the shock. The bony frill of Ceratopsia would have added to their frightening appearance when charging; the neck was strengthened for impact and to support the huge head, with its snipping beak and powerful slicing toothed jaws. A charging ceratops would have been a formidable opponent for even the largest predators. Ceratopsia were among the most abundant herbivorous dinosaurs of the Late Cretaceous period (97–65 million years ago).

EXAMPLES OF SKULLS OF PACHYCEPHALOSAURS

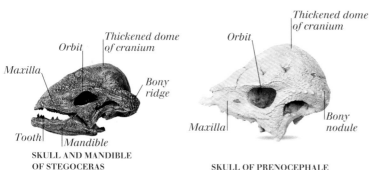

- Orbit
- Thickened dome of cranium
- Maxilla
- Bony ridge
- Tooth
- Mandible

SKULL AND MANDIBLE OF STEGOCERAS

- Thickened dome of cranium
- Orbit
- Maxilla
- Bony nodule

SKULL OF PRENOCEPHALE

- Thickened dome of cranium
- Bony spike
- Maxilla
- Orbit
- Bony nodule

SKULL OF PACHYCEPHALOSAURUS

EXTERNAL FEATURES OF PACHYCEPHALOSAURUS

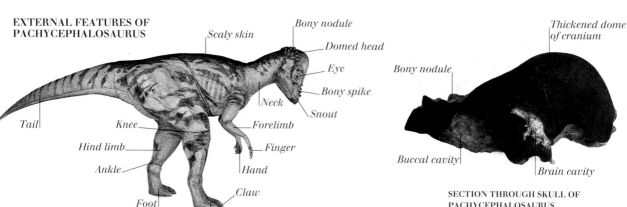

- Scaly skin
- Bony nodule
- Domed head
- Eye
- Bony spike
- Neck
- Snout
- Tail
- Knee
- Forelimb
- Finger
- Hind limb
- Hand
- Ankle
- Claw
- Foot
- Toe

- Thickened dome of cranium
- Bony nodule
- Buccal cavity
- Brain cavity

SECTION THROUGH SKULL OF PACHYCEPHALOSAURUS

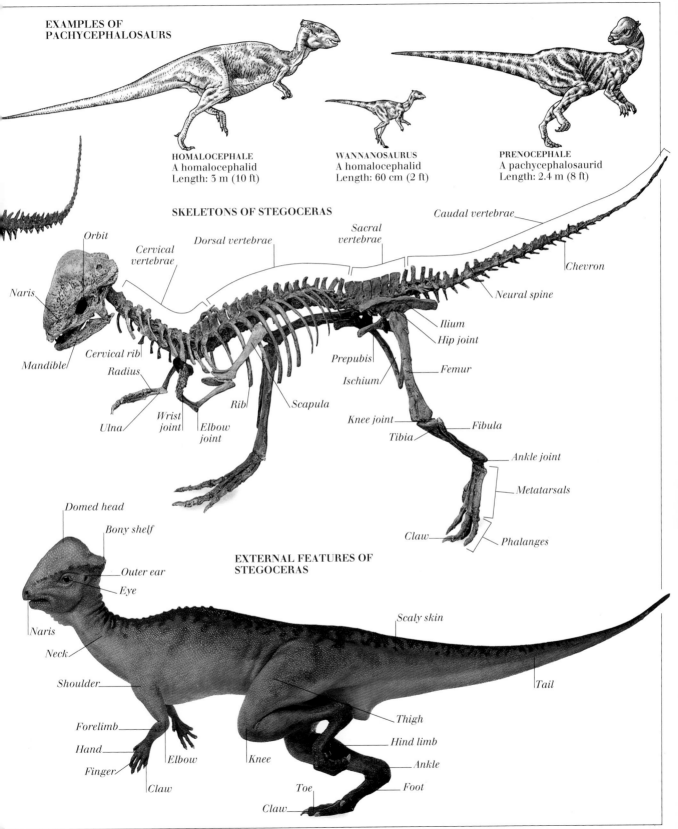

EXAMPLES OF PACHYCEPHALOSAURS

HOMALOCEPHALE
A homalocephalid
Length: 3 m (10 ft)

WANNANOSAURUS
A homalocephalid
Length: 60 cm (2 ft)

PRENOCEPHALE
A pachycephalosaurid
Length: 2.4 m (8 ft)

SKELETONS OF STEGOCERAS

Orbit

Cervical
vertebrae

Dorsal vertebrae

Sacral
vertebrae

Caudal vertebrae

Chevron

Naris

Neural spine

Ilium

Hip joint

Cervical rib

Prepubis

Femur

Mandible

Ischium

Radius

Rib

Scapula

Ulna

Wrist
joint

Elbow
joint

Knee joint

Fibula

Tibia

Ankle joint

Metatarsals

Claw

Phalanges

EXTERNAL FEATURES OF STEGOCERAS

Domed head

Bony shelf

Outer ear

Eye

Scaly skin

Naris

Neck

Tail

Shoulder

Thigh

Forelimb

Hind limb

Hand

Elbow

Knee

Ankle

Finger

Toe

Foot

Claw

Claw

Marginocephalians 2

Brow horn

Parietosquamosal frill

Nose horn

Epoccipital bone

Thick, scaly skin

Thigh

Tail

Ankle

Nail

Hind limb

Elbow

Forelimb

Wrist

Eye

Naris

Toothless beak

EXTERNAL FEATURES OF TRICERATOPS

Parietal fenestra

Epoccipital bone

Parietosquamosal frill

Nose horn core

Supraorbital ridge

Naris

Orbit

Cranium

Mandible

SKULL AND MANDIBLE OF STYRACOSAURUS

Parietosquamosal frill

Cranium

Postorbital bone

Nasal bone

Orbit

Lacrimal bone

Naris

Beak

Rostral bone

Predentary bone

Dentary bone

Tooth

Mandible

Parietal fenestra

Infratemporal fenestra

Jugal bone

Surangular bone

Angular bone

SKULL AND MANDIBLE OF PROTOCERATOPS

Hip joint

Ilium

Prepubis

Dorsal vertebrae

Ischium

Femur

Knee joint

Fibula

Tibia

Ankle joint

Metatarsals

Phalanges

Caudal vertebra

Chevron

Neural spine

Rib

Scapula

Humerus

Elbow joint

Ulna

Sternal bone

Coracoid

Shoulder joint

Radius

SKELETON OF TRICERATOPS

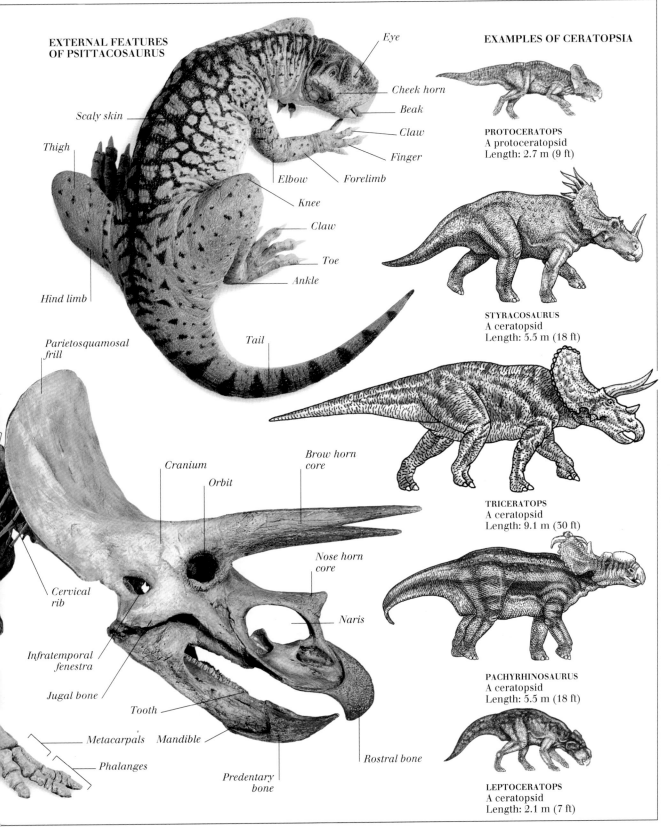

**EXTERNAL FEATURES
OF PSITTACOSAURUS**

Eye

Cheek horn

Beak

Claw

Finger

Scaly skin

Thigh

Elbow

Forelimb

Knee

Claw

Toe

Ankle

Hind limb

Tail

Parietosquamosal
frill

Cranium

Orbit

Brow horn
core

Nose horn
core

Naris

Cervical
rib

Infratemporal
fenestra

Jugal bone

Tooth

Metacarpals   Mandible

Phalanges

Predentary
bone

Rostral bone

EXAMPLES OF CERATOPSIA

PROTOCERATOPS
A protoceratopsid
Length: 2.7 m (9 ft)

STYRACOSAURUS
A ceratopsid
Length: 5.5 m (18 ft)

TRICERATOPS
A ceratopsid
Length: 9.1 m (30 ft)

PACHYRHINOSAURUS
A ceratopsid
Length: 5.5 m (18 ft)

LEPTOCERATOPS
A ceratopsid
Length: 2.1 m (7 ft)

Mammals 1

TETRALOPHODON
CHEEK TEETH

SINCE THE EXTINCTION of the dinosaurs 65 million years ago, mammals have been the dominant vertebrates on land. This class includes terrestrial, aerial, and aquatic forms. Having developed from the reptilian Therapsids, the first true mammals – small, nocturnal, shrew-like creatures, such as *Megazostrodon* – appeared over 200 million years ago during the Triassic period (245–208 million years ago). Mammals had several features that improved on those of their reptilian ancestors: an efficient four-chambered heart allowed these warm-blooded animals to sustain high levels of activity; a covering of hair helped them maintain a constant body temperature; an improved limb structure gave them more efficient locomotion; and the birth of live young and the immediate supply of food from the mother's milk aided their rapid growth. Since the end of the Mesozoic era (65 million years ago), the number of different mammal orders and the abundance of species in each order have varied dramatically. For example, the Perissodactyla (the order that includes *Coelodonta* and modern horses) was a common group during the Early Tertiary period (about 54 million years ago). Today, the mammalian orders with the most species include the Rodentia (rats and mice), the Chiroptera (bats), the Primates (monkeys and apes), the Carnivora (bears, cats, and dogs), and the Artiodactyla (cattle, deer, and pigs), while the Proboscidea order, which formerly included many genera, such as *Phiomia, Moeritherium, Tetralophodon,* and *Mammuthus,* now has only three species of elephant. In Australia and South America, millions of years of continental isolation led to increased diversity of the marsupials, a group of mammals distinct from the placentals (see p. 74) that existed elsewhere.

Long tail aids
balance

Insulating
hair

Neural
spine

Scapula

Cervical
vertebra

Humerus

Nasal horn

Naris

Orbit

Mandible

Predentary
bone

Radius

Ulna

Chisel-edged
molar

Metacarpal

Phalanx

UPPER JAWBONE (MAXILLA) OF A HORSE

Molars

Premolars

HOOFBONE (THIRD PHALANX) OF A HORSE

Articular surface

Tendon insertion

Cranium

Naris

Predentary bone

Molar tooth

SKULL AND MANDIBLE OF A MOERITHERIUM

Nasal tusk

Molar tooth

Shovel-shaped tusk

SKULL AND MANDIBLE OF A PHIOMIA

Trunk

Thick hide

Short tusk used for rooting up plants

MODEL OF A PHIOMIA

Dorsal vertebra

Ilium

Ball and socket joint

Pubis

Rib

Caudal vertebra

Femur

Tibia

Fibula

Metatarsal

Phalanx

SKELETON OF AN ARSINOITHERIUM

Cranium

Mandible

Teeth

Elongated digit

Humerus

Hind limb bone

FOSSIL SKELETON OF A BAT

Mammals 2

LOWER JAW OF A BEAR

Articulation with skull

Large canine

Diastema

Low cusp

Molar

Premolar

Zygomatic arch

Cranium

Orbit

Coronoid process

Maxilla

Cervical vertebra

Nasal bone

Canine

Incisor

Mandible

Molar

Occipital region

SKELETON OF A TOXODON

Scapula

Neural spine

Humerus

Radius

Ulna

Metacarpals

Large breastbone

Phalanx

SKULL OF AN OPOSSUM

Orbit

Cranium

Naris

Occipital region

Canine

Infraorbital foramen

Molar

**FOSSIL SKULL OF
AN HYAENODON**

Orbit

Sagittal crest

Naris

Cranium

Canine

Neck
insertion

Infraorbital
foramen

Mandible

Molar

**LOWER JAW OF AN
AUSTRALOPITHECUS**

Expanded
occlusal
surface

Premolar

Molar

Ilium

Rib

Femur

Knee
joint

Tibia

Fibula

Metatarsals

Phalanx

SKULL OF A SMILODON

Orbit

Muscle scar

Naris

Sagittal crest

Infraorbital
foramen

Occipital
condyle

Canine

Dentary
bone

Slicing
tooth

Zygomatic
arch

Thick,
insulating
coat

Ivory tusk

Woolly
underhair

Hairy trunk

RECONSTRUCTION OF A MAMMOTH

The first hominids

MODERN HUMANS BELONG TO THE MAMMALIAN order of primates
(see pp. 202–203), which originated about 55 million years ago; they
comprise the only extant hominid species. The earliest hominid was
Australopithecus ("southern ape"), a small-brained intermediate between
apes and humans that was capable of standing and walking upright. *Homo
habilis*, the first known human appeared at least 2 million years ago. This
larger-brained "handy man" began making tools for hunting. *Homo erectus*
first appeared in Africa about 1.8 million years ago and spread into Asia about
800,000 years later. Smaller-toothed than *Homo habilis*, it developed fire as a
tool, which enabled it to cook food. Neanderthals, a near relative of modern
humans, originated about 200,000 years ago, and *Homo sapiens* (modern humans)
appeared in Africa about 100,000 years later. The two co-existed for thousands
of years, but by 30,000 years ago, *Homo sapiens* had become dominant and the
Neanderthals had died out. Classification of *Homo sapiens* in relation to its ancestors is
enormously problematic: modern humans must be classified not only by bone structure,
but also by specific behaviour – the ability to plan future action; to follow traditions;
and to use symbolic communication, including complex language and the
ability to use and recognize symbols.

**JAWBONE OF AUSTRALOPITHECUS
(SOUTHERN APE)**

*Larger jawbone
than modern
human*

*Large back
tooth*

*Jutting brow
ridge*

Cranium

Orbit

Naris

*Jutting
jawbone*

**SKULL OF AUSTRALOPITHECUS
(SOUTHERN APE)**

Orbit

Naris

**SKULL OF HOMO HABILIS
(FIRST KNOWN HUMAN)**

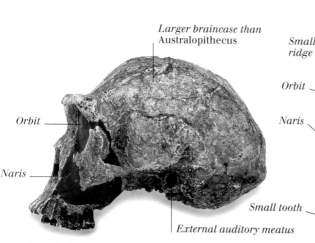

*Larger braincase than
Australopithecus*

Orbit

Naris

External auditory meatus

SKULL OF HOMO ERECTUS (UPRIGHT MAN)

*Well-rounded
cranium*

*Small brow
ridge*

Orbit

Naris

Small tooth

*External
auditory meatus*

SKULL OF HOMO SAPIENS (MODERN HUMAN)

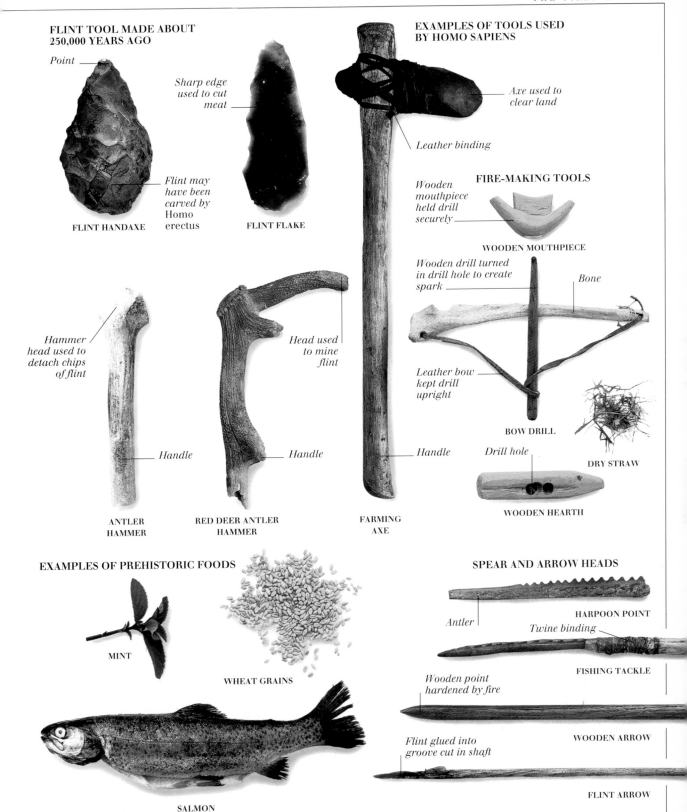

FLINT TOOL MADE ABOUT 250,000 YEARS AGO

Point

Sharp edge used to cut meat

Flint may have been carved by Homo erectus

FLINT HANDAXE

FLINT FLAKE

Hammer head used to detach chips of flint

Head used to mine flint

Handle

Handle

Handle

ANTLER HAMMER

RED DEER ANTLER HAMMER

FARMING AXE

EXAMPLES OF TOOLS USED BY HOMO SAPIENS

Axe used to clear land

Leather binding

FIRE-MAKING TOOLS

Wooden mouthpiece held drill securely

WOODEN MOUTHPIECE

Wooden drill turned in drill hole to create spark

Bone

Leather bow kept drill upright

BOW DRILL

DRY STRAW

Drill hole

WOODEN HEARTH

EXAMPLES OF PREHISTORIC FOODS

MINT

WHEAT GRAINS

SALMON

SPEAR AND ARROW HEADS

Antler

HARPOON POINT

Twine binding

FISHING TACKLE

Wooden point hardened by fire

WOODEN ARROW

Flint glued into groove cut in shaft

FLINT ARROW

PLANTS

PLANT VARIETY · · · · · · · 112

FUNGI AND LICHENS · · · · · 114

ALGAE AND SEAWEEDS · · · · · 116

LIVERWORTS AND MOSSES · · · · 118

HORSETAILS, CLUBMOSSES, AND FERNS · 120

GYMNOSPERMS 1 · · · · · 122

GYMNOSPERMS 2 · · · · · 124

MONOCOTYLEDONS AND DICOTYLEDONS · 126

HERBACEOUS FLOWERING PLANTS · · · 128

WOODY FLOWERING PLANTS · · · 130

ROOTS · · · · · · · · 132

STEMS · · · · · · · · 134

LEAVES · · · · · · · 136

PHOTOSYNTHESIS · · · · · 138

FLOWERS 1 · · · · · · 140

FLOWERS 2 · · · · · · 142

POLLINATION · · · · · 144

FERTILIZATION · · · · · 146

SUCCULENT FRUITS · · · · 148

DRY FRUITS · · · · · · 150

GERMINATION · · · · · 152

VEGETATIVE REPRODUCTION · · · 154

DRYLAND PLANTS · · · · · 156

WETLAND PLANTS · · · · · 158

CARNIVOROUS PLANTS · · · · 160

EPIPHYTIC AND PARASITIC PLANTS · · 162

Plant variety

Leaf

THERE ARE MORE THAN 300,000 SPECIES of plants. They
show a wide diversity of forms and life-styles, ranging, for example, from delicate
liverworts, adapted for life in a damp habitat, to cacti, capable of surviving in the desert, and
from herbaceous plants, such as corn, which completes its life-cycle in one year, to the giant redwood tree,
which can live for thousands of years. This diversity reflects the adaptations of plants to survive in a wide
range of habitats. This is seen most clearly in the flowering plants (phylum Angiospermophyta), which are
the most numerous, with over 250,000 species, and the most widespread, being found from the tropics to the
poles. Despite their diversity, plants share certain characteristics: typically, plants are green, and make their
food by photosynthesis; and most plants live in or on a substrate, such as soil, and do not actively move. Algae
(kingdom Protista) and fungi (kingdom Fungi) have some plant-like characteristics and are
often studied alongside plants, although they are not true plants.

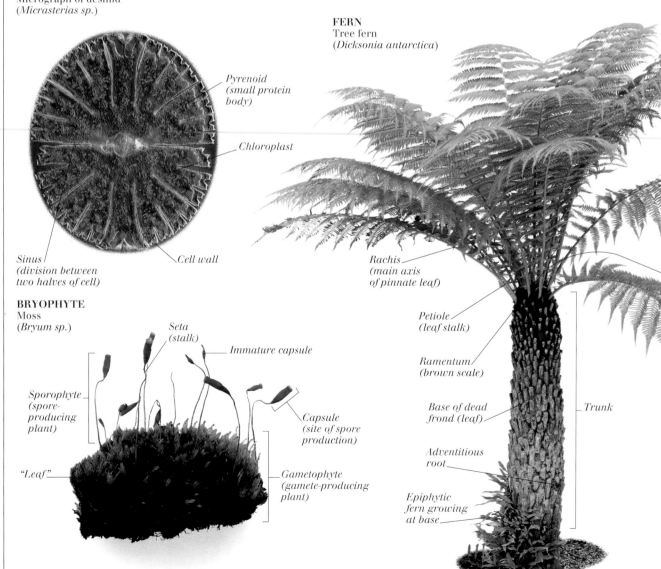

GREEN ALGA
Micrograph of desmid
(*Micrasterias sp.*)

*Pyrenoid
(small protein
body)*

Chloroplast

*Sinus
(division between
two halves of cell)*

Cell wall

FERN
Tree fern
(*Dicksonia antarctica*)

*Rachis
(main axis
of pinnate leaf)*

*Petiole
(leaf stalk)*

*Ramentum
(brown scale)*

*Base of dead
frond (leaf)*

Trunk

*Adventitious
root*

*Epiphytic
fern growing
at base*

BRYOPHYTE
Moss
(*Bryum sp.*)

*Seta
(stalk)*

Immature capsule

*Sporophyte
(spore-
producing
plant)*

*Capsule
(site of spore
production)*

"Leaf"

*Gametophyte
(gamete-producing
plant)*

FLOWERING PLANT
Succulent
(*Kedrostis africana*)

*Petiole
(leaf stalk)*

Leaf

Stem

*Caudex
(swollen
stem
base)*

Root

Spine Flower

*Bract
(leaf-like structure)*

Inflorescence

Stem

FLOWERING PLANT
Micrograph of cross-section
through leaf of marram grass
(*Ammophila arenaria*)

*Sclerenchyma
(strengthening
tissue)*

*Cuticle
(waterproof
covering)*

Xylem   } *Vascular
tissue*

Phloem

*Stiff trichome
(hair)*

*Interlocked
trichomes (hairs)*

*Epidermis
(outer layer
of cells)*

*Hinge cells
(cause curling of leaf to
reduce water loss)*

*Mesophyll
(photosynthetic
tissue)*

*Pinna
(leaflet)*

FLOWERING PLANT
Couch grass
(*Agropyron repens*)

*Caryopsis
(type of
dry fruit)*

FLOWERING PLANT
Pitcher plant
(*Sarracenia purpurea*)

Sepal

*Fruit
surrounded
by floral parts*

*Rachis
(main axis of
grass inflorescence)*

*Umbrella
of style*

*Pitcher (leaf
modified to trap
insects)*

Frond (leaf)

*Pedicel
(flower
stalk)*

Node

Hood

*Downward-pointing
hair (encourages
insect prey into
pitcher)*

*Midrib of
pinna (leaflet)*

Wing

*Lamina
(blade)*

*Round, hollow
stem*

*Sheathing
leaf base*

*Adventitious
root*

*Immature
pitcher*

Fungi and lichens

FUNGI WERE ONCE THOUGHT OF AS PLANTS but are now classified as a separate kingdom. This kingdom includes not only the familiar mushrooms, puffballs, stinkhorns, and moulds, but also yeasts, smuts, rusts, and lichens. Most fungi are multicellular, consisting of a mass of thread-like hyphae that together form a mycelium. However, the simpler fungi (e.g., yeasts) are microscopic, single-celled organisms. Typically, fungi reproduce by means of spores. Most fungi feed on dead or decaying matter, or on living organisms. A few fungi obtain their food from plants or algae, with which they have a symbiotic (mutually advantageous) relationship. Lichens are a symbiotic partnership between algae and fungi. Of the six types of lichens the three most common are crustose (flat and crusty), foliose (leafy), and fruticose (shrub-like). Some lichens (e.g., *Cladonia floerkeana*) are a combination of types. Lichens reproduce by means of spores or soredia (powdery vegetative fragments).

Emerging sporophore (spore-bearing structure)

Pileus (cap) continuous with stipe (stalk)

Bark of dead beech tree

Inrolled margin of pileus (cap)

Gill (site of spore production)

Sporophore (spore-bearing structure)

Stipe (stalk)

Hyphae (fungal filaments)

OYSTER FUNGUS
(Pleurotus pulmonarius)

EXAMPLES OF LICHENS

Secondary fruticose thallus

Branched, hollow stem

Apothecium (spore-producing body)

FRUTICOSE
Cladonia portentosa

Soredia (powdery vegetative fragments) produced at end of lobe

Tree bark

Foliose thallus

FOLIOSE
Hypogymnia physodes

Gleba (spore-producing tissue found in this type of fungus)

Sporophore (spore-bearing structure)

Porous stipe (stalk)

Volva (remains of universal veil)

STINKHORN
(Phallus impudicus)

Toothed branchlet

Branch

Sporophore (spore-bearing structure)

Stipe (stalk)

RAMARIA FORMOSA

Soredia (powdery vegetative fragments) released onto surface of squamulose thallus

Apothecium (spore-producing body)

Basal scale of primary squamulose thallus

Podetium (granular stalk) of secondary fruticose thallus

Moss

SQUAMULOSE (SCALY) AND FRUTICOSE THALLUS
Cladonia floerkeana

SECTION THROUGH FOLIOSE LICHEN SHOWING REPRODUCTION BY SOREDIA

Algal cell

Fungal hypha

Upper cortex

Algal layer

Medulla of fungal hyphae (mycelium)

Lower cortex

Rhizine (bundle of absorptive hyphae)

Soredium (powdery vegetative fragment involved in propagation) released from lichen

Soralium (pore in upper surface of thallus)

Upper surface of thallus

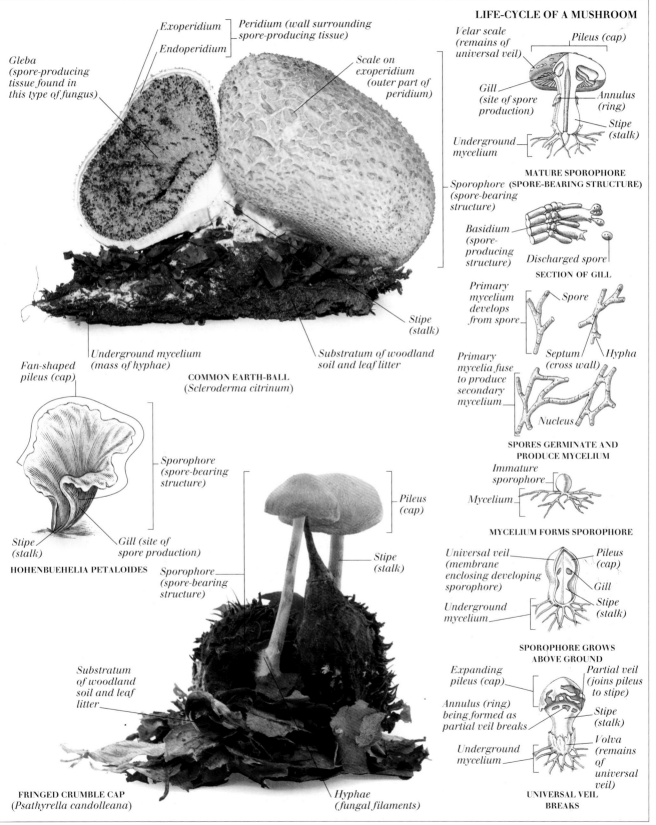

Gleba
(spore-producing
tissue found in
this type of fungus)

Exoperidium

Endoperidium

Peridium (wall surrounding
spore-producing tissue)

Scale on
exoperidium
(outer part of
peridium)

Stipe
(stalk)

Underground mycelium
(mass of hyphae)

Substratum of woodland
soil and leaf litter

COMMON EARTH-BALL
(Scleroderma citrinum)

Fan-shaped
pileus (cap)

Sporophore
(spore-bearing
structure)

Stipe
(stalk)

Gill (site of
spore production)

HOHENBUEHELIA PETALOIDES

Sporophore
(spore-bearing
structure)

Pileus
(cap)

Stipe
(stalk)

Substratum
of woodland
soil and leaf
litter

FRINGED CRUMBLE CAP
(Psathyrella candolleana)

Hyphae
(fungal filaments)

LIFE-CYCLE OF A MUSHROOM

Velar scale
(remains of
universal veil)

Pileus (cap)

Gill
(site of spore
production)

Annulus
(ring)

Stipe
(stalk)

Underground
mycelium

MATURE SPOROPHORE

Sporophore
(spore-bearing
structure)

Basidium
(spore-
producing
structure)

Discharged spore

SECTION OF GILL

Primary
mycelium
develops
from spore

Spore

Primary
mycelia fuse
to produce
secondary
mycelium

Septum
(cross wall)

Hypha

Nucleus

**SPORES GERMINATE AND
PRODUCE MYCELIUM**

Immature
sporophore

Mycelium

MYCELIUM FORMS SPOROPHORE

Universal veil
(membrane
enclosing developing
sporophore)

Pileus
(cap)

Gill

Underground
mycelium

Stipe
(stalk)

**SPOROPHORE GROWS
ABOVE GROUND**

Expanding
pileus (cap)

Partial veil
(joins pileus
to stipe)

Annulus (ring)
being formed as
partial veil breaks

Stipe
(stalk)

Underground
mycelium

Volva
(remains
of
universal
veil)

**UNIVERSAL VEIL
BREAKS**

Algae and seaweeds

ALGAE ARE NOT TRUE PLANTS. They form a diverse group
of plant-like organisms that belong to the kingdom Protista.
Like plants, algae possess the green pigment chlorophyll
and make their own food by photosynthesis (see pp. 138-139).
Many algae also possess other pigments by which they can be
classified; for example, the brown pigment fucoxanthin is
found in the brown algae. Some of the ten phyla of algae are
exclusively unicellular (single-celled); others also contain
aggregates of cells in filaments or colonies. Three phyla –
the Chlorophyta (green algae), Rhodophyta (red algae),
and Phaeophyta (brown algae) – contain larger, multicellular,
thalloid (flat), marine organisms commonly known as seaweeds.
Most algae can reproduce sexually. For
example, in the brown seaweed
Fucus vesiculosus, gametes
(sex cells) are produced in
conceptacles (chambers) in
the receptacles (fertile tips
of fronds); after their release
into the sea, antherozoids
(male gametes) and oospheres
(female gametes) fuse; the
resulting zygote settles on a rock
and develops into a new seaweed.

BROWN SEAWEED
Channelled wrack
(*Pelvetia canaliculata*)

Receptacle
(fertile tip
of frond)

Thallus
(plant
body)

Apical
notch

Margin of
lamina (blade)
rolled inwards
to form channel

Hapteron (holdfast)

BROWN SEAWEED
Spiral wrack
(*Fucus spiralis*)

Apical notch

Conceptacle
(chamber)

Receptacle
(fertile tip
of frond)

Thallus
(plant
body)

Lamina
(blade)

Smooth margin

Midrib

Hapteron (holdfast)

EXAMPLES OF ALGAE

Reproductive
chamber

Cap

Sterile whorl

Cell wall

Stalk

Rhizoid

GREEN ALGA
Acetabularia sp.

Flagellum

Eyespot

Contractile
vacuole

Cytoplasm

Nucleus

Cell
wall

Chloroplast

Pyrenoid
(small protein
body)

Starch
grain

GREEN ALGA
Chlamydomonas sp.

Coenobium
(colony of cells)

Daughter
coenobium

Gelatinous
sheath

Biflagellate cell

GREEN ALGA
Volvox sp.

Spine

Cytoplasm

Girdle

Vacuole

Nucleus

Plastid
(photosynthetic
organelle)

DIATOM
Thalassiosira sp.

Apical notch

Receptacle
(fertile tip
of frond)

Conceptacle
(chamber)
containing
reproductive
structures)

Lamina
(blade)

Midrib

RECEPTACLE
Spiral wrack
(*Fucus spiralis*)

BROWN SEAWEED
Oarweed
(*Laminaria digitata*)

Thallus (plant body)

Lamina (blade)
palmately
divided

GREEN SEAWEED
Enteromorpha linza

Crinkled margin

Thallus (plant body)

Unbranched, spirally twisted frond

Small hapteron (holdfast) attaching seaweed to mussel

RED SEAWEED
Corallina officinalis

Branch

Branched, hard thallus (plant body)

Hapteron (holdfast)

Main stem

LIFE-CYCLE OF BROWN SEAWEED
Bladder wrack
(*Fucus vesiculosus*)

Male receptacle

Female receptacle

Lamina (blade)

Air bladder

Hapteron (holdfast)

Stipe (stalk)

MALE AND FEMALE SEAWEEDS

Male receptacle

Female receptacle

Conceptacle

Ostiole (opening to conceptacle)

MALE AND FEMALE RECEPTACLES

Paraphysis (sterile hair)

Ostiole (opening to conceptacle)

Antheridium (male sex organ)

Oogonium (female sex organ)

SECTIONS THROUGH MALE AND FEMALE CONCEPTACLES

Oogonium

Antherozoid (male gamete)

Antheridium (male sex organ)

Oosphere (female gamete)

PRODUCTION OF GAMETES

RED SEAWEED
Dilsea carnosa

Thallus (plant body)

Lamina (blade)

Hapteron (holdfast)

GREEN ALGA
Spirogyra sp.

Antherozoid (male gamete) swims towards oosphere

Flagellum

Oosphere (female gamete) is fertilized by antherozoid to produce a zygote

FERTILIZATION

Cytoplasm

Cell (cylindrical)

End wall of cell

Cell wall

Filament (strand of linked cells)

Two filaments linked for conjugation (sexual reproduction)

Spirally wound chloroplast

Conjugation tube

End wall of conjugation tube still in place

Flexible stipe (stalk)

Hapteron (holdfast)

Young thallus (plant body)

Hapteron (holdfast)

ZYGOTE DEVELOPS INTO A YOUNG SEAWEED

Liverworts and mosses

LIVERWORTS AND MOSSES ARE SMALL, LOW-GROWING PLANTS that belong to the phylum Bryophyta. Bryophytes do not have true stems, leaves, or roots (they are anchored to the ground by rhizoids), nor do they have the vascular tissues (xylem and phloem) that transport water and nutrients in higher plants. With no outer, waterproof cuticle, bryophytes are susceptible to drying out, and most grow in moist habitats. The bryophyte life-cycle has two stages. In stage one, the green plant (gametophyte) produces male and female gametes (sex cells), which fuse to form a zygote. In stage two, the zygote develops into a sporophyte that remains attached to the gametophyte. The sporophyte produces spores, which are released and germinate into new green plants. Liverworts (class Hepaticae) grow horizontally and may be thalloid (flat and ribbon-like) or "leafy". Mosses (class Musci) typically have an upright "stem" with spirally arranged "leaves".

A LEAFY LIVERWORT
Scapania undulata

"Stem"

"Leaf"

Rhizoid

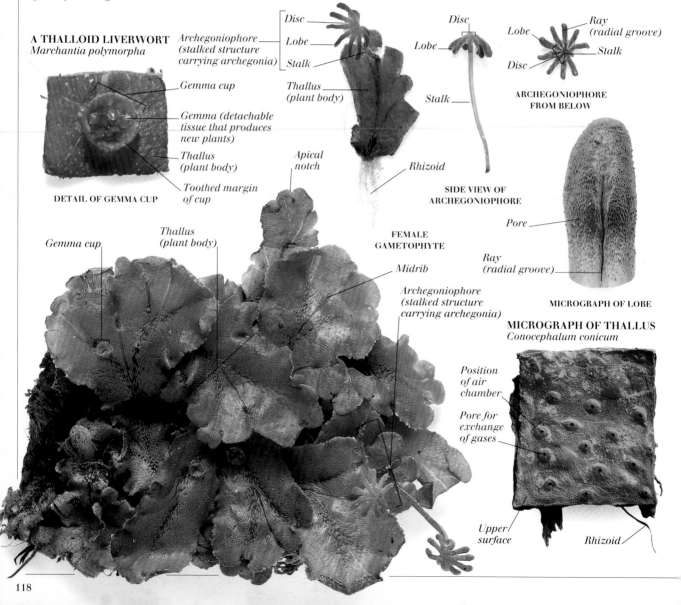

A THALLOID LIVERWORT
Marchantia polymorpha

Gemma cup

Gemma (detachable tissue that produces new plants)

Thallus (plant body)

Toothed margin of cup

DETAIL OF GEMMA CUP

Archegoniophore (stalked structure carrying archegonia)

Disc

Lobe

Stalk

Thallus (plant body)

Apical notch

Rhizoid

FEMALE GAMETOPHYTE

Disc

Lobe

Stalk

SIDE VIEW OF ARCHEGONIOPHORE

Lobe

Disc

Ray (radial groove)

Stalk

ARCHEGONIOPHORE FROM BELOW

Pore

Ray (radial groove)

MICROGRAPH OF LOBE

Gemma cup

Thallus (plant body)

Midrib

Archegoniophore (stalked structure carrying archegonia)

Position of air chamber

Pore for exchange of gases

Upper surface

Rhizoid

MICROGRAPH OF THALLUS
Conocephalum conicum

A COMMON MOSS
Polytrichum commune

"Stem"

Branch of conducting tissue to "leaf"

Cortex

Epidermis (outer layer of cells)

"Leaf"

Central strand of conducting tissue

Midrib

MICROGRAPH OF CROSS-SECTION THROUGH STEM AND LEAF

MICROGRAPH OF MOSS SPORE
Funaria hygrometrica

LIFE-CYCLE OF MOSS
Funaria sp.

Male rosette ("leaves" around antheridia)

Female rosette ("leaves" around archegonia)

Main "stem"

Lateral branch of "stem"

Rhizoid

Archegonium (female sex organ)

GAMETOPHYTE

Antherozoids (male gametes) released from antheridium

Antheridium (male sex organ)

Epidermis of capsule

Remains of spore-forming tissue

SECTION THROUGH MATURE MALE APEX

SECTION THROUGH MATURE FEMALE APEX

Spore-containing space

Columella (central tissue of capsule)

CROSS-SECTION THROUGH CAPSULE

Flagellum

Antherozoid (male gamete) swims to oosphere

Archegonium (female sex organ)

Oosphere (female gamete) fertilized by antherozoid

FERTILIZATION

Capsule

Apophysis (swollen area between seta and capsule)

Columella (central tissue of capsule)

Beak

Operculum (lid)

Calyptra (hood covering capsule)

"Leaf"

Seta (stalk)

"Stem"

EXTERNAL VIEW OF MOSS

Male apex ("leaves" surrounding antheridia)

Young aerial "stem"

"Leaf"

"Stem"

Capsule

Seta (stalk)

Sporophyte grows from fertilized oosphere

Gametophyte

SPOROPHYTE

Capsule

Operculum (lid)

Peristome tooth opens

Apophysis

Seta (stalk)

Air space

Spores dispersed

RIPE CAPSULE

Young gametophyte

Protonema (branched green filament)

Rhizoid

Bud

Spore

DEVELOPING GAMETOPHYTE

119

Horsetails, clubmosses, and ferns

HORSETAILS, CLUBMOSSES, AND FERNS are primitive land plants, which, like higher plants, have stems, roots, and leaves, and vascular systems that transport water, minerals, and food. However, unlike higher plants, they do not produce seeds when reproducing. Their life-cycles involve two stages. In stage one, the sporophyte (green plant) produces spores in sporangia. In stage two, the spores germinate, developing into small, short-lived gametophyte plants that produce male and female gametes (sex cells); the gametes fuse to form a zygote from which a new sporophyte plant develops. Horsetails (phylum Sphenophyta) have erect, green stems with branches arranged in whorls; some stems are fertile and have a single spore-producing strobilus (group of sporangia) at the tip. Clubmosses (phylum Lycopodophyta) typically have small leaves arranged spirally around the stem, with spore-producing strobili at the tip of some stems. Ferns (phylum Filicinophyta) typically have large, pinnate fronds (leaves); sporangia, grouped together in sori, develop on the underside of fertile fronds.

FROND
Male fern
(*Dryopteris filix-mas*)

CLUBMOSS
Lycopodium sp.

Stem with spirally arranged leaves

Branch

Strobilus
(group of sporangia)

CLUBMOSS
Selaginella sp.

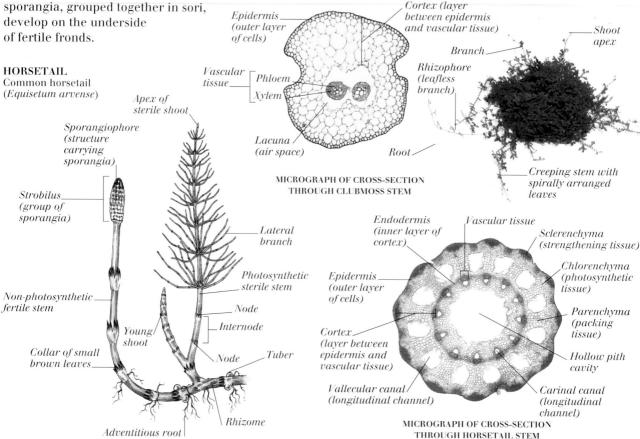

Epidermis
(outer layer of cells)

Cortex (layer between epidermis and vascular tissue)

Vascular tissue — Phloem / Xylem

Lacuna
(air space)

Root

**MICROGRAPH OF CROSS-SECTION
THROUGH CLUBMOSS STEM**

Shoot apex

Branch

Rhizophore
(leafless branch)

Creeping stem with spirally arranged leaves

HORSETAIL
Common horsetail
(*Equisetum arvense*)

Apex of sterile shoot

Sporangiophore
(structure carrying sporangia)

Strobilus
(group of sporangia)

Non-photosynthetic fertile stem

Collar of small brown leaves

Young shoot

Lateral branch

Photosynthetic sterile stem

Node

Internode

Node

Tuber

Rhizome

Adventitious root

Endodermis
(inner layer of cortex)

Vascular tissue

Sclerenchyma
(strengthening tissue)

Chlorenchyma
(photosynthetic tissue)

Epidermis
(outer layer of cells)

Parenchyma
(packing tissue)

Cortex
(layer between epidermis and vascular tissue)

Hollow pith cavity

Vallecular canal
(longitudinal channel)

Carinal canal
(longitudinal channel)

**MICROGRAPH OF CROSS-SECTION
THROUGH HORSETAIL STEM**

SPORE PRODUCTION IN FERN

Bracken
(*Pteridium aquilinum*)

Apex of pinnule

Sporangium (spore-producing structure)

Pinnule (leaflet of pinna)

Spore

Sporangium (spore-producing structure)

Annulus (ring of cells around sporangium)

Spore inside dehisced (split open) sporangium

Abaxial (lower) surface of pinnule

Midrib of pinnule

Sorus (group of sporangia)

MICROGRAPH OF LOWER SURFACE OF FERTILE PINNULE

Midrib of pinnule

MICROGRAPH OF SPORANGIA ON LOWER SURFACE OF FERTILE PINNULE

LIFE-CYCLE OF FERN

Pinna (leaflet)

Pinnule (leaflet of pinna)

Frond (leaf)

Rolled immature frond

SPOROPHYTE

Rhizome

Pinnule (leaflet of pinna)

Placenta

Indusium (flap protecting sorus)

Sporangium (spore-producing structure)

Sorus (group of sporangia)

SECTION THROUGH MATURE PINNULE

Sporangium splits and releases spores

Annulus ruptures at weak point

Spore

RELEASE OF SPORES FROM SPORANGIUM

Spore

Filament develops into prothallus

Rhizoid

GERMINATION OF SPORE

Antheridium (male sex organ)

Archegonium (female sex organ)

Prothallus (free-living gametophyte)

Rhizoid

GAMETOPHYTE PRODUCES GAMETES

Antheridium (male sex organ)

Oosphere (female gamete)

Antherozoid (male gamete) swims to oosphere

Archegonium (female sex organ)

FERTILIZATION

Primary leaf of growing sporophyte

Remains of gametophyte

FERTILIZED OOSPHERE GROWS INTO NEW SPOROPHYTE PLANT

FERN

Male fern
(*Dryopteris filix-mas*)

Midrib of pinna (leaflet)

Apex of frond (leaf)

Pinna (leaflet)

Pinnule (leaflet of pinna)

Frond (leaf)

Young frond (leaf)

Rachis (main axis of pinnate leaf)

Base of old dead frond (leaf)

Young frond (leaf) rolled and covered by ramenta

Ramentum (brown scale)

Rhizome

Vascular bundle

Sclerenchyma (strengthening tissue)

Phloem

Xylem

Vascular tissue

Epidermis (outer layer of cells)

Parenchyma (packing tissue)

MICROGRAPH OF CROSS-SECTION THROUGH FERN RACHIS

Adventitious root

Gymnosperms 1

THE GYMNOSPERMS ARE FOUR RELATED PHYLA of seed-producing plants; their seeds, however, lack the protective, outer covering which surrounds the seeds of flowering plants. Typically, gymnosperms are woody, perennial shrubs or trees, with stems, leaves, and roots, and a well-developed vascular (transport) system. The reproductive structures in most gymnosperms are cones: male cones produce microspores in which male gametes (sex cells) develop; female cones produce megaspores in which female gametes develop. Microspores are blown by the wind to female cones, male and female gametes fuse during fertilization, and a seed develops. The four gymnosperm phyla are the conifers (phylum Coniferophyta), mostly tall trees; cycads (phylum Cycadophyta), small palm-like trees; the ginkgo or maidenhair tree (phylum Ginkgophyta), a tall tree with bilobed leaves; and gnetophytes (phylum Gnetophyta), a diverse group of plants, mainly shrubs, but also including the horizontally growing welwitschia.

LIFE-CYCLE OF SCOTS PINE
(*Pinus sylvestris*)

Needle (*foliage leaf*)

Cone

Ovuliferous scale (*ovule- then seed-bearing structure*)

MALE CONES   **YOUNG FEMALE CONE**

Pollen grain in micropyle (*entrance to ovule*)   Ovuliferous scale

Pollen grain

Nucleus

Air sac

Ovule (*contains female gamete*)

POLLINATION

Integument (*outer part of ovule*)

Archegonium (*containing female gamete*)

Pollen tube (*carries male gamete from pollen grain to ovum*)

FERTILIZATION

SCALE AND SEEDS
Pine
(*Pinus sp.*)

Ovuliferous scale (*ovule- then seed-bearing structure*)

Wing scar

Wing of seed derived from ovuliferous scale

Seed

Seed

Point of attachment to axis of cone

Seed scar

OVULIFEROUS SCALE FROM THIRD-YEAR FEMALE CONE

Ovuliferous scale (*ovule- then seed-bearing structure*)

Seed

Seed

Wing

MATURE FEMALE CONE AND WINGED SEED

Microsporangium (*structure in which pollen grains are formed*)

Microsporophyll (*modified leaf carrying microsporangia*)

Ovule (*contains female gametes*)

Bract scale

Scale leaf

Axis of cone

Ovuliferous scale (*ovule- then seed-bearing structure*)

Axis of cone

MICROGRAPH OF LONGITUDINAL SECTION THROUGH YOUNG MALE CONE

MICROGRAPH OF LONGITUDINAL SECTION THROUGH SECOND-YEAR FEMALE CONE

Plumule (*embryonic shoot*)

Cotyledon (*seed leaf*)

Root

GERMINATION OF PINE SEEDLING

WELWITSCHIA
(*Welwitschia mirabilis*)

Frayed end of leaf

SMOOTH CYPRESS
(*Cupressus glabra*)

Immature female cone

Ovuliferous scale (ovule- then seed-bearing structure)

Mature female cone

Scale-like leaf

Immature male cone

Stem

Ovuliferous scale

Ovule (contains female gamete)

CROSS-SECTION THROUGH IMMATURE CONE

Ovuliferous scale (ovule- then seed-bearing structure)

Seed

CROSS-SECTION THROUGH MATURE CONE

Opening between woody scales through which seeds are released

Woody scale

DISCARDED CONE

YEW
(*Taxus baccata*)

Single ovule (contains female gamete)

Scale

Female "cone"

Scale

Developing seed

Scale

FEMALE "CONES" AT VARIOUS STAGES OF DEVELOPMENT

Seed

Aril (fleshy outgrowth from seed)

Stem

Needle (foliage leaf)

CYCAD
Sago palm
(*Cycas revoluta*)

Pinna (leaflet)

Pinnate leaf

Scale leaf

Old leaf base

Stem covered by scale leaves

MAIDENHAIR TREE
(*Ginkgo biloba*)

Girdle scar

Stem

Petiole (leaf stalk)

Bilobed leaf

Continuously growing leaf

Site of cone growth

Adaxial (upper) surface of leaf

Abaxial (lower) surface of leaf

Frayed end of leaf

Immature cone

Stalk scar

Woody stem

Gymnosperms 2

BRANCH OF BISHOP PINE
(*Pinus muricata*)

Second-year female cone

Ovuliferous scale
(ovule- then seed-bearing
structure)

Needle
(foliage leaf)

Ovuliferous scale
(ovule- then seed-
bearing structure)

Bud
scale

Cone

Cone stalk

Stem

Dwarf shoot

Scale leaf scar

**FEMALE CONE
(FIRST YEAR)**

Apical bud

Stem

Male cone

Needle (foliage leaf)

Dwarf shoot

Scar of
dwarf shoot

Upper surface
of needle
(foliage leaf)

Margin
of needle
(foliage leaf)

Needle
(foliage leaf)

Apical bud

Stem

Dwarf shoot

TERMINAL ZONE OF BRANCH

Stoma
(pore)

Vascular tissue

Phloem   Xylem

Mesophyll
(photosynthetic tissue)

Stoma
(pore)

Epidermis
(outer
layer of
cells)

Female
cone

Woody ovuliferous
scale (ovule- then
seed-bearing structure)

Endodermis
(inner layer
of cortex)

Resin canal

Cuticle
(waterproof
covering)

**FEMALE CONE
(THIRD YEAR)**

**MICROGRAPH OF CROSS-SECTION
THROUGH NEEDLE (FOLIAGE LEAF)**

**MICROGRAPH OF NEEDLE
(FOLIAGE LEAF) OF PINE
(*Pinus sp.*)**

CROSS-SECTION THROUGH
MATURE STEM OF BISHOP PINE
(*Pinus muricata*)

Apical bud scale

Apical bud

Shoot apex

Needle (foliage leaf) bud

Bud scale

Scale leaf

Immature needle (foliage leaf)

Annual ring

Heartwood (supportive, inactive secondary xylem)

Branch trace (vascular bundle supplying branch)

Pith

Sapwood (active secondary xylem)

Phloem

Periderm (outer layer of bark)

Bark

MICROGRAPH OF LONGITUDINAL SECTION
THROUGH SHOOT APEX OF PINE
(*Pinus sp.*)

Medullary ray (extension of pith)

Cortex (layer between epidermis and vascular tissue)

Pith

Hypodermis (cell layer below epidermis)

Base of dwarf shoot

Dwarf shoot trace (vascular bundle supplying dwarf shoot)

Epidermis (outer layer of cells)

Resin canal

Secondary xylem

Phloem

Vascular tissue

Primary xylem

MICROGRAPH OF CROSS-SECTION
THROUGH YOUNG STEM OF PINE
(*Pinus sp.*)

Cortex (layer between phellem and vascular tissue)

Resin canal

Endodermis (inner layer of cortex)

Phloem

Phellem (protective outer layer)

Secondary xylem

Primary xylem

MICROGRAPH OF CROSS-SECTION
THROUGH YOUNG ROOT OF PINE
(*Pinus sp.*)

Cortex (layer between phellem and vascular tissue)

Secondary xylem

Phellem (protective outer layer)

Primary xylem

Resin canal

Phloem

MICROGRAPH OF CROSS-SECTION
THROUGH MATURE ROOT OF PINE
(*Pinus sp.*)

125

Monocotyledons and dicotyledons

FLOWERING PLANTS (PHYLUM ANGIOSPERMOPHYTA) are divided into two classes: monocotyledons (class Monocotyledoneae) and dicotyledons (class Dicotyledoneae). Typically, monocotyledons have seeds with one cotyledon (seed leaf); their foliage leaves are narrow with parallel veins; the flower components occur in multiples of three; sepals and petals are indistinguishable and are known as tepals; vascular (transport) tissues are scattered in random bundles throughout the stem; and, since they lack stem cambium (actively dividing cells that produce wood), most monocotyledons are herbaceous (see pp. 128-129). Dicotyledons have seeds with two cotyledons; leaves are broad with a central midrib and branched veins; flower parts occur in multiples of four or five; sepals are generally small and green; petals are large and colourful; vascular bundles are arranged in a ring around the edge of the stem; and, because many dicotyledons possess wood-producing stem cambium, there are woody forms (see pp. 130-131) as well as herbaceous ones.

CROSS-SECTION THROUGH MONOCOTYLEDONOUS LEAF BASES

COMPARISONS BETWEEN MONOCOTYLEDONS AND DICOTYLEDONS

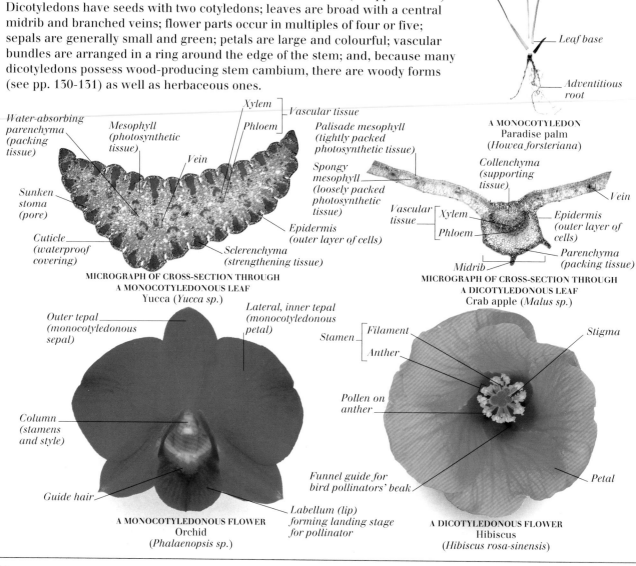

Vein (parallel venation)

Leaflet

Petiole (leaf stalk)

Emerging leaf

Leaf base

Adventitious root

A MONOCOTYLEDON
Paradise palm
(Howea forsteriana)

Water-absorbing parenchyma (packing tissue)

Mesophyll (photosynthetic tissue)

Xylem

Phloem

Vascular tissue

Vein

Sunken stoma (pore)

Cuticle (waterproof covering)

Epidermis (outer layer of cells)

Sclerenchyma (strengthening tissue)

MICROGRAPH OF CROSS-SECTION THROUGH A MONOCOTYLEDONOUS LEAF
Yucca (Yucca sp.)

Palisade mesophyll (tightly packed photosynthetic tissue)

Spongy mesophyll (loosely packed photosynthetic tissue)

Vascular tissue

Xylem

Phloem

Collenchyma (supporting tissue)

Vein

Epidermis (outer layer of cells)

Parenchyma (packing tissue)

Midrib

MICROGRAPH OF CROSS-SECTION THROUGH A DICOTYLEDONOUS LEAF
Crab apple (Malus sp.)

Outer tepal (monocotyledonous sepal)

Lateral, inner tepal (monocotyledonous petal)

Stamen

Filament

Anther

Stigma

Pollen on anther

Column (stamens and style)

Guide hair

Labellum (lip) forming landing stage for pollinator

Funnel guide for bird pollinators' beak

Petal

A MONOCOTYLEDONOUS FLOWER
Orchid
(Phalaenopsis sp.)

A DICOTYLEDONOUS FLOWER
Hibiscus
(Hibiscus rosa-sinensis)

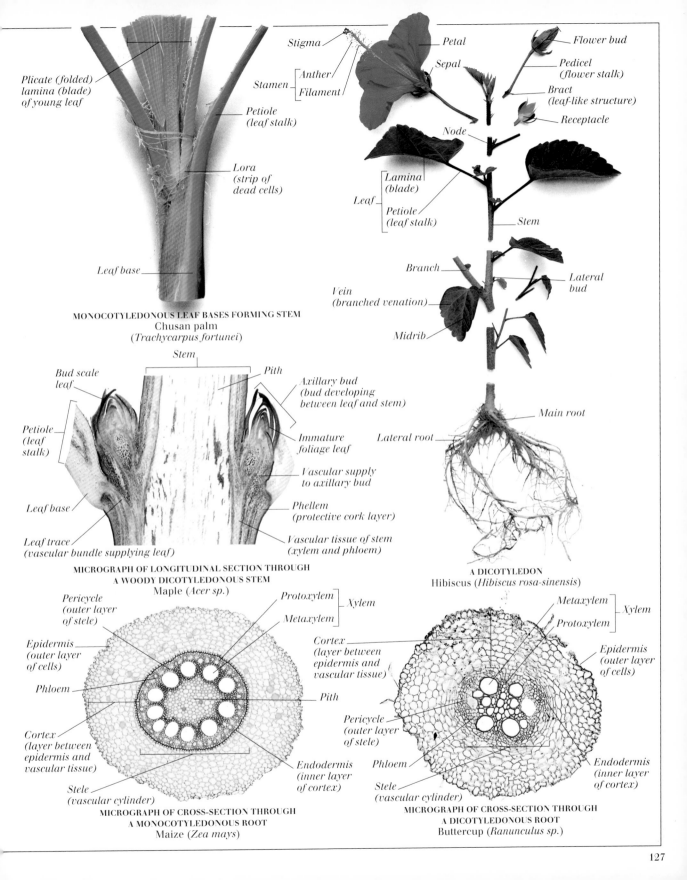

Plicate (folded)
lamina (blade)
of young leaf

Petiole
(leaf stalk)

Lora
(strip of
dead cells)

Leaf base

MONOCOTYLEDONOUS LEAF BASES FORMING STEM
Chusan palm
(*Trachycarpus fortunei*)

Stigma

Stamen { Anther / Filament }

Petal

Sepal

Flower bud

Pedicel
(flower stalk)

Bract
(leaf-like structure)

Receptacle

Node

Lamina
(blade)

Leaf {

Petiole
(leaf stalk)

Stem

Branch

Vein
(branched venation)

Midrib

Lateral
bud

Main root

Lateral root

A DICOTYLEDON
Hibiscus (*Hibiscus rosa-sinensis*)

Stem

Bud scale
leaf

Pith

Axillary bud
(bud developing
between leaf and stem)

Petiole
(leaf
stalk)

Immature
foliage leaf

Vascular supply
to axillary bud

Leaf base

Leaf trace
(vascular bundle supplying leaf)

Phellem
(protective cork layer)

Vascular tissue of stem
(xylem and phloem)

**MICROGRAPH OF LONGITUDINAL SECTION THROUGH
A WOODY DICOTYLEDONOUS STEM**
Maple (*Acer sp.*)

Pericycle
(outer layer
of stele)

Epidermis
(outer layer
of cells)

Phloem

Cortex
(layer between
epidermis and
vascular tissue)

Stele
(vascular cylinder)

Protoxylem
Metaxylem } Xylem

Pith

Endodermis
(inner layer
of cortex)

**MICROGRAPH OF CROSS-SECTION THROUGH
A MONOCOTYLEDONOUS ROOT**
Maize (*Zea mays*)

Cortex
(layer between
epidermis and
vascular tissue)

Metaxylem
Protoxylem } Xylem

Epidermis
(outer layer
of cells)

Pericycle
(outer layer
of stele)

Phloem

Stele
(vascular cylinder)

Endodermis
(inner layer
of cortex)

**MICROGRAPH OF CROSS-SECTION THROUGH
A DICOTYLEDONOUS ROOT**
Buttercup (*Ranunculus sp.*)

Herbaceous flowering plants

HERBACEOUS FLOWERING PLANTS TYPICALLY HAVE GREEN, NON-WOODY STEMS, and tend to be relatively short-lived. Many herbaceous plants live for only one or two years. Annuals (e.g., sweet peas) grow from seed, produce flowers and then seeds, and die within a single year. Biennials (e.g., carrots) have a two-year life cycle. In the first year, seeds grow into plants, which produce leaves and store food in underground storage organs; the stems and foliage then die back in winter. In the second year, new stems grow from the storage organs, produce leaves, flowers, and seeds, and then die. Some herbaceous plants (e.g., potatoes) are perennial. They grow back year after year, producing shoots and flowers in spring, storing food in underground tubers or rhizomes during summer, dying back in autumn, and surviving underground during winter.

Young plant forming

Petiole (stalk) of young leaf

Lateral root

Stipule (structure at base of leaf)

Node

Trifoliate leaf

Simple ovate leaflet

Root nodule

Main root

SWEET PEA
(*Lathyrus odoratus*)

STRAWBERRY
(*Fragaria x ananassa*)

Runner (creeping stem)

Remains of leaves

Lateral root scar

Stem

Leaf scar

Rib

Leaf base

Leaf scar

Petiole (leaf stalk)

Spine (modified leaf)

Lateral root

Tap root

CARROT
(*Daucus carota*)

Slender rhizome

Stem tuber

Adventitious root

Stem

Narrow, succulent leaf

Simple deltoid leaf

POTATO
(*Solanum tuberosum*)

ROCK STONECROP
(*Sedum rupestre*)

Adventitious root

PARTS OF HERBACEOUS FLOWERING PLANTS

Midrib

*Bract
(leaf-like
structure)*

*Bracteole
(small bract)*

*Cyme
(type of inflorescence)*

*Succulent,
simple ovate
leaf*

*Inner, tubular
disc floret*

*Outer, ligulate
ray floret*

Node

Flower bud

*Dentate
margin*

*Peduncle
(inflorescence stalk)*

Internode

**LIVE-FOR-EVER OR
ICE PLANT**
(*Sedum spectabile*)

*Simple lobed
leaf*

*Capitulum
(type of inflorescence)*

Leaf

*Peduncle
(inflorescence
stalk)*

*Flower
bud*

*Petiole
(leaf stalk)*

*Petiole
(leaf
stalk)*

Leaf base

Stem

*Linear
leaf*

FLORISTS' CHRYSANTHEMUM
(*Chrysanthemum morifolium*)

*Succulent
stem*

*Leaf
scar*

*Lateral
bud*

Prickle

*Hollow
stem*

BEGONIA
(*Begonia* x
tuberhybrida)

*Bract
(leaf-like
structure)*

*Capitulum
(type of
inflorescence)*

*Sheath formed
from leaf base*

TOADFLAX
(*Linaria* sp.)

**CEREOID
CACTUS**

*Spinose-dentate
margin*

*Dentate
margin*

*Unwinged rachis
(main axis of
pinnate leaf)*

*Peduncle
(inflorescence
stalk)*

*Winged
stem*

*Rachis
(main axis of
pinnate leaf)*

SLENDER THISTLE
(*Carduus tenuiflorus*)

Flower bud

*Stipule
(structure at
base of leaf)*

Tendril

*Stem
segment*

*Winged
rachis
(main
axis of
pinnate
leaf)*

*Pinna
(leaflet)*

*Margin of
cladode*

*Toothed
notch*

HOGWEED
(*Heracleum sphondylium*)

*Bract
(leaf-like
structure)*

Tepal

PERUVIAN LILY
(*Alstroemeria aurea*)

*Petiole
(leaf stalk)*

*Peduncle
(inflorescence
stalk)*

*Cladode
(flattened stem)*

*Stem
branch*

*Raceme
(type of inflorescence)*

CRAB CACTUS
(*Schlumbergera truncata*)

Petal

Sepal

EVERLASTING PEA
(*Lathyrus latifolius*)

Woody flowering plants

WOODY FLOWERING PLANTS ARE PERENNIAL, that is, they continue to grow and reproduce for many years. They have one or more permanent stems above ground, and numerous smaller branches. The stems and branches have a strong woody core that supports the plant and contains vascular tissue for transporting water and nutrients. Outside the woody core is a layer of tough, protective bark, which has lenticels (tiny pores) in it to enable gases to pass through. Woody flowering plants may be shrubs, which have several stems arising from the soil; bushes, which are shrubs with dense branching and foliage; or trees, which typically have a single upright stem (the trunk) that bears branches. Deciduous woody plants (e.g., roses) shed all their leaves once a year and remain leafless during winter. Evergreen woody plants (e.g., ivy) shed their leaves gradually, so retaining full leaf cover throughout the year.

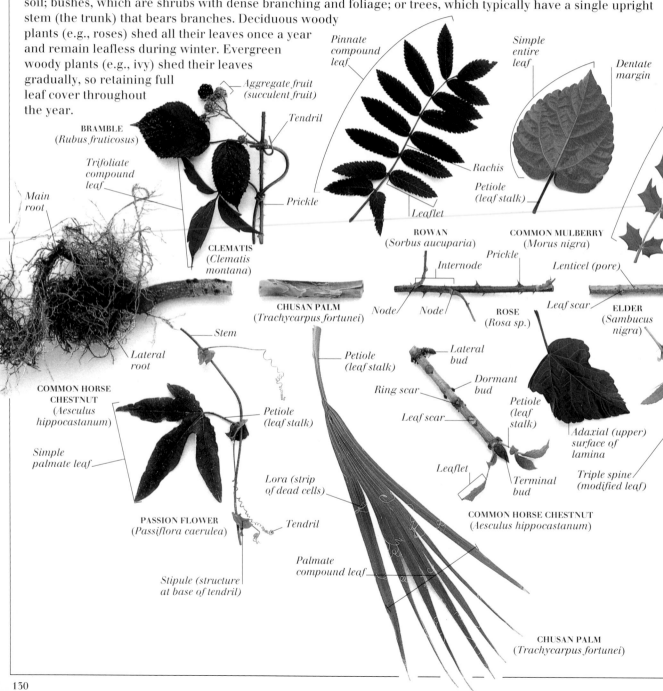

Aggregate fruit (succulent fruit)

BRAMBLE (*Rubus fruticosus*)

Tendril

Trifoliate compound leaf

Prickle

Pinnate compound leaf

Simple entire leaf

Dentate margin

Rachis

Petiole (leaf stalk)

Leaflet

ROWAN (*Sorbus aucuparia*)

COMMON MULBERRY (*Morus nigra*)

Main root

CLEMATIS (*Clematis montana*)

Prickle

Internode

Lenticel (pore)

CHUSAN PALM (*Trachycarpus fortunei*)

Node

Node

ROSE (*Rosa sp.*)

Leaf scar

ELDER (*Sambucus nigra*)

Lateral root

Stem

COMMON HORSE CHESTNUT (*Aesculus hippocastanum*)

Petiole (leaf stalk)

Lateral bud

Dormant bud

Ring scar

Petiole (leaf stalk)

Leaf scar

Petiole (leaf stalk)

Adaxial (upper) surface of lamina

Simple palmate leaf

Lora (strip of dead cells)

Leaflet

Terminal bud

Triple spine (modified leaf)

COMMON HORSE CHESTNUT (*Aesculus hippocastanum*)

PASSION FLOWER (*Passiflora caerulea*)

Tendril

Stipule (structure at base of tendril)

Palmate compound leaf

CHUSAN PALM (*Trachycarpus fortunei*)

PARTS OF WOODY FLOWERING PLANTS

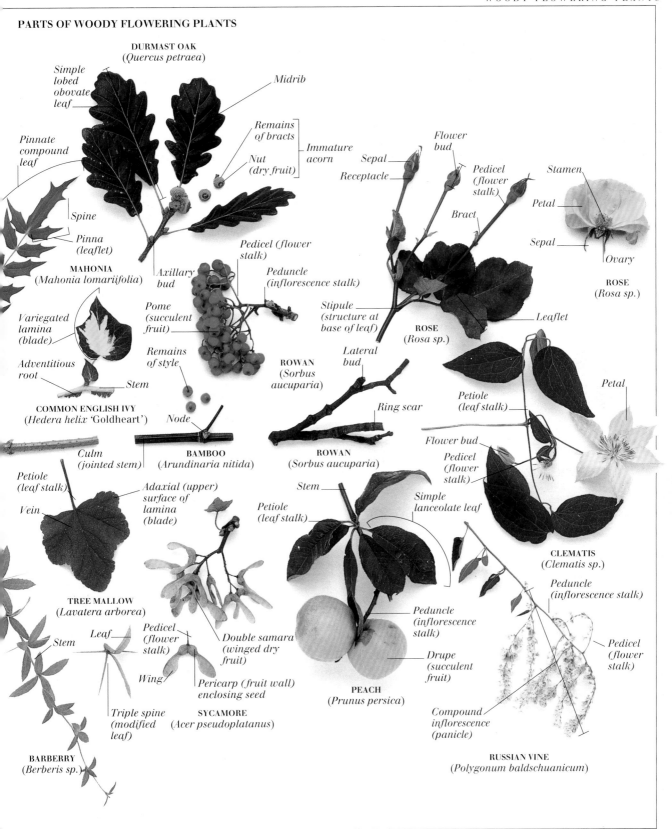

DURMAST OAK
(*Quercus petraea*)

Simple
lobed
obovate
leaf

Midrib

Remains
of bracts

Immature
acorn

Nut
(dry fruit)

Pinnate
compound
leaf

Spine

Pinna
(leaflet)

MAHONIA
(*Mahonia lomariifolia*)

Axillary
bud

Pedicel (flower
stalk)

Peduncle
(inflorescence stalk)

Pome
(succulent
fruit)

Variegated
lamina
(blade)

Remains
of style

Adventitious
root

Stem

COMMON ENGLISH IVY
(*Hedera helix* 'Goldheart')

Node

Culm
(jointed stem)

BAMBOO
(*Arundinaria nitida*)

ROWAN
(*Sorbus
aucuparia*)

Stipule
(structure at
base of leaf)

ROSE
(*Rosa sp.*)

Leaflet

Lateral
bud

Ring scar

ROWAN
(*Sorbus aucuparia*)

Flower
bud

Sepal

Receptacle

Pedicel
(flower
stalk)

Bract

Stamen

Petal

Sepal

Ovary

ROSE
(*Rosa sp.*)

Petiole
(leaf stalk)

Petal

Flower bud

Pedicel
(flower
stalk)

CLEMATIS
(*Clematis sp.*)

Petiole
(leaf stalk)

Vein

Adaxial (upper)
surface of
lamina
(blade)

TREE MALLOW
(*Lavatera arborea*)

Stem

Petiole
(leaf stalk)

Simple
lanceolate leaf

Stem

Leaf

Pedicel
(flower
stalk)

Wing

Triple spine
(modified
leaf)

Double samara
(winged dry
fruit)

Pericarp (fruit wall)
enclosing seed

SYCAMORE
(*Acer pseudoplatanus*)

Peduncle
(inflorescence
stalk)

Drupe
(succulent
fruit)

PEACH
(*Prunus persica*)

Peduncle
(inflorescence stalk)

Pedicel
(flower
stalk)

Compound
inflorescence
(panicle)

RUSSIAN VINE
(*Polygonum baldschuanicum*)

BARBERRY
(*Berberis sp.*)

Roots

ROOTS ARE THE UNDERGROUND PARTS OF PLANTS. They have three main functions. First, they anchor the plant in the soil. Second, they absorb water and minerals from the spaces between soil particles; the roots' absorptive properties are increased by root hairs, which grow behind the root tip, allowing maximum uptake of vital substances. Third, the root is part of the plant's transport system: xylem carries water and minerals from the roots to the stem and leaves, and phloem carries nutrients from the leaves to all parts of the root system. In addition, some roots (e.g., carrots) are food stores. Roots have an outer epidermis covering a cortex of parenchyma (packing tissue), and a central cylinder of vascular tissue. This arrangement helps the roots resist the forces of compression as they grow through the soil.

CARROT
(*Daucus carota*)

MICROGRAPH OF PRIMARY ROOT DEVELOPMENT
Cabbage (*Brassica sp.*)

Split in testa
as seed
germinates

Cotyledon
(seed leaf)

Primary root

Testa
(seed coat)

Root hair

Root tip
(region of
cell division)

FEATURES OF A TYPICAL ROOT
Buttercup
(*Ranunculus sp.*)

Pericycle
(outer layer
of stele)

Root hair

Air space
(allowing gas
diffusion in
the root)

Stele
(vascular cylinder)

Phloem sieve tube
(through which
nutrients are
transported)

Companion cell
(cell associated
with phloem
sieve tube)

Cortex
(layer between
epidermis and
vascular tissue)

Root hair

Epidermis
(outer layer
of cells)

Xylem vessel
(through which water
and minerals are transported)

Endodermis
(inner layer
of cortex)

Cell wall

Nucleus

Cytoplasm

Parenchyma
(packing) cell

PRIMARY ROOT AND MICROGRAPHS OF SECTIONS THROUGH ROOTS

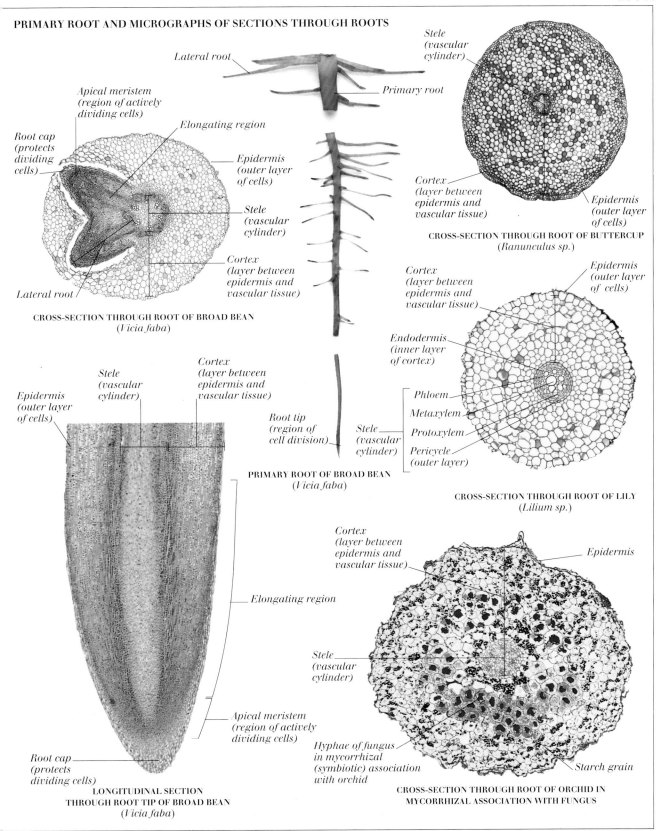

Lateral root

Primary root

Apical meristem (region of actively dividing cells)

Elongating region

Root cap (protects dividing cells)

Epidermis (outer layer of cells)

Stele (vascular cylinder)

Cortex (layer between epidermis and vascular tissue)

Lateral root

CROSS-SECTION THROUGH ROOT OF BROAD BEAN
(*Vicia faba*)

Stele (vascular cylinder)

Cortex (layer between epidermis and vascular tissue)

Epidermis (outer layer of cells)

Root tip (region of cell division)

PRIMARY ROOT OF BROAD BEAN
(*Vicia faba*)

Stele (vascular cylinder)

Cortex (layer between epidermis and vascular tissue)

Epidermis (outer layer of cells)

Elongating region

Apical meristem (region of actively dividing cells)

Root cap (protects dividing cells)

LONGITUDINAL SECTION THROUGH ROOT TIP OF BROAD BEAN
(*Vicia faba*)

Stele (vascular cylinder)

Cortex (layer between epidermis and vascular tissue)

Epidermis (outer layer of cells)

CROSS-SECTION THROUGH ROOT OF BUTTERCUP
(*Ranunculus sp.*)

Cortex (layer between epidermis and vascular tissue)

Epidermis (outer layer of cells)

Endodermis (inner layer of cortex)

Phloem

Metaxylem

Protoxylem

Pericycle (outer layer)

Stele (vascular cylinder)

CROSS-SECTION THROUGH ROOT OF LILY
(*Lilium sp.*)

Cortex (layer between epidermis and vascular tissue)

Epidermis

Stele (vascular cylinder)

Hyphae of fungus in mycorrhizal (symbiotic) association with orchid

Starch grain

CROSS-SECTION THROUGH ROOT OF ORCHID IN MYCORRHIZAL ASSOCIATION WITH FUNGUS

Stems

THE STEM IS THE MAIN SUPPORTIVE PART OF A PLANT that grows above ground. Stems bear leaves (organs of photosynthesis), which grow at nodes; buds (shoots covered by protective scales), which grow at the stem tip (apical or terminal buds) and in the angle between a leaf and the stem (axillary or lateral buds); and flowers (reproductive structures). The stem forms part of the plant's transport system: xylem tissue in the stem transports water and minerals from the roots to the aerial parts of the plant, and phloem tissue transports nutrients manufactured in the leaves to other parts of the plant. Stem tissues are also used for storing water and food. Herbaceous (non-woody) stems have an outer protective epidermis covering a cortex that consists mainly of parenchyma (packing tissue) but also has some collenchyma (supporting tissue). The vascular tissue of such stems is arranged in bundles, each of which consists of xylem, phloem, and sclerenchyma (strengthening tissue). Woody stems have an outer protective layer of tough bark, which is perforated with lenticels (pores) to allow gas exchange. Inside the bark is a ring of secondary phloem, which surrounds an inner core of secondary xylem.

MICROGRAPH OF LONGITUDINAL SECTION THROUGH APEX OF STEM
Coleus sp.

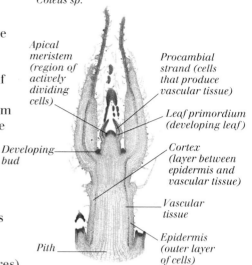

Apical meristem (region of actively dividing cells)

Procambial strand (cells that produce vascular tissue)

Leaf primordium (developing leaf)

Developing bud

Cortex (layer between epidermis and vascular tissue)

Vascular tissue

Pith

Epidermis (outer layer of cells)

YOUNG WOODY STEM
Lime
(Tilia sp.)

EMERGENT BUDS
London plane
(Platanus x acerifolia)

Secondary phloem

Pith

Phellem (protective cork layer)

Cortex (layer between phellem and vascular tissue)

Xylem vessel (through which water and minerals are transported)

Xylem fibre (supporting tissue)

Ray (parenchyma cells)

Phloem sieve tube (through which nutrients are transported)

Phloem fibre (supporting tissue)

Lenticel (pore)

Vascular cambium (actively dividing cells that produce xylem and phloem)

Autumn wood

Spring wood

Secondary xylem

Companion cell (cell associated with phloem sieve tube)

Young leaves emerging

Terminal bud

Lateral bud

Node

Internode

Inner bud scale

Outer bud scale

Node

Leaf scar

Lenticel (pore)

Woody stem

MICROGRAPHS OF CROSS-SECTIONS THROUGH VARIOUS STEMS

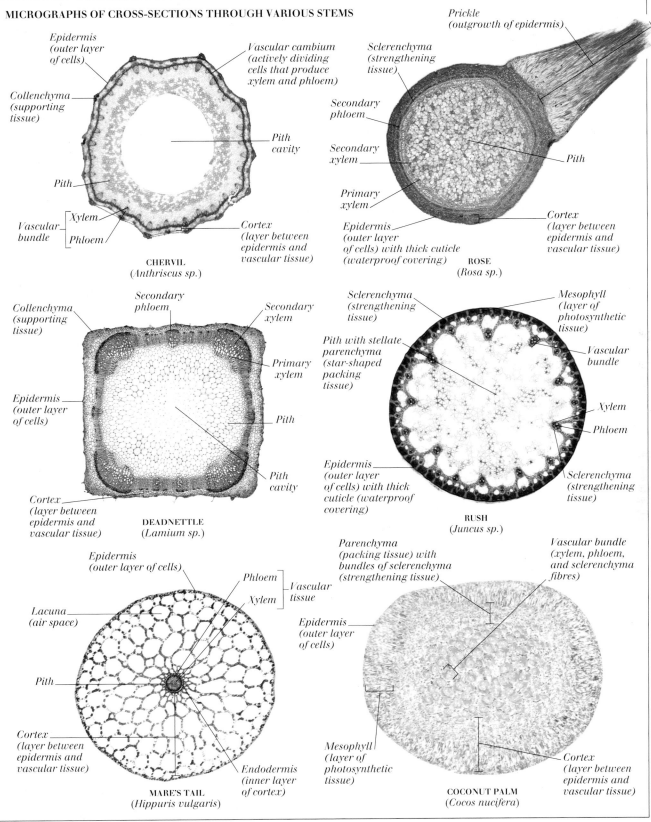

Epidermis (outer layer of cells)

Collenchyma (supporting tissue)

Pith

Vascular bundle — Xylem, Phloem

Vascular cambium (actively dividing cells that produce xylem and phloem)

Pith cavity

Cortex (layer between epidermis and vascular tissue)

CHERVIL (Anthriscus sp.)

Prickle (outgrowth of epidermis)

Sclerenchyma (strengthening tissue)

Secondary phloem

Secondary xylem

Primary xylem

Epidermis (outer layer of cells) with thick cuticle (waterproof covering)

Pith

Cortex (layer between epidermis and vascular tissue)

ROSE (Rosa sp.)

Collenchyma (supporting tissue)

Epidermis (outer layer of cells)

Cortex (layer between epidermis and vascular tissue)

Secondary phloem

Secondary xylem

Primary xylem

Pith

Pith cavity

DEADNETTLE (Lamium sp.)

Sclerenchyma (strengthening tissue)

Pith with stellate parenchyma (star-shaped packing tissue)

Epidermis (outer layer of cells) with thick cuticle (waterproof covering)

Mesophyll (layer of photosynthetic tissue)

Vascular bundle

Xylem

Phloem

Sclerenchyma (strengthening tissue)

RUSH (Juncus sp.)

Epidermis (outer layer of cells)

Lacuna (air space)

Pith

Cortex (layer between epidermis and vascular tissue)

Phloem
Xylem — Vascular tissue

Endodermis (inner layer of cortex)

MARE'S TAIL (Hippuris vulgaris)

Parenchyma (packing tissue) with bundles of sclerenchyma (strengthening tissue)

Epidermis (outer layer of cells)

Mesophyll (layer of photosynthetic tissue)

Vascular bundle (xylem, phloem, and sclerenchyma fibres)

Cortex (layer between epidermis and vascular tissue)

COCONUT PALM (Cocos nucifera)

Leaves

LEAVES ARE THE MAIN SITES OF PHOTOSYNTHESIS (see pp. 138-139) and transpiration (water loss by evaporation) in plants. A typical leaf consists of a thin, flat lamina (blade) supported by a network of veins; a petiole (leaf stalk); and a leaf base, where the petiole joins the stem. Leaves can be classified as simple, in which the lamina is a single unit, or compound, in which the lamina is divided into separate leaflets. Compound leaves may be pinnate, with pinnae (leaflets) on both sides of a rachis (main axis), or palmate, with leaflets arising from a single point at the tip of the petiole. Leaves can be classified further by the overall shape of the lamina, and by the shape of the lamina's apex, margin, and base.

CHECKERBLOOM
(*Sidalcea malviflora*)

SIMPLE LEAF SHAPES

Subacute apex

Acuminate apex

Entire margin

Entire margin

Cuneate base

Cordate base

PANDURIFORM
Croton
(*Codiaeum variegatum*)

LANCEOLATE
Sea buckthorn
(*Hippophae rhamnoides*)

GENERAL LEAF FEATURES

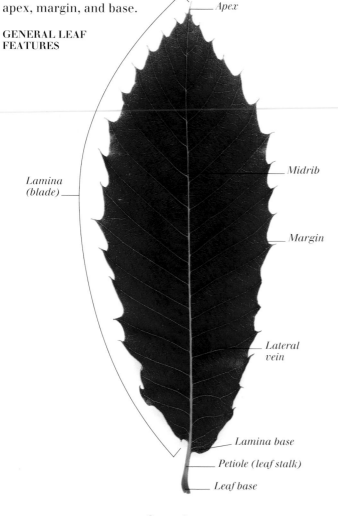

Apex

Lamina (blade)

Midrib

Margin

Lateral vein

Lamina base

Petiole (leaf stalk)

Leaf base

Sweet chestnut
(*Castanea sativa*)

COMPOUND LEAF SHAPES

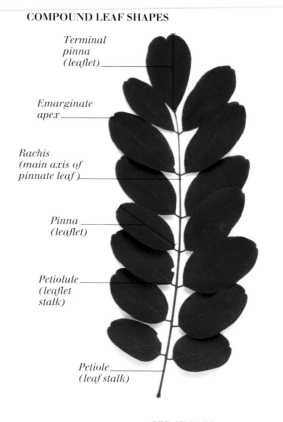

Terminal pinna (leaflet)

Emarginate apex

Rachis (main axis of pinnate leaf)

Pinna (leaflet)

Petiolule (leaflet stalk)

Petiole (leaf stalk)

ODD PINNATE
False acacia
(*Robinia pseudoacacia*)

Subacute apex — Entire margin — Cuneate base

OBOVATE
Tupelo
(*Nyssa sylvatica*)

Acuminate apex — Variegated lamina (blade) — Cuneate base

RHOMBOID
Persian ivy
(*Hedera colchica*
'Sulphur Heart')

Subacute apex — Entire margin — Cuneate base

ELLIPTIC
Fig
(*Ficus sp.*)

Acute apex — Entire margin — Entire margin — Cordate base

PALMATELY LOBED
Common ivy
(*Hedera helix*)

Mucronate apex — Serrulate margin

ORBICULAR
Camellia
(*Camellia japonica*)

Cuspidate apex — Entire margin — Truncate base

DELTOID
Persian ivy
(*Hedera colchica*)

Acuminate apex — Entire margin

LINEAR
Iris
(*Iris lazica*)

Pinna (leaflet) — Petiolule (leaflet stalk) — Rachis (main axis of pinnate leaf) — Petiole (leaf stalk)

EVEN PINNATE
Black walnut
(*Juglans nigra*)

Leaflet — Petiole (leaf stalk)

DIGITATE
Horse chestnut
(*Aesculus parviflora*)

Pinnule (leaflet of pinna) — Pinna (leaflet) — Rachis (main axis of pinnate leaf) — Petiole (leaf stalk) — Rachilla (secondary axis of pinnate leaf)

BIPINNATE
Honey locust
(*Gleditsia triacanthos*)

Leaflet — Rachis — Petiole (leaf stalk)

BITERNATE
Clematis
(*Clematis sp.*)

Leaflet — Petiole (leaf stalk)

TRIFOLIATE
Laburnum
(*Laburnum x watereri*)

Pinnule (leaflet of pinna) — Rachilla (secondary axis of pinnate leaf) — Petiolule (leaflet stalk) — Petiole (leaf stalk) — Pinna (leaflet) — Rachis (main axis of pinnate leaf)

TRIPINNATE
Meadow rue
(*Thalictrum delavayi*)

Photosynthesis

PHOTOSYNTHESIS IS THE PROCESS by which plants make their food using sunlight, water, and carbon dioxide. It takes place inside special structures in leaf cells called chloroplasts. The chloroplasts contain chlorophyll, a green pigment that absorbs energy from sunlight. During photosynthesis, the absorbed energy is used to join together carbon dioxide and water to form the sugar glucose, which is the energy source for the whole plant; oxygen, a waste product, is released into the air. Leaves are the main sites of photosynthesis, and have various adaptations for that purpose: flat laminae (blades) provide a large surface for absorbing sunlight; stomata (pores) in the lower surface of the laminae allow gases (carbon dioxide and oxygen) to pass into and out of the leaves; and an extensive network of veins brings water into the leaves and transports the glucose produced by photosynthesis to the rest of the plant.

MICROGRAPH OF LEAF
Lily (*Lilium sp.*)

Stoma
(pore)

Guard cell
(controls
opening
and closing
of stoma)

Lower
surface of
lamina
(blade)

THE PROCESS OF PHOTOSYNTHESIS

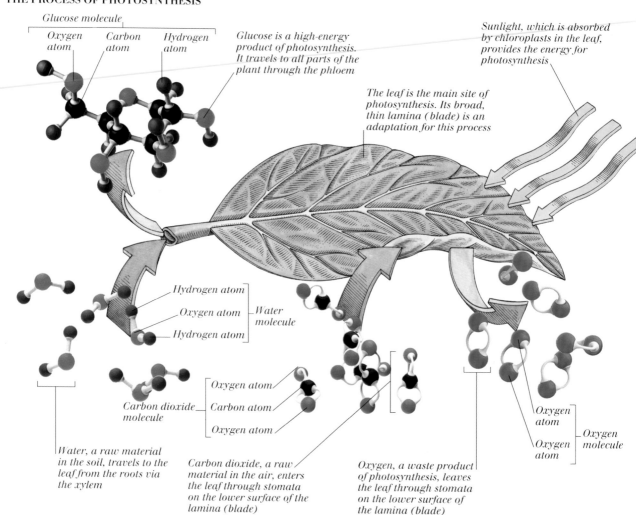

Glucose molecule

Oxygen
atom

Carbon
atom

Hydrogen
atom

Glucose is a high-energy
product of photosynthesis.
It travels to all parts of the
plant through the phloem

Sunlight, which is absorbed
by chloroplasts in the leaf,
provides the energy for
photosynthesis

The leaf is the main site of
photosynthesis. Its broad,
thin lamina (blade) is an
adaptation for this process

Hydrogen atom

Oxygen atom   Water
molecule

Hydrogen atom

Carbon dioxide
molecule

Oxygen atom

Carbon atom

Oxygen atom

Oxygen
atom

Oxygen
molecule

Oxygen
atom

Water, a raw material
in the soil, travels to the
leaf from the roots via
the xylem

Carbon dioxide, a raw
material in the air, enters
the leaf through stomata
on the lower surface of the
lamina (blade)

Oxygen, a waste product
of photosynthesis, leaves
the leaf through stomata
on the lower surface of
the lamina (blade)

CROSS-SECTION THROUGH LEAF
Christmas rose
(*Helleborus niger*)

Cuticle (waterproof covering)

Upper (adaxial) epidermis (outer layer of cells)

Cell wall

Cytoplasm

Vacuole

Chloroplast (photosynthetic organelle)

Palisade mesophyll (tightly packed layer of photosynthetic tissue)

Nucleus

Intercellular space

Sclerenchyma (strengthening tissue)

Xylem (tissue that transports water and mineral salts)

Spongy mesophyll (loosely packed layer of photosynthetic tissue)

Phloem (tissue that transports sugars and other nutrients)

Vein

Lower (abaxial) epidermis (outer layer of cells)

Parenchyma (packing tissue)

Guard cell (controls opening and closing of stoma)

Stoma (pore)

Substomatal chamber

INTERNAL VIEW OF CHLOROPLAST

Granum (stack of thylakoids that hold chlorophyll molecules in position)

Lamella (membrane of thylakoid)

Thylakoid (flat sac of granum)

Stroma (watery matrix)

Deoxyribonucleic acid (DNA) strand

Chloroplast envelope

Outer membrane

Inner membrane

Starch grain

Ribosome (site of protein synthesis)

Stroma thylakoid (link between grana)

Flowers 1

FLOWERS ARE THE SITES OF SEXUAL REPRODUCTION in flowering plants. Their component parts are arranged in whorls around the receptacle (tip of the flower stalk). The sepals (collectively called the calyx) are outermost; typically small and green, they protect the developing flower. The petals (collectively called the corolla) are typically large and brightly coloured; they are found inside the sepals. In monocotyledonous flowers (see pp. 126-127), sepals and petals are indistinguishable; individually they are called tepals (collectively called the perianth). The petals surround the male and female reproductive structures (androecium and gynoecium). The androecium consists of stamens (male organs); each stamen is made up of a filament (stalk) and anther. The gynoecium has one or more carpels (female organs); each carpel consists of an ovary, style, and stigma. Some flowers (e.g., lily) occur singly on a pedicel (flower stalk); others (e.g., elder, sunflower) are arranged in a group (inflorescence) on a peduncle (inflorescence stalk).

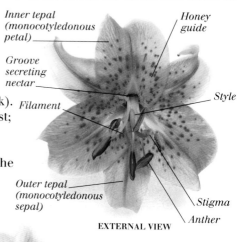

Inner tepal (monocotyledonous petal)
Honey guide
Groove secreting nectar
Filament
Style
Outer tepal (monocotyledonous sepal)
Stigma
Anther

EXTERNAL VIEW

A MONOCOTYLEDONOUS FLOWER
Lily
(*Lilium sp.*)

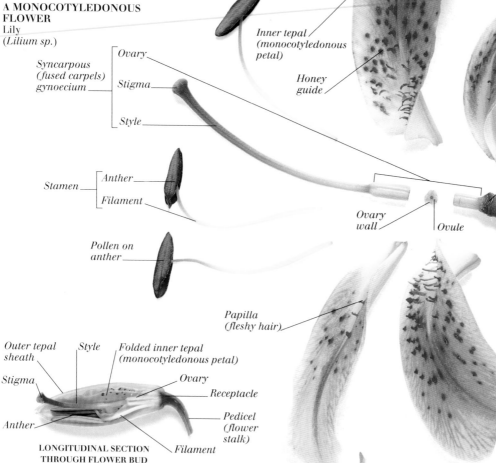

Syncarpous (fused carpels) gynoecium
Ovary
Stigma
Style

Stamen
Anther
Filament

Pollen on anther

Inner tepal (monocotyledonous petal)
Honey guide

Outer tepal (monocotyledonous sepal)

Ovary wall
Ovule

Tepal scar
Receptacle

Pedicel (flower stalk)

Papilla (fleshy hair)

Outer tepal sheath
Style
Folded inner tepal (monocotyledonous petal)
Stigma
Ovary
Receptacle
Anther
Pedicel (flower stalk)
Filament

LONGITUDINAL SECTION THROUGH FLOWER BUD

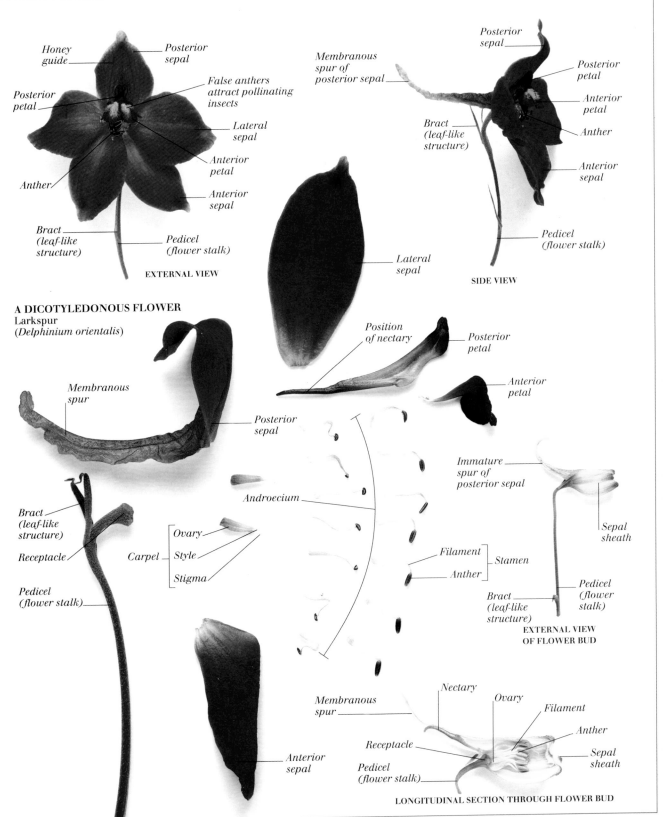

Honey guide

Posterior sepal

Posterior petal

False anthers attract pollinating insects

Lateral sepal

Anterior petal

Anterior sepal

Anther

Bract (leaf-like structure)

Pedicel (flower stalk)

EXTERNAL VIEW

Membranous spur of posterior sepal

Posterior sepal

Posterior petal

Anterior petal

Anther

Bract (leaf-like structure)

Anterior sepal

Pedicel (flower stalk)

SIDE VIEW

Lateral sepal

A DICOTYLEDONOUS FLOWER
Larkspur
(*Delphinium orientalis*)

Membranous spur

Posterior sepal

Position of nectary

Posterior petal

Anterior petal

Immature spur of posterior sepal

Sepal sheath

Bract (leaf-like structure)

Receptacle

Androecium

Carpel
- Ovary
- Style
- Stigma

Filament
Anther
Stamen

Bract (leaf-like structure)

Pedicel (flower stalk)

Pedicel (flower stalk)

EXTERNAL VIEW OF FLOWER BUD

Membranous spur

Anterior sepal

Nectary

Ovary

Filament

Anther

Receptacle

Sepal sheath

Pedicel (flower stalk)

LONGITUDINAL SECTION THROUGH FLOWER BUD

Flowers 2

COMPOUND INFLORESCENCE (CAPITULUM)
Sunflower
(*Helianthus annulus*)

Disc florets

Ray floret

Florets (small flowers) are grouped together to resemble a single large flower

Sterile ray floret to attract pollinating insects

Outer fertilized floret

Two-lobed stigma

Florets with anthers ready to shed pollen

Style

Pollen

Anther

Inner, immature florets

Corolla tube (fused petals)

Pappus (modified sepal)

Ovary

Corolla tube (fused petals)

Ovary

FLORETS FROM SUNFLOWER

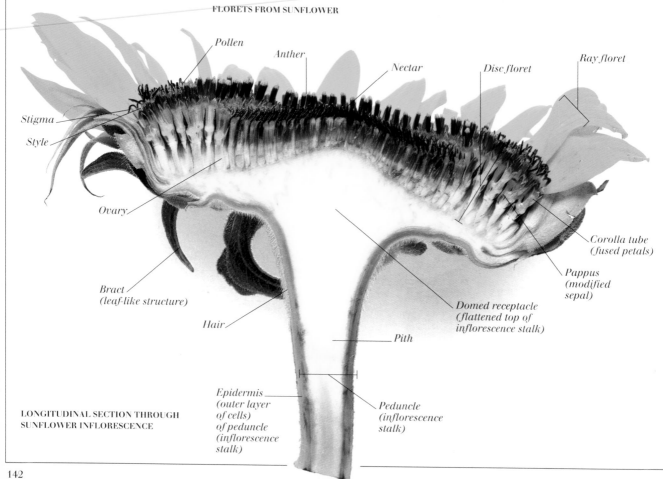

Pollen

Anther

Nectar

Disc floret

Ray floret

Stigma

Style

Ovary

Corolla tube (fused petals)

Pappus (modified sepal)

Bract (leaf-like structure)

Hair

Domed receptacle (flattened top of inflorescence stalk)

Pith

Epidermis (outer layer of cells) of peduncle (inflorescence stalk)

Peduncle (inflorescence stalk)

LONGITUDINAL SECTION THROUGH SUNFLOWER INFLORESCENCE

ARRANGEMENT OF FLOWERS ON STEM

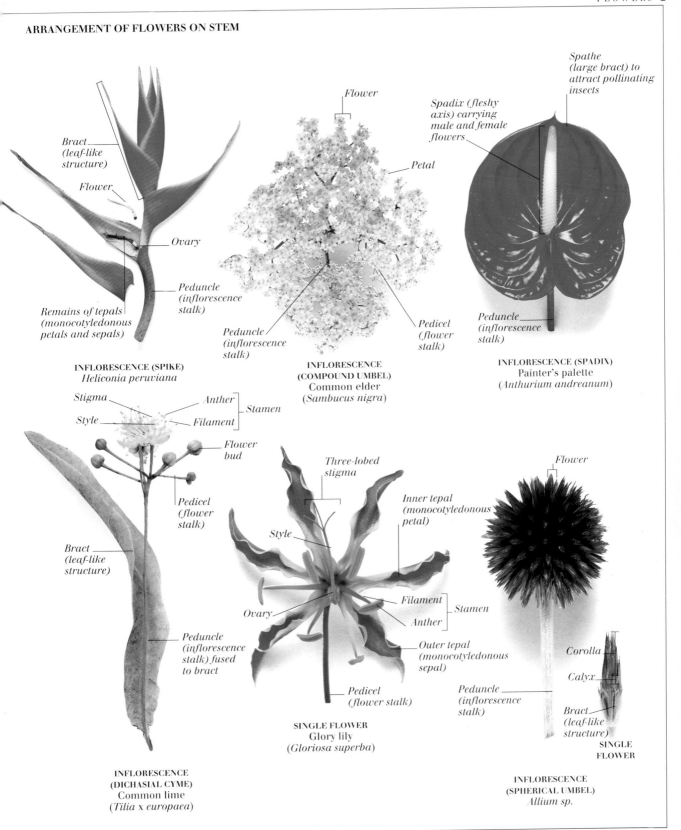

Bract
(leaf-like
structure)

Flower

Ovary

Remains of tepals
(monocotyledonous
petals and sepals)

Peduncle
(inflorescence
stalk)

INFLORESCENCE (SPIKE)
Heliconia peruviana

Flower

Petal

Peduncle
(inflorescence
stalk)

Pedicel
(flower
stalk)

**INFLORESCENCE
(COMPOUND UMBEL)**
Common elder
(*Sambucus nigra*)

Spathe
(large bract) to
attract pollinating
insects

Spadix (fleshy
axis) carrying
male and female
flowers

Peduncle
(inflorescence
stalk)

INFLORESCENCE (SPADIX)
Painter's palette
(*Anthurium andreanum*)

Stigma

Style

Anther

Filament

Stamen

Flower
bud

Pedicel
(flower
stalk)

Bract
(leaf-like
structure)

Peduncle
(inflorescence
stalk) fused
to bract

**INFLORESCENCE
(DICHASIAL CYME)**
Common lime
(*Tilia x europaea*)

Three-lobed
stigma

Inner tepal
(monocotyledonous
petal)

Style

Ovary

Filament

Anther

Stamen

Outer tepal
(monocotyledonous
sepal)

Pedicel
(flower stalk)

SINGLE FLOWER
Glory lily
(*Gloriosa superba*)

Flower

Corolla

Calyx

Bract
(leaf-like
structure)

**SINGLE
FLOWER**

Peduncle
(inflorescence
stalk)

**INFLORESCENCE
(SPHERICAL UMBEL)**
Allium sp.

Pollination

POLLINATION IS THE TRANSFER OF POLLEN (which contains the male sex cells) from an anther (part of the male reproductive organ) to a stigma (part of the female reproductive organ). This process precedes fertilization (see pp. 146-147). Pollination may occur within the same flower (self-pollination), or between flowers on separate plants of the same species (cross-pollination). In most plants, pollination is carried out either by insects (entomophilous pollination) or by the wind (anemophilous pollination). Less commonly, birds, bats, or water are the agents of pollination. Insect-pollinated flowers are typically brightly coloured, scented, and produce nectar, on which insects feed. Such flowers also tend to have patterns that are visible only in ultraviolet light, which many insects can see but which humans cannot. These features attract insects, which become covered with the sticky or hooked pollen grains when they visit one flower, and then transfer the pollen to the next flower they visit. Wind-pollinated flowers are generally small, relatively inconspicuous, and unscented. They produce large quantities of light pollen grains that are easily blown by the wind to other flowers.

REPRODUCTIVE STRUCTURES IN WIND-POLLINATED PLANT
Sweet chestnut
(*Castanea sativa*)

Flower bud

Prominent stigma protrudes from flower

Female flower

Petiole (leaf stalk)

Bract (leaf-like structure)

Peduncle (inflorescence stalk)

FEMALE

Male flower

Part of male catkin (inflorescence adapted for wind pollination)

Peduncle (inflorescence stalk)

Filament

Anther

MALE

REPRODUCTIVE STRUCTURES IN INSECT-POLLINATED PLANTS

Stigma

Style

Dehisced (split open) pollen sac

Boundary between two fused carpels (each carpel consists of a stigma, style, and ovary)

Ovary

Endothecium (pollen sac wall)

Pollen grain

Anther

Filament

Stamen

Calyx (whorl of sepals)

MICROGRAPHS OF POLLEN GRAINS

Exine (outer coat of pollen grain)

Pore

EUROPEAN FIELD ELM
(*Ulmus minor*)

MICROGRAPH OF CARPELS (FEMALE ORGANS)
Yellow-wort
(*Blackstonia perfoliata*)

Colpus (furrow-shaped aperture)

Exine (outer coat of pollen grain)

JUSTICIA AUREA

MICROGRAPH OF STAMENS (MALE ORGANS)
Common centaury
(*Centaurium erythraea*)

Exine (outer coat of pollen grain)

Pore

Baculum (rod-shaped structure)

MEADOW CRANESBILL
(*Geranium pratense*)

Colpus (furrow-shaped aperture)

Exine (outer coat of pollen grain)

Equatorial furrow

BOX-LEAVED MILKWORT
(*Polygala chamaebuxus*)

INSECT POLLINATION OF MEADOW SAGE

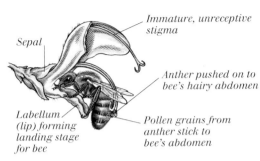

Sepal

Immature, unreceptive stigma

Anther pushed on to bee's hairy abdomen

Labellum (lip) forming landing stage for bee

Pollen grains from anther stick to bee's abdomen

1. BEE VISITS FLOWER WITH MATURE ANTHERS BUT IMMATURE STIGMA

Pollen grains attached to hairy abdomen

Long style curves downwards when bee enters flower

Mature, receptive stigma touches bee's abdomen, picking up pollen

2. BEE FLIES TO OTHER FLOWERS

Sepal

Labellum (lip) forming landing stage for bee

3. BEE VISITS FLOWER WHERE THE ANTHERS HAVE WITHERED AND THE STIGMA IS MATURE

SUNFLOWER UNDER NORMAL AND ULTRAVIOLET LIGHT

Central area of disc florets

Ray floret

NORMAL LIGHT

Petal

Ovary

Stigma

Stamen { Filament / Anther

NORMAL LIGHT

ST JOHN'S WORT UNDER NORMAL AND ULTRAVIOLET LIGHT

Honey guide directs insects to dark, central part of flower

Paler, outer part of ray floret

Darker, inner part of ray floret

Insects attracted to darkest, central part of flower, which contains nectaries, anthers, and stigmas

Dark central area containing nectaries, anthers, and stigmas

ULTRAVIOLET LIGHT

ULTRAVIOLET LIGHT

Colpus (furrow-shaped aperture)

Exine (outer coat of pollen grain)

Columella (small column-shaped structure)

Trilete mark (development scar)

Pore

Exine (outer coat of pollen grain)

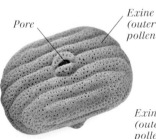

Exine (outer coat of pollen grain)

Exine (outer coat of pollen grain)

Tricolpate (three colpae) pollen grain

MIMULOPSIS SOLMSII

THESIUM ALPINIUM

RUELLIA GRANDIFLORA

CROSSANDRA NILOTICA

Fertilization

FERTILIZATION IS THE FUSION of male and female gametes (sex cells) to produce a zygote (embryo). Following pollination (see pp. 144-145), the pollen grains that contain the male gametes are on the stigma, some distance from the female gamete (ovum) inside the ovule. To enable the gametes to meet, the pollen grain germinates and produces a pollen tube, which grows down and enters the embryo sac (the inner part of the ovule that contains the ovum). Two male gametes, travelling at the tip of the pollen tube, enter the embryo sac. One gamete fuses with the ovum to produce a zygote that will develop into an embryo plant. The other male gamete fuses with two polar nuclei to produce the endosperm, which acts as a food store for the developing embryo. Fertilization also initiates other changes: the integument (outer part of ovule) forms a testa (seed coat) around the embryo and endosperm; the petals fall off; the stigma and style wither; and the ovary wall forms a layer (called the pericarp) around the seed. Together, the pericarp and seed form the fruit, which may be succulent (see pp. 148-149) or dry (see pp. 150-151). In some species (e.g., blackberry), apomixis can occur: the seed develops without fertilization of the ovum by a male gamete but endosperm formation and fruit development take place as in other species.

BANANA
(*Musa 'lacatan'*)

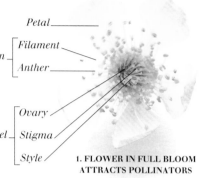

DEVELOPMENT OF A SUCCULENT FRUIT
Blackberry
(*Rubus fruticosus*)

Petal

Stamen { Filament / Anther

Carpel { Ovary / Stigma / Style

**1. FLOWER IN FULL BLOOM
ATTRACTS POLLINATORS**

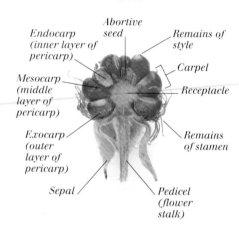

Endocarp
(inner layer of
pericarp)

Abortive
seed

Remains of
style

Carpel

Mesocarp
(middle
layer of
pericarp)

Receptacle

Exocarp
(outer
layer of
pericarp)

Remains
of stamen

Sepal

Pedicel
(flower
stalk)

**4. PERICARP FORMS
FLESH, SKIN, AND A HARD INNER
LAYER (SHOWN IN CROSS-SECTION)**

Exocarp
(outer layer of
pericarp)

Carpel

Remains
of style

Remains
of stamen

Remains
of sepal

Pedicel
(flower
stalk)

**7. MESOCARP (FLESHY PART OF PERICARP)
OF EACH CARPEL STARTS TO
CHANGE COLOUR**

Exocarp
(outer layer of
pericarp)

Drupelet

Remains
of style

Remains
of stamen

Remains
of sepal

Pedicel
(flower
stalk)

**8. CARPELS MATURE INTO DRUPELETS
(SMALL FLESHY FRUITS WITH SINGLE SEEDS
SURROUNDED BY HARD ENDOCARP)**

Exocarp
(outer layer
of pericarp)

Drupelet

Remains
of style

Remains
of sepal

Remains
of stamen

Pedicel
(flower
stalk)

**9. MESOCARP OF DRUPELET BECOMES
DARKER AND SWEETER**

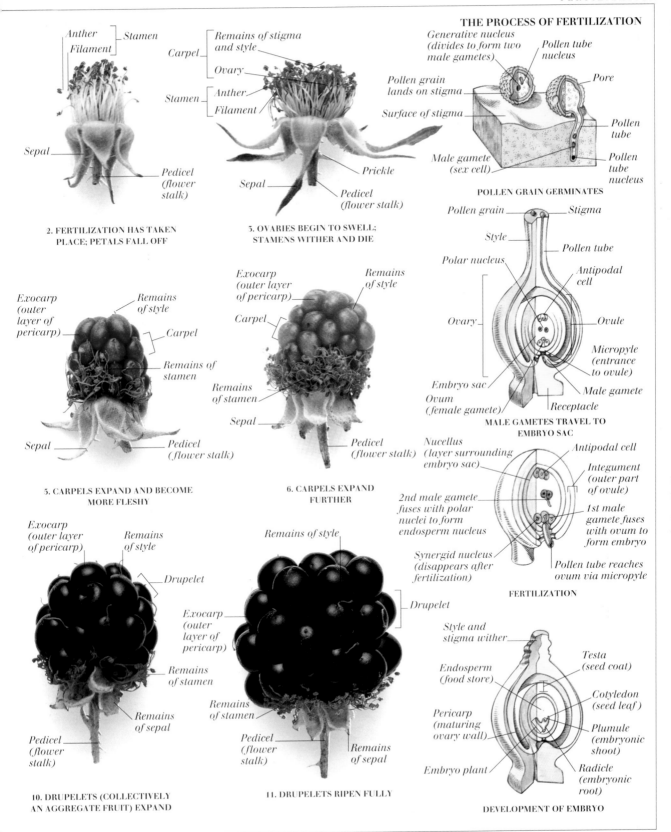

THE PROCESS OF FERTILIZATION

Stamen
Anther
Filament

Sepal

Pedicel (flower stalk)

2. FERTILIZATION HAS TAKEN PLACE; PETALS FALL OFF

Carpel — Remains of stigma and style / Ovary

Stamen — Anther / Filament

Sepal

Prickle

Pedicel (flower stalk)

5. OVARIES BEGIN TO SWELL; STAMENS WITHER AND DIE

Generative nucleus (divides to form two male gametes)
Pollen tube nucleus
Pollen grain lands on stigma
Pore
Surface of stigma
Pollen tube
Male gamete (sex cell)
Pollen tube nucleus

POLLEN GRAIN GERMINATES

Exocarp (outer layer of pericarp)
Remains of style
Carpel
Remains of stamen
Sepal
Pedicel (flower stalk)

5. CARPELS EXPAND AND BECOME MORE FLESHY

Exocarp (outer layer of pericarp)
Remains of style
Carpel
Remains of stamen
Sepal
Pedicel (flower stalk)

6. CARPELS EXPAND FURTHER

Pollen grain
Stigma
Style
Pollen tube
Polar nucleus
Antipodal cell
Ovary
Ovule
Micropyle (entrance to ovule)
Embryo sac
Male gamete
Ovum (female gamete)
Receptacle

MALE GAMETES TRAVEL TO EMBRYO SAC

Nucellus (layer surrounding embryo sac)
Antipodal cell
Integument (outer part of ovule)
2nd male gamete fuses with polar nuclei to form endosperm nucleus
1st male gamete fuses with ovum to form embryo
Synergid nucleus (disappears after fertilization)
Pollen tube reaches ovum via micropyle

FERTILIZATION

Exocarp (outer layer of pericarp)
Remains of style
Drupelet
Remains of stamen
Remains of sepal
Pedicel (flower stalk)

10. DRUPELETS (COLLECTIVELY AN AGGREGATE FRUIT) EXPAND

Remains of style
Drupelet
Exocarp (outer layer of pericarp)
Remains of stamen
Pedicel (flower stalk)
Remains of sepal

11. DRUPELETS RIPEN FULLY

Style and stigma wither
Testa (seed coat)
Endosperm (food store)
Cotyledon (seed leaf)
Pericarp (maturing ovary wall)
Plumule (embryonic shoot)
Embryo plant
Radicle (embryonic root)

DEVELOPMENT OF EMBRYO

Succulent fruits

A FRUIT IS A FULLY DEVELOPED and ripened ovary (seed-producing part of a plant's female reproductive organs). Fruits may be succulent or dry (see pp. 150-151). Succulent fruits are fleshy and brightly coloured, making them attractive to animals, which eat them and so disperse the seeds away from the parent plant. The wall (pericarp) of a succulent fruit has three layers: an outer exocarp, a middle mesocarp, and an inner endocarp. These three layers vary in thickness and texture in different types of fruits and may blend into each other. Succulent fruits can be classed as simple (derived from one ovary) or compound (derived from several ovaries). Simple succulent fruits include berries, which typically have many seeds, and drupes, which typically have a single stone or pip (e.g., cherry and peach). Compound succulent fruits include aggregate fruits, which are formed from many ovaries in one flower, and multiple fruits, which develop from the ovaries of many flowers. Some fruits, known as false fruits or pseudocarps, develop from parts of the flower in addition to the ovaries. For example, the flesh of the apple is formed from the receptacle (the upper end of the flower stalk).

BERRY
Cocoa
(*Theobroma cacao*)

HESPERIDIUM (A TYPE OF BERRY)
Lemon
(*Citrus limon*)

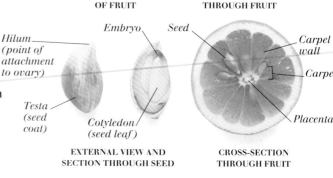

Pedicel (flower stalk)
Endocarp
Mesocarp
Pedicel (flower stalk)
Exocarp
Leathery exocarp
Seed
Oil gland
Vesicle (juice sac)
Remains of style
Remains of style
Placenta

EXTERNAL VIEW OF FRUIT
LONGITUDINAL SECTION THROUGH FRUIT

Hilum (point of attachment to ovary)
Embryo
Seed
Carpel wall
Carpel
Testa (seed coat)
Cotyledon (seed leaf)
Placenta

EXTERNAL VIEW AND SECTION THROUGH SEED
CROSS-SECTION THROUGH FRUIT

SYCONIUM (A TYPE OF FALSE FRUIT)
Fig
(*Ficus carica*)

Peduncle (inflorescence stalk)
Remains of female flowers
Fleshy infolded receptacle
Remains of male flowers
Pip (seed surrounded by endocarp)
Skin
Pore closed by scales

EXTERNAL VIEW OF FRUIT
LONGITUDINAL SECTION THROUGH FRUIT

FRUIT WITH FLESHY ARIL
Lychee
(*Litchi chinensis*)

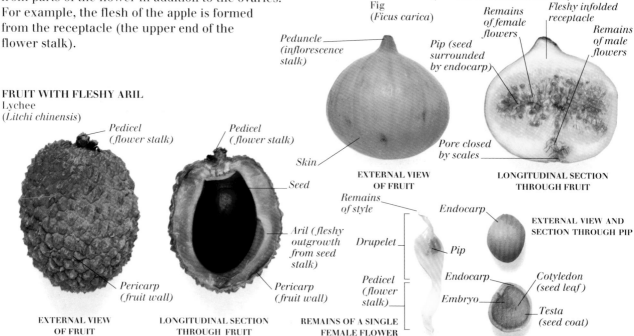

Pedicel (flower stalk)
Pedicel (flower stalk)
Seed
Aril (fleshy outgrowth from seed stalk)
Pericarp (fruit wall)
Pericarp (fruit wall)

Remains of style
Endocarp
Drupelet
Pip
Pedicel (flower stalk)
Endocarp
Embryo
Cotyledon (seed leaf)
Testa (seed coat)

EXTERNAL VIEW AND SECTION THROUGH PIP

EXTERNAL VIEW OF FRUIT
LONGITUDINAL SECTION THROUGH FRUIT
REMAINS OF A SINGLE FEMALE FLOWER

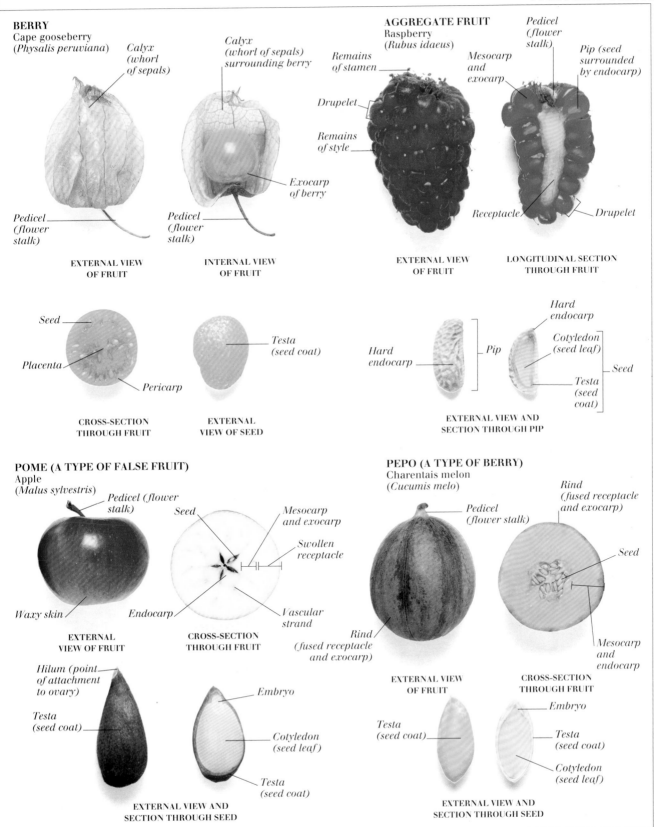

BERRY
Cape gooseberry
(*Physalis peruviana*)

Calyx (whorl of sepals)

Calyx (whorl of sepals) surrounding berry

Pedicel (flower stalk)

Exocarp of berry

Pedicel (flower stalk)

EXTERNAL VIEW
OF FRUIT

INTERNAL VIEW
OF FRUIT

AGGREGATE FRUIT
Raspberry
(*Rubus idaeus*)

Pedicel (flower stalk)

Pip (seed surrounded by endocarp)

Remains of stamen

Mesocarp and exocarp

Drupelet

Remains of style

Receptacle

Drupelet

EXTERNAL VIEW
OF FRUIT

LONGITUDINAL SECTION
THROUGH FRUIT

Seed

Placenta

Pericarp

Testa (seed coat)

CROSS-SECTION
THROUGH FRUIT

EXTERNAL
VIEW OF SEED

Hard endocarp

Hard endocarp

Pip

Cotyledon (seed leaf)

Seed

Testa (seed coat)

EXTERNAL VIEW AND
SECTION THROUGH PIP

POME (A TYPE OF FALSE FRUIT)
Apple
(*Malus sylvestris*)

Pedicel (flower stalk)

Seed

Mesocarp and exocarp

Swollen receptacle

Waxy skin

Endocarp

Vascular strand

EXTERNAL
VIEW OF FRUIT

CROSS-SECTION
THROUGH FRUIT

Hilum (point of attachment to ovary)

Testa (seed coat)

Embryo

Cotyledon (seed leaf)

Testa (seed coat)

EXTERNAL VIEW AND
SECTION THROUGH SEED

PEPO (A TYPE OF BERRY)
Charentais melon
(*Cucumis melo*)

Pedicel (flower stalk)

Rind (fused receptacle and exocarp)

Seed

Rind (fused receptacle and exocarp)

Mesocarp and endocarp

EXTERNAL VIEW
OF FRUIT

CROSS-SECTION
THROUGH FRUIT

Testa (seed coat)

Embryo

Testa (seed coat)

Cotyledon (seed leaf)

EXTERNAL VIEW AND
SECTION THROUGH SEED

Dry fruits

DRY FRUITS HAVE A HARD, DRY PERICARP (fruit wall) around their seeds unlike succulent fruits, which have fleshy pericarps (see pp. 148-149). Dry fruits are divided into three types: dehiscent, in which the pericarp splits open to release the seeds; indehiscent, which do not split open; and schizocarpic, in which the fruit splits but the seeds are not exposed. Dehiscent dry fruits include capsules (e.g., love-in-a-mist), follicles (e.g., delphinium), legumes (e.g., pea), and siliquas (e.g., honesty). Typically, the seeds of dehiscent fruits are dispersed by the wind. Indehiscent dry fruits include nuts (e.g., sweet chestnut), nutlets (e.g., goosegrass), achenes (e.g., strawberry), caryopses (e.g., wheat), samaras (e.g., elm), and cypselas (e.g., dandelion). Some indehiscent dry fruits are dispersed by the wind, assisted by "wings" (e.g., elm) or "parachutes" (e.g., dandelion); others (e.g., goosegrass) have hooked pericarps to aid dispersal on animals' fur. Schizocarpic dry fruits include cremocarps (e.g., hogweed), and double samaras (e.g., sycamore); these are dispersed by the wind.

NUTLET
Goosegrass
(*Galium aparine*)

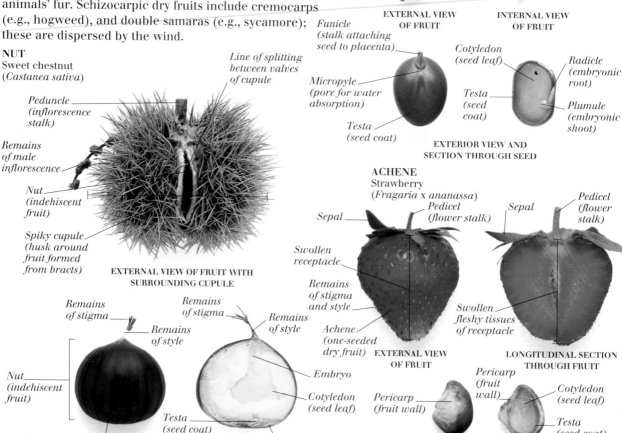

LEGUME
Pea
(*Pisum sativum*)

Pedicel (*flower stalk*)
Receptacle
Remains of sepal
Remains of stamen
Placenta
Pericarp (*fruit wall*)
Remains of style and stigma

Pedicel (*flower stalk*)
Receptacle
Remains of sepal
Funicle (*stalk attaching seed to placenta*)
Pericarp (*fruit wall*)
Seed
Remains of style and stigma

EXTERNAL VIEW OF FRUIT

INTERNAL VIEW OF FRUIT

Funicle (*stalk attaching seed to placenta*)
Micropyle (*pore for water absorption*)
Testa (*seed coat*)

Cotyledon (*seed leaf*)
Radicle (*embryonic root*)
Testa (*seed coat*)
Plumule (*embryonic shoot*)

EXTERIOR VIEW AND SECTION THROUGH SEED

NUT
Sweet chestnut
(*Castanea sativa*)

Line of splitting between valves of cupule

Peduncle (*inflorescence stalk*)

Remains of male inflorescence

Nut (*indehiscent fruit*)

Spiky cupule (*husk around fruit formed from bracts*)

EXTERNAL VIEW OF FRUIT WITH SURROUNDING CUPULE

ACHENE
Strawberry
(*Fragaria x ananassa*)

Sepal
Pedicel (*flower stalk*)

Swollen receptacle

Remains of stigma and style

Achene (*one-seeded dry fruit*)

EXTERNAL VIEW OF FRUIT

Sepal
Pedicel (*flower stalk*)

Swollen fleshy tissues of receptacle

LONGITUDINAL SECTION THROUGH FRUIT

Remains of stigma
Remains of style

Remains of stigma
Remains of style

Nut (*indehiscent fruit*)

Embryo
Cotyledon (*seed leaf*)

Testa (*seed coat*)

Woody pericarp (*fruit wall*)

Woody pericarp (*fruit wall*)

EXTERNAL VIEW AND SECTION THROUGH FRUIT

Pericarp (*fruit wall*)

Pericarp (*fruit wall*)
Cotyledon (*seed leaf*)
Testa (*seed coat*)

EXTERNAL VIEW AND SECTION THROUGH SEED

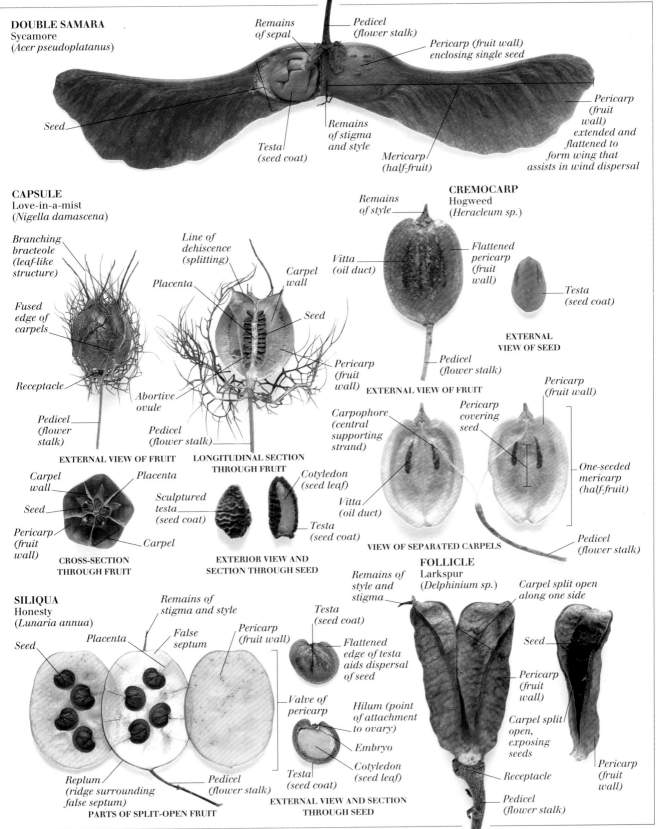

DOUBLE SAMARA
Sycamore
(*Acer pseudoplatanus*)

Remains
of sepal

Pedicel
(flower stalk)

Pericarp (fruit wall)
enclosing single seed

Seed

Testa
(seed coat)

Remains
of stigma
and style

Mericarp
(half-fruit)

Pericarp
(fruit
wall)
extended and
flattened to
form wing that
assists in wind dispersal

CAPSULE
Love-in-a-mist
(*Nigella damascena*)

Branching
bracteole
(leaf-like
structure)

Line of
dehiscence
(splitting)

Placenta

Carpel
wall

Fused
edge of
carpels

Seed

Receptacle

Abortive
ovule

Pericarp
(fruit
wall)

Pedicel
(flower
stalk)

Pedicel
(flower stalk)

EXTERNAL VIEW OF FRUIT

LONGITUDINAL SECTION
THROUGH FRUIT

Carpel
wall

Placenta

Seed

Pericarp
(fruit
wall)

Carpel

CROSS-SECTION
THROUGH FRUIT

Sculptured
testa
(seed coat)

Cotyledon
(seed leaf)

Testa
(seed coat)

EXTERIOR VIEW AND
SECTION THROUGH SEED

CREMOCARP
Hogweed
(*Heracleum sp.*)

Remains
of style

Vitta
(oil duct)

Flattened
pericarp
(fruit
wall)

Testa
(seed coat)

EXTERNAL
VIEW OF SEED

Pedicel
(flower stalk)

EXTERNAL VIEW OF FRUIT

Carpophore
(central
supporting
strand)

Pericarp
covering
seed

Pericarp
(fruit wall)

Vitta
(oil duct)

One-seeded
mericarp
(half-fruit)

Pedicel
(flower
stalk)

VIEW OF SEPARATED CARPELS

SILIQUA
Honesty
(*Lunaria annua*)

Remains of
stigma and style

False
septum

Pericarp
(fruit wall)

Placenta

Seed

Valve of
pericarp

Replum
(ridge surrounding
false septum)

Pedicel
(flower stalk)

PARTS OF SPLIT-OPEN FRUIT

Testa
(seed coat)

Flattened
edge of testa
aids dispersal
of seed

Hilum (point
of attachment
to ovary)

Embryo

Testa
(seed coat)

Cotyledon
(seed leaf)

EXTERNAL VIEW AND SECTION
THROUGH SEED

FOLLICLE
Larkspur
(*Delphinium sp.*)

Remains of
style and
stigma

Carpel split open
along one side

Seed

Pericarp
(fruit
wall)

Carpel split
open,
exposing
seeds

Receptacle

Pedicel
(flower stalk)

Pericarp
(fruit
wall)

Germination

GERMINATION IS THE GROWTH OF SEEDS INTO SEEDLINGS. It starts when seeds become active below ground, and ends when the first foliage leaves appear above ground. A seed consists of an embryo and its food store, surrounded by a testa (seed coat). The embryo is made up of one or two cotyledons (seed leaves) attached to a central axis. The upper part of the axis consists of an epicotyl, which has a plumule (embryonic shoot) at its tip. The lower part of the axis consists of a hypocotyl and a radicle (embryonic root). After dispersal from the parent plant, the seeds dehydrate and enter a period of dormancy. Following this dormant period, germination begins, provided that the seeds have enough water, oxygen, warmth, and, in some cases, light. In the first stages of germination, the seed takes in water; the embryo starts to use its food store; and the radicle swells, breaks through the testa, and grows downwards. Germination then proceeds in one of two ways, depending on the type of seed. In epigeal germination, the hypocotyl lengthens, pulling the plumule and its protective cotyledons out of the soil. In hypogeal germination, the cotyledons remain below ground and the epicotyl lengthens, pushing the plumule upwards.

HYPOGEAL GERMINATION
Broad bean
(*Vicia faba*)

Cotyledon (seed leaf)

Cotyledon (seed leaf)

Testa (seed coat)

Plumule (embryonic shoot)

Epicotyl (upper part of axis)

Hypocotyl (region between epicotyl and radicle)

Radicle (embryonic root)

SEED AT START OF GERMINATION

Cotyledon (seed leaf)

Foliage leaf

Cotyledon (seed leaf)

Stipule (structure at base of leaf)

Epicotyl increases in length and turns green

Cataphyll (scale leaf of plumule)

Epicotyl (upper part of axis)

Hypocotyl (region between epicotyl and radicle)

FOLIAGE LEAVES APPEAR

Split in testa (seed coat) due to expanding cotyledons

Young shoot

Cataphyll (scale leaf of plumule)

Testa (seed coat)

Epicotyl (upper part of axis) lengthens

Plumule (embryonic shoot)

Cotyledons (seed leaves) remain within testa (seed coat) below soil's surface

Primary root

Hilum (point of attachment to ovary)

Cortex

Cotyledons (seed leaves) remain food source for the seedling

Primary root

Radicle (embryonic root)

Lateral root

Vascular tissue (xylem and phloem)

Epidermis

Lateral root system

SHOOT APPEARS ABOVE SOIL

RADICLE BREAKS THROUGH TESTA

Root tip (region of cell division)

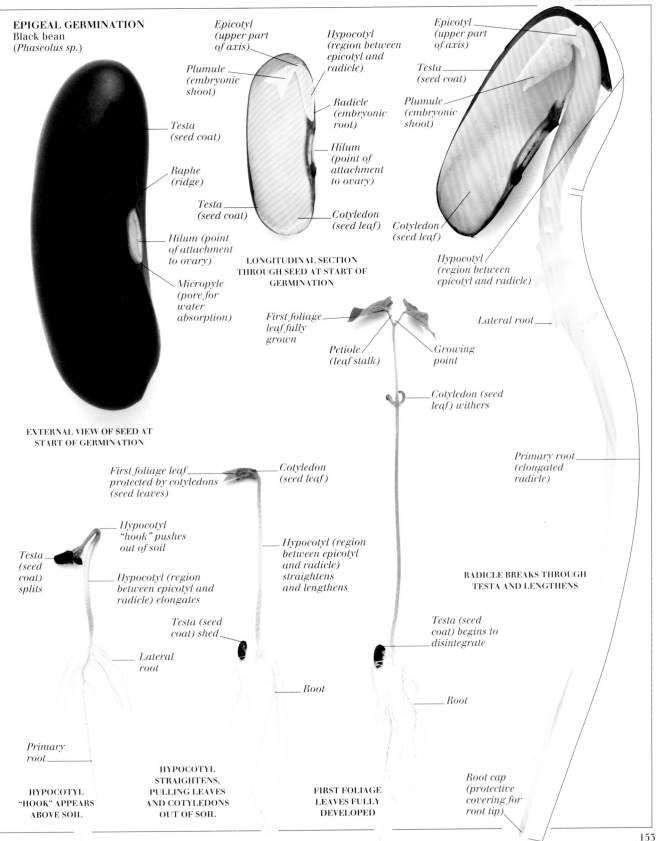

EPIGEAL GERMINATION
Black bean
(*Phaseolus sp.*)

*Epicotyl
(upper part
of axis)*

*Plumule
(embryonic
shoot)*

*Hypocotyl
(region between
epicotyl and
radicle)*

*Radicle
(embryonic
root)*

*Epicotyl
(upper part
of axis)*

*Testa
(seed coat)*

*Plumule
(embryonic
shoot)*

*Testa
(seed coat)*

*Raphe
(ridge)*

*Hilum
(point of
attachment
to ovary)*

*Testa
(seed coat)*

*Cotyledon
(seed leaf)*

*Cotyledon
(seed leaf)*

*Hilum (point
of attachment
to ovary)*

**LONGITUDINAL SECTION
THROUGH SEED AT START OF
GERMINATION**

*Hypocotyl
(region between
epicotyl and radicle)*

*Micropyle
(pore for
water
absorption)*

*First foliage
leaf fully
grown*

Lateral root

*Petiole
(leaf stalk)*

*Growing
point*

*Cotyledon (seed
leaf) withers*

**EXTERNAL VIEW OF SEED AT
START OF GERMINATION**

*Primary root
(elongated
radicle)*

*First foliage leaf
protected by cotyledons
(seed leaves)*

*Cotyledon
(seed leaf)*

*Hypocotyl
"hook" pushes
out of soil*

*Testa
(seed
coat)
splits*

*Hypocotyl (region
between epicotyl and
radicle) elongates*

*Hypocotyl (region
between epicotyl
and radicle)
straightens
and lengthens*

**RADICLE BREAKS THROUGH
TESTA AND LENGTHENS**

*Testa (seed
coat) shed*

*Testa (seed
coat) begins to
disintegrate*

*Lateral
root*

Root

Root

*Primary
root*

**HYPOCOTYL
"HOOK" APPEARS
ABOVE SOIL**

**HYPOCOTYL
STRAIGHTENS,
PULLING LEAVES
AND COTYLEDONS
OUT OF SOIL**

**FIRST FOLIAGE
LEAVES FULLY
DEVELOPED**

*Root cap
(protective
covering for
root tip)*

Vegetative reproduction

MANY PLANTS CAN PROPAGATE THEMSELVES by vegetative reproduction. In this process, part of a plant separates off, takes root, and grows into a new plant. Vegetative reproduction is a type of asexual reproduction; that is, it involves only one parent, and there is no fusion of gametes (sex cells). Plants use various structures to reproduce vegetatively. Some plants use underground storage organs. Such organs include rhizomes (horizontal, underground stems), the branches of which produce new plants; bulbs (swollen leaf bases) and corms (swollen stems), which produce daughter bulbs or corms that separate off from the parent; and stem tubers (thickened underground stems) and root tubers (swollen adventitious roots), which also separate off from the parent. Other propagative structures include runners and stolons, creeping horizontal stems that take root and produce new plants; bulbils, small bulbs that develop on the stem or in the place of flowers, and then drop off and grow into new plants; and adventitious buds, miniature plants that form on leaf margins before dropping to the ground and growing into mature plants.

CORM
Gladiolus
(*Gladiolus sp.*)

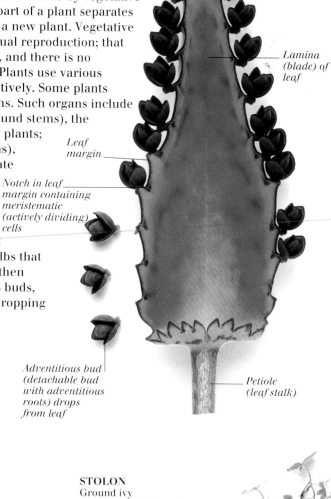

ADVENTITIOUS BUD
Mexican hat plant
(*Kalanchoe daigremontiana*)

Apex of leaf

Lamina (blade) of leaf

Leaf margin

Notch in leaf margin containing meristematic (actively dividing) cells

Adventitious bud (detachable bud with adventitious roots) drops from leaf

Petiole (leaf stalk)

BULBIL IN PLACE OF FLOWER
Orange lily
(*Lilium bulbiferum*)

Scar left by flower

Leaf

Pedicel (flower stalk)

Detachable bulbil formed in place of flower

Peduncle (inflorescence stalk)

STOLON
Ground ivy
(*Glechoma hederacea*)

Terminal bud

Internode

Node

Node

Parent plant

Stolon (creeping stem)

Adventitious root of daughter plant

Daughter plant developed from lateral bud

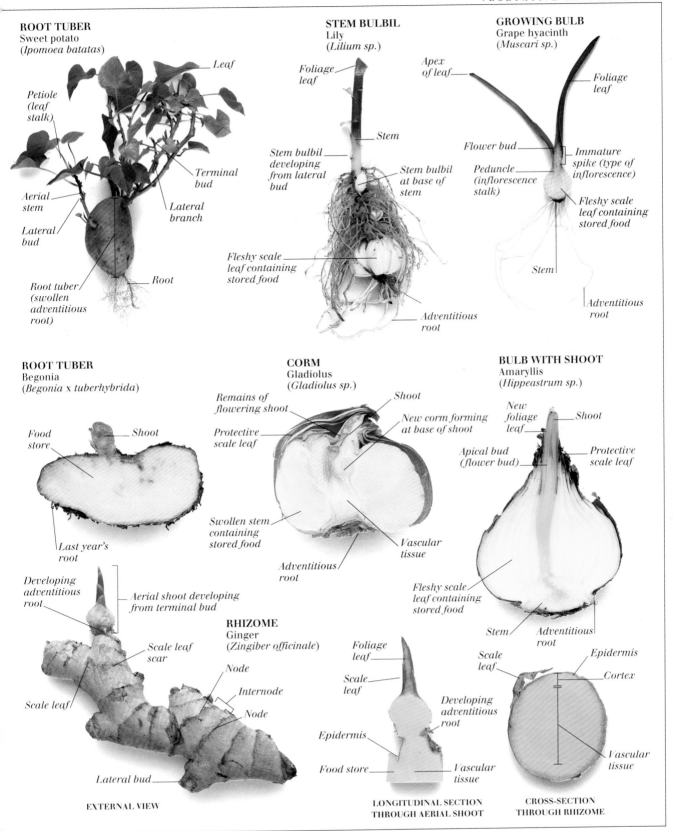

ROOT TUBER
Sweet potato
(*Ipomoea batatas*)

Leaf

Petiole
(leaf
stalk)

Terminal
bud

Aerial
stem

Lateral
branch

Lateral
bud

Root tuber
(swollen
adventitious
root)

Root

STEM BULBIL
Lily
(*Lilium sp.*)

Foliage
leaf

Stem

Stem bulbil
developing
from lateral
bud

Stem bulbil
at base of
stem

Fleshy scale
leaf containing
stored food

Adventitious
root

GROWING BULB
Grape hyacinth
(*Muscari sp.*)

Apex
of leaf

Foliage
leaf

Flower bud

Immature
spike (type of
inflorescence)

Peduncle
(inflorescence
stalk)

Fleshy scale
leaf containing
stored food

Stem

Adventitious
root

ROOT TUBER
Begonia
(*Begonia* x *tuberhybrida*)

Food
store

Shoot

Last year's
root

Developing
adventitious
root

Aerial shoot developing
from terminal bud

Scale leaf
scar

Node

Internode

Node

Scale leaf

Lateral bud

EXTERNAL VIEW

CORM
Gladiolus
(*Gladiolus sp.*)

Remains of
flowering shoot

Shoot

Protective
scale leaf

New corm forming
at base of shoot

Swollen stem
containing
stored food

Vascular
tissue

Adventitious
root

RHIZOME
Ginger
(*Zingiber officinale*)

Foliage
leaf

Scale
leaf

Epidermis

Food store

Developing
adventitious
root

Vascular
tissue

LONGITUDINAL SECTION
THROUGH AERIAL SHOOT

BULB WITH SHOOT
Amaryllis
(*Hippeastrum sp.*)

New
foliage
leaf

Shoot

Apical bud
(flower bud)

Protective
scale leaf

Fleshy scale
leaf containing
stored food

Stem

Adventitious
root

Scale
leaf

Epidermis

Cortex

Vascular
tissue

CROSS-SECTION
THROUGH RHIZOME

Dryland plants

DRYLAND PLANTS (XEROPHYTES) are able to survive in unfavourable habitats. All are found in places where little water is available; some live in high temperatures that cause excessive loss of water from the leaves. Xerophytes show a number of adaptations to dry conditions; these include reduced leaf area, rolled leaves, sunken stomata, hairs, spines, and thick cuticles. One group, succulent plants, stores water in specially enlarged spongy tissues found in leaves, roots, or stems. Leaf succulents have enlarged, fleshy, water-storing leaves. Root succulents have a large, underground water-storage organ with short-lived stems and leaves above ground. Stem succulents are represented by the cacti (family Cactaceae). Cacti stems are fleshy, green, and photosynthetic; they are typically ribbed or covered by tubercles in rows, with leaves being reduced to spines or entirely absent.

LEAF SUCCULENT
Lithops sp.

Areole (modified lateral shoot)

Trichome (hair)

Spine (modified leaf)

Waxy cuticle (waterproof covering)

Water-storing parenchyma (packing tissue)

Tubercle (projection from stem surface)

Vascular cylinder (transport tissue)

Root

LONGITUDINAL SECTION THROUGH STEM

Spine (modified leaf)

Tubercle (projection from stem surface)

Root

EXTERNAL VIEW

Sinuous (wavy) cell wall

Stoma (pore) controlling exchange of gases

MICROGRAPH OF STEM SURFACE

Spine (modified leaf)

Areole (modified lateral shoot)

Tubercle (projection from stem surface)

Waxy cuticle (waterproof covering)

DETAIL OF STEM SURFACE

LEAF SUCCULENT
Haworthia truncata

Translucent "window" allows light to reach base of leaf

Succulent leaf

Root tuber

Root

Translucent "window" allows light to reach base of leaf

Waxy cuticle (waterproof covering)

Water-storing parenchyma (packing tissue)

Photosynthetic region

LONGITUDINAL SECTION THROUGH LEAF

Raised cell surface

Stoma (pore)

Cup surrounding sunken stoma (pore)

MICROGRAPH OF LEAF SURFACE

LEAF SUCCULENT
Lithops bromfieldii

Leaf

Fissure

Mottled surface of leaf

Dead, withered leaf

Dead flower in old fissure

Unified leaf pair

Translucent "window" allows light to reach centre of leaf

Fissure

Waxy cuticle (waterproof covering)

Photosynthetic region

Water-storing parenchyma (packing tissue)

LONGITUDINAL SECTION THROUGH LEAF PAIR

ROOT SUCCULENT
Oxalis sp.

Petiole (leaf stalk)

Flower bud

Pedicel (flower stalk)

Trifoliate leaf

Stem

Root tuber

Root

STEM AND ROOT SUCCULENT
String of hearts
(*Ceropegia woodii*)

Stem

Root tuber

Root

EXTERNAL VIEW

Petiole (leaf stalk)

Succulent trailing stem

Succulent leaf

Root tuber

Water-storing parenchyma

Root

LONGITUDINAL SECTION THROUGH ROOT TUBER

157

Wetland plants

WETLAND PLANTS GROW SUBMERGED IN WATER, either partially (e.g., water hyacinth) or completely (e.g., pond weeds), and show various adaptations to this habitat. Typically, there are numerous air spaces inside the stems, leaves, and roots; these aid gas exchange and buoyancy. Submerged parts generally have no cuticle (waterproof covering), enabling the plants to absorb minerals and gases directly from the water; in addition, being supported by the water, they need little of the supportive tissue found in land plants. Stomata, the gas exchange pores, are absent from plants that are completely submerged; in partially submerged plants with floating leaves (e.g., water lilies), stomata are found on the upper leaf surfaces, where they cannot be flooded.

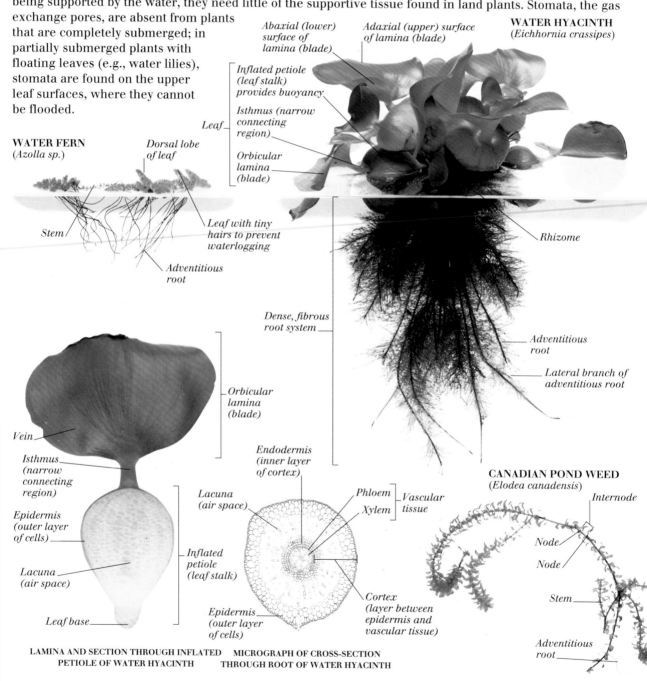

WATER FERN
(*Azolla sp.*)

Dorsal lobe of leaf

Stem

Leaf with tiny hairs to prevent waterlogging

Adventitious root

WATER HYACINTH
(*Eichhornia crassipes*)

Abaxial (lower) surface of lamina (blade)

Adaxial (upper) surface of lamina (blade)

Inflated petiole (leaf stalk) provides buoyancy

Isthmus (narrow connecting region)

Leaf

Orbicular lamina (blade)

Rhizome

Dense, fibrous root system

Adventitious root

Lateral branch of adventitious root

Orbicular lamina (blade)

Vein

Isthmus (narrow connecting region)

Epidermis (outer layer of cells)

Lacuna (air space)

Leaf base

Inflated petiole (leaf stalk)

Endodermis (inner layer of cortex)

Lacuna (air space)

Phloem

Xylem

Vascular tissue

Epidermis (outer layer of cells)

Cortex (layer between epidermis and vascular tissue)

CANADIAN POND WEED
(*Elodea canadensis*)

Internode

Node

Node

Stem

Adventitious root

LAMINA AND SECTION THROUGH INFLATED PETIOLE OF WATER HYACINTH

MICROGRAPH OF CROSS-SECTION THROUGH ROOT OF WATER HYACINTH

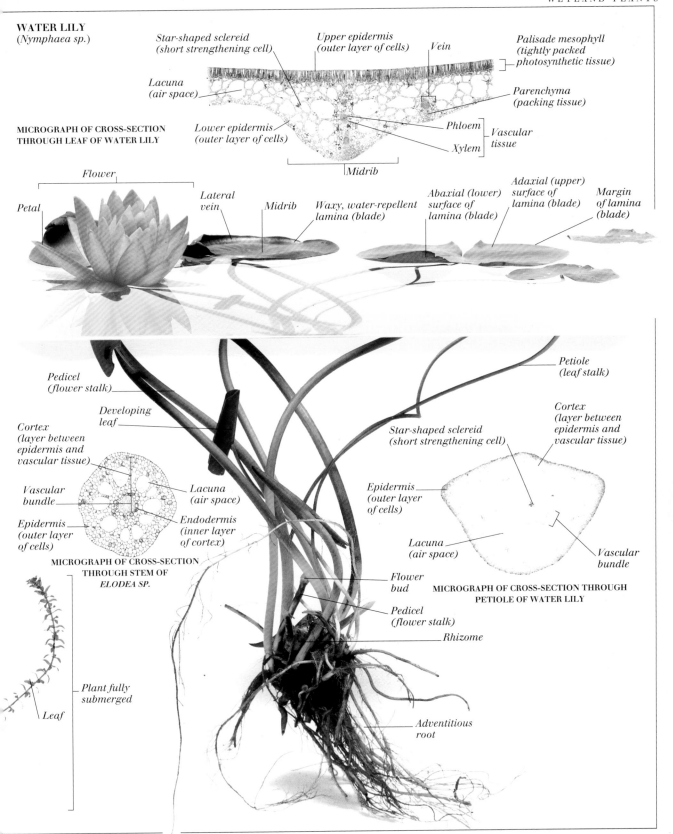

WATER LILY
(Nymphaea sp.)

*Star-shaped sclereid
(short strengthening cell)*

*Upper epidermis
(outer layer of cells)*

Vein

*Palisade mesophyll
(tightly packed
photosynthetic tissue)*

*Lacuna
(air space)*

*Parenchyma
(packing tissue)*

**MICROGRAPH OF CROSS-SECTION
THROUGH LEAF OF WATER LILY**

*Lower epidermis
(outer layer of cells)*

Phloem

Xylem

*Vascular
tissue*

Midrib

Flower

*Lateral
vein*

Midrib

*Waxy, water-repellent
lamina (blade)*

*Abaxial (lower)
surface of
lamina (blade)*

*Adaxial (upper)
surface of
lamina (blade)*

*Margin
of lamina
(blade)*

Petal

*Pedicel
(flower stalk)*

*Petiole
(leaf stalk)*

*Developing
leaf*

*Cortex
(layer between
epidermis and
vascular tissue)*

*Star-shaped sclereid
(short strengthening cell)*

*Cortex
(layer between
epidermis and
vascular tissue)*

*Vascular
bundle*

*Lacuna
(air space)*

*Epidermis
(outer layer
of cells)*

*Epidermis
(outer layer
of cells)*

*Endodermis
(inner layer
of cortex)*

*Lacuna
(air space)*

*Vascular
bundle*

**MICROGRAPH OF CROSS-SECTION
THROUGH STEM OF
ELODEA SP.**

*Flower
bud*

**MICROGRAPH OF CROSS-SECTION THROUGH
PETIOLE OF WATER LILY**

*Pedicel
(flower stalk)*

Rhizome

*Plant fully
submerged*

*Adventitious
root*

Leaf

Carnivorous plants

Areola ("window" of transparent tissue)

Fishtail nectary

Hood

Wing

Pitcher

Tubular petiole (leaf stalk)

Areola ("window" of transparent tissue)

CARNIVOROUS (INSECTIVOROUS) PLANTS FEED ON INSECTS and other small animals, in addition to producing food in their leaves by photosynthesis. The nutrients absorbed from trapped insects enable carnivorous plants to thrive in acid, boggy soils that lack essential minerals, especially nitrates, where most other plants could not survive. All carnivorous plants have some leaves modified as traps; many use bright colours and scented nectar to attract prey; and most use enzymes to digest the prey. There are three types of traps. Pitcher plants, such as the monkey cup and cobra lily, have leaves modified as pitcher-shaped pitfall traps, half-filled with water; once lured inside the mouth of the trap, insects lose their footing on the slippery surface, fall into the liquid, and either decompose or are digested. Venus fly traps use a spring-trap mechanism; when an insect touches trigger hairs on the inner surfaces of the leaves, the two lobes of the trap snap shut. Butterworts and sundews entangle prey by sticky droplets on the leaf surface, while the edges of the leaves slowly curl over to envelop and digest the prey.

Dome-shaped hood develops

Fishtail nectary appears

Immature pitcher

Smooth surface

Nectar roll

Mouth

Wing

Downward pointing hair

DEVELOPMENT OF MODIFIED LEAF IN COBRA LILY

Immature trap

Interlocked teeth

Closed trap

Red colour of trap attracts insects

VENUS FLY TRAP
(*Dionaea muscipula*)

Phyllode (flattened petiole)

Summer petiole (leaf stalk)

Nectary zone (glands secrete nectar)

Digestive zone (glands secrete digestive enzymes)

Tooth

Lobe of trap

Midrib (hinge of trap)

Trigger hair

Trap (twin-lobed leaf blade)

Spring petiole (leaf stalk)

Sensory hinge

Trigger hair

Inner surface of trap

Digestive gland

MICROGRAPH OF LOBE OF VENUS FLY TRAP

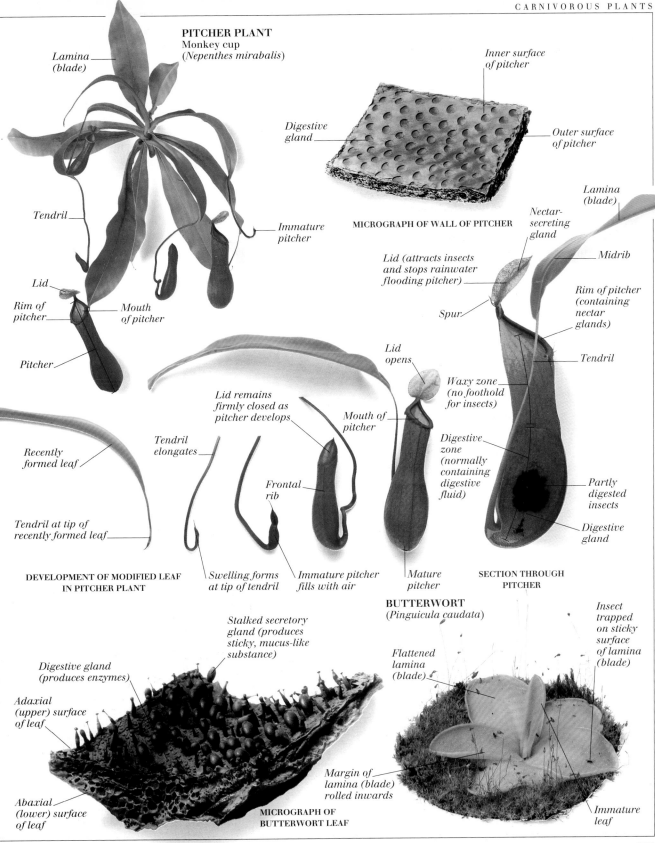

PITCHER PLANT
Monkey cup
(*Nepenthes mirabalis*)

Lamina (blade)

Tendril

Immature pitcher

Lid

Rim of pitcher

Mouth of pitcher

Pitcher

Inner surface of pitcher

Digestive gland

Outer surface of pitcher

MICROGRAPH OF WALL OF PITCHER

Lamina (blade)

Nectar-secreting gland

Midrib

Lid (attracts insects and stops rainwater flooding pitcher)

Rim of pitcher (containing nectar glands)

Spur

Tendril

Waxy zone (no foothold for insects)

Digestive zone (normally containing digestive fluid)

Partly digested insects

Digestive gland

Recently formed leaf

Lid remains firmly closed as pitcher develops

Lid opens

Mouth of pitcher

Tendril at tip of recently formed leaf

Tendril elongates

Frontal rib

Mature pitcher

Swelling forms at tip of tendril

Immature pitcher fills with air

DEVELOPMENT OF MODIFIED LEAF IN PITCHER PLANT

SECTION THROUGH PITCHER

BUTTERWORT
(*Pinguicula caudata*)

Stalked secretory gland (produces sticky, mucus-like substance)

Insect trapped on sticky surface of lamina (blade)

Flattened lamina (blade)

Digestive gland (produces enzymes)

Adaxial (upper) surface of leaf

Abaxial (lower) surface of leaf

Margin of lamina (blade) rolled inwards

Immature leaf

MICROGRAPH OF BUTTERWORT LEAF

Epiphytic and parasitic plants

EPIPHYTIC AND PARASITIC PLANTS GROW ON OTHER LIVING PLANTS. Typically, epiphytic plants are not rooted in the soil; instead, they live above ground level on the stems and branches of other plants. Epiphytes obtain water from trapped rainwater and from moisture in the air, and minerals from organic matter that has accumulated on the surface of the plant on which they are growing. Like other green plants, epiphytes produce their food by photosynthesis. Epiphytes include tropical orchids and bromeliads (air plants), and some mosses that live in temperate regions. Parasitic plants obtain all their nutrient requirements from the host plants on which they grow. The parasites produce haustoria, root-like organs that penetrate the stem or roots of the host and grow inwards to merge with the host's vascular tissue, from which the parasite extracts water, minerals, and manufactured nutrients. As they have no need to produce their own food, parasitic plants lack chlorophyll, the green photosynthetic pigment, and they have no foliage leaves. Partial parasitic plants (e.g., mistletoe) obtain water and minerals from the host plant but have green leaves and stems and are therefore able to produce their own food by photosynthesis.

EPIPHYTIC BROMELIAD
Aechmea miniata

Inflorescence (spike)

Peduncle (inflorescence stalk)

Flower bud

Strap-shaped arching leaf (part of rosette of leaves)

Leaf margin with spines

Overlapping leaf bases in which rainwater is trapped

Mass of adventitious roots

Stem

Bark of tree to which epiphyte is attached

EPIPHYTIC ORCHID
Brassavola nodosa

Peduncle (inflorescence stalk)

Pedicel (flower stalk)

Flower

Scale leaf

Leaf

Aerial root

Node

Stem

Bark of tree to which epiphyte is attached

Velamen (multi-layered epidermis capable of absorbing water from rain or condensation)

Exodermis (outer layer of cortex)

Cortex (layer between epidermis and vascular tissue)

Cortex cell containing chloroplasts

Pith

Vascular tissue { *Xylem* *Phloem*

Endodermis (inner layer of cortex)

**MICROGRAPH OF CROSS-SECTION THROUGH
AERIAL ROOT OF EPIPHYTIC ORCHID**

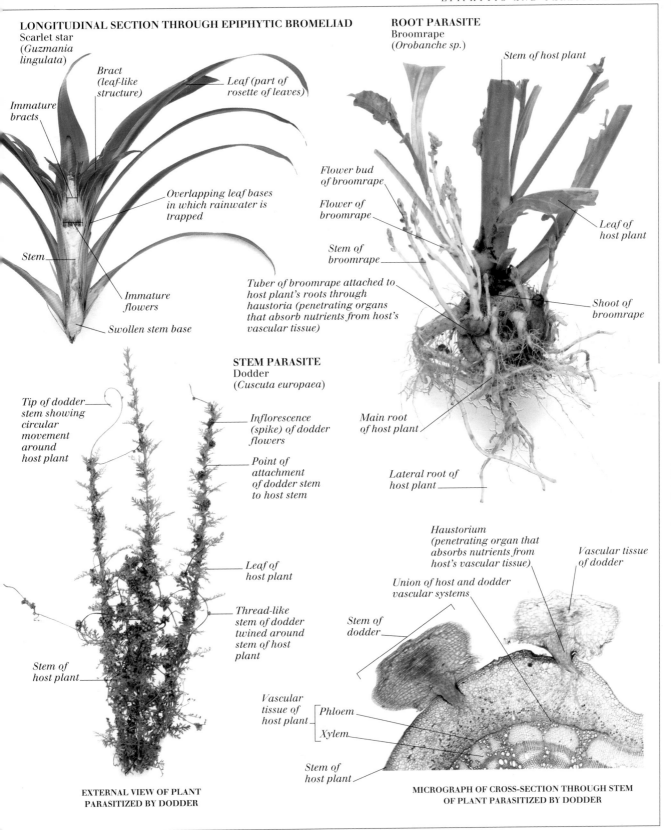

LONGITUDINAL SECTION THROUGH EPIPHYTIC BROMELIAD
Scarlet star
(*Guzmania
lingulata*)

Bract
(leaf-like
structure)

Leaf (part of
rosette of leaves)

Immature
bracts

Overlapping leaf bases
in which rainwater is
trapped

Stem

Immature
flowers

Swollen stem base

ROOT PARASITE
Broomrape
(*Orobanche sp.*)

Stem of host plant

Flower bud
of broomrape

Flower of
broomrape

Stem of
broomrape

Tuber of broomrape attached to
host plant's roots through
haustoria (penetrating organs
that absorb nutrients from host's
vascular tissue)

Leaf of
host plant

Shoot of
broomrape

Main root
of host plant

Lateral root of
host plant

STEM PARASITE
Dodder
(*Cuscuta europaea*)

Tip of dodder
stem showing
circular
movement
around
host plant

Inflorescence
(spike) of dodder
flowers

Point of
attachment
of dodder stem
to host stem

Leaf of
host plant

Thread-like
stem of dodder
twined around
stem of host
plant

Stem of
host plant

Haustorium
(penetrating organ that
absorbs nutrients from
host's vascular tissue)

Vascular tissue
of dodder

Union of host and dodder
vascular systems

Stem of
dodder

Vascular
tissue of
host plant

Phloem

Xylem

Stem of
host plant

**EXTERNAL VIEW OF PLANT
PARASITIZED BY DODDER**

**MICROGRAPH OF CROSS-SECTION THROUGH STEM
OF PLANT PARASITIZED BY DODDER**

ANIMALS

SPONGES, JELLYFISH, AND SEA ANEMONES · · · 166

INSECTS · · · · · · · · · · · · · · · · · · · 168

ARACHNIDS · · · · · · · · · · · · · · · · · · 170

CRUSTACEANS · · · · · · · · · · · · · · · · · 172

STARFISH AND SEA URCHINS · · · · · · · · · · 174

MOLLUSCS · · · · · · · · · · · · · · · · · · · 176

SHARKS AND JAWLESS FISH · · · · · · · · · · 178

BONY FISH · · · · · · · · · · · · · · · · · · 180

AMPHIBIANS · · · · · · · · · · · · · · · · · · 182

LIZARDS AND SNAKES · · · · · · · · · · · · · 184

CROCODILIANS AND TURTLES · · · · · · · · · · 186

BIRDS 1 · · · · · · · · · · · · · · · · · · · 188

BIRDS 2 · · · · · · · · · · · · · · · · · · · 190

EGGS · 192

CARNIVORES · · · · · · · · · · · · · · · · · · 194

RABBITS AND RODENTS · · · · · · · · · · · · · 196

UNGULATES · · · · · · · · · · · · · · · · · · 198

ELEPHANTS · · · · · · · · · · · · · · · · · · 200

PRIMATES · · · · · · · · · · · · · · · · · · · 202

DOPHINS, WHALES, AND SEALS · · · · · · · · · 204

MARSUPIALS AND MONOTREMES · · · · · · · · 206

Sponges, jellyfish, and sea anemones

SPONGES ARE MAINLY MARINE animals that make
up the phylum Porifera. They are among
the simplest of all animals, having no
tissues or organs. Their bodies consist
of two layers of cells separated by a
jelly-like layer (mesohyal) that is strengthened
by mineral spicules or protein fibres. The body
is perforated by a system of pores and water
channels called the aquiferous system. Special
cells (choanocytes) with whip-like structures
(flagella) draw water through the aquiferous
system, thereby bringing tiny food particles
to the sponge's cells. Jellyfish (class Scyphozoa),
sea anemones (class Anthozoa), and corals
(also class Anthozoa) belong to the
phylum Cnidaria, also known as
Coelenterata. More complex than
sponges, coelenterates have simple
tissues, such as nervous tissue;
a radially symmetrical body;
and a mouth surrounded by
tentacles with unique stinging
cells (cnidocytes).

INTERNAL ANATOMY OF A SPONGE

Amoebocyte

Osculum (excurrent pore)

Choanocyte (collar cell)

Ostium (incurrent pore)

Porocyte (pore cell)

Mesohyal

Spongocoel (atrium; paragaster)

Spicule

Pinacocyte (epidermal cell)

Ostium (incurrent pore)

SKELETON OF A SPONGE

Protein matrix

Pore

EXTERNAL FEATURES OF A SEA ANEMONE

Tentacle

EXAMPLES OF SEA ANEMONES

JEWEL ANEMONE
(*Corynactis viridis*)

PARASITIC ANEMONE
(*Calliactis parasitica*)

PLUMOSE ANEMONE
(*Metridium senile*)

MEDITERRANEAN SEA ANEMONE
(*Condylactis sp.*)

GREEN SNAKELOCK
ANEMONE
(*Anemonia viridis*)

BEADLET ANEMONE
(*Actinia equina*)

GHOST ANEMONE
(*Actinothoe
sphyrodeta*)

Sagartia elegans

INTERNAL ANATOMY OF A JELLYFISH

Stomach

Filament

Gonad

Ectoderm

Endoderm

Mesoglea

Radial canal

Hood

Tentacle

Subgenital pit

Rhopalium

Oral arm

Mouth

EXTERNAL APPEARANCE OF A JELLYFISH

EXAMPLES OF CORALS

HONEYCOMB CORAL
(Goniastrea aspera)

MUSHROOM CORAL
(Fungia fungites)

STAR CORAL
(Balanophyllia regia)

STRUCTURE OF A CNIDOCYTE

Operculum

Thread

Cnidocil (trigger)

Spine

Barb (stylet)

Cnidocil (trigger)

Barb (stylet)

Operculum

Thread

Nucleus

Nucleus

BEFORE DISCHARGE

AFTER DISCHARGE

INTERNAL ANATOMY OF A SEA ANEMONE

Oral disc

Mouth

Ostium (mesenteric perforation)

Tentacle

Sphincter muscle

Collar

Siphonoglyph

Mesenteric filament

Complete mesentery

Incomplete mesentery

Retractor muscle

Gonad

Oral disc

Gastrovascular cavity

Mouth

Basal disc (pedal disc)

Pharynx

Insects

PUPA
(CHRYSALIS)

THE WORD INSECT REFERS to small invertebrate creatures, especially those with bodies divided into sections. Insects, including beetles, ants, bees, butterflies, and moths, belong to various orders in the class Insecta, which is a division of the phylum Arthropoda. Features common to all insects are an exoskeleton (external skeleton); three pairs of jointed legs; three body sections (head, thorax, and abdomen); and one pair of sensory antennae. Beetles (order Coleoptera) are the biggest group of insects, with about 300,000 species (about 30 per cent of all known insects). They have a pair of hard elytra (wing cases), which are modified front wings. The principal function of the elytra is to protect the hind wings, which are used for flying. Ants, together with bees and wasps, form the order Hymenoptera, which contains about 200,000 species. This group is characterized by a marked narrowing between the thorax and abdomen. Butterflies and moths form the order Lepidoptera, which has about 150,000 species. They have wings covered with tiny scales, hence the name of their order (Lepidoptera means "scale wings"). The separation of lepidopterans into butterflies and moths is largely artificial as there are no features that categorically distinguish one group from the other. In general, however, most butterflies fly by day, whereas most moths are night-flyers. Some insects, including butterflies and moths, undergo complete metamorphosis (transformation) during their life-cycle. A butterfly metamorphoses from an egg to a larva (caterpillar), then to a pupa (chrysalis), and finally to an imago (adult).

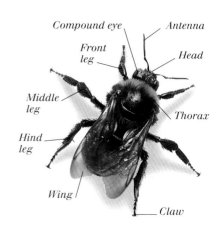

EXAMPLES OF INSECTS

Compound eye — Antenna
Front leg — Head
Middle leg — Thorax
Hind leg
Wing
Claw

BUMBLEBEE

Compound eye
Stigma (spot)
Vein
Abdomen

DAMSELFLY

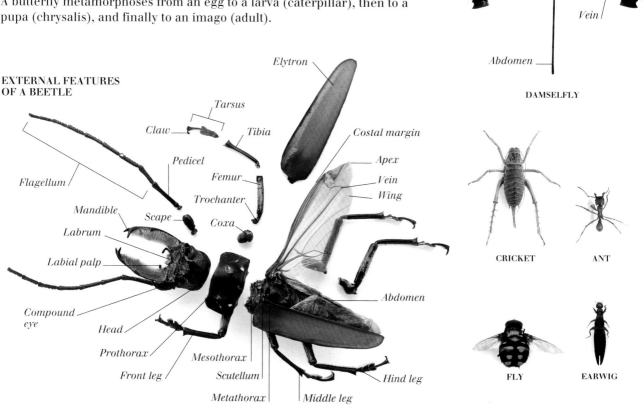

EXTERNAL FEATURES OF A BEETLE

Elytron
Tarsus
Claw — Tibia
Pedicel — Costal margin
Flagellum — Apex
Femur — Vein
Trochanter — Wing
Mandible — Scape — Coxa
Labrum
Labial palp
Abdomen
Compound eye
Head
Prothorax
Mesothorax
Front leg
Scutellum
Metathorax — Middle leg — Hind leg

CRICKET

ANT

FLY

EARWIG

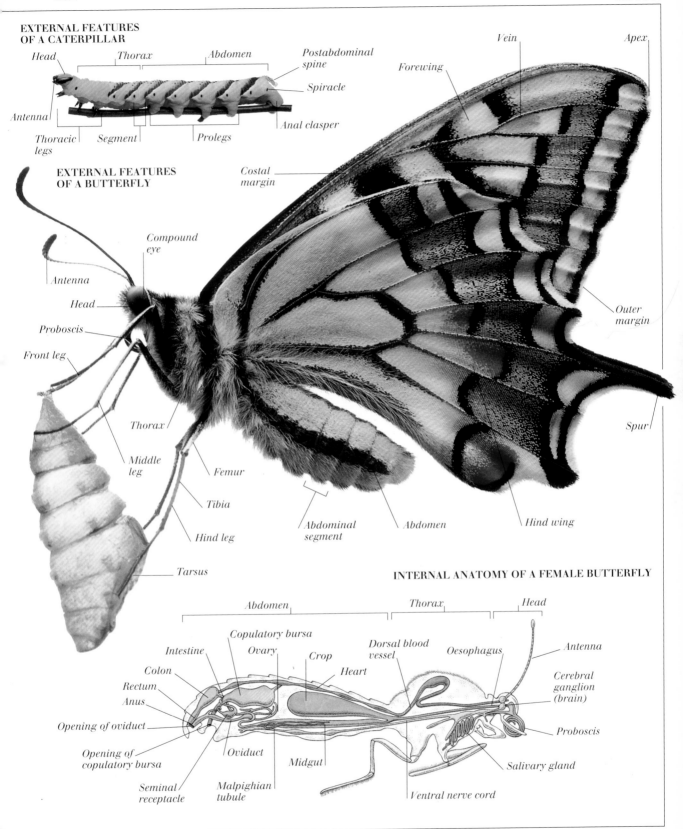

**EXTERNAL FEATURES
OF A CATERPILLAR**

Head

Thorax

Abdomen

Postabdominal
spine

Spiracle

Antenna

Thoracic
legs

Segment

Prolegs

Anal clasper

**EXTERNAL FEATURES
OF A BUTTERFLY**

Vein

Apex

Forewing

Costal
margin

Compound
eye

Antenna

Head

Proboscis

Front leg

Thorax

Middle
leg

Femur

Tibia

Hind leg

Tarsus

Outer
margin

Spur

Abdominal
segment

Abdomen

Hind wing

INTERNAL ANATOMY OF A FEMALE BUTTERFLY

Abdomen

Thorax

Head

Copulatory bursa

Intestine

Ovary

Crop

Dorsal blood
vessel

Oesophagus

Antenna

Colon

Heart

Cerebral
ganglion
(brain)

Rectum

Anus

Proboscis

Opening of oviduct

Opening of
copulatory bursa

Oviduct

Midgut

Malpighian
tubule

Salivary gland

Seminal
receptacle

Ventral nerve cord

Arachnids

THE CLASS ARACHNIDA INCLUDES SPIDERS (order Araneae) and scorpions (order Scorpiones). The class is part of the phylum Arthropoda, which also includes insects and crustaceans.

Spiders and scorpions are characterized by having four pairs of walking legs; a pair of pincer-like mouthparts called chelicerae; another pair of frontal appendages called pedipalps, which are sensory in spiders but used for grasping in scorpions; and a body divided into two sections (a combined head and thorax called a cephalothorax or prosoma, and an abdomen or opisthosoma). Unlike other arthropods, spiders and scorpions lack antennae. Spiders and scorpions are carnivorous. Spiders poison prey by biting with the fanged chelicerae, scorpions by stinging with the end of the metasoma (tail).

MEXICAN TRUE RED-LEGGED TARANTULA
(Euathlus emilia)

INTERNAL ANATOMY OF A FEMALE SPIDER

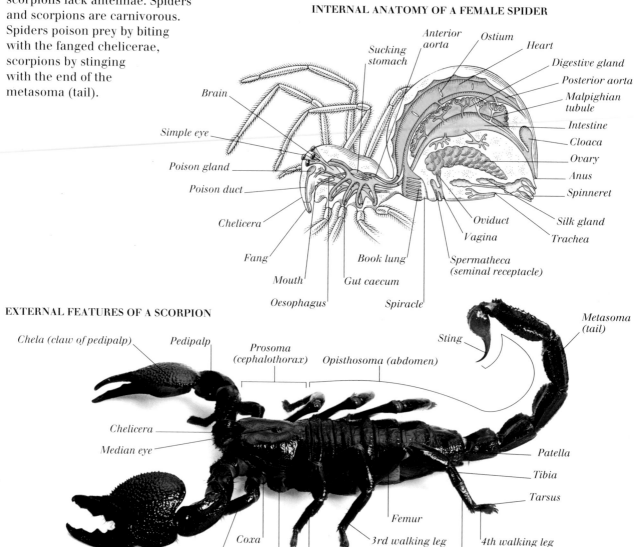

Anterior aorta
Sucking stomach
Ostium
Heart
Digestive gland
Posterior aorta
Malpighian tubule
Intestine
Cloaca
Ovary
Anus
Spinneret
Silk gland
Trachea
Oviduct
Vagina
Spermatheca (seminal receptacle)
Spiracle
Book lung
Gut caecum
Mouth
Oesophagus
Fang
Chelicera
Poison duct
Poison gland
Simple eye
Brain

EXTERNAL FEATURES OF A SCORPION

Chela (claw of pedipalp)
Pedipalp
Prosoma (cephalothorax)
Opisthosoma (abdomen)
Sting
Metasoma (tail)
Chelicera
Median eye
Patella
Tibia
Tarsus
Coxa
1st walking leg
Trochanter
2nd walking leg
Claw
3rd walking leg
Metatarsus
4th walking leg
Femur

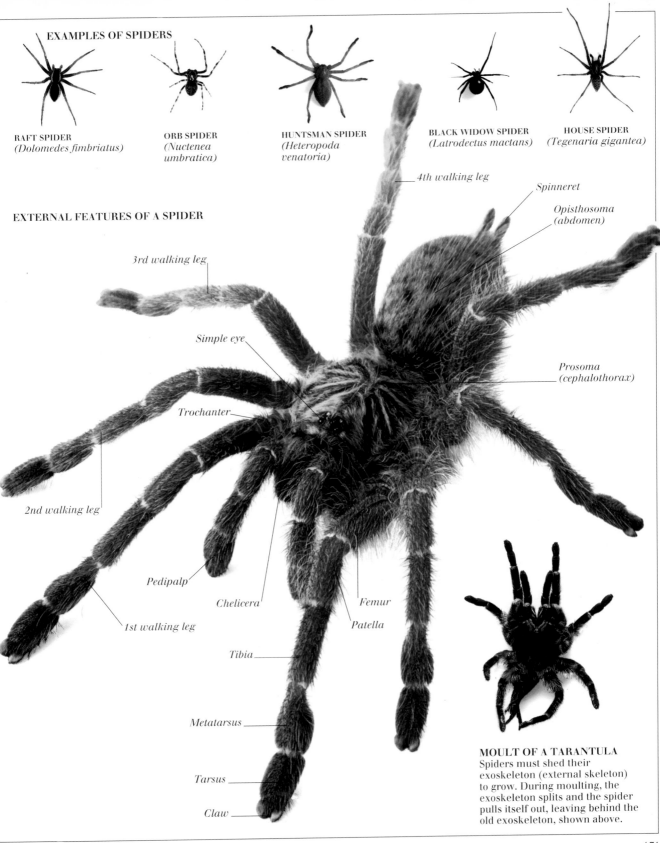

EXAMPLES OF SPIDERS

RAFT SPIDER
(Dolomedes fimbriatus)

ORB SPIDER
(Nuctenea umbratica)

HUNTSMAN SPIDER
(Heteropoda venatoria)

BLACK WIDOW SPIDER
(Latrodectus mactans)

HOUSE SPIDER
(Tegenaria gigantea)

EXTERNAL FEATURES OF A SPIDER

4th walking leg

Spinneret

Opisthosoma (abdomen)

3rd walking leg

Simple eye

Prosoma (cephalothorax)

Trochanter

2nd walking leg

Pedipalp

Chelicera

Femur

1st walking leg

Patella

Tibia

Metatarsus

Tarsus

Claw

MOULT OF A TARANTULA
Spiders must shed their exoskeleton (external skeleton) to grow. During moulting, the exoskeleton splits and the spider pulls itself out, leaving behind the old exoskeleton, shown above.

Crustaceans

THE SUBPHYLUM CRUSTACEA is one of the largest groups in the phylum Arthropoda. The subphylum is divided into several classes, the most important of which are Malacostraca and Cirripedia. The class Malacostraca includes crayfish, crabs, lobsters, and shrimps. Typical features of malacostracans include a body divided into two sections (a combined head and thorax called a cephalothorax, and an abdomen); an exoskeleton (external skeleton) with a large plate (carapace) covering the cephalothorax; stalked, compound eyes; and two pairs of antennae. The class Cirripedia includes barnacles, which, unlike other crustaceans, spend their adult lives attached to a surface, such as a rock. Other characteristics of cirripedes include an exoskeleton of overlapping calcareous plates; a body consisting almost entirely of thorax (the abdomen and head are minute); and six pairs of thoracic appendages (cirri) used for filter feeding.

1st swimmeret (1st pleopod)

2nd swimmeret (2nd pleopod)

3rd swimmeret (3rd pleopod)

4th swimmeret (4th pleopod)

5th swimmeret (5th pleopod)

Telson

Abdomen

Endopod

Exopod

Uropod

Abdominal segment

3rd leg (3rd pereopod)

2nd leg (2nd pereopod)

5th leg (5th pereopod)

4th leg (4th pereopod)

EXTERNAL FEATURES OF A CRAB

Carpus

Propodus

Dactylus

Compound eye

Antenna

Cheliped (chela; claw; 1st leg; 1st pereopod)

Carapace (shell)

Merus

Abdomen

2nd leg (2nd pereopod)

5th leg (5th pereopod)

3rd leg (3rd pereopod)

4th leg (4th pereopod)

EXTERNAL FEATURES OF A SHRIMP

Cephalothorax

Abdomen

Compound eye

Antenna

Leg (pereopod)

Swimmeret (pleopod)

Uropod

Exopod

Endopod

Telson

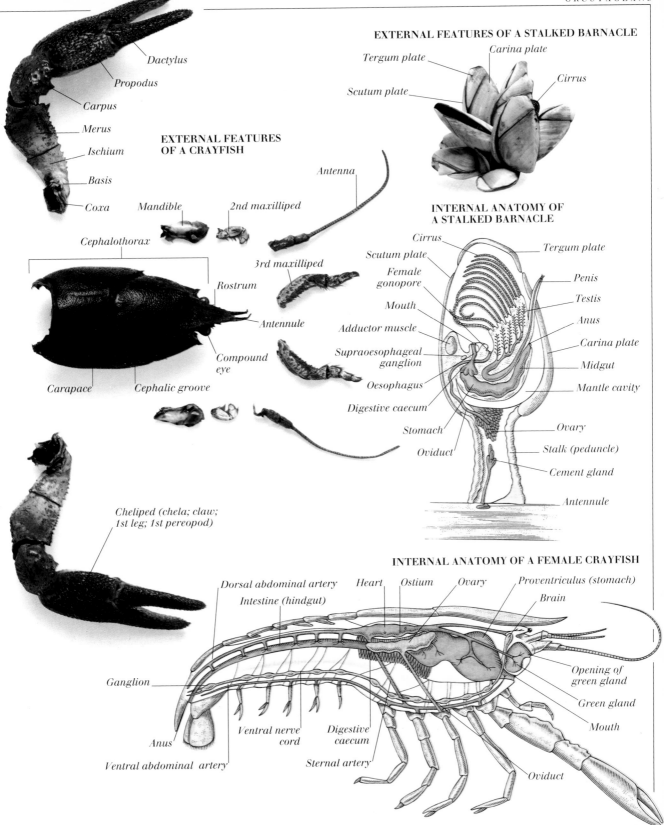

EXTERNAL FEATURES OF A STALKED BARNACLE

Tergum plate
Carina plate
Scutum plate
Cirrus

Dactylus
Propodus
Carpus
Merus
Ischium
Basis
Coxa

EXTERNAL FEATURES OF A CRAYFISH

Mandible
2nd maxilliped
Antenna

Cephalothorax
Rostrum
3rd maxilliped

Antennule
Compound eye

Carapace
Cephalic groove

INTERNAL ANATOMY OF A STALKED BARNACLE

Cirrus
Tergum plate
Scutum plate
Penis
Female gonopore
Testis
Mouth
Anus
Adductor muscle
Carina plate
Supraoesophageal ganglion
Midgut
Oesophagus
Mantle cavity
Digestive caecum
Stomach
Ovary
Oviduct
Stalk (peduncle)
Cement gland
Antennule

Cheliped (chela; claw; 1st leg; 1st pereopod)

INTERNAL ANATOMY OF A FEMALE CRAYFISH

Dorsal abdominal artery
Heart
Ostium
Ovary
Proventriculus (stomach)
Intestine (hindgut)
Brain

Ganglion
Opening of green gland
Green gland
Mouth

Anus
Ventral nerve cord
Digestive caecum
Ventral abdominal artery
Sternal artery
Oviduct

Starfish and sea urchins

STARFISH, SEA URCHINS, AND THEIR relatives (including feather stars, brittle stars, basket stars, sea daisies, sea lilies, and sea cucumbers) make up the phylum Echinodermata. A unique feature of echinoderms is the water vascular system, which consists of a series of water-filled canals from which protrude thousands of tiny tube feet. The tube feet may be used for movement, feeding, or respiration. Other features include pentaradiate symmetry (that is, the body can be divided into five parts radiating from the centre); no head; a diffuse, decentralized nervous system that lacks a brain; and no excretory organs. Typically, echinoderms also have an endoskeleton (internal skeleton) consisting of hard calcite ossicles embedded in the body wall and often bearing protruding spines or tubercles. The ossicles may fit together to form a test (as in sea urchins) or remain separate (as in sea cucumbers).

EXTERNAL FEATURES OF A STARFISH (UPPER, OR ABORAL, SURFACE)

Disc

Madreporite

Spine

Arm

INTERNAL ANATOMY OF A STARFISH

Rectum

Pyloric stomach

Madreporite

Stone canal

Anus

Rectal caecum

Tube foot

Ring canal

Lateral canal

Radial canal

Ampulla

Cardiac stomach

Pyloric duct

Pyloric caecum

Mouth

Oesophagus

Gonad

Gonopore

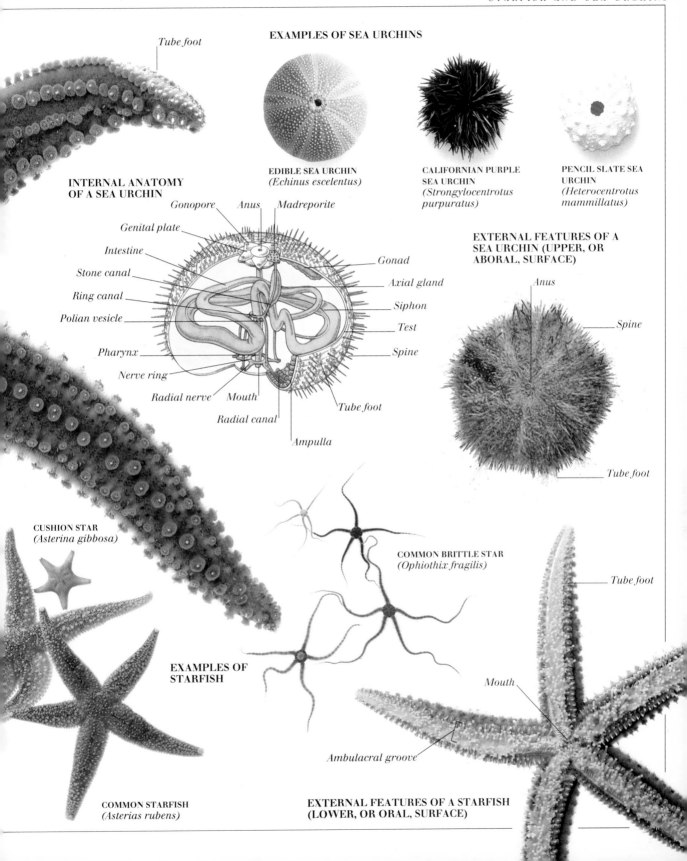

Tube foot

EXAMPLES OF SEA URCHINS

EDIBLE SEA URCHIN
(*Echinus escelentus*)

**CALIFORNIAN PURPLE
SEA URCHIN**
(*Strongylocentrotus
purpuratus*)

**PENCIL SLATE SEA
URCHIN**
(*Heterocentrotus
mammillatus*)

**INTERNAL ANATOMY
OF A SEA URCHIN**

Gonopore

Anus

Madreporite

Genital plate

Intestine

Gonad

Stone canal

Axial gland

Ring canal

Siphon

Polian vesicle

Test

Pharynx

Spine

Nerve ring

Radial nerve

Mouth

Radial canal

Tube foot

Ampulla

**EXTERNAL FEATURES OF A
SEA URCHIN (UPPER, OR
ABORAL, SURFACE)**

Anus

Spine

Tube foot

CUSHION STAR
(*Asterina gibbosa*)

COMMON BRITTLE STAR
(*Ophiothix fragilis*)

Tube foot

**EXAMPLES OF
STARFISH**

Mouth

Ambulacral groove

COMMON STARFISH
(*Asterias rubens*)

**EXTERNAL FEATURES OF A STARFISH
(LOWER, OR ORAL, SURFACE)**

Molluscs

THE PHYLUM MOLLUSCA (MOLLUSCS) is a large group of animals that includes octopuses, snails, and scallops. Octopuses and their relatives —including squid and cuttlefish—form the class Cephalopoda. Cephalopods typically have a head with a radula (a file-like feeding organ) and beak; a well-developed nervous system; sucker-bearing tentacles; a muscular mantle (part of the body wall) that can expel water through the siphon, enabling movement by jet propulsion; and a small shell or no shell. Snails and their relatives—including slugs, limpets, and abalones—make up the class Gastropoda. Gastropods typically have a coiled external shell, although some, such as slugs, have a small internal shell or no shell; a flat foot; and a head with tentacles and a radula. Scallops and their relatives—including clams, mussels, and oysters—make up the class Bivalvia (also called Pelecypoda). Features of bivalves include a shell with two halves (valves); large gills that are used for breathing and filter feeding; and no radula.

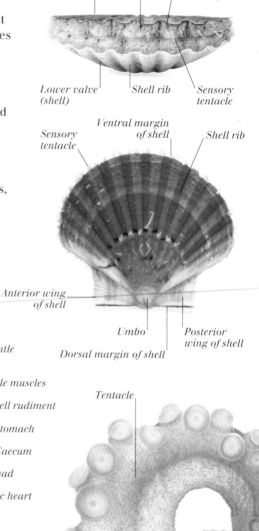

Upper valve (shell)   Mantle   Ocellus (eye)

Lower valve (shell)   Shell rib   Sensory tentacle

Sensory tentacle   Ventral margin of shell   Shell rib

Anterior wing of shell

Umbo   Posterior wing of shell

Dorsal margin of shell

INTERNAL ANATOMY OF AN OCTOPUS

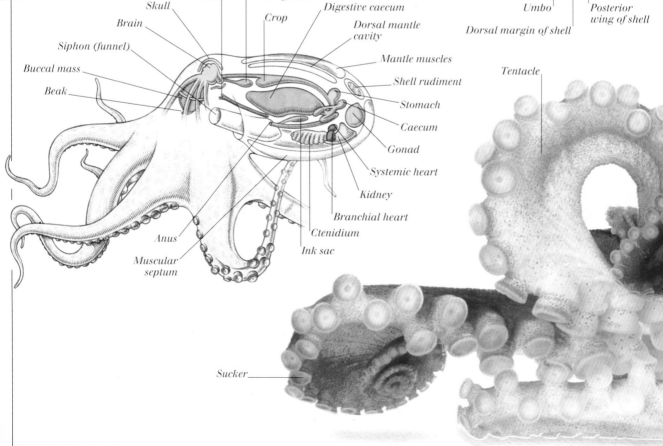

Cephalic vein
Poison gland
Crop
Digestive caecum
Dorsal mantle cavity
Mantle muscles
Shell rudiment
Stomach
Caecum
Gonad
Systemic heart
Kidney
Branchial heart
Ctenidium
Ink sac
Skull
Brain
Siphon (funnel)
Buccal mass
Beak
Anus
Muscular septum

Tentacle

Sucker

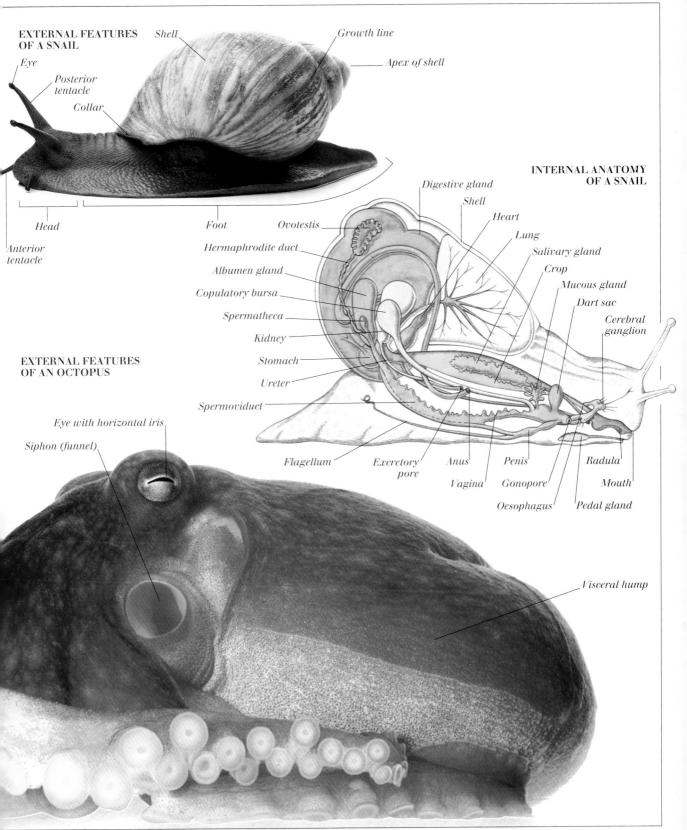

**EXTERNAL FEATURES
OF A SNAIL**

Eye

*Posterior
tentacle*

Collar

Shell

Growth line

Apex of shell

Head

Foot

*Anterior
tentacle*

**INTERNAL ANATOMY
OF A SNAIL**

Digestive gland

Shell

Heart

Lung

Salivary gland

Crop

Mucous gland

Dart sac

*Cerebral
ganglion*

Ovotestis

Hermaphrodite duct

Albumen gland

Copulatory bursa

Spermatheca

Kidney

Stomach

Ureter

Spermoviduct

Flagellum

*Excretory
pore*

Anus

Vagina

Penis

Gonopore

Oesophagus

Radula

Mouth

Pedal gland

**EXTERNAL FEATURES
OF AN OCTOPUS**

Eye with horizontal iris

Siphon (funnel)

Visceral hump

Sharks and jawless fish

SHARKS, DOGFISH (WHICH ARE actually small sharks), skates, and rays belong to a class of fishes called Chondrichthyes, which is a division of the superclass Gnathostomata (meaning "jawed mouths"). Also sometimes known as elasmobranchs, sharks and their relatives have a skeleton made of cartilage (hence their common name, cartilaginous fish), a characteristic that distinguishes them from bony fish (see pp. 180-181). Other important features of cartilaginous fish are extremely tough, tooth-like scales, and lack of a swim bladder. Jawless fish—lampreys and hagfish—are primitive, eel-like fish that make up the order Cyclostomata (meaning "round mouths"), a division of the superclass Agnatha (meaning "without jaws"). In addition to their characteristic round, sucker-like mouths and lack of jaws, cyclostomes also have smooth, slimy skin without scales, and unpaired fins.

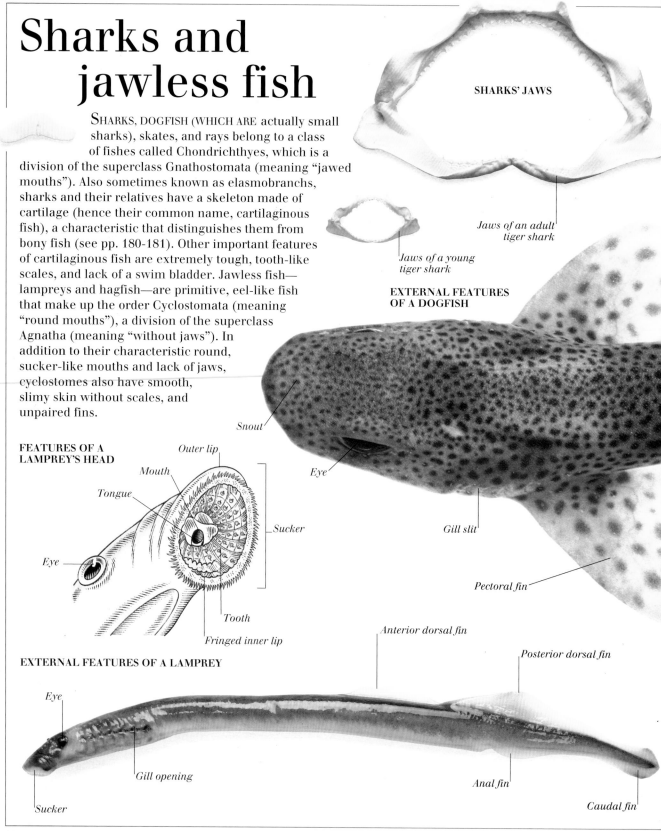

SHARKS' JAWS

Jaws of an adult tiger shark

Jaws of a young tiger shark

EXTERNAL FEATURES OF A DOGFISH

Snout

Eye

Gill slit

Pectoral fin

FEATURES OF A LAMPREY'S HEAD

Outer lip

Mouth

Tongue

Sucker

Eye

Tooth

Fringed inner lip

EXTERNAL FEATURES OF A LAMPREY

Anterior dorsal fin

Posterior dorsal fin

Eye

Gill opening

Anal fin

Caudal fin

Sucker

EXAMPLES OF CARTILAGINOUS FISH

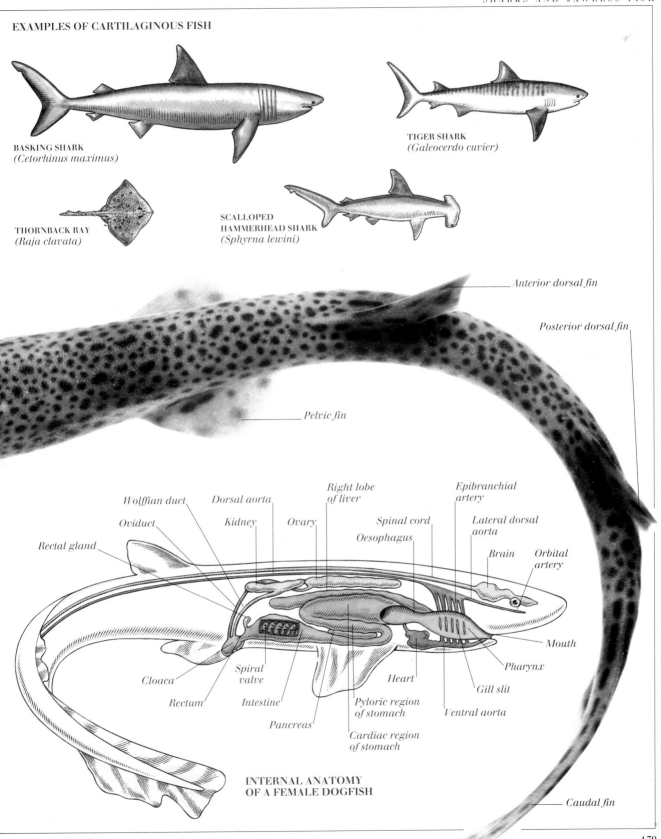

BASKING SHARK
(*Cetorhinus maximus*)

TIGER SHARK
(*Galeocerdo cuvier*)

THORNBACK RAY
(*Raja clavata*)

**SCALLOPED
HAMMERHEAD SHARK**
(*Sphyrna lewini*)

Anterior dorsal fin

Posterior dorsal fin

Pelvic fin

Right lobe
of liver

Wolffian duct

Dorsal aorta

Oviduct

Kidney

Ovary

Epibranchial
artery

Spinal cord

Oesophagus

Lateral dorsal
aorta

Rectal gland

Brain

Orbital
artery

Mouth

Pharynx

Cloaca

Spiral
valve

Gill slit

Heart

Rectum

Intestine

Ventral aorta

Pancreas

Pyloric region
of stomach

Cardiac region
of stomach

**INTERNAL ANATOMY
OF A FEMALE DOGFISH**

Caudal fin

Bony fish

BONY FISH, SUCH AS CARP, TROUT, SALMON, perch, and cod, are by far the best known and largest group of fish, with more than 20,000 species (over 95 per cent of all known fish). As their name suggests, bony fish have skeletons made of bone, in contrast to the cartilaginous skeletons of sharks, jawless fish, and their relatives (see pp. 178-179). Other typical features of bony fish include a swim bladder, which functions as a variable-buoyancy organ, enabling a fish to remain effortlessly at whatever depth it is swimming; relatively thin, bone-like scales; a flap (called an operculum) covering the gills; and paired pelvic and pectoral fins. Scientifically, bony fish belong to the class Osteichthyes, which is a division of the superclass Gnathostomata (meaning "jawed mouths").

HOW FISH BREATHE

Fish "breathe" by extracting oxygen from water through their gills. Water is sucked in through the mouth; simultaneously, the opercula close to prevent the water from escaping. The mouth is then closed, and muscles in the walls of the mouth, pharynx, and opercular cavity contract to pump the water inside over the gills and out through the opercula. Some fish rely on swimming with their mouths open to keep water flowing over the gills.

Gill raker
Pharynx
Water out
Gill slit
Mouth
Water in
Gill filament
Operculum

EXAMPLES OF BONY FISH

MANDARINFISH
(Synchiropus splendidus)

ANGLERFISH
(Caulophryne jordani)

LIONFISH
(Pterois volitans)

OCEANIC SEAHORSE
(Hippocampus kuda)

STURGEON
(Acipenser sturio)

Vertebra
Neural spine
Hypural
Haemal spine
Caudal fin ray
Anal fin ray
Radial cartilage

SNOWFLAKE MORAY EEL
(Echidna nebulosa)

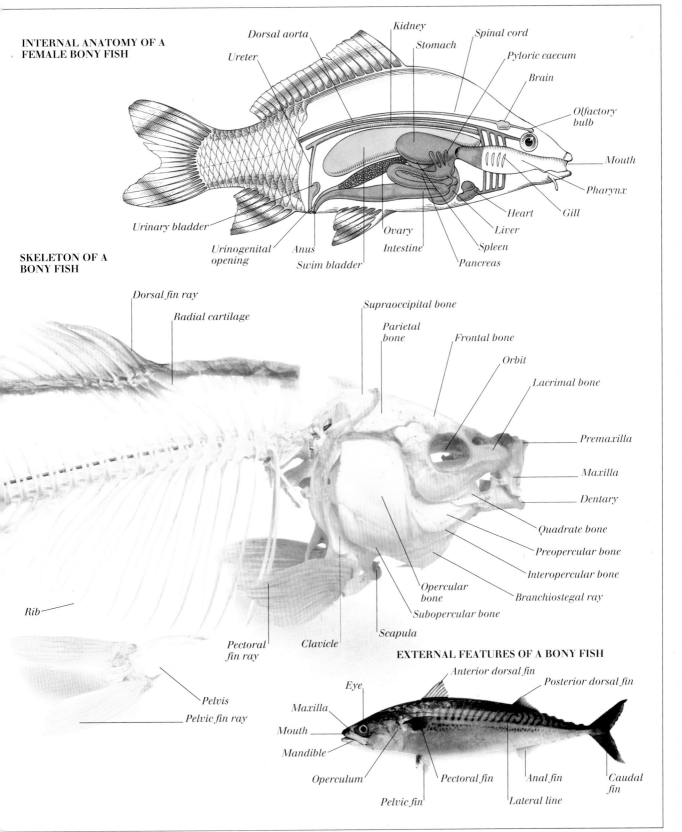

INTERNAL ANATOMY OF A FEMALE BONY FISH

Dorsal aorta

Ureter

Kidney

Stomach

Spinal cord

Pyloric caecum

Brain

Olfactory bulb

Mouth

Pharynx

Gill

Heart

Liver

Spleen

Pancreas

Intestine

Ovary

Swim bladder

Anus

Urinogenital opening

Urinary bladder

SKELETON OF A BONY FISH

Dorsal fin ray

Radial cartilage

Supraoccipital bone

Parietal bone

Frontal bone

Orbit

Lacrimal bone

Premaxilla

Maxilla

Dentary

Quadrate bone

Preopercular bone

Interopercular bone

Branchiostegal ray

Opercular bone

Subopercular bone

Scapula

Clavicle

Pectoral fin ray

Rib

Pelvis

Pelvic fin ray

EXTERNAL FEATURES OF A BONY FISH

Eye

Maxilla

Mouth

Mandible

Operculum

Pelvic fin

Pectoral fin

Anterior dorsal fin

Posterior dorsal fin

Anal fin

Lateral line

Caudal fin

181

Amphibians

THE CLASS AMPHIBIA INCLUDES FROGS and toads (which make up the order Anura), and newts and salamanders (which make up the order Urodela). Amphibians typically have moist, scaleless, hairless skin; lungs; and are cold-blooded. They also undergo complete metamorphosis, from eggs laid in water through various water-living larval stages (such as tadpoles) to land-living adults. Typical features of adult frogs and toads include a squat body with no tail; long, powerful hind legs; and large, often bulging, eyes. Adult newts and salamanders typically have a long body with a well-developed tail; and relatively short, equal-sized legs. However, newts and salamanders show considerable variation; for example, in some species the adults have minute legs, external gills rather than lungs, and spend their entire lives in water.

INTERNAL ANATOMY OF A FEMALE FROG

Larynx

Right bronchus

Stomach

Right lung

Pulmonary artery

Left lung

Heart

Pancreas

Liver

Duodenum

Posterior vena cava

Spleen

Right kidney

Left kidney

Dorsal aorta

Mesentery

Cloaca

Small intestine (ileum)

Rectum

Left ureter

EXTERNAL FEATURES OF A FROG

Hind limb

Trunk

Head

Forelimb

5 digits

External nostril

Tympanum (eardrum)

Mouth

Web

Eye

4 digits

EXTERNAL FEATURES OF A SALAMANDER

Eye

Tail

Forelimb

Hind limb

Digit

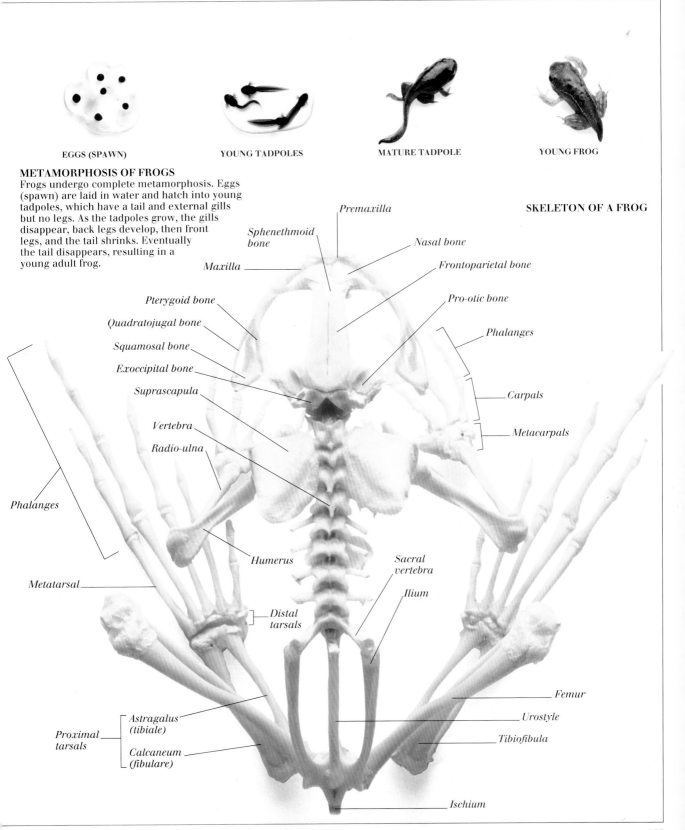

EGGS (SPAWN)

YOUNG TADPOLES

MATURE TADPOLE

YOUNG FROG

METAMORPHOSIS OF FROGS

Frogs undergo complete metamorphosis. Eggs (spawn) are laid in water and hatch into young tadpoles, which have a tail and external gills but no legs. As the tadpoles grow, the gills disappear, back legs develop, then front legs, and the tail shrinks. Eventually the tail disappears, resulting in a young adult frog.

SKELETON OF A FROG

Premaxilla

Sphenethmoid bone

Nasal bone

Maxilla

Frontoparietal bone

Pterygoid bone

Pro-otic bone

Quadratojugal bone

Phalanges

Squamosal bone

Exoccipital bone

Suprascapula

Carpals

Vertebra

Metacarpals

Radio-ulna

Phalanges

Humerus

Sacral vertebra

Ilium

Metatarsal

Distal tarsals

Proximal tarsals

Astragalus (tibiale)

Femur

Calcaneum (fibulare)

Urostyle

Tibiofibula

Ischium

Lizards and snakes

LIZARDS AND SNAKES BELONG to the order Squamata, a division of the class Reptilia. Characteristic reptilian features include scaly skin, lungs, and cold-bloodedness. Most reptiles lay leathery-shelled eggs, although some hatch the eggs inside their bodies and give birth to live young. Lizards belong to the suborder Lacertilia. Typically, they have long tails, and shed their skin in several pieces. Many lizards can regenerate a tail if it is lost; some can change colour; and some are limbless. Snakes make up the suborder Ophidia (also called Serpentes). All snakes have long, limbless bodies; can dislocate their lower jaw to swallow large prey; and have eyelids that are joined together to form a single transparent covering over the front of the eye. Most snakes shed their skin in a single piece. Constrictor snakes kill their prey by squeezing; venomous snakes poison their prey.

EXAMPLES OF SNAKES

MEXICAN MOUNTAIN KING SNAKE (*Lampropeltis triangulum annulata*)

BANDED MILK SNAKE (*Lampropeltis ruthveni*)

EXTERNAL FEATURES OF A LIZARD

Eye

Mouth

Crest

Eardrum

Masseteric scale

Dorsal scale

External nostril

Dewlap

Foreleg

Belly

Ventral scale

SKELETON OF A LIZARD

Skull

Orbit

Scapula

Cervical vertebrae

Phalanges

Carpals

Metacarpal

Humerus

Ulna

Radius

Rib

Thoracolumbar vertebrae

Pelvis

Sacrum

Femur

Tibia

Fibula

Tarsals

Metatarsal

Caudal vertebrae

Phalanges

Toe

Claw

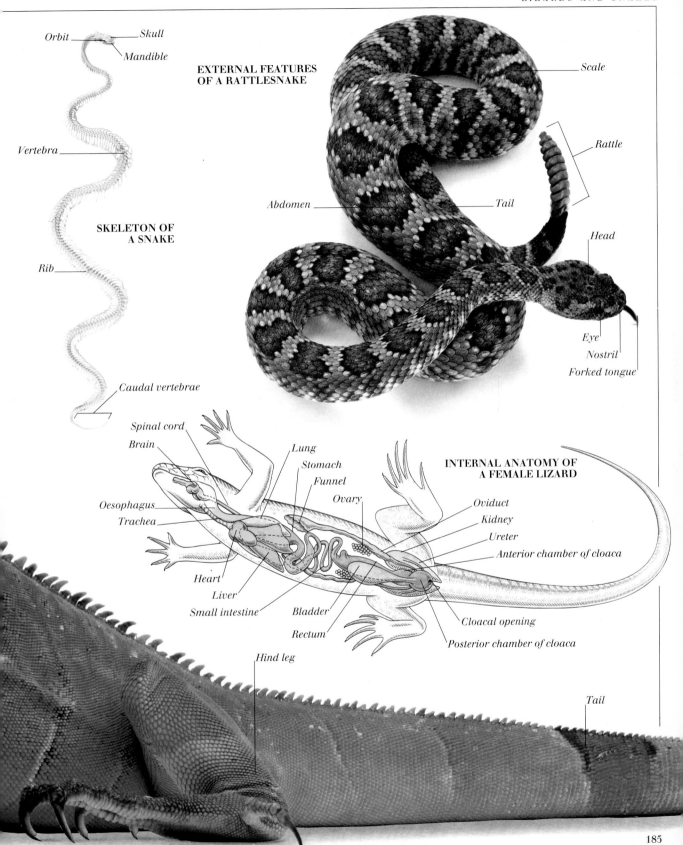

EXTERNAL FEATURES
OF A RATTLESNAKE

Orbit

Skull

Mandible

Scale

Vertebra

Rattle

Abdomen

Tail

SKELETON OF
A SNAKE

Head

Rib

Eye

Nostril

Forked tongue

Caudal vertebrae

Spinal cord

Brain

Lung

Stomach

Funnel

INTERNAL ANATOMY OF
A FEMALE LIZARD

Ovary

Oesophagus

Oviduct

Trachea

Kidney

Ureter

Anterior chamber of cloaca

Heart

Liver

Small intestine

Bladder

Cloacal opening

Rectum

Posterior chamber of cloaca

Hind leg

Tail

185

Crocodilians and turtles

CROCODILIANS AND TURTLES BELONG to different orders in the class Reptilia. The order Crocodilia includes crocodiles, alligators, caimans, and gharials. Typically, crocodilians are carnivores (flesh-eaters), and have a long snout, sharp teeth for gripping prey, and hard, square scales. All crocodilians are adapted to living on land and in water: they have four strong legs for moving on land; a powerful tail for swimming; and their eyes and nostrils are high on the head so that they stay above water while the rest of the body is submerged. The order Chelonia includes marine turtles, terrapins (freshwater turtles), and tortoises (land turtles). Characteristically, chelonians have a short, broad body encased in a bony shell with an outer horny covering, into which the head and limbs can be withdrawn; and a horny beak instead of teeth.

SKULLS OF CROCODILIANS

GHARIAL
(Gavialis gangeticus)

NILE CROCODILE
(Crocodylus niloticus)

AMERICAN ALLIGATOR
(Alligator mississippiensis)

SKELETON OF A CROCODILE

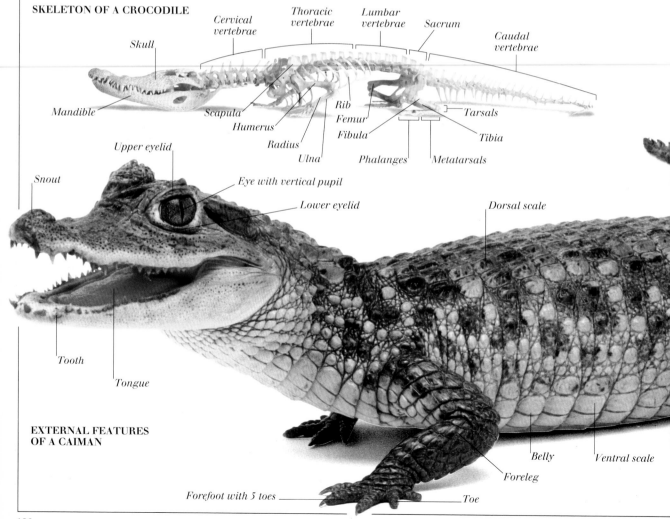

Cervical vertebrae
Thoracic vertebrae
Lumbar vertebrae
Sacrum
Caudal vertebrae
Skull
Mandible
Scapula
Humerus
Radius
Ulna
Rib
Femur
Fibula
Phalanges
Metatarsals
Tarsals
Tibia

Upper eyelid
Eye with vertical pupil
Lower eyelid
Dorsal scale
Snout
Tooth
Tongue

EXTERNAL FEATURES OF A CAIMAN

Belly
Ventral scale
Foreleg
Forefoot with 5 toes
Toe

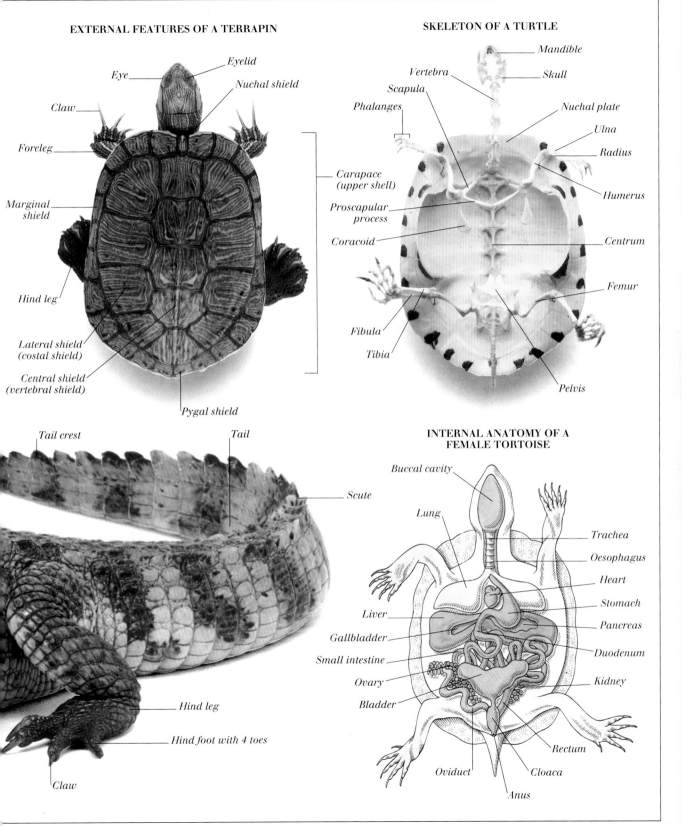

EXTERNAL FEATURES OF A TERRAPIN

- Eyelid
- Eye
- Claw
- Nuchal shield
- Foreleg
- Marginal shield
- Carapace (upper shell)
- Proscapular process
- Coracoid
- Hind leg
- Lateral shield (costal shield)
- Central shield (vertebral shield)
- Pygal shield

SKELETON OF A TURTLE

- Mandible
- Vertebra
- Skull
- Scapula
- Phalanges
- Nuchal plate
- Ulna
- Radius
- Humerus
- Centrum
- Femur
- Fibula
- Tibia
- Pelvis

- Tail crest
- Tail
- Scute
- Hind leg
- Hind foot with 4 toes
- Claw

INTERNAL ANATOMY OF A FEMALE TORTOISE

- Buccal cavity
- Lung
- Trachea
- Oesophagus
- Heart
- Stomach
- Pancreas
- Liver
- Gallbladder
- Duodenum
- Small intestine
- Kidney
- Ovary
- Bladder
- Rectum
- Oviduct
- Cloaca
- Anus

187

Birds 1

BIRDS MAKE UP THE CLASS AVES. There are more than 9,000 species, almost all of which can fly (the only flightless birds are penguins, ostriches, rheas, cassowaries, and kiwis). The ability to fly is reflected in the typical bird features: forelimbs modified as wings; a streamlined body; and hollow bones to reduce weight. All birds lay hard-shelled eggs, which the parents incubate. Birds' beaks and feet vary according to diet and way of life. Beaks range from general-purpose types suitable for a mixed diet (those of thrushes, for example), to types specialized for particular foods (such as the large, curved, sieving beaks of flamingos). Feet range from the webbed "paddles" of ducks, to the talons of birds of prey. Plumage also varies widely, and in many species the male is brightly coloured for courtship display whereas the female is drab.

EXTERNAL FEATURES OF A BIRD

Forehead

Eye

Crown

Nostril

Nape

Upper mandible

Beak

Lower mandible

Chin

Throat

EXAMPLES OF BIRDS

MALE TUFTED DUCK
(*Aythya fuligula*)

WHITE STORK
(*Ciconia ciconia*)

MALE OSTRICH
(*Struthio camelus*)

Minor coverts

Lesser wing coverts

Median wing coverts

Greater wing coverts
(major coverts)

Secondary flight feathers
(secondary remiges)

Primary flight feathers
(primaryremiges)

Breast

Belly

Flank

Thigh

Under tail coverts

Tarsus

Claw

Toe

Tail feathers (retrices)

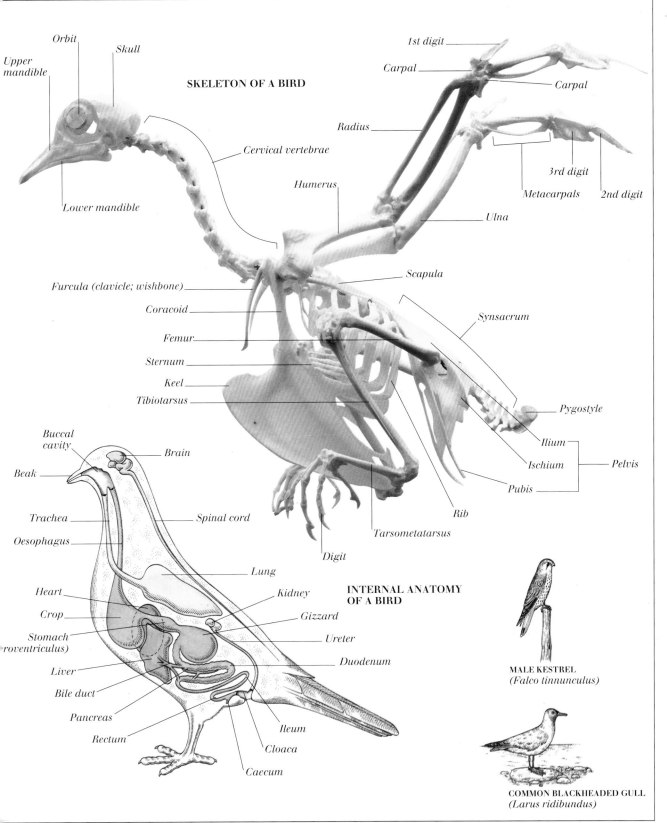

SKELETON OF A BIRD

Upper mandible

Orbit

Skull

1st digit

Carpal

Carpal

Radius

Cervical vertebrae

Humerus

3rd digit

Metacarpals

2nd digit

Lower mandible

Ulna

Furcula (clavicle; wishbone)

Scapula

Coracoid

Synsacrum

Femur

Sternum

Keel

Tibiotarsus

Pygostyle

Ilium

Ischium

Pelvis

Pubis

Rib

Tarsometatarsus

Digit

Buccal cavity

Brain

Beak

Spinal cord

Trachea

Oesophagus

Lung

INTERNAL ANATOMY OF A BIRD

Heart

Kidney

Crop

Gizzard

Stomach (proventriculus)

Ureter

Liver

Duodenum

Bile duct

Pancreas

Ileum

Rectum

Cloaca

Caecum

MALE KESTREL
(Falco tinnunculus)

COMMON BLACKHEADED GULL
(Larus ridibundus)

Birds 2

EXAMPLES OF BIRDS' FEET

KITTIWAKE
(Rissa tridactyla)
The webbed feet are
adapted for paddling
through water.

LITTLE GREBE
(Tachybaptus ruficollis)
The lobed, flattened feet
are adapted for swimming
underwater.

TAWNY OWL
(Strix aluco)
The clawed feet are adapted
for gripping prey.

EXAMPLES OF BIRDS' BEAKS

KING VULTURE
(Sarcorhamphus papa)
The hooked beak is adapted
for pulling apart flesh.

GREATER FLAMINGO
(Phoenicopterus ruber)
In the living bird, the large,
curved beak contains a
cartilaginous "sieve" for
filtering food particles
from water.

MISTLE THRUSH
(Turdus viscivorus)
The general-purpose beak is
suitable for a wide range of animal
and plant foods.

BLUE-AND-YELLOW MACAW
(Ara ararauna)
The broad, powerful, hooked beak
is adapted for crushing seeds and
eating fruit.

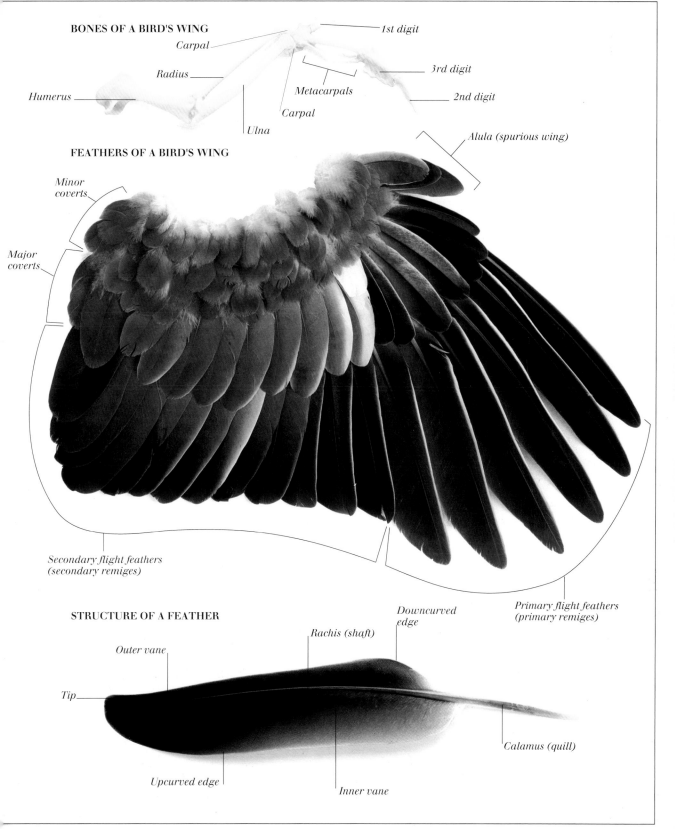

BONES OF A BIRD'S WING

1st digit

Carpal

Radius

3rd digit

Humerus

Metacarpals

2nd digit

Carpal

Ulna

Alula (spurious wing)

FEATHERS OF A BIRD'S WING

Minor coverts

Major coverts

Secondary flight feathers (secondary remiges)

Primary flight feathers (primary remiges)

STRUCTURE OF A FEATHER

Downcurved edge

Rachis (shaft)

Outer vane

Tip

Calamus (quill)

Upcurved edge

Inner vane

Eggs

AN EGG IS A SINGLE CELL, produced by the female, with the capacity to develop into a new individual. Development may take place inside the mother's body (as in most mammals) or outside, in which case the egg has a protective covering such as a shell. Egg yolk nourishes the growing young. Eggs developing inside the mother generally have little yolk, because the young are nourished from her body. Eggs developing outside may also have little yolk if they are produced by animals whose young go through a larval stage (such as a caterpillar) that feeds itself while developing into the adult form. The shelled eggs of birds and reptiles contain enough yolk to sustain the young until it hatches into a juvenile version of the adult.

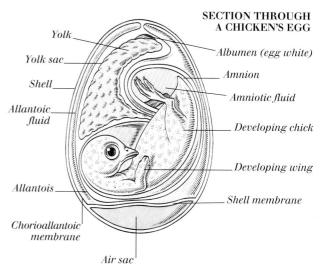

SECTION THROUGH A CHICKEN'S EGG

Yolk

Yolk sac

Shell

Allantoic fluid

Allantois

Chorioallantoic membrane

Air sac

Albumen (egg white)

Amnion

Amniotic fluid

Developing chick

Developing wing

Shell membrane

VARIETY OF EGGS

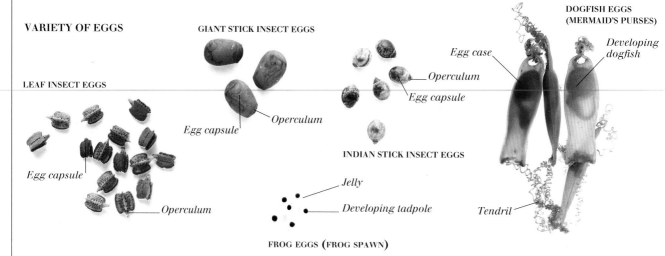

GIANT STICK INSECT EGGS

Egg capsule

Operculum

LEAF INSECT EGGS

Egg capsule

Operculum

Operculum

Egg capsule

INDIAN STICK INSECT EGGS

Jelly

Developing tadpole

FROG EGGS (FROG SPAWN)

DOGFISH EGGS (MERMAID'S PURSES)

Egg case

Operculum

Developing dogfish

Tendril

HATCHING OF A QUAIL'S EGG

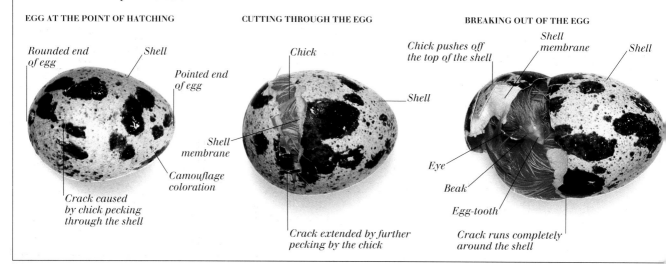

EGG AT THE POINT OF HATCHING

Rounded end of egg

Shell

Pointed end of egg

Camouflage coloration

Crack caused by chick pecking through the shell

CUTTING THROUGH THE EGG

Chick

Shell

Shell membrane

Crack extended by further pecking by the chick

BREAKING OUT OF THE EGG

Chick pushes off the top of the shell

Shell membrane

Shell

Eye

Beak

Egg-tooth

Crack runs completely around the shell

EXAMPLES OF BIRDS' EGGS

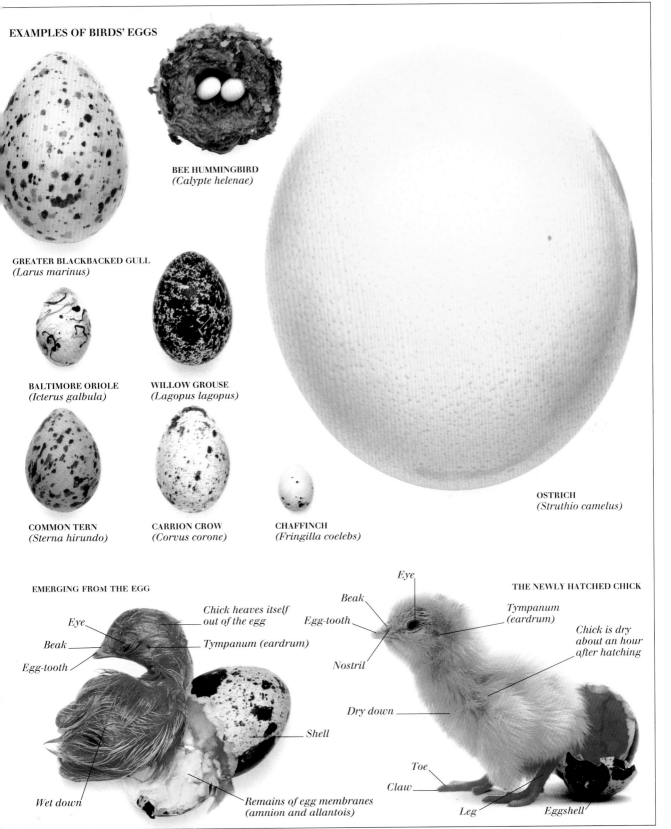

BEE HUMMINGBIRD
(Calypte helenae)

GREATER BLACKBACKED GULL
(Larus marinus)

BALTIMORE ORIOLE
(Icterus galbula)

WILLOW GROUSE
(Lagopus lagopus)

COMMON TERN
(Sterna hirundo)

CARRION CROW
(Corvus corone)

CHAFFINCH
(Fringilla coelebs)

OSTRICH
(Struthio camelus)

EMERGING FROM THE EGG

Eye

Beak

Egg-tooth

Chick heaves itself out of the egg

Tympanum (eardrum)

Shell

Wet down

Remains of egg membranes (amnion and allantois)

THE NEWLY HATCHED CHICK

Eye

Beak

Egg-tooth

Nostril

Tympanum (eardrum)

Chick is dry about an hour after hatching

Dry down

Toe

Claw

Leg

Eggshell

Carnivores

THE MAMMALIAN ORDER CARNIVORA includes cats, dogs, bears, raccoons, pandas, weasels, badgers, skunks, otters, civets, mongooses, and hyenas. The order's name is derived from the fact that most of its members are carnivores (flesh-eaters). Typical carnivore features therefore reflect a hunting life-style: speed and agility; sharp claws and well-developed canine teeth for holding and killing prey; carnassial teeth (cheek teeth) for cutting flesh; and forward-facing eyes for good distance judgment. However, some members of the order—bears, badgers, and foxes, for example—have a more mixed diet, and a few are entirely herbivorous (plant-eating), notably pandas. Such animals have no carnassial teeth and tend to be slower-moving than pure flesh-eaters.

EXTERNAL FEATURES OF A MALE LION

Nose
Eye
Mane
Nostril
Vibrissa (whisker)
Tongue
Canine tooth
Incisor tooth
Chest
Elbow
Lower arm
Toe

SKULL OF A LION

Zygomatic arch
Coronoid process
Sagittal crest
Orbit
Nasal bone
Maxilla
Upper premolars
Upper canine
Lower canine
Mandible
Lower premolars
Occipital condyle
Condyle
Tympanic bulla
Angular process
Upper carnassial tooth (4th upper premolar)

SKULL OF A BEAR

Sagittal crest
Occipital condyle
Zygomatic arch
Orbit
Upper molars
Nasal bone
Upper premolars
Maxilla
Upper canine
Upper incisor
Lower incisor
Lower canine
Mandible
Lower arm
Tympanic bulla
Angular process
Condyle
Lower molars
Lower premolars
Toe

EXAMPLES OF CARNIVORES

ALSATIAN DOG
(Canis familiaris)

MANED WOLF
(Chrysocyon brachyurus)

RACCOON
(Procyon lotor)

AMERICAN BLACK BEAR
(Ursus americanus)

SKELETON OF A DOMESTIC CAT

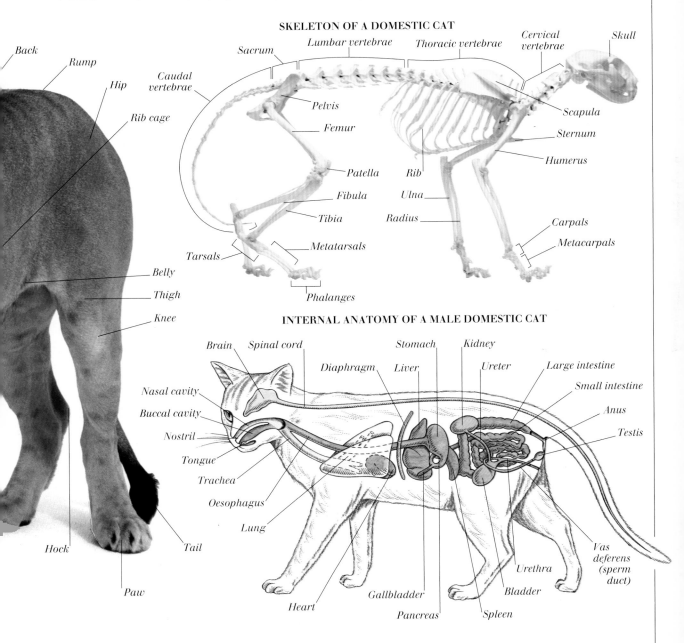

Back

Rump

Hip

Rib cage

Caudal
vertebrae

Sacrum

Lumbar vertebrae

Thoracic vertebrae

Cervical
vertebrae

Skull

Pelvis

Femur

Scapula

Sternum

Humerus

Patella

Rib

Fibula

Ulna

Tibia

Radius

Metatarsals

Carpals

Metacarpals

Tarsals

Belly

Thigh

Knee

Phalanges

INTERNAL ANATOMY OF A MALE DOMESTIC CAT

Brain

Spinal cord

Diaphragm

Stomach

Liver

Kidney

Ureter

Large intestine

Small intestine

Nasal cavity

Buccal cavity

Anus

Nostril

Testis

Tongue

Trachea

Oesophagus

Lung

Hock

Tail

Paw

Heart

Gallbladder

Pancreas

Spleen

Bladder

Urethra

Vas
deferens
(sperm
duct)

Rabbits and rodents

ALTHOUGH RABBITS AND RODENTS belong to different orders of mammals, they have some features in common. These features include chisel-shaped incisor teeth that grow continually, and eating their faeces to extract more nutrients from their plant diet. Rabbits and hares belong to the order Lagomorpha. Characteristically, they have four incisors in the upper jaw and two in the lower jaw; powerful hind legs for jumping; forelimbs adapted for burrowing; long ears; and a small tail. Rodents make up the order Rodentia. This is the largest order of mammals, with more than 1,700 species, including squirrels, beavers, chipmunks, gophers, rats, mice, lemmings, gerbils, porcupines, cavies, and the capybara. Typical rodent features include two incisors in each jaw; short forelimbs for manipulating food; and cheek pouches for storing food.

EXTERNAL FEATURES OF A RAT

Snout
Eye
Ear
Nose
Nostril
Pinna (ear flap)
Vibrissa (whisker)
Neck
Mouth
Tail
Forelimb
5 digits
Hind limb
5 digits

EXTERNAL FEATURES OF A RABBIT

Pinna (ear flap)
Ear
Shoulder
Eye
Nose
Nostril
Vibrissa (whisker)
Forelimb
5 digits

INTERNAL ANATOMY OF A MALE RABBIT

Gallbladder
Brain
Liver
Stomach
Kidney
Nasal cavity
Spinal cord
Colon
Ileum
Ureter
Rectum
Bladder
Mouth
Anus
Buccal cavity
Urethra
Tongue
Testis
Oesophagus
Lung
Vas deferens
Trachea
Diaphragm
Pancreas
Appendix
Heart
Duodenum
Caecum

196

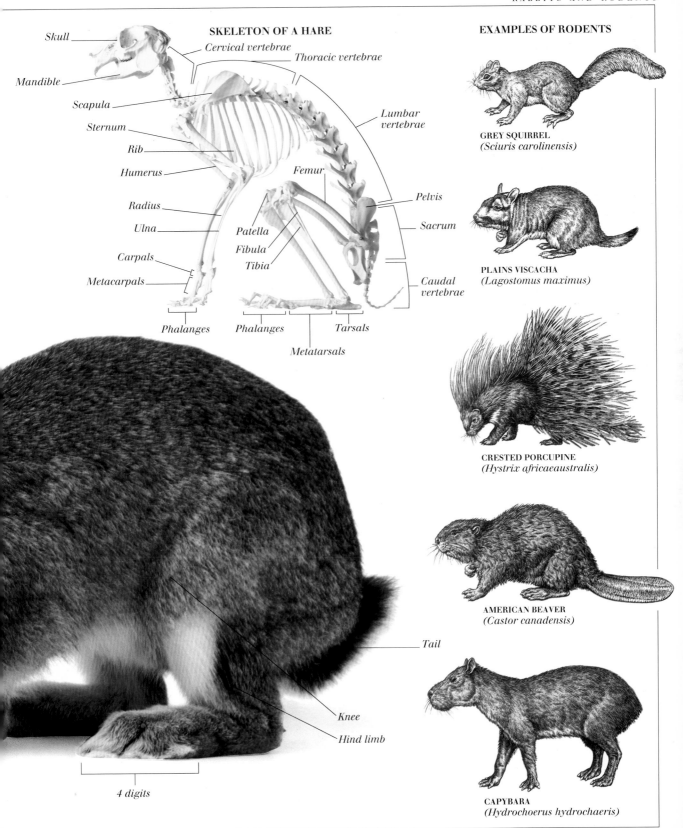

SKELETON OF A HARE

Skull

Cervical vertebrae

Thoracic vertebrae

Mandible

Scapula

Lumbar
vertebrae

Sternum

Rib

Femur

Humerus

Radius

Pelvis

Ulna

Patella

Sacrum

Carpals

Fibula

Metacarpals

Tibia

Caudal
vertebrae

Phalanges

Phalanges

Tarsals

Metatarsals

Tail

Knee

Hind limb

4 digits

EXAMPLES OF RODENTS

GREY SQUIRREL
(Sciuris carolinensis)

PLAINS VISCACHA
(Lagostomus maximus)

CRESTED PORCUPINE
(Hystrix africaeaustralis)

AMERICAN BEAVER
(Castor canadensis)

CAPYBARA
(Hydrochoerus hydrochaeris)

Ungulates

UNGULATES IS A GENERAL TERM FOR a large, varied group of mammals that includes horses, cattle, and their relatives. The ungulates are divided into two orders on the basis of the number of toes. Members of the order Perissodactyla (odd-toed ungulates) have one or three toes. Perissodactyls include horses, asses, and zebras (all of which are one-toed), and rhinoceroses and tapirs (which are three-toed). Members of the order Artiodactyla (even-toed ungulates) have two or four toes. Most artiodactyls have two toes, which are typically encased in hooves to give the so-called cloven hoof. Two-toed, cloven-hoofed artiodactyls include cows and other cattle, sheep, goats, antelopes, deer, and giraffes. The other main two-toed artiodactyls are camels and llamas. Most two-toed artiodactyls are ruminants; that is, they have a four-chambered stomach and chew the cud. The principal four-toed artiodactyls are pigs, peccaries, and hippopotamuses.

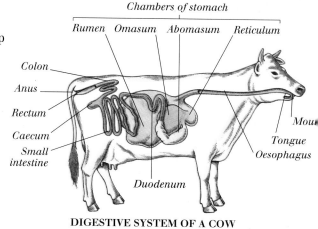

DIGESTIVE SYSTEM OF A COW

Chambers of stomach
Rumen Omasum Abomasum Reticulum
Colon
Anus
Rectum
Caecum
Small intestine
Duodenum
Mou[...]
Tongue
Oesophagus

COMPARISON OF THE FRONT FEET OF A HORSE AND A COW

SKELETON OF THE LEFT FRONT FOOT OF A HORSE

SKELETON OF THE RIGHT FRONT FOOT OF A COW

Fused 3rd and 4th metacarpals

2nd metacarpal (splint bone)

3rd metacarpal (cannon bone)

Sesamoid bone

Sesamoid bone

Phalanges of 3rd digit

Phalanges of 3rd digit

Phalanges of 4th digit

Hoof bone

Hoof bone of 3rd digit

Hoof bone of 4th digit

Croup
Back
Loin
Root of tail
Buttock
Tail
Thigh
Flank
Stifle
Belly
Gaskin
Hock
Chestnut
Shannon bone (cannon bone)
Pastern
Heel
Coronet
Hoof

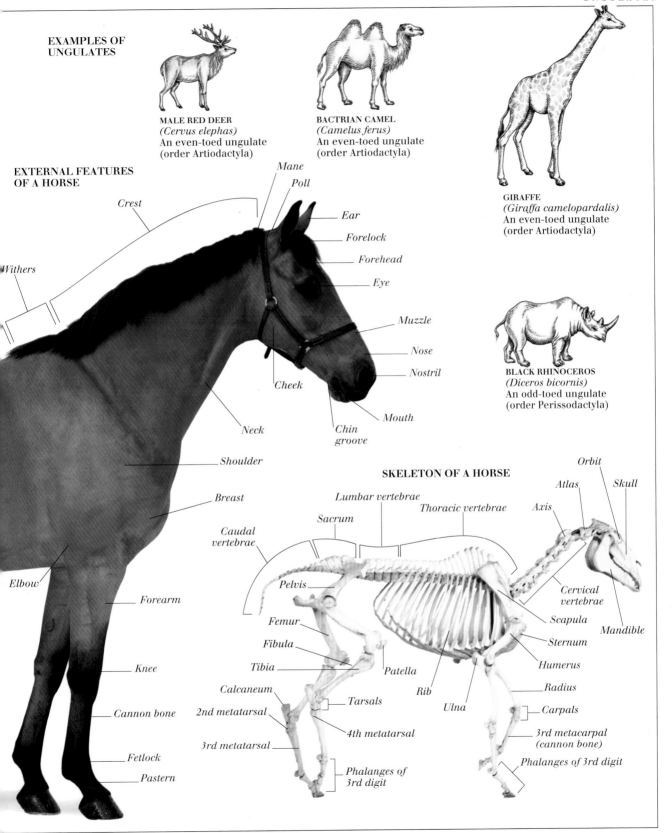

EXAMPLES OF UNGULATES

MALE RED DEER
(Cervus elephas)
An even-toed ungulate
(order Artiodactyla)

BACTRIAN CAMEL
(Camelus ferus)
An even-toed ungulate
(order Artiodactyla)

GIRAFFE
(Giraffa camelopardalis)
An even-toed ungulate
(order Artiodactyla)

BLACK RHINOCEROS
(Diceros bicornis)
An odd-toed ungulate
(order Perissodactyla)

EXTERNAL FEATURES OF A HORSE

Mane
Poll
Crest
Ear
Forelock
Forehead
Eye
Withers
Muzzle
Nose
Nostril
Cheek
Neck
Chin groove
Mouth
Shoulder
Breast
Elbow
Forearm
Knee
Cannon bone
Fetlock
Pastern

SKELETON OF A HORSE

Orbit
Atlas
Skull
Axis
Lumbar vertebrae
Thoracic vertebrae
Sacrum
Caudal vertebrae
Cervical vertebrae
Pelvis
Scapula
Mandible
Femur
Sternum
Fibula
Humerus
Tibia
Patella
Radius
Rib
Carpals
Calcaneum
Tarsals
2nd metatarsal
Ulna
4th metatarsal
3rd metacarpal (cannon bone)
3rd metatarsal
Phalanges of 3rd digit
Phalanges of 3rd digit

Elephants

THE TWO SPECIES OF elephants—African and Asian—are the only members of the mammalian order Proboscidea. The bigger African elephant is the largest land animal: a fully grown male may be up to 4 m (13 ft) tall and weigh as much as 7 tonnes (6.9 tons). A fully grown male Asian elephant may be 3.3 m (11 ft) tall and weigh 5.4 tonnes (5.3 tons). The trunk—an extension of the nose and upper lip—is the elephant's other most obvious feature. It is used for manipulating and lifting, feeding, drinking and spraying water, smelling, touching, and producing trumpeting sounds. Other characteristic features include a pair of tusks, used for defence and for crushing vegetation; thick, pillar-like legs and broad feet to support the massive body; and large ear flaps that act as radiators to keep the elephant cool.

DIFFERENCES BETWEEN AFRICAN AND ASIAN ELEPHANTS

Flat forehead
Very large ears
2 "lips" at the end of the trunk
4 toenails
Concave back
3 toenails

AFRICAN ELEPHANT
(*Loxodonta africana*)

Twin-domed forehead
Smaller ears
1 "lip" at the end of the trunk
5 toenails
Arched back
4 toenails

ASIAN ELEPHANT
(*Elephas maximus*)

INTERNAL ANATOMY OF A FEMALE ELEPHANT

Brain
Nasal cavity
Buccal cavity
Mouth
Tongue
Tusk
Spinal cord
Heart
Stomach
Duodenum
Kidney
Ureter
Uterus
Rectum
Bladder
Anal flap
Anus
Vagina
Epiglottis
Oesophagus
Trachea
Lung
Diaphragm
Nasal passage
Spleen
Vulva
Small intestine
Nostril
Rump
Hind leg
Toenail

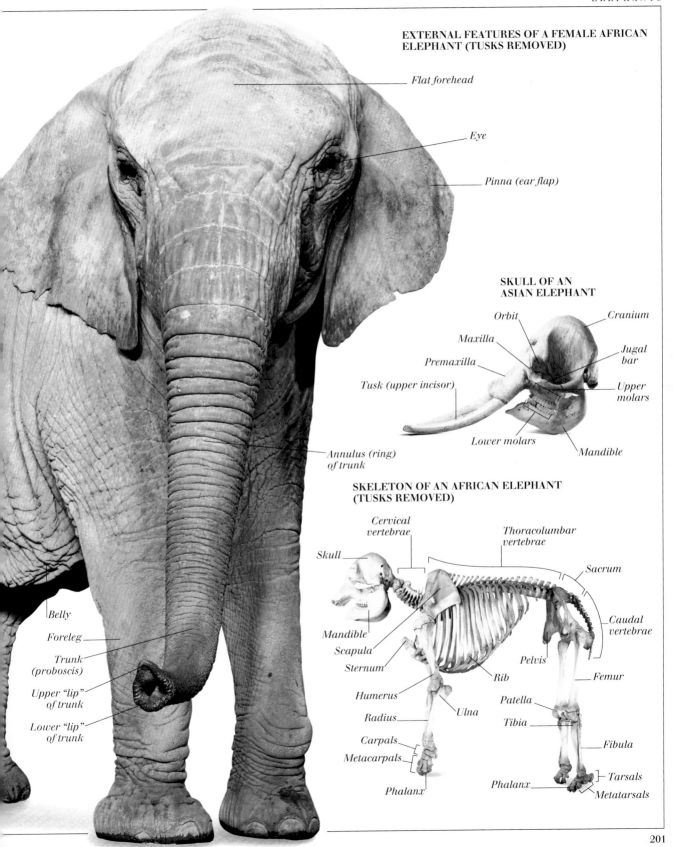

EXTERNAL FEATURES OF A FEMALE AFRICAN ELEPHANT (TUSKS REMOVED)

Flat forehead

Eye

Pinna (ear flap)

Annulus (ring) of trunk

Belly

Foreleg

Trunk (proboscis)

Upper "lip" of trunk

Lower "lip" of trunk

SKULL OF AN ASIAN ELEPHANT

Orbit

Cranium

Maxilla

Premaxilla

Jugal bar

Tusk (upper incisor)

Upper molars

Lower molars

Mandible

SKELETON OF AN AFRICAN ELEPHANT (TUSKS REMOVED)

Cervical vertebrae

Thoracolumbar vertebrae

Skull

Sacrum

Mandible

Caudal vertebrae

Scapula

Sternum

Pelvis

Humerus

Femur

Rib

Radius

Patella

Ulna

Tibia

Carpals

Metacarpals

Fibula

Phalanx

Tarsals

Phalanx

Metatarsals

Primates

THE MAMMALIAN ORDER PRIMATES consists of monkeys, apes, and their relatives (including humans). There are two suborders of primates: Prosimii, the primitive primates, which include lemurs, tarsiers, and lorises; and Anthropoidea, the advanced primates, which include monkeys, apes, and humans. The anthropoids are divided into New World monkeys, Old World monkeys, and hominids. New World monkeys typically have wide-apart nostrils that open to the side; and long tails, which are prehensile (grasping) in some species. This group of monkeys lives in South America, and includes marmosets, tamarins, and howler monkeys. Old World monkeys typically have close-set nostrils that open forwards or downwards; and non-prehensile tails. This group of monkeys lives in Africa and Asia, and includes langurs, mandrills, macaques, and baboons. Hominids typically have large brains, and no tail. This group includes the apes—chimpanzees, gibbons, gorillas, and orangutans—and humans.

INTERNAL ANATOMY OF A FEMALE CHIMPANZEE

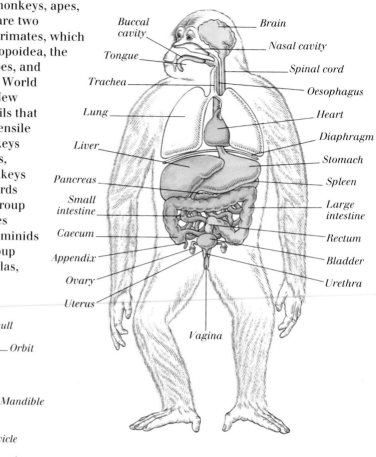

Buccal cavity
Tongue
Trachea
Lung
Liver
Pancreas
Small intestine
Caecum
Appendix
Ovary
Uterus
Vagina

Brain
Nasal cavity
Spinal cord
Oesophagus
Heart
Diaphragm
Stomach
Spleen
Large intestine
Rectum
Bladder
Urethra

SKELETON OF A RHESUS MONKEY

Cervical vertebrae
Thoracic vertebrae
Lumbar vertebrae
Sacrum
Femur
Patella
Fibula
Pelvis
Caudal vertebrae
Tarsals
Metatarsals
Tibia
Phalanges

Skull
Orbit
Mandible
Clavicle
Scapula
Rib
Humerus
Radius
Ulna
Carpals
Metacarpals
Phalanges

SKULL OF A CHIMPANZEE

Temporal bone
Suture
Parietal bone
Occipital bone
Auditory meatus
Zygomatic arch
Mandible
Molar tooth
Premolar tooth
Frontal bone
Supraorbital ridge
Orbit
Maxilla
Premaxilla
Incisor tooth
Canine tooth

EXAMPLES OF PRIMATES

RING-TAILED LEMUR
(Lemur catta)
A prosimian

MALE RED HOWLER MONKEY
(Alouatta seniculus)
A New World monkey

MALE MANDRILL
(Mandrillus sphinx)
An Old World monkey

CHIMPANZEE
(Pan troglodytes)
An ape

EXTERNAL FEATURES OF A YOUNG GORILLA

GOLDEN LION TAMARIN
(Leontopithecus rosalia)
A New World monkey

Pinna (ear flap)

Shoulder

Brow ridge

Eye

Nostril

Mouth

Upper arm

Thigh

Forearm

Chest

Knee

Elbow

Lower leg

Hand

Foot

Toe

Finger

Toenail

Dolphins, whales, and seals

DOLPHINS, WHALES, AND SEALS belong to two orders of mammals adapted to living in water. Dolphins and whales make up the order Cetacea. Typical cetacean features include a streamlined, fish-like shape; forelimbs in the form of flippers; no visible hind limbs; a horizontally flattened tail; and thick blubber under the skin. There are two groups of cetaceans: toothed whales, including sperm whales, white whales, beaked whales, dolphins, and porpoises; and the larger whalebone (baleen) whales, including rorquals, grey whales, and right whales. The blue whale—a rorqual—is the largest living animal: an adult may be up to 30 m (100 ft) long and weigh 130 tonnes (128 tons). Seals and their relatives—sea lions and walruses—make up the order Pinnipedia. Characteristically, they have a streamlined, torpedo-shaped body; forelimbs and hind limbs modified as flippers; thick blubber; and no external ears.

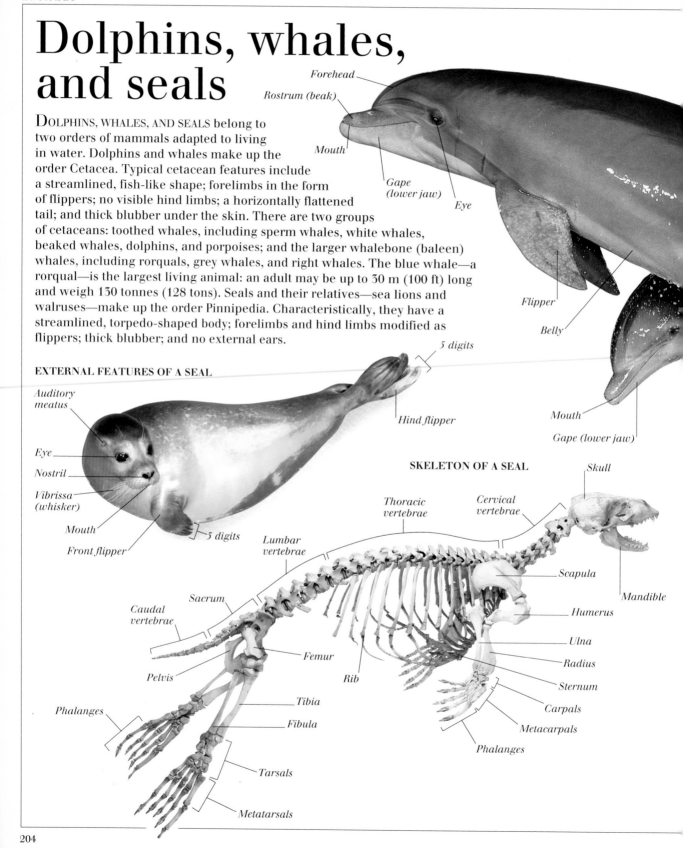

Forehead

Rostrum (beak)

Mouth

Gape (lower jaw)

Eye

Flipper

Belly

5 digits

Hind flipper

Mouth

Gape (lower jaw)

EXTERNAL FEATURES OF A SEAL

Auditory meatus

Eye

Nostril

Vibrissa (whisker)

Mouth

Front flipper

5 digits

SKELETON OF A SEAL

Skull

Thoracic vertebrae

Cervical vertebrae

Mandible

Lumbar vertebrae

Scapula

Humerus

Ulna

Radius

Sternum

Carpals

Metacarpals

Phalanges

Sacrum

Caudal vertebrae

Femur

Rib

Pelvis

Tibia

Fibula

Phalanges

Tarsals

Metatarsals

EXAMPLES OF CETACEANS

EXTERNAL FEATURES
OF A DOLPHIN

Dorsal fin

Tail

Tail fluke

BLUE WHALE
(*Balaenoptera musculus*)

SPERM WHALE
(*Physeter catodon*)

MALE BAIRD'S BEAKED WHALE
(*Berardius bairdi*)

MALE KILLER WHALE
(*Orcinus orca*)

MALE NARWHAL
(*Monodon monoceros*)

INTERNAL ANATOMY OF
A MALE DOLPHIN

Spinal cord

Stomach

Kidney

Intestine

Bladder

Blowhole (nostril)

Brain

Aorta

Nasal plug

Melon

Buccal cavity

Anus

Rectum

Tongue

Penis

Oesophagus

Testis

Trachea

Lung

Liver

Urinogenital opening

Heart

205

Marsupials and Monotremes

MARSUPIALS AND MONOTREMES are two orders of mammals that differ from other mammalian groups in the ways that their young develop. The order Marsupialia, the pouched mammals, is made up of kangaroos and their relatives. Typically, marsupials give birth to their young at a very early stage of development. The young then crawls to the mother's pouch (which is on the outside of her abdomen), where it attaches itself to a nipple and remains until fully developed. Most marsupials live in Australia, although the opossums—which are classified as marsupials despite not having a pouch—live in the Americas. The order Monotremata is made up of the platypus and its relatives (the echidnas, or spiny anteaters). The monotremes are primitive mammals that lay eggs, which the mother incubates. The monotremes are found only in Australia and New Guinea.

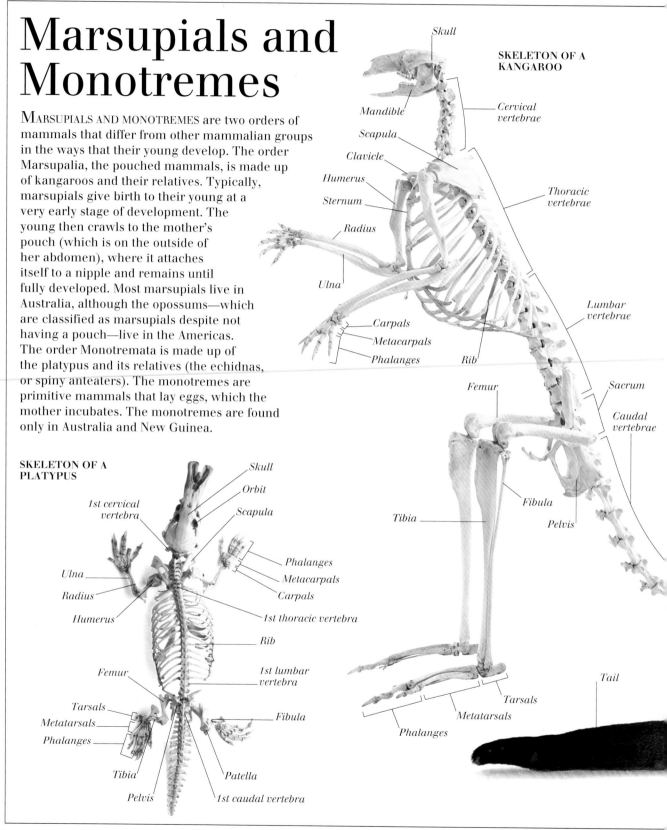

SKELETON OF A KANGAROO

Skull

Mandible

Cervical vertebrae

Scapula

Clavicle

Humerus

Sternum

Thoracic vertebrae

Radius

Ulna

Lumbar vertebrae

Carpals

Metacarpals

Phalanges

Rib

Femur

Sacrum

Caudal vertebrae

Tibia

Fibula

Pelvis

Tail

Tarsals

Metatarsals

Phalanges

SKELETON OF A PLATYPUS

Skull

Orbit

Scapula

1st cervical vertebra

Ulna

Radius

Humerus

Phalanges

Metacarpals

Carpals

1st thoracic vertebra

Rib

Femur

1st lumbar vertebra

Tarsals

Metatarsals

Phalanges

Fibula

Tibia

Patella

Pelvis

1st caudal vertebra

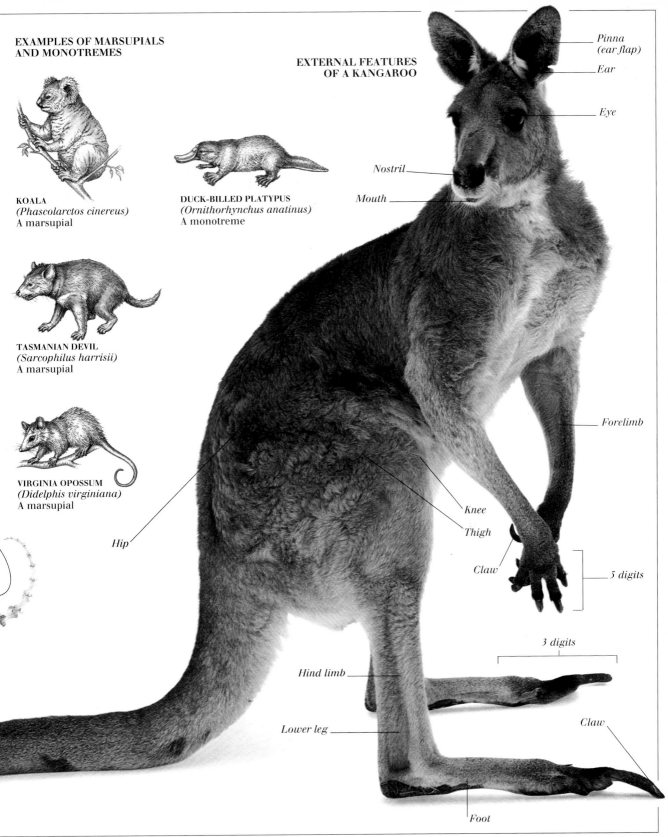

EXAMPLES OF MARSUPIALS AND MONOTREMES

KOALA
(Phascolarctos cinereus)
A marsupial

DUCK-BILLED PLATYPUS
(Ornithorhynchus anatinus)
A monotreme

TASMANIAN DEVIL
(Sarcophilus harrisii)
A marsupial

VIRGINIA OPOSSUM
(Didelphis virginiana)
A marsupial

EXTERNAL FEATURES OF A KANGAROO

Pinna (ear flap)

Ear

Eye

Nostril

Mouth

Forelimb

Hip

Knee

Thigh

Claw

5 digits

3 digits

Hind limb

Lower leg

Claw

Foot

THE
HUMAN BODY

BODY FEATURES · · · · · · · 210

HEAD · · · · · · · 212

BODY ORGANS · · · · · · · 214

BODY CELLS · · · · · · · 216

SKELETON · · · · · · · 218

SKULL · · · · · · · 220

SPINE · · · · · · · 222

BONES AND JOINTS · · · · · · · 224

MUSCLES 1 · · · · · · · 226

MUSCLES 2 · · · · · · · 228

HANDS · · · · · · · 230

FEET · · · · · · · 232

SKIN AND HAIR · · · · · · · 234

BRAIN · · · · · · · 236

NERVOUS SYSTEM · · · · · · · 238

EYE · · · · · · · 240

EAR · · · · · · · 242

NOSE, MOUTH, AND THROAT · · · · · · · 244

TEETH · · · · · · · 246

DIGESTIVE SYSTEM · · · · · · · 248

HEART · · · · · · · 250

CIRCULATORY SYSTEM · · · · · · · 252

RESPIRATORY SYSTEM · · · · · · · 254

URINARY SYSTEM · · · · · · · 256

REPRODUCTIVE SYSTEM · · · · · · · 258

DEVELOPMENT OF A BABY · · · · · · · 260

Body features

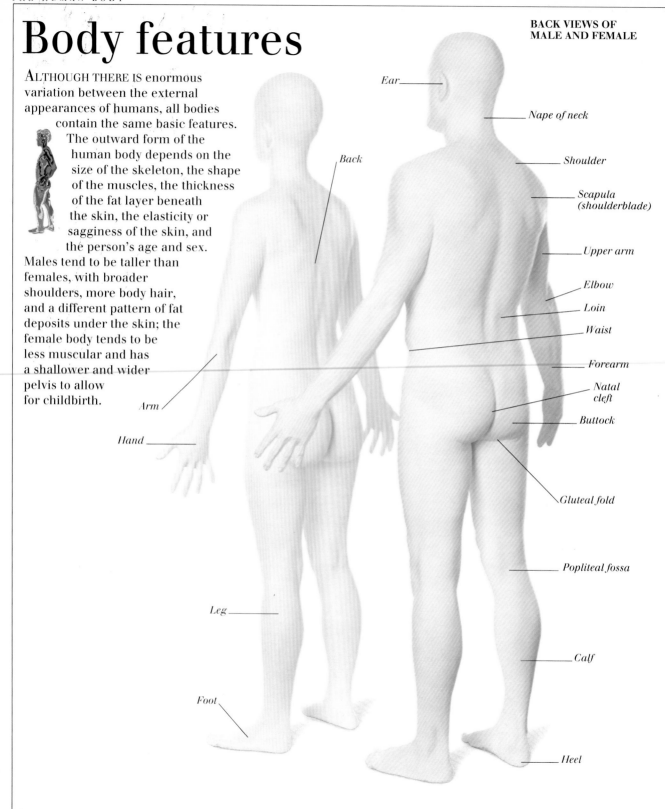

ALTHOUGH THERE IS enormous variation between the external appearances of humans, all bodies contain the same basic features. The outward form of the human body depends on the size of the skeleton, the shape of the muscles, the thickness of the fat layer beneath the skin, the elasticity or sagginess of the skin, and the person's age and sex. Males tend to be taller than females, with broader shoulders, more body hair, and a different pattern of fat deposits under the skin; the female body tends to be less muscular and has a shallower and wider pelvis to allow for childbirth.

BACK VIEWS OF MALE AND FEMALE

Ear

Nape of neck

Shoulder

Scapula (shoulderblade)

Upper arm

Elbow

Loin

Waist

Forearm

Natal cleft

Buttock

Gluteal fold

Popliteal fossa

Calf

Heel

Back

Arm

Hand

Leg

Foot

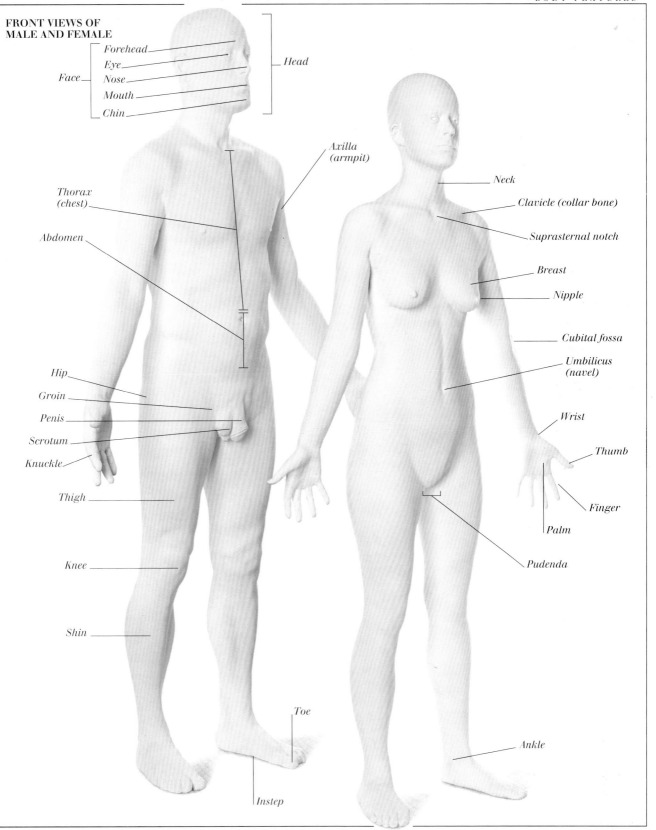

**FRONT VIEWS OF
MALE AND FEMALE**

Face

Forehead
Eye
Nose
Mouth
Chin

Head

Axilla
(armpit)

Neck

Clavicle (collar bone)

Suprasternal notch

Thorax
(chest)

Breast

Nipple

Abdomen

Cubital fossa

Umbilicus
(navel)

Hip

Groin

Penis

Wrist

Scrotum

Thumb

Knuckle

Finger

Thigh

Palm

Knee

Pudenda

Shin

Toe

Ankle

Instep

Head

IN A NEWBORN BABY, the head accounts for one-quarter of the total body length; by adulthood, the proportion has reduced to one-eighth. Contained in the head are the body's main sense organs: eyes, ears, olfactory nerves that detect smells, and the taste buds of the tongue. Signals from these organs pass to the body's great coordination centre: the brain, housed in the protective, bony dome of the skull. Hair on the head insulates against heat loss, and adult males also grow thick facial hair. The face has three important openings: two nostrils through which air passes, and the mouth, which takes in nourishment and helps form speech. Although all heads are basically similar, differences in the size, shape, and colour of features produce an infinite variety of appearances.

SIDE VIEW OF EXTERNAL FEATURES OF HEAD

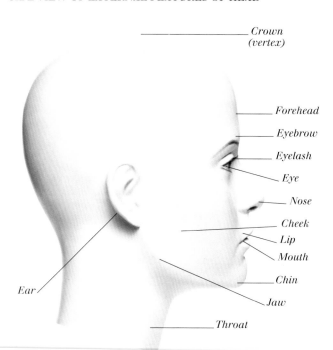

Crown (vertex)

Forehead

Eyebrow

Eyelash

Eye

Nose

Cheek

Lip

Mouth

Chin

Jaw

Ear

Throat

SECTION THROUGH HEAD

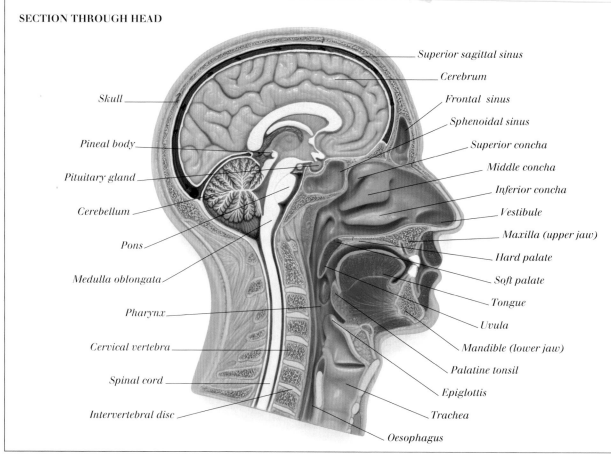

Skull

Pineal body

Pituitary gland

Cerebellum

Pons

Medulla oblongata

Pharynx

Cervical vertebra

Spinal cord

Intervertebral disc

Superior sagittal sinus

Cerebrum

Frontal sinus

Sphenoidal sinus

Superior concha

Middle concha

Inferior concha

Vestibule

Maxilla (upper jaw)

Hard palate

Soft palate

Tongue

Uvula

Mandible (lower jaw)

Palatine tonsil

Epiglottis

Trachea

Oesophagus

**FRONT VIEW OF EXTERNAL
FEATURES OF HEAD**

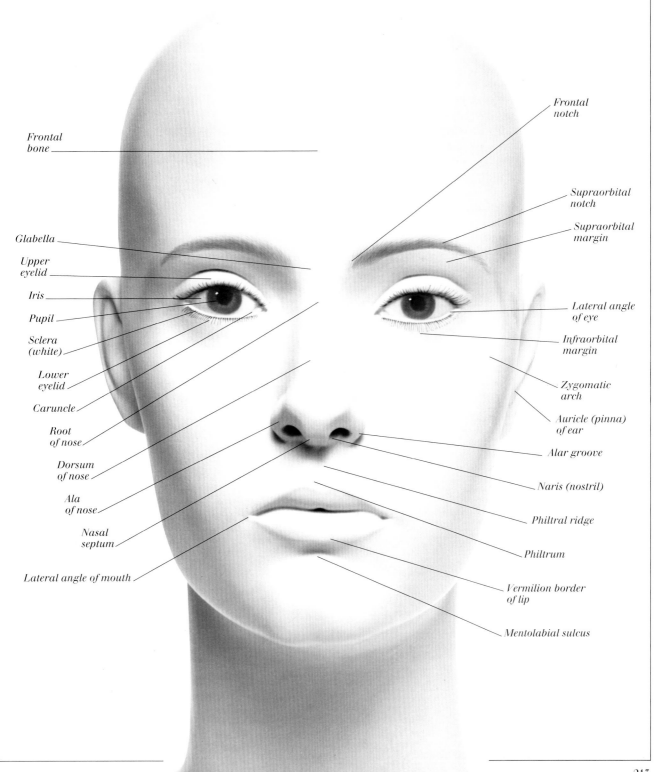

Frontal
notch

Supraorbital
notch

Supraorbital
margin

Lateral angle
of eye

Infraorbital
margin

Zygomatic
arch

Auricle (pinna)
of ear

Alar groove

Naris (nostril)

Philtral ridge

Philtrum

Vermilion border
of lip

Mentolabial sulcus

Frontal
bone

Glabella

Upper
eyelid

Iris

Pupil

Sclera
(white)

Lower
eyelid

Caruncle

Root
of nose

Dorsum
of nose

Ala
of nose

Nasal
septum

Lateral angle of mouth

Body organs

ALL THE VITAL BODY ORGANS except for the brain are enclosed within the trunk or torso (the body apart from the head and limbs). The trunk contains two large cavities separated by a muscular sheet called the diaphragm. The upper cavity, known as the thorax or chest cavity, contains the heart and lungs. The lower cavity, called the abdominal cavity, contains the stomach, intestines, liver, and pancreas, which all play a role in digesting food. Also within the trunk are the kidneys and bladder, which are part of the urinary system, and the reproductive organs, which hold the seeds of new human life. Modern imaging techniques, such as contrast X-rays and different types of scans, make it possible to see and study body organs without the need to cut through their protective coverings of skin, fat, muscle, and bone.

MAJOR INTERNAL STRUCTURES

Thyroid gland

Larynx

Heart

Right lung

Left lung

Diaphragm

Liver

Large intestine

Stomach

Small intestine

Greater omentum

IMAGING THE BODY

SCINTIGRAM OF HEART CHAMBERS

ANGIOGRAM OF RIGHT LUNG

CONTRAST X-RAY OF GALLBLADDER

SCINTIGRAM OF NERVOUS SYSTEM

DOUBLE CONTRAST X-RAY OF COLON

ULTRASOUND SCAN OF TWINS IN UTERUS

ANGIOGRAM OF KIDNEYS

ANGIOGRAM OF ARTERIES OF HEAD

CT SCAN THROUGH FEMALE CHEST

THERMOGRAM OF CHEST REGION

ANGIOGRAM OF ARTERIES OF HEART

MRI SCAN THROUGH HEAD AT EYE LEVEL

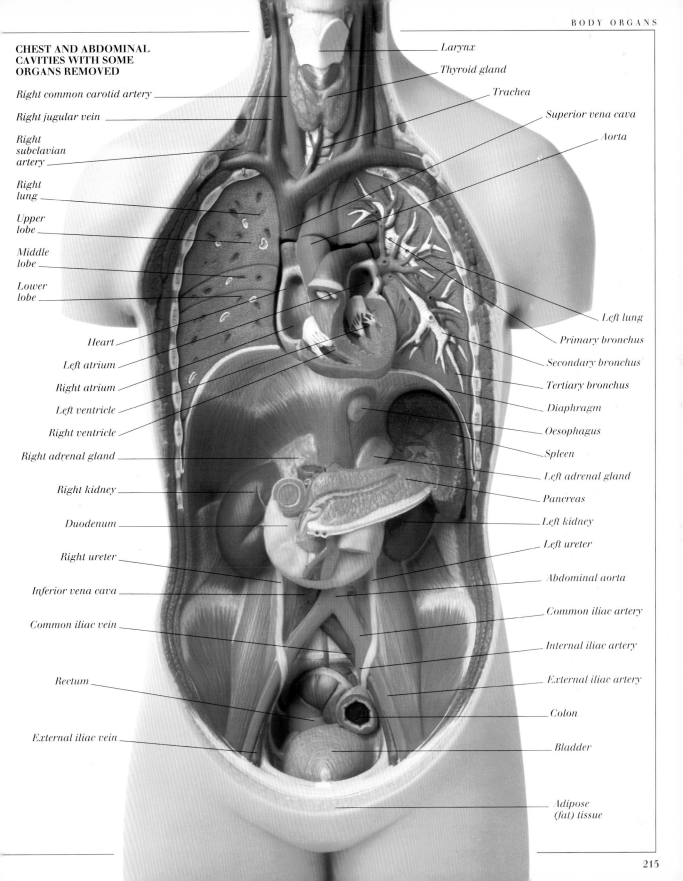

**CHEST AND ABDOMINAL
CAVITIES WITH SOME
ORGANS REMOVED**

Right common carotid artery

Right jugular vein

*Right
subclavian
artery*

*Right
lung*

*Upper
lobe*

*Middle
lobe*

*Lower
lobe*

Heart

Left atrium

Right atrium

Left ventricle

Right ventricle

Right adrenal gland

Right kidney

Duodenum

Right ureter

Inferior vena cava

Common iliac vein

Rectum

External iliac vein

Larynx

Thyroid gland

Trachea

Superior vena cava

Aorta

Left lung

Primary bronchus

Secondary bronchus

Tertiary bronchus

Diaphragm

Oesophagus

Spleen

Left adrenal gland

Pancreas

Left kidney

Left ureter

Abdominal aorta

Common iliac artery

Internal iliac artery

External iliac artery

Colon

Bladder

*Adipose
(fat) tissue*

Body cells

EVERYONE IS MADE UP OF BILLIONS OF CELLS, which are the basic structural units of the body. Bones, muscles, nerves, skin, blood, and all other body tissues are formed from different types of cells. Each cell has a specific function but works with other types of cells to perform the enormous number of tasks needed to sustain life. Most body cells have a similar basic structure. Each cell has an outer layer (called the cell membrane) and contains a fluid material (cytoplasm). Within the cytoplasm are many specialized structures (organelles). The most important organelle is the nucleus, which contains vital genetic material and acts as the cell's control centre.

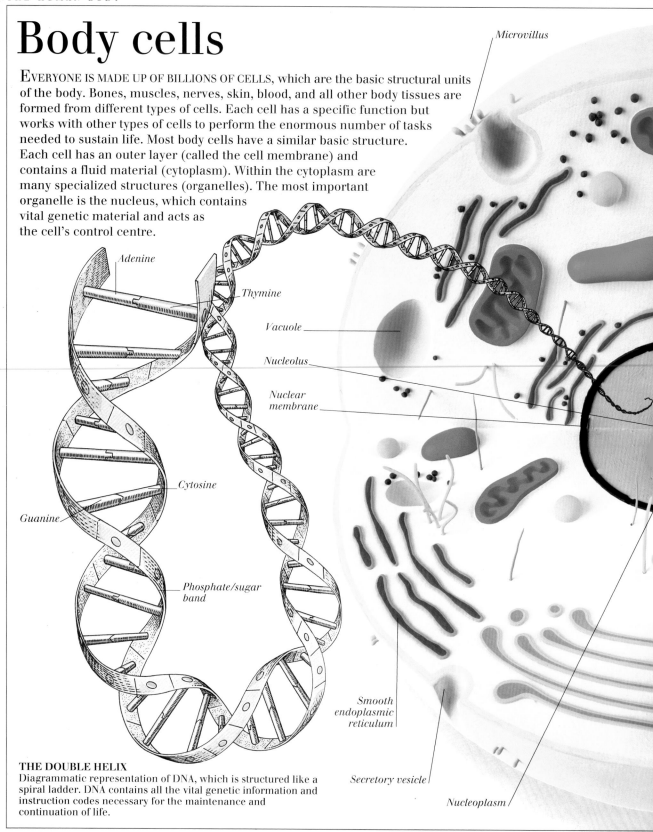

Microvillus

Adenine

Thymine

Vacuole

Nucleolus

Nuclear
membrane

Cytosine

Guanine

Phosphate/sugar
band

Smooth
endoplasmic
reticulum

Secretory vesicle

Nucleoplasm

THE DOUBLE HELIX
Diagrammatic representation of DNA, which is structured like a spiral ladder. DNA contains all the vital genetic information and instruction codes necessary for the maintenance and continuation of life.

GENERALIZED HUMAN CELL

Cytoplasm

Lysosome

Cell membrane

Mitochondrial crista

Nucleus

Rough endoplasmic reticulum

Microfilament

Pore of nuclear membrane

Ribosome

Centriole

Mitochondrion

Microtubule

Peroxisome

Pinocytotic vesicle

Golgi complex (Golgi apparatus; Golgi body)

TYPES OF CELLS

BONE-FORMING CELL

NERVE CELLS IN SPINAL CORD

SPERM CELLS IN SEMEN

SECRETORY THYROID GLAND CELLS

ACID-SECRETING STOMACH CELLS

CONNECTIVE TISSUE CELLS

MUCUS-SECRETING DUODENAL CELLS

RED AND TWO WHITE BLOOD CELLS

FAT CELLS IN ADIPOSE TISSUE

EPITHELIAL CELLS IN CHEEK

Skeleton

THE SKELETON IS A MOBILE FRAMEWORK made up of 206 bones, approximately half of which are in the hands and feet. Although individual bones are rigid, the skeleton as a whole is remarkably flexible and allows the human body a huge range of movement. The skeleton serves as an anchorage for the skeletal muscles, and as a protective cage for the body's internal organs. Female bones are usually smaller and lighter than male bones, and the female pelvis is shallower and has a wider cavity.

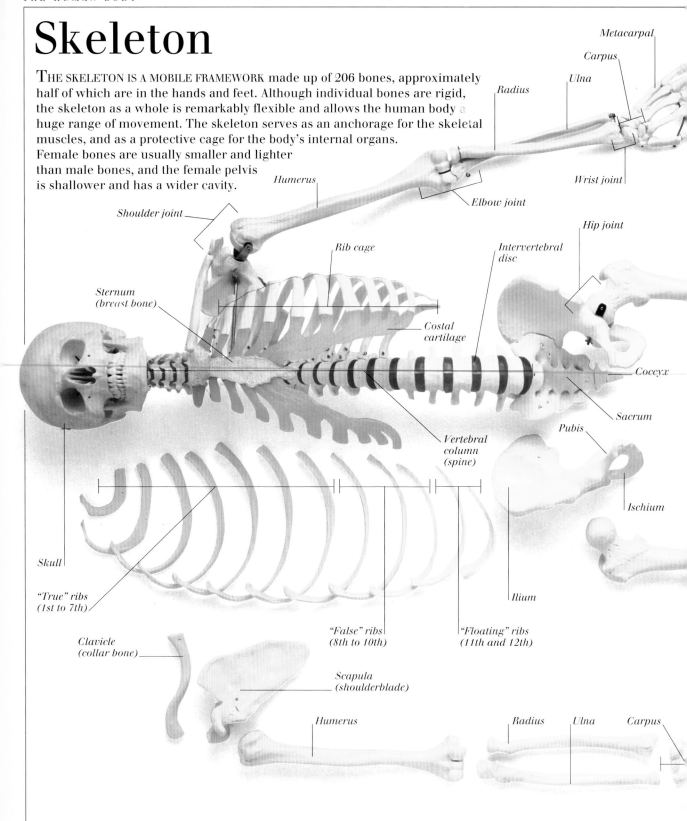

Metacarpal

Carpus

Ulna

Radius

Humerus

Shoulder joint

Elbow joint

Wrist joint

Hip joint

Rib cage

Intervertebral disc

Sternum (breast bone)

Costal cartilage

Coccyx

Sacrum

Pubis

Vertebral column (spine)

Ischium

Skull

Ilium

"True" ribs (1st to 7th)

"False" ribs (8th to 10th)

"Floating" ribs (11th and 12th)

Clavicle (collar bone)

Scapula (shoulderblade)

Humerus

Radius

Ulna

Carpus

Distal phalanx

Middle phalanx

Proximal phalanx

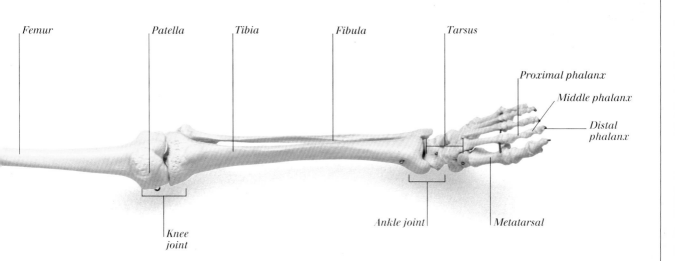

Femur   Patella   Tibia   Fibula   Tarsus

Proximal phalanx

Middle phalanx

Distal phalanx

Knee joint

Ankle joint   Metatarsal

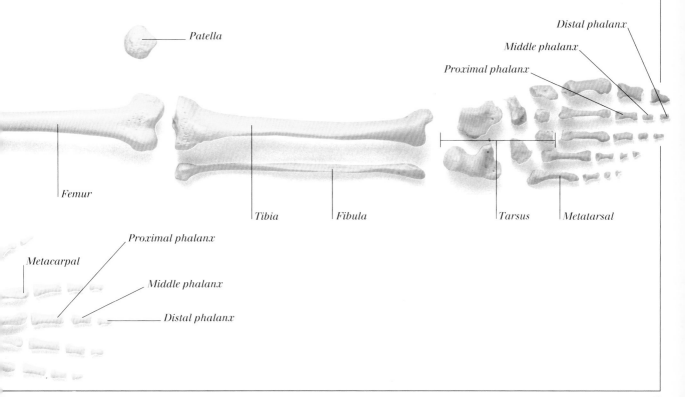

Patella

Distal phalanx

Middle phalanx

Proximal phalanx

Femur

Tibia   Fibula

Tarsus   Metatarsal

Metacarpal

Proximal phalanx

Middle phalanx

Distal phalanx

Skull

THE SKULL is the most complicated bony structure of the body but every feature serves a purpose. Internally, the main hollow chamber of the skull has three levels that support the brain, with every bump and hollow corresponding to the shape of the brain. Underneath and towards the back of the skull is a large round hole, the foramen magnum, through which the spinal cord passes. To the front of this are many smaller openings through which nerves, arteries, and veins pass to and from the brain. The roof of the skull is formed from four thin, curved bones that are firmly fixed together from the age of about two years. At the front of the skull are the two orbits, which contain the eyeballs, and a central hole for the airway of the nose. The jaw bone hinges on either side at ear level.

RIGHT SIDE VIEW OF A FETAL SKULL

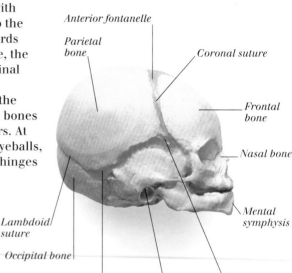

Anterior fontanelle

Parietal bone

Coronal suture

Frontal bone

Nasal bone

Mental symphysis

Lambdoid suture

Occipital bone

Mastoid fontanelle

External auditory meatus

Sphenoidal fontanelle

RIGHT SIDE VIEW OF SKULL

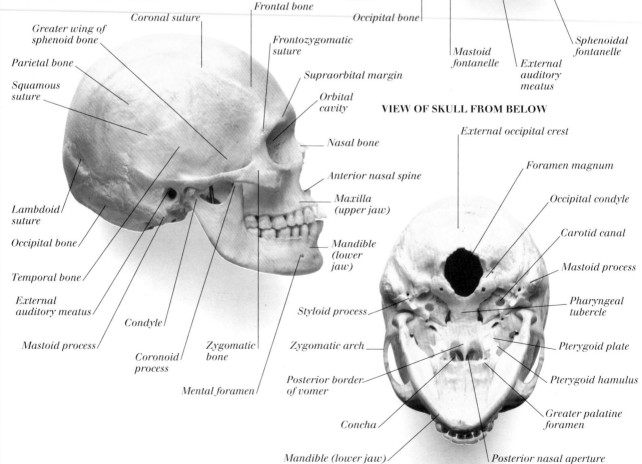

Greater wing of sphenoid bone

Coronal suture

Frontal bone

Frontozygomatic suture

Parietal bone

Squamous suture

Supraorbital margin

Orbital cavity

Nasal bone

Anterior nasal spine

Maxilla (upper jaw)

Mandible (lower jaw)

Lambdoid suture

Occipital bone

Temporal bone

External auditory meatus

Mastoid process

Condyle

Coronoid process

Zygomatic bone

Mental foramen

VIEW OF SKULL FROM BELOW

External occipital crest

Foramen magnum

Occipital condyle

Carotid canal

Mastoid process

Pharyngeal tubercle

Pterygoid plate

Pterygoid hamulus

Greater palatine foramen

Posterior nasal aperture

Styloid process

Zygomatic arch

Posterior border of vomer

Concha

Mandible (lower jaw)

FRONT VIEW OF SKULL

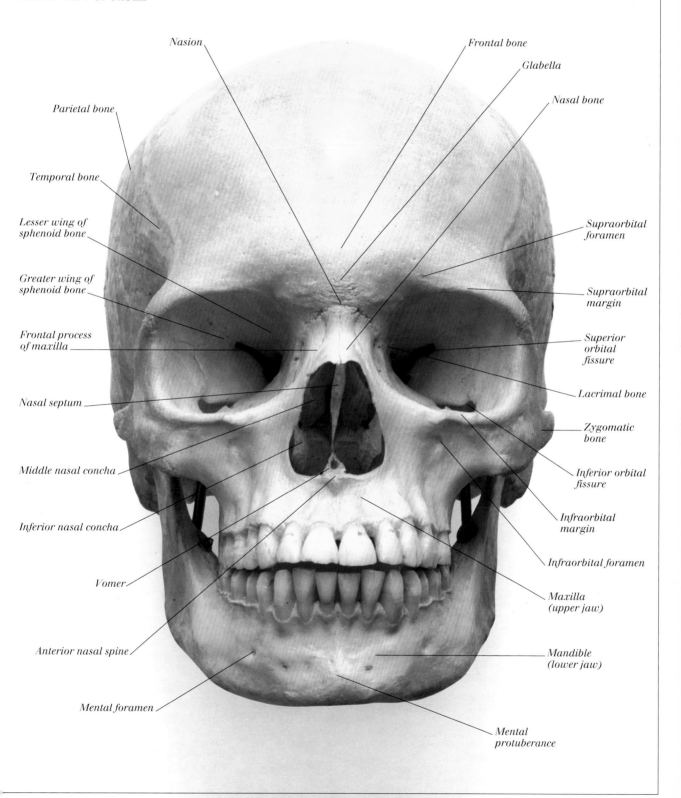

Nasion

Frontal bone

Glabella

Nasal bone

Parietal bone

Temporal bone

Lesser wing of
sphenoid bone

Greater wing of
sphenoid bone

Frontal process
of maxilla

Nasal septum

Middle nasal concha

Inferior nasal concha

Vomer

Anterior nasal spine

Mental foramen

Supraorbital
foramen

Supraorbital
margin

Superior
orbital
fissure

Lacrimal bone

Zygomatic
bone

Inferior orbital
fissure

Infraorbital
margin

Infraorbital foramen

Maxilla
(upper jaw)

Mandible
(lower jaw)

Mental
protuberance

Spine

THE SPINE (OR VERTEBRAL COLUMN) has two main functions: it serves as a protective surrounding for the delicate spinal cord and forms the supporting back bone of the skeleton. The spine consists of 24 separate differently shaped bones (vertebrae) with a curved, triangular bone (the sacrum) at the bottom. The sacrum is made up of fused vertebrae; at its lower end is a small tail-like structure made up of tiny bones collectively called the coccyx. Between each pair of vertebrae is a disc of cartilage that cushions the bones during movement. The top two vertebrae differ in appearance from the others and work as a pair: the first, called the atlas, rotates around a stout vertical peg on the second, the axis. This arrangement allows the skull to move freely up and down, and from side to side.

SPINE DIVIDED INTO VERTEBRAL SECTIONS

FRONT

Cervical vertebrae

Thoracic vertebrae

Lumbar vertebrae

Sacral vertebrae

Coccygeal vertebrae

TYPES OF VERTEBRAE (VIEWED FROM ABOVE)

ATLAS

Anterior arch

Anterior tubercle

Vertebral foramen

Transverse process

Lateral mass with superior articular facet

Posterior arch

Posterior tubercle

Transverse foramen

AXIS

Facet

Dens

Vertebral foramen

Spinous process

Lamina

Transverse process and foramen

CERVICAL VERTEBRA

Body

Anterior tubercle

Posterior tubercle

Superior articular process

Spinous process

Vertebral foramen

Transverse foramen

SKULL AND SPINE

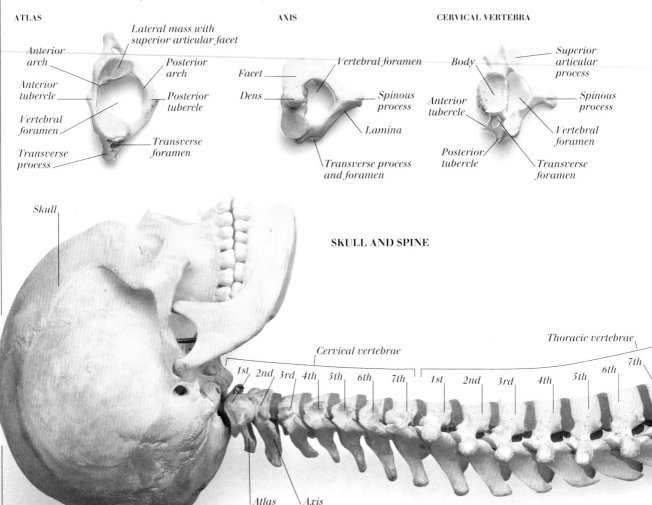

Skull

Cervical vertebrae

1st 2nd 3rd 4th 5th 6th 7th

Thoracic vertebrae

1st 2nd 3rd 4th 5th 6th 7th

Atlas Axis

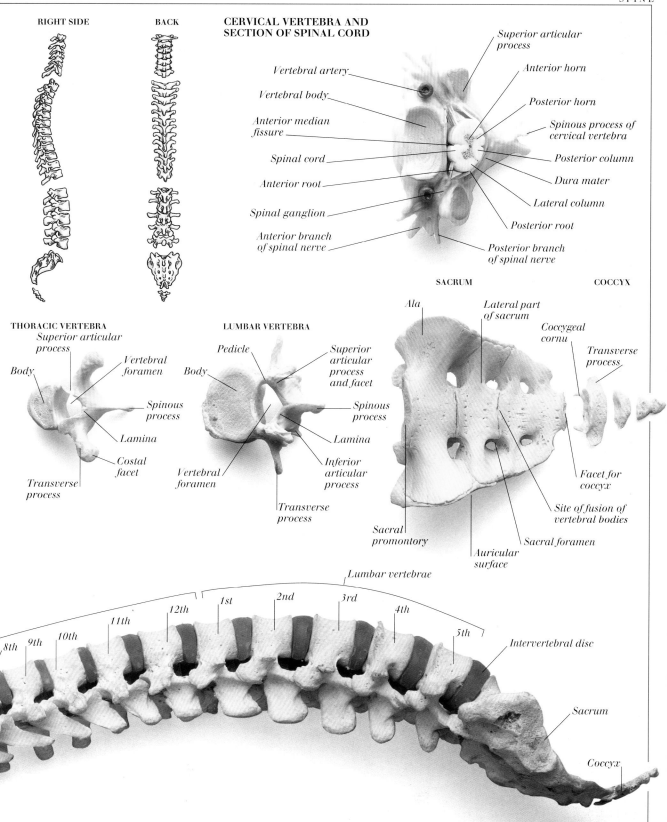

RIGHT SIDE

BACK

CERVICAL VERTEBRA AND SECTION OF SPINAL CORD

Vertebral artery

Vertebral body

Anterior median fissure

Spinal cord

Anterior root

Spinal ganglion

Anterior branch of spinal nerve

Superior articular process

Anterior horn

Posterior horn

Spinous process of cervical vertebra

Posterior column

Dura mater

Lateral column

Posterior root

Posterior branch of spinal nerve

THORACIC VERTEBRA

Superior articular process

Body

Vertebral foramen

Spinous process

Lamina

Costal facet

Transverse process

LUMBAR VERTEBRA

Pedicle

Body

Superior articular process and facet

Spinous process

Lamina

Inferior articular process

Vertebral foramen

Transverse process

SACRUM

Ala

Lateral part of sacrum

Sacral promontory

Auricular surface

Sacral foramen

Site of fusion of vertebral bodies

COCCYX

Coccygeal cornu

Transverse process

Facet for coccyx

Lumbar vertebrae

8th 9th 10th 11th 12th 1st 2nd 3rd 4th 5th

Intervertebral disc

Sacrum

Coccyx

Bones and joints

BONES FORM the body's hard, strong skeletal framework. Each bone has a hard, compact exterior surrounding a spongy, lighter interior. The long bones of the arms and legs, such as the femur (thigh bone), have a central cavity containing bone marrow. Bones are composed chiefly of calcium, phosphorus, and a fibrous substance known as collagen. Bones meet at joints, which are of several different types. For example, the hip is a ball-and-socket joint that allows the femur a wide range of movement, whereas finger joints are simple hinge joints that allow only bending and straightening. Joints are held in place by bands of tissue called ligaments. Movement of joints is facilitated by the smooth hyaline cartilage that covers the bone ends and by the synovial membrane that lines and lubricates the joint.

LIGAMENTS SURROUNDING HIP JOINT

Iliac crest

Iliac fossa

Pubofemoral ligament

Iliac spine

Obturator canal

Superior ramus of pubis

Greater trochanter of femur

Iliofemoral ligament

Body of pubis

Intertrochanteric line

Obturator membrane

Lesser trochanter of femur

Ischial tuberosity

Femur

Ischium

SECTION THROUGH LEFT FEMUR

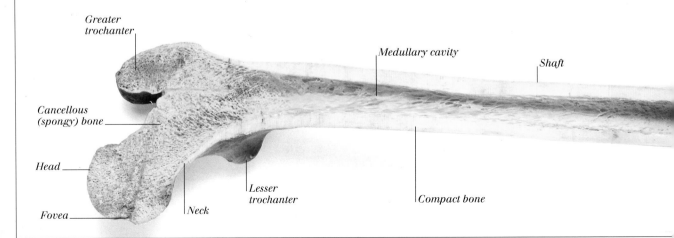

Greater trochanter

Medullary cavity

Shaft

Cancellous (spongy) bone

Head

Lesser trochanter

Compact bone

Fovea

Neck

SECTION THROUGH HIP JOINT

Psoas major muscle

Iliacus muscle

Iliac crest

External iliac artery

Hyaline cartilage of acetabulum

Hyaline cartilage of head of femur

Ligament of head of femur

Femoral artery

Articular cavity

Gluteus minimus muscle

Gluteus medius muscle

Acetabular labrum

Head of femur

Greater trochanter of femur

Neck of femur

Vastus lateralis muscle

Pectineus muscle

Adductor longus muscle

Iliacus muscle

Vastus medialis muscle

Shaft of femur

SECTION OF COMPACT BONE

Parallel rows of concentric bony layers make up this strong material.

BONE MARROW SMEAR

Composed mainly of red and white blood cells, marrow fills the cavities of bones.

SECTION THROUGH LONG BONE

Lateral epicondyle

Patellar surface

Medial epicondyle

Adductor tubercle

Osteon (haversian system)

Osteocyte (bone cell)

Intermediate lamella

Endosteum

Volkmann's vessel

Lacuna

Haversian canal

Periosteum

Sharpey's fibre

Outer lamella

Haversian lamella

225

Muscles 1

THERE ARE THREE MAIN TYPES OF MUSCLE: skeletal muscle (also called voluntary muscle because it can be consciously controlled); smooth muscle (also called involuntary muscle because it is not under voluntary control); and the specialized muscle tissue of the heart. Humans have more than 600 skeletal muscles, which differ in size and shape according to the jobs they do. Skeletal muscles are attached either directly or indirectly (via tendons) to bones, and work in opposing pairs (one muscle in the pair contracts while the other relaxes) to produce body movements as diverse as walking, threading a needle, and an array of facial expressions. Smooth muscles occur in the walls of internal body organs and perform actions such as forcing food through the intestines, contracting the uterus (womb) in childbirth, and pumping blood through the blood vessels.

SOME OTHER MUSCLES IN THE BODY

IRIS
The muscle fibres contract and dilate (expand) to alter pupil size.

Iris
Pupil

TONGUE
Interlacing layers of muscle allow great mobility.

ILEUM
Opposing muscle layers transport semi-digested food.

SUPERFICIAL SKELETAL MUSCLES

FRONT VIEW

Brachioradialis
Flexors of forearm
Brachialis
Frontalis
Orbicularis oculi
Temporalis
Sternocleidomastoid
Trapezius
Pectoralis major
Deltoid
Serratus anterior
Biceps brachii
Rectus abdominis
Linea alba
External oblique
Tensor fasciae latae
Iliopsoas
Pectineus
Adductor longus
Rectus femoris
Gracilis
Sartorius
Vastus lateralis
Vastus medialis
Gastrocnemius
Tibialis anterior

BACK VIEW

Extensors
of hand

Flexors
of hand

MOVEMENT OF THE FOREARM
Controlled movement of the limbs relies
on coordinated relaxation and contraction
of opposing muscles. To raise the forearm,
the biceps (two-rooted muscle) contracts
and shortens while the triceps (three-
rooted muscle) relaxes; the reverse occurs
when the forearm is lowered.

Temporalis

Triceps
brachii

Triceps in
resting phase

Sternocleidomastoid

Teres minor

Biceps in
resting phase

Teres major

Forearm
at rest

Trapezius

Infraspinatus

Rhomboideus major

Deltoid

Latissimus dorsi

Triceps
relaxes

Biceps
contracts

Forearm
half raised

Triceps fully
relaxed

Biceps fully
contracted

Forearm
fully raised

Gluteus
maximus

Adductor
magnus

Gracilis

Triceps
contracts

Biceps
relaxes

Forearm
half lowered

Biceps femoris

Semitendinosus

Gastrocnemius

Soleus

Triceps back in
resting phase

Biceps back in
resting phase

Forearm
back at rest

Peroneus
brevis

Muscles 2

SKELETAL MUSCLE FIBRE

Myofibril

Sarcomere

Motor end plate

Synaptic knob

Nucleus

Sarcoplasmic reticulum

Schwann cell

Sarcolemma

Motor neuron

Endomysium

Node of Ranvier

MUSCLES OF FACIAL EXPRESSION

A single expression is the result of movement of many muscles; the main muscles of expression are shown in action below.

FRONTALIS

CORRUGATOR SUPERCILII

ORBICULARIS ORIS

ZYGOMATICUS MAJOR

DEPRESSOR ANGULI ORIS

TYPES OF MUSCLE

CARDIAC MUSCLE

SKELETAL MUSCLE

SMOOTH MUSCLE

CONTRACTION OF SKELETAL MUSCLE

RELAXED STATE

CONTRACTED STATE

MUSCLES OF
HEAD AND NECK

Frontalis

Corrugator
supercilii

Orbicularis
oculi

Levator labii
superioris

Zygomaticus
major

Masseter

Risorius

Levator anguli oris

Platysma

Depressor anguli oris

Sternocleidomastoid

Omohyoid

Trapezius

Procerus

Temporalis

Nasalis

Orbicularis oris

Buccinator

Depressor labii
inferioris

Mentalis

Thyrohyoid

Scalenus medius

Sternohyoid

Cricothyroid

Hands

THE HUMAN HAND is an extremely versatile tool, capable of delicate manipulation as well as powerful gripping actions. The arrangement of its 27 small bones, moved by 37 skeletal muscles that are connected to the bones by tendons, allows a wide range of movements. Our ability to bring the tips of our thumbs and fingers together, combined with the extraordinary sensitivity of our fingertips due to their rich supply of nerve endings, makes our hands uniquely dextrous.

X-RAY OF LEFT HAND OF A YOUNG CHILD

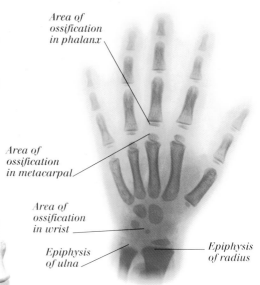

Area of ossification in phalanx

Area of ossification in metacarpal

Area of ossification in wrist

Epiphysis of ulna

Epiphysis of radius

Areas of cartilage in the wrist and at the ends of the finger bones are the sites of growth and have still to ossify.

BONES OF HAND

Ring finger

Middle finger

Index finger

Little finger

Distal phalanx

Middle phalanx

Proximal phalanx

2nd metacarpal

3rd metacarpal

4th metacarpal

5th metacarpal

Hamate

Pisiform

Capitate

Triquetral

Lunate

Ulna

Head

Shaft

Base

Distal phalanx of thumb

Proximal phalanx of thumb

1st metacarpal

Trapezium

Trapezoid

Scaphoid

Radius

STRUCTURES UNDERLYING SKIN OF PALM OF HAND

Flexor pollicis brevis muscle

Opponens pollicis muscle

Abductor pollicis brevis muscle

Adductor pollicis muscle

Flexor retinaculum

2nd lumbrical muscle

Radial artery

Digital artery

Digital nerve

Flexor digitorum tendon

Opponens digiti minimi muscle

Abductor digiti minimi muscle

Ulnar nerve

Ulnar artery

Palmaris longus tendon

EXTERNAL FEATURES OF BACK OF HAND

Little finger

Distal interphalangeal joint

Proximal interphalangeal joint

Ring finger

Extensor digitorum tendon

Head of ulna

Middle finger

Cuticle

Lunule

Index finger

Nail

Metacarpophalangeal joint

Wrist

Distal end of radius

Thumb

Feet

THE FEET AND TOES are essential elements in body movement. They bear and propel the weight of the body during walking and running, and also help to maintain balance during changes of body position. Each foot has 26 bones, more than 100 ligaments, and 33 muscles, some of which are attached to the lower leg. The heel pad and the arch of the foot act as shock absorbers, providing a cushion against the jolts that occur with every step.

BONES OF FOOT

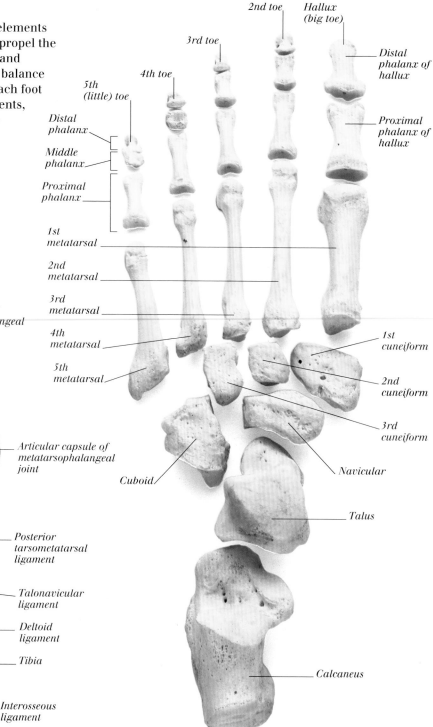

2nd toe

Hallux (big toe)

3rd toe

Distal phalanx of hallux

4th toe

5th (little) toe

Distal phalanx

Proximal phalanx of hallux

Middle phalanx

Proximal phalanx

1st metatarsal

2nd metatarsal

3rd metatarsal

1st cuneiform

4th metatarsal

2nd cuneiform

5th metatarsal

3rd cuneiform

Navicular

Cuboid

Talus

Calcaneus

LIGAMENTS OF FOOT

Posterior cuneonavicular ligament

Articular capsule of interphalangeal joint

Plantar calcaneonavicular ligament

Articular capsule of metatarsophalangeal joint

Posterior tarsometatarsal ligament

Talonavicular ligament

Bifurcate ligament

Deltoid ligament

Fibula

Tibia

Calcanean (Achilles) tendon

Interosseous ligament

STRUCTURES UNDERLYING SKIN OF FOOT

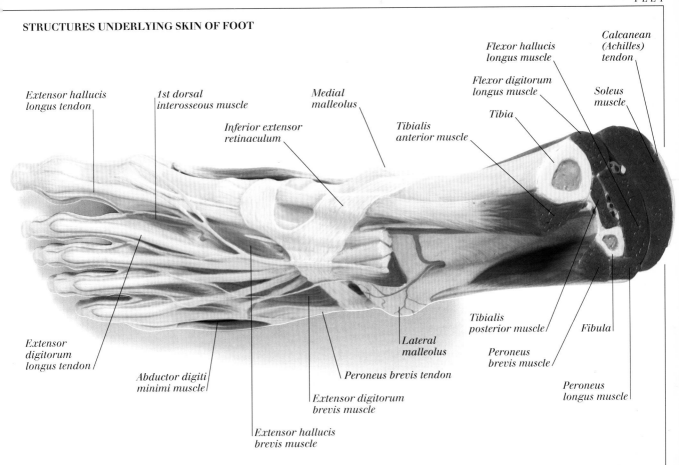

Extensor hallucis
longus tendon

1st dorsal
interosseous muscle

Medial
malleolus

Flexor hallucis
longus muscle

Calcanean
(Achilles)
tendon

Flexor digitorum
longus muscle

Soleus
muscle

Inferior extensor
retinaculum

Tibialis
anterior muscle

Tibia

Extensor
digitorum
longus tendon

Abductor digiti
minimi muscle

Extensor digitorum
brevis muscle

Extensor hallucis
brevis muscle

Lateral
malleolus

Peroneus brevis tendon

Tibialis
posterior muscle

Fibula

Peroneus
brevis muscle

Peroneus
longus muscle

EXTERNAL FEATURES OF FOOT

Toenail

Hallux
(big toe)

Interphalangeal
joint

Extensor hallucis
longus tendon

Extensor digitorum
longus tendon

Medial malleolus

2nd toe

3rd toe

4th toe

5th
(little) toe

Lateral malleolus

233

Skin and hair

SKIN IS THE BODY'S LARGEST ORGAN, a waterproof barrier that protects the internal organs against infection, injury, and harmful sun rays. The skin is also an important sensory organ and helps to control body temperature. The outer layer of the skin, known as the epidermis, is coated with keratin, a tough, horny protein that is also the chief constituent of hair and nails. Dead cells are shed from the skin's surface and are replaced by new cells from the base of the epidermis, the region that also produces the skin pigment, melanin. The dermis contains most of the skin's living structures, and includes nerve endings, blood vessels, elastic fibres, sweat glands that cool the skin, and sebaceous glands that produce oil to keep the skin supple. Beneath the dermis lies the subcutaneous tissue (hypodermis), which is rich in fat and blood vessels. Hair shafts grow from hair follicles situated in the dermis and subcutaneous tissue. Hair grows on every part of the skin apart from the palms of the hands and soles of the feet.

SECTION OF HAIR

Medulla

Cortex

Melanin granule

Cell nucleus residue

Macrofibril

Cuticle

SECTIONS OF DIFFERENT TYPES OF SKIN

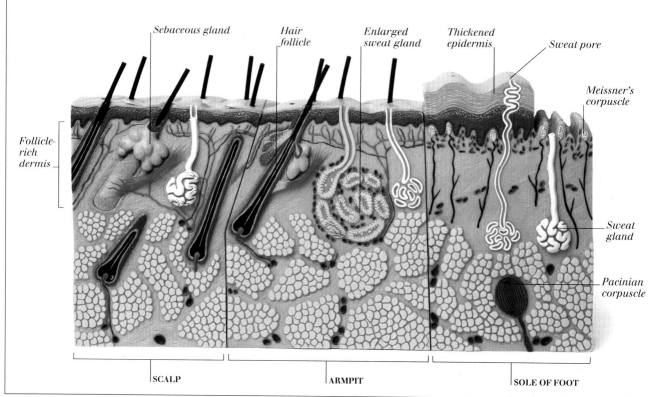

Sebaceous gland

Hair follicle

Enlarged sweat gland

Thickened epidermis

Sweat pore

Meissner's corpuscle

Follicle-rich dermis

Sweat gland

Pacinian corpuscle

SCALP

ARMPIT

SOLE OF FOOT

SECTION OF SKIN

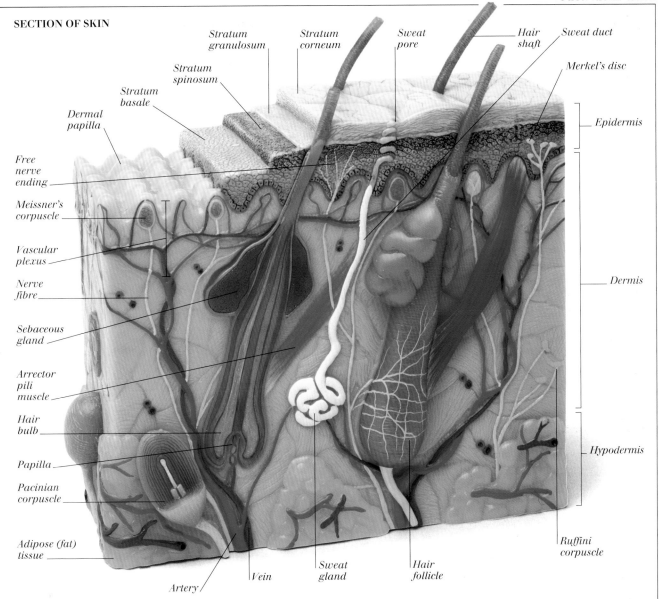

Stratum granulosum
Stratum corneum
Sweat pore
Hair shaft
Sweat duct
Stratum spinosum
Stratum basale
Merkel's disc
Dermal papilla
Free nerve ending
Epidermis
Meissner's corpuscle
Vascular plexus
Nerve fibre
Sebaceous gland
Dermis
Arrector pili muscle
Hair bulb
Papilla
Pacinian corpuscle
Adipose (fat) tissue
Hypodermis
Ruffini corpuscle
Artery
Vein
Sweat gland
Hair follicle

PHOTOMICROGRAPHS OF SKIN AND HAIR

SECTION OF SKIN
The flaky cells at the skin's surface are shed continuously.

SWEAT PORE
This allows loss of fluid as part of temperature control.

SKIN HAIR
Two hairs pushing through the outer layer of skin.

HEAD HAIR
The root and part of the shaft of a hair from the scalp.

Brain

THE BRAIN IS THE MAJOR ORGAN of the central nervous system and the control centre for all the body's voluntary and involuntary activities. It is also responsible for the complexities of thought, memory, emotion, and language. In adults, this complex organ is a mere 1.4 kg (3 lb) in weight, containing over 10 thousand million nerve cells. Three distinct regions can easily be seen – the brainstem, the cerebellum, and the large cerebrum. The brainstem controls vital body functions, such as breathing and digestion. The cerebellum's main functions are the maintenance of posture and the coordination of body movements. The cerebrum, which consists of the right and left cerebral hemispheres joined by the corpus callosum, is the site of most conscious and intelligent activities.

MRI SCAN OF TRANSVERSE SECTION THROUGH BRAIN

White matter

Grey matter

Skull

Scalp

Longitudinal fissure

Lateral ventricle

Coronal section

Sagittal section

SAGITTAL SECTION THROUGH BRAIN

Central sulcus

Fornix

Cerebrum

Parietal lobe

Parieto-occipital sulcus

Corpus callosum

Thalamus

Pineal body

Occipital lobe

Frontal lobe

Aqueduct

Hypothalamus

Cerebellum

Optic chiasma

4th ventricle

Pituitary gland

Mesencephalon (midbrain)

Spinal cord

Pons

Brainstem

Medulla oblongata

SECTION THROUGH SKULL AND BRAIN

Scalp

Epicranial
aponeurosis

Arachnoid
granulation

Pericranium

Skull

Lateral
lacuna

Dura mater

Arachnoid
mater

Superior
sagittal
sinus

Pia mater

Falx
cerebri

Subarachnoid
space

Cerebrum { Grey matter / White matter }

Cerebral
vessel

EXTERNAL ANATOMY OF BRAIN

Parietal lobe

Parieto-occipital
sulcus

Precentral gyrus

Postcentral gyrus

Central sulcus

Frontal lobe

Lateral sulcus

Occipital
lobe

Temporal lobe

Cerebellum

SPECIFIC ROLES OF AREAS OF CEREBRUM

Skilled
movements

Basic
movements

Sensation

Visual
recognition

Behaviour and
emotion

Speech

Vision

Hearing

Balance
and muscle
coordination

CORONAL SECTION THROUGH BRAIN

Corpus
callosum

Longitudinal
fissure

Grey matter

White matter
} Cerebrum

Caudate
nucleus

Lateral
ventricle

Fornix

Lentiform
nucleus

Internal
capsule

Thalamus

Crus
cerebri of
midbrain

3rd
ventricle

Pons

Medulla oblongata

Cerebellum

NERVE CELLS IN BRAIN

The dark cells are Purkinje's
cells, which are among the
largest nerve cells in the body.

Nervous system

THE NERVOUS SYSTEM IS THE BODY'S internal, electrochemical, communications network. Its main parts are the brain, spinal cord, and nerves. The brain and spinal cord form the central nervous system (CNS), the body's chief controlling and coordinating centres. Billions of long neurons, many grouped as nerves, make up the peripheral nervous system, transmitting nerve impulses between the CNS and other regions of the body. Each neuron has three parts: a cell body, branching dendrites that receive chemical signals from other neurons, and a tube-like axon that conveys these signals as electrical impulses.

CENTRAL AND PERIPHERAL NERVOUS SYSTEMS

Cranial nerves

Cerebrum

Cerebellum

Cervical nerves

Brachial plexus

Spinal cord

Thoracic nerves

Radial nerve

Median nerve

Ulnar nerve

Lumbar nerves

Sacral nerves

Sacral plexus

Femoral nerve

Pudendal nerve

Sciatic nerve

Cutaneous nerve

Common peroneal nerve

Posterior tibial nerve

Superficial peroneal nerve

Deep peroneal nerve

SECTION THROUGH SPINAL CORD

Spinal ganglion

Grey matter

Central canal

Posterior root of spinal nerve

Spinal nerve

White matter

Anterior median fissure

Anterior root of spinal nerve

STRUCTURE OF A MOTOR NEURON

Cell body
Nucleus
Synaptic knob
Axon hillock
Axon
Dendrite
Nucleolus
Nissl body

Schwann cell
Node of Ranvier
Mitochondrion
Myelin sheath

STRUCTURE OF A SYNAPTIC KNOB

Presynaptic axon
Microtubule
Neurofilament
Endoplasmic reticulum
Mitochondrion
Synaptic vesicle
Neurotransmitter
Presynaptic membrane

TYPES OF NEURON

MULTIPOLAR
Motor end plate
Node of Ranvier
Schwann cell
Myelin sheath
Axon
Nucleus
Cell body
Dendrite

UNIPOLAR
Dendrite
Axon
Cell body
Nucleus
Receptor

BIPOLAR
Dendrite
Axon
Cell body
Nucleus
Dendrite

TYPES OF NERVE ENDING

FREE NERVE ENDING

MEISSNER'S CORPUSCLE

MERKEL'S DISC

RUFFINI CORPUSCLE

PACINIAN CORPUSCLE

Eye

THE EYE IS THE ORGAN OF SIGHT. The two eyeballs, protected within bony sockets called orbits and on the outside by the eyelids, eyebrows, and tear film, are directly connected to the brain by the optic nerves. Each eye is moved by six muscles, which are attached around the eyeball. Light rays entering the eye through the pupil are focused by the cornea and lens to form an image on the retina. The retina contains millions of light-sensitive cells, called rods and cones, which convert the image into a pattern of nerve impulses. These impulses are transmitted along the optic nerve to the brain. Information from the two optic nerves is processed in the brain to produce a single coordinated image.

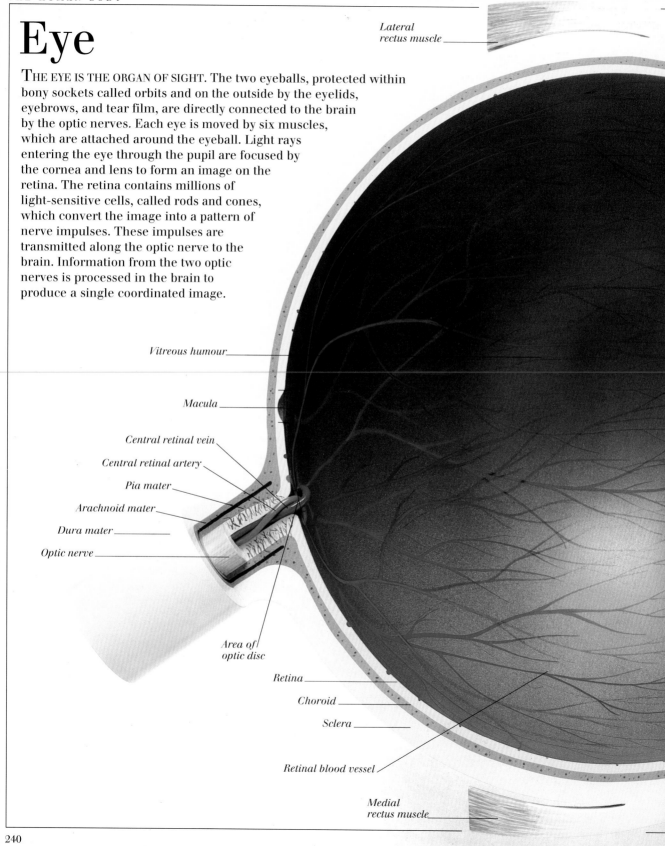

Lateral rectus muscle

Vitreous humour

Macula

Central retinal vein

Central retinal artery

Pia mater

Arachnoid mater

Dura mater

Optic nerve

Area of optic disc

Retina

Choroid

Sclera

Retinal blood vessel

Medial rectus muscle

SECTION THROUGH LEFT EYE

Iris

Anterior chamber
Posterior chamber
} Aqueous humour

Conjunctiva

Pupil

Cornea

Lens

Sphincter muscle

Dilator muscle

Zonular ligament

Sinus venosus sclerae

Iridocorneal angle

Ciliary body

Ora serrata

LACRIMAL (TEAR-PRODUCING) APPARATUS

Lacrimal sac

Lacrimal canaliculus

Lacrimal gland

Middle meatus

Middle nasal concha

Nasal septum

Inferior nasal concha

Nasolacrimal duct

Lacrimal punctum

OPHTHALMOSCOPIC VIEW OF RETINA

Retinal blood vessel

Optic disc

Macula

The blind spot, where the optic nerve leaves the eye, can be clearly seen as a light circular area towards the centre of the image.

MUSCLES SURROUNDING RIGHT EYE

Medial rectus

Superior oblique

Levator palpebrae superioris

Trochlea

Superior rectus

Annular tendon

Inferior rectus

Lateral rectus

Inferior oblique

Ear

THE EAR IS THE ORGAN OF HEARING AND BALANCE. The outer ear consists of a flap called the auricle or pinna and the auditory canal. The main functional parts – the middle and inner ears – are enclosed within the skull. The middle ear consists of three tiny bones, known as auditory ossicles, and the eustachian tube, which links the ear to the back of the nose. The inner ear consists of the spiral-shaped cochlea, and also the semicircular canals and the vestibule, which are the organs of balance. Sound waves entering the ear travel through the auditory canal to the tympanic membrane (eardrum), where they are converted to vibrations that are transmitted via the ossicles to the cochlea. Here, the vibrations are converted by millions of microscopic hairs into electrical nerve signals to be interpreted by the brain.

RIGHT AURICLE (PINNA)

Upper crux of antihelix

Auricle (pinna)

Triangular fossa

Scaphoid fossa

Lower crux of antihelix

Helix

Concha

Antihelix

Auditory canal

Antitragus

Tragus

Intertragic notch

External auditory meatus

Cartilaginous part of meatus

Lobule

Lobule

Temporal bone

Cartilage of auricle

Mastoid process

OSSICLES OF MIDDLE EAR

MALLEUS (HAMMER)   INCUS (ANVIL)   STAPES (STIRRUP)

These three tiny bones connect to form a bridge between the tympanic membrane and the oval window. With a system of membranes they convey sound vibrations to the inner ear.

INTERNAL STRUCTURE OF AMPULLA

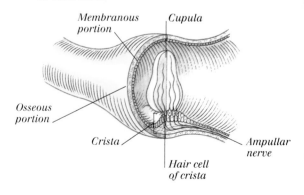

Membranous portion

Cupula

Osseous portion

Crista

Hair cell of crista

Ampullar nerve

LABYRINTH

Osseous (bony)
part of meatus

Tympanic membrane
(eardrum)

Semicircular canal

Vestibulocochlear
nerve

Cochlea

Tensor
tympani muscle

Internal
carotid artery

Eustachian
tube

Styloid process

Utricle

Saccule

Common crus

Anterior
semicircular
canal

Lateral
semicircular
canal

Ampulla

Vestibular
nerve

Tympanic
canal

Median
canal

Vestibular
canal

Cochlea

Cochlear nerve

Oval window

Posterior semicircular
canal

SECTION THROUGH COCHLEA

Organ
of Corti

Median
canal

Vestibular canal

Vestibular
membrane

Spiral
ganglion

Cochlear
nerve

Tympanic canal

Hair cells

Basilar
membrane

Nose, mouth, and throat

WITH EVERY BREATH, air passes through the nasal cavity down the pharynx (throat), larynx ("voice box"), and trachea (windpipe) to the lungs. The nasal cavity warms and moistens air, and the tiny layers in its lining protect the airway against damage by foreign bodies. During swallowing, the tongue moves up and back, the larynx rises, the epiglottis closes off the entrance to the trachea, and the soft palate separates the nasal cavity from the pharynx. Saliva, secreted from three pairs of salivary glands, lubricates food to make swallowing easier; it also begins the chemical breakdown of food, and helps to produce taste. The senses of taste and smell are closely linked. Both depend on the detection of dissolved molecules by sensory receptors in the olfactory nerve endings of the nose and in the taste buds of the tongue.

STRUCTURE OF TONGUE

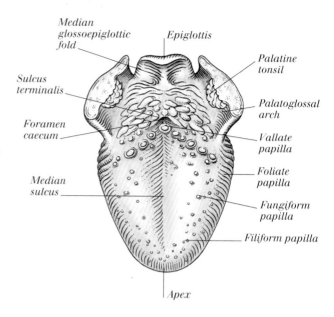

Median glossoepiglottic fold
Epiglottis
Palatine tonsil
Sulcus terminalis
Palatoglossal arch
Foramen caecum
Vallate papilla
Foliate papilla
Median sulcus
Fungiform papilla
Filiform papilla
Apex

TASTE AREAS ON TONGUE

Bitter
Sour
Salt
Sweet

STRUCTURES SURROUNDING PHARYNX

Lingual nerve
Tongue
Styloglossus muscle
Hyoglossus muscle
Sublingual gland
Hypoglossal nerve
Mandible (lower jaw)
Superior laryngeal nerve
Submandibular gland
Superior thyroid artery
Hyoid bone
Laryngeal prominence (Adam's apple)
Thyrohyoid muscle
Thyrohyoid membrane
Cricothyroid muscle
Cricothyroid ligament
Thyroid gland
Trachea

TYPES OF PAPILLAE

FILIFORM PAPILLAE   FUNGIFORM PAPILLAE   VALLATE PAPILLAE

SECTION THROUGH NOSE, MOUTH, AND THROAT

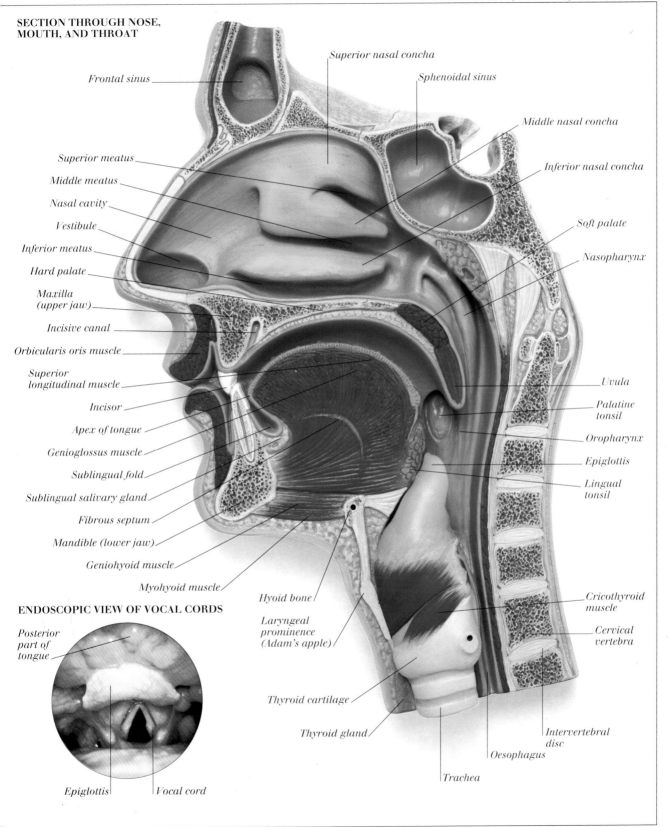

Frontal sinus

Superior nasal concha

Sphenoidal sinus

Middle nasal concha

Inferior nasal concha

Superior meatus

Middle meatus

Nasal cavity

Vestibule

Inferior meatus

Hard palate

Maxilla (upper jaw)

Incisive canal

Orbicularis oris muscle

Superior longitudinal muscle

Incisor

Apex of tongue

Genioglossus muscle

Sublingual fold

Sublingual salivary gland

Fibrous septum

Mandible (lower jaw)

Geniohyoid muscle

Myohyoid muscle

Soft palate

Nasopharynx

Uvula

Palatine tonsil

Oropharynx

Epiglottis

Lingual tonsil

Cricothyroid muscle

Cervical vertebra

Hyoid bone

Laryngeal prominence (Adam's apple)

Thyroid cartilage

Thyroid gland

Trachea

Oesophagus

Intervertebral disc

ENDOSCOPIC VIEW OF VOCAL CORDS

Posterior part of tongue

Epiglottis

Vocal cord

Teeth

THE 20 PRIMARY TEETH (also called deciduous or milk teeth) usually begin to erupt when a baby is about six months old. They start to be replaced by the permanent teeth when the child is about six years old. By the age of 20, most adults have a full set of 32 teeth although the third molars (commonly called wisdom teeth) may never erupt. While teeth help people to speak clearly and give shape to the face, their main function is the chewing of food. Incisors and canines shear and tear the food into pieces; premolars and molars crush and grind it further. Although tooth enamel is the hardest substance in the body, it tends to be eroded and destroyed by acid produced in the mouth during the breakdown of food.

DEVELOPMENT OF TEETH IN A FETUS

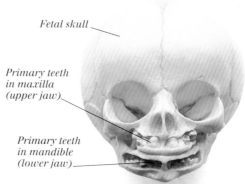

Fetal skull

Primary teeth in maxilla (upper jaw)

Primary teeth in mandible (lower jaw)

FETAL JAWS
By the sixth week of embryonic development areas of thickening occur in each jaw; these areas give rise to tooth buds. By the time the fetus is six months old, enamel has formed on the tooth buds.

DEVELOPMENT OF JAW AND TEETH

Maxilla (upper jaw)

Mandible (lower jaw)

A NEWBORN BABY'S JAWS
The primary teeth can be seen developing in the jaw bones; they begin to erupt around the age of six months.

A FIVE-YEAR-OLD CHILD'S TEETH
There is a full set of 20 erupted primary teeth; the permanent teeth can be seen developing in the upper and lower jaws.

A NINE-YEAR-OLD CHILD'S TEETH
Most of the teeth are primary teeth but the permanent incisors and first molars have now emerged.

AN ADULT'S TEETH
By the age of 20, the full set of 32 permanent teeth (including the wisdom teeth) should be in position.

THE PERMANENT TEETH

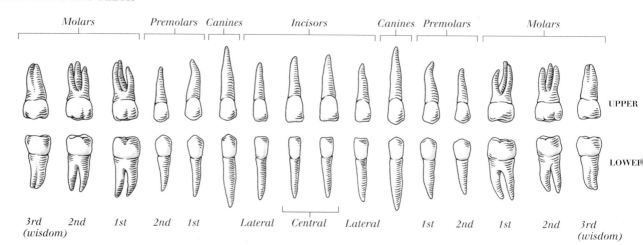

Molars *Premolars* *Canines* *Incisors* *Canines* *Premolars* *Molars*

UPPER

LOWER

3rd (wisdom) *2nd* *1st* *2nd* *1st* *Lateral* *Central* *Lateral* *1st* *2nd* *1st* *2nd* *3rd (wisdom)*

STRUCTURE OF A TOOTH

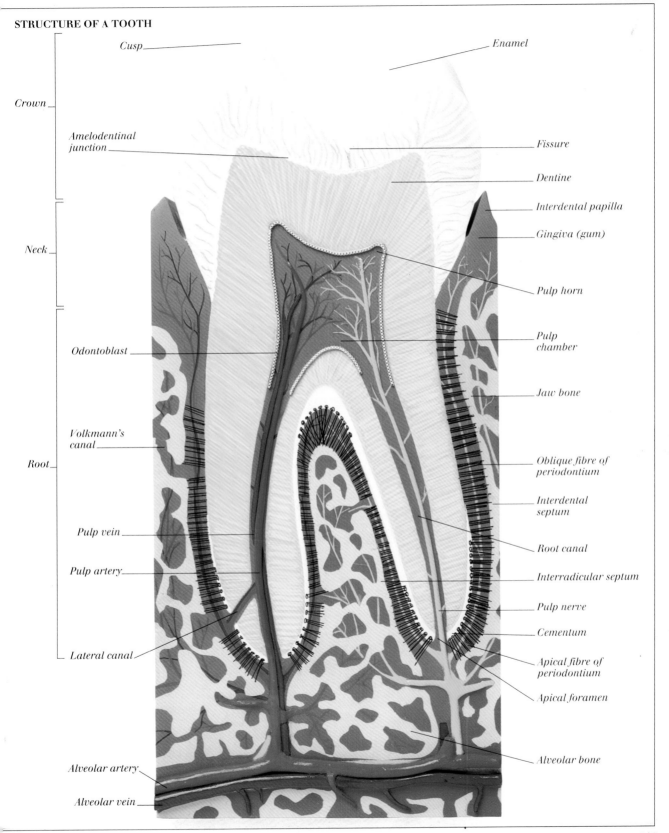

Cusp

Enamel

Crown

Ameloclentinal junction

Fissure

Dentine

Interdental papilla

Gingiva (gum)

Neck

Pulp horn

Odontoblast

Pulp chamber

Jaw bone

Volkmann's canal

Oblique fibre of periodontium

Root

Interdental septum

Pulp vein

Root canal

Pulp artery

Interradicular septum

Pulp nerve

Cementum

Lateral canal

Apical fibre of periodontium

Apical foramen

Alveolar bone

Alveolar artery

Alveolar vein

Digestive system

THE DIGESTIVE SYSTEM BREAKS DOWN FOOD into particles so tiny that blood can take nourishment to all parts of the body. The system's main part is a 9 m (30 ft) tube from mouth to rectum; muscles in this alimentary canal force food along. Chewed food first travels through the oesophagus to the stomach, which churns and liquidizes food before it passes through the duodenum, jejunum, and ileum – the three parts of the long, convoluted small intestine. Here, digestive juices from the gallbladder and pancreas break down food particles; many filter out into the blood through tiny fingerlike villi that line the small intestine's inner wall. Undigested food in the colon forms faeces that leave the body through the anus.

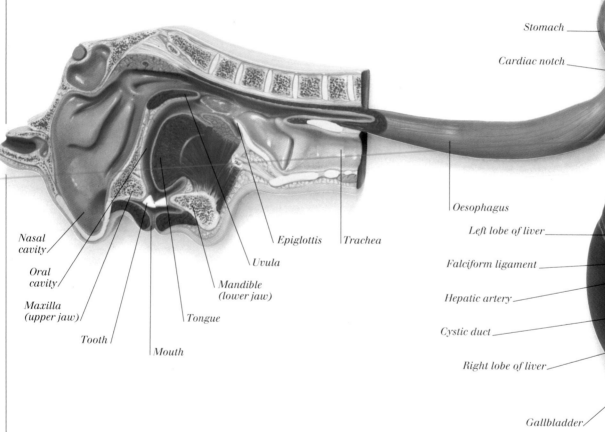

Stomach

Cardiac notch

Nasal cavity

Oral cavity

Maxilla (upper jaw)

Tooth

Mouth

Tongue

Mandible (lower jaw)

Uvula

Epiglottis

Trachea

Oesophagus

Left lobe of liver

Falciform ligament

Hepatic artery

Cystic duct

Right lobe of liver

Gallbladder

ENDOSCOPIC VIEWS INSIDE ALIMENTARY CANAL

OESOPHAGUS

Mucosa

STOMACH ENTRANCE

Cardiac orifice

STOMACH

Ruga

STOMACH EXIT

Pylorus

ALIMENTARY CANAL

Fold of mucous membrane

Angular notch

Spleen

Pancreas

Peritoneum

Transverse colon

Taenia colica

Descending colon

Small intestine (jejunum and ileum)

Haustration of colon

Sigmoid colon

Anal sphincter muscle

Rectum

Anal canal

Anus

Terminal ileum

Appendix

Appendix orifice

Caecum

Ileocaecal fold

Semilunar fold

Ascending colon

Duodenum

Bile duct

Plica circulare

Pyloric sphincter muscle

DUODENUM

Plica circulare

ILEUM

Villi of mucosa

COLON

Semilunar fold

Blood vessel

RECTUM

Mucosa

Heart

THE HEART IS A HOLLOW MUSCLE in the middle of the chest that pumps blood around the body, supplying cells with oxygen and nutrients. A muscular wall, called the septum, divides the heart lengthways into left and right sides. A valve divides each side into two chambers: an upper atrium and a lower ventricle. When the heart muscle contracts, it squeezes blood through the atria and then through the ventricles. Oxygenated blood from the lungs flows from the pulmonary veins into the left atrium, through the left ventricle, and then out via the aorta to all parts of the body. Deoxygenated blood returning from the body flows from the vena cava into the right atrium, through the right ventricle, and then out via the pulmonary artery to the lungs for reoxygenation. At rest the heart beats between 60 and 80 times a minute; during exercise or at times of stress or excitement the rate may increase to 200 beats a minute.

ARTERIES AND VEINS SURROUNDING HEART

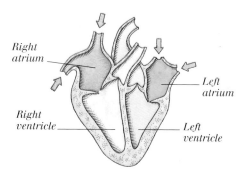

Aorta

Left coronary artery

Cardiac vein

Right coronary artery

Coronary sinus

Main branch of left coronary artery

SECTION THROUGH HEART WALL

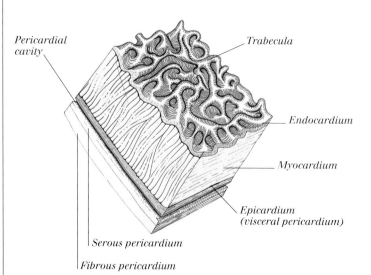

Pericardial cavity

Trabecula

Endocardium

Myocardium

Epicardium (visceral pericardium)

Serous pericardium

Fibrous pericardium

HEARTBEAT SEQUENCE

ATRIAL DIASTOLE

Right atrium

Left atrium

Right ventricle

Left ventricle

Deoxygenated blood enters the right atrium while the left atrium receives oxygenated blood.

STRUCTURE OF HEART

Brachiocephalic trunk

Left subclavian artery

Left common carotid artery

Superior vena cava

Ascending aorta

Right pulmonary artery

Left pulmonary vein

Pulmonary trunk

Fossa ovalis

Pulmonary semilunar valve

Coronary artery

Right pulmonary vein

Right atrium

Chordae tendineae

Opening of inferior vena cava

Muscular part of interventricular septum

Branch of coronary artery

Left ventricle

Tricuspid valve

Papillary muscle

Chordae tendineae

Myocardium of left ventricle

Right ventricle

Trabecula

ATRIAL SYSTOLE (VENTRICULAR DIASTOLE)

Right atrium contracts

Left atrium contracts

Tricuspid valve opens

Mitral valve opens

Right ventricle dilates

Left ventricle dilates

Left and right atria contract, forcing blood into the relaxed ventricles.

VENTRICULAR SYSTOLE

Pulmonary artery

Aorta

Pulmonary valve opens

Aortic valve opens

Tricuspid valve closes

Mitral valve closes

Right ventricle contracts

Left ventricle contracts

Ventricles contract and force blood to the lungs for oxygenation and via the aorta to the rest of the body.

Circulatory system

THE CIRCULATORY SYSTEM consists of the heart and blood vessels, which together maintain a continuous flow of blood around the body. The heart pumps oxygen-rich blood from the lungs to all parts of the body through a network of tubes called arteries, and smaller branches called arterioles. Blood returns to the heart via small vessels called venules, which lead in turn into larger tubes called veins. Arterioles and venules are linked by a network of tiny vessels called capillaries, where the exchange of oxygen and carbon dioxide between blood and body cells takes place. Blood has four main components: red blood cells, white blood cells, platelets, and liquid plasma.

ARTERIAL SYSTEM OF BRAIN

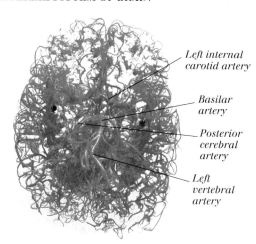

Left internal carotid artery

Basilar artery

Posterior cerebral artery

Left vertebral artery

CIRCULATORY SYSTEM OF HEART AND LUNGS

Superior vena cava

Aorta

Right ventricle

Left ventricle

CIRCULATORY SYSTEM OF LIVER

Inferior vena cava

Portal vein

Common bile duct

Hepatic artery

Gallbladder

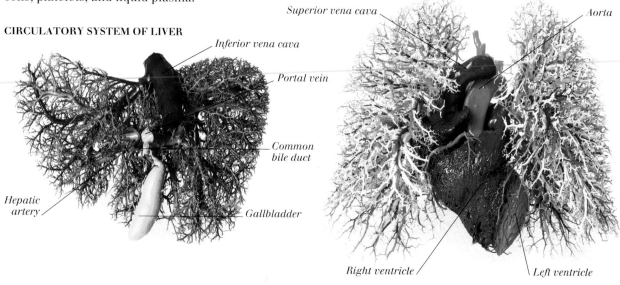

SECTION OF MAIN ARTERY

Tunica media

Collagen and elastic fibres

External elastic lamina

Tunica adventitia

Internal elastic lamina

Tunica intima

Endothelium

Arteriole

SECTION OF MAIN VEIN

Tunica media

Collagen and elastic fibres

External elastic lamina

Tunica adventitia

Valve cusp

Internal elastic lamina

Tunica intima

Endothelium

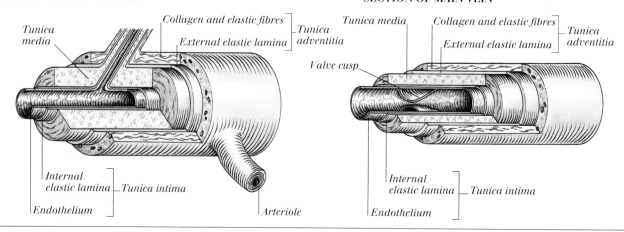

PRINCIPAL ARTERIES AND VEINS OF CIRCULATORY SYSTEM

Common carotid artery

Subclavian artery

Arch of aorta

Axillary artery

Pulmonary artery

Coronary artery

Brachial artery

Gastric artery

Hepatic artery

Splenic artery

Superior mesenteric artery

Radial artery

Ulnar artery

Palmar arch

Digital artery

Common iliac artery

External iliac artery

Internal iliac artery

Femoral artery

Popliteal artery

Peroneal artery

Anterior tibial artery

Posterior tibial artery

Lateral plantar artery

Dorsal metatarsal artery

Internal jugular vein

Brachiocephalic vein

Subclavian vein

Axillary vein

Cephalic vein

Superior vena cava

Pulmonary vein

Basilic vein

Hepatic portal vein

Median cubital vein

Inferior vena cava

Anterior median vein

Gastroepiploic vein

Palmar vein

Digital vein

Inferior mesenteric vein

Superior mesenteric vein

Common iliac vein

External iliac vein

Internal iliac vein

Femoral vein

Great saphenous vein

Short saphenous vein

Dorsal venous arch

Digital vein

TYPES OF BLOOD CELLS

RED BLOOD CELLS
These cells are biconcave in shape to maximize their oxygen-carrying capacity.

WHITE BLOOD CELLS
Lymphocytes are the smallest white blood cells; they form antibodies against disease.

PLATELETS
Tiny cells that are activated whenever blood clotting or repair to vessels is necessary.

BLOOD CLOTTING

Filaments of fibrin enmesh red blood cells as part of the process of blood clotting.

Respiratory system

THE RESPIRATORY SYSTEM supplies the oxygen needed by body cells and carries off their carbon dioxide waste. Inhaled air passes via the trachea (windpipe) through two narrower tubes, the bronchi, to the lungs. Each lung comprises many fine, branching tubes called bronchioles that end in tiny clustered chambers called alveoli. Gases cross the thin alveolar walls to and from a network of tiny blood vessels. Intercostal (rib) muscles and the muscular diaphragm below the lungs operate the lungs like bellows, drawing air in and forcing it out at regular intervals.

BRONCHIOLE AND ALVEOLI

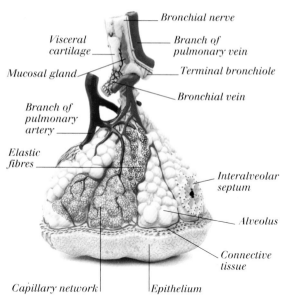

Bronchial nerve

Visceral cartilage

Branch of pulmonary vein

Mucosal gland

Terminal bronchiole

Bronchial vein

Branch of pulmonary artery

Elastic fibres

Interalveolar septum

Alveolus

Connective tissue

Capillary network

Epithelium

SEGMENTS OF BRONCHIAL TREE

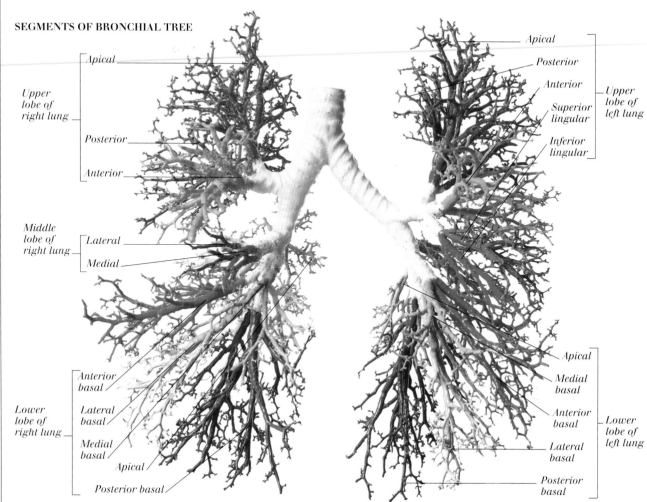

Apical

Apical

Posterior

Upper lobe of right lung

Anterior

Upper lobe of left lung

Superior lingular

Posterior

Inferior lingular

Anterior

Middle lobe of right lung

Lateral

Medial

Anterior basal

Apical

Medial basal

Lateral basal

Lower lobe of right lung

Anterior basal

Medial basal

Lower lobe of left lung

Apical

Lateral basal

Posterior basal

Posterior basal

STRUCTURES OF THORACIC CAVITY

Epiglottis

Hyoid bone

Thyroid cartilage

Thyroid gland

Cricoid cartilage

Apex of lung

Trachea

Superior vena cava

Aorta

Upper lobe of right lung

Upper lobe of left lung

Horizontal fissure

Pulmonary trunk

Oblique fissure

Left pulmonary artery

Heart

Lower lobe of left lung

Secondary bronchus

Tertiary bronchus

Lower lobe of right lung

Middle lobe of right lung

Right crus of diaphragm

Abdominal aorta

Left crus of diaphragm

Oesophagus

Muscular wall of diaphragm

GASEOUS EXCHANGE IN ALVEOLUS

Oxygen diffuses into blood

Oxygenated blood

Alveolus

Deoxygenated blood rich in carbon dioxide

Carbon dioxide diffuses from blood into alveolus

MECHANISM OF RESPIRATION
INSPIRATION

Lung expands

Air drawn into lungs

Diaphragm contracts and flattens

Intercostal muscles contract

EXPIRATION

Lung contracts

Air forced out of lungs

Diaphragm relaxes and moves up

Intercostal muscles relax

Urinary system

THE URINARY SYSTEM FILTERS WASTE PRODUCTS from the blood and removes them from the body via a system of tubes. Blood is filtered in the two kidneys, which are fist-sized, bean-shaped organs. The renal arteries carry blood to the kidneys; the renal veins remove blood after filtering. Each kidney contains about one million tiny units called nephrons. Each nephron is made up of a tubule and a filtering unit called a glomerulus, which consists of a collection of tiny blood vessels surrounded by the hollow Bowman's capsule. The filtering process produces a watery fluid that leaves the kidney as urine. The urine is carried via two tubes called ureters to the bladder, where it is stored until its release from the body through another tube called the urethra.

ARTERIAL SYSTEM OF KIDNEYS

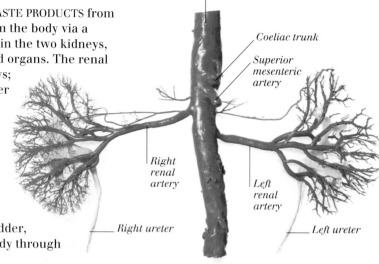

Aorta

Coeliac trunk

Superior mesenteric artery

Right renal artery

Left renal artery

Right ureter

Left ureter

SECTION THROUGH LEFT KIDNEY

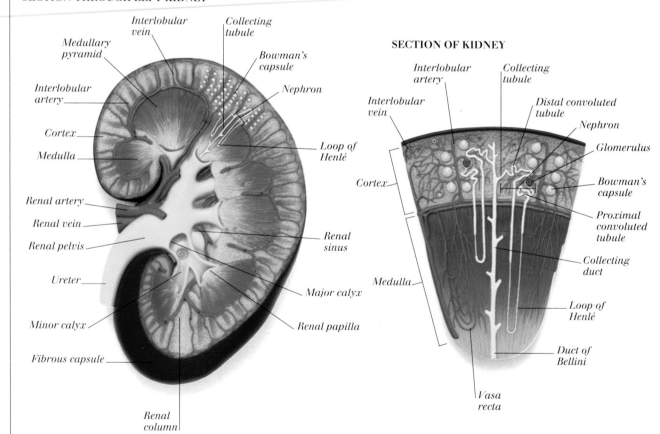

Interlobular vein

Medullary pyramid

Collecting tubule

Bowman's capsule

Nephron

Interlobular artery

Cortex

Medulla

Loop of Henlé

Renal artery

Renal vein

Renal pelvis

Renal sinus

Ureter

Minor calyx

Major calyx

Fibrous capsule

Renal papilla

Renal column

SECTION OF KIDNEY

Interlobular artery

Collecting tubule

Interlobular vein

Distal convoluted tubule

Nephron

Cortex

Glomerulus

Bowman's capsule

Proximal convoluted tubule

Medulla

Collecting duct

Loop of Henlé

Duct of Bellini

Vasa recta

256

MALE URINARY TRACT

Superior mesenteric artery

Coeliac trunk

Left adrenal (suprarenal) gland

Right adrenal (suprarenal) gland

Inferior vena cava

Renal artery

Renal vein

Right kidney

Aorta

Right ureter

Left suprarenal vein

Left renal artery

Left renal vein

Left kidney

Left ureter

Vertebral column

Psoas muscle

Left common iliac artery

Left common iliac vein

Testicular vein and artery

Bladder

Superior pubic ramus

SECTION THROUGH BOWMAN'S CAPSULE

Distal convoluted tubule

Efferent arteriole

Afferent arteriole

Basement membrane of Bowman's capsule

Bowman's space

Bowman's capsule

Glomerulus

Proximal convoluted tubule

SECTION THROUGH MALE BLADDER

Right ureter

Peritoneum

Urachus

Left ureter

Transitional cell mucosa

Right ureteric orifice

Internal urethral orifice

Prostate gland

Muscle layer

Left ureteric orifice

Trigone

Internal urethral sphincter muscle

Urethra

257

Reproductive system

SEX ORGANS LOCATED IN THE PELVIS create new human lives. Each month a ripe egg is released from one of the female's ovaries into a fallopian tube leading to the uterus (womb), a muscular pear-sized organ. A male produces minute tadpole-like sperm in two oval glands called testes. When the male is ready to release sperm into the female's vagina, many millions pass into his urethra and leave his body through the fleshy penis. The sperm travel up through the vagina into the uterus and fallopian tubes, and one sperm may enter and fertilize an egg. The fertilized egg becomes embedded in the uterus wall and starts to grow into a new human being.

SECTION THROUGH OVARY

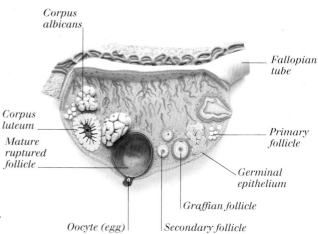

Corpus albicans

Corpus luteum

Mature ruptured follicle

Oocyte (egg)

Fallopian tube

Primary follicle

Germinal epithelium

Graffian follicle

Secondary follicle

SECTION THROUGH FEMALE PELVIC REGION

Ovary

Fundus of uterus

Uterus (womb)

Cervix (neck of uterus)

Os

Rectum

Vagina

Anus

Perineum

Introitus (vaginal opening)

Ureter

Ampulla of fallopian tube

Fimbria of fallopian tube

Isthmus of fallopian tube

Bladder

Pubic symphysis

Urethra

Clitoris

External urinary meatus

Labia minora

Labia majora

FEMALE REPRODUCTIVE ORGANS

Fallopian tube

Fundus of uterus

Isthmus of fallopian tube

Ovarian ligament

Ampulla of fallopian tube

Ovary

Body of uterus (womb)

Os

Fimbria of fallopian tube

Vagina

Cervix (neck of uterus)

MALE REPRODUCTIVE ORGANS

External spermatic fascia

Prostate gland

Ductus (vas) deferens

Seminal vesicle

Cremasteric fascia

Bulbourethral gland

Internal spermatic fascia

Urethra

Epididymis

Corpus spongiosum

Testis (testicle)

Corpus cavernosum

Scrotum

Prepuce (foreskin)

Glans penis

Urethral opening

SECTION THROUGH MALE PELVIC REGION

Intervertebral disc

Ureter

EXTERNAL STRUCTURE OF SPERM

Acrosomal cap

Head

Mitochondrial sheath

Terminal ring

Tailpiece

Flagellum

Colon

Sacrum

Bladder

Pubis of pelvis

Prostate gland

Penis

Seminal vesicle

Corpus cavernosum

Corpus spongiosum

Ejaculatory duct

Urethra

Epididymis

Glans penis

Testis (testicle)

Scrotum

Development of a baby

A FERTILIZED EGG IS NOURISHED AND PROTECTED as it develops into an embryo and then a fetus during the 40 weeks of pregnancy. The placenta, a mass of blood vessels implanted in the uterus lining, delivers nourishment and oxygen, and removes waste through the umbilical cord. Meanwhile, the fetus lies snugly in its amniotic sac, a bag of fluid that protects it against any sudden jolts. In the last weeks of the pregnancy, the rapidly growing fetus turns head-down: a baby ready to be born.

EMBRYO AT FIVE WEEKS

Rudimentary ear

Rudimentary eye

Rudimentary mouth

Heart bulge

Arm bud

Rudimentary liver

Tail bud

Leg bud

Rudimentary vertebra

Amniotic fluid

Umbilicus (navel)

Uterine wall

Fetus

SECTION THROUGH PLACENTA

Umbilical cord

Umbilical vein

Umbilical artery

Fetal blood vessels

Amnion

Chorionic plate

Chorion

Trophoblast

Pool of maternal blood

Septum

Chorionic villus

Decidual plate

Maternal blood vessel

Myometrium

**SECTION THROUGH PELVIS IN
NINTH MONTH OF PREGNANCY**

THE DEVELOPING FETUS

Placenta

Uterine wall

*Fallopian
tube*

SECOND MONTH
All the internal
organs have
developed by
this stage.

Fetus

*Intervertebral
disc*

*Umbilical
cord*

THIRD MONTH
The fetus is
fully formed
and now
begins a
period of rapid
growth.

Vertebra

Spinal cord

FIFTH MONTH
Although the fetus
is here in breech
(bottom down)
position, it
will probably
turn by 180°
before birth. By
the fifth month
the baby is moving
actively and responds
to sound.

Cervix

SEVENTH MONTH
The internal organs
are maturing in
preparation for life
outside the uterus.
The baby has grown
to such a size that
there is less room
for movement
within the uterus.

Bladder

Cervix

Rectum

Anus

*Pubic
bone*

Placenta

Vagina

Urethra

GEOLOGY, GEOGRAPHY, AND METEOROLGY

EARTH'S PHYSICAL FEATURES	264
THE ROCK CYCLE	266
MINERALS	268
MINERAL FEATURES	270
VOLCANOES	272
IGNEOUS AND METAMORPHIC ROCKS	274
SEDIMENTARY ROCKS	276
FOSSILS	278
MINERAL RESOURCES	280
WEATHERING AND EROSION	282
CAVES	284
GLACIERS	286
RIVERS	288
RIVER FEATURES	290
LAKES AND GROUNDWATER	292
COASTLINES	294
OCEANS AND SEAS	296
THE OCEAN FLOOR	298
THE ATMOSPHERE	300
WEATHER	302

Earth's physical features

MOST OF THE EARTH'S SURFACE (about 70 per cent) is covered with water. The largest single body of water, the Pacific Ocean, alone covers about 30 per cent of the surface. Most of the land is distributed as seven continents; these are (from largest to smallest) Asia, Africa, North America, South America, Antarctica, Europe, and Australasia. The physical features of the land are remarkably varied. Among the most notable are mountain ranges, rivers, and deserts. The largest mountain ranges – the Himalayas in Asia and the Andes in South America – extend for thousands of kilometres. The Himalayas include the world's highest mountain, Mount Everest (8,848 metres). The longest rivers are the River Nile in Africa (6,695 kilometres) and the Amazon River in South America (6,437 kilometres). Deserts cover about 20 per cent of the total land area. The largest is the Sahara, which covers nearly a third of Africa. The Earth's surface features can be represented in various ways. Only a globe can correctly represent areas, shapes, sizes, and directions, because there is always distortion when a spherical surface – the Earth's, for example – is projected on to the flat surface of a map. Each map projection is therefore a compromise: it shows some features accurately but distorts others. Even satellite mapping does not produce completely accurate maps, although they can show physical features with great clarity.

EXAMPLES OF MAP PROJECTIONS

CYLINDRICAL PROJECTION

CYLINDRICAL-PROJECTION MAP

SATELLITE MAPPING OF THE EARTH

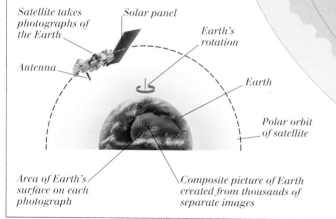

Satellite takes photographs of the Earth

Solar panel

Earth's rotation

Antenna

Earth

Polar orbit of satellite

Area of Earth's surface on each photograph

Composite picture of Earth created from thousands of separate images

180° 160° 120° 80°

Great Slave Lake

Great Bear Lake

Lake Superior

Mackenzie-Peace River

Greenland

Bering Sea

Hudson Bay

Baffin Island

NORTH AMERICA

Rocky Mountains

Sonoran Desert

Lake Huron
Lake Ontario
Lake Erie
Lake Michigan

Sierra Madre

Chihuahuan Desert

Appalachian Mountains

Gulf of Mexico

ATLANTIC OCEAN

Mississippi-Missouri River

Caribbean Sea

Guiana Highlands

Amazon River

Brazilian Highla

PACIFIC OCEAN

AMERICA

Andes

Atacama Desert

Gran Chaco

Parana River

Mato Grosse

Pampas

Patagonia

180° 160° 120° 80°

WEST OF GREENWICH MERIDIAN

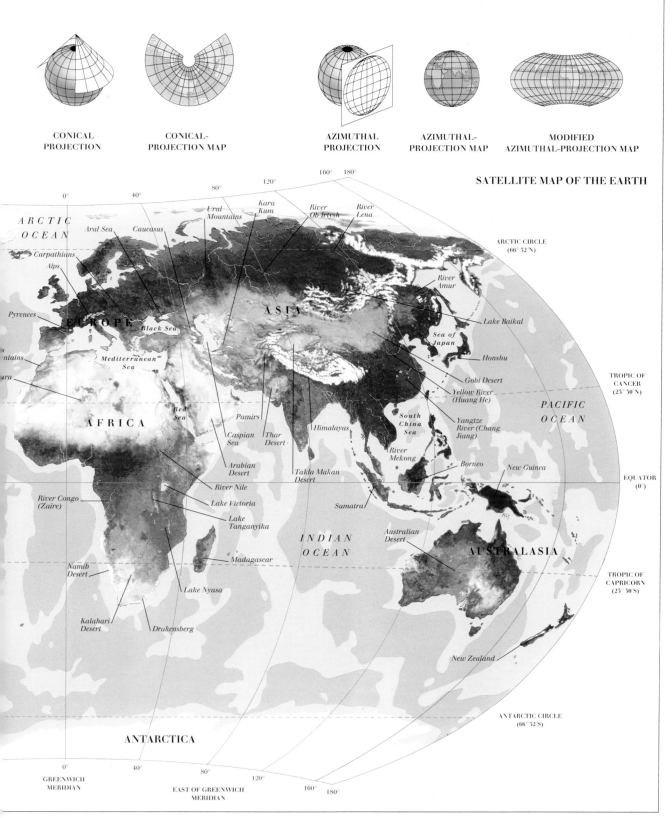

CONICAL
PROJECTION

CONICAL-
PROJECTION MAP

AZIMUTHAL
PROJECTION

AZIMUTHAL-
PROJECTION MAP

MODIFIED
AZIMUTHAL-PROJECTION MAP

SATELLITE MAP OF THE EARTH

160°   180°
120°
80°
40°
0°

*ARCTIC
OCEAN*

ARCTIC CIRCLE
(66° 32'N)

Carpathians
Alps

Aral Sea
Caucasus

Ural
Mountains

Kara
Kum

River
Ob-Irtysh

River
Lena

River
Amur

Pyrenees

EUROPE

Black Sea

A S I A

Lake Baikal

Sea of
Japan

Honshu

ntains

*Mediterranean
Sea*

Gobi Desert

Yellow River
(Huang He)

TROPIC OF
CANCER
(23° 30'N)

*PACIFIC
OCEAN*

ara

AFRICA

Red
Sea

Pamirs

Thar
Desert

Himalayas

South
China
Sea

Yangtze
River (Chang
Jiang)

Caspian
Sea

Arabian
Desert

River Nile

Takla Makan
Desert

River
Mekong

Borneo

New Guinea

EQUATOR
(0°)

*River Congo
(Zaire)*

Lake Victoria

Lake
Tanganyika

Sumatra

*INDIAN
OCEAN*

Australian
Desert

AUSTRALASIA

Madagascar

Namib
Desert

Lake Nyasa

TROPIC OF
CAPRICORN
(23° 30'S)

Kalahari
Desert

Drakensberg

New Zealand

ANTARCTIC CIRCLE
(66° 32'S)

ANTARCTICA

0°
40°
80°
120°
160°   180°

GREENWICH
MERIDIAN

EAST OF GREENWICH
MERIDIAN

The rock cycle

THE ROCK CYCLE IS A CONTINUOUS PROCESS through which old rocks are transformed into new ones. Rocks can be divided into three main groups: igneous, sedimentary, and metamorphic. Igneous rocks are formed when magma (molten rock) from the Earth's interior cools and solidifies (see pp. 274-275). Sedimentary rocks are formed when sediment (rock particles, for example) becomes compressed and cemented together in a process known as lithification (see pp. 276-277). Metamorphic rocks are formed when igneous, sedimentary, or other metamorphic rocks are changed by heat or pressure (see pp. 274-275). Rocks are added to the Earth's surface by crustal movements and volcanic activity. Once exposed on the surface, the rocks are broken down into rock particles by weathering (see pp. 282-283). The particles are then transported by glaciers, rivers, and wind, and deposited as sediment in lakes, deltas, deserts, and on the ocean floor. Some of this sediment undergoes lithification and forms sedimentary rock. This rock may be thrust back to the surface by crustal movements or forced deeper into the Earth's interior, where heat and pressure transform it into metamorphic rock. The metamorphic rock in turn may be pushed up to the surface or may be melted to form magma. Eventually, the magma cools and solidifies – below or on the surface – forming igneous rock. When the sedimentary, igneous, and metamorphic rocks are exposed once more on the Earth's surface, the cycle begins again.

HEXAGONAL BASALT
COLUMNS, ICELAND

THE ROCK CYCLE

Igneous
rock

Cooling and solidification (crystallization)

Weathering, transport,
and deposition

Sediment

Magma

Heat and pressure (metamorphism)

Weathering, transport, and deposition

Weathering, transport, and deposition

Compression and cementation (lithification)

Melting

Heat and pressure
(metamorphism)

Metamorphic
rock

Sedimentary
rock

STAGES IN THE ROCK CYCLE

*Magma extruded as lava,
which solidifies to form
igneous rock*

*Lava
flow*

Vent

Main
conduit

Secondary
conduit

Lava

Ash

*Rock surrounding
magma changed
by heat to form
metamorphic rock*

*Intense heat of rising
magma melts some of
the surrounding rock*

*Sedimentary rock
crushed and folded to
form metamorphic rock*

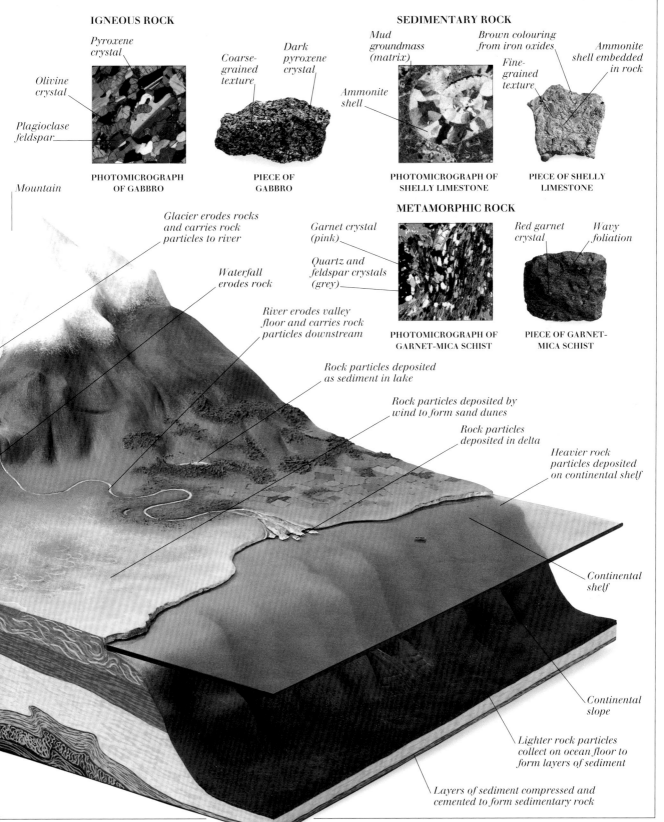

IGNEOUS ROCK

Pyroxene crystal

Olivine crystal

Plagioclase feldspar

Coarse-grained texture

Dark pyroxene crystal

PHOTOMICROGRAPH OF GABBRO

PIECE OF GABBRO

SEDIMENTARY ROCK

Mud groundmass (matrix)

Brown colouring from iron oxides

Ammonite shell embedded in rock

Ammonite shell

Fine-grained texture

PHOTOMICROGRAPH OF SHELLY LIMESTONE

PIECE OF SHELLY LIMESTONE

METAMORPHIC ROCK

Garnet crystal (pink)

Quartz and feldspar crystals (grey)

Red garnet crystal

Wavy foliation

PHOTOMICROGRAPH OF GARNET-MICA SCHIST

PIECE OF GARNET-MICA SCHIST

Mountain

Glacier erodes rocks and carries rock particles to river

Waterfall erodes rock

River erodes valley floor and carries rock particles downstream

Rock particles deposited as sediment in lake

Rock particles deposited by wind to form sand dunes

Rock particles deposited in delta

Heavier rock particles deposited on continental shelf

Continental shelf

Continental slope

Lighter rock particles collect on ocean floor to form layers of sediment

Layers of sediment compressed and cemented to form sedimentary rock

267

Minerals

A MINERAL IS A NATURALLY OCCURRING SUBSTANCE that has a characteristic chemical composition and specific physical properties, such as habit and streak (see pp. 270-271). A rock, by comparison, is an aggregate of minerals and need not have a specific chemical composition. Minerals are made up of elements (substances that cannot be broken down chemically into simpler substances), each of which can be represented by a chemical symbol. Minerals can be divided into two main groups: native elements and compounds. Native elements are made up of a pure element. Examples include gold (chemical symbol Au), silver (Ag), copper (Cu), and carbon (C); carbon occurs as a native element in two forms, diamond and graphite. Compounds are combinations of two or more elements. For example, sulphides are compounds of sulphur (S) and one or more other elements, such as lead (Pb) in the mineral galena, or antimony (Sb) in the mineral stibnite.

NATIVE ELEMENTS

Dendritic (branching) copper

Limonite groundmass (matrix)

COPPER
(Cu)

SULPHIDES

Dendritic (branching) gold

Kimberlite groundmass (matrix)

White diamond

Hexagonal graphite crystal

Quartz vein

GOLD
(Au)

DIAMOND
(C)

GRAPHITE
(C)

Cubic galena crystal

GALENA
(PbS)

OXIDES/HYDROXIDES

Milky quartz groundmass (matrix)

Smoky quartz crystal

SMOKY QUARTZ
(SiO_2)

Rounded bauxite grains in groundmass (matrix)

Mass of specular haematite crystals

SPECULAR HAEMATITE
(Fe_2O_3)

BAUXITE
(FeO(OH) and $Al_2O_3.2H_2O$)

Prismatic stibnite crystal

Quartz groundmass (matrix)

STIBNITE
(Sb_2S_3)

Perfect octahedral pyrites crystal

Quartz crystal

PYRITES
(FeS_2)

Parallel bands of onyx

ONYX
(SiO_2)

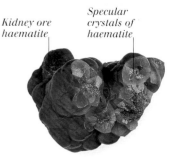

Kidney ore haematite

Specular crystals of haematite

KIDNEY ORE HAEMATITE
(Fe_2O_3)

PHOSPHATES

Limonite groundmass (matrix)

Rock groundmass (matrix)

Radiating wavellite crystals

WAVELLITE
$(Al_3(PO_4)_2(OH,F)_3.5H_2O)$

Prismatic pyromorphite crystals

PYROMORPHITE
$(Pb_5(PO_4)_3Cl)$

CARBONATES

Striated cerussite crystal

Dog tooth calcite crystal

CERUSSITE
$(PbCO_3)$

CALCITE
$(CaCO_3)$

SULPHATES

Rock groundmass (matrix)

Radiating crystal mass of daisy gypsum

Radiating cyanotrichite crystals

CYANOTRICHITE
$(Cu_4Al_2(SO_4)(OH)_{12}.2H_2O)$

DAISY GYPSUM
$(CaSO_4.2H_2O)$

MOLYBDATE

Tabular wulfenite crystal

Dark rock groundmass (matrix)

WULFENITE
$(PbMoO_4)$

SILICATES

Feldspar groundmass (matrix)

Transparent bicolored tourmaline crystal

Dodecahedral sodalite crystal

SODALITE
$(Na_8Al_6Si_6O_{24}Cl_2)$

Striated surface of olivine crystal

TOURMALINE
$(Na(Mg,Fe,Li,Mn,Al)_3Al_6(BO_3)_3Si_6.O_{18}(OH,F)_4)$

OLIVINE
$(Fe_2SiO_4 - Mg_2SiO_4)$

Striated prismatic epidote crystal

Tabular muscovite crystal

EPIDOTE
$(Ca_2(Al,Fe)_3(SiO_4)_3(OH))$

Orthoclase crystal

MUSCOVITE
$(KAl_2(Si_3Al)O_{10}(OH,F)_2)$

ORTHOCLASE
$(KAlSi_3O_8)$

HALIDES

Cubic rock salt crystal

Cubic fluorite crystal

GREEN FLUORITE
(CaF_2)

ORANGE HALITE (ROCK SALT)
$(NaCl)$

Mineral features

MINERALS CAN BE IDENTIFIED BY STUDYING features such as fracture, cleavage, crystal system, habit, hardness, colour, and streak. Minerals can break in different ways. If a mineral breaks in an irregular way, leaving rough surfaces, it possesses fracture. If a mineral breaks along well-defined planes of weakness, it possesses cleavage. Specific minerals have distinctive patterns of cleavage; for example, mica cleaves along one plane. Most minerals form crystals, which can be categorized into crystal systems according to their symmetry and number of faces. Within each system, several different but related forms of crystal are possible; for example, a cubic crystal can have six, eight, or twelve sides. A mineral's habit is the typical form taken by an aggregate of its crystals. Examples of habit include botryoidal (like a bunch of grapes) and massive (no definite form). The relative hardness of a mineral may be assessed by testing its resistance to scratching. This property is usually measured using Mohs scale, which increases in hardness from 1 (talc) to 10 (diamond). The colour of a mineral is not a dependable guide to its identity as some minerals have a range of colours. Streak (the colour the powdered mineral makes when rubbed across an unglazed tile) is a more reliable indicator.

CLEAVAGE

Cleavage in one direction

CLEAVAGE ALONG ONE PLANE

Cleavage in three directions, forming a block cube

CLEAVAGE ALONG THREE PLANES

Horizontal cleavage

Vertical cleavage

CLEAVAGE ALONG TWO PLANES

Cleavage in four directions, forming a double-pyramid crystal

CLEAVAGE ALONG FOUR PLANES

CRYSTAL SYSTEMS

Cubic iron pyrites crystal

Tetragonal idocrase crystal

Representation of tetragonal system

TETRAGONAL SYSTEM

CUBIC SYSTEM

Representation of cubic system

Hexagonal beryl crystal

Representation of hexagonal/ trigonal system

HEXAGONAL/TRIGONAL SYSTEM

Orthorhombic barytes crystal

Representation of orthorhombic system

ORTHORHOMBIC SYSTEM

FRACTURE

Fire opal with conchoidal (shell-like) fracture

Nickel-iron with hackly (jagged) fracture

CONCHOIDAL FRACTURE

HACKLY FRACTURE

Orpiment with uneven fracture

Garnierite with splintery fracture

UNEVEN FRACTURE

SPLINTERY FRACTURE

Monoclinic selenite crystal

Representation of monoclinic system

Triclinic axinite crystal

Representation of triclinic system

MONOCLINIC SYSTEM

TRICLINIC SYSTEM

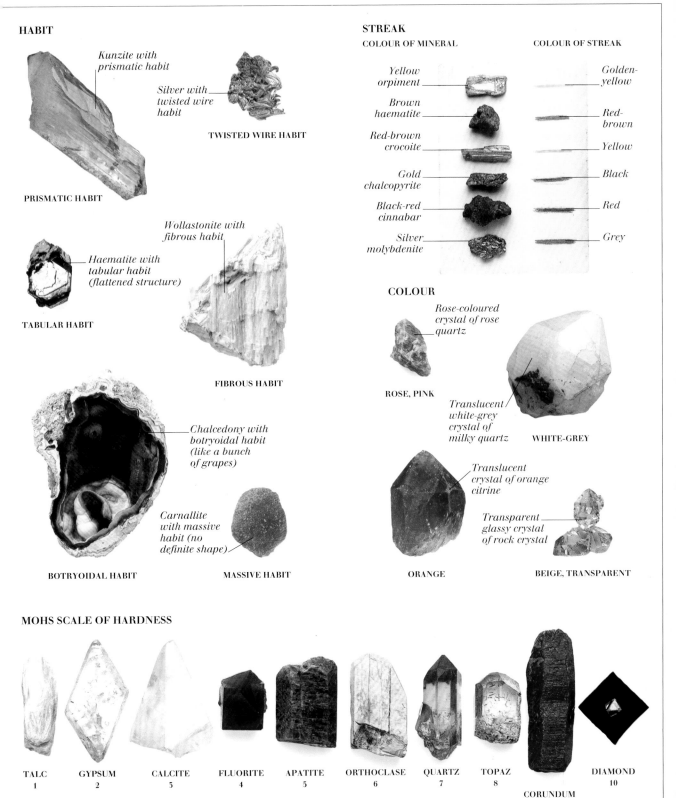

HABIT

Kunzite with prismatic habit

Silver with twisted wire habit

TWISTED WIRE HABIT

PRISMATIC HABIT

Haematite with tabular habit (flattened structure)

TABULAR HABIT

Wollastonite with fibrous habit

FIBROUS HABIT

Chalcedony with botryoidal habit (like a bunch of grapes)

Carnallite with massive habit (no definite shape)

BOTRYOIDAL HABIT

MASSIVE HABIT

STREAK

COLOUR OF MINERAL	COLOUR OF STREAK
Yellow orpiment	Golden-yellow
Brown haematite	Red-brown
Red-brown crocoite	Yellow
Gold chalcopyrite	Black
Black-red cinnabar	Red
Silver molybdenite	Grey

COLOUR

Rose-coloured crystal of rose quartz

ROSE, PINK

Translucent white-grey crystal of milky quartz

WHITE-GREY

Translucent crystal of orange citrine

Transparent glassy crystal of rock crystal

ORANGE

BEIGE, TRANSPARENT

MOHS SCALE OF HARDNESS

TALC 1	GYPSUM 2	CALCITE 3	FLUORITE 4	APATITE 5	ORTHOCLASE 6	QUARTZ 7	TOPAZ 8	CORUNDUM 9	DIAMOND 10

Volcanoes

VOLCANOES ARE VENTS OR FISSURES in the Earth's crust through which magma (molten rock that originates from deep beneath the crust) is forced on to the surface as lava. They occur most commonly along the boundaries of crustal plates; most volcanoes lie in a belt called the "Ring of Fire", which runs along the edge of the Pacific Ocean. Volcanoes can be classified according to the violence and frequency of their eruptions. Non-explosive volcanic eruptions generally occur where crustal plates pull apart. These eruptions produce runny basaltic lava that spreads quickly over a wide area to form relatively flat cones. The most violent eruptions take place where plates collide. Such eruptions produce thick rhyolitic lava and may also blast out clouds of dust and pyroclasts (lava fragments). The lava does not flow far before cooling and therefore builds up steep-sided, conical volcanoes. Some volcanoes produce lava and ash eruptions, which build up composite volcanic cones. Volcanoes that erupt frequently are described as active; those that erupt rarely are termed dormant; and those that have stopped erupting altogether are termed extinct. As well as the volcanoes themselves, other features associated with volcanic regions include geysers, hot mineral springs, solfataras, fumaroles, and bubbling mud pools.

Folded, rope-like surface

PAHOEHOE
(ROPY LAVA)

HORU GEYSER,
NEW ZEALAND

VOLCANO TYPES

Basaltic lava plateau
Fissure created by plates moving apart
Gentle slope

FISSURE VOLCANO

Vent
Gentle slope built up by numerous basaltic lava flows

BASIC SHIELD VOLCANO

Vent
Steep, convex sides caused by thick lava cooling quickly

DOME VOLCANO

Layers of sedimentary rocks

Slightly concave sides
Vent
Cinder
Fine ash

ASH-CINDER VOLCANO

Lava
Vent
Ash
Steep conical shape
Secondary conduit

COMPOSITE VOLCANO

Caldera (volcanic crater)
New cone
Old cone
Ash

CALDERA VOLCANO

Metamorphic rocks (rocks altered by heat and pressure)

HOW VOLCANIC PLUGS BECOME EXPOSED

Extinct volcano
Solidified lava forms plug

PLUG FORMATION

Plug exposed
Volcanic cone slowly eroded away

INITIAL EROSION AROUND PLUG

Resistant lava plug remains
Volcanic cone completely eroded away

COMPLETE DENUDATION OF PLUG

LAPILLI
(LAVA FRAGMENTS)

Small piece of solidified lava

TYPES OF LAVA

Scoria (sharp,
angular
chunks)

AA (BLOCKY LAVA)

Driblets of
lava from roof
of tunnel

REMELTED LAVA

LOCATION OF VOLCANOES

▲ Volcano

⊢┼┼┼ Plate boundary

STRUCTURE OF A VOLCANO

Steeply sloping cone
consisting of numerous
layers of ash and lava

Laccolith

Secondary
conduit

Vent

Plug (solidified lava)

Main conduit

Volcanic ash

Cinder
cone

Mineral
spring

Magma
reservoir

Lava
flow

Groundwater

VOLCANIC FEATURES

Sulphurous
gases

SOLFATARA

Water heated
by hot rocks

Jet of hot water
and steam

Steam
pressure
builds up

GEYSER

Hot
water

Mud and surface
deposits mixed
with hot water

MUD POOL

Superheated
water

Steam

FUMAROLE

Igneous and metamorphic rocks

IGNEOUS ROCKS ARE FORMED WHEN MAGMA (molten rock that originates from deep beneath the Earth's crust) cools and solidifies. There are two main types of igneous rock: intrusive and extrusive. Intrusive rocks are formed deep underground where magma is forced into cracks or between rock layers to form structures such as sills, dykes, and batholiths. The magma cools slowly to form coarse-grained rocks such as gabbro and pegmatite. Extrusive rocks are formed above the Earth's surface from lava (magma that has been ejected in a volcanic eruption). The molten lava cools quickly, producing fine-grained rocks such as rhyolite and basalt. Metamorphic rocks are those that have been altered by intense heat (contact metamorphism) or extreme pressure (regional metamorphism). Contact metamorphism occurs when rocks are changed by heat from, for example, an igneous intrusion or lava flow. Regional metamorphism occurs when rock is crushed in the middle of a folding mountain range. Metamorphic rocks can be formed from igneous rocks, sedimentary rocks, or even from other metamorphic rocks.

BASALT COLUMNS

Cinder cone
Large eroded lava flow
Cedar-tree laccolith
Butte
Plug
Cone sheet
Ring dyke
Batholith
Dyke
Sill
Dyke swarm
Lopolith

IGNEOUS ROCK STRUCTURES

CONTACT METAMORPHISM

Metamorphic aureole (region where contact metamorphism occurs)

Hot igneous intrusion
Limestone
Shale
Marble (metamorphosed limestone)
Slate (metamorphosed shale)

REGIONAL METAMORPHISM

Mountain range
Slate, formed under low pressure and temperature
Compression
Compression
Crust
Schist, formed under medium pressure and temperature
Mantle
Gneiss, formed under high pressure and temperature
Magma

EXAMPLES OF METAMORPHIC ROCKS

Pale feldspar
Dark mica
Dark mineral band
Pale calcite

GNEISS
FOLDED SCHIST
SKARN

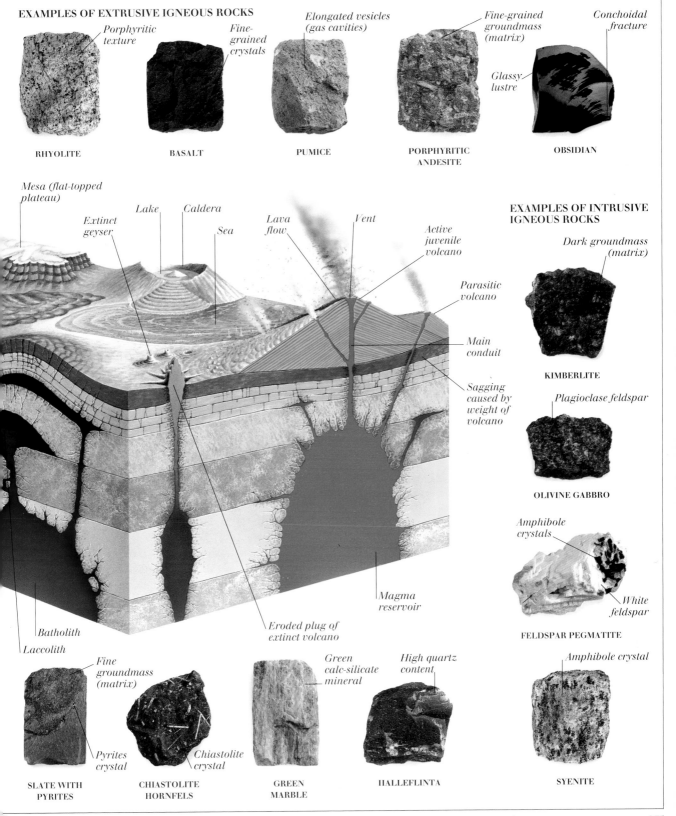

EXAMPLES OF EXTRUSIVE IGNEOUS ROCKS

Porphyritic texture

Fine-grained crystals

Elongated vesicles (gas cavities)

Fine-grained groundmass (matrix)

Conchoidal fracture

Glassy lustre

RHYOLITE

BASALT

PUMICE

PORPHYRITIC ANDESITE

OBSIDIAN

Mesa (flat-topped plateau)

Extinct geyser

Lake

Caldera

Sea

Lava flow

Vent

Active juvenile volcano

Parasitic volcano

Main conduit

Sagging caused by weight of volcano

Magma reservoir

Eroded plug of extinct volcano

Batholith

Laccolith

EXAMPLES OF INTRUSIVE IGNEOUS ROCKS

Dark groundmass (matrix)

KIMBERLITE

Plagioclase feldspar

OLIVINE GABBRO

Amphibole crystals

White feldspar

FELDSPAR PEGMATITE

Amphibole crystal

Fine groundmass (matrix)

Green calc-silicate mineral

High quartz content

Pyrites crystal

Chiastolite crystal

SLATE WITH PYRITES

CHIASTOLITE HORNFELS

GREEN MARBLE

HALLEFLINTA

SYENITE

Sedimentary rocks

SEDIMENTARY ROCKS ARE FORMED BY THE ACCUMULATION and consolidation of sediments (see pp. 266-267). There are three main types of sedimentary rock. Clastic sedimentary rocks, such as breccia or sandstone, are formed from other rocks that have been broken down into fragments by weathering (see pp. 282-283), which have then been transported and deposited elsewhere. Organic sedimentary rocks – for example, coal (see pp. 280-281) – are derived from plant and animal remains. Chemical sedimentary rocks are formed by chemical processes. For example, rock salt is formed when salt dissolved in water is deposited as the water evaporates. Sedimentary rocks are laid down in layers, called beds or strata. Each new layer is laid down horizontally over older ones. There are usually some gaps in the sequence, called unconformities. These represent periods in which no new sediments were being laid down, or when earlier sedimentary layers were raised above sea level and eroded away.

THE GRAND CANYON, USA

EXAMPLES OF UNCONFORMITIES

Early beds tilted and eroded   *Later beds horizontal*

ANGULAR UNCONFORMITY

No bedding in early rocks   *Later beds horizontal*

NONCONFORMITY

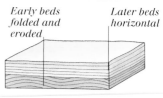

Early beds folded and eroded   *Later beds horizontal*

DISCONFORMITY

SEDIMENTARY LAYERS OF THE GRAND CANYON REGION

Wasatch formation
Kaiparowits formation
Wahweap sandstone
Tropic formation
Dakota sandstone
Carmel formation
Pink Cliffs
Bryce Canyon
Zion Canyon
Gray Cliffs
Sevier fault
White Cliffs
Pipe Spring

Temple Cap sandstone
Navajo sandstone
Kayenta formation
Moenave formation
Chinle formation
Shinarump member
Moenkopi formation
Kaibab limestone
Toroweap formation
Coconino sandstone
Hermit shale

EXAMPLES OF SEDIMENTARY ROCKS

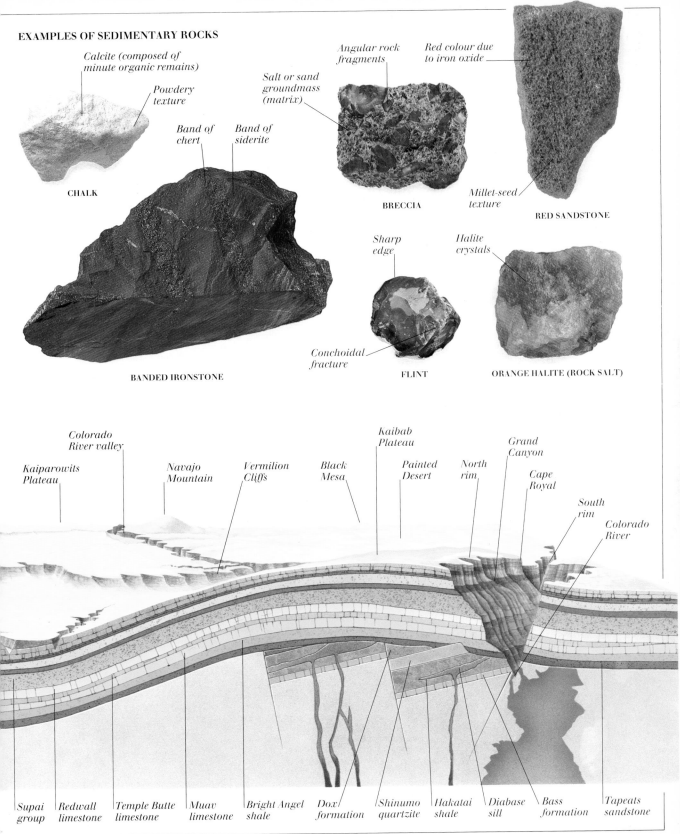

Calcite (composed of minute organic remains)

Powdery texture

CHALK

Band of chert

Band of siderite

BANDED IRONSTONE

Angular rock fragments

Salt or sand groundmass (matrix)

BRECCIA

Red colour due to iron oxide

Millet-seed texture

RED SANDSTONE

Sharp edge

Conchoidal fracture

FLINT

Halite crystals

ORANGE HALITE (ROCK SALT)

Colorado River valley

Kaiparowits Plateau

Navajo Mountain

Vermilion Cliffs

Black Mesa

Kaibab Plateau

Painted Desert

North rim

Grand Canyon

Cape Royal

South rim

Colorado River

Supai group

Redwall limestone

Temple Butte limestone

Muav limestone

Bright Angel shale

Dox formation

Shinumo quartzite

Hakatai shale

Diabase sill

Bass formation

Tapeats sandstone

Fossils

FOSSILS ARE THE REMAINS of plants and animals that have been preserved in rock. A fossil may be the preserved remains of an organism itself, an impression of it in rock, or preserved traces (known as trace fossils) left by an organism while it was alive, such as organic carbon outlines, fossilized footprints, or droppings. Most dead organisms soon rot away or are eaten by scavengers. For fossilization to occur, rapid burial by sediment is necessary. The organism decays, but the harder parts – bones, teeth, and shells, for example – may be preserved and hardened by minerals from the surrounding sediment. Fossilization may also occur even when the hard parts of an organism are dissolved away to leave an impression called a mould. The mould is filled by minerals, thereby creating a cast of the organism. The study of fossils (palaeontology) can not only show how living things have evolved, but can also help to reveal the Earth's geological history – for example, by aiding in the dating of rock strata.

PROCESS OF FOSSILIZATION

ANIMAL DIES

SOFT PARTS ROT

SHELL BURIED

SHELL FOSSILIZED

EXAMPLES OF FOSSILS

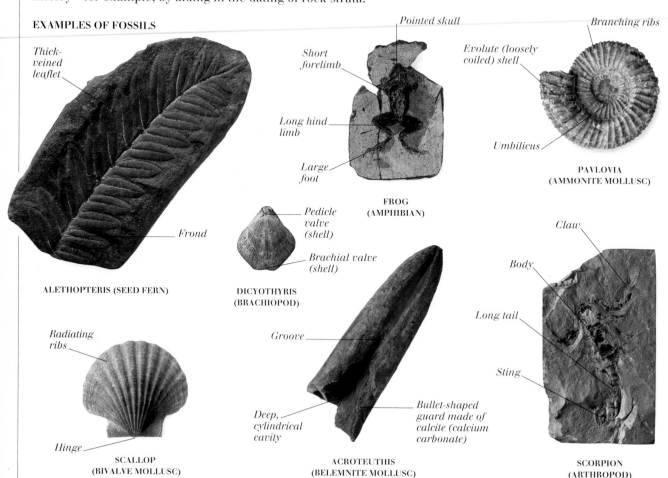

ALETHOPTERIS (SEED FERN)

Thick-veined leaflet

Frond

FROG (AMPHIBIAN)

Pointed skull

Short forelimb

Long hind limb

Large foot

PAVLOVIA (AMMONITE MOLLUSC)

Branching ribs

Evolute (loosely coiled) shell

Umbilicus

DICYOTHYRIS (BRACHIOPOD)

Pedicle valve (shell)

Brachial valve (shell)

SCALLOP (BIVALVE MOLLUSC)

Radiating ribs

Hinge

ACROTEUTHIS (BELEMNITE MOLLUSC)

Groove

Deep, cylindrical cavity

Bullet-shaped guard made of calcite (calcium carbonate)

SCORPION (ARTHROPOD)

Claw

Body

Long tail

Sting

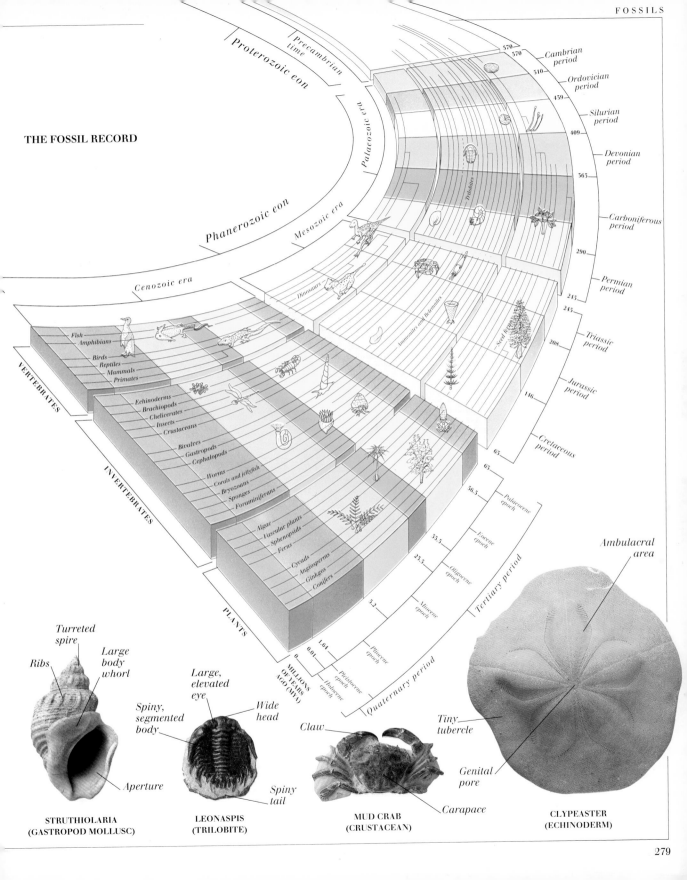

THE FOSSIL RECORD

Precambrian time

Proterozoic eon

Palaeozoic era

Phanerozoic eon

Mesozoic era

Cenozoic era

570 — Cambrian period
510 — Ordovician period
439 — Silurian period
409 — Devonian period
363 — Carboniferous period
290 — Permian period
245 — Permian period

Trilobites

Dinosaurs

Ammonites and Belemnites

Seed ferns

245 — Triassic period
208 — Jurassic period
146 — Cretaceous period
65 —

VERTEBRATES

Fish
Amphibians
Birds
Reptiles
Mammals
Primates

INVERTEBRATES

Echinoderms
Brachiopods
Chelicerates
Insects
Crustaceans
Bivalves
Gastropods
Cephalopods
Worms
Corals and jellyfish
Bryozoans
Sponges
Foraminiferans

PLANTS

Algae
Vascular plants
Sphenopsids
Ferns
Cycads
Angiosperms
Ginkgos
Conifers

65
56.5 — Palaeocene epoch
35.5 — Eocene epoch
23.5 — Oligocene epoch
5.2 — Miocene epoch

Tertiary period

1.64 — Pliocene epoch
0 — 0.01 — Pleistocene epoch
Holocene epoch

MILLIONS OF YEARS AGO (MYA)

Quaternary period

Turreted spire
Ribs
Large body whorl
Aperture

STRUTHIOLARIA (GASTROPOD MOLLUSC)

Large, elevated eye
Spiny, segmented body
Wide head
Spiny tail

LEONASPIS (TRILOBITE)

Claw
Carapace

MUD CRAB (CRUSTACEAN)

Ambulacral area
Tiny tubercle
Genital pore

CLYPEASTER (ECHINODERM)

Mineral resources

MINERAL RESOURCES CAN BE DEFINED AS naturally occurring substances that can be extracted from the Earth and are useful as fuels and raw materials. Coal, oil, and gas – collectively called fossil fuels – are commonly included in this group, but are not strictly minerals, because they are of organic origin. Coal formation begins when vegetation is buried and partly decomposed to form peat. Overlying sediments compress the peat and transform it into lignite (soft brown coal). As the overlying sediments accumulate, increasing pressure and temperature eventually transform the lignite into bituminous and hard anthracite coals. Oil and gas are usually formed from organic matter that was deposited in marine sediments. Under the effects of heat and pressure, the compressed organic matter undergoes complex chemical changes to form oil and gas. The oil and gas percolate upwards through water-saturated, permeable rocks and they may rise to the Earth's surface or accumulate below an impermeable layer of rock that has been folded or faulted to form a trap – an anticline (upfold) trap, for example. Minerals are inorganic substances that may consist of a single chemical element, such as gold, silver, or copper, or combinations of elements (see pp. 268-269). Some minerals are concentrated in mineralization zones in rock associated with crustal movements or volcanic activity. Others may be found in sediments as placer deposits – accumulations of high-density minerals that have been weathered out of rocks, transported, and deposited (on river-beds, for example).

OIL RIG, NORTH SEA

Stalk

Leaf

PLANT MATTER

Decayed plant matter

About 60% carbon

PEAT

About 70% carbon

Crumbly texture

LIGNITE (BROWN COAL)

Powdery texture

About 80% carbon

BITUMINOUS COAL

Shiny surface

About 95% carbon

ANTHRACITE COAL

HOW COAL IS FORMED

Vegetation

Increasing pressure and temperature

Increasing layers of overlying sediment

Increasing pressure and temperature

Increasing layers of overlying sediment

Increasing pressure and temperature

Peat (about 60% carbon)

PEAT

Lignite (about 70% carbon)

LIGNITE (BROWN COAL)

Bituminous coal (about 80% carbon)

BITUMINOUS COAL

EXAMPLES OF OIL AND GAS TRAPS

Impermeable rock

Oil

Water-saturated permeable rock

Fault

FAULT TRAP

Pinch-out

Water-saturated permeable rock

Folded impermeable rock

Fault

Gas

Oil

PINCH-OUT TRAP

Anticline

Folded impermeable rock

Water-saturated permeable rock

Gas

Oil

ANTICLINE TRAP

Folded impermeable rock

Water-saturated permeable rock

Oil

Impermeable salt dome

SALT-DOME TRAP

MAJOR COAL, OIL, AND GAS DEPOSITS

● Coal   ● Oil and gas

HOW AN ANTICLINE TRAP IS FORMED

Layer of sediment containing decayed plant and animal matter

Sea

Old seabed

Oil and gas formed by chemical reactions, heat, and pressure

DEPOSITION OF ORGANIC MATERIAL

Increasing layers of overlying sediment

Sea

FORMATION OF OIL AND GAS

Land

Sea

Anticline

Impermeable rock layer folded to form oil and gas trap

Gas

Oil

Water-saturated permeable rock

COLLECTION OF OIL AND GAS IN ANTICLINE TRAP

MINERALIZATION ZONES

Continental crust

Volcano

Subduction zone

Oceanic crust

Mid-ocean ridge

Tin, tungsten, bismuth, and copper

Copper, zinc, gold, and chromium

Copper, gold, silver, tin, lead, and mercury

Lead, zinc, and copper

Chromium

Manganese, cobalt, and nickel

Copper and zinc

281

Weathering and erosion

WEATHERING IS THE BREAKING DOWN of rocks on the Earth's surface. There are two main types: physical (or mechanical) and chemical. Physical weathering may be caused by temperature changes, such as freezing and thawing, or by abrasion from material carried by winds, rivers, or glaciers. Rocks may also be broken down by the actions of animals and plants, such as the burrowing of animals and the growth of roots. Chemical weathering causes rocks to decompose by changing their chemical composition – for example, rainwater may dissolve certain minerals in a rock. Erosion is the wearing away and removal of land surfaces by water, wind, or ice. It is greatest in areas of little or no surface vegetation, such as deserts, where sand dunes may form.

FORMATION OF A HAMADA (ROCK PAVEMENT)

Wind blows away small particles

Larger particles aggregate

Hamada forms

FIRST STAGE

SECOND STAGE

FINAL STAGE

FEATURES OF WEATHERING AND EROSION

FEATURES PRODUCED BY WIND ACTION

Wind-blown sand

Mushroom-shaped rock

Neck

Rock base eroded by wind-blown sand

ROCK PEDESTAL

Wind-blown sand

Widened joint

Soft rock

Hard rock

ZEUGEN

Wind-blown sand

Furrow

Hard rock

Soft rock eroded by wind-blown sand

YARDANG

Mesa (flat-topped plateau)

Canyon

Zeugen

Joint

Hard rock

Soft rock

Shelf formed of hard rock

Talus (scree)

Alluvial fan (alluvial cone)

Bahada (gentle slope covered with loose rock)

Bolson (alluvium-filled basin)

EXAMPLES OF PHYSICAL WEATHERING PROCESSES

Heated rock surface expands

Exfoliation dome

Flaking rock

Fallen debris

EXFOLIATION (ONION-SKIN WEATHERING)

Joint expands and contracts due to temperature changes

Block of fallen rock

BLOCK DISINTEGRATION

Talus (scree)

Joint widened by frozen water

FROST WEDGING

Crack widened by tree root

Trunk

TREE ROOT ACTION

SECTION THROUGH A BARKHAN DUNE

Strong wind

Weak wind

Windward face

Direction of wind-blown sand

Direction of sand movement

Slip face

Foreset strata

Cross-bed set

Topset strata

Bottomset strata

EXAMPLES OF SAND DUNES

Wind direction

Crescent-shaped dune

BARKHAN DUNE

Wind direction

Dune at right angle to wind

TRANSVERSE DUNE

Wind direction

Point where sand ridges meet

STAR DUNE

Wind direction

Parallel dunes

SEIF (LINEAR) DUNE

Canyon

Wadi (dry wash)

Mesa (flat-topped plateau)

Talus (scree)

Butte (flat-topped mesa remnant)

Eroded arch

Residual hill on pediment

Hamada (rock pavement)

Rock pedestal

Barkhan dune

Parabolic dune

Transverse dune

Seif (linear) dune

Inselberg (isolated, steep-sided hill)

Playa (dry lake bed of salt or desiccated clay)

Faultline

Freshwater lake

Fertile oasis

Deflation hollow created by wind erosion

Hog's-back (steep ridge)

Hard sandstone

Faultline

Cuesta (asymmetric ridge)

Hard granite

Caves

CAVES COMMONLY FORM in areas of limestone, although on coastlines they also occur in other rocks. Limestone is made of calcite (calcium carbonate), which dissolves in the carbonic acid naturally present in rainwater, and in humic acids from the decay of vegetation. The acidic water trickles down through cracks and joints in the limestone and between rock layers, breaking up the surface terrain into clints (blocks of rock), separated by grikes (deep cracks), and punctuated by sink-holes (also called swallow-holes or potholes) into which surface streams may disappear. Underground, the acidic water dissolves the rock around crevices, opening up a network of passages and caves, which can become large caverns if the roofs collapse. Various features are formed when the dissolved calcite is redeposited; for example, it may be redeposited along an underground stream to form a gour (series of calcite ridges), or in caves and passages to form stalactites and stalagmites. Stalactites develop where calcite is left behind as water drips from the roof; where the drops land, stalagmites build up.

MERGED
STALACTITES

STALACTITE WITH
RING MARKS

Ring mark

SURFACE TOPOGRAPHY OF A CAVE SYSTEM

Doline (depression caused by collapse of cave roof)

Sink-hole

Porous limestone

Gorge where cave roof has fallen in

Resurgence

Limestone terrain with clints and grikes

Impermeable rock

STALAGMITE FORMATIONS

Calcite (calcium carbonate) crystallized under water

Thin encrustations of calcite (calcium carbonate)

Scar of bare rock

Former water table

Permeable limestone

CALCAREOUS TUFA

CRYSTALLINE STALAGMITIC FLOOR

Encrustations on dead stems of small plants

Calcite (calcium carbonate)

Calcite (calcium carbonate)

Resurgence

Encrustations with fungoid structure

STALAGMITIC FLOOR

STALAGMITIC BOSS

Layer of impermeable rock

Present water table

DEVELOPMENT OF A CAVE SYSTEM

STRUCTURE OF LIMESTONE STRATA

- Impermeable rock
- Joint
- Bedding plane
- Impermeable rock
- Permeable limestone

INITIAL CAVE

- Water seeps through cracks in rock
- Stream enters permeable rock
- Calcite (calcium carbonate) deposits begin to form
- Resurgence
- Tunnel
- Underground stream

EXTENDED CAVE SYSTEM

- Doline caused by collapse of cave roof
- Sink-hole
- Stalactite
- Stalagmite
- Gorge
- Resurgence
- Cave
- Dry gallery

INTERCONNECTED CAVE SYSTEM

- Stalactite
- Pillar (column)
- Gorge
- Stalactite
- Dry gallery (former course of underground stream)
- Gour (series of calcite ridges) deposited by running water
- Stalagmite
- Joint in rock enlarged by water
- Bedding plane
- Curtain of deposited calcite (calcium carbonate)
- Tunnel
- Cave
- Passage
- Cavern
- Gour (series of calcite ridges)

Glaciers

GLACIER BAY, ALASKA

A VALLEY GLACIER IS A LARGE MASS OF ICE that forms on land and moves slowly downhill under its own weight. It is formed from snow that collects in cirques (mountain hollows also known as corries) and compresses into ice as more and more snow accumulates. The cirque is deepened by frost wedging and abrasion (see pp. 282-283), and arêtes (sharp ridges) develop between adjacent cirques. Eventually, so much ice builds up that the glacier begins to move downhill. As the glacier moves it collects moraine (debris), which may range in size from particles of dust to large boulders. The rocks at the base of the glacier erode the glacial valley, giving it a U-shaped cross-section. Under the glacier, *roches moutonnées* (eroded outcrops of hard rock) and drumlins (rounded mounds of rock and clay) are left behind on the valley floor. The glacier ends at a terminus (the snout), where the ice melts as fast as it arrives. If the temperature increases, the ice melts faster than it arrives, and the glacier retreats. The retreating glacier leaves behind its moraine and also erratics (isolated single boulders). Glacial streams from the melting glacier deposit eskers and kames (ridges and mounds of sand and gravel), but carry away the finer sediment to form a stratified outwash plain. Lumps of ice carried on to this plain melt, creating holes called kettles.

VALLEY GLACIER

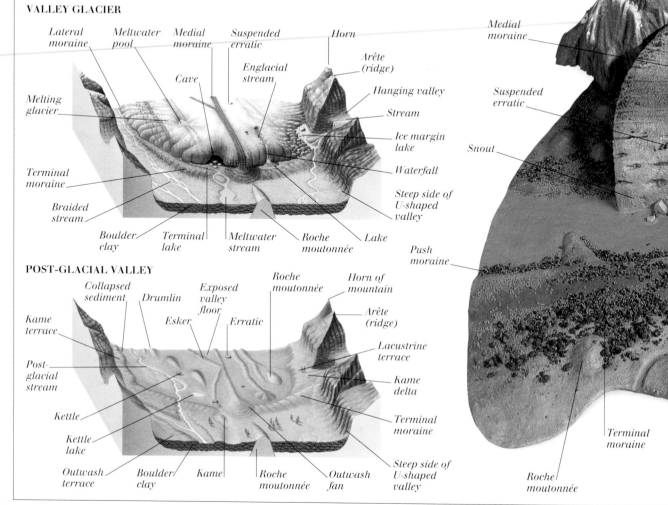

Lateral moraine
Meltwater pool
Medial moraine
Suspended erratic
Horn
Medial moraine
Arête (ridge)
Englacial stream
Cave
Hanging valley
Suspended erratic
Melting glacier
Stream
Ice margin lake
Snout
Terminal moraine
Waterfall
Braided stream
Steep side of U-shaped valley
Boulder clay
Terminal lake
Meltwater stream
Roche moutonnée
Lake
Push moraine

POST-GLACIAL VALLEY

Collapsed sediment
Drumlin
Exposed valley floor
Roche moutonnée
Horn of mountain
Kame terrace
Esker
Erratic
Arête (ridge)
Post-glacial stream
Lacustrine terrace
Kame delta
Kettle
Terminal moraine
Kettle lake
Terminal moraine
Outwash terrace
Boulder clay
Kame
Roche moutonnée
Outwash fan
Steep side of U-shaped valley
Roche moutonnée

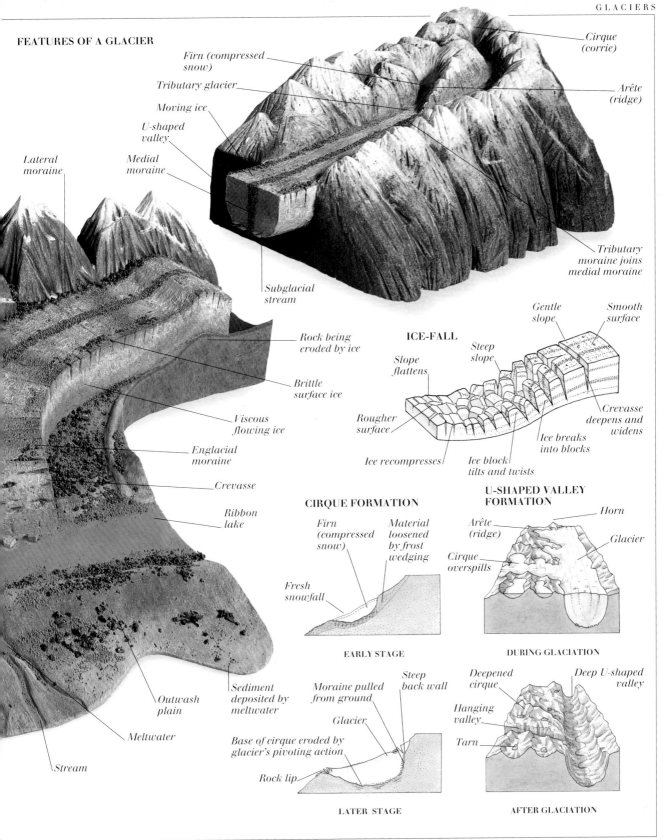

FEATURES OF A GLACIER

Cirque
(corrie)

Firn (compressed
snow)

Tributary glacier

Arête
(ridge)

Moving ice

U-shaped
valley

Medial
moraine

Lateral
moraine

Tributary
moraine joins
medial moraine

Subglacial
stream

Rock being
eroded by ice

ICE-FALL

Gentle
slope

Smooth
surface

Steep
slope

Slope
flattens

Brittle
surface ice

Viscous
flowing ice

Crevasse
deepens and
widens

Englacial
moraine

Rougher
surface

Crevasse

Ice recompresses

Ice block
tilts and twists

Ice breaks
into blocks

Ribbon
lake

CIRQUE FORMATION

U-SHAPED VALLEY
FORMATION

Firn
(compressed
snow)

Material
loosened
by frost
wedging

Horn

Arête
(ridge)

Glacier

Cirque
overspills

Fresh
snowfall

Outwash
plain

Sediment
deposited by
meltwater

EARLY STAGE

DURING GLACIATION

Meltwater

Moraine pulled
from ground

Steep
back wall

Deepened
cirque

Deep U-shaped
valley

Glacier

Hanging
valley

Stream

Base of cirque eroded by
glacier's pivoting action

Tarn

Rock lip

LATER STAGE

AFTER GLACIATION

Rivers

RIVERS FORM PART of the water cycle – the continuous circulation of water between the land, sea, and atmosphere. The source of a river may be a mountain spring or lake, or a melting glacier. The course that the river subsequently takes depends on the slope of the terrain and on the rock types and formations over which it flows. In its early, upland stages, a river tumbles steeply over rocks and boulders and cuts a steep-sided V-shaped valley. Farther downstream, it flows smoothly over sediments and forms winding meanders, eroding sideways to create broad valleys and plains. On reaching the coast, the river may deposit sediment to form an estuary or delta (see pp. 290-291).

RIVER CAPTURE

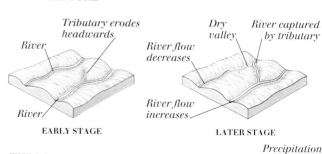

River *Tributary erodes headwards*

River

EARLY STAGE

River flow decreases *Dry valley* *River captured by tributary*

River flow increases

LATER STAGE

SATELLITE IMAGE OF GANGES RIVER DELTA, BANGLADESH

River Ganges

Ganges delta

Infertile swampland *Distributary* *Large volume of sediment*

THE WATER CYCLE

Precipitation falls on high ground

Wind

Water vapour released into atmosphere by trees and other plants

Wind

Water carried downstream by river

Water vapour forms clouds

Water evaporates from sea

Water stored in sea

River flows into sea

Water seeps underground and flows to sea

Water seeps underground and flows to sea

Water evaporates from lake

Water seeps underground and flows to sea

Seabed

Sea

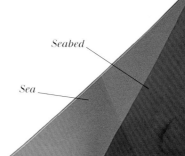

Sediment layers

RIVER DRAINAGE PATTERNS

RADIAL

CENTRIPETAL

PARALLEL

DENDRITIC

DERANGED

TRELLISED

ANNULAR

RECTANGULAR

STAGES IN A RIVER'S DEVELOPMENT

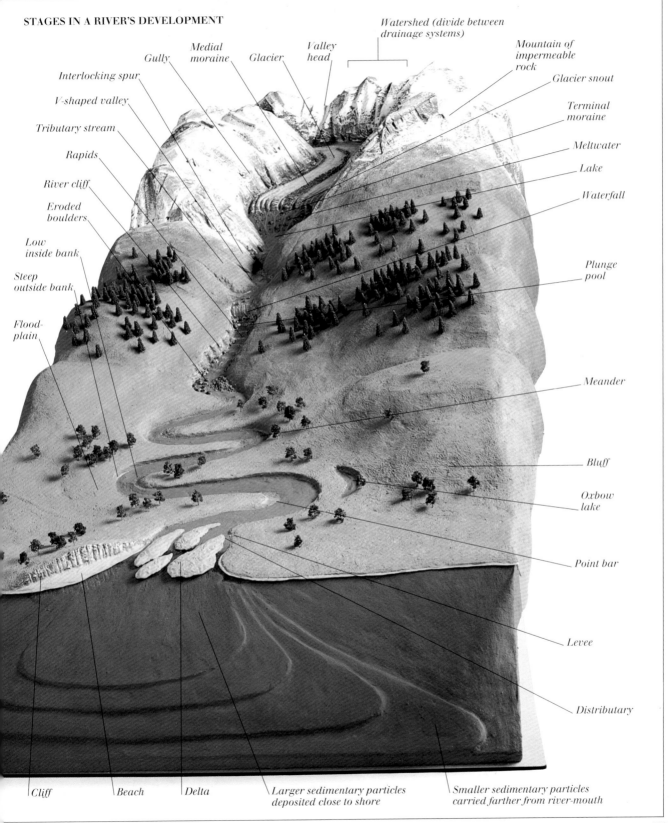

Watershed (divide between drainage systems)

Mountain of impermeable rock

Medial moraine

Glacier

Valley head

Glacier snout

Terminal moraine

Meltwater

Gully

Interlocking spur

V-shaped valley

Tributary stream

Rapids

River cliff

Eroded boulders

Low inside bank

Steep outside bank

Flood-plain

Lake

Waterfall

Plunge pool

Meander

Bluff

Oxbow lake

Point bar

Levee

Distributary

Cliff

Beach

Delta

Larger sedimentary particles deposited close to shore

Smaller sedimentary particles carried farther from river-mouth

River features

RIVERS ARE ONE OF THE MAJOR FORCES that shape the landscape. Near its source, a river is steep (see pp. 288-289). It erodes downwards, carving out V-shaped valleys and deep gorges. Waterfalls and rapids are formed where the river flows from hard rock to softer, more easily eroded rock. Farther downstream, meanders may form and there is greater sideways erosion, resulting in a broad river valley. The river sometimes erodes through the neck of a meander to form an oxbow lake. Sediment deposited on the valley floor by meandering rivers and during floods helps to create a flood-plain. Floods may also deposit sediment on the banks of the river to form levees. As a river spills into the sea or a lake, it deposits large amounts of sediment, and may form a delta. A delta is an area of sand-bars, swamps, and lagoons through which the river flows in several channels called distributaries – the Mississippi delta, for example. Often, a rise in sea level may have flooded the river-mouth to form a broad estuary, a tidal section where seawater mixes with fresh water.

HOW WATERFALLS AND RAPIDS ARE FORMED

Hard rock • *Plunge pool* • *Softer rock*

WATERFALL

Hard rock • *River erodes softer rocks to form rapids* • *Softer rock* • *Gently sloping rock strata*

RAPIDS

A RIVER VALLEY DRAINAGE SYSTEM

Headward erosion — *Waterfall* — *Gorge*

Steep gorge cut by river — *Mountain*

GORGE

Flood-plain — *Stream* — *Sediment bar*

BRAIDING

River erodes headwards

HEADWARD EROSION

Entrenched meander — *Braiding* — *Lake* — *River terrace* — *Levee*

Meander — *River erodes downwards* — *Natural bridge* — *Steep cliffs*

ENTRENCHED MEANDER

Old meander — *Bridge* — *River*

NATURAL BRIDGE

Oxbow lake — *Lake* — *River-mouth* — *Sediment deposited on seabed*

WATERFALL FEATURES

Hard rock

Island

River

Hard rock

Rock undercut by swirling boulders

Plunge pool

Softer rock

Rock undercut by swirling boulders

Flood-plain

River

Levee formed from sediment deposited by floods

Sediment

LEVEE

River

Present flood-plain

Oldest terrace (remnant of previous flood-plain)

Sediment

RIVER TERRACE

Flood-plain

Bay

Sea-cliff

Sea

THE MISSISSIPPI DELTA

Mississippi River

Levee

Distributary

Point bar

Swamp

Sediment plume

Sea

Levee

Freshwater bay

Spit

Sediment plume

FORMATION OF A DELTA

Distributary

Lagoon

Sediment deposited by river

River

Levee

Sea

EARLY STAGE

Earliest deposit of sediment

Bedrock

Latest deposit of sediment

Sea

SECTION THROUGH DELTA

Distributary

Lagoon

Bar

Sediment deposited by river

River

Sea

Levee

Spit

Swamp formed by deposition of sediment in lagoon

MIDDLE STAGE

River

Sediment deposited by river

Distributary

Lagoon

Levee

Infilled swamp

Lagoon

Sea

LATE STAGE

Lakes and groundwater

NATURAL LAKES OCCUR WHERE a large quantity of water collects in a hollow in impermeable rock, or is prevented from draining away by a barrier, such as moraine (glacial deposits) or solidified lava. Lakes are often relatively short-lived landscape features, as they tend to become silted up by sediment from the streams and rivers that feed them. Some of the more long-lasting lakes are found in deep rift valleys formed by vertical movements of the Earth's crust (see pp. 58-59) – for example, Lake Baikal in Russia, the world's largest freshwater lake, and the Dead Sea in the Middle East, one of the world's saltiest lakes. Where water is able to drain away, it sinks into the ground until it reaches a layer of impermeable rock, then accumulates in the permeable rock above it; this water-saturated permeable rock is called an aquifer. The saturated zone varies in depth according to seasonal and climatic changes. In wet conditions, the water stored underground builds up, while in dry periods it becomes depleted. Where the upper edge of the saturated zone – the water table – meets the ground surface, water emerges as springs. In an artesian basin, where the aquifer is below an aquiclude (layer of impermeable rock), the water table throughout the basin is determined by its height at the rim. In the centre of such a basin, the water table is above ground level. The water in the basin is thus trapped below the water table and can rise under its own pressure along faultlines or well shafts.

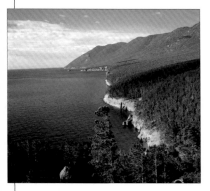

LAKE BAIKAL, RUSSIA

EXAMPLES OF SPRINGS

EXAMPLES OF SPRINGS

Permeable limestone
Water table
Spring line
Stream
Spring
Impermeable shale

LIMESTONE SPRING

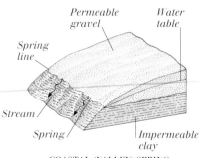

Permeable gravel
Water table
Spring line
Stream
Spring
Impermeable clay

COASTAL (VALLEY) SPRING

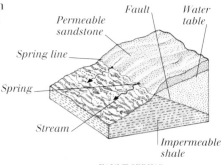

Fault
Water table
Permeable sandstone
Spring line
Spring
Stream
Impermeable shale

FAULT SPRING

STRUCTURE OF AN ARTESIAN BASIN

Recharge area
Water table
Height of water table in recharge area
Artesian spring
Aquiclude (impermeable rock)
Artesian spring
Fault
Artesian well
Aquifer (saturated rock)
Aquiclude (impermeable rock)

Water table
Jointed, solidified lava
Spring
Jointed, solidified lava
Stream
Spring line
Impermeable mudstone

LAVA SPRING

FEATURES OF A GROUNDWATER SYSTEM

Marsh

Lake

Stream

Zone of aeration

Layer of soil moisture

Zone of aeration

Capillary fringe

Water table

Saturated zone

CLOSE-UP OF SURFACE LAYER

Dry-season water table

Present water table (wet season)

Temporarily saturated zone (saturated only in wet season)

Permanently saturated zone (saturated in wet and dry seasons)

EXAMPLES OF LAKES

Glacial deposits

Lake in kettle (former site of ice block)

Oxbow lake (cut-off river meander)

River

KETTLE LAKE

OXBOW LAKE

Caldera (collapsed crater)

Volcanic lake

Movement along strike-slip (lateral) fault

Strike-slip (lateral) fault

Lake in elongated hollow

VOLCANIC LAKE

STRIKE-SLIP (LATERAL) FAULT LAKE

Rift valley

Steep back wall eroded by frost and ice

Moraine or rock lip damming lake

High valley walls

Sinking graben (block fault)

Tarn (circular mountain lake)

GRABEN (BLOCK-FAULT) LAKE

TARN

THE DEAD SEA, ISRAEL/JORDAN

River Jordan

Dead Sea

Steep rift-valley walls

Salt left by evaporation

Israel

Shallow flats

Jordan

Coastlines

COASTLINES ARE AMONG THE MOST RAPIDLY changing landscape features. Some are eroded by waves, wind, and rain, causing cliffs to be undercut and caves to be hollowed out of solid rock. Others are built up by waves transporting sand and small rocks in a process known as longshore drift, and by rivers depositing sediment in deltas. Additional influences include the activities of living organisms such as coral, crustal movements, and sea-level variations due to climatic changes. Rising land or a drop in sea level creates an emergent coastline, with cliffs and beaches stranded above the new shoreline. Sinking land or a rise in sea level produces a drowned coastline, typified by fjords (submerged glacial valleys) or submerged river valleys.

FEATURES OF A SEA-CLIFF

Cliff-top
Cliff-face
High tide level
Low tide level
Offshore deposits
Wave-cut platform
Undercut area of cliff

FEATURES OF WAVES

Wave height *Crest* *Wavelength* *Trough* *Shorter wavelength near beach*

Circular orbit of water and suspended particles
Orbit deformed into ellipse as water gets shallower

Mature river
Headland
Bedding plane
Sea-cliff
Remnants of former headland
Estuary

LONGSHORE DRIFT

Pebble *Backwash* *Movement of material along beach* *Build-up of material against groyne*

Beach
Groyne
Waves approaching shore at an oblique angle

Swash zone
Swash

DEPOSITIONAL FEATURES OF COASTLINES

Bay-head beach *Wave direction* *Headland*

Wave direction *Tombolo* *Island*

Wave direction *Cuspate foreland*

Wave direction *Barrier beach* *Lagoon*

BAY-HEAD BEACH **TOMBOLO** **CUSPATE FORELAND** **BARRIER BEACH**

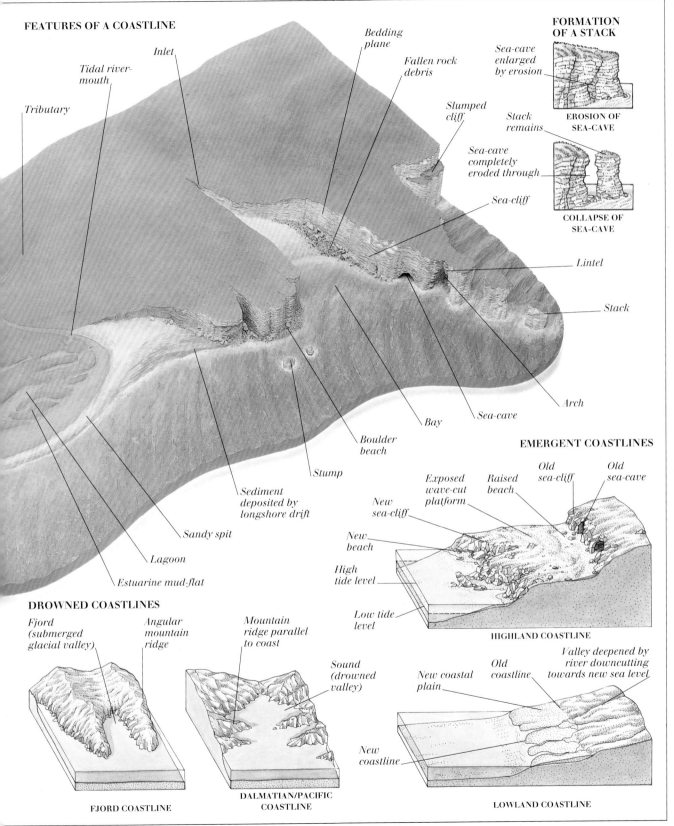

FEATURES OF A COASTLINE

Tributary

Tidal river-mouth

Inlet

Bedding plane

Fallen rock debris

Slumped cliff

Sea-cliff

FORMATION OF A STACK

Sea-cave enlarged by erosion

EROSION OF SEA-CAVE

Stack remains

Sea-cave completely eroded through

COLLAPSE OF SEA-CAVE

Lintel

Stack

Arch

Sea-cave

Bay

Boulder beach

Stump

Sediment deposited by longshore drift

Sandy spit

Lagoon

Estuarine mud-flat

EMERGENT COASTLINES

Exposed wave-cut platform

Raised beach

Old sea-cliff

Old sea-cave

New sea-cliff

New beach

High tide level

Low tide level

HIGHLAND COASTLINE

DROWNED COASTLINES

Fjord (submerged glacial valley)

Angular mountain ridge

Mountain ridge parallel to coast

Sound (drowned valley)

New coastal plain

Old coastline

Valley deepened by river downcutting towards new sea level

New coastline

FJORD COASTLINE

DALMATIAN/PACIFIC COASTLINE

LOWLAND COASTLINE

Oceans and seas

OCEANS AND SEAS COVER ABOUT 70 PER CENT of the Earth's surface and account for about 97 per cent of its total water. These oceans and seas play a crucial role in regulating temperature variations and determining climate. Their waters absorb heat from the Sun, especially in tropical regions, and the surface currents distribute it around the Earth, warming overlying air masses and neighbouring land in winter and cooling them in summer. The oceans are never still. Differences in temperature and salinity drive deep current systems, while surface currents are generated by winds blowing over the oceans. All currents are deflected – to the right in the Northern Hemisphere, to the left in the Southern Hemisphere – as a result of the Earth's rotation. This deflective factor is known as the Coriolis force. A current that begins on the surface is immediately deflected. This current in turn generates a current in the layer of water beneath, which is also deflected. As the movement is transmitted downwards, the deflections form an Ekman spiral. The waters of the oceans and seas are also moved by the constant ebb and flow of tides. These are caused by the gravitational pull of the Moon and Sun. The highest tides (Spring tides) occur at full and new Moon; the lowest tides (neap tides) occur at first and last quarter.

SURFACE CURRENTS

GREENWICH MERIDIAN

North Pacific Current

NORTH PACIFIC GYRE

North Equatorial Current

Equatorial Countercurrent

South Equatorial Current

Alaska Current

East Greenland Current

Gulf Stream

North Atlantic Current

NORTH ATLANTIC GYRE

Florida Current

Canaries Current

North Equatorial Current

South Equatorial Current

Equatorial Countercurrent

Peru Current

Brazil Current

SOUTH ATLANTIC GYRE

SOUTH PACIFIC GYRE

Humboldt Current

Falkland Current

Antarctic Circumpolar Current

GREENWICH MERIDIAN

OFFSHORE CURRENTS

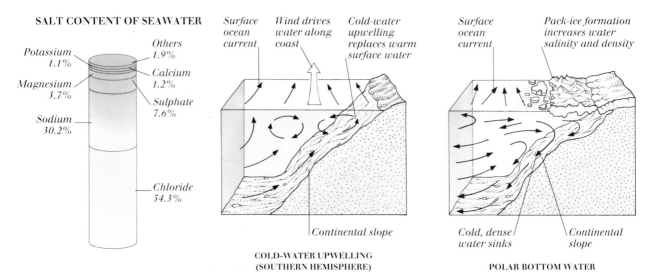

SALT CONTENT OF SEAWATER

Potassium 1.1%

Others 1.9%

Magnesium 3.7%

Calcium 1.2%

Sulphate 7.6%

Sodium 30.2%

Chloride 54.3%

Surface ocean current

Wind drives water along coast

Cold-water upwelling replaces warm surface water

Continental slope

COLD-WATER UPWELLING (SOUTHERN HEMISPHERE)

Surface ocean current

Pack-ice formation increases water salinity and density

Cold, dense water sinks

Continental slope

POLAR BOTTOM WATER

EFFECT OF CORIOLIS FORCE

North Pole

Coriolis force

Winds and currents deflected to right in Northern Hemisphere

Equator

Original direction of wind or current

Winds and currents deflected to left in Southern Hemisphere

Actual direction of wind or current

South Pole

EKMAN SPIRAL (NORTHERN HEMISPHERE)

EQUATOR (0°)

Wind

Surface current caused by wind

Subsurface current slightly deflected by Coriolis force

Deep current at 180° to surface current

Midwater current further deflected by Coriolis force

ARCTIC CIRCLE (66° 52'N)

Oyashio Current

Kuroshio Current

TROPIC OF CANCER (23° 50'N)

North Equatorial Current

Equatorial Countercurrent

North-east Monsoon Drift

North Equatorial Current

Equatorial Countercurrent

South Equatorial Current

South Equatorial Current

SOUTH INDIAN GYRE

East Australian Current

TROPIC OF CAPRICORN (23° 50'S)

West Australian Current

ANTARCTIC CIRCLE (66° 52'S)

HOW TIDES ARE CAUSED

HIGH SPRING TIDE

New Moon

LOW NEAP TIDE

Last quarter

Moon's gravitational pull

HIGH SPRING TIDE

Full Moon

Earth's orbit *Earth*

Tidal bulge caused by Sun's gravitational pull

Tidal bulge caused by Moon's gravitational pull

Sun's gravitational pull

Sun's gravitational pull reinforces centrifugal effect, producing large tidal bulge

Equal and opposite tidal bulge produced by centrifugal effect due to Earth's spin

LOW NEAP TIDE

First quarter

Sun's gravitational pull diminishes Moon's effect

Sun

Moon's orbit

Tidal bulge where Moon's gravitational pull is strongest

Moon

The ocean floor

THE OCEAN FLOOR COMPRISES TWO SECTIONS: the continental shelf and slope, and the deep-ocean floor. The continental shelf and slope are part of the continental crust, but may extend far into the ocean. Sloping quite gently to a depth of about 140 metres, the continental shelf is covered in sandy deposits shaped by waves and tidal currents. At the edge of the continental shelf, the seabed slopes down to the abyssal plain, which lies at an average depth of about 3,800 metres. On this deep-ocean floor is a layer of sediment made up of clays, fine oozes formed from the remains of tiny sea creatures, and occasional mineral-rich deposits. Echo-sounding and remote sensing from satellites has revealed that the abyssal plain is divided by a system of mountain ranges, far bigger than any on land – the mid-ocean ridge. Here, magma (molten rock) wells up from the Earth's interior and solidifies, widening the ocean floor (see pp. 58-59). As the ocean floor spreads, volcanoes that have formed over hot spots in the crust move away from their magma source; they become extinct and are increasingly submerged and eroded. Volcanoes eroded below sea level remain as seamounts (underwater mountains). In warm waters, a volcano that projects above the ocean surface often acquires a fringing coral reef, which may develop into an atoll as the volcano becomes submerged.

CONTINENTAL-SHELF FLOOR

Bedrock exposed by tidal scour

Shoreline

Parallel strips of coarse material left by strong tidal currents

Sand deposited in wavy pattern by weaker currents

Irregular patches of fine sand deposited by weakest currents

FEATURES OF THE OCEAN FLOOR

Sediment

Submarine canyon

Continental shelf

Course of mud river

Continental rise

Continental slope

Seamount (underwater mountain)

Guyot (flat-topped seamount)

Abyssal plain

Continental crust

Ooze (sediment consisting of remains of tiny sea creatures)

Layer of volcanic rock

Pillow lava

Volcanic crystalline rock

Oceanic crust

KEY

- Calcareous ooze
- Pelagic clay
- Glacial sediments
- Siliceous ooze
- Terrigenous sediments
- Continental margin sediments
- Metalliferous muds
- Major nodule fields

DEEP-OCEAN FLOOR SEDIMENTS

ECHO-SOUND PROFILE OF OCEAN FLOOR

Sand wave

Event mark indicates synchronization of survey equipment

Sand wave

Seabed profile

Minor oscillations caused by ship's movement

Velocity of sound in water (1,493 m/sec)

Reference code

Mid-ocean ridge

Ocean trench

Magma (molten rock)

Sediment

DEVELOPMENT OF AN ATOLL

Volcanic island

Sea level

Coral grows on shoreline

FRINGING REEF

Lagoon

Coral continues to grow, forming barrier reef

Eroded volcanic island subsides

BARRIER REEF

Coral continues to grow where waves bring food

Lagoon

Dead coral

Volcanic island becomes submerged

ATOLL

Coral submerged too deeply to grow

Volcanic island is submerged further

SUBMERGED ATOLL

The atmosphere

JET STREAM

THE EARTH IS SURROUNDED BY ITS ATMOSPHERE, a blanket of gases that enables life to exist on the planet. This layer has no definite outer edge, gradually becoming thinner until it merges into space, but over 80 per cent of atmospheric gases are held by gravity within about 20 kilometres of the Earth's surface. The atmosphere blocks out much harmful ultraviolet solar radiation, and insulates the Earth against extremes of temperature by limiting both incoming solar radiation and the escape of re-radiated heat into space. This natural balance may be distorted by the greenhouse effect, as gases such as carbon dioxide have built up in the atmosphere, trapping more heat. Close to the Earth's surface, differences in air temperature and pressure cause air to circulate between the equator and poles. This circulation, together with the Coriolis force, gives rise to the prevailing surface winds and the high-level jet streams.

Exosphere (altitude above about 500 km)

Corona

ATMOSPHERIC CIRCULATION AND WINDS

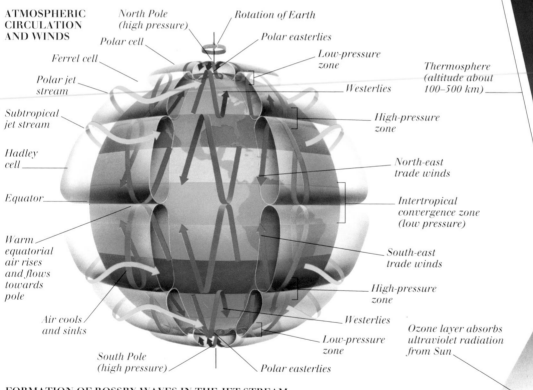

North Pole (high pressure)

Rotation of Earth

Polar cell

Polar easterlies

Ferrel cell

Low-pressure zone

Polar jet stream

Westerlies

Subtropical jet stream

Thermosphere (altitude about 100–500 km)

High-pressure zone

Hadley cell

North-east trade winds

Equator

Intertropical convergence zone (low pressure)

Warm equatorial air rises and flows towards pole

South-east trade winds

High-pressure zone

Air cools and sinks

Westerlies

South Pole (high pressure)

Low-pressure zone

Polar easterlies

Ozone layer absorbs ultraviolet radiation from Sun

FORMATION OF ROSSBY WAVES IN THE JET STREAM

Long Rossby wave develops in polar jet stream

Cold air

Rossby wave becomes more pronounced

Fully developed Rossby wave

Mesosphere (altitude about 50–100 km)

Warm air

INITIAL UNDULATION

DEEPENING WAVE

DEVELOPED WAVE

Stratosphere (altitude about 10–50 km)

Troposphere (altitude up to about 10 km)

STRUCTURE OF THE ATMOSPHERE

GLOBAL WARMING

Solar radiation re-radiated as heat

Some re-radiated heat escapes into space

Sun

Some re-radiated heat reflected back to Earth

Incoming solar radiation

Earth

Atmosphere

NATURALLY MODERATED GREENHOUSE EFFECT

Meteor (shooting star) burns up as it passes through atmosphere

Less re-radiated heat escapes

Solar radiation re-radiated as heat

More re-radiated heat reflected back to Earth

Aurora

Surface temperature rises

"Greenhouse gases" accumulate in atmosphere

Incoming solar radiation

UNBALANCED GREENHOUSE EFFECT

14% of incoming solar radiation absorbed by atmosphere

7% of incoming solar radiation reflected by atmosphere

COMPOSITION OF THE LOWER ATMOSPHERE

24% of incoming solar radiation reflected by clouds

Other elements less than 0.1%

Argon 0.93%

Cosmic rays (high-energy particles from space) penetrate to stratosphere

Oxygen 21%

Some absorbed heat re-radiated by atmosphere

4% of incoming solar radiation reflected by oceans and land

Nitrogen 78%

51% of incoming solar radiation absorbed by Earth's surface

Some absorbed heat re-radiated by clouds

Weather

WEATHER IS DEFINED AS THE ATMOSPHERIC CONDITIONS at a particular time and place; climate is the average weather conditions for a given region over time. Weather is assessed in terms of temperature, wind, cloud cover, and precipitation, such as rain or snow. Fine weather is associated with high-pressure areas, where air is sinking. Cloudy, wet, changeable weather is common in low-pressure zones with rising, unstable air. Such conditions occur at temperate latitudes, where warm air meets cool air along the polar fronts. Here, spiralling low-pressure cells known as depressions (mid-latitude cyclones) often form. A depression usually contains a sector of warmer air, beginning at a warm front and ending at a cold front. If the two fronts merge, forming an occluded front, the warm air is pushed upwards. An extreme form of low-pressure cell is a hurricane (also called a typhoon or tropical cyclone), which brings torrential rain and exceptionally strong winds.

TYPES OF OCCLUDED FRONT

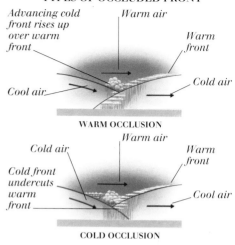

Advancing cold front rises up over warm front

Warm air

Warm front

Cool air

Cold air

WARM OCCLUSION

Cold air

Warm air

Warm front

Cold front undercuts warm front

Cool air

COLD OCCLUSION

FORMS OF PRECIPITATION

Water droplets less than 0.5 mm in diameter fall as drizzle

Water droplets coalesce to form raindrops 0.5–5.0 mm in diameter

Rising air

RAIN FROM CLOUDS NOT REACHING FREEZING LEVEL

Coalesced water droplets fall as rain

Ice crystal

Snowflakes grown from ice crystals fall as snow

Rising air

Snowflakes melt to fall as rain

RAIN AND SNOW FROM CLOUDS REACHING FREEZING LEVEL

Vertical air currents toss frozen water droplets up and down

Alternate freezing and melting builds up layers of ice

Rising air

Ice falls as hailstones

HAIL

TYPES OF CLOUD

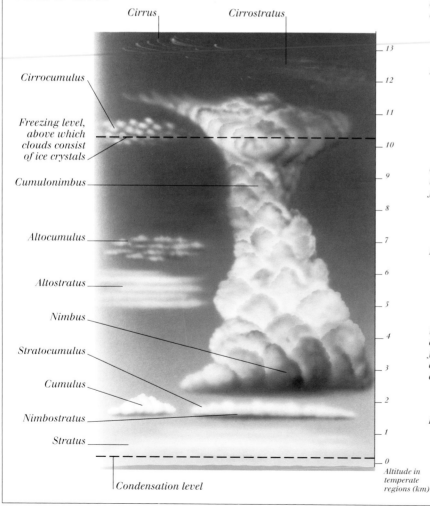

Cirrus

Cirrostratus

Cirrocumulus

Freezing level, above which clouds consist of ice crystals

Cumulonimbus

Altocumulus

Altostratus

Nimbus

Stratocumulus

Cumulus

Nimbostratus

Stratus

Condensation level

13

12

11

10

9

8

7

6

5

4

3

2

1

0

Altitude in temperate regions (km)

STRUCTURE OF A HURRICANE

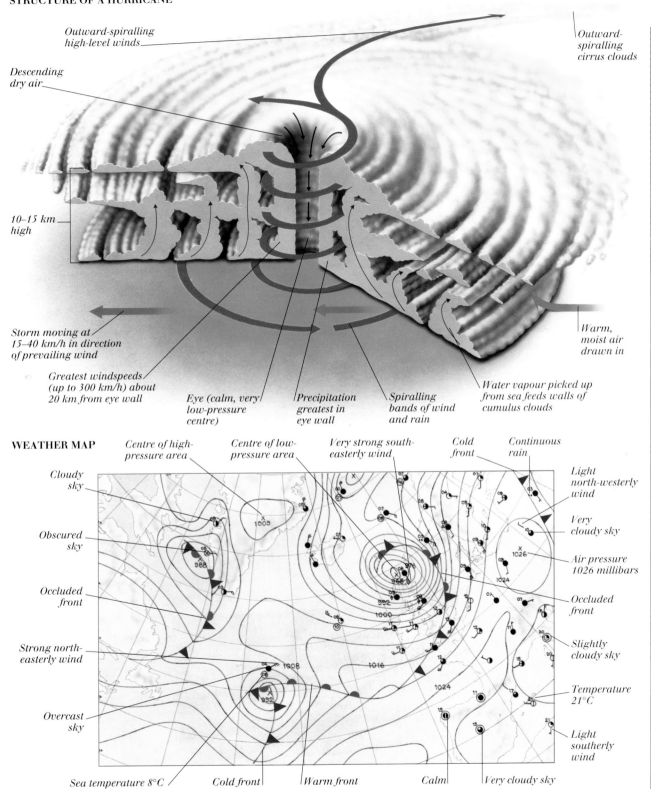

Outward-spiralling
high-level winds

Outward-
spiralling
cirrus clouds

Descending
dry air

10–15 km
high

Storm moving at
15–40 km/h in direction
of prevailing wind

Warm,
moist air
drawn in

Greatest windspeeds
(up to 300 km/h) about
20 km from eye wall

Eye (calm, very
low-pressure
centre)

Precipitation
greatest in
eye wall

Spiralling
bands of wind
and rain

Water vapour picked up
from sea feeds walls of
cumulus clouds

WEATHER MAP

Centre of high-
pressure area

Centre of low-
pressure area

Very strong south-
easterly wind

Cold
front

Continuous
rain

Cloudy
sky

Light
north-westerly
wind

Obscured
sky

Very
cloudy sky

Air pressure
1026 millibars

Occluded
front

Occluded
front

Strong north-
easterly wind

Slightly
cloudy sky

Temperature
21°C

Overcast
sky

Light
southerly
wind

Sea temperature 8°C

Cold front

Warm front

Calm

Very cloudy sky

303

Physics and Chemistry

The Variety of Matter 306

Atoms and Molecules 308

The Periodic Table 310

Chemical Reactions 312

Energy 314

Electricity and Magnetism 316

Light 318

Force and Motion 320

The variety of matter

**PLANT AND INSECT
(LIVING MATTER)**

MATTER IS ANYTHING THAT HAS A MASS. It includes everything from natural substances, such as minerals or living organisms, to synthetic materials. Matter can exist in three distinct states – solid, liquid, and gas. A solid is rigid and retains its shape. A liquid is fluid, has a definite volume, and will take the shape of its container. A gas (also fluid) fills a space, so its volume will be the same as the volume of its container. Most substances can exist as a solid, a liquid, or a gas: the state is determined by temperature. At very high temperatures, matter becomes plasma, often considered to be a fourth state of matter. All matter is composed of microscopic particles, such as atoms and molecules (see pp. 308-309). The arrangement and interactions of these particles give a substance its physical and chemical properties, by which matter can be identified. There is a huge variety of matter because particles can arrange themselves in countless ways, in one substance or by mixing with others. Natural glass, for example, seems to be a solid but is, in fact, a supercool liquid: the atoms are not locked into a pattern and can flow. Pure substances known as elements (see p. 310) combine to form compounds or mixtures. Mixtures called colloids are made up of larger particles of matter suspended in a solid, liquid, or gas, while a solution is one substance dissolved in another.

TYPES OF COLLOID

HAIR GEL (SOLID IN LIQUID)

**SHAVING FOAM
(AIR IN LIQUID)**

**MIST
(LIQUID IN GAS)**

EXAMPLES OF MATTER

The element silicon in pure crystalline form

Polythene is made by combining natural materials in new ways

Low pressure gases

Streaks of plasma (mixture of electrons and charged atoms)

Voltage tears electrons from atoms of low pressure gases inside

Central electrode

**POLYTHENE
(SYNTHETIC POLYMER)**

**PURE SILICON
(SEMICONDUCTOR)**

**BALL CONTAINING
HIGH-TEMPERATURE GAS
(PLASMA)**

Obsidian is molten volcanic rock that cools quickly, so atoms cannot form a regular pattern

Solid crystals dissolve in liquid water

Water

Potassium permanganate crystals

Azurite is found naturally with deposits of copper ore

**OBSIDIAN
(NATURAL GLASS)**

**AZURITE
(CRYSTALLINE MINERAL)**

**POTASSIUM PERMANGANATE AND WATER
(SOLUTION)**

STATES OF MATTER

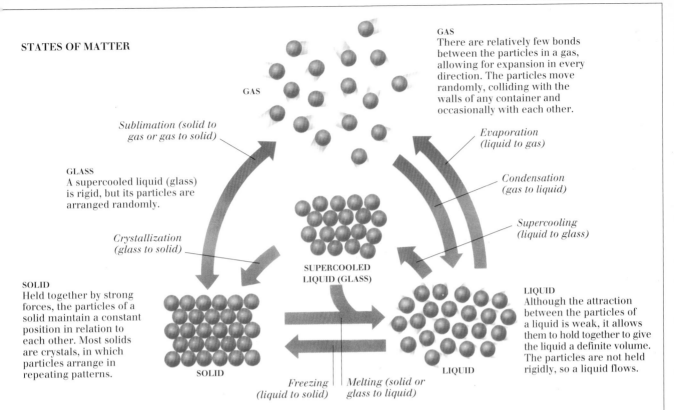

GAS
There are relatively few bonds between the particles in a gas, allowing for expansion in every direction. The particles move randomly, colliding with the walls of any container and occasionally with each other.

GAS

Sublimation (solid to gas or gas to solid)

Evaporation (liquid to gas)

GLASS
A supercooled liquid (glass) is rigid, but its particles are arranged randomly.

Condensation (gas to liquid)

Crystallization (glass to solid)

Supercooling (liquid to glass)

SUPERCOOLED LIQUID (GLASS)

SOLID
Held together by strong forces, the particles of a solid maintain a constant position in relation to each other. Most solids are crystals, in which particles arrange in repeating patterns.

LIQUID
Although the attraction between the particles of a liquid is weak, it allows them to hold together to give the liquid a definite volume. The particles are not held rigidly, so a liquid flows.

SOLID

LIQUID

Freezing (liquid to solid)

Melting (solid or glass to liquid)

CHANGING STATES OF WATER

Round-bottomed glass flask

Ice cubes have a definite shape

Liquid water

Liquid takes the shape of its container

Water remains liquid up to 100 °C (212 °F)

A gas will leave its container

Bubbles of steam form in boiling water

Steam turns back into liquid water where it meets cooler glass

Eventually, all the liquid will become a gas

SOLID STATE: ICE
The solid state of water, ice, forms when liquid water is cooled sufficiently. Ice cubes are rigid, with a definite shape and volume.

LIQUID STATE: WATER
When the temperature of a substance rises above its freezing point, it melts to become a liquid. Ice changes to water.

GASEOUS STATE: STEAM
Above its boiling point, a substance will become a gas. When heated sufficiently, liquid water turns to steam, a colourless gas.

Atoms and molecules

FALSE-COLOUR IMAGE OF ACTUAL GOLD ATOMS

ATOMS ARE THE smallest individual parts of an element (see pp. 310-311). They are tiny, with diameters in the order of one ten-thousand-millionth of a metre (10^{-10} m). Two or more atoms join together (bond) to form a molecule of a substance known as a compound. For example, when atoms of the elements hydrogen and fluorine join together, they form a molecule of the compound hydrogen fluoride. So molecules are the smallest individual parts of a compound. Atoms themselves are not indivisible – they possess an internal structure. At their centre is a dense nucleus, consisting of protons, which have a positive electric charge (see p. 316), and neutrons, which are uncharged. Around the nucleus are the negatively charged electrons. It is the electrons that give a substance most of its physical and chemical properties. They do not follow definite paths around the nucleus. Instead, electrons are said to be found within certain regions, called orbitals. These are arranged around the nucleus in "shells", each containing electrons of a particular energy. For example, the first shell (1) can hold up to two electrons, in a so-called s-orbital (1s). The second shell (2) can hold up to eight electrons, in s-orbitals (2s) and p-orbitals (2p). If an atom loses an electron, it becomes a positive ion (cation). If an electron is gained, an atom becomes a negative ion (anion). Ions of opposite charges will attract and join together, in a type of bonding known as ionic bonding. In covalent bonding, the atoms bond by sharing their electrons in what become molecular orbitals.

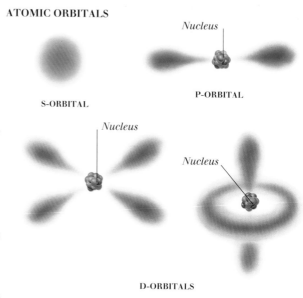

ATOMIC ORBITALS

Nucleus

S-ORBITAL

Nucleus

P-ORBITAL

Nucleus

Nucleus

D-ORBITALS

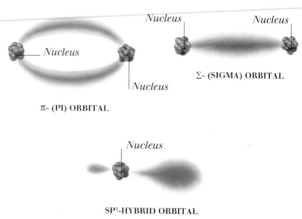

MOLECULAR ORBITALS

Nucleus

Nucleus

π- (PI) ORBITAL

Nucleus

Nucleus

Nucleus

Σ- (SIGMA) ORBITAL

Nucleus

SP⁵-HYBRID ORBITAL

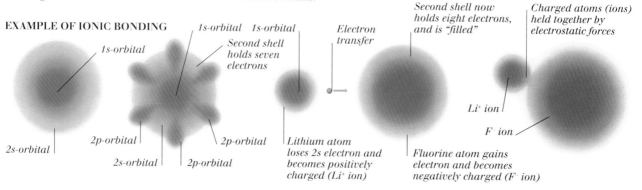

EXAMPLE OF IONIC BONDING

1s-orbital

2s-orbital

1. NEUTRAL LITHIUM ATOM (Li)

1s-orbital   *1s-orbital*
Second shell holds seven electrons

2p-orbital   *2p-orbital*
2s-orbital   *2p-orbital*

NEUTRAL FLUORINE ATOM (F)

Electron transfer

Lithium atom loses 2s electron and becomes positively charged (Li⁺ ion)

Second shell now holds eight electrons, and is "filled"

Fluorine atom gains electron and becomes negatively charged (F⁻ ion)

2. ELECTRON TRANSFER

Charged atoms (ions) held together by electrostatic forces

Li⁺ ion

F⁻ ion

3. IONIC BONDING: LITHIUM FLUORIDE MOLECULE (LiF)

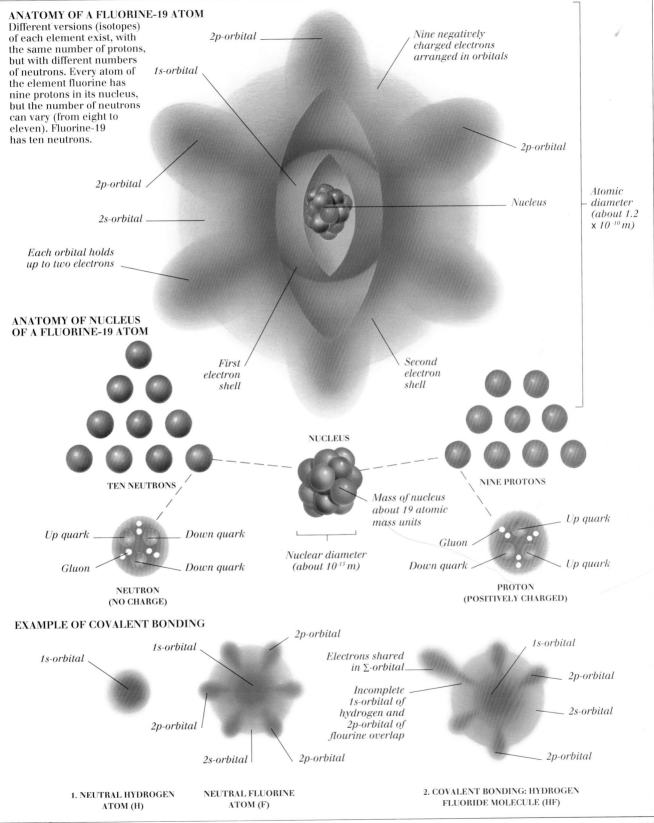

ANATOMY OF A FLUORINE-19 ATOM
Different versions (isotopes) of each element exist, with the same number of protons, but with different numbers of neutrons. Every atom of the element fluorine has nine protons in its nucleus, but the number of neutrons can vary (from eight to eleven). Fluorine-19 has ten neutrons.

2p-orbital

1s-orbital

Nine negatively charged electrons arranged in orbitals

2p-orbital

2p-orbital

2s-orbital

Nucleus

Atomic diameter (about 1.2 x 10^{-10} m)

Each orbital holds up to two electrons

ANATOMY OF NUCLEUS OF A FLUORINE-19 ATOM

First electron shell

Second electron shell

NUCLEUS

TEN NEUTRONS

NINE PROTONS

Mass of nucleus about 19 atomic mass units

Up quark

Down quark

Gluon

Down quark

Nuclear diameter (about 10^{-15} m)

Up quark

Gluon

Down quark

Up quark

NEUTRON (NO CHARGE)

PROTON (POSITIVELY CHARGED)

EXAMPLE OF COVALENT BONDING

1s-orbital

1s-orbital

2p-orbital

2p-orbital

2s-orbital

2p-orbital

Electrons shared in Σ-orbital

Incomplete 1s-orbital of hydrogen and 2p-orbital of flourine overlap

1s-orbital

2p-orbital

2s-orbital

2p-orbital

1. NEUTRAL HYDROGEN ATOM (H)

NEUTRAL FLUORINE ATOM (F)

2. COVALENT BONDING: HYDROGEN FLUORIDE MOLECULE (HF)

The periodic table

AN ELEMENT is a substance that consists of atoms of one type only. The 92 elements that occur naturally, and the 17 elements created artificially, are often arranged into a chart called the periodic table. Each element is defined by its atomic number – the number of protons in the nucleus of each of its atoms (it is also the number of electrons present). Atomic number increases along each row (period) and down each column (group). The shape of the table is determined by the way in which electrons arrange themselves around the nucleus: the positioning of elements in order of increasing atomic number brings together atoms with a similar pattern of orbiting electrons (orbitals). These appear in blocks. Electrons occupy shells of a certain energy (see pp. 308-309). Periods are ordered according to the filling of successive shells with electrons, while groups reflect the number of electrons in the outer shell (valency electrons). These outer electrons are important – they decide the chemical properties of the atom. Elements that appear in the same group have similar properties because they have the same number of electrons in their outer shell. Elements in Group 0 have "filled shells", where the outer shell holds its maximum number of electrons, and are stable. Atoms of Group I elements have just one electron in their outer shell. This makes them unstable – and ready to react with other substances.

METALS AND NON-METALS
Elements at the left-hand side of each period are metals. Metals easily lose electrons and form positive ions. Non-metals, on the right of a period, tend to become negative ions. Semi-metals, which have properties of both metals and non-metals, are between the two.

Atomic number is number of protons in each nucleus

Atomic number goes up by one along each period

1						
H Hydrogen 1.0						

Chemical symbol — **H** — **Chemical name** — Hydrogen — 1.0 — *Relative atomic mass* — *Atomic number* — 1

RELATIVE ATOMIC MASS
Atomic mass (formerly atomic weight) is the mass of each atom of an element. It is equal to the number of protons plus the number of neutrons (electrons have negligible mass). The figures given are the averages for all the different versions (isotopes) of each element, measured relative to the mass of carbon-12.

Group I

Group II

1st transition metals

3 **Li** Lithium 6.9	4 **Be** Beryllium 9.0					
11 **Na** Sodium 23.0	12 **Mg** Magnesium 24.3					
19 **K** Potassium 39.1	20 **Ca** Calcium 40.1	21 **Sc** Scandium 45.0	22 **Ti** Titanium 47.9	23 **V** Vanadium 50.9	24 **Cr** Chromium 52.0	25 **Mn** Manganese 54.9
37 **Rb** Rubidium 85.5	38 **Sr** Strontium 87.6	39 **Y** Yttrium 88.9	40 **Zr** Zirconium 91.2	41 **Nb** Niobium 92.9	42 **Mo** Molybdenum 95.9	43 **Tc** Technetium 99.0
55 **Cs** Caesium 132.9	56 **Ba** Barium 137.4	57-71	72 **Hf** Hafnium 178.5	73 **Ta** Tantalum 181.0	74 **W** Tungsten 183.9	75 **Re** Rhenium 186.2
87 **Fr** Francium 223.0	88 **Ra** Radium 226.0	89-103	104 **Unq** Unnilquadium (261)	105 **Unp** Unnilpentium (262)	106 **Unh** Unnilhexium (263)	107 **Uns** Unnilseptium (262)

s-block

Two series always separated out from the table to give it a coherent shape

d-block

Soft, silvery, and highly reactive metal

SODIUM: GROUP 1 METAL

Silvery, reactive metal

MAGNESIUM: GROUP 2 METAL

Hard, silvery metal

CHROMIUM: 1ST TRANSITION METAL

TYPES OF ELEMENT KEY:

- Alkali metals
- Alkaline earth metals
- Transition metals
- Lanthanides (rare earths)
- Actinides
- Poor metals
- Semi-metals'
- Non-metals
- Noble gases

Radioactive metal

PLUTONIUM: ACTINIDE SERIES METAL

57 **La** Lanthanum 138.9	58 **Ce** Cerium 140.1	59 **Pr** Praseodymium 140.9	60 **Nd** Neodymium 144.2
89 **Ac** Actinium 227.0	90 **Th** Thorium 232.0	91 **Pa** Protactinium 231.0	92 **U** Uranium 238.0

ALLOTROPES OF CARBON
Some elements exist in more than one form – these are known as allotropes. Carbon powder, graphite, and diamond are allotropes of carbon. They all consist of carbon atoms, but have very different physical properties.

DIAMOND

GRAPHITE

CARBON POWDER

Bright yellow crystal

SULPHUR: GROUP 6 SOLID NON-METAL

IODINE: GROUP 7 SOLID NON-METAL

Purple-black solid turns to gas easily

Group 0

Period

						2 **He** Helium 4.0

Boron and carbon groups — *Nitrogen and oxygen groups* — *Halogens*

Group III	*Group IV*	*Group V*	*Group VI*	*Group VII*
5 **B** Boron 10.8	6 **C** Carbon 12.0	7 **N** Nitrogen 14.0	8 **O** Oxygen 16.0	9 **F** Fluorine 19.0

Short period

10
Ne
Neon
20.2

| 13
Al
Aluminium
27.0 | 14
Si
Silicon
28.1 | 15
P
Phosphorus
31.0 | 16
S
Sulphur
32.1 | 17
Cl
Chlorine
55.5 | 18
Ar
Argon
40.0 |

2nd transition metals — *3rd transition metals*

Long period

26 **Fe** Iron 55.9	27 **Co** Cobalt 58.9	28 **Ni** Nickel 58.7	29 **Cu** Copper 63.5	30 **Zn** Zinc 65.4	31 **Ga** Gallium 69.7	32 **Ge** Germanium 72.6	33 **As** Arsenic 74.9	34 **Se** Selenium 79.0	35 **Br** Bromine 79.9	36 **Kr** Krypton 85.8
44 **Ru** Ruthenium 101.0	45 **Rh** Rhodium 102.9	46 **Pd** Palladium 106.4	47 **Ag** Silver 107.9	48 **Cd** Cadmium 112.4	49 **In** Indium 114.8	50 **Sn** Tin 118.7	51 **Sb** Antimony 121.8	52 **Te** Tellurium 127.6	53 **I** Iodine 126.9	54 **Xe** Xenon 131.5
76 **Os** Osmium 190.2	77 **Ir** Iridium 192.2	78 **Pt** Platinum 195.1	79 **Au** Gold 197.0	80 **Hg** Mercury 200.6	81 **Tl** Thallium 204.4	82 **Pb** Lead 207.2	83 **Bi** Bismuth 209.0	84 **Po** Polonium 210.0	85 **At** Astatine 210.0	86 **Rn** Radon 222.0
108 **Uno** Unniloctium (265)	109 **Une** Unnilennium (266)									

d-block — *p-block*

Atomic mass is estimated, as element exists fleetingly

Unreactive, colourless gas glows red in discharge tube

Shiny semi-metal

NOBLE GASES
Group 0 contains elements that have a filled (complete) outer shell of electrons, which means the atoms do not need to lose or gain electrons by bonding with other atoms. This makes them stable and they do not easily form ions or react with other elements. Noble gases are also called rare or inert gases.

Yellow, unreactive precious metal

Soft, shiny, reactive metal

GOLD: 3RD TRANSITION METAL

TIN: GROUP 4 POOR METAL

ANTIMONY: GROUP 5 SEMI-METAL

NEON: GROUP 0 COLOURLESS GAS

61 **Pm** Promethium 147.0	62 **Sm** Samarium 150.4	63 **Eu** Europium 152.0	64 **Gd** Gadolinium 157.3	65 **Tb** Terbium 158.9	66 **Dy** Dysprosium 162.5	67 **Ho** Holmium 164.9	68 **Er** Erbium 167.3	69 **Tm** Thulium 168.9	70 **Yb** Ytterbium 175.0	71 **Lu** Lutetium 175.0
93 **Np** Neptunium 237.0	94 **Pu** Plutonium 242.0	95 **Am** Americium 243.0	96 **Cm** Curium 247.0	97 **Bk** Berkelium 247.0	98 **Cf** Californium 251.0	99 **Es** Einsteinium 254.0	100 **Fm** Fermium 253.0	101 **Md** Mendelevium 256.0	102 **No** Nobelium 254.0	103 **Lr** Lawrencium 257.0

f-block

Chemical reactions

A CHEMICAL REACTION TAKES PLACE whenever bonds between atoms are broken or made. In each case, atoms or groups of atoms rearrange, making new substances (products) from the original ones (reactants). Reactions happen naturally, or can be made to happen; they may take years, or only an instant. Some of the main types are shown here. A reaction usually involves a change in energy (see pp. 314-315). In a burning reaction, for example, the making of new bonds between atoms releases energy as heat and light. This type of reaction, in which heat is given off, is an exothermic reaction. Many reactions, like burning, are irreversible, but some can take place in either direction, and are said to be reversible. Reactions can be used to form solids from solutions: in a double decomposition reaction, two compounds in solution break down and re-form into two new substances, often creating a precipitate (insoluble solid); in displacement, an element (eg. copper) displaces another element (eg. silver) from a solution. The rate (speed) of a reaction is determined by many different factors, such as temperature, and the size and shape of the reactants. To describe and keep track of reactions, internationally recognized chemical symbols and equations are used. Reactions are also used in the laboratory to identify matter. An experiment with candle wax, for example, demonstrates that it contains carbon and hydrogen.

SALT FORMATION (ACID ON METAL)

Glass beaker

Hydrogen gas (H_2) given off

Zinc (Zn) replaces hydrogen in acid (HCl) to form zinc chloride solution ($ZnCl_2$)

Hydrogen in acid driven off when acid meets a reactive metal

Hydrochloric acid (HCl)

Effervescence

Zinc metal chippings (Zn)

Zinc metal chippings (Zn)

THE REACTION
Hydrochloric acid added to zinc produces zinc chloride and hydrogen.
$Zn + 2HCl \rightarrow ZnCl_2 + H_2$

DISPLACEMENT

Copper metal (Cu)

Silver nitrate solution ($AgNO_3$)

Two metals compete for nitrate ions

Glass flask

Copper (Cu) displaces silver ions (Ag^{2+}) from silver nitrate solution ($AgNO_3$)

Blue solution of copper nitrate ($Cu(NO_3)_2$) forms

Needles of silver metal (Ag) form

THE REACTION
Copper metal added to silver nitrate solution produces copper nitrate and silver metal.
$Cu + 2AgNO_3 \rightarrow Cu(NO_3)_2 + 2Ag$

BURNING MATTER

Ammonium dichromate (($NH_4)_2Cr_2O_7$)

Flame

In this burning reaction, atoms form simpler substances and give off heat and light

Ammonium dichromate (($NH_4)_2Cr_2O_7$) converts to chromium oxide (Cr_2O_3)

Nitrogen monoxide (NO) and water vapour (H_2O) given off as colourless gases

THE REACTION
When lit, ammonium dichromate combines with oxygen from air.
$(NH_4)_2Cr_2O_7 + O_2 \rightarrow Cr_2O_3 + 4H_2O + 2NO$

A REVERSIBLE REACTION

Flat-bottomed glass flask

Potassium chromate solution (K_2CrO_4)

Bright yellow solution contains potassium and chromate ions

Pipette

Hydrochloric acid (HCl) added in drops

Acid causes reaction to take place

Chromate ions converted to orange dichromate ions

Potassium dichromate (KCr_2O_7) forms

Pipette

Sodium hydroxide (NaOH) neutralizes the acid

Solution turns to bright orange of potassium dichromate

Potassium dichromate (KCr_2O_7) re-forms to potassium chromate (K_2CrO_4)

Sodium hydroxide (NaOH) added in drops

Solution returns to original bright yellow colour

1. THE REACTANT
Potassium chromate dissolves in water to form potassium ions and chromate ions.
$K_2CrO_4 \rightarrow 2K^+ + CrO_4^{2-}$

2. THE REACTION
Addition of hydrochloric acid changes chromate ions into dichromate ions.
$2CrO_4^{2-} \rightarrow Cr_2O_7^{2-}$

3. REVERSING
Addition of sodium hydroxide changes dichromate ions back into chromate ions.
$Cr_2O_7^{2-} \rightarrow 2CrO_4^{2-}$

FERMENTATION

Airtight stopper

Yeast converts sugar into alcohol (C_2H_5OH) and carbon dioxide gas (CO_2)

Flat-bottomed glass flask

Yeast mixed with warm water and sugar ($C_6H_{12}O_6$)

Carbon dioxide bubbles (CO_2)

THE REACTION
Yeast converts sugar and warm water into alcohol and carbon dioxide.
$$C_6H_{12}O_6 \rightarrow 2C_2H_5OH + 2CO_2$$

DOUBLE DECOMPOSITION

Potassium iodide solution (KI)

Lead nitrate solution ($Pb(NO_3)_2$)

Two solutions swap partners

Potassium iodide solution added to lead nitrate solution

Lead iodide (PbI_2), a yellow solid, forms

Potassium nitrate solution (KNO_3) forms

1. THE REACTANTS
Potassium iodide in water (KI) and lead nitrate in water ($Pb(NO_3)_2$) each form colourless solutions.

2. THE REACTION
When the solutions are mixed, lead iodide, a precipitate, and potassium nitrate solution are formed.
$$2KI + Pb(NO_3)_2 \rightarrow PbI_2 + 2KNO_3$$

TESTING CANDLE WAX, AN ORGANIC COMPOUND

Clamp stand

Burning produces carbon dioxide gas (CO_2) and water vapour (H_2O)

Delivery tube

Gases are trapped in funnel

Delivery tube

Unburned carbon forms soot particles

Bung

Bung

Thistle funnel

U-tube

Bung

Flame

Tube connection to pump that sucks gases through

Burning candle wax

Water vapour condenses to form liquid water (H_2O)

Clamp

Test tube

Water vapour trapped by solid drying agent, anhydrous copper sulphate ($CuSO_4$)

Anhydrous copper sulphate ($CuSO_4$)

Carbon dioxide gas (CO_2) given off

Candle wax ($C_{18}H_{38}$), a hydrocarbon, contains the elements carbon and hydrogen

Anhydrous copper sulphate crystals ($CuSO_4$) combine with water vapour (H_2O) to form darker blue hydrated copper sulphate ($CuSO_4 . 10H_2O$)

Calcium hydroxide ($Ca(OH)_2$) and carbon dioxide (CO_2) form insoluble calcium carbonate ($CaCO_3$): lime water becomes milky

Calcium hydroxide solution (lime water, $Ca(OH)_2$)

1. THE BURNING REACTION
Burning wax produces carbon dioxide gas and water vapour.
$$2C_{18}H_{38} + 55O_2 \rightarrow 36CO_2 + 38H_2O$$

2. TESTING FOR WATER VAPOUR
A solid drying agent traps water vapour, proving the presence of hydrogen in the candle wax.
$$CuSO_4 + 10H_2O \rightarrow CuSO_4 . 10H_2O$$

3. TESTING FOR CARBON DIOXIDE
Calcium hydroxide in solution reacts with carbon dioxide, forming a carbonate and turning milky.
$$Ca(OH)_2 + CO_2 \rightarrow CaCO_3 + H_2O$$

Energy

ANYTHING THAT HAPPENS – from a pin-drop to an explosion – requires energy. Energy is the capacity for "doing work" (making something happen). Various forms of energy exist, including light, heat, sound, electrical, chemical, nuclear, kinetic, and potential energies. The Law of Conservation of Energy states that the total amount of energy in the Universe is fixed – energy cannot be created or destroyed. It means that energy can only change from one form to another (energy transfer). For example, potential energy is energy that is "stored", and can be used in the future. An object gains potential energy when it is lifted; as the object is released, potential energy changes into the energy of motion (kinetic energy). During transference, some of the energy converts into heat. A combined heat and power station can put some of the otherwise "waste" heat to useful effect in local schools and housing. Most of the Earth's energy is provided by the Sun, in the form of electromagnetic radiation (see pp. 316-317). Some of this energy transfers to plant and animal life, and ultimately to fossil fuels, where it is stored in chemical form. Our bodies obtain energy from the food we eat, while energy needed for other tasks, such as heating and transport, can be obtained by burning fossil fuels – or by harnessing natural forces like wind or moving water – to generate electricity. Another source is nuclear power, where energy is released by reactions in the nucleus of an atom. All energy is measured by the international unit, the joule (J). As a guide, one joule is about equal to the amount of energy needed to lift an apple one metre.

SANKEY DIAGRAM SHOWING ENERGY FLOW IN A COAL-FIRED COMBINED HEAT AND POWER STATION

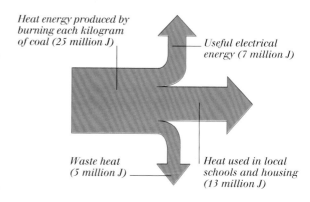

Heat energy produced by burning each kilogram of coal (25 million J)

Useful electrical energy (7 million J)

Waste heat (5 million J)

Heat used in local schools and housing (13 million J)

CROSS-SECTION OF HYDROELECTRIC POWER STATION WITH FRANCIS TURBINE

Transformer

Insulator

High voltage cable

Switch gear including circuit braker

Bushing

Rotor house

Generator unit

Gate

Generator rotor turned by turbine

Shaft

Francis turbine

Curved blade

Gate

Afterbay

Screen

Water in reservoir

Potential energy of water intake turns turbine

Penstock

Draft tube

Tailrace

Water that flows out has lost some energy

CROSS-SECTION OF NUCLEAR POWER STATION WITH PRESSURIZED WATER REACTOR

Steam generator

Concrete shielding

Water pressurizer

Steel girder framework

Control rod

Reactor core

Pump

Moderator (water)

Enriched uranium fuel

Coolant (water) takes heat from reactor core to heat exchanger

Heat exchanger

Water pumped back into steam generator

Pump

Water cools used steam

Steam loses energy to turbine and condenses back to water

Water in heat exchanger turns to steam

Steam drives turbine

Turbine shaft turns generator

Generator produces electric current at 25,000 volts

Transformer increases voltage to 300,000 volts

High voltage cable

Pylon carries high voltage electricity

Hot water to cooling tower

Cold water from cooling tower

ENERGY SYSTEMS

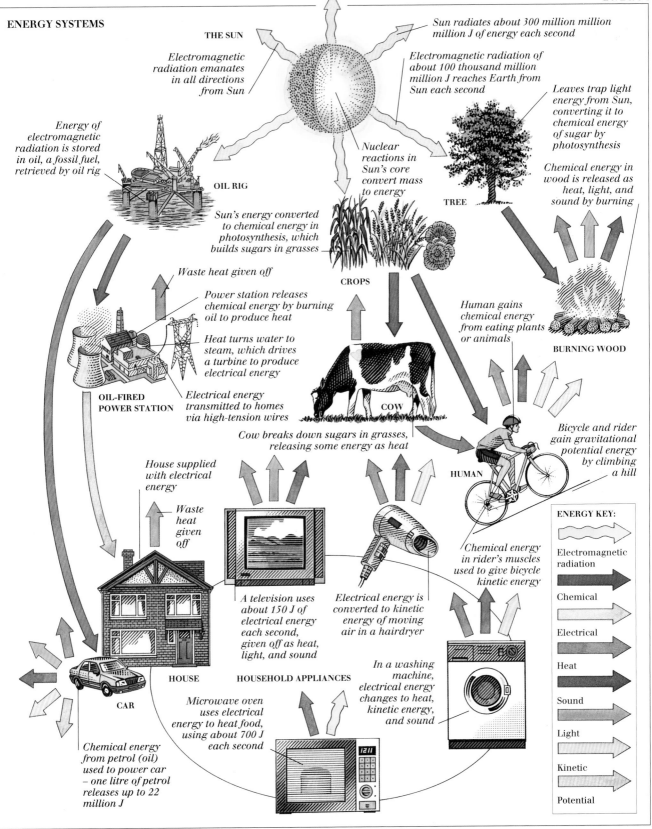

THE SUN

Sun radiates about 300 million million million J of energy each second

Electromagnetic radiation emanates in all directions from Sun

Electromagnetic radiation of about 100 thousand million million J reaches Earth from Sun each second

Leaves trap light energy from Sun, converting it to chemical energy of sugar by photosynthesis

Energy of electromagnetic radiation is stored in oil, a fossil fuel, retrieved by oil rig

OIL RIG

Nuclear reactions in Sun's core convert mass to energy

TREE

Chemical energy in wood is released as heat, light, and sound by burning

Sun's energy converted to chemical energy in photosynthesis, which builds sugars in grasses

CROPS

Waste heat given off

Power station releases chemical energy by burning oil to produce heat

Heat turns water to steam, which drives a turbine to produce electrical energy

OIL-FIRED POWER STATION

Electrical energy transmitted to homes via high-tension wires

Human gains chemical energy from eating plants or animals

BURNING WOOD

COW

Cow breaks down sugars in grasses, releasing some energy as heat

House supplied with electrical energy

Waste heat given off

HUMAN

Bicycle and rider gain gravitational potential energy by climbing a hill

Chemical energy in rider's muscles used to give bicycle kinetic energy

A television uses about 150 J of electrical energy each second, given off as heat, light, and sound

Electrical energy is converted to kinetic energy of moving air in a hairdryer

HOUSE

HOUSEHOLD APPLIANCES

In a washing machine, electrical energy changes to heat, kinetic energy, and sound

CAR

Microwave oven uses electrical energy to heat food, using about 700 J each second

Chemical energy from petrol (oil) used to power car – one litre of petrol releases up to 22 million J

ENERGY KEY:

Electromagnetic radiation

Chemical

Electrical

Heat

Sound

Light

Kinetic

Potential

Electricity and magnetism

ELECTRICAL EFFECTS result from an imbalance of electric charge. There are two types of electric charge, named positive (carried by protons) and negative (carried by electrons). If charges are opposite (unlike), they attract one another, while like charges repel. Forces of attraction and repulsion (electrostatic forces) exist between any two charged particles. Matter is normally uncharged, but if electrons are gained, an object will gain an overall negative charge; if they are removed, it becomes positive. Objects with an overall negative or positive charge are said to have an imbalance of charge, and exert the same forces as individual negative and positive charges. On this larger scale, the forces will always act to regain the balance of charge. This causes static electricity. Lightning, for example, is produced by clouds discharging a huge excess of negative electrons. If charges are "free" – in a wire or material that allows electrons to pass through it – the forces cause a flow of charge called an electric current. Some substances exhibit the strange phenomenon of magnetism – which also produces attractive and repulsive forces. Magnetic substances consist of small regions called domains. Normally unmagnetized, they can be magnetized by being placed in a magnetic field. Magnetism and electricity are inextricably linked, a fact put to use in motors and generators.

LIGHTNING

VAN DE GRAAFF (ELECTROSTATIC) GENERATOR

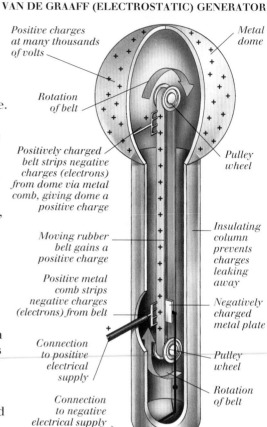

Positive charges at many thousands of volts

Metal dome

Rotation of belt

Positively charged belt strips negative charges (electrons) from dome via metal comb, giving dome a positive charge

Pulley wheel

Moving rubber belt gains a positive charge

Positive metal comb strips negative charges (electrons) from belt

Connection to positive electrical supply

Connection to negative electrical supply

Insulating column prevents charges leaking away

Negatively charged metal plate

Pulley wheel

Rotation of belt

CURRENT ELECTRICITY

Crocodile clip connector

Bulb receives 3 volts

Bulb holder

Metal wire (conductor) coated with plastic (insulator)

Bulb receives 3 volts

Bulb holder

Direction of current, opposite to electron flow by convention

Electrons flow from negative terminal to positive terminal

Switch completes or breaks circuit

Junction

Four 1.5 volt cells (total of 6 volts)

Negative terminal

Positive terminal

VOLTAGE
The higher the voltage, the greater the energy of electrical charges. One volt is one joule (unit of energy) per coulomb (unit of charge).

CURRENT
The greater the number of electrons moving around the circuit, the higher the current. Current is measured in amps (A). One amp equals one coulomb (unit of charge) per second.

Metal wire (conductor) coated with plastic (insulator)

Bulb holder

Bulb receives 6 volts

Bulb has high resistance

RESISTANCE
For a given voltage, the flow of current depends upon the resistance of a circuit. Resistance is the degree to which a substance resists electrical current. It is measured in ohms (Ω).

SERIES ELECTRICAL CIRCUIT

SIMPLE ELECTRICAL CIRCUIT

MAGNETIC FIELDS AND FORCES

Iron filings

North-seeking pole

Profile of magnetic field

Bar magnet

North-seeking pole

South-seeking pole

Unlike poles attract

Direction of force

Like poles repel

North-seeking pole

South-seeking pole

Unlike poles attract

North-seeking pole

South-seeking pole

Like poles repel

South-seeking pole of electromagnet

Electromagnet

Wire to battery

MAGNETIC DOMAINS

Domain

Direction of magnetization within domain is random

Domain boundary

UNMAGNETIZED IRON

Direction of magnetization within domain has aligned

Domain aligned with magnetization has grown

Domain not aligned with magnetization has shrunk

Direction of overall magnetization

MAGNETIZED IRON IN A MAGNETIC FIELD

GENERATING MAGNETISM FROM ELECTRICITY

Direction of magnetic field (from north pole to south pole)

Magnetic field

Coil carries electric current

Direction of current

Electric current produces magnetic field

Metal wire (conductor) coated with plastic (insulator)

Negative terminal

Positive terminal

Four 1.5 volt cells (total of 6 volts)

CIRCUIT WITH ELECTROMAGNET

GENERATING ELECTRICITY FROM MAGNETISM

Terminal box

Coil of wire

Permanent magnet

Bearing

Non-drive end

Coil of wire

Terminal

Stator

Main rotor turns in magnetic field produced by coil of wire in stator

Fan

Drive end

Coil of wire

Shaft

Secondary (exciter) rotor

ELECTRIC GENERATOR
In a generator, the rotor rotates within the magnetic field of the stator to produce an electric current.

Coil of wire rotates within magnetic field of permanent magnet

Permanent magnet

Steel casing

Iron core

Coated copper winding

Commutator

Terminal

Spindle

End of shaft

Terminal

ELECTRIC MOTOR
In a motor, magnetic forces between the winding and permanent magnet produce a rotary motion.

Light

INFRA-RED IMAGE OF A HOUSE

LIGHT IS A FORM OF ENERGY. It is a type of electromagnetic radiation, like X-rays or radio waves. All electromagnetic radiation is produced by electric charges (see pp. 316-317): it is caused by the effects of oscillating electric and magnetic fields as they travel through space. Electromagnetic radiation is considered to have both wave and particle properties. It can be thought of as a wave of electricity and magnetism. In that case, the difference between the various forms of radiation is their wavelength. Radiation can also be said to consist of particles, or packets of energy, called photons. The difference between light and X-rays, for instance, is the amount of energy that each photon carries. The complete range of radiation is referred to as the electromagnetic spectrum, extending from low energy, long wavelength radio waves to high energy, short wavelength gamma rays. Light is the only part of the electromagnetic spectrum that is visible. White light from the Sun is made up of all the visible wavelengths of radiation, which can be seen when it is separated by using a prism. Light, like all forms of electromagnetic radiation, can be reflected (bounced back) and refracted (bent). Different parts of the electromagnetic spectrum are produced in different ways. Sometimes visible light – and infra-red radiation – is generated by the vibrating particles of warm or hot objects. The emission of light in this way is called incandescence. Light can also be produced by fluorescence, a phenomenon in which electrons gain and lose energy within atoms.

MAXWELLIAN DIAGRAM OF ELECTROMAGNETIC RADIATION AS WAVES

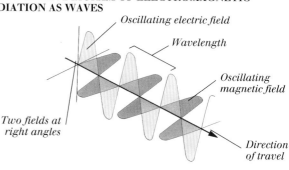

Oscillating electric field

Wavelength

Oscillating magnetic field

Two fields at right angles

Direction of travel

ELECTROMAGNETIC RADIATION AS PARTICLES

Photon thought of as wave packet of energy

Blue light has about twice the energy of red light

Red light has long wavelength

Blue light has shorter wavelength: waves are more tightly packed

PHOTON OF RED LIGHT　　　**PHOTON OF BLUE LIGHT**

SPLITTING WHITE LIGHT INTO THE SPECTRUM

Prism forms spectrum by bending wavelengths at different angles

Glass prism　　White light

Red light (wavelength: 6.2–7.7×10^{-7} m)

Orange light (wavelength: 5.9–6.2×10^{-7} m)

Yellow light (wavelength: 5.7–5.9×10^{-7} m)

Green light (wavelength: 4.9–5.7×10^{-7} m)

Blue light (wavelength: 4.5–4.9×10^{-7} m)

Violet light (wavelength: 3.9–4.5×10^{-7} m)

THE ELECTROMAGNETIC SPECTRUM

ENERGY (JOULES)　10^{-28}|　10^{-27}|　10^{-26}|　10^{-25}|　10^{-24}|　10^{-23}|　10^{-22}|　10^{-21}|　10^{-20}|

WAVELENGTH (METERS)　10^{4}|　10^{3}|　10^{2}|　10|　1|　10^{-1}|　10^{-2}|　10^{-3}|　10^{-4}|　10^{-5}

Long-wave radio　Medium-wave radio　Short-wave radio　Very high-frequency (VHF) radio　Microwaves　Infra-red radiation

Radio waves

ARTIFICIAL LIGHT SOURCES

FLUORESCENT TUBE

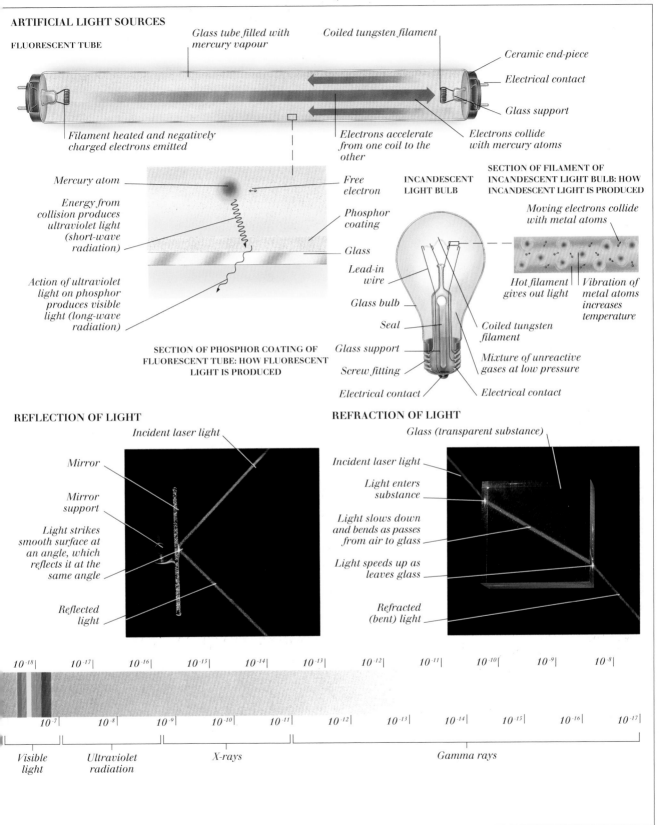

Glass tube filled with mercury vapour

Coiled tungsten filament

Ceramic end-piece

Electrical contact

Glass support

Filament heated and negatively charged electrons emitted

Electrons accelerate from one coil to the other

Electrons collide with mercury atoms

Mercury atom

Energy from collision produces ultraviolet light (short-wave radiation)

Action of ultraviolet light on phosphor produces visible light (long-wave radiation)

Free electron

Phosphor coating

Glass

SECTION OF PHOSPHOR COATING OF FLUORESCENT TUBE: HOW FLUORESCENT LIGHT IS PRODUCED

INCANDESCENT LIGHT BULB

SECTION OF FILAMENT OF INCANDESCENT LIGHT BULB: HOW INCANDESCENT LIGHT IS PRODUCED

Moving electrons collide with metal atoms

Hot filament gives out light

Vibration of metal atoms increases temperature

Lead-in wire

Glass bulb

Seal

Glass support

Screw fitting

Electrical contact

Coiled tungsten filament

Mixture of unreactive gases at low pressure

Electrical contact

REFLECTION OF LIGHT

Incident laser light

Mirror

Mirror support

Light strikes smooth surface at an angle, which reflects it at the same angle

Reflected light

REFRACTION OF LIGHT

Glass (transparent substance)

Incident laser light

Light enters substance

Light slows down and bends as passes from air to glass

Light speeds up as leaves glass

Refracted (bent) light

10^{-18} | 10^{-17} | 10^{-16} | 10^{-15} | 10^{-14} | 10^{-13} | 10^{-12} | 10^{-11} | 10^{-10} | 10^{-9} | 10^{-8} |

10^{-7} | 10^{-8} | 10^{-9} | 10^{-10} | 10^{-11} | 10^{-12} | 10^{-13} | 10^{-14} | 10^{-15} | 10^{-16} | 10^{-17} |

Visible light

Ultraviolet radiation

X-rays

Gamma rays

Force and motion

FORCES ARE PUSHES OR PULLS that change the motion of objects. To make a stationary object move, or a moving object stop, a force is needed. A force is also required to change the speed or direction of an object. This change in speed or direction is known as acceleration. Acceleration depends on the size (magnitude) of the force, and on the mass of the object. The effects of forces were first summarized by Isaac Newton in his three laws of motion. The international unit of force, named after him, is the newton (N), which is approximately equal to the weight of one apple. Gravity – the force of attraction between any two masses – can be measured using a newton meter (spring balance). Forces are put to useful effect in machines. A simple machine, such as a wheel and axle, is a device that changes the size or direction of an applied force. It allows an applied force (the effort) to produce another force (the load). A lever uses a bar that turns on a fulcrum to exert force. In all simple machines, there is a relationship between force and distance. A small force (in a compound pulley, for instance) moves through a large distance to lift a heavy object a small distance. This is called the Law of Simple Machines.

SIMPLE MACHINES

Single-pulley system (simple pulley)

Pulley wheel

Simple pulley only changes direction of a force

Effort is the same size as the load (10 N) and is pulled the same distance

One rope attached to load

Load of 10 N

Two-pulley system (simple pulley)

Pulley wheel

Effort is half the load (5 N), but the rope must be pulled twice the distance

Two ropes share the force and distance

Pulley wheel

Load of 10 N

Four-pulley system (compound pulley)

Two pulley wheels

Effort is one quarter of the load (2.5 N), but the rope must be pulled four times the distance

Four ropes share the force and distance

SIMPLE AND COMPOUND PULLEYS

Two pulley wheels

Load of 10 N

NEWTON METERS (SPRING BALANCES)

Weight is measured using a spring

When weight pulls downwards, pointer moves along scale and measures force

Weight is 10 N

Weight is 20 N

Mass of 1 kg

Mass of 2 kg

WEIGHT AND MASS
The "mass" of an object is a measure of the quantity of matter that it possesses. Mass is usually measured in grams (g) or kilograms (kg). The "weight" of an object is the force exerted on the object's mass by gravity. Since weight is a force, its unit is the newton (N).

Wheel and axle multiplies the effort

Force is transmitted to the wheels by the chain

Pedal

Crank

Effort, provided by cyclist's muscles, is smaller than the load, but moves through a greater distance

A larger force, the load, is produced at the axle

WHEEL AND AXLE

A screw, acting like a wedge wrapped around a shaft, multiplies the effort

Effort, a turning force supplied through a screwdriver

Pitch (the angle of the screw thread)

The smaller the angle of pitch, the less force is required, but more turns are needed to move it through a greater distance

A larger force, the load, pulls the screw into wood

SCREW

Effort pushes axe into wood

A larger force, the load, moves through a smaller distance to push wood apart

Axe blade has wedge shape

Wedge multiplies effort

WEDGE

NEWTON'S THREE LAWS OF MOTION

NEWTON'S FIRST LAW

When no force acts on a body, it will continue in a state of rest or uniform motion.

Mass of 1 kg

Newton meter shows no applied force

Mass of trolley is negligible

Trolley is not in motion, and will remain at rest until a force acts

NO FORCE, NO ACCELERATION: STATE OF REST

Constant speed

Mass of 1 kg

Newton meter shows no applied force

Trolley is in motion, and will continue at a constant speed in a straight line until a force acts

NO FORCE, NO ACCELERATION: UNIFORM MOTION

NEWTON'S SECOND LAW

When a force acts on a body, the motion of the body will change. The size of the change will depend upon the mass of the object and the magnitude of the applied force.

Acceleration is 2 ms⁻²

Trolley and mass (1 kg) gain 2 metres per second of speed each second (2 ms⁻²)

Mass of 1 kg

Newton meter registers force of 2 N

Acceleration is 1 ms⁻²

Trolley and mass (2 kg) gain 1 metre per second of speed each second (1 ms⁻²)

Mass of 2 kg

Newton meter registers force of 2 N

With the same applied force, an object with 2 kg mass accelerates at half the rate of object with 1 kg mass

FORCE AND ACCELERATION: SMALL MASS, LARGE ACCELERATION   **FORCE AND ACCELERATION: LARGE MASS, SMALL ACCELERATION**

NEWTON'S THIRD LAW

If one object exerts a force on another, an equal and opposite force, called the reaction force, is applied by the second object on the first.

Acceleration: the trolley and mass accelerate at 2 ms⁻²

Newton meter registers force of 2 N to the left

Newton meters pull on each other with equal and opposite forces

Newton meter registers force of 2 N to the right

Mass of 1 kg

Person experiences a reaction force

ACTION AND REACTION

THREE CLASSES OF LEVER

Fulcrum, between effort and load

Effort

Load is greater than effort, but moves through smaller distance

CLASS 1 LEVER
Pliers consist of two class 1 levers.

Fulcrum

Load, between effort and fulcrum

Effort is smaller than load, but moves through greater distance

CLASS 2 LEVER
Nutcrackers consist of two class 2 levers.

Load is applied at open end

Effort forces tongs together

Load is smaller than effort, but moves through greater distance

Effort, between fulcrum and load

Fulcrum

CLASS 3 LEVER
Tongs consist of two class 3 levers.

RAIL AND ROAD

STEAM LOCOMOTIVES 324

DIESEL TRAINS 326

ELECTRIC AND HIGH-SPEED TRAINS 328

TRAIN EQUIPMENT 330

TRAMS AND BUSES 332

THE FIRST CARS 334

ELEGANCE AND UTILITY 336

MASS-PRODUCTION 338

THE "PEOPLE'S CAR" 340

EARLY ENGINES 342

MODERN ENGINES 344

ALTERNATIVE ENGINES 346

BODYWORK 348

MECHANICAL COMPONENTS 350

CAR TRIM 352

HYBRID CAR 354

RACING CARS 356

BICYCLE ANATOMY 358

BICYCLES 360

THE MOTORCYCLE 362

THE MOTORCYCLE CHASSIS 364

MOTORCYCLE ENGINES 366

COMPETITION MOTORCYCLES 368

Steam locomotives

WAGONS THAT ARE PULLED along tracks have been used to transport material since the 16th century, but these trains were drawn by men or horses until the invention of the steam locomotive. Steam locomotives enabled the basic railway system to realize its true potential. In 1804, Richard Trevithick built the world's first working steam locomotive in South Wales. It was not entirely successful, but it encouraged others to develop new designs. By 1829, the British engineer Robert Stephenson had built the "Rocket", considered to be the forerunner of the modern locomotive. The "Rocket" was a self-sufficient unit, carrying coal to heat the boiler and a water supply for generating steam. Steam passed from the boiler to force the pistons back and forth, and this movement turned the driving wheels, propelling the train forwards. Used steam was then expelled in characteristic "chuffs". Later steam locomotives, like "Ellerman Lines" and the "Mallard", worked in a similar way, but on a much larger scale. The simple design and reliability of steam locomotives ensured that they changed very little in 120 years of use, before being replaced from the 1950s by more efficient diesel and electric power (see pp. 326-329).

"ROCKET" STEAM LOCOMOTIVE, 1829

Chimney
Smokebox
Pipe takes steam from boiler to cylinder
Leaf spring
Regulator (throttle)
Remains of firebox
"Rocket" nameplate
Wrought iron boiler
Valve chest
Valve setting control
Wooden buffer beam
Wooden driving wheel
Metal tyre
Ballast
Rail chair
Wooden sleeper
Piston rod
Carrying wheel
Axle
Wrought iron rail
Cylinder
Driver's platform

"ELLERMAN LINES", 1949 (CUTAWAY VIEW)

Vacuum reservoir
Panel brace
Water tank
Coal space
Tender hand brake
Cab
Firebox
Brick arch
Stay
Water filler
Panel sheeting
Hand rail
Buffer
Brake vacuum pipe
Wheel guard
Axle
Axle box
Tender wheel
Brake rigging
Water float to indicate water level
Water float lever
Step
Axle box cover
Footplate
Coupling
Coil spring
Trailing wheel
Grate
Fire drawn into fire tubes

TENDER

CAB INTERIOR OF "MALLARD" EXPRESS STEAM LOCOMOTIVE, 1938

Steam sanding control

Blower isolator valve

Pressure gauge isolator valve

Vacuum brake isolator valve

Steam heating isolator valve

Steam chest pressure gauge

Sliding roof vent

Vacuum brake pressure gauge

Boiler pressure gauge

Blower control

Gauge glass to show level of water in boiler

Regulator controls flow of steam to cylinders

Exhaust steam water injector control

Cab side-window

Steam heating pressure gauge

Vacuum brake lever

Glass deflector

Live steam water injector control

Whistle lever

Manual sanding lever

Cylinder drain cock lever

Reverser handle

Control valve for hot water hose

Driver's seat

Fireman's seat

Steam-operated reversing shaft lock control

Oil can warming tray

Firebox

Firehole

Firebox door

Steam heat safety valve

Fire tube

Steam dome

Mechanical lubricator

Chimney

Thermal siphon

Regulator valve

Superheater tube inside flue tube

Boiler

Pipe takes steam from boiler to cylinder

Blast-pipe

Smokebox

Smokebox door

Lubricating pipe

Piston valve

Buffer

Brake shoe

Driving wheel

Expansion lever

Slide bar

Bogie frame

Screw coupling

Brake rigging

Crank

Connecting rod

Combination lever

Piston, linked to connecting rod

Leading wheel

Coupling rod

Cylinder

STEAM LOCOMOTIVE

Diesel trains

RUDOLF DIESEL FIRST DEMONSTRATED the diesel engine in Germany in 1898, but it was not until the 1940s that diesel locomotives were successfully established on both passenger and freight services, in the US. Early diesel locomotives like the "Union Pacific" were more expensive to build than steam locomotives, but were more efficient and cheaper to operate, especially where oil was plentiful. One feature of diesel engines is that the power output cannot be coupled directly to the wheels. To convert the mechanical energy produced by diesel engines, a transmission system is needed. Almost all diesel locomotives have electric transmissions, and are known as "diesel-electric" locomotives. The diesel engine works by drawing air into the cylinders and compressing it to increase its temperature; a small quantity of diesel fuel is then injected into it. The resulting combustion drives the generator (more recently an alternator) to produce electricity, which is fed to electric motors connected to the wheels. Diesel-electric locomotives are essentially electric locomotives that carry their own power plants, and are used worldwide today. The "Deltic" diesel-electric locomotive, similar to the one shown here, replaced classic express steam locomotives, and ran at speeds up to 160 kph (100 mph).

FRONT VIEW OF "UNION PACIFIC" DIESEL-ELECTRIC LOCOMOTIVE, 1950s

Exhaust vent
Windscreen wiper
Horn
Cab front window
Head-light
Cab door
Name of operating railroad
Illuminated locomotive unit number
Railroad crest
Cab step
Step
Motor-driven bogie axle
Air-brake coupling hose
Centre buck-eye coupler

PROTOTYPE "DELTIC" DIESEL-ELECTRIC LOCOMOTIVE, 1956

Engine room vent
Inspection hatch
Engine exhaust port
Radiator fan
Engine room window
Engine room vent

Fuel tank
Water for heating boiler
Inspection socket
Folding step
Drain for radiator coolant
Radiator coolant
Sand box
Telescopic damper
Drain for control reservoir

DIESEL ENGINE OF BRITISH RAIL CLASS 20 DIESEL-ELECTRIC LOCOMOTIVE

EXAMPLES OF FREIGHT CARS

Exhaust vent

Cylinder head (V-four configuration)

Turbo-charged diesel engine drives generator

Generator cooling fan

Generator compartment vent

Auxiliary generator

Main generator produces electricity that drives wheels

Main chassis member

Innermost wheel set on cab-end bogie

Air brake pipe

Brake rigging

Battery box

Engine crankcase

Air reservoir and isolator valves

Lubricating oil primary pump and fuel supply pump

BOX CAR

HOPPER CAR

REFRIGERATOR CAR

LIVESTOCK CAR

FLAT CAR WITH BULKHEADS

Driver's seat

Cab door

Warning horn

Cab

Windscreen

Windscreen wiper

Cab window

Manufacturer's logo

Cab vent

Indicator light

Sand box

Buffer

Brake cylinder

Roller-bearing axle box

Brake shoe

Brake actuating chain

Transverse leaf spring secondary suspension

Coil spring primary suspension

AUTOMOBILE CAR

Electric and high-speed trains

THE FIRST ELECTRIC LOCOMOTIVE ran in 1879 in Berlin, Germany. In Europe, electric trains developed as a more efficient alternative to the steam locomotive and diesel-electric power. Like diesels, electric trains employ electric motors to drive the wheels but, unlike diesels, the electricity is generated externally at a power station. Electric current is picked up either from a catenary (overhead cable) via a pantograph, or from a third rail. Since it does not carry its own power-generating equipment, an electric locomotive has a better power-to-weight ratio and greater acceleration than its diesel-electric equivalent. This makes electric trains suitable for urban routes with many stops. They are also faster, quieter, and less polluting. The latest electric French TGV (Train à Grande Vitesse) reaches 300 kph (186 mph); other trains, like the London to Paris and Brussels "Eurostar", can run at several voltages and operate between different countries. Simpler electric trains perform special duties – the "People Mover" at Gatwick Airport in Britain runs between terminals.

HOW ALTERNATING CURRENT (AC) ELECTRIC TRAINS WORK

Running rail for return current
Feeder station provides current
Catenary
Vacuum circuit breaker
Thyristor converter converts current (ac) to direct current (dc)
Pantograph collects current
Traction motor turns wheel
Transformer steps down voltage
Axle brush
Control circuit

FRONT VIEW OF ITALIAN STATE RAILWAYS CLASS 402 ELECTRIC LOCOMOTIVE

Collector strip for electric current
Double-arm pantograph
Head-light
Windscreen wiper
Italian State Railways crest
Number of electric (E) locomotive (class 402 No. 5)
Buffer
"Jumper" cable
Conventional hook-screw coupling
Front light (white)
Rear light (red)

FRONT VIEW OF PARIS METRO

Route number
Windscreen wiper
Unit number
Operator's initials (Régie Autonome des Transports Parisien)
Rubber running wheel
Guard for rubber wheel
Door open/shut indicator light
Driver's seat
Handle
Front light (white)
Rear light (red)
Buffing pad
Rubber guide wheel

SIDE VIEW OF GATWICK EXPRESS "PEOPLE MOVER"

Pneumatic rubber wheel
Concrete track
Automatic door
No driver (train controlled by central computer)

"EUROSTAR" MULTI-VOLTAGE ELECTRIC TRAIN

Cab window

Grille over warning horn

Rear light (red)

Head-light (white)

Fibreglass reinforced plastic cover

Fibreglass reinforced plastic cover

Aerofoil wheel guard

Aerofoil wheel guard

FRONT VIEW

Sanding pipe

Cab side-window

Cab front window

Electric equipment compartment

Cab door

Side vent

3002

Leading driven axle

Horizontal telescopic damper

Third (electric) rail collector shoe

Coil spring suspension

SIDE VIEW

TGV ELECTRIC HIGH-SPEED TRAIN

Luggage rack

Reading light

Double-glazed and tinted side-window

Sliding curtain

Seat

Main overhead lighting

Automatic electric carriage end door

Antimacassar

Headrest

Armrest

Centre gangway

INTERIOR OF TGV

Cab side-window

Cab front window

Windscreen wiper

Emergency exit door

Access panel for servicing

Nose air deflector dam

Cab door

Hand rail

Side vent

Roof vent

306

SNCF

PARTENAIRE OLYMPIQUE

SNCF

Vertical damper

Horizontal damper

SIDE VIEW OF TGV

Train equipment

MODERN RAILWAY TRACK consists of two parallel steel rails clipped on to a support called a sleeper. Sleepers are usually made of reinforced concrete, although wood and steel are still used. The distance between the inside edges of the rails is the track gauge. It evolved in Britain, which uses a gauge of 1,435 mm (4 ft 8½ in), known as the standard gauge. As engineering grew more sophisticated, narrower gauges were adopted because they cost less to build. The loading gauge, which is equally important, determines the size of the largest loaded vehicle that may pass through tunnels and under bridges with adequate clearance. Safe train operation relies on following a signalling system. At first, signalling was based on a simple time interval between trains, but it now depends on maintaining a safe distance between successive trains travelling in the same direction. Most modern signals are colour lights, but older mechanical semaphore signals are still used. On the latest high-speed lines, train drivers receive control instructions by electronic means. Signalling depends on reliable control of the train by effective braking. For fast, modern trains, which have considerable momentum, it is essential that each vehicle in the train can be braked by the driver or by a train control system, such as Automatic Train Protection (ATP). Braking is achieved by the brake shoe acting on the wheel rim (rim brakes), by disc brakes, or, increasingly, by electrical braking.

MECHANICAL SEMAPHORE SIGNAL

Red, square-ended arm in raised position means "all clear"

Red glass

Green glass

Actuating lever system

Motor operating "home" stop signal

Green glass

Yellow glass

Yellow, "distant" warning arm in horizontal position means "caution"

Tubular steel post

Ladder

Electrical relay box

FOUR-ASPECT COLOUR LIGHT SIGNAL

Glass (yellow)

Glass (green)

Yellow glass (lit)

Glass (red)

FRONT VIEW

Lifting lug

Lamp shield

Clip

Base

SIDE VIEW

HOW A MODERN MAIN-LINE SIGNALLING SYSTEM WORKS

Red "stop" light instructs next train not to enter this section of track

Green "all clear" light instructs train B to proceed into this section of track

Green "all clear" light instructs train B to proceed into this section of track

Green "all clear" light instructs train B to proceed into this section of track

Pantograph

Catenary

Train B

Track

EXAMPLES OF INTERNATIONAL TRACK GAUGES

1,000 mm
(3 ft 3¹/₂ in)
East Africa, India, Malaysia, Chile, and Argentina

1,067 mm
(3 ft 6 in)
Japan, Australia, Sudan, West Africa, South Africa, and New Zealand

1,435 mm
(4 ft 8¹/₂ in)
US, Canada, China, Egypt, Turkey, Iran, Japan, Peru, Britain, Europe, Australia, Brazil, and Mexico

1,524 mm
(5 ft 0 in)
Russia, Spain, Portugal, and Finland

1,600 mm
(5 ft 3 in)
Ireland, Australia, and Brazil

1,676 mm
(5 ft 6 in)
India, Pakistan, and Argentina

EXAMPLES OF INTERNATIONAL LOADING GAUGES

Britain: 2.75 m (9 ft 0 in) x 3.95 m (12 ft 11 in)

Europe: 3.1 m (10 ft 2 in) x 4.5 m (14 ft 9 in)

US: 3.3 m (10 ft 10 in) x 4.9 m (16 ft 2 in)

Russia: 3.4 m (11 ft 2 in) x 5.3 m (17 ft 4 in)

1,435 mm
(4 ft 8¹/₂ in)
Standard track gauge

1,524 mm
(5 ft 0 in)
Track gauge of Russia, with largest loading gauge

FLAT-BOTTOMED RAIL

Flat-bottomed steel rail

Steel spring secures rail to sleeper

Synthetic insulating pad

Sleeper supports track and maintains gauge

BULL-HEAD RAIL

Wooden "key" secures rail in chair

Steel tapered screw fastens chair to sleeper

Bull-head pattern steel rail

Cast-iron chair

Wooden sleeper

DISC BRAKES ON MODERN WAGON BOGIE

Base of wagon

Airbag secondary suspension

HOT BOX
TEST VALVE

Brake disc

Brake calliper

Damper

Hand brake wheel

Axle

Wheel

Two yellow "preliminary caution" lights instruct train B that it must stop in two signals time

Yellow "caution" light instructs train B that it must stop at next signal

Green "all clear" light instructs train A to proceed into this section of track

Red "stop" light instructs train B not to enter this section of track

Braking distance

Train A

Trams and buses

METROLINK TRAM, MANCHESTER, BRITAIN

AS CITY POPULATIONS exploded in the 1800s, there was an urgent need for mass transportation. Trams were an early solution. The first trams, like buses, were horse-drawn, but in 1881, electric street tramways appeared in Berlin, Germany. Electric trams soon became widespread throughout Europe and North America. Trams run on rails along a fixed route, using electric motors that receive power from overhead cables. As road networks developed, motorized buses offered a flexible alternative to trams. By the 1930s, they had replaced tram systems in many cities. City buses typically have doors at both front and rear to make loading and unloading easier. Double-decker designs are popular, occupying the same amount of street space as single-decker buses but able to transport twice the number of people. Buses are also commonly used for inter-city travel and touring. Tour buses have reclining seats, large windows, luggage space, and toilets. Recently, as city traffic has become increasingly congested, many city planners have designed new tram routes to run alongside bus routes as part of an integrated transport system.

EARLY TRAM, c.1900

- Trolley boom
- Trolley base
- Upper deck
- Trolley head
- Drop window
- Quarter light
- Brake
- Stair
- Lower deck
- Underframe
- Platform
- Controller
- Truck
- Lifeguard

L.C.C.

MCW METROBUS, LONDON, BRITAIN

- Window vent
- Upper deck windscreen
- Route information
- Destination screen
- Offside mirror
- Asymmetric windscreen
- Windscreen wiper
- Sidelight
- Head-light
- Grille
- Fog light
- Number plate
- Manufacturer's badge

- Upper deck air intake
- Mirror for driver to see upstairs
- Route number
- Nearside mirror
- Licence holder
- Turning indicator

- Square roof dome
- Operator's logo
- Destination screen
- Nearside mirror
- Front bumper
- Entrance door
- Emergency door control
- Turning indicator

LONDON NORTHERN

Hornsey Rise   Crouch End
Turnpike Lane
West Green Road

41

ARCHWAY STN.

PAY DRIVER

mcw

KYV 739X

LONDON NORTHERN

FRONT VIEW

SINGLE-DECKER BUS, NEW YORK, US

Wheelchair access

Sliding window

Sloped roof dome

Tinted glass

Marker light

Repeater indicator

Entrance door

Side mirror

Route number

Head-light

Bumper

Turning indicator

Air intake

Bumper

Tyre | Axle

Exit door

Access panel

Sidelight

Entrance door

Number plate

SIDE VIEW

Entrance door

FRONT VIEW

DOUBLE-DECKER TOUR BUS, PARIS, FRANCE

Tinted glass

Air intake

Access panel

Skirt

Paris Vision

Raked windscreen

Panoramic window

Turning indicator

Bumper

Plug-style entrance door

Access door

Twin rear axle

Side entrance

Single front axle

Tyre

Sliding window vent

Upper saloon window

Advertising panel

Air intake

Lower saloon window

Fleet number

Engine access panel

Rear bumper

Emergency door control

Two-leaf style exit door

Legal lettering

London Buses logo

Tyre

Axle

Skirt

SIDE VIEW

The first cars

THE EARLIEST ROAD VEHICLE powered by an engine, the Cugnot steam traction engine, was built in 1770. More practical steam carriages, such as the Bordino, were available in the early 19th century, but they were heavy and cumbersome. Restrictive laws and the introduction of railways, faster and able to carry more passengers, saw the decline of "cars" powered by steam. It was not until 1860 that the first practical power unit for road vehicles was developed, with the invention of the internal combustion engine by the Belgian Etienne Lenoir. By around 1890, Karl Benz and Gottlieb Daimler in Germany, and Albert de Dion and Armand Peugeot in France were building cars for sale to the public. These early cars, despite being primitive, expensive, and produced in limited numbers, heralded the age of the motor car.

STEAM-POWERED CUGNOT "FARDIER", 1770

Twin cylinder engine
Steam pipe
Rocking beam
Steering tiller
Wooden wheel (artillery wheel)
Chimney
Brake pedal
Seat
Wooden frame
Load space
Haystack boiler
Carrying fork
Piston rod
Ratchet wheel
Single front driving wheel
Step
Log basket
Broad, rough tyre

BORDINO STEAM CARRIAGE, 1854

Chimney
Hood iron (landau iron)
Landau body
Drop-down window
Leather hood
Fire-tube boiler
Sprung chassis
Safety valve
Water tank
Safety valve weight
Coke hopper
Chauffeur's seat (stoker's seat; spider seat; tiger seat)
Step
Tie bar
Full-elliptic leaf spring
Iron tyre
Wooden spoke
Wooden wheel (artillery wheel)
Hub
Tie rod
Steam chest
Connecting rod
Twin-cylinder steam engine
Unsprung chassis
Steam distributor valve

SIDE VIEW OF PETROL-DRIVEN BENZ MOTORWAGEN, 1886

Steering tiller

Brake quadrant

Brake lever

Cooling water tank

Steering column

Full-elliptic leaf spring

Steering rack

Bevel gear

Steering link

Final drive sprocket

Steering head

Seat spring

Driven pulley

Wheel fork

Tubular chassis

Driving chain

Driving sprocket

Hub

Solid rubber tyre

Tangent-spoked wire wheel

REAR VIEW OF BENZ MOTORWAGEN, 1886

Pinion

Lubricator

Cooling tank

Crown wheel

Driving pulley

Fuel tank

Drive belt

Big-end bearing

Groove for rope starter

Crankshaft

Flywheel

Seat squab

Candle lamp

Driver's seat

Steering tiller

Brake lever

Dashboard

Headlamp

Round pin

Splinter bar

Towing hook

Forecarriage

Steam pipe

Spoke

Frame

OVERHEAD VIEW OF BENZ MOTORWAGEN, 1886

Steering link

Footboard

Steering tiller

Brake lever

Tool and battery box

Trembler coil box

Intake pipe

Single cylinder

Fuel tank

Cooling water tank

Oil-filled lubricator

Flywheel

Crown wheel

Crankshaft

Driving pulley

Drive belt

Elegance and utility

Dᴜʀɪɴɢ ᴛʜᴇ ꜰɪʀꜱᴛ ᴅᴇᴄᴀᴅᴇ ᴏꜰ ᴛʜᴇ 20ᴛʜ ᴄᴇɴᴛᴜʀʏ, the motorist who could afford it had a choice of some of the finest cars ever made. These handbuilt cars were powerful and luxurious, using the finest woods, leathers, and cloths, and bodywork made to the customer's individual requirements; some had six-cylinder engines as big as 15 litres. The price of such cars was several times that of an average house, and their yearly running costs were also very high. As a result, basic, utilitarian cars became popular. Costing perhaps one-tenth of the price of a luxury car, these cars had very little trim and often had only single-cylinder engines.

1904 OLDSMOBILE SINGLE-CYLINDER ENGINE

Oil bottle dripfeed · Crankcase · Starting handle bracket · Exhaust pipe · Cylinder head · Cylinder · Starter cog · Carburettor · Engine timing gear · Crankshaft · Flywheel · Gear band

FRONT VIEW OF 1906 RENAULT

Mahogany framed windscreen · Cast aluminium wheel spider · Canopy · Rear window · British Automobile Association badge · Bedford cord upholstery · Window blind · British Royal Automobile Club badge · Blind pull · Window lift strap · Rear-view mirror · Broad lace trim · Lamp bracket · Oil side lamp · Windscreen support · Dashboard radiator · Mudguard (wing) · Brass bevel · Bonnet catch · Access panel · Bail handle · Lifting handle · Mirror reflector · Acetylene headlamp · Steering spindle · Chevron-tread tyre · Elliott steering knuckle · Dumb iron · Screwdown greaser · Front axle · Starting handle · Track rod

SIDE VIEW OF 1906 RENAULT

Luggage grid · Button-quilted upholstery · Mahogany-framed plate glass window · Round-corner single limousine coachwork · Rear oil lamp · Shock absorber · Hub · Hub cap · Beaded edge tyre · Tyre security bolt

X 825

1904 OLDSMOBILE TRIM AND BODYWORK

Reflector

Rear lamp

Engine cover handle

Engine cover

Mudguard

Mudguard stay

Ignition switch

Seat squab

Seat back rest frame

Dashboard

Tiller

Brake pedal

Throttle pedal

Mirror

1904 OLDSMOBILE CHASSIS

Front steering track-rod

Front spring

Brake rod

Full-elliptic steering spring

Steering wiffletree

Rear spring

Starting handle bracket

Combined spring and chassis unit

Front axle

Non-skid tyre

Brass scrollwork

Blind pull

Canopy

Openable windscreen

Brass bevel

Division

Oil side lamp

Bonnet

Dashboard

Handbrake

Steering wheel

Water pipe

Broad lace trim

Leather upholstery

Gear lever

Plug lead conduit

Acetylene headlamp

Fuel/air intake pipe

Bi-block engine

Bulb horn

Spare tyre

Jump seat (opera seat; strapontin)

Rim clamp

Tyre carrier

Running board

Leather valance

Dashboard radiator

Tyre strap

Bonnet stay

Exhaust manifold

Starting handle

Wooden artillery wheel

Mass-production

THE FIRST CARS WERE HAND-ASSEMBLED from individually built parts, a time-consuming procedure that required skilled mechanics and made cars very expensive. This problem was solved, in America, by a Detroit car manufacturer named Henry Ford; he introduced mass-production by using standardized parts, and later combined these with a moving production line. The work was brought to the workers, each of whom performed one simple task in the construction process as the chassis moved along the line. The first mass-produced car, the Ford Model T, was launched in 1908 and was available in a limited range of body styles and colours. However, when the production line was introduced in 1914, the colour range was cut back; the Model T became available, as Henry Ford said, in "any colour you like, so long as it's black". Ford cut the production time for a car from several days to about 12 hours, and eventually to minutes, making cars much cheaper than before. As a result, by 1920 half the cars in the world were Model T Fords.

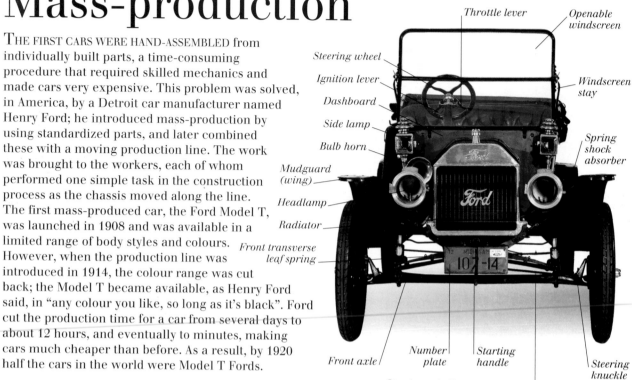

Throttle lever
Openable windscreen
Steering wheel
Ignition lever
Windscreen stay
Dashboard
Side lamp
Spring shock absorber
Bulb horn
Mudguard (wing)
Headlamp
Radiator
Front transverse leaf spring
Front axle
Number plate
Starting handle
Steering knuckle
Steering spindle connecting-rod

STAGES OF FORD MODEL T PRODUCTION

Left half of differential housing
Pinion
Hub bolt
Rear leaf spring (cross-member)
Steering arm
King pin
Demountable wheel
Hub brake shoe
Track rod
Steering wheel
Pinion housing
Front transverse leaf spring
Differential housing
Chassis frame
Rear spring perch
Rear axle
Front cross-member
Battery carrier
Radius rod
Body mount
Bearing sleeve
Half-shaft
King pin
Right half of differential housing
Crown wheel
Bevel pinion
Front axle
Demountable wheel
Radius rod
Rear axle bearing
Torque tube
Running-board stay
Hub brake shoe

SIDE VIEW OF 1913 FORD MODEL T

Hood

Rear seat

Hood frame

Front seat

Rear door

Steering wheel

Steering column

Horn bulb

Windscreen

Side lamp

Bonnet

Radiator filler cap

Radiator filler neck

Front mudguard

Spring shock absorber

Rear mudguard (rear wing)

Tyre valve

Drain plug

Horn

Radius rod

Wooden-spoked wheel

Hub cap

Running board

Valance

Spare tyre

Dummy front door

Radiator shell

Steering column

Drag link

Demountable wheel

Bun lamp burner

Fuel sediment bowl

Running-board bracket

Light switch

Starter switch

Headlamp rim

Headlamp

Ruckstell axle

Bonnet clip

Steering gearbox

Handbrake

Radiator hose

Track rod

Rear cross-member

Brake drum

Starter

Drop arm

Drag link

Crank handle

Cylinder block

Torque tube

Greaser

Brake rod

Transmission casing

Radiator apron

Tank support

Front wing stay

Carburettor

Radiator

Demountable wheel

Steering arm

Clincher wheel

Battery strap

Bonnet clip

Fender eye bolt

Handbrake quadrant

Running-board support

Detachable rim

Reflector

Headlamp shell

Running board

The "people's car"

THE MOST POPULAR CAR in the history of car manufacture is the Volkswagen Beetle, originally called the KdF Wagen. The car was developed in Germany in the 1930s by Dr. Ferdinand Porsche. At that time, Germany had only half the number of cars of Britain or France, and Adolf Hitler took a personal interest in the development of the Volkswagen ("people's car"). The intention was to provide a new industry, new jobs, and a car so cheap that anyone in work could afford it. Dr. Porsche designed a car that was cheap to build and run; its rear-mounted, air-cooled engine cut down the number of parts needed and also reduced weight. However, few civilians managed to obtain the Beetle before the outbreak of the Second World War in 1939. After the war, the Beetle proved so popular that eventually more than 20 million were sold.

CUSTOMIZED VOLKSWAGEN BEETLE

FLAT-FOUR CYLINDER ARRANGEMENT

Fuel tank

Fuel tank sender unit

Windscreen-wiper motor assembly

Steering idler

Steering tie-rod

Fuel filler neck

Steering box assembly

Frame head

Anti-roll bar

Brake back plate

Track control arm

Pedal cluster

Suspension strut

Dust shroud

Front suspension top mount

Gear lever knob

Seat mount

Handbrake

Strut insert (shock absorber)

Front road spring

Front suspension top mount

Floor pan (platform chassis)

Torsion bar cover

Trailing arm

Rear brake drum

Tyre

Sports wheel

Rear shock absorber

Transaxle (gearbox and final drive)

Clutch and flywheel

Flat-four engine

Air filter

Tail pipe

Drive shaft

Heat exchanger

Starter motor

Rear lamp

Air scoop

Quarter light

Bonnet

Indicator

Tail pipe

Pressed steel wheel

Fuel filler cap

Counterweight

Piston

Crankshaft

Big end

Connecting rod (con-rod)

**BODY SHELL OF
VOLKSWAGEN BEETLE**

Front bumper

Bonnet release
handle

Nearside
headlamp unit

Offside headlamp
unit

Nearside front
indicator lens

Chrome
trim strip

Bonnet

Offside front
indicator lens

Nearside front
mudguard
(front wing)

Offside front
mudguard
(front wing)

Front
wing
piping

Spare-
wheel
well

Bonnet
hinge

Front
wing
piping

Blade

Offside
running
board

Quarter light

Mirror

Arm

Nearside
running
board

Door catch

Windscreen wiper

Steering
column

Wind
deflector
(baffle)

Sun roof

Quarter
light

Door
handle

Window winder
handle

Passenger door

Body shell

Window
winder
regulator

Drop glass

Rear
wing
piping

Rear
wing
piping

Air intake
vents

Engine lid
(engine cover)

Rear valance

Air
intake
vents

Nearside rear
mudguard
(rear wing)

Number
plate
light

Offside rear
mudguard
(rear wing)

Number plate

Nearside rear lamp cluster
(rear lamp unit)

Offside rear lamp cluster
(rear lamp unit)

Rear bumper

WRV
408L

Early engines

STEAM AND ELECTRICITY were used to power cars until early this century, but neither power source was ideal. Electric cars had to stop frequently to recharge their heavy batteries, and steam cars gave smooth power delivery but were too complicated for the average motorist to use. A rival power source, the internal combustion engine, was invented in 1860 by Etienne Lenoir (see pp. 334-335). This engine converted the force of a controlled explosion into rotary motion, to turn the wheels of a vehicle. Early variations on this basic model included sleeve valves, separately cast cylinders, and the two-stroke combustion cycle. Today, many internal combustion engines, including the Wankel rotary and diesels (see pp. 346-347), use the four-stroke cycle, first demonstrated by Nikolaus Otto in 1876. The Otto cycle, often described as "suck, squeeze, bang, blow", has proved the best method of ensuring that the engine turns over smoothly and that exhaust emissions are controllable.

TROJAN TWO-STROKE ENGINE, 1927

Port linking combustion chambers of upper and lower cylinders

Water connection

Upper paired cylinder

Spark plug

Wide piston-ring

Transfer port

Wire gauze pad

Upper piston

Flywheel

Flexible, forked connecting-rod

Counterweight

Big end

Crankcase

BERSEY ELECTRIC CAB, 1896

Mounting for tray of 40 batteries

Housing for electric motors

SECTIONED WHITE STEAM CAR, 1903

Steering wheel

Throttle wheel

Brake lever

Reverse lever

Automatic cylinder lubricator

Flash steam generator

Lamp bracket

High-pressure cylinder

Rocking lever

Exhaust pipe

Water pump

Condenser

Low-pressure cylinder

Fuel tank

Semi-elliptic spring

Brake drum

Spiral tubes

Flitch-plated wooden chassis

Drop arm

Water tank

Drag link

Dumb iron

CYCLE OF A FOUR-STROKE INTERNAL COMBUSTION ENGINE

INDUCTION STROKE ("SUCK")

Exhaust port closed
Inlet valve
Inlet port opens
Fuel and air (the "charge") sucked into cylinder
Piston moves downwards
Counterweight
Crankshaft
Crankpin

COMPRESSION STROKE ("SQUEEZE")

Exhaust port closed
Charge compressed by piston
Inlet port closed
Connecting rod (con-rod)
Piston moves upwards

POWER STROKE ("BANG")

Spark plug
Inlet port closed
Exhaust port closed
Charge ignited by spark plug
Explosion pushes piston downwards
Big end

EXHAUST STROKE ("BLOW")

Exhaust valve
Inlet port closed
Exhaust port opens
Burned gases forced out of cylinder
Piston moves upwards

16-HORSEPOWER HUMBER ENGINE, 1911

Brass housing for ignition cable
Inlet port
Water pipe
Valve cap
Spark plug
Side valve (inlet valve)
Pair-cast cylinder
Water jacket
Fan bracket
Tappet
Valve spring
Timing chain
Timing chest
Crankcase
Starting handle
Flywheel
Camshaft
Oil pump
Oil sump

DAIMLER DOUBLE-SLEEVE VALVE ENGINE, 1910

Spark plug socket
Junk ring
Cylinder head
Inlet port
Exhaust port
Inlet manifold
Outer sleeve valve
Water jacket
Cylinder wall
Inner sleeve valve
Piston
Carburettor
Engine bearer
Flywheel

OUTER SLEEVE VALVE

Oil groove

INNER SLEEVE VALVE

Sleeve port
Eye for connecting con-rods to secondary crankshaft

343

Modern engines

TODAY'S PETROL ENGINE WORKS on the same basic principles as the first car engines of a century ago, although it has been greatly refined. Modern engines, often made from special metal alloys, are much lighter than earlier engines. Computerized ignition systems, fuel injectors, and multi-valve cylinder heads achieve a more efficient combustion of the fuel/air mixture (the charge) so that less fuel is wasted. As a result of this greater efficiency, the power and performance of a modern engine are increased, and the level of pollution in the exhaust gases is reduced. Exhaust pollution levels today are also lowered by the increasing use of special filters called catalytic converters, which absorb many exhaust pollutants. The need to produce ever more efficient engines means that it can take up to seven years to develop a new engine for a family car, at a cost of many millions of pounds.

FRONT VIEW OF A FORD COSWORTH V6 12-VALVE

Idle control valve
Plenum chamber
Valve rocker
Power steering pump reservoir
Oil dipstick
Steering pump pulley
High-tension ignition lead (spark plug lead)
Cogged drive belt
Fan
Alternator
Crankshaft pulley
Viscous coupling
Oil sump

FRONT VIEW OF A FORD COSWORTH V6 24-VALVE

Idle control valve
Plenum chamber
Exhaust gas recirculation valve
Camshaft timing gear
Steering pump drive pulley
Camshaft chain
Belt tensioner
Air conditioning pump
Alternator cooling fan
Oil sump
Drive belt
Crankshaft pulley

SECTIONED VIEW OF A JAGUAR STRAIGHT 6

Cam follower (bucket tappet)
Valve spring
Cam lobe
Cam
Combustion chamber
Compression ring
Camshaft
Cam cover
Cylinder head
Distributor
Valve stem
Fan
Exhaust valve
Air conditioning refrigerant pipe
Cylinder liner
Suspension self-levelling pump
Water jacket
Power steering pump
Piston
Swash plate
Connecting rod (con-rod)
Drive belt
Main bearing housing
Compressor piston
Big end
Transmission adaptor plate
Air conditioning compressor
Crankshaft counterweight
Oil sump
Oil pick-up pipe
Anti-surge baffle
Crankcase
Oil-control ring (scraper ring)

FRONT VIEW OF A JAGUAR V12

Air cleaner

Camshaft sprocket

Distributor

Fuel injector nozzle

Inlet manifold tract

Plenum chamber

Camshaft

Cam follower

Piston ring land

Piston ring groove

Exhaust manifold

Piston skirt

Gudgeon pin

Cooling fan

Fan drive shaft

Belt pulley

Coolant outlet

Cam cover

Viscous coupling

Alternator

Alternator pulley

Piston

Crankshaft

STRAIGHT 4 CYLINDER ARRANGEMENT

Counterweight

Connecting rod (con-rod)

V12 CYLINDER ARRANGEMENT

SECTIONED VIEW OF A JAGUAR V12

Distributor drive shaft

Air inlet

Exhaust valve

Inlet valve

Timing chain

Piston crown

Piston ring land

Water pump

Piston

Ancillary drive pulley

Timing chain drive sprocket

Connecting rod (con-rod)

Counterweight (balance weight)

Main bearing

Crankcase

Pipe to oil cooler

Sump

Throttle butterfly

Fuel pipe

Inlet manifold

Ignition amplifier

Throttle linkage

Cam cover

Oil feed pipe

Cylinder head

Coolant rail (water rail)

Exhaust heat shield

Exhaust manifold

Oil pipe banjo

Drive plate

Starter ring

Oil filter

345

Alternative engines

THE MOST COMMON TYPE OF ALTERNATIVE ENGINE is the diesel engine, which, instead of igniting the compressed fuel/air mixture with a spark, uses compression alone, heating the mixture to the point where it explodes. A diesel engine's fuel consumption is low in comparison with similarly sized piston engines, despite its heavier, reinforced moving parts and cylinder block. Another type of engine is the rotary-combustion, first successfully developed by Felix Wankel in the 1950s. Its two trilobate (three-sided) rotors revolve in housings shaped in a fat figure-of-eight. The four sequences of the four-stroke cycle, which occur consecutively in a piston engine, occur simultaneously in a rotary engine, producing power in a continuous stream.

ROTARY-ENGINED MAZDA RX-7

Aerodynamic windscreen

Headrest

Hood bag

Front spoiler (chin spoiler)

Side marker lamp

Rubbing strake

Cast alloy wheel

WANKEL ROTARY ENGINE

OIL-PUMP HOUSING

Distributor fixing point (drive point)

FRONT SIDE HOUSING

Intake port

FRONT ROTOR CHAMBER

Trailing spark-plug hole

INTERMEDIATE HOUSING

Oil filler

Dipstick tube

REAR ROTOR CHAMBER

Intake port

Aluminium alloy backing

Oil-pump drive

Coolant passage

Exhaust port

Leading spark-plug hole

Water drain bolt

Trailing spark-plug hole

Leading spark-plug hole

THE WANKEL ROTARY CYCLE

Exhaust port

Intake port

Fuel/air mixture being compressed

Water passage

Burning gas expands

Trilobate rotor

Gas continues to expand

Stationary gear (fixed gear)

Exhaust port closed

Vacuum sucks in fuel/air mixture

Compression continues

Burnt gas exhausts

Rotor gear

Compressed gas ignites

Fuel/air mixture continues to enter

Burnt gas continues to exhaust

Output shaft turns

Burnt gas begins to expand

Compression begins

FORD TURBOCHARGED DIESEL ENGINE

Engine lifting eye

Rocker cover

Baffle plate

Inlet track

Turbo impeller (inlet rotor)

Turbo propeller (exhaust rotor)

Exhaust

Bell housing

Oil filler cap

Cam follower

Valve return spring

Water jacket

Water pump pulley

Compression ring

Oil-control ring

Piston

Ancillary drive belt

Water jacket

Oil cooler

Oil cooler matrix

Oil filter

Engine block

Oil sump pan

Oil return pipe for turbocharger

REAR SIDE HOUSING

Chrome plating

Exhaust port

ROTOR AND SEALS

Outer oil seal

Inner oil seal spring

Inner oil seal

Rotor bearing

Rotor gear

Side gear

Corner seal spring

Corner seal insert

Corner seal

Rotor

Balancing drilling

Apex seal

Apex seal spring

Apex seal groove

Inner oil seal groove

Outer oil seal groove

Outer oil seal spring

Hole for output shaft

Side seal spring

Side seal

Side seal groove

OUTPUT SHAFT

Front counterweight

Front eccentric rotor journal

Oil hole

Rear stationary gear (fixed gear)

V-belt pulley

Front stationary gear (fixed gear)

Main journal

Eccentric shaft

Oil jet

Rear eccentric rotor journal

Flywheel with balance weight

Bodywork

RENAULT LOGO

THE BODY OF A MODERN mass-produced car is built on the monocoque (single-shell) principle, in which the roof, side panels, and floor are welded into a single integral unit. This bodyshell protects and supports the car's internal parts. Steel and glass are used to construct the bodyshell, creating a unit that is both light and strong. Its lightness helps to conserve energy, while its strength protects the occupants. Modern bodywork is designed with the aid of computers, which are used to predict factors such as aerodynamic efficiency and impact-resistance. High-technology is also employed on the production line, where robots are used to assemble, weld, and paint the body.

Door handle

Door lock

Left-hand door glass

Left-hand quarter glass

Tail-gate support

Window washer jet

Heating element contact

Rear window glass

Tail-gate support

Tail-gate

Rear bumper

Bodyshell

Fuel cap

Right-hand quarter glass

Zinc phosphating

Degreased bare metal

Right-hand door glass

Door key and lock

Door handle

Primer

Base coat colour

Varnish

Cataphoresic coating

Chrome passivation

Left-hand door

Left-hand mirror assembly

Door hinge

Electric window motor

Rear hatch

Aerial

Side marker lamp

SIDE VIEW OF A RENAULT CLIO

Spoiler bumper

Bonnet-release cable

Bonnet

Bonnet catch

Bonnet hinge

Window winder cable

Windscreen glass

Front bumper

Window winder handle

Door hinge

Bonnet

Headrest

Headlamp

Right-hand door

Right-hand mirror assembly

Spoiler bumper

Fog-lamp

FRONT VIEW OF A RENAULT CLIO

Mechanical components

A TYPICAL MODERN CAR has several thousand individual mechanical components. These are assembled to form the car's various mechanical systems: engine and exhaust, transmission, steering, suspension, and brakes. To ensure that each system functions properly, components are manufactured to extremely fine tolerances – to within a five-hundredth of a millimetre (about one ten-thousandth of an inch) in some cases.

Alloy wheel

Hub cap

Hub nut

Hub seal

Exhaust downpipe

Silencer

Catalytic converter

Suspension spring

Rear silencer

Fuel tank

Vent pipe

Torsion bar

Handbrake

Nearside rear suspension arm

Anti-roll bar

Gear lever

Steering wheel

Steering rack

Offside rear suspension arm

Steering column

Shock absorber

Electric fuel pump

Brake cylinder

Brake shoe

Hub seal

Hub nut

Hub and brake drum

Clutch pedal

Brake pedal

Throttle pedal

Brake backplate

Fuel tank filler neck

Hub cap

Clutch cable

Throttle cable

Wheel trim

Steel wheel

MECHANICAL COMPONENTS OF A RENAULT CLIO, 1991

Brake shield

Alloy wheel

Clutch release bearing

Brake disc

Hub

Clutch pressure plate

Nearside drive shaft

Top hose

Track-rod end

Upper suspension arm

Brake hose

Clutch centre plate

Track rod

Brake pad

Power steering pump

Bottom hose

Gearbox (transmission)

Gear-change rod

Lower suspension arm

Anti-roll bar

Starter motor

Flywheel

Fan motor

Power steering belt

Exhaust Manifold

Electronic ignition unit

Subframe

Intake manifold

Brake cylinder

Water pump

Fan motor support

Brake servo

Alternator

Alternator belt

Engine

Brake caliper fixing bolt

Distributor

Suspension strut

Brake caliper locking plate

Air cleaner

Brake caliper

Offside drive shaft

Radiator

Hub carrier

Brake hose

Lock nut and washer

Brake disc

Front hub bearing

Water bottle

Brake shield

Steel wheel

Wheel trim

Car trim

A MODERN CAR HAS TWO TYPES OF TRIM, according to the materials used: hard (chrome and plastics) and soft (upholstery materials). Safety and comfort are priorities in the trim's design: seats help the occupants to maintain a comfortable posture, rubber seals keep out dirt and moisture, and headlamps light the way. Older cars had interior or leather panelling cut and fitted by craftsmen; modern cars use precisely moulded plastics and seat fabrics cut by robot-controlled lasers to reduce costs and production time. Doors are now trimmed off the production line so that complex wiring can be built in.

TRIM OF A RENAULT CLIO, 1991

Rear quarter trim panel

Inner roof trim

Roof seal

Quarter trim panel

Quarter panel moulding

Rear seat belt

Centre seat belt

Rear seat belt stalk (catch)

Split, folding rear seat assembly

Rear shelf

Rear tyre

Tail-gate trim

Rear shelf radio speaker

Rear shelf radio speaker

Gear lever surround

Tail-gate seal

Rear wiper blade

Rear wiper arm

Untrimmed headrest

Number plate lamp

Rear indicator and stop lamp assembly

Rear wheel embellisher (wheel trim)

Rear seat belt

Quarter panel moulding

HALOGEN HEADLAMP BULB

Rear tyre

SPOTLAMP BULB

Filament

MARKER LAMP BULB

Filament

FESTOON BULB

Rear quarter trim panel

Roof seal

Quarter trim panel

Inner roof trim

Contact   Bayonet fixing

Contact   Contact

Roof moulding

Window winder handle

Door seal

Front tyre

Front wheel embellisher (wheel trim)

Door lock handle

Door pull handle

Indicator lamp

Fog-lamp

Inner sill trim

Door moulding (rubbing strip)

Inner windscreen moulding

Front seat belt

Front door radio speaker

Dash radio speaker

Headlamp

Front seat assembly

Sun visor

Dash panel (instrument panel)

Windscreen wiper bracket and spindles

Windscreen wiper blade

Washer jet

Fan blade

Heater unit

Interior light

Radio

Rear-view mirror

Centre console

Steering wheel

Fascia (dash)

Windscreen seal

Sun visor

Headlamp

Front seat frame

Dash radio speaker

Windscreen wiper arm

Front seat belt

Control stalk

Front door radio speaker

Inner windscreen moulding

Door trim panel

Inner sill trim

Door moulding (rubbing strip)

Fog-lamp

Door seal

Door pull handle

Window winder handle

Indicator lamp

Door lock handle

Front tyre

Front wheel embellisher (wheel trim)

Hybrid car

THERE HAVE BEEN SEVERAL proposed alternatives to conventional petrol- or diesel-powered cars, including cars that use solar or battery power. The object is to lower harmful emissions and conserve natural resources. One of the alternatives already in production is the hybrid car. A hybrid vehicle uses two or more fuels. Examples include diesel-electric trains and mopeds. The latter combine the power of a petrol engine with pedal power. In a hybrid car, petrol consumption is reduced by the provision of additional power by an electric motor during acceleration. The motor is driven by power from on-board batteries that are recharged by an engine-driven generator when the car is decelerating or cruising. Some hybrid cars transfer energy from the wheels to a flywheel during braking. The flywheel drives the generator, which recharges the batteries.

HONDA INSIGHT

Aerial

Aerodynamic roof

Windscreen

Wing mirror

Plastic front wings

Front air dam

Plastic bumper

Aerodynamic underside components

Cooling intake

Aluminium bonnet

SIDE VIEW OF 1-LITRE VTEC ENGINE

FRONT VIEW OF 1-LITRE VTEC ENGINE

Motor power cables

Air-intake duct

Ignition coils

Dipstick

Rocker cover

Ignition coils

Water pump

Coolant pipe

Electric motor housing

Lightweight plastic intake manifold

Lightweight magnesium alloy oil sump pan

Oil filter

Air conditioning compressor

Engine drive belt

Belt tensioner

Air conditioning compressor

Crankshaft pulley

Drive belt

HOW HYBRID POWER WORKS

Petrol engine provides power for acceleration and to generator

Inverter

Battery

Inverter controls direction of electrical current

Motor electronic control module (ECM)

Battery electronic control module (ECM)

Battery cooling fan

Inverter cooling fan

REAR VIEW

Electric motor

Power from generator recharges battery during deceleration

Power from battery to motor during acceleration

INVERTER AND BATTERY

High-voltage cables

High-voltage connector

DC converter

Inverter housing

Motor electronic control module (ECM)

Battery electronic control module (ECM)

⚠ **DANGER**
HIGH VOLTAGE

INVERTER ASSEMBLY

BATTERY ASSEMBLY

Inverter cooling fan connector

Magnesium housing for air intake

DC converter connection

Junction board

Cover mounting bracket

Battery cooling fan

Manifold connector

O_2 sensor

Catalyst

Rear exhaust section connector

EXHAUST WITH CATALYTIC CONVERTER

Racing cars

SINCE MOTORING BEGAN, racing cars have been a major
focus of innovation in car design. Features that are now
commonplace, such as disc brakes, turbochargers, and even
safety belts, were used first on competition cars. Research into
racing cars has contributed to a new understanding of engine
performance, aerodynamics, and tyre adhesion, and has led
to the development of ultra-light materials such as carbon-
fibre for car bodies. A modern McLaren Formula One car has
a low, streamlined body and an open cockpit but, unlike its
forerunner, it also has front and rear wings that push the
wheels firmly on to the track, huge tyres for extra grip, and
electronic sensors that continually relay information to the
pits about the car's performance.

72° V10 ENGINE

Fuel injection trumpet guard

Cam cover

Gearbox fixing stud

Water and oil pump assembly

Mercedes-Benz

Harmonically-tuned exhaust system

Cylinder head

Stressed cylinder block

BACK VIEW OF MCLAREN MERCEDES MP4-13

Upper flap

Grooved racing tyre

Warning light

Half-shaft

West

Rear wing end-plate

One-piece side pod and engine cover

BRIDGESTONE   BRIDGESTONE

Side pod air outlet

Diffuser

Exhaust pipe

Differential

SIDE VIEW OF MCLAREN MERCEDES MP4-13

Engine cover

Winglet

Head rest

Engine air intake

On-board TV mini-camera

Hakkinen

BOSS
HUGO BOSS

Mobil 1

E

LOCTITE

Rear wing end-plate

CAMOZZI

WARSTEIN

BRIDGEST

Mercedes-Benz

West

BRIDGESTONE

Alloy wheel

ENKEI

West

Wheel nut

POTENZA

Side pod

OVERHEAD VIEW OF MCLAREN MERCEDES MP4-13

Front wing end-plate

Front wing

Nose cover

Lower wishbone

Front brake duct

Grooved racing tyre

Driver's radio aerial

Rear-view mirror

One-piece side pod and engine cover

Radius arm

Rear wing endplate

Slot

Upper flap

Rear wing upper mainplane

Grooved racing tyre

Driver protection

Safety harness

Turning vane

Upper wishbone

FRONT VIEW OF MCLAREN MERCEDES MP4-13

Rear wing upper mainplane

Rear-view mirror

Radiator air intake

Upper wishbone

Lower wishbone

Engine air intake

Driver's radio aerial

Front brake duct

Grooved racing tyre

End-plate

Front wing

Wing supports

Steering link

Rear-view mirror

Forward rollover structure

Driver's radio aerial

Alloy wheel

High nose

COMPUTER ASSOCIATES 8

BRIDGESTONE POTENZA

Mobil

Turning vane

Wheel nut

Front wing end-plate

Bicycle anatomy

THE BICYCLE IS A TWO-WHEELED, light-weight machine, which is propelled by human power. It is efficient, cheap, easily manufactured, and one of the world's most popular forms of transport. The first pedal-driven bicycle was built in Scotland in 1839. Since then the basic design – of a frame, wheels, brakes, handlebars, and saddle – has been gradually improved, with the addition of a chain, gear system, and pneumatic tyres (tyres inflated with air). The recent invention of the mountain bike (all-terrain bike) has been an important development. With its strong, rugged frame, wide tyres, and 21 gears, a mountain bike enables riders to reach rough and hilly areas that were previously inaccessible to cyclists.

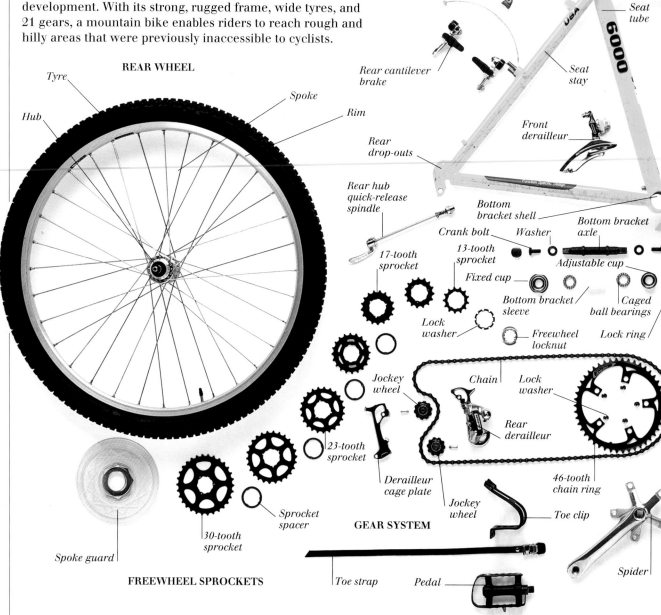

REAR WHEEL

Tyre

Hub

Spoke

Rim

Saddle

Seat post

Cable guide

Seat post quick-release bolt

Straddle wire

Seat tube

Rear cantilever brake

Seat stay

Front derailleur

Rear drop-outs

Rear hub quick-release spindle

Bottom bracket shell

Bottom bracket axle

Crank bolt

Washer

Adjustable cup

17-tooth sprocket

13-tooth sprocket

Fixed cup

Bottom bracket sleeve

Caged ball bearings

Lock ring

Lock washer

Freewheel locknut

Jockey wheel

Chain

Lock washer

Rear derailleur

23-tooth sprocket

Derailleur cage plate

Jockey wheel

46-tooth chain ring

Toe clip

Spoke guard

30-tooth sprocket

Sprocket spacer

GEAR SYSTEM

Spider

FREEWHEEL SPROCKETS

Toe strap

Pedal

Gear cable

Gearshift

Gearshift

Handlebar
stem

Handlebar

Handlebar
grip

Expander
bolt

Lock
nut

Top tube

Rear brake
cable

Top race

Lock
washer

Brake
lever

Brake lever

Cable guide

**BICYCLE
FRAME**

Head
tube

Top cup

Caged ball
bearings

Front brake
cable

Hub

Spoke

Down
tube

Bottom
cup

Rubber
bearing
seal

Straddle wire

Steerer
tube

Bottom
race

Toe clip

Front
cantilever
brake

Cantilever
brake boss

Rim

Inner tube

Toe
strap

Pedal

Fork blade

Left crank
arm

24-tooth
chain ring

Front hub
quick-release
spindle

36-tooth
chain ring

Handlebar

Dust cap

Saddle

Frame

Brake lever
and gearshift

Valve

Tyre

FRONT WHEEL

Pedal

Chain

Bicycles

ALTHOUGH ALL BICYCLES are made up of the same basic components, they can vary greatly in design. A racing bike, such as the Eddy Merckx model, with its light frame and steep head- and seat-angles, is built for speed. Its design forces the rider to adopt the "aerotuck", a crouched, aerodynamic position. While a touring bike resembles the racing bike in many respects, it is designed for comfort and stability on long-distance journeys. Touring bikes are characterized by more relaxed frame angles, heavy chain stays that support the rear panniers, and a long wheelbase (the distance between the wheel axles) for reliable handling. All-round bicycles, known as "hybrids", combine the light weight and speed of sports bikes with the rugged durability of mountain bikes (see pp. 358-359). Bicycles that are not designed for conventional road use include time-trial bikes, which have a short head tube, sloping top tube, "aero" handlebars, and aerodynamic tubing. Most Human Powered Vehicles (HPVs) are recumbents – the rider has a recumbent position – which maximize power output and minimize drag (resistance). Essential to the safety of all riders are helmets, and both front and rear lights; locks protect against theft.

FRONT AND REAR LIGHTS

HELMET

Hard outer shell

Red rear light

Air vent

White front light

Polystyrene padding

Quick-release strap

EDDY MERCKX RACING BICYCLE

Saddle

Seat post

Cable guide

Saddle clamp

Seat-post bolt

Rear brake cable

Top tube (crossbar)

Steel frame

Brake-block bolt

Seat tube

Down tube

Brake block

Seat stay

Water-bottle cage

Tyre

Front derailleur

Tyre tread

Tyre wall

Wheel rim

Freewheel sprocket

STEEL LOCK

Key

Hardened steel

Rear derailleur

Pulley bolt

Tension pulley

Chain

Chain stay

Crank bolt

Chain ring

Crank

Spider

Pedal

Toe clip

Pick-proof lock

CANNONDALE SH600 HYBRID BICYCLE

Gel-filled saddle

Light-weight frame

Straight handlebar

Brake bridge

Cantilever brake

All-surface tyre

CANNONDALE ST1000 TOURING BICYCLE

Rear mudguard

Water bottle

Drop handlebar

Front mudguard

Rear pannier

Front pannier

Long chain stay

Large diameter aluminium tubing

Headset

Stem

Binder bolt

Handlebar

Front brake cable

Brake lever

Head tube

Brake pivot bolt

Brake pad

Fork

Hub quick-release lever

Spoke

Spoke nipple

Presta valve

Hub

ROSSIN ITALIAN TIME-TRIAL BICYCLE

Aero handlebar

Sloping top tube

Steep seat tube

Hollow disc wheel

Short head tube

Clipless pedal

Tri-spoke wheel

Narrow tyre

WINDCHEETAH SL MARK VI "SPEEDY" RACING HPV BICYCLE

Fleecy headrest

Fibreglass bucket seat

Joystick

Brake lever

53-tooth chain ring

Clipless pedal

7-speed freewheel

Aluminium tubing

Drum brake

Extended racing chain

The motorcycle

THE MOTORCYCLE HAS EVOLVED from a motorized cycle – a basic bicycle with an engine – into a sophisticated, high-performance machine. In 1901, the Werner brothers established the most viable location for the engine by positioning it low in the centre of the chassis (see pp. 364-365): the new Werner became the basis for the modern motorcycle. Motorcycles are used for many purposes – for commuting, delivering messages, touring, and racing – and different machines have been developed according to the demands of different types of riders. The Vespa scooter, for instance, which is small-wheeled, economical, and easy-to-ride, was designed to meet the needs of the commuter. Sidecars provided transport for the family until the arrival of cheap cars caused their popularity to decline. Enthusiast riders generally favour larger capacity machines that are capable of greater performance and offer more comfort. Four-cylinder machines have been common since the Honda CB750 appeared in 1969. Despite advances in motorcycle technology, many riders are attracted to the traditional looks of motorcycles like the twin-cylinder Harley-Davidson. The Harley-Davidson Glides exploit the style of the classic American V-twin engine, where the cylinders are placed in a V-formation.

1901 WERNER MOTORCYCLE

Vacuum-operated inlet valve
Fuel tank
Electric ignition control
Bicycle-type saddle
Inlet-over-exhaust (IOE) engine
Pulley rim rear brake
A 2201
Alloy crankcase
Cast iron cylinder barrel
Twisted rawhide drive belt

1988 HARLEY-DAVIDSON FLHS ELECTRA GLIDE

1965 BMW R/60 WITH 1952 STEIB CHAIR

Handlebar
Head-light
Mirror
Windscreen
Adjustable link
Sidecar
Fuel tank
Sidelight
Horizontally opposed engine
Mudguard
Sidecar chassis rail
Indicator
Sidecar wheel
Sidecar lower link
Exhaust pipe
Square-section tyre
Side reflector

FRONT VIEW

Mudguard
Canvas shroud
Speedometer
Ignition lock
Tail-light
Grab handle
Tool tray
Mudguard stay
Lockable luggage boot
Silencer
Suspension linkage
Bullet-shaped sidecar body
Drum brake
Knock-off wheel nut
SIDE VIEW
Long leading-link fork (Earles fork)

Backrest
Passenger seat
Pannier
Passenger grab rail
Luggage rack
Licence plate
Tail-light
Silencer bracket
Disc brake
Crash bar
Exhaust clamp

1969 HONDA CB750

1963 VESPA GRAND SPORT 160 MARK 1

Tail-light

Seat

Mirror

Front brake lever

Seat strap

Indicator

Shock absorber

Oil tank

Telescopic fork

Mudguard stay

Disc brake

Clutch cover

Single overhead camshaft engine

Heat shield

Passenger footrest

Exhaust pipe

Twist grip gear change

Monocoque chassis

Seat strap

Throttle

Front brake lever

Clutch lever

Engine cover

Seat

Head-light

Cooling grille

Horn

Tail-light

Choke

Shock absorber

Petrol tap

Kick-starter

Centre stand

Foot brake

Silencer

Rubber foot mat

Drum brake

Single-sided trailing-link fork

Mirror

Brake master cylinder

Windscreen

Handgrip

Clutch cable

Front brake lever

Throttle cable

Light switch

Windscreen adjustor

Padded seat

Manufacturer's logo

Head-light

Oil tank filler cap

Fuel tank

Fog-lamp

Oil tank

Indicator

Telescopic fork

Side reflector

Mudguard

Passenger footrest

Gearbox

Air filter

45° V-twin engine

Crash bar

Exhaust pipe

Duplex tubular cradle frame

Footrest

Brake calliper

Cast alloy wheel

Brake pedal

Disc brake

The motorcycle chassis

THE MOTORCYCLE CHASSIS is the main "body" of the motorcycle, to which the engine is attached. Consisting of the frame, wheels, suspension, and brakes, the chassis performs various functions. The frame, which is built from steel or alloy, keeps the wheels in line to maintain the handling of the motorcycle, and serves as a structure for mounting other components. The engine and gearbox unit is bolted into place, while items such as the seat, the mudguards, and the fairing are more easily removable. Suspension cushions the rider from irregularities in the road surface. In most suspension systems, coil springs controlled by an oil damper separate the main mass of the motorcycle from the wheels. At the front, the spring and damper are usually incorporated in a telescopic fork; the rear employs a pivoted swingarm. The suspension also helps to retain maximum contact between the tyres and the road, necessary to effective braking and steering. Drum brakes were common until the 1970s, but modern motorcycles use disc brakes, which are more powerful.

1985 HONDA VF750 WITH BODYWORK

Racing number plate
Frame-mounted fairing
Fuel tank
Telescopic fork
Dual seat
Mudguard
Disc brake
Box-section swingarm
V4 engine unit
Box-section tubular cradle frame
Floating disc brake

1985 HONDA VF750 WITH BODYWORK REMOVED

Brake master cylinder
Headstock
Bracing tube
Shock absorber top mounting
Engine mounting plate
Square-section steel tubing
Rear sub-frame
Bodywork mounting point
Shock absorber
Exhaust mounting strap
Exhaust pipe
Light alloy wheel
Axle adjustor
Disc brake
Disc brake calliper
Box-section swingarm
Brake torque arm
Brake master cylinder
Footrest hanger
Brake pedal
Swingarm pivot
Multiplate clutch
Oil level window
Oil sump
Engine cover
Engine mounting bolt
V4 engine unit
Radiator
Oil cooler
Radiator pipe

DRUM BRAKE

EXTERIOR OF DRUM BRAKE

Bolt hole
Torque arm
Air cooling scoop
Axle hole
Cooling fin
Speedometer drive
Cable stop
Brake plate
Operating arm

INTERIOR OF DRUM BRAKE

Torque arm
Bolt hole
Brake shoe
Pivot
Brake shoe return spring
Operating cam
Axle hole
Brake shoe return spring
High-friction material

OPERATING PARTS OF DISC BRAKE SYSTEM

Brake fluid reservoir
Master cylinder
Push-rod
Piston
Hydraulic brake fluid
Wheel disc
Calliper assembly
Piston
Brake pad

Clutch cable
Hydraulic brake hose
Telescopic fork leg
Fork slide
Light alloy wheel
Axle
Floating disc brake
Brake calliper

SPRING/DAMPER UNIT

Rubber mounting bush
Twin rate spring
Damper rod
Damper body
Pre-load adjustor
Rubber mounting bush

HOW A SPRING/DAMPER UNIT WORKS

Rubber mounting bush
Spring
Damper rod
Compressible gas
Non-return valve
Hydraulic fluid
Hydraulic fluid chamber
Rubber mounting bush

TYPES OF TYRE

RACING SLICK TYRE
No tread pattern

TUBELESS SPORTS TYRE
Radial groove

TRIALS TYRE
Knobbly tread pattern

GENERAL -USE TYRE
Hard-wearing rubber compound

Motorcycle engines

MOTORCYCLE ENGINES must be light-weight and compact, and have a good power output. They have between one and six cylinders, can be cooled by air or water, and the capacity of the combustion chamber varies from 49cc (cubic centimetres) to 1500cc. Two types of internal combustion engine are common: the four-stroke, which is used in cars (see pp. 342-343), and the two-stroke. A basic two-stroke engine has only three moving parts – the crankshaft, the connecting rod, and the piston – but the power output is high. The engine fires every two strokes (rather than every four), giving a "power stroke" every revolution (see p. 343). Power is conveyed from the engine to the rear wheel by the transmission system. This usually consists of a clutch, a gearbox, and a final drive system. Clutches are multiplate devices, which run in oil. Gearboxes have five or six speeds and are operated by foot pedal. Shaft and belt drive systems are used in some cases, but chain drive to the rear wheel is most common.

EXTERIOR OF STANDARD TWO-STROKE ENGINE

Spark plug cap
Fuel tap
Carburettor mounting
Kick-starter
Carburettor
Cylinder head
Cooling fin
Exhaust port
Case screw
Clutch activating arm
Engine cover
Gear lever

TRANSMISSION SYSTEM

GEARBOX

Gear lever selector shaft
5th gear
2nd gear
4th gear
3rd gear
1st gear
6th gear
Input shaft
Splines for mounting gear lever
Bearing
Output shaft
Splines for mounting final drive sprocket
Gear tooth
Selector fork
Copper oil feed pipe
Aluminium outer casing

MULTIPLATE CLUTCH

Fibre plate
Outer clutch drum, connected to engine
Pressure plate, connected to inner clutch drum
Springs force plates together
Metal plate
Key locks fibre plate to outer drum
Straight-cut primary-drive gear

MODERN "O RING" DRIVE CHAIN

Small front sprocket
Roller with sealed-in lubricant
Large rear sprocket
Mounting hole
Plate
Sprocket tooth
Hole for retaining bolt

**VELOCETTE OVERHEAD
VALVE (OHV) ENGINE**

Screw and lock nut
tappet adjustor

Oil feed pipe

Inlet port

Spark plug lead

Cam follower

Magneto drive

Camshaft gear

Engine
mounting
bolt hole

Oil passageway

Crankcase

Oil pump

Mounting lug

Rocker arm

Rocker cover
retaining bolt

Cylinder head

Exhaust port

Cylinder head

Combustion chamber

Cooling fin

Piston

Push rod

Valve lifter

Timing gear

Engine
mounting
bolt hole

Crankshaft

Non-return valve

Oil sump

Competition motorcycles

THERE ARE MANY TYPES of motorcycle sport and in each, a specialist machine has evolved to perform to specific requirements. Races take place on roads or tracks or "off-road", in fields, dirt tracks, and even the desert. "Grand Prix" world championships in road-racing are contested by three classes: 125cc, 250cc two-strokes; the top class of 500cc two-strokes; and 900cc four-stroke machines. The latest racing sidecars have more in common with racing cars than motorcycles. The rider and passenger operate within an all-enclosing, aerodynamic fairing. The Suzuki RGV500 shown here, like other Grand Prix machines, carries advertising, which helps to cover the cost of developing motorcycle technology. In Speedway, which originated in the US in 1902, motorcycles operate without brakes or a gearbox. Off-road competition motorcycles have less emphasis on high power output. In Motocross, for example, which is held on rough terrain, they must have high ground clearance, flexible long-travel suspension, and tyres with a chunky tread pattern.

1992 HUSQVARNA MOTOCROSS TC610

Throttle cable
Handlebar brace
Long seat
Racing number
Hand protector
Radiator air vent
Flexible plastic mudguard
Light-weight exhaust system
Telescopic fork
Plastic guard
Axle
Overhead camshaft engine
Gear lever
Shock absorber
Disc brake
Knobbly tyre
Disc brake
Brake calliper
Alloy swingarm
Shock absorber linkage

1992 SUZUKI RGV500
SIDE VIEW

Exhaust pipe
Racing number
Air vent
One-piece seat and tail unit
Shock absorber
Minimal seat padding
Arched alloy swingarm

Exhaust pipe
Vent
Silencer
Shock absorber mounting
Three-spoke alloy wheel
Axle adjustor
Disc brake
Rear brake calliper
Slick racing tyre
Drive chain
Footrest
Brake pedal
Disc brake master cylinder
Light-weight alloy frame

Exhaust pipe
Handlebar
Footrest
Rear brake pedal
Drive chain
Wide, slick tyre
Exhaust pipe

REAR VIEW

1981 WESLAKE SPEEDWAY

Carburettor cover

Throttle

Throttle cable

Fuel tank filler cap

Oil filler cap

Mudguard

Seat

Fuel tank

Mudguard

Wheel cover

Telescopic fork

Narrow tyre

Wide tyre

Brakeless wheel hub

Silencer

Footrest

Oil pump

Overhead valve engine

Tubular open cradle frame

Fairing stay

Throttle cable

Fuel tank breather

Fuel tank

Throttle

Front brake lever

Telescopic fork

Mudguard

Sponsor's logo

Air vent

Braided steel hydraulic hose

Brake calliper

Carbon-fibre disc brake

Three-spoke alloy wheel

Slick tyre

Quickly detachable (QD) fairing

1968 KIRBY BSA RACING SIDECAR

FRONT VIEW

Rev counter

Windscreen

All-enclosing fairing

Fuel tank

Battery

Wheel guard

Square-section tyre

Passenger windscreen

Passenger grab rail

SIDE VIEW

Throttle cable

Exhaust pipe

Rev counter

All-enclosing fairing

Sidecar chassis

Engine

Fibreglass wheel guard

Fuel cap

Windscreen

Racing number

Clutch lever

Fairing

Radiator

Front brake lever

Hydraulic brake hose

Mudguard

Axle

Slick tyre

FRONT VIEW

Sea and Air

Ships of Greece and Rome · · · · · 372

Viking Ships · · · · · 374

Medieval Warships and Traders · · · · · 376

The Expansion of Sail · · · · · 378

A Ship of the Line · · · · · 380

Rigging · · · · · 382

Sails · · · · · 384

Mooring and Anchoring · · · · · 386

Ropes and Knots · · · · · 388

Paddlewheels and Propellers · · · · · 390

Anatomy of an Iron Ship · · · · · 392

The Battleship · · · · · 394

Frigates and Submarines · · · · · 396

Pioneers of Flight · · · · · 398

Early Monoplanes · · · · · 400

Biplanes and Triplanes · · · · · 402

World War I Aircraft · · · · · 404

Early Passenger aircraft · · · · · 406

World War II Aircraft · · · · · 408

Modern Piston Aero-engines · · · · · 410

Modern Jetliners 1 · · · · · 412

Modern Jetliners 2 · · · · · 414

Supersonic Jetliners · · · · · 416

Jet Engines · · · · · 418

Modern Military Aircraft · · · · · 420

Helicopters · · · · · 422

Light Aircraft · · · · · 424

Gliders, Hang-gliders, and Microlights · · · · · 426

Ships of Greece and Rome

ROMAN ANCHOR

Stock

Shank

Palm

Acutely angled arm

Ring

Crown

IN THE EXPANSIVE EMPIRES OF GREECE AND ROME, powerful fleets were needed for battle, trade, and communication. Greek galleys were powered by a sail and many oars. A new armament, the embolos (ram), was fitted on to the galley bow. As ramming duels required fast and manoeuvrable boats, extra rows of oarsmen were added, culminating in the trireme. During the fifth and fourth centuries B.C., the trireme dominated the Mediterranean. It was powered by 170 oarsmen, rowing with one oar each. The oarsmen were ranged on three levels, as the model opposite shows. The trireme also carried archers and soldiers for boarding. Galleys were pulled out of the water when not in use, and were kept in dockyard ship-sheds. The merchant ships of the Greeks and Romans were mighty vessels too. The full-bodied Roman corbita, for example, could hold up to 400 tons and carried a cargo of spices, gems, silk, and animals. The construction of these boats was based on a stout hull with planking secured by mortice and tenon. Some of these ships embarked on long voyages, sailing even as far as India. To make them easier to steer, corbitas set a fore sail called an "artemon". It flew from a forward-leaning mast that was a forerunner of the long bowsprits carried by the great clipper ships of the 19th century.

ATTIC VASE SHOWING A GALLEY

ROMAN CORBITA

Double halyard

Roband (rope band)

Ceruchi (lift)

Bullseye

Fore mast

Heraldic device

Antenna (yard)

Buntline

Ring

Brace

Ruden (brail line)

Artemon (fore sail)

Oculus (eye)

Fore stay

Tabling

Sheet

Anchor

Bolt rope

Prow

Windlass

Scala (ladder)

Bronze mast truck

Keraia (yard)

Catena (riding bitt)

Kalos (brailing rope)

Ancorale (anchor rope; anchor rode)

Mast

Kubernetes (helmsman)

Embolos (ram; beak)

Sternpost

Hatch board

Pedalia (twin rudder)

Deck beam

Ophthalmos (eye)

Oar port sleeve

Zosteres (rubbing strake)

Kope (oar)

Cargo hold

Masthead

Single clump block

Malus (mast)

Rope parrel

Bullet block

Antenna (yard)

Brace block

Timber fairlead

Shroud

Leather reinforcing strip

Scala (ladder)

Velum (main sail)

Sheer pole

Deadeye

Lanyard

Poop break

Poop deck

Main double halyard

Main brace

Main sheet

Hole and peg joint

Poop deck house

Clavus (tiller)

Swan neck ornament

Stern balustrade

Ring bolt

Sternpost

Gubernator (helmsman)

Wale

Planking

Gubernacula (rudders)

Shaft

Blade

Oar lanyard

Bitt

Constratum (deck)

Midships fence

Clew

ROWING POSITIONS ON A GREEK TRIREME (TRIERE)
The katastroma (deck) has been removed from this model to show the positions taken by oarsmen on a trireme.

Thranite (upper level oarsman)

Zygian (middle level oarsman)

Deck rail

Tropeter (leather grommet)

Paraxeiresia (outrigger)

Kope (oar)

Stanchion

Zugon (thwart; seat)

Thalamian (lower level oarsman)

Hyperesion (oarsman's cushion)

Pine hull

MORTICE-AND-TENON FASTENINGS FOR HULL PLANKS

Mortice

Gomphoi (dowel)

Tenon

Hull plank

373

Viking ships

IN THE DARK AGES and early medieval times, the longships of Scandinavia were one of the most feared sights for people of northern Europe. The Vikings launched raids from Scandinavia every summer in longships equipped with a single steering oar on the right, or "steerboard", side (hence "starboard"). A longship had one row of oars on each side and a single sail. The hull had clinker (overlapping) planks. Prowheads adorned fighting ships during campaigns of war. The sailing longship was also used for local coastal travel. The karv below was probably built as transport for an important family, while the smaller faering (top right) was a rowing boat only. The fleet of William of Normandy that invaded England in 1066 owed much to the Viking boatbuilding tradition, and has been depicted in the Bayeux Tapestry (above). Seals used by port towns and royal courts through the ages provide an excellent record of contemporary ship design. The seal opposite shows how ships changed from the Viking period to the end of the Middle Ages. The introduction of the fighting platform – the castle – and the addition of extra masts and sails changed the character of the medieval ship. Note also that the steering oar has been replaced by a centred rudder.

BOATBUILDERS' TOOLS

Shave
Broad axe
Sheer
Breast auger
Master shipwright
Stempost
Hood end
Keel
T-handle auger
Axe
Strake
Tree cut for planking

Zoomorphic head
Eye
Tooth

Roband

Leather diagonal reinforcement

Square sail of homespun yarn

Leech (leach)

Braiding
Snake-tail ornament

Serpentine neck

VIKING KARV (COASTER)

Lozenge-shaped recess

Rectangular cross-band

Tye halyard

Sternpost

Tiller

Foot

Boss (rudder pivot)

DRAGON PROWHEAD

Steering oar (side rudder)

Oar
Starboard (steerboard) side
Keel

FAERING (VIKING ROWING BOAT)

Grommet

Tiller

Clench nail

Knee

Grommet

Plank scarf

Prow

Kabe (oar pivot)

Stepped sternpost

Pivot

Stepped stempost

Side rudder

Sheer strake

Oar

Keel

Thwart (seat)

Double-ended hull

Masthead

Masthead pulley for tye halyard

Yard

Head

Head earing

Parrel

COURT SEAL SHOWING A THREE-MASTED, SQUARE-RIGGED SHIP

Weaponry

Banner/ windvane

Topcastle

Main mast

Furled forecourse sail

Furled lateen mizzen sail

Jack staff

Mizzen mast

Fore mast

Aftercastle

Forecastle

Centred rudder

Stempost

Gudgeon

Leechline

Main sail

Anchor

Mast

Snake-head ornament

Sail foot control line used as a sheet or tack

Open, double-ended hull

Stempost

Main sheet

Oar port

Scroll work

Clinker-built oak planking (overlapping planking)

Stowage crutch for oars

Clench nail

Medieval warships and traders

FROM THE 16TH CENTURY, SHIPS WERE BUILT WITH A NEW FORM OF HULL, constructed from carvel (edge-to-edge) planking. Warships of the time, like King Henry VIII of England's Mary Rose, boasted awesome fire power. This ship carried both long-range cannon in bronze, and short-range, anti-personnel guns in iron. Elsewhere, ships took on a multiformity of shapes. Dhows transported slaves from East Africa to Arabia, their fore-and-aft rigged lateen sails allowing them to sail close to the wind around the lands of the Indian Ocean. The Chinese sailed to East Africa and Arabia in junks, trading goods that were carried in watertight compartments. New astronomical tools helped medieval sailors to find their way. Cross-staves and astrolabes were used to measure the altitude of the sun or stars. One of a choice of four cross-pieces was slid up or down the staff of the cross-stave – which was graduated in degrees of altitude – until its top aligned with the celestial body and its base with the horizon. The sighting rule of the astrolabe was simply lined up with a known body, and its altitude read from marks on the metal disc. With sundials, the sailor could use the shadow of the sun to show the time of day.

DHOW

Main yard
Furled lateen main sail
Mizzen yard
Furled lateen mizzen sail
Parrel
Main mast
Mizzen mast
Tiller
Rudder
Shroud
Parrel tackle
Stem head
Eye
Raking stempost

JUNK

Su-wei (fourth mast)
Wei-wei (mizzen mast)
Halyard
Sail batten
Rudder head
Transom
Rudder
Quarterdeck house
Topsail
Chung-ta-wei (main mast)
Erh-wei (second mast)
T'on-wei (port fore-mast)
Lug sail
Cargo hatch
Oar
Grapnel-type anchor

SAILING WARSHIP

Fore top yard
Fore topmast
Fore topcastle
Lift
Fore yard
Fore mast
Ratline
Shroud
Woolding
Forecastle
Forecastle castle-deck gunport
Fore topmast stay
Bowsprit
Sprit yard
Fore stay
Beakhead
Rigging rail
Chain wale (channel)
Hawse hole
Anchor cable
Stempost

Main topgallant mast

Main topgallant yard

Main topmast topcastle

Main top yard

Mizzen topmast

Mizzen top yard

Main topmast stay

Mizzen topcastle

Main topmast

Lift

Main topcastle

Bonaventure top yard

Lift

Bonaventure topmast

Main yard

Parrel

Bonaventure topcastle

Tye

Jeer

Bonaventure yard

Brace

Bonaventure mast

Main stay

Aftercastle

Mizzen mast

Mizzen yard

Main mast

Swifting tackle

Aftercastle castle-deck gunport

Outrigger

Upper deck gunport

Lid

Chain wale (channel)

Gangway

Deadeye

Gun carriage

Transom

Rudder

Sternpost

Keel

Blindage (removable archery screen)

Wale

Main deck gunport

Carvel planking

Port bower anchor

CROSS-STAVE (CROSS-STAFF)

90 degree cross-piece (transversary)

Clamp

Boxwood staff

60 degree cross-piece

Altitude scale in degrees and minutes

30 degree cross-piece

Ocular end

10 degree cross-piece (dutch shoe)

SUNDIAL

Style of the gnomon (edge)

Needle

Gnomon

Outrigger

Pivot

Hour line

Dial

ASTROLABE

Swivel suspension ring

Graduated ring

Scale of degrees

Pivot

Alidade (sighting rule)

Bottom ballast

Scribed arc decoration

The expansion of sail

BY THE 18TH CENTURY, SAILING SHIPS had become fast and effective floating
fortresses. The navies of the north European powers competed with each
other by building heavily-armed fighting ships called "men-of-war".
The distinctive round stern of the ship below, with its open gallery,
balcony, and elaborate wood carving is typical of the period. Hulls
around this time were semicircular in cross section, although many
boat designers were soon to return to the V-shaped hulls used by the
Vikings. Ships of the period carried more sail than ever before.
A labyrinth of rigging supported the masts and yards from which
the profusion of square sails were set. Ships grew higher,
as extra masts were fitted above the lower mast, and
the bowsprit became longer to allow the ship
to carry staysails, spritsails, and jibsails. Ships
went into battle in single file, so that broadsides
from the multiple decks of guns would have
maximum effect. Ships were classified by rates,
the rating of a vessel depending on how many
guns it had. A first rate ship had more than
100 guns. The guns fired solid round
shot, usually made of iron.

WOODEN SAILING SHIP

BOW

Gilded truck

Main topgallant mast

Main topgallant shroud

Bolster

Trestle trees

Main topmast

Main topmast backstay

Main topmast shroud

Cap

Main top

Mast-head

Mizzen topmast

Mizzen topmast stay

Mizzen top

Main top rail

Lift

Mizzen topmast shroud

Mizzen top

Hounds

Futtock shroud

Mizzen yard

Mizzen backstay

Vang

Fiddle block

Mizzen shroud

Mizzen stay

Mizzen mast

Poop rail

Taffrail

Main shroud

Main mast

Brace

Lift

Foot rope

Studding sail boom

Main top rail

Studding sail yard (stuns'l yard)

Jacob's ladder

Rope preventer

Rudder chain

Rudder

Sternpost

Pintle strap

Gudgeon strap

Wash cant

Knee of the head

Hawse hole

Ship's wheel

Binnacle box

Keel

Channel

Chain

Step

Boat slide

SAIL PATTERN OF A 74-GUN SHIP

Main topgallant stay

Fore topgallant mast

Fore topgallant backstay

Gilded truck

Fore topgallant stay

Mouse and collar

Main topmast stay

Fore topmast shroud

Main topmast preventer stay

Ratline

Fore topmast

Fore top

Fore topmast backstay

Fore shroud

Main stay

Mainstay tackle

Fore hatch tackle

Mizzen topgallant sail

Main topgallant sail

Fore mast topgallant sail

Mizzen topsail

Fore mast topsail

Mizzen course

Fore topsail

Jibsail

Fore mast course

Fore topmast stay

Fore topmast preventer stay

Truck

Jack staff

Jib boom

STERN

Sprit topsail

Spritsail course

Fore staysail

Main course

Main topsail

Fore mast course

Fore mast topmast

Fore mast

Rope woolding

Fore stay

Fish davit

Mainrail head

Anchor buoy

Cap

Bee

Outer spritsail yard

Spritsail yard

Foot rope

Bowsprit

Bobstay

Figurehead

Rail

Trailboard

Draught (draft) mark

Bower anchor

Tallow coating

Capstan   Clewline   Gunport   Gun   Gripe

Main topgallant yard

Fore topgallant yard

Main topsail yard

Yardarm

Fore topsail yard

Main yard

Fore yard

Mizzen topmast yard

Stern lantern

Captain's cabin (great cabin)

Balcony

Upper gallery

Port

Stern quarter gallery

A ship of the line

THE 74-GUN WOODEN SHIP WAS A MAINSTAY of British and French battlefleets in the late 18th and early 19th centuries. This "ship of the line" was heavy enough to fight with the most potent of rivals, yet nimble too. The length of such a ship was determined by the number of guns required for each deck, allowing enough room for crews to man them. The gun deck was about 52 m (170 ft) long. The decks had to be very strong to carry the weight of the guns. The deck planks have been removed on the vessel pictured below, to show just how close together the beams had to be to make the hull strong enough. Only timber with a perfect grain was used. The upper deck was open at the waist, but afore and abaft were officers' cabins. The forecastle and quarterdeck carried light guns and acted as platforms for working rigging and for reconnaissance. The ship's longboats (launches) were carried on booms between the gangways.

UPPER DECK OF A 74-GUN SHIP

LONGBOAT

Truck · Flag halyard · Mast · Backstay · Jib halyard · Topping lift · Fore stay halyard · Peak halyard · Shroud · Main sheet · Fore sail halyard · Gaff · Boom · Parrel · Bowsprit · Traveller · Stempost · Waterline · Deadeye · Oar · Side bench

Thole pin · Windlass bar · Transom · Tiller · Planking · Rabbit line · Sheerplank · Frame · Keel · Rudder · Floor · Thwart (seat)

Stock · Hoop · Steam grating · Cathead · Ring · Timber head · Galley stove chimney · Belfry · Waterway · Gangway · Capstan · Knighthead · Fore bitt · Deadeye · Heads (privy) · Figurehead · Head beam · Head rail · Roundhouse · Boomkin · Anchor cable · Arm · Sheave for cat tackle · Deck beam · Breastwork · Forked beam · Pawl · Skid beam · Fluke · Hoop · Stock · Foremast hole · Carling (carline) · Bulwark · Main companion way

Head · Forecastle (fo'c'sle) · Waist

BOW

Figurehead

Head rail

Headboard

Main rail

Middle rail

Lower rail

Supporter

Cat block

Ekeing

Cheek

Catted anchor

Riband

Hawse piece

Side step

Eye bolt

Stempost

Deadwood

Hawse hole

Frame

Main wale

STERN

Cove

Taffrail

Screen bulkhead

Balcony

Upper counter rail

Drop

Lower counter rail

Gunport lid

Filling transom

Wing transom

Timber under transom

Side counter timber

Counter timber

Tuck

Tuck rail

After fashion piece

Cant frame

Main bitt

Hatch coaming/ shot garland

Ledge

Spirketting

Backstay stool

Companion ladder

Master's sea cabin

Mizzen mast hole

Channel

Great cabin (captain's cabin)

Coaming

Pilaster

Ledge (batten)

Screen bulkhead

Standard knee

Poop rail

Necking

Stern carving

Taffrail

Wardroom

Upper finishing

Quarter gallery

Gunport drip (eyebrow; rigol)

Mizzen bitt

Clerk's cabin

Main mast hole

Mast partner

Grating

Gunport lid

Lodging knee

Rail at break of poop deck

Quarterdeck

Poop deck

Rigging

MOST SAILING SHIPS HAVE TWO TYPES OF RIGGING. Standing rigging – kept taut by rigging screws or old-fashioned lanyards and deadeyes – refers to the ropes, wires, and chains that support the masts and yards (horizontal spars). Running rigging, which includes types of block and tackle, halyards, and sheets, is used to hoist, lower, or trim sails.

BOWSPRIT AND JIB BOOM

Outer jib stay

Inner jib stay

Inner jib tack

Bowsprit cap

Fore topmast staysail tack

Fore stay

Whisker boom

Jib boom

Upper deadeye

Lower deadeye

Butterfly plate

Chain plate

Bowsprit

Boom guy block

Martingale backrope

Martingale (dolphin striker)

Spear

Foot rope

Lizard

Chain bobstay

OTHER RIGGING FITTINGS

Handle

Eye plate lug

Parallel shaft

MAST BAND

BELAYING PIN

STANDING BLOCK

Arse (tail)

Running part

Shoulder

Lug

Eye

SHACKLE

Crown

Clear   Jaw

Crown

Soft eye

Lug

Served eye splice

Standing part

Swivel becket

Shell

Screw thread

Shank

Shoulder

Eye

Hauling part (fall)

SHACKLE PIN

Sailmaker's whipping

RIGGING TOOLS

BLOCK AND TACKLE (PURCHASE; HANDY BILLY)

Cheese (cheesing)

RIGGER'S GAUGE FOR MEASURING THE DIAMETER OF ROPE OR WIRE

Fore royal stay

Flying jib tack

Outer jib tack

Outer martingale stay

Middle martingale stay

Inner martingale stay

Double rope becket

LANYARD AND DEADEYES

RIGGING SCREW (TURNBUCKLE)

Leather pointing

Shroud

Spun yarn serving

DUTCH TRIPLE FIDDLE BLOCK

Eye

Flat seizing

Swallow

Strop

Turk's head

Hitched hauling end

UPPER DEADEYE

Swallow

Flat wire seizing

Solid heart thimble

Cotter pin

SCORED BULLSEYE FAIRLEAD

Eye

Strap

SHEET LEAD

Base

RUNNING BLOCK

Sheave (shiver; shiv)

Standing part

Fork end

Tail

LANYARD

Right hand screw

Shoulder

Back

Shank

HOOK

Crown

Clear

Jaw

SPLICING FID

Open body

Left hand screw

Fixed lug

Bill

ROPE SERVING MALLET

Safe working load mark

Seizing

Penny washer (pin cover plate)

Cheek

LOWER DEADEYE

HEAVER FOR WIRE SERVING

Grooving

Swallow

Binding

Shoulder

Bolt

Face

Eye

PRICKERS

HOLLOW SPIKE FOR WIRE

MARLINSPIKE

Nut

Crown

Sails

THERE ARE TWO MAIN TYPES OF SAIL, often used in combination. Square sails are driving sails. They are usually attached by parrels to yards, square to the mast to catch the following wind. On fore-and-aft sails, such as lateen and lug sails, the luff (leading edge) usually abuts a mast or a stay. The head of the sail may abut a gaff, and the foot a boom. Around the world, a great range of rigs (sail patterns), such as the ketch, lugger, and schooner, have evolved to suit local needs. Sails are made from strips of cloth, cut to give the sail a belly and strong enough to resist the most violent of winds. Cotton and flax are the traditional sail materials, but synthetic fabrics are now commonly used.

SECTION OF A SAIL

Seizing   LUFF (LEADING EDGE)   Luff slide   Bolt rope   Head

Round thimble

Rope strand

Grommet

Head cringle

LEECH (LEACH)

Sharp point

SERVING MALLET

Groove for spunyarn rope

Flat seam

Flatboard

Synthetic flax (duradon)

NEEDLES AND SEAMING TWINE

Tabling

Handle

Seaming twine

Luff cloth

Grip

Rat's tail

Needle packet

SAILMAKER'S FID

SAILCLOTHS

Needle

KEVLAR ON FLEX FILM

HEAVYWEIGHT NYLON CLOTH

SAILMAKER'S PALM

SAIL HOOK

Strap

Thumbhole

Crown

Cowhide face

MYLAR

NYLON AND SILICON CLOTH

Bill

Shank

Metal needle pad

SYNTHETIC FLAX (DURADON)

WOVEN DACRON

BEESWAX

Handle

SAILMAKER'S MALLET

Cheek

Groove made by thread

Whipping

Hide grip

Seizing

SAILMAKING TOOLS

Copper face

Mizzen gaff topsail

Main sail

Main gaff topsail

Fore staysail

Jibsail

Mizzen sail

KETCH

Standing lug mizzen

Mizzen yard topsail

Dipping lug foresail

LUGGER

SAILS AND RUNNING RIGGING OF A DOUBLE TOPSAIL SCHOONER

Fore topmast staysail

SAILING RIGS

Main gaff topsail

Fore sail

Main sail

Fore staysail

Jibsail

FISHERMAN'S SCHOONER (FORE-AND-AFT SCHOONER)

Upper topsail lift

Lower topsail brace

Main topsail halyard

Flying jib halyard

Fore upper topsail

Triatic stay

Foot rope

Upper topsail brace

Outer jib halyard

Fore peak halyard

Lower topsail clewline

Fore yard lift

Fore lower topsail

Inner jib halyard

Fore throat halyard

Fore staysail halyard

Fore sail

Mast hoop

Inner jib downhaul

Outer jib downhaul

Outer jib sheet

Flying jib sheet

Inner jib sheet

Flying jib downhaul

Yard

Head

Gaff

Luff

Boom

Foot

Flying jib

Outer jib

Reef point

Inner jib

Fore staysail

Fore staysail sheet

Mooring and anchoring

FOR LARGE VESSELS IN OPEN WATER, ANCHORAGE IS ESSENTIAL. By holding a ship securely to the seabed, an anchor prevents the vessel from being at the mercy of wave, tide, and current. The earliest anchors were nothing more than stones. In later years, many anchors had a standard design, much like the Admiralty pattern anchor shown on this page. The Danforth anchor is somewhat different. It has particularly deep flukes to give it great holding power. On large sailing ships, anchors were worked by teams of sailors. They turned the drum of a capstan by pushing on bars slotted into the revolving cylinder. This, in turn, lifted or lowered the anchor chain. In calm harbours and estuaries, ships can moor (make fast) without using anchors. Berthing ropes can be attached to bollards both inboard and on the quayside. Berthing ropes are joined to each other by bends, like those opposite.

STONE ANCHOR (KILLICK)

Rope hole

TYPES OF ANCHOR

CLOSE-STOWING ANCHOR

End link

ANCHOR CHAIN

Common link

Patent link

SHACKLE, SWIVELS, AND LINK

CQR ANCHOR (SECURE ANCHOR; PLOUGH ANCHOR)

DANFORTH ANCHOR

Crown

Shank

Bolt

Lug

GALVANIZED "D" SHACKLE

MOORING SWIVEL

CHAIN SWIVEL

Screw thread

MAILLOT (SCREW LINK)

ADMIRALTY ANCHOR TYPE ACII

Pea (bill)

ADMIRALTY PATTERN ANCHOR

Fluke

TWIN BOLLARDS WITH RAKED PILLARS AND A HAWSER (HEAVY ROPE)

Flat

Throat

STOCKLESS ANCHOR

Blade

Rim

Stock

Tripping palm

Crown

Base

MUSHROOM ANCHOR (PERMANENT MOORING ANCHOR)

BERTHING ROPES (HAWSERS)

Ship

Twin bollards

Stern rope

Upper head (drumhead)

Head rope

Quayside

After breast rope

After spring rope

Fore spring rope

Fore breast rope

Bollard

MOORING ROPE BENDS

HAWSER BEND
(TWO DOUBLE ROUND TURNS
AND DOUBLE HALF HITCHES)

Standing part

Seizing

Seizing

CARRICK BEND

Seizing

SINGLE SHEET BEND
(SWAB HITCH)

Bare end (fag end)

Standing part

Thin rope

Thick rope

Outboard end

Three-strand hawser belayed with figure of eight turns

Pillar

Foundry plug

Horn

Bolt hole

Cross piece

Bitter end (inboard end)

Bar hole (pigeon hole)

Cap

Strengthening chock

Barrel

Trenail (treenail)

Strengthening chock

Whelp

Pawl slot

Lignum vitae bearing

WOOD CAPSTAN WITH A VERTICAL SPINDLE

Tapered spindle

Spigot

Pin

Ropes and knots

ALL KINDS OF ROPES ARE USED AT SEA, from thin twines and yarns to thick hawsers. Synthetic fibres have been developed specifically for use at sea. Nylon ropes stretch, and so are ideal for anchoring; polypropylene has little stretch, so is ideal for halyards and sheets. Different types of knots are used for different purposes. Knots that join two ropes are called bends; hitches join a rope to another object; and bowlines produce an eye (loop) in the end of a rope. Ropes can be joined by splicing (unravelling the ends and weaving them together) or seizing (lashing the ropes together side by side).

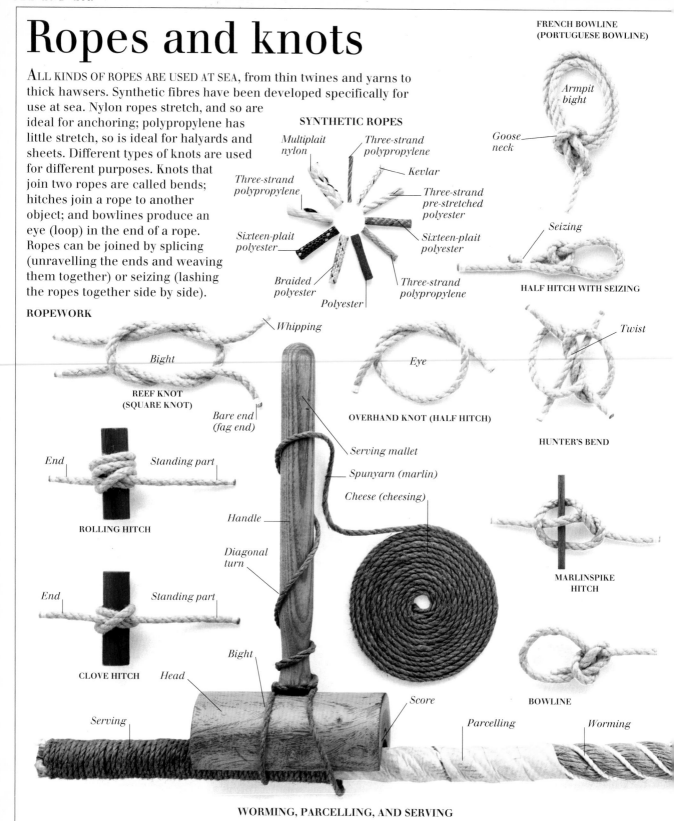

FRENCH BOWLINE (PORTUGUESE BOWLINE)

Armpit bight

Goose neck

Seizing

HALF HITCH WITH SEIZING

SYNTHETIC ROPES

Multiplait nylon

Three-strand polypropylene

Kevlar

Three-strand polypropylene

Three-strand pre-stretched polyester

Sixteen-plait polyester

Sixteen-plait polyester

Braided polyester

Three-strand polypropylene

Polyester

ROPEWORK

Whipping

Bight

REEF KNOT (SQUARE KNOT)

Bare end (fag end)

Eye

OVERHAND KNOT (HALF HITCH)

Twist

HUNTER'S BEND

End   *Standing part*

ROLLING HITCH

Serving mallet

Spunyarn (marlin)

Cheese (cheesing)

Handle

Diagonal turn

MARLINSPIKE HITCH

End   *Standing part*

CLOVE HITCH

Bight

Head

BOWLINE

Serving   *Score*   *Parcelling*   *Worming*

WORMING, PARCELLING, AND SERVING

THUMB KNOT

SPANISH BOWLINE

FLAT SEIZING
(ROUND SEIZING)

DOUBLE CARRICK BEND

End

*Frapped
turn*

*Heaving
line knot*

LIGHTERMAN'S HITCH

HEAVING LINE BEND

*Standing
part*

JURY MAST KNOT
(MAST HEAD BEND)

SHEET BEND (SWAB HITCH)

MANHARNESS KNOT
(BUTTERFLY KNOT;
ARTILLERY LOOP)

Cheese (cheesing)

Marlinspike

HEAVING LINE

PINNED SHEEPSHANK

Jaw

Rat tail

*Hawser laid three-strand manilla
rope with right-handed lay*

Paddle wheels and propellers

THE INVENTION OF THE STEAM ENGINE IN THE 18TH CENTURY made mechanically driven ships fitted with paddle wheels or propellers a viable alternative to sails. Paddle wheels have fixed or feathered floats, and the model shown below features both types. Feathered floats give more propulsive power than fixed floats because they are almost upright at all times in the water. Paddle wheels were superseded by the propeller on ocean-going vessels in the mid-19th century. Propellers are more efficient, work better in rough water, and are less vulnerable in collisions. The first propellers were two-bladed but later three- and four-bladed versions are more powerful; the shape and pitch of blades have also been refined over the years. At the beginning of the 18th century, tillers were superseded on many larger ships by the ship's wheel as a means of steering.

SHIP'S WHEEL

King spoke handle

Handle

Spoke

Rim plate

Felloe (rim section)

Maker's name

Nave plate

Nave

PADDLE WHEEL WITH FIXED FLOATS

Wrist pin

Limb

Fixed float

Hub

Deck beam

OSCILLATING STEAM ENGINE

Slip eccentric for slide valve

Ahead/astern controls

Main crank

Slide valve

THREE-BLADED PROPELLER

Blade

Tapered shaft hole

Hub

Keyway

Strut

Frame

Piston rod (tail rod)

Stuffing box

Oscillating cylinder

Bottom plate (bedplate)

Slide valve rod

Control platform

Propeller blade tip trace

Pitch

Blade

Propeller diameter

Hub

Propeller hub trace

PROPELLER ACTION

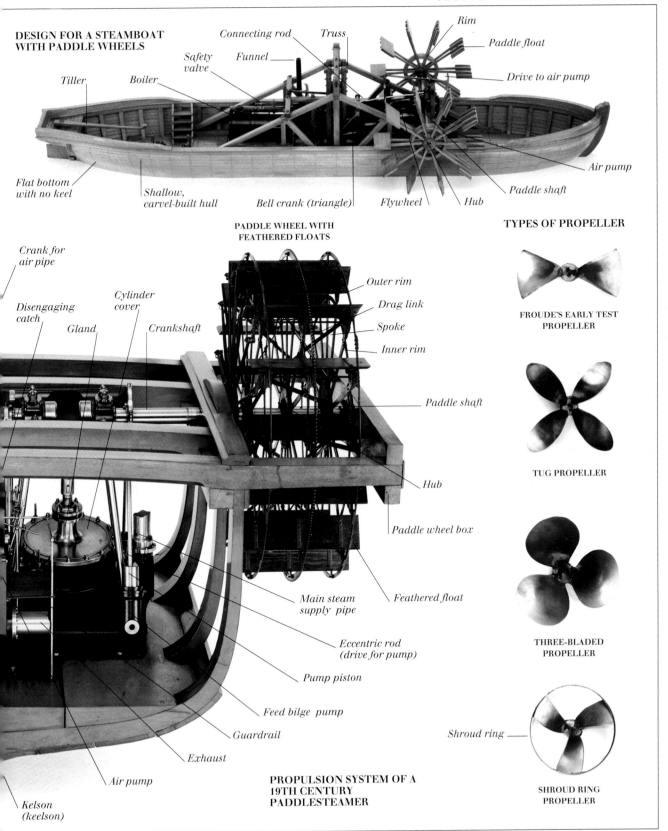

DESIGN FOR A STEAMBOAT WITH PADDLE WHEELS

Rim

Connecting rod

Truss

Paddle float

Safety valve

Funnel

Drive to air pump

Tiller

Boiler

Flat bottom with no keel

Shallow, carvel-built hull

Bell crank (triangle)

Flywheel

Hub

Paddle shaft

Air pump

PADDLE WHEEL WITH FEATHERED FLOATS

Crank for air pipe

Disengaging catch

Cylinder cover

Gland

Crankshaft

Outer rim

Drag link

Spoke

Inner rim

Paddle shaft

Hub

Paddle wheel box

Main steam supply pipe

Feathered float

Eccentric rod (drive for pump)

Pump piston

Feed bilge pump

Guardrail

Exhaust

Air pump

Kelson (keelson)

PROPULSION SYSTEM OF A 19TH CENTURY PADDLESTEAMER

TYPES OF PROPELLER

FROUDE'S EARLY TEST PROPELLER

TUG PROPELLER

THREE-BLADED PROPELLER

Shroud ring

SHROUD RING PROPELLER

Anatomy of an iron ship

IRON PARTS WERE USED IN THE HULLS OF WOODEN SHIPS AS EARLY AS 1675, often in the same form as the wooden parts that they replaced. Eventually, as on the tea clipper Cutty Sark (below), iron rigging was found to be stronger than the traditional rope. The first "ironclads" were warships whose wooden hulls were protected by iron armour plates. Later ironclads actually had iron hulls. The model opposite is based on the British warship HMS Warrior, launched in 1860, the first battleship built entirely of iron. The plan of the iron paddlesteamer (bottom), built somewhat later, shows that this vessel was a sailing ship; but it also boasted a steam propulsion plant amidships that turned two side paddlewheels. Early iron hulls were made from plates that were painstakingly rivetted together (as below), but by the 20th century vessels began to be welded together, whole sections at a time. The Second World War "liberty ship" was one of the first of these "production-line vessels".

TEA CLIPPER

Steel yard

Iron wire stay

Steel lower mast

Steel bowsprit

Wooden planking with copper sheathing

Forged iron anchor

RIVETTED PLATES

Pan head rivet

Plate

Button head rivet (snap head)

Seam

PLAN OF AN IRON PADDLESTEAMER

LIBERTY SHIP

Gun section

Accommodation section

Cargo derrick

Weld line

Stern section

Midships section

Cargo hold

Bow section

Steering position

Steering gear

Stern

Vertical frame ladder

Mast step

Rudder

Rudder post

Heel of rudder post

Mizzen mast

Poop deck

Guardrail

Lounge

Deck lantern

Binnacle

Main mast

State room

Steam whistle

After funnel

Skylight

Crankshaft

Guardrail

Eccentric

Paddle wheel

Connecting rod

Bar keel

Afterpeak

Cabin

Tank

Main mast step

Donkey boiler

Box boiler

Foundation

Reversing wheel

Bottom plate

Side lever

Cylinder

Stern framing

CUTAWAY SECTION OF AN "IRONCLAD"

Bulwark cap

Bulwark

Upper sheer strake

Teak backing

Topside strake

Wrought iron armour plate

Main sheer strake

Main deck tie plate

Lower deck tie plate

Frame

Bilge stringer

Bilge strake

Bilge keelson

Side keelson

Bottom plating

Garboard strake

Waterway

Scupper

Deck planking

Upper deck stringer (tie) plate

Lighting hole

Angle bar (I bar)

Box sister keelson

Keel

Upper deck beam

Upper deck pillar (stanchion)

Main deck beam

Main deck pillar (stanchion)

Lower deck beam

Hold pillar (stanchion)

Centre line keelson

Limber hole

Floor

Forward funnel

Main deck

Fore mast

Ventilator cowl

Skylight

Capstan

Chimney

Hatch

Bowsprit

Hawse pipe

Stem

Beam

Chain locker

Bulkhead stiffener

Deep floor

Forefoot

Deck beam

Smoke box

Combustion chamber

Cabin

'Tween decks ladder

Lower deck

Centre girder

Forepeak

393

The battleship

IN THE EARLY YEARS OF THE 20TH CENTURY, sea warfare – attacking enemy vessels or defending a ship – was revolutionized by the introduction of Dreadnought-type battleships like the Brazilian vessel below. These new ships combined the latest advances in steam propulsion, gunnery, and armour plating. The gun turret was designed to fire shells over huge distances. It was protected by armour 30 cm (12 in) thick. The measurements given for the guns of this ship refer to the bore diameter. Where "weight" is quoted, this is the weight of the shell that the gun fires. Torpedoes – as portrayed on the upper cigarette card (right) – were self-propelled underwater missiles, often steered by gyro-control. Depth charges were designed in the First World War for use against submerged U-boats. They are canisters filled with explosives that are detonated by depth-sensitive pistols. The lower cigarette card shows depth charges being fired by a "thrower", fired from a torpedo tube, and rolled from the stern. Ship's shields were fitted to warships from the late 19th century onwards. The shield shown opposite depicts a traditional ship's cannon.

20TH CENTURY WEAPONRY

Torpedo tube

Sight

Warhead

TORPEDOES

DEPTH CHARGES

Side-thrown canister

Stern-rolled canister

Torpedo-fired canister

Boat handling derrick

BRAZILIAN BATTLESHIP

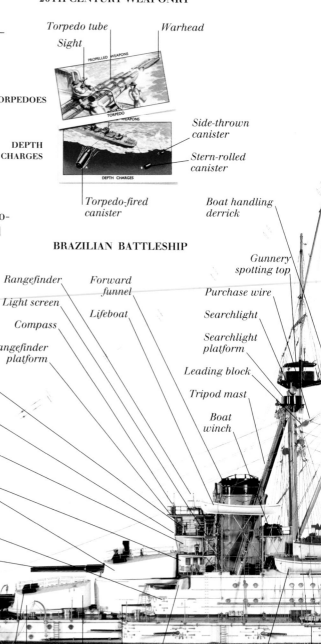

Rangefinder

Forward funnel

Gunnery spotting top

Light screen

Lifeboat

Purchase wire

Compass

Searchlight

Compass and rangefinder platform

Searchlight platform

Ship's wheel

Leading block

Navigating bridge

Tripod mast

Conning tower

Boat winch

Captain's shelter/chart house

Weather shutter for gun

"F" turret

Arms of Brazil

Jack staff

30 cm (12 in) gun

Skylight

Stem (false ram bow)

Porthole

Belt armour

Forward accommodation ladder

Sighting hood

"A" turret

Turret barbette

Open gun mounting

12 cm (4.7 in) gun

Steam launch

Guest boat boom

SHIP'S SHIELD

Rope moulding

Muzzle moulding

Swell of muzzle

Chase

Reinforce

Ogee

Astragal

Trunnion

Lion crest

Radio antenna

Upper wireless and telegraphy yard (Upper W/T yard)

Topgallant mast

Wireless and telegraphy yard (W/T yard)

Lower yard

Signal gear

Ladder way

Brake slip

Davit

Clump cathead

Guardrail

Hawser fairlead

Sheet anchor

Starboard bower anchor

Lifeboat davit

Breakwater

Cable holder

Anchor chain

Bollard

Hawse pipe

Boat boom

Towing fairlead

Port bower anchor

Exhaust pipe

Searchlight

Searchlight platform

After compass platform

After bridge

1.3 kg (3 pound) gun ("three pounder")

"X" turret

"Y" turret

Officer's accommodation ladder

Davit for whaler

Whaler

Flagmast

Vedette boat

Gig

After funnel

Funnel stay

Stern walk

Scarph

Aft anchor

"P" turret

Ash chute

Hen coop

Bilge keel

Gun battery

Torpedo net boom

Turret roof rail

Propeller shaft boss

Torpedo net

Propeller

Propeller shaft

Rudder

Life buoy

Frigates and submarines

FROM THE MID-19TH CENTURY, ARMOURED SHIPS provided a new challenge to enemy craft. In response, huge revolving gun turrets were developed. These could fire in any direction, could be loaded from the breech very rapidly, and, instead of cannonballs, they discharged exploding shells. Modern fighting ships, like the frigate, combine heavy ship-borne armament with light helicopter weaponry. Submarines function below the surface of the sea. Their speed and ability to fire missiles from under water are their major assets. The nuclear submarine can stay under water for several years without refuelling.

Stabilizer fin

Aft hydroplane

Propeller

Lower rudder

Rangefinder

Look out periscope

Local control cabinet

Breech wheel

Breech block

Loading arm

Slide locking lever

Slide

Sighting hood

Recoil cylinder

Elevating wheel

Guide for gun loading cage

Blast bag (breeches)

Rammer lever

Gun loading cage

Floor of gun house

Turret roller

Roller path

Training rack gearing

Working chamber

Training gear

Rammer

GUN TURRET

In this turret for two 37 cm (15 in) guns, shells are carried in a hoisting cage. The shell is rammed into the gun, followed by the propellant (charge). Once the breech is closed, the gun is ready for firing. The whole operation requires around 70 sailors.

Waiting position

Roller path support

Floor

"Walking pipe" (water supply)

Barbette (armour)

Main hoisting cage

Turret trunk

Cordite handling room

Cordite supply shuttle

Ensign staff

FRIGATE

Lynx helicopter

SONAR torpedo decoy

Cordite case

Rudder

Practice projectile

High-explosive projectile

Shell bogie

Shell room

Hydraulic grab

Shell-handling gear

Variable pitch propeller

Ladder way

Steam pipework

Machinery raft

Main turbine

Machinery control room

Switchboard room

Snort mast

Conning tower

Periscope

Electronic warfare mast

Control room

Sonar room

Galley

Officers' mess

NUCLEAR "HUNTER-KILLER" SUBMARINE

SONAR transducer array

Torpedo tube

Forward hydroplane

Junior ratings' bunk space

Senior ratings' mess

Main engine steam condenser

Distiller

Diesel motor compartment

Reactor space

Wireless office

Junior ratings' mess

Carbon dioxide scrubber compartment

Torpedo compartment

Muzzle

Barrel

15 cm (6 in) SHELL
This shell is designed to burst in the air above its target.

Bursting charge (explosive)

Flash tube

Body

Wooden packing

Transit plug

Expelling plate

Driving band

SHELL CASE

CROSS-SECTION OF THE SHELL

Bullet

Surveillance RADAR

Navigation/helicopter control RADAR antenna

Mast

RADAR for gunnery and missile control

Signalling lamp

Jack staff

Seacat missile launcher

Motor whaler

Vent

Aerial rig

Oerlikon gun position

Enclosed bridge

Exocet missile launcher

Stern gallery

Funnel

Gun turret

11 cm (4.5 in) gun

Aerial

F174

RADAR for gunnery and missile control

Stabilizer

Liferaft cylinder

Signal flag compartment

Reel

Fairlead

Anchor

SONAR bulge

Breakwater

Draught (draft) mark

Anti-submarine torpedo tube

Triple "chaff" rocket launcher

Bilge keel

Pennant number

Porthole

Bollard

Pioneers of flight

FLIGHT HAS FASCINATED MANKIND for centuries, and countless unsuccessful flying machines have been designed. The first successful flight was made by the French Montgolfier brothers in 1783, when they flew a balloon over Paris. The next major advance was the development of gliders, notably by the Englishman Sir George Cayley, who in 1845 designed the first glider to make a sustained flight, and by the German Otto Lilienthal, who became known as the world's first pilot because he managed to achieve controlled flights. However, powered flight did not become a practical possibility until the invention of lightweight, petrol-driven internal combustion engines at the end of the 19th century. Then, in 1903, the American brothers Orville and Wilbur Wright made the first powered flight in their Wright Flyer biplane, which used a four-cylinder, petrol-driven engine. Aircraft design advanced rapidly, and in 1909 the Frenchman Louis Blériot made his pioneering flight across the English Channel (see pp. 400-401). The American Glenn Curtiss also achieved several "firsts" in his Model-D Pusher and its variants, most notably winning the world's first competition for airspeed at Reims in 1909.

FRONT VIEW OF WRIGHT FLYER, 1903

Biplane elevator

Pusher propeller (rear-mounted propeller)

Chain drive to starboard propeller

Fuel tank

Propeller-shaft bracing strut

Offset pilot's cradle

Take-off and landing skid

Side-mounted engine to balance pilot's weight

SIDE VIEW OF CURTISS MODEL-D PUSHER, 1911

Nine-cylinder Salmson radial engine

Pusher propeller (rear-mounted propeller)

Aileron operating arm

Wing strut

Fuel filler cap

Oil filler cap

Body cradle that pivots to control ailerons

Fuel and oil tank

Rudder control wheel

Elevator wire for diving

Lap strap

Control column

Throttle

Nose-wheel brake

Footrest

Aileron

Turnbuckle

Fuel pipe

Pneumatic tyre

Seat support strut

Elevator wire for climbing

Thin, cambered lower wing

Rubber-tyred nose-wheel

Pilot's seat

Wing-protecting skid

Starboard main landing gear

Engine and propeller thrust frame

SIDE VIEW OF WRIGHT FLYER, 1903

Plain cotton fabric

Interplane strut

Wing warping wire

Water-filled radiator

Chain drive

Pusher propeller (rear-mounted propeller)

Front diagonal strut

Elevator drive wheel

Water pipe

Rigid leading edge

Steel hub

Steel propeller shaft

Front-mounted biplane elevator

Bracing wire

Rudder

Landing skid

Elevator control cable

Pilot's cradle

Magneto

Braced rudder strut

Warping connection strut

Four-cylinder 12-HP engine

Rudder control cable

Propeller-shaft bracing strut

Softwood strut

Laminated wooden boom

Tailplane

Elevator control wire

Rudder bracing wire

Rudder

Elevator operating arm

Elevator

FRONT VIEW OF CURTISS MODEL-D PUSHER, 1911

Rudder control wheel

Fuel and oil tank

Nine-cylinder Salmson radial engine

Elevator operating arm

Anti-lift wire

Starboard aileron

Aileron operating arm

Port aileron

Carved interplane strut

Wing-protecting skid

Wing-protecting skid

Lift wire

Control column

Seat beam

Footrest

Axle

Tubular steel leg

Main landing gear lateral brace

Interplane strut pin-jointed to front spar

Early monoplanes

RUMPLER MONOPLANE, 1908

MONOPLANES HAVE ONE WING on each side of the fuselage. The principal disadvantage of this arrangement in early, wooden-framed aircraft was that single wings were weak and required strong wires to brace them to king-posts above and below the fuselage. However, single wings also had advantages: they experienced less drag than multiple wings, allowing greater speed; they also made aircraft more manoeuvrable because single wings were easier to warp (twist) than double wings, and warping the wings was how pilots controlled the roll of early aircraft. By 1912, the French pilot Louis Blériot had used a monoplane to make the first flight across the English Channel, and the Briton Robert Blackburn and the Frenchman Armand Deperdussin had proved the greater speed of monoplanes. However, a spate of crashes caused by broken wings discouraged monoplane production, except in Germany, where all-metal monoplanes were developed in 1917. The wings of all-metal monoplanes did not need strengthening by struts or bracing wires, but despite this, such planes were not widely adopted until the 1930s.

FRONT VIEW OF BLACKBURN MONOPLANE, 1912

Taut fabric

Carved wooden propeller

King-post

Nose-ring

Hub bolted to propeller

Pilot's viewing aperture

Exhaust valve push-rod

Gnome seven-cylinder rotary engine

Elevator hinge

Elevator

Landing gear rear cross-member

Wheel fairing

Tailskid

Rubber-sprung wheel

Landing gear front strut

Axle

Landing skid

Landing gear rear strut

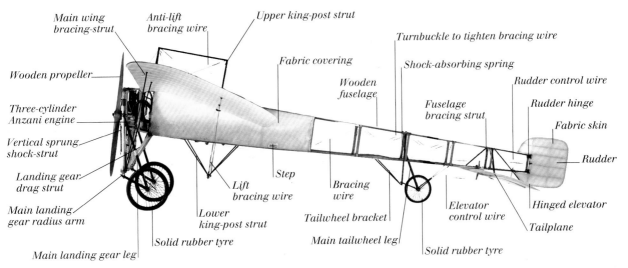

Main wing bracing-strut

Anti-lift bracing wire

Upper king-post strut

Wooden propeller

Fabric covering

Turnbuckle to tighten bracing wire

Shock-absorbing spring

Wooden fuselage

Rudder control wire

Three-cylinder Anzani engine

Fuselage bracing strut

Rudder hinge

Fabric skin

Vertical sprung shock-strut

Rudder

Landing gear drag strut

Step

Main landing gear radius arm

Lift bracing wire

Bracing wire

Elevator control wire

Hinged elevator

Main landing gear leg

Lower king-post strut

Tailwheel bracket

Tailplane

Solid rubber tyre

Main tailwheel leg

Solid rubber tyre

SIDE VIEW OF BLÉRIOT XI, 1909

Anti-lift bracing wire

Leading edge

Rib

Bracing wire anchor bolt

Concave undersurface

Lift bracing wire

Turnbuckle to tighten bracing wire

Warped wing

Carved wooden propeller

King-post

Aluminium cowl

Anti-lift bracing wire

Lateral control wheel

Rudder post

Tailplane

Large fin

Domed topdeck

Hub

Rudder

Engine mount

Elevator

Lift bracing wire

Forward fuselage structure

Diagonal bracing

Triangular-section rear fuselage

Landing gear rear strut

Landing skid

Elevator-operating bracket

Tailskid

Braced landing gear structure

Rubber-sprung wheel

SIDE VIEW OF BLACKBURN MONOPLANE, 1912

Biplanes and triplanes

BIPLANES DOMINATED AIRCRAFT DESIGN until the 1930s, largely because some early monoplanes (see pp. 400-401) were too fragile to withstand the stresses of flight. The struts between biplanes' wings made the wings strong compared with those of early monoplanes, although the greater surface area of biplanes' wings increased drag and reduced speed. Many aircraft designers also developed triplanes, which had a particular advantage over biplanes: more wings meant a shorter wingspan to achieve the same lifting power, and a shorter wingspan gave greater manoeuvrability. Triplanes were most successful as fighters during World War I, the German Fokker triplane being a notable example. However, the greater manoeuvrability of triplanes was no advantage for normal flying and so most manufacturers continued to make biplanes. Many other aircraft designs were attempted. Some were quadruplanes, with four pairs of wings. Some had tandem wings (two pairs of monoplane wings, one behind the other). One of the most bizarre designs was by the Englishman Horatio Phillips: it had 20 sets of narrow wings and looked rather like a Venetian blind.

LAMINATED PROPELLER

Rudder hinge
RAF Central Flying School badge
Rudder
Fin
Navigation light
K 3215
Elevator
Rudder cable
Tailplane
Tailwheel
Bracing strut

SIDE VIEW OF AVRO TRIPLANE IV, 1910

Valve rocker
Air cooling baffle
Magneto
Wing strut
Fuel tank
Throttle
Harness
Pilot's seat

Crankcase breather pipe

Directly driven propeller

Main front strut to engine mount

Skid upper bracing strut

Limit of fuselage skin

Ash skid

Rubber cord suspension

Axle

Turnbuckle

Skid rear strut

Lateral bracing strut

Rubber tyre

Wheel rim

Wire wheel

AVRO TUTOR BIPLANE, 1931

Pin joint

Aileron hinge strut

Aileron control wire

Instructor's cockpit

Padded coaming

Pupil's cockpit

Wooden-domed deck

RAF roundel

Navigation light

Slat-arm fairing

Lift bracing wire

Engine cowling

Nose-ring

Propeller hub

Laminated-wood, fixed-pitch propeller

Metal leading edge

Exhaust collector ring

Exhaust pipe

Main landing gear leg

Inflation valve

Radius rod

Manufacturer's logo

Recessed nose of aileron

Fabric-covered aluminium and steel wing

Inspection cover

Aircraft registration code

Fabric-covered steel-tube fuselage

3215

FRONT VIEW OF AVRO TRIPLANE IV, 1910

Unpainted, varnished fabric

Top wing

Wing strut

Middle wing

Rib

Bottom wing

Leading edge

Fuel filler and vent

Fixed-pitch wooden propeller

Anti-lift bracing wire

Lift bracing wire

Landing skid

Axle

Elevator

Tailplane

Triangular-section fuselage

Lateral bracing strut

Triangular-section fuselage

Fuselage bracing wire

Rudder control cable

Tailplane

Rudder

Metal plate anchorage

Elevator control cable

Longeron

Rubber cord suspension

Tailskid

Tailskid pivot

Elevator

World War I aircraft

FLYING HELMET

WHEN WORLD WAR I STARTED in 1914, the main purpose of military aircraft was reconnaissance. The British-built BE 2, of which the BE 2B was a variant, was well-suited to this duty; it was very stable in flight, allowing the occupants to study the terrain, take photographs, and make notes. The BE 2 was also one of the first aircraft to drop bombs. One of the biggest problems for aircraft designers during the war was mounting machine-guns. On aircraft that had front-mounted propellers, the field of fire was restricted by the propeller and other parts of the aircraft. The problem was solved in 1915 by the Dutchman Anthony Fokker, who designed an interrupter gear that prevented a machine-gun from firing when a propeller blade passed in front of the barrel. The German LVG CVI had a forward-firing gun to the right of the engine, as well as a rear-cockpit gun, and a bombing capability. It was one of the most versatile aircraft of the war.

PORT WINGS FROM A BE 2B

Interplane-strut attachment

Intermediate leading-edge rib

Airspeed-indicator tube

Leading edge

Wingtip

Airspeed-indicator tube

Main rib

Root

Interplane strut

Trailing edge

Airspeed pitot tube

Interplane-strut attachment

Upper side of lower wing

Attachment lug

BE 2B, 1914

Cabane strut fairing

Observer's windscreen

Top-wing centre section

Engine air intake (ram scoop)

Cabane strut

Wooden propeller

Lift bracing wire

Air-cooled V8 engine

Pilot's windscreen

Plywood skin

Crankcase

Control column

Buffed metal cowling

Padded coaming

Silencing heat exchanger

Exhaust pipe

Landing gear front strut

Elevator rocking arm

Ash skid

Step

Step

Reconnaissance camera bracket

Pneumatic rubber tyre

Bomb rack

Lateral control wire

Wheel cover

V-strut

Lower-wing attachment

112 lb (51 kg) bomb

SIDE VIEW OF LVG CVI, 1917

Pilot's cockpit
Observer's cockpit
Cold-water pipe
Exhaust pipe
Starboard aileron
7.92-mm Parabellum machine-gun
230-HP Benz six-cylinder water-cooled engine
Rudder
Fin
Rudder control wire
Laminated wooden propeller
Elevator
Steel drive bracket
Air ventilator inlet
Pitot head
Pivoted, sprung tailskid
Aircraft registration code
Interplane strut
Pneumatic rubber tyre
Elevator control wire
Aircraft type
Aileron control cable
Axle
Bracing wire
Tyre inflation aperture

FRONT VIEW OF LVG CVI, 1917

Lozenge-patterned fabric
Forward-firing machine-gun
Exhaust stack
230-HP Benz six-cylinder water-cooled engine
Wooden propeller
Pitot head
Interplane strut
Anti-lift bracing wire
Lift bracing wire
Main fuel tank
Pneumatic rubber tyre
Axle
Tailskid
Landing gear strut
Gravity-feed fuel tank
Turnbuckle
Multiple rubber-cord suspension

Fixed tailplane
Fabric covering
Elevator
Rib
Rudder
Elevator hinge
Fabric lacing
Tailplane attachment
Rudder post
Steel lug
Spar
Aircraft registration code
Shock-absorbing spring
Steel V-strut
Leading edge
Trailing edge
Pivoted tailskid
National marking
Rib

HORIZONTAL TAIL OF A BE 2B

687

Early passenger aircraft

UNTIL THE 1930s, most passenger aircraft were biplanes, with two pairs of wings and a wooden or metal framework covered with fabric or, sometimes, plywood. Such aircraft were restricted to low speeds and low altitudes because of the drag on their wings. Many had an open cockpit, situated behind or in front of an enclosed – but unpressurized – cabin that carried a maximum of ten people. The passengers usually sat in wicker chairs that were not bolted to the floor, and the journey could be bumpy when flying through turbulence. Warm clothing, and ear plugs to reduce the effects of prolonged noise, were often required. During the 1930s, powerful, streamlined, all-metal monoplanes, such as the Lockheed Electra shown here, became widespread. By 1939, the advent of pressurized cabins allowed fast flights at high altitudes, where there is less turbulence. Flying boats were still necessary on many routes until 1945 because of inadequate runways and the frequency of emergency sea-landings. World War II, however, resulted in enough good runways being built for land-planes to become standard on all major airline routes.

Green starboard navigation light

Flush-riveted metal-skinned wing

Leading edge

Fuel-jettison valve

Static discharge wick

Split flap in landing position

Roof trim panel

PASSENGER CABIN TRIM PANELS

Forward bulkhead upper panel

Passenger service-panel aperture

Ash-tray

Starboard wall forward panel

Cockpit door panel

Forward bulkhead lower panel

Starboard wall mid-forward panel

SIDE VIEW OF LOCKHEED ELECTRA, 1934

Cockpit windscreen

Sliding window

Emergency escape hatch

Steel firewall

Oil tank

Passenger window

Air intake

Ventilator exit

Nose

Propeller pitch-change cylinder

Blade counterweight

Spinner mounting disc

Variable-pitch propeller

Pratt & Whitney nine-cylinder radial engine

Exhaust collector ring

Red port navigation light

Landing gear door

Exhaust pipe

Brake pipe

Electrically driven split flap

Passenger door

Static discharge wick

Aileron

Main landing gear

Aluminium wheel

Mudguard

Metal-skinned wing

Cylinder-cooling gills

Variable-pitch propeller

Cockpit windscreen

High-visibility tip

Pratt & Whitney nine-cylinder radial engine

Valve push-rod tube

Streamlined spinner

Inner wing containing fuel tank

Fixed landing light

Red filter signal light

Exhaust pipe

Single-leg main landing gear

Pitot mast

Tank drain tap

Single-leg main landing gear

Landing gear door

Landing gear fork

Battery compartment

Electrical service compartment

Brake pipe

Axle

Pneumatic rubber tyre

Brake pipe

Inspection cover

Tailwheel

Landing gear fork

Axle

Pneumatic rubber tyre

Disc brake

Landing gear fork

Roof trim

PASSENGER SEAT

Starboard wall aft panel

Bulkhead starboard trim

Backrest

Document panel

Seat button

Bulkhead port trim

Lap strap

Armrest

Starboard wall mid-aft panel

Seat anchor bolthole

Wall anchor

Floor anchor

Seat cushion

Interior cabin trim for aft bulkhead between cabin and luggage hold

PORT ENGINE COWLINGS

Rotating beacon

Starboard rudder

Inspection door

Starboard trimtab

120° nose-ring segment

Fixed tailplane

Tailplane

Port fin

Aluminium flush-riveted skin

Propeller-hub spinner

Port trimtab

NC5171N

Ventilator exit

Tailplane tip

Aircraft registration code

120° cowling panel

Joining latch

Swivelling rubber-tyred tailwheel

World War II aircraft

WHEN WORLD WAR II began in 1939, air forces had already replaced most of their fabric-skinned biplanes with all-metal, stressed-skin monoplanes. Aircraft played a far greater role in military operations during World War II than ever before. The wide range of aircraft duties, and the introduction of radar tracking and guidance systems, put pressure on designers to improve aircraft performance. The main areas of improvement were speed, range, and engine power. Bombers became larger and more powerful – converting from two to four engines – in order to carry a heavier bomb load; the US B-17 Flying Fortress could carry up to 6.2 tonnes (6.1 tons) of bombs over a distance of about 3,200 km (2,000 miles). Some aircraft increased their range by using drop tanks (fuel tanks that were jettisoned when empty to reduce drag). Fighters needed speed and manoeuvrability: the Hawker Tempest shown here had a maximum speed of 700 kph (435 mph), and was one of the few Allied aircraft capable of catching the German jet-powered V1 "flying bomb". By 1944, Britain had introduced its first turbojet-powered aircraft, the Gloster Meteor fighter, and Germany had introduced the fastest fighter in the world, the turbojet-powered Me 262, which had a maximum speed of 868 kph (540 mph).

PROPELLER

High-visibility yellow tip

Light-alloy propeller spinner

Variable-pitch aluminium-alloy blade

COMPONENTS OF A HAWKER TEMPEST MARK V, c.1943

STARBOARD ENGINE COWLINGS

Radiator-access cowling

Lower side-cowling

Upper side-cowling

Cowling fastener

2,400-HP Napier Sabre 24-cylinder engine

Cartridge starter

Propeller governor

Radiator header tank

Propeller drive shaft

Distributor

Ejector exhaust

Magneto

Starter motor

Engine top cowling

Cowling fastener

Upper side-cowling

Lower side-cowling

Radiator-access cowling

PORT ENGINE COWLINGS

SECTIONED B-17G FLYING FORTRESS BOMBER, c.1943

Astronavigation dome

Oxygen bottle

Upper gun turret

Radio operator's seat

Ammunition belt

Dorsal fin

Fin

VHF aerial

Rudder

First pilot's seat

1,000 lb (454 kg) bomb

Ammunition box

"Cheyenne-type" tail-gun turret

Hand-held gun

Plastic nose

Waist gun

Ammunition feed

Entrance door

Retracted tailwheel

Tail gunner's compartment

Bomb aimer's viewing panel

HF radio aerial

Navigator's seat

Sperry ball gun turret

Oxygen bottle

Ammunition feed

Chin gun turret

Bomb door

Direction-finding-aerial fairing

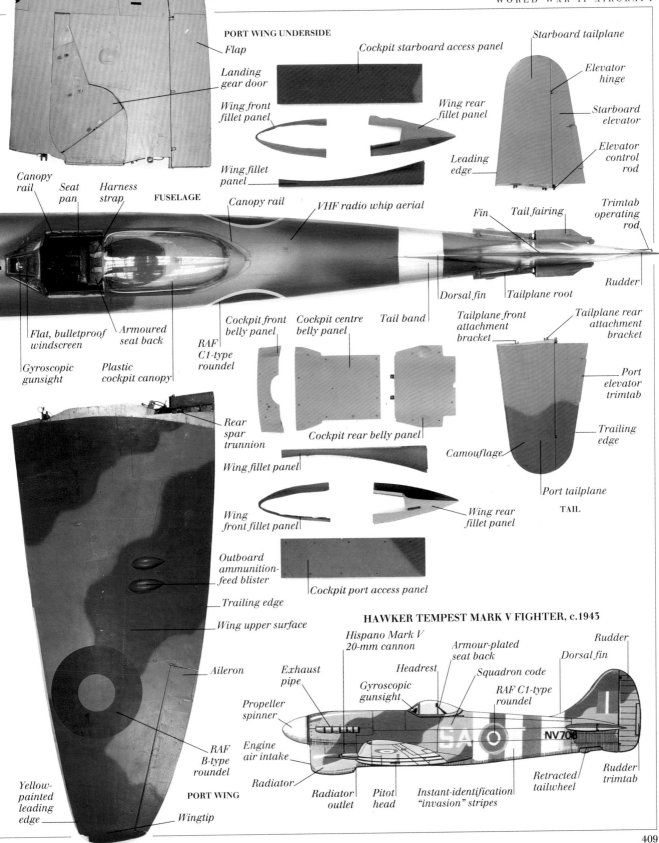

PORT WING UNDERSIDE

Flap

Landing gear door

Cockpit starboard access panel

Wing front fillet panel

Wing rear fillet panel

Wing fillet panel

Starboard tailplane

Elevator hinge

Starboard elevator

Leading edge

Elevator control rod

Canopy rail

Seat pan

Harness strap

FUSELAGE

Canopy rail

VHF radio whip aerial

Fin

Tail fairing

Trimtab operating rod

Dorsal fin

Tailplane root

Rudder

Flat, bulletproof windscreen

Armoured seat back

Gyroscopic gunsight

Plastic cockpit canopy

Cockpit front belly panel

Cockpit centre belly panel

Tail band

Tailplane front attachment bracket

Tailplane rear attachment bracket

RAF C1-type roundel

Rear spar trunnion

Cockpit rear belly panel

Camouflage

Port elevator trimtab

Trailing edge

Port tailplane

TAIL

Wing fillet panel

Wing front fillet panel

Wing rear fillet panel

Outboard ammunition-feed blister

Trailing edge

Wing upper surface

Aileron

Cockpit port access panel

HAWKER TEMPEST MARK V FIGHTER, c.1943

Hispano Mark V 20-mm cannon

Armour-plated seat back

Rudder

Dorsal fin

Exhaust pipe

Headrest

Squadron code

Gyroscopic gunsight

RAF C1-type roundel

Propeller spinner

Engine air intake

Radiator

RAF B-type roundel

Radiator outlet

Pitot head

Instant-identification "invasion" stripes

Retracted tailwheel

Rudder trimtab

Yellow-painted leading edge

Wingtip

PORT WING

Modern piston aero-engines

MID WEST TWO-STROKE, THREE-CYLINDER ENGINE

PISTON ENGINES today are used mainly to power the vast numbers of light aircraft and microlights, as well as crop-sprayers and crop-dusters, small helicopters, and fire-bombers (which dump water on large fires). Virtually all heavier aircraft are now powered by jet engines. Modern piston aero-engines work on the same basic principles as the engine used by the Wright brothers in the first powered flight in 1903. However, today's engines are more sophisticated than earlier engines. For example, modern aero-engines may use a two-stroke or a four-stroke combustion cycle; they may have from one to nine air- or water-cooled cylinders, which may be arranged horizontally, in-line, in V formation, or radially; and they may drive the aircraft's propeller either directly or through a reduction gearbox. One of the more unconventional types of modern aero-engine is the rotary engine shown here, which has a trilobate (three-sided) rotor spinning in a chamber shaped like a fat figure-of-eight.

Spark plug

Coolant outlet

Cylinder head

Piston *Cylinder barrel* *Exhaust manifold*

Exhaust port *Cylinder liner*

Upper crankcase

Reduction gearbox *Driven gear* *Gearbox drive splines* *Pump drive belt* *Coolant pump*

Connecting rod (con-rod)

Small end

Propeller drive flange

Generator rotor

Big end *Counterweight*

Torsional vibration damper

Crankshaft

Sprag clutch

Stator

Ignition trigger housing

Gearbox mounting plate

Engine mounting plate

Lower crankcase

ROTOR AND HOUSINGS OF A MID WEST SINGLE-ROTOR ENGINE

Propeller bolt hole

Dowel

Coolant jacket

Inlet tract

Propeller drive flange

Stud

Stud hole

Roller

Eccentric-shaft bearing

Stud hole

Propeller shaft rear bearing

Coolant jacket

Dowel hole

Dowel

Rotor chamber

Exhaust tract

GEARBOX CASE

FRONT HOUSING (FRONT END-PLATE)

TROCHOID HOUSING

Modern jetliners 1

BAE-146 JETLINER

MODERN JETLINERS HAVE ENABLED ordinary people to travel to places where once only the wealthy could afford to go. Compared with the first jetliners (which were introduced in the 1940s), modern ones are much quieter, burn fuel more efficiently, and produce less air pollution. These advances are largely due to the replacement of turbojet engines with turbofan engines (see pp. 418-419). The greater power of turbofan engines at low speeds enables modern jetliners to carry more fuel and passengers than turbojet aircraft; a modern Boeing 747-400 (popularly known as a "jumbo jet") can fly 400 people for 13,700 km (8,500 miles) without needing to refuel. Jetliners fly at high altitudes, typically cruising at 8,000-11,000 m (26,000-36,000 ft), where they can use fuel efficiently and usually avoid bad weather. The pilot always controls the aircraft during take-off and landing, but at other times the aircraft is usually controlled by an autopilot. Autopilots are complex on-board mechanisms that detect deviations from an aircraft's route and make appropriate adjustments to the flight controls. Flight decks are also equipped with radars that warn pilots of approaching hazards, such as mountain ranges, bad weather, and other aircraft.

Shoulder cowling

Engine pylon

Hinged cowling panel

Nose cowling

Fan duct nozzle

Fire-extinguisher discharge indicator

Core-engine jet pipe

Oil-filler door

Push-in door for hand-held fire-extinguisher

Drain mast

TURBOFAN ENGINE COWLING

STRUCTURAL COMPONENTS OF A BAE-146 JETLINER

Oil-filler door for integrated-drive generator

FUSELAGE NOSE-SECTION

FUSELAGE MID-SECTION

Electrically heated, birdproof windscreen

Side window

Anchor for open door

Rain gutter

Hinge

Peephole

Finger recess

Static air-pressure plate

Forward main door aperture

VHF omni-range and instrument-landing-system aerials

Light-alloy door frame

Passenger window aperture

Main external operating handle

Multiple-pinned lock

Floor level

Radome

Toilet service connector

Anchor for open door

Air temperature probe

Stall warning vane

Pitot head for dynamic air pressure

FORWARD MAIN DOOR

Overwing fuel-filler cap

Systems connector

Overwing fuel-filler cap

STARBOARD WING ASSEMBLY

Fuel contents indicator

Centre-line (spine) of aircraft

Single-piece skin over inboard wing

Rubber sealing strip

Rubber sealing strip

Trailing edge

Trailing edge of fixed wing

Spoiler anchorage

Hydraulic actuator attachment

Pivot point

Flap-track fairing

Screw joint

Aft section

MOVABLE FLAP TRACK AND FAIRING

Hinge

INBOARD LIFT SPOILERS

Stainless-steel flap seal

Track roller

Upper carriage attached to flap

FOWLER FLAP

Anchor bearing

Track

Tab-hinge line

Leading edge

Root

Gearbox mount

Bellcrank lever

Gearbox unit

Flap drive screw

Carriage drive nut

Lower carriage

Skin lap-joint

Leading edge

Main spar bridge

Root rib

Wing-root mount containing central fuel tank

Inboard tab

Attachment structure for wing-to-fuselage fairing

Cabin air-pressure discharge valve

Floor level

Fairing of landing gear bay

Fairing of landing gear pivot

Yellow anti-corrosion paint

Modern jetliners 2

Landing and taxiing light

Heated de-icing leading edge

Roll-spoiler hinge

Roll-spoiler hydraulic actuator attachment

STARBOARD WING

Fixed trailing edge

Aileron hinge

Starboard navigation light

Hinge

Hydraulic actuator attachment

Spoiler arm

Hinge bracket

Aerodynamic balance

Horn balance

Recessed hinge

INTERMEDIATE LIFT SPOILER

Flap seal

OUTBOARD ROLL SPOILER

AILERON

Trimtab

Servo-tab

MAIN FOWLER FLAP

Leading edge

Flap tip

Static discharge wick attachment

Outboard tab

Tab-hinge line

FUSELAGE SPINE FAIRING

Landing gear door

Hydraulic brake pipe

Main pivot

Finger recess

Peephole

Hot-air de-icing duct

Electrical harness

Oleo lock-jack

Skin lap-joint

Passenger window aperture

Light-alloy beam

Direction bar

Hinge

Brake pipe

Main external operating handle

Pneumatic tyre

Shock-strut bearing

Outer wheel axle

Side brace and retraction jack trunnions

Hinge

Wheel hub

Pivoted trailing-link arm

Lower pivot

Hydraulic brake pipe

Anchor for open door

Cabin air-discharge aperture

STARBOARD TWIN-WHEEL MAIN LANDING GEAR

AFT MAIN DOOR

BAE-146 MODERN JETLINER

Tailplane

Logo

Rudder

Fin

Starboard aft
service door

Flap-track
fairing

Core-engine
jet pipe

Main landing
gear fairing

Landing light

Starboard inboard
engine

VHF radio aerial

Forward door for
crew and service

Radome

VHF
aerial

Water-drain
mast

STARBOARD
ELEVATOR

Horn
balance

Tab
hinge

Aerodynamic
balance

Recessed
hinge

Centre-line
(spine)

Root

Trimtab

Servo-tab

**TAILPLANE
FAIRINGS**

Intermediate
fairing (fin tip)

Aft fairing

Fin trailing edge

Forward
fairing

Side
fairing

Elevator
chassis
box

Tailplane attachment
bracket

Heated de-icing
leading edge

FIN

Forward
spar

Fairing panel

Aft spar

Fin-attachment
skin

Access to yaw dampers
and rudder trim jack

TAILPLANE

Rain gutter

Fin leading-edge
attachment

Auxiliary power
unit (APU)
inlet

Heated de-icing
leading edge

Operating arm

Elevator
hinge

Hinge

Skin lap-
joint

Trailing
edge

Tailplane
tip

Auxiliary power unit
(APU) vent

Oil-
cooler
duct

STARBOARD AIR-BRAKE

Aft main door aperture

Heated drain mast

FUSELAGE TAIL-SECTION

Supersonic jetliners

**COMPUTER-
DESIGNED SST**

SUPERSONIC AIRCRAFT FLY FASTER than the speed of sound (Mach 1). There are many supersonic military aircraft, but only two supersonic passenger-carrying aircraft (also called SSTs, or supersonic transports) have been produced: the Russian Tu-144, and Concorde, produced jointly by Britain and France. The Tu-144 was withdrawn in 1978, after only seven months in service. Concorde has remained in service since 1976, with a break for modifications from July 2000 until October 2001. Its features include a droop nose, which is lowered during take-off and landing to aid visibility from the cockpit, and the pumping of fuel between forward and aft trim tanks to help stabilize the aircraft. Concorde has a narrow fuselage and short-span wings to reduce drag during supersonic flight. Its noisy turbojet engines with afterburners enable it to carry 100 passengers at a cruising speed of Mach 2 at 15,000-18,000 m (50,000-60,000 ft). Once an aircraft is flying faster than Mach 1, it produces a continuous air-pressure wave, which is heard as a "sonic boom".

Strake
Fin
Standby pitot head
Starboard outboard engine air-intake
Inboard elevon-jack fairing
Nose-gear leg

FRONT VIEW OF CONCORDE

OVERHEAD VIEW OF CONCORDE

Variable nozzle
Leading edge

Toilets
Electrothermal de-icing panel
Starboard forward trim tank
Overhead hand-baggage bin
Passenger accommodation
Underfloor air-conditioning duct
Seat attachment rail
Life-raft
Wardrobe
VHF aerial
Forward galley
Additional crew's seat
Aluminium-alloy layers and insulation
Third pilot's seat
Erosion-resistant radome
Cockpit windscreen
Retractable visor
"A" frame
Nose-gear leg
Lateral bracing strut
Telescopic strut
Steering actuator
Port forward trim tank
Machined skin panel
Plug-type passenger door
Nose-gear door
Standby flight-control hydraulic jack
Multi-ply high-pressure tyre
Weather radar
Captain's seat
Upper rudder
Fin
Visor jack
Droop-nose hinge
Cockpit air-conditioning duct
Dorsal fin
Emergency exit
Pivoted retractable frame
Tail cone
Aft door
Elevon (combined elevator and aileron)
Hot-section steel and titanium skin
Engine cowling
Landing gear door
Bogie main landing gear

SECTIONED VIEW OF CONCORDE

Fire-suppression bottle access panel

Pressurized keel box

Fuel tank

Main air duct

Emergency exit

Cold-air unit

Static discharge wick

Elevon (combined elevator and aileron)

Cabin air duct

Inspection panel

Flight-control mixing unit

HF radio aerials fairing

Emergency oxygen cylinders

Upper rudder

Auxiliary power unit

VHF omni-range aerial

Lower-rudder power control unit

Servo control-unit fairing

Tail cone

Fuel-jettison pipe

Twin-wheel tail bumper

Air-conditioning duct

Rear bulkhead

Aft galley unit

Rear emergency door

Tank inspection access

Inboard elevon (combined elevator and aileron)

Landing gear hydraulics

Port main landing-gear leg well

Variable nozzle

Nozzle actuator

Heat-exchanger exhaust

Elevon power control unit

Spar

Rib

Leading edge

Middle passenger door

Fuel pipe

VHF aerial

Port engine fuel pumps

Four-wheel bogie

Port main landing gear leg

Forward ramp drive

Main landing gear cross-beam

Upper lip of port engine air intakes

Retraction jack

Honeycomb elevon structure

Fuel tank

Heat exchanger

Rolls-Royce Olympus Mark 610 turbojet

Engine front support link

SIDE VIEW OF CONCORDE

VHF aerial

Emergency exit

Passenger window

Flight deck windscreen

Retracted visor

Nose in drooped position

Standby pitot head

Nose-leg telescopic strut

Nose-gear leg

Starboard forward door

Aerodynamic strake

Radome

Steerable twin-wheel nose-gear

417

Jet engines

JET ENGINES ARE USED BY MOST MILITARY and heavy aircraft, and by many helicopters. The simplest type of jet engine, or gas turbine, is the turbojet. It works by continuously burning a mixture of fuel and air in a combustion chamber to produce a jet of hot exhaust gas that is expelled through a nozzle to produce thrust. The hot gas also spins turbine blades, which, in turn, spin the blades of an air compressor; the compressor forces air into the combustion chamber. Many of the fastest aircraft use turbojets, with additional booster units called afterburners, but their use is restricted by their high noise emission. Most jetliners use turbofan jet engines, which are quieter. An enormous fan, driven by a low-pressure turbine, feeds some air into the compressor but feeds most of it through bypass ducts to join the exhaust jetstream in the tail cone. The bypass stream produces most of the thrust. Many smaller, propeller-driven aircraft use turboprop jet engines, in which the engine powers a propeller.

NPT 301 MODERN TURBOJET

Fuel sprayer
Reverse-flow combustion chamber
Radial diffuser
Turbine rotor
Centrifugal compressor
Exhaust diffuser
Inducer
Tail cone
Air intake
Jet pipe
Exhaust nozzle
Igniter
Nose cone
Alternator
Nozzle guide vane
Air impingement starter
Combustion chamber casing

Temperature and pressure sensor
Low-pressure fan
Inlet cone (rotating spinner)
Pressure line
Fancase with special structure to contain broken fan
Electronic engine control and airframe interface connector
Electronic engine control (EEC) unit
Compressor front bearing
Engine front mount
Electrical wiring harness
Fuel and oil heat exchanger
Oil filter
Compressor air-bleed connection

Plenum ring for hot anti-icing air
Flow splitter
Gearbox bevel drive
Integral oil tank
High-pressure compressor
Combustion chamber
Fuel manifold
High-pressure turbine
Fuel nozzle
Centrifugal compressor
Fan duct

PRATT & WHITNEY CANADA PW120 SERIES MODERN TURBOPROP

Alternator mount pad
Propeller speed probe
Reduction gearbox
Propeller hub flange
Propeller brake pad
Engine front mount
Torquemeter mount
Gearbox oil scavenge line
Autofeather unit
Air intake
Electronic engine control (EEC) unit
Oil filter
Oil tank
Oil-pressure regulating valve
Accessory drive pad
Throttle lever
Fuel-cooled oil cooler
Fuel filter
Fuel heater
Fuel manifold
Intercompressor bleed valve
Intercompressor diffuser pipe
High-pressure bleed venturi connector
Turbine support case
Jet pipe connection
Oil pipe
Thermocouple bus-bar
Fuel nozzle
Igniter plug
Engine rear mount

Low-pressure turbine
Heat shield
Blade tip sealing shroud
Exhaust cone
Core jet pipe (exhaust fairing)
Scavenge oil line
Inter-module bolted joint
Fuel shut-off valve cable

SECTIONED PRATT & WHITNEY CANADA PW305 MODERN TURBOFAN

HOW JET ENGINES WORK

TURBOFAN

Fan sucks air in
Fan blade
Rotating blades compress air
Fuel inlet
Inner drive shaft
Outer drive shaft
Exhaust gases provide extra thrust
Bypass air provides main thrust
High-pressure turbine spins outer drive shaft to drive compressor
Fuel/air mixture ignites

TURBOPROP

Compressor sucks air in
Propeller spins to provide main thrust
Reduction gearbox
Rotating blades compress air
Fuel inlet
Combustion chamber
Three-stage turbine driven by hot gas
Exhaust gases add a little thrust
Turbine shaft drives propeller and compressor

TURBOJET

Compressor sucks air in
Rotating blades compress air
Fuel inlet
Fuel/air mixture ignites
Combustion chamber
Turbine blades driven by hot gas
Exhaust gases provide all the thrust
Turbine drives compressor via drive shaft

Modern military aircraft

MODERN MILITARY AIRCRAFT ARE AMONG THE MOST SOPHISTICATED and expensive products of the 21st century. Fighters need computer-operated controls for manoeuvrability, powerful engines, and effective air-to-air weapons. Most modern fighters also have guided missiles, radar, and passive, infra-red sensors. These developments enable today's fighters to engage in combat with adversaries that are outside visual range. Bombers carry a large weapon load and enough fuel for long-range flights. A few military aircraft, such as the Tornado and the F-14 Tomcat, have variable-sweep ("swing") wings. During take-off and landing their wings are fully extended, but for high-speed flight and low-level attacks the wings are pivoted fully back. A recent development is the "stealth" bomber, which is designed to absorb or deflect enemy radar in order to remain undetected. Earlier bombers, such as the Tornado, use terrain-following radars to fly so close to the ground that they avoid enemy radar detection.

FRONT VIEW OF A PANAVIA TORNADO

Instrument landing system aerial

Birdproof windscreen

Air data probe

Port variable-incidence air intake

Wing-root glove fairing

Starboard inboard stores pylon

Taileron

Starboard main landing gear door

Main landing gear leg

Laser ranger and marked-target seeker

Starboard nose-gear door

Steerable twin-wheel nose-gear

Radome containing ground-mapping, attack, and terrain-following radars

Taxiing light

Wing extended for take-off and landing

Wing pivoted back for high-speed flight

SWING-WING F-14 TOMCAT FIGHTER

SIDE VIEW OF A PANAVIA TORNADO GR1A (RECONNAISSANCE VERSION), 1986

Pilot's cockpit

Navigator's instrument console

Navigator's cockpit

Single canopy over both cockpits

Engine air intake

Navigation light

Flat, birdproof windscreen

High-velocity air duct to disperse rain

Upper "request identification" aerial

Air data probe

Radome containing ground-mapping, attack, and terrain-following radars

UHF aerial

Angle-of-attack probe

Tacan (tactical air navigation) aerial

Emergency canopy release handle

Nose-gear door

Steerable nose-gear leg

Pitot head

Twin nose-wheel

Hinged auxiliary air intake

Cold air intake (ram scoop)

Heat exchanger exhaust duct

Window covering infra-red reconnaissance camera

NORTHROP B-2 ("STEALTH" BOMBER), 1989

Starboard split rudder

Inboard elevons (combined elevators and ailerons)

Refractory (heat-resistant) skin behind exhaust outlet

Variable-incidence gust-alleviator

Wing leading edge coated with radar-absorbent material

Port wingtip rudder

Outboard elevon (combined elevator and aileron)

Leading-edge aerial

Engine aft bulkhead

Wing containing fuel tank

Flight refuelling receptacle

Weapon-bay rear bulkhead

Weapon-bay front bulkhead

Auxiliary air intake

Air intake coated with radar-absorbent material

Ejector-seat roof hatches

Space for extra crew member

Two-seater cockpit

Port outboard stores pylon

Port navigation light

Fin-tip aerial fairing

Radar warning receiver looking forwards

Instrument landing system aerial

Fin

Radar warning receiver looking rearwards

Heat exchanger air intake (ram scoop)

Extended port air-brake

Rudder

Wing-root glove fairing

Wing-root pneumatic seal

Heat exchanger hot-air exhaust

Air-brake jack

Fin-root aerial fairing

Spine end fairing

Thrust-reverser (closed)

Port fully-variable afterburner nozzle

Port inboard stores pylon

Hydraulic hand-pump

Port flap

Port taileron (combined tailplane and aileron)

Wingtip aerial fairing

Port navigation light

Lower "request identification" aerial

Powered leading-edge slat

Main-gear door

Port main landing gear

Port outboard stores pylon

421

Helicopters

HELICOPTERS USE ROTATING BLADES for lift, propulsion, and steering. The first machine to achieve sustained, controlled flight using rotating blades was the autogiro built in the 1920s by the Spaniard Juan de la Cierva. His machine had unpowered blades above the fuselage that relied on the flow of air to rotate them and provide lift as the autogiro was driven forwards by a conventional propeller. Then, in 1939, the Russian-born American Igor Sikorsky produced his VS-300, the forerunner of modern helicopters. Its engine-driven blades provided lift, propulsion, and steering. It could take off vertically, hover, and fly in any direction, and had a tail rotor to prevent the helicopter body from spinning. The introduction of gas turbine jet engines to helicopters in 1955 produced quieter, safer, and more powerful machines. Because of their versatility in flight, helicopters are today used for many purposes, including crop-spraying, traffic surveillance, and transporting crews to deep-sea oil rigs, as well as acting as gunships, air ambulances, and air taxis.

BELL 47G-3B1

BELL 47G-3B1

Blade counterweight
Droop stop
Main rotor hub
Blade-root attachment
Main rotor mast
Stabilizer-bar weight
Direct-vision panel
Fuel vent pipe
Protective gaiter
Frameless plastic canopy
Fuel tank
Fuel tank cradle
Tail-rotor drive shaft
Radio
Exhaust pipe
Air intake pipe
Instrument panel
Electric fuel pump
Cyclic-pitch lever
Battery
Battery overspill
Electrical inverter
Breather pipe
Pitot head
Oil tank
Anti-collision beacon
Carburettor hot-air intake pipe
Landing light
Air filter
Landing skid
Navigation light
Ground handling wheel
Valve-rocker cover
VHF omni-range aerial
Ventilator
Electric power socket
Lycoming six-cylinder engine
Collective-pitch lever
Riveted light-alloy forward fuselage section

SCHWEIZER 300C

Blade-root attachment

Three-blade main rotor

Ventilator

Flight-control rod

Outside air-temperature gauge

Main rotor mast

Anti-collision beacon

Anti-torque tail rotor

Magnetic compass

Navigation aerial

Automatic direction-finding aerial

Plastic canopy

Fuel tank

Cyclic-pitch lever

G-SAND

Tail boom

Engine air intake

Tubular bracing strut

Vertical tail

Tail rotor guard

Pitot head

Tail-rotor drive shaft

Anti-collision beacon

Tail-boom support strut

Exhaust silencer

Landing skid

Transmission drive-pulley cover

Landing gear damper

Landing light

Transponder aerial

Lycoming four-cylinder engine

High-visibility tip

Twin-blade main rotor

Anti-torque tail rotor

Anti-collision beacon

Triangular-section, unskinned rear fuselage

Elevator upper control wire

Synchronized elevator

Tail rotor hub

Tail rotor gearbox

G-BGID

Tubular tail rotor guard

Elevator lower control wire

Tail-rotor pitch control wire

Small fixed fin

Main rotor blade

Droop stop

Main rotor hub

Allison 250-C20J turboshaft engine

Anti-collision beacon

Blade-root attachment

Jet pipe

Main rotor mast

VHF aerial

Upper fin

Air temperature probe

Horizontal stabilizer

Anti-torque tail rotor

Forward-hinged door

G-HUMT

Lower fin

Transponder aerial

Flush-riveted aluminium fuselage

Tail boom

Boarding step

Landing skid

Rear cross-tube

Baggage compartment door

BELL 206 JETRANGER

Light aircraft

Port wingtip

LIGHT AIRCRAFT, SUCH AS THE ARV SUPER 2 shown here, are small, lightweight, and of simple construction. More than a million have been built since World War I, mainly for recreational use by private owners. Virtually all light aircraft have piston engines, most of which are air-cooled, although some are liquid-cooled. Open cockpits, almost universal in the 1920s, have today been replaced by enclosed cabins. The cabins of high-wing aircraft have one or two doors, whereas those of low-wing aircraft usually have a sliding or hinged canopy. Most modern light aircraft are made of aluminium alloy, although some are made of wood or of fibre-reinforced materials. Light aircraft today also usually have navigational instruments, an electrical system, cabin heating, wheel brakes, and a two-way radio.

Aileron mass balance

Aileron torque tube

Port aileron

PORT MAIN LANDING GEAR

Inner tube

Tyre

Hub

Brake disc

Stub axle

Landing gear leg

Brake mount

Brake pipe

Hydraulic brake calliper

Dorsal fin

TAILPLANE AND RUDDER

Elevator

Rudder tip fairing

Rudder mass balance

Fin tip fairing

Rudder

Fin

Rear fuselage top skin

Rear attachment-bracket for wing

REAR FUSELAGE

Longeron

Frame

Battery box

Diaphragm

Side skin

Elevator trimtab

Drive pillar

Attachment plate

Rear fuselage bottom skin

"Skin-grip" pin

Coolant outlet

Aluminium radiator

Air scoop

Tailplane

Coolant inlet

Elevator push-rod

Elevator push-rod

Rocking elevator arm

CONTROL RODS AND CABLES

Flap torque tube

Aileron rod

Aileron torque tube

Rudder cable

Flap drive-rod

Flap drive-rod

SIDE VIEW OF ARV SUPER 2

Canopy

Wing

Communications aerial

Navigational aerial

Fin

Spinner

Engine cowling

Dorsal fin

Rudder

Elevator

G-BNHB

Nose-gear

Step

Wing strut

Radiator

Tailskid

Tailplane

Venturi for instruments

Main landing gear

Aircraft registration code

STARBOARD MAIN LANDING GEAR

Brake mount

Brake calliper

Brake pipe

Landing gear leg

Brake disc

Stub axle

Inner tube

Tyre

Hub

PORT WING

Port top-wing fairing

Wing strut

Port flap

Pitot head

Airspeed-indicator tube

Port underwing fairing

Headrest

Backrest

SEAT ASSEMBLY

Seat cushion

Quick-release mechanism

Lap strap

Lap-strap length adjuster

Bolted anchor

CANOPY

Direct-vision panel

Pressurized strut

Hinge

Leading-edge fairing

Moulded plastic

Canopy latch

Outside air-temperature gauge

COCKPIT

Fibreglass canopy frame

Fuel tank top skin

Forward attachment bracket for wing

Rudder pedal

Control-column aperture

Semi-bulkhead

Cockpit coaming

Engine mount

Nose-leg upper mount

Firewall

"Skin-grip" pin

Fibreglass fuel tank

Bulkhead

Lap-strap attachment bracket

THREE-CYLINDER ENGINE

Port engine cowling

Air intake box

Water outlet

Carburettor

Backplate

Fuel hose

Cylinder head

Exhaust manifold

Gearbox

Propeller drive flange

PROPELLER

Spinner

Flanged plate

Starboard engine cowling

CONTROL COLUMN AND FLAP LEVER

Elevator arm

Torque tube assembly

Control column

Throttle lever

Brake lever

Elevator push-rod

Flap lever

Elevator trimtab lever

Flap lever detent box

Release button

Carburettor hot air lever

Bearing assembly

Pilot's handgrip

STARBOARD WING

Wing strut

Starboard underwing fairing

Starboard top-wing fairing

INSTRUMENT PANEL

Flight instruments

Engine instruments

Glove box

Radio plugs

NOSE-GEAR

Steering stop

Nose-leg down tube

Rubber bungee (elasticated cord) shock absorber

Damper unit

Hoop

Pivoted fork

Axle bolt

Nose-wheel

Gliders, hang-gliders, and microlights

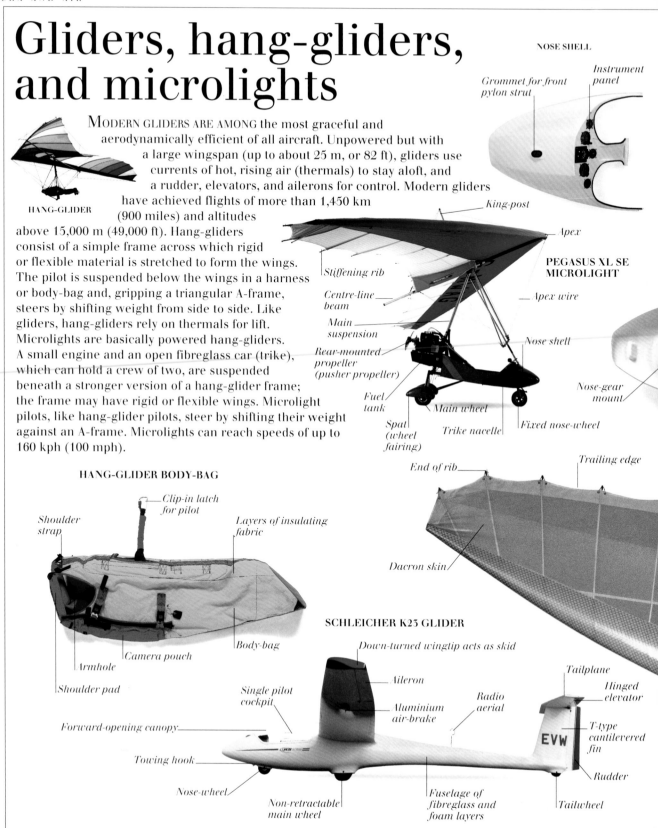

NOSE SHELL

Grommet for front pylon strut

Instrument panel

MODERN GLIDERS ARE AMONG the most graceful and aerodynamically efficient of all aircraft. Unpowered but with a large wingspan (up to about 25 m, or 82 ft), gliders use currents of hot, rising air (thermals) to stay aloft, and a rudder, elevators, and ailerons for control. Modern gliders have achieved flights of more than 1,450 km (900 miles) and altitudes above 15,000 m (49,000 ft). Hang-gliders consist of a simple frame across which rigid or flexible material is stretched to form the wings. The pilot is suspended below the wings in a harness or body-bag and, gripping a triangular A-frame, steers by shifting weight from side to side. Like gliders, hang-gliders rely on thermals for lift. Microlights are basically powered hang-gliders. A small engine and an open fibreglass car (trike), which can hold a crew of two, are suspended beneath a stronger version of a hang-glider frame; the frame may have rigid or flexible wings. Microlight pilots, like hang-glider pilots, steer by shifting their weight against an A-frame. Microlights can reach speeds of up to 160 kph (100 mph).

HANG-GLIDER

King-post

Apex

PEGASUS XL SE MICROLIGHT

Stiffening rib

Centre-line beam

Main suspension

Rear-mounted propeller (pusher propeller)

Apex wire

Nose shell

Nose-gear mount

Fuel tank

Spat (wheel fairing)

Main wheel

Trike nacelle

Fixed nose-wheel

End of rib

Trailing edge

HANG-GLIDER BODY-BAG

Clip-in latch for pilot

Shoulder strap

Layers of insulating fabric

Dacron skin

Body-bag

Armhole

Camera pouch

Shoulder pad

SCHLEICHER K23 GLIDER

Down-turned wingtip acts as skid

Aileron

Single pilot cockpit

Radio aerial

Tailplane

Aluminium air-brake

Hinged elevator

Forward-opening canopy

T-type cantilevered fin

Towing hook

EVW

Rudder

Nose-wheel

Non-retractable main wheel

Fuselage of fibreglass and foam layers

Tailwheel

SOLAR WINGS PEGASUS QUASAR MICROLIGHT

Foot throttle

Pilot's steering bar

Passenger's steering bar and footrest

Lap strap

Fuel tank filler nozzle

Spat (wheel fairing)

Engine mount

Pylon fairing

Aircraft name

Air outlet

Rear engine cowling

Pylon strut

Footbrake

Pilot's seat

Hand throttle

Pylon-strut strap

Passenger's seat

Main wing-strut

TRIKE UNIT

Leading edge

Trailing edge

TWIN-CYLINDER ENGINE

Propeller drive gearbox

Sealed lid

Twin carburettors

Air filter

Dual ignition plug

Air cooling fan

Exhaust connection

Engine rear mount

Metal hub

Waterproof stowage box

TRIKE NACELLE

EXHAUST PIPE

PROPELLER

WINGFRAME

Centre-line beam

After silencer

Main exhaust silencer

Eyelet tensioning trailing edge to rib

Bracing cable

Single spar

King-post

Rib

Leading edge

Semi-rigid fibreglass skin

Lift bracing wire

427

THE VISUAL ARTS

DRAWING	430
TEMPERA	432
FRESCO	434
OILS	436
WATERCOLOUR	438
PASTELS	440
ACRYLICS	442
CALLIGRAPHY	444
PRINTMAKING 1	446
PRINTMAKING 2	448
MOSAIC	450
SCULPTURE 1	452
SCULPTURE 2	454

Drawing

DRAWINGS CAN BE FINISHED WORKS OF ART, or preparatory studies for paintings and other visual arts. They can be made using a wide variety of drawing instruments such as pencils, graphite sticks, chalks, charcoal, pens and inks, and silver wires. The most common drawing instrument is the graphite pencil. A graphite pencil consists of a thin rod of graphite mixed with clay, encased in wood. Charcoal is one of the oldest drawing instruments. It is produced by firing twigs of willow, vine, or other woods at high temperatures in airtight containers. Erasers can be used to rub out marks made by drawing materials such as graphite pencils or charcoal, or to achieve a particular effect – such as smudging. Fixative is often applied – using a mouth diffuser or aerosol spray fixative – to prevent smudging once a drawing is finished. Silver lines can be produced by drawing silver wire across specially prepared paper – a technique known as silverpoint. The lines are permanent and cannot be erased. In time the silver lines oxidize and turn brown.

FIXATIVE AND MOUTH DIFFUSER

Hinge

Liquid fixative consisting of dissolved resin

Fixative is sucked into tube and sprayed on to drawing

CHALK, CRAYON, AND CHARCOAL

Calcite (calcium carbonate) mixed with pigment

BLUE CHALK

Iron oxide mixed with chalk

SANGUINE CRAYON

Carbonized wood

WILLOW CHARCOAL

ERASERS

Hard texture

Medium-soft, light line

PLASTIC ERASER

Soft texture

Very soft, dark line

PUTTY ERASER

DRAWING INSTRUMENTS

2B GRAPHITE PENCIL

8B GRAPHITE PENCIL

SILVER WIRE IN A METAL HOLDER

DRAWING BOARD

Drawing board

Paper

Drawing clip

DRAWING MATERIALS

Coloured pencil

Graphite stick

Bulldog clip

Dip pen

Pencil sharpener

Sketch book

Ink bottle

Silver lines
oxidize to a
light brown
colour

Figures drawn
in ink on top
of lines

Line drawn
in silverpoint
using a rule

Vanishing
point located
on head of
man riding
rearing horse

Lines of
squared
pavement slabs
recede toward
a single
vanishing
point

Complex perspective
drawing done as a
preparatory study
for a painting

EXAMPLE OF A SILVERPOINT DRAWING
The Adoration of the Magi, Leonardo da Vinci, 1481
Pen and ink over silverpoint on paper
16.5 x 29.2 cm (6½ x 11½ in)

Paper prepared
with size (glue)
and pigment

One of a series
of drawings
recording
London during
1944–1945

Charcoal lines
softened by
rubbing and
smudging

Charcoal
gives strong,
expressive lines

Handmade, tinted
paper

Broad charcoal
mark

Lines rapidly
drawn on site

EXAMPLE OF A CHARCOAL DRAWING
St. Paul's and the River, David Bomberg, 1945
Charcoal on paper
50.8 x 65.8 cm (20 x 25⅛ in)

Tempera

ILLUMINATED MANUSCRIPT

THE TERM TEMPERA is applied to any paint in which pigment is tempered (mixed) with a water-based binding medium – usually egg yolk. Egg tempera is applied to a smooth surface such as vellum (for illuminated manuscripts) or more commonly to hardwood panels prepared with gesso – a mixture of chalk and size (glue). Hog hair brushes are used to apply the gesso. A layer of gesso grosso (coarse gesso) is followed by successive layers of gesso sotile (fine gesso) that are sanded between coats to provide a smooth, yet absorbent ground. The paint is applied with fine sable brushes in thin layers, using light brushstrokes. Tempera dries quickly to form a tough skin with a satin sheen. The luminous white surface of the gesso combined with the overlaid paint produces the brilliant crispness and rich colours particular to this medium. Egg tempera paintings are frequently gilded with gold. Leaves of finely beaten gold are applied to a bole (reddish-brown clay) base and polished by burnishing.

MATERIALS FOR GILDING

Parchment for protecting gold leaf from draughts

Brush

Bowl containing diluted bole

Gold leaf

Gilder's knife

Gilder's tip for picking up gold leaf

Gold leaf smoothed and polished with a burnisher

Gilder's cushion

Surface prepared with gesso

Gold leaf applied in overlapping layers

Burnisher

Agate tip

Bole brushed on to gesso

MATERIALS FOR TEMPERA PANEL PAINTING

Yolk

EGG

White

SIZE (GLUE)

GESSO

MORTAR AND PESTLE

Mortar

Lip

Pestle for crushing and grinding pigments

EGG YOLK BINDING MEDIUM

EXAMPLES OF BRUSHES

FLAT HOG HAIR BRUSH

SABLE BRUSH SIZE 6

SABLE BRUSH SIZE 1

EXAMPLE OF A TEMPERA PAINTING
Presentation in the Temple, Ambrogio Lorenzetti, 1342
Tempera on wood, 257 x 168 cm (8 ft 5⅛ in x 5 ft 6⅛ in)

PIGMENTS FOR FLESH-COLOUR PAINTING

Altarpiece
commissioned for
Siena Cathedral, Italy

Textured gold ornament made
by punching motifs into the
gilded surface

The red tinge of
the bole is just
visible beneath
the gold

Edge of a sheet
of gold leaf

Crisp edge
characteristic of
tempera painting

Vine black used
to create the
dim cathedral
interior

Highlights on
the beard made
by applying thin
layers of white
over dried paint

Red drapery
painted in
vermilion

Raised right hand
and pointing finger
is the gesture of
prophecy

Receding floor
tiles create the
impression of
depth

Patch of discoloured
varnish, left from
last cleaning

VERDACCIO

**VERMILION AND
LEAD WHITE**

VERMILION

**RED EARTH
(IRON OXIDE)**

EXAMPLES OF PIGMENTS

Warm flesh
tones achieved
by layering
vermilion and
white over an
undercoat of
verdaccio

Patterned gold
halo glitters in
candlelight

MALACHITE

**ULTRAMARINE
LAPIS LAZULI**

Ultramarine
lapis lazuli, as
costly as gold,
was reserved for
significant
figures such as
the Virgin Mary

Craquelure
(pattern of
cracks in
the paint)

VINE BLACK

LEAD TIN YELLOW

**DETAIL FROM "PRESENTATION
IN THE TEMPLE"**

Fresco

FRESCO IS A METHOD OF WALL PAINTING. In buon fresco (true fresco), pigments are mixed with water and applied to an intonaco (layer of fresh, damp lime-plaster). The intonaco absorbs and binds the pigments as it dries making the picture a permanent part of the wall surface. The intonaco is applied in sections called giornate (daily sections). The size of each giornata depends on the artist's estimate of how much can be painted before the plaster sets. The junctions between giornate are sometimes visible on a finished fresco. The range of colours used in buon fresco are limited to lime-resistant pigments such as earth colours (below). Slaked lime (burnt lime mixed with water), bianco di San Giovanni (slaked lime that has been partly exposed to air), and chalk can be used to produce fresco whites. In fresco secco (dry fresco), pigments are mixed with a binding medium and applied to dry plaster. The pigments are not completely absorbed into the plaster and may flake off over time.

CROSS-SECTION SHOWING FRESCO LAYERS

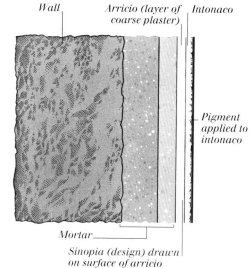

Wall

Arricio (layer of coarse plaster)

Intonaco

Pigment applied to intonaco

Mortar

Sinopia (design) drawn on surface of arricio

EXAMPLES OF EARTH COLOUR PIGMENTS

RAW UMBER

RED EARTH (IRON OXIDE)

GREEN EARTH

RAW SIENNA

INGREDIENTS FOR FRESCO WHITES

Chalk

Marble slab for mixing ingredients

Bianco di San Giovanni

Slaked lime

EXAMPLES OF FRESCO BRUSHES

Round hog hair brush

Rust-resistant twine binding

Dome-shaped hog hair brush

Pointed hog hair brush

TONDO

MUCCINI

RIGA

EXAMPLE OF A FRESCO
The Expulsion of the Merchants from the Temple, Giotto, c.1306
Fresco, 200 x 185 cm (78 x 72 in)

*One of a series
of frescoes in the
Arena Chapel,
Padua, Italy*

*Temple acts as
a backdrop for
the action*

*Bianco di San
Giovanni often
used for fresco
whites*

*Gold leaf applied
to apostle's halo*

*Green earth
pigment applied
to robe*

*Child painted
on top of
apostle's robe*

*Patches of azurite
blue have turned
green due to
reaction with
carbon dioxide*

*Hairline junction
between giornate
is visible*

*Red earth
pigment applied
in buon fresco
has retained
rich hue*

*Azurite blue applied in fresco secco has
flaked off to reveal the plaster beneath*

*Dry, matt surface characteristic
of buon fresco*

*Artist has to finish giornata
before plaster dries*

Junction between giornate

*Paint applied
in buon fresco
to child's face*

*White dove
represents
the Holy Ghost*

*Paint applied
in fresco secco
to child's body
has flaked off*

*A fresco was
generally
worked in
zones from
the top down*

*Area with little
detail can be
painted quickly,
allowing a
larger giornata
to be completed*

*Highly detailed
area takes a
longer time to
paint, restricting
the size of the
giornata*

*Sinopia (design)
sketched in
red earth*

**DETAIL FROM "THE
EXPULSION"**

GIORNATE (DAILY SECTIONS) IN "THE EXPULSION"

Oils

OIL PAINTS ARE MADE BY MIXING and grinding pigment with a drying vegetable oil such as linseed oil. The paint can be applied to many different surfaces and textures – the most common being canvas. Before painting, the canvas is stretched on a wooden frame and its surface is prepared with layers of size (glue) and primer. The two main types of brushes used in oil painting are stiff hog hair bristle brushes – generally used for covering large areas; and soft hair brushes made from sable or synthetic material – generally used for fine detail. Other tools, including painting knives, can also be used to achieve different effects. Oil paint can be applied thickly (a technique known as impasto), or can be thinned down using a solvent – such as turpentine or white spirit. Varnishes are sometimes applied to finished paintings to protect their surface and to give them a matt or gloss finish.

KIDNEY-SHAPED PALETTE

DAMMAR RESIN VARNISH

Crystals are dissolved and applied to painting to protect its surface

COMMERCIAL OIL PAINTS

CADMIUM RED

Lightfast opaque colour

ULTRAMARINE

Transparent colour

LINSEED OIL

EXAMPLES OF PIGMENTS

CADMIUM RED

DOUBLE DIPPER (PALETTE ATTACHMENT)

Screw-top lid

HOG HAIR BRISTLE BRUSHES

Flat hog hair brush

Filbert hog hair brush

Flat hog hair brush

Filbert hog hair brush

Oil derived from seeds of flax plant

CERULEAN BLUE

Container for storing solvent or drying oil

SYNTHETIC BRUSH

EXAMPLES OF BRUSHES

Round hog hair brush

EQUIPMENT FOR MAKING OIL PAINT

Airtight jar for storing paint

PAINTING KNIVES

SABLE BRUSH

Palette knife for mixing drying oil and pigment

TROWEL-SHAPED PAINTING KNIFE

DIAMOND-SHAPED PAINTING KNIFE

Blade

Blade

Long, wooden handle

Glass muller for grinding drying oil and pigment

Glass slab with abrasive surface

Cranked, steel shank

Cranked, steel shank

Protective, plastic case

EXAMPLE OF AN OIL PAINTING
Fritillarias, Vincent van Gogh, 1886
Oil on canvas, 73.5 x 60.5 cm (29 x 24 in)

Artist's signature
scratched in wet
paint with the
end of the brush

Background
enlivened by
dabs of white
and green

Each leaf
painted
in a single,
rapid stroke

Orange and blue
(complementary
colours) placed
together to give
maximum contrast
and enhance
one another to
appear brighter

Impasto
(deep ridges
of paint applied
in thick strokes)

Strong
directional
brushstrokes
on table draw
attention to
the vase

Features of vase highlighted
by generous touches of yellow

RADIAL STUDIO EASEL

Top sliding-
block adjusts
to canvas
height

Canvas
support

Height
adjustment
key

Angle
adjustment
key

Tripod

CANVAS STRETCHED ON WOODEN FRAME (VIEWED FROM THE BACK)

Staple

Canvas prepared
with glue (size)
and primer

Wooden
frame

Unprimed
canvas

EXAMPLES OF CANVASES

COTTON DUCK

FINE LINEN

COARSE LINEN

Watercolour

WATERCOLOUR PAINT IS MADE OF GROUND PIGMENT mixed with a water-soluble binding medium, usually gum arabic. It is usually applied to paper using soft hair brushes such as sable, goat hair, squirrel, and synthetic brushes. Watercolours are often diluted and applied as overlaying washes (thin, transparent layers) to build up depth of colour. Washes can be laid in a variety of ways to create a range of different effects. For example, a wet-in-wet wash can be achieved by laying a wash on top of another wet wash. The two washes blend together to give a fused effect. Sponges are used to modify washes by soaking up paint so that areas of pigment are lightened or removed from the paper. Watercolours can also be applied undiluted – a technique known as dry brush – to create a broken-colour effect. Watercolours are generally transparent and allow light to reflect from the surface of the paper through the layers of paint to give a luminous effect. They can be thickened and made opaque by adding body colour (Chinese white).

Natural sap from acacia tree

NATURAL SPONGE

ANATOMY OF A SABLE BRUSH

Soft red sable hair

Toe (tip)

Wooden handle

SOFT HAIR BRUSHES

Hair trimmed and cemented into ferrule

ROUND SABLE BRUSH (SIZE 6)

Round ferrule

Hair tied with clove hitch knot

ROUND SABLE BRUSH (SIZE 1)

TUBES OF WATERCOLOUR PAINT

SYNTHETIC WASH BRUSH

WINSOR GREEN

SQUIRREL MOP WASH BRUSH

PORTABLE BOX OF WATERCOLOUR PAINTS

CADMIUM YELLOW

Painted colour swatch

Chinese white

Pan of watercolour paint

Lid can be used for mixing colours

LARGE GOAT HAKE WASH BRUSH

EXAMPLE OF A WATERCOLOUR
Burning of the Houses of Parliament, Turner, 1834
Watercolour on paper, 29.2 x 44.5 cm (11½ x 17½ in)

Transparent washes laid on top of each other to create tonal depth

Transparent washes allow light to reflect off the surface of the paper to give a luminous effect

Highlight scratched out with a scalpel

Paper shows through thin wash to give flames added highlight

Crowd painted with thin strokes laid over a pale wash

Undiluted paint applied, then partly washed out, to create the impression of water

EXAMPLES OF WASHES

WASH OVER DRY BRUSH
Wash laid over paint applied with dry brush gives two-tone effect

GRADED WASH
Strong wash applied to tilted paper gives graded effect

DRY BRUSH
Undiluted paint dragged across surface of paper gives broken effect

EXAMPLES OF WATERCOLOUR PAPERS

SMOOTH-TEXTURED PAPER

MEDIUM-TEXTURED PAPER

ROUGH-TEXTURED PAPER

WET-IN-WET
Two diluted washes left to run together to give fused effect

COLOUR WHEEL OF WATERCOLOUR PAINTS

Yellow (primary colour)

Secondary colours made by mixing yellow and blue

Secondary colours made by mixing red and yellow

Blue (primary colour)

Red (primary colour)

Secondary colours made by mixing blue and red

Pastels

PASTELS ARE STICKS OF PIGMENT made by mixing ground pigment with chalk and a binding medium, such as gum arabic. They vary in hardness depending on the proportion of the binding medium to the chalk. Soft pastel – the most common form of pastel – contains just enough binding medium to hold the pigment in stick form. Pastels can be applied directly to any support (surface) with sufficient tooth (texture). When a pastel is drawn over a textured surface, the pigment crumbles and lodges in the fibres of the support. Pastel marks have a particular soft, matt quality and are suitable for techniques such as blending, scumbling, and feathering. Blending is a technique of rubbing and fusing two or more colours on the support using fingers or various tools such as tortillons (paper stumps), soft hair brushes, putty erasers, and soft bread. Scumbling is a technique of building up layers of pastel colours. The side or blunted tip of a soft pastel is lightly drawn over an underpainted area so that patches of the colour beneath show through. Feathering is a technique of applying parallel strokes of colour with the point of a pastel, usually over an existing layer of pastel colour. A thin spray of fixative can be applied – using a mouth diffuser (see pp. 430-431) or aerosol spray fixative – to a finished pastel painting, or in between layers of colour, to prevent smudging.

EQUIPMENT FOR MAKING PASTELS

Glass muller

Chalk

Glass slab with abrasive surface

Gum arabic

Ivory-black pigment

Cobalt-blue pigment

EXAMPLES OF SOFT PASTELS

COBALT-BLUE HALF PASTEL

VERMILION HALF PASTEL

OLIVE-GREEN FULL PASTEL

MAUVE FULL PASTEL

BOXED PASTEL SET

EQUIPMENT USED WITH PASTELS

Boxed set containing a mixture of portrait and landscape colours

Foam compartments protect the pastels

Soft pastel

Wooden tray

PUTTY ERASER

AEROSOL SPRAY FIXATIVE

SOFT HAIR BRUSH

BREAD

Soft bread suitable for erasing and blending

TORTILLONS (PAPER STUMPS)

Soft point used for blending

Tight roll of paper

EXAMPLE OF A PASTEL PAINTING
Woman Drying her Neck, Edgar Degas, c.1898
Pastel on cardboard, 62.5 x 65.5 cm (24½ x 25½ in)

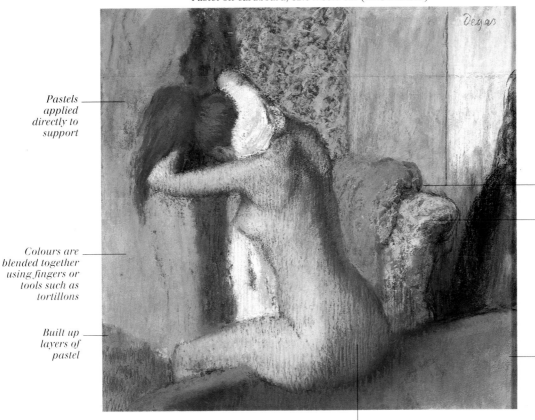

Pastels applied directly to support

Rich colour of fabric created by overlaying yellows and oranges

Broken colours, characteristic of scumbling technique

Colours are blended together using fingers or tools such as tortillons

Built up layers of pastel

Toned colour of paper visible beneath thinly applied pastels

Pure bright colours laid side by side produce strong contrasts

DETAIL FROM "WOMAN DRYING HER NECK"

Feathering technique used to produce skin tones

EXAMPLES OF TEXTURED PAPERS AND PASTEL BOARDS

WATERCOLOUR PAPER (ROUGH TEXTURE)

GLASS PAPER

WATERCOLOUR PAPER (MEDIUM TEXTURE)

INGRES PAPER

FLOCKED PASTEL BOARD

CANSON PAPER

EXAMPLES OF COLOURED AND TINTED PAPERS

Acrylics

ACRYLIC PAINT IS MADE BY MIXING PIGMENT with a synthetic resin. It can be thinned with water but dries to become water insoluble. Acrylics are applied to many surfaces, such as paper and acrylic-primed board and canvas. A variety of brushes, painting knives, rollers, air-brushes, plastic scrapers, and other tools are used in acrylic painting. The versatility of acrylics makes them suitable for a wide range of techniques. They can be used opaquely or – by adding water – in a transparent, watercolour style. Acrylic mediums can be added to the paint to adjust its consistency for special effects such as glazing and impasto (ridges of paint applied in thick strokes) or to make it more matt or glossy. Acrylics are quick-drying, which allows layers of paint to be applied on top of each other almost immediately.

EXAMPLES OF BRUSHES

Sable brush

Hog hair sash brush

Synthetic hog hair brush

Synthetic sable brush

Hog hair brush

Goat hair brush

Synthetic wash brush

Ox hair brush

EXAMPLES OF PAINTS USED IN ACRYLICS

Azo yellow

Phthalo green

Cerulean blue

Phthalo blue

Quinacridone red

Titanium white

Pad of disposable paper palettes

Yellow ochre

Burnt umber

Burnt sienna

PAINTING TOOLS

Flexible, plastic blade

PLASTIC PAINTING KNIFE

Stippled effect achieved using thick paint

Striated effect

Glue spreader

Credit card

Paint spread evenly

PLASTIC SCRAPERS

Plastic handle

SPONGE ROLLER

Blended tones

Uniform tone

Paint cup

Nozzle

Main lever

AIR-BRUSH

Air hose

EXAMPLE OF AN ACRYLIC PAINTING
A Bigger Splash, David Hockney, 1967
Acrylic on canvas, 242.5 x 243.8 cm (95½ x 96 in)

Paint applied evenly using a roller

Cotton duck canvas support (surface)

Flatness of rollered areas enhanced by adding gel medium to the paint

Masking tape stuck on to canvas to define main shapes, and paint applied within these areas using a roller

Thin strip of pool edge left unpainted

Splash painted using thicker paint and small brush

Imprecise edge on end of spring board where paint has seeped under masking tape

EXAMPLES OF ACRYLIC PAINTS AND TECHNIQUES

Opaque effect

Extruded (squeezed) effect

Paint applied using painting knife

PURPLE ACRYLIC PAINT

YELLOW ACRYLIC PAINT

ORANGE ACRYLIC PAINT

Transparent, watercolour effect

Translucent, impasto glaze

Thick impasto with coarse texture

BLUE ACRYLIC PAINT DILUTED WITH WATER

GREEN ACRYLIC PAINT MIXED WITH GEL MEDIUM

RED ACRYLIC PAINT MIXED WITH TEXTURE PASTE

Calligraphy

CALLIGRAPHY IS BEAUTIFULLY FORMED LETTERING. The term applies to written text and illumination (the decoration of manuscripts using gold leaf and colour). The essential materials needed to practise calligraphy are a writing tool, ink, and a writing surface. Quills are among the oldest writing tools. They are usually made from goose or turkey feathers, and are noted for their flexibility and ability to produce fine lines. A quill point, however, is not very durable and constant recutting and trimming is required. The most commonly used writing instrument in western calligraphy is a detachable, metal nib held in a penholder. The metal nib is very durable, and there are a wide range of different types. Particular types of nibs – such as copperplate, speedball, and roundhand nibs – are used for specific styles of lettering. Some nibs have integral ink reservoirs and others have reservoirs that are detachable. Brushes are also used for writing, and for filling in outlined letters and painting decoration. Other writing tools used in calligraphy are fountain pens, felt-tip pens, rotring pens, and reed pens. Calligraphy inks may come in liquid form, or as a solid ink stick. Ink sticks are ground down in distilled water to form a liquid ink. The most common writing surfaces for calligraphy are good quality, smooth -surfaced papers. To achieve the best writing position, the calligrapher places the paper on a drawing board set at an angle.

EQUIPMENT USED IN BRUSH LETTERING

Brush rest

Wolf hair brush

Goat hair brush

BRUSHES AND BRUSH REST

Liquid ink made by grinding down ink stick in distilled water

Solid carbon ink stick

Ink stone

INK STICK AND STONE

Feather

PENS, NIBS, AND BRUSHES USED IN CALLIGRAPHY

PENHOLDER

COPPERPLATE NIB

SPEEDBALL NIB

FELT-TIP PEN

ROUNDHAND NIB AND DETACHABLE INK RESERVOIR

AUTOMATICPEN

Feather stripped for better handling

REED PEN

Barrel

SQUARE SABLE BRUSH

POINTED SABLE BRUSH

Hand-cut point

GOOSE-FEATHER QUILL

GOAT HAIR BRUSH

WOLF HAIR BRUSH

FOUNTAIN PEN AND INK

Bottle of permanent black ink

Barrel

Clip

Nib

Outer cap

EXAMPLES OF LETTERING STYLES

Apex
Bowl
Curved stroke
Stem
Inner counter
Stem
Stem
Arm
Counter
Crossbar
Inner counter
Counter
Inner counter

ROMAN CAPITALS

Cap line
X line
Base line
Descender line
Ascender
Curved stroke
Ear
Arch
Crossbar
Serif
Neck
Descender
Height of letter determined by ladder of nib widths

ITALIC ROMAN

Slightly pinched (curved) vertical stroke
Letter filled in using brush
Inner counter
Tail
Spine
Pointed apex

VERSAL

CHINESE LETTERING

Rice paper
Broad brush stroke
Chinese character meaning long life
Artist's stamped signature

ARTIST'S STAMP

Stamp
Stamped signature of the artist
Ink pad

DRAWING BOARD

Adjustable set square
Blade with parallel motion

AN ILLUMINATED MANUSCRIPT

Style of lettering called Gothic book script
Large decorative letter used to mark the opening of a chapter
Words written carefully by hand
Gold leaf
Grid lines provide guide to position of words and pictures

EXAMPLES OF CALLIGRAPHY PAPERS

Standard European paper
Indian handmade paper
Flecked, tinted paper
Imitation parchment paper

Printmaking 1

PRINTS ARE MADE BY FOUR BASIC printing processes – intaglio, lithographic, relief, and screen. In intaglio printing, lines are engraved or etched into the surface of a metal plate. Lines are engraved by hand using sharp metal tools. They are etched by corroding the metal plate with acid, using acid-resistant ground to protect the areas not to be etched. The plate is then inked and wiped, leaving the grooves filled with ink and the surface clean. Dampened paper is laid over the plate, and both paper and plate are passed through the rollers of an etching press. The pressure of the rollers forces the paper into the grooves, so that it takes up the ink, leaving an impression on the paper. Lithographic printing is based on the antipathy between grease and water. An image is drawn on a surface – usually a stone or metal plate – with a greasy medium, such as tusche (lihographic ink). The greasy drawing is fixed on to the plate by applying an acidic solution, such as gum arabic. The surface is then dampened and rolled with ink. The ink adheres only to the greasy areas and is repelled by the water. Paper is laid on the plate and pressure is applied by means of a press. In relief printing, the non-printing areas of a wood or linoleum block are cut away using gouges, knives, and other tools. The printing areas are left raised in relief and are rolled with ink. Paper is laid on the inked block and pressure is applied by means of a press or by burnishing (rubbing) the back of the paper. The most common forms of relief printing are woodcut, wood engraving, and linocut. In screen printing, the printing surface is a mesh stretched across a wooden frame. A stencil is applied to the mesh to seal the non-printing areas and ink is scraped through the mesh to produce an image.

THE FOUR MAIN PRINTING PROCESSES

Paper

Printed image

Engraved or etched image

Metal plate

Inked area

INTAGLIO

Printed image

Paper

Damp surface rejects ink

Image drawn on stone with greasy medium

Ink adheres to greasy image

LITHOGRAPHIC

Paper

Printed image

Raised figure

Inked surface

Wood block

RELIEF

Wooden frame

Ink forced through mesh

Stencil

Printed image

Paper

SCREEN

LEATHER
INK DABBER

EQUIPMENT USED IN INTAGLIO PRINTING

ROCKER

SCRIBER

ROULETTE

SCRAPER

BURNISHER

CLAMP

ETCHING PRESS USED FOR INTAGLIO PRINTMAKING

Flywheel

Paper

Felt blanket cushions and distributes pressure exerted by rollers

Spoke

Screw pressure adjustor

Handle

Printed image

Top roller

Position guide

Sliding bed (plank) is wound between steel rollers

Inked-up copper plate

GROUND

Acid-resistant ground rolled on to metal plate before etching

EXAMPLES OF PRINTING PAPERS

GROUND ROLLER

Gelatine roller

Wooden handle

EXAMPLE OF AN INTAGLIO PRINT
Annie with a Sun Hat, Jock McFadyen, 1993
Etched copper plate, 41 x 40 cm (16 x 15¾ in)

Printmaking 2

EXAMPLE OF A LITHOGRAPHIC STONE AND PRINT
Crown Gateway 2, Mandy Bonnell, 1987
Lithograph, 50 x 40 cm (19½ x 15¾ in)

IMAGE DRAWN ON STONE

LITHOGRAPIC PRINT

EXAMPLE OF A SCREEN PRINT
Sea Change, Patrick Hughes, 1992
Screen print, 77 x 94.5 cm (30 x 37 in)

SCREEN AND SQUEEGEE

Squeegee

Rubber blade

Mesh

Wooden frame

EQUIPMENT USED IN LITHOGRAPHIC PRINTING

CRAYON AND HOLDER

LITHOGRAPHIC PENCIL

TUSCHE (LITHOGRAPHIC INK) PEN

ERASING STICK

EXPANDABLE SPONGE

TUSCHE (LITHOGRAPHIC INK) STICK

RUBBING INK

INK ROLLER

MILD ACIDIC SOLUTION

GUM ARABIC SOLUTION

WATER-BASED SCREEN PRINTING INKS

BLUE ACRYLIC INK

RED ACRYLIC INK

BROWN TEXTILE INK

EQUIPMENT USED IN RELIEF PRINTING

V-SHAPED GOUGE

INK ROLLER

Rubber roller

LINOLEUM AND WOODCUT BLOCK

U-SHAPED GOUGE

GRAVER

Linoleum

KNIFE

SCORPER

WOOD ENGRAVING

Side-grain wood block

END-GRAIN WOOD BLOCK

INKED-UP ENGRAVED BLOCK

WOOD ENGRAVING PRINT

RELIEF-PRINTING PRESS

Spiral spring

Crown

Piston

Tympan lowered on to printing block

Printed image

Staple (frame)

Platen

Bar (pressure handle)

Printing block

Bed is rolled under platen

Drum handle

Rail

Counterweight

Drum (rounce)

Leg

Pillar (post)

Foot

Mosaic

MOSAIC IS THE ART OF MAKING patterns and pictures from tesserae (small, coloured pieces of glass, marble, and other materials). Different materials are cut into tesserae using different tools. Smalti (glass enamel) and marble are cut into pieces using a hammer and a hardy (a pointed blade) embedded in a log. Vitreous glass is cut into pieces using a pair of nippers. Mosaics can be made using a direct or indirect method. In the direct method, the tesserae are laid directly into a bed of cement–based adhesive. In the indirect method, the design is drawn in reverse on paper or cloth. The tesserae are then stuck face-down on the paper or cloth using water-soluble glue. Adhesive is spread with a trowel on to a solid surface – such as a wall – and the back of the mosaic is laid into the adhesive. Finally, the paper or cloth is soaked off to reveal the mosaic. Gaps between tesserae can be filled with grout. Grout is forced into gaps by dragging a grouting squeegee across the face of the mosaic. Mosaics are usually used to decorate walls and floors, but they can also be applied to smaller objects.

EQUIPMENT FOR BREAKING MARBLE

Sawn strip of marble, ready for breaking into cubes

Mosaic hammer

Hardwearing, tungsten carbide tip

NIPPERS

Alicante (red marble) pieces

Hardy (pointed blade) embedded in a log

MOSAIC TOOLS

CEMENT-BASED ADHESIVE

GROUT

SMALTI (GLASS ENAMEL)

RED SMALTI

EXAMPLE OF A MOSAIC (DIRECT METHOD)
Seascape, Tessa Hunkin, 1993
Smalti mosaic on board
80 cm (31½ in) diameter

Handle with rubber grip

YELLOW SMALTI

BLUE SMALTI

TROWEL

Notch

GROUTING SQUEEGEE

Wooden handle

Steel blade

Rubber blade

Wooden handle

Gold-leaf smalti

STAGES IN THE CREATION OF A MOSAIC (INDIRECT METHOD)

COLOUR SKETCH
A colour sketch is drawn
in oil pastel to give a clear
impression of how the finished
mosaic will look.

REVERSE IMAGE
Tesserae are glued face-down
on reverse image on paper.
Mosaic is then attached to solid
surface and paper is removed.

MOSAIC POT

Geometric design

Grout

MOSAIC MOSQUE DESIGN

Floral design

Geometric border

*Andamenti
(line along
which tesserae
are laid)*

*Grout fills
the gaps
between the
tesserae*

*Mosaic
mounted
on board*

*Vitreous
glass cut into
triangular
shape with
nippers*

*Gold tessera
with ripple
finish*

*Gold tessera
placed upside-
down*

VITREOUS GLASS

**GREEN VITREOUS
GLASS WITH GOLD LEAF**

*Plain
finish*

**RED VITREOUS
GLASS**

*Ripple
finish*

SHEETS OF VITREOUS GLASS

**BLUE VITREOUS
GLASS**

FINISHED MOSAIC
Goldfish, Tessa Hunkin, 1993
Vitreous glass mosaic on board
35.5 x 25.5 cm (14 x 10 in)

*Border of square
vitreous glass*

Sculpture 1

THE TWO TRADITIONAL METHODS OF MAKING SCULPTURE are carving and modelling. A carved sculpture is made by cutting away the surplus from a block of hard material such as stone, marble, or wood. The tools used for carving vary according to the material being carved. Heavy steel points, claws, and chisels that are struck with a lump hammer are generally used for stone and marble. Sharp gouges and chisels that are struck with a wooden mallet are used for wood. Sculptures formed from hard materials are generally finished by filing with rasps, rifflers, and other abrasive implements. Modelling is a process by which shapes are built up, using malleable materials such as clay, plaster, and wax. The material is cut with wire-ended tools and modelled with the fingers or a variety of hardwood and metal implements. For large or intricate modelled sculptures an armature (frame), made from metal or wood, is used to provide internal support. Sculptures formed in soft materials may harden naturally or can be made more durable by firing in a kiln. Modelled sculptures are often first designed in wax or another material to be cast later in a metal (see pp. 454-455) such as bronze. The development of many new materials in the 20th century has enabled sculptors to experiment with new techniques such as construction (joining preformed pieces of material such as machine components, mirrors, and furniture) and kinetic (mobile) sculpture.

EXAMPLES OF MARBLE CARVING TOOLS

1.1 kg (2½ lb) iron head

Ash handle

LUMP HAMMER

EXAMPLES OF WOODCARVING TOOLS

CABINET RASP

STRAIGHT GOUGE

SALMON BEND GOUGE

CHISEL

Stone for sharpening woodcarving tools

Cedar box

ARKANSAS HONE-STONE

CARVING MALLET

CALLIPERS

Curved leg

Gap measures distance between two points on a sculpture

Wing nut

WIDE MARBLE CLAW

NARROW MARBLE CLAW

POINT

FLAT CHISEL

BULLNOSE CHISEL

EXAMPLES OF RIFFLERS (FOR STONE, MARBLE, AND WOOD)

30 CM (12 IN) RIFFLER

15 CM (6 IN) RIFFLER

Surface for sharpening stonecarving tools

DIAMOND WHETSTONE

*Tiny holes along
the hairline made
with a point*

*Soft skin texture tooled
with a fine-toothed
marble claw*

**DETAIL OF
SLAVE'S HEAD**

EXAMPLE OF A CARVED WOOD SCULPTURE
Mary Magdalene, Donatello, 1454-1455
Poplar wood, height 188 cm (6 ft 2 in)

EXAMPLE OF A CARVED MARBLE SCULPTURE
The Rebel Slave, Michelangelo, 1513-1516
Marble, height 213 cm (7ft)

*Hair worked
with a narrow
claw*

*Delicately
modelled
hand carved
with a chisel*

*Hair
highlighted
with gold
leaf*

*Translucent white
marble, quarried at
Carrara, Italy*

*Figure cut
from single
length of
poplar*

*Deep
ridges of
hair cut
with a
gouge*

*Surface rubbed
smooth with
rifflers and
pumice*

*Strut gives added
support to long
slender limb*

*Wood prepared
with gesso
(chalk and glue)
and painted*

*Series of tiny
punch holes,
made with a
fine point,
outline the
form*

*Base scored with
jagged parallel
cuts made with
point and lump
hammer*

*Foot carved in
deep relief*

*Rough surface
made by driving
a point into the
marble at an
oblique angle*

*The dimensions of the marble block
determine the size of the sculpture*

DETAIL OF SLAVE'S FOOT

Sculpture 2

EXAMPLES OF MODELLING TOOLS

WIRE-ENDED CUTTING TOOL

CURVED MOULDING TOOL

SPATULA-ENDED WAX MODELLING TOOL

ROUNDED WAX MODELLING TOOL

EXAMPLES OF BRONZE FINISHING TOOLS

HOOKED RIFFLER   **POINTED RIFFLER**

SPIRIT LAMP (FOR HEATING WAX MODELLING TOOLS)

Wick

Brass holder

Glass bowl

Methylated spirit

STAGES IN THE LOST-WAX METHOD OF CASTING
Based on Mars, Giambologna, c.1546

Wax-covered wire armature

Wax riser (vertical, hollow rod)

Chaplet (iron nail)

Wax runner (horizontal, hollow rod)

Fire-resistant clay

ORIGINAL MODEL
An original, solid wax model is made and preserved so that numerous replicas can be cast.

HOLLOW WAX FIGURE IS CAST
A new, hollow wax model is cast from the original model. It is filled with a plaster core that is held in place with nails. Wax runners and risers are attached.

FIGURE IS BAKED IN CASTING MOULD
The model is encased in clay and baked. The wax melts away (through the channels made by the wax rods) and is replaced by molten bronze.

MODELLING STAND AND ARMATURE

Aluminium wire figure

Fixed iron armature support

Marine ply modelling board

Rotating table top

Tripod

Screw-hole for fastening the iron to modelling board

Aluminium table stand

Height adjustor

Clay smoothed to create the effect of soft skin

Incision made with serrated tool

Strips of clay, added to the model, give the effect of folded drapery

EXAMPLE OF A CLAY MODEL
Madonna and Child, Henry Moore, 1945
Terracotta, height 18.4 cm (7¼ in)

Maquette (small sketch) modelled from a solid lump of clay

Terracotta clay, fires at 1,000°C to 1,050°C (1,832°F to 1,922°F)

Model for a much larger bronze sculpture

Roughly worked clay

Metal riser

Metal runner

Stump left by rod will be filed down

Hole left by nail will be plugged with bronze

Golden brown colour of untreated bronze

Dark brown patina

STATUE IS STRIPPED OF CLAY
When the bronze has cooled, the clay mould is broken open to reveal the bronze statue with solid metal runners and risers.

STATUE IS FINISHED
The nails are pulled out and a large hole is made to remove the plaster core. When the metal rods have been sawn off, the sculpture is filed to refine the surface.

STATUE IS CLEANED
Finally the work is cleaned and polished. An artificial patina (colouring) is achieved by treating the surface with chemicals.

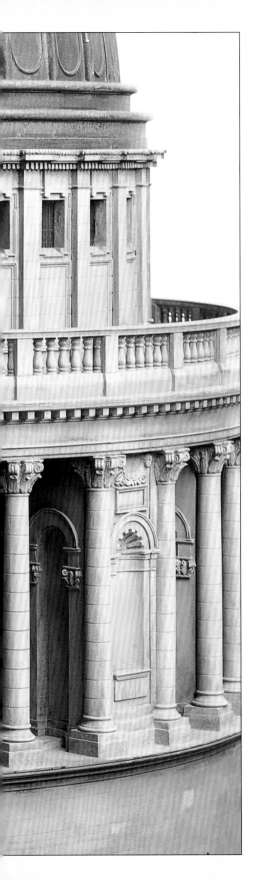

ARCHITECTURE

ANCIENT EGYPT 458

ANCIENT GREECE 460

ANCIENT ROME 1 462

ANCIENT ROME 2 464

MEDIEVAL CASTLES AND HOUSES 466

MEDIEVAL CHURCHES 468

GOTHIC 1 470

GOTHIC 2 472

RENAISSANCE 1 474

RENAISSANCE 2 476

BAROQUE AND NEOCLASSICAL 1 478

BAROQUE AND NEOCLASSICAL 2 480

BAROQUE AND NEOCLASSICAL 3 482

ARCHES AND VAULTS 484

DOMES 486

ISLAMIC BUILDINGS 488

SOUTH AND EAST ASIA 490

THE 19TH CENTURY 492

THE EARLY 20TH CENTURY 494

MODERN BUILDINGS 1 496

MODERN BUILDINGS 2 498

Ancient Egypt

THE CIVILIZATION OF THE ANCIENT EGYPTIANS (which lasted from about 3100 BC until it was finally absorbed into the Roman empire in 30 BC) is famous for its temples and tombs. Egyptian temples were often huge and geometric, like the Temple of Amon-Re (below and right). They were usually decorated with hieroglyphs (sacred characters used for picture-writing) and painted reliefs depicting gods, Pharaohs (kings), and queens. Tombs were particularly important to the Egyptians, who believed that the dead were resurrected in the after-life. The tombs were often decorated – as, for example, the surround of the false door opposite – in order to give comfort to the dead. The best-known ancient Egyptian tombs are the pyramids, which were designed to symbolize the rays of the sun. Many of the architectural forms used by the ancient Egyptians were later adopted by other civilizations; for example, columns and capitals were later used by the ancient Greeks (see pp. 460-461) and ancient Romans (see pp. 462-465).

Cornice decorated with cavetto moulding

Campaniform (open papyrus) capital

Architrave

Papyrus-bud capital

Socle

Side aisle   *Central nave*   *Side aisle*

SIDE VIEW OF HYPOSTYLE HALL, TEMPLE OF AMON-RE, KARNAK, EGYPT, c.1290 BC

Horus, the sun-god   *Architrave*   *Stone slab forming flat roof of side aisle*

Kepresh crown with disc

Chons, the moon-god   *Amon-Re, king of the gods*   *Hathor, the sky-goddess*   *Papyrus motif*   *Cartouche (oval border) containing the titles of the Pharaoh (king)*   *Socle*   *Aisle running north-south*

LIMESTONE FALSE DOOR WITH HIEROGLYPHS, TOMB OF KING TJETJI, GIZA, EGYPT, c.2400 BC

Lintel

Hieroglyph representing a house

Disc representing sun or light

Eroded image of Tjetji

Limestone stela (slab)

Hoe-shaped hieroglyph representing "mr" sound

Head of false door

Image of Tjetji's wife

Image of Tjetji's daughter

PLANT CAPITAL OF THE PTOLEMAIC-ROMAN PERIOD, EGYPT, 332-30 BC

Palm leaf

Papyrus flower

Papyrus leaf

Papyrus stem

Lotus bud

Lotus stem

Cornice decorated with cavetto moulding

Bead moulding

Trellis window

Rectangular pier decorated with hieroglyphs

Elevated roof of central nave

Clerestory

Disc representing sun or light

Architrave

Square abacus

Papyrus-bud capital

Papyriform column

Shaft

Scene depicting a Pharaoh (king) paying homage to the god Amon-Re

Central nave

ANCIENT EGYPTIAN BUILDING DECORATION

DECORATED WINDOW, MEDINET HABU, EGYPT, C.1198 BC

ROPE AND PATERAE DECORATION

CAPITAL WITH THE HEAD OF THE SKY-GODDESS HATHOR, TEMPLE OF ISIS, PHILAE, EGYPT, 283-47 BC

LOTUS AND PAPYRUS FRIEZE DECORATION

Ancient Greece

THE CLASSICAL TEMPLES OF ANCIENT GREECE were built according to the belief that certain forms and proportions were pleasing to the gods. There were three main ancient Greek architectural orders (styles), which can be distinguished by the decoration and proportions of their columns, capitals (column tops), and entablatures (structures resting on the capitals). The oldest is the Doric order, which dates from the seventh century BC and was used mainly on the Greek mainland and in the western colonies, such as Sicily and southern Italy. The Temple of Neptune, shown here, is a classic example of this order. It is hypaethral (roofless) and peripteral (surrounded by a single row of columns). About a century later, the more decorative Ionic order developed on the Aegean Islands. Features of this order include volutes (spiral scrolls) on capitals and acroteria (pediment ornaments). The Corinthian order was invented in Athens in the fifth century BC and is typically identified by an acanthus leaf on the capitals. This order was later widely used in ancient Roman architecture.

Abacus

Echinus

Annulet   *Trachelion (neck)*

**DORIC CAPITAL, THE PROPYLAEUM (GATEWAY), THE
ACROPOLIS, ATHENS, GREECE, 449 BC**

Abacus   *Lesbian leaf pattern*

*Coussinet
(cushion)*

*Cyma reversa
profile*

Volute

*Echinus with
egg and dart
decoration*

Eye   *Palmette*

**IONIC CAPITAL, THE PROPYLAEUM (GATEWAY), TEMPLE OF
ATHENA POLIAS, PRIENE, GREECE, c.534 BC**

Mask

Abacus

Volute

Cauliculus

*Acanthus
leaf*

Bell-shaped core

**CORINTHIAN CAPITAL FROM A STOA (PORTICO),
PROBABLY FROM ASIA MINOR**

TEMPLE OF NEPTUNE, PAESTUM, ITALY, c.460 BC

Raking cornice

Trachelion (neck)   *Taenia*   *Triglyph*   *Metope*   *Glyph (channel)*

Pediment

*Doric
entablature*

*Pteron
(external
colonnade)*

Euthynteria   *Drum*   *Stylobate*   *Column of the Doric order*

PLAN OF THE TEMPLE OF NEPTUNE, PAESTUM

Pronaos (vestibule)

Naos wall

Anta (pilaster
terminating
naos wall)

Naos (cella)

Peristyle

Opisthodomos
(rear portico)

Pteron
(external
colonnade)

Hexastyle pteron
(colonnade of six columns)

ANCIENT GREEK BUILDING DECORATION

Volute

FACADE, TREASURY OF ATREUS, MYCENAE,
GREECE, 1350-1250 BC

Meander

FRETWORK, PARTHENON, ATHENS,
GREECE, 447-436 BC

ACROTERION,
TEMPLE OF
APHAIA, AEGINA,
GREECE, 490 BC

Griffon
(gryphon)

Raking
cornice

ANTEFIXA,
TEMPLE
OF APHAIA,
AEGINA,
GREECE,
490 BC

Palmette

Volute

Regula (short fillet beneath taenia)   Eaves

Cornice

Frieze

Architrave

Capital

Shaft

Crepidoma
(stepped
base)

Entasis (slight curve of a column)   Intercolumniation   Fluting

Ancient Rome 1

IN THE EARLY PERIOD OF THE ROMAN EMPIRE extensive use
was made of ancient Greek architectural ideas, particularly
those of the Corinthian order (see pp. 460-461). As a result,
many early Roman buildings – such as the Temple of Vesta
(opposite) – closely resemble ancient Greek buildings. A
distinctive Roman style began to evolve in the first century
AD. This style developed the interiors of buildings (the Greeks
had concentrated on the exterior) by using arches, vaults, and
domes inside the buildings, and by ornamenting internal walls.
Many of these features can be seen in the Pantheon. Exterior
columns were often used for decorative, rather than structural,
purposes, as in the Colosseum and the Porta Nigra (see
pp. 464-465). Smaller buildings had timber frames with
wattle-and-daub walls, as in the mill (see pp. 464-465).
Roman architecture remained influential for many centuries,
with some of its principles being used in the 11th century in
Romanesque buildings (see pp. 468-469) and also in the 15th
and 16th centuries in Renaissance buildings (see pp. 474-477).

ANCIENT ROMAN BUILDING DECORATION

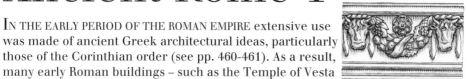

FESTOON, TEMPLE OF VESTA,
TIVOLI, ITALY, C.80 BC

RICHLY DECORATED
ROMAN OVUM

INTERIOR OF THE PANTHEON,
ROME, ITALY, 118-c.128

Inner dome,
following the
curve of a
depressed arch

Outer
saucer
dome

Entablature

Curved
cornice

Lesene

Cornice

Triangular
pediment

Concave
niche

Marble veneer   Segmental pediment   Pedestal

FRONT VIEW OF THE PANTHEON

Oculus

Series of concentric,
step-like rings

Dentil ornament

Engaged
pediment

Raking
cornice

Pediment

Rotunda

Outer saucer dome

Intermediate
block

Entablature
with
inscription

Octastyle portico
(eight-column portico)

SIDE VIEW OF THE PANTHEON

Entablature

Pitched roof

Eaves

Intermediate
block

Upper
cornice

Relieving
arch

Opening for
ventilation

Cornice

Colonnade

Ornamental
band decorated
with festoons

Attached
fluted pilaster

TEMPLE OF VESTA, TIVOLI, ITALY, c.80 BC

Circular naos (cella) — Architrave — Ceiling — Fascia

Corinthian entablature

Corinthian capital

Pteron (colonnade)

Naos (cella) window

Opus incertum (concrete wall faced with irregularly shaped stones)

Egg and dart decoration

Upper torus

Scotia

Lower torus

Jamb with corrugated surface

Naos (cella) door

Cornice

Threshold

Podium

FRIEZE, FORUM OF TRAJAN, ROME, ITALY, 98-113

KEYSTONE, ARCH OF TITUS, ROME, ITALY, 81

Oculus illuminating interior of rotunda

Coffer

Stepped side of coffer

Step-like ring

Frieze decorated with arabesques, urns, and winged horses

Barrel vault

Passageway

Coffer

Engaged pediment

Monolithic shaft (shaft made from a single stone)

Barrel vault

Raking cornice

Pediment

Entablature

Corinthian column

Entablature

Aedicule (tabernacle)

Festoon

Fluting

Corinthian pilaster

Base

Corinthian capital

Rotunda

Portico

463

Ancient Rome 2

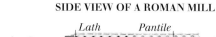

SIDE VIEW OF A ROMAN MILL

Principal rafter
Wall-plate
Wall-post
Top-plate
Floorboard
Intermediate floor-joist
Sill
Stud
Foundation

Lath
Pantile

Verge
Eaves
Plain fascia
Plaster coating

Grille
Joist
Boarding

FRONT VIEW OF A ROMAN MILL, 1ST CENTURY BC

Half-round ridge tile
Pitched roof
Ashlar post
Plain fascia
Flat soffit
Mill wheel
Wattle-and-daub wall with plaster coating

King-strut
Lath
Principal rafter
Tie-beam
Wall-plate
Intermediate floor-joist
Top-plate
Wall-post
Sill
Binder

Supporting post
Floor-joist
Foundation post

THE COLOSSEUM (FLAVIAN AMPHITHEATRE), ROME, ITALY, 70-82

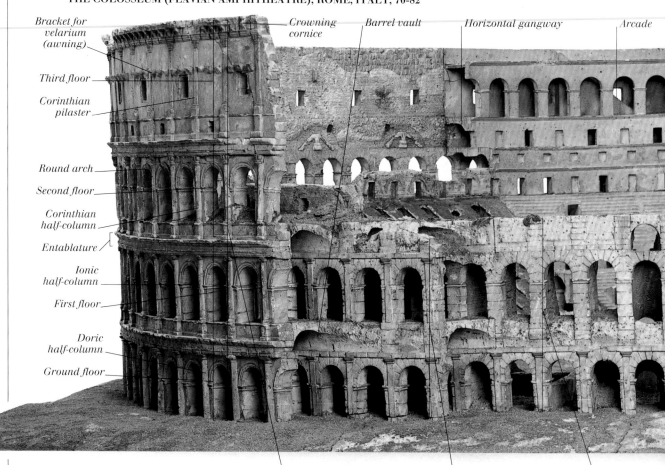

Bracket for velarium (awning)
Third floor
Corinthian pilaster
Round arch
Second floor
Corinthian half-column
Entablature
Ionic half-column
First floor
Doric half-column
Ground floor

Crowning cornice
Barrel vault
Horizontal gangway
Arcade

External travertine shell
Intermediate shell
Inner shell

PORTA NIGRA, TRIER, GERMANY, c.240-260

Crowning cornice

Impost

Semicircular tower

Parapet

Keystone

Arcaded passageway

Round-arched window

Lesene

Voussoir

Semicircular tower

Cornice

Entablature

Frieze

Relieving arch

Architrave

Arcading

Apse (added in Middle Ages)

Attached column

Courtyard

Round arch

Entrance to town

Capital

Shaft

Base

Facade

ROMAN WATTLE-AND-DAUB WALL, 1ST CENTURY BC

Hazel twig framework

Clay mixture

Paintwork

Plaster

Opening to staircase

Maenianum summum (gallery)

Rectangular window

String course

Cuneus (wedge of seating)

Opus quadratum (square masonry)

Arched opening to staircase

Radiating, wedge-shaped chamber

Radial wall

Opus incertum (concrete wall faced with irregularly shaped stones)

Cornice

Ambulatory corridor

Attached rectangular pier

Keystone

Impost

Tuscan capital

Voussoir

Tuscan pilaster

Medieval castles and houses

WARFARE WAS COMMON IN EUROPE in the Middle Ages, and many monarchs and nobles built castles as a form of defence. Typical medieval castles have outer walls surrounding a moat. Inside the moat is a bailey (courtyard), protected by a chemise (jacket-wall). The innermost and strongest part of a medieval castle is the keep. There are two main types of keep: towers called donjons, such as the Tour de César and Coucy-le-Château, and rectangular keeps ("hall-keeps"), such as the Tower of London. Castles were often guarded by salients (projecting fortifications), like those of the Bastille. Medieval houses typically had timber cruck (tent-like) frames, wattle-and-daub walls, and pitched roofs, like those on medieval London Bridge (opposite).

DONJON, TOUR DE CESAR, PROVINS, FRANCE, 12TH CENTURY

- Oculus
- Loophole
- Conical spire
- Flying buttress
- Hexahedral hall
- Semicircular turret
- Fireplace
- Bailey
- Embrasure
- Chemise (jacket-wall)
- Plain impost
- Battlements (crenellations)
- Hemispherical cupola
- Gallery
- Squinch
- Vaulted room
- Main entrance
- Staircase to chemise (jacket-wall)
- Depressed cupola
- Vaulted staircase
- Motte

- Loophole

SALIENT, CAERNARVON CASTLE, BRITAIN, 1283-1323

- Timber cruck frame

CRUCK-FRAMED HOUSE, BRITAIN, c.1200

- Blind, rounded relieving arch
- Tetrahedral spire
- Rectangular turret
- Quoin
- Cornice
- Buttress
- Round-arched window with twin openings
- Merlon
- Crenel
- Battlements (crenellations)
- Loophole
- Wooden staircase leading to entrance above ground level
- Timber-framed house
- Cruck frame
- Paling

TOWER OF LONDON, BRITAIN, FROM 1070

- Curtain wall
- Pointed relieving arch
- Semicircular relieving arch
- Plain string course
- Bracket decorated with scroll moulding
- Rectangular window
- Sunken rectangular panel
- Round-arched window
- Semicircular salient
- Loophole
- Lateral circular salient

THE BASTILLE, PARIS, FRANCE, 14TH CENTURY

MEDIEVAL LONDON BRIDGE, BRITAIN, 1176 (WITH 14TH-CENTURY BATTLEMENTED BUILDING, NONESUCH HOUSE, AND TWO-TOWERED GATE)

Gate-house
Battlemented building
Chapel pier
Railing
Onion-shaped dome
Pitched roof
Shaped gable
Nonesuch House
Crypt of Becket Chapel
Starling
Two-towered gate
Oriel window
Timber framing with ornamental woodwork
Pier
Pointed Gothic stone arch
Timber framing

DONJON, COUCY-LE-CHATEAU, AISNE, FRANCE, 1225-1245

Cornice
Pointed arch
Loophole
Round arch
Parapet
Passageway
Gallery
Pointed arch
Inner hall
Tribune (elevated platform)
Springing point of rib vault
Projecting rectangular pier
Window opening
Chimney-shaft
Rectangular opening
Fireplace
Archivolt decorated with torus and fascia
Bridge to castle entrance
Steps
Mezzanine (entresol) housing drawbridge windlass
Entrance
Moat
Dodecahedral second floor
Engaged colonette
Dodecahedral first floor
Embrasure
Dodecahedral ground floor
Passageway inside structure of outer wall
Four-centred relieving arch
Niche
Corbel with sculptural decoration
Capital
String course
Ruin of segmental ramp leading to chemise (jacket-wall)

Medieval churches

DURING THE MIDDLE AGES, large numbers of churches were built in Europe. European churches of this period typically have high vaults supported by massive piers and columns. In the 10th century, the Romanesque style developed. Romanesque architects adopted many Roman or early Christian architectural ideas, such as cross-shaped ground-plans – like that of Angoulême Cathedral (opposite) – and the basilican system of a nave with a central vessel and side aisles. In the mid-12th century, flying buttresses and pointed vaults appeared. These features later became widely used in Gothic architecture (see pp. 470-471). Bagneux Church (opposite) has both styles: a Romanesque tower, and a Gothic nave and choir.

Finial

Incline

Circular staircase-turret

Loophole

Octahedral spire

Octahedral crossing tower

Round-arched window

Series of archivolts decorated with tori

Series of jambs decorated with colonettes

CHURCH-ROOF BOSS, BRITAIN

ROMANESQUE CAPITALS

"THE FLIGHT INTO EGYPT" CAPITAL, CATHEDRAL OF ST. LAZARE, AUTUN, FRANCE, 1120-1150

"CHRIST IN MAJESTY" CAPITAL, BASILICA OF ST. MADELEINE, VEZELAY, FRANCE, 1120-1140

Pitched roof

Tribune (elevated platform)

Semicircular transverse arch

Vaulting shaft

Attached half-column

Round arcade arch

Romanesque capital

Arcade

Square central shaft

Twin opening of gallery bays

Compound pier

Barrel vault

Lean-to roof

Transept

Quadrant arch

Colonette

Round stilted arch

Attached half-column

Side aisle

Main vessel

Side aisle

GROUND-PLAN OF ANGOULEME CATHEDRAL, FRANCE, FROM c.1105

Heavily moulded transverse arch

Crossing

Transept chapel

Chevet (choir with round apse and chapels)

Transept

Engaged column

Dome

Buttress

Transverse arch with plain fascia

Nave

Nave bay

Clustered column

Vestibule

CHOIR, CHURCH OF ST. SERGE, ANGERS, FRANCE, c.1215-1220

Historiated boss

Longitudinal ridge-rib

Loophole

Diagonal rib with torus moulding

Cell

Gable

Domed rib-vault

Transverse arch

Lierne

Historiated keystone

Formeret

Tas-de-charge

Round-arched window

Polyhedral abacus

Cubic abacus

Foliated capital

Attached colonette

Embrasure

Rectangular apse

Cornice

Vaulting shaft

Rectangular side-chapel

Impost with foliated frieze

Arcade column

Bay of main vessel

Octahedral socle

BAGNEUX CHURCH, FRANCE, 1170-1190

Moulded rib with an arris between two tori

Flying buttress

Roof space

Cell

Polyhedral abacus

Transverse arch

Oculus

Tower vault

Square-roofed pinnacle

Lean-to roof

Exterior wall

Triforium

Tower

Foliated capital

Pointed arch

Triple vaulting-shaft

Torus moulding

Quadripartite vault

Colonette

Formeret

Tower-vault oculus

Attached compound pier

Recessed panel

Corbel

Round arch

Pier buttress

Impost

Embrasure

Pier supporting tower

Weathering

Attached half-column

Side aisle

Base

Square socle

Intrados of arch with flat band between two tori

Nave column

Compound pier

Arcade

Nave

Choir

Octahedral socle

Bay

Attached colonette

Gothic 1

GOTHIC STAINED GLASS WITH FOLIATED SCROLL MOTIF, ON WOODEN FORM

GOTHIC BUILDINGS are characterized by rib vaults, pointed or lancet arches, flying buttresses, decorative tracery and gables, and stained-glass windows. Typical Gothic buildings include the Cathedrals of Salisbury and old St. Paul's in England, and Notre Dame de Paris in France (see pp. 472-473). The Gothic style developed out of Romanesque architecture in France (see pp. 468-469) in the mid-12th century, and then spread throughout Europe. The decorative elements of Gothic architecture became highly developed in buildings of the English Decorated style (late 13th-14th century) and the French Flamboyant style (15th-16th century). These styles are exemplified by the tower of Salisbury Cathedral and the staircase in the Church of St. Maclou (see pp. 472-473), respectively. In both of these styles, embellishments such as ballflowers and curvilinear (flowing) tracery were used liberally. The English Perpendicular style (late 14th-15th century), which followed the Decorated style, emphasized the vertical and horizontal elements of a building. A notable feature of this style is the hammer-beam roof.

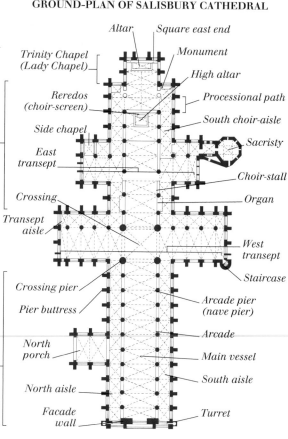

Altar
Square east end
Trinity Chapel (Lady Chapel)
Monument
High altar
Reredos (choir-screen)
Processional path
Side chapel
South choir-aisle
Choir
Sacristy
East transept
Choir-stall
Crossing
Organ
Transept aisle
West transept
Crossing pier
Staircase
Pier buttress
Arcade pier (nave pier)
Arcade
North porch
Main vessel
Nave
South aisle
North aisle
Facade wall
Turret

GOTHIC TORUS WITH BALLFLOWERS

Limestone block
Block members carved into rolls
Block members cut polygonally
Pencil guideline
Early stage of ballflower carving

BLOCK AFTER INITIAL CUTTING

BLOCK WITH MEMBERS CUT INTO ROLLS

Torus
Ballflower
Fillet
Mason's mark

FINISHED BLOCK

Trinity Chapel (Lady Chapel)
Choir
Octahedral pinnacle with small spire
Finial
Blind semi-arch
Staggered triple lancet windows
Turret-like pinnacle
Parapet decorated with blind arches filled with trefoils
Mullion
Stained glass
Base
Cornice
Lean-to roof
East transept facade
Buttress

NORTH SIDE, SALISBURY CATHEDRAL, BRITAIN, 1220-1280 (STEEPLE AND SPIRE ADDED DURING 14TH CENTURY)

WEST FACADE, SALISBURY CATHEDRAL

Weather-vane

Orb

Spire

Band with lozenge decoration

Semi-attached gable with small pilasters

Turret-like pinnacle

Ballflower decoration

Spire-like pinnacle

Traceried parapet with lozenge decoration

Blind gabled arch

Octahedral turret

Gable

Row of blind arches filled with trefoils

Octafoil

Battlemented cornice

Cinquefoil moulding

Blind lancet

Flying buttress

Nave

Angle buttress

West transept facade

Weathering

Pier buttress

Trefoil decoration

North porch

Archivolt

Twin lancet window under pointed arch, crowned by a quatrefoil

Trefoil in a spandrel

Blind rhombus tracery filled with a quatrefoil

Finial

Pitched roof

Staggered triple lancet window

Parapet

Small gable crowning buttress

Angle buttress

North porch

Blind semi-arch

Lateral porch

Main porch

Crocket

Niche under small gabled roof

Aureole

Gable

Staggered triple lancet window

Spire

Parapet

Row of blind trefoil arches

Blind pointed arches filled with twin lancets and quatrefoils

Projecting turret

Row of gabled niches under trefoil arches

Spire

Moulded side of gable

Spire-like pinnacle

Pitched roof

Flying buttress

Lateral turret

Small gable crowning buttress

Crocket

Buttress

471

Gothic 2

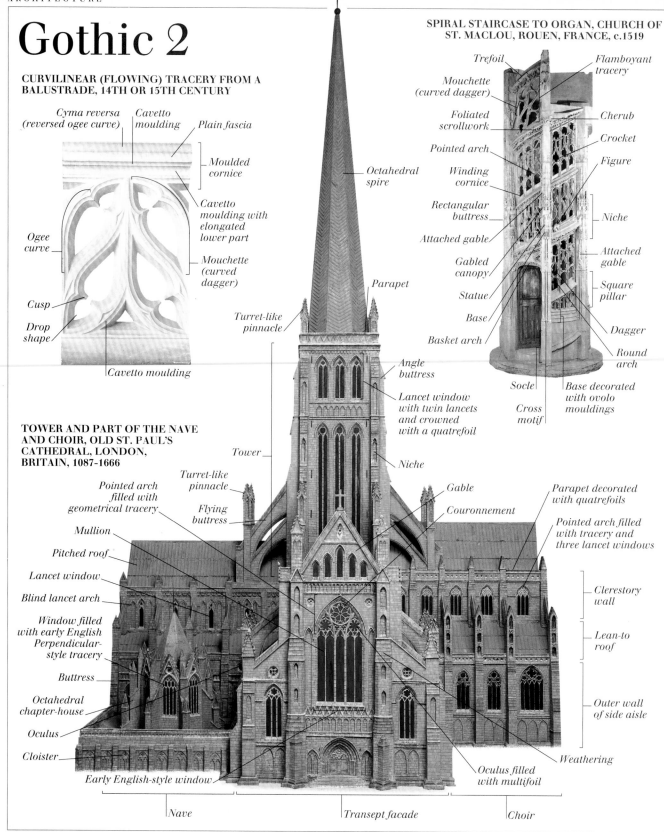

CURVILINEAR (FLOWING) TRACERY FROM A BALUSTRADE, 14TH OR 15TH CENTURY

Cyma reversa (reversed ogee curve)

Cavetto moulding

Plain fascia

Moulded cornice

Cavetto moulding with elongated lower part

Mouchette (curved dagger)

Ogee curve

Cusp

Drop shape

Cavetto moulding

SPIRAL STAIRCASE TO ORGAN, CHURCH OF ST. MACLOU, ROUEN, FRANCE, c.1519

Trefoil

Flamboyant tracery

Mouchette (curved dagger)

Cherub

Foliated scrollwork

Crocket

Pointed arch

Figure

Winding cornice

Rectangular buttress

Niche

Attached gable

Attached gable

Gabled canopy

Square pillar

Statue

Base

Dagger

Basket arch

Round arch

Socle

Base decorated with ovolo mouldings

Cross motif

Octahedral spire

Parapet

Turret-like pinnacle

Angle buttress

Lancet window with twin lancets and crowned with a quatrefoil

TOWER AND PART OF THE NAVE AND CHOIR, OLD ST. PAUL'S CATHEDRAL, LONDON, BRITAIN, 1087-1666

Tower

Niche

Pointed arch filled with geometrical tracery

Turret-like pinnacle

Flying buttress

Gable

Couronnement

Parapet decorated with quatrefoils

Mullion

Pitched roof

Lancet window

Blind lancet arch

Window filled with early English Perpendicular-style tracery

Buttress

Octahedral chapter-house

Oculus

Cloister

Early English-style window

Nave

Pointed arch filled with tracery and three lancet windows

Clerestory wall

Lean-to roof

Outer wall of side aisle

Weathering

Oculus filled with multifoil

Transept facade

Choir

Ridge

Common rafter

Architrave of window zone, also acting as collar-beam

Principal

Attached baluster

Attached column

Strut

Raised surface

Hammer-post

Bevelled edge

Arched brace

Wooden panel

Hammer-beam

Gothic window tracery

Collar-beam decorated with pearl motif

Gothic window

Arched brace

Brace

Bracket

Impost

TRUSS OF HAMMER-BEAM ROOF, THE UPPER FRATER (LATER BLACKFRIARS' PLAYHOUSE), LONDON, BRITAIN, PROBABLY 14TH CENTURY

SPIRE AND TRANSEPT ROOF, CATHEDRAL OF NOTRE DAME DE PARIS, FRANCE, c.1163–1250

Rafter

Straight brace

Beam

Gable

Round arch

Pinnacle

Oculus

Blind trefoil

Lancet arch

Trefoil arch

Cusp

Quatrefoil

Colonette

Pointed arch

Lesene

Lancet arch

Balustrade

Mullion

Triangular cornice

Cornice with chamfered edge

Geometrical tracery

Trefoil arch

Stud

Balustrade

Scissor brace

Upper collar

Principal rafter

Ridge-board

Octahedral spire

Common rafter

Roof truss of nave and transept

TYPICAL GOTHIC FEATURES

FLYING BUTTRESS OVER SIDE AISLES, MILAN CATHEDRAL, ITALY, C.1385–1485

GARGOYLE, HORSLEY CHURCH, DERBYSHIRE, BRITAIN, C.1450

Vertical strut

Intermediate collar

Raised valley-rafter

Beam

Jack-rafter

Clasped purlin

Lower collar

Scissor-beam

King-post

Queen-post

Tie-beam

Passing brace

HAMMER-BEAM ROOF, CHURCH OF ST. BOTOLPH, TRUNCH, NORFOLK, BRITAIN, 1360–1380

Renaissance 1

THE RENAISSANCE was a European movement – lasting roughly from the 14th century to the mid-17th century – in which the arts and sciences underwent great changes. In architecture, these changes were marked by a return to the classical forms and proportions of ancient Roman buildings. The Renaissance originated in Italy, and the buildings most characteristic of its style can be found there, such as the Palazzo Strozzi shown here. Mannerism is a branch of the Renaissance style that distorts the classical forms; an example is the Laurentian Library staircase. As the Renaissance style spread to other European countries, many of its features were incorporated into the local architecture; for example, the Château de Montal in France (see pp. 476-477) incorporates aedicules (tabernacles).

FACADE ON TO PIAZZA, PALAZZO STROZZI

Crowning cornice

Arched window

Round arch

Light

Rustication

Arched doorway

Rectangular window

SIDE VIEW OF PALAZZO STROZZI, FLORENCE, ITALY, 1489 (BY G. DA SANGALLO, B. DA MAIANO, AND CRONACA)

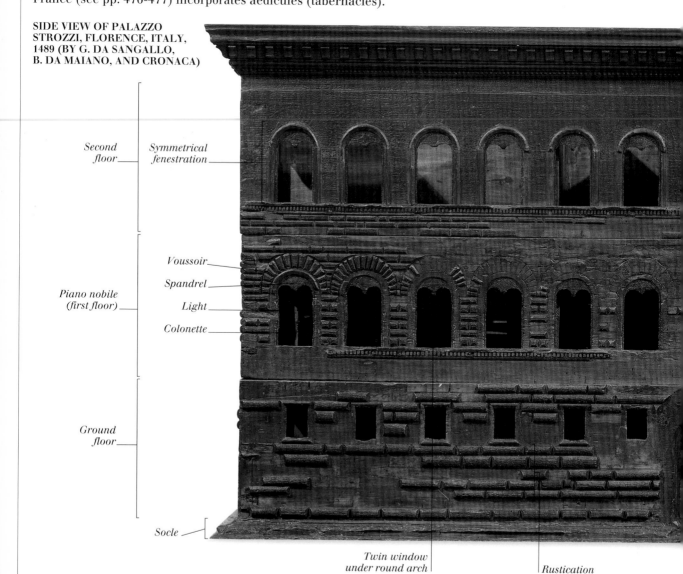

Second floor

Symmetrical fenestration

Piano nobile (first floor)

Voussoir

Spandrel

Light

Colonette

Ground floor

Socle

Twin window under round arch

Rustication

DETAILS FROM ITALIAN RENAISSANCE BUILDINGS

PANEL FROM DRUM OF DOME,
FLORENCE CATHEDRAL, 1420-1436

COFFERING IN DOME,
PAZZI CHAPEL,
FLORENCE, 1429-1461

STAIRCASE,
LAURENTIAN LIBRARY,
FLORENCE, 1559

PORTICO, VILLA ROTUNDA,
VICENZA, 1567-1569

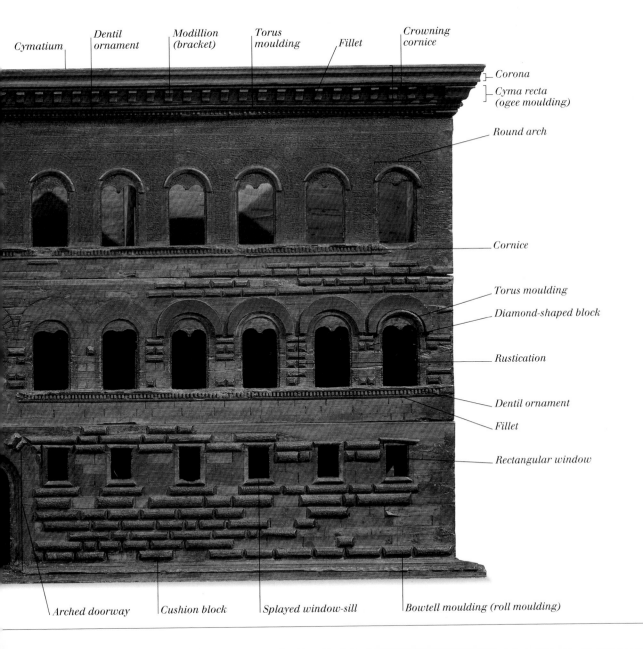

Cymatium

Dentil ornament

Modillion (bracket)

Torus moulding

Fillet

Crowning cornice

Corona

Cyma recta (ogee moulding)

Round arch

Cornice

Torus moulding

Diamond-shaped block

Rustication

Dentil ornament

Fillet

Rectangular window

Arched doorway

Cushion block

Splayed window-sill

Bowtell moulding (roll moulding)

Renaissance 2

DETAILS FROM EUROPEAN RENAISSANCE BUILDINGS

STONE WALL, QUOINS, AND SHELL DECORATION, CASA DE LAS CONCHAS, SALAMANCA, SPAIN, 1475-1483

SPIRAL-STAIRCASE TOWER, CHATEAU DE BLOIS, FRANCE, 1514-1530

CONICAL DOME, CHATEAU DE CHAMBORD, FRANCE, 1519-1547

PAIR OF CHIMNEY-STACKS, PALAIS DE FONTAINEBLEAU, FRANCE, FROM 1528

NORTH WING, CHATEAU DE MONTAL, LOT, FRANCE, FROM 1523

Chimney-stack

Ridge of half-round tiles

Pitched roof

Finial

Medallion

Pinnacle

Foliated volute with dolphin head

Gable

Head-shaped keystone

Dormer window

Frieze with shell-pattern decoration

Finial

Ionic capital with head-shaped decoration

Putto holding candelabrum

Blind pediment

Grotesque figure

Medallion with bust of Robert de Montal

Lesene decorated with paterae

Frieze decorated with sculptural wreaths, tendrils, and grotesque figures

Lesene

Pedestal

Dado

Hipped roof

Conical spire of turret

Fish-scale tile

Belvedere

Keystone decorated with scroll ornament

Cornice decorated with fascias and an ogee moulding

Rectangular window

Transom

Aedicule (tabernacle)

Double pilaster

Mullion

Shell

Concave, arched niche

Small pier decorated with statuette in concave niche

Cornice

Frieze with scroll motif

Pseudo-Corinthian capital

Plinth   Cornice   Architrave   Portal   Pilaster

NORTH-WING STAIRCASE, CHATEAU DE MONTAL

Hipped roof

Conical spire

Turret

Eaves with oversailing fascias and fillets

Loophole

Cornice with fascias and ogee mouldings

Rib vault

Column

Second-floor landing

First-floor landing

Conical corbel

Flight of stairs

Lesene

Handrail

Pier supporting flight of stairs

Pier supporting first-floor landing

Riser

Tread

CAMPANILE, CHURCH OF ST. EUSTACHE, PARIS, FRANCE, 1532-1640

Weather-vane

Orb

Fish-scale tile

Hemispherical dome

Semicircular torus moulding

Fillet

Weathering

Plain fascia

Ogee moulding

Small architrave

Archivolt

Volute

Plain fascia

Emphasized keystone

Cavetto moulding

Cincture

Capital

Zinc plating

Fillet

Square pillar

GLOBE THEATRE, LONDON, BRITAIN, 1599

Hipped roof

Turret

Timber-framed hut, housing windlass

Ornamental panelling

Pitched roof

Music gallery

Ornamental panelling with concave brace decoration

Balustrade

Balcony stage

Stage cover

Light curtain

Door to dressing-rooms

Thatched roof

Box (gentlemen's room)

Loft used as storage room

Window stage

Upper gallery (twopenny gallery)

Outer wall

Railing

Middle gallery

Post supporting bay window

Upper-gallery support

Stage-door

Lower gallery

Standing room

Bench

Round pillar (stage-post)

Square, carved base

Study (inner stage) with traverse (crossing)

Platform stage

Paling

Partition separating galleries from boxes

Low balustrade

Door to tiring-house

Baroque and neoclassical 1

THE BAROQUE STYLE EVOLVED IN THE EARLY 17TH CENTURY in Rome. It is characterized by curved outlines and ostentatious decoration, as can be seen in the Italian church details (right). The baroque style was particularly widely favoured in Italy, Spain, and Germany. It was also adopted in Britain and France, but with adaptations. The British architects Sir Christopher Wren and Nicholas Hawksmoor, for example, used baroque features – such as the concave walls of St. Paul's Cathedral and the curved buttresses of the Church of St. George in the East (see pp. 480-481) – but they did so with restraint. Similarly, the curved buttresses and volutes of the Parisian Church of St. Paul-St. Louis are relatively plain. In the second half of the 17th century, a distinct classical style (known as neoclassicism) developed in northern Europe as a reaction to the excesses of baroque. Typical of this new style were churches such as the Madeleine (a proposed facade is shown below), as well as secular buildings such as the Cirque Napoleon (opposite) and the buildings of the British architect Sir John Soane (see pp. 482-483). In early 18th-century France, an extremely lavish form of baroque developed, known as rococo. The balcony from Nantes (see pp. 482-483) with its twisted ironwork and head-shaped corbels is typical of this style.

DETAILS FROM ITALIAN
BAROQUE CHURCHES

SCROLLED BUTTRESS,
CHURCH OF ST. MARIA DELLA
SALUTE, VENICE, 1631-1682

STATUE OF THE ECSTASY OF
ST. THERESA, CHURCH OF ST. MARIA
DELLA VITTORIA, ROME, 1645-1652

Round-arched window
Twin pilaster
Coved dome
Triple keystone
Triangular pediment
Attic storey
Balustrade
Re-entrant entablature
Composite capital
Attached triangular pediment
Blind window
Composite column
Composite pilaster
Socle

Raking cornice
Frieze
Panel

Attached segmental pediment
Lantern
Parapet
Cornice
Finial

Dentil ornament
Urn
Modillion (bracket)
Cornice
Entablature
Raised panel
Festoon
Intermediate cornice
Volute
Fluted shaft
Base

Door jamb
Architrave
Blind door

PROPOSED FACADE, THE MADELEINE (NEOCLASSICAL), PARIS, FRANCE, 1764 (BY P. CONTANT D'IVRY)

CIRQUE NAPOLEON (NEOCLASSICAL), PARIS, FRANCE, 1852 (BY J.I. HITTORFF)

EXTERIOR

Rectangular panel
Small polyhedral roof
Attached colonette
Polyhedral iron roof
Projecting entablature
Palmette
Sculpted frieze
Cornice
Pedestal
Smooth, vertical rustication
Projecting pedestal
Statue of Amazon on horseback
Hanging wreath
Dado (die)
Plinth
Smooth rustication
Eagle carrying festoons

INTERIOR

King-post
Statue of Minerva
Tie-beam
Orb
Painted inner roof
Brace
Polyhedral lantern
Roll moulding
Strut
Straight brace
Projecting entablature
Crest
Projecting socle
Outer wall
Attached Corinthian column
Frieze painted with scenes from classical mythology
Circle (auditorium)

Finial with cavetto moulding
Foliated panel
Transverse arch
Window hood-mould
Crowning cornice
Fascia
Volute
Dentil
Barrel vault
Raised window jamb
Clerestory level
Rectangular door leading to roofed space
Groin vault
Semi-parabolic curve
Short pilaster
Curved buttress
Gallery level
Modillion (bracket)
Pier-shaped pinnacle
Architrave decorated with oversailing fascias
Semicircular arched window
Cornice
Corinthian capital
Gallery
Cornice
Foliated frieze
Small cupola
Depressed arch
Balustrade
Pendentive
Oeil-de-boeuf ("ox-eye") window
Keystone decorated with scroll ornament
Archivolt
Formeret (wall rib)
Cornice
Archivolt decorated with plain fascias
Window jamb
Arcade
Window-sill
Arcade level
Round arch
Round arch
Buttress
Outer wall
Re-entrant corner
Base
Socle
Doorway connecting chapels
Side chapels
Main vessel
Side chapels

NAVE, CHURCH OF ST. PAUL-ST. LOUIS (FRENCH BAROQUE), PARIS, FRANCE, FROM 1627 (BY E. MARTELLANGE)

Baroque and neoclassical 2

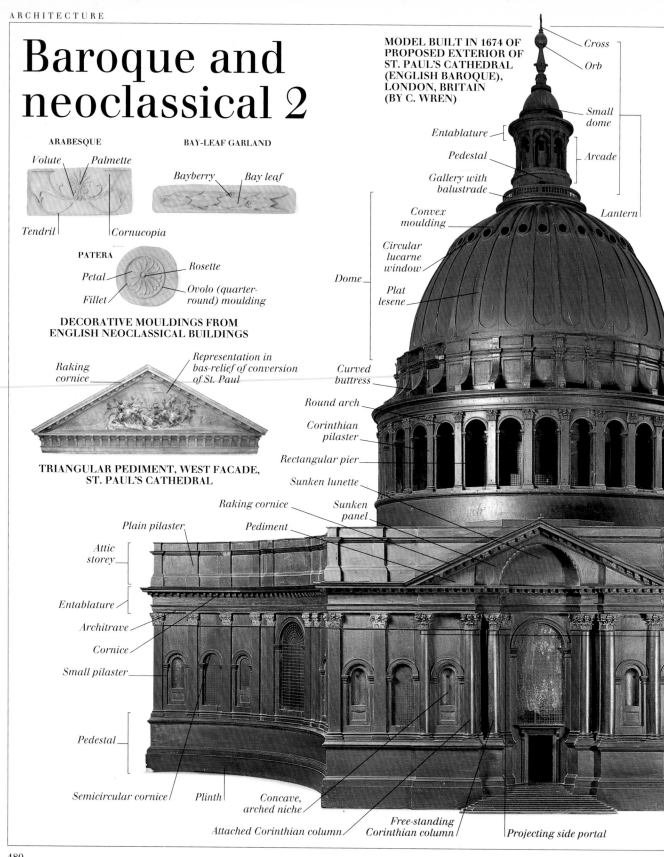

ARABESQUE

Volute
Palmette
Tendril
Cornucopia

BAY-LEAF GARLAND

Bayberry
Bay leaf

PATERA

Petal
Rosette
Fillet
Ovolo (quarter-round) moulding

DECORATIVE MOULDINGS FROM ENGLISH NEOCLASSICAL BUILDINGS

Raking cornice
Representation in bas-relief of conversion of St. Paul

TRIANGULAR PEDIMENT, WEST FACADE, ST. PAUL'S CATHEDRAL

Plain pilaster
Attic storey
Entablature
Architrave
Cornice
Small pilaster
Pedestal
Semicircular cornice
Plinth
Concave, arched niche
Attached Corinthian column
Free-standing Corinthian column
Projecting side portal

Raking cornice
Pediment
Sunken panel

MODEL BUILT IN 1674 OF PROPOSED EXTERIOR OF ST. PAUL'S CATHEDRAL (ENGLISH BAROQUE), LONDON, BRITAIN (BY C. WREN)

Cross
Orb
Small dome
Entablature
Pedestal
Gallery with balustrade
Arcade
Lantern
Convex moulding
Circular lucarne window
Dome
Plat lesene
Curved buttress
Round arch
Corinthian pilaster
Rectangular pier
Sunken lunette

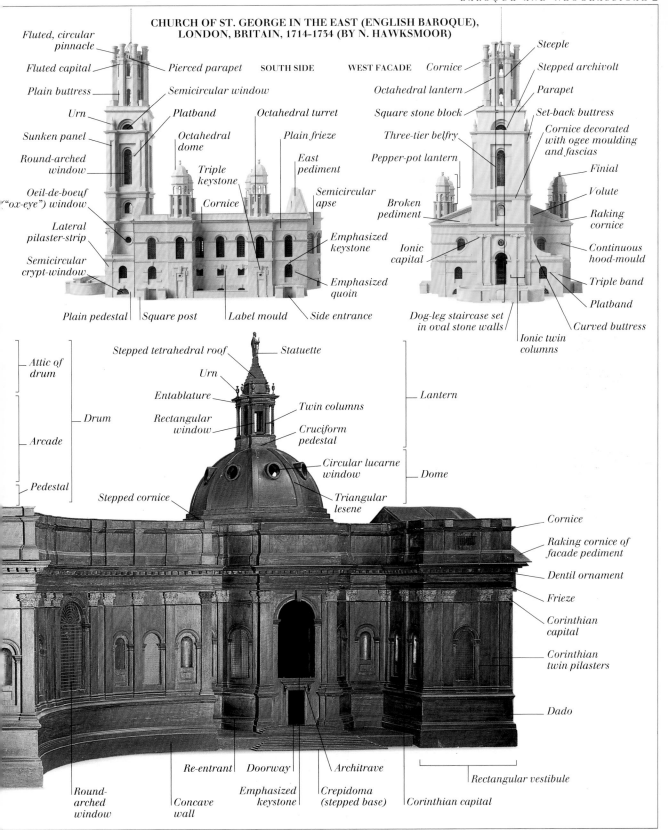

CHURCH OF ST. GEORGE IN THE EAST (ENGLISH BAROQUE), LONDON, BRITAIN, 1714-1734 (BY N. HAWKSMOOR)

SOUTH SIDE   WEST FACADE

Fluted, circular pinnacle

Fluted capital

Plain buttress

Urn

Sunken panel

Round-arched window

Oeil-de-boeuf ("ox-eye") window

Lateral pilaster-strip

Semicircular crypt-window

Pierced parapet

Semicircular window

Platband

Octahedral dome

Triple keystone

Cornice

Plain pedestal

Square post

Octahedral turret

Plain frieze

East pediment

Semicircular apse

Emphasized keystone

Emphasized quoin

Label mould

Side entrance

Cornice

Octahedral lantern

Square stone block

Three-tier belfry

Pepper-pot lantern

Broken pediment

Ionic capital

Steeple

Stepped archivolt

Parapet

Set-back buttress

Cornice decorated with ogee moulding and fascias

Finial

Volute

Raking cornice

Continuous hood-mould

Triple band

Platband

Curved buttress

Dog-leg staircase set in oval stone walls

Ionic twin columns

Attic of drum

Drum

Arcade

Pedestal

Stepped tetrahedral roof

Urn

Entablature

Rectangular window

Stepped cornice

Statuette

Twin columns

Cruciform pedestal

Circular lucarne window

Triangular lesene

Lantern

Dome

Cornice

Raking cornice of facade pediment

Dentil ornament

Frieze

Corinthian capital

Corinthian twin pilasters

Dado

Round-arched window

Concave wall

Re-entrant

Doorway

Emphasized keystone

Architrave

Crepidoma (stepped base)

Corinthian capital

Rectangular vestibule

481

Baroque and neoclassical 3

DETAILS FROM BAROQUE, NEOCLASSICAL, AND ROCOCO BUILDINGS

PORTICO, THE VYNE, HAMPSHIRE, BRITAIN, 1654 (NEOCLASSICAL)

GILT IRONWORK FROM SCREEN, PALAIS DE VERSAILLES, FRANCE, 1669-1674 (FRENCH BAROQUE)

WINDOW, PALAZZO STANGA, CREMONA, ITALY, EARLY 18TH CENTURY (ROCOCO)

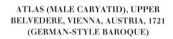

ATLAS (MALE CARYATID), UPPER BELVEDERE, VIENNA, AUSTRIA, 1721 (GERMAN-STYLE BAROQUE)

BALCONY, NANTES, FRANCE, 1730-1740 (ROCOCO)

MASONRY OF A NICHE IN THE ROTUNDA (NEOCLASSICAL), BANK OF ENGLAND, LONDON, BRITAIN, 1794 (BY J. SOANE)

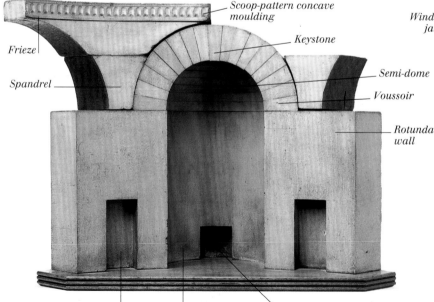

- Scoop-pattern concave moulding
- Keystone
- Semi-dome
- Voussoir
- Rotunda wall
- Frieze
- Spandrel
- Flat, rectangular niche
- Rounded niche
- Flat, square niche

CORNER OF THE NEW STATE PAPER OFFICE (NEOCLASSICAL), LONDON, BRITAIN, 1830-1831 (BY J. SOANE)

- Classical-style entablature
- Cornice
- Frieze
- Architrave
- Pantile (S-shaped roofing tile)
- Fascia
- Eaves
- Scroll-shaped corbel
- Curved corbel
- Smooth rustication
- Second-floor window
- Cornice
- Drip-cap
- Cornice
- Frieze
- Window architrave
- Window jamb
- First-floor window
- Window-sill in the form of a frieze
- Ground-floor window
- Splayed window-sill
- Vermiculated rustication

TYRINGHAM HOUSE (NEOCLASSICAL), BUCKINGHAMSHIRE, BRITAIN, 1793-1797 (BY J. SOANE)

ROOF LEVEL (ATTIC LEVEL)

Space for illumination above unroofed central hall

Chimney-stack

Space above unroofed main staircase

Oculus illuminating secondary staircase

Flat roof

Parapet rail

Baluster

Cornice

Attic storey of convex portico

Balustrade

Cornice

FIRST-FLOOR LEVEL (CHAMBER FLOOR)

Upper level of central hall, open to floor below

Main staircase

Secondary staircase

Abacus

Pilaster capital

Attached Tuscan twin pilasters

Window-sill

Triangular pilaster

First-floor storey of convex portico

Bow front

GROUND-FLOOR LEVEL (PRINCIPAL FLOOR)

Withdrawing-room

Central hall

Library and breakfast-room

Main staircase

Water-closet (toilet)

Secondary staircase

Eating-room

Segmented lintel course

Window-sill

Window architrave

Base

Plinth

Horizontal rustication

Vestibule (entrance hall)

Ground-floor storey of convex portico

Band incised with Greek-style fret ornament

Window jamb

Basement

FACADE OF TYRINGHAM HOUSE

Chimney-stack

Voussoir

Basement window

Entrance door

Circular entrance steps

Rail

Baluster

Parapet

Balustrade

Cornice

Entablature

Capital

Shaft

Ionic column

Base

PROSTYLE COLONNADE

Arches and vaults

ARCHES ARE CURVED STRUCTURES used to bridge spans and to support the weight of upper parts of buildings, such as domes, as in St. Paul's Cathedral (below) and the antique temple (opposite). The voussoirs (wedge-shaped blocks) that form an arch (right) support each other and convert the downward force of the weight of the building into an outward force. This outward force is in turn transferred to buttresses, piers, or abutments. A vault is an arched roof or ceiling. There are four main types of vault (opposite). A barrel vault is a single vault, semicircular in cross-section; a groin vault consists of two barrel vaults intersecting at right-angles; a rib vault is a groin vault reinforced by ribs; and a fan vault is a rib vault in which the ribs radiate from the springing point (where the arch begins) like a fan.

PARTS OF AN ARCH

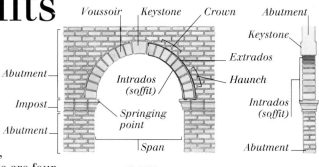

Voussoir Keystone Crown Abutment
Abutment
Keystone
Extrados
Intrados
(soffit) Haunch
Impost
Abutment Springing
point
Intrados
(soffit)
Span Abutment

FRONT **SIDE**

ARCHES AND BASE OF DOME, ST. PAUL'S CATHEDRAL, LONDON, BRITAIN, 1675-1710 (BY C. WREN)

Inner dome
Colonnade
Pilaster Passageway
Base Cornice
Pendentive Opening to passageway Pedestal of outer dome
"Whispering Gallery"
Upper arch (concealing difference in heights between main arch and minor arches) Triangular buttress
Moulded bracket
Round arch
Extrados Semi-dome
Intrados (soffit) Upper barrel-vaulted passage opening on to side aisle
Springing point
Impost Barrel vault
Abutment
Passage leading to side aisle Strut built into masonry to strengthen pier (added in the 20th century)
Minor arch leading to side aisle Main arch leading to nave Pier Minor arch

TYPES OF ARCH

HORSESHOE ARCH (MOORISH ARCH), GREAT MOSQUE, CORDOBA, SPAIN, 785

BASKET ARCH (SEMI-ELLIPTICAL ARCH), PALATINE CHAPEL, AIX-LA-CHAPELLE, FRANCE, 790-798

TUDOR ARCH, TOWER OF LONDON, BRITAIN, C.1086-1097

LANCET ARCH, WESTMINSTER ABBEY, LONDON, BRITAIN, 1503-1519

TREFOIL ARCH, BEVERLEY MINSTER, YORKSHIRE, BRITAIN, C.1300

TYPES OF VAULT

Transverse rib
Temporary brace
Temporary structure used to centre vault
Horizontal abutment

BARREL VAULT (TUNNEL VAULT; WAGON VAULT)

Barrel vault
Transverse arch
Voussoir
Right-angled intersection
Groin

GROIN VAULT

Transverse ridge-rib
Longitudinal ridge-rib
Diagonal rib

RIB VAULT

Tierceron (secondary rib)
Ridge-rib
Springing point
Concave-sided lozenge
Panel

FAN VAULT

COMPOSITE MODEL OF ANTIQUE FRENCH TEMPLE

Coved dome
Lesene
Pedestal of lantern
Archivolt decorated with plain fascias
Abutment
Dentil

Series of plain fascias
Re-entrant angle
Cavetto moulding
Fillet
Cornice
Plain frieze
Architrave
Ionic capital
Chamfered corner
Keystone decorated with scroll
Plain Ionic column
Shaft
Scotia
Plinth
Dado

Round arch
Cornice
Horizontal band
Twisted vertical band
Naos (cella)

Lantern
Coved dome
Pedestal of dome
Entablature
Fluted Ionic column
Pedestal of column

Base
Intercolumniation
Ionic column with twisted vertical bands (wreaths) and horizontal bands

ENGLISH BOND BRICKWORK OF GROIN VAULT AND RIB VAULT

Right-angled intersection
Groin
Header
Stretcher
Cell of barrel vault
Springing point

EXTRADOS OF GROIN VAULT

Stretcher
Header
Cell
Extrados of diagonal rib
Springing point

EXTRADOS OF RIB VAULT

INTERIOR DECORATION OF COFFERED VAULT

Compass
Coffer (square sunken panel)
Square
Hammer
Chamfered edge
Arris moulding
Mason's tools

Domes

A DOME IS A CONVEX ROOF. Domes are categorized according to the shapes of both the base and the section through the centre of the dome. The base may be circular, square, or polygonal (many-sided), depending on the plan of the drum (the walls on which the dome rests). The section of a dome may be the same shape as any arch (see pp. 484-485). Various types of dome are illustrated here: a hemispherical dome, which has a circular base and a semicircular section; a saucer dome, which has a circular base and a segmental (less than a semicircle) section; a polyhedral dome, which is a dome on a polygonal base whose sides meet at the top of the dome; and an onion dome, which has a circular or polygonal base and an ogee-shaped section. Many domes have a lantern (a turret with windows) to provide light inside.

LANTERN AND UPPER DOME TIMBERING, ST. PAUL'S CATHEDRAL

DOME TIMBERING, CHURCH OF THE SORBONNE, PARIS, FRANCE, 1635-1642 (BY J. LEMERCIER)

- Ogee-curved dome
- Window zone
- Pedestal
- Floorboard
- Ashlar piece
- Pin
- Short strut
- Mortise-and-tenon joint
- Principal rafter
- Vertical post
- Straight brace
- Tie-beam
- Circular baseplate
- Common rafter
- Straight brace
- Deeply projecting pier buttress
- Cornice
- Depressed hood-mould
- Circular lucarne window
- Floor-joist
- Hood-mould
- Waisted-oval lucarne window
- Ogee-curved window-frame
- Shaft connecting lantern and church interior

ROOF WITH LANTERN AND ONION DOME

- Weathercock
- Ellipsoid orb
- Keeled lesene
- Onion dome
- Fish-scale tile
- Octahedral base
- Sloping roof
- Round arch
- Attached pillar
- Vertical band
- Oversailing fascia
- Octahedral base of lantern
- Oversailing fascia
- Tetrahedral capital
- Return
- Window
- Torus
- Fillet
- Lantern
- Tetrahedral roof

REPRESENTATION OF DOME METALLING, CHURCH OF THE SORBONNE

- Cross
- Orb
- Square rib
- Inverted ovolo (quarter-round)
- Astragal
- Volute
- Fillet
- Roll moulding
- Plain fascia
- Buttress
- Lantern
- Round-arched window
- Volute
- Ovolo (quarter-round)
- Cornice
- Fillet
- Projecting pier buttress
- Dome on a circular base
- Fish-scale tile
- Inverted demi-heart torus moulding
- Hood-mould
- Waisted-oval lucarne window
- Small volute
- Gutter
- Parapet
- Semicircular torus moulding
- Small roll
- Fillet
- Plain fascia
- Triple lesene

TYPES OF DOME

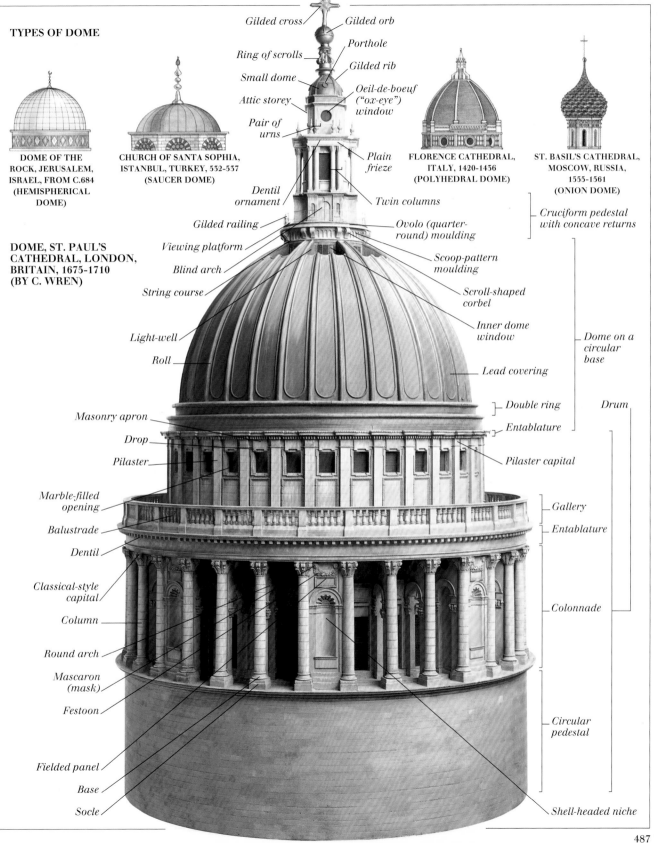

DOME OF THE ROCK, JERUSALEM, ISRAEL, FROM C.684 (HEMISPHERICAL DOME)

CHURCH OF SANTA SOPHIA, ISTANBUL, TURKEY, 532-537 (SAUCER DOME)

FLORENCE CATHEDRAL, ITALY, 1420-1436 (POLYHEDRAL DOME)

ST. BASIL'S CATHEDRAL, MOSCOW, RUSSIA, 1555-1561 (ONION DOME)

DOME, ST. PAUL'S CATHEDRAL, LONDON, BRITAIN, 1675-1710 (BY C. WREN)

Gilded cross · Gilded orb · Porthole · Gilded rib · Small dome · Oeil-de-boeuf ("ox-eye") window · Ring of scrolls · Attic storey · Pair of urns · Plain frieze · Dentil ornament · Gilded railing · Viewing platform · Blind arch · String course · Light-well · Roll · Twin columns · Ovolo (quarter-round) moulding · Scoop-pattern moulding · Scroll-shaped corbel · Inner dome window · Lead covering · Cruciform pedestal with concave returns · Dome on a circular base · Masonry apron · Drop · Pilaster · Marble-filled opening · Balustrade · Dentil · Classical-style capital · Column · Round arch · Mascaron (mask) · Festoon · Fielded panel · Base · Socle · Double ring · Entablature · Pilaster capital · Drum · Gallery · Entablature · Colonnade · Circular pedestal · Shell-headed niche

487

Islamic buildings

OPUS SECTILE MOSAIC DESIGN

THE ISLAMIC RELIGION was founded by the prophet Mohammed, who was born in Mecca (in present-day Saudi Arabia) about 570 AD. In the following three centuries, Islam spread from Arabia to North Africa and Spain, as well as to India and much of the rest of Asia. The worldwide influence of Islam remains strong today. Common characteristics of Islamic buildings include ogee arches and roofs, onion domes, and walls decorated with carved stone, paintings, inlays, or mosaics. The most important type of Islamic building is the mosque – the place of worship – which generally has a minaret (tower) from which the muezzin (official crier) calls Muslims to prayer. Most mosques have a mihrab (decorative niche) that indicates the direction of Mecca. As figurative art is not allowed in Islam, buildings are ornamented with geometric and arabesque motifs, and inscriptions (frequently Koranic verses).

Bud-like onion dome

Depressed arch surrounding mihrab

Painted roof pavilion

Lotus-flower pendentive

Turkish-crescent finial

Arabic inscription

Crest

Painted minaret with censer (incense burner)

Spandrel

Series of recessed arches

Semi-dome

Arched niche within a niche

Mural resembling tomb

Polyhedral niche

Recessed colonettes

MIHRAB, JAMI MASJID (PRINCIPAL OR CONGREGATIONAL MOSQUE), BIJAPUR, INDIA, c.1636

Tablet flower

Shield

Herring-bone pattern

Spandrel with floral design

Ogee arch

Carved stone

Undulating band

Cusp

Volute

Impost

Capital with stylized floral design

Panel with fret pattern

Jali (latticed screen) with geometrical patterns

Band with Arabic inscriptions praising Allah (God)

Attached colonette

ARCH, THE ALHAMBRA, GRANADA, SPAIN, 1333-1354

Enamelled turquoise earthenware tile

Trigon

Cube with chamfered corners

Polygonal capital

Niche

Enamelled white earthenware tile

Column shaft

Arabesques of stylized plants

Enamelled lapis blue earthenware tile

MIHRAB WITH COLUMN, EL-AINYI MOSQUE, CAIRO, EGYPT, 15TH CENTURY

EXAMPLES OF ISLAMIC MOSAICS, EGYPT AND SYRIA

Star-shaped motif

Triangle of yellow marble

Rhombus of black marble

Stone band

Greek cross of red marble

STAR AND GREEK-CROSS MOSAIC

Stone

Black marble

Turquoise glass

Mosaic tessellation

Tessera (small mosaic piece)

FRET-PATTERN MOSAIC

Greek cross of black and yellow marble

Star-shaped motif

Stone band

Rhombus of red marble

STAR AND GREEK-CROSS MOSAIC

Parallelogram of black marble

Triangle of yellow marble

Rhombus of red marble

Symmetrical quadrilateral of stone

Star-shaped motif

MOSAIC OF HEXAGONS, TRIANGLES, AND SYMMETRICAL QUADRILATERALS

Hexagonal design

Band of black marble

Band of stone

HEXAGON AND BAND MOSAIC

Triangle of turquoise glass

Parallelogram of mother-of-pearl

DANCETTE-PATTERN MOSAIC

Symmetrical quadrilateral of black marble

Triangle of stone

Hexagon of red marble

MOSAIC OF HEXAGONS, TRIANGLES, AND SYMMETRICAL QUADRILATERALS

MARBLE TOMB OF ITIMAD-UD-DAULA, AGRA, INDIA, c.1622-1628

Kalasa finial (finial with orbs)

Padmakosa (lotus petal)

Circular top of minaret

Parapet decorated with lattice-work

Ogee-curved roof

Chajya (deep eaves)

Balcony

Roof pavilion

Domed roof

Cusped arch

Pietra dura inlay (slices of semi-precious stone laid in sockets)

Cornice

Bracket

Spandrel decorated with arabesque

Octahedral base of minaret

Star-pattern inlay

Sandstone plinth

Sandstone parapet decorated with lattice-work

Jali (latticed screen) with geometrical patterns

Depressed entrance arch

Sandstone stairway

Opus sectile mosaic (geometric mosaic) of stone, tile, glass, and enamel

South and east Asia

THE TRADITIONAL ARCHITECTURE of south and east Asia has been profoundly influenced by the spread from India of Buddhism and Hinduism. This influence is shown both by the abundance and by the architectural styles of temples and shrines in the region. Many early Hindu temples consist of rooms carved from solid rock-faces. However, free-standing structures began to be built in southern India from about the eighth century AD. Many were built in the Dravidian style, like the Temple of Virupaksha (opposite) with its characteristic antarala (terraced tower), perforated windows, and numerous arches, pilasters, and carvings. The earliest Buddhist religious monuments were Indian stupas, which consisted of a single hemispherical dome surmounted by a chattravali (shaft) and surrounded by railings with ornate gates. Later Indian stupas and those built elsewhere were sometimes modified; for example, in Sri Lanka, the dome became bell-shaped, and was called a dagoba. Buddhist pagodas, such as the Burmese example (right), are multistoreyed temples, each storey having a projecting roof. The form of these buildings probably derived from the yasti (pointed spire) of the stupa. Another feature of many traditional Asian buildings is their imaginative roof-forms, such as gambrel (mansard) roofs, and roofs with angle-rafters (below).

DETAILS FROM EAST ASIAN BUILDINGS

KASUGA-STYLE ROOF WITH SUMIGI (ANGLE-RAFTERS), KASUGADO SHRINE OF ENJOJI, NARA, JAPAN, 12TH-14TH CENTURY

TERRACES, TEMPLE OF HEAVEN, BEIJING, CHINA, 15TH CENTURY

GAMBREL (MANSARD) ROOF WITH UPSWEPT EAVES AND UNDULATING GABLES, HIMEJI CASTLE, HIMEJI, JAPAN, 1608-1609

CORNER CAPITAL WITH ROOF BEAMS, POPCHU-SA TEMPLE, POPCHU-SA, SOUTH KOREA, 17TH CENTURY

Gilded band

Gilded iron hti (crown)

Dubika (mast)

Arrow motif

Torus moulding with spiral carving

Decorative eaves board

Ogee-arched motif with decorative carvings

Ogee-arched motif forming horn

Hip-rafter

Pentroof

Undulating moulding

Engaged pillar

Baluster finial

Arched entrance

Balustrade

Rectangular window

Pillar

Baluster

Straight brace

PERFORATED STONE WINDOWS, TEMPLES OF VIRUPAKSHA AND MALLIKARJUNA, PATTADAKAL, INDIA, 8TH CENTURY

Tablet flower

Fret motif

Chain motif

Floral pattern

Sickle motif

Semicircle

Leaf

Scroll motif

DAGOBA STUPA, KANDY, SRI LANKA, c.2ND CENTURY BC–7TH CENTURY AD

Chattra (umbrella)

Hanging ornament

Chattravali (shaft)

Ring with indentations symbolizing chattras

Ornamental metalwork

Yasti (tee; pointed spire)

Harmika (stylized square railing)

Auda (bell-shaped dome)

Trimala (series of three circular courses)

Circular base

SIDE VIEW AND PLAN VIEW, TEMPLE OF VIRUPAKSHA, PATTADAKAL, INDIA, c.746

Stupica (small stupa) of the Dravidian order

Dravidian finial

Blind chataya arch

Antarala (terraced tower)

Perforated window

Gopuram finial (wagon-like finial)

Bracketed capital

Small gopuram (gate-head)

Parapet

Roll cornice

Niche with statue

Gate

Panel with bas-relief carving

Plan view

Pillar

Twin pilasters

Pradakshina (circumambulatory passage around shrine)

Shrine

Shrine chamber

Niche

Gate

Mandapa (pillared hall)

491

The 19th century

BUILDINGS OF THE 19TH CENTURY are characterized by the use of new materials and by a great diversity of architectural styles. From the end of the 18th century, iron and steel became widely used as alternatives to wood for the framework of buildings, as in the flax-spinning mill shown here. Built in Britain in 1796, this mill exemplifies an architectural style that became common throughout the industrialized world for more than a century. The Industrial Revolution also brought mass-production of building parts – a development that enabled the British architect Sir Joseph Paxton to erect London's Crystal Palace (a building made entirely of iron and glass) in only nine months, ready for the Great Exhibition of 1851. The 19th century saw a widespread revival of older architectural styles. For example, in the USA and Germany, Neo-Greek architecture was fashionable; in Britain and France, Neo-Baroque, Neo-Byzantine, and Neo-Gothic styles (as seen in the Palace of Westminster and Tower Bridge) were dominant.

SECTION THROUGH A FLAX-SPINNING MILL

Cast-iron wall-plate
Pitched roof
Ridge
Machinery space
Verge
Gutter
Cast-iron mortise-and-tenon joint
Anchor-joint
Inverted T-section cast-iron beam
Drain-pipe
Segmentally arched brick vault
End flange
Concrete floor
Tapering part of column
Paved ground floor
Strengthened central column

FLAX-SPINNING MILL, SHREWSBURY, BRITAIN, 1796 (BY C. BAGE)

Multi-gabled roof (ridge and furrow roof)
Ridge
Furrow
Verge
Timber rafter
Cast-iron wall-plate
Gutter
Gable
Drain-pipe
Tapering part of column
Three courses of stretchers
Segmentally-arched brick vault
Course of headers
Cast-iron mortise-and-tenon joint
Course of decorative headers
Tie-rod
Cast-iron cruciform column
Cast-iron lattice window
Inverted T-section cast-iron beam
Cast-iron tenon
Anchor-joint
Strengthened central column
Bonded brick wall
Stone foundation
Quoin
Jamb
Gauged arch (segmental arch of tapered bricks)

CLOCK TOWER ("BIG BEN"), PALACE OF WESTMINSTER, LONDON, BRITAIN, 1836-1868 (BY C. BARRY AND A.W.N. PUGIN)

Finial

Spire

Skylight

Cornice decorated with shields

Iron railing

Small orb

Orb

Iron tracery

Dormer window

Round arch filled with open tracery

Tetrahedral spire

Bell chamber

Balustrade

Ogee tracery arch filled with trefoil

Flying buttress

Pinnacle

Spandrel

Octahedral shaft with billet decoration

Dial

Cornice

Moulded corbel

Star-shaped corner buttress

Panelled field filled with tracery

Slender diagonal buttress

Narrow window

String course

Carved panel

Stepped storeys

DETAILS FROM BUILDINGS IN REVIVALIST STYLES

CUPOLA, MERCHANTS' EXCHANGE, PHILADELPHIA, USA, 1832-1834 (NEO-GREEK)

SCULPTURE AND PEDIMENT, OPERA HOUSE, PARIS, FRANCE, 1861-1874 (NEO-BAROQUE)

DOMED TURRET, WESTMINSTER CATHEDRAL, LONDON, BRITAIN, 1894-1903 (NEO-BYZANTINE)

Tetrahedral spire

Finial

Spire

Cornice

Archway

Dormer head (gable) filled with blind tracery

Finial

Parapet

Parapet of balcony

Octahedral upper turret

Wedge-shaped corbel

String course

Stone panel

Pier

High-level footbridge

Lattice-work

Cast-iron tracery

Heraldic shield

Cast-iron panelling

Moulded corbel

Drawbridge (bascule)

Steel brace

Circular turret/buttress

Archway

TOWER BRIDGE, LONDON, BRITAIN, 1886-1894 (BY H. JONES)

CRYSTAL PALACE EXHIBITION HALL, LONDON, BRITAIN, 1851 (BY J. PAXTON)

Longitudinal girder

Window

Ridge and furrow glass roof-windows

Crest

Cast-iron ornamental arch-plate

Arched facade

Semicircular barrel vault

Cast-iron trapezium

Octahedral column

Side exit

Sheet-iron louvre

Strengthened support

Entrance

The early 20th century

ARCHITECTURE OF THE EARLY 20TH CENTURY is notable for radical new types of steel-and-glass buildings – particularly skyscrapers – and the widespread use of steel-reinforced concrete. The steel-framed skyscraper was pioneered in Chicago in the 1880s, but did not become widespread until the first decades of the 20th century. As construction techniques were refined, skyscrapers became higher and higher; for example, the Empire State Building (right) of 1929-1931 has 102 storeys. Many buildings of this period were constructed from lightweight concrete slabs, which could be supported by cantilever beams or by pilotis (stilts), as in the Villa Savoye (below). The early 20th century also produced a great variety of architectural styles, some of which are illustrated opposite. Despite their diversity, the styles of this period generally had one thing in common: they were completely new, with few links to past architectural styles. This originality is in marked contrast to 19th-century architecture (see pp. 492-493), much of which was revivalist.

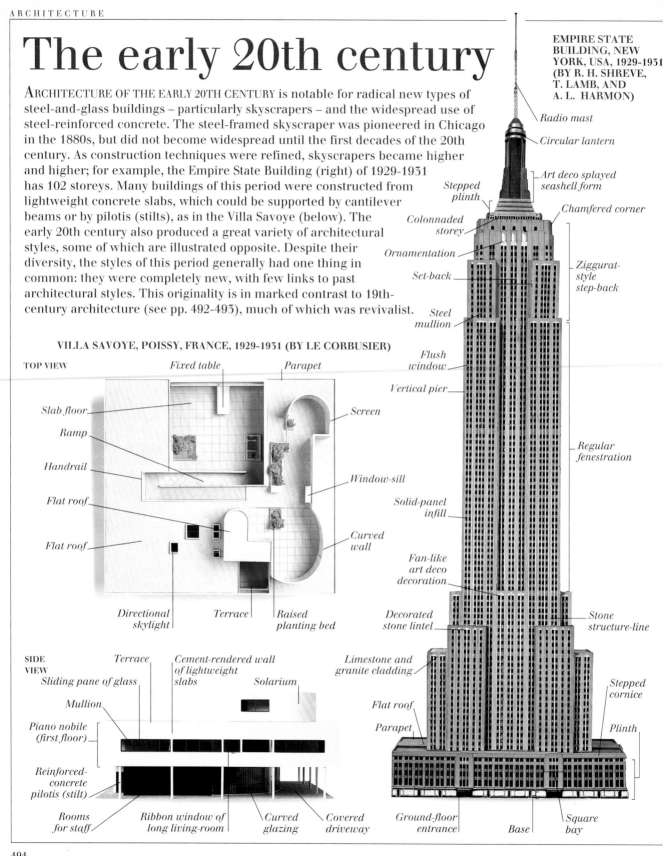

EMPIRE STATE BUILDING, NEW YORK, USA, 1929-1931 (BY R. H. SHREVE, T. LAMB, AND A. L. HARMON)

- Radio mast
- Circular lantern
- Art deco splayed seashell form
- Stepped plinth
- Chamfered corner
- Colonnaded storey
- Ornamentation
- Ziggurat-style step-back
- Set-back
- Steel mullion
- Flush window
- Vertical pier
- Regular fenestration
- Solid-panel infill
- Fan-like art deco decoration
- Decorated stone lintel
- Stone structure-line
- Limestone and granite cladding
- Stepped cornice
- Flat roof
- Plinth
- Parapet
- Ground-floor entrance
- Base
- Square bay

VILLA SAVOYE, POISSY, FRANCE, 1929-1931 (BY LE CORBUSIER)

TOP VIEW
- Fixed table
- Parapet
- Slab floor
- Ramp
- Handrail
- Screen
- Flat roof
- Window-sill
- Flat roof
- Curved wall
- Directional skylight
- Terrace
- Raised planting bed

SIDE VIEW
- Terrace
- Cement-rendered wall of lightweight slabs
- Solarium
- Sliding pane of glass
- Mullion
- Piano nobile (first floor)
- Reinforced-concrete pilotis (stilt)
- Rooms for staff
- Ribbon window of long living-room
- Curved glazing
- Covered driveway

MIDWAY GARDENS, CHICAGO, USA, 1914 (BY F. L. WRIGHT)

Flagpole

Plain coping-stone

Main floor

Decorated cement frieze

Terrace

Steps

Stage

Orchestra shell

Tiled, shallow pitched roof

Ridge

Projecting balustrade

Hip

Ornamental light

Main pavilion

Arcade

Terrace

Octagonal window

Ornamental sculpture

Flat roof

Stone plinth

EAST SIDE

Tiled frieze

NORTH SIDE

Cantilevered, latticed shade

Deep-set window

Planting bed

Brick pier

Slit window

Stepped flat-roofs

Terrace

Ornamented coping-stone

EARLY 20TH-CENTURY ARCHITECTURAL STYLES

DORMER WINDOW, STUDIO ELVIRA, MUNICH, GERMANY, 1902 (ART NOUVEAU)

AEG TURBINE HALL, BERLIN, GERMANY, 1909 (DEUTSCHER WERKBUND)

ROBIE HOUSE, CHICAGO, USA, 1909-1910 (PRAIRIE STYLE)

GRUNDTVIG CHURCH, COPENHAGEN, DENMARK, 1920 (EXPRESSIONIST)

VERTEX, CHRYSLER BUILDING, NEW YORK, USA, 1928-1930 (ART DECO)

TOWER, TOWN HALL, HILVERSUM, NETHERLANDS, 1930 (DUTCH CUBIST)

CASA DEL FASCIO, COMO, ITALY, 1932-1936 (GRUPPO SEVEN CUBIST)

MOTIF ABOVE DOORWAY, HOOVER FACTORY, LONDON, BRITAIN, 1933 (ART DECO)

Modern buildings 1

**KAWANA HOUSE, JAPAN,
FROM 1987 (BY N. FOSTER)**

ARCHITECTURE SINCE ABOUT THE 1950s is generally known as modern architecture. One of its main influences has been functionalism – a belief that a building's function should be apparent in its design. Both the Centre Georges Pompidou (below and opposite) and the Hong Kong and Shanghai Bank (see pp. 498-499) are functionalist buildings: on each, elements of engineering and the building's services are clearly visible on the outside. In the 1980s, some architects rejected functionalism in favour of post-modernism, in which historical styles – particularly neoclassicism – were revived, using modern building materials and techniques. In many modern buildings, walls are made of glass or concrete hung from a frame, as in the Kawana House (right); this type of wall construction is known as curtain walling. Other modern construction techniques include the intricate interlocking of concrete vaults – as in the Sydney Opera House (see pp. 498-499) – and the use of high-tension beams to create complex roof shapes, such as the paraboloid roof of the Church of St. Pierre de Libreville (see pp. 498-499).

Solar panel
Concrete frame
Pile foundation
Raft
Composite cladding-panel

SIDE VIEW

Rocker-beam
Curtain walling
Lattice-beam
Floor-beam connection
Floor

FRONT VIEW

**SERVICES FACADE, CENTRE GEORGES POMPIDOU,
PARIS, FRANCE, 1977 (BY R. PIANO AND R. ROGERS)**

Metal-faced, fire-resistant panel
Air-conditioning duct
Cooling tower
Water-pipe

Grand gallery level
Main gallery levels
Library level
Administrative level
Mezzanine gallery level
Reception level

Staircase to grand hall
Electrical plant
Water-cooled, fire-resistant column
Continuous glazing
Tinted glass
Services entrance

PRINCIPAL FACADE, CENTRE GEORGES POMPIDOU

Gallery space

External walkway

Electronically operated roller-blind

Cooling tower

Continuous glazing

Steel lattice-beam

Terrace

Main truss

Cradle support for escalator

Gerberette (cast-steel rocker-beam)

Cross-bracing

Double fire-escape staircase

Suspended fire-resistant glass curtain

Reinforced-concrete and steel floor-plate

Double floor-height

Main entrance

Glazed escalator tube

Node

Water-cooled, fire-resistant steel column

Exposed "plug-in" services

Steel lattice-beam

Dual air-conditioning unit for roof

Elevator

Elevator-motor room

Vertical-duct distribution zone

Metal sandwich-panel (insulating panel)

Gerberette (cast-steel rocker-beam)

Rose connection

Outer tension-column

External steel-lattice mullion

Water-cooled, fire-resistant cross-beam

Double fire-escape staircase

Water storage tank

Cross-bracing

Open gallery floor

Water-pipe

Steel-framed services column

Double cross-bracing

Modern buildings 2

HONG KONG AND SHANGHAI BANK, HONG KONG, 1981-1985 (BY N. FOSTER)

SOUTH FACADE

Inverted top-truss
Mast
Illuminated fascia
External maintenance crane
Soffit
Curved glazing
Cockpit
Counterweight
Boom
Circular access platform
Steel column
Face panel
Hanger
Handrail
Top beam
Outer diagonal beam
Outer bottom boom
Inner diagonal beam
Inner bottom boom
Pin joint
Refuge terrace
Hanger
Two-storey stability truss (coathanger truss)
Flange
Lightweight, column-free, steel and concrete floor
Glazed soffit
Plaza

Sun-shade louvre
Mullion
Composite cladding-panel
Escalator
Fire-escape staircase
External staircase
Double floor-height
Full-height glazing
Sun scoop
Glazed curtain wall
Vertical, glazed typhoon screen
Entrance lobby

EAST SIDE

Soffit
Helicopter landing-pad
Navigation light
Stepped elevation
Face panel
Horizontal window
Vertical window
External maintenance crane
Cross-bracing
Service shaft
Double floor-height
Sun scoop
10-floor-high atrium
Internal bridge

**CHURCH OF ST. PIERRE,
LIBREVILLE, GABON, 1990**

Lattice-truss

Cross-bracing

Mullion

Plate connector

Paraboloid roof

Concave curve

Convex curve

Tension member

Rafter

Bolt

Full-height glazing

Eaves

Rendered, splayed outer wall

Entrance

Tinted glass

Circular steps

Reinforced plinth

Concrete shoe

Inner diagonal beam

Beam housing

Pin joint

Glulam wall-plate (glued and laminated wall-plate)

Secondary hall

Main hall

**OPERA HOUSE, SYDNEY, AUSTRALIA,
1959-1973 (BY J. UTZON)**

Vaults with curved ribs

Precast concrete rib

Glass wall

Mullion

Main hall

Bronze glazing bar

Precast concrete rib-segment

Ridge

Continuous glazing

Solid podium

Ribbon window

HARBOUR FACADE

Vault roof constructed of chevron-shaped, precast tiles

Vault over restaurant

Staircase

Solid podium

Pink cladding

Pink granite-aggregate paving slab

Main line of support

Awning

Staircase

Terrace

WEST SIDE

MUSIC

MUSICAL NOTATION 502

ORCHESTRAS 504

BRASS INSTRUMENTS 506

WOODWIND INSTRUMENTS 508

STRINGED INSTRUMENTS 510

GUITARS 512

KEYBOARD INSTRUMENTS 514

PERCUSSION INSTRUMENTS 516

DRUMS 518

ELECTRONIC INSTRUMENTS 520

Musical notation

MUSICAL NOTATION IS ANY METHOD by which sounds are written down so that they can be read and performed by others. The present-day conventional system of notation uses a five-line stave (staff) – divided by vertical lines into sections known as bars – on which notes, rests, clefs, key signatures, time signatures, accidentals, and other symbols are written. A note indicates the duration of a sound and, according to its position on the stave, its pitch. Notes can be arranged on the stave in order of pitch to form a scale. A silence in the music is indicated by a rest. The clef, which is placed at the begininng of a stave, fixes the pitch. The key signature, which is placed after the clef, indicates the key. The time signature, placed after the key signature, shows the number of beats in a bar. Accidentals are used to indicate the raising or lowering of the pitch of a note.

ELEMENTS OF MUSICAL NOTATION

CLEFS
Treble (or G) clef
Alto (or C) clef
Bass (or F) clef

TIME SIGNATURES
Six-eight time
Three-four time
Stave (staff)

NOTES
Breve
Minim
Quaver
Semibreve
Crotchet
Semiquaver

RESTS
Breve rest
Minim rest
Quaver rest
Semibreve rest
Crotchet rest
Semiquaver rest

SCALE
C D E F G A B C

ACCIDENTALS
Sharp
Natural
Double sharp
Flat
Double flat
Key signature

Moderately fast and quiet
Tie (bind)
Repeat the previous bar
Treble clef
Bass clef
Four-four time (common time)
Key signature
Alto clef
Treble voice
Alto voice
Tenor voice
Bass voice
Organ part for right hand
Organ part for left hand
Organ pedal line
Instruments of the orchestra written in Italian
Bar line
Bass clef
Bar
Crotchet

Accidental sharp

Tie (bind)

Accidental natural

Unison (both clarinets play the same note)

Semibreve

Crotchet

FLUTES

OBOES

CLARINETS IN A

BASSOONS

HORNS IN D

TRUMPETS IN D

TIMPANI IN D AND A

FIRST AND SECOND VIOLINS

VIOLAS

VOICES

CELLOS

ORGAN

DOUBLE BASSES

Semibreve rest

Accidental sharp

Piano (play softly)

Slur

Pianissimo (play very softly)

Crotchet rest

Orchestras

AN ORCHESTRA IS A GROUP of musicians that plays music written for a specific combination of instruments. The number and type of instruments included in the orchestra depends on the style of music being played. The modern orchestra (also known as a symphony orchestra) is made up of four sections of instruments – stringed, woodwind, brass, and percussion. The stringed section consists of violins, violas, cellos (violoncellos), double basses, and sometimes a harp (see pp. 510-511). The main instruments of the woodwind section are flutes, oboes, clarinets, and bassoons – the piccolo, cor anglais, bass clarinet, saxophone, and double bassoon (contrabassoon) can also be included if the music requires them (see pp. 508-509). The brass section usually consists of horns, trumpets, trombones, and the tuba (see pp. 506-507). The main instruments of the percussion section are the timpani (see pp. 518-519). The side drum, bass drum, cymbals, tambourine, triangle, tubular bells, xylophone, vibraphone, tam-tam (gong), castanets, and maracas can also be included in the percussion section (see pp. 516-517). The musicians are usually arranged in a semi-circle – strings spread along the front, woodwind and brass in the centre, and percussion at the back. A conductor stands in front of the musicians and controls the tempo (speed) of the music and the overall balance of the sound, ensuring that no instruments are too loud or too soft in relation to the others.

TUBULAR BELLS

TAM-TAM (GONG)

VIBRAPHONE

XYLOPHONE

CASTANETS

TAMBOURINE

MARACAS

TRIANGLE

TRUMPETS

HORNS

CLARINETS

BASS CLARINET

HARP

SAXOPHONE

PICCOLO

SECOND VIOLINS

FIRST VIOLINS

CYMBALS SIDE DRUM BASS DRUM

TIMPANI

EXAMPLE OF A LAYOUT OF THE INSTRUMENTS FOR A MODERN (SYMPHONY) ORCHESTRA

TROMBONES

TUBA

BASSOONS

DOUBLE BASSOON

DOUBLE BASSES

FLUTES

OBOES

COR ANGLAIS

VIOLAS

Score

CONDUCTOR'S STAND

CELLOS

505

Brass instruments

BUGLE

BRASS INSTRUMENTS ARE WIND INSTRUMENTS that are made of metal, usually brass. Although they appear in many different shapes and sizes, all brass instruments have a mouthpiece, a length of hollow tube, and a flared bell. The mouthpiece of a brass instrument may be cup-shaped, as in the cornet, or cone-shaped, as in the horn. The tube may be wide or narrow, mainly conical, as in the horn and tuba, or mainly cylindrical, as in the trumpet and trombone. The sound of a brass instrument is made by the player's lips vibrating against the mouthpiece, so that the air vibrates in the tube. By changing lip tension, the player can vary the vibrations and produce notes of different pitches. The range of notes produced by a brass instrument can be extended by means of a valve system. Most brass instruments, such as the trumpet, have piston valves that divert the air in the instrument along an extra piece of tubing (known as a valve slide) when pressed down. The total length of the tube is increased and the pitch of the note produced is lowered. Instead of valves, the trombone has a movable slide that can be pushed away from or drawn toward the player. The sound of a brass instrument can also be changed by inserting a mute into the bell of the instrument.

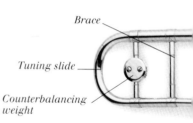

Brace

Tuning slide

Counterbalancing weight

SIMPLIFIED DIAGRAM SHOWING HOW A PISTON VALVE SYSTEM WORKS

Piston valves at rest

Air bypasses piston valves

PISTON VALVES AT REST

First piston valve pressed down

Second and third piston valves at rest

Air diverted through first valve slide

PISTON VALVE PRESSED DOWN

TRUMPET

Finger button

First piston valve

Spring returns piston valve to rest position

Second piston valve

Third piston valve

Holes divert air into valve slides

Cup-shaped mouthpiece

Mouthpiece receiver

Little finger support

Music stand holder

Narrow, cylindrical tube

Flared bell

Tuning slide

First valve slide

First valve slide thumb hook

Second valve slide

Third valve slide finger ring

Third valve slide

Third valve slide water key

Tuning slide water key

SECTIONS OF A TROMBONE

Flared bell

EXAMPLES OF MUTES

CUP MUTE

TENOR MUTE

ALTO MUTE

Inner tube

Outer tube of slide

Cup-shaped mouthpiece

Mouthpiece brace held by the left hand

Slide brace held by the right hand

Narrow, cylindrical tube

Water key

TROMBONE

Flared bell

Outer tube of slide

Cup-shaped mouthpiece

FLUGELHORN

Piston valves

Little finger support

Flared bell

Cup-shaped mouthpiece

Valve slide

Conical tube

HORN

Cone-shaped mouthpiece

Finger key

Rotary valves

Narrow, conical bore

Large, flared bell

CORNET

Piston valves

Little finger support

Flared bell

Cup-shaped mouthpiece

Bore widens after valves

Valve slide

TUBA

Large, flared bell

Piston valves

Cup-shaped mouthpiece

Valve slide

Wide, conical tube

507

Woodwind instruments

Woodwind instruments are wind instruments that are generally made of wood, although some are made of metal or plastic. The sound of a woodwind instrument is produced by the vibration of air in a hollow tube. The air is made to vibrate by blowing across a blow hole – as in the flute and piccolo – or by blowing through a single reed – as in the clarinet and saxophone – or a double reed – as in the bassoon, cor anglais, and oboe. The pitch of a woodwind instrument can be changed by opening or closing holes cut into the tube of the instrument.

Bell

Double reed

Bell joint

Curved crook

Conical, wooden tube

Tenor joint

Conical, wooden tube

Upper joint

Bass joint

Key

Double reed

Crook

Cylindrical, metal tube

Key

Body joint

Blow hole

Head joint

Lip plate

PICCOLO

Right-hand rest

Key

Double reed

Cork

Upper joint

Key

Finger hole

Foot joint

Key

Mouthpiece with single reed

Ligature

Barrel joint

Butt

Key

Middle joint

Key

Middle joint

Cylindrical, metal tube

Body joint

Cylindrical, wooden tube

Key

Upper joint

BASSOON

Finger hole

Conical, wooden tube

Lip plate

Head joint

Bell joint

Bulb-shaped bell

Blow hole

COR ANGLAIS

Flared bell

Bell joint

OBOE

FLUTE

Bell joint

Middle joint

Flared bell

CLARINET

TENOR SAXOPHONE

Mouthpiece with single reed

Conical, metal tube

Upturned, flared bell

SECTIONS OF A TENOR SAXOPHONE

Mouthpiece with single reed

Ligature

Neck

Upper octave key

Key rod

KEYS FOR THE LEFT THUMB

Lower octave key

Key

Key

KEYS FOR THE LEFT HAND

Key rod

Key

Key rod

KEYS FOR THE LEFT PALM

Mother-of-pearl touchpiece (button)

KEYS FOR THE RIGHT HAND

Key

Key rod

MAIN BODY OF SAXOPHONE

Conical, metal tube

KEYS FOR THE RIGHT PALM

Tonehole

Upturned, flared bell

Mother-of-pearl touchpiece (button)

Tonehole

Pad made up of layers of felt and cork

Roller

Key guard

Cup

Key rod

Key

Metal centre of pad reflects sound

Key guard

KEYS FOR THE RIGHT LITTLE FINGER

Padded key

KEYS FOR THE LEFT LITTLE FINGER

Key guard

509

Stringed instruments

STRINGED INSTRUMENTS PRODUCE SOUND by the vibration of stretched strings. This may be done by drawing a bow across the strings, as in the violin; or by plucking the strings, as in the harp and guitar (see pp. 512-513). The four modern members of the bowed string family are the violin, viola, cello (violoncello), and double bass. Each consists of a hollow, wooden body, a long neck, and four strings. The bow is a wooden stick with horsehair stretched across its length. The vibrations made by drawing the bow across the strings are transmitted to the hollow body, and this itself vibrates, amplifying and enriching the sound produced. The harp consists of a set of strings of different lengths stretched across a wooden frame. The strings are plucked by the player's thumbs and fingers – except the little finger of each hand – which produces vibrations that are amplified by the harp's soundboard. The pitch of the note produced by any stringed instrument depends on the length, weight, and tension of the string. A shorter, lighter, or tighter string gives a higher note.

Scroll eye

Scroll

Peg-hole

Ebony tuning-pegs

Neck made of maple wood

Fingerboard

Rounded shoulder

Strings

Belly (soundboard)

Waist

Sound-hole

Rib

Purfling

Bridge

Tailpiece

Chin rest

Tailpiece loop fits around end-pin

SECTIONS OF A VIOLIN

End-pin (tail-pin)

Head

Point

Stick

Scroll

Scroll eye

Peg-box

Tuning-peg

Horsehair

Nut

String

Fingerboard

Rounded shoulder

Purfling

Belly (soundboard)

Waist

Sound-hole

Bridge

Tuning adjustor

Frog

Tailpiece

Screw

Chin rest

VIOLIN BOW

VIOLIN

Crown

Tuning-peg

Neck (string arm)

Shoulder

String

Soundboard

Pillar

Pedestal

Foot

Pedal

HARP

Scroll

Scroll eye

Peg-box

Tuning-peg

Nut

Fingerboard

String

Rounded shoulder

Belly (soundboard)

Sound-hole

Bridge

Tuning adjustor

Tailpiece

Spike

CELLO (VIOLONCELLO)

Head

Point

Inward-curving stick

Horsehair

Frog

Screw

DOUBLE BASS BOW

Scroll

Scroll eye

Tuning-pegs at back of peg-box

Nut

Fingerboard

String

Sloping shoulder

Belly (soundboard)

Purfling

Waist

Sound-hole

Sound-hole

Bridge

Rib

Tailpiece

Spike

DOUBLE BASS

Scroll

Scroll eye

Tuning-peg

Peg-box

Nut

Fingerboard

String

Belly (soundboard)

Rounded shoulder

Purfling

Waist

Bridge

Waist

Sound-hole

Chin rest

Tuning adjustor

Tailpiece

VIOLA

Guitars

THE GUITAR IS A PLUCKED stringed instrument (see pp. 510-511). There are two types of guitar – acoustic and electric. Acoustic guitars have hollow bodies and six or twelve strings. Plucking the strings produces vibrations that are amplified by their hollow bodies. Electric guitars usually have solid bodies and six strings. Pick-ups placed under the strings convert their vibrations into electronic signals that are magnified by an amplifier, and sent to a loudspeaker where they are converted into sounds (see pp. 520-521). Electric bass guitars are very similar in structure to electric guitars, and produce sound in the same way, but have four strings and play bass notes.

String

Fret

Machine head

Hollow body

Neck

Headstock

Sound-hole

B string

G string

D string

A string

Low E string

Maker's label

Bridge

Lining glued along top and bottom edge of rib

Rib

End block

Strap peg

Joint

Transverse (crosswise) strut strengthens back

Back made of two pieces of cherry wood joined together

Bridge pin

Saddle

Bridge

Binding

COMPONENTS OF AN ACOUSTIC GUITAR

Top E string

Nut

Truss rod cover

Screws

Machine heads

Headstock

Machine head

Truss rod slot

Fingerboard

Truss rod

Fretwire slot

Position dots

Fretwire

Sound-hole

Bracing

Soundboard made of two pieces of spruce joined together

EXAMPLES OF ACOUSTIC GUITARS

Rose

Sound-hole

Hollow body

String

Machine head

Bridge

Neck

Headstock

Scratchplate

WASHBURN TWELVE-STRING

Hollow, metal body

Sound-hole

Tailpiece

String

Machine head

Neck

Headstock

Resonator

DOBRO RESONATOR

EXAMPLES OF ELECTRIC GUITARS

Pick-up

Scratchplate

Solid body

String

Machine head

Bridge

Neck

Headstock

Output socket

Vibrato arm

FENDER STRATOCASTER

Pick-up

Toggle switch

Solid body

String

Machine head

Bridge

Neck

Headstock

Scratchplate

GIBSON LES PAUL

Pick-up

Solid body

String

Machine head

Bridge

Neck

Headstock

Output socket

Scratchplate

FENDER JAZZ BASS

Keyboard instruments

KEYBOARD INSTRUMENTS are instruments that are sounded by means of a keyboard. The organ and piano are two of the principal members of the keyboard family. The organ consists of pipes which are operated by one or more manuals (keyboards) and a pedal board. The pipes are lined up in rows (known as ranks or registers) on top of a wind chest. The sound of the organ is made when air is admitted into a pipe by pressing a key or pedal. The piano consists of wire strings stretched over a metal frame, and a keyboard and pedals that operate hammers and dampers. The piano frame is either vertical – as in the upright piano – or horizontal – as in the grand piano. When a key is at rest, a damper lies against the string to stop it vibrating. When a key is pressed down, the damper moves away from the string as the hammer strikes it, causing the string to vibrate and sound a note.

ORGAN PIPE

UPRIGHT PIANO

Muffler felt | Pressure bar | Tuning pin | Pin block
Hammer
Hammer rail
88–note keyboard
Wood case
Keybed
Soundboard
Metal frame
String
Hitch pin
Treble bridge
Bass bridge
Una corda (soft) pedal
Sostenuto pedal
Damper (sustaining) pedal

UPRIGHT PIANO ACTION

KEY AT REST

String
Hammer
Damper lies against string, and stops it vibrating
Hammer rest
Back check
Damper lever
Action lever
Jack
Capstan screw
Key released

ORGAN CONSOLE

Pipe
Pedal stop
Music stand
Swell stop
Choir stop
Swell manual (keyboard)
Great stop
Great manual (keyboard)
Thumb piston
Choir manual (keyboard)
Toe piston
Pedal board | Foot pedal
Swell pedal

KEY PRESSED DOWN

String
Hammer strikes string
Damper moves away from string, allowing it to vibrate
Hammer rest
Back check
Damper lever
Action lever
Jack
Capstan screw
Key pressed down

CONCERT GRAND PIANO (VIEWED FROM ABOVE)

Soundboard

Bass bridge

Hitch pin

Metal frame

Single bass note string

Long bridge

CONCERT GRAND PIANO (FRONT VIEW)

Lid

String

Wooden case

Keyboard

Una corda (soft) pedal

Sostenuto pedal

Damper (sustaining) pedal

Tenor note strings (two strings for each note)

Treble note strings (three strings for each note)

Wooden case

Hammer

Tuning pin

Wrest plank

Keyboard lid

88-note keyboard

STEINWAY & SONS
NEW YORK HAMBURG

STEINWAY

Percussion instruments

PERCUSSION INSTRUMENTS are a large group
of instruments that produce sound by being
struck, shaken, scraped, or clashed together.
Most percussion instruments – such as the
tam-tam (gong), cymbals, and maracas – do
not have a definite pitch and are used for
rhythm and impact, and the distinctive

TEMPLE BLOCKS

timbre (colour) of their sound. Other percussion instruments –
such as the xylophone, vibraphone, and tubular bells – are tuned
to a definite pitch and can play melody, harmony, and rhythms.
The xylophone and vibraphone each have two rows of bars that
are arranged in a similar way to the black and white keys of a
piano. Metal tubes are suspended below the bars to amplify the
sound. The vibraphone has electrically operated fans that rotate
in the tubes and produce a vibrato (wavering pitch) effect.

EXAMPLES OF BEATERS

SOFT-HEADED BEATER   *Felt-covered head*

HARD-HEADED BEATER   *Rosewood head*

MALLET   *Leather-covered head*

*Row of bars graduated
in length and pitch*   **XYLOPHONE**

*Wooden bar
struck with hard-
headed beater*

*Hollow,
metal tube*

Metal stand

TUBULAR BELLS

*Tube struck
with mallet*

*Hollow,
metal tube*

*Damper
bar*

*Metal
frame*

*Mechanism
linking pedal
and damper
bar*

*Row of tubes
graduated in
length and pitch*

Damper pedal

TAM-TAM (GONG)

*Tam-tam struck in
centre with soft-
headed beater*   *Cord*

*Metal
frame*

Rim

*Large,
metal disc*

CYMBALS

Leather strap fits around player's hand

Pad protects hands from vibrations

Thin, convex disc of copper and tin alloy

Zildjian

SECTIONS OF A MARACA

Wooden handle

Lead shot

Hollow, wooden head

TRIANGLE

Steel rod bent into triangular shape

Steel beater

CLAVES

Hardwood sticks clashed together to give a sharp crack

CASTANETS

Cord

Hollowed wood

VIBRAPHONE

Row of bars graduated in length and pitch

Metal bar struck with soft-headed beater

MUSSER

Metal frame

Damper pedal

Metal tube containing electrically operated fan that produces vibrato (wavering pitch) effect

Electric cable

Drums

A DRUM IS A percussion instrument that consists of a drumhead, made of skin or plastic, stretched over one or both ends of a hollow vessel (the body-shell). Drums are played in most parts of the world and are made in a number of different shapes and sizes. They can be divided into three groups according to the shape of the body-shell: frame drums (e.g., tambourines), bowl-shaped drums (e.g., timpani), and tubular drums (e.g., congas). Drums are usually sounded by striking the drumhead with the hands or with beaters, such as a hard-headed stick. The drumhead vibrates, and its vibrations are amplified by the hollow body-shell. The snare drum has wires – known as snares – stretched across the lower drumhead; the snares vibrate against the lower drumhead when the drum is played. Most drums, such as congas, do not have a definite pitch and can play only rhythms (see pp. 516-517). Other drums, such as timpani, have a definite pitch and can play melody, harmony, and rhythms. They can be tuned by adjusting the tension of the drumhead. Different types of drum can be combined together with other percussion instruments to form a drum kit. The basic components of the drum kit are bass drum, tom-toms, floor tom (tenor drum), snare drum, and cymbals.

TAMBOURINE

Crash cymbal

Tension key

DRUM KIT

Tension rod

Tom-tom

Lug

Hi-hat cymbal

Snare drum

Tripod stand

Chain

Tension screw

Felt-covered beater

Pedal

Pedal

SNARE DRUM (VIEWED FROM BELOW)

Snare mounting

Adjustable damper

Lug

Transparent lower drumhead

Upper drumhead

Snare

Stick

Snare release lever

EXAMPLES OF BEATERS

Acorn

HARD-HEADED STICK

Taper

SOFT-HEADED STICK

Felt-covered head

WIRE BRUSH

Wire bristles

Ride cymbal

Tension key

Tom-tom

Tension rod

Lug

Height adjustment key

Floor tom (tenor drum)

Tension rod

Lug

Wooden body-shell

Height adjustment key

Leg

Bass drum

Rubber foot

CONGAS

Metal hoop

Drumhead

Tension rod

Wooden body-shell

Tripod stand

Leg

TIMPANUM (KETTLE DRUM)

Drumhead

Tension rod

Metal hoop

Tuning gauge

Copper body-shell

Strut

Tension rod

Crown

Tuning pedal

Castor

Electronic instruments

ELECTRONIC DRUMS

ELECTRONIC INSTRUMENTS generate electronic signals
that are magnified by an amplifier, and sent to a loudspeaker
where they are converted into sounds. Synthesizers, and other
electronic instruments, simulate the characteristic sounds of
conventional instruments, and also create entirely new sounds.
Most electronic instruments are keyboard instruments, but electronic
wind and percussion instruments are also popular. A digital sampler
records and stores sounds from musical instruments or other sources.
When the sound is played back, the pitch of the original sound can be
altered. A keyboard can be connected to the sampler so that a tune can
be played using the sampled sounds. With a MIDI (Musical Instrument
Digital Interface) system, a computer can be linked with other electronic
instruments, such as keyboards and electronic drums, to make sounds
together or in sequence. It is also possible, using music software, to
compose and play music on a home computer.

Drum pad

*Height
adjustment key*

Tripod

HOME KEYBOARD

*Power
button* *Volume
control* *Function
display* *Memory record
button* *Tone editor
control*

*Demonstration
tune button*

*Pitch
modulator* *Multi-accompaniment
system control* *Tone and rhythm
pattern selector* *Key*

SYNTHESIZER

*Memory
card slot* *Joystick* *Function
display* *Edit control* *Data entry
key pad*

*Sound structure
guide*

*Volume
control*

*Pitch
modulator* *Sound selection control* *Key*

WIND SYNTHESIZER

Keys for left hand

Mouthpiece

WIND CONTROLLER

Keys for right hand

DIGITAL SAMPLER

Contrast control

Function display

Power button

Data increment control

POWER PACK

MIDI (Musical Instrument Digital Interface) cable

Connecting cable

SOUND MODULE

Record trigger

Floppy-disc drive

Play button

Data entry key pad

Microphone input

Store button

Input connector socket

Data entry key pad

Volume control

COMPUTER WITH MIDI AND AUDIO SOFTWARE SEQUENCER

Start and stop controls

Audio clock settings

Surround sound special effect plug-in

Edit control

Play button

Function display

Effect balance control

COMPUTER DISPLAY

Software effect plug-in

APPLE MACINTOSH G4 COMPUTER

Recorded information

CD-drive

Virtual mixing board

SPEAKER

KEYBOARD

MOUSE

SPEAKER

SPORTS

SOCCER · · · · · · · · · · · · · · · · · 524

AMERICAN FOOTBALL · · · · · · · · · · 526

AUSTRALIAN RULES AND GAELIC FOOTBALL · 528

RUGBY · · · · · · · · · · · · · · · · · · 530

BASKETBALL · · · · · · · · · · · · · · · 532

VOLLEYBALL, NETBALL, AND HANDBALL · · 534

BASEBALL · · · · · · · · · · · · · · · · · 536

CRICKET · · · · · · · · · · · · · · · · · · 538

HOCKEY, LACROSSE, AND HURLING · · · · 540

ATHLETICS · · · · · · · · · · · · · · · · · 542

RACKET SPORTS · · · · · · · · · · · · · · 544

GOLF · 546

ARCHERY AND SHOOTING · · · · · · · · · 548

ICE HOCKEY · · · · · · · · · · · · · · · · 550

ALPINE SKIING · · · · · · · · · · · · · · · 552

EQUESTRIAN SPORTS · · · · · · · · · · · 554

JUDO AND FENCING · · · · · · · · · · · · 556

SWIMMING AND DIVING · · · · · · · · · · 558

CANOEING, ROWING, AND SAILING · · · · 560

ANGLING · · · · · · · · · · · · · · · · · · 562

Soccer

GAMES INVOLVING KICKING A BALL have a long history and were recorded in China as early as 300 BC; in medieval Europe, street football was banned as a menace to the public; only in 1863 were the rules established, specifically banning carrying the ball for all players except the goalkeeper, and separating rugby from soccer. Soccer, officially termed association football, is a team sport in which players attempt to score goals by passing and dribbling the ball down the field past opposing defenders, and kicking or heading the ball into the goal net, outwitting the defending goalkeeper. Each team consists of ten outfield players (defenders, midfielders, and strikers) and a goalkeeper. Players from the opposing team may challenge the player in possession of the ball, but an illegal or foul tackle results in a penalty if a foul occurs inside the penalty area or a free kick if outside the penalty area. The round ball used in soccer is more easily controlled than the oval balls used in American, Canadian, and Australian rules football and in rugby. The result is a more "open" or flowing game which is played and watched by millions of people worldwide.

ASSISTANT REFEREE'S FLAG

Lightweight, brightly coloured fabric

Handle with rubber grip

REFEREE'S EQUIPMENT

Red card

Yellow card

Referee's whistle

Stop-watch

SOCCER PITCH

46–91 m (150–300 ft)

Corner flag

Goal-line

Corner arc

Penalty area

Penalty mark

Referee

Halfway-line flag

Striker

Striker

Left midfielder

Central midfielder

Left back

Touch-line

Central defender

Goal

Goalkeeper

Penalty arc

Assistant referee

Centre circle

Centre spot

Halfway line

Striker

Right midfielder

Right back

Central defender

Goal area

PITCH MARKINGS

Halfway line

1.5 m (5 ft)

HALFWAY-LINE FLAG

Corner arc

CORNER FLAG

7.3 m (24 ft)

Goal-line

GOAL

GOALKEEPER

Goalkeeper's shirt

Glove

Shin guard

Shorts

Sock

Soccer boot

SOCCER STRIP

Open-neck collar

Lightweight, man-made fabric team shirt

Team logo

Manufacturer's logo

Ribbed welt

Sponsor's logo

MAKING A SOCCER BALL

Hole punched in panel for stitching

Ball size number

Manufacturer's name

Edge cut to fit perfectly

Mitre

F.I.F.A. APPROVED

MULTIPLEX

Waxed thread

22–23 cm (8 1/2–9 in)

Needle

Bladder valve

Bladder made from latex rubber

Panels sewn together with ball inside out

Laminated panel

Long cotton sock

Club crest

Team shorts

Synthetic bootlace

Interchangeable nylon stud

SOCCER BOOT

American football

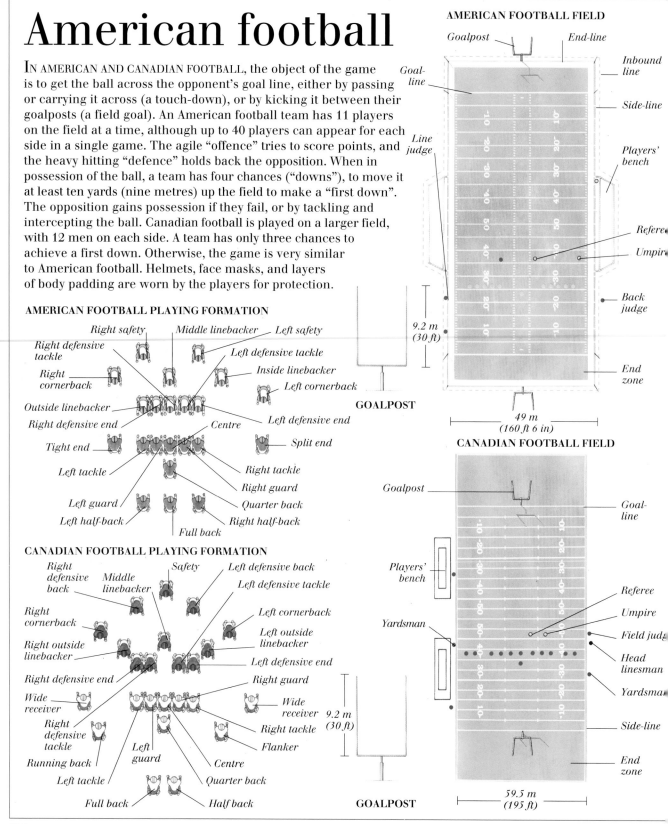

IN AMERICAN AND CANADIAN FOOTBALL, the object of the game is to get the ball across the opponent's goal line, either by passing or carrying it across (a touch-down), or by kicking it between their goalposts (a field goal). An American football team has 11 players on the field at a time, although up to 40 players can appear for each side in a single game. The agile "offence" tries to score points, and the heavy hitting "defence" holds back the opposition. When in possession of the ball, a team has four chances ("downs"), to move it at least ten yards (nine metres) up the field to make a "first down". The opposition gains possession if they fail, or by tackling and intercepting the ball. Canadian football is played on a larger field, with 12 men on each side. A team has only three chances to achieve a first down. Otherwise, the game is very similar to American football. Helmets, face masks, and layers of body padding are worn by the players for protection.

AMERICAN FOOTBALL FIELD

Goalpost
End-line
Inbound line
Goal-line
Side-line
Line judge
Players' bench
Referee
Umpire
Back judge
End zone

9.2 m (30 ft)

GOALPOST

49 m (160 ft 6 in)

AMERICAN FOOTBALL PLAYING FORMATION

Right safety
Middle linebacker
Left safety
Right defensive tackle
Left defensive tackle
Right cornerback
Inside linebacker
Left cornerback
Outside linebacker
Right defensive end
Centre
Left defensive end
Tight end
Split end
Left tackle
Right tackle
Right guard
Left guard
Quarter back
Left half-back
Right half-back
Full back

CANADIAN FOOTBALL FIELD

Goalpost
Goal-line
Players' bench
Referee
Umpire
Yardsman
Field judge
Head linesman
Yardsman
Side-line
End zone

9.2 m (30 ft)

GOALPOST

59.5 m (195 ft)

CANADIAN FOOTBALL PLAYING FORMATION

Right defensive back
Middle linebacker
Safety
Left defensive back
Left defensive tackle
Right cornerback
Left cornerback
Left outside linebacker
Right outside linebacker
Left defensive end
Right defensive end
Wide receiver
Right guard
Wide receiver
Right defensive tackle
Right tackle
Flanker
Running back
Left guard
Centre
Left tackle
Quarter back
Full back
Half back

PLAYER

Team logo

Helmet

Wrist pad

Player's number

Thigh pad

Pants

Tie to shoulder pads

Studded shoe

PROTECTIVE EQUIPMENT

28 cm (11 in)

Painted white ring

Lace

Brown pebbled leather

195

FOOTBALL

HELMET

Non-breakable plastic

Rubber-coated plastic

Shock absorber

Riddell

SHOULDER PAD

BIKE MADE IN USA

BIKE MADE IN USA

AIR·LITE

BLUE·LASER 40-42

Chest protector weight up to 2.5 kg (5 lb 8 oz)

REFEREE'S SIGNALS

TIME OUT

TOUCH-DOWN OR FIELD GOAL

PERSONAL FOUL

OFFSIDE OR ENCROACHMENT

HOLDING

ILLEGAL MOTION

FIRST DOWN

PASS INTERFERENCE

BIKE

UPPER ARM PAD

BIKE

ELBOW PAD

FINGERLESS GLOVE

Screw-in stud

PONY

PONY

BOOT

Fold-over leather tongue

RIB PADS

Strap ties on to shoulder pad

Tail bone pad

Foam-sponge filling

BIKE AL80

BIKE AL80

HIP PAD

Rigid plastic covering

BIKE AL82

BIKE AL82

THIGH PAD

PANTS

KNEE PAD

Australian rules and Gaelic football

VARIETIES OF FOOTBALL have developed all over the world and Australian rules football is considered to be one of the roughest versions, allowing full body tackles although participants wear no protective padding. The game is played on a large, oval pitch by two sides, each of 18 players. Players can kick or punch the ball, which is shaped like a rugby ball, but cannot throw it. Running with the ball is permitted, as long as the ball touches the ground at least once every ten metres. The full backs defend two sets of posts. Teams try to score "goals" (six points) between the inner posts or "behinds" (one point) inside the outer posts. Each game has four quarters of 25 minutes, and the team with the most points at the end of the allotted time is the winner. In Gaelic football, an Irish version of soccer (see pp. 524–525), a size 5 soccer ball is used. Each team can have 15 players on the field at a time. Players are allowed to catch, fist, and kick the ball, or dribble it using their hands or feet, but cannot throw it. Teams are awarded three points for getting the ball into the net, and one point for getting it through the posts above the crossbar. Gaelic football is rarely played outside of Ireland.

START OF PLAY

Field umpire

Centre circle

SCORING

GOAL (6 POINTS)

BEHIND (1 POINT)

AUSTRALIAN RULES FOOTBALL FIELD

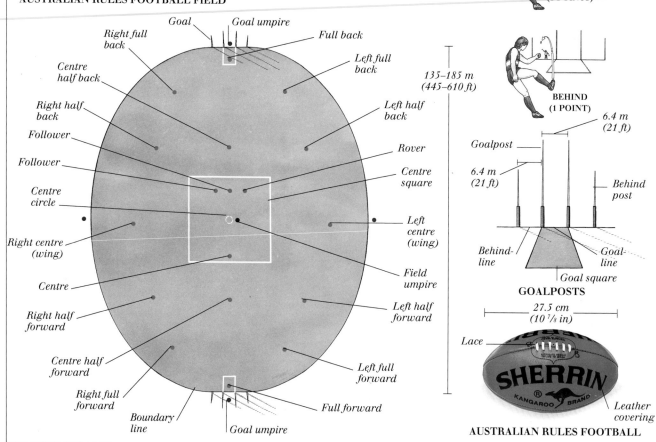

Goal

Goal umpire

Right full back

Full back

Centre half back

Left full back

Right half back

Left half back

Follower

Rover

Follower

Centre square

Centre circle

Left centre (wing)

Right centre (wing)

Field umpire

Centre

Left half forward

Right half forward

Left full forward

Centre half forward

Right full forward

Full forward

Boundary line

Goal umpire

135–185 m (445–610 ft)

6.4 m (21 ft)

Goalpost

6.4 m (21 ft)

Behind post

Behind-line

Goal-line

Goal square

GOALPOSTS

27.5 cm (10 ⅞ in)

Lace

SHERRIN

KANGAROO BRAND

Leather covering

AUSTRALIAN RULES FOOTBALL

AUSTRALIAN RULES FOOTBALL SKILLS

RUNNING WITH THE BALL

KICKING

TACKLING

TAKING A MARK

PASSING THE BALL

AUSTRALIAN RULES FOOTBALL DRESS

Australian Football League logo

Team colours

Sleeveless team guernsey

Sock

Shorts

GAELIC FOOTBALL PITCH

Corner flag

Goalkeeper

Goal umpire

Goal area

Right full back

Left full back

Full back

Right half-back

Left half-back

Centre half-back

Centre flag

Linesman

Linesman

Left midfielder

Right midfielder

Midfield line

Referee

Right half-forward

Left half-forward

Right full-forward

Centre half-forward

Full forward

Left full-forward

80–90 m
260–295 ft)

CONTROLLING THE BALL

SCORING IN GAELIC FOOTBALL

GOAL (3 POINTS)

POINT (1 POINT)

22–23 cm
(8 1/2–9 in)

6.4 m
(21ft)

Goalpost

Crossbar

Parallelogram

GOAL

oneills
all-ireland

GAELIC FOOTBALL

Rugby

RUGBY IS PLAYED WITH AN OVAL BALL, which may be carried, thrown, or kicked. There are two codes of rugby, both played at amateur and professional levels. Rugby Union is played by two teams of 15 players. They can score points in two ways: by placing the ball by hand over the opponents' goal-line (a try, scoring four points) or by kicking it over the crossbar of the opponent's goal (a conversion of a try, scoring two points; a penalty kick, scoring three points; or a drop-kick, scoring three points). Rugby League developed from the Union game but is played by 13 players. In League games, a try scores four points; a conversion scores two points; a drop goal scores one point, and a penalty kick scores two points. Scrummages occur in both codes when play stops following an infringement.

RUGBY UNION PITCH

Touch in-goal line
Goal
Dead-ball line
Goal-line
Touch-line
5 m line
Referee
Scrum-half
Hooker
10 m line
Tight-head prop
Loose-head prop
Touch judge
Flanker
Flanker
Lock forward
Lock forward
Centre
Right wing
Left wing
Centre
Number 8
Full back
Fly-half
In-goal area

68 m
(225 ft)
maximum

RUGBY UNION SCRUMMAGE

Loose-head prop
Hooker
Tight-head prop
Scrum-half
Flanker
Flanker
Lock forward
Lock forward
Number 8

RUGBY UNION GOALPOST

5.5 m (18 ft)
Upright
Crossbar
Protective padding
3 m (9 ft 10 in)

RUGBY LEAGUE SCRUMMAGE

Blind-side prop
Hooker
Open-side prop
Scrum-half
Second-row forward
Second-row forward
Loose forward

RUGBY LEAGUE GOALPOST

5.5 m (18 ft)
Upright
Crossbar
Protective padding

RUGBY LEAGUE PITCH

Goal
Dead-ball line
Touch in-goal
Touch in-goal line
Goal-line
Touch-line
10 m line
Hooker
Referee
Open-side prop
Touch judge
Touch judge
Blind-side prop
Second-row forward
Second-row forward
Scrum-half
Loose forward
Stand-off half
Left wing
Centre
Full back
Centre
Right wing

68m
(225 ft)
maximum

RUGBY SCORING AND SKILLS

GOAL

Goal-line

TRY

PASS

PLACE KICK

FLYING TACKLE

Ankle support

Circular stud

RUGBY BOOT

RUGBY UNION PLAYER

Shirt in team colour

Knee-high sock

Team shorts

Studded boot

RUGBY UNION BALL

Laminated leather panel covered with textured plastic

GILBERT

REPLICA

official ENGLAND replica ball

SIZE 5

Four-panel construction

28–30 cm (11–12 in)

RUGBY LEAGUE BALL

Eight-panel construction

TETLEY'S

GILBERT

official TETLEY'S replica ball SIZE 5

Laminated leather panel covered with textured plastic

28 cm (11 in)

Button-up collar

Team crest

RUGBY LEAGUE SHIRT

Short sleeve

BLUE HALIFAX

GILBERT

BEDFORD BLUES 1886

CITY

RUGBY UNION SHIRT

Team crest

Team colour   **RUGBY SHIRTS**

Basketball

BASKETBALL IS A BALL GAME for two teams of five players, originally devised in 1890 by James Naismath for the Y.M.C.A. in Springfield, Massachusetts, U.S.A. The object of the game is to take possession of the ball and score points by throwing the ball into the opposing team's basket. A player moves the ball up and down the court by bouncing it along the ground or "dribbling"; the ball may be passed between players by throwing, bouncing, or rolling. Players may not run with or kick the ball, although pivoting on one foot is allowed. The game begins with the referee throwing the ball into the air and a player from each team jumping up to try and "tip" the ball to a team-mate. The length of the game and the number of periods played varies at different levels. There are amateur, professional, and international rules. No game ends in a draw. An extra period of five minutes is played, plus as many extra periods as are necessary to break the tie. In addition to the five players on court, each team has up to seven substitutes, but players may only leave the court with the permission of the referee. Basketball is a non-contact sport and fouls on other players are penalized by a throw-in awarded against the offending team; a free throw at the basket is awarded when a player is fouled in the act of shooting. Basketball is a fast-moving game, requiring both physical and mental coordination. Skilful tactical play matters more than simple physical strength and the agility of the players makes the game an excellent spectator sport.

BASKETBALL SKILLS

CHEST PASS

DRIBBLE

OVERHEAD PASS

INTERNATIONAL BASKETBALL COURT

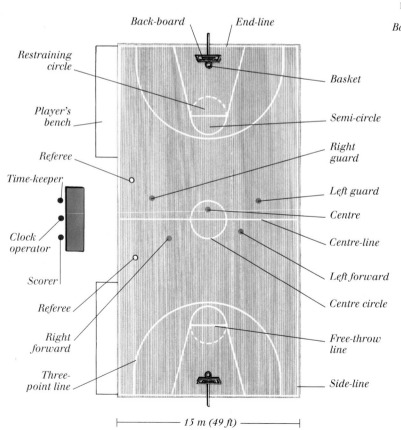

Back-board
End-line
Restraining circle
Player's bench
Referee
Time-keeper
Clock operator
Scorer
Referee
Right forward
Three-point line

Basket
Semi-circle
Right guard
Left guard
Centre
Centre-line
Left forward
Centre circle
Free-throw line
Side-line

15 m (49 ft)

BASKET AND BACK-BOARD

Back-board

Metal rim
Cord net

1.8 m (6 ft)

LAY-UP SHOT

JUMP SHOT

BASKET AND BACK-BOARD STRUCTURE

3.05 m (10 ft)

LONG PASS

ZONE DEFENCES

Point man

Free-throw line

1 – 2 – 2 ZONE

1 – 3 – 1 ZONE

2 – 3 ZONE

AMERICAN BASKETBALL VEST

Cool, lightweight fabric

Team name

Player's number

24–5 cm
(9 ¹/₂ – 9 ³/₄ in)

Textured surface for good grip

Cushioned sole

Low heel profile

BASKETBALL

BASKETBALL SHOE

INTERNATIONAL REFEREE'S SIGNALS

TECHNICAL FOUL

INTENTIONAL FOUL

JUMP BALL

STOP CLOCK FOR FOUL

SUBSTITUTION

PERSONAL FOUL: NO FREE THROWS

TRAVELLING

ILLEGAL DRIBBLE

CHARGING WITH THE BALL

ONE FREE THROW

STOP CLOCK

Volleyball, netball, and handball

VOLLEYBALL, NETBALL, AND HANDBALL are fast-moving team sports played with balls on courts with a hard surface. In volleyball, the object of the game is to hit the ball over a net strung across the centre of the court so that it touches the ground on the opponent's side. The team of six players can take three hits to direct the ball over the net, although the same player cannot hit the ball twice in a row. Players can hit the ball with their arms, hands or any other part of their upper body. Teams score points only while serving. The first team to score 15 points, with a two-point margin over their opponent, wins the game. Netball is one of the few sports played exclusively by women. Similar to basketball (see pp.532–533), it is played on a slightly larger court with seven players instead of five. A team moves the ball towards the goal by throwing, passing, and catching it with the aim of throwing the ball through the opponents' goal net. Players are confined by their playing position to specific areas of the court. Team handball is one of the world's fastest games. Each side has seven players. A team moves the ball by dribbling, passing, or bouncing it as they run. Players may stop, catch, throw, bounce, or strike the ball with any part of the body above the knees. Each team tries to score goals by directing the ball past the opposition's goalkeeper into the net, which is similar to a soccer net.

VOLLEYBALL SHOTS

OVERHAND SERVE   SPIKE (SMASH)

UNDERHAND SERVE   FOREARM PASS (DIG)

VOLLEYBALL KIT

Team colours

Ribbed cuff

Cotton-knit jersey

Elasticated waist

Shorts

Elasticated knit fabric

Injected moulded padding

VOLLEYBALL COURT

End-line

Linesman

Clear space

Linesman

Side-line

Players' bench

Referee

Scorer

Net

Left forward

Back zone

Left back

Linesman

Attack zone

Attack line

Umpire

Centre forward

Right forward

Centre back

Linesman

Service area

Server

9 m (29 ft 6 in)

VOLLEYBALL

Leather covering

21 cm (8¹/₄ in)

VOLLEYBALL NET

Tape   Net   Antenna

Men's: 2.4 m (8 ft)
Women's: 2.2 m (7 ft 4 in)

Post

KNEE PADS

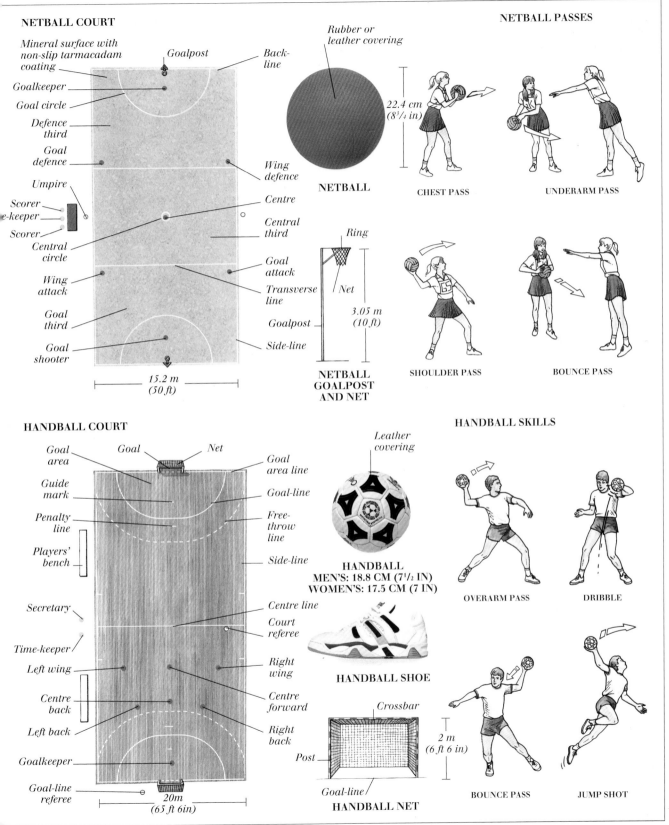

NETBALL COURT

Mineral surface with non-slip tarmacadam coating

Goalkeeper

Goal circle

Defence third

Goal defence

Umpire

Scorer e-keeper

Scorer

Central circle

Wing attack

Goal third

Goal shooter

Goalpost

Back-line

Wing defence

Centre

Central third

Goal attack

Transverse line

Goalpost

Side-line

15.2 m (50 ft)

NETBALL PASSES

Rubber or leather covering

22.4 cm (8³/₄ in)

NETBALL

CHEST PASS

UNDERARM PASS

Ring

Net

3.05 m (10 ft)

NETBALL GOALPOST AND NET

SHOULDER PASS

BOUNCE PASS

HANDBALL COURT

Goal area

Guide mark

Penalty line

Players' bench

Secretary

Time-keeper

Left wing

Centre back

Left back

Goalkeeper

Goal-line referee

Goal

Net

Goal area line

Goal-line

Free-throw line

Side-line

Centre line

Court referee

Right wing

Centre forward

Right back

20m (65 ft 6in)

HANDBALL SKILLS

Leather covering

HANDBALL
MEN'S: 18.8 CM (7¹/₂ IN)
WOMEN'S: 17.5 CM (7 IN)

OVERARM PASS

DRIBBLE

HANDBALL SHOE

Crossbar

2 m (6 ft 6 in)

Post

Goal-line

HANDBALL NET

BOUNCE PASS

JUMP SHOT

Baseball

BASEBALL IS A BALL GAME for two teams of nine players. The batter hits the ball thrown by the opposing team's pitcher, into the area between the foul lines. He then runs round all four fixed bases in order to score a run, touching or "tagging" each base in turn. The pitcher must throw the ball at a height between the batter's armpits and knees, a height which is called the "strike zone". A ball pitched in this area that crosses over the "home plate" is called a "strike" and the batter has three strikes in which to try and hit the ball (otherwise he is "struck out"). The fielding team tries to get the batting team out by catching the ball before it bounces, tagging a player of the batting team with the ball who is running between bases, or by tagging a base before the player has reached it. Members of the batting team may stop safely at a base as long as it is not occupied by another member of their team. When the batter runs to first base, his team-mate at first base must run on to second – this is called "force play". A game consists of nine innings and each team will bat once during an inning. When three members of the batting team are out, the teams swap roles. The team with the greatest number of runs wins the game.

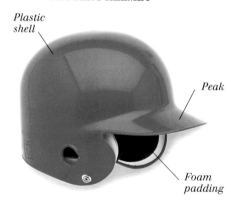

BATTER'S HELMET

Plastic shell

Peak

Foam padding

Wire coated in strong nylon

Plastic-coated foam padding

CATCHER'S MASK

BASEBALL PITCH

Centre field

Centre fielder

Warning track

Left fielder

Right fielder

Left field

Second baseman

Right field

Foul line

Outfield

Shortstop

First baseman

Umpire

First base

Third baseman

Infield

Third base

Coach's box

Home run

Second base

Dugout

On-deck circle

Pitcher's mound

100 m (325 ft) minimum

Pitcher

Pitcher's rubber

PITCHER'S MOUND

Batter

Home plate

Catcher

Home-plate umpire

HOME PLATE

MAKING A BASEBALL

Woollen yarn

Rubber inner casing

Horsehide strip

Cork centre

Cotton thread outer casing

Woollen strand

Red outer stitching

THE PITCHING SEQUENCE

THE WIND-UP 1   THE WIND-UP 2   THE WIND-UP 3

THE WIND-UP 4   THE RELEASE   THE FOLLOW-THROUGH

UMPIRING SIGNALS

BALL   INFIELD   STRIKE

FAIR BALL   RUNNER IS SAFE   FOUL TIP

BASEBALL EQUIPMENT

Webbed pocket

Fingers laced together

Strap

Thumb

Palm

Leather stitching

Heel

STEERHIDE LEATHER

FIELDER'S GLOVE AND BALL

PONY

Metal heel plate

AMERICAN BASEBALL BOOT

Metal toe plate

Batter's helmet

Bat

Batting glove

Team shirt

Undershirt

Pants

Spiked shoe

BATTER

Hitting area

Crest

Official Baseball

1.1 m (3 ft 6 in) maximum

Handle

Knob

BAT

Cricket

CRICKET IS A BALL GAME PLAYED by two teams of eleven players on a pitch with two sets of three stumps (wickets). The bowler bowls the ball down the pitch to the batsman of the opposing team, who must defend the wicket in front of which he stands. The object of the game is to score as many runs as possible. Runs can be scored individually by running the length of the playing strip, or by hitting a ball which lands outside the boundary ("six"), or which lands inside the boundary but bounces or rolls outside ("four"); the opposing team will bowl and field, attempting to dismiss the batsmen. A batsman can be dismissed in one of several ways: by the bowler hitting the wicket with the ball ("bowled"); by a fielder catching the ball hit by the batsman before it touches the ground ("caught"); by the wicket-keeper or another fielder breaking the wicket while the batsman is attempting a run and is therefore out of his ground ("stumped" or "run out"); by the batsman breaking the wicket with his own bat or body ("hit wicket"); by a part of the batsman's body being hit by a ball that would otherwise have hit the wicket ("leg before wicket" ["lbw"]). A match consists of one or two innings and each innings ends when the tenth batsman of the batting team is out, when a certain number of overs (a series of six balls bowled) have been played, or when the captain of the batting team "declares" ending the innings voluntarily.

CRICKET STROKES

FORWARD DEFENSIVE STROKE

BACKWARD DEFENSIVE STROKE

ON-DRIVE

OFF-DRIVE

PULL

HOOK

SQUARE CUT

LEG GLANCE

POSSIBLE FIELD POSITIONS FOR AN AWAY SWING BOWLER TO A RIGHT-HANDED BATSMAN (IN RED) AND OTHER FIELD POSITIONS

Long on
Umpire
Long off
Boundary line
Bowler
Deep mid-wicket
Non-striking batsman
Mid-on
Extra cover
Silly mid-on
Forward short leg
Mid-off
Square leg
Silly mid-off
Deep square leg
Cover
Square-leg umpire
Point
Batsman
Long leg
Gulley
Leg slip
Third man
Wicket-keeper
Second slip
Fine leg
First slip
Sight screen

CRICKET PITCH

Wicket-keeper
Batsman
Wicket
Bowling crease
20 m (66 ft)
Bowler
Return crease
Umpire
Non-striking batsman

CRICKET BALL AND WICKET

Leather skin
Seam
BALL
Bail
WICKET
Stump

MAKING A BAT HANDLE

Sarawak cane

Twine wrapped around handle

Rubber strip

LAMINATING THE WOOD

BINDING THE HANDLE

PROTECTIVE CLOTHING

Slit in leather for greater flexibility

Padding protects knuckles from injury

Mesh covering for ventilation

BATTING GLOVE

Dimpled rubber improves grip

Wrist strap

WICKET-KEEPER'S GLOVES

Polycarbonate shell with cloth covering

Peak

Foam cheek-piece for comfort and good fit

Protective plastic ear piece

HELMET

MAKING A BAT BLADE

V-shaped splice

Kiln-dried willow

SEASONING THE TIMBER

Blade planed by hand

CUTTING THE SPLICE

ADDING THE HANDLE TO THE BAT

Rubber grip

Shoulder of bat

Handle glued into splice

Scoop

Toe of the bat shaped

FITTING THE HANDLE

Grip rolled onto handle

Sanded and polished bat

FINISHING TOUCHES

GRAY-NICOLLS

PLACEMENT POWER

BATSMAN

Bat

Padded glove

Wristband

Cap

White shirt

White sweater

Stripes in team colours

Thigh pad under white trousers

Knee roll

Cricket shoe

Leg pad

Dimpled rubber sole

Hockey, lacrosse, and hurling

ALL OVER THE WORLD, TEAM GAMES have evolved which require that a ball be struck or carried, and tossed at the end of a stick. Early forms of these games include hurling, shinty, bandy, and pelota. Hockey is played by men and women: two teams of eleven players try to gain and keep possession of the ball and score goals by using the hockey stick to propel the ball into their opponents' goal net. Skills such as passing, pushing, or hitting the ball by slapping or lifting it in a flicking movement, and shooting at goal are crucial. Hockey is played indoors and outdoors on grass or synthetic pitches. Lacrosse is played internationally as a 12-a-side game for women and as 10-a-side game for men. The women's pitch has no absolute boundaries but the men's pitch has clearly defined side-lines and end-lines. The ball is kept in play by being carried, thrown or batted with the crosse, and rolled or kicked in any direction. In men's and women's lacrosse, play can continue behind the marked goal areas. Similar skills are required in hurling – a Gaelic field game played on the same pitch as Gaelic football (see pp. 528–529), using the same goalposts and net. In hurling, the ball may be struck with or carried on the hurley and, when off the ground, may be struck with the hand or kicked. Goals (three points) are scored when the ball passes between the posts and under the crossbar; one point is scored when it passes between the posts and over the crossbar.

GOALKEEPER'S EQUIPMENT

Air vent

Hard shell

Face mask

HELMET

Strap

Rigid palm

Padded wrist

GAUNTLET

HOCKEY STICK AND BALL

STICK

Handle

Tape

Blade

Steam-bent ash head

Stitched seam

7–7.5 cm (2³⁄₄–3 in)

91 cm (3 ft)

BALL

HOCKEY FIELD

Side-line

Centre forward

Inside right

Right wing

Right half

Right back

Corner flag

Shooting circle

Goal

Penalty spot

Five yard mark

Goal-line

Inside left

Left wing

Umpire

Centre half

Left half

Left back

Goalkeeper

55 m (180 ft)

Protective overshoe

Padding protects toes against the hard ball

Strap

GOALKEEPER'S KICKER

2.1 m (7 ft)

HOCKEY GOAL

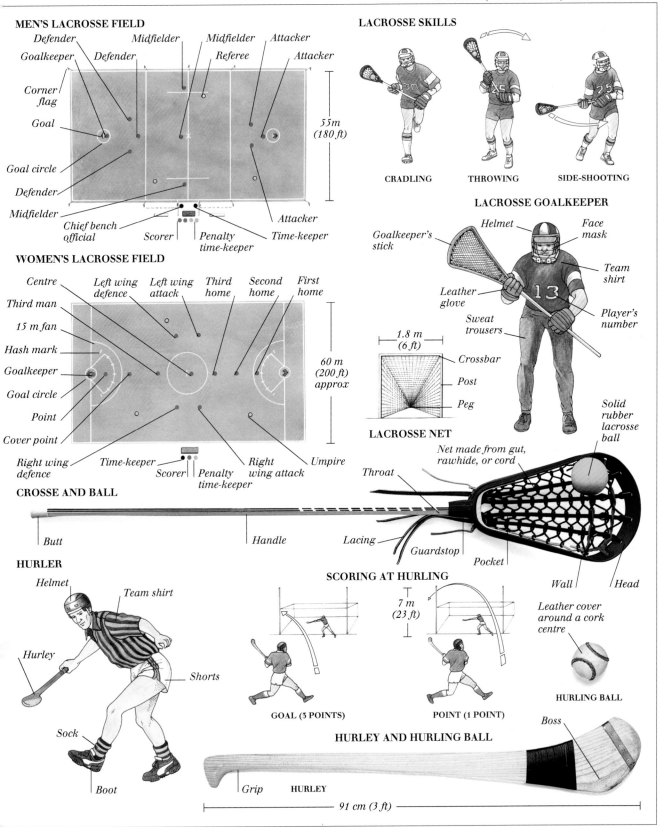

MEN'S LACROSSE FIELD

Defender
Goalkeeper
Defender
Midfielder
Midfielder
Referee
Attacker
Attacker

Corner
flag

Goal

Goal circle

Defender

Midfielder

Chief bench
official
Scorer
Penalty
time-keeper
Attacker
Time-keeper

55m
(180 ft)

LACROSSE SKILLS

CRADLING
THROWING
SIDE-SHOOTING

WOMEN'S LACROSSE FIELD

Centre
Third man
15 m fan
Hash mark
Goalkeeper
Goal circle
Point
Cover point
Right wing
defence

Left wing
defence
Left wing
attack
Third
home
Second
home
First
home

Time-keeper
Scorer
Penalty
time-keeper
Right
wing attack
Umpire

60 m
(200 ft)
approx

LACROSSE GOALKEEPER

Goalkeeper's
stick
Helmet
Face
mask
Team
shirt
Leather
glove
Player's
number
Sweat
trousers

13

1.8 m
(6 ft)
Crossbar
Post
Peg

Solid
rubber
lacrosse
ball

LACROSSE NET

CROSSE AND BALL

Butt
Handle
Throat
Lacing
Guardstop
Pocket
Net made from gut,
rawhide, or cord
Wall
Head

HURLER

Helmet
Team shirt
Hurley
Shorts
Sock
Boot

SCORING AT HURLING

7 m
(23 ft)

GOAL (3 POINTS)
POINT (1 POINT)

Leather cover
around a cork
centre

HURLING BALL

HURLEY AND HURLING BALL

Boss

Grip
HURLEY
91 cm (3 ft)

Athletics

THE SPORTS that make up athletics are divided into two main groups: track events – which include sprinting, middle, and long distance running, relay running, hurdling, and walking – and field events which require jumping and throwing skills. Contests designed to test the speed, strength, agility, and stamina of athletes were held by the ancient Greeks over 4,000 years ago. However, the abolition of the Olympic Games in 393 AD meant that athletics were neglected until the revival of large-scale competitions in the mid-nineteenth century. Modern stadia offer areas reserved for the long jump, triple jump, and pole vault usually situated outside the running track. The javelin, shot, hammer, and discus are thrown within the track area. Most athletes specialize in one or two events but, in the heptathlon, women compete in seven events, held over two days: 200 m and 800 m races, 100 m hurdles, javelin, shot put, high jump, and long jump. In the decathlon, men compete in ten events over two days: 100 m, 400 m, and 1,500 m races, 110 m hurdles, javelin, discus, shot put, pole vault, high jump, and long jump.

FIELD EVENT EQUIPMENT

Steel wire

Head

Swivel

HAMMER 7 KG (16 LB)

Body

Metal rim

Centre weight

DISCUS MEN: 2 KG (4 LB 7 OZ) WOMEN: 1 KG (2 LB 3 OZ)

Hammer handle

Rubber coating

Shot-pellet filling

12.7 cm (5 in)

10 cm (4 in)

MEN'S SHOT 7 KG (16 LB)

WOMEN'S SHOT 4 KG (8 LB 12 OZ)

JAVELIN

Cord grip   *Shaft*   *Tip*

Men: 2.6 m (8 ft 6 in)
Women: 2.3 m (7 ft 6 in)

ATHLETICS TRACK AND FIELD

Finishing post   *Pole-vault mat*   *Pole-vault runway*   *100 m starting line*

Finishing line

Javelin fan

Steeplechase water jump

Hammer circle

Discus circle

Javelin runway

Lane

One lap is 400 m

Shot-put fan

Shot-put circle

High-jump fan

Discus fan

High-jump mat

Hammer fan

Triple-jump take-off board   *Triple-jump take-off line*   *Indicator board*   *Triple-jump runway*   *Long-jump take-off board*   *Landing area*

Hollow plastic tube

RELAY BATONS

TYPES OF SHOE

Lightweight construction

Spiked sole

TRACK SHOE

Reflective side strip

Wedge heel

Air-cushioned sole

RUNNING SHOE

DISCUS THROW

Swing · *Shift* · *Twist* · *Release*

Drive · *Arch*

Take-off

Approach · *Landing*

SHOT PUT

Crouch · *Shift* · *Thrust* · *Release*

HIGH JUMP

HAMMER THROW

Swing · *Entry* · *Lift* · *Release*

JAVELIN THROW

Withdrawal stride · *Half turn* · *Step* · *Drive forward* · *Release*

Handstand

Push-pull · *Release*

Rock-back

Hang

Take-off

Plant

Landing

LONG JUMP

Take-off · *Flight* · *Hitch-kick* · *Stretch* · *Landing*

Take-off board

POLE VAULT

TRIPLE JUMP

Hop · *Skip* · *Jump*

Take-off

Take-off board · *Land on foot used for take-off* · *Land on opposite foot*

Racket sports

PROTECTIVE EYEWEAR

THE OBJECT OF ALL RACKET SPORTS is to make shots the opponent cannot return. Games are played by two players (singles) or four players (doubles). Racket shape and size is tailored to each sport, but all rackets are constructed of wood, plastic, aluminium, or high-performance materials such as fibreglass and carbon graphite. Racket strings are usually synthetic, although natural gut is still used. Tennis is played on a court divided by a low net. Opposing players serve alternate games. At least six games must be won to gain a set, and two or sometimes three sets are needed to win a match. Tennis courts may be concrete, grass, clay, or synthetic, each surface requiring a different style of play. Badminton is an indoor sport that is played with light, flexible rackets and a feather shuttlecock on a court with a high net. Players can score points only on their serve. The first to reach 15 points (11 points for women's singles) wins the game. Two games are needed to win a match. Squash and racketball are both played in enclosed courts. One player hits the ball against the front wall, and the other tries to return it before it bounces on the floor more than once. Squash rackets have smaller, rounder heads and stiffer frames than badminton rackets. In America, the game is played on a narrower court than an international court using a much harder ball. Squash games are played to nine points (international) or 15 points (American). In racketball, players use a ball that is larger and bouncier than a squash ball. The racket is thick and sturdy, with a large head, short handle, and a thong that loops around the wrist. Points can be won only when serving, and the first player to reach 21 points wins.

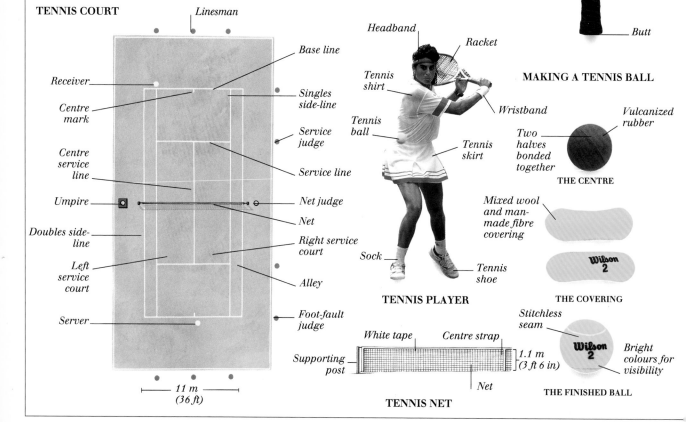

TENNIS RACKET

Synthetic string
Frame
Head
Logo
Throat
Grip
Butt

TENNIS COURT

Linesman
Base line
Receiver
Singles side-line
Centre mark
Service judge
Centre service line
Service line
Umpire
Net judge
Net
Doubles side-line
Right service court
Left service court
Alley
Server
Foot-fault judge

11 m
(36 ft)

TENNIS PLAYER

Headband
Racket
Tennis shirt
Wristband
Tennis ball
Tennis skirt
Sock
Tennis shoe

TENNIS NET

White tape
Centre strap
Supporting post
1.1 m
(3 ft 6 in)
Net

MAKING A TENNIS BALL

Vulcanized rubber
Two halves bonded together

THE CENTRE

Mixed wool and man-made fibre covering

THE COVERING

Stitchless seam
Bright colours for visibility

THE FINISHED BALL

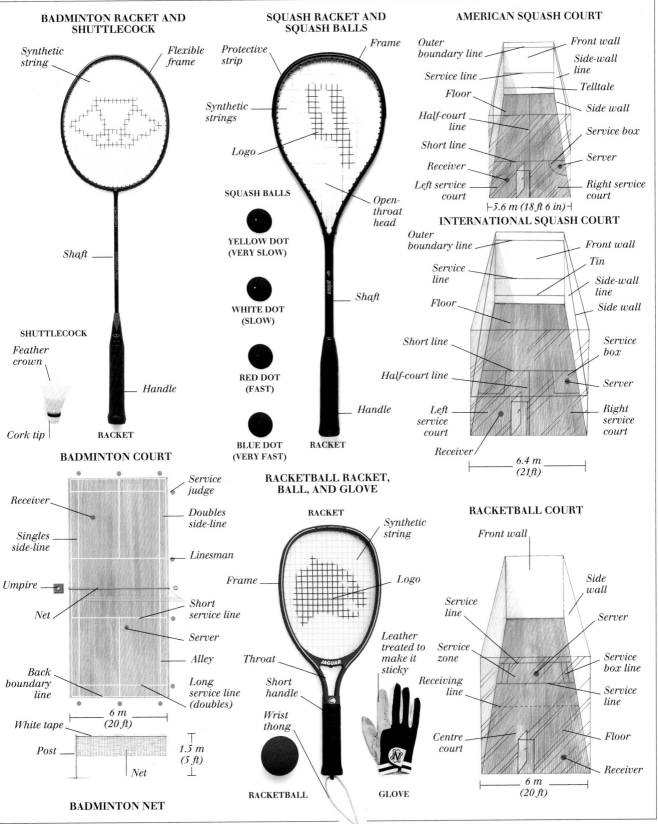

BADMINTON RACKET AND SHUTTLECOCK

Synthetic string

Flexible frame

Shaft

SHUTTLECOCK

Feather crown

Handle

Cork tip

RACKET

BADMINTON COURT

Receiver

Service judge

Doubles side-line

Singles side-line

Linesman

Umpire

Net

Short service line

Server

Alley

Back boundary line

Long service line (doubles)

6 m (20 ft)

White tape

Post

1.5 m (5 ft)

Net

Net

BADMINTON NET

SQUASH RACKET AND SQUASH BALLS

Protective strip

Frame

Synthetic strings

Logo

Open-throat head

Shaft

Handle

RACKET

SQUASH BALLS

YELLOW DOT (VERY SLOW)

WHITE DOT (SLOW)

RED DOT (FAST)

BLUE DOT (VERY FAST)

RACKETBALL RACKET, BALL, AND GLOVE

RACKET

Synthetic string

Frame

Logo

Leather treated to make it sticky

Throat

Short handle

Wrist thong

RACKETBALL

GLOVE

AMERICAN SQUASH COURT

Outer boundary line

Front wall

Service line

Side-wall line

Floor

Telltale

Half-court line

Side wall

Short line

Service box

Receiver

Server

Left service court

Right service court

5.6 m (18 ft 6 in)

INTERNATIONAL SQUASH COURT

Outer boundary line

Front wall

Service line

Tin

Side-wall line

Floor

Side wall

Short line

Service box

Half-court line

Server

Left service court

Right service court

Receiver

6.4 m (21 ft)

RACKETBALL COURT

Front wall

Side wall

Service line

Server

Service zone

Service box line

Receiving line

Service line

Centre court

Floor

Receiver

6 m (20 ft)

545

Golf

GOLF BALL AND TEE

THE GAME OF GOLF was first played in Scotland some 400 years ago. Players are required to hit a ball, using a wooden or iron club, from a smooth level point or "teeing ground", down the "fairway", and on to a putting green where the target hole is located. The fairway is a strip of clear land along which there are natural hazards – such as ponds and streams, man-made hazards – such as bunkers (sand-pits), and rough (areas of uncut grass). Championship golf courses have 18 holes. The object of the game is to hit the ball into each hole in turn, and to complete the "round" using as few strokes as possible. Players compete individually or in teams, playing the course together in groups of two, three, or four. The two basic forms of competition are match play and stroke play. In match play, the side winning the majority of holes over a certain number of rounds wins the match. In stroke play, the winner is the player who finishes a certain number of rounds having made the fewest strokes.

GOLF BALL WITH BALATA SURFACE

Dimpled surface

Wound yarn

Liquid

Balata cover

Membrane to contain liquid

Water obstacle

Putting green

Elevated green

Dog-leg hole

Putting green

Bridge

Clubhouse

Pond

Bunker

Hole

Practice area

Teeing ground

Rough

Pathway

AUGUSTA NATIONAL GOLF COURSE, AUGUSTA, GEORGIA, U.S.A.

Fairway

Screen of trees

A TYPICAL HOLE

Teeing ground

Water obstacle | Bridge | Fairway | Wood | Rough

MAKING A WOODEN CLUB

Close grain of wood

Streamlined back

Plastic insert on face

Sand, stain, and varnish finish

Persimmon wood

Slot cut for plate

Metal sole plate protects the wood

Outline of head

RAW MATERIAL

CREATING THE BASIC SHAPE

ADDING THE LEAD WEIGHT

THE FINISHED CLUB HEAD

PUTTER, WOOD, AND IRON

WOOD

Textured vulcanized rubber grip

IRON

PUTTER

RANGE OF WOODEN CLUBS

10 degree loft

15 degree loft

21 degree loft

DRIVER

3-WOOD

5-WOOD

RANGE OF IRON CLUBS

22 degree loft

26 degree loft

3-IRON

4-IRON

30 degree loft

34 degree loft

38 degree loft

42 degree loft

46 degree loft

50 degree loft

56 degree loft

5-IRON

6-IRON

7-IRON

8-IRON

9-IRON

PITCHING WEDGE

SAND WEDGE

Shaped pistol grip

GOLF ACCESSORIES

GOLF SCORE RECORD

BALL MARKERS

Spiked sole

SCORECARD AND PENCIL

TEE PEGS

PITCHMARK REPAIRER

PRACTICE BALL

LIGHTWEIGHT SHOE

Stainless steel shaft

Steel shaft

Steel shaft

84 cm (33 in)

94 cm (37 in)

109 cm (43 in)

Neck

Neck

Angled neck

Face

Heel

Toe

Heel

Flag pole or pin

Green

Toe

Toe

Groove

Sole

Heel

Bunker (sand -pit)

Blade

547

Archery and shooting

TARGET SHOOTING AND ARCHERY EVOLVED as practice for hunting and battle skills. Modern bows, although designed according to the principles of early hunting bows, use laminates, fibreglass, dacron, and carbon, and are equipped with sights and stabilizers. Competitors in target archery shoot over distances of 30 m (100 ft), 50 m (165 ft), 70 m (230 ft), and 90 m (300 ft) for men, and 30 m (100 ft), 50 m (165 ft), 60 m (200 ft), and 70 m (230 ft) for women. The closer the shot is to the centre of the target, the higher the score. The individual scores are added up, and the archer with the highest total wins the competition. Crossbows are used in match competitions over 10 m (33 ft), and 30 m (100 ft). Rifle shooting is divided into three categories: smallbore, bigbore, and air rifle. Contests take place over a variety of distances and further subdivisions are based on the type of shooting position used: prone, kneeling, or standing. The Olympic biathlon combines cross-country skiing and rifle shooting over a course of approximately 20 km (12 1/2 miles). Additional magazines of ammunition are carried in the butt of the rifles. Bigbore rifles fitted with a telescopic sight can be used for hunting and running game target shooting. Pistol shooting events, using rapid-fire pistols, target pistols, and air pistols, take place over 10 m (33 ft), 25 m (82 ft), and 50 m (165 ft) distances. In rapid-fire pistol shooting, a total of 60 shots are fired from a distance of 25 m (83 ft).

CROSSBOW AND BOLT

Laminated fibreglass bow

Bolt

Bolt rest

45 mm (1 3/4 in)

CROSSBOW TARGET

Stirrup held between feet when drawing bow

Sight

Hardwood laminate limb

Dacron string

Sight

MODERN BOW

Pressure button

Grip

V-bar stabilizers

Magnesium riser

Plastic fletch

Nock

Forearm guard

Finger hole

Aluminium shaft

BRACER

Strap

FINGER TAB

ARCHER'S GLOVE

Wristband

Weight

Velcro fastening

Waistband

Accessory pouch

ARCHERY EQUIPMENT

QUIVER

**SMALLBORE
BIATHLON RIFLE**

*Rifle sight without
magnifying lens*

Barrel

Fore sight

Trigger

*5.6 mm (0.22 in)
calibre bullet*

*Trigger
guard*

Magazine

*Extra magazine
stored in rifle butt*

*155 mm
(6 in)*

**SMALLBORE
FREE RIFLE
TARGET FOR
50 M (165 FT)
RANGE**

**BIGBORE
HUNTING RIFLE**

Bolt

*Bolt
handle*

Telescopic sight

Open sight

Open sight

*7.62 mm
(0.3 in)
calibre
bullet*

Sling fixing point

*1 m
(39 in)*

**BIGBORE
RIFLE
TARGET FOR
300 M (1000 FT)
RANGE**

AIR PISTOL

*Wooden grip
shaped to fit
the hand*

*Cocking
lever and
barrel*

Piston

*155 mm
(6 in)*

TARGET PISTOL

Back sight

Fore sight

Hammer

Sight pin

*Firing
pin*

*197 mm
(7¾ in)*

**AIR-PISTOL
TARGET FOR
10 M (33 FT)
RANGE**

*Sight ring
attachment*

**PISTOL
TARGET FOR
18 M (60 FT)
RANGE**

Magazine

*9 mm
(0.35 in)
calibre
bullet*

Trigger

*Air-pistol
pellet*

Nock

FIELD ARROW

Metal tip

Feathering

Wooden shaft

Straw butt

*White inner
2 points*

*Aluminium
longrod stabilizer*

*Blue outer
5 points*

*Yellow inner 10
points (bull's-eye)*

ARCHERY TARGET

Ice hockey

ICE HOCKEY IS PLAYED by two teams of six players on an ice rink, with a goal net at each end. The object of this fast, and often dangerous, game is to hit a frozen rubber puck into the opposing team's net with a ice hockey stick. The game begins when the referee drops the puck between the sticks of two players from opposing teams, who "face off". The rink is divided into three areas: defending, neutral, and attacking zones. Players may move with the puck and pass the puck to one another along the ice, but may not pass it more than two zones across the rink markings. A goal is scored when the puck entirely crosses the goal-line between the posts and under the crossbar of the goal. A team may field up to 20 players although only six players are allowed on the ice at one time; substitutions occur frequently. Each game consists of three periods of 20 minutes, divided by breaks of 15 minutes.

GOALKEEPER

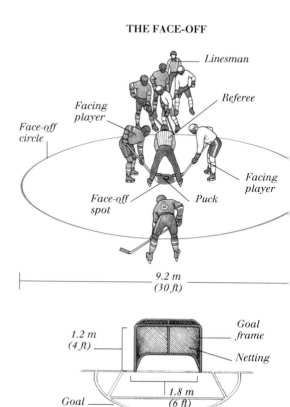

Helmet

Face mask

Throat protector

Team shirt

Butt end

Pants

Catch glove

Blocking pad

Goalkeeper's pad

Skate

Blade

Goalkeeper's stick

Heel

Blade

ICE HOCKEY RINK

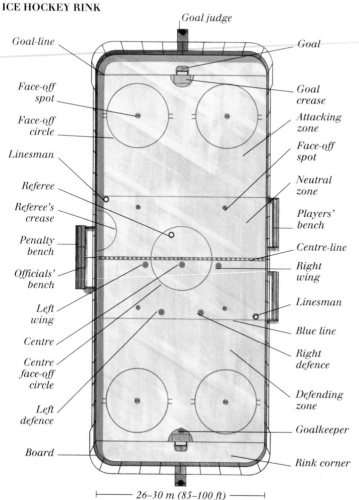

Goal judge

Goal-line

Goal

Face-off spot

Goal crease

Face-off circle

Attacking zone

Linesman

Face-off spot

Referee

Neutral zone

Referee's crease

Penalty bench

Players' bench

Officials' bench

Centre-line

Left wing

Right wing

Centre

Linesman

Centre face-off circle

Blue line

Left defence

Right defence

Board

Defending zone

Goalkeeper

Rink corner

26–30 m (85–100 ft)

THE FACE-OFF

Linesman

Facing player

Referee

Face-off circle

Face-off spot

Facing player

Puck

9.2 m (30 ft)

1.2 m (4 ft)

Goal frame

Netting

1.8 m (6 ft)

Goal crease

ICE HOCKEY GOAL

GOALKEEPER'S HELMET

Customized
paintwork

Face
guard

Chin
protection

PLAYER'S BODY
ARMOUR

Air vents

Rigid
plastic
shell

Manufacturer's
logo

Chin
strap

Foam
padding

PLAYER'S
HELMET

CANADIEN

Shoulder
padding

ELBOW
PADS

DR

DAIGNAULT
ROLLAND

3075N
GRAND/LARGE

Heavy
padding

Flexible
gusset

Rigid
finger cap

TORSPO
20

GLOVE

Strap

DR
Daignault · Rolland
4355 M
DÉFENSE-PRO-DEFENCE

Chest
padding

Wrist
protection

LEG PROTECTOR

Knee
protection

Rigid
plastic
casing

Thick
foam
backing

DR
Daignault · Rolland
16.5"
43cm CENTURION-J

Leg pad

Puck stopper

ICE HOCKEY
STICKS

GOALKEEPER'S
STICK

SHOULDER
AND CHEST
PADDING

MADE IN FINLAND
TORSPO
Pro 5000

OUTFIELD
PLAYER'S
STICK

147 cm
(4 ft 9 in)

TORSPO
Pro 500

Thin
shaft

Wide
lower
shaft

Vulcanized
rubber

7.6 cm
(3 in)

FROZEN
PUCK

TORSPO

TORSPO

39 cm
(15 in)

32 cm
(12 1/2 in)

Thick
blade

Heel

Ankle
support

Safety
heel tip

Blade   SKATE

Alpine skiing

COMPETITIVE ALPINE SKIING is divided into four disciplines: downhill, slalom, giant slalom, and super-giant slalom (Super-G). Each one tests different skills. In downhill skiing, competitors race down a slope marked out by control flags, known as "gates", and are timed on a single run only. Competitors wear crash helmets, one-piece Lycra suits, and long skis with flattened tips to minimize air resistance. Slalom and giant slalom skiers negotiate a twisting course requiring balance, agility, and quick reactions. Courses are defined by pairs of gates. Racers must pass through each pair of gates to complete the course successfully. Competitors are timed on two runs over different courses, and the skier who completes the courses in the shortest time wins. The equipment and protective guards used by slalom skiers are shown opposite. In Super-G races, competitors ski a single run that combines the technical challenge of slalom with the speed of downhill. The course requires skiers to complete medium-to-long radius turns at high speed, and contain up to two jumps. Clothing is the same as for downhill, but slightly shorter skis are used.

DOWNHILL SKIER

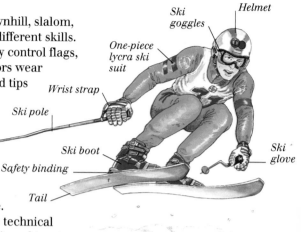

Ski goggles • Helmet • One-piece lycra ski suit • Wrist strap • Ski pole • Basket • Ski boot • Safety binding • Tail • Ski glove

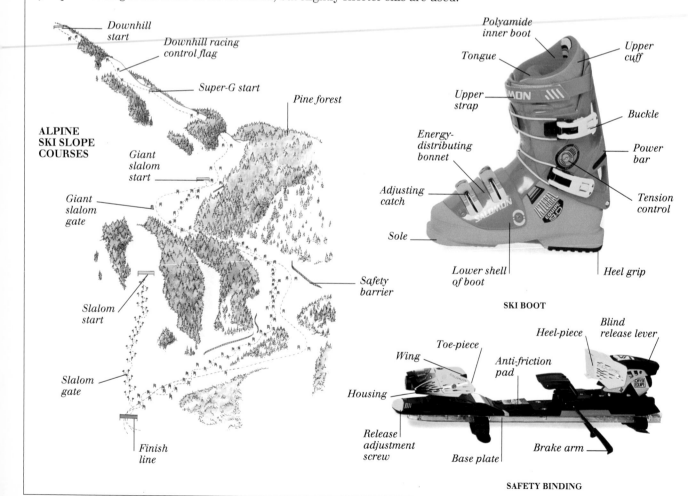

ALPINE SKI SLOPE COURSES

Downhill start • Downhill racing control flag • Super-G start • Pine forest • Giant slalom start • Giant slalom gate • Safety barrier • Slalom start • Slalom gate • Finish line

Polyamide inner boot • Tongue • Upper cuff • Upper strap • Buckle • Energy-distributing bonnet • Power bar • Adjusting catch • Tension control • Sole • Lower shell of boot • Heel grip

SKI BOOT

Toe-piece • Heel-piece • Blind release lever • Wing • Anti-friction pad • Housing • Release adjustment screw • Base plate • Brake arm

SAFETY BINDING

SLALOM CLOTHING AND EQUIPMENT

GOGGLES

Elasticated strap

Anti-glare lens

SLALOM HELMET

Hard nylon shell

Padding

Strap

Chin guard

SKI GLOVE

Extended cuff

Wrist strap

Rigid pad for hand protection

PADDED SWEATER

High collar

Double-knit wool and polyester fabric

PADDED SKI TROUSERS

Adjustable shoulder strap

Ribbed cuff

Zip pocket

Front zip fastening

Waterproof fabric

Cuff fits over ski boot

HAND GUARD

Moulded polypropylene

LEG GUARD

Tough polypropylene shell deflects the shaft of the slalom gate

Velcro strap

SLALOM SKI POLE

Wrist strap

Grip

Shock-absorbing platform under boot

Edge

Shaft

Basket

SLALOM SKI

Tail

188–203 cm (74–80 in)

Tip

Equestrian sports

EQUESTRIAN SPORTS HAVE TAKEN place throughout the world for centuries: events involving mounted horses were recorded in the Olympic Games of 642 BC. Showjumping, however, is a much more recent innovation, and the first competitions were held at the beginning of the 1900s. In this sport, horse and rider must negotiate a course of variable, unfixed obstacles, making as few mistakes as possible. Showjumping fences consist of wooden stands, known as standards or wings, that support planks or poles. Parts of the fence are designed to collapse on impact, preventing injury to the horse and rider. Judges penalise competitors for errors, such as knocking down obstacles, refusing jumps, or deviating from the course. Depending on the type of competition, the rider with the fewest faults, most points, or fastest time wins. There are two basic forms of horse racing – flat races and races with jumps, such as steeplechase or hurdle-races. Thoroughbred horses are used in this sport, as they have great strength and stamina and can achieve speeds of up to 65 kph (40 mph). Jockeys wear "silks" – caps and jackets designed in distinctive colours and patterns which help identify the horses. In harness racing, the horse is driven from a light, two-wheeled carriage called a sulky. Horses are trained to trot and to pace, and different races are held for each of these types of gait. In pacing races, the horses wear hobbles to prevent them from breaking into a trot or gallop. Breeds such as the Standardbred and the French Trotter have been developed especially for this sport.

SHOWJUMPING SADDLE

High cantle

Deep seat

Pommel

Forward-cut flap

Knee roll

SHOWJUMPING FENCES

Standard — Foot

Plank

UPRIGHT PLANKS

Standard — Foot

Pole

UPRIGHT POLES

Back pole

Standard

Foot — Pole

TRIPLE BAR (STAIRCASE)

Standard

Pole

Foot

HOG'S-BACK

Pillar

Wooden block painted to resemble a brick

WALL

Hard hat

Riding jacket

Browband

Throat-latch

Rein

Jodhpurs

Cheek-piece

Showjumping saddle

Hindquarters

Dock

Running martingale

Noseband

Brushing boot

Sheepskin numnah

Girth

Stirrup iron

Riding boot

Hoof

Gaskin

Hock joint

Fetlock joint

Pastern

Coronet

SHOWJUMPING HORSE WITH RIDER

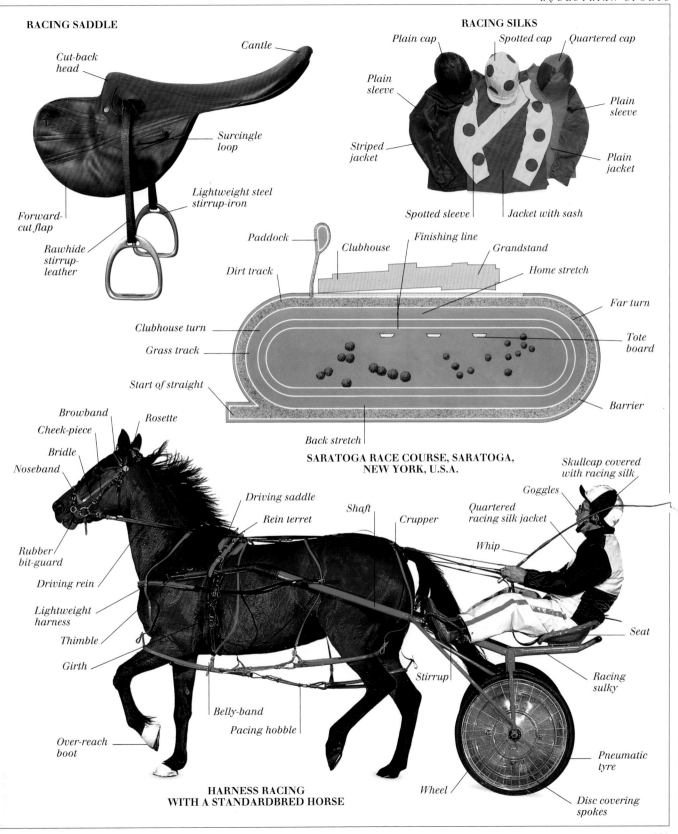

RACING SADDLE

Cut-back head

Cantle

Surcingle loop

Lightweight steel stirrup-iron

Forward-cut flap

Rawhide stirrup-leather

RACING SILKS

Plain cap

Spotted cap

Quartered cap

Plain sleeve

Plain sleeve

Striped jacket

Plain jacket

Spotted sleeve

Jacket with sash

Paddock

Finishing line

Clubhouse

Grandstand

Dirt track

Home stretch

Clubhouse turn

Far turn

Grass track

Tote board

Start of straight

Barrier

Back stretch

SARATOGA RACE COURSE, SARATOGA, NEW YORK, U.S.A.

Browband

Rosette

Cheek-piece

Bridle

Noseband

Driving saddle

Rein terret

Shaft

Crupper

Skullcap covered with racing silk

Goggles

Quartered racing silk jacket

Whip

Rubber bit-guard

Driving rein

Lightweight harness

Thimble

Seat

Girth

Racing sulky

Belly-band

Stirrup

Over-reach boot

Pacing hobble

Pneumatic tyre

Wheel

Disc covering spokes

HARNESS RACING WITH A STANDARDBRED HORSE

Judo and fencing

COMBAT SPORTS ARE BASED ON THE SKILLS used in fighting. In these sports, the competitors may be unarmed – as in judo and boxing – or armed – as in fencing and kendo. Judo is a system of unarmed combat developed in the East. Translated from the Japanese the name means "the gentle way". Students learn how to turn an opponent's force to their own advantage. The usual costume is loose white trousers and a jacket, fastened with a cloth belt. The colour of belt indicates the student's level of expertise, from white-belted novices to the expert "black belts". Competitions take place on a mat or "shiaijo", 9 or 10 m (30 or 33 ft) square in size, bounded by "danger" and "safety" areas to prevent injury. Competitors try to throw, pin, or master their opponent by applying pressure to the arm joints or neck. Judo bouts are strictly monitored, and competitors receive points for superior technique, not for injuring their opponent. Fencing is a combat sport using swords, which takes place on a narrow "piste" 14 m (46 ft) long. Competitors try to touch specific target areas on their opponent with their sword or "foil" while avoiding being touched themselves. The winner is the one who scores the greatest number of hits. Fencers wear clothing made from strong white material, which affords maximum protection while allowing freedom of movement, steel mesh masks with padded bibs to protect the fencer's neck, and a long white glove on their sword hand. Fencing foils do not have sharpened blades, and their tips end in a blunt button to prevent injuries. Three types of swords are used – foils, épées, and sabres. Official foil and épée competitions always use an electric scoring system. The sword tips are connected to lights by a long wire that passes underneath each fencer's jacket. A bulb flashes when a hit is made.

JUDO HOLDS AND THROWS

SIDE FOUR QUARTER HOLD

SINGLE WING

BODY DROP

ONE ARM SHOULDER THROW

SHOULDER WHEEL

SWEEPING LOW THROW

STOMACH THROW

KNEE WHEEL

JUDO KIT

JUDO MAT

16 m
(52 ft 6 in)

Judge

Scorer

Holding time-keeper

Time-keeper

Danger area Contestant

Draw-string

Contestant

Referee

Contest area

Safety area

Cotton trousers

Black belt Heavy-duty cotton jacket

FENCING PISTE

Rear limit line

14 m (46 ft)

Sabre and épéé warning line

Scorer

Electrical scoring apparatus

Centre line

President

Time-keeper

On-guard line

Body wire

Reel

FENCING TARGET AREAS

SABREUR

FOILIST

EPEEIST

FENCING EQUIPMENT

Steel wire mesh

Padded bib

MESH MASK

Woven metal thread

METAL JACKET

Cuff

Glove

GAUNTLET

TARGET AREAS ON THE UPPER BODY

Mask
Wire mesh
Bib
Tierce
Sixte
Gauntlet
Seconde
Octave

Under plastron
Quinte
Quarte
Prime
Septime

Metal over-jacket

Breeches

Stocking

Fencing shoe

THE SABRE

THE FOIL

Martingale

THE EPEE

Button

Blade

PARTS OF THE SWORD

Guard

Tang

Leather pad

Alternative pistol-grip handle

Brass screw

Steel foil pommel

Swimming and diving

SWIMMING GOGGLES

SWIMMING WAS INCLUDED in the first modern Olympic Games in 1896 and diving events were added in 1904. Swimming is both an individual and a team sport and races take place over a predetermined distance in one of the four major categories of stroke – freestyle (usually front crawl), butterfly, breaststroke, and backstroke. Competition pools are clearly marked for racing and anti-turbulence lane lines are used to separate the swimmers and help keep the water calm. The first team or individual to finish the race is the winner. Competitive diving is divided into men's and women's springboard and platform (highboard) events. There are six official groups of dives: forward dives, backward dives, armstand dives, twist dives, reverse dives, and inward dives. Competitors perform a set number of dives and after each one a panel of judges awards marks according to the quality of execution and the degree of difficulty.

STYLES OF DIVES

Starting position
Hands above head
Legs fully stretched
Flight
Arched back
Toes pointed
Entry
Feet together
Hands close together

FORWARD DIVE   **BACKWARD DIVE**

SWIMWEAR

Latex rubber moulds to shape of head

CAPS

Rubber-covered wire

NOSE CLIP

Moulded rubber

EARPLUG

High neckline

Man-made stretch fabric

Drawstring

High-cut leg

Strong seam

SWIMSUIT   **TRUNKS**

SWIMMING POOL

Swimmer
Lane number
Starting block
Chief time-keeper
Lane time-keeper
Placing judge
End wall
Starter
Recorder
Side wall
Backstroke marker 15 m (49 ft) from end of pool
Anti-turbulence lane line
Referee
Stroke judge
Backstroke turn indicator 5 m (16 ft) from end of pool
Bottom line
Turning judge
Turning wall
Lane
23 m (75 ft 6 in)

Perfectly steady armstand

Arms and legs align throughout flight and entry

ARMSTAND DIVE

Arms spread wide apart

Body and legs straighten for flight and entry

TWIST DIVE

Pike position

Height of dive

Shoulders fall backwards for vertical entry

REVERSE DIVE PIKED

Pike position

Hands touch toes

Feet lift up for straight entry

INWARD DIVE PIKED

FRONT CRAWL
Flutter kick

FULL BODY STRETCH

Arm pulls like a paddle

LOWER ARM PULL

Arrow-like position

STREAMLINED ARM ENTRY

Body rolls on a central axis

SIDE-TO-SIDE BODY ROLL

BREASTSTROKE
Straight leg

BODY GLIDE

Knees together

DOUBLE ARM PULL

Elbows tucked in

SQUEEZING THE WATER

Arm fully extended

FROG KICK

BACKSTROKE
Little finger enters first

BODY ROLL

Arm comes up straight

PULLING THROUGH

Recovering hand

STRAIGHTENING OUT

Shoulder exits water first

SHOULDER LIFT

BUTTERFLY
Palm turned outwards

CATCHING THE WATER

Legs ready to kick down

DOUBLE ARM PULL

Head clears the water

KICKING DOWN

Shoulders power the stroke

WHOLE BODY UNDULATION

Canoeing, rowing, and sailing

WATERBORNE SPORTS are as varied as the crafts used. There are two disciplines in rowing; sweep rowing, in which each rower has one oar and sculling, in which rowers use two oars. There are a number of different Olympic and competitive rowing events for both men and women. The number of rowers and weight classes vary. Some rowing events use a coxswain; a steersman who does not row but directs the crew. Kayaks and canoes are used in straight sprint and slalom races. Slalom races take place over a course consisting of 20 to 25 gates, including at least six upstream gates. In yacht racing, competitors must complete prescribed courses, organized by the race committees, in the shortest possible time, using sail power only. Olympic events include classes for keel boats, dinghies, and catamarans.

SAILING GEAR

Buoyancy aid

Sleeveless long johns

Long-sleeved jacket

Neoprene material

Belt

GLOVE

Bootlace

Ribbed top

Non-slip sole

BOOT

ONE-PERSON KAYAK AND PADDLE

Blade

Rim

Shaft

Nose cone

Right rail

Cockpit

Back strap

Stern

High density polythene

Toggle

Bow

Left rail

Seat

Cockpit rim

380

SINGLE SCULL AND OARS
(WITH CLOTH DECKING REMOVED)

Neck

Shaft

Stroke-side oar

Spoon

Blade

Colours

Gate

Adjusting screw

Gate clamp

Grip

Bow-side oar

Button

Loom

Rigger

Stretcher

Sycamore beam

Water shoot

Bung

Aft shoulder

Shoe

Keel

Sternpost

Spruce beam

Diagonal frame

Aluminium beam

Kelson (keelson)

LIFEJACKET

Backstrap/
rescue
strap

Reinforced
seam

Neck
opening

Whistle

Topping-
up valve

Lanyard

Waistband

SAILING DINGHY

Elastic control line

Boom

Rudder

Mast

Mainsheet

Standing
rigging

Spreader

Bow

Stern

Tiller

Toestrap

Centre-board

Cockpit

Shroud

SCULLS

Jib fairlead

DOUBLE SCULL

SINGLE SCULL

Non-slip deck
surface

SWEEP-ROWING BOATS

Slide track

Wheel

COXLESS FOUR

COXED PAIR

COXLESS PAIR

Sliding seat

Main deck

Saxboard

EIGHT

COXED FOUR

Wheel
spacer

Forward deck

Hatch

Breakwater

In-board

Bowball

Bowpost

Angling

ANGLING MEANS FISHING WITH A ROD, reel, line, and lure. There are several different types of angling: freshwater coarse angling, for members of the carp family and pike; freshwater game angling, for salmon and trout; and sea angling, for sea fish such as flatfish, bass, and mackerel. Anglers use a variety of methods of catching fish. These include bait fishing, in which bait (food to allure the fish) is placed on a hook and cast into the water; fly fishing, in which a natural or artificial fly is used to lure the fish; and spinning, in which a lure that looks like a small fish revolves as it is pulled through the water. The angler uses the rod, reel, and line to cast the lure over the water. The reel controls the line as it spills off the spool and as it is wound back. Weights may be fixed to the line so that it will sink. Swivels are attached to prevent the line from twisting. When a fish bites, the hook must become embedded in its mouth and remain there while the catch is reeled in.

Keeper ring

Drag spindle

Disk drag

Handgrip

Drag washer

Disk spring

Gear retainer

Dual click gear

Retaining screw

Check slide

Check pawl cover

Check pawl

Check spring

REELS

Spool-release button

Reel foot (reel scoop)

Plate-nut

Click mechanism

Mechanical brake

Side plate

Centrifugal brake

Spool

Handle

Star drag

Level-wind system

MULTIPLIER REEL

Reel foot (reel scoop)

Unskirted spool

Handle

Line

Tension nut (drag adjustment)

Ratchet (anti-reverse device)

Handgrip

Reel

Bail arm

FIXED-SPOOL REEL

HOOKS, SWIVELS, AND WEIGHTS

Eye

Shank

ANATOMY OF A HOOK

Gape

Bend

Throat

Point

Barb

TREBLE HOOK

ABERDEEN HOOK

REVERSED BEND HOOK

EXAMPLES OF BARREL SWIVELS

HILLMAN ANTI-KINK WEIGHT

FLY ROD AND REEL

Intermediate ring

TIP SECTION

Reel seat

Screw locking nut

Tip ring

Disk drag housing

Reel foot (reel scoop)

Butt cap

Line

Drag knob screw

Butt extension

Release lever

Spool screw

Clicker plate

Drag knob

DragonFly 100

Disc Drag

Release spring

Spool cover

Spool-release button

Line guide

ARTIFICIAL FLIES

Handle

DUNKELD WET FLY

Body

Tail

Cheek

Line guide cover

Head

Hackle

ARTIFICIAL LURES

Retaining screw

Ribbing

DEVON MINNOW

Fin

Eye

Treble hook

Swivel

Tulip mount

DEER HOPPER DRY FLY

JOINTED PLUG

Front hackle

Eye

Tail

Adjustable vane

Joint

Treble hook

Hook

Head

Wing

THE MODERN WORLD

PERSONAL COMPUTER · · · · · · · · · · · · · · · · 566

HAND-HELD COMPUTER · · · · · · · · · · · · · 568

FLATBED SCANNER · · · · · · · · · · · · · · · 570

FAX MACHINE · · · · · · · · · · · · · · · · · 572

INKJET PRINTER · · · · · · · · · · · · · · · · 574

THE INTERNET · · · · · · · · · · · · · · · · 576

ELECTRONIC GAMES · · · · · · · · · · · · · · 578

DIGITAL CAMERA · · · · · · · · · · · · · · · 580

DIGITAL VIDEO CAMERA · · · · · · · · · · · 582

HOME CINEMA · · · · · · · · · · · · · · · · 584

PERSONAL MUSIC · · · · · · · · · · · · · · · 586

MOBILE PHONE · · · · · · · · · · · · · · · · 588

GLOBAL POSITIONING SYSTEM · · · · · · · 590

VACUUM CLEANER · · · · · · · · · · · · · · 592

IRON AND WASHER-DRYER · · · · · · · · · 594

MICROWAVE COMBINATION OVEN · · · · · · 596

TOASTER · · · · · · · · · · · · · · · · · · · 598

DRILL · 600

HOUSE OF THE FUTURE · · · · · · · · · · · · 602

RENEWABLE ENERGY · · · · · · · · · · · · · 604

CLONING TECHNOLOGY · · · · · · · · · · · · 606

ROBOTS · 608

HIGH-PERFORMANCE MICROSCOPES · · · · · 610

SPACE TELESCOPE · · · · · · · · · · · · · · · 612

PROBING THE UNIVERSE · · · · · · · · · · · 614

Personal computer

PERSONAL COMPUTERS (PCs) fall into two main types: IBM-compatible PCs, known simply as PCs, and Apple Macintosh PCs, known as "Macs". They differ in the way files and programs, and the user's access to them, are organized, and programs must be tailored for each type. However, in most other respects PCs and Macs have much in common. Both contain microchips, or integrated circuits, that store and process data. The "brain" of any PC is a chip known as the central processing unit (CPU), which performs mathematical operations in order to run program instructions and receive, store, and output data. The most powerful CPUs today perform over a billion calculations a second. Data can be input via CDs and other storage media, as well as via modems. Highly portable laptop PCs are also in widespread use. Most PCs are able to communicate with many other devices, from video cameras (see pp. 582–83) to personal data assistants (see pp. 568–69).

APPLE POWER MAC G4 1GHz DUAL PROCESSOR

Liquid crystal display (LCD)

System unit

Keyboard

Mouse

REAR VIEW OF SYSTEM UNIT

Lockable cover latch

Headphone socket

Modem port

Speaker socket

Ethernet network

Firewire ports

Universal serial bus (USB) ports

Access covers for PCI expansion slots

FRONT VIEW OF SYSTEM UNIT

Carrying handle

CD/DVD drive

Cooling vent

Zip expansion bay

Power socket

Cooling vent

Security lock port

Power button

Reset button

Speaker

COMPONENTS OF APPLE POWER MAC G4 1GHz DUAL PROCESSOR

Carrying handle

Case

Power supply

Cooling fan

Hard disk drive

PCI expansion slots

Video card

Processor heat sink

Processor cooling fan

Modem

Internal power cable

Headphone socket

Temperature warning

Processor card

Backup battery

Motherboard

Legal information

SAMSUNG VM8000 LAPTOP

Liquid crystal display (LCD)

Speaker

Touchpad left button

Power button

Cover latch slot

Scroll button

Touchpad right button

Touchpad

REAR VIEW OF SAMSUNG VM8000 LAPTOP

Modem port

Personal System/2 (PS/2) port

VGA monitor port

Ethernet Local Area Network (LAN) port

Universal serial bus (USB) port

Security lock port

Universal serial bus (USB) port

Headphone jack

Microphone jack

Parallel printer port

Hand-held computer

PERSONAL DIGITAL ASSISTANTS (PDAs), or hand-held computers, are one of the many small electronic devices that began to be developed during the last years of the 20th century. There are two main types of PDA: those with integral keyboards and those without. PDAs with keyboards are larger and heavier than their keyboardless counterparts, which can be easily held in one hand. The latter employ a combination of touch-screen technology and handwriting-recognition programs to receive instructions and data. In order to write data into the PDA screen with a stylus, users must usually learn to use a special alphabet that the computer understands. PDAs are not intended to replace personal computers (PCs) – there is a high risk of losing data if the batteries are not recharged or replaced before they go flat. The contents of a PDA's memory needs to be regularly backed up on to a PC. Besides their basic programs, such as address book, calendar, and note pad, PDAs are increasingly absorbing the functions of other small electronic devices, such as MP3 players (see pp. 586–587), Global Positioning System (GPS) receivers (see pp. 590–591), and mobile phones (see pp. 588–589). Some can also access e-mail and the Internet.

Backlit liquid crystal display (LCD)

Power button/ backlight control/light-emitting diode (LED) indicator

Applications launcher icon

Calculator icon

Menu icon

Zoom in/out icon

Writing area

PALM M500 PDA

Alarm vibrator motor

FRONT CASE

Front bezel

Power button/ backlight control/ light-emitting diode (LED) indicator

BOTTOM VIEW OF PALM M500 PDA

Date book button *Scroll down buttton* *"To Do" list button*

Front case

Rear case

Address book button *HotSync™ connector* *Note pad button*

APPLICATION BUTTON ASSEMBLY

Date book button *Scroll up button* *Note pad button*

Address book button

Scroll down buttton *"To Do" list button*

Writing tip

STYLUS

EXAMPLES OF SOFTWARE

COMPONENTS OF A PALM M500 PDA

GAMES SOFTWARE

BACK OF EXPANSION CARD

FRONT OF EXPANSION CARD

Rear bezel

Accessory locator

Connectors

BUSINESS APPLICATION

MAIN CIRCUIT BOARD

Expansion card slot

Reset button

Printed circuit board (PCB)

BACK OF LCD ASSEMBLY

Underside of screen

Power socket

Rechargeable battery

HotSync™ connector slot

Manufacturing code

Microprocessor

Screen connector socket

PDA MOUNTED ON CRADLE

Power supply to circuit board

HotSync™ connector

Screen connector

HotSync™ cradle provides connection to PC

Liquid crystal display (LCD) circuit board

Connector

HotSync™ button

Flatbed scanner

SCANNERS CONVERT physical images into electronic form, allowing them to be sent over the Internet, displayed on a website, stored on a computer, and manipulated using specialized software. Scanners work by detecting and analysing light reflected from an opaque image, such as a photographic print. Some can also scan photographic transparencies by analysing light that has passed through the image. Flatbed scanners contain a unit, called the scan head, that contains a lamp, mirrors, a lens, and an array of CCDs (Charge-Coupled Devices). The carriage passes beneath the image; the lamp shines light on to or through the original; the mirrors reflect the light on to the lens, which focuses it on to the CCD array. Each CCD detects the brightness of light from a particular pixel (picture element) along a horizontal strip and converts this data into an electric signal. For colour images, the light is usually passed through red, green, and blue filters and then directed to the CCD array so that it can be broken down into its component colours. This information is then converted to digital form. The quality of the image depends on its resolution, measured in dpi (Dots Per Inch).

EPSON PERFECTION 1650 SCANNER

Integrated transparency unit (TPU)

Glass plate

Start button and indicator light

Photo print button

Scan to e-mail button

Scan to Web button

Reflective document mat

Power supply cable

Direct current (DC) inlet

Lock

Inverter board

Lamp power supply connector

TPU connector port

FILM AND SLIDE HOLDER

35mm-slide holder

35mm film strip holder

Shield plate

Panel board connector

HOW A FLATBED SCANNER WORKS

Original image (photograph or artwork)

Lamp

Lens focuses light on to CCD array

Glass plate

The electronic image is converted to digital form and transmitted to a computer

Light beam is reflected from the original to a series of mirrors

Carriage is moved beneath the original by a stepper motor in a rapid series of tiny steps

CCD array builds up electric charges that vary according to the brightness of the light beam

Cover support

UNDERSIDE OF SCAN HEAD COVER

COMPONENTS OF AN EPSON PERFECTION 1650 SCANNER

Underside of lamp housing

TPU connector

LID ASSEMBLY

Hinge

Glass plate

Lens assembly

Universal serial bus (USB) port

Ferrite core

Integrated transparency unit (TPU)

Scan head

Reflective document mat

Mirror

FCC cable

Carriage shaft

FCC cable slot

Finger recess

UNDERSIDE OF COVER

Underside of control panel

OVERHEAD VIEW

Idler pulley

Control panel circuit board

THE EFFECT OF SCANNING AT DIFFERENT RESOLUTIONS

Pixel

15 DPI
Lowest resolution at which you may scan.

72 DPI
Used for websites and screen images.

300 DPI
Used for printing books and magazines.

Fax machine

FAX (FACSIMILE) MACHINES TRANSMIT and receive images of documents over the telephone network. Like a scanner (see pp. 570–571, a fax machine scans the original document in a series of horizontal strips, each composed of many pixels (picture elements). A page fed into the machine passes over a lamp whose light is reflected off the page on to an array of about 1,800 tiny CCDs (Charge-Coupled Devices). Each CCD detects the brightness of light reflected from a pixel in the current horizontal strip of the page and produces a corresponding electric signal. The signals are processed and transmitted to another fax machine, which reproduces the pixellated image as a series of black dots interspersed with unprinted, white areas.

COMPONENTS OF BROTHER T-78 FAX MACHINE

UNDERSIDE OF CONTROL PANEL CASING

Document pressure bar assembly

BROTHER T-78 FAX MACHINE

Liquid crystal display (LCD)

Paper guides

Roller

Call hold button

Handset

Call transfer button

Redial/pause button

Handset cord

Speakerphone button

Telephone line cord

Printhead wiring harness

Rotary dial phone book index and function navigator

Message manager launch button

Stop button

Copy button

Start button

ROM cover

Rear clamshell

HANDSET

Speaker

Telephone "on hook" wiring harness

Speaker

Weight

Drive gear assembly

Handset front clamshell

Handset cradle

Motor

Handset cord

HANDSET MOUNT

INSIDE OF MAIN FRAME

Rear panel cover

Paper tray

Control panel frame

Circuit board

Underside of keypad

Cover stopper link

Spring plate

Power supply cord

CONTROL PANEL CASING

PRINTING CARTRIDGE

Spring

Recorder frame

PRINTING ASSEMBLY

Recording head assembly

Printhead power wiring harness

Head protector

Document pinch roller

Document feed roller

PAPER FEED ROLLERS

Document ejection roller

Paper ejection roller

Scanning unit

Inkjet printer

INKJET PRINTERS EXPEL ink droplets from hundreds of tiny jets, or nozzles, on to a medium, such as paper, to print an image. Each droplet corresponds to a single pixel (picture element). Black-and-white printers use only black ink, while colour printers overprint combinations of the printing colours (cyan, yellow, magenta, and black) to create a full colour range. The printhead containing the nozzles moves sideways across the paper, creating a line of pixels, before the paper moves slightly forward so the next line can be printed. Two basic methods are used to eject ink: thermal, in which ink is heated to form an expanding bubble that expels a droplet from the nozzle, and piezoelectric, in which an electric current expands a crystal causing it to push out the ink droplet. The printer shown here can print digital photographs directly from a memory card.

EPSON STYLUS PHOTO 895 COLOUR INKJET PRINTER

Printer cover

Colour ink-cartridge clamp

Black ink-cartridge clamp

Output tray

Output tray extension

Carriage drive belt

Settings display

Settings control panel

Power button

PC card adapter

Ink-cartridge replacement button

Roll paper manipulation button

Maintenance button

OVERHEAD VIEW WITH OUTER CASING REMOVED

Paper hopper

Head data cable support

Preview monitor socket

Motor assembly

Paper thickness adjust lever

Colour ink-cartridge clamp

Spur gear

Head data cable

Paper output stacker

Black ink-cartridge clamp

Ink outlet hole

Colour ink cartridge

Ink outlet hole

Black ink cartridge

INK CARTRIDGES

PC CARD ADAPTER

PAPER FEED COMPONENTS

ROLL PAPER HOLDER ADAPTER

Attachment clip

ROLL PAPER HOLDER

Attachment clip

PAPER SUPPORT

OVERHEAD VIEW OF CASING

Left edge guide

Sheet feeder

Right edge guide

Printer cover

Preview monitor slot

Settings display

Photo select button

Cancel button

Start print button

Print Mode   All Index One Set
Paper Type   Photo Matte Plain
Paper Size   A4 100x150 100 127 Roll
Page Layout
Select Photo IPF No.
Copies   Far Brighness
Quality   High Normal
PhotoEnhance On Off

Select Photo Brightness
Cancel
Print

Processing light   *Setting select buttons*

HOW A PIEZOELECTRIC INKJET PRINTHEAD WORKS

Uncharged piezoelectric crystal

Ink reservoir

Firing chamber

INKJET NOZZLE

Charged crystal expands, increasing pressure in reservoir

Ink droplet forced out of firing chamber by increased pressure in reservoir

DROPLET EJECTED

Ink sucked into reservoir by lowered pressure

Uncharged crystal contracts, lowering pressure in reservoir

CHAMBER REFILLED

EPSON

The Internet

THE INTERNET CONSISTS OF TENS of thousands of computer networks linked together to form one huge, global network, allowing any computer on one network to communicate with any computer on another. The two main services used on the Internet are e-mail and the World Wide Web. E-mail allows text messages to be sent – along with attached computer files, images, or video clips, for example – to other computers on the Internet. The Web consists of billions of pages made up of digital files that are stored on computers across the world and can be viewed using a Web browser. The Web also provides interactive access to various services, such as banking and shopping.

Sender's Internet service provider (ISP) directs message into the Internet

Recipient's ISP receives message and stores it until retrieved by the recipient

Telephone line

Server guides message to its intended destination

HOW E-MAIL WORKS

E-MAIL SENDER

Screen displays e-mail program

Modem encodes and sends message via the telephone line

E-MAIL ADDRESS

User name　　*Domain name*

anna@merlin.provider.co.uk

Separator　　*Country code*

Reply all icon

E-MAIL PROGRAM

Reply icon

Forward icon

Print icon

Send/receive icon

Find icon

File menu

New mail icon

Toolbar

View selector panel

Addresses icon

Inbox icon

Delete icon

Outbox icon

Message list

Sent items icon

Deleted items icon

Preview panel

Drafts icon

E-MAIL RECIPIENT

Modem

E-mail program on screen displays received message

Computer with e-mail program installed

Mouse

STREAMED INTERNET VIDEO ON-SCREEN DISPLAY

Window controls

Screen

Programme file name

DSCF0005.AVI

Playhead indicates which part of programme segment is playing

Streaming allows video to start playing before it has all downloaded

00:02:20

Volume control

Previous frame

Rewind control

Play/pause control

Forward control

Next frame

STREAMED INTERNET RADIO ON-SCREEN DISPLAY

Window controls

Elapsed time display

Volume control

Programme display

Pause/play control

TV selector

Graphic equalizer display

WCPE 89.7 Classical Radio

00:41:54

Live Broadcast

UNIVERSAL RESOURCE LOCATOR (URL) ADDRESS

Prefix

Page locator

http://www.dk.com/store_select.asp

Main website address

WEB PAGES

Browser menu with navigation buttons

Universal Resource Locator (URL) or web page address

Home page

Rollover button provides links to subsidiary page

Browser icon

Navigation area contains links to other parts of the site

Subsidiary page

Hyperlink text allows direct access to another web page or website

Link to external website

Dorling Kindersley

Back Forward Stop Refresh Home AutoFill Print Mail

Address http://www.dk.com/store_select.asp

Live Home Page   Apple Computer   Apple Support   Apple Store   Microsoft MacTopia   Office for Macintosh   Internet Explorer

DK

DORLING KINDERSLEY

VISIONARY PUBLISHING FOR THE 21st C

UNITED KINGDOM   UNITED STATES   AUSTRALIA & NEW ZEALAND   INDIA   GERMANY   FRANCE

UNITED KINGDOM

DORLING KINDERSLEY   19th May 2002

BIRDS OF BRITAIN AND EUROPE

WIN £100 WORTH OF YOUR CHOICE DK BOOKS

Electronic games

VIDEO GAMES HAVE BEEN around since the early 1970s. They are played on PCs, arcade machines, home consoles, and portable handheld players. All these types of players have certain components in common. They need devices such as joysticks and control pads with buttons for controlling movement and action on screen. The game itself is stored in the form of digital information on CD, DVD or microchip – which may be integral or stored in a removable cartridge – or on an internal hard disk. A central processing unit (CPU) (see pp. 566–567) is needed to process commands from the player, while specialized graphics chips are used to process the complex mapping and texturing functions that make modern games appear so realistic.

GAME BOY ADVANCE

Left shoulder button

Directional button pad

Screen

Outside of lower clamshell

Right shoulder button

'A' button

'B' button

Battery terminal

Start button

Select button

Speaker panel

LOWER CLAMSHELL

Ribbon cable connector

Left shoulder button

Button contact

On/off switch

UPPER CLAMSHELL AND DISPLAY

GAME BOY ADVANCE GAMES

Fantasy quest story line

High-resolution colour graphics

BREATH OF FIRE

WARIO LAND 4

Score panel

DOOM

Left shoulder button

Directional button membrane

Directional button pad

Left side trim piece

Start button

Select button

Game cartridge

PLAYSTATION 2

Memory card slot

Console

Dual shock controller

CD

Controller port

Disc loading tray

Wrist-strap attachment

Battery tray

MOTHERBOARD

Right shoulder button

Memory microchip

Mylar cone speaker

Right shoulder button

32-bit central processing unit (CPU)

Colour liquid crystal display (LCD) screen

Volume control dial

"B" button

"A" button

A and B button membrane

Right side trim piece

MICROSOFT XBOX

CONSOLE

Disc tray

Power button

Analogue thumbstick

Universal serial bus (USB) ports

8-way D-pad

Analogue action buttons

CONTROLLER

NINTENDO CUBE

Power indicator light

Name plate

CD eject button

Cooling vent

Power button

Handle

TV connector

ADVANCE

Digital camera

FOR MORE THAN 200 YEARS, CAMERAS recorded
pictures as chemical changes in silver-containing
substances, on a strip of flexible, celluloid film. The
digital camera records pictures in electronic form.
At its heart is a specialized integrated circuit
known as a charge-coupled device (CCD). This has
millions of micro-units known as pixels. It works in
the opposite way to a miniature computer or TV
screen. Instead of electric signals making pixels
shine, when light hits a pixel it generates a tiny
electrical signal, according to the light's colour and
brightness. The signals from the CCD's millions of
pixels are analogue: they vary continuously in a
wave-like fashion. They are converted by a
microchip to digital codes of numbers,
represented as on-off electronic pulses. The
digital signals are processed and fed both to
the in-camera memory chip, which holds a
temporary version, and the memory stick,
which can be removed to
download its contents into a
computer or television. The
rest of the camera is similar
to the traditional design.

**FRONT VIEW OF SONY CYBER-SHOT
DSC-P1 DIGITAL CAMERA**

- Program mode selector
- Light level sensor
- Viewing window objective lens aperture
- Memory stick and battery recess
- Finger grip
- Flash unit
- Lens cover
- Lens bezel

LENS ZOOM AND FOCUS

- CCD ribbon connector
- CCD window
- Lens mounting bracket
- CCD board
- CCD microchip
- Drive gear access hole
- Locating pin
- Zoom motor
- 09BB
- Drive pin
- Lens inner barrel (zoom/focus)
- Achromatic multi-lens
- Viewing window objective lens aperture
- Flash unit aperture

HOW A DIGITAL CAMERA WORKS

- CCD turns light into electronic signals
- Lens focuses light
- Light from scene
- Analogue signals
- Analogue to digital converter microchip
- Microprocessor
- Digital signals
- LCD screen
- Memory stick
- In-camera memory chip
- Finger grip

FRONT PANEL

SONY
Cyber-shot
3.3 MEGA PIXELS

REAR VIEW

Program selector
Macro button
Flash button
Viewing window
Screen display button
Program mode selector
Lens zoom in/out toggle
Cover for USB and recharger jack sockets
Speaker
Screen light on/off
Volume up/down toggle
Image viewing screen
On-screen menu selector

UNDERSIDE OF TOP PANEL

Shutter button
Display screen aperture
Program mode selector
Power on/off slider

Power on light
Display screen
Program mode selector control
Ribbon socket connector
Microphone

DISPLAY SCREEN AND TOP PANEL CIRCUIT BOARD

Plastic body containing memory chip

MEMORY STICK

Contact array

FRONT VIEW (COVER REMOVED)

Ribbon connector
Ribbon connector
Memory stick and battery recess
Universal serial bus (USB) socket
Recharger jack socket
Zoom control microchip
CCD connector socket
Universal serial bus (USB) plug
Main ribbon loom socket

Fixed objective lens
Dual sliding zoom lens

VIEWING WINDOW ASSEMBLY

INSIDE VIEW OF BACK PLATE ASSEMBLY

USB socket access hole
Image screen processor microchip
Rear of image viewing screen

BASE PLATE

Tripod screw socket

581

Digital video camera

A VIDEO CAMERA, OR CAMCORDER, records a scene as a sequence of 25 still images per second, along with sound. It comprises a camera to capture light from the scene, a viewfinder through which the scene may be viewed, a screen on which the recorded scene may be viewed, charge-coupled devices (CCDs) to convert the visual data into an electric signal, and a means of storing the signal. Digital video cameras convert the signal into digital form – a series of separate measurements of the initial analogue (continuously varying) signal. They record the digital signal on tape, hard disk, or DVD. Digital recordings can be copied accurately, whereas analogue recordings tend to "fade" with each copy.

SONY DIGITAL HANDYCAM

Accessory shoe

Viewfinder

Lock

Power switch

Memory stick slot

Cassette compartment lid

Liquid crystal display (LCD) panel

Battery release

Battery

SCREEN ASSEMBLY

LEFT SIDE ASSEMBLY

REAR ASSEMBLY

Ribbon connector

Power clip

Underside of touch panel

Start/stop button

Power switch

Rear cabinet

Printed circuit board (PCB)

Power supply wiring

Digital video jack cover

Battery lock

Focus ring

Viewfinder

Start/stop button

Headphone jack

Memory stick slot

Liquid crystal display (LCD) panel

Accessory shoe

Viewfinder

Battery

Power lead

SONY

Outer cover

LCD panel open button

LCD circuit board

Ribbon connector

TAPE READER

Tape reading head

Cassette drive wheel

Microchip

MAIN CIRCUIT BOARD

VIDEO CASSETTE

Video tape

Outer case

TOP ASSEMBLY

Ribbon connector

Microphone block

Microphone cover

Shoe accessory

LENS AND VIEWFINDER ASSEMBLY

Focus ring

Printed circuit board (PCB)

Viewfinder lens

Viewfinder sleeve

Viewfinder ring

Lens cap

CASSETTE COMPARTMENT ASSEMBLY

Speaker

A/V jack

MIC jack

RIGHT SIDE ASSEMBLY

Ribbon connector

Memory stick connector

Memory stick

FRONT ASSEMBLY

Ribbon connector

Light-emitting diode

Video jack

Cabinet underside

Video port cover

Memory stick slot

Window accessory

Frame

Cover front

Cassette compartment cover

Super nightshot control

Backlight control

Nightshot control

Photo control

Lens

Recording light

Speaker

Zoom control

Focus ring

Display/ touch panel button

Focus control

Base plate

Handle attachment

Eject knob

Tripod mount

Memory stick eject button

Home cinema

HOME CINEMA REPLICATES a real "movie theatre" with visuals from a plasma wide-screen, and acoustics from strategically sited loudspeakers that give the viewer/listener the sense of being surrounded by sound. The source for sound and vision is a DVD (Digital Versatile Disc). Its player uses standard CD (Compact Disc) digital technology, but with a higher density of laser-read microscopic pits – more than 20 billion such pits in multi-level spiral tracks that, stretched out, would extend for about 40 kilometres. It is hard for the human ear to discern the direction of low-pitched sounds, so these emanate from a central bass speaker, often built into or below the screen unit. The direction of high-pitched sounds, like people screaming and tyres squealing, is easier to detect. Mid- and high-frequency speakers are positioned around the viewer, so these sounds fit the location of the action. Plasma screens use fluorescent tube ("strip-light") technology. Tiny three-cell pixels, each about one millimetre across, contain red, green and blue phosphor chemicals and a gas mix. Where electric pulses coincide for a split second in the criss-cross matrix of wire electrodes, the gas energizes and emits ultraviolet light, which in turn makes the phosphor glow.

SPEAKER UNITS

Small cabinet for discrete mounting on stand or shelf

Large, heavy cabinet emphasizes deep-pitched sounds

Bass ports emit vibrating air of low-frequency sound waves

Acoustically transparent covering allows all sounds to pass through

TWEETER (MID AND HIGH NOTES)

WOOFER (DEEP NOTES)

HOW SURROUND SOUND WORKS

Woofer (bass unit)

Front left sound channel

Rear left sound channel

DVD player under screen

Plasma screen

Front right sound channel

Region of most realistic sound reception

Rear right sound channel

WIDE-SCREEN PLASMA DISPLAY

Mid-grey bezel

Damped anti-shock swivel base

16:9 (width:height) screen proportions fit human field of vision

HOW A PLASMA SCREEN WORKS

Rear dielectric sandwich

Phosphor lining cell

Front dielectric sandwich

Red cell

Green cell

Blue cell (glowing)

Inert gas in cell

Main screen

Anti-glare screen surface

Rear panel

Rear energized electrode

Rear un-energized electrode

Cell barrier

Pixel boundary

Front energized electrode

Front un-energized electrode

INTERNAL VIEW OF SONY DAV-S300

Mains electricity supply lead

Internal fuse overload protection

Voltage reduction and regulation circuits

Power transistors

Power transistor heat sink (dissipator)

DVD/CD drive turntable

DVD/CD laser-reader (within compartment)

Enclosed DVD/CD compartment

DVD/CD sliding tray

Tweeter loudspeaker connectors

Woofer loudspeaker connector

VCR (video cassette recorder) connections

Radio tuner aerial socket (FM)

Internal radio tuner aerial (AM)

Video input/output circuit board

Tuner settings memory microchip

Tuner/amplifier link cables

DVD/CD processor microchip

Display screen and control circuits

Display screen

Control buttons

Ribbon connectors transfer DVD/CD signals

Enter button activates menu choices

Volume control

Access slot in tray for reading underside of DVD/CD

FRONT VIEW

Mains power on/off switch

DVD/CD sliding tray

Vibration-reducing damper foot

Remote control sensor

Display screen

Radio tuner FM/AM selector

Muting button

DVD/CD control buttons

Volume control

Headphones socket

REMOTE CONTROL

Power button

Sleep button

TV power button

Function button

Display button

Previous/next track buttons

Play button

Enter button

DVD display button

Personal music

THE FIRST SOURCE OF SOUND and music small and light enough to carry, and functioning without external electricity, was the transistor radio of the 1950s. In the 1970s, the magnetic audio cassette tape allowed recorded music to be played via portable tape players such as Sony's *Walkman*. Also, new metal alloys permitted the tiny but high-power magnets needed for lightweight earphones. In the mid 1980s optical CDs (compact discs) brought recorded sound into the digital era. Sony's MD or minidisc introduced re-recordable CDs combining magnetic and optical technology. From the mid 1990s music could be stored in all-electronic digital form in a memory "chip", usually in the file format called MP3. These files can be sent to and from computers and via the Internet.

SONY PORTABLE MINIDISC PLAYER MZ-EP11

Disc tray shutter

Upper panel

Battery cover

MINIDISC

SONY HEADPHONES

Earpiece cover

Earpiece

Speaker

AVLS (automatic volume limiter) control

Mega bass control

Access window sliding cover

Central drive hole

Sliding cover mechanism

Lower cover

Central drive access

Write-protect tab

Read/write access window

Upper cover

Micropits in CD surface

Headphone socket

Terminal

Limiter switch

Digital mega bass switch

Ornamental strip

DC socket

Battery cover

Battery case

SONY PORTABLE MINIDISC PLAYER COVER

Lower panel

Upper panel

AVLS

NORM   LIMIT

DIGITAL MEGA BASS

0   1   2

SONY

PORTABLE MINIDISC PLAYER MZ-EP11

DC : 1.5V EXTERNAL DC SUPPLY
BATTERY SUPPLY : 1.5V×1 IEC, JIS LR6 SIZE AA OR EQUIV.
SONY CORP. ソニー株式会社 MADE IN JAPAN
US AND FOREIGN PATENTS LICENSED FROM
DOLBY LABORATORIES LICENSING CORPORATION

〈高温にご注意〉夏季の直射日光の当る所や閉め切った自
動車内、または熱器具の近くには放置しないで下さい。
〈高温により変形・変色・故障の原因になることがあります。〉

CE

COMPONENTS OF A SONY MINIDISC PLAYER

Forward control

Reverse control

Play control

Stop control

Disc tray shutter

Volume reduction control

Volume increase control

Plate clip

Volume reduction control

Shield

Volume increase control

Diode assembly

Reading head assembly

Disc drive motor

Slider release

Laser

Coil base

Sled bearing

Sled gear

Sled motor

Capacitor

Flexible board

Ornamental strip

AUDIO CASSETTE PLAYER

Display

Volume increase control

Volume reduction control

Lid assembly

SONY

WALKMAN

AUDIO CASSETTE

Feed spool

Audio tape controls

Take-up spool

Tape guide

PORTABLE CD PLAYER

Liquid crystal display (LCD)

EQ button

Mode selector

Play/pause button

Memory recall

Volume controls

Power button

Previous track button

Next track button

Panasonic
SL-CT480

AUDIO CD

Centre hole

Protective transparent plastic surface

Shutter open knob

APPLE IPOD

Hold button

Earphone socket

Firewire socket

TOP VIEW

Menu roll-on scroll wheel

Previous track control

Play/pause control

menu

Display screen

Menu selector

Next track control

Select/enter option

FRONT VIEW

Mobile phone

IN THE EARLY 1990S, THE MOBILE PHONE (or cellphone) was still a rare luxury, but by the end of the decade it outsold almost every other electrical gadget – as a professional tool, domestic convenience, and even a fashion accessory. A typical mobile phone has also shrunk in size, due to improvements in rechargeable batteries, which now store more electricity for longer in a smaller package, and to smaller, more efficient electronics that use less electricity. A "mobile" is basically a low-power radio receiver-transmitter, plus a tiny microphone to convert sounds into electrical signals, and a small speaker that does the reverse. A liquid crystal display (LCD) shows numbers, letters, and symbols. Newer models have a larger screen for more complex images in colour, and some incorporate other functions such as Internet access, radio, and an audio player. When the mobile phone is activated, it sends out a radio pulse that is answered by nearby mast transmitter-receivers. The phone locks onto the clearest signal and uses this while within range (the range of each transmitter is known as a cell). The phone continuously monitors signal strength and switches to an alternative transmitter when necessary.

NOKIA 3510

Exchangeable cover

On/off button

Screen

Earpiece

Cancel button

Screen bezel

Number buttons double as letter buttons for text messages

Send/select button

Menu select forward/ back button

"Hash" special function button

"Star" special function button

NOKIA 5510

Upper number pad

Letter keys

Special function buttons

Screen surround

Power button

Call-send button

Menu select up/down button

Liquid crystal display (LCD)

Speaker

SONY ERICSSON T68

Earpiece

Colour screen

Call and select option button

Number pad

Cordless battery charger

HOW A MOBILE PHONE WORKS

Phone locks onto signals from local mast within home cell

Caller sends call signal to nearest cell tower

Recipient's non-mobile phone (fixed at wall socket or cordless with base-set) emits ring tone

Cells are smaller in areas where many calls occur simultaneously (cities, suburbs)

Phone out of signal range – no reception

Activated phone auto-switches to signals from next cell as it moves across cell boundary

Landlines (or tower-to-tower links) carry phone signals to local exchange

Local mobile phone network exchange

Main telephone network exchange

Signals forwarded to non-mobile phone

Recipient's mobile phone emits ring tone

Signals forwarded to relevant cell for transmission

COMPONENTS OF A NOKIA 3310

Rear clamshell

On/off button

MAIN CIRCUIT BOARD

Earphone connector

Screen connector

Screen power connector

Underside of battery recess

Cancel button connectors

Keypad connectors

Vibrator motor

Simm card connectors

Mains power connectors

Microphone

BATTERY COMPARTMENT

Earpiece perforations

NOKIA

Screen bezel

Send/select button connector

Keypad button aperture

Menu select forward/ back button connectors

FRONT FACIA

Speaker

Monochrome liquid crystal display (LCD) screen

Cancel button

Send/select button

Menu select forward/ back button

Keypad button

KEYPAD AND SCREEN ASSEMBLY

Keypad contacts (on underside)

FRONT OF KEYPAD

Contact strip

SIMM CARD

Battery identification

NOKIA

Battery charger connector

3.6-VOLT RECHARGEABLE BATTERY

Global positioning system

THE GLOBAL POSITIONING SYSTEM (GPS) is a network of 24 navigation satellites orbiting the Earth that people can use to pinpoint their position. The satellites orbit at a height of 20,000 kilometres (12,500 miles). A GPS receiver picks up signals from any of these satellites that are above the horizon. It uses information in each signal to work out how far away it is from the satellite. It can calculate its position on the Earth's surface when it has information from at least three satellites. A basic GPS receiver shows the latitude and longitude of its position on its screen. A more advanced receiver shows the position on a digital map. Some receivers display extra information, such the distance that has been travelled and the average speed of the vehicle in which the receiver is installed.

Cigarette lighter adapter and speaker cable

Antenna

GARMIN STREET PILOT III GPS

Page key

On/off and screen control button

Enter key

Quit key

Rocker pad

Menu key

Speak key

Liquid crystal display (LCD) screen

Find key

Zoom keys

Route key

HOW GPS WORKS

Satellite 1

Satellite 2

The receiver takes a reading of its distance from two satellites. The receiver is located along the plane where the two resultant spheres meet

Earth

Satellite 3

A signal from a third satellite defines two positions on that plane. The position on the earth's surface is read as the correct location

Locking lever

Release catch

IN-CAR MOUNTING BRACKET ASSEMBLY

QUICK-RELEASE BASE

MOUNTING BRACKET

Ratcheted base

Speaker
plug

Power plug

GARMIN GPS V

Adjustable
antenna

Power
backlight key

Rocker keypad

COMPONENTS OF A GARMIN
STREET PILOT III GPS

Data plug

Antenna

Liquid crystal
display (LCD)
screen

Memory
battery

Data plug
socket

Main printed
circuit board
(PCB)

Rear case

USB PROGRAMMER ASSEMBLY

Shielded
receiver

Data
cartridge

Universal serial
bus (USB)
programmer

Front case

Liquid crystal
display (LCD)
assembly

Underside
of control
pad

SPARE FUSES

Vacuum cleaner

IN A CONVENTIONAL VACUUM CLEANER, an electric motor spins a fan that sucks in air carrying dust and debris. The air is forced through tiny pores in a dust bag, trapping most particles. In the 1990s, James Dyson's dual cyclone "bag-less" design did away with the dust bag – and the reduced airflow caused by clogging of its pores. An electrically-driven fan creates a partial vacuum within the machine. Air is forced at more than 100 kilometres per hour past a rotating brush that loosens dirt. The airflow passes along the wand and hose to the outer part of a cylinder-shaped bin. As the air whirls around at 300 kilometres per hour (like a mini-hurricane or cyclone), centrifugal force flings larger particles outwards, to fall to the bin's base. The air then passes through perforations into the cone-shaped, narrower inner bin, where a second cyclone spins even faster, almost 1,000 kilometres per hour, flinging off yet smaller particles. The now almost-clean air exits via two microporous filters.

DYSON DC05 MOTORHEAD

Wand handle and brushbar controls

Upper wand

Lower wand

Motorized brushbar floor tool

CYCLONE ASSEMBLY

Air intake from hose

Inner cyclone cone

Air exit to bin/cyclone cover

Hose electricity connector

Hose slider

Bin upper seal seating

Perforated shroud

Bin handle clip

Hose slider seating

Hose electricity supply

Post-motor micropore filter

Filter rim casing

WASHABLE PRE-MOTOR FILTER

Microporous filter

Central retaining screw

DUST COLLECTION BIN

Inner bin fin

Bin upper seal

Bin base

Bin lower seal

Inner bin dust collection area

Polycarbonate plastic bin body

Bin handle

Bin cover retaining clip

OVERHEAD VIEW OF DYSON DC05 MOTORHEAD

Suction reduction control

On/off and brushbar motor control

Hose cuff electrical link

Flexible hose shrouding

Tool or wand cuff

Accessory holder

Electricity connector to brushbar motor

Hose base

Main motor casing

Hinged bin/cyclone cover

Air intake to bin/cyclone cover

Bin cover retaining clip

Bin cover handle

Motor air intake

Wheel guard and flex rewind

Main wheel

ACCESSORIES

Tool/ brushbar connector

Nozzle

Textured scraper

STAIR TOOL

CREVICE TOOL

Wand telescopic link

Brush tool articulation

UPHOLSTERY BRUSH

Flexible hose shrouding

WAND

MOTORIZED BRUSHBAR FLOOR TOOL

Wand/handle connector

Handle connector

Roller

Brushbar drive motor cover

Sole plate roller

Brushbar drive belt cover

Rotating brushbar

Sole plate

Iron and washer-dryer

IN THE DAYS BEFORE WASHING MACHINES, laundry was done by hand – washed in a barrel, squeezed in a roller-mangle, hung on a line, and smoothed with an iron heated on the hob or stove. In the 1880s electrically heated irons were one of the first home electrical appliances. Today's iron still applies heat, sometimes moistened with steam, to dampen and flatten garment fibres. Machines with electric heaters and motors took the strain out of washing from the 1910s. Up to the 1960s, three machines were needed to wash, spin, and dry. Now clothes are swirled in a rotating ribbed tub of hot water, then spun fast to throw off most of the water, before slowly tumbling in electrically heated air to dry – all in one appliance.

FRONT VIEW OF A MIELE WASHER-DRYER

Detergent tray

Control panels

Door

Filter access flap

COMPONENTS OF A STEAM IRON

Steam control knob

Spray barrel

Nose

Steam barrel

Spray nozzle aperture

Spray pump

Spray nozzle

Steam release activator

Nose

Water tank

Handle

Temperature and steam control dial

Soleplate surround

Heating elements

Pilot light

Mains spade contacts

Earth wire

Pilot light supply wire

SIDE VIEW OF STEAM IRON

Flex kink guard

Steam control knob

Spray and steam knobs

Temperature and steam control dial

Water tank

Soleplate

Securing screw mounting

Heel moulding

Mains flex clamp

Mains supply lead

Mains flex

COMPONENTS OF A MIELE WASHER-DRYER

Waste water anti-siphon pipe hook

Drum suspension springs

Water inlet hose

Detergent tray holder

Water inlet valves

Waste water pipe

Water inlet connector

Detergent tray recess

Control panel

Control panel wiring

Water inlet pipe

Drum and door seal

Stainless steel rotating drum

Drum inlet elbow

Door catch with safety cut-out

Door metal cap

Filter seal

Fluff filter impeller

Door porthole

Drain tap

Door wiring loom

Detergent tray

Fabric softener section

Filter screw cover

Hinged front panel

Water-softener dial

Filter

Tray fascia

Water hardness adjustment and filter flap lever

Microwave combination oven

CONVENTIONAL OVENS use electrically warmed elements or a flame to heat food. In a microwave oven heat energy is created by electromagnetic waves produced by a magnetron and led by waveguides into the oven compartment. These microwaves cannot pass through the compartment's metal casing, being reflected within and spread evenly by a fan. But they do pass through most types of plastic, ceramics, and glass. Therefore platters or containers made from these materials are suitable for use in microwave ovens. A combination oven also has conventional heating elements, to grill and "brown" in the traditional fashion, either alone or in conjunction with microwaves.

MICROWAVE COMBINATION OVEN

Turntable rotator

Door lock

Display screen

Control panel

Metal cook/grill tray (non-microwave)

Rollers

Glass cooking turntable

Metal turntable cover (non-microwave)

Metal grill/griddle (non-microwave)

Under-turntable roller ring (non-microwave)

Water molecules spin with energy from microwaves

HOW MICROWAVES HEAT FOOD

Hydrogen atom

Oxygen atom

Each water molecule in food has two hydrogen atoms and one oxygen atom

Microwaves make water molecules vibrate

Friction from spinning molecules creates heat

SIDE VIEW OF MICROWAVE COMBINATION OVEN

Magnetron assembly

Waveguide

Voltage regulators

Wiring loom

Mains earthing wire to case and chassis

Door

Fan electricity supply

Control panel circuitry

Main fan

Rigid metal chassis

Magnetron cooling fan

Voltage transformers

Door safety cut-out mechanism

Thermal/electrical insulation

Low-voltage supply for control circuits

Mains electrical lead

Circuit board plug

Electricity supply to magnetron

High-voltage magnetron supply

TOP VIEW OF MICROWAVE COMBINATION OVEN

Waveguide backing

Heating element cover

Heating element terminal cover

Electric heating elements

Oven compartment casing

Outer casing fitment

Microwave-proof door seals

Thermal/electrical insulation

Overheat cut-out sensor supply

Chassis earth terminal

Voltage stabilizer

Magnetron assembly

Voltage circuitry

Door

Control panel fascia

BACK VIEW OF MICROWAVE COMBINATION OVEN

Main fan electrical supply

Magnetron cooling fan

Magnetron cooling fan mounting

Magnetron perforated heat sink (dissipates warmth)

Mains electrical lead

Thermal/electrical insulation

Fan transformer

Vibration-reducing fan mounting

Cooling perforations for heating elements

Back of oven compartment

Fan dust shield

Main fan (scatters microwaves and circulates hot air)

Rear chassis plate

Toaster

MOST ELECTRIC TOASTERS not only grill slices of bread, they also pop them up when ready. While the slices rest on a spring-loaded rack, electric heating elements toast the bread. At the same time, a bimetallic strip heats and expands. One of the two metals in this strip expands more quickly than the other, causing the strip to curve. As it bends, it completes an electrical circuit and activates an electromagnet. The magnet attracts a catch, releasing the spring that holds the rack down in the toaster. The elements switch off, and the toasted slices pop up.

Connecting wire

Ejector bracket

Time switch

Variable time control knob

Selector switch

Screw

Screw

Switch end casting

Crumb tray

End baffle plate

Screw

Screw

Earth connection point

Foot

Cable entry point

End element connecting link

End element

Baseplate

End element wire guard

Screw

Washer

Mains input lead

Cable retaining gland

Ejector knob

Screw

Spring

Nut

Ejector bracket

Ejector assembly

Plain end casting

Switch end casting

Stainless steel cover

Selector switch

Ejector knob

Variable time control knob

Foot

Crumb tray

Fixing screw

Screw

Foot

Centre element wire cage

Inner cage assembly

End baffle plate

Stainless steel cover

Foot

Plain end casting

Screw

Screw

Element retaining stop

Nut

Washer

Screw

Element connecting link

End element

Nut

Washer

Screw

Centre element

End element wire guard

Drills

THE ELECTRICALLY POWERED MOTOR OF A POWER DRILL, cooled by a fan, turns a shaft at high speed. The shaft connects, in turn, to a system of gears that rotates a chuck even faster. Clamped by the chuck, a sharp bit cuts out the hole, and at the same time the bit's screw-shaped grooves channel the waste out of the hole. For drilling hard materials, many power drills have a hammer mechanism: when this is operated a ratchet in the gearcase causes the chuck and bit to pound in and out as they drill. A hand drill, although slower and less forceful than a power drill, is easier to control. For cutting wide holes, carpenters often prefer a brace-and-bit. This acts like a lever: the bowed handle of the brace moves a larger distance than the bit, turning the bit with extra force.

MOTOR ASSEMBLY

Commutator

Armature

Armature spindle

Fan

Motor case

Field coils

Motor case

Motor case

Spring

Brush

Screw

Washer

Lead wire

Brush holder

Hammer mechanism actuator

Top insert blank

Screw hole

Electromagnetic induction capacitor

Triac device

Chuck key holder

Hammer actuator position

Gearcase position

Screw

INTERNAL VIEW OF CLAMSHELL

Motor position

Lock button

On/off trigger

Trigger position

Washer

Cable

TRIGGER MECHANISM

Spring

600

GEAR MECHANISM

Thrust plate

Ratchet mechanism

Spindle

Gearcase cover

Chuck key

Jaw

Bit

Gearcase

Chuck keyhole

Washer

Spring washer

Gearcase cover screw

Gearcase screw

POWER DRILL

Hammer mechanism actuator

Chuck

On/off trigger

Chuck key holder

Cable

HAND DRILL

Main handle

Turning handle

Side handle

Drive wheel

Pinion

Chuck

Jaw

Bit

EXTERNAL VIEW OF CLAMSHELL

Screw hole

Exhaust vent

Air inlet

Clamshell screw

BRACE-AND-BIT

Quill

Head

Crank

Handle

Ratchet

Chuck

Jaw

Bit

House of the future

HOUSES IN THE FUTURE are likely to be more environmentally friendly and energy-efficient than older dwellings, by making better use of materials and intelligent control systems. The Integer house was designed by Cole Thompson Associates, Bree Day Partnership, and Paul Hodgkins Associates, and built in conjunction with the Building Research Establishment in the UK. One of its key features is a large conservatory that warms one side of the house. Extensive use is made of recycled, natural, and renewable materials and energy. The walls are made from timber and insulated with fibre from recycled newspaper; waste water from the bathrooms is saved and used to flush the toilets; and a wind turbine and solar panels contribute some of the electricity requirements. Many elements were prefabricated off site for ease of construction. The Integer house uses only half the energy and a third less water than a traditionally built house.

WALL CONSTRUCTION

Cellulose fibre insulation

Vertical batten

Plasterboard

Red cedar boarding

Vertical batten

Noggin

Skirting board

Breather paper

Floating floor

Cables and ducting

Wooden boarding

SIDE AND REAR VIEW OF THE INTEGER HOUSE

Single-glazed conservatory

Gutter collects rain water for use in the garden

Composter for recycling kitchen waste

FRONT VIEW OF THE INTEGER HOUSE

Turfed roof helps to regulate temperature

Passive stack vents from bathroom and toilet

Automatic louvres cool conservatory

Small windows reduce heat loss

Red cedar walls that do not require painting or staining

Intelligent electronic door-lock

Hatch for home deliveries

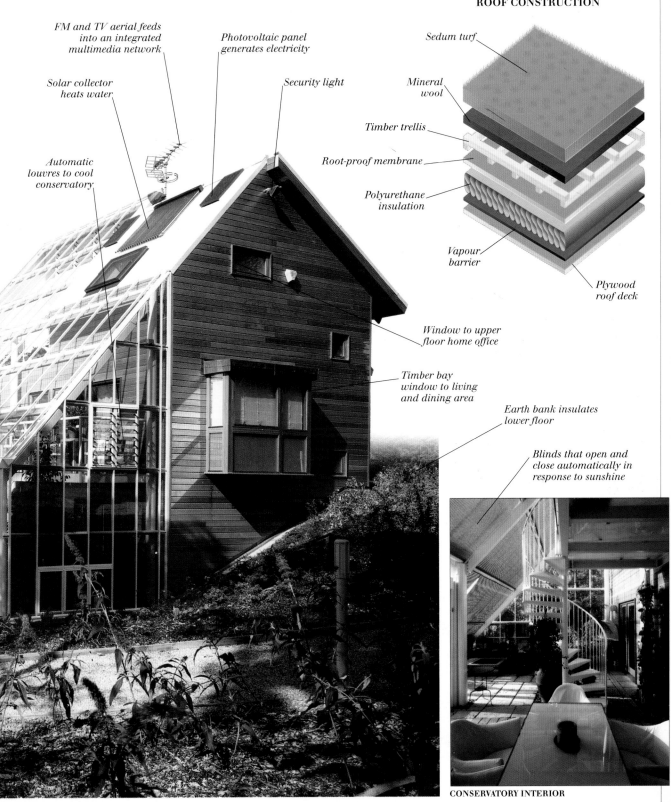

ROOF CONSTRUCTION

Sedum turf

Mineral wool

Timber trellis

Root-proof membrane

Polyurethane insulation

Vapour barrier

Plywood roof deck

FM and TV aerial feeds into an integrated multimedia network

Photovoltaic panel generates electricity

Security light

Solar collector heats water

Automatic louvres to cool conservatory

Window to upper floor home office

Timber bay window to living and dining area

Earth bank insulates lower floor

Blinds that open and close automatically in response to sunshine

CONSERVATORY INTERIOR

Renewable energy

RENEWABLE ENERGY COMES from sources that do not become depleted as we use the energy. When a fossil fuel such as coal is burned, it is gone forever, but a renewable source remains available no matter how much is used. The tides, waves, flowing water, sunlight, and the wind are all renewable sources of energy. Wind and water energy are captured by a device called a turbine. The turbine spins and drives an electricity generator. Energy from sunlight, or solar energy, is changed into electricity in two main ways. One uses mirrors to concentrate solar energy and magnify its heating effect which is used to change water into steam to drive turbines. Photovoltaic cells change sunlight directly into electricity. A cell is made from two layers of silicon. One gives out electrons (negative particles) and the other receives them. Sunlight knocks electrons out of atoms where the two layers meet, separating them from the positive particles. The electrons are attracted to one layer of the cell, the positive particles to the other layer. Electrons are naturally attracted to the positive particles, but to come together again, the electrons must flow out of the cell, through an external electric circuit, or load, and back to the other side of the cell, creating a charge. The cell supplies electric current for as long as light keeps falling on it.

VESTAS V47 WIND TURBINE

Blade pitch control

Blade

Hub controller

Aerodynamic hub cover

Blade bearing

Blade hub

Rotor lock

TIDAL POWER

Open sea

Road bridge across an estuary

Winch operates turbine floodgate

Rising tide passes through main floodgate into estuary

Turbine floodgate closed, trapping water behind it

RISING TIDE

Turbine floodgate opened by winch allows trapped water to flow out to the open sea

Main floodgate closed as tide falls

Escaping water drives turbine

FALLING TIDE

Gearbox

Oil cooler

Generator

Anemometer

Wind vane

Service crane

Hydraulic unit

Electronic controller

Yaw ring

Yaw control

WIND TURBINES IN A WIND FARM

HOW A GENERATOR WORKS

Slip ring collects current from coil

Carbon brush collects current from slip ring

N polarity magnet

Wire coil rotates inside magnet

Wind or water flow through turbine rotates shaft

S polarity magnet

Proximity to magnet causes electric current to flow through coil

FIRST HALF TURN

N polarity magnet

Coil makes half a turn

S polarity magnet

Direction of current reverses every half turn owing to proximity to opposite polarity magnet

SECOND HALF TURN

SOLAR POWER

Anti-reflective coating

Glass

Electrons flow out of cell

Electric current powers external load

Sunlight

Contact grid

N-type silicon

Junction

P-type silicon

Back contact grid

Light knocks electrons out of atoms

Electrons flow back to cell

Solar cell containing photovoltaic cells

Power lead-out wires

Waterproof cable connector

HOW A PHOTOVOLTAIC CELL WORKS

SOLAR PANEL

Cloning technology

IN A LIVING CELL THE GENETIC MATERIAL DNA (deoxyribonucleic acid) contains thousands of units called genes that carry instructions for development, growth, and repair of the living creature. During normal reproduction, half the mother's genetic material contained in an egg cell joins with half the genetic material from the father carried in a sperm cell, to form a unique new genome (set of genes) for a new life. During the early stages of embryo development, the fertilized egg divides into stem cells, which have the potential to become specialized into the hundreds of cell types in a body. Through therapeutic cloning, stem cells can be produced in a laboratory. It is hoped that in the future this technology can be used to grow new tissue that can be transplanted back into the donor to treat illness, without fear of rejection – when the body recognizes a transplanted part as "foreign" because it has different genes, and tries to destroy it. In another form of cloning, performed experimentally using animals, genetic material from a donor animal has been inserted into an egg from another animal that has been emptied of its own genetic material, to produce an animal genetically identical to the donor.

NORMAL REPRODUCTION

Spare cells from egg development

Nucleus with mother's genetic material

Egg cell membrane

Egg cell

Nucleus with mother's genetic material

Polar body (spare genetic material) forms as part of final egg cell division

THERAPEUTIC CLONING

Egg cell with polar body

Zona pellucida (outer casing of egg cell)

Fragments of DNA stain as dark "bar code" bands

GEL IMAGE SHOWING DNA PROFILE

"Plug" of zona removed

Suction through micro-pipette holds egg steady

Gentle suction through micro-needle

Micro-needle inserted through egg cell membrane

Zona plug discarded

Polar body removed

Egg genetic material in nucleus removed

Discarded parts no longer needed

Egg cell provides conditions for multiplication

Zona (casing)

Egg cell

Egg cell nucleus containing genetic material

GENETIC MATERIAL REMOVED FROM EGG

"Enucleated" egg cell (lacks nucleus with genetic material)

Stem cells (unspecialized or undifferentiated cells) collected from donor

Donor genetic material introduced into egg cell

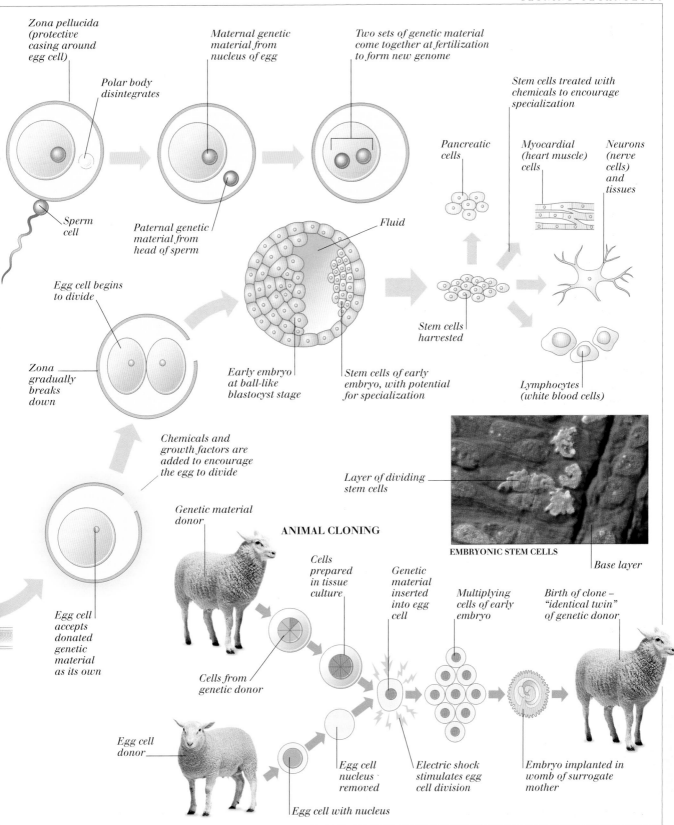

Zona pellucida (protective casing around egg cell)

Polar body disintegrates

Maternal genetic material from nucleus of egg

Two sets of genetic material come together at fertilization to form new genome

Stem cells treated with chemicals to encourage specialization

Pancreatic cells

Myocardial (heart muscle) cells

Neurons (nerve cells) and tissues

Sperm cell

Paternal genetic material from head of sperm

Fluid

Egg cell begins to divide

Stem cells harvested

Zona gradually breaks down

Early embryo at ball-like blastocyst stage

Stem cells of early embryo, with potential for specialization

Lymphocytes (white blood cells)

Chemicals and growth factors are added to encourage the egg to divide

Layer of dividing stem cells

Genetic material donor

ANIMAL CLONING

EMBRYONIC STEM CELLS

Base layer

Cells prepared in tissue culture

Genetic material inserted into egg cell

Multiplying cells of early embryo

Birth of clone – "identical twin" of genetic donor

Egg cell accepts donated genetic material as its own

Cells from genetic donor

Egg cell donor

Egg cell nucleus removed

Electric shock stimulates egg cell division

Embryo implanted in womb of surrogate mother

Egg cell with nucleus

Robots

ROBOTS ARE MACHINES THAT CAN carry out a variety of tasks on their own, with little or no human control. Most robots are mechanical arms used to build things in factories. The end of the robot's arm can be fitted with different tools for gripping, drilling, cutting, welding, and painting. Robot toys have become popular, too. They incorporate sensors that respond to sounds and sometimes touch. Some of them can even understand spoken words. The Aibo robot dog can understand 75 voice commands. Scientists are also trying to create more advanced human-like robots that can see, hear, learn, and make their own decisions. Cog, a robot that has been progressively developed at the Massachusetts Institute of Technology since the 1990s, is one of these "humanoid" robots.

CAR-BUILDING ROBOTS

Welding tool

Vehicle body

INDUSTRIAL ROBOTS

Arm up-down joint

Wrist joints

End effector

Arm out-in joint

Arm rotation joint

Floor-mounted base

KAWASAKI INDUSRIAL ROBOT

SONY AIBO ROBOT DOG

Head sensor

Stereo microphone

Retractable head light

Back sensor

Infra-red distance sensor

Tail sensors

Tail light

Face sensor

Back indicator

Face light

Pause button

Chest light

Foot pad

ELEMENTS OF ROBOT ACTION

CENTRAL PROCESSING UNIT (CPU)

Information from sensors

Information from sensors interpreted by CPU to modify actions

Pre-programmed instructions

SENSORS

LIGHT

SOUND

TOUCH

PROXIMITY

SMELL

TASTE

MECHANICAL ACTIONS

COG HUMANOID ROBOT

Right eye pan motor

Left eye pan motor

Motor cabling

Peripheral view

Foveal view

Left

Right

VIEWS FROM COG'S FOUR CAMERA EYES

Eye tilt motor

Cable to off-board computer

Foveal camera "eye"

Peripheral camera "eye"

Neck roll motor

Neck tilt motor

Sensor signal boards

Shoulder motor

Touch-sensitive fingertips

Torso frame

Sensor cables

Series elastic actuator (for wrist motor)

Elbow motor

Torso roll motor

High-performance microscopes

FEI TECNAI G² TRANSMISSION ELECTRON MICROSCOPE

OPTICAL MICROSCOPES FORM A MAGNIFIED image by using lenses to bend light. Some special-purpose optical microscopes used in industry and research are designed for observing particular materials, such as living cells. They produce magnifications of up to about 1,000. Electron microscopes produce magnifications of as much as 1.5 million. Their images are formed by means of electrons focused by magnetic lenses. There are two main types: scanning electron microscopes (SEMs) scan electrons back and forth across the surface of a specimen; transmission electron microscopes (TEMs) transmit electrons through a thin slice of the specimen.

TEM IMAGE OF A VIRUS

OPTICAL MICROSCOPE IMAGE OF DYING NERVE CELLS

Video camera

Right eyepiece

Filter turret

Objective lens

Manipulator

Left eyepiece

Manipulator

Specimen

Specimen stage

OLYMPUS BX51W1 OPTICAL MICROSCOPE

Electron gun housing

Evacuated column

Condenser aperture

Condenser housing

Objective lens and specimen stage

Objective aperture

Imaging system housing

Vacuum valve

Detector

Binocular eyepieces

Viewing screen

HOW A TEM WORKS

Electron gun

Electron stream

Aperture plate

Aperture creates electron beam

Condenser focuses electron beam

Specimen stage

Specimen

Objective lens refocuses image formed by electron beam

Projector lens enlarges and projects the image

Binocular eyepieces

Specimen airlock

Phosphor imaging screen glows when hit by electrons to create the image

Cooling device

Camera

Screen

Image controls

Mouse

Keyboard

TECNAI

HITACHI S-3500H SCANNING ELECTRON MICROSCOPE

Evacuated column

Screen

Image controls

Vacuum pump cabinet

S-3500H

Keyboard

HOW A SEM WORKS

Electron stream

Electron gun

Aperture plate

Aperture creates electron beam

Condenser lens focuses primary electron beam

Scanning coils direct electron beam across the specimen

Screen

Objective lens refocuses electron beam

Electron detector assembly

Specimen stage

Secondary electrons from the specimen surface

Specimen surface hit by primary electrons

Underside of caterpillar body

Caterpillar foot

SEM IMAGE OF A CATERPILLAR

611

Space telescope

SPACE TELESCOPES ORBIT THE EARTH hundreds of kilometres above the ground, their instruments collecting light from stars and galaxies. Telescopes in space have a clearer view than those on Earth, because they are unaffected by the Earth's atmosphere, which absorbs or distorts much of this radiation. There are a variety of types of space telescopes designed to observe different types of light. The Hubble Space Telescope observes infra-red, ultraviolet, and visible light. It can detect objects that are 100 times fainter than those any telescopes on Earth can see. When this 11,000-kilogram (242-ton), 13-metre (50-foot) long telescope was launched by the Space Shuttle in 1990, it was found that its primary mirror was faulty and its images were blurred. Astronauts fitted extra optics to correct the problem in 1993.

IMAGES TAKEN FROM HUBBLE

Pillar of gas

CONE NEBULA

VIEW FROM COLUMBIA SPACE SHUTTLE

Space shuttle remote manipulator system (robot arm)

Solar array

Axial instrument unit

Central deflector

High-gain radio antenna

Rotating joint

Crew handrail

Aft shroud

Guidance control sensor

2.4-metre primary mirror

Aperture door mounting

Light shield

33-centimetre secondary mirror

Secondary baffle

Aperture

Aperture door

Epoxy resin frame

Crew handrail

Door hinge

Aluminium shield

Light shield

EXPLODED VIEW OF HUBBLE SPACE TELESCOPE

Hydrogen gas emissions

Young star

"WHIRLPOOL" GALAXY

"Tadpole" galaxy

DRACO CONSTELLATION

Newly formed stars

OMEGA NEBULA

"Spirograph" nebula

LEPUS CONSTELLATION

Interstellar cloud remains

Young star – LL Ori

PLEIADES STAR CLUSTER

GREAT NEBULA, ORION

COSTAR device slot

Batteries

Space shuttle remote manipulator system (robot arm)

Space shuttle astronaut

COSTAR corrective optical device

Space shuttle astronaut

HUBBLE SPACE TELESCOPE

Solar array supporting arm

Solar array collects solar power for operating instruments

Crew handrail for astronauts to hold during maintenance operations

Solar array

Aft shroud

Crew handrail

High-gain radio antenna for communication with satellites

Primary mirror housing

Aperture door acts like a camera lens cap

Aperture allows light into the mirror housing

Light shield blocks out peripheral light

Thermal insulation to protect against extremes of temperature

High-gain radio antenna

Probing the Universe

SPACE PROBES HAVE VISITED every planet in the Solar System except Pluto. They take close-up photographs and gather information that cannot be collected from Earth-based equipment. Some probes fly past or go into orbit around planets or moons. Others are designed to land. Two Voyager space probes flew past most of the outer planets in the 1970s and 1980s. Two Viking spacecraft landed on Mars in 1976. The Magellan spacecraft orbited Venus from 1989 and mapped its surface. The Pathfinder spacecraft landed on Mars in 1997 and released a rover vehicle to explore the surface. The Cassini space probe with a mini-probe called Huygens is due to arrive at Saturn in 2004. Huygens will be dropped onto Titan, one of Saturn's moons.

High-gain antenna

Fields and particles intruments

Ganymede photographed by Voyager

Huygens mini probe

Propulsion module

Heat shield

THE LAUNCH OF THE CASSINI SPACE PROBE ON OCTOBER 10TH, 1997

JUPITER AND ITS MOON IO PHOTOGRAPHED BY CASSINI

A MAP OF JUPITER'S VAST MAGNETIC FIELD PRODUCED BY CASSINI'S INSTRUMENTS

Ganymede photographed by Cassini

IMPROVING CLARITY
Cassini provides clearer images than earlier probes as shown by these views of Ganymede, a moon of Jupiter.

CASSINI SPACE PROBE AND HUYGENS MINI PROBE

Heat shield

Hydrazine propellant tank

Lander unit

Backshell

Helium tank

Visible amd infrared spectrometers

Remote sensing palette

Wide-angle camera

PAM-D upper stage booster

Radio-isotope thermoelectric generator

Delta II expendable launch vehicle

MARS PATHFINDER SPACECRAFT

Camera

Solar panel

Instrument package

Rocker-bogie assembly

Attitude control thruster

MARS PATHFINDER ROVER "SOUJOURNER"

Main engines

Lower equipment module

Mars Lander

PATHFINDER MISSION TO MARS (SIMULATION)

Political map of the world

This map depicts the political boundaries of the world's nations. There are currently 193 independent countries in the world – a marked increase from the 82 that existed in 1950. With the trend towards greater fragmentation, this figure is likely to increase. There are also some 60 overseas dependencies still in existence, with various forms of local administration, but all belonging to a sovereign state. The largest country in the world is the Russian Federation, which covers 17,075,400 sq. km (6,592,800 sq. mi.), while the smallest is the Vatican City, covering 0.44 sq. km (0.17 sq. mi.). Under the Antarctic Treaty of 1959, no countries are permitted territorial claims in Antarctica.

ABBREVIATIONS	
AFGH.	Afghanistan
ALB.	Albania
AUT.	Austria
AZ. OR AZERB.	Azerbaijan
B. & H.	Bosnia & Herzegovina
BELG.	Belgium
BELO.	Belorussia
BOTS.	Botswana
BULG.	Bulgaria
CAMB.	Cambodia
C.A.R.	Central African Republic
CRO.	Croatia
CZ. REP.	Czech Republic
DOM. REP.	Dominican Republic
EST.	Estonia
HUNG.	Hungary
KYRG.	Kyrgyzstan
LAT.	Latvia
LIECH.	Liechtenstein
LITH.	Lithuania
LUX.	Luxemburg
MACED.	Macedonia
MOLD.	Moldavia
NETH.	Netherlands
NETH. ANT.	Netherlands Antilles
PORT.	Portugal
ROM.	Romania
RUSS. FED.	Russian Federation
SERB. & MON.	Serbia & Montenegro
SLVK.	Slovakia
SLVN.	Slovenia
S.M.	San Marino
SWITZ.	Switzerland
TAJ.	Tajikistan
THAI.	Thailand
TURKMEN.	Turkmenistan
U.A.E.	United Arab Emirates
UZBEK.	Uzbekistan
VAT. CITY	Vatican City
ZIMB.	Zimbabwe

Time zones

The world is divided into 24 time zones, measured in relation to 12 noon Greenwich Mean Time (GMT), on the Greenwich Meridian (0°). Time advances by one hour for every 15° longitude east of Greenwich (and goes back one hour for every 15° west), but the system is adjusted in line with administrative boundaries. Numbers on the map indicate the number of hours that must be added to, or subtracted from GMT to calculate the time in each zone. Thus, eastern USA (–5) is 5 hours behind GMT.

TYPES OF CALENDAR

GREGORIAN
The 365-day Gregorian calendar was introduced by Pope Gregory XIII in 1582 and is now in use throughout most of the Western world. Every four years (leap year) an extra day is added. Below are the names of the months (and number of days).

January (31)	July (31)
February (28, 29 in leap years)	August (31)
	September (30)
March (31)	October (31)
April (30)	November (30)
May (31)	December (31)
June (30)	

JEWISH
The Jewish calendar is a lunar calendar adapted to the solar year. It normally has 12 months but in leap years, which occur seven times in every cycle of 19 years, there are 13 months. The years are reckoned from the Creation (which is placed at 3761 BC); the months are Nisan, Iyyar, Sivan, Thammuz, Ab, Elul, Tishri, Hesvan, Kislev, Tebet, Sebat, and Adar, with an intercalary month (First Adar) being added in leap years.

MUSLIM
The Muslim calendar is based on a year of 12 months, each month beginning roughly at the time of the New Moon. The months are Muharram, Safar, Rabi'I, Rabi'II, Jumada I, Jumada II, Rajab, Sha'ban, Ramadan, Shawwal, Dhu l-Qa'dah, and Dhu l-Hijja.

CHINESE
The Chinese calendar is a lunar calendar, with a year consisting of 12 months. Intercalary months are added to keep the calendar in step with the solar year of 365 days. Months are referred to by a number within a year, but also by animal names that, from ancient times, have been attached to years and hours of the day.

+8　+9　+10　+11　+12　–12　–11　–10　–9　–8　–7　–6　–5　–4　–3　–2

A R C T I C　O C E A N

International Dateline

+10

+11

–9

+12

+10

–8

–4

–3

Arctic Circle

–1

+9

+10

+10

–12

–7

–3

*P A C I F I C
O C E A N*

+9

+10

–5

–4

–3½

+9

–6

–3

*A T L A N T I C
· O C E A N*

–11

*Tropic of
Cancer*

–10

–5

+10

+12

–10

–4

+9

+11

–10

Equator

+8

+12　+12

–5

+11

–9½

–4

–10　–10

–3

Tropic of Capricorn

+8

+10

–8½

–6

+9½

+10½

–11½

+10½

–4

+11

+12

*P A C I F I C
O C E A N*

+12¾

–3　–4

–2

–3

20:00　21:00　22:00　23:00　24:00　01:00　02:00　03:00　04:00　05:00　06:00　07:00　08:00　09:00　10:00

Antarctic Circle

–3

Useful data

UNITS OF MEASUREMENT

METRIC UNIT	EQUIVALENT
Length	
1 centimetre (cm)	10 millimetres (mm)
1 metre (m)	100 centimetres
1 kilometre (km)	1,000 metres
Mass	
1 kilogram (kg)	1,000 grams (g)
1 tonne (t)	1,000 kilograms
Area	
1 square centimetre (cm²)	100 square millimetres (mm²)
1 square metre (m²)	10,000 square centimetres
1 hectare	10,000 square metres
1 square kilometre (km²)	1,000,000 square metres
Volume	
1 cubic centimetre (cc)	1 millilitre (ml)
1 litre (l)	1,000 millilitres
1 cubic metre (m³)	1,000 litres
Capacity (liquid and dry measures)	
1 centilitre (cl)	10 millilitres (ml)
1 decilitre (dl)	10 centilitres
1 litre (l)	10 decilitres
1 decalitre (dal)	10 litres
1 hectolitre (hi)	10 decalitres
1 kilolitre (kl)	10 hectolitres

IMPERIAL UNIT	EQUIVALENT
Length	
1 foot (ft)	12 inches (in)
1 yard (yd)	3 feet
1 rod (rd)	5.5 yards
1 mile (mi)	1,760 yards
Mass	
1 dram (dr)	27.344 grains (gr)
1 ounce (oz)	16 drams
1 pound (lb)	16 ounces
1 hundredweight (cwt) (long)	112 pounds
1 hundredweight (cwt) (short)	100 pounds
1 ton (long)	2,240 pounds
1 ton (short)	2,000 pounds
Area	
1 square foot (ft²)	144 square inches (in²)
9 square feet	1 square yard (yd²)
1 acre	4,840 square yards
1 square mile	640 acres
Volume	
1 cubic foot	1,728 cubic inches
1 cubic yard	27 cubic feet
Capacity (liquid and dry measures)	
1 fluidram (fl dr)	60 minims (min)
1 fluid ounce (fl oz)	8 fluidrams
1 gill (gi)	5 fluid ounces
1 pint (pt)	4 gills
1 quart (qt)	2 pints
1 gallon (gal)	4 quarts
1 peck (pk)	2 gallons
1 bushel (bu)	4 pecks

NUMBER SYSTEMS

ROMAN	ARABIC
I	1
II	2
III	3
IV	4
V	5
VI	6
VII	7
VIII	8
IX	9
X	10
XI	11
XII	12
XIII	13
XIV	14
XV	15
XX	20
XXI	21
XXX	30
XL	40
L	50
LX	60
LXX	70
LXXX	80
XC	90
C	100
CI	101
CC	200
CCC	300
CD	400
D	500
DC	600
DCC	700
DCCC	800
CM	900
M	1,000
MM	2,000

METRIC - IMPERIAL CONVERSIONS

TO CONVERT	INTO	MULTIPLY BY
Length		
Centimetres	inches	0.3937
Metres	feet	3.2810
Kilometres	miles	0.6214
Metres	yards	1.0940
Mass		
Grams	ounces	0.0352
Kilograms	pounds	2.2050
Tonnes	long tons	0.9843
Tonnes	short tons	1.1025
Area		
Square centimetres	square inches	0.1550
Square metres	square feet	10.7600
Hectares	acres	2.4710
Square kilometres	square miles	0.3861
Square metres	square yards	1.1960
Volume		
Cubic centimetres	cubic inches	0.0610
Cubic metres	cubic feet	35.3100
Capacity		
Litres	pints	1.7600
Litres	gallons	0.2200

IMPERIAL - METRIC CONVERSIONS

TO CONVERT	INTO	MULTIPLY BY
Length		
Inches	centimetres	2.5400
Feet	metres	0.3048
Miles	kilometres	1.6090
Yards	metres	0.9144
Mass		
Ounces	grams	28.3500
Pounds	kilograms	0.4536
Long tons	tonnes	1.0160
Short tons	tonnes	0.9070
Area		
Square inches	square centimetres	6.4520
Square feet	square metres	0.0929
Acres	hectares	0.4047
Square miles	square kilometres	2.5900
Square yards	square metres	0.8361
Volume		
Cubic inches	cubic centimetres	16.3900
Cubic feet	cubic metres	0.0283
Capacity		
Pints	litres	0.5683
Gallons	litres	4.5460

RULES OF ALGEBRA

EXPRESSION	COMMENTS	EXPRESSION BECOMES
$a + a$	Simple addition	$2a$
$a + b = c + d$	Subtract b from either side	$a = c + d - b$
$ab = cd$	Divide both sides by b	$a = cd \div b$
$(a + b)(c + d)$	Multiplication of bracketed terms	$ac + ad + bc + bd$
$a^2 + ab$	Use parentheses	$a(a + b)$
$(a + b)^2$	Expand brackets	$a^2 + 2ab + b^2$
$a^2 - b^2$	Difference of two squares	$(a + b)(a - b)$
$1/a + 1/b$	Find common denominator	$(a + b)/ab$
$a/b \div c/d$	Dividing by a fraction is the same as multiplying by its reciprocal	$a/b \times d/c$

POWERS OF TEN USED WITH SCIENTIFIC UNITS

FACTOR	NAME	PREFIX	SYMBOL
10^{18}	quintillion	exa-	E
10^{15}	quadrillion	peta-	P
10^{12}	trillion	tera-	T
10^{9}	billion	giga-	G
10^{6}	million	mega-	M
10^{3}	thousand	kilo-	k
10^{2}	hundred	hecto-	h
10^{1}	ten	deca-	da
10^{-1}	one tenth	deci-	d
10^{-2}	one hundredth	centi-	c
10^{-3}	one thousandth	milli-	m
10^{-6}	one millionth	micro-	μ
10^{-9}	one billionth	nano-	n
10^{-12}	one trillionth	pico-	p
10^{-15}	one quadrillionth	femto-	f
10^{-18}	one quintillionth	atto-	a

Note: The American system of numeration for denominations above one million is used in this book. In this system, each of the denominations above one billion (1,000 millions) is 1,000 times the preceding one.

BIOLOGY SYMBOLS

SYMBOL	MEANING
○	female individual (used in inheritance charts)
□	male individual (used in inheritance charts)
♀	female
♂	male
×	crossed with; hybrid
+	wild type
F_1	offspring of the first generation
F_2	offspring of the second generation

TEMPERATURE SCALES

To convert from Celsius (C) to Fahrenheit (F): $F = (C \times 9 \div 5) + 32$
To convert from Fahrenheit to Celsius: $C = (F - 32) \times 5 \div 9$
To convert from Celsius to Kelvin (K): $K = C + 273$
To convert from Kelvin to Celsius: $C = K - 273$

Celsius	-20	-10	0	10	20	30	40	50	60	70	80	90	100
Fahrenheit	-4	14	32	50	68	86	104	122	140	158	176	194	212
Kelvin	253	263	273	283	293	303	313	323	333	343	353	363	373

PHYSICS SYMBOLS

SYMBOL	MEANING
α	alpha particle
β	beta ray
γ	gamma ray; photon
ε	electromotive force
η	efficiency; viscosity
λ	wavelength
μ	micro-; permeability
ν	frequency; neutrino
ρ	density; resistivity
σ	conductivity
c	velocity of light
e	electronic charge

SCIENTIFIC NOTATION

NUMBER	NUMBER BETWEEN 1 AND 10	POWER OF TEN	SCIENTIFIC NOTATION
10	1	10^1	1×10^1
150	1.5	$10^2 (= 100)$	1.5×10^2
274,000,000	2.74	$10^8 (= 100,000,000)$	2.74×10^8
0.0023	2.3	$10^{-3} (= 0.001)$	2.3×10^{-3}

MATHEMATICAL SYMBOLS

SYMBOL	EXPLANATION
+	addition
−	subtraction
×	multiplication
÷	division
=	equals
≠	does not equal
>	greater than
<	less than
≥	greater than or equal to
≤	less than or equal to
∞	infinity
%	per cent
π	pi (3.1416)
°	degree
≈	is approximately equal to
∠	angle
∥	parallel to
Σ	summation
u,u	vectors
f(x)	function
!	factorial
√	square root
ℰ	universal set
$A \cap B$	intersection
$A \cup B$	unison
$A \subset B$	subset
∅	null set

CHEMISTRY SYMBOLS

SYMBOL	MEANING
+	plus; together with
−	single bond
•	single bond; single unpaired electron; two separate parts or compounds regarded as loosely joined
=	double bond
≡	triple bond
R	group
X	halogen atom
Z	atomic number

TRIGONOMETRY

Angle A (degrees)	sin A	cos A	tan A
0	0	1	0
30	1/2	$\sqrt{3}/2$	$1/\sqrt{3}$
45	$1/\sqrt{2}$	$1/\sqrt{2}$	1
60	$\sqrt{3}/2$	1/2	$\sqrt{3}$
90	1	0	∞

Shapes: Plane

Two-dimensional shapes are termed plane (or flat) shapes. Plane shapes constructed with straight sides, as illustrated here, are called polygons. They are categorized according to the number of sides they have – for example, three-sided polygons are known as triangles. A polygon that has sides of equal length and internal angles of equal size, such as a square, is said to be regular.

AREAS AND PERIMETERS

The formulae for calculating the areas and perimeters of simple plane shapes were devised by Classical Greek mathematicians.

SCALENE TRIANGLE
A triangle (three-sided polygon) with no equal sides or angles.

ISOSCELES TRIANGLE
A triangle with only two sides and two angles equal.

RIGHT-ANGLED TRIANGLE
A triangle with one angle as a right angle (90°).

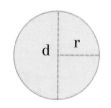

CIRCLE
r = radius
d = diameter = 2 × r

Circumference = 2 × π × r
Area = π × r²
(π = 3.1416)

EQUILATERAL TRIANGLE
A regular triangle.
All angles are 60°.

SQUARE
A regular quadrilateral.
All angles are 90°.

RHOMBUS
A quadrilateral with all sides equal and two pairs of equal angles.

RECTANGLE
A quadrilateral with four right angles and opposite sides of equal length.

PARALLELOGRAM
A quadrilateral with two pairs of parallel sides.

TRAPEZIUM
A quadrilateral with one pair of parallel sides.

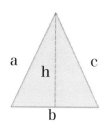

TRIANGLE
Height = h
Sides = a, b, c

Perimeter = a + b + c
Area = ½ × b × h

PENTAGON
A five-sided polygon. A regular pentagon is shown above.

HEXAGON
A six-sided polygon. A regular hexagon is shown above.

OCTAGON
An eight-sided polygon. A regular octagon is shown above.

RECTANGLE
Sides = a, b

Perimeter = 2 × (a + b)
Area = a × b

Shapes: Solid

Three-dimensional shapes are known as solid shapes, and include spheres, cubes, and pyramids. A solid shape with a polygon at each face is called a polyhedron.

SURFACE AREAS AND VOLUMES

Volume refers to the amount of space that a solid object occupies. Its surface area is the sum of the area of each of its faces.

TETRAHEDRON
A four-sided polyhedron. A regular tetrahedron is shown.

CUBE
A regular hexahedron. All sides are equal and all angles are 90°.

OCTAHEDRON
A polyhedron with eight sides.

CYLINDER
Surface area =
$2 \times \pi \times r \times h + 2\pi r^2$
Volume = $\pi \times r^2 \times h$

Height = h
Radius = r

PRISM
A polyhedron of constant cross-sections in planes perpendicular to its longitudinal axis.

PYRAMID
A polygonal base and triangular sides that meet at a point.

TORUS
A doughnut-like, ring shape.

SPHERE
A round shape, as in a ball or an orange.

HEMISPHERE
Formed when a sphere is cut exactly in half.

SPHEROID
An egg-shaped solid object whose cross-section is a circle or an ellipse.

CONE
Surface area =
$\pi \times r \times l + \pi r^2$
Volume = $\frac{1}{3} \times \pi \times r^2 \times l$

Height = h
Radius = r
Side = l

CONE
An elliptical or circular base with sides tapering to a single point.

RIGHT CYLINDER
A tube-shaped, solid figure. A right cylinder has parallel faces.

HELIX
A twisted curve. The distance moved in one revolution is its pitch.

RECTANGULAR BLOCK
Surface area =
$2 (a \times b + b \times c + a \times c)$
Volume = $a \times b \times c$

Sides = a, b, c

Index

A

Aa lava 273
A and B button membrane 579
Abacus
  Ancient Egyptian temple 459
  Ancient Greek building 460
  Medieval church 469
  Neoclassical building 483
Abalone 176
Abaxial epidermis 139
Abaxial surface
  Butterwort leaf 161
  Fern pinnule 121
  Mulberry leaf 130
  Water hyacinth leaf 158
  Water lily leaf 159
  Welwitschia leaf 123
Abbey of St. Foi 468
Abdomen
  Crab 172
  Crayfish 172
  Human 211
  Insect 168-169
  Rattlesnake 185
  Scorpion 170
  Shrimp 172
  Spider 171
Abdominal aorta 215, 255
Abdominal artery 173
Abdominal cavity 215
Abdominal segment
  Butterfly 169
  Crayfish 172
  Eurypterid fossil 79
  Extinct shrimp 79
Abductor digiti minimus muscle 231, 233
Abductor pollicis brevis muscle 231
Aberdeen hook 562
Abies Concolor 66
Abomasum 198
Aboral surface
  Sea urchin 175
  Starfish 174
Abortive ovule 151
Abortive seed 146
Abrasion
  Glacier 286
  Weathering and erosion 282
Absolute magnitude
  Hertzsprung-Russell diagram 23
  Stars 22
Absorption lines 22-23
Absorptive hyphae 114
Abutment 484-485
Abyssal plain 298
Acacia tree sap 438
Acadagnostus 64
Acamar 19
Acanthostachys strobilacea 112-113
Acanthostega 80
Acanthus leaf 460
Accelerated electron 319
Acceleration 320-321
  Electric train 328
  Motorcycle 364
Access door 333
Accessory drive pad 419
Accessory locator 569
Accessory pouch 548
Accessory shoe 582, 583
Access slot 585
Access window sliding cover 586

Access panel 329, 333
Accidentals 502-503
Accretion disc 27-29
AC electric train 328
Acer pseudoplatanus 131, 151
Acer sp. 127
Acetabularia sp. 116
Acetabular labrum 225
Acetabulum
  Eryops 81
  Ornithischian 82
  Saurischian 82
Acetylene headlamp 336-337
Achenes 150
Achernar 20
Achilles tendon 232-233
Achromatic multi-lens 580
Acid
  Intaglio printing 446
  Reversible reaction 312
  Salt formation 312
Acidalia Planitia 43
Acidic solution 446, 448
Acid-resistant ground 446-447
Acid-secreting stomach cell 217
Acipenser sturio 180
Acorn 131
Acoustic guitar 512-513
Acropolis 460
Acrosomal cap 259
Acroterion 460-461
Acroteuthis 278
Acrux
  Centaurus and Crux 21
  Southern stars 21
Acrylic ink 448
Acrylic paint techniques 443
Acrylic-primed board 442
Acrylics 442-443
Actinia equina 166
Actinides 310
Actinium 310
Actinothoe sphyrodeta 166
Action 321
Action lever 514
Active galaxy 12
Active volcano 272
  Igneous and metamorphic rocks 275
  Mountain building 62
Actuating lever system 330
Acuminate leaf apex 136-137
Acute leaf apex 137
Adam's apple 212, 244-245
Adam's ring
  Neptune's rings 50
  Structure of Neptune 51
Adaptation 112
  Dryland plants 156-157
  Wetland plants 158-159
Adaxial epidermis 139
Adaxial surface
  Butterwort leaf 161
  Mulberry leaf 130
  Tree mallow leaf 131
  Water hyacinth leaf 158
  Water lily leaf 159
  Welwitschia leaf 123
Addresses icon 576
Adjustable antenna 591
Adductor longus muscle 225, 226
Adductor magnus muscle 227
Adductor muscle 173

Adductor pollicis muscle 251
Adductor tubercle 225
Adenine 216
Adhara 18, 21
Adipose tissue 215, 235
Address book button 568
Addresses icon 576
Adjustable antenna 591
Adjustable damper 518
Adjustable link 362
Adjustable vane 563
Adjusting screw 560
Admiralty anchor Type ACII 386
Admiralty pattern anchor 386
Adrenal gland 215, 257
Adventitious buds 154
Adventitious roots
  Aechmea miniata 162
  Canadian pond weed 158
  Couch grass 113
  Fern 121
  Horsetail 120
  Ivy 131
  Monocotyledon 126
  Potato 128
  Rock stonecrop 128
  Tree fern 112
  Vegetative reproduction 154-155
  Water fern 158
  Water hyacinth 158
  Water lily 159
Advertising 368
Advertising panel 333
Aechmea miniata 162
Aedicule
  Ancient Roman building 463
  Renaissance building 474, 476
AEG Turbine Hall 495
Aegyptopithecus 75
Aeration zone 293
Aerial
  Frigate 397
  Honda Insight 354
  Renault Clio 349
Aerial mammals 104
Aerial rig 397
Aerial root 162
Aerial shoot 155
Aerial stem 119, 155
Aerodynamic balance 414-415
Aerodynamic hub cover 604
Aerodynamic roof 354
Aerodynamic tubing 360
Aerodynamic underside components 354
Aerodynamic windscreen 346
Aerofoil guard 329
"Aero" handlebars 360-361
Aerosol spray fixative 430, 440
"Aerotuck" position 360
Aesculus hippocastanum 130
Aesculus parviflora 137
Afferent arteriole 257
A-frame
  Concorde 416
  Gliders, hang-gliders, and microlights 426
Africa
  Cretaceous period 72-73
  Earth's physical features 264-265
  Great Rift Valley 60
  Jurassic period 70
  Late Carboniferous period 66
  Middle Ordovician

period 64
  Quaternary period 76-77
  Tertiary period 74-75
  Triassic period 68
African elephant 200-201
African plate 59
Aft anchor 395
Aft door 416
Afterbay 314
After breast rope 387
After bridge 395
Afterburner
  Jet engine 418
  Supersonic jetliner 416
Afterburner nozzle 421
Aftercastle
  Sailing warship 377
  Square-rigged ship 375
Aftercastle castle-deck gunport 377
After compass platform 395
After fashion piece 381
After funnel
  Battleship 395
  Iron paddlesteamer 392
Afterpeak 392
After silencer 427
After spring rope 387
Aft fairing 415
Aft galley unit 417
Aft hydroplane 396
Aft main door 414-415
Aft shoulder 560
Aft shroud 612, 613
Aft spar 415
Agate burnisher tip 432
Aghulas current 297
Agnatha 178
Agropyron repens 113
Ahead/astern controls 590
Aileron
  ARV light aircraft 424
  BAe-146 components 414
  Curtiss biplane 398-399
  Hawker Tempest components 409
  Lockheed Electra airliner 406
  LVG CVI fighter 405
  Schleicher glider 426
Aileron control wire 403
Aileron hinge strut 403
Aileron mass balance 424
Aileron operating arm 598
Aino Planitia 36-37
Air
  Atmosphere 300
  Oceans and seas 296
  Weather 302-303
Air ambulance 422
Airbag suspension 331
Air bladder 117
Air-brake
  BAe-146 components 415
  Schleicher glider 426
  Tornado 421
Air-brake coupling hose 526
Air-brake jack 421
Air brushes 442
Air chamber 118
Air cleaner
  Jaguar V12 engine 345
  Renault Clio 351
Air compression 326
Air-conditioning 496-497
Air conditioning compressor 344, 354
Air-conditioning duct 417
Air conditioning pump 344
Air conditioning refrigerant pipe 344

Air-cooled engine
  Motorcycle engine 366
  V8 engine 404
Air cooling baffle 402
Air cooling fan 427
Air cooling scoop 365
Air-cushioned sole 543
Air data probe 420
Air exit 592
Air filter
  Bell-47 helicopter 422
  Harley Davidson FLHS Electra Glide 363
  Pegasus Quasar microlight 427
  Volkswagen Beetle 340
Air hose 442
Air impingement starter 418
Air inlet
  Jaguar V12 engine 345
  Power drill 601
Air intake
  Concorde 416
  Double-decker tour bus 333
  Formula One racing car 356, 357
  Lockheed Electra airliner 406
  MCW Metrobus 332-333
  Modern military aircraft 420-421
  Single-decker bus 333
  Turbojet engine 418
  Turboprop engine 419
  Vacuum cleaner 592, 593
Air intake box 425
Air-intake duct 354
Air intake vent 341
Air mass 296
Air outlet 356, 427
Air passage
  Lambeosaurus 99
  Parasaurolophus 99
Air pistol 548-549
Air pressure 303
Air pump
  Oscillating steam engine 391
  Steamboat 391
Air reservoir valve 327
Air resistance 552
Air rifle shooting 548
Air sac
  Chicken's egg 192
  Scots pine 122
Air scoop
  ARV Super 2 424
  Volkswagen Beetle 340
Air spaces
  Clubmoss stem 120
  Mare's tail stem 135
  Moss 119
  Root 132
  Stem 135
  Wetland plants 158-159
Airspeed-indicator tube 404
Airspeed pitot tube 404
Air taxi 422
Air temperature 300
Air temperature probe
  BAe-146 components 412
  Bell Jetranger helicopter 423
Air vent
  Bicycle helmet 360
  Hockey helmet 540
  Suzuki RGV500 368-369
Air ventilator inlet 405
Aisle
  Ancient Egyptian temple 458
  Cathedral dome 484

Gothic church 470, 472-473
  Medieval church 468-469
Akna Montes 37
Ala 213, 223
Alar groove 213
Alarm vibrator motor 558
Alba Fossae 43
Alba Patera 43
Albategnius 40
Albertosaurus 84
Albireo 20
Albumen 192
Albumen gland 177
Alcohol fermentation 313
Alcor 19
Alcyone 20
Aldebaran 18, 19
Alderamin 19
Alethopteris 67, 278
Algae 56, 112, 116-117
  Desmid 112
  Earth's evolution 56
  Fossil record 279
  Lichen symbiote 114
Algal cell 114
Algal layer 114
Algebra 621
Algedi 20
Algenib 19, 20
Algieba 18
Algol 19, 20
Alhambra 488
Alhena 18, 21
Alicante 450
Alidade 377
Alimentary canal 248-249
Alioth 18
  The Plough 19
Alkaid 18
  The Plough 19
Alkali metals 310
Allantoic fluid 192
Allantois 192-193
"All clear" position 330
All-enclosing fairing 369
Alley 544-545
Alligator 186
Allison 250-C20J turboshaft engine 423
Allium sp. 143
Allosaurus 71, 85
Allotropes 511
Alloy disc 517
Alloy frame 368
Alloy wheel
  Formula One racing car 356, 357
  Honda VF750 364-365
  Renault Clio 350-351
  Suzuki RGV500 368-369
All-round bicycle 360
All-terrain bicycle 358
Alluvial cone 282
Alluvial fan 282
Alluvium-filled basin 282
Almach 19, 20
  Pegasus and Andromeda 19
Al Nair 19, 20
Alnilam 18
Alnitak
  Horsehead Nebula 16
  Orion 18
Alouatta seniculus 203
Alpha Centauri 21
Alpha Hydri 20
Alpha Mensae 20
Alphard 18, 21
Alpha Regio 36-37
Alpha ring 48
Alphecca 18, 21
Alpheratz 19, 20
  Pegasus and Andromeda 19
Alphonsus 40
Alpine skiing 552-553
Alps 60, 265

Alrami 21
Alsatian dog 195
Alstroemeria aurea 129
Altair 19, 20
Altar 470
Alternating current 328
Alternative engines 346-347
Alternator
　Diesel train 326
　Ford V6 12-valve engine 344
　Jaguar V12 engine 345
　NPT 301 turbojet 418
　Renault Clio 351
Alternator belt 351
Altitude scale 377
Alto clef 502
Altocumulus cloud 302
Alto mute 507
Altostratus cloud 302
Alto voice 502
Aludra 21
Alula 191
Aluminium 311
　Earth's composition 39
　Earth's crust 58
Aluminium alloy backing 346
Aluminium arrow shaft 548
Aluminium beam 560
Aluminium bonnet 354
Aluminium cowl 401
Aluminium flush-riveted skin 407
Aluminium gearbox casing 366
Aluminium racket 544
Aluminium shield 612
Aluminium wheel 406
Aluminium wire figure 455
Alveolar artery and vein 247
Alveolar bone 247
Alveoli 254-255
Amaryllis 155
Amateur rules 552
Amazon Basin 39
Amazonis Planitia 43
Amazon River 264
Ambiens muscle
　Albertosaurus 84
　Iguanodon 97
Ambulacral groove 79, 175
Ambulatory corridor 465
Amelodentinal junction 247
American alligator 186
American beaver 197
American black bear 195
American football 524, 526-527
American squash court 545
American squash game 544
Americium 311
Ammonia
　Jupiter's atmosphere 45
　Saturn's atmosphere 47
　Structure of Neptune 51
　Structure of Uranus 49
Ammonite 278-279
Ammonite shell 267
Ammonium dichromate 312
Ammonium hydrosulphide
　Jupiter's atmosphere 45
　Saturn's atmosphere 47
Ammophila arenaria 113
Ammunition 548-549
Ammunition box 408
Amnion 192-193, 260
Amniotic egg 80
Amniotic fluid 192, 260

Amniotic sac 260
Amoebocyte 166
Amphibia 182
Amphibian 80-81, 182-183
　Fossil 278-279
　Primitive 68-69, 78
Amphibole 275
Amphitheatre 464-465
Amplification
　Drums 518
　Electronic instruments 520
　Guitar 512
　Stringed instruments 510
　Vibraphone 516
　Xylophone 516
Amplifier 520
Amps 316
Ampulla
　Ear 242-243
　Fallopian tube 258-259
　Sea urchin 175
　Starfish 174
Ampullar nerve 242
Anal canal 249
Anal clasper 169
Anal fin
　Bony fish 180-181
　Lamprey 178
Anal fin ray 180
Anal flap 200
Analogue action buttons 579
Analogue thumb stick 579
Anal sphincter muscle 249
Anchisaurus 88-89
Anchor
　74-gun ship 380
　BAe-146 components 412, 414
　Battleship 394-395
　Frigate 397
　Junk 376
　Roman corbita 372
　Square-rigged ship 375
　Tea clipper 392
　Types 386
　Wooden sailing ship 379
Anchor bearing 413
Anchor buoy 579
Anchor cable
　74-gun ship 380
　Sailing warship 376
Anchor chain 386, 595
Anchoring 386-387
Anchor-joint 492
Anchor rode 372
Anchor rope 372-373
Ancient Egyptian building 458-459
Ancient Greek building 460-461, 462
Ancient Greeks 542
Ancient Roman building 462-465, 474
Ancillary drive belt 347
Ancillary drive pulley 345
Ancorale 372
Andamenti 451
Andes
　Cretaceous period 73
　Earth's external features 39
　Jurassic period 71
　Quaternary period 77
　Satellite map 264
　Tertiary period 75
　Triassic period 69
Andröecium 140-141, 143
Andromeda 19, 20
Andromeda Galaxy 14, 19
Anemometer 605
Anemonia viridis 166
Anemophilous pollination 144

Angiogram 214
Angiospermophyta 112, 126
Angiosperms 279
Angle 572
Angle bar 393
Angle buttress 471, 472
Angle-of-attack probe 420
Anglerfish 180
Angling 562-563
Angoulême Cathedral 468-469
Angular mountain ridge 295
Angular notch 249
Angular process 194
Angular unconformity 276
Anhydrous copper sulphate 313
Animal cloning 607
Animal life
　Electromagnetic radiation 314
　Primitive 78
Animal remains
　Fossils 278
　Sedimentary rocks 276
Animal stances 82
Animals 56, 67, 78
Anions 308
Ankle
　Anchisaurus 89
　Corythosaurus 98
　Edmontonia 95
　Herrerasaurus 86
　Human 211
　Iguanodon 96
　Pachycephalosaurus 100
　Psittacosaurus 103
　Stegoceras 101
　Stegosaurus 92
　Triceratops 102
　Tyrannosaurus 84
Ankle joint
　Brachiosaurus 90
　Diplodocus 90
　Euoplocephalus 94
　Human 219
　Parasaurolophus 98
　Plateosaurus 88
　Stegoceras 101
　Struthiomimus 87
　Triceratops 102
　Tyrannosaurus 84
Ankylosaurs 85, 92, 94-95
Anne's Spot 47
Annual growth ring 125
Annuals 128
Annular river drainage 288
Annular tendon 241
Annulet 460
Annulus
　Fern 121
　Mushroom 115
Annulus of trunk 201
Ant 168
Anta 461
Antarala 490-491
Antarctica
　Cretaceous period 72-73
　Earth's physical features 264-265
　Jurassic period 70
　Late Carboniferous period 66
　Quaternary period 76-77
　Tertiary period 74-75
　Triassic period 68
Antarctic Circle
　Satellite map 265
　Surface currents 297
Antarctic circumpolar current 296
Antares 18, 21
Antefixa 461

Antelope 198
Antenna
　Battleship 395
　Crab 172
　Crayfish 173
　Frigate 397
　Global positioning system 590, 591
　Insects 168-169
　Malacostraca 172
　Roman corbita 372-373
　Shrimp 172
　Volleyball net 534
Antennule 173
Anterior antebrachial muscle 86
Anterior aorta 170
Anterior arch 222
Anterior brachial muscle
　Brachiosaurus 91
　Gallimimus 86
Anterior branch of spinal nerve 223
Anterior chamber 241
Anterior chamber of cloaca 185
Anterior crural muscle
　Brachiosaurus 90
　Gallimimus 86
Anterior dorsal fin
　Bony fish 181
　Dogfish 179
　Lamprey 178
Anterior fontanelle 220
Anterior horn 223
Anterior median fissure 223, 238
Anterior median vein 253
Anterior nasal spine 220-221
Anterior petal 141
Anterior root 238
Anterior semicircular canal 243
Anterior sepal 141
Anterior tentacle 177
Anterior tibial artery 253
Anterior tibial muscle
　Albertosaurus 84
　Iguanodon 97
Anterior tubercle 222
Anterior wing of shell 176
Antheridium 117
　Fern 121
　Moss 119
Antherozoids 116-117
　Fern 121
　Moss 119
Anthers 140-143, 145
　Dicotyledons 126-127
　Fertilization 146-147
　Pollination process 144-145
Anthozoa 166
Anthracite coal 280
Anthriscus sp. 135
Anthropoids 202
Anthurium andreanum 143
Antibodies 253
Anticlinal fold 60
Anticline 60-61, 62
Anticline trap 280-281
Anticlinorium 61
Anti-collision beacon 422-423
Anti-corrosion paint 413
Anticyclonic storm system
　Cloud features of Neptune 50
　Jupiter 44-45
　Structure of Saturn 47
Anti-friction pad 552
Anti-glare lens 553
Anti-glare screen surface 584
Antihelix 242
Anti-lift bracing wire
　Avro triplane 403

Blackburn monoplane 401
Blériot XI monoplane 401
LVG CVI fighter 405
Anti-lift wire 599
Antimacassar 329
Antimony 311
Antipodal cell 147
Anti-reflective coating 605
Anti-reverse drive 562
Anti-roll bar
　Renault Clio 350-351
　Volkswagen Beetle 340
Anti-submarine torpedo tube 397
Anti-surge baffle 344
Anti-torque tail rotor 423
Antitragus 242
Anti-vibration engine mount 411
Antler hammer 109
Antler harpoon 109
Antlia 18, 21
Antoniadi 41
Antorbital fenestra
　Baryonyx 83
　Camarasaurus 91
　Diplodocus 90
　Plateosaurus 88
Anura 182
Anus
　Barnacle 173
　Bony fish 181
　Butterfly 169
　Cow 187
　Crayfish 173
　Dolphin 205
　Domestic cat 195
　Elephant 200
　Human 249, 258, 261
　Octopus 176
　Rabbit 196
　Sea urchin 175
　Snail 177
　Spider 170
　Starfish 174
　Tortoise 187
Anvil 242
Aorta
　Anterior 170
　Bony fish 181
　Dogfish 179
　Dolphin 205
　Dorsal 179, 181, 182
　Human 215, 250-251, 252, 255, 256-257
　Posterior 170
　Spider 170
　Ventral 179
Apatite 271
Ape 108, 202-203
Aperture 610, 612, 613
Aperture door 612, 613
Aperture door mounting 612
Aperture plate 611
Apex
　Beetle wing 168
　Butterfly wing 169
　Calligraphy characters 445
　Clubmoss shoot 120
　Fern frond 121
　Fern pinnule 121
　Horsetail shoot 120
　Leaf 136-137, 154-155
　Lung 255
　Moss 119
　Pegasus XL SE microlight 426
　Pine shoot 125
　Snail shell 177
　Tongue 244-245
Apex wire 426
Aphelion 30-31
Aphrodite Terra 36-37
Apical bud
　Bulb 155

Pine shoot 125
Apical foramen 247
Apical meristem 134
Apical notch
　Seaweed 116
　Thalloid liverwort 118
Apollo 41
Apomixis 146
Apophysis 119
Apothecium 114
Appalachian mountains
　Late Cretaceous period 67
　Mountain building 62
　Quaternary period 77
　Satellite map 264
　Tertiary period 75
　Triassic period 69
Apparent magnitude 22
Appendix
　Chimpanzee 202
　Human 249
　Rabbit 196
Appendix orifice 249
Apple 148-149
Apple Ipod 587
Apple Macintosh G4 computer 585
Apple Macintosh PCs 566
Apple Power Mac G4 1GHz dual processor 567
Application button assembly 568
Applications launcher icon 568
Approach 543
Apse 465, 469, 481
Aquarius 19, 20
Aquatic mammals 104
Aqueduct 256
Aqueous humour 241
Aquiclude 292
Aquifer 292
Aquiferous system 166
Aquila 19, 20
Ara 20
Ara ararauna 190
Arabesque
　Islamic building 488-489
　Neoclassical moulding 480
Arabia
　Cretaceous period 72
　Jurassic period 70
Arabian Desert 265
Arabic number system 591
Arachnids 170-171
Arachnoid granulation 237
Arachnoid mater 237, 240
Aral Sea 265
Araneae 170
Araucaria araucana 68
Arcade
　Ancient Roman building 464-465
　Baroque church 479-481
　Gothic building 470-471
　Medieval church 468-469
　Twentieth-century building 495
Arcadia Planitia 43
Arch 484-485
　Ancient Roman building 462, 464-465
　Asian building 490-491
　Baroque church 479, 480
　Calligraphy characters 445
　Cathedral dome 487
　Features of a coastline 295
　French temple 484-485
　Gothic church 470-473

High jump 545
Islamic building 488-489
Medieval building 466-469
Nineteenth-century building 492-493
Renaissance building 474-475
Archaeopteryx 57, 84, 85
Arched brace 473
Arched doorway 474, 475
Arched facade 493
Archegoniophore 118
Archegonium
Fern 121
Liverwort 118
Moss 119
Scots pine 122
Archery 548-549
Archery screen 377
Archimedes 40
Architrave
Ancient Egyptian temple 458-459
Ancient Greek temple 461
Ancient Roman building 463, 465
Baroque church 479-481
French temple 485
Gothic building 473
Neoclassical building 478, 482-483
Renaissance building 476-477
Archivolt
Baroque church 479, 481
French temple 485
Gothic church 471
Medieval building 467-468
Renaissance building 477
Arch of aorta 253
Arch of Titus 463
Arch-plate 493
Archway 493
Medieval church 469
Moulding 485
Arctic Circle
Satellite map 265
Surface currents 297
Arctic Ocean 265
Arcturus 18, 21
Hertzsprung-Russell diagram 23
Area measurements 590
Areas 622, 623
Areola 160
Areole 156
Arête 286-287
Argentina 331
Argon
Atmospheric composition 301
Mars' atmosphere 43
Mercury's atmosphere 35
Periodic table 311
Venus' atmosphere 37
Argyre Planitia 43
Ariel 48
Aries 19, 20
Aril
Lychee fruit 148
Yew seed 123
A ring 46-47
Aristarchus 40
Aristillus 40
Aristoteles 40
Arkab Prior 21
Arkansas hone-stone 452
Arm
74-gun ship 380
Calligraphy characters 445

Gorilla 203
Human 210
Lion 194
Roman anchor 372
Starfish 174
Volkswagen Beetle 341
Armature
Power drill motor 600
Sculpture 452, 454-455
Armature spindle 600
Arm bud 260
Armed sports 556-557
Armour
Battleship 394
Gun turret 396
Ironclad 393
Armoured dinosaurs 92
Armoured seat back 409
Arm out-in joint 608
Armpit 211, 234
Armpit bight 388
Armrest 329, 407
Arm rotation joint 608
Arms of Brazil 394
Armstand dive 558-559
Arm up-down joint 608
Arrector pili muscle 235
Arricio 454
Arrow head 109
Arse 382
Arsenic 311
Arsia Mons 43
Arsinoitherium 57, 75, 104-105
Art deco style 495
Twentieth-century building 494, 495
Artemon 372
Arterial system
Brain 252
Kidney 256
Arteriole 252
Artery
Abdominal 173
Alveolar 247
Anterior tibial 253
Axillary 253
Basilar 252
Brachial 253
Central retinal 240
Common carotid 215, 251, 253
Common iliac 215, 253, 257
Coronary 250-251, 253
Digital 231, 253
Dorsal metatarsal 253
Epibranchial 179
External iliac 215, 225, 253
Femoral 225, 253
Gastric 253
Hepatic 248, 252-253
Interlobular 256
Internal carotid 243, 252
Internal iliac 215, 253
Lateral plantar 253
Orbital 179
Peroneal 253
Popliteal 253
Posterior cerebral 252
Posterior tibial 253
Pulmonary 182, 251, 253, 254-255
Pulp 247
Radial 251, 253
Renal 256-257
Splenic 253
Sternal 173
Subclavian 215, 251, 253
Superior mesenteric 253, 256
Superior thyroid 244
Testicular 257
Ulnar 251, 253
Umbilical 260
Vertebral 223, 252

Artesian water 292
Arthropoda 168, 170, 172, 278
Articular capsule 232
Articular cavity
Hip joint 225
Metatarsophalangeal joint 252
Artificial elements 310
Artificial fly 562-563
Artificial light 319
Artificial lure 563
Artillery loop 389
Artillery wheel 354
Artiodactyla 104, 198-199
Artist's easel 437
Artist's signature 437, 445
Artist's stamp 445
Art nouveau style 495
Arundinaria nitida 151
ARV Super 2 light aircraft 424-425
Arzachel 40
Ascender 445
Ascending aorta 251
Ascending colon 249
Ascraeus Mons 43
Asexual reproduction 154
Ash
Mountain building 62
Rock cycle 266
Volcano 272-273
Ash chute 395
Ash-cinder volcano 272
Ash eruptions 272
Ash head 540
Ashlar 464, 486
Asia
Cretaceous period 72-73
Earth's physical features 264-265
Himalaya formation 62-63
Hominids 108
Jurassic period 70
Middle Ordovician period 64
Quaternary period 76-77
Tertiary period 74-75
Triassic period 68
Asian buildings 490-491
Asian elephant 200-201
Asparagus setaceous 64
Ass 198
Association football 524-525
Astatine 311
Asterias rubens 175
Asterina gibbosa 175
Asteroids 52-53
Solar System 30
Asteroxylon 78-79
Asthenosphere 58-59
Astragal
Church of the Sorbonne 486
Ship's shield 395
Astragalus 183
Astrolabe 376, 377
Astronavigation dome 408
Asymmetric ridge 283
Atacama Desert 264
Atalanta Planitia 36
Athletics 542-543
Atlantic Ocean 264-265
Quaternary period 77
Tertiary period 75
Atlas
Baroque building 482
Horse 199
Human 222
Moon 40
Atlas mountains
Earth's external features 39
Quaternary period 77
Satellite map 265

Atmosphere
Earth 38-39, 64, 300-301
Jupiter 45
Mars 43
Mercury 34-35
Neptune 51
Pluto 51
Saturn 47
Uranus 49
Venus 37
Water cycle 288
Atoll 298-299
Atoll development 299
Atomic mass 309, 310
Atomic number 310
Atomic weight 310
Atoms 306, 308-309, 596
Chemical properties 310
Chemical reactions 312
Periodic table 310
Atrial diastole 250
Atrial systole 251
Atrium
Hong Kong and Shanghai Bank 498
Human 215, 250-251
Sponge 166
Attached column
Ancient Roman building 465
Baroque church 480
Gothic building 473
Medieval building 468-469
Neoclassical building 479
Attachment-bracket 424
Attachment clip 575
Attachment lug 404
Attachment plate 424
Attack line 534
Attack radar 420
Attic
Baroque church 480-481
Cathedral dome 487
Neoclassical building 478, 483
Attic vase 572
Attitude control thruster 615
Attraction 316-317
"A" turret 394
Auda 491
Audio cassette 587
Audio cassette player 587
Audio clock settings 521
Audio software sequencer 521
Audio tape controls 587
Auditorium 479
Auditory canal 242
Auditory meatus
Chimpanzee 202
Seal 204
Auger 574
Augusta National Golf course 546
Aureole 471
Auricle 242
Auricular surface 223
Auriga 18, 21
Aurora 38, 301
Australasia 264-265
Australia
Cretaceous period 72-73
Jurassic period 70
Late Carboniferous period 66
Middle Ordovician period 64
Quaternary period 76-77
Railway track gauge 331
Satellite map 265
Tertiary period 74-75

Triassic period 68
Australian Desert 265
Australian rules football 524, 528-529
Australopithecus 77, 108
Lower jaw 107
Tertiary period 74
Autofeather unit 419
Autogiro 422
Automatic cylinder lubricator 342
Automatic direction-finding aerial 423
Automatic door 328-329
Automatic louvres 602, 603
Automatic pen 444
Automatic Train Protection (ATP) 330
Automobile freight car 327
Autopilot 412
Autumn wood xylem 134
Auxiliary air intake 420-421
Auxiliary generator 327
Auxiliary power unit 417
Auxiliary power unit inlet 415
Aves 188
Avimimus 87
AVLS (automatic volume limiter control) 586
Avogadro 41
Avro triplane IV 402-403
Avro Tutor biplane 402-403
Away swing bowler 538
Awning 499
Axe 109, 374
Axial gland 175
Axial instrument unit 612
Axial tilt
Earth 38
Jupiter 44
Mars 42
Mercury 34
Moon 40
Neptune 50
Pluto 51
Saturn 46
Uranus 48
Venus 36
Axilla 211
Axillary artery 253
Axillary bud 134
Dicotyledon stem 127
Durmast oak 131
Leaf scars 154
Axillary vein 253
Axinite 270
Axis
Azolla sp. 158
Horse 199
Human 222
Seed 152-153
Pine cone 122
Axis of rotation
Jupiter 44
Mars 42
Mercury 34
Moon 40
Neptune 50
Pluto 51
Pulsar 28
Saturn 46
Uranus 48
Venus 36
Axle
Avro triplane 402-403
Blackburn monoplane 400
Bus 333
Curtiss biplane 399
Honda VF750 365
Lockheed Electra airliner 407
LVG CVI fighter 405
Steam locomotive 324

Axle bolt 425
Axon 239
Aythya fuligula 188
Azimuthal map projection 265
Azo yellow 442
Azurite 306

B

B-17G Flying Fortress bomber 408
Baboon 202
Bach 35
Back
Block and tackle 383
Elephant 200
Horse 198
Human 210
Lion 195
Back-board 532
Back bone 222
Back check 514
Back contact grid 605
Background radiation 10
Back judge 526
Backlight control 583
Back line 535
Backlit liquid crystal display (LCD) 568
Back pocket 528
Backrest
ARV light aircraft 425
Lockheed Electra passenger seat 407
Backs
Handball 535
Hockey 540
Soccer 524
Volleyball 534
Back sight 549
Backstay 378, 379, 380
Backstay stool 381
Back strap 560, 561
Backstroke 558-559
Backup battery 567
Backward defensive stroke 538
Backward dive 558
Backwash 294
Back zones 534
Bacteria 56
Bactrian camel 199
Baculum 144
Badger 194
Badminton 544-545
BAe-146 jetliner components 412-415
Baffin Island 264
Baffle 341
Baffle plate 347
Bage, C. 492
Baggage compartment door 423
Bagneux Church 468-469
Bahada 282
Bail 538
Bail arm 562
Bailey 466
Bail handle 336
Bailly 40
Baird's beaked whale 205
Bait fishing 562
Balaenoptera musculus 205
Balance 232
Balance and muscle coordination 237
Balance weight
Jaguar V12 engine 345
Mid West rotary engine 411
Balancing drilling
Mid West rotary engine 411
Wankel rotary engine 347
Balanophyllia regia 167
Balata surface 546

Balcony 493
  Islamic tomb 489
  Nineteenth-century
    building 493
  Renaissance theatre
    477
  Rococo style 478, 482
  Sailing ship 378, 379,
    381
Baleen whale 204
Ball
  American football 526
  Australian rules football
    528
  Baseball 537
  Basketball 533
  Cricket 538
  Gaelic football 528-529
  Golf 546
  Handball 535
  Hockey 540
  Hurling 541
  Lacrosse 541
  Netball 535
  Racketball 545
  Rugby 524, 530-531
  Soccer 524
  Squash 545
  Tennis 544
  Volleyball 554
Ballast 324
Ball bearings 358-359
Ballflowers 470-471
Ball marker 547
Ball size number 525
Baltica 65
Baltimore oriole 193
Baluster
  Asian building 490
  Gothic building 473
  Neoclassical building
    485
Balustrade
  Asian building 490
  Baroque church 479-
    480
  Cathedral dome 487
  Gothic church 472-473
  Neoclassical building
    478, 483
  Nineteenth-century
    building 493
  Renaissance theatre
    477
  Twentieth-century
    building 495
Balzac 35
Bamboo 131
Banana 146
Banded ironstone 277
Banded milk snake 184
Bandy 540
Bank of England 482
Banner 375
Bar
  Musical notation 502
  Relief-printing press
    449
Barb
  Angling 562
  Cnidocyte 167
Barberry 130-131
Barbette
  Battleship 394
  Gun turret 396
Bar code 606
Bare end
  Reef knot 388
  Single sheet bend 387
Barium 310
Bark
  Bishop pine stem 125
  Epiphyte 162
  Lichen 114
  Perennials 130-131
  Stem 134
  Woody plants 130-131
Bar keel 392
Barkhan dune 283

Bar line 502
Barnacle 172-173
Barnard's Star 23
Baroque style 478-483
Barosaurus 82
Barrel
  Gun turret 397
  Wood capstan 387
Barrel joint 508
Barrel vault 484-485
  Ancient Roman
    building 463-464
  Baroque church 479
  Medieval church 468
  Nineteenth-century
    building 493
Barrier beach 294
Barrier reef 299
Barry, C. 493
Bars 516-517
Bar swivel 562
Baryonyx 85, 84-85
Baryte 270
Basal disc 167
Basal scale 114
Basalt 274-275
Basaltic lava 272
Bascule 493
Base
  Ancient Greek temple
    461
  Ancient Roman
    building 465, 465
  Asian building 491
  Baroque church 479,
    481
  Dome 484, 486, 487
  French temple 485
  Gothic church 470, 472
  Medieval church 469
  Neoclassical building
    478, 483
  Renaissance theatre
    477
  Sheet lead 383
  Twentieth-century
    building 494
  Twin bollards 386
Baseball 536-537
Base line
  Calligraphy lettering
    445
  Tennis 544
Basement 483
Basement membrane of
  Bowman's capsule 257
Base of phalanx 230
Base plate 552, 581
Bases 556
Basic movements 237
Basic shield volcano 272
Basidium 115
Basilar artery 252
Basilar membrane 243
Basilican system 468
Basilica of St. Madeleine
  468
Basilic vein 253
Basket
  Basketball 532
  Ski pole 552-553
Basket arch 472, 484
Basketball 552-533
Basket star 174
Basking shark 179
Bas-relief carving 491
Bass angling 562
Bass bridge
  Concert grand piano
    515
  Upright piano 514
Bass clarinet 504
Bass clef 502
Bass drum 504-505, 518-
  519
Bass formation 277
Bass joint 508
Bass notes 512
Bassoon 503, 504-505, 508

Bass ports 584
Bass voice 502
Bastille 466
Bat
  Baseball 537
  Cricket 539
Bat (animal) 105
Batholiths 274-275
Batsman 538-539
Batten
  74-gun ship 381
  Junk 376
  Wall construction 602
Batter 536-537
Battery
  Bell-47 helicopter 422
  Bersey electric cab 342
  Digital video camera
    582
  Hubble space Telescope
    613
  Inverter 355
  Kirby BSA racing
    sidecar 369
Battery assembly 355
Battery box 327, 424
Battery carrier 338
Battery case 586
Battery charger connector
  589
Battery clip 581
Battery compartment 407
Battery cooling fan 355
Battery electronic control
  module (ECM) 355
Battery identification 589
Battery lock 582
Battery lid 586
Battery overspill 422
Battery release 582
Battery strap 339
Battery terminal 578
Battery tray 579
Batting gloves
  Baseball 537
  Cricket 539
Battlemented cornice 471
Battlements 466-467
Battleship 394-395
Bauxite 268
Bay
  Building 468, 469, 494
  Coastline features 295
  River features 291
Bay-head beach 294
Bay-leaf garland 480
Bayonet fixing 352
Bay window 477
"B" button 578-579
BE 2B bomber 404-405
Beach
  Coastline 294-295
  River development 289
Beacon 407, 422-423
Beaded edge tyre 336
Beadlet anemone 166
Bead moulding 459
Beak
  Ankylosaurus 94
  Attic vase 372
  Bird 188-190
  Ceratopsian 100
  Chelonian 186
  Dolphin 204
  Euoplocephalus 94
  Hatching chick 192-193
  Iguanodon 97
  Moss 119
  Octopus 176
  Ornithopod 96
  Panoplosaurus 94
  Protoceratops 102
  Psittacosaurus 105
  Stegosaurus 92
Beaked whale 204
Beaker 312
Beam
  BAe-146 jetliner 414
  Gothic church 473

High-tension 496
  Iron paddlesteamer 393
  Modern building 497-
    499
  Nineteenth-century
    building 492
  Single skull 560
Bean
  Black 153
  Broad 152
Bear 104, 106, 194-195
Bearing
  Electric generator 317
  Jaguar V12 engine 345
  Motorcycle gearbox 366
  Rotary engine output
    shaft 411
Bearing assembly 425
Bearing housing 344
Bearing mount 411
Bearing seal 359
Bearing sleeve 338
"Beast feet" 84
Beaten gold 432
Beaters 516, 518-519
Beats 502
Beaver 196-197
Becket 383
Becket Chapel 467
Bed
  Relief printing press
    449
  Sedimentary rocks 276
Bedding plane
  Cave system 285
  Coastline 294-295
Bedford cord upholstery
  336
Bedplate 390
Bedrock 298
  Delta formation 291
Bee 168, 379
Bee hummingbird 193
Bee pollination 144-145
Beeswax 384
Beethoven 35
Beetle 168
Begonia 129, 155
Begonia x tuberhybrida
  129, 155
Behaviour 108, 237
Belaying pin 382
Belemnites 71, 278-279
Belfry
  74-gun ship 380
  Church of St. George in
    the East 481
Bell 508
Bell 206 Jetranger 423
Bell 47G-3B1 422-423
Bellatrix 18
Bell chamber 493
Bell crank 591
Bell housing 347
Bell joint 508
Bello 35
Bell Regio
  Radar map of Venus 36
  Structure of Venus 37
Belly
  Bird 188
  Caiman 186
  Dolphin 204
  Elephant 201
  Horse 198
  Lion 195
  Lizard 184
  Sail 384
  Viola 511
  Violin 510
Belly-band 555
Belt
  Jupiter 44-45
  Structure of Saturn 47
Belt armour 394
Belt colour 556
Belt drive 366
Belt pulley 345
Belt tensioner 344, 364

Belvedere 476
Bench officials
  Ice hockey 550
  Lacrosse 541
Bending 318
Bends 387
Benguela current 297
  Satellite map 264
Benz, Karl 334
Benz Motorwagen 335
Benz six-cylinder engine
  405
Berardius bairdii 205
Berberis sp. 130-131
Berkelium 311
Berries 148-149
Beryl 270
Beryllium 310
Beta Hydri 20
Beta Mensae 20
Beta Pictoris 21
Beta ring 48
Betelgeuse 18, 21
  Hertzsprung-Russell
    diagram 23
  Orion 18
  Universe 10-11
Betula grossa 74
Betula lenta 76
Betulites 74
Bevel gear 335
Bevel pinion 338
Beverley Minster 484
Bezel 584
Bhagirathi Parbat 62
Bianco di San Giovanni
  434-435
Biathlon rifle 549
Bib 568
Bi-block engine 337
Biceps brachii muscle 226
Biceps femoris muscle
  227
Bicycle 360-361
Bicycle anatomy 358-359
Bicycle riding 315
Biennials 128
Biflagellate cell 116
Bifurcate ligament 252
"Big Ben" 493
Bighorn rifle shooting
  548-549
Big end
  Flat-four cylinder
    arrangement 340
  Four-stroke cycle 343
  Jaguar straight six
    engine 344
  Mid West engine 410
  Trojan engine 342
Big-end bearing 355
Big toe 232-233
Bile duct 189, 249
Bilge keel 595, 397
Bilge keelson 393
Bill
  Danforth anchor 386
  Running block 383
  Sail hook 384
Bilobed leaves 123
Bin base 592
Bin cover handle 593
Bin cover retaining clip
  592, 593
Binder 464
Binder bolt 361
Binding 383
  Acoustic guitar 512
  Iron paddlesteamer 392
Binding medium 440
Bin handle 592
Bin handle clip 592
Bin lower seal 592
Binnacle box 378
Binocular eyepieces 610,
  611

Bin upper seal 592
Bin upper seal seating 592
Biology symbols 591, 621
Bipedal dinosaur 84, 96,
  100
Bipinnate leaf 137
Biplane elevator 398-399
Biplanes 402-403, 408
Bipolar neuron 239
Birch 74, 76
Bird 84, 188-191
  Beak 190
  Earth's evolution 57
  Feathers 191
  Feet 190
  Fossil record 279
  Wing 191
"Bird feet" 96
Bird-hipped dinosaur 82,
  92, 96
Bird of prey 188
Bird pollination 144
Bishop pine 124-125
Bismuth 281, 311
Bit 601
Biternate leaves 137
Bit-guard 555
Bitt
  74-gun ship 380-381
  Roman corbita 373
Bitter end, Hawser 387
Bituminous coal 280
Bivalves 79, 176, 278-279
Blackbacked gull 193
Black bean 153
Black belt 556
Blackberry 130, 146-147
Blackburn monoplane
  400-401
Blackburn, Robert 400
Black dwarf 24-25
Blackheaded gull 189
Black ink cartridge 574
Black ink-cartridge clamp
  574
Black holes 28-29
  Galaxies 12
  Massive stars 26-27
Black Mesa 277
Black rhinoceros 199
Black Sea 265
Blackstonia perfoliata 144
Black walnut 137
Black widow spider 171
Bladder
  Bony fish 181
  Chimpanzee 202
  Dolphin 205
  Domestic cat 195
  Elephant 200
  Human 215, 257, 258-
    259, 261
  Lizard 185
  Rabbit 196
  Soccer ball 525
  Swim 178, 180-181
  Tortoise 187
  Urinary 181
Bladder wrack 117
Blade
  Butterwort 161
  Calligraphy drawing
    board 445
  Danforth anchor 386
  Dicotyledon leaf 127
  Fencing foil 557
  Golf clubs 547
  Hockey stick 540
  Kayak paddle 560
  Leaf surfaces 136, 138
  Monocotyledon leaf 127
  Propeller 390
  Roman rudder 373
  Sculling oar 560
  Seaweed 116-117
  Vegetative reproduction
    154
  Venus fly trap 160
  Volkswagen Beetle 341

Wetland plants 158-159
Wind turbine 604
Blade bearing 604
Blade counterweight 406, 422
Blade hub 604
Blade pitch control 604
Blade-root attachment 422-423
Blade tip sealing shroud 419
Blanking plate 411
Blast bag 396
Blastocyst 607
Blast-pipe 325
Blending 440
Blériot XI monoplane 401
Blériot, Louis
    Early monoplane 400
    Pioneers of flight 398
Blindage 377
Blind arch
    Asian building 491
    Cathedral dome 487
    Gothic church 470
Blind door 478
Blind pull 336-337
Blind release bar 552
Blinds 603
Blind-side prop 530
Blind spot 241
Blind tracery 493
Blind trefoil 473
Blind window 478
Block and tackle 382-383
Block carving 470
Block cube 270
Block disintegration 282
Block-fault lake 293
Block-fault mountain 62
Blocking pad 550
Blocks 310
Blood cells 253
Blood clotting 253
Blower control 325
Blower isolator valve 325
Blow hole 508
Blowhole 205
Blubber 204
Blue-and-yellow macaw 190
Blue cell 584
Blue-green alga 56, 78
Blue light 318
Blue line 550
Blue supergiant star
    Hertzsprung-Russell diagram 23
    Stellar black hole 29
Blue whale 204-205
Bluff 289
Blunt button 556-557
BMW R/60 motorcycle 362
Board
    Ice hockey rink 550
    Modelling 455
    Pastels 441
Boarding 464
Board mounting 450-451
Boat boom 395
Boatbuilder's tools 374
Boat handling derrick 395
Boat slide 378
Boat winch 394
Bobstay 379
Body
    Anchisaurus 89
    Discus 542
    Dunkeld wet fly 563
    Motorcycle 364-365
    Sauropodomorpha 88
    Stringed instruments 510
Body-bag 426
Body cells 216-217
Body cradle 398
Body drop 556
Body joint
    Flute 508

Piccolo 508
Body mount 338
Body organs 214-215
Body padding 526
Body sections
    Insect 168
    Scorpion 170
    Spider 170-171
Body-shell 518-519
Bodyshell
    Renault Clio 348-349
    Volkswagen Beetle 341
Body tackles 528
Body temperature regulation
    Dinosaurs 92
    Mammals 104
Body wire 557
Bodywork 348-349
    Racing cars 356
    Volkswagen Beetle 341
Bodywork mounting point 364
Boeing 747-400 412
Bogie axle 326
Bogie frame 325
Bogie main landing gear 416
Boiler
    Box boiler 392
    Donkey boiler 392
    Steamboat with paddle wheels 392
    Steam locomotives 324-325
Boiler pressure gauge 325
Boiler water level 325
Bole base 432-433
Bollard
    Battleship 395
    Frigate 397
    Mooring and anchoring 386-387
Bolson 282
Bolster 378
Bolt
    Church of St. Pierre 499
    Lower deadeye 383
    Shackle 386
    Toaster 598
Bolted anchor 425
Bolt hole
    Drum brake 365
    Mid West rotary engine 411
    Twin bollards 387
Bolt rest 548
Bolt rope 372, 384
Bolts 548-549
Bomb 404, 408
Bomb aimer's viewing panel 408
Bomb door 408
Bomber
    Modern military aircraft 420
    World War I aircraft 404-405
    World War II aircraft 408-409
Bomb rack 404
Bonaventure mast 377
Bonaventure topcastle 377
Bonaventure topmast 377
Bonaventure top yard 377
Bonaventure yard 377
Bonded brick wall 492
Bonding
    Chemical reactions 312
    Covalent 309
    English bond 485
    Gases 307
    Ionic 308
    Liquids 307
Bone cell 217, 225
Bone marrow smear 225
Bones
    Fossil 278

Human 224-225, 230, 232
Bone structure 108
Bone surface 80
Bonnet
    1906 Renault 337
    Ford Model T 339
    Renault Clio 349
    Volkswagen Beetle 340-341
Bonnet catch 336, 349
Bonnet clip 339
Bonnet-release cable 349
Bonnet-release handle 341
Bonnet stay 337
Bony crest
    Baryonyx 83
    Corythosaurus 98
    Lambeosaurus 99
    Parasaurolophus 99
Bony dorsal shield 78
Bony fish 180-181
Bony frill 100
Bony nodule
    Pachycephalosaurus 100
    Prenocephale 100
Bony ridge 100
Bony shelf 100, 101
Bony spike 100
Bony strut 83
Bony studs 91
Bony tendons 96
Boom
    Battleship 394-395
    Curtiss Model-D pusher 399
    Double topsail schooner 385
    Guest boat boom 394
    Hong Kong and Shanghai Bank 498
    Longboat 380
    Rigging 382
    Sailing dinghy 561
Boom guy block 382
Boomkin 380
Boötes 18, 21
Boots
    American football 527
    Baseball 557
    Hurling 541
    Riding 554
    Rugby 551
    Sailing 560
    Ski 552
    Soccer 525
Bordino Steam Carriage 334-335
Borealis Planitia 35
Borneo 265
Boron 311
Boss
    Church roof 468-469
    Hurley 541
    Viking karv 374
Bothriolepis 65
Botryoidal habit 270-271
Bottom ballast 377
Bottom bracket 358
Bottom hose 351
Bottom plate 390, 592-593
Bottom race 359
Bottomset strata 283
Boudin 60-61
Boulder beach 295
Boulder clay 286
Bounce pass 535
Boundary
    Cricket 538
    Mantle-crust 39
    Outer core-mantle 39
Boundary line
    Australian rules football 528
    Badminton 545
    Cricket 538
    Squash 545

Bow
    74-gun ship 381
    Kayak 560
    Sailing dinghy 561
    Stringed instruments 510
    Wooden sailing ship 378
Bowball 561
Bow drill 109
Bower anchor
    Battleship 395
    Sailing warship 377
    Wooden sailing ship 379
Bow front 483
Bowl 445
Bowline 388, 389
Bowling crease 538
Bowman's capsule 256
Bowman's space 257
Bow ornament 375
Bowpost 561
Bowsprit cap 382
Bowtell moulding 475
Box 477
Box boiler 392
Box fold 61
Box freight car 327
Boxing 556
Box-leaved milkwort 144
Box-section tubular cradle frame 364
Box sister keelson 393
Boxwood staff 377
Brace
    Asian building 490
    Barrel vault 485
    Dome 486
    Double topsail schooner 385
    "Ellerman Lines" steam locomotive 324
    Gothic building 473
    Neoclassical building 479
    Nineteenth-century building 493
    Roman corbita 372
    Sailing warship 377
    Trombone 506
    Wooden sailing ship 378
Brace-and-bit 600-601
Brace block 573
Bracer 548
Brachial artery 253
Brachialis muscle 226
Brachial plexus 238
Brachial valve 278
Brachiocephalic trunk 251
Brachiocephalic vein 253
Brachiopods 278-279
Brachioradialis muscle 226
Brachiosaurus 88, 90-91
Brachylophosaurus 98
Bracing 513
Bracing cable 427
Bracing strut 401-402, 423
Bracing tube 364
Bracing wire
    Blériot XI monoplane 401
    LVG CVI fighter 405
    Wright Flyer 399
Bracken 121

Bracket
    Baroque church 479
    Cathedral dome 484
    Gothic building 473
    Islamic tomb 489
    Medieval building 466
    Neoclassical building 478
    Renaissance building 475
Bracket shell 58
Bracteoles
    Dehiscent fruit 151
    Ice-plant 129
    Live-for-ever 129
Bracts 141-143
    Bromeliad 113
    Dicotyledon flower 127
    Durmast oak 131
    Florists' chrysanthemum 129
    Guzmania lingulata 163
    Ice-plant 129
    Indehiscent fruit 150
    Live-for-ever 129
    Peruvian lily 129
    Rose 131
    Slender thistle 129
    Wind-pollinated plant 144
Bract scales 122
Braided polyester 388
Braided stream 286
Braiding
    Dragon prowhead 374
    River features 290
Brailing rope 372
Brail line 372
Brain
    Bird 189
    Bony fish 181
    Butterfly 169
    Chimpanzee 202
    Crayfish 173
    Dogfish 179
    Dolphin 205
    Domestic cat 195
    Elephant 200
    Hominid 108
    Human 236-237
    Lizard 185
    Octopus 176
    Rabbit 196
    Spider 170
Braincase 108
Brain cavity 100
Brainstem 236
Brake 332, 350
Brake actuating chain 327
Brake arm 552
Brake back plate 340, 350
Brake block 560
Brake bridge 361
Brake cable 365
Brake calliper
    ARV light aircraft 424
    Disc brake 365
    Harley-Davidson FLHS Electra Glide 363
    Honda VF750 364-365
    Husqvarna Motocross TC610 368
    Renault Clio 351
    Suzuki RGV500 368-369
    Wagon bogie 331
Brake cylinder 327, 550-351
Brake disc
    ARV light aircraft 424
    Renault Clio 351
    Wagon bogie 331
Brake drum 339-340, 342
Brake duct 357
Brake fluid 365
Brake hose 351
Brakeless wheel hub 369
Brake lever
    ARV light aircraft 425

Benz Motorwagen 335
Bicycle 359
Eddy Merckx racing bicycle 361
Harley-Davidson FLHS Electra Glide 363
Kirby BSA 369
Suzuki RGV500 369
White Steam Car 342
"Windcheetah" racing HPV bicycle 561
Brake master cylinder
    Harley-Davidson FLHS Electra Glide 363
    Honda VF750 364
    Suzuki RGV500 368
Brake mount 424
Brake pad
    Disc brake 365
    Eddy Merckx racing bicycle 361
    Renault Clio 351
    Wagon bogie 331
Brake pedal
    Harley-Davidson FLHS Electra Glide 363
    Honda VF750 364
    Oldsmobile bodywork 337
    Renault Clio 350
    Steam-powered Cugnot 334
    Suzuki RGV500 368
Brake pipe
    ARV light aircraft 424
    BAe-146 components 414
    Lockheed Electra airliner 406-407
Brake pivot bolt 361
Brake plate 365
Brake quadrant 335
Brake rigging
    British Rail Class 20 diesel engine 327
    "Ellerman Lines" steam locomotive 324-325
Brake rod 337, 339
Brake servo 351
Brake shield 351
Brake shoe 330
    "Deltic" diesel-electric locomotive 327
    Drum brake 365
    "Ellerman Lines" steam locomotive 325
    Renault Clio 350
Brake slip 395
Brake torque arm 564
Brake vacuum pump 324
Braking
    Motorcycle 364
    Train 330
Braking control system 330
Braking distance 331
Bramante 35
Bramble 130, 146-147
Branched leaf venation 127
Branches
    Bishop pine 124
    Clubmoss 120
    Crab cactus 129
    Dicotyledons 127
    Horsetail 120
    Perennials 130-131
    Seaweed 117
    Sporophore 114
    Woody plants 130-131
Branchial heart 176
Branching bracteole 151
Branchiostegal ray 181
Branchlet 114
Branch trace 125
Brassavola nodosa 162
Brass bevel 336-337
Brass housing for ignition cable 343

Brassica sp. 132
Brass instruments 504-505, 506-507
Brazil 331
Brazilian battleship 394-395
Brazilian current 296
Brazilian Highlands 264
Bread 598
Breakfast-room 483
Breakwater
  Battleship 395
  Frigate 397
  Single scull 561
Breast
  Bird 188
  Horse 199
  Human 211
Breast auger 374
Breast bone 218
Breast stroke 558-559
Breastwork 380
Breather paper 602
Breather pipe 422
Breccia 276-277
Breech 396
Breech block 396
Breeches 557
Breech wheel 396
Breve rest 502
Brick arch 524
Brick pier 495
Brick vault 492
Brick wall 492
Bridge
  Acoustic guitar 512-513
  Battleship 394-395
  Cello 511
  Double bass 511
  Electric guitar 513
  Frigate 397
  Golf course 546
  London Bridge 466-467
  Medieval castle 467
  Modern building 498
  Viola 511
  Violin 510
Bridge pin 512
Bridges 330
Bridle 555
Bright Angel shale 277
B ring 46-47
Britain 331
Brittle stars 174-175
Broad axe 374
Broad bean 133, 152
Broad disc 79
Broad lace trim 336-337
Broadside 378
Broken pediment 481
Bromeliads 112-113
  Epiphytic 162-163
Bromine 311
Bronchi 254
Bronchial nerve 254
Bronchial tree 254
Bronchial vein 254
Bronchiole and alveoli 254
Bronchus
  Frog 182
  Human 215, 255
Bronze casting 452
Bronze finishing tools 454
Bronze mast truck 372
Bronze statue 455
Broomrape 163
Brother T-78 fax machine 572, 573
Browband 554-555
Brow horn 102
Brow horn core 103
Brown alga 116
Brown scales 121
Brown seaweed 116-117
Brow ridge
  Australopithecus 108
  Gorilla 203
  Homo sapiens 108

Browser icon 577
Browser menu 577
Brush 432, 444, 600
Brushbar 592, 593
Brushbar drive belt cover 593
Brushbar motor control 593
Brush holder 600
Brushing boot 554
Brush lettering equipment 444
Brush rest 444
Brush tool articulation 593
Bryce Canyon 276
Bryophyta 118
Bryophytes 112, 118-119
Bryozoans 279
Bryum sp. 112
Buccal cavity
  Bird 189
  Chimpanzee 202
  Dolphin 205
  Domestic cat 195
  Elephant 200
  Pachycephalosaurus 100
  Rabbit 196
  Tortoise 187
Buccal mass 176
Buccinator muscle 229
Bucket seat 361
Bucket tappet 344
Bud
  Adventitious 154
  Aechmea miniata 162
  Apical meristem 134
  Begonia 129
  Bishop pine 124
  Broomrape 163
  Clematis flower 131
  Dicotyledons 127
  Durmast oak 131
  Florists' chrysanthemum 129
  Horse chestnut 130
  Larkspur 141
  Lily 140
  Lime 143
  London plane 134
  Moss 119
  Oxalis sp. 121
  Pine needle 125
  Rhizome 155
  Root tuber 154-155
  Rose 131
  Rowan twig 131
  Stolon 154
  Water lily 159
Buddhist style 490
Budh Planitia 35
Bud scale
  Bishop pine 124
  Dicotyledon stem 127
  London plane 134
  Pine shoot apex 125
Buffer
  "Deltic" diesel-electric locomotive 327
  "Ellerman Lines" steam locomotive 324-325
  Italian State Railways Class 402 328
  "Rocket" steam locomotive 324
Buffing pad 328
Bugle 506
Bulb
  Renault Clio 352
  Vegetative reproduction 154-155
Bulb horn
  1906 Renault 337
  Ford Model T 338
Bulbil 154-155
Bulbourethral gland 259
Bulkhead
  ARV Super 2 425

Flat freight car 327
Bulkhead stiffener 393
Bulkhead trim 407
Bulldog clip 430
Bullet 397, 549
Bullet block 373
Bullet-shaped guard 278
Bull-head rail 331
Bullnose chisel 452
Bull's-eye 549
Bulwark
  74-gun ship 380
  Ironclad 393
Bumblebee 168
Bumper
  Bus 332-333
  Honda Insight 354
  Renault Clio 348-349
  Volkswagen Beetle 341
Bung 313, 560
Bunkers 546-547
Bunk space 397
Bun lamp burner 339
Buntline 372
Buon fresco 434-435
Buoy 379
Buoyant wetland plants 158
Burmese pagoda 490
Burning reaction 312, 313, 315
Burnisher 432, 446
Bursting charge 397
Buses 332-335
Bush 605
Bushes 130-131
Bushing 314
Butt
  Bassoon 508
  Lacrosse crosse 541
  Tennis racket 544
Butt cap 563
Butte
  Igneous rock structures 274
  Weathering and erosion 283
Buttercup 127, 132-133
Butterfly 168
Butterfly knot 389
Butterfly plate 582
Butterfly swimming stroke 558-559
Butterwort 160-161
Butt extension 563
Buttock
  Horse 198
  Human 210
Button contact 578
Button head rivet 392
Button-quilted upholstery 336
Buttress 484
  Baroque church 478-481
  Dome 486
  Gothic church 470-473
  Medieval building 466, 468-469
  Nineteenth-century building 493
Butt section 562

C

3C275 (quasar) 11
Caarduus tenuiflorus 129
Cab 324, 327
Cabane strut 404
Cabbage 132
Cab-end bogie 327
Cabin
  74-gun ship 380-381
  Iron paddlesteamer 392-393
  Wooden sailing ship 379
Cabin air-discharge aperture 414

Cabin air duct 417
Cabin air-pressure discharge valve 413
Cabinet rasp 452
Cabinet underside 583
Cabin trim 406-407
Cable 600-601
Cable entry point 598
Cable guide 558-359, 360
Cable holder 395
Cable retaining gland 598
Cables and ducting 602
Cable stop 365
Cacti
  Desert survivors 112
  Dryland adaptation 156
  Herbaceous flowering plants 129
Cadmium 311
Cadmium red 436
Cadmium yellow 438
Caecum
  Bird 189
  Brachiosaurus 90
  Chimpanzee 202
  Cow 198
  Digestive 176, 173
  Gut 170
  Human 249
  Octopus 176
  Pyloric 181-174
  Rabbit 196
  Rectal 174
Caelum 18
Caernarvon Castle 466
Caesium 310
Caiman 186-187
Calamus 191
Calcanean tendon 252-233
Calcaneum 183, 199
Calcareous ooze 299
Calcareous plates 172
Calcareous tufa 284
Calcite (calcium carbonate)
  Blue chalk 450
  Carbonates 269
  Cave 284-285
  Fossils 278
  Mohs scale 271
  Sedimentary rocks 277
  Testing candle wax 313
Calcite curtain 285
Calcite ossicle 174
Calcite ridge 284-285
Calcium 310
  Earth's composition 39
  Earth's crust 58
  Seawater salt content 296
Calcium line 23
Calculator icon 568
Caldera
  Igneous rock structures 275
  Lake formation 293
  Volcano 272
Caledonian mountains
  Late Carboniferous period 67
  Triassic period 69
Calendars 618
Calf 210
Californian purple sea urchin 175
Californium 311
Call and select option button 588
Call hold button 572
Calliactis parasitica 166
Calligraphy 444-445
Caliper assembly 365
Calipers 452
Callisto 44
Call-send button 588
Call transfer button 572
Caloris Basin 34-35
Caloris Montes 35

Calypte helenae 193
Calyptra 119
Calyx 140
  Allium sp. 143
  Centaury 144
  Human 256
  Simple succulent berry 149
Cam 344
Camarasaurus 91
Cambium 126
Cambrian period
  Fossil record 279
  Geological timescale 56
Camcorder 582
Cam cover
  Jaguar straight six engine 344
  Jaguar V12 engine 345
  72° VTO engine 356
Camellia 157
Camels 198-199
Camera 611, 615
  Digital 580-581
  Digital video 582-583
Camera pouch 426
Cam follower
  Ford diesel engine 347
  Jaguar straight six engine 344
  Jaguar V12 engine 345
  Velocette OHV engine 367
Cam lobe 344
Camouflage 409
Camouflage coloration 192
Campaniform capital 458
Campanile 477
Camptosaurus 70, 97
Camshaft 343-345
Camshaft gear 367
Camshaft sprocket 345
Camshaft timing gear 344
Canada 331
Canadian football 524, 526-527
Canadian pond weed 158-159
Canal
  Sea urchin 175
  Starfish 174
Canals 42
Canaries current 296
Cancel button 575, 588
Cancel button connectors 589
Cancellous bone 224
Cancer 18, 21
Candelabrum 476
Candle lamp 335
Candle wax 312-313
Canes Venatici 18, 21
Canine tooth
  Bear 106, 194
  Chimpanzee 202
  Human 246
  Hyaenodon 107
  Lion 194
  Opossum 106
  Smilodon 107
  Toxodon 106
Canis familiaris 195
Canis Major 18, 21
Canis Minor 18, 21
Canister 594
Cannon 376, 394
Cannon bone 198-199
Cannondale bicycle 361
Canoeing 560-561
Canopus 15
Canopy
  1906 Renault 336-337
  ARV light aircraft 424-425
  Bell-47 helicopter 422
  Daimler engine 343
  Ford Model T 339
  Hawker Tempest

components 409
Oldsmobile engine 336
Schleicher glider 426
Schweizer helicopter 423
Canopy latch 425
Canopy rail 409
Canson paper 441
Cant frame 381
Cantilever beam 494
Cantilever brake 358, 361
Cantilever brake boss 359
Cantilevered shade 495
Cantle
  Racing saddle 555
  Showjumping saddle 554
Canvas
  Acrylic paint 442
  Oil paint 436
  Preparation 437
Canvas shroud 362
Canvas support 437
Canyon
  Sedimentary rocks 276-277
  Weathering and erosion 282-283
Cap
  Alga 116
  Fungus 114-115
  Radicle tip 153
  Wood capstan 387
  Wooden sailing ship 378-379
Capacitor 587
Capacity measurements 590
Cape gooseberry 149
Capella 18, 21
Cape Royal 277
Capillary fringe 293
Capillary network 254
Capital
  Ancient Egyptian building 458-459
  Ancient Greek building 458, 460-461
  Ancient Roman building 458, 463, 465
  Asian building 490, 491
  Baroque church 479, 481
  Cathedral dome 487
  Domed roof 486
  French temple 485
  Islamic mosque 488
  Medieval building 467-469
  Neoclassical building 478, 483
  Ptolemaic-Roman period 459
  Renaissance building 476-477
  Romanesque style 468
Capitate bone 230
Capitulum 129, 142
Cap line 445
Capricornus 19, 20
Capstan 387
  74-gun ship 380
  Iron paddlesteamer 393
  Wooden sailing ship 379
Capstan screw 514
Capsule
  Dry fruit 150-151
  Moss 112, 119
Captain's cabin 379, 381
Captain's seat 416
Captain's shelter 394
Capybara 196-197
Carapace 172-173, 187
Carbon
  Atomic mass 310
  Bows 548
  Candle wax 312-313
  Coal formation 280

Minerals 268
Periodic table 311
Small stars 24-25
Structure of red supergiant 26
Carbonates 269
Carbon atom 138
Carbon bush 605
Carbon dioxide
  Earth's atmosphere 300
  Gas 312-313
  Mars' atmosphere 43
  Photosynthesis 138
  Respiratory system 255
  Scrubber compartment 397
  Structure of comet 53
  Venus' atmosphere 37
Carbon graphite racket 544
Carbonic acid 284
Carboniferous period 56-57, 66-67
  Reptiles 80
Carbon ink stick 444
Carbonized wood 430
Carbon monoxide
  Mars' atmosphere 45
  Venus' atmosphere 37
Carbon powder 311
Carbon-rich earth layers 66
Car-building robots 608
Carburettor
  ARV light aircraft 425
  Mid West twin-rotor engine 411
  Pegasus Quasar microlight 427
  Two-stroke engine 366
Carburettor cover 369
Carburettor hot-air intake pipe 422
Carburettor hot air lever 425
Cardiac notch 248
Cardiac region of stomach 179
Cardiac stomach 174
Cardiac vein 250
Carduus tenuiflorus 129
Cargo-carrying boat
  Dhow 376
  Junk 376
  Liberty ship 392
  Roman corbita 372-373
  Tea clipper 392
Cargo derrick 392
Cargo hatch 376
Cargo hold 372, 392
Car, hybrid 354
Caribbean plate 59
Caribbean Sea 264
Carina 21
Carinal canal 120
Carina plate 173
Carling 380
Carmel formation 276
Carnallite 271
Carnassial teeth 194
Carnivores 104, 194-195
  Jurassic period 70
  Theropod 84
  Triassic period 68
Carnivorous plants 160-161
  Pitcher plant 113
Carotid canal 220
Carp 180
Carpals
  Bird 189
  Bird's wing 191
  Domestic cat 195
  Elephant 201
  Frog 183
  Hare 197
  Horse 199
  Kangaroo 206
  Lizard 184

Platypus 206
Rhesus monkey 202
Seal 204
Carp angling 562
Carpathian mountains 77, 265
Carpels 140-141
  Dehiscent fruit 151
  Fertilization 146-147
  Fruit development 148-149
  Insect-pollinated plant 144
  Lemon fruit 148
  Ovary 140
  Stigma 140
  Style 140
Carpel wall 148, 151
Carpophore 151
Carpus
  Crab 172
  Crayfish 173
  Human 218
Carrara white marble 453
Carriage 413, 570
Carriage drivebelt 574
Carriage shaft 571
Carrick bend 387, 389
Carrion crow 195
Carrot 128, 132
Carrying fork 354
Carrying handle 566, 567
Carrying wheel 324
Cartilage
  Auricle 242
  Bony fish 180
  Meatus 242
  Wrist 230
Cartilaginous fish 178-179, 180
  Parasaurolophus 98
  Plateosaurus 89
  Platypus 206
  Rhesus monkey 202
  Seal 204
  Stegoceras 101
  Stegosaurus 93
  Struthiomimus 87
  Triceratops 102
  Tuojiangosaurus 93
  Tyrannosaurus 84-85
  Westlothiana 81
Cartouche 458
Cartridge starter 408
Caruncle 215
Carved sculpture 452, 453
Carved stone 488
Carvel-built hull 576, 391
Carvel planking 376, 377
Carving
  Asian building 490-491
  Gothic building 470
  Sculpture 452
Carving mallet 452
Caryopses 113, 150
Casa de las Conchas 476
Casa del Fascio 495
Case 567
Caspian Sea 265
Cassette compartment assembly 83
Cassette compartment cover 583
Cassette compartment lid 582
Cassini Division 46, 47
Cassini space probe 614-615
Cassiopeia 19
Cassowaries 188
Cast alloy wheel 546
Cast aluminium wheel spider 336
Castanea sativa 136, 150
Castanets 504, 517
Casting 452, 454
Cast-iron 492-493
Cast-iron chair 331
Cast iron cylinder barrel 363
Castle-deck gunport 376-377
Castles, 374, 466-467
Castor 18, 21
Castor canadensis 197
Cat 104, 194-195
Catalyst 355
Catalytic converter 344, 350, 356
Catamaran 560
Cataphoresic coating 548

Cataphyll 152
Cat block 381
Catcher's mask 536
Catch glove 550
Catena 572
Catenary 328, 330
Caterpillar 168, 169, 611
  Eggs 192
Catharina 40
Cathead
  74-gun ship 380
  Battleship 395
Cathedral of St. Lazare 468
Cations 308
Catkin 144
Catted anchor 381
Cattle 104, 198
Caucasus 265
Caudal fin 178, 179, 180-181
Caudal musculature 90, 95
Caudal plate 92-93
Caudal spike 92-93
Caudal vertebrae
  Ankylosaurus 95
  Archaeopteryx 85
  Crocodile 186
  Diplodocus 90
  Domestic cat 195
  Elephant 201
  Eryops 81
  Euoplocephalus 95
  Gallimimus 86
  Hare 197
  Horse 199
  Iguanodon 96
  Kangaroo 206
  Kentrosaurus 93
  Lizard 184-185
  Parasaurolophus 98
  Plateosaurus 89
  Platypus 206
  Rhesus monkey 202
  Seal 204
  Stegoceras 101
  Stegosaurus 93
  Struthiomimus 87
  Tuojiangosaurus 93
  Tyrannosaurus 84-85
  Westlothiana 81
Caudate nucleus 237
Caudex 151
Caudo-femoral muscle 97
Cauliculus 460
Caulophryne jordani 180
Cave bear skull 77
Caves 284-285
  Coastline 294-295
  Glacier 286
Cavetto moulding
  Ancient Egyptian building 458-459
  Baroque church 479
  French temple 485
  Gothic building 472
  Renaissance building 477
Cavies 196
Cayley, Sir George 398
CCD board 580
CCD connector socket 581
CCD microchip 580
CCD ribbon connector 580
CCD (Charge-Coupled Devices) 570, 572
CCD window 589
C clef 502
CD 579
CD-drive 521
CD/DVD drive 566
CDs 586, 587
Cedar-tree laccolith 274
Ceilings 463, 484
Celestial equator
  Stars of northern skies 18-19

Stars of southern skies 20-21
Celestial poles 18
Celestial sphere 18
Cell
  Alga 116-117
  Body 217
  Building 469, 485
  Chusan palm leaf 130
  Clubmoss stem 120
  Collar 166
  Dicotyledon 126-127
  Epidermal 166
  Epiphytic orchid 162
  Fern rachis 121
  Horsetail stem 120
  Leaf 126, 159
  Marram grass 113
  Monocotyledon 126-127
  Moss 119
  Mushroom 115
  Photosynthesis 138-139
  Pine 124-125
  Pore 166
  Root 132-133
  Root tip 152
  Spirogyra sp. 117
  Stem 134-135
  Wetland plants 158-159
Cella 461, 463, 485
Cell body 239
Cell membrane 217
Cell nuclear membrane 216
Cell nucleus 217
Cell nucleus residue 234
Cello 503-505, 510
Cells 607
Cell wall
  Alga 112, 116
  Leaf 159
  Palisade mesophyll 139
  Root 132
  Spirogyra sp. 117
  Stem surface 156
Celsius temperature scale 590
Cement-based adhesive 450
Cement gland 173
Cement-rendered wall 494
Cenozoic era 57, 74, 76
  Fossil record 279
Censer 488
Centaurium erythraea 144
Centaurus 18, 21
Centaurus A (radio galaxy) 13
Centaurus and Crux 21
Central Asia 64
Central bulge 12, 14
Central canal 238
Central computer control 328
Central deflector 612
Central drive access 586
Central drive hole 586
Central electrode 306
Central nervous system 238
Central peak
  Degas and Brontë 34
  Venus' craters 36
Central processing unit 566, 579
Central retinal artery 240
Central retinal vein 240
Central shield 187
Central sulcus 236-237
Centre
  American football 526
  Australian football 528
  Basketball 532
  Canadian football 526
  Lacrosse 541

Netball 535
Rugby 530
Centre-board 561
Centre buck-eye coupler 326
Centre circle
  Australian rules football 528
  Basketball 532
  Ice hockey 550
  Netball 535
  Soccer 524
Centre console 553
Centre court 545
Centred rudder 375
Centre element 599
Centre field 536
Centre flag 529
Centre forward 540
Centre gangway 329
Centre Georges Pompidou 496-497
Centre girder 393
Centre half 540
Centre half-back 528, 529
Centre half-forward 528, 529
Centre hole 587
Centre line 413, 415
  Fencing piste 557
  Ice hockey 550
  Soccer 524
Centre-line beam 426-427
Centre line keelson 393
Centrifugal brake 562
Centrifugal compressor 418
Centrifugal effect 297
Centriole 217
Centripetal river drainage 288
Centrum 187
Cephalapsis 65
Cephalic groove 173
Cephalic vein
  Human 253
  Octopus 176
Cephalopods 176, 279
Cephalothorax
  Crayfish 173
  Malacostraca 172
  Scorpion 170
  Shrimp 172
  Spider 170-171
Cepheus 19
Ceramic end-piece 319
Ceratopsia 83, 103
Ceratosauria 83
Ceraunius Tholus 43
Cercidyphyllum sp. 72
Cerebellum 212, 236-237, 238
Cerebral areas 237
Cerebral ganglion 169, 177
Cerebral vessel 257
Cerebrum 212, 236-237, 238
Cereoid cactus 129
Cerium 310
Ceropegia woodii 157
Ceruchi 372
Cerussite 269
Cervical musculature
  Euoplocephalus 94
  Gallimimus 86
Cervical nerves 258
Cervical plate 92-93
Cervical rib 84, 96, 100-101, 103
Cervical vertebrae
  Archaeopteryx 85
  Arsinoitherium 104
  Bird 189
  Brachiosaurus 91
  Crocodile 186
  Domestic cat 195
  Elephant 201
  Eryops 80

Hare 197
Horse 199
Human 212, 222, 245
Iguanodon 96
Kangaroo 206
Kentrosaurus 93
Lizard 184
Parasaurolophus 99
Plateosaurus 88
Platypus 206
Rhesus monkey 202
Seal 204
Stegoceras 101
Stegosaurus 93
Struthiomimus 87
Toxodon 106
Tuojiangosaurus 93
Tyrannosaurus 84
Cervix 258-259
Cervus elephas 199
Cetaceans 204-205
Cetiosaurus 91
Cetorhinus maximus 179
Cetus 19, 20
Chaffinch 193
Chain
  Bicycle 358-359, 360-361
  Drum kit 518
  Motorcycle 366
  Wheel and axle 320
  Wooden sailing ship 378
Chain bobstay 382
Chain drive
  Motorcycle clutch 362
  Werner motorcycle 366
  Wright Flyer 398-399
Chain locker 393
Chain motif 491
Chain plate 382
Chain swivel 386
Chain wale 376-377
Chajya 489
Chalcedony 271
Chalk 450
  Tempera 432
  Gesso 434
  Pastel making 440
  Fresco 434
  Sedimentary rocks 277
Chamber
  Building 465, 491
  Gun turret 396
Chambers
  Seaweed 116
  Stomach 198
  Substomatal 139
Chamfered corner 485, 488, 494
Championship golf courses 546
Change 321
Chang Jiang 265
Channel
  74-gun ship 381
  Sailing warship 376-377
  Temple of Neptune 460
  Wooden sailing ship 378
Channelled wrack 116
Chapel
  Baroque church 479
  Gothic church 470
  Medieval church 469
Chapel pier 467
Chaplet 454
Chapter-house 472
Charcoal drawing 430-431
Charentais melon 149
Charge
  Four-stroke cycle 343
  Modern engines 344
Charged atom 306, 308
Charged particle 316
Charging with ball 553
Charon 50
Chart house 394
Chase 395

Chassis
First cars 334-335
Ford Model T 338
Kirby BSA sidecar 369
Microwave
combination oven 596
Monocoque 363
Motorcycle 362, 364-365
Oldsmobile chassis 337
Panhard-system
Volkswagen Beetle 340
White Steam Car 342
Chassis earth terminal 597
Chassis electrical plug 357
Chassis frame 338
Chassis number 327
Chataya arch 491
Châteaux 474, 476-477
Chattra 491
Chattravali 490-491
Chauffeur's seat 334
Checkerbloom 136
Check pawl 562
Cheek
74-gun ship 381
Dunkeld wet fly 563
Horse 199
Human 212
Running block 383
Sailmaker's mallet 384
Stegosaurus 92
Check horn 103
Cheek-piece
Harness racer 555
Showjumper 554
Cheek pouch 98, 196
Cheek teeth
Ankylosaurs 92
Carnivores 194
Ornithopods 96
Tetralophodon 104
Theropods 84
Cheese 382, 388-389
Cheiracanthus 65
Cheirolepis 65
Chekhov 35
Chela 170, 172, 173
Chelicera 79
Chelicerae 170-171
Chelicerates 279
Cheliped
Crab 172
Crayfish 173
Chelonia 186
Chemical bond 307
Chemical change 280-281
Chemical energy 314-315
Chemical equations 312
Chemical properties
Electrons 308, 310
Substances 306
Chemical reactions 312-313
Chemical sedimentary rocks 276
Chemical symbols 312, 591
Periodic table 510-511
Chemical weathering 282
Chemise 466-467
Chemistry symbols 621
Cherry 148
Cherry wood 512
Chert 277
Cherub 472
Chervil 135
Chest
Gorilla 205
Human 211, 214
Lion 194
Chestnut 198
Chest padding 551
Chest pass 532, 535
Chest protector 527
Chevet 469

Chevron 81, 85, 87, 89, 93, 95-96, 98, 101-102
Chevron fold 61
Chevron-tread tyre 336
Chi1 Orionis 18
Chi2 Orionis 18
Chiastolite hornfels 275
Chihuahuan Desert 264
Chile 331
Chimney
Bordino Steam Carriage 334
"Ellerman Lines" steam locomotive 325
Iron paddlesteamer 393
"Rocket" steam locomotive 324
Chimney-shaft 467
Chimney-stack 476, 483
Chimpanzee 202-203
Chin
Bird 188
Human 211, 212
China
Ball games 524
Late Carboniferous period 66-67
Middle Ordovician period 64-65
Ornithopod 96
Railway track gauge 331
Thyreophorans 92
Chinese calendar 618
Chinese characters 445
Chinese junk 376
Chinese white 438
Chin groove 199
Chin guard 553
Chin gun turret 408
Chinle formation 276
Chin rest 510-511
Chin spoiler 546
Chipmunk 196
Chirostenotes 87
Chisel 452-453
Chlamydomonas sp. 116
Chlorenchyma 120
Chloride 296
Chlorine 311
Chlorophyll 138
Chloroplast 139
Photosynthesis pigment 116, 138, 162
Chlorophyta 116
Chloroplast 138-139
Alga 112
Chlamydomonas sp. 116
Envelope 139
Epiphytic orchid 162
Internal view 139
Spirogyra sp. 117
Choanocyte 166
Choir 468-469, 470, 472
Choir manual 514
Choir-screen 470
Choir-stall 470
Choir stop 514
Chondrichthyes 178
Chondrostean fish 69
Chong Ch'ol 35
Chordae tendineae 251
Chorioallantoic membrane 192
Chorion 260
Choroid 240
Christian architecture 468
Christmas rose 139
Chromate ion 312
Chrome passivation 348
Chrome plating 347
Chrome trim strip 341
Chromium
Mineralization zones 281
Oxide 312
Periodic table 310
Chromosphere 32-33

Chrysalis 168
Chrysanthemum morifolium 129
Chryse Planitia 43
Chrysler Building 495
Chrysocyon brachyurus 195
Chuck 601
Chuck key 601
Chung-ta-wei 376
Church
Santa Sophia 487
Sorbonne 486
St. Botolph 473
St. Eustache 477
St. George in the East 478, 481
St. Maclou 470, 472
St. Maria della Salute 478
St. Maria della Vittoria 478
St. Paul-St. Louis 478-479
St. Pierre de Libreville 496, 499
St. Serge 469
Church-roof boss 468
Chusan palm 127, 130
Ciconia ciconia 188
Cigarette lighter adapter and speaker cable 590
Ciliary body 241
Cincture 477
Cinder 272
Cinder cone
Igneous rock structures 274
Volcanic structure 273
Cinema, home 584-585
Cinnabar 271
Cinquefoil moulding 471
Circle 479, 622
Circle area measurement 590
Circuit 316
Circuit board 573, 581, 582, 585, 589
Circuit board plug 596
Circuit breaker 314
Circular mountain lake 293
Circulatory system 252-255
Circumference 622
Cirque 286-287
Cirque formation 287
Cirque Napoleon 478-479
Cirri 172
Cirrocumulus cloud 302
Cirrostratus cloud 302
Cirrus 173
Cirrus cloud
Neptune 50
Structure of Mars 43
Weather 302-303
Citrus limon 148
City bus 332
Civet 194
Cladding 494, 496, 498-499
Cladode 129
Cladonia floerkeana 114
Cladonia portentosa 114
Clam 176
Clamp
Cross-stave 377
Intaglio printing 313
U-tube 446
Clamshell 572, 578, 589
Clarinet 503-504, 508
Classical-style architecture 474, 478, 482
Clastic sedimentary rocks 276
Claves 517
Clavicle
Bird 189

Bony fish 181
Eryops 80
Human 211, 218
Kangaroo 206
Rhesus monkey 202
Clavius 40
Clavus 373
Claw
Albertosaurus 84
Anchisaurus 89
Archaeopteryx 85
Beetle 168
Bird 188
Bumblebee 168
Caiman 187
Chick 193
Crab 172
Crayfish 173
Dinosaur 87
Herrerasaurus 86
Kangaroo 207
Lizard 184
Marble sculpture 452
Pachycephalosaurus 100
Psittacosaurus 103
Scorpion 170
Spider 171
Stegoceras 101
Terrapin 187
Tyrannosaurus 84
Clawed feet 190, 206
Clay 298
Clay daub 465
Clay modelling 452, 455
Clay mounds 286
Clear space 534
Cleavage 270
Clef 502
Cleithrolepis granulatus 69
Cleithrum 80
Clematis 130-131, 137
Clench nail 375
Cleomedes 40
Cleopatra Patera 37
Clerestory 459, 472, 479
Clew 373
Clewline 379, 385
Cliffs
Coastlines 294-295
River's stages 289
Sedimentary rocks 276-277
Climate
Carboniferous period 66
Geological time 56
Oceans and seas 296
Weather 302
Climatic change
Coastline 294
Geological time 56
Clincher wheel 359
Clinker-built hull 375
Clinker-built oak planking 375
Clints 284-285
Clitoris 258
Cloaca
Bird 189
Brachiosaurus 90
Dogfish 179
Euoplocephalus 95
Frog 182
Lizard 185
Tortoise 187
Cloacal opening 185
Clock operator 532
Clock tower 493
Cloister 472
Cloning technology 606-607
Close-stowing anchor 386
Cloud deck 50-51
Cloud features
Neptune 50

Saturn 46
Venus 36
Clouds
Earth's atmosphere 301
Jupiter 44-45
Mars 42-43
Neptune 50-51
Saturn 46-47
Uranus 48-49
Venus 36-37
Water cycle 288
Weather 302-303
Cloud shadow 50
Clouds of dust and gas
Life of massive star 24
Milky Way 14-15
Nebulae and star clusters 16-17
Origin and expansion of Universe 11
Small stars 24
Cloud-top temperature
Structure of Jupiter 45
Structure of Neptune 51
Structure of Saturn 47
Structure of Uranus 49
Clove hitch 388
Cloven hoof 198
Clubmosses 64, 66, 120-121
Clump cathead 395
Clustered column 469
Clutch 364, 366
Clutch and flywheel 340
Clutch cable 350, 363, 365
Clutch centre plate 351
Clutch cover 363
Clutch lever 363, 369
Clutch pedal 350
Clutch pressure plate 351
Clutch release bearing 351
Clypeaster 279
Cnidocytes 166-167
CNS 238
Coal
Earth's evolution 57
Mineral resources 280-281
Power stations 314
Sedimentary rocks 276
Steam locomotive 324
Coal-forming forests 57
Coal measures 61
Coaming 381
Coastal spring 292
Coaster 374-375
Coastlines 294-295
Cave 284
Cobalt
Mineralization zones 281
Periodic table 311
Cobra lily 160-161
Coccosteus 65
Coccygeal cornu 223
Coccygeal vertebrae 222
Coccyx 218, 222
Cochlea 242-243
Cocking lever 549
Cockpit
Avro biplane 403
Kayak 560
LVG CVI fighter 405
Modern military aircraft 420-421
Sailing dinghy 561
Schleicher glider 426
Cockpit canopy 409
Cockpit coaming 425
Cocoa 148
Coconino sandstone 276
Cocos nucifera 135
Cocos plate 59
Cod 180
Codiaeum variegatum 136
Coelenterata 166
Coeliac trunk 256-257
Coelodonta 76-77, 104

Coelophysids 68
Coelurus 87
Coenobium 116
Coffer 463, 485
Coffered vault 485
Coffering 475
Cogged drive belt 344
Cog humanoid robot 609
Coil base 587
Coil spring
"Ellerman Lines" steam locomotive 324
Motorcycle 364
Coil suspension spring
"Deltic" diesel-electric locomotive 327
"Eurostar" multi-voltage electric train 329
Wagon bogie 331
Coke hopper 334
Cold air intake 420
Cold-air unit 417
Cold front 302-303
Cold occlusion 502
Cold-water pipe 405
Cold-water upwelling 296
Coleoptera 168
Coleus sp. 134
Collagen and elastic fibres 252
Collapsed crater 293
Collar
Cathedral of Notre Dame de Paris 473
Sea anemone 167
Snail 177
Collar-beam 473
Collar bone 211, 218
Collar cell 166
Collar of horsetail 120
Collecting duct 256
Collecting tubule 256
Collective lever 422
Collenchyma 126, 154-135
Colliding plates 272
Colloids 306
Colon
Butterfly 169
Cow 198
Human 215, 249, 259
Rabbit 196
Colonette
Gothic church 473
Islamic building 488
Medieval building 467-469
Neoclassical building 479
Renaissance building 474
Colonnade
Ancient Greek building 460-461
Ancient Roman building 462-463
Cathedral dome 484, 487
Neoclassical building 483
Colonnaded storey 494
Colorado River
Earth's evolution 57
Grand Canyon 277
Valley 277
Colosseum 462, 464-465
Colour 270
Colour changes 312-313
Colour ink cartridge 574
Colour ink-cartridge clamp 574
Colour light signals 330
Colour liquid crystal display (LCD) screen 579
Colour screen 588
Colour wheel 439
Colpus 144
Columba 18, 21

Columella 119, 145
Column
Ancient Egyptian building 458-459
Ancient Greek building 458, 460
Ancient Roman building 458, 462-463, 465
Baroque church 480-481
Cathedral dome 487
Cave system 285
French temple 485
Gothic church 473
Islamic mosque 488
Medieval church 468-469
Modern building 496-498
Monocotyledonous flower 126
Neoclassical building 478-479, 483
Nineteenth-century building 492-493
Renaissance building 477
Coma 52-53
Coma Berenices 18, 21
Combat sports 556-557
Combination lever 325
Combustion 326
Combustion chamber
Capacity 366-367
Iron paddlesteamer 393
Jaguar straight six engine 344
Jet engines 418-419
Combustion cycle 410
Comets 30, 52-53
Common bile duct 252
Common blackheaded gull 189
Common carotid artery 215, 251, 253
Common centaury 144
Common crus 243
Common digital extensor muscle 84, 97
Common elder 143
Common English ivy 131
Common horse chestnut 130
Common horsetail 120
Common Iguana 82
Common iliac artery 215, 253, 257
Common iliac vein 215, 253, 257
Common ivy 137
Common lime 143
Common link 386
Common mulberry 130
Common peroneal nerve 238
Common rafter 473, 486
Common starfish 175
Common tern 193
Common time 502
Communication 108
Communications aerial 424
Commutator 600
Commuters 363
Compact bone 224-225
Compact disc 584, 586, 587
Companion cells 132-134
Companion ladder 381
Companion way 380
Compass
Battleship 394
Vault decoration 485
Compass and rangefinder platform 394
Competent bed rock 61

Competition motorcycles 368-369
Competitions
Archery 548
Diving 558
Judo 556
Rowing 560
Skiing 552-553
Complete mesentery 167
Composite capital 478
Composite column 478
Composite pilaster 478
Composite volcano 272
Composter 602
Compound eye
Beetle 168
Bumblebee 168
Butterfly 169
Crab 172
Crayfish 173
Damselfly 168
Malacostraca 172
Shrimp 172
Compound inflorescence 131, 142
Compound leaf 130-131, 136
Compound pier 468-469
Compound pulleys 320
Compound succulent fruit 148-149
Compound umbel 143
Compressible gas 365
Compression
Faults and folds 60
Glacier 286
Igneous and metamorphic rocks 274
Mineral resources 280
Mountain building 62
Rock cycle 266
Compression ring
Ford diesel engine 347
Jaguar straight six engine 344
Compression stroke 343
Compressor 418
Compressor piston 344
Compsognathus 70
Computer
and E-mail program 677
Electronic instruments 520
Hand-held 568-569
Modern bodywork 348
Computer display 521
Computerized ignition system 344
Concave brace 477
Concave moulding 482
Concave wall 478, 481
Conceptacles 116-117
Concert grand piano 515
Concha
Ear 242
Nasal 221, 241
Conchoidal fracture
Extrusive igneous rocks 275
Fracture 270
Sedimentary rocks 277
Concorde 416-417
Concrete 492, 494, 496-499
Concrete shielding 314
Concrete shoe 499
Concrete track 328
Concrete wall 463, 465, 496
Condensation 307
Nuclear power station 314
Testing candle wax 313
Condensation level 302
Condenser 342
Condenser aperture 610
Condenser housing 611

Condenser lens 611
Conducting tissue 119
Conductor
Electrical circuit 316
Generating magnetism 317
Orchestra 504
Conductor's stand 505
Condylactis sp. 166
Condyle
Carnivore 194
Human 220
Cone 623
Cones
Bishop pine 124
Gymnosperms 122
Igneous and metamorphic rocks 274
Pine 122
Scots pine 122
Smooth cypress 123
Volcanoes 272-273
Welwitschia 123
Yew 123
Cone sheet 274
Cone stalk 124
Cone surface area measurement 590
Cone volume measurement 590
Congas 519
Congo Basin 39
Conical bore 507
Conical dome 476
Conical map projection 265
Conical spire 466, 476
Conical volcano 272
Conifer
Cretaceous period 72
Earth's evolution 57
Fossil record 279
Gymnosperm 122-125
Jurassic period 70
Triassic period 68
Coniferophyta 122
Conjugation 117
Conjunctiva 241
Connecting rod
Bordino Steam Carriage 334
Flat-four cylinder arrangement 340
Four-stroke cycle 343
Iron paddlesteamer 392
Jaguar straight six engine 344
Jaguar V12 engine 345
Mid West two-stroke engine 410
Steamboat with paddle wheels 391
Connecting wire 598
Connective tissue cells 582
Connectors 569
Conning tower 394, 397
Conocephalum conicum 118
Con-rod 340, 343-345
Conservation of Energy Law 314
Conservatory 602, 603
Console 579
Constellations 18-21, 613
Constratum 373
Constrictor snakes 184
Construction sculpture 452
Contact 352
Contact array 581
Contact grid 605
Contact metamorphism 274
Contact strip 589
Contant d'Ivry 478
Contest area 556
Contests
Head-butting 100
Shooting 548

Continental crust 58-59
Mineralization zones 281
Mountain building 62-63
Ocean floor 298
Continental drift 58
Continental margin sediments 299
Continental rise 298
Continental Sea 73, 75
Continental shelf
Ocean floor 298
Prehistoric Earth 69, 71
Rock cycle 267
Continental slope
Ocean floor 298
Offshore currents 296
Rock cycle stages 267
Continents
Formation of the Earth 38, 56
Earth's physical features 264-265
Geological time 56
Contrabassoon 504-505
Contractile vacuole 116
Contrast control 521
Control cabinet 396
Control circuit 328
Control buttons 585
Control column
ARV light aircraft 425
BE 2B bomber 404
Curtiss biplane 398-399
Control-column aperture 425
Control flag 552
Controller 332, 579
Control line 561
Control panel 571, 595, 596
Control panel boards 597
Control panel casing 573
Control panel fascia 597
Control panel microchips 596
Control panel frame 573
Control panel wiring 595
Control panels 594
Control platform 390
Control reservoir drain 326
Control rod 314, 424
Control room 397
Control stalk 353
Convection cell 33
Convection current 38
Convective zone 24, 33
Converging plates 63
Conversion 530
Convex portico 483
Cook/grill tray 596
Cooking 108
Cooksonia 56
Cooksonia hemispherica 64
Coolant 314
Coolant inlet 424
Coolant jacket 410-411
Coolant outlet
ARV light aircraft 424
Jaguar V12 engine 345
Mid West two-stroke engine 410
Coolant passage 346
Coolant pipe 354
Coolant pump 410
Coolant rail 345
Cooling device 611
Cooling fan 345, 567
Cooling fin
Drum brake 365
Mid West rotary engine 411
Two-stroke engine 366
Velocette OHV engine 367
Cooling intake 534

Cooling perforations 597
Cooling tank 335
Cooling tower
Centre Georges Pompidou 496-497
Nuclear power station 314
Cooling vent 566
Cooling water tank 335
Co-orbital moons 46
Coping-stone 495
Copper
Mineral resources 280-281
Minerals 268
Periodic table 311-312
Copper body-shell 519
Copper face 384
Copper nitrate solution 312
Copper ore 306
Copper plate nib 444
Copper sheathing 392
Copper sulphate 313
Coprates Chasma 43
Copulatory bursa
Butterfly 169
Snail 177
Copy button 572
Coracoid
Bird 189
Diplodocus 90
Euoplocephalus 94
Gallimimus 86
Triceratops 102
Turtle 187
Tyrannosaurus 84
Coral 78, 166-167
Atoll development 299
Fossil record 279
Corallina officinalis 117
Coral reef
Earth's evolution 56
Ocean floor 298
Cor Anglais 504-505, 508
Corbel
Cathedral dome 487
Medieval building 467, 469
Neoclassical building 482
Nineteenth-century building 493
Renaissance building 477
Rococo style 478
Corbita 372-373
Cor Caroli 18, 21
Cordaites 70
Cordaites leaf bases 136-137
Cordite case 396
Cordite handling room 396
Cordite supply shuttle 396
Cordless battery charger 588
Core
Earth 38-39
Helix Nebula 17
Massive stars 26-27
Moon 40
Neutron stars and black holes 28-29
Small stars 24-25
Structure of comet 53
Structure of Earth 63
Structure of Jupiter 45
Structure of Mars 43
Structure of Mercury 35
Structure of Neptune 51
Structure of Pluto 51
Structure of Saturn 47
Structure of Uranus 49
Structure of Venus 37
Core-engine jet pipe 412, 415
Core jet pipe 419
Core temperature
Structure of Earth 39

Structure of Jupiter 45
Structure of main sequence star 24
Structure of red giant 25
Structure of red supergiant 26
Structure of Saturn 47
Structure of Sun 33
Structure of Uranus 49
Corinthian capital 460, 463, 479, 481
Corinthian column 463-464, 479-480
Corinthian entablature 463
Corinthian order 460, 462
Corinthian pilaster 463-464, 480-481
Coriolis force 296-297, 300
Cork
Oboe 508
Stems 134-135
Woody dicotyledons 127
Corms 154-155
Corn 112
Cornea 241
Corner arc 524
Corner seal 347
Cornet 506
Cornice
Ancient Egyptian temple 458-459
Ancient Greek building 460-461
Ancient Roman building 462-465
Asian building 491
Baroque church 479-481
Dome 484, 486
French temple 485
Gothic church 470-473
Islamic tomb 489
Medieval building 466-467, 469
Neoclassical building 478-479, 482-483
Nineteenth-century building 493
Renaissance building 474-477
Twentieth-century building 494
Cornucopia 480
Corolla 140, 142-143
Corona
Earth's atmosphere 300
Palazzo Strozzi 475
Sun's atmosphere 32-33
Corona Australis 19
Corona Borealis 18, 21
Coronal section through brain 236-237
Coronal suture 220
Coronary artery 250-251, 253
Coronary sinus 250
Corona temperature 33
Coronet 198, 554
Coronoid process 96, 106, 194, 220
Corpus albicans 258
Corpus callosum 236-237
Corpus cavernosum 259
Corpus luteum 258
Corpus spongiosum 259
Corridor 465
Corries 286-287
Corrugator supercilii muscle 228-229
Cortex
Apical meristem 134
Canadian pond weed 158-159
Clubmoss stem 120
Dicotyledon 127
Epiphytic orchid 162

Hair 254
Horsetail stem 120
Kidney 256
Lichen 114
Monocotyledon 127
Moss 119
Pine 125
Radicle 152
Rhizome 155
Root 152-153
Stems 134-135
Water hyacinth 158
Water lily 159
Corundum 271
Corvus 18, 21
Corvus corone 193
Corynactis viridis 166
Corythosaurus 96, 98
Cosmic background
radiation 10
Cosmic ray 301
COSTAR corrective optical
device 613
COSTAR device slot 613
Costal cartilage 218
Costal facet 223
Costal margin 168, 169
Costal shield 187
Cotter pin 583
Cotton duck canvas 437,
443
Cotyledon 126, 152-153
Development 132
Dicotyledon 126
Dry fruit seed 150-151
Embryo development
147
Epigeal germination
153
Hypogeal germination
152
Monocotyledon 126
Pine 122
Root development 132
Seed 152-153
Succulent fruit seed
148-149
Couch grass 113
Coucy-le-Château 466-467
Coulomb 316
Counter
Calligraphy lettering
445
Counterbalancing weight
506
Counter rail 381
Counter timber 381
Counterweight
Flat-four cylinder
arrangement 340
Four-stroke cycle 343
Hong Kong and
Shanghai Bank 498
Jaguar V12 engine 345
Output shaft 347
Relief printing press
449
Rotary engine output
shaft 410
Trojan engine 342
V12 cylinder
arrangement 345
Country code 576
Coupling
Conventional hook-
screw 328
"Ellerman Lines" steam
locomotive 324
Coupling rod 325
Couronnement 472
Course
Asian building 491
Medieval building 466-
467
Neoclassical building
483
Nineteenth-century
building 492-493
Court referee 535

Court
Basketball 532
Handball 535
Netball 535
Volleyball 534
Court seal 375
Courtship display 188
Courtyard 465, 466
Coussinet 460
Covalent bonding 308-309
Cove 381
Coved dome 478, 485
Cover 582
Cover for USB and
recharger jack sockets
581
Cover front 583
Cover latch 566
Cover latch port 567
Cover point 541
Cover stopper link 573
Cover support 570
Coverts 188, 191
Cow 198
Cowhide face 384
Cowling fastener 408
Cowling panel 407, 412
Coxa
Beetle 168
Crayfish 173
Scorpion 170
Coxswain 560
CPU 566, 579
CQR anchor 386
Crab 172
Crab apple 126
Crab cactus 129
Crab Nebula 28
Cracks 284-285
Cradle frame
Honda VF750 364
Weslake Speedway
motorcycle 369
Cradling 541
Crane 498
Cranial nerves 238
Cranium
Ankylosaurus 94
Archaeopteryx 85
Australopithecus 108
Bat 105
Camarasaurus 91
Diplodocus 90
Elephant 201
Eryops 80
Euoplocephalus 94
Homo sapiens 108
Hyaenodon 107
Iguanodon 96
Kentrosaurus 93
Lambeosaurus 99
Moeritherium 105
Opossum 106
Pachycephalosaurus
100
Panoplosaurus 94
Parasaurolophus 99
Plateosaurus 88
Prenocephale 100
Protoceratops 102
Stegoceras 100
Stegosaurus 93
Struthiomimus 87
Styracosaurus 102
Toxodon 106
Triceratops 103
Tuojiangosaurus 93
Tyrannosaurus 84
Crank 320
Brace-and-bit 601
Eddy Merckx racing
bicycle 360
"Ellerman Lines" steam
locomotive 325
Crank bolt 558, 360
Crankcase
BE 2B bomber 404
British Rail Class 20
diesel engine 327

Humber engine 343
Jaguar straight six
engine 344
Jaguar V12 engine 345
Mid West two-stroke
engine 410
Oldsmobile engine 336
Trojan engine 342
Velocette OHV engine
367
Werner motorcycle 362
Crankcase breather pipe
402
Crank handle 339
Crankpin 343
Crankshaft
Benz Motorwagen 335
Flat-four cylinder
arrangement 340
Four-stroke cycle 343
Iron paddlesteamer 392
Mid West two-stroke
engine 410
Oldsmobile engine 336
Oscillating steam
engine 391
Straight four cylinder
arrangement 345
Two-stroke engine 366
Velocette OHV engine
367
Crankshaft counterweight
344
Crankshaft pulley 344,
355
Crash bar 362-363
Crash cymbal 518
Crash helmet 552
Crater
Mercury's North Pole 35
Northern stars 18
Oceanus Procellarum
40
Southern stars 21
Surface features of
Mars 42
Crayfish 172-173
Crayon 448
Creeping stems 154
Clubmoss 120
Strawberry 128
Cremasteric fascia 259
Cremocarp 150-151
Crenellation 466
Crepidoma 461, 481
Crescent-shaped dune
283
Crest
Building 479, 488, 493
Fold formation 60
Horse 199
Lizard 184
Ship's shield 395
Crested porcupine 197
Cretaceous period 72-73
Fossil record 279
Geological time 56-57
Crevasse 287
Crevice 284
Crevice tool 593
Crew handrail 612, 613
Crew's seat 416
Cricket (animal) 168
Cricket (game) 538-539
Cricoid cartilage 255
Cricothyroid ligament 244
Cricothyroid muscle 229,
244-245
C ring 46-47
Cringle 384
Crista 242
Crocket 471-472
Crocodile clip connector
316
Crocodiles 68, 73, 186-187
Crocodylus niloticus 186
Crocoite 271
Cronaca 474
Crook 508

Crop
Bird 189
Butterfly 169
Octopus 176
Snail 177
Crop-duster 410
Crops 315
Crop-sprayer 410, 422
Cross
Baroque church 480
Dome 486-487
Motif 472
Crossandra nilotica 145
Crossbar
Calligraphy characters
445
Eddy Merckx racing
bicycle 360
Gaelic football 529
Handball 535
Hurling 540
Rugby 530
Cross-bed set 283
Crossbow 548
Cross-bracing 497-499
Cross-country skiing 548
Crosse 540-541
Crossing 469-470, 477
Crossing tower 468
Cross-member 338-339
Cross-piece 376-377, 387
Cross-pollination 144
Cross-staff 377
Cross-stave 376-377
Cross tube 423
Cross wall of hypha 115
Crosswise strut 512
Crotchet rest 502-503
Croton 136
Crouch 543
Croup 198
Crow 193
Crown
Bird 188
Building 484, 490
Danforth anchor 386
Harp 511
Head 212
Relief-printing press
449
Rigging 382-383
Roman anchor 372
Sail hook 384
Shackle 386
Teeth 247
Timpanum 519
Crowning cornice
Ancient Roman
building 464, 465
Baroque church 479
Renaissance building
474-475
Crown wheel
Benz Motorwagen 335
Ford Model T 338
Cruciform column 492
Cruciform pedestal 481,
487
Cruck frame 466
Crumb tray 598-599
Crupper 555
Crusafontia 56
Crus cerebri of midbrain
237
Crus of diaphragm 255
Crust
Moon 41
Ocean floor 298
Pulsar 28
Regional
metamorphism 274
Structure of comet 53
Structure of Earth 38-
39
Structure of Mars 43
Structure of Mercury 35
Structure of Venus 37
Crustaceans 172-173
Arthropoda 170

Cretaceous period 72-
73
Fossil 279
Crustal movement
Coastline 294
Faults and folds 60
Mineralization zones
280
Mountain building 62
Rock cycle 266
Volcano 272
Crustal plate boundary 39
Crustal plates 58-59, 60
Crustose lichen 114
Crutch
Viking karv 375
Crux-Centaurus Arm 14
Crypt 467
Crypt-window 481
Crystalline external crust
28
Crystalline stalagmitic
floor 284
Crystallization 307
Crystal Palace Exhibition
Hall 492-493
Crystals
Faults 60
Intrusive igneous rocks
275
Mineral features 270-
271
Minerals 268-269
Solids 307
Crystal systems 270
Ctenidium 176
CT scan 214
Cube 623
Cubic crystal 270
Cubic system 270
Cubital fossa 211
Cuboid bone 232
Cucumis melo 149
Cud 198
Cuesta 283
Culm 131
Cumulonimbus cloud 302
Cumulus cloud 302
Cuneate leaf base 136-137
Cuneus 465
Cup 509
Cup mute 507
Cupola 466, 479, 493
Cupressus glabra 123
Cup-shaped mouthpiece
506-507
Cup surrounding stomata
157
Cupula 242
Cupule 150
Curium 311
Current 296-297
Current electricity 316
Curtain 477, 497
Curtain wall 466, 496, 498
Curtiss, Glenn 398
Curtiss Model-D Pusher
398-399
Curved buttress 478-481
Curved cornice 462
Curvilinear tracery 470,
472
Cuscuta europaea 163
Cushion
Doric capital 460
Rowing positions 373
Cushion star 175
Cusp
Asian building 488
Gothic building 472-473
Structure of a tooth 247
Cuspate fold 61
Cuspate foreland 294
Cusped arch 489
Cuspidate leaf apex 137
Cutaneous nerve 238
Cuticle
Bishop pine needle 124
Dryland plants 156

Golden barrel cactus
156
Hair 234
Haworthia truncata 157
Leaf 139
Lithops bromfieldii 157
Marram grass 113
Monocotyledon leaf 126
Nail 231
Rose stem 135
Rush stem 135
Wetland plants 158
Cuttlefish 176
Cutty Sark 392
Cyanotrichite 269
Cycadophyta 122
Cycads 68, 122-123, 279
Cycas revoluta 68, 123
Cycas sp. 68
Cyclic-pitch lever 422-423
Cyclone assembly 592
Cyclonic storm
Structure of Earth 39
Structure of Mars 43
Structure of Neptune 50
Cyclostomata 178
Cygnus 19, 20
Cylinder
Diesel train 326
Early engines 342-343
"Ellerman Lines" steam
locomotive 325
Iron paddlesteamer 392
Modern piston aero-
engines 410
Motorcycle 362, 366
Oldsmobile engine 336
"Rocket" steam
locomotive 324
Cylinder barrel
Mid West two-stroke
engine 410
Werner motorcycle 362
Cylinder block 339
Cylinder-cooling gills 407
Cylinder drain cock lever
325
Cylinder head
72° V10 engine 356
ARV light aircraft 425
British Rail Class 20
diesel engine 327
Daimler engine 343
Jaguar straight six
engine 344
Jaguar V12 engine 345
Mid West two-stroke
engine 410
Oldsmobile engine 336
Two-stroke engine 366
Velocette OHV engine
367
Cylinder liner
Jaguar Straight six
engine 344
Mid West two-stroke
engine 410
cylinder shape 623
Cylinder surface area
measurement 590
Cylinder volume
measurement 590
Cylinder wall 343
Cylindrical fault 61
Cylindrical map
projection 264
Cyma recta 475
Cyma reversa 460, 472
Cymatium 475
Cymbals 504-505, 516-517
Drum kit 518
Cyme 129, 143
Cypress 123
Cypselas 150
Cyrillus 40
Cystic duct 248
Cytoplasm
Chlamydomonas sp. 116
Diatom 116

Human 217
  Palisade mesophyll 139
  Root cell 132
  Thalassiosira sp. 116
Cytosine 216

D

Dacron 548
Dacron sailcloth 384
Dacron skin 426
Dactylus 172-173
Dado
  Baroque church 481
  French temple 485
  Neoclassical building 479
  Renaissance building 476
Dagger 472
Dagoba stupa 490-491
Daimler double-sleeve valve engine 343
Daimler, Gottlieb 334
Daisy gypsum 269
Dakota sandstone 276
D'Alembert 41
Dalmatian coastline 295
Da Maiano, B. 474
Damped anti-shock swivel base 584
Damper
  Piano 514
  TGV electric high-speed train 329
  Wagon bogie 331
Damper bar 516
Damper body 365
Damper pedal
  Concert grand piano 515
  Tubular bells 516
  Upright piano 514
  Vibraphone 517
Damper unit 425
Damp lime-plaster 434
Damselfly 168
Dancette-pattern mosaic 489
Dandelion 150
Danforth anchor 386
Danger area 556
Danilova 36
Dark mica 274
Dark nebulae 16
Darlingtonia californica 160-161
Dart sac 177
Darwin 43
Da Sangallo, G. 474
Dash 553
Dashboard
  1906 Renault 337
  Bordino Steam Carriage 335
  Ford Model T 338
Dashboard radiator 336-337
Dash panel 353
Dash radio speaker 353
Data cartridge 591
Data entry key pad
  Digital sampler 521
  Synthesizer 520
  Wind synthesizer 521
Data increment control 521
Data plug 591
Data plug socket 591
Date book button 568
Daucus carota 128, 132
Daughter bulbs 154
Daughter plants 154
Davit 395
D-block 310-311
DC converter 355
DC converter connection 355

DC current 328
DC socket 586
Dead-ball line 550
Deadeye
  74-gun ship 380
  Longboat 380
  Rigging 382-383
  Roman corbita 373
  Sailing warship 377
Deadnettle 135
Dead organisms 278
Dead plant encrustations 284
Dead Sea 292-293
Deadwood 381
Debris
  Glacier 286-287
  Mountain building 62
  Ray crater 34
Decathlon 542
Decidual plate 260
Deciduous plants 150-151
Deciduous teeth 246
Deciduous trees 72
Deck
  Greek trireme 373
  Roman corbita 373
Deck beam
  74-gun ship 380
  Ironclad 393
  Paddle steamer 390, 393
  Roman corbita 372
Deck house 373, 376
Deck lantern 392
Deck planking 393
Deck rail 373
Decorative letter 445
Deep cracks 284-285
Deep current systems 296-297
Deepened valley 295
Deep floor 393
Deep mid wicket 538
Deep-ocean floor 298
Deep-ocean floor sediments 299
Deep peroneal nerve 238
Deep relief carving 453
Deep square leg 538
Deer 104, 198-199
Deer hopper dry fly 563
Defence 526, 535
Defenders
  Ice hockey 550
  Lacrosse 541
  Soccer 524
Defending zones 550
Defensive back 526
Defensive end 526
Defensive tackle 526
Deflation hollow 283
Degreased bare metal 348
Dehiscence 150-151
  Fern spore 121
  Pollen sac 144
Dehiscent fruits 150-151
Dehydration 152
De-icing leading edge 414, 415
Deimos 42
Deinonychus 73
Deinotherium 77
Dekla Tessera 37
de la Cierva, Juan 422
Deleted items icon 576
Delete icon 576
Delphinium 150
Delphinium orientalis 141
Delphinium sp. 151
Delphinus 19, 20
Delta
  Coastline 294
  River features 290
  River 288-289
  Rock cycle 266-267
Delta Andromedae 19
Delta Crucis 21
Delta formation 291

Delta Hydri 20
Delta II expendable launch vehicle 615
Delta ring 48
Deltavjatia vjatkensis 81
"Deltic" diesel-electric locomotive 326-327
Deltoid leaf 137
Deltoid ligament 252
Deltoid muscle 226-227
Demountable wheel 338-339
Dendrite 259
Dendritic copper 268
Dendritic gold 268
Dendritic river drainage 288
Deneb 19, 20
  Hertzsprung-Russell diagram 23
Deneb Algedi 19, 20
Deneb Kaitos 19, 20
Denebola 18, 21
Dens 222
Density
  Formation of black hole 29
  Massive stars 26-27
  Small stars 24-25
  Stellar black hole 29
Dentary 181
Dentary bone 96, 102, 107
Dentate leaf margin
  Hogweed 129
  Ice-plant 129
  Live-for-ever 129
  Mulberry 130
  Rock stonecrop 128
Dentil
  Ancient Roman building 462
  Baroque church 479, 481
  Cathedral dome 487
  French temple 485
  Neoclassical building 478
  Renaissance building 475
Dentine 247
Deoxyribonucleic acid strand 139
Deperdussin, Armand 400
Depressed arch
  Ancient Roman building 462
  Islamic building 488-489
Depressions 302
Depressor anguli oris muscle 228-229
Depressor labii inferioris muscle 229
Depth charge 394
Derailleur cage plate 358
Deranged river drainage 288
Dermal armour 95
Dermal papilla 235
Dermis 234-235
Derrick 392, 395
Descender 445
Descending colon 249
Desert 39, 57
  Carboniferous to Permian period 66
  Earth's physical features 264-265
  Rock cycle 266
  Weathering and erosion 282-283
Desertification 57, 76
Desiccated clay 283
Design
  Fresco 434-435
  Modelled sculpture 452
  Mosaic 449
Deslandres 40
Desmid 112

Destination screen 352
Detachable bud 154
Detachable ink reservoir 444
Detachable rim 339
Detector 610
Detergent tray 594, 595
Detergent tray holder 595
Detergent tray recess 595
Deuterium nucleus 22
Deutscher Werkbund style 495
Devonian fish 65
Devonian period 64-65, 80
  Fossil record 279
  Geological time 56
  Primitive life 78
Devon minnow 563
Dewlap 184
Dextral strike-slip fault 61
Dhow 376
Diabase sill 277
Diagonal bracing 401
Diagonal reinforcement 374
Diagonal strut 399
Diagonal turn 388
Dial
  Clocktower 493
  Sundial 377
Diameter 622
  Atoms 308
  Earth 30
  Fluorine-19 atom 309
  Fluorine-19 nucleus 309
  Jupiter 26, 44
  Jupiter's moons 44
  Life of massive star 26-27
  Life of small star 21-26
  Mars 30
  Mars' moons 42
  Mercury 30
  Moon 40
  Neptune 31
  Neptune's moons 50
  Planets 30-31
  Pluto 31
  Saturn 27, 46
  Saturn's moons 46
  Stars 22
  Sun 32
  Uranus 27, 48
  Uranus' moons 48
  Venus 30
Diamond 311
  Mineral features 270-271
  Native elements 268
Diamond-shaped painting knife 436
Diamond whetstone 452
Diaphragm
  ARV Super 2 424
  Chimpanzee 202
  Domestic cat 195
  Elephant 200
  Human 215, 254-255
  Rabbit 196
Diastema 106
Diatom 116
Diceros bicornis 199
Dichasial cyme 143
Dicksonia antarctica 70, 112-113
Dicloelosia bilobata 65
Dicotyledon 126-127, 141-145
Dicyothyris 278
Didelphis 106
Didelphis virginiana 207
Dielectric sandwich 584
Diesel-electric train 326
Diesel fuel injection 326
Diesel motor compartment 397
Diesel, Rudolph 326
Diesel train 324, 326-327

Differential 356
Differential housing 338
Diffuser 356
Digestive caecum 173, 176
Digestive enzymes 160
Digestive gland
  Snail 177
  Spider 170
Digestive glands/zones
  Butterwort 161
  Monkey cup 161
  Venus fly trap 160
Digestive system
  Cow 198
  Human 248-249
Digit 105
Digital artery 231, 253
Digital camera 580-581
Digital extensor muscle 94
Digital flexor muscle 84
Digital nerve 231
Digital sampler 520-521
Digital vein 253
Digital video camera 582-585
Digital video jack cover 582
Digitate leaf 137
Digits
  Bird 189
  Bird's wing 191
  Frog 182
  Kangaroo 207
  Rabbit 196-197
  Rat 196
  Salamander 182
  Seal 204
Dilator muscle 241
Dilsea carnosa 117
Dimetrodon loomisi 67
Dinghy 560
Dinosaur cladogram 83
Dinosaur 56-57, 80, 82-83
  Fossil record 279
Diode assembly 587
Dionaea muscipula 160
Dione 46
Dip 60
Diplodocus 70, 88, 90-91
Dip pen 450
Dipping bed rock 60-61
Dipping lug foresail 385
Diprotodon 76
Dip-slip fault 61
Dipstick 354
Dipstick tube 346, 356
Dipterus valenciennesi 81
Direct current 328
Direct current (DC) inlet 571
Directional button membrane 578
Directional button pad 578
Direction bar 414
Direction-finding-aerial fairing 408
Direct method mosaic creation 450
Direct-vision panel
  ARV light aircraft 425
  Bell-47 helicopter 422
Dirt track motorcycle racing 368
Disc
  Basal 167
  Crab 166-167
  Liverwort 118
  Pedal 167
  Sea anemone 166-167
  Starfish 174
  Starfish fossil 79
Disc brake
  Harley-Davidson FLHS Electra Glide 362-363
  Honda CB750 563
  Honda VF750 364

Husqvarna Motocross TC610 368
Lockheed Electra airliner 407
Motorcycle 364-365
Suzuki RGV500 368-369
Disc brake calliper 364, 368-369
Disc cover 579
Disc drive motor 587
Disc florets 129, 142, 145
Disc loading tray 579
Disconformity 276
Discovery Rupes 35
Disc tray 579
Disc tray shutter 586, 587
Discus 542-543
Disk drag 562-563
Displacement reactions 312
Display 578, 587
Display button 585
Display screen 581, 585, 587, 596
Display screen and control circuits 585
Display/touch panel button 583
Distal convoluted tubule 256-257
Distal end of radius 231
Distal interphalangeal joint 231
Distal phalanx 219, 230, 252
Distal tarsal 183
Distance lines
  Gaelic football 529
  Rugby 530
Distance running 542
Distance signalling 330
Distilled water 444
Distiller 397
Distributary
  River features 290-291
  Rivers 288-289
Distributor
  Hawker Tempest Mark V 408
  Jaguar straight six engine 344
  Jaguar V12 engine 345
  Renault Clio 351
Distributor drive shaft 345
Distributor fixing point 346
Diving 558-559
DNA 139, 216, 606
Dobro resonator 513
Dock 554
Document ejection roller 573
Document feed roller 573
Document panel 407
Document pinch roller 573
Document pressure bar assembly 572
Document table 571
Dodder 163
Dog 104, 194-195
Dogfish 178-179, 192
Dog-leg hole 546
Dog-leg staircase 481
Doline 284-285
Dolomedes fimbriatus 171
Dolphins 204-205
Dolphin striker 382
Domain name 576
Dome 484, 486-487
  Ancient Roman building 462
  Asian building 490-491
  Baroque church 480-481
  French temple 485
  Islamic building 488
  Medieval building 467, 469

Neoclassical building 478
Renaissance building 475-477
Domed receptacle 142
Domed roof 489
Domed topdeck 401
Domed turret 493
Dome metalling 486
Dome of the Rock 487
Dome timbering 486
Dome volcano 62, 272
Donjon 466-467
Donkey boiler 392
Donor genetic material 606, 607
Door
Ancient Egyptian tomb 458-459
Ancient Roman building 463
Baroque church 479
Bell 206 jetliner 423
Double-decker touring bus 333
Gatwick Express "People Mover" 328
MCW Metrobus 332-333
Microwave combination oven 596
Neoclassical building 478
Renaissance theatre 477
Renault Clio 349
Single-decker bus 333
TGV electric high-speed train 329
Washer-dryer 594
Door catch 341
Door catch with safety cut-out 595
Door frame 412
Door glass 348
Door handle 341, 348
Door hinge 612
Door jamb 478
Door key and lock 348
Door lock 596, 602
Door metal cap 595
Door moulding 353
Door porthole 595
Door safety cut-out mechanism 596
Door trim panel 353
Doorway 474-475, 479, 481, 495
Door wiring loom 595
Doppler 41
Dorado 21
Doric capital 460
Doric column 460, 464
Doric half-column 464
Doric order 460
Dormancy
Horse chestnut bud 130
Seed 152
Dormant volcano 272
Dormer head 493
Dormer window 476, 493, 495
Dorsal abdominal artery 173
Dorsal aorta
Bony fish 181
Dogfish 179
Frog 182
Dorsal blood vessel 169
Dorsal fin
ARV light aircraft 424
Bony fish 181
Concorde 416
Dogfish 179
Dolphin 205
Lamprey 178
World War II aircraft 408-409
Dorsal fin ray 181
Dorsal interosseous muscle 233

Dorsal lobe 158
Dorsal mantle cavity 176
Dorsal margin of shell 176
Dorsal metatarsal artery 253
Dorsal plate 78, 92-93
Dorsal scale 184, 186
Dorsal scute 95
Dorsal spine base 78
Dorsal venous arch 253
Dorsal vertebrae
Archaeopteryx 85
Brachiosaurus 90
Diplodocus 90
Eryops 80
Euoplocephalus 94
Gallimimus 86
Iguanodon 96
Kentrosaurus 93
Parasaurolophus 99
Pareiasaur 81
Plateosaurus 88
Stegoceras 101
Stegosaurus 93
Struthiomimus 87
Tuojiangosaurus 93
Tyrannosaurus 84
Dorsum 213
Double-arm pantograph 328
Double bass 503-505, 510, 511
Double bassoon 504-505
Double-decker bus 332-333
Double decomposition reaction 312-313
Double-dipper palette attachment 436
Double-ended hull 375
Double flat 502
Double halyard 373
Double helix 216
Double-planet system
Earth 38
Pluto 50
Double-pyramid crystal 270
Double reed 508
Double rope becket 383
Doubles 544
Double samaras
Dry fruit 150-151
Sycamore 131
Double scull 561
Double sharp 502
Double topsail schooner 385
Dowel
Mid West single rotor engine 410
Mortice-and-tenon fastening 373
Dowel hole 410-411
Downfolds 60
Downhaul 385
Downhill skiing 552
"Downs" 526
Downthrow 60
Down tube 360
Dox formation 277
Dpad, 8-way 579
Dpi (Dots Per Inch) 570
Draco 19, 20
Draft mark
Frigate 397
Wooden sailing ship 379
Drafts icon 576
Draft tube 314
Drag
Biplanes and triplanes 402
Cycling 360
Early monoplane 400
Early passenger aircraft 406
Drag knob 563

Drag link
19th century paddlesteamer 391
Ford Model T 339
White Steam Car 342
Dragon prowhead 374
Drag spindle 562
Drag washer 562
Drainage systems divide 289
Drain mast 412, 415
Drain-pipe 492
Drain plug 339
Drakensberg 265
Draught mark 379, 397
Dravidian finial 491
Dravidian style 490
Drawbridge 493
Drawbridge windlass 467
Drawing 430-431
Drawing board 430, 444-445
Drawing instruments 430
Drawing materials 430
Dreadnought-type battleship 394
Dressing-room 477
Dribbling
Basketball 552
Gaelic football 528
Handball 534-535
Soccer 524
Drill 600-601
D ring 46-47
Drip-cap 482
Drive 543
Drive belt 354, 335, 344, 562
Drive bracket 405
Drive chain 366, 368
Drive end 317
Drive gear 411
Drive gear access hole 580
Drive gear assembly 572
Driven gear 410
Driven pulley 335
Drive pillar 424
Drive pin 580
Drive plate 345
Drive point 346
Driver 547
Driver protection 357
Driverless train 328
Driver's platform 324
Driver's radio aerial 357
Driver's seat
Bordino Steam Carriage 335
"Deltic" diesel-electric locomotive 327
"Mallard" express steam locomotive 325
Paris Metro 328
Drive shaft
Jet engine 419
Renault Clio 351
Volkswagen Beetle 340
Drive sprocket mounting spline 366
Drive-wheel 601
Driving band 397
Driving chain 335
Driving pulley 335
Driving rein 555
Driving saddle 555
Driving sprocket 335
Driving wheel 324-325
Drizzle 302
Dromiceiomimus 86
Droop nose 416
Droop stop 422-423
Drop 381
Drop arm
Ford Model T 339
White Steam Car 542
Drop-down window 334
Drop glass 341
Drop goal 530

Drop handlebar 361
Drop-kick 530
Drop tank 408
Drop window 332
Drowned coastline 294-295
Drowned valley 295
Drum 486
Ancient Greek building 460
Baroque church 481
Cathedral dome 487
Relief printing press 449
Washer-dryer 595
Drum and door seal 595
Drum brake
BMW R/60 362
Motorcycle 364-365
Vespa Grand Sport 160 Mark 1 363
"Windcheetah" racing HPV bicycle 361
Drumhead 387
Drum inlet elbow 595
Drumlins 286
Drum pad 520
Drums 518-519, 520
Drum suspension springs 595
Drupelets 146-149
Drupes 131, 148-149
Dry air 303
Dry brush 458-439
Dry capacity measurements 590
Dry fresco 434-435
Dry fruits 150-151
Couch grass 113
Durmast oak 131
Sycamore 131
Dry gallery 284-285
Drying agent 313
Dry lake bed 283
Dryland plants 156-157
Dryopteris filix-mas 120-121
Dryosaurus 70
Dry pericarps 150
Dry season 293
Dry wash 283
Dual click gear 562
Dual ignition plug 427
Dual seat 364
Dual shock controller 579
Dual sliding zoom lens 581
Dubhe 18
The Plough 19
Dubika 490
Duck 188
Duck-billed platypus 206-207
"Duckbills" 96
Duct 496, 497
Duct of Bellini 256
Ductus deferens 259
Dugout 536
Dumb iron 336, 342
Dummy front door 339
Dunkeld wet fly 563
Duodenum
Bird 189
Cow 198
Elephant 200
Frog 182
Human 215, 248-249
Rabbit 196
Tortoise 187
Duplex tubular cradle frame 363
Duradon 384
Dura mater 223, 237, 240
Durmast oak 131
Dust
Asteroids, comets, and meteoroids 52-53
Mars 42-43
Moon 41

Nebulae and star clusters 16-17
NGC 2997 (spiral galaxy) 12
Overhead view of our galaxy 14
Solar system 30
Venus' atmosphere 37
Dust cap 559
Dust cloud
Geological time 56
Large Magellanic Cloud 12
Mars 42-43
Milky Way 14-15
Nebulae and star clusters 16-17
Origin and expansion of Universe 11
Volcano 272
Dust collection bin 592
Dust lane
Centaurus A 13
Horsehead Nebula 16
NGC 2997 (spiral galaxy) 12
Optical image of Rings and dust lanes 48
Trifid Nebula 16
Dust particles 53
Dust shroud 340
Dust storm 43
Dust tail 52-53
Dutch cubist style 495
Dutch shoe 377
Dutch triple fiddle block 383
DVD/CD control buttons 585
DVD/CD drive turntable 585
DVD/CD laser-reader 585
DVD/CD on-screen menu display button 585
DVD/CD processor microchip 585
DVD/CD sliding tray 585
DVD/CD stop button 585
DVD display button 585
DVD player 584-585
Dwarf crocodile 82
Dwarf shoot 124-125
Dyke 274
Dyke swarm 274
Dynastes hercules 12
Dyson DC05 vacuum cleaner 592-593
Dysprosium 311

E
Ear
Calligraphy characters 445
Elephant 200
Gorilla 203
Hare 196
Horse 198
Human 210, 212, 242-243
Kangaroo 207
Rabbit 196
Rat 196
Eardrum
Chick 193
Frog 182
Human 243
Lizard 184
Earles fork 562
Early desertification 57
Early engines 342-343
Early English
Perpendicular-style tracery 472
Early English-style window 472
Early monoplanes 400-401

Early passenger aircraft 406-407
Early tram 332
Early voyagers 374-375
Earphone connector 589
Earphone socket 587
Earpiece 586, 588
Earpiece cover 586
Earplug 558
Earth 38-39
Cretaceous period 73
Energy emission from Sun 22
Jurassic period 71
Objects in Universe 11
Phases of the Moon 41
Primitive life 78-79
Quaternary period 77
Solar eclipse 32
Solar System 30
Tertiary period 75
Tides 297
Triassic period 69
Earth-ball fungus 115
Earth bank 603
Earth connection 598
Earth formation 56-57
Earth pigments 434
Earthquake anatomy 63
Earthquake region 39
Earthquakes
Crustal movement 58
Faults and folds 60
Mountain building 62-63
Earth's atmosphere 38-39, 78, 300-301
Earth's composition 39
Earth's core 38-39, 63
Earth's crust 38-39, 58-59
Igneous and metamorphic rocks 274
Lake formation 292
Volcano 272
Earth's crustal plates 62, 64
Earth's energy 314
Earth's evolution 56-57
Earth's external features 39
Earth's formation 38, 56, 64
Earth's interior
Ocean floor 298
Rock cycle 266
Structure 39
Earth's layers 38
Earth's magnetic field 38
Earth's mantle 38-39, 58-59
Earth's orbit 297
Earth's physical features 264-265
Earth's rotation 38
Atmospheric circulation and winds 300
Oceans and seas 296
Satellite mapping 264
Earth's satellite 38
Earth's surface
Atmosphere 300-301
Earth's physical features 264
Formation of the Earth 38-39
Geological time 56
Mineral resources 280
Mountain building 62
Oceans and seas 296
Precambrian to Devonian period 64
Rock cycle 266
Earth's tilt 58
Earth wire 594
Earwig 168
East Africa 331
East Asian buildings 490-491
East Australian current 297

East Greenland current 296
Eaves
 Ancient Greek building 461
 Ancient Roman building 462, 464
 Islamic tomb 489
 Modern building 499
 Neoclassical building 482
 Renaissance building 477
Eaves board 490
Eccentric 392
Eccentric rod 391
Eccentric rotor journal 347
Eccentric shaft 347, 411
Eccentric-shaft bearing 410
Echidna nebulosa 180
Echidnas 206
Echinocactus grusonii 156
Echinoderms 174, 279
Echinus 460
Echinus esculentus 175
Echo-sounding 298
Ecliptic
 Inclination of planetary orbits 31
 Stars of northern skies 18-19
 Stars of southern skies 20-21
ECM 355
Ecphora 75
Ectoderm 167
Eddy Merckx racing bicycle 360-361
Edible sea urchin 175
Edmontonia 95
Eel 180
Efferent arteriole 256-257
Effervescence 512
Effort 520-521
Egg cells 606-607
Eggs 192-193
 Amphibian 78, 80
 Baltimore oriole 193
 Bee hummingbird 193
 Bird 188
 Butterfly 168
 Capsule 192
 Carrion crow 193
 Case 192
 Chaffinch 193
 Chicken 192
 Common tern 193
 Dinosaur 82
 Dogfish 192
 Frog 182-183, 192
 Giant stick insect 192
 Greater backblacked gull 193
 Hatching 192-193
 Human 258, 260
 Indian stick insect 192
 Leaf insect 192
 Maiasaura 98
 Membrane 193
 Ostrich 193
 Quail 192-193
 Reptile 66, 184
 Titanosaurid 91
 Willow grouse 193
Egg tempera 432
Egg-tooth 192-193
Egg white 192
Egg yolk binding medium 432
Egypt 331
Egyptian building 458-459
Eichhornia crassipes 158
Eighteenth-century building 492
 Baroque 481
 Neoclassical 478, 482-483

Eighth-century building 490-491
Einsteinium 311
Eisila Regio 36-37
Ejaculatory duct 259
Ejecta
 Degas and Brönte 34
 Features of supernova 27
 Ray crater 34
 Venusian craters 32
Eject knob 583
Ejector assembly 599
Ejector exhaust 408
Ejector-seat roof hatches 421
Ekeing 381
Ekman spiral 296-297
El-Ainyi Mosque 488
Elapsed time display 577
Elasmobranchs 178
Elastic fibre 252, 254
Elastic rocks 60
Elbow
 Anchisaurus 89
 Corythosaurus 98
 Edmontonia 95
 Gorilla 203
 Horse 199
 Human 210
 Iguanodon 97
 Lion 194
 Psittacosaurus 103
 Stegoceras 101
 Stegosaurus 92
 Triceratops 102
Elbow guard 553
Elbow joint
 Brachiosaurus 91
 Diplodocus 90
 Eryops 80
 Euoplocephalus 94
 Human 218
 Parasaurolophus 99
 Plateosaurus 88
 Stegoceras 101
 Triceratops 102
 Tyrannosaurus 84
Elbow motor 609
Elbow pad 527, 551
Elder 150-131, 140 143
Electrical braking 330
Electrical cells 316-317
Electrical charge imbalance 316
Electrical circuit 316
 Toaster 598
Electrical contact 319
Electrical effects 316
Electrical energy 314-315
Electrical harness 414
Electrical inverter 422
Electrical plant 496
Electrical relay 596
Electrical relay box 350
Electrical service compartment 407
Electrical supply 316
Electrical wiring harness 418
Electric bass guitars 512
Electric cable 517
Electric car 342
Electric charge 308
Electric coil 517
Electric current 316-317, 328. 603
Electric equipment compartment 329
Electric fuel pump 422
Electric generator 317
Electric guitar 512-513
Electric heating elements 597
Electric ignition control 362
Electricity 316-317
Electricity connector to brushbar motor 593

Electricity generation
 Diesel train 326
 Electric train 326
 Magnetism 317
Electricity supply 590
Electric locomotive 324, 328-329
Electric motor
 Diesel train 326
 Electric train 328
 Tram 332
Electric motor/generator 357
Electric motor housing 354
Electric power line 328, 402
Electric power socket 422
Electric scoring system 556-557
Electric street tramway 332
Electric toaster 598
Electric train 328-329
Electric tram 332
Electric transmission 326
Electric window motor 349
Electrode 306
Electromagnet 317, 598
Electromagnetic induction capacitor 600
Electromagnetic radiation 314-315, 318
Electromagnetic spectrum 318-319
Electron 308, 316
 Atomic number 310
 Fluorine-19 309
Electron beam 611
Electron detector assembly 611
Electron gun 611
Electron gun housing 610
Electronic controller 605
Electronic control signals 330
Electronic control-unit connector 356
Electronic drums 520
Electronic engine control (EEC) unit 418-419
Electronic games 578-579
Electronic ignition unit 351
Electronic impulses 584
Electronic instruments 520-521
Electronic signals 512
Electronic warfare mast 397
Electrons 605
Electron shell 308-309, 310
Electron stream 611
Electron transfer 308
Electrostatic forces 308, 316
Electrostatic generator 316
Electrothermal de-icing panel 416
Element retaining stop 599
Elements 306, 308
 Atomic mass 310
 Minerals 268
 Periodic table 310-311
Elephant 90, 104, 200-201
Elephas maximus 200
Elevated green 546
Elevating wheel 396
Elevation 498
Elevator
 ARV light aircraft 424
 BAe-146 components 415
 Bell-47 helicopter 423

Biplanes and triplanes 402-403
 Curtiss biplane 399
 Early monoplanes 400-401
 Hawker Tempest components 409
 Schleicher glider 426
 World War I aircraft 405
 Wright Flyer 399
Elevator arm 425
Elevator chassis box 415
Elevator control cable 399, 403
Elevator control rod 409
Elevator control wire
 Bell-47 helicopter 423
 Blériot XI monoplane 401
 Curtiss biplane 399
 LVG CVI fighter 405
Elevator drive wheel 399
Elevator hinge
 BAe-146 components 415
 BE 2B tail 405
 Blackburn monoplane 400
 Hawker Tempest components 409
Elevator operating arm 399
Elevator-operating bracket 401
Elevator push-rod 424-425
Elevator rocking arm 404
Elevator trimtab 424, 409
Elevator wire 398
Eleventh-century building 466, 468
Elevon 416-417, 421
Elevon-jack fairing 416
Elevon power control unit 417
"Ellerman Lines" steam locomotive 324-325
Elliott steering knuckle 336
Ellipsoid orb 486
Elliptical galaxy 11-12
Elliptical orbit 30
Elliptic leaf 137
Elm 144, 150
El Nath 18, 21
Elodea canadensis 158-159
Elodea sp. 159
Elongating root 133, 153
Eltanin 19
Elytron 168
E-mail 576, 577
E-mail address 576
E-mail program 576, 577
E-mail sender 576
Emarginate apex 136
Embellisher 553
Embolos 372
Embrasure 466-467, 469
Embryo 607
 Cotyledon 152-153
 Dry fruit seed 150-151
 Fertilization 146-147
 Germination 152-153
 Human 260
 Reptile 80
 Seed leaf 152
 Succulent fruit seed 148-149
Embryonic root 150, 152-153
Embryonic shoot 147
 Epigeal germination 153
 Hypogeal germination 152
 Pea seed 150
 Pine 122
 Seed axis 152-153

Embryo sac 146-147
Emergency canopy release handle 420
Emergency door control 332-333
Emergency escape hatch 406
Emergency exit 416-417
Emergency oxygen cylinder 417
Emergent coastlines 294-295
Emission nebula 11-12, 14, 16-17
Empire State Building 494
Enamel
 Islamic buildings 488, 489
 Teeth 247
Enceladus 46
Encke 40
Encke Division 46-47
Enclosed bridge 397
Enclosed DVD/CD compartment 585
Encroachment 527
End 388-389
End baffle plate 598-599
End block 512
End effector 608
End element 598-599
End-grain wood block 449
End-line
 American football 526
 Basketball 552
 Men's Lacrosse 540
 Volleyball 554
End link 586
Endocardium 250
Endocarp 146-147, 148-149
Endoderm 167
Endodermis
 Bishop pine needle 124
 Canadian pond weed stem 158-159
 Dicotyledon 127
 Epiphytic orchid 162
 Fern rachis 121
 Horsetail stem 120
 Mare's tail stem 135
 Monocotyledon 127
 Pine root 125
 Root 132-133
 Water hyacinth root 158
Endomysium 228
Endoperidium 115
Endoplasmic reticulum 239
Endopod 172
Endoscopic view
 Alimentary canal 248
 Vocal cords 245
Endoskeleton 174
Endosperm 147
Endosteum 225
Endothecium 144
Endothelium 252
End-pin 510
End-plate
 Formula One racing car 356-357
 Modern piston aero-engine 410-411
End-plate aerodynamic skirt 357
End zone 526
En échelon fractures 60-61
Energized electrode 584
Energy 314-315
 Chemical reactions 512
 Electron shells 310
 Light 318
 Renewable 604-605
Energy conversion 138
Energy emission from Sun 22
Engaged column 469

Engaged pediment 462-463
Engine 342-347, 410-411, 418-419
 1906 Renault 337
 1-litre VTEC 354
 72° V10 556
 ARV light aircraft 425
 BAe-146 jetliner 415
 BMW R/60 362
 Bordino Steam Carriage 334
 Diesel 326
 Early monoplane 400-401
 Hawker Tempest components 408
 Helicopter 422-423
 Honda CB750 363
 Honda VF750 364
 Kirby BSA 369
 Lockheed Electra airliner 406-407
 Motorcycles 362, 364, 366-367
 Oldsmobile engine 336
 Pegasus Quasar microlight 427
 Pioneers of flight 398-399
 Renault Clio 350-351
 Velocette overhead valve (OHV) 367
 Volkswagen Beetle 340
Engine aft bulkhead 421
Engine air intake
 BE 2B bomber 404
 Concorde 416
 Formula One racing car 356, 357
 Hawker Tempest fighter 409
 Schweizer helicopter 423
 Tornado 420
Engine and propeller thrust frame 398
Engine bearer 343
Engine block 347
Engine cover
 Formula One racing car 356, 357
 Honda VF750 374
 Oldsmobile bodywork 337
 Two-stroke engine 366
 Vespa Grand Sport 160 Mark 1 363
 Volkswagen Beetle 341
Engine cowling
 ARV light aircraft 424-425
 Avro biplane 403
 Concorde 416
 Hawker Tempest components 408
 Lockheed Electra airliner 407
 Pegasus Quasar microlight 427
Engine crankcase 327
Engine drive belt 554
Engineering 496
Engine front mount 418-419
Engine front support link 417
Engine fuel pump 417
Engine instruments 425
Engine lid 341
Engine lifting eye 347
Engine mounting
 ARV light aircraft 425
 Blackburn monoplane 401
 Honda VF750 364
 Modern piston aero-engine 411

Pegasus Quasar microlight 427
Velocette OHV engine 367
Engine pylon 412
Engine rear mount
  Pegasus Quasar microlight 427
  Turboprop engine 419
Engine room 326
Engine timing gear 336
Englacial moraine 287
Englacial stream 286
England 92
English baroque style 480-481
English bond brickwork 485
English Decorated style 470
English ivy 151
English Perpendicular style 470, 472
Engraving 446
Enif 19, 20
  Pegasus and Andromeda 19
Ensign staff 596
Entablature
  Ancient Greek building 460
  Ancient Roman building 462-465
  Baroque church 480-481
  Cathedral dome 487
  French temple 485
  Neoclassical building 478-479, 482-483
Entasis 461
Enter button 585
Enter key 590
Enteromorpha linza 117
Entomophilous pollination 144
Entrance
  Islamic tomb 489
  Medieval building 466-467
  Modern building 496-499
  Neoclassical building 483
  Nineteenth-century building 495
  Twentieth-century building 494
Entrenched meander 290
Entresol 467
Enucleated egg cell 606
Enzyme 160
Eocene epoch
  Fossil record 279
  Geological timescale 57
Eon
  Fossil record 279
  Geological time 56-57
Epée 556-557
Epibranchial artery 179
Epicardium 250
Epicentre 63
Epicotyl 152-153
Epicranial aponeurosis 237
Epidermal cell 166
Epidermis
  Apical meristem 134
  Canadian pond weed stem 159
  Clubmoss stem 120
  Dicotyledon 126-127
  Epiphytic orchid 162
  Fern rachis 121
  Flower 142
  Horsetail stem 120
  Human 234-235
  Leaf 139
  Marram grass 113
  Monocotyledon 126-127

Moss 119
Multi-layered 162
Pine needle 124
Pine stem 125
Prickle 135
Radicle 152
Rhizome 155
Root 132-133
Stem 134-135
Water hyacinth 158
Water lily 159
Epididymis 259
Epidote 269
Epigeal germination 152-153
Epiglottis
  Elephant 200
  Human 212, 244-245, 248, 255
Epiphysis 230
Epiphytes 112, 162-163
Epithelial cell 217
Epithelium 254
Epocciptal bone 102
Epoch
  Fossil record 279
  Geological time 56-57
Epoxy resin frame 612
Epsilon Centauri 21
Epsilon Crucis 21
Epsilon Hydri 20
Epsilon ring 48-49
Epson Perfection 1650 scanner 570, 571
Epson Stylus Photo 895 colour inkjet printer 574
EQ button 587
Equal-shock intensity lines 63
Equator
  Atmosphere 300
  Quaternary period 76
  Saturn 47
  Satellite map 265
  Surface currents 297
Equatorial air 300
Equatorial current 296-297
Equatorial furrow 144
Equatorial Zone 45
Equestrian sports 554-555
Equisetites sp. 66
Equilateral triangle 622
Equisetum arvense 70, 120
Equuleus 19, 20
Era
  Fossil record 279
  Geological time 56-57
Eraser 430
Erasing stick 448
Erbium 311
Erect limb stance 82
Erh-wei 376
Eridanus 19, 20
E ring 46
Erosion 282-283
  Coastline 294-295
  Lake formation 293
  Ocean floor 298
  River features 290-291
  Rock cycle 267
  Sedimentary rocks 276
Eryops 80-81
Escalator 497-498
Esker 286
Estonioceras perforatum 65
Estuarine mud-flat 295
Estuary 288, 290-294
Eta Centauri 21
Eta Mensae 20
Eta Orionis 18
Eta ring 48
Eta Sagittarii 21
Etching 446
Ethernet Local Area Network (LAN) port 567
Ethernet network 566

Euathlus emilia 170
Euoplocephalus 94-95
Eurasia 76
Eurasian plate 59
Europa 44
Europe
  Cretaceous period 72-73
  Earth's physical features 264-265
  Electric train 326
  Electric tram 332
  Jurassic period 70
  Loading gauge 331
  Middle Ordovician period 64
  Quaternary period 76
  Railway track gauge 331
  Tertiary period 74-75
  Triassic period 68
European field elm 144
European hard-screw coupling 402
Europium 311
"Eurostar" multi-voltage electric train 328-329
Eurypterid fossil 79
Eustachian tube 243
Eustreptospondylus 85
Euthynteria 460
Evacuated column 610, 611
Evaporation 307
Event horizon 28-29
Evergreens 130-131
Everlasting pea 129
Evolute shell 278
Evolution
  Earth 56-57
  Living things 278
Exchangeable cover 588
Excretory pore 177
Excurrent pore 166
Exfoliation 282
Exhaust
  Catalytic converter 555
  Ford diesel engine 347
  Modern mechanics 350-351
  Paddlesteamer 391
Exhaust clamp 362
Exhaust collector ring 403, 406
Exhaust cone 419
Exhaust connection 427
Exhaust diffuser 418
Exhaust downpipe 350
Exhaust fairing 419
Exhaust gas recirculation valve 344
Exhaust heat shield 345
Exhaust manifold
  1906 Renault 337
  ARV light aircraft 425
  Jaguar V12 engine 345
  Mid West two-stroke engine 410
  Renault Clio 351
Exhaust nozzle 418
Exhaust pipe
  Avro biplane 403
  Bell-47 helicopter 422
  BMW R/60 362
  Brazilian battleship 395
  Harley-Davidson FLHS Electra Glide 363
  Formula One racing car 356
  Hawker Tempest fighter 409
  Honda CB750 363
  Honda VF750 364
  Kirby BSA 369
  Lockheed Electra airliner 406-407
  Oldsmobile engine 336
  Pegasus Quasar microlight 427
  Suzuki RGV500 368

White Steam Car 342
World War I aircraft 404-405
Exhaust pipe flange 411
Exhaust port
  "Deltic" diesel-electric locomotive 326
  Four-stroke cycle 343
  Mid West 75-HP engine 410
  Two-stroke engine 367
  Velocette OHV engine 367
  Wankel engine 347
  Wankel rotary cycle 346
Exhaust silencer 423, 427
Exhaust stack 405
Exhaust steam water injector control 325
Exhaust stroke 343
Exhaust system 368
Exhaust tract 410
Exhaust valve 343-345
Exhaust valve push-rod 400
Exhaust vent
  British Rail Class 20 diesel engine 327
  Drill 601
  "Union Pacific" locomotive 326
Exine 144-145
Exit door 333
Exocarp 146-149
Exocciptal bone 183
Exocet missile launcher 597
Exodermis 162
Exoperidium 115
Exopod 172
Exoskeleton
  Insect 168
  Malacostraca 172
  Spider 171
Exosphere 300
Exothermic reactions 312
Expander bolt 359
Expandible sponge 448
Expansile jaw 85
Expansion card 569
Expansion card slot 569
Expansion lever 325
Expansion of sail 378-379
Expelling plate 597
Expiration 255
Exploding shell 396, 397
Expressionist style 495
Extended cave system 285
Extended port air-brake 421
Extensor digitorum brevis muscle 233
Extensor digitorum longus tendon 233
Extensor digitorum tendon 231
Extensor hallucis brevis muscle 233
Extensor hallucis longus tendon 233
Extensors of hand 227
External anatomy
  Body 210-211
  Brain 257
  Ear 242-243
  Foot 233
  Hand 231
  Sperm 259
External auditory meatus
  Homo erectus 108
  Homo sapiens 108, 220, 242
External crust 28
External elastic lamina 252
External iliac artery 215, 225, 253
External iliac vein 215, 253

External nostril 184
External oblique muscle 226
External occipital crest 220
External pubo-ischio-femoral muscle 97
External skeleton
  Insect 168
  Malacostraca 172
  Spider 171
External spermatic fascia 259
External urinary meatus 258
Extinct geyser 275
Extinction
  Dinosaur 56, 74, 82, 104
  Life 66
  Pleistocene mammals 76
Extinct volcano 62, 272
  Igneous rock structures 275
  Mountain building 62
  Ocean floor 298
Extrados 484-485
Extra period 552
Extrusive rocks 274, 275
Eye
  Allosaurus 85
  Amphibian 182
  Anchisaurus 89
  Angling hook 562
  Beetle 168
  Bird 188
  Bony fish 181
  Brachiosaurus 91
  Bumblebee 168
  Butterfly 169
  Caiman 186
  Carnivore 194
  Chick 192-193
  Corythosaurus 98
  Crab 172
  Crayfish 173
  Crocodilian 186
  Deer hopper dry fly 563
  Devon minnow 563
  Dhow 376
  Dogfish 178
  Dolphin 204
  Elephant 201
  Figurehead 374
  Forward-facing 194
  Frog 182
  Gallimimus 86
  Gorilla 203
  Greek and Roman ships 372
  Herrerasaurus 86
  Horse 198
  Human 211, 212, 240-241
  Iguanodon 97
  Kangaroo 207
  Knot 588
  Lamprey 178
  Lion 194
  Lizard 184
  Median 170
  Octopus 177
  Pachycephalosaurus 100
  Psittacosaurus 103
  Rabbit 196
  Rat 196
  Rattlesnake 185
  Rigging 382-383
  Salamander 182
  Scallop 176
  Scorpion 170
  Seal 204
  Shrimp 172
  Simple 170-171
  Snail 177
  Snake 185
  Spider 170
  Stegoceras 101

Stegosaurus 92
Terrapin 187
Triceratops 102
Trilobite fossil 78
Tyrannosaurus 84
Westlothiana 87
Eyeball 241
Eye bolt 381
Eyebrow
  74-gun ship 581
  Human 212
Eyelash 212
Eyelid
  Caiman 186
  Human 213
  Snake 184
  Terrapin 187
Eye pan motor 609
Eyepieces 610, 611
Eye plate lug 382
Eyespot 116
Eye tilt motor 609

F

F-14 Tomcat fighter 420
Fabric 384
Fabric covering
  Aluminium and steel wing 403
  BE 2B tail 405
  Blériot XI monoplane 401
  Steel-tube fuselage 403
Fabric lacing 405
Fabric skin 401
Fabric softener section 595
Fabry 41
Facade
  Ancient Greek building 461
  Ancient Roman building 465
  Baroque church 480-481
  Gothic church 470-472
  Modern building 496-499
  Neoclassical building 478, 485
  Nineteenth-century building 493
  Renaissance building 474
Facade pediment 481
Facade wall 470
Face
  Deadeye 383
  Human 211
  Sailmaker's mallet 384
Face mask
  American football 526
  Fencing 557
  Hockey goalkeeper 540
  Ice hockey goalkeeper 550
  Lacrosse goalkeeper 541
  Slalom skiing 553
Facet 222-223
Facia 589
"Facing off" 550
Faering 374-375
Fag end 387, 388
Fahrenheit temperature scale 590
Fairing 364, 369
Fairing of landing gear 413
Fairing panel 415
Fairlead
  Battleship 395
  Frigate 397
  Rigging 385
  Roman corbita 373
Fairway 546
Falciform ligament 248

Falco tinnunculus 189
Falkland current 296
Fall 382
Fallopian tube 258-259, 261
False acacia 136
False anthers 141
False door 458-459
False fruit 148-149
False ram bow 394
"False ribs" 218
False septum 151
Falx cerebri 237
Fan
  Jaguar straight six engine 344
  Jet engines 418-419
  Microwave combination oven 596-597
  Power drill 600
Fan blade
  Renault Clio 353
  Turbofan 419
Fancase 418
Fan drive shaft 545
Fan duct nozzle 412
Fan dust shield 597
Fan fold 61
Fang 170
Fan transformer 597
Fan motor 351
Fan vault 484-485
Farming axe 109
Fascia
  Ancient Roman building 463-464
  Baroque church 479, 481
  Dome 486
  French temple 485
  Gothic building 472
  Medieval building 467, 469
  Modern building 498
  Neoclassical building 482
  Renaissance building 476-477
  Renault Clio 353
Fat
  Cells 217
  Tissue 215, 235
Faultline
  Lake formation 292
  Mountain building 62-63
  Weathering and erosion 283
Fault plane 60
Faults 60-61, 292
  Mineral resources 280
  Mountain building 62
  Oil and gas traps 281
  Showjumping competitions 554
Fault spring 292
Fault structure 60
Fault trap 281
Fax machine 572-573
F-block 311
FCC cable 571
F clef 502
Feather 188, 191
Feathered float 391
Feathering 440-441
Feather shuttlecock 544-545
Feather star 174
Feed bilge pump 391
Feeder station 328
Feed spool 587
Feet
  Human 232-233
  Theropods 84
Fei Tecnai G2 transmission electron microscope 610
Feldspar 267, 269, 275

Felloe 390
Felt blanket 447
Felt-covered beater 516, 518-519
Felt-tip pen 444
Female
  Body 210, 211
  Pelvis 218, 258
  Reproductive organs 259
Female apex 119
Female cones
  Bishop pine 124
  Gymnosperm 122
  Pine 122, 124
  Smooth cypress 123
  Yew 123
Female flower organs 140-143
Female flower remains 148
Female flowers 143, 144, 148
Female gametes
  Fertilization 146-147
  Gymnosperm 122
  Scots pine 122
  Seaweed 116-117
  Yew 123
Female receptacles 117
Female reproductive organs
  Fern 121
  Fruit 148
  Moss 119
  Plants 144
Femoral artery 225, 253
Femoral musculature 86
Femoral nerve 238
Femoral vein 271
Femoro-tibial muscle 84
Femur
  Albertosaurus 84
  Archaeopteryx 85
  Beetle 168
  Bird 189
  Brachiosaurus 90
  Butterfly 169
  Crocodile 186
  Dinosaur 82
  Domestic cat 195
  Elephant 201
  Eryops 81
  Euoplocephalus 94
  Frog 183
  Gallimimus 86
  Hare 197
  Horse 199
  Human 218-219, 224-225
  Iguanodon 96-97
  Kangaroo 206
  Kentrosaurus 93
  Lizard 184
  Parasaurolophus 98
  Plateosaurus 88
  Platypus 206
  Rhesus monkey 202
  Scorpion 170
  Seal 204
  Spider 171
  Stegoceras 101
  Stegosaurus 93
  Struthiomimus 87
  Toxodon 107
  Triceratops 102
  Tuojiangosaurus 93
  Turtle 187
  Tyrannosaurus 84
Fencing 556-557
Fender eye bolt 339
Fender jazz bass guitar 513
Fender stratocaster guitar 513
Fenestration 474, 494
Fermentation 313
Fermium 311

Fern 120-121
  Fossil 66, 279
  Life-cycle 121
  Prehistoric Earth 68, 70, 72
  Tree fern 112-113
Ferrel cell 300
Ferrite core 571
Fertile horsetail stem 120
Fertile oasis 287
Fertilization 146-147
  Fern 121
  Gymnosperm 122
  Scots pine 122
  Seaweed 117
Festoon
  Ancient Roman building 462-463
  Cathedral dome 487
  Neoclassical building 478-479
Fetal skull 220
Fetlock 199, 554
Fetus 260-261
Fibre 134-135
Fibreglass 548
  Bow 548
  Bucket seat 361
  Canopy frame 425
  Fuel tank 425
  Racket 544
  Reinforced plastic cover 529
  Wheel guard 369
Fibre insulation 602
Fibre plate 366
Fibrils 32
Fibrin 253
Fibrous capsule 256
Fibrous habit 271
Fibrous pericardium 250
Fibrous septum 245
Fibula
  Albertosaurus 84
  Brachiosaurus 90
  Crocodile 186
  Diplodocus 90
  Domestic cat 195
  Elephant 201
  Eryops 81
  Euoplocephalus 94, 87
  Hare 197
  Horse 199
  Human 219, 232-233
  Iguanodon 96-97
  Kangaroo 206
  Lizard 184
  Parasaurolophus 99
  Platypus 206
  Rhesus monkey 202
  Seal 204
  Stegoceras 101
  Stegosaurus 93
  Struthiomimus 87
  Toxodon 107
  Triceratops 102
  Turtle 187
  Tyrannosaurus 84
Fibulare 183
Ficus carica 148
Ficus sp. 137
Fid 385, 384
Fiddle block 378, 383
Field arrow 549
Field coil 600
Fielder's glove 537
Field events 542
Field goal 526-527
Fielding 538
Fielding team 536
Field judge 526
Field positions 538
Fields and particles instruments 614
Field umpire 528
Fifteenth century
  Mihrab 488

Renaissance building 474-475
  Style 462, 470
  Terrace 490
  Tracery 472
Fig 137, 148
Fighters 404-405, 408-409, 420
Fighting 556
Fighting platform 374
Figurehead
  74-gun ship 380-381
  Wooden sailing ship 379
Figure of eight turns 387
Filament
  Alga 116
  Dicotyledon flower 126-127
  Fern 121
  Fertilization 146-147
  Flowers 140-141, 143
  Fungal 114-115
  Jellyfish 167
  Light bulb 319
  Nebulae and star clusters 16-17
  Sun 32-33
  Moss 119
  Pollination 144
Filbert hog hair brush 436
File menu 576
Filicinophyta 120
Filiform papilla 244
Filing 455
Filled shell 310-311
Fillet
  Ancient Greek temple 461
  Dome 486
  French temple 485
  Gothic building 470
  Neoclassical moulding 480
  Renaissance building 475, 477
Filling transom 381
Film and transparency holder 570
Filter 576
Filter access flap 594
Filter rim casing 592
Filter seal 595
Filter screw cover 595
Filter turret 610
Fimbria 258-259
Fin
  Anal 178, 181
  ARV light aircraft 424
  Avro biplane 402
  BAe-146 components 415
  Blackburn monoplane 401
  Caudal 178-181
  Concorde 416
  Devon minnow 563
  Dorsal 178-179, 181, 205
  Helicopter 423
  Lockheed Electra airliner 407
  Lungfish 81
  LVG CVI fighter 405
  Pectoral 178, 180-181
  Pelvic 179-181
  Schleicher glider 426
  Tornado 421
  Ventral 179
  World War II aircraft 408-409
Final drive and gearbox 340
Final-drive sprocket 335
Fin-attachment skin 415
Find icon 576
Find key 590
Fine leg 538
Fine linen canvas 437

Fine-toothed marble claw 453
Finger
  Anchisaurus 89
  Gorilla 203
  Human 211
  Iguanodon 97
  Pachycephalosaurus 100
  Psittacosaurus 103
  Stegoceras 101
  Theropod 84
Fingerboard 510-511, 513
Finger-claw 83, 85
Finger grip 580
Finger hole 508
Finger key 507
Fingerless glove 527
Fingernail 231
Finger recess 571
Finger tab 548
Finial
  Asian building 490-491
  Baroque church 479, 481
  Gothic church 470-471
  Islamic building 488-489
  Medieval building 468
  Neoclassical building 478
  Nineteenth-century building 493
  Renaissance building 476
Finishing line 542, 554-555
Fin leading-edge attachment 415
Finned tail 80
Fin-root aerial fairing 421
Fin tip 415
Fin tip fairing 421, 424
Fin trailing edge 415
Fir 66
Fire 108
Fireball 10
Firebox 324-325
Fire-escape 497-498
Fire extinguisher 328
Fire-extinguisher discharge indicator 412
Fire-hole 325
Fire-making tools 109
Fireman's seat 325
Fire opal 270
Fireplace 466-467
Fire-resistant clay 454
Fire-resistant curtain 497
Fire-resistant panel 496
Fire-tube boiler 334
Fire tubes 324-325
Firewall 406, 425
Firewire ports 560
Firewire socket 587
Firing 452
Firewire ports 560
Firewire socket 587
Firing chamber 575
Firing pin 549
Firn 287
First century 462-464
"First down" 526- 527
First pilot's seat 408
First quarter 41
First rate ship 378
First slip 538
First transition metals 310
First violin 503, 504-505
First wheel set 329
Fish
  Bony 180-181
  Breathing 180
  Cartilaginous 178
  Fossil 279
  Holostean 73
  Jawless 178-179
Fish davit 379
Fisherman's schooner 385
Fishing tackle 109

Fish-scale tile 476-477, 486
Fishtail nectaries 160
Fissure 247
Fissures 157
Fissure volcano 272
Five-line stave 502
Five yard mark 540
Fixative 430, 440
Fixed float 390
Fixed gear 346-347, 411
Fixed lug 383
Fixed objective lens 581
Fixed-spool reel 562
Fixing screw 599
Fjord 294-295
Flagella 166
Flagellum
  Beetle 168
  Chlamydomonas sp. 116
  Moss 119
  Seaweed gametes 117
  Snail 177
  Sperm 259
Flag halyard 379
Flagmast 395
Flag pin 547
Flagpole 495
Flaking rock 282
Flamboyant tracery 472
Flame 312-313
Flamingo 188, 190
Flamsteed 40
Flange 492, 498
Flanged plate 425
Flank
  Bird 188
  Cow 198
Flanker
  Canadian football 526
  Rugby 530
Flank spike 95
Flap
  ARV light aircraft 425
  Formula One racing car 356, 357
  Hawker Tempest components 409
  Lockheed Electra airliner 406
  Tornado 421
Flap drive screw 413
Flap lever 425
Flap seal 413, 414
Flap tip 414
Flap torque tube 424
Flap track 413
Flap-track fairing 413, 415
Flared bell
  Brass instruments 506-507
  Woodwind instruments 508-509
Flash steam generator 342
Flash tube 397
Flash unit 580
Flask 312-313
Flat
  Musical notation 502
  Twin bollards 586
Flatbed scanner 570-571
Flatboard 384
Flat bottom 391
Flat-bottomed rail 331
Flat chisel 452
Flat cone 272
Flatfish angling 562
Flat-four engine 340
Flat freight car 327
Flat horse-races 554
Flat laminae 138
Flat roof
  Ancient Egyptian building 458
  Neoclassical building 483
  Twentieth-century building 494-495

Flat seam 384
Flat seizing 383, 389
Flat soffit 464
Flattened pericarp 151
Flattened petiole 160
Flattened stem 129
Flat-topped plateau 275, 282
Flat-topped seamount 298
Flat wire seizing 383
Flavian amphitheatre 464
Flax-spinning mill 492
Fleet number 333
Flesh-eaters 194
Flesh-eating dinosaur 70
Flesh tones 433
Fleshy aril 148
Fleshy axis 143
Fleshy fruit 146-147
Fleshy hair 140
Fleshy infolded receptacle 148
Fleshy scale leaf 155
Fletch 548
Flexible hose shrouding 595
Flex kink guard 594
Flexor digitorum longus muscle 233
Flexor digitorum tendon 231
Flexor hallucis longus muscle 233
Flexor pollicis brevis muscle 231
Flexor retinaculum muscle 231
Flexors of forearm 226
Flexors of hand 227
Flexor tubercle 85
Flex rewind 593
Flight 543
Flight-control hydraulic jack 416
Flight-control mixing unit 417
Flight-control rod 423
Flight controls 412
Flight feathers 188, 191
Flight instruments 425
Flight refuelling receptacle 421
Flint 277
Flint tools 108-109
Flipper
  Dolphin 204
  Seal 204
Flitch-plated wooden chassis 542
Float 590-591
Floating disc brake 364-365
Floating floor 602
"Floating" rib 218
Flocked pastel board 441
Floodgate 604
Flood-plain 289-291
Floods 290
Floor
  Gun turret 396
  Ironclad 393
  Longboat 380
  Modern building 496-498
  Nineteenth-century building 492
  Twentieth-century building 494-495
Floor anchor 407
Floorboard 464, 486
Floor-joist 464
Floor-mounted base 608
Floor pan 340
Floor tom 518-519
Florence Cathedral 475, 487
Florets 142
  Florists' chrysanthemum 129

Ultraviolet light 145
Florida current 296
Florists' chrysanthemum 129
Flower bud
  Aechmea miniata 162
  Broomrape 163
  Bulb 155
  Clematis 131
  Florists' chrysanthemum 129
  Hibiscus 127
  Ice-plant 129
  Live-for-ever 129
  Oxalis sp. 157
  Peruvian lily 129
  Rose 131
  Water lily 159
  Wind pollination 144
Flowering plant 57, 70, 72
Flowering shoot 155
Flowers 140-143
  Brassavola nodosa 162
  Bromeliad 113
  Broomrape 163
  Buds 140-141, 143
  Clematis 131
  Colour 140, 144-145
  Dicotyledons 126-127, 141-143
  Dodder 163
  Epiphytes 162-163
  Everlasting pea 129
  Florists' chrysanthemum 129
  Guzmania lingulata 163
  Ice-plant 129
  Involucre 129
  Monocotyledons 126, 140-141, 145
  Peruvian lily 129
  Pollination 144-145
  Rose 131
  Russian vine 131
  Scented 144
  Stem arrangements 143
  Ultraviolet light 145
  Vegetative reproduction 154
  Water lily 159
  Yew 123
Flower scars 154
Flower spike 143, 155
Flower stalk
  Brassavola nodosa 162
  Bulbil 154
  Clematis 131
  Dry fruit 150-151
  Fertilization 146-147
  Florists' chrysanthemum 129
  Fruit development 146-147
  Monocotyledons 140-141, 145
  Oxalis sp. 157
  Rose 131
  Rowan 131
  Russian vine 131
  Succulent fruit 148-149
  Sycamore 151
  Water lily 159
  Yew 123
Flow splitter 418
Fluff filter impeller 595
Fluid 306
Fluke
  74-gun ship 380
  Danforth anchor 386
Fluorescent light 318-319
Fluorine 308-309, 311
Fluorite 271
  Halides 269
Flush-riveted aluminium fuselage 423
Flush-riveted metal-skinned wing 406
Flush window 494
Flute 503, 504-505, 508

Fluted pilaster 462
Fluted pinnacle 481
Fluted shaft 478
Flute tube 525
Fluting 461, 463
Flutter kick 559
Fly 168
Fly fishing 562
Fly-half 550
Flying boat 406
Flying buttress
  Gothic building 470-473
  Medieval building 466, 468-469
  Nineteenth-century building 493
Flying Fortress bomber 408
Flying helmet 404
Flying jib 385
Flying reptile 70
Flying tackle 531
Fly rod 562-563
Flywheel
  Benz Motorwagen 335
  Early engines 342-343
  Etching press 447
  Mid West rotary engine 411
  Oldsmobile engine 336
  Renault Clio 351
  Steamboat 391
Flywheel retaining thread 411
Flywheel with balance weight 347
FM and TV aerial 603
Focker, Anthony 404
Fo'c'sle 380
Focus 63
Focus control 583
Focus ring 583
Fog 42-43
Fog-lamp 349, 353
Fog light 332, 363
Foil 556-557
Foilist 557
Foil pommel 557
Folded rock 60, 266
  Impermeable rock 281
  Mineral resources 280
  Strata 60-61
Folded schist 274
Folding mountain range 274
Folding step 326
Fold mountains 62
Fold of mucous membrane 249
Folds 60-61
Foliage leaf
  Bishop pine 124
  Bud 124
  Bulb 155
  Germination 152-153
  Monocotyledon 126
  Parasitic plant 162
  Pine 124-125
  Rhizome 155
  Seedling 152-153
  Stem bulbil 155
  Yew 123
Foliated capital 469
Foliated frieze 469, 479
Foliated panel 479
Foliated scrollwork 472
Foliated volute 476
Foliate papilla 244
Foliose lichen 114
Foliose thallus 114
Follicle
  Dehiscent dry fruit 150-151
  Hair 235
  Ovary 258
Fomalhaut 19, 20
Fontanelle 220
Food storage
  Bulb 155

Corm 155
Embryo 147
Rhizome 155
Root tuber 155
Scale leaf 155
Seed 152
Succulent 156-157
Swollen stem 113, 155
Foot
  Anchisaurus 89
  Bird 190
  Caiman 186-187
  Corythosaurus 98
  Cow 198
  Diplodocus 90
  Duck 188
  Elephant 90
  Gorilla 203
  Harp 511
  Herrerasaurus 86
  Horse 198
  Human 210
  Iguanodon 96
  Kangaroo 207
  Pachycephalosaurus 100
  Relief-printing press 449
  Sails 374, 385
  Slug 176
  Snail 177
  Stegoceras 101
  Stegosaurus 92
  Toaster 598-599
  Tyrannosaurus 84
  Tube 174
  Webbed 188
  Westlothiana 81
Football 524-525
Footboard 335
Foot brake 363
Footbridge 465
Foot-fault judge 544
Foot mat 363
Foot pad 608
Foot pedal 366, 514
Footplate 324
Footrest
  Curtiss biplane 598-599
  Suzuki RGV500 368
  Weslake Speedway motorcycle 369
Footrest hanger 364
Foot rope 378-379, 382, 385
Foot throttle 427
Foramen caecum 244
Foramen magnum 220
Foraminiferans 279
Force 320-321
"Force play" 536
Ford Cosworth V6 12-valve engine 344
Ford Cosworth V6 24-valve engine 344
Ford, Henry 338
Ford Model T 338-339
Ford turbocharged diesel engine 347
Fore-and-aft rigged lateen sails 376
Fore-and-aft sails 384
Fore-and-aft schooner 385
Forearm
  Gorilla 203
  Horse 199
  Human 210
  Movement 227
Forearm guard 548
Forearm pass 554
Fore bitt 380
Fore breast rope 387
Forecarriage 335
Forecastle
  74-gun ship 380
  Sailing warship 376
  Square-rigged ship 375
Forecastle castle-deck gunport 376

Forefoot
  Caiman 186
  Diplodocus 90
  Edmontonia 95
  Elephant 90
  Iron paddlesteamer 393
  Stegosaurus 92
Fore hatch tackle 379
Forehead
  Bird 188
  Dolphin 204
  Elephant 200-201
  Horse 199
  Human 211, 212
Foreleg
  Caiman 186
  Elephant 201
  Lizard 184
  Terrapin 187
Forelimb
  Anchisaurus 89
  Bird 188
  Corythosaurus 98
  Edmontonia 95
  Frog 182
  Hare 196
  Herrerasaurus 86
  Iguanodon 97
  Kangaroo 207
  Pachycephalosaurus 100
  Psittacosaurus 103
  Rabbit 196
  Rat 196
  Salamander 182
  Stegoceras 101
  Stegosaurus 92
  Thyreophorans 92
  Triceratops 102
  Tyrannosaurus 84
Forelock 199
Fore lower topsail 385
Fore mast
  Iron paddlesteamer 392
  Roman corbita 372
  Sailing warship 376
  Square-rigged ship 375
  Wooden sailing ship 379
Fore mast course 379
Foremast hole 380
Fore mast topgallant sail 379
Fore mast topsail 379
Forepeak 393
Fore royal stay 383
Fore sail 372, 385
Fore sail halyard 380
Foreset strata 283
Fore shroud 379
Foresight
  Rifle 549
  Target pistol 549
Foreskin 259
Fore spring rope 387
Fore stay
  Rigging 382
  Roman corbita 372
  Sailing warship 376
  Wooden sailing ship 379
Fore staysail 379, 385
Forest-dwelling mammals 74
Fore throat halyard 385
Fore top 379
Fore topcastle 376
Fore topgallant mast 379
Fore topmast 376, 379
Fore topmast stay 376, 379
Fore topmast staysail 385
Fore topmast staysail tack 382
Fore topsail 379
Fore upper topsail 385
Forewing 169
Fore yard 376, 379
Fore yard lift 385
Forged iron anchor 392

Fork
  ARV Super 2 425
  Eddy Merckx racing bicycle 361
  Harley-Davidson FLHS Electra Glide 363
  Honda CB750 363
  Motorcycle 364
  Vespa Grand Sport 160
  Mark 1 363
Fork blade 359
Forked beam 380
Forked connecting-rod 342
Fork end 383
Fork slide 565
Formeret 469, 479
Fornax 19, 20
Fornix 256-257
Fortifications 466
Forum of Trajan 463
Forward bulkhead panel 406
Forward control 577, 587
Forward deck 561
Forward defensive stroke 558
Forward dive 558
Forward door 415, 417
Forward-facing eyes 194
Forward fairing 415
Forward-firing machine-gun 405
Forward funnel 393, 395
Forward fuselage structure 401
Forward galley 416
Forward hydroplane 397
Forward main door 412
Forward ramp drive 417
Forward rollover structure 357
Forwards 532, 534-535
Forward short leg 538
Forward spar 415
Fossa ovalis 251
Fossil fuel 280-281, 314-315
Fossilization 278
Fossil record 279
Fossils 278-279
  Acanthostega skull 80
  Ankylosaurus tail club 95
  Birch leaf 74, 76
  Blue-green algae 78
  Brachiopod 65
  Clubmoss 66
  Eurypterid 79
  Fern 66
  Graptolite 65
  Horsetail 66
  Hyaenodon skull 107
  Jawless fish 78
  Land plant 64
  Lungfish 81
  Nautiloid 65
  Palm bark 74
  Shark teeth 67
  Starfish 79
  Swamp plant 64
  Sweetgum leaf 76
  Titanosaurid egg 91
  Trilobite 78
Fossil skeleton
  Archaeopteryx 85
  Bat 105
  Parasaurolophus 98
  Pareiasaur 81
  Struthiomimus 87
  Westlothiana 81
Foster, N. 496, 498
Foul lines 536
Fouls 552
Foul tackle 524
Foul tip 537
Foundation
  Ancient Roman building 464

Iron paddlesteamer 392
Modern building 496
Nineteenth-century building 492
Foundry plug 587
Fountain pen 444
Four-aspect colour light signal 330
Four-chambered heart 104
Four-cylinder 12-HP engine 399
Four-cylinder motorcycle 363
Four-footed dinosaur 88, 92, 96, 100
Four-pulley system 520
Four-stroke combustion engine 366
Four-stroke cycle 343
Fourteenth century 474
  Arch 488
  Gothic building 471-473
  Medieval building 466-467
  Roof 490
  Style 470
Fourth mast 376
Four-wheel bogie 417
Fovea 224
Foveal camera 609
Foveal view 609
Fowler flap 413, 414
Foxes 194
Fracastorius 40
Fracture 270
Fractured rock 34
Fragaria x ananassa 128, 150
Fra Mauro 40
Frame
  74-gun ship 381
  ARV light aircraft 424
  Bicycle 558-559
  Cannondale SH600 Digital video 583
  Hybrid bicycle 361
  Concert grand piano 515
  Concorde 416
  Harley-Davidson FLHS Electra Glide 363
  Honda VF750 564
  Ironclad 393
  Longboat 380
  Medieval house 466
  Minidisc player 587
  Modelled sculpture 452
  Modern building 496
  Motorcycle 364
  Oscillating steam engine 390
  Racing bicycle 360
  Racket 544-545
  Relief-printing press 449
  Single scull 560
  Steam-powered Cugnot 335
  Steel 494
  Upright piano 514
  Weslake Speedway motorcycle 369
Frame angle 360
Frame drum 518
Frame head 340
Frame-mounted fairing 564
Fram Rupes 35
Francis turbine 314
Francium 310
Frapped turn 389
Free nerve ending 235, 239
Freestyle swimming stroke 558
Free-throw line 532-533, 535
Freewheel 361

Freewheel lock nut 358
Freewheel sprocket 360
Freezing 307
Freezing level 302
Freight car 527
Freight service 326
French baroque style 479, 482
French bowline 388
French Flamboyant style 470
French TGV train 528-529
French trotter 554
Fresco 434-435
Freshwater bay 291
Freshwater angling 562
Freshwater lake
  Lakes and groundwater 292
  Weathering and erosion 283
Freshwater turtle 186
Fret 512-513
Fret-pattern mosaic 488-489
Fretwork 461, 491
Frieze
  Ancient Egyptian building 459
  Ancient Greek building 461
  Ancient Roman building 463, 465
  Baroque church 479, 481
  Cathedral dome 487
  French temple 485
  Medieval church 469
  Neoclassical building 478-479, 482
  Renaissance building 476
  Twentieth-century building 495
Frigate 396-397
F ring 46-47
Fringed crumble cap 115
Fringilla coelebs 193
Fringing reef 299
Frog 182-183
  Double bass bow 511
  Eggs 183, 192
  Fossil 278
  Violin bow 510
Frog kick 559
Frond
  Fern 120-121
  Seaweed 116-117
  Tree fern 112-113
Front air dam 354
Frontal bone
  Bony fish 181
  Chimpanzee 202
  Human 212-213, 220-221
Frontalis muscle 226, 228-229
Frontal lobe 236-237
Frontal notch 213
Frontal process 221
Frontal rib 161
Frontal sinus 212, 245
Front axle
  1906 Renault 336-337
  Ford Model T 338
  Honda VF750 565
  Husqvarna Motocross TC610 368
  Kirby BSA 369
Front bezel 568, 584
Front brake cable
  Bicycle 359
  Eddy Merckx racing bicycle 361
Front brake lever 363
Front bumper 332
Front cantilever brake 359
Front case 568
Front crawl 558-559

Front cylinder exhaust pipe 368
Front derailleur 358-360
Front leg 168-169
Front light
  Bicycle 360
  Paris Metro 328
  Italian State Railways Class 402 328
Frontoparietal bone 183
Frontozygomatic suture 220
Front spring 337
Front wheel
  Bicycle 359
Front wing 168
Frost wedging 282, 286-287
Froude's early test propeller 391
Frozen rubber puck 550-551
Fruit
  Bramble 130
  Couch grass 113
  Development 146-147
  Dry 150-151
  Durmast oak 131
  Peach 131
  Pitcher plant 113
  Rowan 131
  Succulent 148-149
  Sycamore 151
Fruit wall 148-149, 150-151
Fruticose lichen 114
Fruticose thallus 114
"F" turret 394
Fucoxanthin 116
Fucus spiralis 116
Fucus vesiculosus 116, 117
Fuel/air intake pipe 337
Fuel and oil heat exchanger 418
Fuel and oil tank 398-399
Fuel cap 548, 369
Fuel contents indicator 413
Fuel-cooled oil cooler 419
Fuel drip tray 411
Fuel filler and vent 403
Fuel filler cap
  Curtiss biplane 398
  Volkswagen Beetle 340
Fuel filler neck 340
Fuel filter 419
Fuel heater 419
Fuel hose 425
Fuel injection 344, 356
Fuel inlet 419
Fuel-jettison pipe 417
Fuel-jettison valve 406
Fuel manifold 418-419
Fuel nozzle 418-419
Fuel pipe
  Concorde 417
  Curtiss biplane 398
  Jaguar V12 345
Fuel reservoir 368
Fuel sediment bowl 339
Fuel shut-off valve cable 419
Fuel sprayer 418
Fuel supply pump 327
Fuel tank
  Avro triplane 402
  Benz Motorwagen 335
  BMW R/60 362
  Concorde 417
  "Deltic" diesel-electric locomotive 326
  Harley-Davidson FLHS Electra Glide 363
  Helicopter 422-423
  Honda VF750 565
  Lockheed Electra airliner 407
  LVG CVI fighter 405
  Pegasus XL SE microlight 426

Renault Clio 350
Suzuki RGV500 369
Volkswagen Beetle 340
Werner motorcycle 362
Weslake Speedway motorcycle 369
White Steam Car 342
Wright Flyer 398
Fuel tank breather 369
Fuel tank cradle 422
Fuel tank filler cap 369
Fuel tank filler neck 350
Fuel tank filler nozzle 427
Fuel tank sender unit 340
Fuel tank top skin 425
Fuel tap 366
Fuel vent pipe 422
Fulcrum 320-321
Full back
  American football 526
  Australian rules football 527
  Canadian football 526
  Gaelic football 529
  Rugby 530
Full back line 529
Full-elliptic leaf spring 334-335
Full-elliptic steering spring 337
Full forward 528-529
Fumaroles 272-273
Funaria hygrometrica 119
Funaria sp. 119
Functionalism 496
Function button 585
Function display 520-521
Fundus 258
Fungal filament 114-115
Fungi 112, 114-115, 133
Fungia fungites 167
Fungiform papilla 244
Fungoid-structure encrustations 284
Funicle 150
Funnel
  Battleship 395
  Frigate 397
  Iron paddlesteamer 392-393
  Lizard 185
  Octopus 176-177
  Steamboat with paddle wheels 391
Funnel guide 126
Funnel stay 395
Furcula 189
Furled forecourse sail 375
Furled lateen main sail 576
Furled lateen mizzen sail 375, 376
Furnerius 40
Furrow 282
Furud 21
Fused carpels 140, 144, 151
Fused petals 142, 145
Fused receptacles 149
Fuselage 401, 409, 424
Fuselage bottom skin 424
Fuselage bracing wire 403, 426
Fuselage mid-section 412
Fuselage nose-section 412
Fuselage skin 402
Fuselage spine fairing 414
Fuselage tail-section 415
Fuselage top skin 424
Fuses 591
Fusion crust 52
Futtock shroud 378

G

Gabbro 267, 274
Gable
  Gothic building 470-473

Medieval building 467, 469
  Nineteenth-century building 492-493
  Renaissance building 476
Gabled arch 471
Gacrux 21
Gadolium 311
Gaelic football 528-529
Gaff 380, 385
Gagarin 41
Galactic centre 14, 18, 20
Galactic nucleus 12-13
Galactic plane 14-15
Galaxy 10-15, 613
Galena 268
Galeocerdo cuvier 179
Galilean moons 44
Galium aparine 150
Gallbladder
  Domestic cat 195
  Human 248, 252
  Rabbit 196
  Tortoise 187
Galle ring 50-51
Gallery
  74-gun ship 381
  Ancient Roman building 465
  Baroque church 479-480
  Cathedral dome 487
  Frigate 397
  Medieval building 466-468
  Modern building 496-497
  Renaissance theatre 477
  Wooden sailing ship 378-379
Galley 372-397
Gallimimus 82, 84, 86-87
Gallium 311
Galois 41
Galvanized "D" shackle 386
Gambrel roof 490
Game Boy Advance 578, 579
Game Boy Advance games 578
Game cartridge 579
Game target shooting 548
Gamete 154
  Brown seaweed 116-117
  Bryophyte 118-119
  Fern 120-121
  Fertilization 146-147
  Gymnosperm 122
  Moss 112
  Pine 122
  Vegetative reproduction 154
  Yew 123
Gametophyte
  Bryophyte 118-119
  Fern 120-121
  Liverwort 118
  Moss 112, 119
Gamma 18, 21
Gamma Centauri 21
Gamma Hydri 20
Gamma Mensae 20
Gamma radiation 10
Gamma ray 22, 318-319
Gamma ring 48
Ganges bridge 63
Ganges River delta 288
Ganglion 173, 177
Gangway
  74-gun ship 380
  Colosseum 464
  Sailing warship 377
Ganymede 44, 614

Gape
  Angling hook 562
  Dolphin 204
Garboard strake 393
Gargoyle 473
Garmin GPS V 591
Garmin Street Pilot III GPS 590, 591
Garnet 267
Garnet-mica schist 267
Garnierite 270
Garudimimus 86
Gas 306-307
  Asteroids, comets, and meteoroids 52-53
  Chemical reactions 313
  Massive stars 26-27
  Mineral resources 280-281
  NGC 2997 (spiral galaxy) 12
  Small stars 24-25
  Stellar black hole 29
Gas blanket 300
Gas cloud
  Earth's formation 56
  Milky Way 14
  Nebulae and star clusters 16-17
  Origin and expansion of Universe 10-11
Gas current 29
Gas deposit 57, 281
Gaseous exchange in alveolus 255
Gaseous water 49
Gas exchange 134
  Leaf 138-139
  Photosynthesis process 138
  Root 132
  Sunken stoma 156-157
  Wetland plants 158
Gas formation 280-281
Gas giants
  Jupiter 44-45
  Neptune 50-51
  Saturn 46-47
  Solar System 30-31
  Uranus 48-49
Gaskin 198, 554
Gas loop 32-33
Gas molecule 53
Gassendi 40
Gas shell 16-17, 25
Gas tail 52-53
Gastralia 85, 87
Gas traps 281
Gastric artery 253
Gastrocnemius muscle
  Albertosaurus 84
  Euoplocephalus 94
  Human 226-227
  Iguanodon 97
Gastroepiploic vein 253
Gastropod mollusc 75
Gastropods 176, 279
Gastrovascular cavity 167
Gas turbine 418
Gate
  Building 467, 490-491
  Canoeing 560
  Downhill skiing 552
  Hydroelectric power station 314
Gate clamp 560
Gate-house 467
Gateway 460
Gatwick Express "People Mover" 328
Gauge 330-331
Gauge class 525
Gauged arch 492
Gauntlet 540, 557
Gavialis gangeticus 186
G clef 502
Gear 587
Gear band 336

Gearbox
  ARV light aircraft 425
  Ford Model T 339
  Harley-Davidson FLHS
    Electra Glide 363
  Motorcycle 364, 366
  Renault Clio 351
  Volkswagen Beetle 340
  Wind turbine 605
Gearbox bevel drive 418
Gearbox case 410
Gearbox drive spline 410
Gearbox fixing stud 356
Gearbox mount 413
Gearbox oil scavenge line
  419
Gearbox unit 413
Gear cable 359
Gearcase 601
Gearcase position 600
Gear change 363
Gear-change rod 351
Gear lever
  1906 Renault 337
  Husqvarna Motocross
    TC610 568
  Renault Clio 350
  Two-stroke engine 366
Gear lever knob 340
Gear lever surround 352
Gear ratios 361
Gear retainer 562
Gear shift 359
Gear system 358, 366
Gears
  Drills 600
  Motorcycle 366
Gelatine roller 447
Gemini 18
Gemma 118
Generative nucleus 147
Generator 317
  British Rail class 20
    diesel engine 327
  Diesel train 326
  Electric train 326
  Nuclear power station
    314
  Van de Graaff 316
  Wind turbine 605
Generator cooling fan 327
Generator housing 411
Generator rotor
  Hydroelectric power
    station 314
  Mid West engine 411
Generator unit 314
Genetic material 606, 607
Genioglossus muscle 245
Geniohyoid muscle 245
Genome 607
Genital plate 175
Gentlemen's room 477
Geographic pole 38
Geological time 56-57, 279
Geranium pratense 144
Gerberette 497
Gerbil 196
Germanium 311
German-style baroque
  482
Germany 326
Germinal epithelium 258
Germination 152-153
  Cabbage seed 132
  Epigeal 152-153
  Fern spore 121
  Hypogeal 152-153
  Mushroom spore 115
  Pine 122
  Pollen grain 146-147
Gesso 452, 453
Geyser 272-273, 275
Gharial 186
Ghost anemone 166
Giant redwood 112
Giant slalom 552
Giant stars 22-23, 26
Gibbon 202

Gibson Les Paul guitar
  513
Gig 395
Gilded band 490
Gilded cross 487
Gilded orb 487
Gilded rib 487
Gilded truck 378-379
Gilding materials 451,
  452
Gill
  Bivalves 176
  Bony fish 180-181
  Dogfish 178-179
  Fungi 114-115
  Lamprey 178
  Newt 182
  Salamander 182
  Tadpole 183
Gill filament 180
Gill opening 178
Gill raker 180
Gill slit 178-180
Gilt ironwork 482, 490
Ginger 155
Gingiva 247
Ginkgo 68, 70, 72, 122-
  123, 279
Ginkgo biloba 68, 123
Ginkgophyta 122
Ginkgo pluripartita 72
Giornate 434-435
Giraffa camelopardalis
  199
Giraffe 198-199
Girder 493
Girdle 116
Girdle scar 123
Girth
  Harness racer 555
  Showjumper 554
Gizzard
  Bird 189
  Brachiosaurus 91
  Euoplocephalus 94
  Gallimimus 86
Glabella
  Human skull 213, 221
  Trilobite fossil 78
Glacial deposits 286-287,
  292-293
Glacial periods 56-57, 76
Glacial sediments 299
Glacial streams 286
Glacier Bay 286
Glacier features 286-287
Glaciers 286-287
  Prehistoric Earth 66, 76
  River's stages 289
  Rock cycle 266-267
  Weathering and erosion
    282
Glacier snout 286, 289
Gladiolus 154-155
Gland
  19th century
    paddlesteamer 391
  Axial 175
  Butterwort 161
  Cement 173
  Green 173
  Monkey cup 161
  Mucous 177
  Pedal 177
  Poison 170, 176
  Rectal 179
  Salivary 177
  Silk 170
  Venus fly trap 160
Glans penis 259
Glass 307
  Buildings 492, 494
  Photovoltaic cell 605
  Tesserae 450
Glass bulb 319
Glass cooking turntable
  596
Glass curtain 497
Glass deflector 325

Glass enamel 450
Glass flask 312
Glass mosaic 489
Glass muller 436, 440
Glass pane 494
Glass paper 441
Glass plate 570, 571
Glass prism 318
Glass slab 456, 440
Glass tube 319
Glass wall 496, 499
Glazing
  Acrylic paints 442
  Modern building 496-
    499
  Twentieth-century
    building 494
Glazing bar 499
Gleba 114-115
Glechoma hederacea 154
Gleditsia triacanthos 137
Glenoid cavity 80
Gliders 426-427
Global positioning system
  (GPS) 590-591
Global warming 301
Globe 264
Globe Theatre 477
Globular cluster 12, 16, 21
Globule 24, 26
Glomerulus 256-257
Gloriosa superba 143
Glory lily 143
Gloss finish
  Acrylics 442
  Oil painting 436
Glossopteris 67
Gloster Meteor fighter 408
Glove box 425
Gloves
  American football 527
  Baseball fielder 537
  Cricket batsman 539
  Cricket wicket-keeper
    539
  Fencing 556-557
  Ice hockey 551
  Lacrosse goalkeeper
    541
  Racketball 545
  Sailing 560
  Skiing 552-553
  Soccer goalkeeper 525
Glucose 158
Glulam wall-plate 499
Gluon 309
Gluteal fold 210
Gluteus maximus muscle
  227
Gluteus medius muscle
  225
Gluteus minimus muscle
  225
Glyph 460
Gnathostomata 178, 180
Gneiss 274
Gnetophytes 122
Gnome seven-cylinder
  rotary engine 400
Gnomon 377
Goal
  Australian rules football
    528
  Gaelic football 529
  Hockey 540
  Hurling 541
  Ice hockey 550
  Lacrosse 541
  Rugby 530-531
  Soccer 524
Goal area
  Gaelic football 529
  Handball 535
  Soccer 524
Goal attack 535
Goal circle 535, 541
Goal crease 541, 550
Goal defence 535
Goal judge 550

Goalkeeper
  Australian rules football
    528
  Football rules 524
  Gaelic football 529
  Handball 534-535
  Hockey 540
  Ice hockey 550
  Lacrosse 541
  Netball 535
  Soccer 525
Goalkeeper's equipment
  540
Goalkeeper's gloves 525
Goalkeeper's helmet 550-
  551
Goalkeeper's kicker 540
Goalkeeper's pad 550
Goalkeeper's shirt 525,
  550
Goalkeeper's stick 550
Goal line
  American football 526
  Australian rules football
    528
  Handball 535
  Hockey 540
  Ice hockey 550
  Rugby 530
  Soccer 524
Goal line referee 535
Goal net 524, 534, 550
Goalposts
  American football 526
  Australian rules football
    528
  Gaelic football 529
  Netball 535
  Rugby 530
Goal shooter 535
Goal square 528
Goal third 535
Goal umpire 528-529
Goat 198
Goat hair brush 438, 442
  Calligraphy 444
Goat hake wash brush 438
Gobi Desert 265
Goggles
  Harness racing 555
  Skiing 552-553
  Swimming 558
Gold 31, 268, 280-281, 438
Gold chalcopyrite 271
Golden barrel cactus 156
Golden lion tamarin 203
Gold leaf 432
  Fresco 435
  Illumination 444-445
  Smalti 450
  Vitreous glass 451
  Wood sculpture
    highlighting 453
Golf 546-547
Golgi complex 217
Gomphoi 373
Gonad
  Jellyfish 167
  Octopus 176
  Sea anemone 167
  Sea urchin 175
  Starfish 174
Gondwanaland
  Cretaceous period 72
  Jurassic period 70-71
  Late Carboniferous
    period 66-67
  Middle Ordovician
    period 64-65
Gong 504, 516
Goniastrea aspera 167
Gonopore
  Barnacle 173
  Sea urchin 175
  Snail 177
  Starfish 174
Goose-feather quill 444
Goosegrass 150
Goose neck 388

Gopher 196
Gopuram finial 491
Gorge
  Cave 284-285
  River features 290
Gorilla 202-203
Gothic architecture 468,
  470-473
Gothic book script
  lettering 445
Gothic stone arch 467
Gothic torus 470
Gouge
  Relief printing 446, 449
  Woodcarving 454-453
Gour 284-285
Goya 35
GPS 590-591
Grab handle 362
Graben 61
Graben lake 293
Gracilis muscle 226-227
Graded wash 439
Graffian follicle 258
Graffias 21
Gran Chaco 264
Grand Canyon 57, 226-227
Grand piano 514-515
"Grand Prix" world
  championships 368
Grandstand 555
Granite-aggregate slab
  499
Granite cladding 494
Granular stalk 114
Granulation 139
Granum 139
Grape hyacinth 155
Graphic equalizer display
  577
Graphite 268, 311
Graphite pencil 430
Graphite stick 430
Grapnel-type anchor 376
Grasping tail 202
Grass 113
Grate 524
Grating 380-381
Graver 449
Gravitation (gravity)
  Atmosphere 300
  Force and motion 320
  Neutron stars and black
    holes 28
  Oceans and seas 296-
    297
  Universe 10
Gravitational pull 296-297
Gravity-feed fuel tank 405
Gray Cliffs 276
Grease 446
Greaser 359
Great Bear Lake 264
Great cabin 379, 381
Great Dark Spot 50-51
Greater blackbacked gull
  193
Greater flamingo 190
Greater omentum 214
Greater palatine foramen
  220
Greater trochanter of
  femur 224-225
Greater wing coverts 188
Greater wing of sphenoid
  bone 220-221
Great Lakes 264
Great manual 514
Great Mosque 484
Great Red Spot 44-45
Great Rift Valley 60
Great saphenous vein 253
Great ship 372-373
Greek-style fret ornament
  483
Green (golf) 547
Green alga 112, 116-117
Green calc-silicate
  mineral 275

Green cell 584
Green chlorophyll
  pigment 116, 138
Green earth 454-435
Green fluorite 269
Green gland 173
Greenhouse effect 36,
  300-301
"Greenhouse gas" 301
Greenland
  Cretaceous period 73
  Late Carboniferous
    period 66
  Middle Ordovician
    period 64
  Satellite map 264
Green light 318, 330-331
Green seaweed 117
Green snakelock
  anemone 166
Green starboard
  navigation light 406
Greenwich Meridian
  Satellite map 264-265
  Surface currents 296
Gregorian calendar 681
Grey matter 236-237, 238
Grey squirrel 197
Grey whale 204
Grid lines 445
Griffon 461
Grikes 284
Grille
  "Eurostar" warning
    horn 329
  Roman Mill 464
Grill/griddle 596
Grimaldi 40
Grip
  Sailmaker's fid 384
  Sailmaker's mallet 384
Gripe 379
Groin
  Arches and vaults 485
  Human body 211
Groin pad 527
Groin vault 479, 484-485
Grommet 373, 375, 384,
  426
Groove
  Rope starter 335
  Serving mallet 384
Grooved racing tyre 356,
  357
Groove for FCC cable 571
Grooving 383
Grotesque figure 476
Ground handling wheel
  422
Ground ivy 154
Ground-mapping radar
  420
Groundmass 268-269
Ground roller 447
Groundwater 292-293
  Volcanic structure 273
Grout 450-451
Growing point 153
Growing tip 79
Growth line
  Fossilized jawless fish
    78
  Snail 177
Groyne 294
Grundtvig Church 495
Gruppo Seven Cubist 495
Grus 19, 20
Gryphon 461
Gryposaurus 96, 99
Guanine 216
Guard
  American football 526
  Basketball 552
  Fencing foot 557
Guard cell 138-139
Guardrail 391-392, 395
Guardstop 541
Gubernator 373
Gudgeon 375

Gudgeon pin 345
Gudgeon strap 378
Guest boat boom 394
Guiana Highlands 264
Guidance control sensor 612
Guide hair 126
Guide mark 555
Guide wheel 328
Guinevere Planitia 36, 37
Guitars 510, 512-513
Gula Mons 37
Gulf of Mexico 264
Gulf Stream 296
Gull 189, 193
Gulley 538
Gully 289
Gum 247
Gum arabic 438
  Lithographic printing 446, 448
  Pastel making 440
Gun
  1.5 kg gun 395
  3 pound gun 395
  4.5 in gun 397
  4.7 in gun 394
  11 cm gun 397
  12 cm gun 394
  12 in gun 394
  30 cm gun 394
  Battleship 394
  Frigate 397
  Measurements 394
  Sailing warship 376
  Wooden sailing ship 378, 379
Gun battery 395
Gun carriage 377
Gun deck 380
Gun loading cage 396
Gunnery control radar dish 612
Gunnery spotting top 394
Gunport 381
  Sailing warship 376-377
  Wooden sailing ship 379
Gun position 397
Gun section 392
Gunship 422
Gun turret 396-397
  Battleship 394
  Frigate 397
  World War II aircraft 408
Gut caecum 170
Gutenberg discontinuity 39
Gutter 486, 492, 602
Guyot 298
Guzmania lingulata 162-163
Gymnosperm 122-125
Gynoecium 140
Gypsum 271
Gyroscopic gunsight 409

H

Habit 270-271
Habitat 112
  Dryland plants 156-157
  Wetland plants 158-159
Hackle 563
Hackly fracture 270
Hadar 21
Hadley cell 300
Hadrosaur 96, 98-99
Hadrosaurus 96, 99
Haemal spine 180
Haematite 268
Hafnium 310
Hagfish 178
Hail 302
Hair 234-235
  Cobra lily 160

Golden barrel cactus 156
Inflorescence 140, 142
Insulating 104, 107
Mammal 104
Marram grass 113
Monocotyledon 126
Pitcher plant 113
Root 132
Venus fly trap 160
Water fern leaf 158
Hair bulb 235
Hair cell 242-243
Hairdryer 315
Hair follicle 234-235
Hair gel 306
Hair-like sepal 142
Hair shaft 235
Hakatai shale 277
Half-back 526, 529
Half-back flank 528
Half-column 464, 468-469
Half-court line 545
Half-forward 529
Half-forward flank 528
Half-fruit 151
Half hitch 388
Half-shaft
  Ford Model T 338
  Formula One racing car 356
  Half turn 543
Halide 269
Halite crystal 277
Hall
  Asian building 491
  Hypostyle 458
  Medieval building 466-467
  Modern building 496, 499
  Neoclassical building 483
Halleflinta 275
Halley's Comet 52
"Hall-keeps" 466
Hallux
  Anchisaurus 89
  Archaeopteryx 85
  Herrerasaurus 86
  Human 232
  Tyrannosaurus 84
Halo 14
Halogen headlamp bulb 352
Halogens 311
Halo ring 44
Halyard
  Double topsail schooner 385
  Junk 376
  Longboat 380
  Rigging 382
  Roman corbita 372, 373
  Viking karv 374
Hamada 282-283
Hamal 19, 20
Hamate bone 230
Hammer 242, 285
  Antler 109
  Athletics 542
  Concert grand piano 515
  Mosaic 450
  Target pistol 549
  Upright piano 514
Hammer actuator 600-601
Hammer-beam roof 470, 473
Hammerhead shark 179
Hammer throw 543
Hand
  Anchisaurus 89
  Human 210
  Iguanodon 97
  Pachycephalosaurus 100
  Primate 203
  Stegoceras 101

Tyrannosaurus 84
Handball 554-555
Handbrake 337, 339-340, 550
Handbrake control shaft 338
Handbrake quadrant 339
Hand brake wheel 331
Hand drill 600-601
Hand-held computer 568
Hand-held gun 408
Handle
  Belaying pin 382
  Brace-and-bit 601
  Nintendo Cube 579
  Steam iron 594
Handlebars
  Bicycle 558-559
  BMW R/60 362
  Cannondale SH600 hybrid bicycle 361
  Cannondale ST 1000 touring bicycle 361
  Eddy Merckx racing bicycle 361
  Suzuki RGV500 368
Handle connector 593
Handle attachment 583
Handling
  Motorcycle 360
  Touring bicycle 364
Hand protector 368
Hand rail
  "Ellerman Lines" steam locomotive 324
  Modern building 498
  Renaissance building 477
  Sailmaker's mallet 384
  Serving mallet 384, 388
  Ship's wheel 390
  TGV electric high-speed train 329
  Twentieth-century building 494
Hands 250 -251
Handset 572
Handset cord 572
Handset cradle 572
Handset mount 572
Handstand 543
Hand throttle 427
Handy Billy 582-583
"Handy man" 108
Hanger 498
Hang-gliders 426-427
Hanging valley 286-287
Hapteron 116-117
Hard disk drive 567
Hard endocarp 146-147, 149
Hard granite 283
Hard hat 554
Hard-headed beater 516, 518-519
Hard metals 310
Hardness 270-271
Hard palate 212, 245
Hard rock 60
  Faults and folds 60
  Glacier 286
  River features 290-291
  Weathering and erosion 282
Hard trim 352
Hardwood implements 452
Hardwood laminate limb 548
Hardwood panels 452
Hardwood sticks 517
Hardy 450
Hare 196-197
Harley-Davidson FLHS Electra Glide 362-363
Harmika 491
Harmon, A.L. 494
Harmonically-tuned exhaust system 356

Harmony
  Drums 518
  Percussion instruments 516
Harness
  Avro triplane IV 402
  Equestrian sports 555
Harness racing 554
Harness strap 409
Harp 504, 510-511
Harpoon point 109
Harpsichord score 521
Hash mark 541
Hash special function button 588
Hastate leaf 128
Hatch
  Cargo 376
  For home deliveries 602
  Iron paddlesteamer 393
  Single scull 561
Hatch board 372
Hatch coaming 381
Hatching egg 192-193
Hatchling 98
Hathor Mons 37
Haunch 484
Haustoria 163
Haustration of colon 249
Haversian system 225
Hawker Tempest 408-409
Hawksmoor, N. 478, 481
Haworthia truncata 157
Hawse hole
  74-gun ship 381
  Sailing warship 376
  Wooden sailing ship 378
Hawse piece 381
Hawse pipe 393, 395
Hawser 386-387
Hawser fairlead 395
Hawthorne 35
Haystack boiler 334
Haze 37, 47
Head
  74-gun ship 380
  Allosaurus 85
  Beetle 168
  Brace-and-bit 601
  Bumblebee 168
  Butterfly 169
  Caterpillar 169
  Ceratopsian 100
  Deer hopper dry fly 563
  Double bass bow 511
  Double topsail schooner 385
  Dunkeld wet fly 563
  Femur 224-225
  Frog 182
  Hammer 542
  Human 211, 212-213
  Insect 168
  Lacrosse crosse 541
  Lamprey 178
  Pachycephalosaurus 100
  Phalanx 230
  Prosauropod 88
  Racing bicycle 360
  Racing saddle 554
  Rattlesnake 185
  Sail 375, 384
  Sauropodomorph 88
  Serving mallet 388
  Snail 177
  Sperm 259
  Stegoceras 101
  Stegosaurus 92
  Tennis racket 544
  Thyreophoran 92
  Ulna 231
  Violin bow 510
Headband 544
Head beam 380
Headboard 581
Head-butting contest 100
Head crest 96

Head cringle 384
Head data cable 574
Head data cable support 574
Head earing 375
Headers
  Brickwork 485
  Nineteenth-century building 492
Head horn 94
Head joint 508
Headlamp
  Bordino Steam Carriage 335
  Bulbs 352
  Ford Model T 338-339
  Renault Clio 349, 353
  Volkswagen Beetle 341
Headland 294
Head-light
  BMW R/60 362
  "Eurostar" multi-voltage electric train 329
  Harley-Davidson FLHS Electra Glide 363
  Italian State Railways Class 402 528
  MCW Metrobus 332
  Single-decker bus 333
  "Union Pacific" locomotive 326
  Vespa Grand Sport 160 Mark 1 363
Head lineman 526
Headphone jack 567, 582
Headphones 586
Headphone socket 566, 567, 585, 586
Head protector 573
Head rail 380-581
Headrest
  ARV light aircraft 425
  Formula One racing car 356
  Hawker Tempest fighter 409
  Mazda RX-7 346
  Renault Clio 349, 352
  TGV electric high-speed train 329
  "Windcheetah" racing HPV bicycle 361
Head rope 387
Headset 361
Headstock
  Acoustic guitar 512-513
  Electric guitar 513
  Honda VF750 564
Head tube 359-361
Headward erosion 290
Headwaters 288
Hearing 237, 242
Heart
  Bird 189
  Bony fish 181
  Branchial 176
  Butterfly 169
  Chimpanzee 202
  Crayfish 173
  Dogfish 179
  Dolphin 205
  Domestic cat 195
  Elephant 200
  Euoplocephalus 94
  Frog 182
  Gallimimus 86
  Human 214-215, 250-251
  Lizard 185
  Mammal 104
  Octopus 176
  Rabbit 196
  Snail 177
  Spider 170
  Systemic 176
  Tortoise 187
Heartbeat sequence 250-251

Heart bulge 260
Heartwood 125
Heat 314-315
  Chemical reactions 312
  Global warming 300-301
  Igneous and metamorphic rocks 274
Heat absorption 92
Heated filament 319
Heater element contacts 548
Heater unit 353
Heat exchanger
  Concorde 417
  Nuclear power station 314
  Volkswagen Beetle 340
Heat exchanger air intake 421
Heat exchanger exhaust duct 420
Heat exchanger hot-air exhaust 421
Heating element cover 597
Heating elements 594
Heating element terminal cover 597
Heat radiation 92
Heat shield
  Jet engine 419
  Motorcycle 363
  Space probes 614, 615
Heat trapping 300
Heaver for wire serving 383
Heaving line 389
Heavy chemical elements 27
Hedera colchica 137
Hedera helix 131, 137
Heel
  Horse 198
  Human 210
  Rudder post 392
Heel moulding 594
Heine 35
Heka 18
Helen Planitia 36
Helianthus annulus 142
Heliconia peruviana 143
Helicoprion bessonowi 67
Helicopter landing-pad 498
Helicopters 396, 410, 422-423
Helium
  Jupiter 44-45
  Massive stars 26
  Mercury's atmosphere 35
  Neptune's atmosphere 51
  Pluto's atmosphere 51
  Periodic table 311
  Saturn 46-47
  Small stars 24-25
  Sun 32
  Uranus' atmosphere 49
Helium-3 nucleus 22
Helium-4 nucleus 22
Helium line 23
Helix 242, 625
Helix Nebula 17
Helleborus niger 139
Hellenic plate 59
Helmet
  American football 526-527
  Baseball batter 556
  Bicycle 360
  Cricket 539
  Hockey goal keeper 540
  Hurling 541
  Ice hockey 550-551
  Lacrosse goalkeeper 541
  Skiing 542

Helmsman 372-373
Hemicyclapsis 56
Hemisphere 623
Hemispherical dome 477, 486-487, 490-491
Hen coop 395
Hepaticae 118
Hepatic artery 248, 252-253
Hepatic portal vein 253
Heptathlon 542
Heracleum sp. 151
Heracleum sphondylium 129
Heraldic device 372
Herbaceous plants 126, 128-129
 Structure 112-113
 Woody 130-131
Herbaceous stems 134
Herbivores
 Carnivora 194
 Jurassic period 70
 Marginocephalian 100
 Ornithopodian 96
 Prosauropods 88-89
 Sauropodomorphian 88
 Triassic period 68
Hercules 19, 20, 40
Herds 88
Hermaphrodite duct 177
Hermit shale 276
Herodotus 40
Herrerasaurids 68, 86
Herring-bone pattern 488
Hertzsprung 41
Hertzsprung-Russell diagram 22-23
Hesperidium 148
Hestia Rupes 37
Heterocentrotus mammillatus 175
Heterodontosaurus 83
Heteropoda venatoria 171
Hexagon 622
Hexagonal system 270
HF radio aerial 408
HF radio aerials fairing 417
Hibiscus 126-127
Hide 105
Hide grip 384
Hieroglyphs 458-459
High altar 470
High-altitude cloud 45, 50
Highboard diving 558
High-density minerals 280
High-energy particle 301
High-energy radiation 22
High-explosive projectile 396
High-gain antenna 614
High-gain radio antenna 612, 613
High-jump 542
Highland coastline 295
High-level jet streams 300
High nose 357
High-performance microscopes 610-611High-pressure areas 302-303
High-pressure bleed venturi connector 419
High-pressure compressor 418
High-pressure cylinder 342
High-pressure turbine 418
High-pressure zone 300
High-resolution colour graphics 578
High-speed trains 328-329
High Spring tide 296-297
High temperature gas 506
High-tension beam 496
High-tension ignition lead 344
High tension wire 315

High tide 296-297
High-velocity air duct 420
High voltage cable 314, 355
High-voltage connector 355
High-voltage magnetron supply 596
Hi-hat cymbal 518
Hilbert 41
Hillman anti-kink weight 562
Hilum
 Dehiscent fruit seed 151
 Epigeal germination 153
 Hypogeal germination 152
 Succulent fruit seed 148-149
Himalayas
 Earth's physical features 264-265
 Geological time 56-57
 Formation 60, 62-62
 Mountain building 62-63
 Quaternary period 77
 Tertiary period 74
Himeji Castle 490
Hind foot
 Caiman 187
 Stegosaurus 92
Hindgut 173
Hind leg
 Amphibian 182
 Beetle 168
 Bumblebee 168
 Butterfly 169
 Caiman 187
 Elephant 200
 Frog 182
 Hare 196
 Iguanodon 97
 Lizard 185
 Rabbit 196
 Terrapin 187
Hind limb
 Anchisaurus 89
 Corythosaurus 98
 Edmontonia 95
 Frog 182
 Iguanodon 96
 Kangaroo 207
 Pachycephalosaurus 100
 Prosauropod 88
 Psittacosaurus 103
 Rabbit 197
 Rat 196
 Salamander 182
 Stegoceras 101
 Stegosaurus 92
 Theropods 84
 Thyreophoran 92
 Triceratops 102
 Tyrannosaurus 84
Hindlimb bone 105
Hind wing 168-169
 ARV light aircraft 425
 BAe-146 components 412-413
Hinge 571
Hinge bracket 414
Hinge cell 113, 160
Hinged bin/cyclone cover 593
Hingeless bivalve shell 79
Hingeline 60
Hip
 Anchisaurus 89
 Human 211
 Kangaroo 207
 Lion 195
 Midway Gardens 495
 Stegosaurus 92
Hip joint 218, 224-225

Brachiosaurus 90
Diplodocus 90
Gallimimus 86
Parasaurolophus 98
Plateosaurus 88
Stegoceras 101
Struthiomimus 87
Hip pad 527
Hippeastrum sp. 155
Hipped roof 476-477
Hippocampus kuda 180
Hippophae rhamnoides 136
Hippopotamus 198
Hippopotamus amphibius 77
Hippuris vulgaris 135
Hip-rafter 490
Hispano Mark V 20-mm cannon 409
Historiated boss 469
Historiated keystone 469
Hitachi S-3500H scanning electron microscope 611
Hitched hauling end 383
Hitch-kick 543
Hitch pin
 Concert grand piano 515
 Upright piano 514
Hittorff, J.I. 479
Hobbles 554
Hock 195, 198
Hockey 540-541
Hock joint 554
Hog marlin 432, 434
Hog's-back 283
Hog's back jump 554
Hogweed 129, 150-151
Hohenbuehelia petaloides 115
Hoisting cage 396
Hold button 587
Holden 43
Holdfast 116-117
Holding 527
Holding timekeeper 556
Hold pillar 393
Hole and peg joint 373
Hollow disc wheel 361
Hollow pith cavity 120
Holmium 311
Holocene epoch
 Fossil record 279
 Geological timescale 57
Holstean fish 73
Homarus sp. 73
Home cinema 584-585
Home computer system 520-521
Homeosaurus pulchellus 71
Home page 577
Home plate 536
Home run 536
"Home" signal 330
Hominid 74-75, 108-109, 202
Homocephale 101
Homo erectus 108
Homo habilis 108
Homo sapiens 57, 76, 108-109
Honda CB750 362-363
Honda Insight 354
Honda VF750 364-365
Hone-stone 452
Honesty 150-151
Honeycomb coral 167
Honey guides 140-141, 145
Honey locust 137
Hong Kong and Shanghai Bank 496, 498
Honshu 265
Hood
 Battleship 394
 Ford Model T 339

Gun turret 396
Jellyfish 167
 Pitcher plant 160
Hood bag 346
Hood end 374
Hood frame 339
Hood iron 334
Hood-mould 479, 481, 486
Hoof 198, 554
Hoofbone 105, 198
Hoof-like nail 36-37
Hook
 Angling 562
 Cricket 538
 Deer hopper dry fly 563
 Devon minnow 563
 Rigging 383
 Sail 384
Hooked beak 190
Hooked pericarps 150
Hooked riffler 454
Hooker 530
Hoop 380, 425
Hoover Factory 495
Hop 543
Hopper freight car 327
Horizon 376
Horizontal bed rock 61
Horizontal cleavage 270
Horizontal damper 329
Horizontal fissure 255
Horizontally opposed engine 362
Horizontal movement 60
Horizontal stabilizer 423
Horn
 Ford Model T 339
 Glacier 286-287
 Mooring 387
 Musical instrument 503, 504
 "Union Pacific" locomotive 326
 Vespa Grand Sport 160
 Mark 1 363
Horn balance 414, 415
Horn bulb 339
"Horned faces" 100
Horny beak 96
Horse 104-105, 198-199
Horse chestnut 130, 137
Horse-drawn vehicle 332
Horsehair bow 510-511
Horsehead Nebula 16
Horse riding 554-555
Horsetail 120-121
Horsley Church 473
Horst 61
Horu Geyser 272
Hose base 593
Hose cuff electrical link 593
Hose electricity supply connector 592
Hose slider 592
Hose slider seating 592
Hot-air de-icing duct 414
Hot mineral springs 272
Hot spot
 Black holes 29
 Earth's crust 58
 Ocean floor 298
HotSync™ button 569
HotSync™ connector 568, 569
HotSync™ connector slot 569
Hot Sync™ cradle 569
Hot water jet 273
Hound 378
Hour line 377
Household appliances 315
House of the future 602-603
Housing
 Alpine skiing 552
 Electric motor 542

House spider 171
Howe 36
Howea forsteriana 126
Howler monkey 202
Hti 490
Huang He 265
Huayangosaurus 93
Hub
 1906 Renault 336
 ARV light aircraft 424
 Benz Motorwagen 335
 Bicycle wheels 358-359
 Blackburn monoplane 400-401
 Bordino Steam Carriage 334
 Eddy Merckx racing bicycle 361
 Paddle wheel 390-391
 Pegasus Quasar microlight 427
 Propellers 390
 Renault Clio 351
 Wright Flyer 399
Hub and brake drum 350
Hub bearing 351
Hubble Space Telescope 612-613
Hub bolt 338
Hub brake shoe 338
Hub cap
 1906 Renault 336
 Ford Model T 339
 Renault Clio 350
Hub carrier 351
Hub controller 604
Hub nut 350
Hub quick release lever 361
Hub seal 550
Hudson Bay 264
Hull
 Carvel-built 376, 391
 Clinker-built 375
 Cross-section 378
 Double-ended 375
 Greek and Roman ships 372-373
 Iron and wood 392
Hull plank 373
Human body 210-211
Human classification 108
Human Powered Vehicles (HPV) 358, 360
Humans 57, 76, 108, 202, 315
Humber engine 343
Humboldt current 296
Humerus
 Archaeopteryx 85
 Arsinoitherium 104
 Bird 189, 191
 Brachiosaurus 91
 Crocodile 186
 Diplodocus 90
 Domestic cat 195
 Elephant 201
 Eryops 80
 Euoplocephalus 94
 Frog 183
 Gallimimus 86
 Hare 197
 Horse 199
 Human 218
 Iguanodon 96
 Kangaroo 206
 Kentrosaurus 93
 Pareiasaur 81
 Plateosaurus 88
 Stegoceras 100
 Struthiomimus 87
 Toxodon 106
 Triceratops 102
 Tyrannosaurus 84
Humic acid 284
Hunter-killer submarine 396-397
Hunter's bend 388
Hunting 108, 548

Huntsman spider 171
Hurdle races 554
Hurdling 542
Hurling 540-541
Hurricane 302-303
Husk 150
Husqvarna Motocross TC610 368
Huygens space probe 614
Hyaenodon 74, 107
Hyaline cartilage 225
Hybrid bicycle 360-361
Hybrid car 554
Hybrid power 355
Hydra 18, 21
Hydrated copper sulphate 313
Hydraulic actuator attachment 413, 414
Hydraulic brake calliper 424
Hydraulic brake hose 369
Hydraulic brake pipe 414
Hydraulic fluid
 Disc brake 365
 Spring/damper unit 365
Hydraulic grab 396
Hydraulic hand-pump 421
Hydraulic hose 369
Hydraulic unit 605
Hydrazine propellant tank 615
Hydrocarbon 313
Hydrochloric acid 312
Hydrochoerus hydrochaeris 197
Hydroelectric power station 314
Hydrogen 308, 310
 Candle wax 312-313
 Covalent bonding 309
 Jupiter's atmosphere 45
 Massive stars 26
 Mercury's atmosphere 35
 Nebulae and star clusters 16-17
 Neptune's atmosphere 51
 Nuclear fusion in Sun 22
 Salt formation 312
 Saturn's atmosphere 47
 Small stars 24-25
 Sun 32
 Uranus' atmosphere 49
Hydrogen alpha line 23
Hydrogen atom 138, 596
Hydrogen beta line 23
Hydrogen fluoride 308
Hydrogen gamma line 23
Hydrogen gas 312
Hydrogen nucleus 22
Hydrogen requirement 138
Hydrogen sulphide 51
Hydroplane 396-397
Hydroxide 268
Hydrus 20
Hyena 194
Hymenoptera 168
Hyoglossus muscle 244
Hyoid bone 244-245, 255
Hypacrosaurus 99
Hypaethral temple 460-461
Hyperesion 373
Hyperlink 577
Hyphae
 Fungus 114-115
 Mycorrhizal association 133
Hypocotyl 152-153
Hypodermis
 Gynosperm 125
 Human 235
Hypogeal germination 152-153
Hypoglossal nerve 244

Hypogymnia physodes 114
Hypostyle hall 458-459
Hypothalamus 236
Hypsilophodon 72, 82
Hypural 180
Hystrix africaeaustralis 197

I

I bar 393
IBM-compatible PCs 566
Ice 66, 307
  Glacier 286-287
  Weathering and erosion 282
Ice age 56
Ice-age mammals 76
Ice block
  Ice-fall 287
  Lake formation 293
Ice-cap 287
Ice crystal 302
Ice cube 307
Ice erosion 287
Ice-fall 287
Ice hockey 550-551
Ice margin lake 286
Ice-plant 128-129
Ice sheet 76
Ichthyosaur 70-71
Ichthyostega 56, 80
Icons 576
Icterus galbula 193
Idle control valve 344
Idocrase 270
Igneous intrusion 274
Igneous rock 266-267, 274-275
Igniter 418
Igniter plug 419
Ignition amplifier 345
Ignition coils 554
Ignition control 362
Ignition lever 338
Ignition lock 362
Ignition switch 337
Ignition trigger housing 410
Iguana iguana 82
Iguanodon 75, 96-97
Ileocaecal fold 249
Ileum
  Bird 189
  Frog 182
  Human 226, 249
  Rabbit 196
Iliac crest 224-225
Iliac fossa 224
Iliac spine 224
Iliacus muscle 225
Ilio-femoral muscle 84, 97
Ilio-fibular muscle 84, 97
Ilio-ischial joint 82
Iliopsoas muscle 226
Ilio-pubic joint 82
Ilio-tibial muscle
  Albertosaurus 84
  Euoplocephalus 94
  Iguanodon 97
Ilium
  Archaeopteryx 85
  Bird 189
  Diplodocus 90
  Eryops 81
  Euoplocephalus 94
  Frog 183
  Gallimimus 86
  Human 218
  Iguanodon 96-97
  Kentrosaurus 93
  Ornithischian 82
  Parasaurolophus 98
  Plateosaurus 88
  Saurischian 82
  Stegoceras 100-101
  Stegosaurus 93
  Struthiomimus 87

Toxodon 107
Tuojiangosaurus 93
Tyrannosaurus 84
Illuminated manuscript 432
Illumination 444-445
Image controls 611
Image screen processor microchip 581
Image viewing screen 581
Imaging system housing 610
Imaging the body 214
Imago 168
Immature pitcher 161
Immature spur 141
Impasto 436-437, 442
Impeller 347
Imperial-Metric conversions 591, 620
Imperial unit measurements 590
Impermeable clay 292
Impermeable mudstone 292
Impermeable rock
  Cave 284-285
  Lake 292
  Mineral resources 280-281
  River's stages 289
Impermeable salt dome 281
Impermeable shale 292
Impost
  Ancient Roman building 465
  Cathedral dome 484
  Gothic building 473
  Islamic building 488
  Medieval building 466, 469
In-board 561
Inboard elevon 417, 421
Inboard elevon-jack fairing 416
Inboard end 387
Inboard engine 415
Inboard lift spoilers 413
Inboard trimtab 413
Inbound lane 526
Inbox icon 576
Incandescent light 318-319
In-car mounting bracket assembly 590
Incident laser light 319
Incisive canal 245
Incisor teeth
  Bear 194
  Chimpanzee 202
  Elephant 201
  Human 245, 246
  Lion 194
  Rabbit 196
  Rodent 196
  Toxodon 106
Incline 468
Incompetent bed rock 61
Incomplete mesentery 167
Incurrent pore 166
Incus 242
Indehiscent fruit 150
Index finger 230-231
India
  Cretaceous period 72-73
  Jurassic period 70
  Himalaya formation 62-63
  Late Carboniferous period 66
  Middle Ordovician period 64
  Mountain building 62-63
  Quaternary period 76-77
  Railway track gauge 331

Tertiary period 74-75
Thyreophorans 92
Triassic period 68
Indian ocean 73, 75, 77, 265
Indian stick insect 192
Indicator
  "Deltic" diesel-electric locomotive 327
  Bus 333
  Harley-Davidson FLHS Electra Glide 363
  Honda CB750 363
  MCW Metrobus 332
  Volkswagen Beetle 340
Indicator assembly 352
Indicator board 542
Indicator lamp 353
Indicator lens 341
Indirect method mosaic creation 450-451
Indium 311
Indo-Australian plate 59
Inducer 418
Induction stroke 343
Indus 20
Indusium 121
Industrial Revolution 492
Industrial robots 608
Inert gas 311, 584
Inferior articular process 223
Inferior concha 212, 241
Inferior extensor retinaculum 233
Inferior meatus 245
Inferior mesenteric vein 253
Inferior nasal concha 221, 241, 245
Inferior oblique muscle 241
Inferior orbital fissure 221
Inferior rectus muscle 241
Inferior vena cava 215, 252-253, 257
Infertile swamp 288
Infield 536-537
Infilled swamp 291
Inflated petiole 158
Inflation valve 405
Inflorescences 140
  Aechmea miniata 162
  Bromeliad 113
  Catkin 144
  Compound 142-143
  Couch grass 113
  Dodder 163
  Stem arrangements 143
Inflorescence stalk 140-143
  Aechmea miniata 162
  Brassavola nodosa 162
  Everlasting pea 129
  Indehiscent fruit 150
  Peach 131
  Peruvian lily 129
  Rowan 131
  Russian vine 131
  Succulent fruit 148
  Vegetative reproduction 154-155
  Wind-pollinated plant 144
Inflorescence types
  Capitulum 129, 142
  Compound umbel 143
  Dichasial cyme 143
  Raceme 129
  Single flower 143
  Spadix 143
  Spherical umbel 143
  Spike 143, 155, 162
Infraorbital foramen 221
Infraorbital margin 213, 221
Infra-red radiation 318-319

Energy emission from Sun 22
Infra-red map of our galaxy 15
Infra-red sensor 608
Infraspinatus muscle 227
Infratemporal fenestra
  Baryonyx 83
  Camarasaurus 91
  Diplodocus 90
  Heterodontosaurus 83
  Lambeosaurus 99
  Panoplosaurus 94
  Parasaurolophus 99
  Plateosaurus 88
  Protoceratops 102
  Triceratops 103
Infratemporal foramen 106-107
Ingres paper 441
Initial cave 285
Ink 430, 444
Ink-cartridge replacement button 574
Ink cartridges 574
Ink dabber 446
Inkjet nozzle 575
Inkjet printer 574-575
Ink outlet hole 574
Ink pad 445
Ink reservoir 444, 575
Ink roller 448, 449
Ink sac 176
Ink stick 444
Ink stone 444
Inlay 488-489
Inlet 295
Inlet cone 418
Inlet manifold
  Daimler engine 343
  Jaguar V12 engine 345
  Mid West single-rotor engine 411
Inlet manifold tract 545
Inlet-over-exhaust (IOE) engine 362
Inlet port 343, 367
Inlet rotor 547
Inlet tract 410
Inlet valve 343, 345, 362
Inner bin fin 592
Inner bud scales 134
Inner cage assembly 599
Inner clutch drum 366
Inner core 38-39, 41
Inner counter 445
Inner cyclone cone 592
Inner dome 484
Inner floret 129, 142
Inner jib downhaul 385
Inner jib halyard 385
Inner jib stay 382
Inner jib tack 382
Inner layer of cortex
  Dicotyledon 127
  Epiphytic orchid 162
  Monocotyledon 127
  Wetland plants 158-159
Inner mantle 44-47
Inner martingale stay 383
Inner membrane 139
Inner planetary orbits 31
Inner posts 528
Inner tepal 126, 140, 143
Inner tube 359, 424, 507
Inner vane 191
Innings 536, 538
Inorganic substances 280
Inscription 488
Insectivorous plants 113, 160-161
Insects 168-169, 279
  Cretaceous 72-73
  Plant food 160-161
  Pollinators 144-145
Inselberg 283
Insoluble solids 312
Inspection cover
  Avro biplane 403

Lockheed Electra airliner 407
Inspection door 407
Inspection panel 417
Inspiration 255
Instep 211
Instructor's cockpit 403
Instrument console 420
Instrument landing system aerial 420-421
Instrument package 615
Instrument panel
  ARV light aircraft 425
  Bell-47 helicopter 422
  Renault Clio 353
  Schweizer helicopter 426
Insulating column 316
Insulating hair 104, 107
Insulation 300
Insulator
  Electric circuit 316
  Generating magnetism 317
  Hydroelectric power station 314
Intaglio printing 446-447, 448
Intake manifold 351, 354
Intake pipe 335
Intake port 346
Integral ink reservoir 444
Integrated transparency unit (TPU) 570, 571
Integrated transport system 332
Integument
  Ovule 147
  Scots pine 122
Intelligent electronic door-lock 602
Intentional foul 533
Interalveolar septum 254
Intercellular leaf space 139
Interception 526
Inter-City travel 332
Intercolumniation 461, 485
Intercompressor bleed valve 419
Intercompressor diffuser pipe 419
Intercostal muscle 91, 255
Interdental papilla 247
Interdental septum 247
Interglacial period 76
Integer house 602, 603
Interior light 353
Interlobular artery 256
Interlobular vein 256
Interlocking spur 289
Intermediate housing 346
Intermediate lamella 225
Intermediate ring 563
Internal capsule 237
Internal carotid artery 243, 252
Internal combustion engine
  First cars 334
  Motorcycle engine 366
  Pioneers of flight 398
Internal crust 28
Internal elastic lamina 252
Internal fuse overload protection 585
Internal iliac artery 215, 253
Internal iliac vein 253
Internal jugular vein 253
Internal power cable 567
Internal skeleton 174
Internal spermatic fascia 259
Internal urethral orifice 257
Internal urethral sphincter muscle 257

International referees signals 533
International rules 532
International squash 544-545
International track gauge 331
Internet 576-577
Internet service provider (ISP) 576
Internode
  Canadian pond weed 158-159
  Horsetail 120
  Ice-plant 129
  Live-for-ever 129
  London plane 134
  Rhizome 155
  Rock stonecrop 128
  Rose stem 130
  Stem 134
  Stolon 154
Interopercular bone 181
Interosseous ligament 232
Interphalangeal joint
  Baryonyx 85
  Human 231, 233
Interplane strut 399, 404-405
Interradicular septum 247
Interrupter gear 404
Interstellar cloud remains 613
Intertragic notch 242
Intertrochanteric line 225
Intertropical convergence zone 300
Interventricular septum 251
Intervertebral disc 212, 218, 223, 245, 261
Intestinal muscle 226
Intestine
  Bony fish 181
  Butterfly 169
  Chimpanzee 202
  Cow 198
  Crayfish 173
  Dogfish 179
  Dolphin 205
  Elephant 200
  Frog 182
  Gallimimus 86
  Human 214
  Large 195, 202
  Lizard 185
  Sea urchin 175
  Small 182, 185, 187, 195, 198, 200, 202
  Spider 170
  Tortoise 187
Intrados 469, 484
Introitus 258
Intrusive rocks 26, 275
Invasion stripes 409
Invertebrates
  Earth's evolution 56
  Fossil record 279
  Insects 168-169
  Marine 65
Inverted ovolo 486
Inverter 355
Inverter board 570
Inverter cooling fan 355
Inverter cooling fan connector 355
Inverter housing 355
Inward dive 558, 559
Io 44
Iodine 311
Ion 308
Ionic bonding 308
Ionic capital 460
  Baroque church 481
  French temple 485
  Renaissance building 476
Ionic column
  Baroque church 481

French temple 485
Neoclassical building 483
Ionic half-column 464
Ionic order 460
Iota Centauri 21
Iota Pegasi 19
Iota Sagittarii 21
Ipomoea batatas 154
Iran 351
Ireland 351
Iridium 311
Iridocorneal angle 241
Iris
  Human 213, 226, 241
  Linear leaf 137
  Octopus 177
Iris lazica 137
Iron 311
  Earth's composition 39
  Earth's crust 58
  Golf club 547
  Magnetic domains 317
  Meteorite 52
  Nineteenth-century buildings 492
  Structure of Mercury 35
  Structure of Venus 37
Iron armature support 455
Ironclad 392-393
Iron club 546-547
Iron filings 317
Iron hull 392-393
Iron oxide
  Earth pigments 454
  Flesh-coloured pigments 433
  Sanguine crayon 430
  Sedimentary rocks 267, 277
Iron oxide dust 42
Iron paddlesteamer 392-393
Iron pyrite 79, 270
Iron railing 493
Iron roof 479
Iron ship 392-393
Iron, steam 594
Iron tracery 493
Iron tyre 334
Ironwork 478, 482
Irregular galaxy 10-12, 15
Irreversible reactions 312
Ischial tuberosity 224
Ischium
  Archaeopteryx 85
  Bird 189
  Crayfish 173
  Diplodocus 90
  Eryops 81
  Euoplocephalus 94
  Frog 183
  Human 218, 224
  Iguanodon 96
  Ornithischian 82
  Parasaurolophus 98
  Plateosaurus 88
  Saurischian 82
  Stegoceras 100-101
  Stegosaurus 93
  Struthiomimus 87
  Triceratops 102
  Tyrannosaurus 84
Ishtar Terra 36-37
Islamic buildings 488-489, 491
Islamic mosaic 489
Islands 291, 294
Isocline 61
Isolated single boulders 286
Isolated steep-sided hill 283
Isolator valve 325, 327
Isosceles triangle 622
Isoseismal lines 63
Isotopes 310
ISP 576
Israel 293

Isthmus
  Reproductive system 258-259
  Water hyacinth 158
Italian State Railways Class 402 328
Italic Roman lettering 445
Itonaco 454
Ivy 130-131, 137

J

Jack 514
Jacket-wall 466
Jack-rafter 473
Jack staff
  Battleship 394
  Frigate 397
  Square-rigged ship 375
  Wooden sailing ship 379
Jacob's ladder 378
Jagged fracture 270
Jaguar straight six engine 344
Jaguar V12 engine 345
Jali 488-489
Jamb
  Ancient Roman temple 463
  Baroque church 479
  Medieval church 468
  Neoclassical building 478, 482-483
  Nineteenth-century building 492
Jami Masjid 488
Javelin 542-543
Justicia aurea 144
Jaw
  Brace-and-bit 601
  Hand drill 601
  Human 212, 220-221
  Power drill 601
  Rope 389
Jawbone
  Allosaurus 85
  Australopithecus 107-108
  Ceratopsian 100
  Dolphin 204
  Horse 105
  Human 220, 247
  Ornithopod 96
  Shark 178
  Snake 184
  Theropods 84
Jawless fish 78, 178-179, 180
Jeer 377
Jejunum 249
Jelly 192
Jellyfish 78, 166-167
  Earth's evolution 56
  Fossil record 279
Jet engine 412, 418-419
Jetliners 412-415
Jet pipe 418-419, 423
Jet pipe connection 419
Jetstream 300, 418
Jewel anemone 166
Jewel Box 11
Jewish calendar 618
Jib boom 379, 382
Jib fairhead 561
Jib halyard 380
Jibsail 378, 379, 385
Jib sheet 585
Jib stay 382
Jib tack 382, 383
Jockey 554-555
Jockey wheel 358
Jodhpurs 554
Joint
  Cave 284-285
  Coastline 295
  Faults and folds 61
  Jointed plug 19
  Weathering and erosion 282

Jointed leg 79, 168
Jointed pincer 79
Jointed solidified lava 292
Jointed stem 131
Joints 224-225, 608
Joist 464, 486
Jones, H. 493
Jordan 293
Joule 314, 316
Journal 347
Joystick 361, 520
Judo 556-557
Jugal bar 201
Jugal bone 96, 102-103
Jugal plate 94
Juglans nigra 137
Jugular vein 215
Juice sac 148
"Jumbo jet" 412
Jumps 552, 554
Jump seat 337
Jump shot 532, 535
Junction
  Electrical circuit 316
  Giornata 454-435
  Photovoltaic cell 605
Junction board 355
Juncus sp. 135
Junior ratings' mess 397
Junk 376
Junk ring 343
Jupiter 30-31, 44-45, 614
Jurassic period 70-71
  Fossil record 279
  Geological time 57
Jury mast knot 389
Justicia aurea 144
Juvenile volcano 275

K

Kabe 375
Kaibab limestone 276
Kaibab Plateau 277
Kaiparowits formation 276
Kaiparowits Plateau 277
Kalahari Desert 265
Kalanchoe daigremontiana 154
Kalasa finial 489
Kalos 372
Kame delta 286
Kame terrace 286
Kangaroo 206-207
Kappa Pegasi 19
Kara Kum 265
Karv 374
Kasugado Shrine of Enjoji 490
Kasuga-style roof 490
Katastroma 373
Kaus Australis 19, 20
  Sagittarius 21
Kaus Borealis 21
Kaus Meridionalis 21
Kawana House 496
Kawasaki industrial robot 608
Kayak 560
Kayenta formation 276
Kazakstania 65
Kedrostis africana 113
Keel
  Battleship 395
  Bird 189
  Frigate 397
  Ironclad 393
  Iron paddlesteamer 392
  Longboat 380
  Sailing warship 377
  Viking ship 374-375
  Wooden sailing ship 378
Keel boat 560
Keeled lesene 486
Keeler 41
Keelson (Kelson) 560
  19th century paddle

steamer 391
Ironclad 393
Keep 466
Keeper ring 562
Kelvin temperature scale 590
Kendo 556
Kentrosaurus 92-93
Kepler 40
Keraia 372
Keratin 254
Kestrel 189
Ketch 384, 385
Kettle 286
Kettle drum 519
Kettle lake 293
  Post-glacial valley 286
Kevlar 384, 388
Key
  Concert grand piano 515
  Home keyboard 520
  Motorcycle clutch 366
  Musical notation 502
  Steel lock 560
  Synthesizer 520
  Upright piano 514
  Woodwind instruments 508-509
Keyboard 521, 566, 611
Keyboard instruments 514-515, 520
Key guard 509
Key pad button 589
Key pad button aperture 589
Key pad connectors 589
Key pad contacts 589
Key rod 509
Key signature 502
Keystone 484
  Ancient Roman building 463, 465
  Baroque church 479, 481
  French temple 485
  Medieval church 469
  Neoclassical building 478, 482
  Renaissance building 476-477
Keyway 390
Kick-stand 363
Kick-starter 363, 366
Kidney
  Bird 189
  Bony fish 181
  Brachiosaurus 90
  Dogfish 179
  Dolphin 205
  Domestic cat 195
  Elephant 200
  Frog 182
  Gallimimus 86
  Human 215, 256-257
  Lizard 185
  Octopus 176
  Rabbit 196
  Snail 177
  Tortoise 187
Kidney ore haematite 268
Kidney-shaped palette 436
Killer whale 205
Killick 586
Kiln 452
Kimberlite 268, 275
Kinetic energy 314-315
Kinetic sculpture 452
King pin 338
King-post 473, 479
  Early monoplane 400-401
  Pegasus Quasar microlight 427
  Pegasus XL SE microlight 426
King-post strut 401
King spoke handle 390
King strut 464

King vulture 190
Kirby BSA racing sidecar 369
Kittiwake 190
Kiwis 188
Knee
  Anchisaurus 89
  Corythosaurus 98
  Faering 375
  Gorilla 203
  Horse 199
  Human 211
  Iguanodon 96
  Kangaroo 207
  Lion 195
  Pachycephalosaurus 100
  Psittacosaurus 103
  Rabbit 197
  Stegoceras 101
  Stegosaurus 92
  Tyrannosaurus 84
Knee joint
  Brachiosaurus 90
  Diplodocus 90
  Euoplocephalus 94
  Human 219
  Parasaurolophus 98
  Plateosaurus 88
  Stegoceras 101
  Struthiomimus 87
  Toxodon 107
  Triceratops 102
  Tyrannosaurus 84
Knee of the head 378
Knee pad 527, 554
Knee roll 539, 554
Knife
  Palette 436
  Relief printing 446, 449
Knighthead 380
Knots 388-389
Knuckle 210
Koala 207
Kochab 18
Kope 372-373
Korolev 41
Krypton 311
Kuan Han-ch'ing 35
Kubernetes 372
Kunzite 271
Kuroshio current 297

L

Labellum 126, 145
Label mould 481
Labia 258
Labial palp 168
Labrum 168
Laburnum x watereri 137
Laccolith 273-275
Lacerta 19, 20
Lacertilia 184
Lacrimal apparatus 241
Lacrimal bone
  Bony fish 181
  Human 221
  Protoceratops 102
Lacrimal canaliculus 241
Lacrimal gland 241
Lacrimal punctum 241
Lacrimal sac 241
Lacrosse 540-541
Lacuna
  Bones and joints 225
  Clubmoss 120
  Mare's tail 135
  Wetland plants 158-159
Lacustrine terrace 286
Lada Terra 36, 37
Ladder
  74-gun ship 381
  Battleship 394
  Frigate 396
  Iron paddlesteamer 392, 393

Roman corbita 372-373
Train equipment 330
Wooden sailing ship 378
Ladder way 395-396
Lady Chapel, Salisbury Cathedral 470
Lagomorpha 196
Lagoon
  Atoll development 299
  Coastline 294-295
  River features 290-291
Lagoon Nebula 21
Lagopus lagopus 193
Lagostomus maximus 197
Lake Baikal 265
Lake Erie 264
Lake Huron 264
Lake Michigan 264
Lake Nyasa 265
Lake Ontario 264
Lakes 292-293
  Glacier 286-287
  Groundwater system 293
  Igneous rock structures 275
  River features 290
  River's stages 289
  Rock cycle 266-267
  Weathering and erosion 283
Lake Superior 264
Lake Tanganyika 265
Lake Victoria 265
Lakshmi Planum 37
Lambda Andromedae 19
Lambda Pegasi 19
Lambdoid suture 220
Lambeosaurus 96, 98-99
Lamb, T. 494
Lamella 139
Lamina 156
  Butterwort 161
  Couch grass 113
  Dicotyledon leaf 127
  Human 222-223
  Leaf 138
  Monocotyledon leaf 127
  Seaweed 116-117
  Succulent 113
  Vegetative reproduction 154
  Water hyacinth leaf 158
  Water lily leaf 159
Laminaria digitata 116-117
Laminates 548
Lamium sp. 155
Lamp 570, 571
Lamp bracket 336, 342
Lamp cluster 341
Lampland 43
Lamprey 178
Lampropeltis ruthveni 184
Lampropeltis triangulum annulata 184
Lamp shield 330
Lanceolate leaf 120, 131, 136
Lancet 471
Lancet arch 473, 484
Lancet window 470-472
Land 39
  Amphibians 80
  Animals 64
  Atmosphere 301
  Plants 56, 64
  Rivers 288
  Vertebrates 82
Lander unit 615
Landau body 334
Landau iron 334
Landing 477
Landing and taxiing light 414
Landing gear 406-407, 424-425
Landing-gear damper 423

645

Landing gear door
BAe-146 components 414
Concorde 416
Hawker Tempest components 409
Lockheed Electra airliner 406-407
Landing gear drag strut 401
Landing gear fork 407
Landing gear front strut 400, 404
Landing gear hydraulics 417
Landing gear leg 424
Landing gear rear cross-member 400
Landing gear rear strut 400-401
Landing gear strut 405
Landing light
BAe-146 jetliner components 414-415
Bell-47 helicopter 422
Lockheed Electra airliner 407
Schweizer helicopter 423
Landing skid
Avro triplane 403
Blackburn monoplane 400-401
Helicopter 422-423
Wright Flyer 399
Land movement 59
Land plants 56, 78
Landscape features 290-291, 294
Land surface removal 282
Land turtle 186
Lane
Athletic track 542
Swimming pool 558
Lane time-keeper 558
Langrenus 40
Language 108
Langur 202
Lantern 486
Baroque church 480-481
French temple 485
Neoclassical building 478-479
Twentieth-century building 494
Wooden sailing ship 379
Lanthanides 310
Lanthanum 310
Lanyard
Lifejacket 561
Oar 373
Rigging 382-383
Roman corbita 373
Lap 542
Lapilli 272
Lap strap
ARV light aircraft 425
Curtiss biplane 398
Lockheed Electra passenger seat 407
Pegasus Quasar microlight 427
Laptop computer 566, 567
Large intestine
Brachiosaurus 90
Chimpanzee 202
Domestic cat 195
Euoplocephalus 94
Human 214
Large Magellanic Cloud
Hydrus and Mensa 20
Our galaxy and nearby galaxies 15
Stars of southern skies 20-21
Large mammals 57
Larkspur 141, 151

Larus marinus 193
Larus ridibundus 193
Larva 168
Laryngeal prominence 212, 244-245
Larynx
Amphibian 182
Human 214-215, 244
Laser 587
Laser ranger 420
Lateen sail 375, 376, 384
Lateral angle 213
Lateral bracing strut 402-403, 416
Lateral branch
Adventitious roots 158-159
Horsetail 120
Vegetative reproduction 154
Lateral bud 134
Begonia 129
Dicotyledon 127
Horse chestnut 130
Leaf scars 154
London plane tree 134
Rhizome 155
Rowan twig 131
Stem bulbil 155
Stolon 154
Lateral canal
Human 247
Starfish 174
Lateral caudal musculature 87
Lateral column 223
Lateral control wheel 401
Lateral control wire 404
Lateral dorsal aorta 179
Lateral epicondyle 225
Lateral fault 61
Lateral fault lake 293
Lateral lacuna 237
Lateral line 181
Lateral malleolus 233
Lateral mass 222
Lateral moraine 286-287
Lateral plantar artery 253
Lateral plate 78
Lateral rectus muscle 240-241
Lateral root 133
Broomrape host 163
Carrot 128
Dicotyledon 127
Germination 152-153
Horse chestnut 130
Seedling 152-153
Strawberry 128
Sweet pea 128
Lateral root scar 128
Lateral sepal 141
Lateral shield 187
Lateral shoot 156
Lateral strike-slip fault 61
Lateral sulcus 237
Lateral tepal 126
Lateral vein 136, 159
Lateral ventricle 237
Lath 464
Lathyrus latifolius 129
Lathyrus odoratus 128
Latissimus dorsi muscle 227
Latrodectus mactans 171
Lattice-beam 496-497
Latticed screen 488-489
Latticed shade 495
Lattice-truss 499
Lattice window 492
Lattice-work 493
Laurasia
Cretaceous period 62
Jurassic period 70-71
Late Carboniferous period 66-67
Laurentia 69
Laurentian Library 474-475

Lava 62
Igneous and metamorphic rocks 274-275
Mountain building 62
Rock cycle 266
Volcano 272-273
Lava eruptions 272
Lava flow 273
Contact metamorphism 274-275
Mars 42
Rock cycle 266
Lava fragments 272
Lavatera arborea 131
Lava types 273
Lavinia Planitia 36-37
Lawrencium 311
Layering
Fresco 434-435
Pastel colours 440
Lay-up shot 552
LCD circuit board 582
LCD panel open button 582
LCD see Liquid crystal display (LCD)
Leach 374, 384
Lead
Mineralization zones 281
Minerals 268
Periodic table 311
Lead covering 487
Leading block 394
Leading edge
Avro biplane 403
Avro triplane 403
BAe-146 components 413, 414-415
BE 2B tail 405
BE 2B wings 404
Blackburn monoplane 401
Concorde 416-417
Hawker Tempest components 409
Lockheed Electra airliner 406
Northrop B-2 bomber 421
Pegasus Quasar microlight 427
Wright Flyer 399
Leading-edge aerial 421
Leading-edge fairing 425
Lead-in wire 319
Lead iodide 313
Lead nitrate 313
Lead shot 517
Lead wire 600
Leaf axis 137
Leaf bases 128, 136-137
Aechmea miniata 162
Couch grass 113
Dicotyledon 127
Florists' chrysanthemum 129
Guzmania lingulata 162-163
Hogweed 129
Monocotyledon 126-127
Sago palm 123
Seedling leaf 152
Water hyacinth 158
Leaf blade
Butterwort 161
Dicotyledon 127
Leaf surface 136, 138
Monocotyledon 127
Vegetative reproduction 154
Venus fly trap 160
Wetland plants 158-159
Leaf insect 192
Leafless branch 120
Leaflets 136-137
Everlasting pea 129
Fern 120-121

Horse chestnut leaf 130
Mahonia 130-131
Monocotyledon 126
Pinna 121, 136-137
Rose 131
Rowan 130
Sago palm 123
Tree fern 112-113
Leaflet stalk 137
Leaf-like structures 141-143
Dehiscent fruit 151
Dicotyledon flower 127
Guzmania lingulata 163
Ice-plant 129
Live-for-ever 129
Peruvian lily 129
Slender thistle 129
Wind pollination 144
Leaf margin 129
Aechmea miniata 162
Slender thistle 129
Vegetative reproduction 154
Leaf notch 154
Leaf primordium 134
Leaf scar
Begonia 129
Elder 130
Horse chestnut 130
Ice-plant 128-129
London plane 134
Rock stonecrop 128
Leaf shape 136-137
Leaf sheath 129
Leaf spring 338
Leaf spring suspension 327
Leaf stalk 128, 136-137
Chusan palm 130
Clematis 131
Cobra lily 160
Common horse chestnut 130
Dicotyledon 127
Everlasting pea 129
Florists' chrysanthemum 129
Kedrostis africana 113
Maidenhair tree 123
Monocotyledon 126-127
Mulberry 130
Oxalis sp. 157
Passion flower 130
Peach 131
Seedling 153
Strawberry 128
String of hearts 157
Tree fern 112
Tree mallow 131
Vegetative reproduction 154-155
Venus fly trap 160
Water lily 159
Wind pollination 144
Leaf succulents
Haworthia truncata 157
Lithops bromfieldii 157
Lithops sp. 156
Leaf trace 127
Leaf venation 129
Leafy liverwort 118
Leafy thallus 114
Lean-to roof 468-470, 472
Leather ball making 525
Leather grommet 373
Leather hood 334
Leather ink dabber 446
Leather pad 557
Leather upholstery 337
Leather valance 337
Leathery exocarps 148
Leaves 136-137
Abaxial surface 123, 130
Adaxial surface 123, 130
Aechmea miniata 162
Apex 136-137

Apical meristem 134
Barberry 130-131
Bishop pine 124
Brassavola nodosa 162
Bromeliad 112-113
Broomrape 163
Butterwort 161
Canadian pond weed 158-159
Carnivorous plants 160-161
Checkerbloom 136
Chusan palm 130
Classification 136-137
Clematis 130-131
Clubmoss 120
Cobra lily 160
Couch grass 113
Dicotyledon 126-127
Dryland plants 156-157
Durmast oak 131
Epiphyte 162-163
Fern 120-121
Florists' chrysanthemum 129
Germination 152-153
Guzmania lingulata 162-163
Haworthia truncata 157
Hinge cell 113
Hogweed 129
Horsetail 120
Intercellular space 139
Ivy 131
Kedrostis africana 113
Lamina 156
Lithops bromfieldii 157
Liverwort 118
London plane tree 134
Maidenhair tree 123
Margin 136
Marram grass 113
Midrib 136
Monkey cup 161
Monocotyledon 126-127
Moss 112, 119
Mulberry 130
Orange lily 154
Oxalis sp. 157
Parasite host 163
Passion flower 130
Peach 131
Photosynthesis 134, 138-139
Pine 122, 124-125
Pitcher development 161
Pitcher plant 113, 160-161
Primordia 134
Rock stonecrop 128
Rose 130-131
Rosettes 162-163
Rowan 130
Sago palm 123
Scots pine 122
Seedling 152-153
Slender thistle 129
Smooth cypress 123
Stomata 139
Strawberry 128
Tendrils 161
Toadflax 129
Tree fern 112-113
Tree mallow 131
Vegetative reproduction 154-155
Veins 136, 138-139
Venus fly trap 160
Water fern 158
Water hyacinth 158
Water lily 159
Welwitschia 122-123
Xerophyte 156-157
Yew 123
Le Corbusier 494
Leda Planitia 36, 37
Ledge 381
Leech 374, 384

Leechline 375
Left edge guide 575
Leg
Amphibian 182
Caiman 186-187
Crab 172
Crayfish 172-173
Crocodilian 186
Elephant 200
Frog 182
Gorilla 203
Human 210
Kangaroo 207
Lizard 184-185
Relief-printing press 449
Salamander 182
Scorpion 170
Shrimp 172
Spider 170-171
Tadpole 183
Terrapin 187
Tripod congas stand 519
"Leg before wicket" 538
Leg bud 260
Leg pad 539, 551
Leg protector 551
Leg slip 538
Legumes 150
Leibnitz 41
Lemercier, J. 486
Lemming 196
Lemon 148
Lemur 202-203
Lemur catta 203
Lenoir, Etienne
Early engines 342
First cars 334
Lens
Digital camera 585
Digital video 583
Flatbed scanner 570
Human body 241
Microscope 610, 611
Lens assembly 583
Lens bezel 580
Lens cap 583
Lens inner barrel (zoom/focus) 580
Lens mounting bracket 580
Lens zoom and focus 580
Lens zoom in/out toggle 581
Lenticels 133, 134
Lentiform nucleus 237
Leo 18, 21
Leo Minor 18, 21
Leonaspsis 279
Leonid meteor shower 52
Leontopithecus rosalia 203
Lepidodendron 66-67
Lepidoptera 168
Lepidotes maximus 73
Leptoceratops 103
Lepus 21
Lesbian leaf pattern 460
Lesene
Ancient Roman building 462, 465
Baroque church 480-481
Dome 486
French temple 485
Gothic church 473
Renaissance building 476-477
Lesser trochanter of femur 225
Lesser wing covert 188
Lesser wing of sphenoid bone 221
Letronne 40
Letter buttons 588
Lettering 444-445
Letter keys 588
Levator anguli oris muscle 229

Levator labii superioris
muscle 229
Levator palpebrae
superioris muscle 241
Levee 289-291
Level-wind system 562
Lever 320-321
Le Verrier ring 50-51
Liang K'ai 35
Libellulium longialatum
73
Liberty ship 392
Libra 18, 21
Library 483, 496
Licence holder 332
Lichens 114-115
Lid
Moss 119
Pitchers 161
Ships for war and trade
377
Lid assembly 571, 587
Lierne 469
Life 56, 78-79, 300
Lifeboat 394
Lifeboat davit 395
Life buoy 395
Life-cycle
Brown seaweed 117
Fern 121
Insect 168
Moss 119
Mushroom 115
Plants 112
Scots pine 122
Lifeguard 532
Lifejacket 561
Life of massive star 26-27
Life of small star 24-25
Life-raft 416
Liferaft cylinder 397
Lift
Athletics 543
Centre Georges
Pompidou 497
Double topsail
schooner 385
Roman corbita 372
Sailing warship 376-
377
Wooden sailing ship
378
Lift bracing wire
Biplanes and triplanes
403
Early monoplane 400-
401
Pegasus Quasar
microlight 427
World War I aircraft
404-405
Lifting handle 336
Lifting lug 330
Lift spoiler 413, 414
Lift wire 399
Ligament
Bifurcate 232
Cricothyroid 244
Deltoid 252
Falciform 248
Foot 232
Hip joint 224
Iliofemoral 224
Interosseus 232
Ovarian 258
Periodontal 247
Plantar
calcaneonavicular 232
Posterior
cuneonavicular 232
Posterior
tarsometatarsal 252
Pubofemoral 224
Talonavicular 232
Zonular 241
Ligature 508, 509
Light 314-315, 318-319
Chemical reactions
512

Renaissance building
474
Seed germination 152
Translucent "window"
157
Twentieth-century
building 495
Ultraviolet 145
Light aircraft 410, 424-425
Light Emitting Diode 583
Lighterman's hitch 389
Light hour 14
Lighting hole 393
Light level sensor 581
Lightning 45, 316
Lights
Bicycle 360
MCW Metrobus 332
Light screen 394
Light shield 612, 613
Light switch 339
Lightweight plastic intake
manifold 354
Light-well 487
Light year 14
Lignite 280
Lignum vitae bearing
387
Ligulate ray floret 129
Lilienthal, Otto 398
Lilium bulbiferum 154
Lilium sp. 133, 138, 140-
141, 155
Lily
Bulbil 154-155
Flower 140-141
Leaf surface 138
Limb
Mammal 104
Paddlesteamer 390
Reptile 80
Structure of a fold 60
Limber hole 393
Lime 143
Lime-resistant pigment
434
Limestone
Cave 284
Contact metamorphism
274
Faults and folds 60
Fossilized blue-green
alga 78
Lower Carboniferous
60
Limestone block 470
Limestone cladding 494
Limestone false door 459
Limestone spring 292
Limestone strata 284
Lime water 313
Limiter switch 586
Limonite groundmass
268-269
Limpet 176
Linaria sp. 129
Line 562
Linea alba 226
Linear dune 285
Linear leaf 129, 137
Linebacker 526
Line guide 563
Line judge 526
Line of sight 41
Linesman
Badminton 545
Gaelic football 529
Ice hockey 550
Soccer 524
Tennis 544
Volleyball 534
Lingual nerve 244
Lingual tonsil 245
Link 386
Link to external website
577
Linocut 446
Linoleum block 446, 449
Linseed oil 436

Lintel
Building 459, 494
Coastline 295
Lintel course 483
Lion 194-195
Lion crest 395
Lionfish 180
Lip
Flower 126, 145
Human 212-213
Lamprey 178
Pollination 145
Lip of trunk 200-201
Lip plate 508, 508
Lip tension 506
Liquidambar styraciflua
76
Liquid capacity
measurements 590
Liquid crystal display
(LCD)
Apple Power Mac G4
1GHz dual processor
566
Brother T-78 fax
machine 572
Game Boy Advance 579
Garmin Street Pilot III
GPS 590, 591
Nokia 5510 588
Portable CD player 587
Samsung VM800 laptop
567
Sony digital handycam
582
Liquid crystal display
(LCD) assembly 591
(LCD) circuit board 569
Liquid helium 45
Liquid hydrogen 44-47
Liquid ink 444
Liquids 306-307
Litchi chinensis 148
Lithification 266
Lithium 308, 310
Lithium fluoride molecule
308
Lithographic printing 446
Lithographic printing
equipment 448
Lithops bromfieldii 157
Lithops sp. 156
Lithosphere 58-59
Little finger 230 -231
Little grebe 190
Little toe 232-233
Live-for-ever 128-129
Liver
Bird 189
Bony fish 181
Chimpanzee 202
Dogfish 179
Dolphin 205
Domestic cat 195
Euoplocephalus 94
Frog 182
Gallimimus 86
Human 214, 248, 252
Lizard 185
Rabbit 196
Tortoise 187
Liverworts 112, 118-119
Livestock freight car 327
Living organisms 306
Lizard 184-185, 382
"Lizard-feet forms" 88
Lizard-hipped dinosaurs
82, 88-89
Llama 198
Load 320-521
Loading arm 396
Loading gauge 330-331
Load space 334
Lobby 498
Lobe
Liverwort 118
Venus fly trap 160
Lobed leaf 129, 131
Lobsters 172

Lobule 242
Local Arm 14
Local control cabinet 396
Locating pin 580
Lock 582
Lockable cover latch 566
Lock button 600
Lock forward 530
Lockheed Electra airliner
406-407
Locking lever 590
Lock nut 351, 359
Locks 360
Lock washer 358-359
Locomotion 104
Locomotives 324-329
Lodging knee 381
Loft 477
Log basket 334
Loin
Horse 198
Human 210
London Bridge 466-467
London plane tree 134
Longboat 380
Long bridge 515
Long-distance cycling 360
Long-distance running
542
Longeron 403, 424
Longitudinal channels
120
Longitudinal fissure 236-
257
Long jump 542-543
Long leading-link fork
362
Long leg 538
Long off 538
Long on 538
Long pass 532
Long radius turns 552
Longrod stabilizer 549
Longship 374-375
Longshore drift 294-295
Long-travel suspension
368
Long-wave radio 318
Look out periscope 396
Loom 560
Loop 388-389
Looped prominence 32-33
Loophole
Medieval building 466-
469
Renaissance building
477
Loop of Henlé 256
Loose forward 530
Loose-head prop 530
Lopolith 274
Lora 127, 130
Lorises 202
Lost-wax casting method
454
Lotus flower 488
Lotus petal 489
Loudspeaker 520
Lounge 392
Louvre 493, 498
Love-in-a-mist 150-151
Lowell 43
Lower Carboniferous
Limestone 60
Lower crankcase 410
Lower crux of antihelix
242
Lower deadeye 382-383
Lower deck 393
Lower-energy radiation
22
Lower epidermis 139, 159
Lower eyelid 213
Lower fin 423
Lower haze 37
Lower lobe of lung 215,
254-255

Lower seed axis 152-153
Lower topsail 385
Lower-wing attachment
404
Lower yard 395
Lowland coastline 295
Low Neap tide 297
Low pressure areas 300,
302-303
Low pressure gases 306
Low tides 296-297
Low-voltage supply 596
Loxodonta africana 200
Lozenge 471, 485
Lubricant 566
Lucarne window 480-481,
486
Lufengosaurus 89
Luff 384-385
Lug 382, 386
Lugger 384
Lug sail
Junk 376
Sail types 384
Lumbar nerves 258
Lumbar vertebrae
Crocodile 186
Domestic cat 195
Hare 197
Horse 199
Human 222-223
Kangaroo 206
Platypus 206
Rhesus monkey 202
Seal 204
Lumbrical muscle 231
Lump hammer 452-453
Lunae Planum 43
Lunaria annua 151
Lunate bone 250
Lunette 480
Lung
Amphibian 182
Bird 189
Brachiosaurus 91
Chimpanzee 202
Dolphin 205
Domestic cat 195
Elephant 200
Euoplocephalus 94
Frog 182
Gallimimus 86
Human 214-215, 252,
254-255
Lizard 184-185
Rabbit 196
Snail 177
Snake 184
Spider 170
Tortoise 187
Lungfish 80, 81
Lunule 231
Lures 562-563
Lutetium 311
LVG CVI fighter 405
Lychee 148
Lycoming four-cylinder
engine 423
Lycoming six-cylinder
engine 422
Lycopodiophyta 64, 120
Lymphocytes 253
Lynx 18, 21
Lynx helicopter 396
Lyra 19, 20
Lysosome 217

M

M22 (globular cluster) 21
Macaques 202
Macaws 190
Mach 41
Machine-gun 404-405
Machine heads 512-513
Mackenzie-Peace River
264
Mackerel angling 562

Maquette 455
Macrobius 40
Macrofibril 234
Macrospicule 33
Macs 566
Macula 240-241
Madagascar 265
Madreporite 174, 175
Madrillus sphinx 203
Maenianum summum 465
Magazine 548-549
Magellanic Cloud 15, 20
Maginus 40
Magma
Igneous and
metamorphic rocks 26
Mountain building 63
Ocean floor 298-299
Rock cycle 266
Volcanoes 272
Magma reservoir
Igneous rock structures
275
Volcanic structure 273
Magnesium 310
Earth's composition 39
Earth's crust 58
Seawater salt content
296
Magnesium alloy oil sump
pan 354
Magnesium housing for
air intake 355
Magnesium riser 548
Magnet 598, 605
Magnetic axis 28
Magnetic compass 423
Magnetic field 38
Magnetism 316-317
Magneto
Avro triplane 402
Hawker Tempest
components 408
Wright Flyer 399
Magneto drive 367
Magneto-optical circuits
587
Magnetosphere 38
Magnetron assembly 596,
597
Magnetron cooling fan
596, 597
Magnetron cooling fan
mounting 597
Magnetron perforated
heat sink 597
Magnitude 22
Magnolia 57, 72
Mahonia 130-131
Maidenhair tree 122-123
Maillot 386
Main circuit board 569,
582
Main engines 615
Main fan 596, 597
Main fan electrical supply
597
Main frame 572
Main-line signalling
system 330-331
Main motor casing 593
Main printed circuit board
(PCB) 591
Mainrail head 379
Main ribbon loom socket
581
Main sail
Dhow 376
Roman corbita 373
Sailing rigs 385
Square-rigged ship 375
Main screen 584
Mains earthing wire 596
Mains electricity supply
lead 585
Main sequence star
Massive stars 26
Objects in Universe 11
Small stars 24

Stars 22-23
Mains flex 594
Mains flex clamp 594
Main sheer strake 393
Main sheet
  Longboat 380
  Roman corbita 373
  Sailing dinghy 561
  Viking karv 375
Main shroud 378
Mains lead 597-598
Main spar bridge 413
Mains power connectors 589
Mains power on/off switch 585
Mains spade contacts 594
Main stay 377, 379
Mains supply lead 594
Maintenance button 574
Main topcastle 377
Main topgallant mast 377, 378
Main topgallant sail 379
Main topgallant stay 379
Main topmast 377, 379
Main topmast topcastle 377
Main topsail 379
Main topsail halyard 385
Main topsail yard 379
Main top yard 377
Main turbine 397
Main wale 381
Main wheel 426, 595
Main wing bracing-strut 401
Main wing-strut 427
Main yard
  Dhow 376
  Sailing warship 377
  Wooden sailing ship 379
Maize 127
Major calyx 256
Major coverts 188, 191
Malachite 433
Malacostraca 172
Malaysia 331
Male
  Bladder 257
  Body 210, 211
  Pelvis 259
  Reproductive organs 259
  Urinary tract 257
Male apex 119
Male catkin 144
Male cone 122-123, 24
Male fern 120-121
Male flower organs 140-143
Male flowers
  Fertilization 146-147
  Gymnosperms 122
  Painter's palette 143
  Seaweed 116-117
  Succulent fruit 148
  Wind-pollinated plant 144
"Mallard" express steam locomotive 324-325
Mallet
  Marble carving 452
  Ships and sailing 383, 384, 588
  Tubular bells 516
Malleus 242
Malpighian tubule
  Butterfly 169
  Spider 170
Malus 373
Malus sp. 126
Malus sylvestris 149
Mammals 104-107
  Carnivora 194
  Cetacea 204
  Cretaceous period 72
  Earth's evolution 56-57

Fossil record 279
Jurassic period 70
Lagomorpha 196
Large 57
Marsupalia 206
Monotremata 206
Pinnipedia 204
Primates 202
Proboscidea 200
Rodentia 196
Shrew-like 70
Small 56
Tertiary period 74-75
Ungulates 198
Mammoth 107
Mammut 75
Mammuthus 76, 77, 104
Mandapa 491
Mandarinfish 180
Mandible
  Acanthostega 80
  Ankylosaurus 94
  Arsinoitherium 104
  Baryonyx 83
  Bat 105
  Bear 194
  Beetle 168
  Bird 188-189
  Bony fish 181
  Camarasaurus 91
  Chimpanzee 202
  Crayfish 173
  Crocodile 186
  Diplodocus 90
  Elephant 201
  Eryops 80
  Euoplocephalus 94
  Hare 197
  Heterodontosaurus 83
  Horse 199
  Human 220-221, 244-245
  Hyaenodon 107
  Iguanodon 96
  Kangaroo 206
  Lambeosaurus 99
  Lion 194
  Moeritherium 105
  Panoplosaurus 94
  Parasaurolophus 99
  Phiomia 105
  Plateosaurus 88
  Protoceratops 102
  Rattlesnake 185
  Rhesus monkey 202
  Seal 204
  Stegoceras 100-101
  Styracosaurus 102
  Toxodon 106
  Triceratops 103
  Turtle 187
  Tyrannosaurus 84
Mandrills 202-203
Mane 194, 199
Manganese 281, 310
Manharness knot 389
Manifold connector 355
Manilla rope 589
Manipulator 610
Man-of-war 378
Mansard roof 490
Mantle
  Earth 38-39, 58-59, 63
  Mars 43
  Mercury 35
  Moon 41
  Molluscs 176-177
  Neptune 51
  Pluto 51
  Regional metamorphism 274
  Uranus 49
  Venus 37
Manufacturing code 569
Maple 127
Map projections 264-265
Maracas 504, 516-517
Marble 274
Marble block 453

Marble breaking equipment 450
Marble mosaic 489
Marble sculpture 452
Marble tessera 450
Marble veneer 462
Marchantia polymorpha 118
Mare Crisium 40
Mare Fecunditatis 40
Mare Frigoris 40
Mare Humorum 40
Mare Imbrium 40
Mare Ingenii 41
Mare Moscoviense 41
Mare Nectaris 40
Mare Nubium 40
Mare Orientale 41
Mareotis Fossae 43
Mare Serenitatis 40
Mare Smithii 41
Mare Tranquillitatis 40
Mare Vaporum 40
Margaritifer Sinus 43
Margin
  Lamina 116-117, 161
  Leaf 129, 136-137
  Needle 124
  Water lily leaf 159
Marginal shield 187
"Margined heads" 100
Marginocephalians 83, 100-103
Maria 40
Marine invertebrates 65
Marine plants 56
Marine reptiles 57, 70
Marine sediments 280
Marine turtles 186
Mariopteris 66
Markab 19, 20
Markeb 21
Marlin 388
Marlinspike 383, 389
Marmosets 202
Marram grass 113
Mars 30, 42-43
Mars Lander 615
Mars Pathfinder space probe 615
Marsh 293
Marsupials 104, 206-207
Martellange, E. 479
Martingale 382, 557
Martingale stay 383
Mary Rose 376
Mascaron 487
Mask 460, 487, 536
  Ancient Roman building 465
  Cathedral dome 484
  Neoclassical building 482
Masonry apron 487
Mason's mark 470
Mason's tools 485
Mass
  Atoms and molecules 309, 320
  Earth 30
  Jupiter 26, 44
  Mars 30
  Mercury 30
  Neptune 31
  Planets 30-31
  Pluto 31
  Saturn 31
  Stars 22
  Uranus 31
  Venus 30
Massive habit 270-271
Massive stars 26-27
Mass measurements 590
Massospondylus 89
Mass-production 338-339, 492
Mass transportation 332

Mast
  Battleship 394
  Frigate 397
  Greek galley 372
  Iron paddlesteamer 392
  Junk 376
  Longboat 380
  Roman corbita 373
  Sailing 561
  Sailing warship 376-377
  Submarine 397
  Tea clipper 392
  Three-masted square-rigged ship 375
  Viking karv 375
  Wooden sailing ship 378-379
Mast band 382
Master cylinder
  Disc brake 365
  Harley-Davidson FLHS Electra Glide 363
  Honda VF750 364
Master shipwright 374
Master's sea cabin 381
Masthead
  Roman corbita 373
  Viking karv 375
  Wooden sailing ship 378
Mast head bend 389
Masthead pulley for tye halyard 375
Mast hoop 385
Mastoid fontanelle 220
Mastoid process 220, 242
Mast partner 381
Mast step 392
Mast truck 372
Matar 19
Match play 546
Maternal blood pool 260
Maternal blood vessel 260
Mathematical symbols 621
Mato Grosso 264
Matter 306-307
  Electrical charge 316
  Identification 312
Mature ruptured follicle 258
Mawsonites spriggi 65
Maxilla
  Ankylosaurus 94
  Baryonyx 83
  Bear 194
  Bony fish 181
  Camarasaurus 91
  Chimpanzee 202
  Diplodocus 90
  Elephant 201
  Eryops 80
  Euoplocephalus 94
  Frog 183
  Horse 105
  Human 212, 220-221, 244-245, 246, 248
  Iguanodon 96
  Lion 194
  Pachycephalosaurus 100
  Prenocephale 100
  Stegoceras 100
  Toxodon 106
Maxillary fenestra 90
Maxilliped 173
Maxwellian diagram 318
Maxwell Montes 36, 37
Mazda RX-7 346
McLaren Mercedes MP4-13 356-357
MCW Metrobus 332-333
ME 262 fighter 408
Meadow cranesbill 144
Meadow rue 137
Meadow sage 145
Meander 461
Meanders 288-289, 290
Measurement units 620
Meatus 242-243

Mechanical semaphore signal 330
Mechanical weathering 282
Mechanics 350-351
Mechanism of respiration 255
Medallion 476
Medial epicondyle 225
Medial malleolus 233
Medial moraine
  Glaciers 286-287
  River's stages 289
Medial rectus muscle 240-241
Median canal 243
Median cubital vein 253
Median eye 170
Median glossoepiglottic fold 244
Median nerve 238
Median sulcus 244
Median wing coverts 188
Medieval castles 466-467
Medieval churches 468-469
Medieval houses 466-467
Medinet Habu, Egypt 459
Mediterranean Sea 74, 265
Mediterranean sea anemone 166
Medium-wave radio 318
Medulla 114, 234, 256
Medulla oblongata 212, 236-237
Medullary cavity 224
Medullary pyramid 256
Medullary ray 125
Medullosa 66
Mega bass control 586
Megaspores 122
Megazostrodon 104
Megrez 19
Meiolania 77
Meissner's corpuscle 234-235, 239
Melanin 234
Melanosaurus 68, 88-89
Melon 149, 205
Melting glacier 286, 289
Meltwater 287, 289
Meltwater pool 286
Membrane
  Chloroplasts 139
  Chorioallantoic 192
  Egg 193
  Shell 192
  Thylakoid 139
Memory card 579
Memory microchip 579
Memory stick 581, 583
Memory stick connector 583
Memory stick cover recess 589
Memory stick eject button 583
Memory stick slot 583
Mendel 41
Mendeleev 41
Mendelevium 311
Meninges 237
Menkalinan 21
Menkar 19, 20
Menkent 21
Mensa 20, 21
Mental foramen 213, 220-221
Mentalis muscle 229
Mental protuberance 221
Mental symphysis 220
Mentolabial sulcus 213
Menu icon 568
Menu key 590
Menu roll-on scroll/wheel 587
Menu select forward/back button 588

Menu select forward/back button connectors 589
Menu selector 587
Menu select up/down button 588
Merak 19
Merchants' Exchange 493
Mercury 30, 34-35
Mercury (metal) 281, 311, 319
Mericarp 151
Meristematic cells 154
Merlon 466
Mermaid's purses 192
Mersenius 40
Merus 172, 173
Merycoidodon 75
Mesa 275, 277, 282
Mesentery 167, 182
Mesocarp 146-147, 148, 148-149
Mesoglea 167
Mesohyal 166
Mesophyll 135
  Bishop pine needle 124
  Dicotyledon leaf 126
  Marram grass 113
  Monocotyledon leaf 126
  Palisade layer 139
  Spongy layer 139
Mesosphere 300
Mesothorax 168
Mesozoic era
  Cretaceous period 72
  Dinosaurs 82
  Fossil record 279
  Geological timescale 57
  Jurassic period 70
  Reptiles 80
  Triassic period 68
Mess 397
Message list 576
Message manager launch button 572
Metacarpals
  Archaeopteryx 85
  Arsinoitherium 104
  Baryonyx 85
  Bird 189, 91
  Brachiosaurus 91
  Cow 198
  Diplodocus 90
  Domestic cat 195
  Elephant 90, 201
  Eryops 80
  Euoplocephalus 94
  Frog 183
  Gallimimus 86
  Hare 197
  Horse 198-199
  Human 218-219, 230
  Kangaroo 206
  Lizard 184
  Parasaurolophus 99
  Plateosaurus 88
  Platypus 206
  Rhesus monkey 202
  Seal 204
  Stegoceras 100
  Toxodon 106
  Triceratops 103
  Tyrannosaurus 84
Metacarpophalangeal joint 85
Metal cook/grill tray 596
Metal grill/griddle 596
Metalliferous muds 299
Metalling 486
Metal modelling implements 452
Metal needle pad 384
Metal nib 444
Metal riser 455
Metal runner 455
Metals 310
Metal tyre 324
Metal wire conductor 316-317

Metamorphic aureole 26
Metamorphic rocks 26, 274-275, 266-267
Metamorphosis
Amphibian 182
Frog 183
Insect 168
Metasoma 170
Metatarsals
Albertosaurus 84
Archaeopteryx 85
Brachiosaurus 90
Crocodile 186
Domestic cat 195
Elephant 201
Eryops 81
Euoplocephalus 94
Frog 183
Hare 197
Horse 199
Human 218-219, 232
Iguanodon 96-97
Kangaroo 206
Lizard 184
Parasaurolophus 98
Plateosaurus 88
Platypus 206
Rhesus monkey 202
Scorpion 170
Seal 204
Spider 171
Stegoceras 100-101
Struthiomimus 87
Toxodon 107
Triceratops 102
Metathorax 168
Metaxylem 127, 132-133
Meteor 52, 301
Meteorite
Asteroids, comets, and meteoroids 52
Earth's atmosphere 38
Moon 41
Ray crater 34
Meteorite impact 34, 40
Meteoroids 52-53
Solar System 30
Methane
Jupiter 45
Neptune and Pluto 50-51
Saturn 47
Uranus 48-49
Methane cirrus clouds 50-51
Metis Regio 36
Metope 460
Metric-Imperial conversions 620
Metric unit measurements 590
Metridium senile 166
Metrobus 332-333
Metrolink tram 332
Mexican hat plant 154
Mexican mountain king snake 184
Mexican true red-legged tarantula 170
Mexico 331
Mezzanine 467, 496
Miaplacidus 21
Mica 26, 270
Mice 104, 196
Michelangelo 35
Micrasterias sp. 112
Microchip 582
Microfilament 217
Microlights 410, 426-427
Micro-needle 606
Micro-organisms 38, 78
Microphone 581, 589
Microphone block 583
Microphone cover 583
Microphone jack 567
Micro-pipette 606
Micropits 586
Microporous filter 592
Microprocessor 569

Microscopes 610-611
Microsoft XBox 579
Microsporangium 122
Microspores 122
Microsporophyll 122
Microtubule 217, 239
Microwave oven 315
Microwave radiation 10
Microwave combination oven 596-597
Microwaves 318, 596
Midbrain 236
Middle ear ossicles 242
Middle finger 230-231
Middle leg
Beetle 168
Bumblebee 168
Butterfly 169
Middle lobe of lung 215, 254-255
Middle meatus 241, 245
Middle nasal concha 212, 221, 241, 245
Middle phalanx 219, 230, 232
Middle rail 381
Midfielders
Gaelic football 529
Lacrosse 541
Soccer 524
Midgut173
Mid-latitude band 36
Mid-latitude cyclones 302
Mid-ocean ridge 281, 298-299
Mid-off 538
Mid-on 538
Midrib
Dicotyledon leaf 126-127
Durmast oak leaf 131
Fern fronds 121
Hogweed leaf 129
Ice-plant leaf 129
Live-for-ever leaf 129
Liverwort 118
Monkey cup 161
Moss leaf 119
Spiral wrack 116
Sweet chestnut leaf 136
Tree fern 113
Venus fly trap 160
Water lily leaf 159
Midships fence 373
Midships section 392
Midwater current 297
Midway Gardens 495
Mid West single-rotor engine 411
Mid West twin-rotor engine 411
Mid West two-stroke engine 410
Miele washer-dryer 594, 595
Mihrab 488
Milan Cathedral 473
Milankovic 43
Milk snake 184
Milk teeth 246
Milky quartz 268, 271
Milky Way 14-15
Northern stars 18
Solar System 30
Stars of southern skies 20
Mill 462, 464, 492
Millstone grit 60-61
Milne 41
Milton 35
Mimas 46
Mimosa 21
Mimulopsis solmsii 145
Minaret 488-489
Mineral-filled fault 60-61
Mineral-rich deposits 298
Minerals 268-269
Carnivorous plants 160

Epiphytes 162
Fossils 278
Mineral features 270-271
Mineral resources 280-281
Photosynthesis 138-139
Wetland plants 158
Xylem vessel 134
Mineral spicules 166
Mineral spring 273
Mineral wool 603
Minidisc 586
Minidisc player 586, 587
Minim 502
Minor calyx 256
Minor coverts 188, 191
Mint 109
Mintaka 18
Miocene epoch
Fossil record 279
Geological timescale 57
Mira 19, 20
Mirach 19, 20
Miranda 48
Mirfak 19, 20
Mirzam 18, 21
Missile launcher 397
Mississippian period 56
Mississippi Delta 290-291
Mississippi-Missouri River 264
Mississippi River 291
Mist 306
Mistle thrush 190
Mistletoe 162
Mitochondrial crista 217
Mitochondrial sheath 259
Mitochondrion 217, 239
Mitral valve 251
Mixosaurus 57
Mizar 19
Mizzen backstay 378
Mizzen bitt 381
Mizzen course 379
Mizzen mast
Dhow 376
Iron paddlesteamer 392
Junk 376
Sailing warship 377
Square-rigged ship 375
Wooden sailing ship 378
Mizzen sail 375, 385
Mizzen shroud 378
Mizzen stay 378
Mizzen top 378
Mizzen topcastle 377
Mizzen topgallant sail 379
Mizzen topmast 377, 378
Mizzen topsail 379
Mizzen yard 376-377, 378
Moat 466-467
Mobile phone 588-589
Mobile sculpture 452
Modelling 452
Modelling tools 454
Modem 567, 576, 577
Modem port 566, 567
Moderator 314
Mode selector 587
Modified cuticle 157
Modified lateral shoots 156
Modified leaflets 129
Modified leaves
Barberry 130-131
Cobra lily 160
Dryland plants 156-157
Everlasting pea 129

Golden barrel cactus 156
Pitcher development 161
Spines 156
Strawberry 128
Modified shoots 156
Modified stipules 128-129
Modillion
Baroque church 479
Neoclassical building 478
Renaissance building 475
Moenave formation 276
Moenkopi formation 276
Moeritherium 104
Mohorovic discontinuity 39
Mohs scale 270-271
Molar tooth
Arsinoitherium 104
Australopithecus 107
Bear 106, 194
Chimpanzee 202
Elephant 201
Horse 105
Human 246
Hyaenodon 107
Moeritherium 105
Opossum 106
Phiomia 105
Toxodon 106
Molecular orbitals 308
Molecules 306, 308-309
Molluscs 176-177
Belemnite 71
Nautiloid 69
Molten bronze 454
Molten core 39
Molten rock
Igneous and metamorphic rocks 274
Matter 306
Ocean floor 298
Plate movements 58
Rock cycle 266
Volcanoes 272
Molybdate 269
Molybdenum 310
Mongooses 194
Monkey cup 161
Monkeys 202-203
Monoceros 18, 21
Monoclinal fold 60
Monocline 61
Monoclinic system 270
Monocoque chassis 363
Monocoque shell 348
Monocotyledonous petals 140, 143
Monocotyledonous sepals 126, 140, 143
Monocotyledons 126-127, 140-141, 143
Monodon monoceros 205
Monograptus convolutus 65
Monolithic shaft 463
Monoplanes 400-401, 402, 406
Monotremes 206-207
Montes Apenninus 40
Montes Cordillera 41
Montes Jura 40
Montes Rook 41
Monteverdi 35
Montgolfier brothers 398
Monument 470
Moon 40-41
Objects in Universe 11
Solar eclipse 32
Tides 296-297
Moonquake region 41
Moons
Jupiter 44
Mars 42
Neptune 50
Saturn 46

Solar System 30
Uranus 48
Mooring 386-387
Moorish arch 484
Moraine 286-287, 292-293
Moray eel 180
Mortar 432
Mortice 373
Mortise 486, 492
Morus nigra 130
Mosaic 450-451
Islamic building 488-489
Tools 450
Mosque 484, 488
Mosses 112, 114, 118-119
Epiphytic 162
Life-cycle 119
Structure 119
Moth 168
Motherboard 567, 579
Mother's milk 104
Motion 320-321
Motocross motorcycle racing 368
Motor 355, 572, 609
Motor air intake 593
Motor assembly 574
Motorcycle chassis 362, 364-365
Motorcycle engines 366-367
Motorcycle racing 368
Motorcycles 362-363
Motorcycle sidecar 362, 369
Motor-driven bogie axle 326
Motor electronic control module (ECM) 355
Motor end plate 228, 239
Motorhead 592, 593
Motorized buses 332
Motor neuron 228, 239
Motor operating signal 330
Motor whaler 397
Motte 466
Mouchette 472
Mould 278
Moulded bracket 484
Moulded corbel 493
Moulding 485
Ancient Egyptian temple 458-459
Asian building 490
Baroque church 480-481
Dome 486-487
Gothic church 471-472
Medieval building 466, 469
Neoclassical building 479-480, 482
Renaissance building 475-477
Ship's shield 395
Moulding tool 454
Moulds 114
Moulting 171
Mounds 286
Mountain bikes 358, 360
Mountain building 56, 58, 62-63
Mountain hollows 286
Mountain lake 288
Mountain ranges
Earth's physical features 264
Faults and folds 60
Geological time 56
Igneous and metamorphic rocks 274
Mountain building 62
Ocean floor 298
Plate movements 59
Mountain ridge 295
Mountain ring 54
Mountains 62-63, 267

Mountain spring 288
Mounting bracket 590
Mounting bush 365
Mounting splines 366
Mouse 521, 566, 611
Mouse and collar 379
Mouth
Barnacle 173
Bony fish 180-181
Cobra lily 160
Cow 198
Crayfish 173
Dogfish 179
Dolphin 204
Elephant 200
Frog 182
Gorilla 203
Horse 199
Human 211, 212, 244-245, 248
Jellyfish 167
Kangaroo 204
Lamprey 178
Lizard 184
Pitcher plant 161
Rabbit 196
Rat 196
Sea anemone 166-167
Seal 204
Sea urchin 175
Snail 177
Spider 170
Starfish 174-175
Mouth diffuser 430, 440
Mouthpiece
Brass instruments 506
Clarinet 508
Tenor saxophone 509
Trumpet 506
Wind synthesizer 521
Movement
Gas particles 307
Objects 320
MP3 586
MRI scan
Head 214
Brain 236
Mt. Everest 264
Mu Andromedae 19
Muav limestone 277
Muccini brush 454
Mucosa 248
Mucosal gland 254
Mucous gland 177
Mucronate leaf apex 137
Mucus-secreting duodenal cells 217
Mud 267, 273
Mud crab 175
Mud-flat 295
Mudguard
1906 Renault 336-337
BMW R/60 with Steib chair 362
Cannondale ST 1000 touring bicycle 361
Ford Model T 338-339
Harley-Davidson FLHS Electra Glide 363
Honda VF750 364
Husqvarna Motocross TC610 368
Kirby BSA 369
Lockheed Electra 406
Motorcycle 364
Suzuki RGV500 369
Volkswagen Beetle 341
Weslake Speedway motorcycle 369
Mudguard stay 337, 362, 363
Mud pools 272-273
Mud river 298
Mulberry 130
Muliphen 21
Mullion
Gothic church 470, 472-473
Modern building 497-499

Renaissance building 476
Small-scale rock formation 60-61
Twentieth-century building 494
Multicellular animals 56
Multicellular organisms 78
Multicellular soft-bodied animals 56
Multifoil 472
Multi-gabled roof 492
Multiplait nylon 388
Multiplate clutch 364, 366
Multiple fruits 148-149
Multiplier reel 562
Multi-ply tyre 416
Multipolar neuron 239
Mu Orionis 18
Mu Pegasi 19
Musa 'lacatan' 146
Muscari sp. 155
Musci 118
Muscle 226-229
  Abductor digiti minimus 231, 233
  Adductor longus 225
  Adductor magnus 227
  Adductor pollicis 231
  Abductor pollicis brevis 231
  Anal sphincter 249
  Arrector pili 235
  Cricothyroid 244-245
  Dilator 241
  Dorsal interosseous 233
  Energy system 315
  Extensor digitorum brevis 233
  Extensor hallucis brevis 233
  Flexor digitorum longus 233
  Flexor hallucis longus 233
  Flexor pollicis brevis 231
  Flexor retinaculum 231
  Genioglossus 245
  Geniohyoid 245
  Gluteus medius 225
  Gluteus minimus 225
  Hyoglossus 244
  Iliacus 225
  Inferior oblique 241
  Inferior rectus 241
  Intercostal 255
  Internal urethral sphincter 257
  Lateral rectus 240-241
  Levator palpebrae superioris 241
  Lumbrical 231
  Medial rectus 240-241
  Myohyoid 245
  Opponens digiti minimi 231
  Opponens pollicis 231
  Orbicularis oris 245
  Papillary 251
  Pectineus 225
  Peroneus brevis 233
  Peroneus longus 233
  Psoas major 225, 257
  Pyloric sphincter 249
  Soleus 233
  Sphincter 241
  Styloglossus 244
  Superior longitudinal 245
  Superior oblique 241
  Superior rectus 241
  Tensor tympani 243
  Thyrohyoid 244
  Tibialis anterior 233
  Tibialis posterior 233
  Urethral sphincter 257
  Vastus lateralis 225

Vastus medialis 225
Muscovite 269
Muscular septum 176
Mushroom anchor 386
Mushroom coral 167
Mushrooms 114, 115
Music 514, 586
Musical Instrument Digital Interface (MIDI) system 520-521
Musical manuscript 502-503
Musical notation 502-503
Musical score 502-503, 505
Music gallery 477
Musicians 504
Music software 520
Muslim calendar 618
Mussels 176
Mussosaurus 68
Mutes 506-507
Muttaburrasaurus 97
Muzzle 199, 397
Mycelium 114-115
Mycorrhizal association 133
Myelin sheath 239
Mylar 384
Mylar cone speaker 579
Myocardium 250-251
Myofibril 228
Myohyoid muscle 245
Myometrium 260

N

Nail
  Corythosaurus 98
  Edmontonia 95
  Elephant 90
  Human 231
  Iguanodon 96-97
  Stegosaurus 92
  Triceratops 102
Nair Al Zaurak 19, 20
Naismath, James 552
Namib Desert 265
Naos 461, 463, 485
Nape 188, 210
Napier Sabre 24-cylinder engine 408
Naris
  Anchisaurus 89
  Ankylosaurus 94
  Arsinoitherium 104
  Australopithecus 108
  Baryonyx 83
  Brachiosaurus 91
  Camarasaurus 91
  Corythosaurus 98
  Edmontonia 95
  Eryops 80
  Euoplocephalus 94
  Homo erectus 108
  Homo habilis 108
  Homo sapiens 108
  Hyaenodon 107
  Iguanodon 96
  Lambeosaurus 99
  Moeritherium 105
  Opossum 106
  Panoplosaurus 94
  Parasaurolophus 99
  Plateosaurus 88
  Protoceratops 102
  Smilodon 107
  Stegoceras 100-101
  Stegosaurus 92
  Styracosaurus 102
  Triceratops 102-103
  Tyrannosaurus 84
Narrow gauge track 331
Narwhal 205
Nasal bone
  Ankylosaurus 94
  Bear 194
  Frog 183

Human 220-221
Lion 194
Panoplosaurus 94
Protoceratops 102
Toxodon 106
Nasal cavity
  Chimpanzee 202
  Domestic cat 195
  Elephant 200
  Human 245, 248
  Rabbit 196
Nasal horn 104
Nasalis 229
Nasal passage 200
Nasal plug 205
Nasal septum 213, 221, 241
Nasal tusk 105
Nash 21
Nasion 221
Nasolacrimal duct 241
Nasopharynx 245
Natal cleft 210
Natal cocoon 24, 26
Native elements 268
Natural bridge 290
Natural elements 310
Natural fly 562
Natural forces 314
Natural glass 306
Natural gut strings 544
Natural lakes 292
Natural satellites 40
Natural sponge 438
Nautiloid mollusc 69
  Fossil 65
Navajo Mountain 277
Navajo sandstone 276
Nave
  Ancient Egyptian temple 458-459
  Baroque church 479
  Cathedral dome 484
  Gothic church 470-473
  Medieval church 468-469
  Ship's wheel 390
Navel 211, 260
Nave plate 390
Navicular bone 232
Navigating bridge 394
Navigational aerial 423-424
Navigation area 577
Navigation buttons 577
Navigator's cockpit 420
Navigator's seat 408
Navka 37
Nazea plate 59
Neanderthals 108
Neap tides 296-297
Nebulae 16-17
  Cone 612
  Galaxies 12-13
  Great, Orion 613
  Life of massive star 26
  Milky Way 14-15
  NGC 1566 (Seyfert galaxy) 13
  Omega 613
  Small stars 24
  Structure of nebula 24
Neck
  Acoustic guitar 512-513
  Anchisaurus 89
  Calligraphy character 445
  Corythosaurus 98
  Electric guitar 513
  Golf club 547
  Harp 511
  Horse 199
  Human 211, 224-225, 247, 258-259
  Iguanodon 97
  Pachycephalosaurus 100
  Rat 196
  Sauropodomorpha 88

Sculling oar 560
Stegoceras 101
Stegosaurus 92
Stringed instruments 510
Tenor saxophone 509
Theropod 84
Violin 510
Necking 381
Neck roll motor 609
Neck tilt motor 609
Nectar 142, 160-161
Nectaries 141, 144-145, 160-161
Needles
  Bishop pine 124
  Pine 124-125
  Scots pine 122
  Yew 123
Nefertiti Corona 37
Negative electric charge 316
Negative ions 308, 310
Neo-Baroque style 492-493
Neo-Byzantine style 492-493
Neoclassical style 478-483, 496
Neodymium 310
Neo-Gothic style 492-493
Neo-Greek style 492-493
Neon 35, 311
Nepenthes mirabilis 161
Nephron 256
Neptune 31, 50-51
Neptunides polychromus 12
Neptunium 311
Nerve
  Ampullar 242
  Bronchial 254
  Cervical 238
  Cochlear 243
  Common peroneal 238
  Cranial 238
  Cutaneous 238
  Deep peroneal 238
  Digital 231
  Femoral 238
  Hypoglossal 244
  Lingual 244
  Lumbar 238
  Median 238
  Optic 240
  Posterior tibial 238
  Pudendal 238
  Pulp 247
  Radial 238
  Sacral 238
  Sciatic 238
  Spinal 223, 238
  Superficial peroneal 238
  Superior laryngeal 244
  Thoracic 238
  Ulnar 231, 238
  Vestibular 243
  Vestibulocochlear 243
Nerve cell 217, 237, 239
Nerve cord 173
Nerve fibre 235
Nerve ring 173
Nervous system 176, 238-239
Nervous tissue 166
Netball 554-555
Neural spine
  Arsinoitherium 104
  Bony fish 180
  Brachiosaurus 90
  Eryops 81
  Euoplocephalus 95, 87
  Iguanodon 96
  Parasaurolophus 98
  Plateosaurus 89
  Stegoceras 100-101
  Stegosaurus 93

Toxodon 106
Triceratops 102
Tuojiangosaurus 93
Tyrannosaurus 85
Neurofilament 239
Neuron 239
Neurotransmitter 239
Neutralization 312
Neutrino 22
Neutron 22, 28
Neutrons 308, 309, 310
Neutron stars 28-29, 26-27
New Guinea 265
New Moon 41
New State Paper Office 482
Newton (N) 320
Newton, Isaac 320
Newton meter 320-321
Newton's Motion laws 320-321
Newts 182
New World monkeys 202-203
New Zealand 265, 272
NGC 1566 (Seyfert galaxy) 13
NGC 2997 (spiral galaxy) 12
NGC 4406 (elliptical galaxy) 11
NGC 4486 (elliptical galaxy) 12
NGC 5236 (spiral galaxy) 11
NGC 5754 (colliding galaxies) 9
NGC 6656 (globular cluster) 21
NGC 6822 (irregular galaxy) 11
Nib types 444
Niche
  Ancient Roman building 462
  Asian temple 491
  Baroque church 480
  Cathedral dome 487
  Gothic church 471-472
  Islamic building 488
  Medieval building 467
  Neoclassical building 482
  Renaissance building 476
Nickel 37, 49, 281, 311
Nickel-iron 270
Nigella damascena 151
Nightshot control 583
Nile crocodile 186
Nimbostratus cloud 302
Nimbus cloud 302
Nineteenth-century buildings 479, 482, 492-493, 494
Nintendo Cube 579
Ninth-century building 490
Niobe Planitia 36, 37
Niobium 310
Nipple
  Human 211
  Marsupials 206
Nissl body 239
Nitrate ions 312
Nitrates 160
Nitrogen
  Atmospheric composition 301
  Helix Nebula 17
  Mars' atmosphere 43
  Periodic table 311
  Pluto's atmosphere 51
  Venus' atmosphere 37
Nitrogen dioxide gas 312
Nobelium 311
Noble gases 310-311
Nock 548

Noctis Labryrinthus 42, 43
Nocturnal mammals 104
Node
  Bamboo 131
  Brassavola nodosa 162
  Canadian pond weed 158-159
  Couch grass 113
  Dicotyledons 127
  Horsetail 120
  Ice-plant 129
  Live-for-ever 129
  Modern buildings 497
  Rhizome 155
  Rock stonecrop 128
  Rose stem 130
  Stems 154
  Stolon 154
  Strawberry 128
Node of Ranvier 228, 239
Nodule fields 299
Nodules 128
Noggin 602
Nokia 3310 588, 589
Nokia 5510 588
Nonconformity 276
Non-drive end 317
Nonesuch House 467
Non-explosive eruptions 272
Non-flowering plants 68
Non-metals 310
Non-return valve 367
Non-skid tyre 337
North America
  Appalachian Mountains 62
  Cretaceous period 72-73
  Earth's physical features 264
  Jurassic period 70
  Late Carboniferous period 66
  Middle Ordivician period 64
  Quaternary period 76-77
  Tertiary period 74-75
  Triassic period 68
North American Cordillera 71
North American period 56
North American plate 59
North Atlantic current 296
North Atlantic Gyre 296
North Atlantic Ocean 39, 71, 73
North East Africa 64
North-easterly wind 303
North-east monsoon 297
North-east trade winds 300
North Equatorial Belt 45
North Equatorial current 296-297
Northern Hemisphere 296-297
North Galactic Pole 15
North magnetic polar region 28
North Pacific current 296
North Pacific Gyre 296
North polar aurora 45
North polar ice-cap 43
North Pole
  Atmospheric circulation and winds 300
  Coriolis force 297
  Jupiter 44
  Mars 42
  Mercury 34
  The Moon 40
  Neptune 50
  Pluto 51
  Pulsar 28
  Saturn 46
  Uranus 48
  Venus 36

North rim 277
North Temperate Zone 45
North Tropical Zone 45
North-westerly wind 303
Nose
  B-17 bomber 408
  Concorde 416-417
  Iron 594
  Horse 198
  Human 211-212, 244-245
  Lion 194
  Lockheed Electra airliner 406
  Rabbit 196
  Rat 196
Noseband 554, 555
Nose clip 558
Nose cone 418, 560
Nose cover 557
Nose cowling 412
Nose-end bogie 327
Nose-gear
  ARV light aircraft 424-425
  Concorde 417
  Tornado 420
Nose horn 102, 103
Nose-ring
  Avro biplane 403
  Blackburn monoplane 400
Nose-wheel
  ARV light aircraft 425
  Curtiss biplane 398
  Pegasus XL SE microlight 426
  Tornado 420
Nostril
  Bird 188
  Chick 193
  Crocodilians 186
  Dolphin 205
  Domestic cat 195
  Elephant 200
  Frog 182
  Gorilla 203
  Horse 198
  Human 213
  Kangaroo 207
  Lion 194
  Lizard 184
  Monkey 202
  Rat 196
  Rattlesnake 185
  Seal 204
Nostril pocket 80
Note pad button 568
Notes 502, 506
Nothosaurian reptile 69
Notre Dame de Paris 470, 473
Nozzle
  Concorde 416-417
  Jet engines 418-419
  Tornado 421
  Vacuum cleaner 593
NPT 301 turbojet 418
N-type silicon 605
Nu Andromedae 19
Nucellus 147
Nuchal plate 187
Nuchal ring 95
Nuchal shield 187
Nuclear energy 314
Nuclear fusion
  Massive stars 26
  Small stars 24
  Stars 22
  Sun 32
Nuclear "hunter-killer" submarine 396-397
Nuclear power station 314
Nuclear reactions 315
Nucleolus 216, 259
Nucleoplasm 216
Nucleus
  Asteroids, comets, and meteoroids 52-53

Atoms and molecules 308, 309
Chlamydomonas sp. 116
Cnidocytes 167
Egg cell 606, 607
Endosperm 147
Fungal cell 115
Galaxies 12-13
Generalized human cell 216
Muscle cell 228
Neuron 239
Overhead view of our galaxy 14
Palisade mesophyll cell 139
Pollen 122
Pollen tube 147
Roots 132
Scots pine pollen 122
Side view of our galaxy 14
Synergid 147
Thalassiosira sp. 116
Nuctenea umbratica 171
Number systems 620
Nunki 19, 20-21
Nu Orionis 18
Nut
  Deadeye 383
  Dry fruit 150
  Durmast oak 131
  Toaster 598
Nutcrackers 321
Nutlets 150
Nutrients
  Carnivorous plants 160
  Epiphyte supply 162
  Phloem sieve tube 134
  Plant transport 139
Nylon and silicon cloth 384
Nymphaea sp. 159
Nyssa sylvatica 137

O

O₂ sensor 355
Oak 74
Oar
  Greek and Roman ships 372-373
  Junk 376
  Longboat 380
  Viking ships 374-375
Oarweed 116-117
Oasis 283
Oberon 48
Objective aperture 610
Objective lens 610, 611
Object mass 320
Oblique-slip fault 61
Oboe 504-505, 508
Obovate leaves 137
Observer's cockpit 405
Observer's windscreen 404
Obsidian 275, 306
Obturator canal 224
Obturator membrane 224
Occipital bone 202, 220
Occipital condyle 107, 194, 220
Occipital lobe 236-237
Occipital region 106
Occluded fronts 302-303
Ocean currents 296-297
Ocean floor 298-299, 266-267
Oceanic crust
  Earth's crust 58-59
  Mineralization zones 281
  Mountain building 62-63
  Ocean floor 298
Oceanic seahorse 180

Ocean ridges 58-59
Oceans 39, 296-297, 301
Ocean trenches
  Ocean floor features 299
  Offshore currents 296
  Plate movements 58
Oceanus Procellarum 40
Ocellus 176
Octafoil 471
Octahedron 623
Octastyle portico 462
Octave 557
Octopus 176-177
Ocular end 377
Oculus
  Ancient Roman building 462-463
  Gothic church 472-473
  Medieval building 466, 469
  Neoclassical building 483
  Roman corbita 372
Odd-toed ungulates 198-199
Odontoblast 247
Oeil-de-boeuf window
  Baroque church 479, 481
  Cathedral dome 487
Oerlikon gun position 397
Oesophagus
  Barnacle 173
  Bird 189
  Brachiosaurus 91
  Butterfly 169
  Chimpanzee 202
  Cow 198
  Dogfish 179
  Dolphin 205
  Domestic cat 195
  Elephant 200
  Human 212, 215, 245, 248
  Lizard 185
  Rabbit 196
  Snail 177
  Spider 170
  Starfish 174
  Tortoise 187
Off-road motorcycle racing 368
Offshore deposits 294
Ogee 395
Ogee arch 488
Ogee-arched motif 490
Ogee curve 472
Ogee-curved dome 486
Ogee-curved roof 489
Ogee moulding 475-477, 481
Ogee tracery 493
Ohms 316
Oil
  Clutches 366
  Diesel trains 326
  Energy storage 315
  Mineral resources 280-281
Oil bottle dripfeed 336
Oil cooler 347, 364, 605
Oil-cooler duct 415
Oil cooler matrix 347
Oil damper 364
Oil deposit formation 57
Oil deposits 281
Oil dipstick 344
Oil duct 151
Oil feed 411
Oil feed pipe 345, 366, 367
Oil filter
  1-litre VTEC engine 354
  Ford diesel engine 347
  Jaguar V12 engine 345
  Turbofan engine 418
  Turboprop engine 419

Oil-fired power station 315
Oil formation 280-281
Oil paints 436-457
Oil pipe banjo 345
Oil-pressure regulating valve 419
Oil pump
  Humber engine 343
  Mid West single-rotor engine 411
  Velocette OHV engine 367
  Weslake speedway bike 369
Oil rig 315
Oil side lamp 336-337
Oil sump
  Honda VF750 364
  Humber engine 343
  Modern engines 344-345
  Velocette OHV engine 367
Oil tank
  Bell-47 helicopter components 422
  Harley-Davidson FLHS Electra Glide 363
  Lockheed Electra airliner 406
  Turbofan engine 418
  Turboprop engine 419
Oil traps 281
Oldsmobile 336-337
Old World monkeys 202-203
Olecranon 85
Olenellus 64
Oleo lock-jack 414
Olfactory bulb 181
Oligocene epoch
  Fossil record 279
  Geological timescale 57
Olivine
  Igneous rock 267
  Meteorites 52
  Silicates 269
Olivine gabbro 275
Olympus BX51W1 optical microscope 610
Olympus Mons 42-43
Omasum 198
Omega Centauri 21
Omicron Andromedae 19
Omicron1 Canis Majoris 21
Omicron2 Canis Majoris 21
Omicron Orionis 18
Omicron Sagittarii 21
Omnivores 84
Omohyoid muscle 229
One-toed ungulates 198
Onion dome 467, 486-488
Onion-skin weathering 282
On-screen display 577
Onyx 268
Oocyte 258
Oogonium 117
Oosphere 116-117
  Fern 121
  Moss 119
Ooze 298
Open cluster 16
Open gun mounting 394
Opera House, Paris 493
Opera House, Sydney 496, 499
Opercula 180
Opercular bone 181
Operculum
  Bony fish 180-181
  Cnidocyte 167
  Giant stick insect eggs 192
  Indian stick insect eggs 192

Leaf insect eggs 192
Moss 119
Ophidia 184
Ophiothix fragilis 175
Ophiuchus 19, 20
Ophthalmos 372
Opisthodomos 461
Opisthosoma 170-171
Opossums 206, 207
Opponens digiti minimi muscle 231
Opponens pollicis muscle 231
Optical map of our galaxy 14-15
Optical microscope 610
Optic chiasma 256
Optic disc 240-241
Optic nerve 240
Option connector 571
Opus incertum 463, 465
Opus quadratum 465
Opus sectile mosaic 488-489
Oral arm 167
Oral cavity 248
Oral disc 166-167
Oral surface 175
Orange citrine 271
Orange halite 269, 277
Orange light 318
Orangutans 202
Ora serrata 241
Orb 486
  Baroque church 480
  Cathedral dome 487
  Gothic church 471
  Neoclassical building 479
  Nineteenth-century building 493
  Renaissance building 477
Orbicularis oculi muscle 226, 229
Orbicularis oris muscle 228-229, 245
Orbicular lamina 158
Orbicular leaves 137
Orbit
  Acanthostega 80
  Ankylosaurus 94
  Archaeopteryx 85
  Arsinoitherium 104
  Australopithecus 108
  Baryonyx 83
  Bear 194
  Bird 189
  Bony fish 181
  Camarasaurus 91
  Chimpanzee 202
  Diplodocus 90
  Elephant 201
  Eryops 80
  Euoplocephalus 94
  Heterodontosaurus 83
  Homo erectus 108
  Homo habilis 108
  Homo sapiens 108
  Horse 199
  Hyaenodon 107
  Iguanodon 96
  Inner planetary 30
  Lambeosaurus 99
  Lion 194
  Lizard 184
  Opossum 106
  Outer planetary 31
  Pachycephalosaurus 100
  Panoplosaurus 94
  Parasaurolophus 99
  Plateosaurus 88
  Platypus 206
  Prenocephale 100
  Protoceratops 102
  Rattlesnake 185
  Rhesus monkey 202
  Smilodon 107

Stars of northern skies 18
Stars of southern skies 20
Stegoceras 100-101
Styracosaurus 102
Toxodon 106
Triceratops 103
Tyrannosaurus 84
Orbital artery 179
Orbital cavity 220
Orbital motion 31, 52
Orbital plane
  Earth 38
  Jupiter 44
  Mars 42
  Mercury 34
  Neptune 50
  Pluto 51
  Saturn 46
  The Moon 40
  Uranus 48
  Venus 36
Orbitals 308-309, 310
Orbital speed (velocity)
  Mercury 34
  Solar System 30-31
Orb spider 171
Orchestra layout 504-505
Orchestral instruments 504-505
  Musical notation 502-503
Orchestras 504-505
Orchestra shell 495
Orchids 126, 133, 162
Orcinus orca 205
Ordovician period 64-65
  Fossil record 279
  Geological time 56
  Primitive life 78
Organ 514, 502-503
Organic compound 313
Organic material deposition 281
Organic remains 276-277, 280
Organ of Corti 243
Oriel window 467
"O Ring" drive chain 366
Orion 18, 21, 24
Orion Arm 14
Orion Nebula 15, 17, 18
Orion's belt 15-16
Ornament
  Asian building 491
  Baroque church 479, 481
  Cathedral dome 487
  Islamic building 488
  Neoclassical building 483
Ornamental strip 586, 587
Ornithischians 68-69, 82-83
  Marginocephalians 100
  Ornithopods 96
  Stegosaurs 92-93
  Thyreophorans 92
Ornithomimosaurs 86-87
Ornithopoda 83
Ornithopods 96-97, 98-99
Ornithorhynchus anatinus 207
Orobanche sp. 163
Orogenesis 62-63
Oropharynx 245
Orpiment 270-271
Orthoclase 269, 271
Orthorhombic system 270
Os 258-259
Oscillating cylinder 390
Oscillating electric field 318
Oscillating magnetic field 318
Oscillating steam engine 390-391
Osculum 166

Osmium 311
Ossicles 79, 174
Ossicles of middle ear 242
Osteichthyes 180
Osteocyte 225
Osteolaemus tetraspis 82
Osteon 225
Ostiole 117
Ostium
  Crayfish 173
  Dogfish 179
  Sea anemone 167
  Spider 170
  Sponge 166
Ostrich 188, 195
Otters 194
Otto cycle 342
Otto, Nikolaus 342
Ouranosaurus 97
Outboard ammunition-
  feed blister 409
Outboard elevon 421
Outbox icon 576
Outer bud scale 134
Outer casing fitment 597
Outer core 38-39, 41
Outer ear
  Brachiosaurus 91
  Stegoceras 101
  Stegosaurus 101
Outer electrons 510-511
Outer envelope 25-26
Outer fertilized floret 142
Outer jib downhaul 385
Outer jib halyard 385
Outer jib sheet 385
Outer jib stay 382
Outer lamella 225
Outer mantle
  Jupiter 44-45
  Saturn 46-47
Outer tepals
  Glory lily 143
  Lily 140
  Monocotyledons 126
Outfield 536
Outlet manifold 411
Output tray 574
Outrigger 373, 377
Outwash fan 286
Outwash plain 287
Outwash terrace 286
Ovary
  Barnacle 173
  Bony fish 181
  Brachiosaurus 90
  Butterfly 169
  Chimpanzee 202
  Crayfish 173
  Dogfish 179
  Epigeal germination
  153
  Fertilization 146-147
  Flower 140-143
  Gallimimus 86
  Human 258-259
  Hypogeal germination
  152
  Insect pollination 144
  Lizard 185
  Rose 131
  Spider 170
  Succulent fruit 148-149
  Tortoise 188
Ovate leaf
  Ice-plant 129
  Live-for-ever 129
  Strawberry 128
Ovda Regio 36, 37
Oven compartment 597
Overarm pass 555
Overhand knot 388
Overhand serve 554
Overhead camshaft
  engine 368
Overhead pass 532
Overhead valve engine
  (OHV) 367, 369
Over-reach boot 555
Overs 538

Oversailing fascia 477,
  482, 486
Overthrust fold 61
Overturned fold 61
Oviduct
  Barnacle 173
  Brachiosaurus 90
  Butterfly 169
  Crayfish 173
  Dogfish 179
  Lizard 185
  Spider 170
  Tortoise 187
Ovolo 486
Ovolo moulding
  Cathedral dome 487
  Gothic church 472
  Neoclassical building
  480
Ovotestis 177
Ovules 140-143
  Bishop pine 124
  Dehiscent fruit 151
  Fertilization 146
  Pine 122
  Scots pine 122
  Smooth cypress 123
  Yew 123
Ovuliferous scales
  Bishop pine 124
  Pine 122
  Scots pine 122
  Smooth cypress 123
  Yew 123
Ovum
  Ancient Roman
  building 462
  Fertilization 146-147
  Scots pine 122
  Oxalis sp. 157
Oxbow lake 293
  River features 290
  River's stages 289
"Ox-eye" window
  Baroque church 479,
  481
  Cathedral dome 487
Oxides 268
Oxygen
  Atmospheric
  Atom 596
  Composition 301
  Early micro-organisms
  78
  Earth's composition 39
  Earth's crust 58
  Earth's formation 38, 64
  Helix Nebula 17
  Mars' atmosphere 43
  Mercury's atmosphere
  35
  Periodic table 311
  Photosynthesis 138
  Seed germination 152
  Structure of red
  supergiant 26
  Respiration 255
Oxygenated blood 255
Oxygen bottle 408
Oxygen group 311
Oyashio current 297
Oyster fungus 114
Oysters 176
Ozone 64
Ozone layer 300

P

Pachycephalosaurus 69,
  85, 100
Pachypteris sp. 68
Pacific coastline 295
Pacific Ocean 264-265,
  272
Pacific plate 59
Pacing races 554
Pacing sulky 554-555

Pacinian corpuscle 254-
  255
Pack-ice 296
Packing tissue
  Dicotyledon leaf 126
  Fern rachis 121
  Golden barrel cactus
  156
  Haworthia truncata 157
  Horsetail stem 120
  Leaf succulents 157
  Lithops bromfieldii 157
  Monocotyledon leaf 126
  Roots 132-133
  Stem 134-135
  Stem succulents 156
  String of hearts 157
  Water lily leaf 159
Padded coaming
  Avro biplane 403
  BE 2B bomber 404
Paddle
  Eurypterid fossil 79
  Kayak 560
Paddlesteamer
  19th century 390-391
  Iron 392-393
Paddle wheels 390-391,
  392
Padmakosa 489
Page key 590
Page locator 577
Pagoda 490
Pahoehoe 272
Painted Desert 277
Painting knives 436, 442
Painting tools 442
Pair-cast cylinder 343
Paired cylinder 342
Palace of Westminster
  492-493
Palaeocene epoch
  Fossil record 279
  Geological timescale 57
Palaeontology 278
Palaeozoic era
  Fossil record 279
  Geological time 56
Palais de Fontainebleau
  476
Palais de Versailles 482
Palatine Chapel,
  Aix-le-Chapelle 484
Palatine tonsil 212, 244-
  245
Palatoglossal arch 244
Palazzo Stanga 482
Palazzo Strozzi 474-475
Pale calcite 26
Pale feldspar 26
Palette 143, 436
Palette knife 436
Paling 466, 477
Palisade mesophyll 126,
  159
Palladium 311
Palm
  Danforth anchor 386
  Hand 211
  Roman anchor 372
  Sailmaker's 384
  Tertiary plant 74
Palm M500 PDA 568-569
Palmar arch 253
Palmaris longus tendon
  231
Palmar vein 253
Palmate leaves 130, 136
Palmate venation 129
Palmette 460-461, 479-480
Palmoxylon 74
Pam-D upper stage
  booster 615
Pamirs 265
Pampas 264
Panavia Tornado GR1A
  420-421
Pancreas
  Bird 189

Bony fish 181
Chimpanzee 202
Dogfish 179
Domestic cat 195
Frog 182
Human 215, 249
Rabbit 196
Tortoise 187
Pandas 194
Panduriform leaves 136
Pane 494
Panel 485
  Asian building 491
  Baroque church 479-
  481
  Cathedral dome 487
  Gothic building 473
  Islamic building 488
  Medieval building 466,
  469
  Modern building 496-
  498
  Neoclassical building
  478-479
  Nineteenth-century
  building 493
  Renaissance building
  475
  Twentieth-century
  building 494
Panel board connector
  570
Pangaea 66, 68-69, 70
Panniers 360, 361, 362
Panoplosaurus 94
Panicle 131
Pantheon 462-463
Pantile 464, 482
Pantograph 328, 330
Pan troglodytes 202
Paper
  Acrylic paint 442
  Calligraphy 444, 445
  Pastels 440
  Printing processes 446,
  447
  Watercolours 438
Paper ejection roller 573
Paper feed components
  575
Paper feed rollers 573
Paper hopper 574
Paper output stacker 574
Paper stumps 440
Paper support 575
Paper tray 573
Papilla
  Flower 140
  Hair 235
  Renal 256
  Tongue 244
Papillary muscle 251
Pappus 142
Papyriform column 459
Parabellum machine-gun
  405
Parabolic dune 283
Paraboloid roof 496, 499
Parachute seed dispersal
  150
Paradise palm 126
Paragaster 166
Parallel dunes 283
Parallelogram 622
Parallel printer port 567
Parallel river drainage
  288
Parallel shaft 382
Parallel venation 126
Parana River 264
Parapet
  Ancient Roman
  building 465
  Asian building 491
  Baroque church 481
  Dome 486
  Gothic church 470-472
  Islamic tomb 489
  Medieval building 467

Neoclassical building
  478, 483
Nineteenth-century
  building 493
Twentieth-century
  building 494
Parapet rail 483
Paraphysis 117, 119
Parasaurolophus 98-99
Parasitic anemone 166
Parasitic cone 272-273
Parasitic plants 162-163
Parasitic volcano 275
Paraxeiresia 373
Parcelling 388
Parchment
  Gilding 432
  Imitation 445
Pareiasaur 81
Parenchyma
  Dicotyledon leaf 126
  Dryland plants 156-157
  Fern rachis 121
  Golden barrel cactus
  156
  Horsetail stem 120
  Monocotyledon leaf 126
  Pine stem 125
  Roots 132
  Stems 134-135
  Water lily leaf 159
Parent plant 154
Parietal bone
  Bony fish 181
  Chimpanzee 202
  Human 220-221
Parietal fenestra 102
Parietal lobe 236-237
Parieto-occipital sulcus
  236-237
Parietosquamosal frill
  102-103
Paripteris 66
Paris Metro 328
Paroccipital process
  Iguanodon 96
  Plateosaurus 88
Parrel
  Dhow 376
  Longboat 380
  Sailing warship 377
  Viking karv 375
Parrel beads 384
Parrel tackle 376
Parthenon 461
Partial solar eclipse 32
Partial veil 115
Particle attraction 307
Particle properties 318
Passiflora caerulea 130
Passing brace 473
Passion flower 130
Passive stack vents 602
Pastels 440-441
Pastern 198-199, 554
Pasteur 41
Patagonia 264
Patella
  Domestic cat 195
  Elephant 201
  Hare 197
  Horse 199
  Human 219
  Platypus 206
  Rhesus monkey 202
  Scorpion 170
  Spider 171
Patellar surface 225
Patera
  Neoclassical building
  480
  Renaissance building
  476
Pause button 608
Paved floor 492
Pavilion 489, 495
Paving slab 499
Pavlova 37
Pavlovia 278

Pavo 20
Pavonis Mons 43
Paw 195
Pawl 380
Pawl slot 387
Paxton, J. 492-493
Pazzi Chapel 475
PCB *see* printed circuit
  board (PCB)
PC card adapter 574
PCI expansion slots 566,
  567
PCs 566
PDAs 568
Pea
  Dry fruit 150
  Danforth anchor 386
Peach 131, 148
Peacock 20
Peak halyard 380
Peat 280
Peccaries 198
Pecopteris 66
Pectineus muscle 225-
  226
Pectoral fin
  Bony fish 180-181
  Lamprey 178
Pectoral fin ray 181
Pectoralis major muscle
  226
Pedal board 514
Pedal cluster 340
Pedal-damper bar
  mechanism 516
Pedal disc 167
Pedal-driven bicycle 358
Pedal gland 177
Pedalia 372
Pedals
  Bass drum 518
  Bicycle 320, 358-359
  Eddy Merckx racing
  bicycle 360
  Harp 511
  Hi-hat cymbal 518
  Piano 514
  Rossin Italian time-trial
  bicycle 361
Pedal stop 514
Pedestal
  Ancient Roman
  building 462
  Baroque church 480-
  481
  Dome 484, 486-487
  French temple 485
  Harp 511
  Neoclassical building
  479
  Renaissance building
  476
Pedice 168
Pedicel
  Brassavola nodosa 162
  Clematis 131
  Dicotyledon flower 127
  Dry fruit 150-151
  Fertilization 146-147
  Florists'
  chrysanthemum 129
  Flowers 140-141, 143
  Fruit development 146-
  147
  Oxalis sp. 157
  Pitcher plant 113
  Rose 131
  Rowan 131
  Russian vine 131
  Succulent fruit 148-149
  Sycamore 131
  Vegetative reproduction
  154
  Water lily 159
Pedicle of vertebra 223
Pedicle valve 278
Pediment
  Ancient Greek building
  460

Ancient Roman building 462-463
Baroque church 480-481
Neo-Baroque building 493
Neoclassical building 478
Renaissance building 476
Pedipalp 170-171
Peduncle 140, 142-143
Aechmea miniata 162
Brassavola nodosa 162
Everlasting pea 129
Florists' chrysanthemum 129
Indehiscent fruit 150
Peach 131
Peruvian lily 129
Rowan 131
Russian vine 131
Succulent fruit 148-149
Toadflax 129
Vegetative reproduction 154
Wind-pollinated plant 144
Peephole 412, 414
Pegasus 19, 20
Pegasus Quasar microlight 426-427
Pegasus XL SE microlight 427
Peg-box 510-511
Pegmatite 26
Peg of vertebrae 222
Pelagic clay 299
Pelecypoda 176
Peloneustes philarcus 71
Pelota 540
Pelvetia canaliculata 116
Pelvic fin
Bony fish 180-181
Dogfish 179
Pelvis
Bird 189
Bony fish 181
Dinosaur 81
Domestic cat 195
Elephant 201
Hare 197
Horse 199
Human 256, 258, 259
Kangaroo 206
Lizard 184
Platypus 206
Rhesus monkey 202
Seal 204
Turtle 187
Penalty area 524
Penalty box 524
Penalty kick 530
Penalty spot 529, 540
Pencils 430
Pencil sharpener 430
Pencil slate sea urchin 175
Pendentive 479, 484, 488
Penguins 188
Penis
Barnacle 173
Dolphin 205
Human 211, 259
Snail 177
Pennant number 397
Pennsylvanian period 56
Penny washer 383
Pens 430
Penstock 514
Pentagon 622
Pentaradiate symmetry 174
Pentroof 490
Penumbra 32
Pepo 149
Pepper-pot lantern 481
Perch 180
Percolation 280

Percussion instruments 516-517
Drums 518-519
Electronic 520
Orchestral arrangement 504-505
Perennials 128, 130-131
Pereopod 172-173
Perforated shroud 592
Perianth 140
Pericardial cavity 250
Pericarp 148
Dry fruit 150-151
Embryo development 147
Fruit development 146-147
Succulent fruit 148-149
Sycamore 151
Pericranium 257
Pericycle 127, 152
Periderm 125
Peridium 115
Perihelion 30-31
Perimeters 622
Perineum 258
Periodic table 310-311
Periodontal ligament 247
Periodontium 247
Periosteum 225
Peripheral camera 609
Peripheral nervous system 238
Peripteral temple 460-461
Periscope 396, 397
Perissodactyla 104, 198-199
Peristome tooth 119
Peristyle 461
Peritoneum 249, 257
Permeable limestone
Caves 284-285
Lake formation 292
Permeable rock 292
Permeable sandstone 292
Permian period 66-67
Fossil record 279
Geological time 57
Peroneal artery 253
Peroneus brevis muscle 227, 253
Peroneus brevis tendon 253
Peroneus longus muscle 253
Peroxisome 217
Perseus 19, 20
Perseus Arm 14-15
Persian ivy 137
Personal computer 566-567
Personal digital assistants (PDAs) 568
Personal music 586-587
Personal System/2 (PS/2) port 567
Perspective drawing 431
Peru current 296
Peruvian lily 129
Petal moulding 480
Petals 140-143
Clematis 151
Colour 140, 144-145
Dicotyledons 126-127
Everlasting pea 129
Fertilization 146
Insect pollination 145
Monocotyledons 126
Peruvian lily 129
Rose 131
Water lily 159
Petavius 40
Petiole 128, 136-137
Chusan palm 130
Clematis 151
Cobra lily 160
Dicotyledons 127
Everlasting pea 129
Florists'

chrysanthemum 129
Horse chestnut 130
Kedrostis africana 113
Maidenhair tree 123
Monocotyledons 126-127
Mulberry 130
Oxalis sp. 157
Passion flower 130
Peach 131
Rock stonecrop 128
Seedling 153
Strawberry 128
String of hearts 157
Tree fern 112
Tree mallow 131
Vegetative reproduction 154
Venus fly trap 160
Water hyacinth 158
Water lily 159
Wind-pollinated plant 144
Petiolule 137
Petrol 315
Peugeot, Armand 354
Phacops 64
Phaeophyta 16
Phaet 21
Phalaenopsis sp. 126
Phalanges
Cow 198
Crocodile 186
Diplodocus 90
Domestic cat 195
Elephant 90
Eryops 80-81
Frog 183
Hare 197
Horse 198-199
Kangaroo 206
Lizard 184
Parasaurolophus 99
Plateosaurus 88
Platypus 206
Rhesus monkey 202
Seal 204
Stegoceras 100-101
Triceratops 102-103
Turtle 187
Tyrannosaurus 84
Phalanx
African elephant 201
Archaeopteryx 85
Arsinoitherium 104
Baryonyx 85, 87
Horse 105
Human 219, 230
Plateosaurus 88
Stegoceras 100
Struthiomimus 87
Toxodon 107
Phallus impudicus 114
Phanerozoic eon 279
Pharyngeal tubercle 220
Pharynx
Bony fish 180-181
Dogfish 179
Human 212, 244
Sea anemone 167
Sea urchin 175
Phascolarctos cinereus 207
Phaseolus sp. 153
Phases of the Moon 41
Phekda 19
Phellem
Pine root 125
Stem 134-135
Woody dicotyledon 127
Phi Andromedae 19
Phidias 35
Philippine plate 59
Phillips, Horatio 402
Philoxenus 35
Philtral ridge 213
Philtrum 213
Phiomia 104
Phloem 138
Bishop pine 124-125

Clubmoss stem 120
Dicotyledons 126-127
Dodder host 163
Epiphytic orchid 162
Fern rachis 121
Horsetail stem 120
Marram grass 113
Monocotyledons 126-127
Parasite host 163
Photosynthesis 138
Pine root/stem 125
Radicle 152
Root 132-133
Sieve tube 154
Stem 134-135
Water hyacinth root 158
Water lily leaf 159
Phloem fibres 134-135
Phloem sieve tube 154
Phobos 42
Phoebe Regio 36
Phoenicopterus ruber 190
Phoenix 19, 20
Phorusrhacus 74
Phosphates 269
Phosphate/sugar band 216
Phosphor imaging screen 611
Phosphor lining cell 584
Phosphorus 311
Photomicrographs of skin and hair 235
Photons 318
Photo print button 570
Photo select button 575
Photosphere 32-33
Photosynthesis 112, 116, 154, 136, 138-139
Carnivorous plants 160-161
Organelle 116, 139
Photosynthetic cells 139
Bishop pine 124
Coconut palm stem 135
Water lily leaf 159
Photosynthetic region 157
Photosynthetic tissue
Cacti 156
Dicotyledon leaf 126
Horsetail stem 120
Marram grass 113
Monocotyledon leaf 126
Rush stem 135
Photovoltaic cell 605
Photovoltaic panel 603
Phyla 116
Phyllode 160
Phyllum 116
Physalis peruviana 149
Physeter catodon 205
Physical weathering 282
Physics symbols 621
Pi2 Orionis 18
Pi3 Orionis 18
Pi4 Orionis 18
Pi5 Orionis 18
Pi6 Orionis 18
Pia mater 237, 240
Piano 503, 514
Piano nobile 474, 494
Piano, R. 496
Piazza 474
Pi Canis Majoris 21
Piccolo 504, 508
Pictor 21
Pier 484
Ancient Egyptian temple 459
Ancient Roman building 465
Baroque church 480
Gothic church 470
Medieval building 467-469
Renaissance building 476-477
Twentieth-century building 494-495

Pier buttress 469-471, 486
Pietra dura inlay 489
Piezoelectric inkjet printhead 575
Pigments 433, 434, 436
Pigs 104, 198
Pilaster
74-gun ship 381
Ancient Greek building 461
Ancient Roman building 463-465
Asian temple 490-491
Baroque church 479-481
Cathedral dome 484, 487
Gothic church 471
Neoclassical building 478, 483
Renaissance building 476
Pileus 114-115
Pillar
Asian buildings 490-491
Domed roof 486
Gothic church 472
Ironclad 393
Renaissance building 477
Twin bollards 387
Pillow lava 298
Pilotis 494
Pilot light 594
Pilot's cockpit
LVG CVI fighter 405
Tornado 420
Pilot's cradle 398-399
Pilot's seat
Avro biplane 402
Curtiss biplane 398
Pegasus Quasar microlight 427
Pin
Capstan 387
Dome timbering 486
Pinacocyte 166
Pineal body 212, 236
Pine hull 373
Pines 122, 124-125
Pinguicula caudata 161
Pinion
Benz Motorwagen 355
Ford Model T 358
Hand drill 601
Pinna
Elephant 201
Everlasting pea 129
Fern 121
Gorilla 203
Human 242-243
Kangaroo 207
Leaves 136-137
Rabbit 196
Rat 196
Sago palm 123
Tree fern 112-113
Pinnacle
Baroque church 479, 481
Gothic church 470, 472-473
Medieval church 469
Nineteenth-century building 493
Renaissance building 476
Pinnate leaves 136-137
Mahonia 130-131
Rowan 130
Sago palm 123
Pinned sheepshank 389
Pinnipedia 204
Pinnule 131, 137
Pinocytotic vesicle 217
Pintle strap 378
Pinus muricata 72, 124-125
Pinus sp. 122, 124-125

Pinus sylvestris 122
Pi Pegasi 19
Pipette 312
Pips 148-149
Pi Sagittarii 21
Pisanosaurus 68
Pisces 19, 20
Pisces Austrinus 19, 20
Pisiform bone 230
Piste 556, 557
Pistol shooting 548
Piston
Disc brake 365
Early engines 342-343
"Ellerman Lines" steam locomotive 325
Ford diesel engine 347
Mid West two-stroke engine 410
Modern engines 344-345
Relief-printing press 449
Steam locomotive 324
Two-stroke engine 366
Velocette OHV engine 367
Volkswagen Beetle 340
Piston engines 410-411, 424
Piston rod 324, 334, 390
Piston valves
Brass instruments 506
Cornet 507
"Ellerman Lines" steam locomotive 325
Flugelhorn 507
Stringed instruments 510
Trumpet 506
Tuba 507
Pisum sativum 150
Pitatus 40
Pitch
Brass instruments 506
Drums 518
Musical notation 502
Percussion instruments 516
Propeller action 390
Screw thread angle 320
Woodwind instruments 508
Pitched roof
Ancient Roman building 462, 464
Gothic church 471-472
Medieval building 466-468
Nineteenth-century building 492
Renaissance building 476-477
Twentieth-century building 495
Pitcher 536
Pitcher plants 113, 160-161
Pitches
Australian rules football 528
Baseball 536
Cricket 538
Gaelic football 529
Lacrosse 540
Pitching wedge
Baseball 537
Golf 547
Pitfall traps 160
Pith
Apical meristem 134
Bishop pine stem 125
Dicotyledon stem 127
Epiphytic orchid 162
Horsetail stem 120
Monocotyledon root 127
Pine stem 125
Stems 134-135
Pith cavity 135

Pitot head
  ARV light aircraft 425
  BAe-146 jetliner
    components 412
  Bell-47 helicopter 422
  Concorde 416-417
  Hawker Tempest
    fighter 409
  LVG CVI fighter 405
  Schweizer helicopter
    423
  Tornado 420
Pitot mast 407
Pituitary gland 212, 236
Pivot
  Astrolabe 377
  BAe-146 jetliner
    components 414
  Drum brake 365
  Sundial 377
  Viking ships 374-375
Pixel 570, 571
Place kick 550
Placenta
  Dry fruit 150-151
  Fern pinnule 121
  Human 260
  Succulent fruit 148-
    149
Placental mammals 74,
  104
Placer deposits 280
Plagioclase feldspar 275
Plains viscacha 197
Planck 18
Plane shapes 622
Planetary nebula
  Nebulae and star
    clusters 17
  Small stars 24-25
Planetary orbits 30-31
Planetary rotation 30
Planets
  Jupiter 44-45
  Mars 42-43
  Mercury 34-35
  Neptune 50-51
  Pluto 50-51
  Saturn 46-47
  Solar System 30-31
  Uranus 48-49
  Venus 36-37
Planking
  Ironclad 393
  Longboat 380
  Roman corbita 373
  Sailing warship 377
  Tea clipper 392
Plantar calcaneonavicular
  ligament 232
Plant bodies 116
Plant capital 459
Plant-eating dinosaurs 68,
  70
Plant matter 280
Plant remains
  Fossils 278-279
  Mineral resources 280
  Sedimentary rocks 276
Plants 56, 66
  Electromagnetic
    radiation 314
  Flowering 57, 70, 72
  Fossil record 279
  Non-flowering 68
Plant variety 112-113
Plasma 306
Plasma display 584
Plasma screen 584
Plaster 452, 464-465
Plasterboard 602
Plastic bumper 354
Plastic fletch 548
Plastic front wings 354
Plastic insulator 316, 317
Plastic rackets 544
Plastid 116
Platanus x acerifolia 134
Platband 481

Plate
  Etching press 477
  Motorcycle clutch 366
  "O Ring" drive chain
    366
Plateau
  Neptune's rings 50
  Structure of Neptune 51
Plateaus 276-277
Plate boundaries 62, 273
Plate clip 587
Platelets 253
Plate movements 58-59
  Faults and folds 60
  Mountain building 62-
    63
Platen 449
Plateosaurus 69, 88-89
Plate tectonics 58-59
Platform
  Cathedral dome 487
  Early tram 332
  Medieval building 467-
    468
  Modern building 498
Platform diving 558
Platform stage 477
Platinum 311
Plat lesene 480
Plato 40
Platypus 206-207
Platysma 229
Playa 283
Play button 585
Play control 587
Player's bench
  American football 526
  Basketball 532
  Handball 535
  Ice hockey 550
  Volleyball 534
Playhead 577
Play/pause button 587
Play/pause control 577,
  587
Playstation 2 579
Plaza 498
Pleiades 14, 16, 19, 20
Pleistocene epoch
  Fossil record 279
  Geological timescale 57
Pleistocene period 76
Plenum chamber 344-345
Plenum ring 418
Pleopod 172
Plesiochelys latiscutata 73
Plesiosaurs 70-71
Pleurotus pulmonarius
  114
Plica circulare 249
Plicate lamina 127
Pliers 521
Plinth
  Baroque church 480
  French temple 485
  Islamic tomb 489
  Modern building 499
  Neoclassical building
    479, 483
  Renaissance building
    476
  Twentieth-century
    building 494-495
Pliocene epoch
  Fossil record 279
  Geological timescale 57
Plough anchor 386
Plug-ins 521
Plug lead conduit 337
Plugs 272-273
  Igneous rock structures
    274
Plumage 188
Plume 45
Plumose anemone 166
Plumule 147, 152-153
Plunge 60
Plunge pool 289, 291
Pluto 31, 50-51

Plutonium 310-311
Plywood roof deck 603
Plywood skin 404
Pneumatic tyres 358, 555
Podetium 114
Podium 463, 499
Point
  Angling hook 562
  Cricket 538
  Double bass bow 511
  Sailmaker's fid 384
  Sculpting tool 452-453
  Violin bow 510
Point bar
  Mississippi Delta 291
  River's stages 289
Pointed arch 466, 467,
  469, 472
Pointed hog hair brush
  454
Pointed riffler 454
Pointed sable brush 444
Pointing 383
Poison duct 170
Poison gland
  Octopus 176
  Spider 170
Polacanthus 95
Polar band 36
Polar body 606, 607
Polar bottom water 296
Polar easterlies 300
Polar fronts 302
Polar hood 36
Polaris 14, 18-19
Polar jet stream 300
Polar nuclei 146
Poles 297, 300
Pole star 14, 18
Pole vault 542
Polian vesicle 175
Political map of the world
  616-617
Poll 199
Pollen 140, 142, 144-145
  Dicotyledon flower 126
  Fertilization 146-147
Pollen-forming structures
  122
Pollen grains 144-145
  Fertilization 146-147
  Pine 122
  Scots pine 122
Pollen sac wall 144
Pollen tubes
  Fertilization 146-147
  Scots pine 122
Pollination 144-145, 122
Pollux 18, 21
Polonium 311
Polycarbonate plastic bin
  592
Polyester 388
Polygala chamaebuxus
  144
Polygnotus 35
*Polygonum
  baldschuanicum* 131
Polyhedral dome 486-487
Polypropylene rope 388
Polythene 306
Polytrichum commune 119
Polyurethane insulation
  603
Pome 131, 149
Pommel 554
Pond weeds 158
Pons 212, 236-237
Pontabdominal spine 169
Poop break 373
Poop deck
  74-gun ship 381
  Iron paddlesteamer 392
  Roman corbita 373
Poop rail
  74-gun ship 381
  Wooden sailing ship
    378
Poor metals 310-311
Popchu-Sa Temple 490

Popliteal artery 253
Popliteal fossa 210
Porch 470-471
Porcupines 196-197
Pore
  Bishop pine needle 124
  Blackberry 147
  Dryland plants 156-157
  Elder stem 130
  Epigeal germination
    153
  False fruit 148
  Gas exchange 138, 158
  Golden barrel cactus
    156
  Haworthia truncata 157
  Leaf 138-139
  Liverwort 118
  Monocotyledon leaf 126
  Nuclear membrane 217
  Perennial bark 130-131
  Pollen grain 144-145
  Seed 153
  Sponge 166
  Water absorption 150,
    153
  Wetland plants 158
  Woody plants 130-131
  Woody stems 134
Porifera 166
Porocyte 166
Porous limestone 284
Porous stipe 114
Porphyritic andesite 275
Porpoises 204
Porrima 21
Porsche, Ferdinand 340
Port
  Trojan two-stroke
    engine 342
  Wooden sailing ship
    379
Portable CD player 587
Portable minidisc player
  586
Portal 476, 480
Portal vein 252
Porta Nigra 462, 465
Port bower anchor 377,
  395
Port foremast 376
Porthole
  Battleship 394
  Dome 487
  Frigate 397
Portico
  Ancient Greek building
    460-461
  Ancient Roman
    building 462-463
  Neoclassical building
    482-483
  Renaissance building
    475
Portugal 331
Portuguese bowline 388
Position guide 447
Positive electric charge
  316
Positive ions 308, 310
Positive metal comb 316
Positive terminal 316, 317
Positron 22
Post 481, 486
Postabdominal spine 169
Postacetabular process 82
Postcentral gyrus 237
Post-crural musculature
  90
Posterior antebrachial
  musculature 86, 91
Posterior aorta 170
Posterior arch 222
Posterior border of vomer
  220
Posterior brachial muscle
  86, 91
Posterior branch of spinal
  nerve 223

Posterior cerebral artery
  252
Posterior chamber 241
Posterior chamber of
  cloaca 185
Posterior column 223
Posterior crural muscle 87
Posterior cuneonavicular
  ligament 232
Posterior dorsal fin
  Bony fish 181
  Dogfish 179
  Lamprey 178
Posterior horn 223
Posterior nasal aperture
  220
Posterior nasal spine 220
Posterior part of tongue
  245
Posterior petal 141
Posterior root 223, 238
Posterior semicircular
  canal 243
Posterior sepal 141
Posterior tarsometatarsal
  ligament 232
Posterior tentacle 177
Posterior tibial artery 253
Posterior tibial nerve 258
Posterior tubercle 222
Posterior vena cava 182
Posterior wing of shell 176
Posterolateral horn 94
Post-glacial stream 286
Post-glacial valley 286
Post-modernism 296, 496
Post-motor micropore
  filter 592
Potassium 35, 58, 286, 310
Potassium chromate
  solution 312
Potassium dichromate
  ions 312
Potassium iodide 312-313
Potassium nitrate 313
Potassium permanganate
  306
Potato 128
Potential energy 314, 315
Potholes 284
Pouch 206
Power bar 552
Power drill 600-601
Power button
  Hand-held computer
    568
  Home cinema 585
  Inkjet printer 574
  Microsoft Xbox 579
  Mobile phone 587-588
  Personal computer
    566-567
Power clip 582
Power indicator light 579
Power lead 582
Power on light 581
Power on/off slider 581
Power output 360, 366
Power plug 591
Power socket 566, 569
Power stations 314, 315
Power steering belt 351
Power steering pump 344,
  351
Power stroke 343
Power supply 567, 569
Power supply cord 570,
  573
Power supply wiring 582
Power switch 582
Power switch control 582
Power-to-weight ratio
  528
Power transistor heat sink
  (dissipator) 585
Power transistors 585
Practice projectile 596
Pradakshina 491
Praesepe 18

Prairie style 495
Praseodynium 310
Pratt & Whitney Canada
  turbofan engine 418-
  419
Pratt & Whitney Canada
  turboprop engine 419
Pratt & Whitney radial
  engine 406-407
Praxiteles 35
Precambrian period 56,
  64-65, 279
Precambrian seas 78
Precentral gyrus 237
Precious metals 311
Precipitate 312
Precipitation 288, 302-303
Predatory dinosaurs 84
Predatory theropods 88
Predenary bone
  Arsinoitherium 104
  Iguanodon 96
  Lambeosaurus 99
  Moeritherium 105
  Protoceratops 102
  Triceratops 103
Prefix 577
Prehensile tail 202
Prehistoric foods 109
Pre-load adjustor 365
Premaxilla
  Baryonyx 83
  Bony fish 181
  Chimpanzee 202
  Elephant 201
  Frog 183
  Iguanodon 96
  Lambeosaurus 99
Premolars
  Australopithecus 107
  Bear 106, 194
  Chimpanzee 202
  Horse 105
  Human 246
  Lion 194
Prenocephale 100-101
Preopercular bone 181
Preparatory drawing 430-
  431
Prepubic process
  Iguanodon 96
  Parasaurolophus 98
  Stegosaurus 93
Prepubis
  Ornithischian 82
  Stegoceras 100-101
Prepuce 259
Preserved remains 278
Press
  Etching 447
  Lithographic printing
    446
  Relief-printing 449
Pressed steel wheel 340
Pressure
  Formation of black hole
    29
  Igneous and
    metamorphic rocks 274
  Mineral resources 280
  Stellar black hole 29
  Volcanic features 273
Pressure line 418
Pressure plate 366
Pressurized cabin 406
Pressurized keel box 417
Pressurized strut 425
Pressurized water reactor
  314
Presta valve 361
Presynaptic axon 239
Presynaptic membrane
  239
Preview monitor slot 575
Preview panel 576
Preview monitor socket
  574
Previous frame 577

Previous/next track
buttons 585
Previous track button 587
Previous track control 587
Prickers 383
Prickle
Blackberry 147
Bramble stem 130
Rose stem 130
Slender thistle 129
Primary bronchus 215
Primary colours 439
Primary-drive gear 366
Primary flight feathers
188, 191
Primary follicle 258
Primary leaf 121
Primary mirror 612
Primary mirror housing
613
Primary mycelium 115
Primary remiges 188, 191
Primary root 132-133
Germination 152-153
Seedling 152-153
Primary teeth 246
Primary thallus 114
Primary xylem 125, 135
Primates 108, 202-203,
279
Primer 348, 456
Primitive crocodilians 68
Primitive life-forms 64
Primitive mammals 206
Principal arteries and
veins 253
Principal rafter
Ancient Roman mill 464
Dome 486
Gothic building 473
Printed circuit board
(PCB)
Digital video camera
582-583
Hand-held computer
569
Printer 574-575
Printer cover 574, 575
Printhead power wiring
harness 573
Printhead wiring harness
572
Print icon 576
Printing assembly 573
Printing block 449
Printing cartridge 573
Printing papers 447
Print making 446-447,
448-449
Prism 318, 623
Prismatic habit 271
Privy 380
Probactosaurus 97
Probes, space 614-615
Proboscidea 104
Proboscis 169, 201
Procambial strand 134
Procerus muscle 229
Processing cooling fan
567
Processing light 575
Processional path 470
Processor card 567
Processor heat sink 567
Procompsognathus 87
Procoptodon 76
Procyon 8, 21
Procyon lotor 195
Production line
Mass-production 338
Modern bodywork 348
Modern trim 352
Programme display 577
Programme file name 577
Program mode selector
580, 581
Program mode selector
control 581
Program selector 581

Projectile 396
Projector lens 611
Prokaryotes 78
Prolegs 169
Promethium 311
Prominence 32-33
Pronaos 461
Pro-otic bone 183
Propagative structures
154-155
Propellant 396
Propeller 390-391
ARV light aircraft 425
Battleship 395
Biplanes and triplanes
402-403
Early monoplanes 400-
401
Ford diesel engine 347
Frigate 396
Hawker Tempest
components 408
Lockheed Electra
airliner 406-407
Pegasus Quasar
microlight 427
Pioneers of flight 398-
399
Submarine 396
World War I aircraft
404-405
Propeller-bolt collar 411
Propeller brake pad 419
Propeller drive flange
ARV light aircraft 425
Modern piston aero-
engines 410-411
Propeller drive gearbox
427
Propeller drive shaft 408
Propeller-hub spinner 407
Propeller shaft
Brazilian battleship 395
Wright Flyer 599
Propeller-shaft boss 395
Propeller-shaft bracing
strut 398-399
Propeller shaft rear
bearing 410
Propeller speed probe 419
Propeller spinner 408, 409
Propodus 172, 173
Propylaeum 460
Prosauropoda 83
Prosauropods 88
Proscapular process 187
Prosimians 203
Prosimii 202
Prosoma 170, 171
Prostate gland 257, 259
Prostyle colonnade 483
Protactinium 310
Protective clothing
American football 528
Cricket 539
Ice hockey 550-551
Protective eyewear 544
Protective gaiter 422
Protective outer layer 125
Protective root covering
153
Protective scale 134
Protective scale leaf 155
Protein body 112
Protein fibres 166
Protein matrix 166
Protein synthesis site 139
Proterozoic eon 279
Proteus 50
Prothallus 121
Prothorax 168
Protista 112, 116
Protoceratops 102-103
Protogalaxies 10-11
Proton 308, 316
Atomic mass 310
Atomic number 310
Fluorine-19 309
Nuclear fusion 22

Protonema 119
Protostar 24, 26
Protoxylem
Dicotyledon root 127
Monocotyledon root 127
Root 132-133
Proventriculus
Bird 189
Crayfish 173
Prow 372, 375
Prowhead 374
Proxima Centauri 18
Proximal convoluted
tubule 256-257
Proximal interphalangeal
joint 231
Proximal phalanx 230, 232
Prunus persica 131
Psathyrella candolleana
115
Pseudocarps 148-149
Pseudo-Corinthian capital
476
Psi Sagittarii 21
Psittacosaurus 100, 103
Psoas major muscle 225,
257
Pterapsis 65
Pterichthyodes 65
Pteridium aquilinum 121
Pterois volitans 180
Pteron 460-461, 463
Pterosaurs 70-71
Pterygoid bone 183
Pterygoid hamulus 220
Pterygoid plate 220
Ptolemaeus 40
Ptolemaic-Roman period
459
"P" turret 395
P-type silicon 605
Pubic bone 261
Pubic ramus 257
Pubic symphysis 258
Pubis
Archaeopteryx 85
Bird 189
Diplodocus 90
Eryops 81
Gallimimus 86
Human 218, 224, 259
Iguanodon 96
Ornithischian 82
Plateosaurus 88
Saurischian 82
Stegosaurus 93
Struthiomimus 87
Tyrannosaurus 84
Pubofemoral ligament 224
Pudenda 211
Pudendal nerve 238
Puffballs 114
Pugin, A.W.N. 493
Pulley bolt 360
Pulley rim rear brake 362
Pulley wheel
Simple pulleys 320
Van de Graaff generator
316
Pulmonary artery
Frog 182
Human 251, 253, 254-
255
Pulmonary semilunar
valve 251
Pulmonary trunk 251, 255
Pulmonary vein 251, 253,
254
Pulp artery and vein 247
Pulp chamber 247
Pulp horn 247
Pulp nerve 247
Pulpit 379
Protoceratops 102-103
Pumice 275
Pump
Nuclear power station
314
Testing candle wax 313

Pump drive belt 410
Pump drive shaft 411
Pump piston 391
Pupa 168
Pupil
Caiman 186
Human 213, 226, 241
Pupil's cockpit 403
Puppis 18, 21
Purchase 382-383
Purchase wire 394
Pure substances 306
Purfling 510, 511
Purkinje's cells 237
Purlin 473
Pusher propeller
Pegasus Quasar
microlight 426
Pioneers of flight 398-
399
Push moraine 286
Push-rod 365, 367
Putter 547
Putting green 546
Putto 476
Putty eraser 430, 440
"P" wave 63
Pygal shield 187
Pygostyle 189
Pylon 314
Pylon fairing 427
Pylon strut 427
Pyloric caecum
Bony fish 181
Starfish 174
Pyloric duct 174
Pyloric region of stomach
179
Pyloric sphincter muscle
249
Pyloric stomach 174
Pyramid 458, 623
Pyrenees 77, 265
Pyrenoid 112, 116
Pyrites 268
Pyroclasts 272
Pyromorphite 269
Pyroxene 52, 267
Pyxis 18

Q

Quadrant arch 468
Quadrate bone 181
Quadratojugal bone
Frog 183
Heterodontosaurus 83
Quadrilateral 489
Quadripartite vault 469
Quadrupedal dinosaurs
88, 92, 96, 100
Quadruplanes 402
Quark 309
Quarter back 526
Quarterdeck 380-381
Quarterdeck house 376
Quarter gallery 381
Quarter glass 348
Quarter light 340-341
Quarter panel moulding
352
Quarter trim panel 352
Quartz
Colour 271
Metamorphic rock 267
Oxides/hydroxides 268
Quasar (quasi-stellar
object)
Galaxies 12
Objects in Universe 11
Origin and expansion of
Universe 10-11
Quasar nucleus 13
Quaternary period 57, 76-
77
Fossil record 279

Pump drive belt 410
Quatrefoil 471-473
Quaver 502
Quayside 387
Queen-post 473
Quercus palustris 74
Quercus petraea 131
Quick-release base 590
Quick-release mechanism
425
Quick-release strap 360
Quill
Drill 601
Feather 191
Writing tool 444
Quinacridone red 442
Quit key 587
Quiver 548
Quoin
Baroque church 481
Medieval building 466
Nineteenth-century
building 492
Renaissance building
476

R

Rabbit line 380
Rabbits 196-197
Raccoons 194-195
Raceme 129
Rachilla 137
Rachis 136-137
Bipinnate leaf 137
Couch grass 113
Everlasting pea 129
Feather 191
Fern 121
Hogweed 129
Pinnate leaf 136-137
Rowan leaf 130
Tree fern 112
Tripinnate leaf 137
Racing bicycle 360
Racing car 356-357
Racing chain 361
Racing colours 554-555
Racing saddle 554
Racing sidecar 368-369
Racing "silks" 554-555
Racing tyre 365
Formula One racing car
356-357
Suzuki RGV500 368-369
Racketball 544-545
Racket sports 544-545
Radar
Modern jetliners 412
Modern military
aircraft 420-421
World War II aircraft
408
RADAR 397
RADAR for gunnery and
missile control 397
Radial artery 231, 253
Radial canal
Jellyfish 167
Sea urchin 175
Starfish 174
Radial cartilage 180
Radial diffuser 418
Radial engine
Curtiss biplane 398-399
Lockheed Electra
airliner 406-407
Radial groove 365
Radial nerve
Human 238
Sea urchin 175
Radial river drainage 288
Radial spoke 47
Radial studio easel 437
Radial wall 465
Radiation 38
Electromagnetic 314
Energy emission from
Sun 22

Galaxies 12-13
Nebulae and star
clusters 16
Ozone formation 64
Universe 10
Radiative zone
Structure of main
sequence star 24
Structure of Sun 33
Radiator
1906 Renault 336-337
ARV light aircraft 424
Ford Model T 338-339
Hawker Tempest
fighter 409
Honda VF750 364
Kirby BSA 369
Renault Clio 351
Wright Flyer 399
Radiator-access cowling
408
Radiator air vent 368
Radiator apron 339
Radiator coolant 326
Radiator fan 326
Radiator filler neck 339
Radiator header tank 408
Radiator hose 339
Radiator outlet 409
Radiator pipe 364
Radiator shell 339
Radicle
Dry fruit 150
Embryo development
147
Epigeal germination
153
Hypogeal germination
152
Radio
Bell-47 helicopter 422
Renault Clio 353
Streamed Internet 577
Radio aerial 426
Radio antenna 395
Radio galaxies 12-13
Radio image 13
Radio-isotope thermo-
electric generator 615
Radio lobe 13
Radio mast 494
Radio operator's seat 408
Radio plugs 425
Radio speaker 353
Radio tuner aerial socket
(FM) 585
Radio tuner FM/AM
selector 585
Radio-ulna 183
Radio wave beam 28
Radio-wave emission 15
Radio waves
Electromagnetic
spectrum 318
Pulsar 28
Radio image of
Centaurus A 13
Radium 310
Radius
Archaeopteryx 85
Arsinoitherium 104
Baryonyx 85
Bird 189, 191
Circle 622
Crocodile 186
Diplodocus 90
Domestic cat 195
Elephant 90, 201
Eryops 80
Euoplocephalus 94
Hare 197
Horse 199
Human 218, 230-231
Iguanodon 96
Kangaroo 206
Lizard 184
Parasaurolophus 99
Pareiasaur 81
Plateosaurus 88

Platypus 206
Rhesus monkey 202
Seal 204
Stegoceras 100-101
Struthiomimus 87
Toxodon 106
Triceratops 102
Turtle 187
Radius arm 357
Radius rod
  Avro Tutor biplane 403
  Ford Model T 338-339
Radome
  BAe-146 jetliner 415
  Concorde 416-417
  Tornado 420
Radon 311
Radula 176-177
RAF Central Flying School
  badge 402
RAF roundels 403, 409
Raft 496
Rafter
  Ancient Roman mill 464
  Dome 486
  Gothic building 473
  Modern building 499
  Nineteenth-century
  building 492
Raft spider 171
Rail
  Electric tram 332
  Kayak 560
  Neoclassical building
  483
  Relief-printing press
  449
  Train 330-331
  Wooden sailing ship
  379
Rail chair 324
Railing
  Asian building 490-491
  Cathedral dome 487
  Medieval building 467
  Nineteenth-century
  building 493
  Renaissance theatre 477
Railroad crest 326
Railway system 324
Rain 302
Rain erosion 294
Rain gutter 412, 415
Rainwater
  Caves 284
  Weathering and erosion
  282
Raised beach 295
Raja clavata 179
Raked windscreen 333
Raking cornice
  Ancient Greek building
  460-461
  Ancient Roman
  building 462-463
  Baroque church 480-
  481
  Neoclassical building
  478
Raking stempost 376
Ram 372
Ramaria formosa 114
Rammer 396
Ramp 467, 494
Ram scoop
  BE 2B bomber 404
  Tornado 420-421
Rangefinder
  Battleship 394
  Gun turret 396
Ranks 514
Ranunculus sp. 127, 132-
  133
Raphe 153
Rapid-fire pistols 548
Rapids
  River features 290
  River's stages 289

Rare earths 310
Rare gases 311
Ras Algethi 20
Ras Alhague 19, 20
Rasp 452
Raspberry 149
Rat 104, 196
Ratchet
  Brace-and-bit 601
  Fixed-spool reel 562
Ratcheted base 590
Ratchet mechanism 601
Ratchet wheel 334
Rating 378
Ratings' mess 397
Ratline 376, 379
Rat's tail 384
Rat tail 589
Rattlesnake 185
Raw sienna 454
Raw umber 434
Ray
  Branchiostegal 181
  Caudal fin 180
  Dorsal fin 181
  Jawless fish 178
  Liverwort 118
  Mercury 34
  Near side of the Moon
  40
  Parenchyma cells 134
  Pectoral fin 181
Ray crater 34
Ray florets
  Florists'
  chrysanthemum 129
  Sunflower 142, 145
Reactants 312
Reactive metals 310-311
Reactor core 314
Reactor space 397
Read/write access
  window 586
Rear axle 338
Rear axle adjustor 364,
  368
Rear bearing 411
Rear bezel 569
Rear brake 362
Rear brake cable 359, 360
Rear brake calliper 368
Rear brake pedal 368
Rear bulkhead 417
Rear cabinet 582
Rear cantilever brake 358
Rear case 568, 591
Rear chassis plate 597
Rear cylinder exhaust
  pipe 568
Rear derailleur 358, 360
Rear door 339
Rear drop-outs 358
Rear hatch 349
Rear hub quick-release
  spindle 358
Rear indicator 362
Rear lamp
  Oldsmobile trim 337
  Volkswagen Beetle 340
Rear leaf spring 338
Rear light
  Bicycle 360
  Italian State Railways
  Class 402 328
  Paris Metro 328
Rear limit line 557
Rear-mounted propeller
  Pegasus Quasar
  microlight 426
  Pioneers of flight 398-
  399
Rear panel cover 573
Rear oil lamp 336
Rear shelf 352
Rear shock absorber 340
Rear sub-frame 364
Rear tail light 329
Rear-view mirror
  1906 Renault 336

Formula One racing car
  357
Redial/pause button 572
Renault Clio 353
Receiver
  American squash 545
  Badminton 545
  International squash
  545
  Racketball 545
  Tennis 544
Receiving line 545
Receptacles
  Algae 116
  Dicotyledon flower 127
  Dry fruit 150-151
  Fertilization 147
  Flower 140-36
  Rose 131
  Seaweed 116-117
  Succulent fruit 148-149
Recessed arch 488
Recessed hinge 414, 415
Rechargeable battery
  Digital camera 581
  Hand-held computer
  569
  Mobile phone 589
Recharge area 292
Recharge jack socket 581
Recoil cylinder 396
Reconnaissance camera
  420
Recorded information 521
Recorder frame 573
Recording head assembly
  573
Recording light 583
Record trigger 521
Rectal caecum 174
Rectal gland 179
Rectangle 622
Rectangular block 625
Rectangular cross-band
  374
Rectangular pier 465, 467,
  480
Rectangular river
  drainage 288
Rectangular window
  Ancient Roman
  building 465
  Asian building 490
  Baroque church 481
  Medieval building 466
  Renaissance building
  474, 476
Rectum
  Bird 189
  Butterfly 169
  Chimpanzee 202
  Cow 198
  Dogfish 179
  Dolphin 205
  Elephant 200
  Frog 182
  Human 215, 248-249,
  258-259, 261
  Lizard 185
  Rabbit 196
  Starfish 174
  Tortoise 187
Rectus abdominis muscle
  226
Rectus femoris muscle
  226
Recumbent fold 61
Red algae 116
Red blood cells 217, 253
Red-brown crocoite 271
Red card 524
Red cedar boarding 602
Red cell 584
Red deer 199
Red dwarf 23
Red earth 433, 434-435
Red filter signal light 407
Red giant
  Small stars 24-25
  Stars 22-23

Red howler monkey 203
Red light 318
  Main-line signalling
  system 330, 331
Red light photon 318
Red marble 450
Red port navigation light
  406
Red sandstone 277
Red seaweeds 117
Red spot 44-45
Red supergiant
  Massive stars 26-27
  Stars 22-23
Reduction gearbox
  Early piston aero-
  engines 410-411
  Jet engines 419
  Turboprop engine 419
Redwall limestone 277
Red warning light
  Italian State Railways
  Class 402 328
  Paris Metro 328
Redwood trees 70
Reed pen 444
Reef knot 388
Reef point 385
Reel
  Angling equipment 562-
  563
  Fencing piste 557
  Frigate 397
Reel foot 562-563
Reel scoop 562-563
Reel seat 563
Re-entrant angle 485
Re-entrant corner 479
Referee
  American football 526
  Basketball 532
  Gaelic football 529
  Ice hockey 550
  Judo 556
  Lacrosse 541
  Rugby 530
  Soccer 524
  Swimming 558
  Volleyball 534
Referee's crease 550
Referee's equipment 524
Referee's signals
  American football 527
  Basketball 533
Reflection 318
Reflection nebula 16
Reflector
  Ford Model T 339
  Oldsmobile trim 337
Refraction 318-519
Refractory (heat-resistant)
  skin 421
Refrigerator freight car
  327
Régie Autonome des
  Transports Parisien 328
Regional metamorphism
  274
Regional weather 302
Registers 514
Regolith (soil) 41
Regula 461
Regulator
  "Mallard" express
  steam locomotive 325
  "Rocket" steam
  locomotive 324
Regulator valve 325
Regulus 18, 21
Rein 554
Reinforce 395
Reinforced concrete 494,
  497
  Sleepers 330
Reinforced plinth 499
Rein terret 555
Relative atomic mass 310
Relay baton 543

Relay running 542
Release 537, 543
Release adjustment screw
  552
Release button 425
Release catch 590
Release lever 563
Release spring 563
Relief 458
Relief printing 446
Relief printing equipment
  449
Relieving arch
  Ancient Roman
  building 462, 465
  Medieval building 466-
  467
Remiges 188, 191
Remote control 585
Remote control 587
Remote control sensor
  585
Remote sensing palette
  615
Removable archery
  screen 377
Renaissance buildings
  474-477
Renal artery 256-257
Renal column 256
Renal papilla 256
Renal pelvis 256
Renal sinus 256
Renal vein 256-257
Renault (1906) 336-337
Renault Clio 348-353
Renault logo 348
Renewable energy 604-
  605
Renoir 35
Repeater indicator 333
Repeating pattern 307
Replum 151
Reply all icon 576
Reply icon 576
Reproduction
  Algae 116-117
  Cloning 606-607
  Fertilization 146-147
  Flowering plants 140
  Liverwort 118
  Moss 118-119
  Vegetative 154-155
Reproductive canal 94
Reproductive chamber
  116
Reproductive organs
  259
Reproductive structures
  Flower 140-143
  Pollination 144
Reproductive system 258-
  259
Reptiles 80-81, 184-187
  Carboniferous period
  66
  Dinosaurs 82-83
  Fossil record 279
  Jurassic period 70
  Present-day 82
  Rhynchosaurian 71
  Synapsid skull 67
  Triassic period 68
Reptilia 184, 186
Repulsion 316-317
"Request identification"
  aerial 421
Re-radiated heat 300-301
Reredos 470
Rescue strap 561
Reservoir 314
Reset button 560, 569
Resin canal
  Bishop pine needle 124
  Pine root/stem 125
Resistance 316
Resonator 513
Respiration 255
Respiratory system 254-
  255

Rest
  Musical notation 502
  Newton's first motion
  law 321
Resurgence 284-285
Retaining bolt hole 366
Retaining screw 562, 563
Reticulum
  Digestive system of a
  cow 198
  Southern stars 20
Retina 240-241
Retractable head light 608
Retraction jack 417
Retractor muscle 167
Retreating glacier 286
Retrices 188
Retroarticular process 83
Return 486-487
Rev counter 369
Reversed bend hook 562
Reverse control 587
Reversed dive piked 559
Reverse dip-slip fault 61
Reverse dive 558
Reverse-flow combustion
  chamber 418
Reverse lever 342
Reverser handle 325
Reverse shock wave 27
Reversible reactions 312
Reversing shaft lock
  control 325
Reversing wheel 392
Revivalist style 493-494
Rewind control 577
Rhamphodopsis 65
Rhamphorhynchus sp. 71
Rheas 188
Rhenium 310
Rhesus monkey 202
Rhinoceroses 198-199
Rhizine 114
Rhizoids 118-119
  Alga 116
  Fern 121
  Liverwort 118
  Moss 119
Rhizomes 154-155
  Fern 121
  Herbaceous flowering
  plants 128
  Horsetail 120
  Water hyacinth 158
  Water lily 159
Rhizophore 120
Rhoı Sagittarii 21
Rhodium 311
Rhodophyta 116
Rhomboideus major
  muscle 227
Rhomboid leaves 137
Rhombus 622
Rhopalium 167
Rhynchosaurian reptile 71
Rhynchosaurs 68-69, 71
Rhyolite 274-275
Rhyolitic lava 272
Rhythm
  Drums 518
  Percussion instruments
  516
Rhythm pattern selector
  520
Rib
  Acoustic guitar 512
  Archaeopteryx 85
  Avro triplane 403
  Baroque church 479
  BE 2B tail 405
  BE 2B wings 404
  Bird 189
  Blackburn monoplane
  401
  Bony fish 181
  Brachiosaurus 90
  Concorde 417
  Crocodile 186
  Diplodocus 90

Dome 486-487
Domestic cat 195
Double bass 511
Elephant 201
Eryops 80
Euoplocephalus 94
Gallimimus 86
Hare 197
Herbaceous flowering
plant 128
Horse 199
Kangaroo 206
Lizard 184
Medieval church 469
Modern building 499
Pareiasaur 81
Pegasus Quasar
microlight 426-427
Pegasus XL SE
microlight 426
Plateosaurus 88
Platypus 206
Rhesus monkey 202
Seal 204
Snake 185
Stegoceras 101
Struthiomimus 87
Toxodon 107
Triceratops 102
Tyrannosaurus 84
Violin 510
Westlothiana 81
Riband 381
Ribbon cable connector
578
Ribbon connectors 585,
581
Ribbon Lake 287
Ribbon socket connector
581
Ribbon window 499
Rib cage
Carnivores 195
Human 218
Ribosome
Chloroplast 139
Human cell 217
Rib vault 469, 484-485
Gothic building 470
Medieval building 467
Renaissance building
477
Rice paper 445
Ride cymbal 519
Ridge
Epigeal germination 153
False septum 151
Gothic building 473
Modern building 499
Nineteenth-century
building 492
Seed 153
Twentieth-century
building 495
Ridge and furrow roof 492
Ridge-board 473
Ridge-rib 469, 485
Ridges 286-287
Ridge tile 464, 476
Riding bitt 372
Riding jacket 554
Riffler 452, 453, 454
Rifle 548, 549
Rift valley 58
Lake formation 292-293
Rig 584-585
Riga brush 434
Rigel
Northern stars 18
Orion 18
Southern stars 21
Star magnitudes 22
Rigger 560
Rigger's gauge 382
Rigging 582-583
Iron 392
Sailing dinghy 561
Wooden sailing ship
378-379

Rigging rail 376
Rigging tools 582-583
Right-angled triangle 622
Right cylinder 623
Right edge guide 575
Right whales 204
Rigid rock 60
Rigol 381
Rim
Bicycle wheel 358-359
Kayak paddle 560
Paddle wheel 391
Tam-tam 516
Twin bollards 586
Rim brake 330
Rim clamp 337
Rim of pitcher 161
Rim plate 390
Rim section 390
Rind 149
Ring
74-gun ship 380
Mushroom 115
Roman corbita 372
Ring 1986 U1R 48
Ring 1986 U2R 48
Ring 6 48
Ring bolt 373
Ring canal
Sea urchin 175
Starfish 174
Ring dyke 26
Ring finger 230 -231
"Ring of Fire" 272
Ring of trunk 201
Rings
Jupiter 44-45
Neptune 50-51
Saturn 46-47
Uranus 48-49
Rings 4 and 5 48
Ring scar 130,131
Ring-tailed lemur 203
Rink corner 550
Riojasaurus 89
Ripple finish 451
Riser
Bronze casting 454, 455
Staircase 477
Rising air
Atmospheric circulation
and winds 300
Precipitation 302
Rising land 294
Risorius muscle 229
Rissa tridactyla 190
Ritchey 43
River Amur 265
River banks 289, 290
River-bed 289
River capture 288
River cliff 289, 290
River Congo 265
River course 288
River development 289
River drainage patterns
288
River features 290-291
River flow 290
River Ganges 288
River Jordan 293
River Lena 265
River Mekong 265
River-mouth 290
River Nile 264-265
River Ob-Irtysh 265
Rivers 288-289
Earth's physical
features 264
River features 290-291
Rock cycle 266-267
Weathering and erosion
282
River source
River features 290
Rivers 288
River's stages 288-289
River terrace 290-291
River valley 288, 289, 290

Rivetted plates 392
Road spring 340
Roband 372, 574
Robie House 495
Robinia pseudoacacia 136
Robots 608-609
Roche 41
Roches moutonnées 286
Rock compression 60
Rock crystal 271
Rock cycle 266-267
Rock debris 295
Rock deformations 60, 61
Rocker 446
Rocker arm 366
Rocker-beam 496-497
Rocker-bogie assembly
615
Rocker cover 347, 354
Rock erosion 282
Rocker keypad 591
Rocker pad 590
"Rocket" steam
locomotive 324
Rocket launcher 397
Rock fracture 60
Rock groundmass 269
Rocking beam 334
Rocking elevator arm 424
Rocking lever 342
Rock layer
Caves 284
Faults and folds 60
Rock lip
Cirque formation 287
Tarn lake 293
Rock mounds 286
Rock particles 266-267
Rock pavement 282-283
Rock pedestal 282-283
Rock prisms 61
Rocks
Faults and folds 60-61
Fossils 278-279
Igneous and
metamorphic rocks
274-275
Mineral resources 280
Minerals 268
Rock cycle 266-267
Sedimentary rocks 276
Weathering and erosion
282
Rock salt
Halides 269
Sedimentary rocks 276-
277
Rock scar 284
Rock stonecrop 128
Rock strata 60, 61
Fossils 278
Rock stress 60, 61
Rock tension 60, 61
Rocky Mountains 73, 75,
77, 264
Rocky planets
Mars 42-43
Mercury 34-35
Solar System 30-31
Venus 36-37
Rococo style 478
Rod 562-563
Rodentia 104, 196
Rodents 196-197.
Rod-shaped structure 144
Rogers, R. 496
Roll 400
Roller
Fax machine 572, 573
Mid West single-rotor
engine 410
Motorized brushbar
floor tool 593
"O Ring" drive chain
366
Painting tool 442
Printing equipment 447,
449
Tenor saxophone 509

Roller-bearing axle box
327
Roller-blind 497
Roller path 596
Rollers 596
Roll 41
Rolling hitch 388
Rollover button 577
Roll paper holder 575
Roll paper holder adapter
575
Roll paper manipulation
button 574
Roll spoiler 414
Roll-spoiler hydraulic
actuator attachment
414
Rolls-Royce Olympus
Mark 610 turbojet 417
Roman anchor 372
Roman architecture 462-
465
Roman corbita 572-573
Romanesque style 468,
470
Roman mill 464
Roman number system
591
Roman ships 372-373
ROM cover 572
Roof boss 468
Roof construction 603
Roof dome 332, 333
Roofed space 479
Roofing tile 482
Roofless temple 460
Roof moulding 352
Roofs 484
Ancient Egyptian
temple 458-459
Ancient Roman
building 462
Asian building 490
Baroque church 481
Dome 486
Gothic building 470-473
Hammer-beam 470, 473
Islamic building 488-
489
Medieval building 467,
468
Modern building 496-
499
Neoclassical building
479, 483
Nineteenth-century
building 492
Renaissance building
476-477
Twentieth-century
building 494-495
Root
BAe-146 jetliner
components 413, 415
BE 2B wings 404
Tooth 247
Root canal 247
Root cap
Broad bean 133
Radicle 153
Root growth 282
Root hairs 152
Root nodule 128
Root of tail 198
Root parasite 163
Root-proof membrane 603
Root rib 413
Roots 132-133
Adventitious 112-113
Amaryllis 155
Begonia 155
Brassavola nodosa 162
Broomrape host 163
Carrot 128
Cell division 133
Clubmoss 120
Couch grass 113
Dehiscent fruit 150
Dicotyledons 127
Elongation region 153

Embryo 147
Epigeal germination
153
Epiphytes 162-163
Fern 121
Germination 152-153
Ginger 155
Gladiolus 155
Golden barrel cactus
156
Grape hyacinth 155
Horse chestnut 130
Horsetail 120
Hypogeal germination
152
Ivy 131
Kedrostis africana 113
Lily 155
Monocotyledons 126-
127
Mycorrhizal association
133
Oxalis sp. 157
Pine seedling 122
Potato 128
Rock stonecrop 128
Seedling 152-153
String of hearts 157
Sweet pea 128
Sweet potato 155
Vegetative reproduction
154-155
Water hyacinth 158
Water transport 138
Root scar 128
Root succulents 157
Root tip 132-133
Radicle 152-153
Root tubers 154-155, 157
Rope and paterae
decoration 459
Rope band 372
Rope hole 386
Rope moulding 395
Rope parrel 373
Rope preventer 378
Ropes 388-389
Rope serving mallet 383
Rope strand 384
Rope wooding 379
Ropework 388
Rorquals 204
Rorqua sp. 130-131, 135
Rosa sp. 130-131
Rose 130-131
Rose quartz 271
Rosette
Epiphytic plants 162-163
Neoclassical building
480
Rosette Nebula 11
Rossby waves 300
Rossin Italian time-trial
bicycle 361
Rostellum 16
Rostral bone 102, 103
Rostrum
Crayfish 173
Dolphin 204
Rotary engine 346-347
Blackburn monoplane
400
Modern piston aero-
engines 410-411
Rotary valves 507
Rotating beacon 407
Rotating drum 595
Rotating joint 612
Rotational period 36
Rotor
Mid West rotary engine
411
Rotor and seals 347
Rotor blade 423
Rotor chamber
Mid West single-rotor
engine 410
Wankel rotary engine
346
Rotor gear 546-547

Rotor gear teeth 411
Rotor house 314
Rotor hub
Bell-47 helicopter 422
Schweizer helicopter
423
Rotor journal 347
Rotor lock 604
Rotor mast 422-423
Rotunda 462-463, 482
Rough 546
Rough endoplasmic
reticulum 217
Rough terrain motorcycle
racing 368
Rough-textured paper
439, 441
Roulette 446
Rounce 449
Round arch
Ancient Roman
building 464-465
Baroque church 479-
480
Dome 484, 486-487
French temple 485
Gothic church 473
Medieval building 467-
469
Nineteenth-century
building 493
Renaissance building
474-475
Round-arched window
Ancient Roman
building 465
Baroque church 481
Dome 486
Medieval building 466,
468-469
Neoclassical building
478
Round ball 524
Round-corner single
limousine coachwork
336
Roundel
Avro biplane 403
Hawker Tempest
fighter 409
Roundhead nib 444
Roundhouse 380
Round pin 335
Round shot 378
Round thimble 384
Route information 332
Route key 590
Rover 528
Rowan 130-131
Rowing 560-561
Rowing boat 375
Rowing positions on a
Greek trireme 373
Rubber bungee shock
absorber 425
Rubber cord suspension
402-403
Rubber guide wheel 328
Rubber mounting bush
365
Rubber puck 550-551
Rubber roller 449
Rubber sealing strip 413
Rubber-sprung wheel
400-401
Rubber tyre 402
Rubber-tyred running
wheel 328
Rubber wheel-guard 328
Rubber wheels
Paris Metro 328
"People Mover" 328
Rubbing
Charcoal drawing 431
Relief printing 446
Rubbing ink 448
Rubbing strake
Mazda RX-7 346
Roman corbita 372

Rubbing strip 353
Rubens 35
Rubidium 310
Rubus fruticosus 150, 146-147
Rubus idaeus 149
Ruckman 528
Rucknover 528
Ruckstell axle 339
Rudder
    ARV light aircraft 424
    Avro biplane 402
    Avro triplane 403
    BAe-146 jetliner 415
    Battleship 395
    BE 2B bomber 405
    Blackburn monoplane 401
    Blériot XI 401
    Concorde 416-417
    Curtiss biplane 399
    Dhow 376
    Frigate 396
    Greek and Roman ships 372-373
    Iron paddlesteamer 392
    Junk 376
    Lockheed Electra airliner 407
    Longboat 380
    LVG CVI fighter 405
    Northrop B-2 bomber 421
    Sailing dinghy 561
    Sailing warship 377
    Schleicher glider 426
    Submarine 396
    Tornado 421
    Viking boats 374-375
    Wooden sailing ship 378
    World War II aircraft 408-409
    Wright Flyer 399
Rudder cable
    ARV light aircraft 424
    Avro biplane 402
Rudder chain 378
Rudder head 376
Rudder hinge
    Avro biplane 402
    Blériot XI monoplane 401
Rudder mass balance 424
Rudder pedal 425
Rudder post
    BE 2B bomber 405
    Blackburn monoplane 401
    Iron paddlesteamer 392
Rudder power control unit 417
Rudder strut 399
Rudder tip fairing 424
Rudder trimtab 409
Ruden 372
Rudimentary ear 260
Rudimentary eye 260
Rudimentary liver 260
Rudimentary mouth 260
Rudimentary vertebra 260
Ruellia grandiflora 145
Ruffini corpuscle 235, 239
Ruga 248
Rugby 524, 530-531
Rugby League 530-531
Rugby Union 530
Rules of algebra 621
Rumen 198
Ruminants 198
Rumpler monoplane 400
Run 556
Runners
    Bronze casting 454-455
    Rock stonecrop 128
    Strawberry 128
    Vegetative reproduction 154

Running 542
Running back 526
Running block 383
Running board
    Ford Model T 339
    1906 Renault 337
    Volkswagen Beetle 341
Running martingale 554
Running part 382
Running rail 328
Running rigging 382-383, 385
Running shoe 543
Running track 542
Running wheel 328
Runs 558
Rupes 34
Rupes Altai 40
Rush 155
Russian vine 131
Rustication
    Neoclassical building 479, 482-485
    Renaissance building 474-475
Rusts 114
Ruthenium 311

S

62 Sagittarii 21
Sabik 20
Sable brush
    Acrylics 442
    Calligraphy 444
    Oil paints 436
    Tempera 432
    Watercolours 438
Sabres 556-557
Sabreur 557
Sabre warning line 557
Sacajawea 37
Saccule 243
Sacral foramen 223
Sacral nerves 238
Sacral plexus 238
Sacral promontory 223
Sacral vertebra 183
Sacral vertebrae
    Diplodocus 90
    Eryops 81
    Human 223
    Iguanodon 96
    Parasaurolophus 98
    Plateosaurus 88
    Stegoceras 101
Sacristy 470
Sacrum
    Crocodile 186
    Domestic cat 195
    Elephant 201
    Hare 197
    Horse 199
    Human 218, 223, 259
    Kangaroo 206
    Lizard 184
    Rhesus monkey 202
    Seal 204
Saddle
    Acoustic guitar 512
    Bicycle 358-359
    Cannondale SH600 hybrid bicycle 361
    Eddy Merckx racing bicycle 360
    Horse racing 555
    Showjumping 554
    Werner motorcycle 362
Saddle clamp 360
Safety area 556
Safety barrier 552
Safety belt 356
Safety binding 552
Safety harness 357
Safety valve
    Bordino steam carriage 334
    Steamboat 391

Safe working load mark 383
Sagartia elegans 166
Sagitta 20
Sagittal crest 107, 194
Sagittal section through brain 236
Sagittarius 19-21
Sagittarius Arm 14
Sago palm 123
Sahara 39, 264-265
Sail
    Roman corbita 372-373
    Square-rigged ship 375
    Types 384-385
    Viking karv 374
Sail batten 376
Sailcloths 384
Sail foot control line 375
Sail hook 384
Sailing 560-561
Sailing rigs 384-385
Sailing warship 376-377
Sailmaker's whipping 382
Sailmaking tools 384
Sail patterns 379, 384
Saiph 18
Salamanders 182
Salient 466
Salisbury Cathedral 470-471
Saliva 244
Salivary gland
    Butterfly 169
    Snail 177
Salmon 109, 180
Salmon angling 562
Salmon bend gouge 452
Salmson radial engine 398-399
Salt
    Dead Sea 293
    Seawater salt content 296
Saltasaurus 72, 91
Salt-dome trap 281
Salt formation 312
Salt groundmass 277
Salt lakes 292
Samaras
    Dry fruit 150
    Sycamore 131, 150
Samarium 311
Sambucus nigra 130-131, 143
Samotherium 74
Samsung VM8000 laptop 567
San Andreas fault 58, 62-63
Sand-bars 290
Sand box 326, 327
Sand dunes
    Rock cycle 267
    Weathering and erosion 282-283
Sand groundmass 277
Sanding pipe 329
Sand-pits 546
Sandstone
    Marble tomb of Itimad-Ud-Daula 489
    Sedimentary rocks 276
Sand wave 299
Sand wedge 547
Sandy deposits 298
Sandy spit 295
Sappho Patera 37
Sapwood 125
Saratoga Race Course 555
Sarcolemma 228
Sarcomere 24
Sarcophilus harrisii 207
Sarcoplasmic reticulum 24
Sarcorhamphus papa 190
Sarracenia purpurea 113

Sartorius muscle 226
Satellite 264
Satellite map 264-265
Saturated zone 292-293
Saturn 46-47
    Solar System 31
Saucer dome 486-487
    Ancient Roman building 462
Saurischia 82-83, 84, 88
Sauropoda 83
Sauropodomorpha 83, 88
Sauropodomorphs 88-91
Sauropods 70, 88
Savannah 74
Saxboard 561
Saxophone 504, 508-509
Scala 372-373
Scale (musical) 502
Scale leaf scar 124, 155
Scale leaves
    Bishop pine 124
    Bulb 155
    Corm 155
    Epiphytic orchid 162
    Hypogeal germination 152
    Pine 122, 125
    Plumule 152
    Rhizome 155
    Sago palm 123
    Stem bulbil 155
Scalene triangle 622
Scalenus medius muscle 229
Scale of degrees 377
Scales
    Asteroxylon 79
    Bishop pine 124
    Bony fish 180
    Bract 122
    Brassavola nodosa 162
    Caiman 186
    Cartilaginous fish 178
    Crocodilians 186
    Dicotyledons 127
    False fruit 148
    Fern fronds 121
    Insects 168
    Lepidoptera wings 168
    Lizard 184
    Mushroom 115
    Ovuliferous 122-124
    Pine cone 122
    Pine shoot apex 125
    Rattlesnake 185
    Sago palm 122
    Tree fern 112
    Yew 123
Scallop 176
    Fossil 278
Scalloped hammerhead shark 179
Scalp 234, 236-237
Scaly lichens 114
Scaly skin
    Anchisaurus 89
    Corythosaurus 98
    Dinosaurs 82
    Edmontonia 95
    Ichthyostega 80
    Iguanodon 97
    Pachycephalosaurus 100
    Psittacosaurus 103
    Reptile 80
    Snake 184
    Stegosaurus 92
    Triceratops 102
    Tyrannosaurus 84
    Westlothiana 81
Scandinavia 64, 69
Scandium 310
Scan head 571
Scanner 570-571
Scanning coils 611
Scanning electron microscope (SEM) 610, 611

Scanning unit 573
Scan to e-mail button 570
Scan to web button 570
Scapania undulata 118
Scape 168
Scaphoid bone 230
Scaphoid fossa 242
Scaphonyx fischeri 69
Scapula
    Archaeopteryx 85
    Arsinoitherium 104
    Bird 189
    Bony fish 181
    Brachiosaurus 91
    Crocodile 186
    Diplodocus 90
    Domestic cat 195
    Elephant 201
    Eryops 80
    Euoplocephalus 94
    Gallimimus 86
    Hare 197
    Horse 199
    Human 210, 218
    Iguanodon 96
    Kangaroo 206
    Lizard 184
    Parasaurolophus 99
    Pareiasaur 81
    Plateosaurus 88
    Platypus 206
    Rhesus monkey 202
    Seal 204
    Stegoceras 101
    Struthiomimus 87
    Toxodon 106
    Triceratops 102
    Tuojiangosaurus 93
    Turtle 187
    Tyrannosaurus 84
Scapular muscle 91
Scarlet star 162-163
Scarph 395
Scars
    Horse chestnut 130
    Leaf 128-30, 134
    Rowan twig 131
    Scavenge oil line 419
    Scelidosauridae 83
    Scelidosaurids 71
    Scelidosaurus 71
Scent 144
Scheat 19,20
Schedar 19
Schickard 40
Schist 26
Schizocarpic dry fruits 150-151
Schleicher K23 glider 426
Schlumbergera truncata 129
Schooner 384-385
Schrödinger 41
Schubert 35
Schwann cell 228, 239
Schweizer 300c 423
Sciatic nerve 238
Scientific notation 621
Scintigram 214
Scissor brace 473
Sciurus carolinensis 197
Sclera 213, 240
Sclereid 159
Sclerenchyma
    Fern rachis 121
    Horsetail stem 120
    Marram grass 113
    Monocotyledon leaf 126
    Stems 134-135
Sclerenchyma fibres 135
Scleroderma citrinum 115
Sclerotic ring 90, 99
Scooter 50-51
Score 588
Scorecard 547
Score panel 578
Scorer
    Basketball 532
    Fencing contest 557

Judo contest 556
Lacrosse 541
Netball 535
Volleyball 534
Scoria 273
Scoring
    Australian rules football 528
    Badminton 544
    Baseball 536
    Basketball 532
    Cricket 538
    Gaelic football 529
    Hockey 540
    Hurling 540-541
    Netball 534
    Rugby 530-531
    Tennis 544
    Volleyball 534
Scorper 449
Scorpion 170, 278
Scorpiones 170
Scorpius 19, 20
Scotia 463, 485
Scots pine 122
Scraper 46
Scraper ring 344
Scratchplate 513
Scree 282-283
Screen
    Computer 576, 577, 611
    French baroque building 482
    Game Boy Advance 578
    Hydroelectric power station 314
    Islamic building 488-489
    Mobile phone 588
    Screen printing 448
    Streamed Internet video 577
    Twentieth-century building 494
Screen assembly 582
Screen bezel 588, 589
Screen bulkhead 581
Screen connector 569, 589
Screen connector socket 569
Screen display button 581
Screen light on/off 581
Screen panel 581
Screen power connector 589
Screen printing 446, 448
Screen surround 588
Screw 320
    Acoustic guitar 513
    Double bass bow 511
    Power drill 600
    Toaster 598
    Violin bow 510
Screw and lock nut tappet adjustor 367
Screw coupling 325
Screwdown greaser 336
Screw fitting 519
Screw hole 600
Screw joint 413
Screw link 386
Screw locking nut 563
Screw pressure adjustor 447
Scriber 446
Scroll
    Cello 511
    Double bass 511
    Viola 511
    Violin 510
Scroll button 567
Scroll down button 568
Scrolled buttress 478
Scroll motif 470, 491
Scroll moulding 466
Scroll ornament 476, 479, 485
Scroll-shaped corbel 482, 487

Scroll up button 567
Scrollwork 472
Scrotum 211, 259
Scrum-half 530
Scrummages 530
Scull 561
Sculling 560
Scull oar 560
Sculptor 19, 20
Sculptural decoration 467
Sculpture 452-455, 493, 495
Sculptured testa 151
Scumbling 440-441
Scupper 393
Scute 186
Scutellum 168
Scutum 19
Scutum plate 173
Scyphozoa 166
Sea
   Anticline trap 281
   Fossils 278
   Hurricane structure 303
   River features 290-291
Sea anemone 166-167
Sea angling 562
Seabed
   Fossils 278
   Ocean floor 298
   River features 290
   Rivers 288
Seabed profile 299
Sea buckthorn 136
Seacat missile launcher 397
Sea-cave 295
Sea-cliff 294-295
   River features 291
Sea creature remains 298
Sea cucumber 174
Sea daisies 174
Sea-dwelling organic structures 78
Sea-floor spread 58
Seahorse 180
Sea level 66
Sea-level variations 294
Sea lilies 174
Sea lion 204
Seals 204-205
Seam
   Rivetted plates 392
   Sail 384
Seaming twine 384
Seamounts 298
Sea of Japan 265
Searchlight 394-395
Seas 296-297
   Igneous and metamorphic rocks 275
   Rivers 288
   Satellite map 265
Seasons 72
Seat
   1906 Renault 337
   Driver's 325, 528
   Faering 375
   Fireman's 325
   First cars 334-335
   Ford Model T 339
   Greek trireme 373
   Harley-Davidson FLHS Electra Glide 363
   Honda CB750 363
   Honda VF750 364
   Husqvarna Motocross TC610 368
   Kayak 560
   Longboat 380
   Motorcycle 364
   Racing sulky 555
   Renault Clio 352-353
   Showjumping saddle 554
   Suzuki RGV500 368
   TGV electric high-speed train 329
   Vespa Grand Sport 160

Mark 1 363
Weslake Speedway motorcycle 369
Seat angle 360
Seat assembly 425, 353
Seat attachment rail 416
Seat back rest frame 337, 352-353
Seat beam 399
Seat belt catch 552
Seat cushion 407, 425
Sea temperature 303
Seat frame 353
Seating 465
Seat mount 340
Seat pan 409
Seat post 358, 360
Seat post quick-release bolt 358
Seat spring 335
Seat squab 335, 337
Seat stay 358, 360
Seat support strut 398
Seat tube 358, 360, 361
Sea urchins 174-175
Seawater
   River features 290
   Salt content 296
Seaweeds 116-117
Seaworm 78
Sebaceous gland 234-235
Secondary baffle 612
Secondary bronchus 215
Secondary colours 459
Secondary conduit 272-273
   Rock cycle 266
Secondary crater 34
Secondary flight feathers 188, 191
Secondary follicle 258
Secondary mirror 612
Secondary mycelium 115
Secondary phloem 134-135
Secondary remiges 188, 191
Secondary rotor 317
Secondary suspension 327
Secondary thallus 114
Secondary vascular tissue 134
Secondary xylem 125, 134-135
Second-century building 462
Second electron shell 309
Second mast 376
Second-row forward 530
Second slip 538
Second toe 232
Second violins 503, 504-505
Second wheel set 329
Secretory gland 161
Secretory thyroid gland cells 217
Secretory vesicle 216
Secure anchor 386
Security light 603
Security lock port 566, 567
Sediment
   Coastlines 294-295
   Fossils 278
   Glaciers 286-287
   Lakes 292
   Mineral resources 280
   Mountain building 62-63
   Ocean floor 298-299
   River features 290-291
   Rivers 288
   Rock cycle 266-267
Sedimentary rocks 276-277
   Igneous and metamorphic rocks 274
   Rock cycle 266-267
Sedna Planitia 36-37

Sedum rupestre 128
Sedum spectabile 128-129
Seed
   Apomixis 146
   Apple 149
   Cape gooseberry 149
   Dehydration 152
   Dispersal 148-151
   Dormancy 152
   Dry fruit 150-151
   Embryo development 147
   Fig 148
   Germination 132, 152-153
   Goosegrass 150
   Gymnosperms 122
   Hilum 148-149, 151-153
   Hogweed 151
   Honesty 151
   Larkspur 151
   Lemon 148
   Love-in-a-mist 151
   Lychee 148
   Melon 149
   Parts 152-153
   Pea 150
   Pine 122
   Raspberry 149
   Root development 132
   Scots pine 122
   Smooth cypress 123
   Strawberry 150
   Succulent fruit 148-149
   Sweet chestnut 150
   Sycamore 131, 151
   Wind dispersal 150
   Wings 150-151
   Yew 123
Seed axis 152-153
Seed coat 132, 152-153
   Dry fruit 150-151
   Embryo development 147
   Epigeal germination 153
   Hypogeal germination 152
   Succulent fruit 148-149
Seed fern 278
Seed leaves 126, 152-153
   Dry fruit 150-151
   Embryo development 147
   Epigeal germination 153
   Hypogeal germination 152
   Pine 122
   Succulent fruit 148-149
Seedlings
   Epigeal germination 153
   Hypogeal germination 152
   Pine 122
Seed-producing organs 148-149
Seed scar 122
Seed stalks 150
Seed wings 151
Segmental arch 492
Segmental pediment 462, 478
Segnosauria 83
Seif dune 283
Seismic activity 58
Seizing 383, 384, 387, 388-389
Selaginella sp. 120Select button 578
Select/enter option 587
Selector fork 366
Selector switch 598-599
Selenite 270
Selenium 311
Self-pollination 144
SEM 601, 611
Semaphore signal 330

Semen 217
Semi-arch 470-471
Semibreve 502-503
Semi-bulkhead 425
Semi-circle 532
Semicircular canals 243
Semicircular tower 465
Semi-conductor 306
Semi-dome 484, 482, 488
Semi-elliptical arch 484
Semi-elliptic leaf spring 342
Semilunar fold 249
Semi-metals 310-311
Seminal receptacle 169
   Spider 170
Seminal vesicle 259
Semiquaver 502
Semi-solid core 37
Semi-solid outer core 41
Semi-sprawling stance 82
   Westlothiana 81
Semitendinosus muscle 227
Send/receive icon 576
Send/select button 588
Send/select button connector 589
Senior ratings' mess 397
Sensor cables 609
Sensors 608
Sensor signal boards 609
Sensory antenna 168
Sensory hinge 160
Sensory tentacle 176
Sent items icon 576
Sepal 140-143
   Clematis 131
   Dicotyledons 126-127
   Dry fruit 150-151
   Everlasting pea 129
   Fertilization 146-147
   Monocotyledons 126
   Peruvian lily 129
   Pitcher plant 113
   Pollination 145
   Rose 131
   Succulent fruit 149
Sepal remains 146-147
Sepal sheath 141
Separated carpels 151
Separator 576
Septime 557
Septum 115
   False 151
   Interventricular 251
   Nasal 213, 241
   Placenta 260
Sequencer 521
Sequoiadendron sp. 70
Series elastic actuator 609
Series electrical circuit 316
Serif 445
Serous pericardium 250
Serpens Caput 18, 21
Serpens Cauda 19, 20
Serpentes 184
Serpentine neck 374
Serrated tooth 84, 85, 88
Serrate leaf margins 129
Serratus anterior muscle 226
Server 534, 544 , 545, 576
Server Service 544
Service area 554
Service box line 545
Service court 544, 545
Service crane 605
Service door 415
Service judge 544, 545
Service line 544, 545
Service shaft 498
Service zone 545
Serving 388
Serving mallet 383, 384, 588
Servo control-unit fairing 417

Servo-tab 414, 415
Sesamoid bone 198
Seta 112, 119
Set-back buttress 481
Set square 445
Settings control panel 574
Settings display 574, 575
Setting select buttons 575
Seven Sisters 14
Seventeenth century 474
   Building 479-481, 488
   Capital 490
   Dome 486-487
   Roof 490
   Style 478
   Tomb 489
Seventh century
   Building 491
Sevier fault 276
Sex cells 154
   Fertilization 146-147
   Gametophyte plants 120
   Gymnosperms 122
   Liverwort 118
   Moss 118-119
Sextans 21
Sexual reproduction
   Algae 116-117
   Bryophytes 119
   Flowering plants 140-147
   Mosses 118-119
   Seaweed 116-117
   Spirogyra sp. 117
Seyfert 41
Seyfert galaxies 12-13
Shackle 382, 386
Shackle pin 382
Shaft
   Ancient Egyptian column 459
   Ancient Greek temple 461
   Ancient Roman building 463, 465
   Arrow 548
   Asian building 490-491
   Badminton racket 545
   Electric generator 317
   Feather 191
   Femur 225
   French temple 485
   Golf club 547
   Harness racer 555
   Hydroelectric power station 314
   Javelin 542
   Kayak paddle 560
   Medieval church 468-469
   Modern building 498
   Neoclassical building 478, 483
   Nineteenth-century building 493
   Phalanx 230
   Power drill 600
   Roman Corbita 373
   Sculling oar 560
   Ski pole 553
   Squash racket 545
Shaft drive 366
Shale
   Contact metamorphism 274
   Grand Canyon 277
Shallow carvel-built hull 391
Shallow flats 293
Shank
   Anatomy of a hook 562
   Danforth anchor 386
   Hook 583
   Roman anchor 372
   Sail hook 384
   Shackle pin 382
Shannon bone 198
Shape
   Chemical reactants 312

Matter 306-307
Periodic table 310
Shapes (plane; solid) 622
Sharks 178-179, 180
Sharp 502
Sharpey's fibre 225
Shaula 19, 20
Shave 374
Shaving foam 306
Shearing 61
Sheave 383
Sheave for cat tackle 380
Sheep 198
Sheepskin numnah 554
Sheer 371
Sheerplank 380
Sheer pole 373
Sheer strake 375, 393
Sheet 372, 375, 382
Sheet anchor 395
Sheet bend 389
Sheet feeder 575
Sheet-iron louvre 493
Sheet lead 383
Shelf formation 282
Shell
   379 cm shell 397
   6 in shell 397
   Building 464, 476
   Chelonians 186
   Crab 172
   Dorsal margin 176
   Egg 192-193
   Exploding 394, 396-397
   Fossil 278
   Massive stars 26
   Mollusc 176-177
   Octopus 176
   Rib 176
   Rudiment 176
   Scallop 176
   Small stars 24-25
   Snail 177
   Standing block 382
   Terrapin 187
   Ventral margin 176
Shell bogie 396
Shell case 397
Shelled invertebrates 56
Shelley 35
Shell-like fracture 270
Shell room 396
Shelly limestone 267
"Shiaijo" 556
Shield 394-395
"Shield bearers" 92
Shielded receiver 591
Shield plate 570
Shield volcano 42
Shin
   Herrerasaurus 86
   Human 211
Shinarump member 276
Shin guard
   Slalom skiing 553
   Soccer 525
Shinty 540
Shinumo quartzite 277
Ship 587
   74-gun ship 379, 380-381
Ship of the line 380-381
Ship's cannon 376, 394
Ships of Greece and Rome 372-373
Ship's shield 394-395
Ship's wheel 378, 390, 394
Shipwright 374
Shiv 383
Shiver 383
Shock absorber
   1906 Renault 336
   American football helmet 527
   ARV light aircraft 425
   Honda CB750 363
   Honda VF750 364
   Renault Clio 350
   Suzuki RGV500 368

Vespa Grand Sport 160
Mark 1 363
Volkswagen Beetle 340
Shock-absorbing platform
553
Shock-absorbing spring
401, 405
Shock-strut 401
Shock waves 27
Path 63
Athletics 543
Basketball 553
Golf 547
Handball 535
Rowing 560
Shoot
Broomrape 163
Embryo 147
Horsetail 120
Hypogeal germination
152
Pine 125
Vegetative reproduction
155
Shoot apex 125
Shooting 548-549
Shooting circle 540
Shooting positions 548
Shoreline
Coastlines 294
Continental-shelf floor
298
Short line 545
Shorts
Australian rules football
529
Hurling 541
Soccer 525
Volleyball 534
Short saphenous vein 253
Shortstop 536
Short-wave radio 318
Shot
Field events equipment
542
Gun 378
Shot garland 381
Shot put 543
Shot-put circle 542
Shot-put fan 542
Shoulder
Anchisaurus 89
Cello 511
Corythosaurus 98
Double bass 511
Gorilla 203
Harp 511
Horse 199
Human 210
Iguanodon 97
Rabbit 196
Rigging 382-383
Stegoceras 101
Stegosaurus 92
Viola 511
Violin 510
Shoulderblade 210, 218
Shoulder button 578, 579
Shoulder cowling 412
Shoulder girdle 80
Shoulder joint
Brachiosaurus 91
Gallimimus 86
Human 218
Parasaurolophus 99
Plateosaurus 88
Triceratops 102
Tyrannosaurus 84
Shoulder motor 609
Shoulder pad 426
Shoulder padding 551
Shoulder pass 535
Shoulder spikes
Edmontonia 95
Euoplocephalus 94
Shoulder wheel throw 556
Showjumping 554
Shreve, R.H. 494
Shrew-like mammals 70

Shrimp 172
Fossil 79
Shrine 490-491
Shroud
Dhow 376
Longboat 380
Rigging 383
Roman corbita 373
Sailing dinghy 561
Sailing warship 376
Shrubs 130-131
Shutter button 581
Shutter for gun 394
Shutter open knob 587
Shuttlecock 544-545
Sickle motif 491
Sidalcea malviflora 136
Side aisle
Cathedral dome 484
Gothic church 472-473
Medieval church 469
Side bench 380
Side brace and retraction
jack trunnions 414
Sidecar
BMW R/60 362
Motorcycle racing 368-
369
Side chapel 469-470, 479
Side counter timber 381
Side-cowling 408
Side drum 504-505
Side fairing 415
Side forequarter hold 556
Side gear 347
Side housing 346-347
Side lamp 338-339
Sidelight 332, 333, 362
Side-line
American football 526
Badminton 545
Basketball 552
Handball 535
Hockey 540
Men's lacrosse 540
Netball 555
Tennis 541
Volleyball 534
Side marker lamp 346,
349
Side-mounted engine 398
Side plate 562
Side pod 356, 357
Side reflector 362, 363
Siderite band 277
Side rudder 374-375
Side-shooting 541
Side vent 329
Side wall 545, 558
Side-wall line 545
Sideways erosion
River features 290
Rivers 288
Sierra Madre 264
Sierra Nevada 57, 75
Sieve tubes 154
Sieving beak 188
Sif Mons 37
Sight 594
Sight pin 549
Sight screen 558
Sighting hood
Battleship 594
Gun turret 396
Sighting rule 376-377
Sights 548-549
Sigma Canis Majoris 21
Sigmoid colon 249
Signal flag compartment
397
Signal gear 395
Signalling systems 330-
331
Sikorsky, Igor 422
Silence 502
Silencer
Harley-Davidson FLHS
Electra Glide 362
Renault Clio 350

Suzuki RGV500 368
Vespa Grand Sport 160
Mark 1 363
Weslake Speedway
motorcycle 369
Silencing heat exchanger
404
Silicate core 51
Silicate dust 53
Silicate material 39
Silicate rock 39
Silicates 269
Siliceous ooze 299
Silicon 26
Earth's composition 39
Earth's crust 58
Periodic table 311
Variety of matter 306
Siliquas 150-151
Silk gland 170
Sill 26
Ancient Roman mill 464
Renaissance building
475
Twentieth-century
building 494
Sill trim 353
Silly mid-off 538
Silly mid-on 538
Silurian period
Fossil record 279
Geological time 56
Silver
Mineral resources 280-
281
Minerals 268
Periodic table 311-312
Streak 271
Silver lines 430-431
Silverpoint 430, 451
Silver wire 430
Silvery metals 310
Simm card 589
Simm card connectors 589
Simple electrical circuit
316
Simple eye 170-171
Simple leaves 156-157
Entire 130
Hastate 128
Herbaceous flowering
plants 128-129
Lanceolate 131
Lobed 131
Simple machines 320
Simple Machines Law 320
Simple pulleys 320
Simple succulent fruits
148-149
Simulated sound 520
Single bass note string
515
Single-celled micro-
organisms 78
Single clump block 373
Single cylinder 335
Single-decker bus 332,
333
Single flowers 140-141,
143
Single front driving wheel
334
Single-glazed
conservatory 602
Single-leg main landing
gear 407
Single overhead cam
engine 363
Single-piece skin 413
Single-pulley system 320
Single reed 508, 509
Singles 544
Single scull 560, 561
Single sheet bend 387
Single-sided trailing-link
fork 363
Single wing hold 556

Singularity
Formation of black hole
29
Stellar black hole 29
Sinistral strike-slip fault
61
Sink-holes 284-285
Sinking land 294
Sinopia 454, 455
Sinous venosus sclerae
241
Sinuous cell wall 156
Sinus
Frontal, 212, 245
Green alga 112
Renal 256
Superior sagittal 212
Sinus Borealis 69
Sinus Iridum 40
Siphon
Octopus 176-177
Sea urchin 175
Siphonoglyph 167
Sirius
Canis Major 21
Northern stars 18
Our galaxy and nearby
galaxies 15
Southern stars 21
Spectral absroption
lines 23
Star magnitudes 22
Sirius A 23
Sirius B 23
Sixteenth century
Building 476-477
Staircase 472
Style 462, 470
Size (glue) 431, 452, 456
Skarn 26
Skate
Chondrichthyes 178
Ice hockey 550, 551
Skeletal muscle 228
Skeletal muscle fibre 228
Skeleton
Archaeopteryx 85
Arsinoitherium 104-105
Baryonyx hand 85
Bat 105
Bird 189
Bony fish 180-181
Cow's foot 198
Crocodile 186
Diplodocus 90
Domestic cat 195
Elephant 201
Eryops 80-81
Frog 183
Hare 197
Horse 199
Human 218-219
Iguanodon 96
Kangaroo 206
Kentrosaurus 93
Lizard 184
Parasaurolophus 98-99
Pareiasaur 81
Plateosaurus 88-89
Platypus 206
Rhesus monkey 202
Seal 204
Snake 185
Spider 171
Sponge 166
Stegoceras 100-101
Stegosaurus 93
Struthiomimus 87
Toxodon 106
Tuojiangosaurus 93
Turtle 187
Tyrannosaurus 84-85
Westlothiana 81
Sketch book 430
Skid 402, 404
Skid beam 380
Ski goggles 552, 553
Skiing 552, 553

Skilled movements 237
Skin
Amphibian 80, 182
Drumhead 518
Lizard 184
Reptile 80
Snake 184
Succulent fruits 148-149
Waterproof 81
Skin and hair 234-235
"Skin-grip" pin 424-425
Skin lap-joint 413, 414,
415
Skin tones 441
Ski pole 552
Skirting board 602
Skis 552
Skull
Acanthostega 80
Alligator 186
Ankylosaurus 94
Australopithecus 108
Baryonyx 83
Bear 194
Camarasaurus 91
Chimpanzee 202
Crocodilians 186
Diplodocus 90
Domestic cat 195
Elephant 201
Euoplocephalus 94
Fetal 220
Gharial 186
Hadrosaurs 96
Hare 197
Heterodontosaurus 83
Homo erectus 108
Homo habilis 108
Horse 199
Human 108, 212, 218,
220-221, 222, 256-257
Hyaenodon 107
Iguanodon 96
Kangaroo 206
Lambeosaurus 99
Lion 194
Lizard 184
Marginocephalian 100
Moeritherium 105
Octopus 176
Opossum 106
Pachycephalosaurs 100
Pachycephalosaurus
100
Phiomia 105
Plateosaurus 88
Platypus 206
Prenocephale 100
Protoceratops 102
Rattlesnake 185
Rhesus monkey 202
Seal 204
Smilodon 107
Stegoceras 100
Styracosaurus 102
Synapsid reptile 67
Tortoise 77
Turtle 187
Skull bones 81
Skullcap 555
Skunks 194
Skylight
Battleship 594
Building 493, 494
Iron paddlesteamer
392-393
Skyscraper 494
Slab
Ancient Egyptian
building 458-459
Modern building 499
Twentieth-century
building 494
Slaked lime 454
Slalom
Skiing 552
Canoeing 560
Slalom clothing 553

Slalom equipment 553
Slalom gate 552
Slat 421
Slate 274, 275
Sleep button 585
Sleeper 324, 331
Sleeve port 543
Sleeve valve 543
Slender thistle 129
Slick racing tyre 365
Kirby BSA 369
Suzuki RCV500 369
Slide 396
Slide bar 325
Slide brace 507
Slide locking lever 396
Slider release 587
Slide track 561
Slide valve 390
Sliding bed 447
Sliding curtain 329
Sliding seat 561
Sliding window 333
Sling fixing point 549
Slip face 283
Slip faults 61
Slipher 43
Slope structure 60
Sloping roof 486
Slug 176
Slumped cliff 295
Slur 503
Smallbore rifle shooting
548
Smallbore rifle target 549
Small intestine
Brachiosaurus 90
Chimpanzee 202
Cow 198
Domestic cat 195
Elephant 200
Euoplocephalus 94
Frog 182
Human 214, 249
Lizard 185
Tortoise 187
Small Magellanic Cloud
Hydrus and Mensa 20
Our galaxy and nearby
galaxies 15
Stars of southern skies
20
Small stars 24-25
Small theropods 87
Small-scale rock
deformities 61
Smalti 450
Smalti mosaic 450
Smash 534
Smell 244
Smilodon 107
Smokebox 524, 525
Smoky quartz 268
Smooth cypress 123
Smooth endoplasmic
reticulum 216
Smudging 430, 431
Smuts 114
Snail 176-177
Snake-head ornament 375
Snakes 184-185
Snap head 392
Snare 518
Snare drum 518
Snort mast 397
Snout
Anchisaurus 89
Caiman 186
Crocodilians 186
Dogfish 178
Edmontonia 95
Herrerasaurus 86
Iguanodonts 96
Jawless fish fossil 78
Pachycephalosaurus
100
Rat 196
Snow
Glaciers 286-287

Weather 302
Snowflake moray eel 180
Snowflakes 302
Soane, J. 478, 482-483
Sobkou Planitia 35
Soccer 524-525
Soccer kit 525
Socket 573
Socle
  Ancient Egyptian
    temple 458
  Baroque church 479
  Cathedral dome 487
  Gothic church 472
  Medieval church 469
  Neoclassical building
    478-479
  Renaissance building
    474
Sodalite 269
Sodium 35, 58
  Periodic table 310
  Seawater salt content
    296
Sodium hydroxide 312
Sodium lines 23
Soffit 464, 484, 498
Soft eye 382
Soft hair brush 436, 438,
  440
Soft-headed beater 516,
  517, 519
Soft metals 310
Soft palate 212, 245
Soft pastels 440
Soft pedal 514, 515
Soft rock
  River features 290
  Weathering and erosion
    282
Software 569
Software effect plug-in
  521
Solanum tuberosum 128
Solar array 612, 613
Solar array supporting
  arm 613
Solar cell 605
Solar collector 603
Solar day 34
Solar eclipse 32
Solar flare 32-33
Solar panel 496, 605, 615
Solar power 605
Solar radiation 300-301
Solar system 38, 30-31
Solar wind
  Earth's magnetosphere
    38
  Structure of comet 53
  Sun 32
Solarium 494
Solar Wings Pegasus
  Quasar microlight 427
Sole of foot 234
Soleplate 593
Soleplate roller 593
Soleplate surround 594
Soleus muscle 227, 233
Solfataras 272-273
Solid body 512, 513
Solid crystals 306
Solid heart thimble 383
Solidified lava
  Lake formation 292
  Volcanoes 272-273
Solid ink stick 444
Solid rubber tyre 335
Solids 306-307
  Chemical reactions 312
Solid shapes 622
Solutions 306, 312-313
Sombrero 12
Somites 79
SONAR bulge 397
SONAR torpedo decoy 396
SONAR transducer array
  397
Sonic boom 416

Sonoran Desert 264
Sony Aibo robot dog 608
Sony Cyber-Shot DSC-P1
  digital camera 580
Sony DAV-S300 585
Sony Ericsson T68 588
Sony digital handycam
  582
Sony Portable Minidisk
  Player MZ- 586-587
Soot particles 513
Sophocles 35
Soralium 114
Sorbus aucuparia 130-131
Soredia 114
Sori 120-121
Sostenuto pedal 514, 515
Sound 314-315
  Coastline 295
  Electronic instruments
    520
  Musical notation 502
Soundboard
  Acoustic guitar 513
  Concert grand piano
    515
  Harp 511
  Upright piano 514
  Viola 511
  Violin 510
Sound channels 584
Sound-hole
  Acoustic guitar 512-513
  Cello 511
  Double bass 511
  Viola 511
  Violin 510
Sound module 521
South Africa 64
South America 264
  Cretaceous period 72-
    73
  Jurassic period 70
  Late Carboniferous
    period 66
  Middle Ordivician
    period 64
  Quaternary period 76-
    77
  Tertiary period 74-75
  Triassic period 68
South American plate 59
South Asian buildings
  490-491
South Atlantic Gyre 296
  Satellite map 265
South Atlantic Ocean 39,
  73
South-east trade winds
  300
South-easterly wind 303
South Equatorial Belt 45
South equatorial current
  296-297
Southerly wind 303
Southern Hemisphere
  296-297
Southern polar region 64
South Galactic Pole 15
South Indian Gyre 297
South magnetic polar
  region 28
South Pacific Gyre 296
South Pacific Ocean 39
South polar ice-cap
  Structure of Mars 43
  Surface of Mars 42
South Pole
  Atmospheric circulation
    and winds 300
  Coriolis force 297
  Earth 38
  Jupiter 44
  Mars 42
  Mercury 34
  The Moon 40
  Neptune 50
  Pluto 51
  Pulsar 28

Saturn 46
  Uranus 48-49
  Venus 36
South rim 277
South seeking pole 317
South Temperate Belt 45
South Temperate Zone
  45
South Tropical Zone 45
Space 300-301
Space probes 614-615
Space shuttle astronaut
  613
Space shuttle remote
  manipulator system
  (robot arm) 612, 613
Space telescope 612-613
Spadix 143
Span 484
Spandrel
  Gothic church 471
  Islamic building 488-
    489
  Neoclassical building
    482
  Nineteenth-century
    building 493
  Renaissance building
    474
Spanish bowline 389
Spar
  BAe-146 jetliner
    components 415
  BE 2B tail 405
  Concorde 417
  Pegasus Quasar
    microlight 427
Spare tyre 337, 339
Spare wheel well 341
Spark plug 342-343, 410
Spark plug cap 366
Spark plug hole 346
Spark plug lead 344
Spar trunnion 409
Spat 426-427
Spathe 143
  Horsetails 120
Spawn 182-183, 192
Speaker
  Digital video 585
  Electronic music
    system 521
  Fax machine 572
  Headphones 586
  Nokia mobile phone
    588, 589
  Samsung laptop 567
  Sony digital camera 581
  System unit 566
Speaker panel 578
Speakerphone button 572
Speaker plug 591
Speaker socket 566
Speaker units 584
Speak key 590
Spear 382
Spear head 109
Special function buttons
  588
Specimen 610, 611
Specimen airlock 611
Specimen stage 610, 611
Spectral absorption lines
  22-23
Spectral type 22-23
Specular haematite 268
Speech 257
Speed
  Forces 320
  Gearbox 366
Speedball nib 444
Speedometer 362
Speedometer drive 365
Speedway motorcycle
  racing 368
Sperm 258-259
Spermatheca
  Snail 177
  Spider 170

Sperm cell 217, 607
Sperm duct 195
Spermoviduct 177
Sperm whale 204-205
Sperry-ball gun turret
  408
Sphenethmoid bone 183
Sphenoidal fontanelle 220
Sphenoidal sinus 212, 245
Sphenoid bone 220
Sphenopsids 279
Sphenopteris latiloba 72
Sphere 623
Spherical umbel 143
Spheroid 623
Sphincter muscle
  Anal 249
  Iris 241
  Pyloric 249
  Sea anemone 167
  Urethral 257
Sphyrna lewini 179
Spica 18, 21
Spicule 52, 53
Spicules 166
Spider
  Arachnid 170-171
  Bicycle 358, 360
Spider seat 334
Spigot 387
Spike
  Aechmea miniata 162
  Dodder 163
  Double bass 511
  Flower 143
  Grape hyacinth 155
  Thyreophorans 92-93
  Volleyball 534
Spiky cupule 150
Spinal column 238
Spinal cord
  Bird 189
  Bony fish 181
  Chimpanzee 202
  Dogfish 179
  Dolphin 205
  Domestic cat 195
  Elephant 200
  Human 212, 217, 223,
    236, 238, 261
  Lizard 185
  Rabbit 196
Spinal ganglion 223, 238,
  243
Spinal nerve 223, 238
Spindle 601
Spine
  Aechmea miniata 162
  Barberry 130-131
  Bromeliad 113
  Calligraphy character
    445
  Cnidocyte 167
  Diatom 116
  Dryland plants 156
  Golden barrel cactus
    156
  Haemal 180
  Herbaceous flowering
    plants 128-129
  Human 218, 222-223
  Mahonia 130-131
  Modern jetliners 413,
    415
  Neural 180
  Sea urchin 174
  Starfish 174
Spine end fairing 421
Spinner
  ARV light aircraft 424-
    425
  Hawker Tempest
    components 408
  Hawker Tempest
    fighter 409
  Lockheed Electra
    airliner 407
  Turbofan engine 418
Spinneret 170-171

Spinner mounting disc
  406
Spinning lure 562
Spinose-dentate margin
  129
Spinous process 222-223
Spiny anteaters 206
Spiny leaflets 130-131
Spiracle
  Acanthostega 80
  Caterpillar 169
  Spider 170
Spiral arm
  Galaxies 12-13
  Milky Way 14
Spiral galaxy
  Galaxies 12-13
  Milky Way 14-15
  Objects in Universe 11
  Origin and expansion of
    Universe 10-11
Spiral ganglion 243
Spiralling clouds 302
Spiralling low-pressure
  cells 302
Spiralling rain 303
Spiralling winds 302-303
Spiral scroll 460
Spiral spring 449
Spiral staircase 472, 476
Spiral tubes 342
Spiral valve 179
Spiral wrack 116
Spire
  Asian building 490-491
  Gothic church 470-471,
    473
  Medieval building 466,
    468
  Nineteenth-century
    building 493
  Renaissance building
    476-477
Spirit lamp 454
Spirketting 381
Spirogyra sp. 117
Spit 291
Splayed window-sill 475,
  482
Spleen
  Bony fish 181
  Chimpanzee 202
  Domestic cat 195
  Elephant 200
  Frog 182
  Human 215, 249
Splenic artery 253
Splicing fid 383
Splint bone 198
Splinter bar 335
Splintery fracture 270
Split flap 406
Split line 151
Split-open pollen sac 144
Split rudder 421
Spoiler 346, 349
Spoiler anchorage 413
Spoiler arm 414
Spoke
  Bicycle wheel 358-359
  Bordino Steam Carriage
    335
  Eddy Merckx racing
    bicycle 361
  Etching press 447
  Paddle wheel 391
  Ship's wheel 390
Spoked wheel
  Bicycle 358-359
  Pacing sulky 555
Spoke guard 358
Spoke nipple 361
Sponge roller 442
Sponges 166-167
  Fossils 279
Spongocoel 166
Spongy bone 224
Spongy mesophyll 126,
  139

Spongy tissues 156
Spool 562
Spoon 560
Spoon-shaped tooth 91
Sporangia 120-121
Sporangiophore 120
Sporangium 79
Spore-case 79
Spore-producing
  structures
  Fern 121
  Fungi 114-115
  Lichen 114
  Moss 112
Spores
  Clubmoss 120
  Fern 120-121
  Fungi 114-115
  Horsetail 120
  Lichen 114
  Liverworts 118
  Mosses 118-119
  Mushroom 115
Sporophores 114-115
Sporophytes
  Clubmoss 120
  Fern 120-121
  Horsetail 120
  Liverworts 118
  Moss 112, 118-119
Sports tyre 365
Sports wheel 340
Sprag clutch 410
Spray and steam knobs
  594
Spray barrel 594
Spray nozzle 594
Spray pump 594
Spreader 561
Spring
  Lakes and
    Groundwater 292
  Motorcycle 366
  Power drill 600
  Toaster 599
Spring and chassis unit
  357
Spring balance 320
Springboard diving 558
Spring/damper unit 365
Springing point 467, 484-
  485
Spring line 292
Spring perch 338
Spring petiole 160
Spring shock absorber
  358-359
Spring tides 296-297
Spring-trap mechanism
  160
Spring washer 601
Spring wood xylem 134
Sprint races 560
Sprinting 542
Spritsail 378
Sprit yard 376
Sprocket 358, 366
Spruce 513
Spruce beam 560
Sprung chassis 354
Spunyarn 388
Spun yarn serving 383
Spur 169
Spur gear 574
Spurious wing 191
Squadron code 409
Squamata 184
Squamosal bone 183
Squamous suture 220
Squamulose lichens 114
Squamulose thallus 114
Square 622
Square cut 538
Square knot 388
Square leg 538
Square-leg umpire 538
Square masonry 465
Square rib 486
Square-rigged ship 375

Square sail 374, 378, 384
Square-section steel tubing 364
Square-section tyre 362, 369
Squash 544, 545
Squeegee 448
Squid 176
Squinch 466
Squirrel 196-197
Squirrel hair brush 438
Squirrel mop wash brush 438
SST 416-417
St. John's wort 145
St. Basil's Cathedral 487
St. Paul's Cathedral
    Arch 484
    Baroque style 478, 480-481
    Dome 480, 486-487
    Old 470, 472
Stabilizer 397, 548
Stabilizer-bar weight 422
Stabilizer fin 396
Stable elements 310, 311
Stack 295
Staff 577, 596
Stage 477, 495
Stage-door 477
Stained glass 470
Stainless steel cover 599
Staircase
    Ancient Roman building 465
    Baroque church 481
    Gothic church 470, 472
    Medieval building 466
    Modern building 496-497, 499
    Neoclassical building 483
    Renaissance building 474-477
Staircase turret 468
Stairs 477
Stair tool 593
Stairway 489
Stalactites 284-285
Stalagmites 284-285
Stalagmitic boss 284
Stalagmitic floor 284
Stalk
    Algae 116
    Barnacle 173
    Dicotyledons 127
    Flower 140
    Fungi 114-115
    Liverwort 118
    Monocotyledons 128
    Moss 112, 119
    Pitcher plant 113
    Seaweed 117
    Stem succulent 113
    Water lily 159
Stalked barnacle 173
Stalked secretory glands 161
Stalk scar 123
Stall warning vane 412
Stamen remains 146-147, 150
Stamens 140-143
    Anther 140-143
    Dicotyledon flower 126-127
    Fertilization 146-147
    Filament 140-143
    Insect-pollination 144
    Monocotyledon flower 126
    Rose 131
Stamp 445
Stance
    Dinosaurs 82
    Hominids 108
    Westlothiana 81
Stanchion 373, 393
Standard 554

Standardbred horse 554, 555
Standard European paper 445
Standard knee 381
Standby pitot head 416-417
Standing block 382
Standing lug mizzen 385
Standing part
    Hawser bend 387
    Knots 388, 389
    Rigging 382-383
    Single sheet bend 387
Standing position 548
Standing rigging 382-383
Stand-off half 530
Stapes 242
Staple 449
Starbirth region 16
Starboard side 574
Starch grains 139
    Chlamydomonas sp. 116
    Orchid root 133
Star clusters 16-17, 613
    Objects in Universe 11
    Our galaxy and nearby galaxies 14
Star coral 167
Star drag 562
Star dune 283
Starfish 174-175
    Fossil 79
Star formation in Orion 24
Starling 467
Star magnitudes 22
Stars 22-23, 613
    Massive stars 26-27
    Milky Way 14-15
    Neutron stars and black holes 28-29
    Small stars 24-25
    Star clusters 16, 613
    Sun 32-33
Star-shaped parenchyma 135
Star-shaped sclereids 159
Stars of northern skies 18-19
Stars of southern skies 20-21
Start button 572, 578
Start button and indicator light 570
Starter 339, 558
Starter cog 336
Starter motor
    Hawker Tempest components 408
    Mid West twin-rotor engine 411
    Renault Clio 351
    Volkswagen Beetle 340
Starter ring 345
Starting block 558
Starting handle 336-337, 338, 343
Starting line (100m) 542
Start print button 575
State room 592
Static air-pressure plate 412
Static discharge wick 406
Static electricity 316
Stationary gear 346-347, 411
Stator 410
Statue 472, 478
Statue creation 455
Statuette 476, 481
Staurikosaurids 69
Staurikosaurus 69
Stay 325, 392
Staysail 378, 385
"Stealth" bomber 420-421
Steam 273, 507
    Locomotives 324, 325

Nuclear power station 314
Oil-fired power station 315
Steam barrel 594
Steamboat with paddle wheels 391
Steam car 334, 342
Steam chest 334
Steam chest pressure gauge 325
Steam condenser 397
Steam control knob 594
Steam dome 325
Steam engine 390-391
Steam generator 314
Steam grating 380
Steam iron 594
Steam launch 394
Steam locomotive 324, 325
Steam pipe 334-335
Steam pipework 397
Steam-powered Cugnot "Fardier" 334
Steam release activator 594
Steam whistle 392
Steel 492
Steel and concrete floor 498
Steel and titanium skin 416
Steel beater 517
Steel brace 493
Steel column 497-498
Steel floor-plate 497
Steel frame 360, 364
Steel girder framework 314
Steel lattice-beam 497
Steel lock 360
Steel mullion 494
Steel point 452
Steel rails 330
Steel-reinforced concrete 494
Steel sleeper 330
Steel wheel 340, 350-351
Steeple 471, 481
Steeplechase 554
Steep ridge 283
Steerboard side 374
Steerer tube 359
Steering 350, 364
Steering actuator 416
Steering arm 338-339
Steering box assembly 340
Steering column
    Benz Motorwagen 335
    Ford Model T 339
    Renault Clio 350
    Volkswagen Beetle 541
Steering gear 592
Steering gearbox 339
Steering head 335
Steering idler 340
Steering knuckle 338
Steering link 335
Steering oar 374
Steering pump pulley 344
Steering rack 335, 350
Steering spindle 336
Steering stop 425
Steering tie-rod 340
Steering tiller 334-335, 337
Steering track-rod 337
Steering wheel
    1906 Renault 337
    Ford Model T 338-339
    Renault Clio 350, 353
    White Steam Car 342
Steering wiffletree 337
Steersman 560
Stegoceras 100-101
Stegosauria 83
Stegosaur 71, 92
Stegosaurus 71, 92

Steib chair 362
Stela 459
Stele
    Dicotyledons 127
    Monocotyledons 127
    Root 132-133
Stellar core 17
Stellar spectral absorption lines 22-23
Stellate parenchyma 135
Stem 134-135
    Aechmea miniata 162
    Asteroxylon 79
    Bamboo 131
    Barberry 130-131
    Battleship 394
    Begonia 129
    Bishop pine 124-125
    Brassavola nodosa 162
    Bromeliad 113
    Broomrape 163
    Calligraphy character 445
    Canadian pond weed 158-159
    Chusan palm 130
    Clubmoss 120
    Corallina officinalis 117
    Couch grass 113
    Crab cactus 129
    Dicotyledons 126-127
    Dodder 163
    Eddy Merckx racing bicycle 361
    Epiphytes 162-163
    Everlasting pea 129
    Florists' chrysanthemum 129
    Flower arrangements 143
    Golden barrel cactus 156
    Guzmania lingulata 162-163
    Hogweed 129
    Horsetail 120
    Ice-plant 128-129
    Iron paddlesteamer 393
    Ivy 131
    Kedrostis africana 113
    Live-for-ever 128-129
    Liverwort 118
    Maidenhair tree 123
    Maple 127
    Monocotyledons 126-127
    Moss 119
    Parasitic plants 163
    Passion flower 130
    Peach 131
    Perennials 130-131
    Sago palm 123
    Strawberry 128
    String of hearts 157
    Vegetative reproduction 154-155
    Water fern 158
    Welwitschia 123
    Woody plants 130-131
    Woody stem 134
    Yew 123
Stem bases
    Bulbil 155
    Guzmania lingulata 162-163
Stem branch 129
Stem bulbils 155
Stem cambium 126
Stem cells 606, 607
Stem head 376
Stempost
    74-gun ship 381
    Dhow 376
    Longboat 380
    Sailing warship 376
    Viking ships 374-375
Stem projections 156
Stem segments 129
Stem succulents 113, 156-157

Stem tubers 128, 154
Stencil 446
Step
    74-gun ship 381
    ARV light aircraft 424
    BE 2B bomber 404
    Blériot XI monoplane 401
    Medieval building 467
    Modern building 499
    Neoclassical building 483
    Steam-powered Cugnot 334
    Twentieth-century building 495
    Wooden sailing ship 378
Stephenson, Robert 324
Stepped roof 481
Stepped stempost 375
Stepped sternpost 375
Sterile hairs 117, 119
Sterile ray 119
Sterile ray floret 142
Sterile shoot 120
Sterile whorl 116
Stern
    74-gun ship 381
    Iron paddlesteamer 392
    Kayak 560
    Sailing dinghy 561
    Wooden sailing ship 378-379
Sterna hirundo 193
Sternal artery 173
Sternal bone 96, 102
Stern balustrade 373
Stern carving 381
Stern framing 392
Stern gallery 397
Stern lantern 379
Sternocleidomastoid muscle 226-227, 229
Sternohyoid muscle 229
Sternpost
    Greek galley 572
    Roman corbita 373
    Sailing warship 377
    Single scull 560
    Viking ships 374-375
    Wooden sailing ship 378
Stern quarter gallery 379
Stern rope 387
Stern section 392
Sternum
    Bird 189
    Domestic cat 195
    Elephant 201
    Hare 197
    Horse 199
    Human 218
    Kangaroo 206
    Seal 204
Stern walk 395
Stibnite 268
Stick insect 192
Stiff brush 436
Stifle 198
Stigma
    Damselfly 168
    Dicotyledon flower 126-127
    Fertilization 146-147
    Flower 140-143
    Pollination 144-145
Stigma remains 146-147, 150-151
Stilt 494
Stilted arch 468
Sting 170
Stinging cells 166
Stinkhorn 114
Stipe 114-115, 116-117
Stippled effect 442
Stipule
    Begonia 129
    Everlasting pea 129

Passion flower 130
Rose 131
Seedling leaf 152
St. John's wort 145
Strawberry 128
Stirrup
    Crossbow 548
    Ossicles of middle ear 242
    Saddle 555
Stoa 460
    Ancient Roman building 463, 465
    Islamic building 488
Stock
    74-gun ship 380
    Danforth anchor 386
    Roman anchor 372
Stockless anchor 386
Stöfler 40
Stoker's seat 334
Stolons 154
Stomach
    Barnacle 173
    Bird 189
    Bony fish 181
    Chimpanzee 202
    Cow 198
    Crayfish 173
    Dogfish 179
    Dolphin 205
    Domestic cat 195
    Elephant 200
    Frog 182
    Human 214, 248
    Jellyfish 167
    Lizard 185
    Octopus 176
    Rabbit 196
    Ruminants 198
    Snail 177
    Starfish 174
    Tortoise 187
Stomach throw 556
Stomata
    Dryland plants 156-157
    Golden barrel cactus 156
    Haworthia truncata 157
    Monocotyledon leaf 126
    Photosynthesis role 138-139
    Pine needle 124
    Wetland plants 158
Stone
    Succulent fruits 148
    Lithographic printing 446, 448
    Sculpture 452
Stone canal 174, 175
Stone plate 446, 448
Stony-iron meteorite 52
Stony meteorite 52
Stop button 572
Stop control 587
Stop lamp assembly 352
Stop signal 330
Stopwatch 524
Storage organs
    Bulb 155
    Corm 155
    Rhizome 155
    Scale leaf 155
    Seed 152
    Succulent tissue 156-157
    Swollen stem 113, 155
    Tubers 128, 155
    Underground 154-155
Store button 521
Stores pylon 420-421
Stork 188
Storm 303
Straddle wire 358, 359
Straight 555
Straight four cylinder arrangement 345
Straight gouge 452
Straight handlebar 361

Strake
  Concorde 416-417
  Ironclad 393
  Roman corbita 372
  Viking ships 374-375
Strapontin 337
Strap-shaped leaf 162
Strata 276
  Faults and folds 60-61
  Sedimentary rocks 276
Stratocumulus cloud 302
Stratosphere
  Earth's atmosphere 300-301
  Jupiter's atmosphere 45
  Mars' atmosphere 43
  Saturn's atmosphere 47
Stratum basale 235
Stratum corneum 255
Stratum granulosum 235
Stratum spinosum 235
Stratus cloud 302
Strawberry 128, 150
Straw butt 549
Streak 270-271
Stream
  Glaciers 286-287
  Groundwater system 293
  Spring examples 292
Streamed Internet radio on-screen display 577
Streamed Internet video on-screen display 577
Streaming 577
Streamlined spinner 407
Strengthening tissue
  Fern rachis 121
  Horsetail stem 120
  Marram grass 113
  Monocotyledon leaf 126
  Stems 134-135
  Water lily leaf 159
Stress 61
Stretcher
  Brickwork 485
  Nineteenth-century building 492
  Single scull 560
Stretches 555
Striated effect 442
Striation 46
Strike
  Baseball 536
  Baseball umpire signal 537
  Slope structure 60
Striker 524
Strike-slip fault 61
Strike-slip fault lake 293
Strike zone 536
Strindberg 35
String
  Acoustic guitar 512-513
  Cello 511
  Concert grand piano 515
  Double bass 511
  Electric guitar 513
  Harp 511
  Upright piano 514
  Viola 511
String arm 511
String course
  Ancient Roman building 465
  Cathedral dome 487
  Medieval building 466-467
  Nineteenth-century building 493
Stringed instruments 510, 511
  Guitar 512, 513
  Orchestral arrangement 504, 505
Strings
  Guitar 512-513
  Racket 544

Violin 510
Strix aluco 190
Strobili 120
Stroke judge 558
Stroke play 546
Strokes 546
Stroke-side oar 560
Stroma 139
Stroma thylakoid 139
Strongylocentrotus purpuratus 175
Strontium 310
Strop 383
Strut 383
  Dome 484, 486
  Gothic building 473
  Marble sculpture support 453
  Neoclassical building 479
  Paddlesteamer 390
  Timpanum 519
Strut insert 540
Struthio camelus 188
  Egg 193
Struthiolaria 279
Struthiomimus 84, 87
Stub axle 424
Stud
  Ancient Roman mill 464
  Gothic building 473
  Mid West single rotor engine 410
Studding sail boom 378
Studding sail yard 378
Studio Elvira 495
Study 477
Stuffing box 390
Stump
  Coastline 295
  Wicket 558
Stupa 490-491
Stupica 491
Sturgeon 180
Style 140-143
  Fertilization 146-147
  Monocotyledon flower 126
  Pitcher plant 113
  Pollination 144-145
  Rowan fruit 131
Style of the gnomon 377
Style remains
  Dry fruit 150-151
  Fruit development 146-147
  Succulent fruit 148-149
Stylet 167
Stylobate 460
Styloglossus muscle 244
Styloid process 220, 243
Stylus 568
Styracosaurus 102, 103
Subacute leaf apex 136-137
Subarachnoid space 237
Subclavian artery 215, 251, 253
Subclavian vein 253
Subduction 58
Subduction zone 281
Subframe 351
Subgenital pit 167
Subglacial stream 287
Sublimation 307
Sublingual fold 245
Sublingual gland 244-245
Submandibular gland 244
Submarine 396-397
Submarine canyon 298
Submerged atoll 299
Submerged glacial valleys 294-295
Submerged river valleys 294
Subopercular bone 181
Substitutions 552, 550
Superheater 325
Substrate 112
Substratum 115

Subsurface current 297
Subtropical jet stream 300
Succulent fruits 148-149, 150
  Bramble 130
  Development 146-147
  Peach 131
  Rowan 131
Succulent leaves 128, 157
Succulent plants 156-157
Succulents 112
  Leaf 157
  Stem 156-157
  Stem and root 157
  Trailing stem 157
Succulent stem 129
Sucker
  Lamprey 178
  Octopus 176
Sucking stomach 170
Suction reduction control 593
Sugar
  Fermentation 312
  Formation 138
  Photosynthesis 315
  Transport 139
Sulcus terminalis 244
Sulky 554-555
Sulphates 269, 296
Sulphides 268
Sulphur 39, 268
  Periodic table 311
Sulphur dioxide 37
Sulphuric acid 36-37
Sulphurous gases 273
Sumatra 265
Sumigi 490
Summer petiole 160
Summit caldera 42
Sump 343, 344-345
Sump pan 354
Sun 32-33, 38
  Atmosphere 301
  Comet tails 48
  Earth's energy 314
  Electromagnetic radiation 314-315
  Energy emission from Sun 22
  Light 318
  Milky Way 14
  Objects in Universe 11
  Oceans and seas 296-297
  Ozone formation 64
  Solar eclipse 32
  Solar System 30-31
  Stars 22-23
Sundew 160
Sundial 376, 377
Sunflower 140, 142, 145
Sunken stoma 157
Sunlight and photosynthesis 138
  solar power 605
Sun roof 341
Sun scoop 498
Sunspots 32-33
Sun visor 350, 353
Supai group 277
Superclusters 10
Supercooling 307
Supercool liquid 306-307
Superficial peroneal nerve 238
Superficial skeletal muscles 226-227
Superfluid neutrons 28
Super-giant slalom (Super-G) skiing 552
Supergiant stars
  Massive stars 26
  Stars 22-23
  Stellar black hole 29
Supergranule 33
Superheater 325
Superior articular facet 222

Superior articular process 222-223
Superior concha 212
Superior laryngeal nerve 244
Superior longitudinal muscle 245
Superior meatus 245
Superior mesenteric artery 253, 256
Superior mesenteric trunk 257
Superior mesenteric vein 253
Superior nasal concha 245
Superior oblique muscle 241
Superior orbital fissure 221
Superior ramus of pubis 224, 257
Superior rectus muscle 241
Superior sagittal sinus 212, 237
Superior thyroid artery 244
Superior vena cava 215, 251, 252-253, 255
Supernova
  Massive stars 26-27
  Nebulae and star clusters 16
  Neutron stars and black holes 29
Supernova remnant
  Nebulae and star clusters 16-17
  X-ray image of Crab Nebula 28
Supersonic flight 416
Supersonic jetliners 416-417
Supersonic transport 416-417
Supporter 381
Supporting tissue
  Bishop pine stem 125
  Dicotyledon leaf 126
  Stems 134-135
Supraoccipital bone 181
Supraoccipital crest 84
Supraesophageal ganglion 173
Supraorbital fissure 221
Supraorbital foramen 221
Supraorbital margin 213, 220, 221
Supraorbital notch 213
Supraorbital ridge
  Chimpanzee 202
  Stegaceras 100
  Styracosaurus 102
Suprarenal gland 257
Suprarenal vein 257
Suprascapula 183
Suprasternal notch 211
Surangular bone 102
Surcingle loop 555
Surface areas 623
Surface currents 296-297
Surface deposits 273
Surface layer 293
Surface ocean current 296
Surface streams 284
Surface temperature 39
  Stars 22
  Structure of main sequence star 24
  Structure of Mars 43
  Structure of Mercury 35
  Structure of Neptune 51
  Structure of red giant 25
  Structure of red supergiant 26
  Structure of Venus 37
  Sun 33
Surface terrain 284

Surface vegetation 282
Surface winds 300
Surrogate mother 607
Surround sound 584
Surround sound special effect plug-in 521
Surveillance RADAR 397
Suspended erratic 286
Suspension
  "Deltic" diesel-electric locomotive 327
  Microlight 426
  Motocross racing 368
  Motorcycle 364
Suspension arm 350-351
Suspension linkage 362
Suspension spring 350
Suspension strut 340, 351
Suspension top mount 340
Sustaining pedal 514, 515
Suture 202
Su-wei 376
Suzuki RGV500 368, 369
Swab hitch 387, 389
Swallow 383
Swallow-hole 284
Swamp 290-291
Swan neck ornament 373
Swash plate 344
Swash zone 294
S waves 63
Sweat duct 235
Sweat gland 234-235
Sweat pore 234-235
Sweep rowing 560
Sweep-rowing boat 561
Sweeping low throw 556
Sweet chestnut 136, 144, 150
Sweetgum 76
Sweet pea 128
Sweet potato 154
Swell manual 514
Swell of muzzle 395
Swell pedal 514
Swell stop 514
Swifting tackle 377
Swim bladder 178, 180-181
Swimmeret 172
Swimming 558, 559
Swimming pool 558
Swimwear 558
Swingarm 364, 368
"Swing-wings" 420
Switch 316
Switchboard room 397
Switch end casting 598-599
Switch gear 314
Swivel becket 382
Swivels
  Mooring and anchoring 386
  Angling 562, 563
Swivel suspension ring 377
Swollen leaf base 154-155
Swollen stem base
  Guzmania lingulata 163
  Kedrostis africana 113
  Oxalis sp. 157
Swollen stem 154-155
Sword 556-557
Sycamore 131, 150-151
Sycamore beam 560
Syconium 148
Syenite 275
Symbiosis
  Lichens 114
  Mycorrhizal association 133
Symbols
  Biology 591
  Chemistry 591
  Communication 108
  Mathematics 591
  Music 502, 503

Physics 591
Symphony orchestra 504, 505
Synapsid reptile skull 67
Synaptic knob 228, 239
Synaptic vesicle 259
Syncarpous gynoecium 140
Synchiropus splendidus 180
Synchronized elevator 423
Syncline 60, 61, 62
Synclinorium 61
Synergid nucleus 147
Synsacrum 189
Synthesizer 520
Synthetic brush 436, 438
Synthetic flax 384
Synthetic hog hair brush 442
Synthetic materials 306
Synthetic polymer 306
Synthetic resin 442
Synthetic ropes 388
Synthetic sable brush 442
Synthetic strings 544, 545
Synthetic wash brush 438, 442
Syria Planum 42, 43
Systems connector 413
System unit 566

T
Tabernacle 463, 474, 476
Tab hinge 415
Tablet flower 488, 491
Tabling 372, 384
Tabular habit 271
Tacan aerial 420
Tachybaptus ruficollis 190
Tack 375
Tackling
  American football 526
  Australian rules football 528, 529
  Rugby 551
  Soccer 524
Tactical air navigation (Tacan) aerial 420
Tadpoles 182-183, 192
Taenia 460
Taenia colica 249
Taffrail 378, 381
Tail
  Amphibian 182
  Anchisaurus 89
  BE 2B bomber 404
  Caiman 187
  Calligraphy character 445
  Corythosaurus 98
  Crocodilians 186
  Deer hopper dry fly 563
  Dolphin 205
  Dunkeld wet fly 563
  87
  Hare 196
  Hawker Tempest components 409
  Herrerasaurus 86
  Horse 198
  Ichthyostega 80
  Iguanodon 96
  Iguanodonts 96
  Kangaroo 206
  Lion 195
  Lizard 184-185
  Lungfish 81
  Monkey 202
  Ornithopods 96
  Pachycephalosaurus 100
  Prehensile 202
  Rabbit 196-197
  Rat 196
  Rattlesnake 185
  Rigging 382-383

Salamander 182
Sauropodomorpha 88
Schweizer helicopter 423
Scorpion 170
Ski 552-553
Stegoceras 101
Stegosaurus 93
Tadpole 185
Triceratops 102
Tyrannosaurus 84
Westlothiana 81
Tail area 78
Tail boom 425
Tail bud 260
Tail bumper 417
Tail club 95
Tail cone 416-417, 418
Tail crest 187
Taileron 420-421
Tail fairing 409
Tail feathers 188
Tail fluke 205
Tail-gate 348
Tail gunner's compartment 408
Tail-gun turret 408
Tail-light
  BMW R/60 362
  Harley-Davidson FLHS Electra Glide 362
  Honda CB750 363
  Vespa Grand Sport 160 Mark 1 363
Tailpiece 510, 511
Tail-pin 510
Tail pipe 340
Tailplane
  ARV light aircraft 424
  BAe-146 jetliner 415
  BE 2B tail 405
  Biplanes and triplanes 402-403
  Blackburn monoplane 401
  Blériot XI monoplane 401
  Curtiss biplane 399
  Hawker Tempest 409
  Lockheed Electra airliner 407
  Schleicher glider 426
Tailplane fairing 415
Tailplane root 409
Tailplane tip 407, 415
Tailrace 314
Tail rod 390
Tail rotor 422-423
Tail-rotor drive shaft 422, 423
Tail rotor gearbox 423
Tail shield 78
Tailskid
  ARV light aircraft 424
  Avro triplane 403
  BE 2B bomber 405
  Blackburn monoplane 400-401
  LVG CVI fighter 405
Tail spike 92
Tail spine 79
Tail unit 568
Tailwheel
  Avro biplane 402
  B-17 bomber 408
  Hawker Tempest fighter 409
  Lockheed Electra airliner 407
  Schleicher glider 426
Tailwheel leg 401
Take-off and landing skid 398
Take-up spool 587
Takla Makan Desert 265
Talc 270-271
Tallow coating 379
Talonavicular ligament 232

Talons 188
Talus 282-283
Talus bone 232
Tamarins 202, 203
Tambourine 504, 518
Tam-tam 504, 516
Tandem wings 402
Tank 392
Tank drain tap 407
Tank inspection access 417
Tank support 339
Tantalum 510
Tantalus Fossae 43
Tapeats sandstone 277
Tape guide 587
Tape reader 582
Tape reading head 582
Tapir 198
Tappet 343
Tappet adjustor 367
Tap root 128
Tarantula Nebula 26-27
  Large Magellanic Cloud 12
Tarantulas 170-171
Target areas 556, 557
Target hole 546
Target pistol 548, 549
Target shooting 548, 549
Tarn 293
  U-shaped valley formation 287
Tarsal bone
  Albertosaurus 84 87
  Iguanodon 97
Tarsals
  Crocodile 186
  Domestic cat 195
  Elephant 201
  Frog 183
  Hare 197
  Horse 199
  Kangaroo 206
  Lizard 184
  Platypus 206
  Rhesus monkey 202
  Seal 204
Tarsiers 202
Tarsomere 13
Tarsometatarsus 189
Tarsus
  Beetle 168
  Bird 188
  Human 219
  Scorpion 170
  Spider 171
Tas-de-charge 469
Tasmanian devil 207
Taste 244
Taste bud 244
Tau Orionis 18
Taurus 19, 20
Taurus mountains 77
Tau Sagittarii 21
Tawny owl 190
Taxiing light 414, 420
Taxus baccata 70, 123
Tea clipper 392
Team crest 531
Team jersey 529
Team name 533
Tear fault 61
Technetium 510
Technosaurus 69
Tee 546
Teeing ground 546
Tee peg 547
Teeth
  Ankylosaurus 92
  Bear 106
  Caiman 186
  Canine 194, 202
  Carnassial 194
  Carnivores 194
  Ceratopsian 100
  Cheek 194
  Chimpanzee 202

Crocodilians 186
  Extinct shark 67
  Hadrosaur 96
  Hominid 108
  Horse 105
  Human 246-247
  Iguanodont 96
  Incisor 194, 196, 201, 202
  Lamprey 178
  Leaf-shaped 88-89
  Molar 194, 201, 202
  Ornithopod 96
  Premolar 194, 202
  Rabbit 196
  Rodents 196
  Theropod 84
  Thyreophoran 92
  Venus fly-trap 160
Teeth development 246
Tegenaria gigantea 171
Telephone line 576
Telephone line cord 572
Telephone on hook wiring harness 572
Telescope, space 612-613
Telescopic damper 326, 329
Telescopic fork
  Harley-Davidson FLHS Electra Glide 363
  Honda CB750 363
  Honda VF750 364
  Husqvarna Motocross TC610 368
  Motorcycle 364
  Suzuki RGV500 368
  Weslake Speedway motorcycle 369
Telescopic sight 548, 549
Telescopic strut 416
Television 315
Telltale 545
Tellurium 311
Tellus Regio 36, 37
Tellus Tessera 37
Telson 172
  Fossil 79
TEM 610, 611
Tempe Fossae 43
Tempera 432, 433
Temperate latitudes 302
Temperature
  Atmosphere 300-301
  Chemical reactions 312-313
  Formation of black hole 29
  Germination 152
  Matter 306-307
  Mineral resources 280
  Oceans and seas 296
  Stellar black hole 29
  Weather 302-303
Temperature and pressure sensor 418
Temperature and steam control dial 594
Temperature changes
  Atmosphere 301
  Oceans and seas 296
  Weathering and erosion 282
Temperature scales 621
Temperature warning 567
Tempered pigment 432
Temple 484-485
  Ancient Egyptian 458
  Ancient Greek 460-461
  Ancient Roman 462-463
  Asian 490
Temple blocks 516
Temple Butte limestone 277
Temple Cap sandstone 276
Temple of Amon-Re 458-459
Temple of Aphaia 461

Temple of Athena Polias 460
Temple of Heaven 490
Temple of Isis 459
Temple of Mallikarjuna 491
Temple of Neptune 460-461
Temple of Vesta 462-463
Temple of Virupaksha 490-491
Tempo 504
Temporal bone
  Chimpanzee 202
  Human 220-221, 242
Temporal lobe 257
Temporalis muscle 226-227, 229
Tendon
  Achilles 232-233
  Annular 241
  Calcanean 232-233
  Extensor digitorum longus 233
  Extensor digitorum 231
  Extensor hallucis longus 233
  Flexor digitorum 231, 87
  Palmaris longus 231
  Peroneus brevis 233
Tendril
  Arabesque 480
  Clematis 130
  Dogfish egg 192
  Everlasting pea 129
  Monkey cup 161
  Passion flower 130
Tennis 544
Tennis racket 544
Tenon
  Flax spinning mill 492
  Hull plank fastening 373
Tenor drum 518-519
Tenor joint 508
Tenor mute 507
Tenor note strings 515
Tenor saxophone 509
Tenor voice 502
Tension
  Drums 518
  Faults and folds 60-61
  Mountain building 62
Tension-column 497
Tension control 552
Tension key 518, 519
Tension member 499
Tension pulley 360
Tension rod 518, 519
Tension screw 518
Tensor fasciae latae muscle 226
Tensor tympani muscle 243
Tentacle
  Coelentrates 166
  Jellyfish 167
  Molluscs 176-177
  Scallop 176
  Sea anemone 166-167
  Snail 177
Tenth century
  Building 490
  Style 468
Tepal scar 140
Tepal
  Flower parts 140, 143
  Monocotyledons 126
  Peruvian lily 129
Terbium 311
Teres major muscle 227
Teres minor muscle 227
Tergum plate 173
  Egg 193
Terminal 586
Terminal box 317
Terminal bronchiole 254
Terminal bud
  Bishop pine 124

Horse chestnut 130
London plane 134
Rhizome 155
Root tuber 154-155
Stems 154
Stolon 154
Terminal ileum 249
Terminal lake 286
Terminal moraine
  Glaciers 286
  Rivers 289
Terminal pinna 136
Terminal ring 259
Terminus 286
Terrace
  Asian building 490-491
  Modern building 497-499
  Twentieth-century building 494-495
Terracotta clay 455
Terrain-following radar 420
Terrapin 186-187
Terrestrial animal 74
Terrestrial mammal 104
Terrigenous sediment 299
Tertiary bronchus 215
Tertiary period 57, 74, 75
  Fossil record 279
Tessellation 489
Tessera 450, 489
Test 174-175
Testa 152
  Dry fruit 150-151
  Embryo development 147
  Epigeal germination 153
  Hypogeal germination 152
  Succulent fruit seed 148-149
Testicle 259
Testicular artery 257
Testicular vein 257
Testis
  Barnacle 173
  Dolphin 205
  Domestic cat 195
  Human 259
  Rabbit 196
Test tube 313
Tetanurae 83
Tethus Regio 36
Tethys 46
Tethys Sea
  Cretaceous period 73
  Jurassic period 71
  Tertiary period 74, 75
  Triassic period 69
Tetragonal system 270
Tetrahedron 623
Tetralophodon 75, 104
Text 444
Text messages 588
Textured papers 441
Textured scraper 593
TGV electric high-speed train 329
Thalamian 373
Thalamus 236-237
Thalassiosira sp. 116
Thalictrum delavayi 137
Thallium 311
Thalloid liverwort 118
Thallus
  Algae 116-117
  Lichen 114
  Liverwort 118
  Seaweed 116-117
T-handle auger 374
Thar Desert 265
Tharsis Tholus 43
Thatched roof 477
Thaumasia Fossae 43
Themis Regio 36
The Plough 19
Therapeutic cloning 606

Theobroma cacao 148
Therapsids 104
Thermal/electrical insulation 596, 597
Thermal insulation 613
Thermals 426
Thermocouple bus-bar 419
Thermogram 214
Thermosphere
  Earth's atmosphere 300
  Mars' atmosphere 43
  Venus' atmosphere 37
Thermostat 411
Theropoda 83
Theropods 84-87
Thesium alpinium 145
Theta1 Sagittarii 21
Theta Andromedae 19
Theta Pegasi 19
Thetis Regio 36
Thick skull 46
Thigh
  Anchisaurus 89
  Bird 188
  Corythosaurus 98
  Gorilla 203
  Horse 198
  Human 211
  Iguanodon 96
  Kangaroo 207
  Lion 195
  Psittacosaurus 103
  Stegoceras 101
  Stegosaurus 92
  Triceratops 102
  Tyrannosaurus 84
Thigh musculature 90
Thigh pad 527
Thimble
  Harness racing 555
  Rigging 383, 384
Third-century building 465
Third home 541
Third man 538, 541
Third rail 328
Thirteenth century
  Building 467, 469-471
  Style 470
Thirty-five mm file strip holder 570
Thistle funnel 313
Thole pin 380
Thoracic cavity 255
Thoracic leg 169
Thoracic nerve 238
Thoracic pleura 78
Thoracic segment 79
Thoracic vertebrae
  Crocodile 186
  Domestic cat 195
  Hare 197
  Horse 199
  Human 222
  Kangaroo 206
  Platypus 206
  Rhesus monkey 202
  Seal 204
Thoracolumbar vertebrae
  Elephant 201
  Lizard 184
Thorax
  Cirripedia 172
  Human 211
  Insects 168-169
Thorium 310
Thornback ray 179
Thoroughbred horse 554
Thranite 373
Thread 167
Three-blade main rotor 423
Three-cylinder Anzani engine 401
Three-cylinder engine 425
Three-lobed stigma 143

Three-masted square-rigged ship 375
Three-point line 532
Three pounder 395
Three-toed ungulates 198
Threshold 463
Throat
  Angling hook 562
  Bird 188
  Danforth anchor 386
  Human 212, 244-245
  Lacrosse crosse 541
  Racketball racket 545
  Squash racket 545
  Tennis racket 544
Throatlatch 199
Throttle
  Avro triplane 402
  Curtiss biplane 398
  "Rocket" steam locomotive 324
  Suzuki RGV500 363
  Vespa Grand Sport 160
  Mark 1 363
  Weslake Speedway motorcycle 369
Throttle butterfly 345
Throttle cable 350
  Harley-Davidson FLHS Electra Glide 363
  Husqvarna Motocross TC610 368
  Kirby BSA racing sidecar 369
  Suzuki RGV500 369
  Weslake Speedway motorcycle 369
Throttle lever 419, 425
Throttle linkage
  Ford Model T 338
  Jaguar V12 engine 345
  Oldsmobile trim 337
  Renault Clio 351
Throttle wheel 342
Throw
  Judo 556
  Structure of a fault 60
Thrower 394
Throw-in 532
Thrushes 188
Thrust 543
Thrust fault 61
Thrust plate 601
Thrust-reverser 421
Thulium 311
Thumb 211, 230-231
Thumb-claw
  Anchisaurus 89
  Apatosaurus 83
  Baryonyx 85, 85
  Massospondylus 83, 89
  Plateosaurus 88
Thumbhole 384
Thumb knot 389
Thumb piston 514
Thumb-spike 96-97
Thwart 373, 375, 380
Thylakoid 139
Thymine 216
Thyreophora 83
Thyreophorans 92-93, 94-95
Thyristor converter 328
Thyrohyoid membrane 244
Thyrohyoid muscle 229, 244
Thyroid cartilage 245, 255
Thyroid gland 214-215, 217, 244-245, 255
Tibetan plateau 63
Tibia
  Archaeopteryx 85
  Beetle 168
  Butterfly 169
  Crocodile 186
  Diplodocus 90
  Domestic cat 195

Elephant 201
Eryops 81
Gallimimus 86
Hare 197
Horse 199
Human 219, 232-233
Iguanodon 96-97
Kangaroo 206
Lizard 184
Parasaurolophus 99
Plateosaurus 88
Platypus 206
Rhesus monkey 202
Scorpion 170
Seal 204
Spider 171
Stegoceras 101
Stegosaurus 95
Struthiomimus 87
Toxodon 107
Triceratops 102
Turtle 187
Tyrannosaurus 84
Tibiale 183
Tibial flexor muscle 97
Tibialis anterior muscle 226, 233
Tibialis posterior muscle 233
Tibiofibula 183
Tibiotarsus 189
Tidal bulge 297
Tidal currents 296-297, 298
Tidal flow 296
Tidal levels 295
Tidal power 604
Tidal river-mouth 295
Tidal scour 298
Tidal waves 58
Tides 294, 297
Tie
  Basketball match 532
  Bordino Steam Carriage 334
  Musical notation 502, 503
  Tie-beam
    Ancient Roman mill 464
    Dome 486
    Gothic church 473
    Neoclassical building 479
Tie plate 393
Tierceron 485
Tie rod 354, 340
Tiger seat 334
Tiger shark 178-179
Tight end 526
Tight-head prop 550
Tile
  Dome 486
  Islamic mosque 488
  Modern building 499
  Neoclassical building 482
  Renaissance building 476-477
Tiled roof 495
Tilia sp. 134
Tilia x europaea 143
Tiller
  Dhow 376
  First cars 334-335
  Longboat 380
  Oldsmobile trim 337
  Roman corbita 373
  Sailing dinghy 561
  Steamboat with paddle wheels 391
  Viking ships 374-375
Tilt and rotation
  Jupiter 44
  Mars 42
  Mercury 34
  The Moon 40
  Neptune 50
  Pluto 51
  Saturn 46

Uranus 48
Venus 36
Timber frame
  Ancient Roman building 462, 464-465
  Dome 486
  Medieval building 466-467
  Renaissance building 477
Timber head 380
Timber rafter 492
Timber trellis 603
Timbre 516
Time interval signal 330
Timekeeper
  Basketball 532
  Fencing contest 557
  Handball 535
  Judo contest 556
  Lacrosse 541
  Netball 535
  Swimming 558
Time signature 502
Time switch 598
Time-trial bicycle 360
Time zones 618-619
Timing chain 343, 345
Timing chest 343
Timing gear 367
Timpani 503, 504, 505, 518
Timpanum 519
Tin 311
  Mineralization zones 281
  Squash 545
Tinatin Planitia 37
Tinted paper 441
Tip of dodder stem 163
Tip ring 563
Tip section 563
Tissue culture 607
Titania 48
Titanium 310
Titanohyrax 74
Toad 182
Toadflax 129
Toaster 598-599
To Do list button 568
Toe
  Albertosaurus 84
  Anchisaurus 89
  Archaeopteryx 85
  Bird 188
  Caiman 186-187
  Corythosaurus 98
  Golf club 547
  Gorilla 203
  Herrerasaurus 86
  Human 211, 232-233
  Iguanodon 96-97
  Lion 194
  Lizard 184
  Pachycephalosaurus 100
  Psittacosaurus 103
  Stegoceras 101
  Tyrannosaurus 84
Toe clip 360
Toenail
  Elephant 200
  Gorilla 203
  Human 233
Toe piston 514
Toe strap 358-359
Toggle switch 513
Toilet 416, 483
Tolstoj 35
Tomb 458-459, 489
Tomb of Itimad-ud-daula 489
Tomb of King Tjetji 459
Tombolo 294
Tom-toms 518-519
Tondo brush 434
Tone editor control 520
Tonehole 509
Tone pattern selector 520

Tongs 321
Tongue
  Allosaurus 85
  Caiman 186
  Chimpanzee 202
  Corythosaurus 98
  Cow 198
  Dolphin 205
  Domestic cat 195
  Elephant 200
  Human 212, 226, 244, 248
  Iguanodon 97
  Lamprey 178
  Lion 194
  Rabbit 196
  Rattlesnake 185
  Ski boot 552
T'on-wei 376
Tool and battery box 335
Toolbar 576
Tool/brush-head connector 593
Tool or wand cuff 593
Tools
  Rigging 382-383
  Sailmaking 384
  Viking boatbuilding 374
Tooth
  Acanthostega 80
  Anchisaurus 89
  Ankylosaurus 94
  Arsinoitherium 104
  Australopithecus 108
  Baryonyx 83
  Camarasaurus 91
  Diplodocus 90
  Dragon prowhead 374
  Eryops 80
  Euoplocephalus 94
  Heterodontosaurus 83
  Homo habilis 108
  Human 108, 246-247, 248
  Iguanodon 96
  Lambeosaurus 99
  Moeritherium 105
  Pastels application 440
  Phiomia 105
  Plateosaurus 88
  Protoceratops 102
  Smilodon 107
  Triceratops 103
  Tyrannosaurus 84
Toothless beak
  Ankylosaurs 92
  Corythosaurus 98
  Euoplocephalus 94
  Gallimimus 86
  Theropods 84
  Triceratops 102
Topaz 271
Topcastle 375, 377
Topgallant mast
  Battleship 395
  Sailing warship 377
  Wooden sailing ship 378-379
Top hose 351
Topmast 377, 378
Topping lift 380
Topping-up valve 561
Top-plate 464
Top race 359
Topsail
  74-gun ship 379
  Double topsail schooner 385
  Junk 376
Topset strata 283
Topside strake 393
Top sliding block 437
Tornado GR1A 420-421
Torosaurus 73
Toroweap formation 276
Torpedo 394-397
Torque arm 364, 365
Torquemeter mount 419
Torque tube 338-339

Torque tube assembly 425
Torrential rain 302
Torsional vibration damper 410-411
Torsion bar 350
Torso frame 609
Torso roll motor 609
Tortillon 440, 441
Tortoise 186
Tortoise skull 77
Torus
  Ancient Roman building 463
  Asian building 490
  Dome 486
  Gothic building 470
  Medieval building 467-469
  Renaissance building 475, 477
  Shapes: solid 623
Total solar eclipse 32
Tote board 555
Touch-down 526
Touch-in goal line 530
Touch judge 530
Touch line
  Rugby 530
  Soccer 524
Touchpad 567
Touchpiece 509
Touch-sensitive fingertips 609
Tour buses 332
Tour de César 466
Touring bicycle 360, 361
Tourmaline 269
Tower
  Ancient Roman building 465
  Asian building 490-491
  Clock 493
  Gothic church 472
  Islamic building 488
  Medieval building 466-467, 468-469
  Modern building 496-497
  Nineteenth-century building 492-493
  Renaissance building 476
  Twentieth-century building 495
Tower Bridge 492-493
Tower vault 469
Towing fairlead 395
Towing hook 355, 426
Town Hall 495
Toxodon 76, 106, 107
TPU connector 571
Trabecula 250-251
Trace fossils 278
Tracery
  Gothic building 470-473
  Nineteenth-century building 493
Trachea
  Bird 189
  Brachiosaurus 91
  Chimpanzee 202
  Dolphin 205
  Domestic cat 195
  Elephant 200
  Gallimimus 86
  Human 212, 215, 244-245, 248, 255
  Lizard 185
  Rabbit 196
  Spider 170
  Tortoise 187
Trachelion 460
Trachycarpus fortunei 127, 130
Track 413
Track control arm 340
Track events 542, 543
Track gauge 330, 331

Track rod
  Elegance and utility 336-337
  Ford Model T 338-339
  Renault Clio 351
Track shoe 543
Traction motor 328
Trade winds 300
Traffic congestion 332
Traffic surveillance 422
Tragus 242
Trailboard 379
Trailing arm 340
Trailing edge
  BAe-146 jetliner components 413, 414, 415
  BE 2B tail 405
  BE 2B wings 404
  Hawker Tempest components 409
  Pegasus Quasar microlight 426-427
Trailing-link arm 414
Trailing wheel 324
Train equipment 330-331
Training gear 396
Trains
  Diesel 326-327
  Electric 328-329
  High-speed 328-329
  Steam 324-325
Trams 332-333
Transaxle 340
Transept
  Gothic church 470, 473
  Medieval church 468-469
Transfer port 542
Transformation 168
Transformer 314, 328
Transform fault 59
Transistor 584
Transitional cell mucosa 257
Transition metals 310, 311
Transit plug 397
Translucent crystal 271
Translucent impasto glaze 443
Translucent white marble 453
Translucent "window" 157
Transmission 350-351
Transmission adaptor plate 344
Transmission electron microscope (TEM) 610, 611
Transmission system 326, 366
Transom
  74-gun ship 381
  Junk 376
  Longboat 380
  North wing, Chateau de Montal 476
  Sailing warship 377
Transparency holder 570
Transparent glassy crystal 271
Transparent lower drumhead 518
Transparent tissue 160
Transparent wash 439
Transpiration 136
Transponder aerial 423
Transportation lock 571
Transport system 332
Transport tissue
  Golden barrel cactus 156
  Monocotyledons 126
  Photosynthesis 138-139
Transversary 377
Transverse arch 485
  Baroque church 479
  Medieval church 468-469

Transverse colon 249
Transverse dune 283
Transverse foramen 222
Transverse leaf spring 338
Transverse line 535
Transverse process
  Human 222-223
  Plateosaurus 89
  Tyrannosaurus 85
Transverse rib 485
Transverse strut 512
Trapezium 17, 622
Trapezium bone 230
Trapezius muscle 226-227, 229
Trapezoid bone 230
Traps
  Butterwort 161
  Cobra lily 160
  Monkey cup 161
  Pitcher plant 113, 160-161
  Sundew 160
  Venus fly trap 160
Traveller 380
Travelling 553
Travertine shell 464
Tray fascia 595
Tread 477
Tread pattern 365
Treasury of Atreus 461
Treble bridge 514
Treble clef 502
Treble hook 562-563
Treble note strings 515
Treble voice 502
Tree 66-67, 130-131
  Energy storage 315
  Epiphytes 162-163
  Gymnosperms 122-125
Tree fern 112-113
Tree mallow 131
Tree root action 282
Treenail 387
Trefoil
  Gothic church 470-473
  Nineteenth-century building 493
Trefoil arch 473, 484
Trellis window 459
Trellised river drainage 288
Trembler coil box 335
Trenail 387
Trestle trees 378
Trevithick, Richard 324
Triac device 600
Trials tyre 365
Triangle
  Shapes: plane 622
  Musical instrument 504, 517
  Steamboat with paddle wheels 391
Triangle mosaic 489
Triangular buttress 484
Triangular fossa 242
Triangular horn 85
Triangular lesene 481
Triangular pediment 462
Triangular-section fuselage
  Avro triplane 403
  Bell-47 helicopter 423
  Blackburn monoplane 401
Triangulum 19, 20
Triangulum Australe 21
Triassic period 68-69
  Fossil record 279
  Geological time 57
Triatic stay 385
Tribune 467-468
Tributary
  Coastlines 295
  Rivers 288
Tributary moraine 287
Tributary stream 289

Triceps brachii muscle 227
Triceratops 100, 102-103
Trichome 156
  Marram grass 113
Triclinic system 270
Tricolpate pollen grain 145
Tricuspid valve 251
Triere 373
Trifid Nebula 16
Trifoliate leaves 128, 130
  Laburnum 137
  Oxalis sp. 157
Triforium 469
Trigger
  Air pistol 549
  Biathlon smallbore rifle 549
  Cnidocyte structure 167
Trigger hair 160
Trigger mechanism 600
Trigger position 600
Triglyph 460
Trigon 488
Trigonal system 270
Trigone 257
Trigonometry 621
Trike nacelle 426-427
Trilete mark 145
Trilobate rotor 346
Tri-lobed tail 81
Trilobites 64, 78
  Earth's evolution 56
  Fossil record 279
Trim 352-353
  1906 Renault 336-337
  Oldsmobile trim 337
  Renault Clio 350-351
  Volkswagen Beetle 341
Trimala 491
Trim piece 579
Trimtab 407, 414, 415
Trim tank 416-417
Trinity Chapel, Salisbury Cathedral 470
Tripinnate leaves 137
Triplanes 402-403
Triple bar jump 554
Triple jump 542
Triple spine 130-131
Tripod mast 394
Tripod mount 583
Tripod screw socket 581
Tripod stand
  Congas 519
  Drum kit 518
  Electronic drums 520
  Modelling stand 455
  Radial studio easel 437
Tripping palm 386
Tripping ring 372
Triquetral bone 230
Trireme 372-373
Tri-spoke wheel 361, 368, 369
Triton 50
Trochanter
  Beetle 168
  Scorpion 170
  Spider 171
Trochlea
  Baryonyx 85
  Human 241
Trochoid housing 410
Trojan two-stroke engine 342
Trolley 332
Trombone 504, 505, 506, 507
Tropeter 373
Trophoblast 260
Tropic formation 276
Tropic of Cancer
  Satellite map 265
  Surface currents 297
Tropic of Capricorn
  Satellite map 265
  Surface currents 297

Tropical cyclone 302
Tropical orchids 162
Tropical rainforest 39, 66
Troposphere
  Earth's atmosphere 300
  Jupiter's atmosphere 45
  Mars' atmosphere 43
  Saturn's atmosphere 47
  Venus' atmosphere 37
Trout 180
Trout angling 562
Truck
  Early tram 332
  Greek galley 372
  Longboat 380
  Wooden sailing ship 378-379
Trumpet 504, 506, 503
Truncate leaf base 137
Trunk
  Elephant 200-201
  Mammoth 107
  Phiomia 105
  Tree fern 112
  Woody flowering plant 130-131
Trunnion 395
Truss
  Gothic church 473
  Modern building 497-499
  Steam boat with paddle wheels 391
Truss rod 513
Try 530, 531
T-section beam 492
Tsiolkovsky 41
T-type cantilevered fin 426
Tu-144 416
Tuba 504, 505
Tube feet 174, 175
Tubeless sports tyre 365
Tuber
  Broomrape 143
  Dryland plants 157
  Horsetail 120
  Potato 128
  Vegetative reproduction 155
Tubercle
  Corythosaurus 98
  Golden barrel cactus 156
  Sea urchins 174
  Starfish 174
  Stem projections 156
Tubular bells 504, 516
Tubular chassis 355
Tubular drums 518
Tubular open cradle frame 369
Tubular petioles 160
Tuck 381
Tudor arch 484
Tufted duck 188
Tug propeller 391
Tulip mount 563
Tuner/amplifier link cables 585
Tuner settings memory microchip 585
Tungsten
  Mineralization zones 281
  Periodic table 310
Tungsten carbide tip 450
Tungsten filament 319
Tunica adventitia 252
Tunica intima 252
Tunica media 252
Tuning adjustor 510-511
Tuning pedal 519
Tuning peg 510, 511
Tuning pin 514, 515
Tuning slide 506
Tunnel
  Cave 285
  Trains 330

Tunnel vault 485
Tuojiangosaurus 92
Tupelo 137
Turbine
  Energy 314-315
  Floodgate 604
  Jet engines 418-419
  Nuclear "Hunter-Killer" submarine 397
Turbo-charged diesel engine 327
Turbocharger 356
Turbofan engine 418-419
  Landing gear 412
Turbo impeller 347
Turbojet engine 418-419
  Landing gear 412
  Supersonic jetliner 416
Turbo propeller 347
Turboprop engine 418-419
Turdus viscivorus 190
Turfed roof 602, 603
Turgai strait 71
Turkish crescent finial 488
Turk's head 383
Turnbuckle
  Avro triplane 402
  Blackburn monoplane 401
  Curtiss biplane 398
  LVG CVI fighter 405
  Rigging screw 383
Turn indicator 558
Turning force 320
Turning indicator 332, 333
Turning judge 558
Turning vane 557
Turns 555
Turntable 596
Turntable rotator 596
Turpentine 436
Turret 486
  Baroque church 481
  Battleship 394-395
  Gothic church 470-471
  Gun turret 596
  Medieval building 466, 468
  Nineteenth-century building 493
  Renaissance building 476-477
Turtle 72-73, 186-187
Tuscan capital 465
Tuscan pilaster 465, 483
Tusche 448
Tusche pen 448
Tusche stick 448
Tusk
  Elephant 200-201
  Mammoth 107
  Phiomia 105
TV mini-camera 356
TV power button 585
TV selector 577
Tweeter 584
Tweeter loudspeaker connectors 585
Twelfth century
  Building 466-467
  Church 469, 473
  Roof 490
  Style 468, 470
Twentieth-century buildings 494-495
Twin-blade main rotor 423
Twin carbon-fibre disc brake 369
Twin carburettors 427
Twin-cylinder engine
  Harley-Davidson 362
  Pegasus Quasar microlight 427
  Steam-powered Cugnot 334
Twin-domed forehead 200
Twine 384
Twin-lobed leaf blade 160

Twin nose-wheel 420
Twin rate spring 365
Twin rear axle 333
Twin rudder 372
Twin-wheel main landing gear 414
Twin-wheel nose-gear 417, 420
Twist 388
Twist dive 558, 559
Twisted wire habit 271
Two-lobed stigma 142
Two-pulley system 520
Two-seater cockpit 421
Two-stroke combustion engine 366
Two-toed ungulates 198
Two-towered gate 467
Tyagaraja 35
Tycho 40
Tye 377
Tye halyard 374
Tympan 449
Tympanic bulla 194
Tympanic canal 243
Tympanic membrane 243
Tympanum
  Frog 182
  Quail chick 193
Typhoon 302
Tyrannosaurus 73, 84-85
Tyre
  1906 Renault 336-337
  ARV light aircraft 424
  Avro triplane 402
  BAe-146 jetliner 414
  Bicycle 358-359
  Blériot XI monoplane 401
  BMW R/60 362
  Cannondale SH600 hybrid bicycle 361
  Curtiss biplane 398
  Double-decker tour bus 333
  Eddy Merckx racing bicycle 360
  First cars 334-335
  General use 365
  Lockheed Electra airliner 407
  MCW Metrobus 333
  Metal 324
  Motocross racing 368
  Motorcycle 365
  Pacing sulky 555
  Pneumatic 358, 555
  Racing car 356-357
  Renault Clio 352-353
  "Rocket" steam locomotive 324
  Rossin Italian time-trial bicycle 361
  Single-decker bus 333
  Slick racing 365
  Suzuki RGV500 368-369
  Trials 365
  Tubeless sports 365
  Volkswagen Beetle 540
  Weslake Speedway motorcycle 369
  World War I aircraft 404-405
Tyre carrier 337
Tyre tread 360, 365, 368
Tyre wall 360
Tyringham House 483

U

UHF aerial 420
UK loading gauges 331
Ulmus minor 144
Ulna
  Archaeopteryx 85
  Arsinoitherium 104
  Baryonyx 85
  Bird 189, 191

Brachiosaurus 91
Crocodile 186
Diplodocus 90
Domestic cat 195
Elephant 90, 201
Eryops 80
Euoplocephalus 94
Gallimimus 86
Hare 197
Horse 199
Human 218, 230
Iguanodon 96
Kangaroo 206
Kentrosaurus 93
Lizard 184
Parasaurolophus 99
Pareiasaur 81
Plateosaurus 88
Platypus 206
Rhesus monkey 202
Seal 204
Stegoceras 100, 101
Stegosaurus 93
Struthiomimus 87
Toxodon 106
Triceratops 102
Tuojiangosaurus 93
Turtle 187
Tyrannosaurus 84
Ulnar artery 251, 253
Ulnar nerve 251, 238
Ultramarine lapis lazuli 433
Ultrasound scan 214
Ultraviolet light 145, 319
Ultraviolet radiation 22, 319
Ultraviolet solar radiation 300
Umbels 143
Umbilical artery and vein 260
Umbilical cord 260-261
Umbilicus 211, 260
Umbo 176
Umbra 32
Umbrella 491
Umbriel 48
Umpire
  American football 526
  Badminton 545
  Baseball 536
  Cricket 538
  Hockey 540
  Lacrosse 541
  Netball 535
  Tennis 544
  Volleyball 534
Umpire signals 537
Una corda pedal 514, 515
Unarmed combat 556
Underarm pass 535
Underframe 332
Underground mycelium 115
Underground stem 154
Underground storage organs 154-155
Underground stream 284-285
Underground water
  Lake formation 292
  Rivers 288
Underhand serve 534
Under plastron 557
Under-turntable roller ring 596
Underwater mountains 298
Underwing fairing 425
Unenergized electrode 584
Ungulates 198-199
Unicellular organisms 56
Unified leaf pair 157
Uniform motion 321
"Union Pacific" diesel train 326
Unipolar neuron 239

Unison 505
Unit number 328
Units of measurement 620
Universal resource
  locator (URL) address
  577
Universal serial bus (USB)
  plug 581
Universal serial bus (USB)
  ports 566, 567, 570, 579
Universal serial bus (USB)
  programmer 591
Universal serial bus (USB)
  socket 581
USB socket access hole
  581
Universal veil 114-115
Universe 10-11
Unmapped region
  Degas and Brönte 34
  Structure of Mercury 35
Unnilennium 311
Unnilhexium 310
Unniloctium 311
Unnilpentium 310
Unnilquandium 310
Unnilseptium 310
Unreactive gas mixture
  319
Unreactive metals 311
Unstable elements 310
Unukalhai 21
Upcurved edge 191
Upfold 60
Upfold trap 280
Upholstery 336-337
Upholstery brush 593
Uplifted block fault
  mountain 62
Upper arm 210
Upper Belvedere 482
Upper Carboniferous Coal
  Measures 61
Upper Carboniferous
  Millstone Grit 60-61
Upper crankcase 410
Upper crux of antihelix
  242
Upper deadeye 382-383
Upper deck 380
Upper epidermis 159
Upper eyelid 213
Upper fin 423
Upper finishing 381
Upper Frater 473
Upper gallery 379
Upper head 387
Upper jaw 212, 220-221,
  244-245, 246, 248
Upper joint
  Clarinet 508
  Cor Anglais 508
  Oboe 508
Upper lobe of lung 215,
  254-255
Upper number pad 588
Upper octave key 509
Upper rudder 416-417
Upper seed axis 152-153
Upper sheer strake 393
Upper topsail 385
Upper wireless and
  telegraphy yard 395
Upright man 108
Upright piano 514
Upright planks jump 554
Upright poles jump 554
Upsilon Sagittarii 21
Upstream gates 560
Upthrow 60
Urachus 257
Ural mountains
  Cretaceous period 73
  Earth's physical
  features 265
  Jurassic period 71
  Late Carboniferous
  period 67
  Triassic period 69

Uranium 310
Uranium fuel 314
Uranius Tholus 43
Uranus 48-49
  Solar System 31
Ureter
  Bird 189
  Bony fish 181
  Domestic cat 195
  Elephant 200
  Frog 182
  Human 215, 256-259
  Lizard 185
  Rabbit 196
  Snail 177
Ureteric orifice 257
Urethra
  Chimpanzee 202
  Domestic cat 195
  Human 256-257, 259,
  261
  Rabbit 196
Urethral opening 259
Urethral sphincter muscle
  257
Urinary bladder 181
Urinary system 256-257
Urinogenital opening
  Bony fish 181
  Dolphin 205
URL 577
Urn 478, 481, 487
Urodela 182
Uropod 172
Urostyle 183
Ursa Major 18, 19
Ursa Minor 18, 21
Ursus americanus 195
Ursus spelaeus 77, 106
U-shaped gouge 449
USB programmer
  assembly 591
USB see Universal serial
  bus (USB)
User name 576
U-shaped valley 286-287
Uterine wall 260-261
Uterus
  Chimpanzee 202
  Elephant 200
  Human 258-259
Utricle 243
U-tube 313
Utzon, J. 499
Uvula 212, 245, 248

V
V1 "flying bomb" 408
V12 cylinder arrangement
  345
V4 engine unit
  British Rail Class 20
  diesel 327
  Honda VF750 364
Vacuole
  Chlamydomonas sp.
  116
  Diatom 116
  Human cell 216
  Palisade mesophyll
  139
Vacuum brake lever 325
Vacuum circuit braker
  328
Vacuum cleaner 592-593
Vacuum operated inlet
  valve 562
Vacuum pump cabinet
  611
Vacuum reservoir 324
Vacuum valve 610
Vagina
  Chimpanzee 202
  Elephant 200
  Human 258-259, 261
  Snail 177
  Spider 170

Valance
  1906 Renault 337
  Ford Model T 339
  Volkswagen Beetle 341
Valency electrons 310
Vallate papillae 244
Vallecular canal 120
Valles Marineris 43
Valley
  Coastline 294
  Glacier 286-287
  Grand Canyon 277
  Mountain 62
  River features 290
  River 288-289
  Rock cycle stages 267
Valley floor erosion 267
Valley head 289
Valley rafter 473
Valley spring 292
Vālmiki 35
Valve 359
Valve chest 324
Valve cusp 252
Valve lifter 367
Valve return spring 347
Valve rocker 344, 402
Valves
  Bivalves 176
  Dehiscent fruit 151
  Indehiscent fruit 150
  Scallop 176
Valve slide 506, 507
Valve spring 343, 344
Valve system 506
Vanadium 310
Van Allen radiation belt 58
Van de Graaff 41
Van de Graaff generator
  316
Vane 191
Van Eyck 35
Vang 378
Vanishing point 431
Vapour barrier 603
Variable incidence air
  intake 420
Variable incidence gust-
  alleviator 421
Variable nozzle 416-417
Variable pitch aluminium-
  alloy blade 408
Variable pitch propeller
  396
Variable time control
  knob 598-599
Variegated lamina 131,
  137
Varnish 348, 436
Vasa recta 256
Vascular cambium 134-
  135
Vascular plants 279
Vascular plexus 255
Vascular strand 149
Vascular system 162-163
Vascular tissue 130
  Aerial shoot 155
  Apical meristem 134
  Bishop pine 124
  Canadian pond weed
  159
  Clubmoss stem 120
  Corm 155
  Dicotyledon 127
  Dodder 163
  Epiphytic orchid 162
  Fern rachis 121
  Higher plants 118-119
  Horsetail stem 120
  Marram grass 113
  Monocotyledon 126-127
  Parasite host 163
  Perennials 130-131
  Pine needle 124
  Pine root/stem 125
  Radicle 152
  Rhizome 155
  Root 132-133

Stem 134-135
  Water hyacinth root 158
  Water lily leaf 159
  Woody plants 130-131
Vas deferens
  Domestic cat 195
  Human 259
  Rabbit 196
Vastitas Borealis 43
Vastus lateralis muscle
  225-226
Vastus medialis muscle
  225-226
Vault 484-485, 496
  Ancient Roman
  building 462-464
  Baroque church 479
  Gothic building 470
  Medieval building 467-
  469
  Modern building 496,
  499
  Nineteenth-century
  building 492-493
  Renaissance building
  477
Vaulting shaft 468-469
V-belt pulley 347
VCR connections 585
Vedette boat 395
Vega 19, 20
  Our galaxy and nearby
  galaxies 15
Vegetable oil 436
Vegetative reproduction
  154-155
Veil 114-115
Vein
  Alveolar 247
  Anterior median 253
  Axillary 253
  Basilic 253
  Brachiocephalic 253
  Bronchial 254
  Cardiac 250
  Central retinal 240
  Cephalic 176, 253
  Common iliac 215, 253,
  257
  Dicotyledon leaf 126-
  127
  Digital 253
  External iliac 215, 253
  Femoral 253
  Gastroepiploic 253
  Great saphenous 253
  Hepatic portal 253
  Hogweed leaf 129
  Inferior mesenteric 253
  Inferior vena cava 215,
  252-253, 257
  Insect 168, 169
  Interlobular 256
  Internal iliac 253
  Internal jugular 253
  Jugular 215
  Leaf 136, 138-139
  Median cubital 253
  Monocotyledon leaf 126
  Palmar 253
  Portal 252
  Pulmonary 251, 253, 254
  Pulp 247
  Renal 256-257
  Short saphenous 253
  Subclavian 253
  Superior mesenteric
  253
  Superior vena cava 215,
  251, 252-253, 255
  Suprarenal 257
  Testicular 257
  Tree mallow leaf 131
  Umbilical 260
  Water hyacinth leaf 158
  Water lily leaf 159
Vela 18, 21
Velamen 162
Velarium 464

Velar scale 115
Vela Supernova Remnant
  17
Vellum 432
Velocette overhead valve
  (OHV) engine 367
Velum 373
Vena cava
  Frog 182
  Inferior 215, 252-253,
  257
  Superior 215, 251, 252-
  253, 255
Vendelinus 40
Veneer 462
Venomous snake 184
Vent
  Frigate 397
  Igneous rock structures
  275
  Mountain building 62
  Rock cycle 266
  Suzuki RGV500 368
  Volcano 272-273
Ventilation 462
Ventilator 422, 423
Ventilator exit 406-407
Ventral abdominal artery
  173
Ventral antebrachial
  muscle 94
Ventral aorta 179
Ventral fin 179
Ventral margin of shell
  176
Ventral nerve cord 169,
  173
Ventral scale 184, 186
Ventricle
  Brain 236-237
  Heart 215, 250-251, 252
Ventricular diastole 251
Ventricular systole 251
Venturi 424
Venus 36-37
  Solar System 30
Venus fly trap 160
Verdaccio 433
Verge 464, 492
Vermiculated rustication
  482
Vermilion 433
Vermilion border of lip
  213
Vermilion Cliffs 277
Versal lettering 445
Vertebra 261
  Bony fish 180
  Cervical 212, 222
  Frog 183
  Lumbar 222-223
  Rattlesnake 185
  Rudimentary 260
  Thoracic 222-223
  Turtle 187
  Westlothiana 81
Vertebral artery 223, 252
Vertebral body 223
Vertebral column 218,
  222, 257
Vertebral foramen 222-
  223
Vertebral shield 187
Vertebrates 56, 64, 104
  Fossil record 279
Vertex
  Building 495
  Human body 212
Vertical air current 302
Vertical batten 602
Vertical cleavage 270
Vertical damper 329
Vertical frame ladder 392
Vertical movement
  Faults and folds 60
  Lake formation 292
Vertical pupil 186
Vertical ridge 129
Vertical spindle 387

Velar scale 115
Vertical stroke 445
Very high frequency
  (VHF) radio 318
Vesicle 148
Vespa Grand Sport 160
  Mark 1 363
Vespa scooter 362, 363
Vessel
  Baroque church 479
  Gothic church 470
  Medieval church 468-
  469
Vesta Rupes 37
Vesta A47 wind turbine
  604
Vestibular canal 243
Vestibular membrane 243
Vestibular nerve 243
Vestibule
  Ancient Greek temple
  461
  Baroque church 481
  Human body 212, 245
  Medieval church 469
  Neoclassical building
  483
Vestibulocochlear nerve
  243
VGA monitor port 567
VHF aerial
  B-17 bomber 408-409
  BAe-146 jetliner 415
  Bell Jetranger
  helicopter 423
  Concorde 416-417
  VHF radio 318
VHF omni-range aerial
  Bell-47 helicopter 422
  Concorde 417
VHF omni-range and
  instrument-landing-
  system aerial 412
Vibraphone 504, 516, 517
Vibration-reducing
  damper foot 58
Vibration-reducing fan
  mounting 597
Vibrations
  Brass instruments 506
  Stringed instruments
  510
Vibrato arm 513
Vibrato effect 516, 517
Vibrator motor 589
Vibrissa
  Lion 194
  Rabbit 196
  Rat 196
  Seal 204
Vicia faba 133, 152
Video
  Digital 582-583
  Streamed Internet 577
Video camera 610
Video card 567
Video cassette 583
Video input/output circuit
  board 585
Video jack port 583
Video port cover 583
Video tape 583
Viewfinder 582
Viewfinder lens 583
Viewfinder ring 583
Viewfinder sleeve 583
Viewing screen 610
Viewing window 581
Viewing window objective
  lens aperture 580
Viewselector panel 576
Viking ships 374-375
Villa Rotunda 475
Villa Savoye 494
Villi of mucosa 248
Viola 503, 504, 505, 510,
  511
Violent eruptions 272
Violet light 318
Violin 503, 504, 505, 510

Violoncello 510-511
Virginia opossum 207
Virgo 18, 21
Virtual mixing board 521
Visceral cartilage 254
Visceral hump 177
Visceral pericardium 250
Viscous coupling 344-345
Visible and infrared
    spectrometers 615
Visible light 318-319
Vision 237
Visor 416-417
Visual recognition 237
Vitreous glass mosaic 451
Vitreous glass tessera 450,
    451
Vitreous humour 240
Vitta 151
Vivaldi 35
Vocal cords 245
Voices 503
Volans 21
Volcanic activity
    Mineralization zones
        280
    Rock cycle 266
Volcanic eruption 26
Volcanic gases 64
Volcanic island 58, 299
Volcanic lake 293
Volcanic lava
    Jupiter 44
    Mars 42
    The Moon 40
    Venus 36
Volcanic mountain 62
Volcanic rock 298, 306
Volcano 58, 63, 272-273
    Jupiter 44
    Locations 273
    Mars 42
    Mineralization zones
        281
    Mountain building 62-
        63
    Ocean floor 298
    Vent 62
    Venus 36
Volkmann's canal 247
Volkmann's vessel 225
Volkswagen Beetle 340-
    341
Volleyball 534-535
Voltage 306, 316
Voltage circuitry 597
Voltage reduction and
    regulation circuits 585
Voltage regulators 596
Voltage stabilizer 597
Voltage transformers 596
Volume 306, 307
Volume control
    Electronic instruments
        520, 521
    Streamed internet radio
        577
    Home cinema 585
    Personal music 587
Volume increase control
    587
Volume reduction control
    587
Volumes 623
Volume up/down toggle
    581
Volute
    Ancient Greek building
        460-461
    Baroque church 479,
        481
    Dome 486
    Islamic building 488
    Neoclassical building
        478, 480
    Renaissance building
        476-477
Volva 114-115
Volvox sp. 116

Vomer 221
Von Kármàn 41
Voussoir 484-485
    Ancient Roman
        building 465
    Neoclassical building
        482
    Renaissance building
        474
V-shaped gouge 449
V-shaped valley
    River features 290
    Rivers 288-289
V-strut 404-405
VTEC engine 354
V-twin engine 362, 363
Vulpecula 19
Vulture 190
Vulva 200
Vyāsa 35
Vyne 482

W

Wadi 283
Wagner 35
Wagon 324
Wagon bogie 330
Wagon vault 485
Wahweap sandstone 276
Waist
    74-gun ship 380-381
    Human 210
    Stringed instruments
        510-511
Waistband 548
Waist gun 408
Wale
    74-gun ship 381
    Roman corbita 373
    Sailing warship 376-377
Walkway 497
Wall
    Ancient Greek temple
        461
    Ancient Roman
        building 462, 465
    Baroque building 478-
        479, 481
    Carpel 148, 151
    Cell 112, 117, 132, 139
    Concrete 496
    Fruit 148-151
    Fungal tissue 115
    Glass 496
    Gothic church 470
    Islamic building 488
    Medieval building 466-
        467, 469
    Modern building 498-
        499
    Neoclassical building
        479, 482
    Nineteenth-century mill
        492
    Ovary 140, 150
    Renaissance building
        476-477
    Twentieth-century
        building 494
Wall anchor 407
Wall construction 602
Wall panel 406-407
Wall painting 434
Walrus 204
Walter 40
Wand 592, 593
Wand handle and
    brushbar controls 592
Wand/handle connector
    593
Wand telescopic link 593
Wankel, Felix 346
Wankel rotary engine
    346-347
Wannanosaurus 101
Wardrobe 416
Wardroom 381

Warhead 394
Warm air 300, 302-303
Warm blood
    Mammals 104
    Theropods 84
Warm front 302-303
Warm occlusion 302
Warm periods 56
Warning horn 327, 329
Warning light 328, 356
Warship
    74-gun ship 379, 380-
        381
    Battleship 394-395
    Frigate 396-397
    Ironclad 392-393
    Man-of-war 378-379,
    Sailing warship 376-377
    Submarine 396-397
Wasatch formation 276
Washable pre-motor filter
    592
Wash cant 378
Washer-dryer 594-595
Wash over dry brush 439
Washburn twelve-string
    guitar 513
Washer
    Bicycle 358
    Power drill 600-601
    Toaster 598-599
Washer jet 353
Washes 458, 439
Washing machine 315
Wasp 168
Waste heat 314-315
Waste water anti-siphon
    pipe hook 595
Waste water pipe 595
Water 38, 66
    Absorption 150
    Amphibian 80
    Changing states 307
    "Deltic" diesel-electric
        locomotive 326
    Energy generation 314-
        315
    Epiphyte supply 162
    Fermentation 313
    Lithographic printing
        446
    Mars 42
    Molecule 138
    Oceans and seas 296
    Photosynthesis 138
    Pollination 144
    Reversible reactions
        312
    Seed germination 152-
        153
    Solutions 306
    Storage organs 156-157
    Transport 134, 139
Water and oil pump
    assembly 356
Waterborne sports 560-
    561
Water-closet 483
Watercolour 438-439
Watercolour paint pan 438
Watercolour paper 439,
    441
Watercolour-style acrylic
    painting 442, 443
Water connection 342
Water-cooled engine 366
Water cycle 288
Water density 296
Water distribution 264
Water droplets 45
Waterfall 291
    Glacier 286
    River 289-290
    Rock cycle 267
Water fern 158
Water float 324
Water hardness
    adjustment and filter
    flap lever 595

Water hyacinth 158
Water ice
    Jupiter's atmosphere
        45
    Mercury's atmosphere
        47
    Structure of comet 53
    Structure of Mars 43
    Structure of Neptune 51
Water-ice fog 42
Water-ice permafrost 43
Water inlet connector 595
Water inlet hose 595
Water inlet pipe 595
Water inlet valves 595
Water jacket
    Daimler engine 343
    Ford diesel engine 347
    Humber engine 343
    Jaguar straight six
        engine 344
Water key 506, 507
Water lily 158-159
Waterline 380
Water obstacle 546
Water outlet 425
Water passage 346
Water pipe
    1906 Renault 337
    Humber engine 343
    Wright Flyer 399
Water pressurizer 314
Waterproof acrylic paint
    442
Waterproof cable
    connector 605
Waterproof covering
    Bishop pine needles
        124
    Golden barrel cactus
        156
    Haworthia truncata 157
    Lithops bromfieldii 157
    Monocotyledon leaf 126
    Rush stem 135
    Wetland plants 158
Waterproof shell 80
Waterproof ski clothing
    553
Waterproof skin 81
Waterproof stowage box
    427
Water pump
    Hybrid car 354
    Jaguar V12 engine 345
    Renault Clio 351
    White Steam Car 342
Water pump pulley 347
Water rail 345
Water reactor 314
Water-retaining cuticle 78
Water salinity 296
Water-saturated
    permeable rock
    Lakes and groundwater
        292
    Mineral resources 280-
        281
Watershed 289
Water shoot 560
Water softener dial 595
Water-soluble glue 450
Water storage tank 497
Water-storing
    parenchyma 156-157
Water supply
    Gun turret 396
    Steam locomotive 324
Water table
    Cave system 284
    Lake formation 292
Water tank
    Bordino Steam Carriage
        334
    "Ellerman Lines" steam
        locomotive 324
    Steam iron 594
    White Steam Car 342
Water vapour

Chemical reactions
    312-313
    Hurricane structure 303
    Jupiter's atmosphere 45
    Mars' atmosphere 43
    Saturn's atmosphere 47
    Venus' atmosphere 37
    Water cycle 288
Water vascular system
    174
Waterway 380, 393
Wattle-and-daub
    Ancient Roman
        building 462, 464-465
    Medieval house 466
Wave 294, 298
    Erosion 294
    Features 294
    Properties 318
Wave-cut platform 295
Waveguide 596, 597
Wavelength 318
Wavellite 269
Wavering pitch 516, 517
Wavy foliation 267
Wax modelling 452
Wax riser 454
Wax runner 454
Waxy cuticle 156, 157
Waxy fruit skin 149
Waxy laminae 159
Waxy zone 161
Weapon-bay bulkhead 421
Weaponry 375
Weasel 194
Weather 302-303
Weathercock 486
Weathering 282-283
    Gothic church 471-472
    Medieval church 469
    Mineral deposits 280
    Renaissance building
        477
    Rock cycle 266
    Sedimentary rocks 276
Weather radar 416
Weather shutter for gun
    394
Weather-vane 471, 477
Web
    Frog 182
    Internet 576
    Webbed feet 188, 190
    Web pages 577
Website address 577
Weight
    Arch 484
    All-round bicycle 360
    Bolts 548
    Fax machine handset
        572
    Measurement 320, 590
    Motorcycle engine 366
    Newton meters 320
Weights 562
Wei-wei 376
Welding tool 608
Weld line 392
Welt 122-123
Welwitschia mirabilis 122-
    123
Werner motorcycle 362
Weslake Speedway
    motorcycle 369
West Africa 73
West Australian current
    297
Westerlies 300
Westlothiana 67, 80-81
Westminster Abbey 484
Westminster Cathedral
    493
Wet-in-wet wash 438, 439
Wetland plants 158-159
Wet season 293
Wet wash 438
Wezen 18
    Canis Major 21
Whaler 395

Whales 204-205
Wheat 109, 150
Wheel
    1906 Renault 337
    Alloy 356, 357
    Bicycle 358-359
    Diesel motor output 326
    First cars 334-335
    Force/motion 320
    Ford Model T 338-339
    Harley-Davidson FLHS
        Electra Glide 363
    Mazda RX-7 346
    Motorcycle 364
    Pacing sulky 555
    Paddle 390-391
    Renault Clio 350-351
    Rossin Italian time-trial
        bicycle 361
    Ship 378, 390, 394
    Single scull 561
    Volkswagen Beetle 340
    Weslake Speedway
        motorcycle 369
Wheel axle
    BAe-146 jetliner 414
    Touring bicycle 360
Wheelbase 360
Wheelchair access 333
Wheel fairing
    Blackburn monoplane
        400
    Pegasus Quasar
        microlight 427
    Pegasus XL SE
        microlight 426
Wheel fork 335
Wheel guard 324, 369, 593
Wheel hub 414
Wheel nut 356, 357
Wheel sets 327, 329
Wheel spacer 561
Whelp 587
Whetstone 452
Whip 555
Whipping 384, 388
Whisker
    Lion 194
    Rabbit 196
    Rat 196
    Seal 204
Whisker boom 382
"Whispering Gallery" 484
Whistle
    Iron paddlesteamer 392
    Life jacket 561
    Referee 524
Whistle lever 325
White belt 556
White blood cells 217, 253
White Cliffs 276
White diamond 268
White dwarfs
    Small stars 24-25
    Stars 22-23
White feldspar 275
White-grey crystal 271
White light 318
White matter
    Cerebrum 236-237
    Spinal cord 238
White of eye 213
White oval
    Jupiter 44-45
    Saturn 46
White spirit 436
White Steam Car 342
White stork 188
White warning light 328
White whale 204
Whorls
    Flower 140
    Green alga cell 116
    Sepals 144, 149
Wicket 538
Wicket-keeper 538
Wide-angle camera 615
Widened joint 282
Wide receiver 526

Wide-screen plasma display 584
Wiener 41
Willow grouse 193
Wind
  Atmosphere 300
  Ekman spiral 297
  Energy generation 314
  Oceans and seas 296-297
  Rock cycle 266-267
  Water cycle 288
  Weather 302
  Weathering and erosion 282-283
  Windspeed 303
Windcheetah SL Mark VI "Speedy" racing HPV bicycle 361
Wind chest 514
Wind controller 521
Wind deflector 341
Wind-dispersed seeds 150-151
Wind erosion 282-283
  Coastline 294
Winding cornice 472
Wind instruments 508, 509
  Brass 506, 507
  Electronic 520
  Woodwind 508, 509
Windlass
  Buildings 467, 477
  Roman corbita 372
Windlass bar 380
Window
  Ancient Egyptian building 459
  Ancient Roman building 463, 465
  Asian building 490-491
  Baroque church 479-481
  Dome 486-487
  Dormer 495
  Double-decker tour bus 333
  "Eurostar" multi-voltage electric train 329
  Gothic building 470-473
  MCW Metrobus 333
  Medieval building 466-469
  Modern building 498, 499
  Neoclassical building 478, 482-483
  Nineteenth-century building 492-493
  Renaissance building 474, 476
  Rococo style 482
  Single-decker bus 333
  TGV electric high-speed train 329
  Twentieth-century building 494-495
Window accessory 583
Window blind 336
Window controls 577
Window-frame 486
Window glass 348
Window jamb 479, 482, 483
Window-sill
  Baroque church 479
  Neoclassical building 482-483
  Twentieth-century building 494
Window stage 477
Wind-pollinated plants 144
Windscreen
  BAe-146 jetliner components 412
  BE 2B bomber 404

BMW R/60 sidecar 362
Concorde 416-417
"Deltic" diesel-electric locomotive 327
Double-decker tour bus 333
Ford Model T 339
Harley-Davidson FLHS 363
Honda Insight 354
Electra Glide 363
Hawker Tempest components 409
Kirby BSA racing sidecar 362
Lockheed Electra airliner 406-407
Tornado 420
Windscreen wiper
  "Deltic" diesel-electric locomotive 327
  "Eurostar" multi-voltage electric train 329
  Italian State Railways Class 402 328
  MCW Metrobus 332
  Paris Metro 328
  TGV electric high-speed train 329
  "Union Pacific" locomotive 326
  Volkswagen Beetle 341
Windsor green 438
Windspeed 303
Wind synthesizer 521
Wind turbine 604, 605
Wind-up 537
Windvane 375, 605
Windward face 283
Wing
  1906 Renault 336
  Alula 191
  ARV light aircraft 424-425
  Australian rules football 528
  Avro biplane 403
  BAe-146 jetliner components 413, 414
  BE 2B wings 404
  Beetle 168
  Biplanes and triplanes 402
  Bird 188, 191
  Blackburn monoplane 401
  Bones 191
  Bumblebee 168
  Butterfly 169
  Cobra lily 160
  Coverts 188
  Curtiss biplane 398
  Deer hopper dry fly 563
  Developing 192
  Dry fruit 150-151
  Early monoplanes 400
  Feather 188, 191
  Ford Model T 338
  Formula One racing car 357
  Gliders, hang-gliders, and microlights 426
  Handball 535
  Hawker Tempest components 409
  Hockey 540
  Ice hockey 550
  Lockheed Electra airliner 406
  Pine seed 122
  Pitcher plant 113
  Rugby 531
  Scots pine seed 122
  Showjumping fence 554
  Ski boot safety binding 552
  Spurious 191
  Sycamore 131

Wing assembly 413
Wing attack 535, 541
Wing case 168
Wing defence
  Lacrosse 541
  Netball 535
Winged seeds
  Scots pine 122
  Sycamore 131, 151
Winged stem 129
Wing end-plate 357
Wing-feather impression 85
Wing fillet panel 409
Wingframe 427
Winglet 556
Wing mirror 354
Wing piping 341
Wing-protecting skid 398-399
Wing-root glove fairing 420-421
Wing-root mount 413
Wing scar 122
Wing stay 539
Wing strut
  ARV light aircraft 424-425
  Avro triplane 402-403
  Curtiss biplane 398
Wing supports 357
Wingtip
  ARV light aircraft 424
  BE 2B wings 404
  Hawker Tempest components 409
  Schleicher glider 426
Wingtip aerial fairing 421
Wing transom 381
Wing vein 168, 169
Wing warping 400
Wire armature 454, 455
Wire bristle brush 519
Wire coil 605
Wire-ended cutting tool 454
Wire-end tools 452
Wire gauze ball 342
Wireless and telegraphy yard 395
Wireless office 397
Wires 518
Wire wheel 402
Wiring loom 596
Wishbone
  Bird 189
  Formula One racing car 357
Withdrawal stride 543
Withdrawing-room 483
Withers 199
Wolf 195
Wolffian duct 179
Wolf hair brush 444
Wollastonite 271
Womb 258-259
Women's lacrosse field 540, 541
Women's shot 542
Wood
  Golf club 547
  Sculpture 454
Wood block 446, 449
Wood capstan 387
Woodcarving 452, 453
Woodcut 446
Wooden arrow 109
Wooden artillery wheel 337
Wooden bar 516
Wooden boarding 602
Wooden body 510
Wooden body-shell 519
Wooden buffer 324
Wooden case 514, 515
Wooden-domed deck 403
Wooden driving wheel 324
Wooden frame
  Harp 511

Printing mesh 446, 448
Sculpture 452
Steam-powered Cugnot "Fardier" 334
Wooden golf clubs 546, 547
Wood engraving 446, 447
Wood engraving print 449
Wooden grip 549
Wooden hearth 109
Wooden "key" 531
Wooden packing 397
Wooden panel 473
Wooden sailing ship 378-379
Wooden sleeper 324, 331
Wooden spoke 334
Wooden-spoked wheel 339
Wooden stands 554
Wooden wheel 334
Woodwind instruments 504, 505, 508, 509
Woodwork 467
Woody flowering plants 126, 130-131
Woody pericarps 150
Woody plants 126
Woody scales
  Bishop pine cone 124
  Smooth cypress 123
Woody stem 134-135
Woofer 584
Woofer loudspeaker connector 585
Woolding 376
Work 314
Working chamber 396
World War I aircraft 404-405
World War II aircraft 408-409
World Wide Web 576
Worming 388
Worms
  Earth's evolution 56
  Fossil record 279
Woven dacron 384
Wrack 116-117
Wren, C. 478
  Baroque church 480
  Cathedral dome 484, 487
Wrest plank
  Concert grand piano 515
  Upright piano 514
Wright brothers
  Modern piston aero-engines 410
  Pioneers of flight 398-399
Wright, F. L. 495
Wright Flyer 398-399
Wrist
  Corythosaurus 98
  Elephant 90
  Human 211, 230-231
  Iguanodon 97
  Stegosaurus 92
  Triceratops 102
Wrist joint
  Baryonyx 85
  Brachiosaurus 91
  Diplodocus 90
  Euoplocephalus 94
  Human 218
  Parasaurolophus 99
  Plateosaurus 88
  Robot 608
  Stegoceras 100, 101
  Tyrannosaurus 84
Wrist pin 390
Wrist position 444
Wrist-strap attachment 579
Write-protect tab 586
Writing area 568
Writing tip 568

Writing tools 444
Wrought iron boiler 324
Wrought iron rail 324
Wuerhosaurus 93
Wulfenite 269

X

Xerophytes 156-157
Xi2 Sagittarii 21
Xi Orionis 18
Xi Pegasi 19
X line 445
X-ray 518-519
  Colon 214
  Gallbladder 214
  Hand 230
X-ray emission 28
X-ray image of Crab Nebula 28
"X" turret 395
Xylem
  Bishop pine 124
  Clubmoss stem 120
  Dicotyledons 126-127
  Dodder host 163
  Epiphytic orchid 162
  Fern rachis 121
  Higher plants 118-119
  Horsetail stem 120
  Marram grass 113
  Monocotyledons 126-127
  Pine needle 124
  Pine root/stem 125
  Radicle 152
  Root 132
  Stem 134-135
  Water hyacinth root 158
  Water lily leaf 159
Xylem fibres 134-135

Y

Yacht racing 560
Yangchuanosaurus 85
Yangtze River 265
Yard 382
  Battleship 395
  Double topsail schooner 385
  Greek and Roman ships 372, 373
  Steel 392
  Tea clipper 392
  Viking karv 375
Yardang 282
Yardarm 379
Yardsman 526
Yasti 490, 491
Yaw control 605
Yaw ring 605
Year
  Earth 30
  Jupiter 31
  Mars 30
  Mercury 26, 34
  Neptune 31
  Planets 30-31
  Pluto 31
  Saturn 31
  Uranus 31
  Venus 30
Yeast
  Fermentation 313
  Fungi 114
Yellow card 524
Yellow light 318, 331
Yellow ochre 442
Yellow orpiment 271
Yellow River 265
Yellow warning arm 330
Yellow-wort 144
Yew 123
Y.M.C.A. 532
Yolk 192
Yolk sac 192

Ytterbium 311
Yttrium 310
"Y" turret 395
Yucca 126
Yucca sp. 126

Z

Zagros Mountains 75
Zaire 265
Zea mays 127
Zeami 35
Zebra 198
Zeeman 41
Zeilleria frenzlii 66
Zeta Centauri 21
Zeta Sagittarii 21
Zeugen 282
Ziggurat-style step-back 494
Zinc 281, 312
Zinc phosphating 348
Zinc plating 477
Zingiber officinale 155
Zion Canyon 276
Zip expansion bay 566
Zirconium 310
Zona pellucida 606, 607
Zone
  Jupiter 44-45
  Structure of Saturn 47
Zone defences 533
Zonular ligament 241
Zoom control 583
Zoom control microchip 581
Zoom in/out icon 568
Zoom keys 590
Zoom motor 580
Zoomorphic head 374
Zosteres 372
Zosterophyllum llanoveranum 64
Zubenelgenubi 18, 21
Zubeneschamali 18, 21
Zugon 373
Zygian 375
Zygomatic arch
  Bear 194
  Chimpanzee 202
  Human 213, 220
  Lion 194
  Smilodon 106
  Toxodon 107
Zygomatic bone 220-221
Zygomaticus major muscle 228-229
Zygote
  Bryophyte 118-119
  Fertilization 146-147
  Plant formation 146
  Primitive land plants 120
  Seaweed 116-117

Acknowledgments

Dorling Kindersley would like to thank (in order of sections):

**The Universe
(consultant editors – Sue Becklake, Gevorkyan Tatyana Alekseyevna):**
John Becklake; the Memorial Museum of Cosmonautics, Moscow; The Cosmos Pavilion, Moscow; The United States Space and Rocket Centre, Alabama; Broadhurst, Clarkson and Fuller Ltd; Susannah Massey

**Prehistoric Earth
(consultant editors – William Lindsay, Martyn Bramwell, Dr Ralph E. Molnar, David Lambert):**
Dr Monty Reid, Andrew Neuman, and the staff of the Royal Tyrrell Museum of Palaeontology, Drumheller, Alberta; Dr Angela Milner and the staff of the Department of Palaeontology, the Natural History Museum, London; Professor W. Ziegler and the staff, in particular Michael Loderstaedt, of the Naturmuseum Senckenburg, Frankfurt; Dr Alexander Liebau, Axel Hunghrebüller, Reiner Schoch, and the staff of the Institut und Museum für Geologie und Paläontologie der Universität, Tübingen; Rupert Wild of the Institut für Paläontologie, Staatliches Museum für Naturkunde, Stuttgart; Dr Scheiber of the Stadtmuseum, Nördlingen; Professor Dr Dietrich Herm of Staatssammlung für Paläontologie und Historische Geologie, München; Dr Michael Keith-Lucas of the Department of Botany, University of Reading; Richard Walker; American Museum of Natural History, New York

**Plants
(consultant editor – Richard Walker):**
Diana Miller; Lawrie Springate; Karen Sidwell; Chris Thody; Michelle End; Susan Barnes and Chris Jones of the EMU Unit of the Natural History Museum, London; Jenny Evans of Kew Gardens, London; Kate Biggs of the Royal Horticultural Society Gardens, Wisley, Surrey; Spike Walker of Microworld Services; Neil Fletcher; John Bryant of Bedgebury Pinetum, Kent; Dean Franklin

**Animals
(consultant editor – Richard Walker):**
David Manning's Animal Ark; Intellectual Animals; Howletts Zoo, Canterbury; John Dunlop; Alexander O'Donnell; Sue Evans of the Royal Veterinary College, London; Dr Geoff Potts and Fred Frettsome of the Marine Biological Association of the United Kingdom, Plymouth; Jeremy Adams of the Booth Museum of Natural History, Brighton; Derek Telling of the Department of Anatomy, University of Bristol; the Natural History Museum, London; Andy Highfield of the Tortoise Trust; Brian Harris of the Aquarium, London Zoo; the Invertebrate Department, London Zoo; Dr Harold McClure of the Yerkes Regional Primate Research Center, Emory University, Atlanta, Georgia; Nielson Lausen of the Harvard Medical School, New England Regional Primates Research

Centre, Southborough, Massachusetts; Dr Paul Hopwood of the Department of Veterinary Anatomy, University of Sydney; Dean Franklin

**The Human Body
(consultant editors – Dr Frances Williams, Dr Fiona Payne, Richard Cummins FRCS):**
Derek Edwards and Dr Martin Collins, British School of Osteopathy; Dr M.C.E. Hutchinson of the Department of Anatomy, United Medical and Dental Schools of Guy's and St Thomas' Hospitals, London. Models – Barry O'Rorke (Bodyline Agency) and Pauline Swaine (MOT Model Agency)

**Geology, Geography, and Meteorology
(consultant editor – Martyn Bramwell):**
Dr John Nudds of the Manchester Museum, Manchester; Dr Alan Wooley and Dr Andrew Clark of the Natural History Museum, London; Graham Bartlett of the National Meteorological Library and Archive, Bracknell; Tony Drake of BP Exploration, Uxbridge; Jane Davies of the Royal Society of Chemistry, Cambridge; Dr Tony Waltham of Nottingham Trent University, Nottingham; staff of the Smithsonian Institute, Washington; staff of the United States Geological Survey, Washington; staff of the National Geographic Society, Washington; staff of Edward Lawrence Associates (Export Ltd), Midhurst; John Farndon; David Lambert

**Rail and Road
Rail (consultant editor – John Coiley)**
Michael Ashworth of the London Transport Museum

Road (consultant editors – David Burgess-Wise, Hugo Wilson)
The National Motor Museum, Beaulieu; Alf Newell of Renault UK Ltd; David Suter of Cheltenham Cutaway Exhibits Ltd; Francesca Riccini of the Science Museum, London. Signore Amadelli of the Museo dell' Automobile Carlo Biscaretti di Ruffia; Paul Bolton of the Mazda MCL Group; Duncan Bradford of Reg Mills Wire Wheels; John and Leslie Brewster of Autocavan; David Burgess-Wise; Trevor Cass of Garrett Turbo Service; John Corbett of The Patrick Collection; Gary Crumpler of Williams Grand Prix Engineering Ltd; Mollie Easterbrooke and Duncan Gough of Overland Ltd; Arthur Fairley of the Vauxhall Motor Company; Paul Foulkes-Halbard of Filching Manor Motor Museum; Frank Gilbert of I. Wilkinson and Son Ltd; Paolo Gratton of Gratton Museum; Colvin Gunn of Gunn and Son; Judy Hogg of Ecurie Bertelli; Milton Holman of Dream Cars; Ian Matthews of IMAT Electronics; Eric Neal of Jaguar Cars Ltd; Paul Niblett, Keith Davidson, Mark Reumel, and David Woolf of Michelin Tyre plc; Doug Nye; Kevin O'Keefe of O'Keefe Cars; Seat UK; Ian Whitley, Raj Johal and Andy Faiers of the Honda Institute; Roger Smith; Jim Stirling of Ironbridge Gorge Museum, Staffordshire; Jon Taylor; Doug Thompson; Martyn Watkins of Ford Motor Company Ltd; John Cattermole, Customer Services Manager at London Northern Buses; F. W. Evans Cycles Ltd; Trek UK Ltd (Bicycle); Sam Grimmer; Colin Uttley

**Physics and Chemistry
(consultant editor – Jack Challoner)**

**Sea and Air
Sea (consultant editors – Geoff Hales and Harvey B. Loomis):**
David Spence, Gillian Hutchinson, David Topliss, Simon Stephens, Robert Baldwin, Jonathan Betts, all of the National Maritime Museum, London; Ian Friel; Simon Turnage of Captain O.M. Watts of London Ltd; Davey and Company Ltd, Great Dunmow; Avon Inflatables Ltd, Llanelli; Musto Ltd, Benfleet; Peter Martin of Spencer Rigging Ltd, Southampton; Peter Rowson of Ratseys Sailmakers, Southampton; Swiftech Ltd, Wallingford; Colin Scattergood of the Barrow Boat Company Ltd, Colchester; Professor J.S. Morrison of the Trireme Trust, Cambridge; The Cutty Sark Maritime Trust; Adrian Daniels of Kelvin Hughes Marine Instruments, London; Arthur Credland of Hull City Council Museums and Art Galleries; The Hull Maritime Society; Gerald Clark; Peter Fitzgerald of the Science Museum, London; Alec Michael of HMB Subwork Ltd, Great Yarmouth, and Ray Ward of the OSEL Group, Great Yarmouth; Richard Bird of UWI, Weybridge; Walker Marine Instruments, Birmingham; The International Sailing Craft Association; The Exeter Maritime Museum; Jane Wilson of the Trinity Lighthouse Company, London; The Imperial War Museum Collections; Thorn Security Ltd; Michael Bach

***Air* (consultant editor – Bill Gunston):**
Aeromega Helicopters, Stapleford; Aero Shopping, London; Avionics Mobile Services Ltd, Watford; Roy Barber and John Chapman of the RAF Museum, Hendon; Mitch Barnes Aviation, London; Mike Beach; British Caledonian Flight Training Ltd; Fred Coates of Helitech (Luton) Ltd; Michael Cuttell and CSE Aviation Ltd, Oxford; Dowty Aerospace Landing Gear, Gloucester; Guy Hartcup of the Airship Association; Anthony Hooley, Chris Walsh, and David Cord of British Aerospace Regional Aircraft Ltd; Ken Huntley of Mid-West Aero Engines Ltd; Imperial War Museum, Duxford; The London Gliding Club, Dunstable; Musée des Ballons, Calvados; Noel Penny Turbines Ltd; Andy Pavey of Aviation Scotland Ltd; Tony Pavey of Thermal Aircraft Developments, London; the Commanding Officer and personnel of RAF St Athan; the Commanding Officer and personnel of RAF Wittering; The Science Museum, London; Ross Sharp of the Science Museum, Wroughton; The Shuttleworth Collection; Skysport Engineering; Mike Smith; Solar Wings Ltd, Marlborough; Julian Temple of Brooklands Museum Trust Ltd; Kelvin Wilson of Flying Start

**Architecture
(consultant editor – Alexandra Kennedy):**
Stephen Cutler for advice and text; Gavin Morgan of the Museum of London, London; Chris Zeuner of the Weald and Downland Museum, Singleton, Sussex; Alan Hills and James Putnam of the British Museum, London; Dr Simon Penn and Michael Thomas of the Avoncroft Museum of Buildings, Bromsgrove,

Worcestershire; Christina Scull of Sir John Soane's Museum, London; Paul Kennedy and John Williamson of the London Door Company, London; Lou Davis of The Original Box Sash Window Company, Windsor; Goddard and Gibbs Studios Ltd, London, for access to stained glass windows; The Royal Courts of Justice, Strand, London; Charles Brooking and Peter Dalton for access to the doors and windows in the Charles Brooking Collection, University of Greenwich, Dartford, Kent; Clare O'Brien of the Shakespeare Globe Trust, Shakespeare's Globe Museum, Bear Gardens, Southwark, London; Ken Teague of the Horniman Museum, London; Canon Haliburton, Mike Payton, Ken Stones, and Anthony Webb of St Paul's Cathedral, London; Roy Spring of Salisbury Cathedral; Reverend Gillean Craig of the Church of St George in the East, London; the Science Museum, London; Dr Neil Bingham; Lin Kennedy of Historic Royal Palaces; Katy Harris of Sir Norman Foster and Partners; Production Design, Thames Television plc, London; Dominique Reynier of Le Centre Georges Pompidou, Paris; Denis Roche of Le Musée National des Monuments Français, Paris; Franck Gioria and students of Les Compagnons du Devoir, Paris, for access to construction models; Frank Folliot of Le Musée Carnavalet, Paris; Dr Martina Harms of Hessische Landesmuseums, Darmstadt; Jefferson Chapman of the University of Tennessee, Knoxville, for access to the model of the Hypostyle Hall, Temple of Amon-Re; staff of the Palazzo Strozzi, Florence; staff of the Sydney Opera House, Sydney; staff of the Empire State Building, New York; Nick Jackson; Ann Terrell

The Visual Arts
(consultant editor – Pip Seymour):
Rosemary Simmons; Michael Taylor of Paupers Press, London; Tessa Hunkin and Emma Biggs of Mosaic Workshop, London; John Tiranti, Jonathan Lyons of Alec Tiranti Ltd, London; Chris Hough; Dr Ashok Roy; Satwinder Sehmi of Alphabet Soup, London; Phillip Poole of Cornelissens, London; George Weil and Sons Ltd, London; The National Gallery, London; Chris Webster of the Tate Gallery, London; China Art Cultural Centre, London; London Graphic Centre, London; A.P. Fitzpatrick, London; Flowers Graphics, London; Intaglio Printmaker, London; Falkiner Papers, London; Edgar Udny and Co, London; John Green

Music
(consultant editor – Susan Sturrock):
Boosey and Hawkes Music Publishers Ltd, London, for permission to reproduce extract from The Prodigal Son by Arthur Sullivan; The Bass and Drum Cellar, London; Empire Drums and Percussion, London; Argents (part of World of Music), London; Bill Lewington Ltd, London; Frobenius organ at Kingston Parish Church, Surrey; Yamaha-Kemble Music (UK) Ltd, Tilbrook, Milton Keynes; Yamaha Atelier, London; Akai (UK) Ltd, Hounslow, Middlesex; Casio Electronics Co. Ltd, London; Roland (UK) Ltd, Fleet, Hampshire; Richard Schulman; Andy Brown of Musictrack

Sports
The Sports Council Information Centre, London; The British Olympic Games Committee; Brian Crennell of Black's Leisure Group (First Sport); Lillywhites of Piccadilly, London; Mitre Sports International Ltd, Huddersfield; David Bloomfield of the Football Association; Denver Athletics Ltd, Norfolk; Greg Everest and Keith Birley of the British League of Australian Rules Football; Peter McNally of the Gaelic Athletic Association; Jeremy Garman of James Gilbert Ltd.; Rex King of the Rugby Football Union, Twickenham; Neil Tunnicliffe and John Huxley of the Rugby Football League, Leeds; Wayne Patterson of the Basketball Hall of Fame, Springfield, Connecticut; Brian Coleman of the English Basketball Association; All American Imports, Northampton; George Bulman of the English Volleyball Association; Julie Longdon of Mizuno Mallory (UK) Ltd; Juliet Stanford of the All-England Netball Association; Jeff Rowland of the British Handball Association; Cally Melin of Adidas UK Ltd; Patrick Donnely of the Baseball Hall of Fame, Cooperstown, New York; Ian Lepage and Stephen Barlow of the Hockey Association, Milton Keynes; Alison Taylor and Anita Mason of the All England Women's Lacrosse Association, Birmingham; David Shuttleworth of the English Lacrosse Union; Les Barnett and Jock Bentley of the British Athletic Federation Ltd, Birmingham; Mike Gilks of the Badminton Association of England; Gurinder Purewall for advice on archery; Chris McCartney of the US Archery Association; Geoff Doe of the National Smallbore Rifle Association, Bisley, Surrey, for information and reference material on shooting; Fagan Sports Goods Distributors, Surrey; Konrad Bartelski for advice on skiing; The British Ski Federation, Edinburgh; Mike Barnett of Snow and Rock of London; Sally Spurway of Mast-Co. Ltd, Reading; Sarah Morgan for advice on equestrian sports; Steve Brown and the New York Racing Association Inc, New York; Danrho of London; Alan Skipp and James Chambers of the Amateur Fencing Association, London; Carla Richards of the US Fencing Association; Hamilton Bland and John Dryer of the Amateur Swimming Association, Loughborough; Cotswold Camping Ltd, London; Tim Spalton of Glyn Locke (Racing Shells) Ltd, Chalgrove; Terry Friel of the US Rowing Association; House of Hardy; Leeda Fishing Tackle

The Modern World
John Lewis, Brent Cross, for the loan of products for photography; Apple Computers UK; Palm Inc.; Epson UK; Naynesh Mistry of Brother UK; Nintendo; Sony UK; Nokia Mobile Phones Ltd; Sony Ericsson; Tony Broad of Garmin Europe; Dualit Ltd; Black and Decker Ltd; James Honour of the Buildings Research Establishment; Craig Anders of Cole Thompson Associates; Vestas Wind Systems; Bryan Adams of MIT; Dr Julian Heath of *Microscopy and Analysis*; Fei UK Ltd; Steve Parker; Ian Graham

PHOTOGRAPHY:
M. Alexander; Peter Anderson; Colin Bowling; Charles Brooks; Jane Burton; Peter Chadwick; Simon Clay; Gordon Clayton; John Coiley; Andy Crawford; Geoff Dann; Philip Dowell; John Downs; Mike Dunning; Torla Evans; David Exton; Paul Forrester; Robert and Anthony Fretwell of Fretwell Photography Ltd.; Philip Gatward; Steve Gorton; Anna Hodgson; Gary Kevin; J. Heseltine; Cyril Laubscher; John Lepine; Lynton Gardiner (American Museum of Natural History, New York); Steve Gorton; Michelangelo Gratton; Judith Harrington; Peter Hayman; Anna Hodgson; Colin Keates; Gary Kevin; Dave King; Bob Langrish; Brian D.Morgan; Nick Nicholls; Nick Parfitt; Tim Parmenter and Colin Keates (Natural History Museum, London); Tim Ridley; Dave Rudkin; Philippe Sebert; James Stevenson; Clive Streeter; Harry Taylor; Matthew Ward; Jerry Young

PHOTOGRAPHIC ASSISTANCE:
Kevin Zak; Gary Ombler

ILLUSTRATORS:
Julian Baum; Rick Blakeley; Kuo Kang Chen; Karen Cochrane; Simone End; Ian Fleming; Roy Flooks; Mark Franklin; David Gardner; Will Giles; Mick Gillah; David Hopkins; Selwyn Hutchinson; Mei Lim; Linden Artists; Nick Loates; Chris Lyon; Kathleen McDougall; Coral Mula; Sandra Pond; Dave Pugh; Colin Rose; Graham Rosewarne; John Temperton; Halli Verrinder; John Woodcock; Chris Woolmer

MODEL MAKERS:
Roby Braun; David Donkin; Morrison Frederick; Gordon Models; John Holmes; Graham High and Jeremy Hunt of Centaur Studios; Richard Kemp; Kelvin Thatcher; Paul Wilkinson

ADDITIONAL DESIGN ASSISTANCE:
Stefan Morris; Ulysses Santos; Suchada Smith

ADDITIONAL EDITORIAL ASSISTANCE:
Helen Castle; Colette Connolly; Camela Decaire; Nick Harris; Andrea Horth; Stewart McEwen; Damien Moore; Melanie Tham

INDEX: Kay Wright; Lynn Bresler

Picture credits:

Action Plus 530tc; Anglo Australian Telescope Board 11cl, 11cra, 11cbl, 12tr, 12bc, 13tl, 13bl, 14tl, 16b, 17tc, 17bl, 22tl/D.Malin 16tl, 26tr, 27tl; Apple Computer Inc. 521b; Austin Brown and the Aviation Picture Library 426tl; Baptistery, Florence/Alison Harris 453r; Biophoto Associates 217ca, 217cra, 228cbc, 228cbc 230tr; BRE Imaging 602bl, 602r, 603tr, 603br; Paul Brierley 311bra; British Aerospace/Anthony Hooley 412tl, 415tl; British Aerospace (Commercial Aircraft) Ltd 416tl; By prmission of the British Library 432tl, 445bl; British Museum 459tl, 459tr, 460tr, 460tc, 460tb, 489b; BP Exploration 299; Duncan Brown 25tl; Frank Lloyd Wright, American, 1867-1959, Model of Midway Gardens, 1914, executed by Richard Tickner, mixed media, 1987, 41.9 x 81.3 x 76.2, 1989.48. view 1. Photography courtesy of the Art Intitute of Chicago 495t; J.A. Coiley 331cr; Bruce Coleman Ltd/Andy Price 272tl; Courtesy of the Board of Trustees of the Victoria and Albert Museum, London 454-455b; Dyson 592tr; European Passenger Services 329tl; ESA /PLV 11bl; Fei Co. 610tc, 610r; French Railways 329c; Garmin Europe 590c; Geoscience Features 311cla; Robert Harding Picture Library 62tl; Hitachi High-Technologies Co. Ltd 611tr; Michael Holford/British Museum 372bl, Michael Holford 374tr; Honda 354tr, 355b; Hutchison Picture Library 60cl; The Image Bank/Edward Bower 306tr; Jet Propulsion Laboratory 11cbr; 30bc; 31bc; 31bcr; 38tl; 42crb; 44cb; 44cbr; 44bc; 44br; 46tl; 46cr; 46cb; 46bc; 46br; 50tl; 50cra; 50cl; 50c; 50cr; 50br; KeyMed Ltd 248bl, 249bl, 249bcl; Department of Prints and Drawings, Uffizi, Florence/Philip Gatward 431cl/Uffizi, Florence/Philip Gatward 433tl; Robin Kerrod/Spacecharts 615br; Dr D.N. Landon (Institute of Neurology) 228bl,br; Life Science Images/Ron Boardman 244bl, 244br; The Lund Observatory 15bc; Microsoft Coporation 579cr; Brian Morrison 329tl, 329r; © The Henry Moore Foundation 455tr; Musée d'Orsay, Paris/Philippe Sebert 437tc, 441tc;

Musée du Louvre, Paris/Philippe Sebert 453tl, 453l, 453br; Musictrack/MOTU Digital performer 521bcl; NASA/AUI 13tr; NASA/JPL 11 cbr, 11br, 30tl, 30bl, 30br, 30bc, 31bc, 31bcr, 31bl, 34cr, 38tl, 40tl, 40cr, 42cr, 44tl, 44cb, 44cbr, 44bc, 44br, 44cr, 46crb, 46tl, 46cr, 46cb, 46bc, 46br, 48tl, 48cra, 48bca, 48bc, 48br, 50tl, 50bc, 50bc, 50cbr, 50br, 50cr, 52cr, 612cr, 612tr, 613tl, 613tcl, 613tcr, 613tr, 613c, 613cr, 614cl, 614cbl, 614bl, 614c, 614r, 615tr, 615cr; National Maritime Museum 373br, 392-393b; National Medical Slide Bank 217cr; Nature Photographers/Paul Sterry 286tl; Newage International 317bl; Nintendo Co. Ltd 579br; Nintendo Magazine 578tc,578cl, 578cbl,578bl; Olympus 610cl, 610bl; Oxford Scientific Films/Breck P. Kent 166tl; Planet Earth 274tr; Quadrant 326tr; Margaret Robinson 332tl; Giotto The Expulsion of the Merchants from the Temple Scala 435tc, 435bl, 435br; Science Photo Library 10bl, 13tr, 28tr, 214bcr, 214bl, 236tr/Michael Abbey 225tc/ Agema Infrared Systems 318tl/AGFA 220tl/Alex Barte 605tr/David Becker 607cr/Biophoto Associates: 217crb/Dr Jeremy Burgess/Science Photo Library 132tr; Dr Jeremy Burgess 235bcl/ CNRI 214tl, 214cl, 214c, 214cr, 214bl, 214clb, 214crb, 214blc, 214br, 217cb, 235bcr, 238tl, 249bcr, 253tr, 253cra, 256tl; Science Photo library /Earth Satellite Corporation 288cl, 293br/Dr Brian Eyden 228cbr/Professor C. Ferlaud 245bl/Vaughan Fleming 311tl/Simon Fraser/U.S. Dept.of Energy 214bcl, 266tl/Eric Grave 217br/Hale Observatories 32br/Max Planck Institute for Radio Astronomy 15tl/Jan Hinsch 225tc/Jodrell Bank 11 tr, 13c /Manfred Kage 217c, 235br, 237br/Dr William C. Keel 13br/Keith Kent 564c/James King-Holmes 316tl, 606bl/Russ Lappa 310bra/John Mead 605br/Astrid & Hans-Freider Michler 217tr/ Dennis Milon 52bl/NASA 11cla, 12tl, 15tr, 30c, 31br, 32tl, 35tl, 36tl, 36cl, 36cr, 36bc, 42br, 42tr, 44tl 52tl, 291tr, 300tl/National Optical Astro Observatory 52tr/NIBSC 253crb/Novosti Press Agency 42bc/Sam Ogden 609c, 609tr/Omikron 244bc/David Parker 63bl, 304-305, 308br/Alfred Pasieka 606cr/Philippe Plailly 308tl/Quest

611br/Roussel-UCLAF/CNRI 217tc/Rev Ronald Royer 32cr/Royal Observatory, Edinburgh/D Malin 11tl, 11cr,12c, 16cl, 16cr, 17br/David Scharf 235bl/Dr Kaus Schiller 248bcl, 248bcr, 248br/Secchi-Lecaque/Roussel-UCLAF/CNRI 253br/H. Sochurek 214cb/Stammers/Thompson 230tl/Sheila Terry 234tl/US Department of Energy 310bc/U.S Geological Survey/Science Photo Library 8-9, 30bcr, 42tl, 42bl/Tom Van Sant/Geosphere Project, Santa Monica/Science Photo Library 273tr, 281tr, 296tr, 297tl/Dr Christopher B. Williams/(Saint Marks Hospital) 249br; Oxford Scientific Films/Animals Animals/Breck P. Kent 167tl; Palm 568tc, 568cl,569tl,569tcl,569tc; Pratt & Whitney Canada 418-419b, 419t; Science Museum 306bl,306bcl. 306 bcr, 324t, 326-327b, 330tr, 331ct, 331 cb; Sony Corporation 579tr, 608bl; Sony Ericsson 588cr; Sporting Pictures 524tl, 544cr; Tony Stone Worldwide 280tl; David Bomberg St Pauls and River 1945/Dinora Davies-Rees/Tate Gallery 431bc; David Hockney A Bigger Splash 1967/ © David Hockney/Tate Gallery 443tc; J.M.W. Turner The Burning of the Houses of Parliament Tate Gallery 439tc; Vision 26tr, 27c; Jerry Young 306tl; Dr Robert Youngson 241cr; courtesy of Vestas Wind Systems 604t; Zefa 217bc/Janicek 276tl/H. Sochurek 210tl, 250tl, 254tl,/ G. Steenmans 292tl

Jacket:
Indianapolis Motor Speedway Foundation front cover bc; NASA background to 2001 on spine, front cover, front inside flap

(t=top, b=bottom, a=above, l-left, r=right, c=centre)

Every effort has been made to trace the copyright holders. Dorling Kindersley apologises for any unintentional omissions and would be pleased, in any such cases, to add an acknowledgment in future editions.

Some pages in this book previously appeared in the *Visual Dictionary* series published by Dorling Kindersley. Contributors to this series include:

Project Art Editors: Duncan Brown, Ross George, Nicola Liddiard, Andrew Nash, Clare Shedden, Bryn Walls

Designers: Lesley Betts, Paul Calver, Simone End, Ellen Woodward

Additional design assistance: Sandra Archer, Christina Betts, Alexandra Brown, Nick Jackson, Susan Knight

Project Editors: Fiona Courtney-Thompson, Paul Docherty, Tim Fraser, Stephanie Jackson, Mary Lindsay

Editorial Assistant: Emily Hill

Additional editorial assistance: Susan Bosanko, Edward Bunting, Candace Burch, Deirdre Clark, Jeanette Cossar, Danièle Guitton, Jacqui Hand, David Harding, Nicholas Jackson, Edwina Johnson, David Lambert, Gail Lawther, David Learmount, Paul Jackson, Christine Murdock, Bob Ogden, Cathy Rubinstein, Louise Tucker, Dr Robert Youngson

Picture Researchers: Vere Dodds, Danièle Guitton, Anna Lord, Catherine O'Rourke, Christine Rista, Sandra Schneider, Vanessa Smith, Clive Webster

Series Editor: Martyn Page

Series Art Editor: Paul Wilkinson

Managing Art Editors: Philip Gilderdale, Steve Knowlden

Art Director: Chez Picthall

Managing Editor: Ruth Midgley

Production: Jayne Simpson